STATISTICS FOR BUSINESS AND ECONOMICS

SIXTH EDITION

DAVID R. ANDERSON
University of Cincinnati

DENNIS J. SWEENEY
University of Cincinnati

THOMAS A. WILLIAMS
Rochester Institute of Technology

West Publishing Company
Minneapolis/St. Paul • New York
Los Angeles • San Francisco

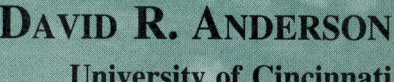

To Marcia, Cherri, and Robbie

Editorial Services: Emily P. McNamara
Proofreading: Lynn Reichel
Text and Cover Design: LightSource Images
Composition: Carlisle Communications
Artwork: Miyake Illustration
Indexing: Schroeder Indexing Services

Minitab is a registered trademark of Minitab, Inc., 3081 Enterprise Drive, State College, PA, 16801 (telephone 814/238–3280; telex 881612; fax 814/238–4383).

WEST'S COMMITMENT TO THE ENVIRONMENT

In 1906, West Publishing Company began recycling materials left over from the production of books. This began a tradition of efficient and responsible use of resources. Today, 100% of our legal bound volumes are printed on acid-free, recycled paper consisting of 50% new paper pulp and 50% paper that has undergone a de-inking process. We also use vegetable-based inks to print all of our books. West recycles nearly 22,650,000 pounds of scrap paper annually—the equivalent of 187,500 trees. Since the 1960s, West has devised ways to capture and recycle waste inks, solvents, oils, and vapors created in the printing process. We also recycle plastics of all kinds, wood, glass, corrugated cardboard, and batteries, and have eliminated the use of polystyrene book packaging. We at West are proud of the longevity and the scope of our commitment to our environment.

West pocket parts and advance sheets are printed on recyclable paper and can be collected and recycled with newspapers. Staples do not have to be removed. Bound volumes can be recycled after removing the cover.

Production, Printing and Binding by West Publishing Company.

 TEXT IS PRINTED ON 10% POST CONSUMER RECYCLED PAPER

British Library Cataloguing-in-Publication Data. A catalogue record for this book is available from the British Library.

COPYRIGHT ©1981, 1984, 1987, 1990, 1993   By WEST PUBLISHING COMPANY
COPYRIGHT ©1996   By WEST PUBLISHING COMPANY
610 Opperman Drive
P.O. Box 64526
St. Paul, MN 55164-0526

Printed in the United States of America

03   02   01   00   99   98   97   96   8   7   6   5   4   3   2

Library of Congress Cataloging-in-Publication Data

Anderson, David Ray, 1941–
      Statistics for business and economics / David R. Anderson, Dennis
   J. Sweeney, Thomas A. Williams.—6th ed.
          p.   cm.
      Includes bibliographical references and index.
      ISBN 0-314-06378-1 student edition (hard: alk. paper)
          0-314-07043-5 instructor's edition (hard: alk. paper)
      1. Commercial statistics.   2. Economics—Statistical methods.
   3. Statistics.   I. Sweeney, Dennis J.   II. Williams, Thomas Arthur,
   1944-   .   III. Title.
   HF1017.A6   1996
   519.5—dc20   95-41209
                                                                       CIP

CONTENTS

Chapter 3 DESCRIPTIVE STATISTICS II: NUMERICAL METHODS • 62

Chapter 4   INTRODUCTION TO PROBABILITY • 116

Chapter 5   DISCRETE PROBABILITY DISTRIBUTIONS • 161

Chapter 6   CONTINUOUS PROBABILITY DISTRIBUTIONS • 197

Chapter 7   SAMPLING AND SAMPLING DISTRIBUTIONS • 231

Chapter 8   INTERVAL ESTIMATION • 276

Chapter 9 HYPOTHESIS TESTING • 313

Chapter 10	**STATISTICAL INFERENCE ABOUT MEANS AND PROPORTIONS WITH TWO POPULATIONS • 366**

Chapter 11 INFERENCES ABOUT POPULATION VARIANCES • 402

Chapter 12 TESTS OF GOODNESS OF FIT AND INDEPENDENCE • 424

Chapter 13 ANALYSIS OF VARIANCE AND EXPERIMENTAL DESIGN • 450

Chapter 14 · SIMPLE LINEAR REGRESSION • 506

Chapter 15   MULTIPLE REGRESSION • 577

Chapter 16 REGRESSION ANALYSIS: MODEL BUILDING • 630

Chapter 19 NONPARAMETRIC METHODS • 744

Appendixes   A-1

PREFACE

The purpose of this book is to give students, primarily those in the fields of business administration and economics, a conceptual introduction to the field of statistics and its many applications. The text is applications oriented and written with the needs of the nonmathematician in mind; the mathematical prerequisite is knowledge of algebra.

APPLICATIONS AND METHODOLOGY

Applications of data analysis and statistical methodology are an integral part of the organization and presentation of the text material. The discussion and development of each technique is presented in an application setting, with the statistical results providing insights to decisions and solutions to problems.

Although the book is applications oriented, we have taken care to provide sound methodological development and to use notation that is generally accepted for the topic being covered. Hence, students will find that this text provides good preparation for the study of more advanced statistical material. A bibliography to guide further study is included as an appendix.

CHANGES IN THE SIXTH EDITION

We appreciate the acceptance of and positive response to the previous editions of this text. Accordingly, in making modifications for this new edition, we have maintained the presentation style and readability of those editions. The significant changes are summarized here.

MORE EXAMPLES AND MANY EXERCISES BASED ON REAL DATA

We have continued the emphasis on helping students understand the wide range of statistical applications by updating and expanding the examples and exercises based on real data and actual statistical studies. Sources such as *The Wall Street Journal, Business Week, USA Today, Fortune, Forbes, Financial World, and Barrons* are used to provide referenced applications and exercises that demonstrate uses of statistics in business and economics. The use of real data enables students to learn about not only the statistical methodology, but also the application.

MINITAB AND EXCEL SPREADSHEET APPENDIXES

The illustrations of computer output within the main body of the text were generated by using the Minitab statistical software package. Today most statistical packages are similar enough in output format that users of other software packages should have little difficulty with interpretation. However, as requested by instructors not using Minitab, the main body of the text does not include the detailed instructions necessary to generate the computer output. Chapter appendixes have been added that describe the Minitab instructions used to generate the output shown in the chapter.

Spreadsheet appendixes have been added to selected chapters to show the statistical capabilities of modern spreadsheet systems. Microsoft Excel is used to illustrate and step-by-step instructions are included.

QUALITY MANAGEMENT APPLICATIONS THROUGHOUT THE TEXT

The use of statistics for the improvement of quality is demonstrated throughout the text. In many chapters, examples and exercises are based on such applications as improving customer service and improving production processes. Chapter 20 is devoted exclusively to the topic of quality control.

TYPES OF DATA

The introduction to data measurement in Chapter 1 has been simplified to the distinction between quantitative and qualitative data. Detailed discussion of nominal, ordinal, interval, and ratio data is left to Chapter 19, Nonparametric Methods. Although the emphasis on data measurement has been reduced, a discussion of cross-sectional and time series data has been added to Chapter 1 because of the importance of such data in business and economics.

BIVARIATE DATA AND CORRELATION APPEAR EARLIER

We present bivariate data in Chapter 2 with crosstabulations and scatter diagrams to help students begin the important process of understanding the relationship between variables. In Chapter 3 we introduce covariance and correlation as descriptive measures for bivariate data.

ADDITIONAL SAMPLING METHODS PRESENTED IN CHAPTER 7

Chapter 7 is used to introduce sampling and sampling distributions. The emphasis is on simple random sampling, but a new section at the end provides an overview of additional sampling methods. Included are stratified simple random sampling, cluster sampling, and systematic random sampling. The importance of probability sampling methods and the drawbacks of convenience and judgmental sampling are noted. A more detailed discussion of these topics and presentation of the appropriate methodology are deferred to Chapter 21, Sample Survey.

MULTIPLE COMPARISON SECTION IN CHAPTER 13 REVISED

Previously, we covered three methods of conducting multiple-comparison tests based on analysis of variance. The section has now been shortened and simplified with an emphasis on Fisher's least significant difference method.

CHANGES TO REGRESSION ANALYSIS IN CHAPTERS 14, 15, AND 16

Chapters 14 and 15 have been revised to provide parallel treatments of simple linear regression and multiple regression. Both chapters begin with the regression model followed by the regression equation and the use of the least squares method to develop the estimated regression equation. The coefficient of determination follows as a measure of how well the estimated regression equation fits the data. Then we provide a full discussion of the model assumptions. Both chapters conclude with the standard tests for significance, residual analysis, and the identification of outliers. Chapter 16 on model building continues to be an important part of the complete regression package; it includes issues that may be of interest to instructors and students who have the time and desire to study regression analysis in more depth.

NEW STATISTICS IN PRACTICE APPLICATIONS

To emphasize the application of statistics, we open each chapter with an actual situation supplied by practitioners in business and economics. Each Statistics in Practice briefly describes an organization and a problem in which the statistical methodology introduced in the chapter has been applied. New applications from *Business Week,* Nevada Occupational Health Clinic, and Fisons Corporation have been added to other applications featuring Procter & Gamble, Polaroid, Monsanto, Xerox, Dow Chemical, and Colgate-Palmolive. The table at the end of this preface lists the organizations and applications described.

NEW CHAPTER ON DECISION ANALYSIS

Chapter 22 has undergone a significant revision. A new application involving construction of condominiums is presented to guide the student through the fundamentals of using probability and expected value in the decision analysis process.

FEATURES AND PEDAGOGY

We have continued many of the features that appeared in previous editions. Some of the important ones follow.

METHODS EXERCISES AND APPLICATIONS EXERCISES

The end-of-section exercises are split into two parts, Methods and Applications. The Methods exercises require students to use the formulas and make the necessary computations. The Applications exercises require students to use the chapter material in real-world situations. Thus, students first focus on the computational "nuts and bolts," then move on to the subtleties of statistical application and interpretation.

SELF-TEST EXERCISES

Certain exercises are identified as self-test exercises. Completely worked-out solutions for those exercises are provided in an appendix at the end of the text. Students can attempt the self-test exercises and immediately check the solution to evaluate their understanding of the concepts presented in the chapter.

NOTES & COMMENTS

At the end of many sections, we provide Notes & Comments designed to give the student additional insights about the statistical methodology and its application. Notes & Comments include warnings about or limitations of the methodology, recommendations for application, brief descriptions of additional technical considerations, and other matters.

COMPUTER CASES

Many chapters have computer cases, which contain problem scenarios accompanied by data sets of modest size. Computer solution by Minitab, The Data Analyst, a spreadsheet, or another statistical software package is required. Each case outlines a managerial report that the student prepares to summarize statistical results as well as present interpretations and recommendations. The data sets for all computer cases are available on a data disk that accompanies the text.

COMPUTER SOFTWARE

The text contains numerous examples and discussions of the important role of statistical software packages in the computation and presentation of statistical results. Use and interpretation of the computer output provided by Minitab are illustrated in the main body of the text. Chapter appendixes have been added that provide the Minitab instructions necessary to generate the within-chapter illustrations. Additional appendixes show how some of those analyses can be conducted with modern spreadsheet packages. Microsoft Excel is used.

DATA DISK

Data sets for text examples, exercises, and computer cases are available on a special data disk accompanying the text. Data disks containing the data sets in a format acceptable to Minitab, Microsoft Excel, and The Data Analyst can be obtained shrink-wrapped with the text.

FLEXIBILITY

The text gives the instructor a reasonable amount of flexibility in selecting material to satisfy specific course needs. A possible outline for a two-quarter sequence follows.

Possible Two-Quarter Course Outline	
First Quarter	**Second Quarter**
Data and Statistics (Chapter 1)	Hypothesis Testing (Chapter 9)
Descriptive Statistics (Chapters 2 and 3)	Two-Population Cases (Chapter 10)
Introduction to Probability (Chapter 4)	Inferences about Population Variances (Chapter 11)
Probability Distributions (Chapters 5 and 6)	Tests of Goodness of Fit and Independence (Chapter 12)
Sampling and Sampling Distributions (Chapter 7)	Analysis of Variance and Experimental Design (Chapter 13)
Interval Estimation (Chapter 8)	Regression Analysis (Chapters 14 and 15)

Other possibilities for such a course depend on the time available and the background of the students. Topics such as model building in regression analysis (Chapter 16), index numbers (Chapter 17), forecasting (Chapter 18), nonparametric methods (Chapter 19), quality control (Chapter 20), sample surveys (Chapter 21), and decision analysis (Chapter 22) can be selected at the option of the instructor to meet the special needs of a particular academic program. However, it is not possible to cover all the material in one semester or in two quarters unless some of the topics have been studied previously.

ACKNOWLEDGMENTS

We owe a debt to many of our colleagues and friends for their helpful comments and suggestions in the development of this text. Among them are:

Mohammad Ahmadi	Jamshid C. Hasseini	Bill Seaver
Cheryl Asher	C. Thomas Innis	Alan Smith
Robert Balough	Ben Isselhardt	Stephen Smith
Abdul Basti	Jeffrey Jarrett	Suzanne Smith
Harry Benham	Robert Bruce Jones	William E. Stein
Michael Bernkopf	Frank Kelly	Willban Terpening
John Bryant	David Krueger	Ted Tsukahara
Peter Bryant	Martin S. Levy	Hiroki Tsurumi
Terri L. Byczkowski	Thomas McCullough	Victor Ukpolo
Michael Cicero	Bette Midgarden	Ebenge Usip
Robert Cochran	Glenn Milligan	Cindy van Es
Robert Collins	David Muse	Andrew Welki
John Cooke	Roger Myerson	Ari Wijetunga
David W. Cravens	Richard O'Connell	Donald Williams
George Dery	Al Palachek	Roy Williams
Gopal Dorai	Diane Petersen-Salameh	J. E. Willis
Edward Fagerlund	Tom Pray	Mustafa Yilmaz
Nicholas Farnum	Ruby Ramirez	Gary Yoshimoto
Sharon Fitzgibbons	Tom Ryan	Charles Zimmerman
Jerome Geaun	James R. Schwenke	Greg Zimmerman
Paul Guy		

A special thanks is owed to our associates from business and industry who supplied the Statistics in Practice features. We recognize them individually by a credit line on each Statistics in Practice article. In addition, we acknowledge the cooperation of Minitab, Inc., in permitting the use of Minitab statistical software in this text. Finally, we are also indebted to our editor, Mary C. Schiller, and others at West Publishing Company for their editorial counsel and support during the preparation of this text.

David R. Anderson
Dennis J. Sweeney
Thomas A. Williams

February 1996

An Overview of Statistics in Practice Features

Chapter Number	Chapter Title	Organization Featured	Application Topic
1	Data and Statistics	*Business Week*	Subscriber sample survey and use of statistics
2	Descriptive Statistics I. Tabular and Graphical Approaches	Colgate-Palmolive	Quality assurance for heavy duty detergents
3	Descriptive Statistics II. Measures of Location and Dispersion	Barnes Hospital	Time spent in hospice program
4	Introduction to Probability	Morton International	Evaluation of customer service testing program
5	Discrete Probability Distributions	Xerox	Performance test of an on-line computerized publication system
6	Continuous Probability Distributions	Procter & Gamble	Manufacturing strategy
7	Sampling and Sampling Distributions	Mead	Estimating the value of Mead forest ownership
8	Interval Estimation	Dollar General	Sampling for estimation of LIFO inventory costs
9	Hypothesis Testing	Harris	Testing for defective plating
10	Statistical Inference about Means and Proportions with Two Populations	Fisons	Evaluation of new drugs
11	Inferences about Population Variances	U.S. General Accounting Office	Water pollution control
12	Tests of Goodness of Fit and Independence	United Way	Determining community perceptions of charities
13	Analysis of Variance and Experimental Design	Burke Marketing Services	New product design
14	Simple Linear Regression and Correlation	Polaroid Corporation	Aging study of film
15	Multiple Regression	Champion International	Control of pulp bleaching process
16	Regression Analysis: Model Building	Monsanto	Feed development for chickens
17	Index Numbers	U.S. Department of Labor, Bureau of Labor Statistics	Consumer price index
18	Time Series Analysis and Forecasting	Nevada Occupational Health Clinic	Forecasting revenue
19	Nonparametric Methods	West Shell Realtors	Comparison of real estate prices across neighborhoods
20	Statistical Methods for Quality Control	Dow Chemical U.S.A.	Statistical process control
21	Sample Survey	Cincinnati Gas & Electric	Survey of commercial customers
22	Decision Analysis	Ohio Edison	Choice of best type of particulate control equipment

ABOUT THE AUTHORS

DAVID R. ANDERSON.   David R. Anderson is Professor of Quantitative Analysis in the College of Business Administrationn at the University of Cincinnati. Born in Grand Forks, North Dakota, he earned his B.S., M.S., and Ph.D. degrees from Purdue University. Professor Anderson has served as Head of the Department of Quantitative Analysis and Operations Management and as Associate Dean of the College of Business Administration. In addition, he was the coordinator of the College's first Executive Program.

At the University of Cincinnati, Professor Anderson has taught introductory statistics for business students as well as graduate level courses in regression analysis, multivariate analysis, and management science. He has also taught statistical courses at the Department of Labor in Washington, D.C. He has been honored with nominations and awards for excellence in teaching and excellence in service to student organizations.

Professor Anderson has coauthored six textbooks in the areas of statistics, management science, linear programming, and production and operations management. He is an active consultant in the field of sampling and statistical methods.

DENNIS J. SWEENEY.   Dennis J. Sweeney is Professor of Quantitative Analysis and Director of the Center for Productivity Improvement at the University of Cincinnati. Born in Des Moines, Iowa, he earned a BSBA degree from Drake University, graduating summa cum laude. He received his MBA and DBA degrees from Indiana University where he was an NDEA Fellow. Since receiving his doctorate in 1971, Professor Sweeney has spent all but 2 years at the University of Cincinnati. During 1978–79, he spent a year working in the management science group at Procter & Gamble; during 1981–82, he was a visiting professor at Duke University. Professor Sweeney has served as Head of the Department of Quantitative Analysis and as Associate Dean at the University of Cincinnati.

Professor Sweeney has published over 30 articles and monographs in the general area of management science. The National Science Foundation, IBM, Procter & Gamble, Federated Department Stores, Kroger, and Cincinnati Gas & Electric have funded his research, which has been published in *Managment Science, Operations Research, Mathematical Programming, Decision Sciences,* and other journals.

Professor Sweeney has coauthored six textbooks in the areas of statistics, management science, linear programming, and production and operations management.

THOMAS A. WILLIAMS.   Thomas A. Williams is Professor of Management Science in the College of Business at Rochester Institute of Technology. Born in Elmira, New York, he earned his B.S. degree at Clarkson University. He did his graduate work at Rensselaer Polytechnic Institute, where he received his M.S. and Ph.D. degrees.

Before joining the College of Business at RIT, Professor Williams served for 7 years as a faculty member in the College of Business Administration at the University of Cincinnati, where he developed the undergraduate program in Information Systems and then served as its coordinator. At RIT he was the first chairman of the Decision Sciences Department. He teaches courses in management science and statistics, as well as more advanced cources in regression and decision analysis.

Professor Williams is the coauthor of seven textbooks in the areas of management science, statistics, production and operations management, and mathematics. He has been a consultant for numerous Fortune 500 companies and has worked on projects ranging from the use of elementary data analysis to the development of large-scale regression models. His current research focuses on the application of total quality management in an academic setting.

1

DATA AND STATISTICS

STATISTICS IN PRACTICE

Business Week

Business Week*
New York, New York

Business Week, published weekly by McGraw-Hill, Inc., is a well-known magazine that offers a variety of articles of interest to the business and economics community. In addition to feature articles on current topics, the magazine includes regular sections on International Business, Economic Analysis, Information Processing, and Science & Technology. The feature articles and regular sections help readers keep abreast of current developments and assess the impact of the developments on the business and economic future.

Most issues of *Business Week* provide an in-depth report on a topic of current interest. For instance, the September 5, 1994 issue contained a special report on database marketing, the October 24, 1994 issue contained a study on the best college and university business schools, and the March 27, 1995 issue contained data on America's most valuable companies and how they rank in terms of market value. Other features that attract reader interest are the annual executive compensation survey and the weekly *Business Week* Index that contains statistics on the state of the economy such as production indexes, stock prices, real estate loan values, and interest rates.

In addition to using statistics and statistical information in its magazine articles, *Business Week* collects and uses statistics to help manage its own business. For example, *Business Week* conducts a survey of its subscribers to learn about their personal profiles, reading habits, shopping

*Charlene Trentham, Research Manager at *Business Week,* provided this Statistics in Practice.

practices, lifestyles, and so on. Managers use statistical summaries generated from the survey to provide better service to subscribers and advertisers. For instance, the 1993 U.S. Subscriber Study indicated that 87% of *Business Week* subscribers own a personal computer and that 44% of the subscribers were planning to purchase a new personal computer within the next 12 months. Such statistics alert managers to the fact that subscribers should be interested in articles about personal computers. In addition, the results of the survey are made available to potential advertisers. The high percentage of subscribers indicating an intention to purchase a new personal computer within the next 12 months would be an incentive for personal computer manufacturers to consider advertising in *Business Week.*

In this chapter, we discuss the types of data available for statistical analysis and how the data are obtained. We then introduce descriptive statistics and statistical inference as two ways of converting data into meaningful and easily interpreted statistical information.

Business Week uses business and economic statistics in many of its articles.

● Frequently, we see the following kinds of statements in newspaper and magazine articles:

- Sales of new homes are occurring at a rate of 703,000 homes per year (*Business Week,* October 1994).
- Crude oil is averaging $17.37 per barrel (*British Petroleum Annual Report,* 1993).
- The unemployment rate has dropped to 5.9% (*Barron's,* October 10, 1994).

- The Dow Jones Industrial Average closed at 4510.79 (*The Wall Street Journal,* June 19, 1995).
- Stock funds account for 29% of investors' portfolios (*The American Association of Individual Investors Journal,* July 1993).
- Airlines have raised the round-trip discount fare to an average of $270 per trip (*USA Today,* March 30, 1995).

The numerical facts in the preceding statements (703,000, $17.37, 5.9%, 4510.79, 29%, and $270) are called statistics. Thus, in everyday usage, the term "statistics" refers to numerical facts. However, the field or subject of statistics involves much more than numerical facts. In a broad sense, *statistics* is the art and science of collecting, analyzing, presenting, and interpreting data. Particularly in business and economics, a major reason for collecting, analyzing, presenting, and interpreting data is to give managers and decision makers a better understanding of the business and economic environment and thus enable them to make more informed and better decisions. In this text, we emphasize the use of statistics for business and economic decision making.

Chapter 1 begins with some illustrations of the application of statistics in business and economics. A discussion of how data, the raw material of statistics, are acquired and used follows. The use of data in developing descriptive statistics and in making statistical inferences is described in Sections 1.4 and 1.5.

1.1   APPLICATIONS IN BUSINESS AND ECONOMICS

In today's global business and economic environment, vast amounts of statistical information are available. The most successful managers and decision makers are the ones who can understand the information and use it effectively. In this section, we provide examples that illustrate some of the uses of statistics for business and economics.

ACCOUNTING

Public accounting firms use statistical sampling procedures when conducting audits for their clients. For instance, suppose an accounting firm wants to determine whether or not the amount of accounts receivable shown on a client's balance sheet fairly represents the actual amount of accounts receivable. Usually the number of individual accounts receivable is so large that reviewing and validating every account would be too time-consuming and expensive. In such situations, it is common practice for the audit staff to select a subset of the accounts called a sample. After reviewing the accuracy of the sampled accounts, the auditors draw a conclusion as to whether or not the accounts receivable amount shown on the client's balance sheet is acceptable.

FINANCE

Financial advisors use a variety of statistical information to guide their investment recommendations. In the case of stocks, the advisors review a variety of financial data including price–earnings ratios and dividend yields. By comparing the information for an individual stock with information about the stock market averages, a financial advisor can begin to draw a conclusion as to whether an individual stock is over- or undervalued. For example, *Barron's* (October 10, 1994) reported that the average price–earnings ratio for the 30 stocks in the Dow Jones Industrial Average was 20.1. On the same day, Philip Morris had a price–earnings ratio of 14. In this case, the statistical information on price–earnings ratios showed that Philip Morris had a lower price in comparison to its earnings than the average for the Dow Jones stocks. A financial advisor therefore might have concluded that Philip Morris was currently underpriced. This and other information about Philip Morris would help the advisor make buy, sell, or hold recommendations for the stock.

MARKETING

Electronic scanners at retail checkout counters are being used to collect data for a variety of marketing research applications. For example, data suppliers such as A. C. Nielsen and Information Resources, Inc. purchase point-of-sale scanner data from grocery stores, process the data, and then sell statistical summaries of the data to manufacturers. In 1992, manufacturers spent an average of $310,000 per product category to obtain this type of scanner data (Scanner Data User Survey, Mercer Management Consulting, Inc., August 1993). Manufacturers also purchase data and statistical summaries on promotional activities such as special pricing and the use of in-store displays. Product brand managers can review the scanner statistics and the promotional activity statistics to gain a better understanding of the relationship between promotional activities and sales. Such analyses are helpful in establishing future marketing strategies for the various products.

PRODUCTION

With today's emphasis on quality, quality control is an important application of statistics in production. A variety of statistical quality control charts are used to monitor the output of a production process. In particular, an x-bar chart is used to monitor the average output. Suppose, for example, that a machine is being used to fill containers with 12 ounces of a well-known soft drink. Periodically, a sample of containers is selected and the average contents of the sample containers determined. This average, or x-bar value, is plotted on an x-bar chart. A plotted value above the chart's upper control limit indicates overfilling and a plotted value below the chart's lower control limit indicates underfilling. Thus, the x-bar chart shows when adjustments are necessary to correct the production process. The process is termed "in control" and allowed to continue as long as the plotted x-bar values are between the chart's upper and lower control limits.

ECONOMICS

Economists are frequently asked to provide forecasts about the future of the economy or some aspect of it. They use a variety of statistical information in making such forecasts. For instance, in forecasting inflation rates, economists use statistical information on such indicators as the Producer Price Index, the unemployment rate, and the manufacturing capacity utilization. Often these statistical indicators are entered into computerized forecasting models that predict inflation rates.

Applications of statistics such as those described in this section are an integral part of this text. Such examples provide an overview of the breadth of statistical applications. To supplement these examples, we have asked practitioners in the fields of business and economics to provide chapter-opening Statistics in Practice articles that serve to introduce the material covered in each chapter. The Statistics in Practice applications show the importance of statistics in a wide variety of decision-making situations.

1.2 DATA

Data are the facts and figures that are collected, analyzed, and summarized for presentation and interpretation. Together, the data collected in a particular study are referred to as the *data set* for the study. Table 1.1 is a data set for 25 shadow stocks. The term "shadow" is used to indicate that the stocks are for small to medium-size firms that are not followed closely by the major brokerage houses. The data set in Table 1.1 was provided by the American Association of Individual Investors (*AAII Journal*, April 1994).

ELEMENTS, VARIABLES, AND OBSERVATIONS

The *elements* are the entities on which data are collected. For the data set in Table 1.1, each individual stock is an element. With 25 stocks, there are 25 elements in the data set.

A *variable* is a characteristic of interest for the elements. The data set in Table 1.1 has the following five variables:

- *Exchange:* Where the stock is traded—NYSE (New York Stock Exchange), AMEX (American Stock Exchange), and OTC (over the counter).
- *Ticker Symbol:* The abbreviation used to identify the stock on the exchange listing.
- *Annual Sales:* Total sales for the most recent 12 months in millions of dollars.

TABLE 1.1 A Data Set for 25 Shadow Stocks

Stock	Exchange	Ticker Symbol	Annual Sales ($ Million)	Earnings Per Share ($)	Price-Earnings Ratio
Alcide Corp.	OTC	ALCD	7.4	.52	22.1
ARX Inc.	NYSE	ARX	54.7	.32	14.1
Bowmar	AMEX	BOM	20.7	.10	32.5
Cache Inc.	OTC	CACH	86.6	.25	28.5
CCA Industries	OTC	CCAM	44.3	.32	25.4
Concord Fabrics	AMEX	CIS	197.3	1.54	6.2
DBA Systems	OTC	DBAS	30.6	.38	16.1
Diodes Inc.	AMEX	DIO	26.4	.34	27.6
Gen Magnaplate	OTC	GMCC	10.4	.48	11.7
Harlyn Products	AMEX	HRN	32.0	.40	11.3
Kimmins Environmental	NYSE	KVN	81.9	.21	13.1
Koss Corp.	OTC	KOSS	36.1	.89	14.6
MagneTech Corp.	OTC	MTCC	22.7	.21	28.0
Media Logic Inc.	AMEX	TST	21.2	.79	5.1
Max & Erma's	OTC	MAXE	43.5	.38	23.7
MHI Group Inc.	NYSE	MH	16.7	.95	8.4
Par Technology	NYSE	PTC	81.2	.32	25.0
Penril DataComm	OTC	PNRL	69.6	.26	25.0
Reflectone Inc.	OTC	RFTN	63.1	.86	12.9
Scientific Tech.	OTC	STIZ	17.3	.46	28.8
Stage II Apparel	AMEX	SA	64.1	.23	21.2
Trans Leasing	OTC	TLII	25.5	.13	27.9
Uni-Marts Inc.	AMEX	UNI	336.9	.48	13.0
Western Beef	OTC	BEEF	273.7	.78	12.2
Zygo Corp.	OTC	ZIGO	23.5	.27	28.7

SOURCE: *American Association of Individual Investors Journal,* April 1994.

- *Earnings Per Share:* Net income for the most recent 12 months divided by the number of common shares outstanding.
- *Price-Earnings Ratio:* Market price per share divided by the most recent 12 months' earnings per share.

Data are obtained by collecting measurements on each variable for every element in the study. The set of measurements collected for a particular element is called an *observation.* Referring to Table 1.1, we see that the first element (Alcide Corp.) provides the observation OTC, ALCD, 7.4, .52, and 22.1. With 25 elements, there are 25 observations; with five variables for each observation, there are 125 data values in the data set.

QUALITATIVE AND QUANTITATIVE DATA

The statistical analysis that is appropriate for a particular variable depends on whether the data for the variable are qualitative or quantitative. *Qualitative data* are labels or names used to identify an attribute of each element. For example, referring to the shadow stocks in Table 1.1, we see that the data values for the exchange variable (NYSE, AMEX, and OTC) are labels used to identify where the stocks are traded. Hence, the data are qualitative and exchange is referred to as a qualitative variable. Ticker symbol is also a qualitative variable, with the data values ALCD, ARX, BOM, and so on being the labels used to identify the corresponding stock.

Quantitative data indicate either how much or how many. For example, the data values for annual sales in Table 1.1 are quantitative, with the values 7.4, 54.7, 20.7, and so on indicating how many millions of dollars of sales the company had during the most recent 12-month period. Since the data are quantitative, annual sales is referred to as a quantitative variable. Earnings per share and price–earnings ratio are also quantitative variables.

Quantitative data are always numeric, but qualitative data may be *either numeric or nonnumeric.* For example, to facilitate data collection and prepare the data for easy entry into a computer database, we might decide to use numeric codes for exchange, letting 1 denote a stock traded on the New York Stock exchange, 2 denote a stock traded on the American Stock exchange, and 3 denote a stock traded over the counter. In this case, the numeric values are the labels or codes used to identify where the stock is traded. The data are qualitative and exchange is a qualitative variable even though the data are shown as numeric values. Social security numbers such as 310-22-7924 consist of numeric values. However, social security numbers are qualitative because the data are actually labels that identify particular individuals. Automobile license plate numbers such as CWX802 and product part codes such as A132 are qualitative data, with the combined numeric and nonnumeric entries being the labels used to identify the particular automobile or particular part.

For purposes of statistical analysis, the important distinguishing difference between qualitative and quantitative data is that *ordinary arithmetic operations are meaningful only with quantitative data.* For example, with quantitative data, the data values can be added together and then divided by the number of data values to compute the average value for the data. This average is meaningful and usually easily interpreted. However, when qualitative data are recorded as numeric values, such arithmetic operations provide meaningless results.

CROSS-SECTIONAL AND TIME SERIES DATA

For purposes of statistical analysis, distinguishing between cross-sectional data and time series data is important. *Cross-sectional data* are data collected at the same or

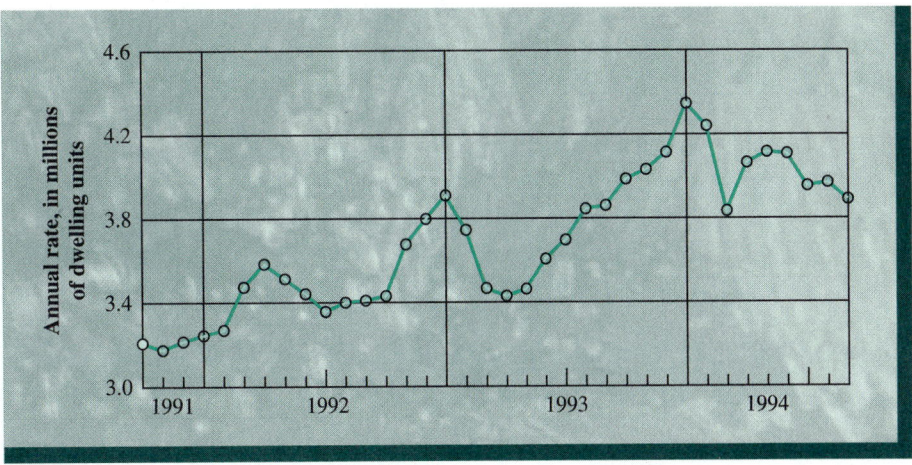

FIGURE 1.1 Time Series Data on Existing Single-Family Home Sales, September 1991 through August 1994
SOURCE: *The Wall Street Journal,* September 2, 1994

approximately the same point in time. The data in Table 1.1 are cross-sectional because they describe the five variables for the 25 shadow stocks at the same point in time, April 1994. *Time series data* are data collected over several time periods. For example, Figure 1.1 is a graph of data for existing single-family home sales over the three-year period from September 1991 to August 1994. There are 36 monthly data values for this time series. Most of the statistical methods presented in this text apply to cross-sectional data. Chapters 17 (Index Numbers) and 18 (Forecasting) provide statistical methods that apply to time series data.

NOTES AND COMMENTS

An observation is the set of measurements obtained for each element in a data set. Hence, the number of observations is always the same as the number of elements. The number of measurements obtained on each element is equal to the number of variables. Hence, the total number of data values in a data set is the number of elements multiplied by the number of variables.

1.3 DATA SOURCES

Data can be collected from existing sources or obtained through surveys and experimental studies designed to obtain new data.

EXISTING SOURCES

In some cases, data needed for a particular application may already exist within a firm or organization. All companies maintain a variety of databases about their employees, customers, and business operations. Data on employee salaries, ages, and years of service can usually be obtained from internal personnel records. Data on sales, advertising expenditures, distribution costs, inventory levels, and production quantities are generally available from other internal record-keeping systems. Many companies

TABLE 1.2 Examples of Data Available from Internal Company Records

Source	Some of the Data Typically Available
Employee records	Name, address, social security number, salary, number of vacation days, number of sick days, and bonus
Production records	Part or product number, quantity produced, direct labor cost, and materials cost
Inventory records	Part or product number, number of units on hand, reorder level, economic order quantity, and discount schedule
Sales records	Product number, sales volume, sales volume by region, and sales volume by customer type
Credit records	Customer name, address, phone number, credit limit, and accounts receivable balance
Customer profile	Age, gender, income level, household size, address, and preferences

also maintain detailed data about their customers. Table 1.2 shows some of the data commonly available from the internal information sources of most companies.

Substantial amounts of business and economic data are available from organizations that specialize in collecting and maintaining data. Companies obtain access to these external data sources through leasing arrangements or by purchase. Dun & Bradstreet and Dow Jones & Company are two firms that provide extensive business database services to clients. A. C. Nielsen and Information Resources, Inc. have built $100-million businesses collecting and processing retail checkout-counter scanner data that they sell to product manufacturers.

Government agencies are another important source of existing data. For instance, the U.S. Department of Labor maintains considerable data on employment rates, wage rates, size of the labor force, and union membership. Table 1.3 lists other selected governmental agencies and some of the data they provide. Data are also available from a variety of industry associations and special-interest organizations. The Travel Industry Association of America maintains travel-related information such as the number of tourists and travel expenditures by state. Such data would be of interest to firms and individuals in the travel industry. The Graduate Management Admission Council maintains data on student characteristics and graduate management education programs. Most of the data from sources such as these are available to qualified users at a modest cost.

TABLE 1.3 Examples of Data Available from Selected Government Agencies

Government Agency	Some of the Data Available
Bureau of the Census	Population data and its distribution, data on number of households and their distribution, data on household income and its distribution
Federal Reserve Board	Data on the money supply, installment credit, exchange rates, and discount rates
Office of Management and Budget	Data on revenue, expenditures, and debt of the federal government
Department of Commerce	Data on business activity—value of shipments by industry, level of profits by industry, and data on growing and declining industries

STATISTICAL STUDIES

Sometimes data are not readily available from existing sources. If the data are considered necessary, a statistical study can be conducted to obtain them. Such statistical studies can be classified as either *experimental* or *observational.*

In an experimental study, the variables of interest are first identified. Then one or more factors in the study are controlled so that data can be obtained about how the factors influence the variables. For example, a pharmaceutical firm might be interested in conducting an experiment to learn about how a new drug affects blood pressure. Blood pressure is the variable of interest in the study. The new drug is the factor that influences the blood pressure. To obtain data about the effect of the new drug, a sample of individuals will be selected. The dosage level of the new drug will be controlled, with different groups of individuals being given different dosage levels. Data on blood pressure will be collected for each group. Statistical analysis of the experimental data will help determine how the new drug affects blood pressure.

In nonexperimental, or observational, statistical studies, no attempt is made to control or influence the variables of interest. A survey is perhaps the most common type of observational study. For instance, in a personal interview survey, research questions are first identified. Then a questionnaire is designed and administered to a sample of individuals. Data are obtained about the research variables but no attempt is made to control the factors that influence the variables. Some restaurants use observational studies to obtain data about their customers' opinions of the quality of food, service, atmosphere, and so on. A questionnaire used by the Lobster Pot Restaurant in Redington Shores, Florida, is shown in Figure 1.2. Note that the customers completing the

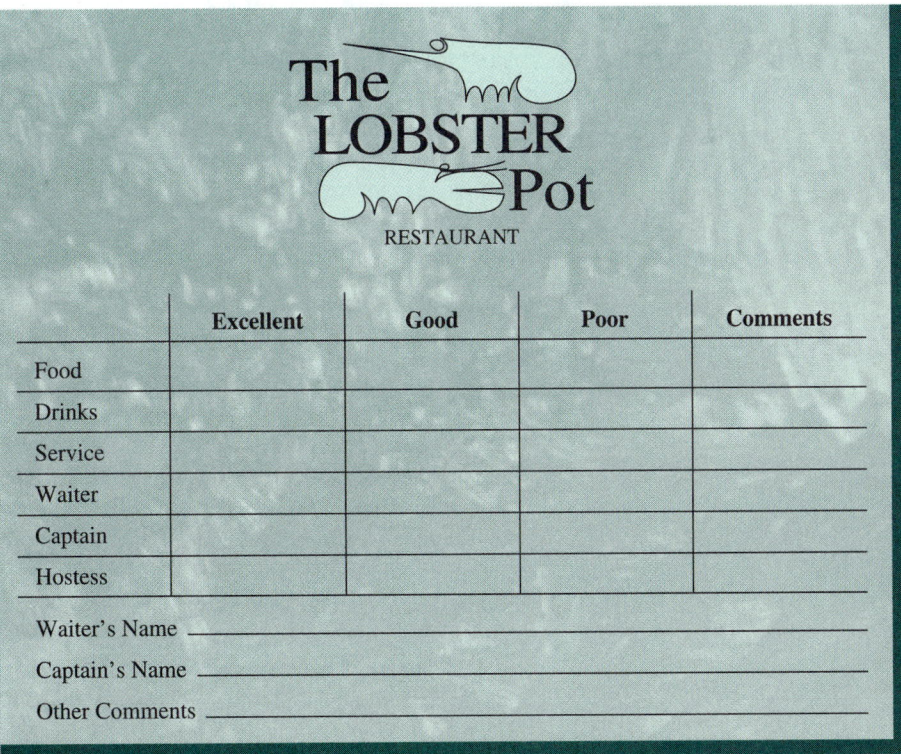

FIGURE 1.2 Customer Opinion Questionnaire Used by the Lobster Pot Restaurant, Redington Shores, Florida (*used with permission*)

questionnaire are asked to provide ratings for six variables: food, drinks, service, waiter, captain, and hostess. The response categories of excellent, good, and poor provide data that enable Lobster Pot's managers to assess the quality of the restaurant's operation.

Managers wanting to use data and statistical analyses as an aid to decision making must be aware of the time and cost required to obtain the data. The use of existing data sources is desirable when data must be obtained in a relatively short period of time. If the data are not readily available from an existing source, the additional time and cost involved in obtaining the data must be taken into account. In all cases, the decision maker should consider the contribution of the statistical analysis to the decision-making process. The cost of data acquisition and the subsequent statistical analysis should not exceed the savings generated by using the information to make a better decision.

DATA-ACQUISITION ERRORS

Managers should always be aware of the possibility of data errors in statistical studies. Using erroneous data could be worse than not using the data and statistical information at all. An error in data acquisition occurs whenever the data value obtained is not equal to the true or actual value that would have been obtained with a correct procedure. Such errors can occur in a number of ways. For example, an interviewer might make a recording error, such as writing the age of a 24-year-old person as 42, or the person answering an interview question might misinterpret the question and make an incorrect response.

Experienced data analysts take great care in collecting and recording data to ensure that errors are not made. Special procedures can be used to check for internal consistency of the data. For instance, such procedures would indicate that the analyst should review data for a respondent who is shown to be 22 years of age but who reports 20 years of work experience. Data analysts also review data for unusually large and small values, called outliers, which are candidates for possible data errors. In Chapter 3, we present some of the methods statisticians use to identify outliers.

The point of this discussion is to alert users of data to the fact that errors can occur during data acquisition. Blindly using any data that happen to be available or using data that were acquired with little care can lead to poor and misleading information. However, taking steps to acquire accurate data can help ensure reliable and valuable decision-making information.

1.4   DESCRIPTIVE STATISTICS

Most of the statistical information in newspapers, magazines, reports, and other publications consists of data that are summarized and presented in a form that is easy for the reader to understand. Such summaries of data, which may be tabular, graphical, or numerical, are referred to as *descriptive statistics*.

Refer again to the data set in Table 1.1 where 25 shadow stocks are listed. Methods of descriptive statistics can be used to provide summaries of the information in this data set. For example, a tabular summary of the data for the exchange variable is shown in Table 1.4. A graphical summary of the same data is shown in Figure 1.3. The purpose of tabular and graphical summaries such as these is to make the data easier to interpret. Referring to Table 1.4 and Figure 1.3, we can see easily that the majority of the stocks in the data set are traded over the counter. On a percentage basis, 56% of the stocks are traded over the counter, 28% are traded on the American Stock Exchange, and only 16% are traded on the New York Stock Exchange.

TABLE 1.4 Frequencies and Percentages for the
Exchange of 25 Shadow Stocks

Exchange	Frequency	Percent
New York Stock Exchange	4	16
American Stock Exchange	7	28
Over the counter	14	56
Total	25	100

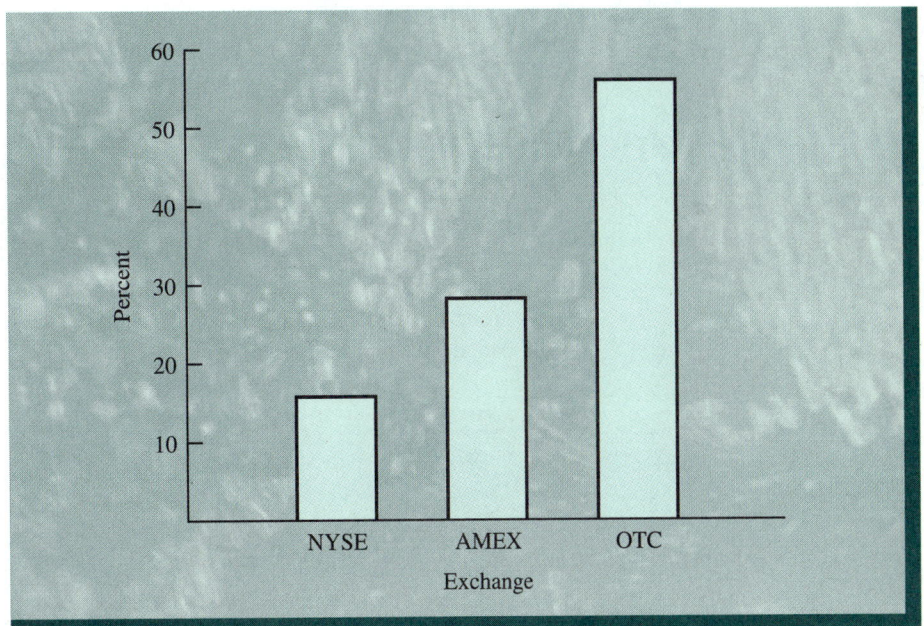

FIGURE 1.3 Bar Graph of Exchange for Shadow Stocks

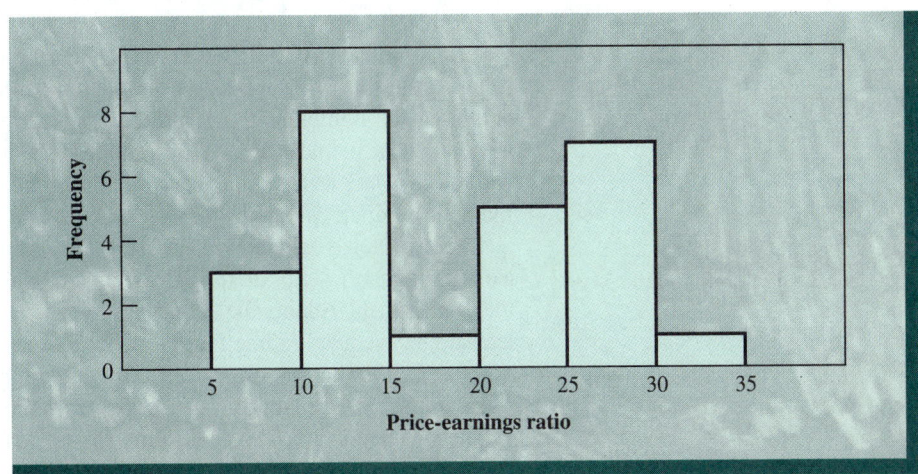

FIGURE 1.4 Price–Earnings Ratio for 25 Shadow Stocks in Table 1.1

A graphical summary of the data on price–earnings ratio for the stocks in Table 1.1 is provided by the histogram in Figure 1.4. From the histogram, it is easy to see that the price–earnings ratios range from 5 to 35, with the highest concentrations being between 10 and 15 and between 25 and 30.

In addition to tabular and graphical displays, numerical descriptive statistics are used to summarize data. The most common numerical descriptive statistic is the *average* or *mean*. Using the data on annual sales in Table 1.1, we can compute the average annual sales by adding the annual sales for all 25 stocks and dividing the sum by 25. Doing so tells us that the average annual sales for the stocks is $67.5 million. This average is taken as a measure of the central value, or central location, of the data.

In recent years there has been a growing interest in statistical methods that can be used for developing and presenting descriptive statistics. Chapters 2 and 3 are devoted to the tabular, graphical, and numerical methods of descriptive statistics.

1.5   STATISTICAL INFERENCE

In many situations, data are sought for a large group of elements (individuals, stocks, voters, households, products, customers, and so on). Because of time, cost, and other considerations, data are collected from only a small portion of the group. The larger group of elements in a particular study is called the *population* and the smaller group is called the *sample*. Formally, we use the following definitions.

POPULATION
A *population* is the set of all elements of interest in a particular study.

SAMPLE
A *sample* is a subset of the population.

A major contribution of statistics is that data from a sample can be used to make estimates and test hypotheses about the characteristics of a population. This process is referred to as *statistical inference*.

As an example of statistical inference, let us consider the study conducted by Norris Electronics. Norris manufactures a high-intensity lightbulb that is used in a variety of electrical products. In an attempt to increase the useful life of the lightbulb, the product design group has developed a new lightbulb filament. In this case, the population is defined as all lightbulbs that could be produced with the new filament. To evaluate the advantages of the new filament, a sample of 200 new-filament bulbs was manufactured and tested. Data were collected on the number of hours each lightbulb operated before filament burnout. The data from the sample are reported in Table 1.5.

Suppose Norris is interested in using the sample data to make an inference about the average hours of useful life for the population of all lightbulbs that could be produced with the new filament. Adding the 200 values in Table 1.5 and dividing the total by 200 provides the sample average lifetime for the lightbulbs: 76 hours. We can use this sample result to estimate that the average lifetime for the lightbulbs in the population is 76 hours. Figure 1.5 is a graphical summary of the statistical inference process for Norris Electronics.

Whenever statisticians use a sample to make an inference about a characteristic of a population, they provide a statement of the quality, or precision, associated with the inference. For the Norris example, the statistician might state that the estimate of the

TABLE 1.5 Hours until Burnout for a Sample of 200 Lightbulbs for Norris Electronics

107	73	68	97	76	79	94	59	98	57
54	65	71	70	84	88	62	61	79	98
66	62	79	86	68	74	61	82	65	98
62	116	65	88	64	79	78	79	77	86
74	85	73	80	68	78	89	72	58	69
92	78	88	77	103	88	63	68	88	81
75	90	62	89	71	71	74	70	74	70
65	81	75	62	94	71	85	84	83	63
81	62	79	83	93	61	65	62	92	65
83	70	70	81	77	72	84	67	59	58
78	66	66	94	77	63	66	75	68	76
90	78	71	101	78	43	59	67	61	71
96	75	64	76	72	77	74	65	82	86
66	86	96	89	81	71	85	99	59	92
68	72	77	60	87	84	75	77	51	45
85	67	87	80	84	93	69	76	89	75
83	68	72	67	92	89	82	96	77	102
74	91	76	83	66	68	61	73	72	76
73	77	79	94	63	59	62	71	81	65
73	63	63	89	82	64	85	92	64	73

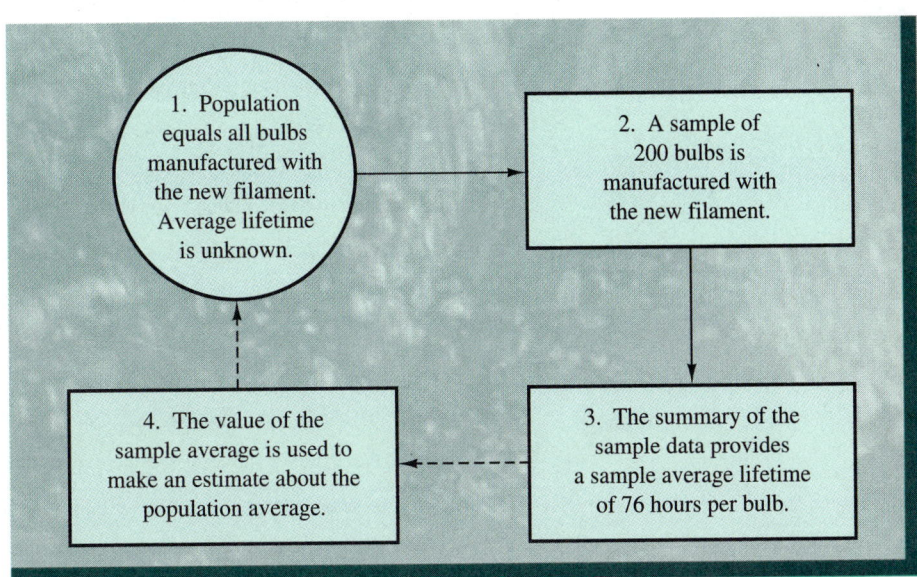

FIGURE 1.5 The Process of Statistical Inference for the Norris Electronics Example

average lifetime for the population of new lightbulbs is 76 hours with a precision of ±4 hours. Thus, 72 hours to 80 hours is an interval estimate of the average lifetime. The statistician can also state how confident he or she is that the interval from 72 hours to 80 hours contains the population average.

SUMMARY

In everyday usage, the term "statistics" refers to numerical facts. However, the field of statistics requires a broader definition of statistics as the art and science of collecting, analyzing, presenting, and interpreting data. Nearly every college student majoring in business or economics is required to take a course in statistics. We began the chapter by describing typical statistical applications for business and economics.

Data are the facts and figures that are collected, analyzed, presented, and interpreted. For purposes of statistical analysis, data are classified as either qualitative or quantitative. Qualitative data consist of labels or names that are used to identify an attribute of an element. Qualitative data may be numeric or nonnumeric. Quantitative data are always numeric and indicate how much or how many for the variable of interest. Ordinary arithmetic operations are meaningful only if the data are *quantitative*. Therefore, statistical computations that are used for quantitative data are not appropriate for qualitative data.

In Sections 1.4 and 1.5 we introduced the topics of descriptive statistics and statistical inference. Descriptive statistics are the tabular, graphical, and numerical methods used to summarize data. Statistical inference is the process of using data obtained from a sample to make estimates or test claims about the characteristics of a population.

GLOSSARY

Data   The facts and figures that are collected, analyzed, and interpreted.

Data set   All the data collected in a particular study.

Elements   The entities on which data are collected.

Variable   A characteristic of interest for the elements.

Observation   The set of measurements obtained for a single element.

Qualitative data   Data that provide labels or names for a characteristic of an element. Qualitative data may be nonnumeric or numeric.

Qualitative variable   A variable with qualitative data.

Quantitative data   Data that indicate how much or how many of something. Quantitative data are always numeric.

Quantitative variable   A variable with quantitative data.

Cross-sectional data   Data collected at the same or approximately the same point in time.

Time series data   Data collected at several successive periods of time.

Descriptive statistics   Tabular, graphical, and numerical methods used to summarize data.

Population   The set of all elements of interest in a particular study.

Sample   A subset of the population.

Statistical inference   The process of using data obtained from a sample to make estimates or test hypotheses about the characteristics of a population.

EXERCISES

1. Discuss the differences between statistics as numerical facts and statistics as a discipline or field of study.

2. Table 1.6 shows the chief executive officer (CEO) compensation, industry classification, annual sales, and the CEO compensation versus shareholder return rating data for 10

TABLE 1.6 Executive Compensation for a Sample of 10 Companies

Company	CEO Compensation ($1000s)	Industry	Sales ($ millions)	CEO Compensation vs. Shareholder Return Rating
Bankers Trust	8866	Banking	7800	5
Coca Cola	3654	Beverages	13957	5
General Motors	1375	Automotive	138219	1
Intel	2184	Electronics	8782	3
Motorola	1736	Electronics	16963	4
Readers Digest	1708	Publishing	2821	4
Sears	3095	Retailing	50838	3
Sprint	1692	Telecomm.	11368	3
Walgreen	1145	Retailing	8498	2
Wells Fargo	2125	Banking	4854	2

SOURCE: Business Week, April 24, 1994.

companies (*Business Week*, April 24, 1994). A CEO compensation versus shareholder return rating of 1 indicates that the company is among the group of companies that have the best ratio of CEO compensation to shareholder return. A rating of 2 indicates that the company is similar to companies that have a very good, but not the best, ratio of CEO compensation to shareholder return. Companies with the worst ratio of CEO compensation to shareholder return have a rating of 5.

a. How many elements are in this data set?
b. How many variables are in this data set?
c. Which variables are qualitative and which variables are quantitative?

Self-Test

3. Refer to the data in Table 1.6 (*Business Week*, April 24, 1994).
   a. Compute the average compensation for the chief executive officers (CEOs).
   b. What percentage of the firms are in the banking industry?
   c. What percentage of the firms have a value of 3 on the CEO compensation versus shareholder return rating?

Self-Test

4. *Fortune* magazine provides data on how the 500 largest U.S. industrial corporations rank in terms of sales and profits. Data for a sample of *Fortune* 500 companies are given in Table 1.7 (*Fortune*, April 18, 1994).
   a. How many elements are in this data set?
   b. What is the population?
   c. Compute the average sales for the sample.
   d. Using the results in part (c), what is the estimate of the average sales for the population?

TABLE 1.7 A Sample of 10 *Fortune* 500 Companies

Company	Sales ($ millions)	Profit ($ millions)	Industry Code
Coastal	10136	115.1	18
CPC Intl.	6738	454.5	8
Del Monte	1555	(188.0)	8
J. M. Huber	1238	29.7	7
Ivax	645	84.7	19
Northrup	5063	96.0	1
Sealy	683	25.7	10
Unisys	7743	565.4	6
Westvaco	2330	104.3	9
Wrigley	1429	174.9	8

SOURCE: Fortune, April 18, 1994.

5. Consider the data set for the sample of *Fortune* 500 companies in Table 1.7 (*Fortune,* April 18, 1994).
   a. How many variables are in the data set?
   b. Which of the variables are qualitative and which are quantitative?
   c. Compute the average profit for the companies.
   d. What percentage of the companies earned a profit over $100 million?
   e. What percentage of the companies have an industry code of 8?

6. Columbia House provides CDs, tapes, and records to its mail-order club members. A Columbia House Music Survey conducted in 1992 asked new club members to complete an 11-question survey. Some of the questions asked were:
   a. How many albums (CDs, tapes, or records) have you bought in the last 12 months?
   b. Are you currently a member of a national mail-order book club? (Yes or No)
   c. What is your age?
   d. Including yourself, how many people (adults and children) are in your household?
   e. What kind of music are you interested in buying? (15 categories were listed, including hard rock, soft rock, adult contemporary, heavy metal, rap, and country.)

   Comment on whether each question provides qualitative or quantitative data.

7. A California state agency classifies worker occupations as professional, white collar, or blue collar. The data are recorded with 1 denoting professional, 2 denoting white collar, and 3 denoting blue collar. The variable is worker occupation. Is it a qualitative or quantitative variable?

8. A Bruskin-Goldring research poll asked 1000 people, "Where is the best place to meet a 'suitable companion'?" (*USA Today,* February 13, 1992) Response categories were religious gathering, friend's home, evening class, work, nightspot, or other.
   a. What was the sample size in this survey?
   b. Are the data qualitative or quantitative?
   c. Would it make more sense to use averages or percentages as a summary of the data in this survey?
   d. Nightspot was the least preferred choice, with 170 people selecting it as the best place to meet a "suitable companion." What percentage was reported for the nightspot category?

9. The Commerce Department reported that of 1994 applications for the Malcolm Baldrige National Quality Award, 23 were from large manufacturing firms, 18 were from large service firms, and 30 were from small businesses.
   a. Is type of business a qualitative or quantitative variable?
   b. What percentage of the applications came from small businesses?

10. State whether each of the following variables is qualitative or quantitative.
    a. Age   b. Gender   c. Class rank   d. Make of automobile
    e. Number of people favoring the death penalty

11. State whether each of the following variables is qualitative or quantitative.
    a. Annual sales
    b. Soft-drink size (small, medium, or large)
    c. Employee classification (GS1 through GS18)
    d. Earnings per share
    e. Method of payment (cash, check, credit card)

12. The Hawaii Visitors Bureau collects data on visitors to Hawaii. The following questions were among 16 asked in a questionnaire handed out to passengers during incoming airline flights in August 1994.
    1. This trip to Hawaii is my: 1st, 2nd, 3rd, 4th, etc.
    2. The primary reason for this trip is: (10 categories including vacation, convention, honeymoon)
    3. Where I plan to stay: (11 categories including hotel, apartment, relatives, camping)
    4. Total days in Hawaii

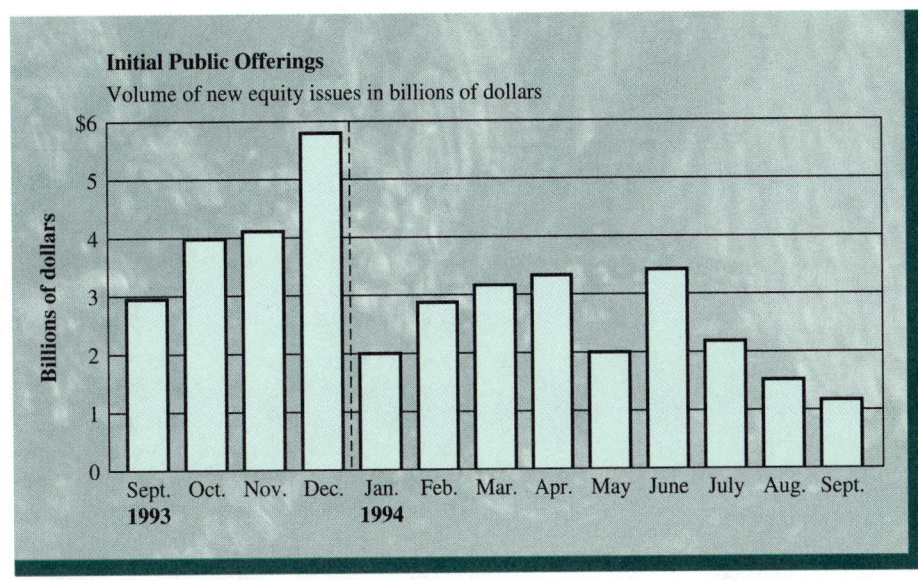

FIGURE 1.6   Initial Public Offerings Volume of new equity issues in billions of dollars.
SOURCE: *The Wall Street Journal,* October 19, 1994.

a. What is the population being studied?

b. Is the use of a questionnaire a good way to reach the population of passengers on incoming airline flights?

c. Comment on each of the four questions above in terms of whether it will provide qualitative or quantitative data.

Self-Test ➤

13. Figure 1.6 is a bar graph providing data on new stock offerings (initial public offerings) by companies over the period September 1993 through September 1994 (*The Wall Street Journal,* October 19, 1994).

a. Are the data qualitative or quantitative?

b. Are they time series or cross-sectional data?

c. What is the variable of interest?

d. Comment on the trend in initial public offerings over time. Would you expect to see an increase or a decrease in October 1994?

14. The following data set provides a snapshot of the recent financial performance of Whirlpool Corporation (*Barrons,* September 26, 1994).

	1990	1991	1992	1993
EARNINGS Per Share	$1.04	$2.45	$2.90	$3.19
REVENUES (billions)	$6.623	$6.770	$7.301	$7.533
NET INCOME (millions)	$72	$170	$205	$231
BOOK VALUE Per Share	$14.20	$8.71	$11.50	$12.31

a. How many variables are there?

b. Are the data qualitative or quantitative?

c. Are they cross-sectional or time series data? Why?

15. Refer again to the data in Table 1.7 for *Fortune* 500 companies (*Fortune,* April 18, 1994). Are they cross-sectional or time series data? Why?

16. The marketing group at your company has come up with a new diet soft drink that it claims will capture a large share of the young adult market.
   a. What data would you want to see before deciding to invest substantial funds in introducing the new product into the marketplace?
   b. How would you expect the data mentioned in (a) to be obtained?

17. A manager of a large corporation has recommended that a $10,000 raise be given to keep a valued subordinate from moving to another company. What internal and external sources of data might be used to decide whether such a salary increase is appropriate?

18. In a recent study of causes of death in men 60 years of age and older, a sample of 120 men indicated that 48 died as a result of some form of heart disease.
   a. Develop a descriptive statistic that can be used as an estimate of the percentage of men 60 years of age or older who die from some form of heart disease.
   b. Are the data on cause of death qualitative or quantitative?
   c. Discuss the role of statistical inference in this type of medical research.

19. The *Business Week* 1993 U.S. Subscriber Study collected data from a sample of 1597 subscribers. Sixty-six percent of the respondents indicated that their annual income was $50,000 or more and 51% reported having an American Express credit card.
   a. What is the population of interest in this study?
   b. Is annual income a qualitative or quantitative variable?
   c. Is ownership of an American Express card a qualitative or quantitative variable?
   d. Does this study involve cross-sectional or time series data?
   e. Describe any statistical inferences *Business Week* might make on the basis of the survey.

20. The 1992 Scanner Data User Survey of 52 companies provided the following findings (Mercer Management Consulting, Inc., August 5, 1993):

   • 56% percent of users are food manufacturers.
   • 12% percent of users are manufacturers of health and beauty aids.
   • On a scale of 1 (very dissatisfied) to 5 (very satisfied), the average level of overall satisfaction with scanner data was 3.6.

   a. Cite two descriptive statistics.
   b. Make an inference of the overall satisfaction in the population of all users of scanner data.
   c. Make an inference about the percentage of the population of all scanner data users that are manufacturers of health and beauty aids.

21. A seven-year medical research study (*Journal of the American Medical Association,* December 1984) reported that women whose mothers took the drug DES during pregnancy were *twice* as likely to develop tissue abnormalities that might lead to cancer as women whose mothers did not take the drug.
   a. This study involved the comparison of two populations. What were the populations?
   b. Do you suppose the data were obtained in a survey or an experiment?
   c. For the population of women whose mothers took the drug DES during pregnancy, a sample of 3980 women showed 63 developed tissue abnormalities that might lead to cancer. Provide a descriptive statistic that could be used to estimate the number of women out of 1000 in this population who have tissue abnormalities.
   d. For the population of women whose mothers did not take the drug DES during pregnancy, what is the estimate of the number of women out of 1000 who would be expected to have tissue abnormalities?
   e. Medical studies of disease and disease occurrence often use a relatively large sample (in this case, 3980). Why?

22. A firm is interested in testing the advertising effectiveness of a new television commercial. As part of the test, the commercial is shown on a 6:30 P.M. local news program in Denver,

Colorado. Two days later a market research firm conducts a telephone survey to obtain information on recall rates (percentage of viewers who recall seeing the commercial) and impressions of the commercial.

a. What is the population for this study?

b. What is the sample for this study?

c. Why would a sample be used in this situation? Explain.

23. The Nielsen organization conducts weekly surveys of television viewing throughout the United States. The Nielsen statistical ratings indicate the size of the viewing audience for each major network television program. Rankings of the television programs and of the viewing-audience market shares for each network are published each week.

a. What is the Nielsen organization attempting to measure?

b. What is the population?

c. Why would a sample be used for this situation?

d. What kinds of decisions or actions are based on the Nielsen studies?

24. A sample of midterm grades for five students showed the following results: 72, 65, 82, 90, 76. Which of the following statements are correct, and which should be challenged as being too generalized?

a. The average midterm grade for the sample of five students is 77.

b. The average midterm grade for all students who took the exam is 77.

c. An estimate of the average midterm grade for all students who took the exam is 77.

d. More than half of the students who take this exam will score between 70 and 85.

e. If five other students are included in the sample, their grades will be between 65 and 90.

2

DESCRIPTIVE STATISTICS I: TABULAR AND GRAPHICAL METHODS

CONTENTS

$\bar{x}$

STATISTICS IN PRACTICE ●●●●●●●●●●●●●●●●●●●●●●●●

Colgate-Palmolive Company*

New York, New York

The Colgate-Palmolive Company started as a small soap and candle shop in New York City in 1806. Today, Colgate-Palmolive products can be found around the world. The company has international operations in 55 countries, and annual sales are in excess of $7 billion. International operations exist in 70 countries, and annual sales are in excess of $7 billion. While best known for its traditional line of soaps, detergents, and toothpastes, subsidiary operations include Mennen, Softsoap, Hills Pet Foods, and others.

The Colgate-Palmolive Company uses statistics in its quality assurance program for home laundry detergent products. One concern is customer satisfaction with the quantity of detergent in a carton. Every carton in each size category is filled with the same amount of detergent by weight, but the volume of detergent is affected by the density of the detergent powder. For instance, if the powder density is on the heavy side, a smaller volume of detergent is needed to reach the carton's specified weight. As a result, the carton may appear to be underfilled when opened by the consumer.

To control the problem of heavy detergent powder, limits are placed on the acceptable range of powder density. Statistical samples are taken periodically and the density of each powder sample is measured. Data summaries are then provided for operating personnel so that corrective action can be taken if necessary to keep the density within the desired quality specifications.

A frequency distribution for the densities of 150 samples taken over a one-week period and a histogram are shown in the accompanying table and figure. Density levels above .40 are unacceptably high. The frequency distribution and histogram show that the operation is meeting its quality guidelines with all of the densities less than or equal to .40. Managers viewing these statistical summaries would be pleased with the quality of the detergent production process.

In this chapter, you will learn about tabular and graphical methods of descriptive statistics such as frequency distributions, bar graphs, histograms, stem-and-leaf displays, dot plots, crosstabulations, and others. The goal of these methods is to summarize data so that they can be easily understood and interpreted.

Frequency Distribution of Density Data

Density	Frequency
.29–.30	30
.31–.32	75
.33–.34	32
.35–.36	9
.37–.38	3
.39–.40	1
Total	150

Histogram of Density Data

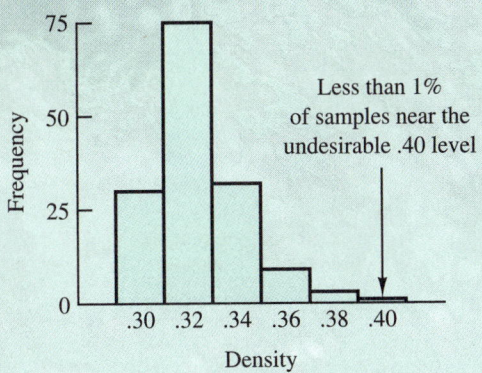

Less than 1% of samples near the undesirable .40 level

*William R. Fowle, Manager of Quality Assurance, Colgate-Palmolive Company, provided this Statistics in Practice.

Managers use statistical summaries to help maintain the quality of Colgate's leading products.

● As indicated in Chapter 1, data can be classified as either *qualitative* or *quantitative*. Qualitative data provide labels or names for categories of like items. Quantitative data indicate how much or how many.

The purpose of this chapter is to introduce several tabular and graphical procedures commonly used to summarize both qualitative and quantitative data. Tabular and graphical summaries of data can be found in annual reports, newspaper articles, and research studies. Everyone is exposed to these types of presentations. Hence, it is important to understand how they are prepared and to know how they should be interpreted. We begin with tabular and graphical methods for summarizing qualitative data. Methods for summarizing quantitative data are presented in Section 2.2. Methods for summarizing data involving the relationship between two variables are presented in Section 2.5.

2.1　SUMMARIZING QUALITATIVE DATA

FREQUENCY DISTRIBUTION

We begin the discussion of how tabular and graphical methods can be used to summarize qualitative data with the definition of a *frequency distribution*.

> **FREQUENCY DISTRIBUTION**
> A frequency distribution is a tabular summary of a set of data showing the frequency (or number) of items in each of several nonoverlapping classes.

The objective in developing a frequency distribution is to provide insights about the data that cannot be quickly obtained by looking only at the original data. To see how frequency distributions can be used with qualitative data, consider the data set in Table 2.1.

TABLE 2.1　Data from a Sample of 50 Computer Purchases

IBM	IBM	Packard Bell
Compaq	IBM	Packard Bell
Apple	Apple	Gateway 2000
Packard Bell	Compaq	Compaq
Gateway 2000	Packard Bell	Compaq
IBM	IBM	Apple
Apple	Compaq	IBM
Packard Bell	Apple	Packard Bell
Packard Bell	Apple	Compaq
Gateway 2000	Compaq	Packard Bell
Compaq	Gateway 2000	Compaq
Compaq	Packard Bell	Packard Bell
Apple	IBM	Compaq
Compaq	IBM	Apple
Apple	Gateway 2000	Packard Bell
Apple	Apple	Apple
Apple	IBM	

What company sells the most personal computers? Dataquest, Inc. reported that, on the basis of third-quarter 1994 sales, Apple, Compaq, Gateway 2000, IBM, and Packard Bell were the top five personal computer vendors (*The Wall Street Journal,* November 15, 1994). Assume that the data in Table 2.1 are from a sample of 50 purchases of personal computers from these five companies. The data shown are qualitative in that each entry is the name of the company supplying the personal computer.

To develop a frequency distribution for these data, we count the number of times each of the five companies appears in the data set. Apple appears 13 times, Compaq appears 12 times, Gateway 2000 appears five times, IBM appears nine times, and Packard Bell appears 11 times. These counts are summarized in the frequency distribution in Table 2.2.

The advantage of the frequency distribution is that it provides a data summary that is easier to understand than the original data as shown in Table 2.1. Using the frequency distribution, we see that Apple, Compaq, and Packard Bell are the very close first, second, and third choices for personal computers. IBM and Gateway 2000 lag behind in fourth and fifth places. The frequency distribution provides a data summary showing how the sample of 50 personal computer purchases are distributed across the five vendors.

TABLE 2.2 Frequency Distribution of Computer Purchases

Company	Frequency
Apple	13
Compaq	12
Gateway 2000	5
IBM	9
Packard Bell	11
Total	50

RELATIVE FREQUENCY AND PERCENT FREQUENCY DISTRIBUTIONS

A frequency distribution shows the number (frequency) of data items in each of several nonoverlapping classes. However, we are often interested in knowing the proportion, or percentage, of the data items in each class. The *relative frequency* of a class is the proportion of the total number of data items belonging to the class. For a data set with n observations, the relative frequency of each class is given by the following formula.

RELATIVE FREQUENCY

$$\text{Relative Frequency of a Class} = \frac{\text{Frequency of the Class}}{n} \qquad \text{(2.1)}$$

The *percent frequency* of a class is the relative frequency multiplied by 100.

A *relative frequency distribution* is a tabular summary of a set of data showing the relative frequency for each class. A *percent frequency distribution* is a tabular summary of a set of data showing the percent frequency for each class. Using (2.1), we can develop a relative frequency distribution for the personal computer data. In Table 2.3 we see that the relative frequency for Apple is 13/50 = .26, the relative frequency for

TABLE 2.3 Relative and Percent Frequency Distributions of Computer Purchases

Company	Relative Frequency	Percent Frequency
Apple	.26	26
Compaq	.24	24
Gateway 2000	.10	10
IBM	.18	18
Packard Bell	.22	22
Total	1.00	100

Compaq is 12/50 = .24, and so on. Computing the relative frequencies for the other computer manufacturers provides the relative frequency distribution in Table 2.3. Multiplying each of the relative frequencies by 100 provides the percent frequency distribution in Table 2.3. From these distributions, we see that on the basis of the sample data, 26% of the purchases were Apple, 24% of the purchases were Compaq, 22% of the purchases were Packard Bell, and so on. We can also note that 26% + 24% + 22% = 72% of the purchases were from the top three manufacturers.

BAR GRAPHS AND PIE CHARTS

A *bar graph* is a graphical device for depicting qualitative data that have been summarized in a frequency, relative frequency, or percent frequency distribution. On the horizontal axis of the graph, we specify the labels that are used for each of the classes. A frequency, relative frequency, or percent frequency scale can be used for the vertical axis of the graph. Then, using a bar of fixed width drawn above each class label, we extend the height of the bar until we reach the frequency, relative frequency, or percent frequency of the class as indicated by the vertical axis. The bars are separated to emphasize the fact that each class is a separate category. Figure 2.1 is a bar graph of the frequency distribution for the 50 computer purchases. Note how the graphical presentation shows Apple, Compaq, and Packard Bell to be the most preferred brands.

The pie chart is a commonly used graphical device for presenting relative frequency distributions for qualitative data. To draw a pie chart, we first draw a circle; then use the relative frequencies to subdivide the circle into sectors, or parts, that correspond to the relative frequency for each class. For example, since there are 360 degrees in a circle and since Apple has a relative frequency of .26, the sector of the pie chart labeled Apple should consist of .26 × 360 = 93.6 degrees. Similar calculations for the other classes yield the pie chart in Figure 2.2. The numerical values shown for each sector can be frequencies, relative frequencies, or percentages.

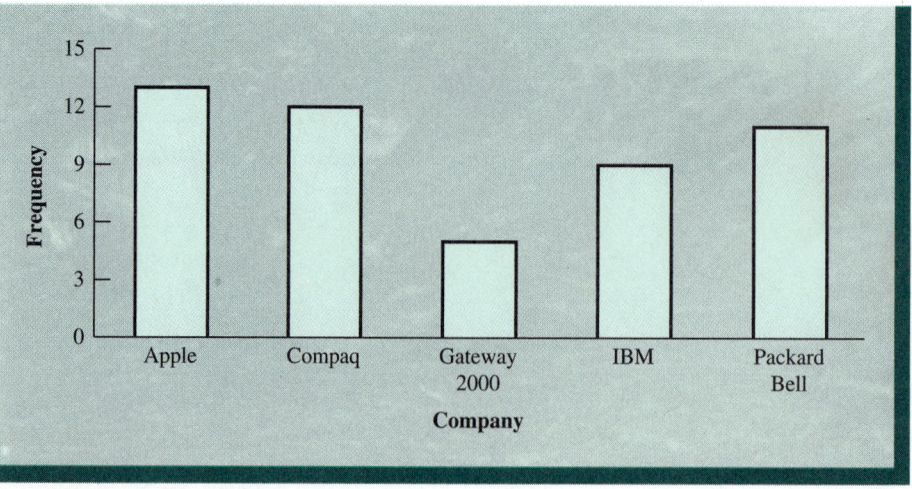

FIGURE 2.1   Bar Graph of Computer Purchases

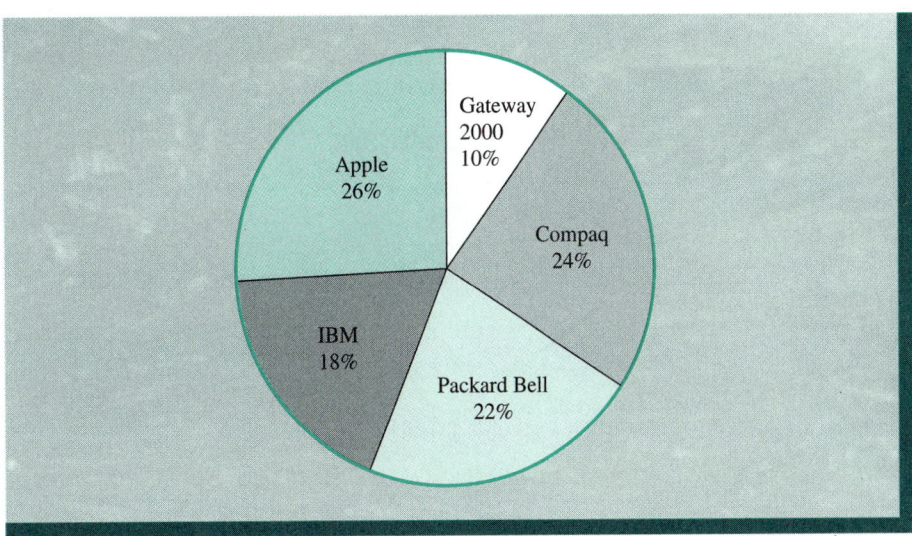

FIGURE 2.2 Pie Chart of Computer Purchases

NOTES AND COMMENTS

1. Often the number of classes in a frequency distribution is the same as the number of categories found in the data, as is the case for the computer purchase data in this section. The data involve only five computer companies, and a separate frequency distribution class was defined for each one. If the data included all types of personal computers, there would be more models with small numbers of purchases. In such cases the categories with smaller frequencies can be grouped into an aggregate class called "other." Most statisticians recommend that from five to 20 classes be used in a frequency distribution; classes with smaller frequencies should normally be grouped.

2. The sum of the frequencies in any frequency distribution always equals the total number of items in the data set. The sum of the relative frequencies in any relative frequency distribution always equals 1.00 and the sum of the percentages in a percent frequency distribution always equals 100.

TABLE 2.4 Exercise 2

Class	Relative Frequency
A	.22
B	.18
C	.40
D	

EXERCISES

METHODS

1. The response to a question has three alternatives: A, B, and C. A sample of 120 responses provides 60 A, 24 B, and 36 C. Show the frequency and relative frequency distributions.

2. A partial relative frequency distribution is given in Table 2.4.
   a. What is the relative frequency of class D?
   b. The total sample size is 200. What is the frequency of class D?
   c. Show the frequency distribution.
   d. Show the percent frequency distribution.

3. A questionnaire provides 58 yes, 42 no, and 20 no-opinion answers.
   a. In the construction of a pie chart, how many degrees would be in the section of the pie showing the yes answers?

b. How many degrees would be in the section of the pie showing the no answers?

c. Construct a pie chart.

d. Construct a bar graph.

APPLICATIONS

4. According to Ward's Automotive Reports, five of the 10 top-selling vehicles in the United States are trucks (*Business Week,* December 5, 1994). The five best-selling trucks in 1994 were Chevy C/K pickup, Dodge Caravan, Ford Explorer, Ford F-Series pickup, and Ford Ranger. Data for a sample of 50 recent purchases follow.

C/K pickup	F-Series pickup	C/K pickup	F-Series pickup	Ford Explorer
Dodge Caravan	C/K pickup	C/K pickup	C/K pickup	Dodge Caravan
Ford Ranger	Dodge Caravan	Ford Ranger	Dodge Caravan	F-Series pickup
C/K pickup	C/K pickup	C/K pickup	F-Series pickup	F-Series pickup
Ford Explorer	F-Series pickup	Ford Ranger	F-Series pickup	Ford Ranger
C/K pickup	F-Series pickup	Dodge Caravan	F-Series pickup	C/K pickup
Ford Ranger	Ford Explorer	F-Series pickup	Ford Explorer	F-Series pickup
F-Series pickup	C/K pickup	Dodge Caravan	C/K pickup	F-Series pickup
Ford Ranger	Ford Explorer	Ford Explorer	Ford Explorer	C/K pickup
F-Series pickup	Ford Ranger	Dodge Caravan	Ford Ranger	Ford Ranger

a. Are these qualitative or quantitative data?

b. Provide frequency and percent frequency distributions for the data.

c. Construct a bar graph and a pie chart for the data.

d. On the basis of the sample, what is America's favorite truck? Is it a close call?

5. Freshmen entering the College of Business at Eastern University were asked to indicate their preferred major. The data in Table 2.5 were obtained. Summarize the data by constructing:
a. Relative and percent frequency distributions. b. A bar graph c. A pie chart.

TABLE 2.5 Exercise 5

Major	Number
Management	55
Accounting	51
Finance	28
Marketing	82

6. The six best-selling fiction books in November 1994 are listed in Table 2.6 (*The Wall Street Journal,* November 23, 1994). Suppose a sample of book purchases in the Houston, Texas, area provided the following data for these six books.

W	D	W	C	I	P	C	W
P	I	W	W	P	C	P	C
L	C	P	C	W	W	P	W
W	C	I	P	L	D	D	
I	P	D	W	C	I	L	
C	D	L	D	I	L	I	

TABLE 2.6 Exercise 6

Book	Code
Celestine Prophecy	C
Debt of Honor	D
Insomnia	I
The Lottery Winner	L
Politically Correct	P
Wings	W

a. Construct frequency and percent frequency distributions for the data.

b. Rank the top six best-selling books.

c. What percentages of the sales are reflected by *Debt of Honor* and *The Lottery Winner?*

Self-Test ••••••••••▶

7. Leverock's Waterfront Steakhouse in Maderia Beach, Florida, uses a questionnaire to ask customers how they rate the server, food quality, cocktails, prices, and atmosphere at the restaurant. Each characteristic is rated on a scale of outstanding (O), very good (V), good (G), average (A), and poor (P). Use descriptive statistics to summarize the following data collected on food quality. What is your feeling about the food quality ratings at the restaurant?

G	O	V	G	A	O	V	O	V	G	O	V	A
V	O	P	V	O	G	A	O	O	O	G	O	V
V	A	G	O	V	P	V	O	O	G	O	O	V
O	G	A	O	V	O	O	G	V	A	G		

8. Position-by-position data for a sample of 55 members of the Baseball Hall of Fame in Cooperstown, New York, are given below (*Sports Illustrated,* April 6, 1992). Each data item

indicates the primary position played by the Hall of Famers: pitcher (P), catcher (H), 1st base (1), 2nd base (2), 3rd base (3), shortstop (S), left field (L), center field (C), and right field (R).

L	P	C	H	2	P	R	1	S	S	1	L	P	R	P
P	P	P	R	C	S	L	R	P	C	C	P	P	R	P
2	3	P	H	L	P	1	C	P	P	P	S	1	L	R
R	1	2	H	S	3	H	2	L	P					

a. Use frequency and relative frequency distributions to summarize the data for the nine positions.
b. What position provides the most Hall of Famers?
c. What position provides the fewest Hall of Famers?
d. What outfield position (L, C, or R) provides the most Hall of Famers?
e. Compare infielders (1, 2, 3, and S) to outfielders (L, C, and R).

9. Employees at Electronics Associates are on a flextime system; they can begin their working day at 7:00, 7:30, 8:00, 8:30, or 9:00 A.M. The following data represent a sample of the starting times selected by the employees.

7:00	8:30	9:00	8:00	7:30	7:30	8:30	8:30	7:30	7:00
8:30	8:30	8:00	8:00	7:30	8:30	7:00	9:00	8:30	8:00

Summarize the data by constructing:
a. A frequency distribution.   b. A percent frequency distribution.
c. A bar graph.   d. A pie chart.
e. What do the summaries tell you about employee preferences in the flextime system?

10. Students in the College of Business Administration at the University of Cincinnati are asked to fill out a course-evaluation questionnaire upon completion of their courses. It consists of a variety of questions that have a five-category response scale. One of the questions follows.

Compared to other courses that you have taken, what is the overall quality of the course you are now completing?

____	____	____	____	____
Poor	Fair	Good	Very Good	Excellent

A sample of 60 students completing a course in business statistics during the spring quarter of 1994 provided the following responses. To aid in computer processing of the questionnaire results, a numeric scale was used with 1 = poor, 2 = fair, 3 = good, 4 = very good, and 5 = excellent.

3	4	4	5	1	5	3	4	5	2	4	5	3	4	4
4	5	5	4	1	4	5	4	2	5	4	2	4	4	4
5	5	3	4	5	5	2	4	3	4	5	4	3	5	4
4	3	5	4	5	4	3	5	3	4	4	3	5	3	3

a. Comment on why these are qualitative data.
b. Provide a frequency distribution and a relative frequency distribution summary of the data.
c. Provide a bar graph and a pie chart summary of the data.
d. On the basis of your summaries, comment on the students' overall evaluation of the course.

2.2 SUMMARIZING QUANTITATIVE DATA

FREQUENCY DISTRIBUTION

As defined in Section 2.1, a frequency distribution is a tabular summary of a set of data showing the frequency (or number) of items in each of several nonoverlapping classes.

TABLE 2.7 Year-End Audit Times (in days)

12	14	19	18
15	15	18	17
20	27	22	23
22	21	33	28
14	18	16	13

This definition holds for quantitative as well as qualitative data. However, with quantitative data we have to be more careful in defining the nonoverlapping classes to be used in the frequency distribution.

For example, consider the quantitative data in Table 2.7. These data provide the time in days required to complete year-end audits for a sample of 20 clients of Sanderson and Clifford, a small public accounting firm. The three steps necessary to define the classes for a frequency distribution with quantitative data are:

1. Determine the number of nonoverlapping classes.
2. Determine the width of each class.
3. Determine the class limits.

Let us demonstrate these steps by developing a frequency distribution for the audit-time data in Table 2.7.

Number of Classes   Classes are formed by specifying ranges of data values that will be used to group the elements in the data set. As a general guideline, we recommend using between five and 20 classes. Data sets with a larger number of elements usually require a larger number of classes. Data sets with a smaller number of elements can often be summarized easily with as few as five or six classes. The goal is to use enough classes to show the variation in the data, but not so many classes that they contain only a few elements. Since the data set in Table 2.7 is relatively small ($n = 20$), we chose to develop a frequency distribution with five classes.

Width of the Classes   The second step in constructing a frequency distribution for quantitative data is to choose a width for the classes. As a general guideline, we recommend that the width be the same for each class. Thus the choices of the number of classes and the width of the classes are not independent decisions. A larger number of classes means a smaller class width and vice versa. To determine an approximate class width, we begin by identifying the largest and smallest data values in the data set. Then, once the desired number of classes has been specified, we can use the following expression to determine the approximate class width.

$$\text{Approximate Class Width} = \frac{\text{Largest Data Value} - \text{Smallest Data Value}}{\text{Number of Classes}} \quad \textbf{(2.2)}$$

The class width given by (2.2) can be adjusted to a convenient width based on the preference of the person developing the frequency distribution. For example, a computed class width of 9.28 might be adjusted to a class width of 10 simply because 10 is a more convenient class width to use in constructing a frequency distribution.

For the data set involving the year-end audit times, the largest value is 33 and the smallest value is 12. Since we have decided to summarize the data set with five classes, using (2.2) provides an approximate class width of $(33 - 12)/5 = 4.2$. We therefore decided to use a class width of five in the frequency distribution.

In practice, the number of classes and the appropriate class width are determined by trial and error. Once a possible number of classes is chosen, (2.2) is used to find the approximate class width. The process can be repeated for a different number of classes. Ultimately, the analyst uses judgment to determine the combination of number of classes and class width that provides the best means for summarizing the data.

For the audit-time data in Table 2.7, we have decided to use five classes, each with a width of five days, to summarize the data. The next task is to specify the class limits for each of the classes.

Class Limits   The *lower class limit* identifies the smallest possible data value assigned to the class. The *upper class limit* identifies the largest possible data value assigned to the class. Again, the analyst uses judgment, and a variety of acceptable class limits are possible.

For the data in Table 2.7, we defined the class limits as 10–14, 15–19, 20–24, 25–29, and 30–34. The smallest data value, 12, is included in the 10–14 class. The largest data value, 33, is included in the 30–34 class. For the 10–14 class, 10 is the lower class limit and 14 is the upper class limit. The difference between the lower class limits of adjacent classes provides the class width. Using the first two lower class limits of 10 and 15, we see that the class width is $15 - 10 = 5$.

The form of each lower class limit and each upper class limit depends on the number of places to the right of the decimal point contained in the data. Since the audit times in Table 2.7 are integer, integer class limits of 10–14, 15–19, and so on are acceptable. If the audit times were recorded in tenths of days, such as 12.3, 14.4, 19.3, and so on, the class limits would also be stated in tenths. In that case, class limits of 10.0–14.9, 15.0–19.9, 20.0–24.9, and so on would be appropriate. If the data were in hundredths, which is often the case with dollar-and-cents data, the class limits 10.00–14.99, 15.00–19.99, 20.00–24.99, and so on would be appropriate. Regardless of how the class limits are chosen, they should be defined in such a way that *each data value belongs to one and only one class*. For instance, class limits of 10–15, 15–20, and 20–25 are unacceptable for the audit-time data because the data values of 15 and 20 would be included in two different classes.

Once the number of classes, class width, and class limits have been determined, a frequency distribution can be obtained by *counting* the number of data items belonging to each class. For example, the data in Table 2.7 show that four values—12, 14, 14, and 13—belong to the 10–14 class. Thus, the frequency for the 10–14 class is 4. Continuing this counting process for the 15–19, 20–24, 25–29, and 30–34 classes provides the frequency distribution in Table 2.8. Using this frequency distribution, we can observe that:

1. The most frequently occurring audit times are in the class of 15–19 days. Eight of the 20 audit times belong to this class.
2. Only one audit required 30 or more days.

Other relevant observations are possible, depending on the interests of the person viewing the frequency distribution. The value of a frequency distribution is that it provides insights about the data that are not easily obtained by viewing the data in their original unorganized form.

TABLE 2.8   Frequency Distribution for the Audit-Time Data

Audit Time (days)	Frequency
10–14	4
15–19	8
20–24	5
25–29	2
30–34	1
Total	20

RELATIVE FREQUENCY AND PERCENT FREQUENCY DISTRIBUTIONS

We define the relative frequency and percent frequency distributions for quantitative data in the same manner as for qualitative data. First, recall that the relative frequency is simply the proportion of the total number of items belonging to a class. For a data set having n items,

$$\text{Relative Frequency of Class} = \frac{\text{Frequency of the Class}}{n}.$$

The percent frequency of a class is the relative frequency multiplied by 100.

Based on the class frequencies in Table 2.8 and with $n = 20$, Table 2.9 shows the relative frequency distribution and percent frequency distribution for the audit-time

TABLE 2.9 Relative and Percent Frequency Distributions for the Audit-Time Data

Audit-Time (days)	Relative Frequency	Percent Frequency
10–14	.20	20
15–19	.40	40
20–24	.25	25
25–29	.10	10
30–34	.05	5
Total	1.00	100

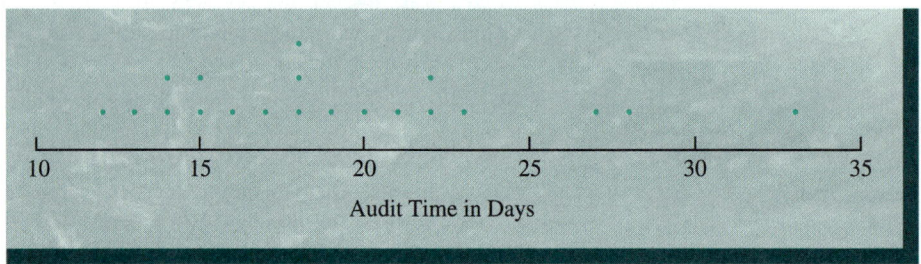

FIGURE 2.3 Dot Plot for the Audit-Time Data in Table 2.7

data. Note that .40 of the audits, or 40%, required from 15 to 19 days. Only .05 of the audits, or 5%, required 30 or more days. Again, additional interpretations and insights can be obtained by using Table 2.9.

DOT PLOT

One of the simplest graphical summaries of data is a *dot plot.* A horizontal axis shows the range of values for the data. Then each data value is represented by a dot placed above the axis. Figure 2.3 is the dot plot for the audit-time data in Table 2.7. The three dots located at the value of 18 indicate that 18 occurs three times in the data set. Dot plots show the details of the data and are useful for comparing two or more sets of data.

HISTOGRAM

Another common graphical presentation of quantitative data is the *histogram.* This graphical summary can be prepared for data that have been previously summarized in either a frequency, relative frequency, or percent frequency distribution. A histogram is constructed by placing the variable of interest on the horizontal axis and the frequency, relative frequency, or percent frequency on the vertical axis. The frequency, relative frequency, or percent frequency of each class is shown by drawing a rectangle whose base is the class interval on the horizontal axis and whose height is the corresponding frequency, relative frequency, or percent frequency.

Figure 2.4 is a histogram for the audit-time data. Note that the class with the greatest frequency is shown by the rectangle appearing above the class of 15–19 days. The height of the rectangle shows that the frequency of this class is 8. A histogram for the relative or percent frequency distribution of this data would look the same as the histogram in Figure 2.4 with the exception that the vertical axis would be labeled with relative or percent frequency values.

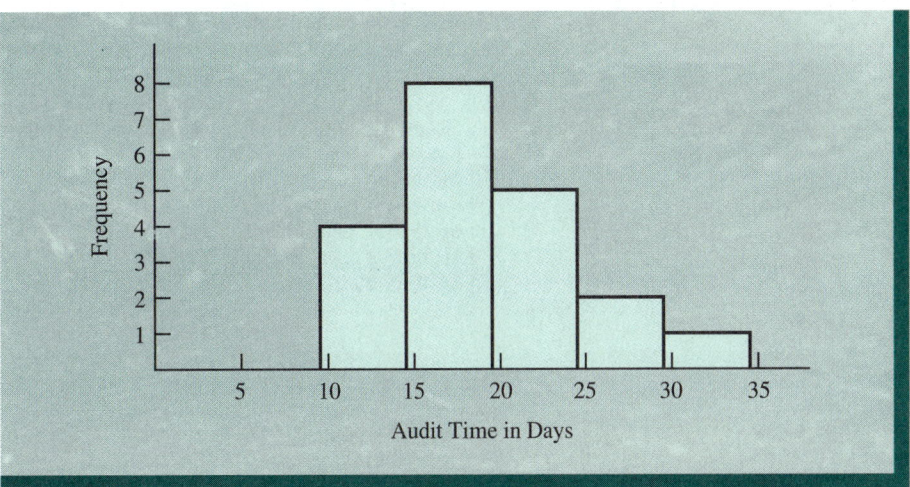

FIGURE 2.4 Histogram for the Audit-Time Data in Table 2.7

As Figure 2.4 shows, the adjacent rectangles of a histogram touch one another. Unlike a bar graph, a histogram has no natural separation between the rectangles of adjacent classes. This is the usual convention for histograms. Since the class limits for the audit-time data are stated as 10–14, 15–19, 20–24, 25–29, and 30–34, there appear to be one-unit intervals of 14 to 15, 19 to 20, 24 to 25, and 29 to 30 between the classes. These spaces are eliminated by drawing the vertical lines of the histogram halfway between the class limits. For example, the vertical lines for the 15–19 class were drawn upward from the values 14.5 and 19.5. Using this procedure for all classes, we drew the vertical lines for the histogram in Figure 2.4 upward from the values 9.5, 14.5, 19.5, 24.5, 29.5, and 34.5. This minor adjustment to eliminate the spaces in a histogram helps show that, even though the data are rounded, all values between the lower limit of the first class and the upper limit of the last class are possible.

CUMULATIVE DISTRIBUTIONS

A variation of the frequency distribution that provides another tabular summary of quantitative data is the *cumulative frequency distribution.* The cumulative frequency distribution uses the number of classes, class widths, and class limits that were developed for the frequency distribution. However, rather than showing the frequency of each class, the cumulative frequency distribution shows the number of items *less than or equal to the upper class limit* of each class. The first two columns of Table 2.10 provide the cumulative frequency distribution for the audit-time data.

To understand how the cumulative frequencies are determined, consider the class with the description "less than or equal to 24." The cumulative frequency for this class is simply the sum of the frequencies for all classes with data values less than or equal to 24. For the frequency distribution in Table 2.8, the sum of the frequencies for classes 10–14, 15–19, and 20–24 indicates that there are 4 + 8 + 5 = 17 items with values less than or equal to 24. Hence, the cumulative frequency for this class is 17. Other observations based on the cumulative frequency distribution in Table 2.10 show that 4 audits were completed in 14 days or less and 19 audits were completed in 29 days or less.

As a final point, we note that a *cumulative relative frequency distribution* shows the proportion of items and a cumulative percent frequency distribution shows the percentage of items with values less than or equal to the upper limit of each class.

TABLE 2.10 Cumulative Frequency, Cumulative Relative Frequency, and Cumulative Percent Frequency Distributions for the Audit-Time Data

Audit Time (days)	Cumulative Frequency	Cumulative Relative Frequency	Cumulative Percent Frequency
Less than or equal to 14	4	.20	20
Less than or equal to 19	12	.60	60
Less than or equal to 24	17	.85	85
Less than or equal to 29	19	.95	95
Less than or equal to 34	20	1.00	100

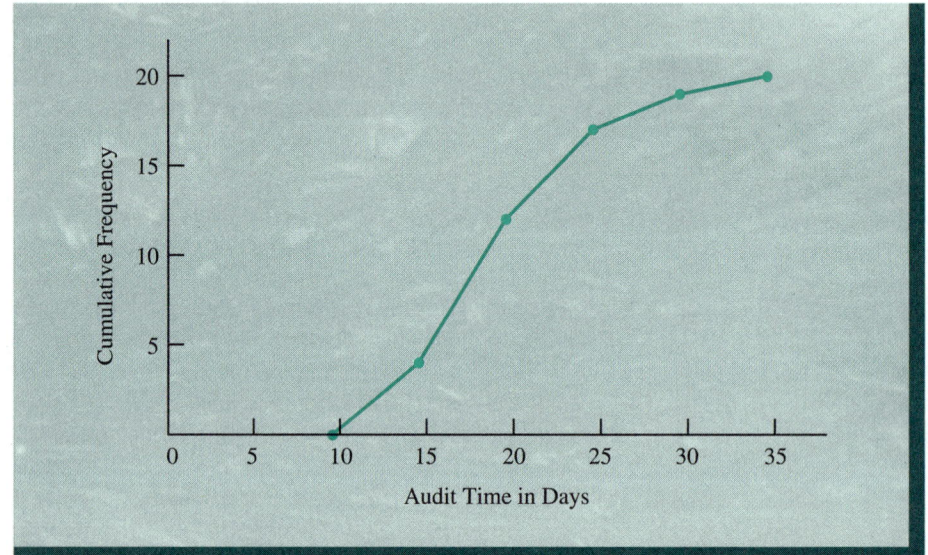

FIGURE 2.5 Ogive for the Audit-Time Data of Table 2.10

The cumulative relative frequency distribution can be computed either by summing the relative frequencies in the relative frequency distribution or by dividing the cumulative frequencies by the total number of items. Using the latter approach, we found the cumulative relative frequencies in column 3 of Table 2.10 by dividing the cumulative frequencies in column 2 by the total number of items ($n = 20$). The cumulative percent frequencies were again computed by multiplying the relative frequencies by 100. The cumulative relative and percent frequency distributions show that .85 of the audits, or 85%, were completed in 24 days or less, .95 of the audits, or 95%, were completed in 29 days or less, and so on.

OGIVE

A graph of a cumulative distribution is called an *ogive*. The data values are shown on the horizontal axis and either the cumulative frequencies, the cumulative relative frequencies, or the cumulative percent frequencies are shown on the vertical axis. Figure 2.5 is the ogive for the cumulative frequencies of the audit-time data in Table 2.10.

The ogive is constructed by plotting a point corresponding to the cumulative frequency of each class. Since the class limits for the audit-time data are 10–14, 15–19, 20–24, and so on, there appear to be one-unit intervals for 14 to 15, 19 to 20, and so on. As with the histogram, these spaces are eliminated by plotting points halfway between the class limits. Thus, 14.5 is used for the 10–14 class, 19.5 is used for the 15–19 class, and so on. The "less than or equal to 14" class with a cumulative frequency of 4 is shown on the ogive in Figure 2.5 by the point located at 14.5 on the horizontal axis and 4 on the vertical axis. The "less than or equal to 19" class with a cumulative frequency of 12 is shown by the point located at 19.5 on the horizontal axis and 12 on the vertical axis. Note that one additional point is plotted at the left end of the ogive. This point starts the ogive by showing that there are no data values below the 10–14 class. It is plotted at 9.5 on the horizontal axis and 0 on the vertical axis. The plotted points are connected by straight lines to complete the ogive.

NOTES AND COMMENTS

1. In some applications, we will want to know the *midpoints* of the classes in a frequency distribution for quantitative data. Each class midpoint is simply halfway between the lower and upper class limits. For example, with the class limits of 10–14, 15–19, 20–24, 25–29, and 30–34 in the audit-time example, the five class midpoints would be 12, 17, 22, 27, and 32, respectively.

2. An *open-end* class is one that has only a lower class limit or upper class limit. For example, in the audit-time data of Table 2.7, suppose two of the audits had taken 58 and 65 days. Rather than continue with the classes of width 5 with class intervals 35–39, 40–44, 45–49, and so on, we could simplify the frequency distribution to show an open-end class of "35 or more." This class would have a frequency of 2. Most often the open-end class appears at the upper end of the distribution. Sometimes an open-end class appears at the lower end of the distribution, and occasionally such classes appear at both ends.

3. The last entry in a cumulative frequency distribution is always the total number of elements in the data set. The last entry in a cumulative relative frequency distribution is always 1.00 and the last entry in a cumulative percent frequency distribution is always 100.

EXERCISES

METHODS

11. Consider the following data.

14	21	23	21	16
19	22	25	16	16
24	24	25	19	16
19	18	19	21	12
16	17	18	23	25
20	23	16	20	19
24	26	15	22	24
20	22	24	22	20

a. Develop a frequency distribution using class limits of 12–14, 15–17, 18–20, 21–23, and 24–26.

b. Develop a relative frequency distribution and a percent frequency distribution using the class limits in part (a).

Self-Test

12. Consider the following frequency distribution.

Class	Frequency
10–19	10
20–29	14
30–39	17
40–49	7
50–59	2

Construct a cumulative frequency distribution and a cumulative relative frequency distribution.

13. Construct a histogram and an ogive for the data in Exercise 12.

14. Consider the following data.

8.9	10.2	11.5	7.8	10.0	12.2	13.5	14.1	10.0	12.2
6.8	9.5	11.5	11.2	14.9	7.5	10.0	6.0	15.8	11.5

a. Construct a dot plot.   b. Construct a frequency distribution.
c. Construct a percent frequency distribution.

APPLICATIONS

Self-Test

15. A doctor's office staff has studied the waiting times for patients who arrive at the office with a request for emergency service. The following data were collected over a one-month period (the waiting times are in minutes).

2 5 10 12 4 4 5 17 11 8 9 8 12 21 6 8 7 13 18 3

Use classes of 0–4, 5–9, and so on.
a. Show the frequency distribution.
b. Show the relative frequency distribution.
c. Show the cumulative frequency distribution.
d. Show the cumulative relative frequency distribution.
e. What proportion of patients needing emergency service have a waiting time of nine minutes or less?

RETURN

16. Data on the 600 largest publicly held U.S. corporations were provided by *Financial World* (December 6, 1994). Return on equity for the most recent 12 months and the five-year average return on equity for 28 insurance companies follow.

	Return on Equity (%)			**Return on Equity (%)**	
Company	**12 Month**	**5-Year Avg.**	**Company**	**12 Month**	**5-Year Avg.**
Allstate	6	5	Loews	6	10
Unitron	5	6	General Re	14	16
Aetna	3	5	Geico	15	18
Chubb	13	16	Cigna	10	7
Safeco	12	14	ITT	11	7
Cinti. Fincl.	11	11	Lincoln Natl.	8	10
Aflac	19	16	MGIC Invst.	20	16
Travelers	17	13	UNUM	15	14
Am. Intl. Grp.	14	13	St. Paul	16	9
Torchmark	21	22	Marsh & McL.	28	27
Transamerica	12	9	MBIA	16	14

	Return on Equity (%)			Return on Equity (%)	
Company	**12 Month**	**5-Year Avg.**	**Company**	**12 Month**	**5-Year Avg.**
Jefferson-Pilot	14	12	Aon	15	13
Progressive	24	21	Providian	14	13
American General	13	11	Berkshire	8	6
SOURCE: Financial World, December 6, 1994.					

TABLE 2.11 Exercise 17

2.1	4.8	5.5	10.4
3.3	3.5	4.8	5.8
5.3	5.5	2.8	3.6
5.9	6.6	7.8	10.5
7.5	6.0	4.5	4.8

a. Develop tabular summaries and a histogram for the 12-month return-on-equity data. Comment on typical returns and their distribution.

b. Develop tabular summaries and a histogram for the data on the five-year average return on equity.

c. Compare returns over the past 12 months with average returns over the last five years.

17. National Airlines accepts flight reservations by telephone. Shown in Table 2.11 are the call durations (in minutes) for a sample of 20 telephone reservations. Construct the frequency and relative frequency distributions for the data. Also provide a histogram.

18. The Roth Young Personnel Service reported that annual salaries for department store assistant managers range from $28,000 to $57,000 (*National Business Employment Weekly*, October 16–22, 1994). Assume the following data are a sample of the annual salaries for 40 department store assistant managers (data are in thousands of dollars).

RETAIL

48	35	57	48	52	56	51	44
40	40	50	31	52	37	51	41
47	45	46	42	53	43	44	39
50	50	44	49	45	45	50	42
52	55	46	54	45	41	45	47

a. What are the lowest and highest salaries reported?

b. Use a class width of $5,000 and prepare tabular summaries of the annual salary data.

c. What proportion of the annual salaries are $35,000 or less?

d. What percentage of the annual salaries are more than $50,000?

e. Prepare a histogram of the data.

TABLE 2.12 Exercise 19

160	170	181	156	176
148	198	179	162	150
162	156	179	178	151
157	154	179	148	156

19. The data in Table 2.12 are the numbers of units produced by a production employee for the most recent 20 days. Summarize the data by constructing:

a. A frequency distribution.

b. A relative frequency distribution.

c. A cumulative frequency distribution.

d. A cumulative relative frequency distribution.

e. An ogive.

20. *Fortune* magazine conducted a survey to learn about its subscribers in the United States and Canada. One survey question asked the value of subscribers' investment portfolios (stocks, bonds, mutual funds, and certificates of deposit). The following percent frequency distribution was prepared from responses to this question (*Fortune* National Subscriber Portrait, 1994).

Value of Investments	**Percent Frequency**
Under $25,000	17
$25,000–49,999	9
$50,000–99,999	12
$100,000–249,999	20
$250,000–499,999	13
$500,000–999,999	13
$1,000,000 or over	16
Total	100

a. What percentage of subscribers have investments of less than $100,000?
b. What percentage of subscribers have investments in the $100,000–499,999 range?
c. What percentage of subscribers have investments of $500,000 or more?
d. The percent frequency distribution is based on 816 responses. How many of the respondents reported having investments of $100,000 to $249,999?
e. Estimate the number of respondents reporting investments of less than $100,000.

21. The personal computer has brought computer convenience and power into the home environment. But just how many hours a week are people actually using their home computers? A study designed to determine the usage of personal computers at home (*U.S. News & World Report,* December 26, 1988) provided the following data in hours per week.

.5	1.2	4.8	10.3	7.0	13.1	16.0	12.7	11.6	5.1
2.2	8.2	.7	9.0	7.8	2.2	1.8	12.8	12.5	14.1
15.5	13.6	12.2	12.5	12.8	13.5	1.3	5.5	5.0	10.8
2.5	3.9	6.5	4.2	8.8	2.8	2.5	14.4	16.0	12.4
2.8	9.5	1.5	10.5	2.2	7.5	10.5	14.1	14.9	.3

Summarize the data by constructing:

a. A frequency distribution (use a class width of three hours).
b. A relative frequency distribution.
c. A histogram.
d. An ogive.
e. Comment on what the data indicate about personal computer usage at home.

2.3   THE ROLE OF THE COMPUTER

Computers play an important role in statistical analysis. Several large-scale statistical software packages such as Minitab, SAS, SPSS, and SYSTAT are widely available. They offer extensive data-handling capabilities and numerous statistical analysis routines that can analyze small to very large data sets. Smaller scale statistical software packages, often developed for instructional purposes, are also available. They have limited data-handling capabilities and are intended to be used for smaller data sets. Finally, general-purpose spreadsheet packages such as Microsoft Excel, Lotus 1-2-3, and QuattroPro have statistical analysis capabilities. In all, a variety of options are available for individuals who want to use computers to assist with the presentation and statistical analysis of data.

In this text, we show how computer software packages can assist in the summarization of data. We use Minitab to illustrate the types of output information that can be provided by statistical packages. In the text discussion we focus on the presentation and interpretation of the computer output. In selected chapter appendixes we show the detailed steps necessary to obtain the Minitab output as well as those necessary to obtain similar statistical output with Microsoft Excel spreadsheets. These appendixes are optional and are intended for readers who want to pursue hands-on usage of Minitab and/or Excel.

Let us now examine the Minitab output for the dot plot, frequency distribution, and histogram of the audit-time data presented in Section 2.2. Minitab uses a worksheet of rows (elements) and columns (variables) to store the data for a particular application. The data can be keyed directly into the worksheet or can be imported from elsewhere, such as from a data disk. We began the session with Minitab by entering the audit-time data from Table 2.7 into a Minitab worksheet. We then instructed Minitab to provide the descriptive statistics output shown in Figure 2.6. Panel A is the dot plot of the audit-time data. Note that this output is very similar to the dot plot in Figure 2.3. Panel B is the histogram output. Note that the histogram provided by Minitab is essentially identical to the one in Figure 2.4. Appendix 2.1 at the end of the chapter describes the step-by-step procedures used to obtain the Minitab output in Figure 2.6.

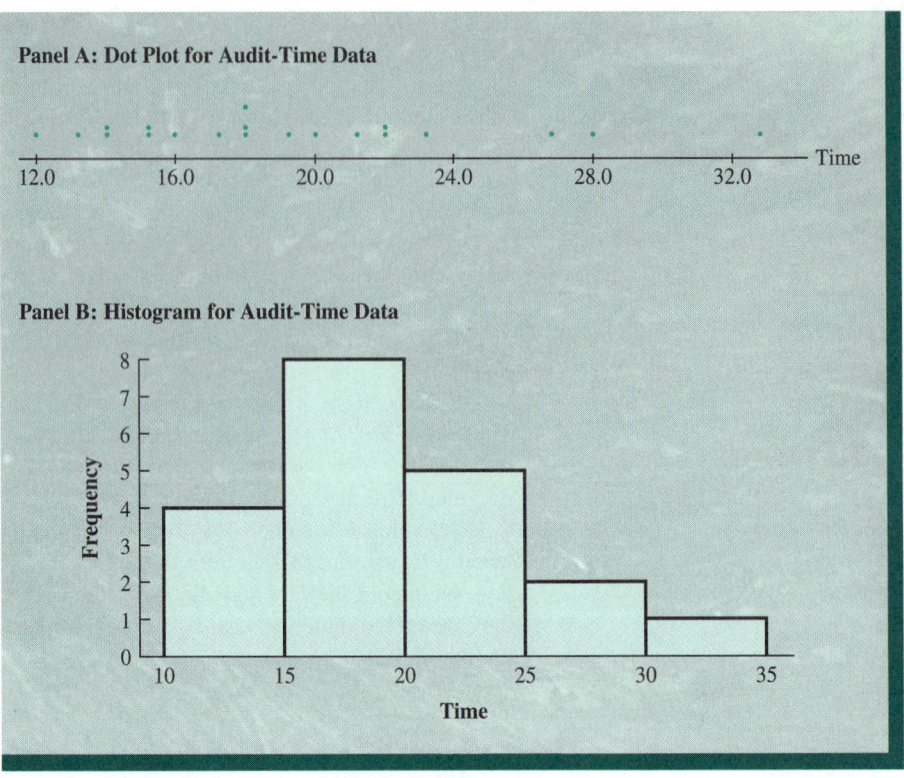

Panel A: Dot Plot for Audit-Time Data

Panel B: Histogram for Audit-Time Data

FIGURE 2.6 Minitab Output for the Audit-Time Data

NOTES AND COMMENTS

This section has described the use of Minitab to summarize the quantitative audit-time data in Table 2.7. Statistical software packages such as Minitab often handle qualitative data by using numeric codes to represent the data. For example, the qualitative data on personal computer purchases in Table 2.1 could have been entered into a Minitab worksheet by using numeric codes such as 1 for Apple, 2 for Compaq, 3 for Gateway 2000, 4 for IBM, and 5 for Packard Bell. With those codes, the Minitab output would appear in the following form.

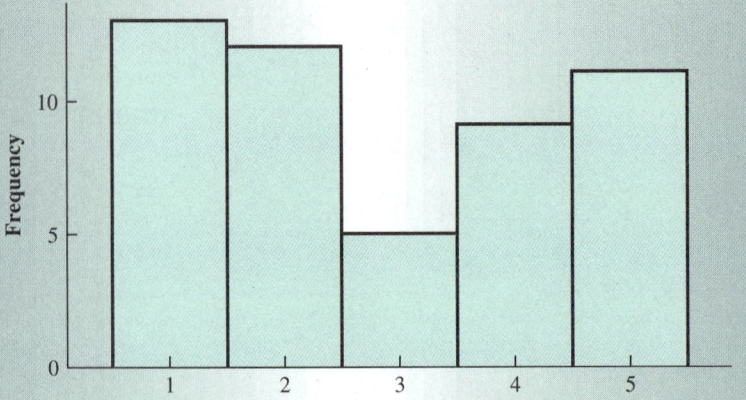

Knowing that the numeric codes are 1 for Apple, 2 for Compaq, and so on, we see that the output provides the bar graph shown previously in Section 2.1.

2.4 EXPLORATORY DATA ANALYSIS

The techniques of *exploratory data analysis* consist of simple arithmetic and easy-to-draw pictures that can be used to summarize data quickly. In this section we show how one such technique—referred to as a *stem-and-leaf display*—can be used to rank order data and provide an idea of the shape of the distribution of a set of quantitative data.

One simple method of displaying data is to arrange them in ascending or descending order. This process, referred to as rank ordering of data, provides some degree of organization. However, such an approach provides little insight about the shape of the distribution of data values. A stem-and-leaf display is a device that shows both rank order and shape simultaneously.

To illustrate the use of a stem-and-leaf display, consider the data set in Table 2.13. These data are the results of a 150-question aptitude test given to 50 individuals who were recently interviewed for a position at Haskens Manufacturing. The data indicate the number of questions answered correctly.

To develop a stem-and-leaf display for the data in Table 2.13, we first arrange the leading digits of each data item to the left of a vertical line. To the right of the vertical line, we record the last digit for each item as we pass through the scores in the order they were recorded. The last digit for each item is placed on the line corresponding to its first digit.

```
 6 | 9  8
 7 | 2  3  6  3  6  5
 8 | 6  2  3  1  1  0  4  5
 9 | 7  2  2  6  2  1  5  8  8  5  4
10 | 7  4  8  0  2  6  6  0  6
11 | 2  8  5  9  3  5  9
12 | 6  8  7  4
13 | 2  4
14 | 1
```

With this organization of the data, sorting the digits on each line into rank order is simple. Doing so leads to the stem-and-leaf display shown on page 39.

APTEST

TABLE 2.13 Number of Questions
Answered Correctly on an Aptitude Test

112	72	69	97	107
73	92	76	86	73
126	128	118	127	124
82	104	132	134	83
92	108	96	100	92
115	76	91	102	81
95	141	81	80	106
84	119	113	98	75
68	98	115	106	95
100	85	94	106	119

```
 6 | 8   9
 7 | 2   3   3   5   6   6
 8 | 0   1   1   2   3   4   5   6
 9 | 1   2   2   2   4   5   5   6   7   8   8
10 | 0   0   2   4   6   6   6   7   8
11 | 2   3   5   5   8   9   9
12 | 4   6   7   8
13 | 2   4
14 | 1
```

Each line in this display is referred to as a *stem,* and each digit on the stem is a *leaf.* For example, consider the first line.

$$6 \mid 8 \quad 9$$

The meaning attached to this line is that there are two items in the data set whose first digit is six: 68 and 69. Similarly, the second line

$$7 \mid 2 \quad 3 \quad 3 \quad 5 \quad 6 \quad 6$$

indicates that there are six items whose first digit is seven: 72, 73, 73, 75, 76, and 76. Thus, we see that the data values in this stem-and-leaf display are separated into two parts. The label for each stem is the one or two leading digits of the number (that is, 6, 7, 8, 9, 10, 11, 12, 13, or 14) and the leaf is the single last digit (that is, 0, 1, 2, . . ., 8, 9). The vertical line simply serves to separate the two parts of each number listed.

To focus on the shape indicated by the stem-and-leaf display, let us use a rectangle to depict the "length" of each stem. Doing so, we obtain the following representation.

```
 6 | 8   9
 7 | 2   3   3   5   6   6
 8 | 0   1   1   2   3   4   5   6
 9 | 1   2   2   2   4   5   5   6   7   8   8
10 | 0   0   2   4   6   6   6   7   8
11 | 2   3   5   5   8   9   9
12 | 4   6   7   8
13 | 2   4
14 | 1
```

Rotating this page counterclockwise onto its side provides a picture of the data very similar to that provided by a histogram with classes of 60–69, 70–79, 80–89, and so on.

Although the stem-and-leaf display may appear to offer the same information as a histogram, it has two primary advantages.

1. The stem-and-leaf display is easier to construct.
2. Within a class interval, the stem-and-leaf display provides more information than the histogram because the stem-and-leaf shows the actual data values.

Just as there is no right number of classes in a frequency distribution or histogram, there is no right number of rows or stems in a stem-and-leaf display. If we believe that our original stem-and-leaf display has condensed the data too much, we can easily stretch the display by using two or more stems for each leading digit(s). For example, to use two lines for each leading digit(s), we would place all data values ending in 0, 1, 2, 3, and 4 on one line and all values ending in 5, 6, 7, 8, and 9 on a second line. The following stretched stem-and-leaf display illustrates this approach.

```
 6 |
 6 | 8  9
 7 | 2  3  3
 7 | 5  6  6
 8 | 0  1  1  2  3  4
 8 | 5  6
 9 | 1  2  2  2  4
 9 | 5  5  6  7  8  8
10 | 0  0  2  4
10 | 6  6  6  7  8
11 | 2  3
11 | 5  5  8  9  9
12 | 4
12 | 6  7  8
13 | 2  4
13 |
14 | 1
14 |
```

Note that data 72, 73, and 73 have leaves in the 0–4 range and are shown with the first stem value of 7. The data 75, 76, and 76 have leaves in the 5–9 range and are shown with the second stem value of 7. This stretched stem-and-leaf display is similar to a frequency distribution with intervals of 60–64, 65–69, 70–74, 75–79, and so on.

Figure 2.7 is a portion of the stem-and-leaf output provided by the Minitab computer software package. Note that the output is identical to the stretched stem-and-leaf display we have just discussed.

The above example has shown a stem-and-leaf display for data having up to three digits. Stem-and-leaf displays for data with more digits are possible. For example, consider the following data, which show the number of hamburgers sold by a fast-food restaurant for each of 15 weeks.

1852	1644	1766	1888	1912	2044	1812	1790
1679	2008	1565	1852	1967	1954	1733	

```
          Stem-and-leaf of C1          N = 50
          Leaf Unit = 1.0

                6   89
                7   233
                7   566
                8   011234
                8   56
                9   12224
                9   556788
               10   0024
               10   66678
               11   23
               11   55899
               12   4
               12   678
               13   24
               13
               14   1
```

FIGURE 2.7   Minitab Stem-and-Leaf Display of the Aptitude Test Scores

A stem-and-leaf display of these data follows.

Leaf Unit = 10

```
 15 | 6
 16 | 4  7
 17 | 3  6  9
 18 | 1  5  5  8
 19 | 1  5  6
 20 | 0  4
```

Only the first three digits of each data value are used in the display. The wording "Leaf Unit = 10" indicates that a leaf value of 1 represents 10–19, a leaf value of 2 represents 20–29, and so on. For example, the leaf value of 6 on the first line of the display represents a number from 60 to 69, indicating that the data values have four digits and that the data value corresponding to the first line is between 1560 and 1569.

EXERCISES

METHODS

22. Construct a stem-and-leaf display for the following data.

70	72	75	64	58	83	80	82
76	75	68	65	57	78	85	72

Self-Test

23. Construct a stem-and-leaf display for the following data.

11.3	9.6	10.4	7.5	8.3	10.5	10.0
9.3	8.1	7.7	7.5	8.4	6.3	8.8

24. Construct a stem-and-leaf display for the following data. Use the first two digits as the stem and the third digit as the leaf.

1161	1206	1478	1300	1604	1725	1361	1422
1221	1378	1623	1426	1557	1730	1706	1689

APPLICATIONS

Self-Test

25. A psychologist developed a new test of adult intelligence. The test was administered to 20 individuals, and the following data were obtained.

114	99	131	124	117	102	106	127	119	115
98	104	144	151	132	106	125	122	118	118

Construct a stem-and-leaf display for the data.

26. The earnings-per-share data for a sample of 20 companies from the *Fortune* 500 largest U.S. industrial corporations follow (*Fortune,* April 18, 1994):

Company	Earnings per Share ($)	Company	Earnings per Share ($)
Apple Computer	.73	Hewlitt-Packard	4.65
Procter & Gamble	−1.11	Sara Lee	1.40
Goodyear	2.64	General Dynamics	14.01
Chiquita Brands	−.99	Compaq Computer	5.45
Hershey Foods	2.15	Sunstrand	3.97
Data General	−1.73	Briggs & Stratton	4.86
Helene Curtis	2.33	Interlake	−1.18
Huffy	−.38	Dell Computer	2.59
Quaker State	.50	Harley-Davidson	−.31
Snap-On Tools	2.02	Zenith Electronics	−3.01

Develop a stem-and-leaf display for the data. Comment on what you learned about the earnings per share for these companies.

JOBSAT

27. In a study of job satisfaction, a series of tests were administered to 50 subjects. The following data were obtained; higher scores represent greater dissatisfaction.

87	76	67	58	92	59	41	50	90	75	80	81	70
73	69	61	88	46	85	97	50	47	81	87	75	60
65	92	77	71	70	74	53	43	61	89	84	83	70
46	84	76	78	64	69	76	78	67	74	64		

Construct a stem-and-leaf display for the data.

28. Periodically *Barron's* publishes earnings forecasts for the companies listed in the Dow Jones Industrial Average. Shown below are the 1995 forecasts of price–earnings (P/E) ratios for these companies implied by *Barron's* earnings forecasts (*Barron's,* December 12, 1994).

Company	1995 P/E Forecast	Company	1995 P/E Forecast
AT&T	13.6	Alcoa	13.8
Allied Signal	10.4	American Express	9.5
Bethlehem Steel	5.2	Boeing	22.7
Caterpillar	9.4	Chevron	13.5
Coca-Cola	21.6	Disney	16.8
Dupont	11.7	Eastman Kodak	12.8
Exxon	14.7	General Electric	12.0
General Motors	4.7	Goodyear	8.0
IBM	11.3	International Paper	11.5
McDonald's	14.9	Merck	13.8
Minnesota Mining	14.0	J.P. Morgan	8.0
Philip Morris	9.1	Procter & Gamble	15.4
Sears	8.1	Texaco	14.6
Union Carbide	9.8	United Technologies	11.3
Westinghouse	14.8	Woolworth	9.8

PEFORCST

a. Develop a stem-and-leaf display for the data.
b. Use the results of the stem-and-leaf display to develop a frequency distribution and percent frequency distribution for the data.

2.5 CROSSTABULATIONS AND SCATTER DIAGRAMS

Thus far in this chapter we have focused on tabular and graphical methods that are used to summarize the data for *one variable at a time.* Often a manager or decision maker is interested in tabular and graphical methods that will assist in the understanding of the *relationship between two variables.* Crosstabulation is a tabular method that can be used to summarize the data for two variables simultaneously. A scatter diagram is a graphical method that has a similar purpose.

Let us illustrate the use of a crosstabulation by considering an application. Zagat's Restaurant Review is a service that provides data on restaurants located throughout the world. Data on a variety of variables such as the restaurant's quality rating and typical meal price are reported. Quality rating is a qualitative variable with rating categories of good, very good, and excellent. Meal price is a quantitative variable that generally ranges from $10 to $49. The quality rating and the meal price data were obtained from Compuserve (January 1995) for a sample of 300 restaurants located in the Los Angeles area.

The general format of a crosstabulation for this application is shown in Table 2.14. The left and top margin labels define the classes for the two variables. In the left margin,

TABLE 2.14 Crosstabulation Format for 300 Los Angeles Restaurants

Quality Rating	Meal Price				Total
	$10–19	$20–$29	$30–39	$40–49	
Good					
Very good					
Excellent					
Total					

TABLE 2.15   Crosstabulation of Quality Rating and Meal Price for 300 Los Angeles Restaurants

Quality Rating	Meal Price				Total
	$10–19	**$20–29**	**$30–39**	**$40–49**	
Good	42	40	2	0	84
Very good	34	64	46	6	150
Excellent	2	14	28	22	66
Total	78	118	76	28	300

TABLE 2.16   Row Percentages for Each Quality Rating Category

Quality Rating	Meal Price				Total
	$10–19	**$20–29**	**$30–39**	**$40–49**	
Good	50.0	47.6	2.4	0.0	100
Very good	22.7	42.7	30.6	4.0	100
Excellent	3.0	21.2	42.4	33.4	100

the row labels (good, very good, and excellent) correspond to the three classes of the quality rating variable. In the top margin, the column labels ($10–19, $20–29, $30–39, and $40–49) correspond to the four classes of the meal price variable. Each restaurant in the sample provides a quality rating and a meal price. Thus, every restaurant in the sample is associated with a cell appearing in one of the rows and one of the columns of the crosstabulation. For example, an Italian restaurant located near Malibu is identified as having a very good quality rating and typical meal price of $32. This restaurant belongs to the cell in row 2 and column 3 of Table 2.14. In constructing a crosstabulation, we simply count the number of restaurants that belong to each of the cells in the crosstabulation table.

Completing the crosstabulation of the data for the sample of 300 restaurants provided the results in Table 2.15. We see that the greatest number of restaurants in the sample (64) have a very good rating and a meal price in the $20–29 range. Only two restaurants have an excellent rating and a meal price in the $10–19 range. Similar interpretations of the other frequencies can be made. In addition, note that the right and bottom margins of the crosstabulation provide the frequency distributions for quality rating and meal price separately. From the frequency distribution in the right margin, we see that data on quality ratings show 84 good restaurants, 150 very good restaurants, and 66 excellent restaurants. Similarly, the bottom margin shows the frequency distribution for the meal price variable.

The value of a crosstabulation is that it provides insight about the relationship between the variables. From the results in Table 2.15, higher meal prices appear to be associated with the higher quality restaurants and the lower meal prices appear to be associated with the lower quality restaurants.

Converting the entries in the table into row percentages or column percentages can afford additional insight about the relationship between the variables. For example, the results of dividing each frequency in Table 2.15 by its corresponding row total and expressing the values as percentages are shown in Table 2.16. For the lowest quality category (good), we see that the greatest percentages are for the less expensive restaurants (50.0% have $10–19 meal prices and 47.6% have $20–29 meal prices). For the highest quality category (excellent), we see that the greatest percentages are for the more expensive restaurants (42.4% have $30–39 meal prices and 33.4% have $40–49 meal prices). Thus, we continue to see that the more expensive meals are associated with the higher quality restaurants.

Crosstabulation is widely used for examining the relationship between two variables. In practice, final reports for many statistical surveys include a large number of crosstabulation tables. In the Los Angeles restaurant sample, the crosstabulation is based on one qualitative variable (quality rating) and one quantitative variable (meal price). Crosstabulations can also be developed when both variables are qualitative and when both variables are quantitative.

A scatter diagram is a graphical presentation of the relationship between two quantitative variables. As an illustration of a scatter diagram, consider the situation of a stereo and sound equipment store in San Francisco. On 10 occasions during the past three months, the store has used weekend television commercials to promote sales at its stores. The managers want to investigate whether there is a relationship between the number of commercials shown and the sales at the store during the following week. Sample data for the 10 weeks with sales in hundreds of dollars are shown in Table 2.17.

Figure 2.8 is the scatter diagram for the data in Table 2.17. The number of commercials (x) is shown on the horizontal axis and the sales (y) is shown on the vertical axis. For week 1, $x = 2$ and $y = 50$. A point with those coordinates is plotted on the scatter diagram. Similar points are plotted for the other nine weeks. The completed scatter diagram in Figure 2.8 indicates a positive relationship between the number of commercials and sales. Higher sales are associated with a higher number of commercials. The relationship is not perfect in that all points are not on a straight line. However, the general pattern of the points suggests that the overall relationship is positive.

TABLE 2.17 Sample Data for the Stereo and Sound Equipment Store

Week	No. of Commercials x	Sales Volume ($100s) y
1	2	50
2	5	57
3	1	41
4	3	54
5	4	54
6	1	38
7	5	63
8	3	48
9	4	59
10	2	46

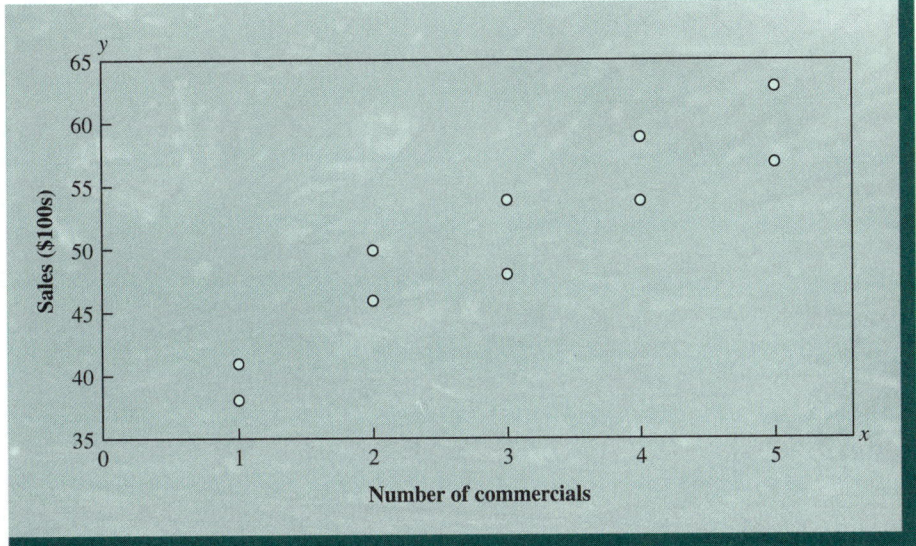

FIGURE 2.8 Scatter Diagram for the Stereo and Sound Equipment Store

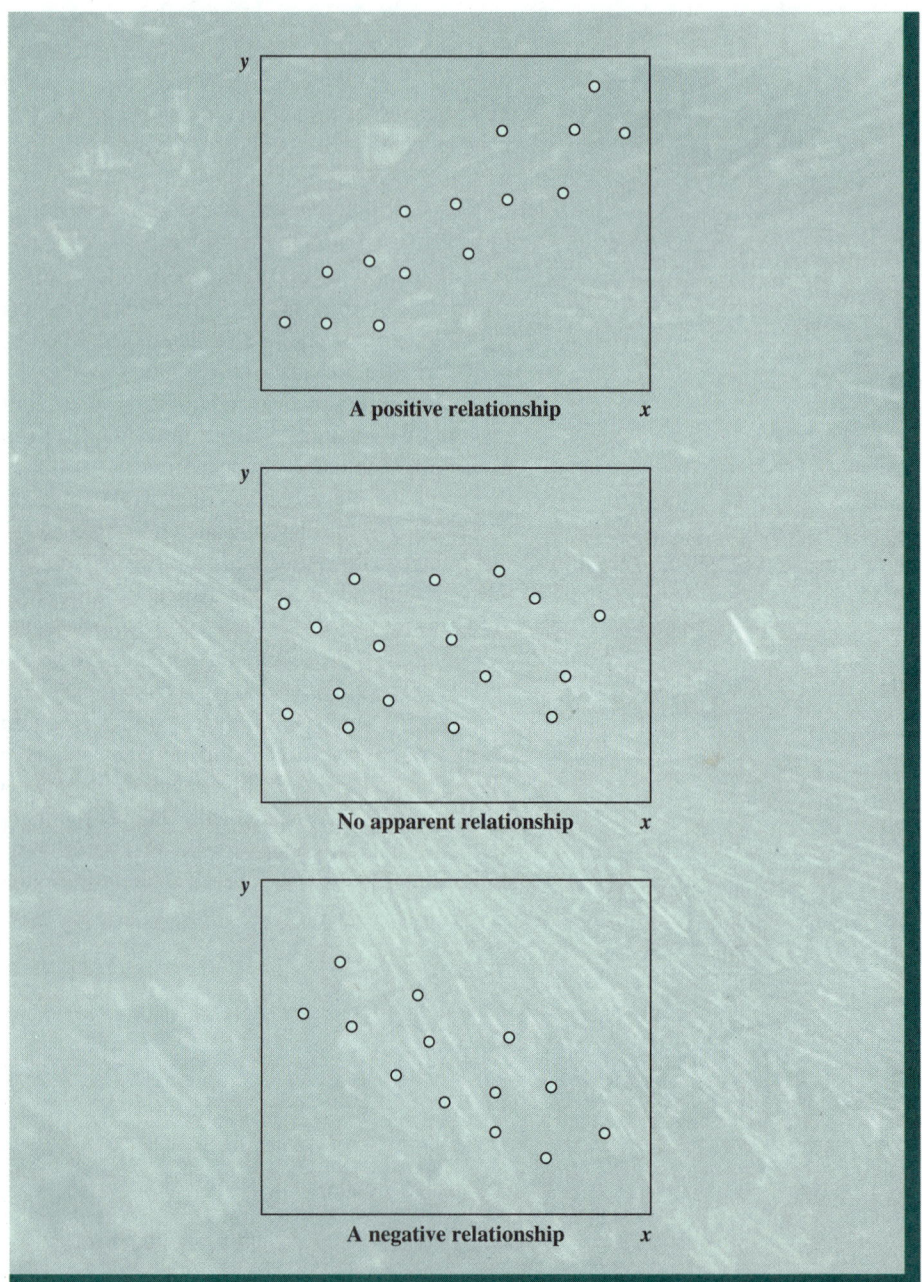

FIGURE 2.9   Types of Relationships Depicted by Scatter Diagrams

Some general scatter diagram patterns and the types of relationships they suggest are shown in Figure 2.9. The top panel depicts a positive relationship similar to the one we saw for the number of commercials and sales example. In the second panel, the scatter diagram shows no apparent relationship between the variables. The third panel depicts a negative relationship where y tends to decrease as x increases.

EXERCISES

METHODS

29. The following data are for 30 observations on two qualitative variables, x and y. The categories for x are A, B, and C; the categories for y are 1 and 2.

Observation	x	y	Observation	x	y
1	A	1	16	B	2
2	B	1	17	C	1
3	B	1	18	B	1
4	C	2	19	C	1
5	B	1	20	B	1
6	C	2	21	C	2
7	B	1	22	B	1
8	C	2	23	C	2
9	A	1	24	A	1
10	B	1	25	B	1
11	A	1	26	C	2
12	B	1	27	C	2
13	C	2	28	A	1
14	C	2	29	B	1
15	C	2	30	B	2

a. Develop a crosstabulation for the data, using x in the rows and y in the columns.
b. Compute the row percentages.
c. Compute column percentages.
d. What is the relationship, if any, between x and y?

30. The following 20 observations are for two quantitative variables, x and y.

SCATTER

Observation	x	y	Observation	x	y
1	−22	22	11	−37	48
2	−33	49	12	34	−29
3	2	8	13	9	−18
4	29	−16	14	−33	31
5	−13	10	15	20	−16
6	21	−28	16	−3	14
7	−13	27	17	−15	18
8	−23	35	18	12	17
9	14	−5	19	−20	−11
10	3	−3	20	−7	−22

a. Develop a scatter diagram for the relationship between x and y.
b. What is the apparent relationship, if any, between x and y?

APPLICATIONS

31. Compute column percentages for the restaurant data in Table 2.15. What is the relationship between quality rating and meal price?

Self-Test ▶

32. Shown in Table 2.18 are financial data for a 30-company sample of the largest U.S. companies whose stock is traded over the counter (*Financial World*, September 1, 1994).
  a. Prepare a crosstabulation of the data on earnings (rows) and book value (columns). Use classes 0.00–0.99, 1.00–1.99, and 2.00–2.99 for earnings per share and classes 0.00–4.99, 5.00–9.99, 10.00–14.99, and 15.00–15.99 for book value per share.
  b. Compute row percentages and comment on any relationship that you see between the variables.

33. Refer to the data in Table 2.18.
  a. Prepare a crosstabulation of the data on book value and stock price.
  b. Compute column percentages and comment on any relationship that you see between the variables.

34. Refer to the data in Table 2.18.
  a. Prepare a scatter diagram of the data on earnings per share and book value.
  b. Comment on any relationship that you see between the variables.

35. Refer to the data in Table 2.18.
  a. Prepare a scatter diagram of the data on earnings per share and stock price.
  b. Does there appear to be a relationship between the variables? Comment.

SUMMARY

A set of data, even if modest in size, is often difficult to interpret directly in the form in which it is gathered. Tabular and graphical procedures provide means of organizing and summarizing data so that patterns are revealed and the data are more easily interpreted. Frequency distributions, relative frequency distributions, percent frequency distributions, bar graphs, and pie charts were presented as tabular and graphical procedures for summarizing qualitative data. Frequency distributions, relative frequency distributions, percent frequency distributions, dot plots, histograms, cumulative frequency distributions, cumulative relative frequency distributions, cumulative percent frequency distributions, and ogives were presented as ways of summarizing quantitative data. A stem-and-leaf display was presented as an exploratory data analysis technique that can be used to summarize quantitative data.

Crosstabulation was presented as a tabular method for summarizing data for two variables. The scatter diagram was introduced as a graphical method for showing the relationship between two quantitative variables. Figure 2.10 is a summary of the tabular and graphical methods presented in this chapter.

GLOSSARY

Qualitative data Data that provide labels or names for categories of like items.

Quantitative data Data that indicate how much or how many.

Frequency distribution A tabular summary of a set of data showing the frequency (or number) of items in each of several nonoverlapping classes.

Relative frequency distribution A tabular summary of a set of data showing the relative frequency—that is, the fraction or proportion—of the total number of items in each of several nonoverlapping classes.

TABLE 2.18 Financial Data for a Sample of 30 Companies

Company	Earnings per Share ($)	Book Value per Share ($)	Stock Price ($)
Acme	2.59	15.00	25.50
Aldus	1.41	9.22	29.50
Am. Fed. Bk.	1.26	7.75	11.63
Applebees	.49	3.60	14.75
Banta Corp.	2.16	14.89	32.75
Bob Evans	1.15	7.41	21.50
Cintas Corp.	1.12	5.64	31.00
Comm. Clr. Hse.	.72	5.76	19.00
Cracker Brl.	.89	6.09	23.13
Devon Group	2.01	8.86	19.50
Duracraft	1.69	5.41	40.00
First Alert	.79	3.18	25.75
Food Lion	.26	3.71	5.94
Gentex	.83	3.09	21.00
Gould Pumps	1.12	8.80	20.25
Haggar Corp.	2.80	15.26	29.00
Hubco, Inc.	2.27	11.74	21.13
Info. Res.	.74	8.59	13.75
Irwin Fincl.	2.82	12.08	21.75
Kelly Srvcs.	1.35	11.06	28.75
Lone Star	.62	4.44	20.00
Mark Twain	2.40	13.75	27.50
Micro Sys.	1.03	4.01	28.50
Novell	.98	3.58	16.13
Pacific Phy.	.55	5.00	11.50
Proffitts Inc.	.50	13.39	18.75
Rival	1.44	6.57	20.38
Sybase	1.07	3.81	37.00
Tyson Foods	1.23	17.06	23.88
Zenith Labs	.85	3.63	15.63

SOURCE: *Financial World,* September 1, 1994.

Percent frequency distribution A tabular summary of a set of data showing the percentage of the total number of items in each of several nonoverlapping classes.

Bar graph A graphical device for depicting the information presented in a frequency distribution, relative frequency distribution, or percent frequency distribution of qualitative data.

Pie chart A graphical device for presenting qualitative data summaries based on subdivision of a circle into sectors that correspond to the relative frequency for each class.

Histogram A graphical presentation of a frequency distribution, relative frequency distribution, or percent frequency distribution of quantitative data constructed by placing the class intervals on the horizontal axis and the frequencies on the vertical axis.

Cumulative frequency distribution A tabular summary of a set of quantitative data showing the number of items having values less than or equal to the upper class limit of each class.

Cumulative relative frequency distribution A tabular summary of a set of quantitative data showing the fraction or proportion of the items having values less than or equal to the upper class limit of each class.

Cumulative percent frequency distribution A tabular summary of a set of quantitative data showing the percentage of the items having values less than or equal to the upper class limit of each class.

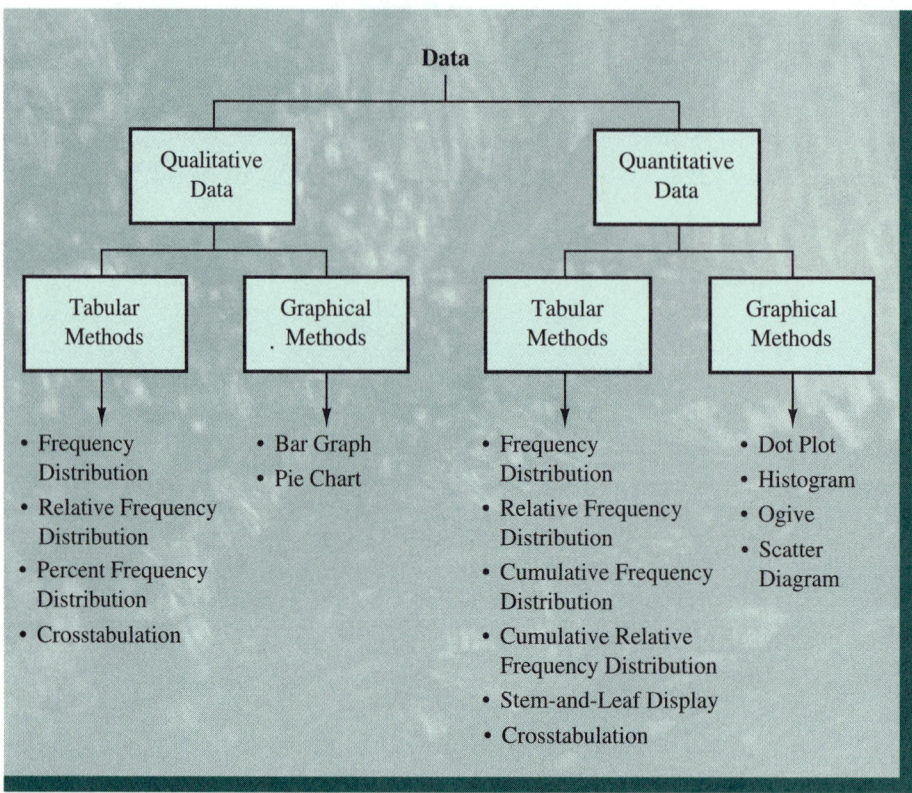

FIGURE 2.10   Tabular and Graphical Procedures for Summarizing Data

Class midpoint   The point in each class that is halfway between the lower and upper class limits.

Stem-and-leaf display   An exploratory data analysis technique that simultaneously rank orders quantitative data and provides insight about the shape of the distribution.

Crosstabulation   A tabular summary of data for two variables. The classes for one variable are represented by the rows; the classes for the other variable are represented by the columns.

Scatter diagram   A graphical means of showing the relationship between two quantitative variables. One variable is shown on the horizontal axis and the other variable is shown on the vertical axis.

KEY FORMULAS

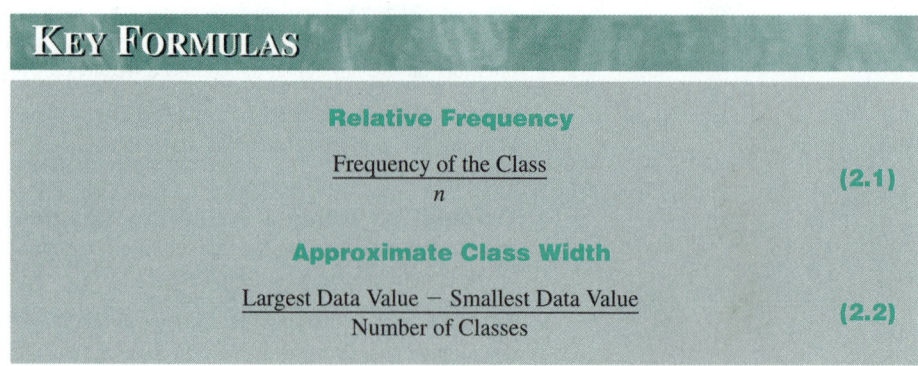

Relative Frequency

$$\frac{\text{Frequency of the Class}}{n} \tag{2.1}$$

Approximate Class Width

$$\frac{\text{Largest Data Value} - \text{Smallest Data Value}}{\text{Number of Classes}} \tag{2.2}$$

SUPPLEMENTARY EXERCISES

36. The Gallup Poll News Service selected a random sample of adults to learn what sports fans select as their favorite sport to watch, in person or on television (*USA Today,* December 12, 1990). The following sample results are consistent with the findings of the Gallup poll. In the data, B is baseball, K is basketball, F is football, I is ice hockey, T is tennis, and O is other sports.

O	F	B	O	B	F	F	K	O	K	F	F	O	F
T	F	F	B	K	F	F	O	F	B	F	O	O	B
I	F	O	B	F	K	B	K	O	O	O	K		

a. Show a frequency distribution.
b. Show a relative frequency distribution. What is the favorite spectator sport?
c. Show a pie chart summary of the data.

37. Each of the *Fortune* 500 companies is classified as belonging to one of several industries (*Fortune,* April 18, 1994). A sample of 20 companies with their corresponding industry classification follows.

Company	Industry Classification	Company	Industry Classification
IBP	Food	Del Monte	Food
Intel	Electronics	McDonnell Douglas	Aerospace
Coca-Cola	Beverage	Morton International	Chemicals
Union Carbide	Chemicals	Quaker Oats	Food
General Electric	Electronics	Pepsico	Beverage
Motorola	Electronics	Maytag	Electronics
Kellogg	Food	Lockheed	Aerospace
Dow Chemical	Chemicals	Pet	Food
Campbell Soup	Food	Westinghouse	Electronics
Ralston Purina	Food	Raychem	Electronics

a. Provide a frequency distribution showing the number of companies in each industry.
b. Provide a percent frequency distribution.
c. Provide a bar graph for the data.

38. Voters participating in a recent election exit poll in Michigan were asked to state their political party affiliation. The collected data, coded 1 for Democrat, 2 for Republican, and 3 for Independent, follow.

1	2	2	1	3	1	2	2	2	1	2	3	2	3	2	1	1	2	1	2
2	1	1	1	2	1	2	3	1	1	2	1	3	1	1	2	1	2	3	2

a. Show a frequency distribution and a relative frequency distribution for the data.
b. Show a bar graph for the data.
c. Comment on what the data suggest about the strengths of the political parties in this voting area.

39. The International Organization for Standardization in Geneva, Switzerland, has developed a widely accepted set of quality standards: ISO 9000. Companies all over the world have become ISO 9000 certified. A Grant Thornton survey (*Fifth Annual Grant Thornton Survey of American Manufacturers Report,* 1994) asked American manufacturers about their plans for obtaining certification. Let C = already certified, P = already pursuing certification, W = will pursue certification, N = will not pursue certification, and U = uncertain. The following sample data are consistent with the responses obtained by Grant Thornton.

W	P	N	N	W	P	C	W	W	N
N	W	U	W	P	W	P	C	N	P
P	N	W	W	N	W	N	W	W	N
C	W	P	W	N	N	C	W	P	N
W	W	N	W	N	U	N	W	N	W

a. Prepare a frequency distribution and a percent frequency distribution for the data set.

b. Prepare a pie chart for the data set.

c. Grant Thornton reported that less than 1% of the companies were certified in 1993. Comment on the trend in obtaining ISO certification based on the 1994 sample data.

40. An international survey was conducted by the Union Bank of Switzerland to obtain data on the hourly wages of blue- and white-collar workers throughout the world (*Newsweek*, February 17, 1992). Workers in Los Angeles ranked seventh in the world in terms of highest hourly wage. Assume that the following 25 values indicate hourly wages for workers in Los Angeles.

LAWAGES

11.50	8.40	11.75	10.05	10.25	8.00	13.65	7.05	9.05
11.90	9.90	6.85	15.35	11.10	14.70	13.15	13.10	6.65
13.10	9.20	9.15	12.05	8.45	5.85	9.80		

a. Construct a frequency distribution using classes of 4.00–5.99, 6.00–7.99, and so on.

b. Construct a relative frequency distribution.

c. Construct cumulative frequency and cumulative relative frequency distributions.

d. Use these distributions to comment on what you have learned about the hourly wages of workers in Los Angeles.

41. The data in Table 2.19 represent sales in millions of dollars for 17 companies in the health care services industry (The 1992 *Business Week* 1000).

a. Construct a frequency distribution to summarize the data. Use a class width of 1000.

b. Develop a relative frequency distribution for the data.

c. Construct a cumulative frequency distribution for the data.

d. Construct a cumulative relative frequency distribution for the data.

e. Construct a histogram as a graphical representation of the data.

TABLE 2.19   Exercise 41

6099	1709	847
3973	604	2104
166	282	170
233	868	230
225	491	2452
2301	393	

42. The closing prices of 40 common stocks follow (*Investor's Daily*, April 25, 1992).

COMSTOCK

29⅝	34	43¼	8¾	37⅞	8⅝	7⅝	30⅜	35¼	19⅜
9¼	16½	38	53⅜	16⅝	1¼	48⅜	18	9⅜	9¼
10	37	18	8	28½	24¼	21⅝	18½	33⅝	31⅛
32¼	29⅝	79⅜	11⅜	38⅞	11½	52	14	9	33½

a. Construct frequency and relative frequency distributions for the data.

b. Construct cumulative frequency and cumulative relative frequency distributions for the data.

c. Construct a histogram for the data.

d. Using your summaries, make comments and observations about the price of common stock.

43. The grade point averages for 30 students majoring in economics follow.

GRADEAVE

2.21	3.01	2.68	2.68	2.74	2.60	1.76	2.77	2.46	2.49
2.89	2.19	3.11	2.93	2.38	2.76	2.93	2.55	2.10	2.41
3.53	3.22	2.34	3.30	2.59	2.18	2.87	2.71	2.80	2.63

a. Construct a relative frequency distribution for the data.

b. Construct a cumulative relative frequency distribution for the data.

c. Construct a histogram for the data.

44. A *Business Week*/Harris poll surveyed business executives for their opinions about the economic outlook for 1995 (*Business Week*, January 9, 1995). Concerning inflation, 57% said it would go up, 18% said it would go down, 24% said it would stay the same, and 1% were not sure. Construct a bar graph and a pie chart for the 1995 inflation outlook of these executives.

45. Seventy-nine new shadow stocks were reported by the American Association of Individual Investors (*AAII Journal,* April 1992). The term "shadow" indicates stocks for small to medium-size firms not followed closely by the major brokerage houses. Information on where the stock was traded—New York Stock Exchange (NYSE), American Stock Exchange (AMEX), and over the counter (OTC)—the earnings per share, and the price–earnings ratio was provided for the following sample of 15 shadow stocks.

SHADOW

Stock	Exchange	Earnings per Share ($)	Price–Earnings Ratio
Selas Corp of America	AMEX	1.61	7.1
CE Software Holdings	OTC	4.13	7.5
Shult Homes Corp	AMEX	1.05	11.0
Basic American Medical	OTC	1.06	12.0
Titan Corporation	NYSE	.24	18.3
First Team Sports	OTC	.51	18.6
Cooker Restaurant Corp	OTC	.76	43.1
Chempower	OTC	.22	20.5
Benchmark Electronics	AMEX	.62	25.0
Mylex Corp	OTC	.11	37.5
Pharmacy Mgmt Service	OTC	.22	50.0
Arrow Automotive Indus.	AMEX	.23	38.6
U.S. Filter Corp	AMEX	.23	73.4
Sun Sportswear	OTC	.21	28.6
Village Supermarket	OTC	.61	13.5

a. Provide frequency and relative frequency distributions for the exchange data. Where are most shadow stocks listed?

b. Provide frequency and relative frequency distributions for the earnings-per-share and price–earnings ratio data. Use class limits of .00–.49, .50–.99, and so on, for the earnings-per-share data and class limits of 0.0–9.9, 10.0–19.9, and so on for the price–earnings ratio data. What observations and comments can you make about the shadow stocks?

STATES

46. A state-by-state listing of per capita incomes for 1991 follows (*The Wall Street Journal,* April 23, 1992).

State	Income	State	Income	State	Income
Ala.	$15,567	Ky.	$15,539	N.D.	$16,088
Alaska	21,932	La.	15,143	Ohio	17,916
Ariz.	16,401	Maine	17,306	Okla.	15,827
Ark.	14,753	Md.	22,080	Ore.	17,592
Calif.	20,952	Mass.	22,897	Pa.	19,128
Colo.	19,440	Mich.	18,679	R.I.	18,840
Conn.	25,881	Minn.	19,107	S.C.	15,420
Del.	20,349	Miss.	13,343	S.D.	16,392
D.C.	24,439	Mo.	17,842	Tenn.	16,325
Fla.	18,880	Mont.	16,043	Texas	17,305
Ga.	17,364	Neb.	17,852	Utah	14,529
Hawaii	21,306	Nev.	19,175	Vt.	17,747
Idaho	15,401	N.H.	20,951	Va.	19,976
Ill.	20,824	N.J.	25,372	Wash.	19,442
Ind.	17,217	N.M.	14,844	W.Va.	14,174
Iowa	17,505	N.Y.	22,456	Wis.	18,046
Kan.	18,511	N.C.	16,642	Wyo.	17,118

Develop a frequency distribution, a relative frequency distribution, and a histogram for the data.

47. The conclusion from a 40-state poll conducted by the Joint Council on Economic Education (*Time,* January 9, 1989) is that students do not learn enough economics. The findings were based on test results from 11th- and 12th-grade students who took a 46-question, multiple-choice test on basic economic concepts such as profit and the law of supply and demand. The following table gives sample data on the number of questions answered correctly.

12	16	22	17	18	23
31	18	24	20	24	28
24	25	19	26	18	18
22	16	13	33	19	14
8	15	16	14	22	19
10	21	15	9	16	
14	30	12	12	17	

Summarize these data using:
a. A stem-and-leaf display.   **b.** A frequency distribution.
c. A relative frequency distribution.   **d.** A cumulative frequency distribution.
e. On the basis of these data, do you agree with the claim that students are not learning enough economics? Explain.

48. The daily high and low temperatures for 24 cities follow (*USA Today,* January 9, 1995).

CITIES

City	High	Low	City	High	Low
Tampa	68	45	Birmingham	58	34
Kansas City	37	28	Minneapolis	17	10
Boise	52	41	Portland	51	48
Los Angeles	66	59	Memphis	54	34
Philadelphia	42	26	Buffalo	26	10
Milwaukee	25	12	Cincinnati	37	24
Chicago	27	16	Charlotte	52	33
Albany	31	9	Boston	38	19
Houston	72	49	Tulsa	54	35
Salt Lake City	51	39	Washington, D.C.	43	28
Miami	75	57	Las Vegas	58	48
Cheyenne	49	35	Detroit	27	13

a. Prepare a stem-and-leaf display for the high temperatures.
b. Prepare a stem-and-leaf display for the low temperatures.
c. Compare the stem-and-leaf displays from (a) and (b) and make some comments about the differences between daily high and low temperatures.
d. Use the stem-and-leaf display from (b) to determine the number of cities having a low temperature of freezing (32°F) or below.
e. Provide frequency distributions for both the high- and low-temperature data.

49. Refer to the data set for high and low temperatures at 24 cities in Exercise 48.
a. Develop a scatter diagram to show the relationship between the two variables, high temperature and low temperature.
b. Comment on the relationship between high and low temperature.

50. Following are financial data for 20 companies in the banking and consumer products industries (*Business Week,* August 15, 1994).

BWDATA

Company	Industry	Price–Earnings Ratio	Profit Margin
Avon Products	Consumer	16	7.2
Bankers Trust	Bank	6	11.1
CoreStates	Bank	15	10.3
Fruit of Loom	Consumer	11	6.1
Mellon Bank	Bank	9	15.4
Liz Claiborne	Consumer	17	3.2
Russell	Consumer	26	5.2
Circuit City	Consumer	16	1.9
State Street	Bank	15	13.5
Banc One	Bank	10	16.7
Maytag	Consumer	19	4.7
First Chicago	Bank	6	15.3
Norwest	Bank	11	13.6
Whirlpool	Consumer	13	4.2
NationsBank	Bank	9	14.6
Wachovia	Bank	11	19.0
Coca-Cola	Consumer	24	17.5
Colgate	Consumer	15	7.5
BankAmerica	Bank	10	14.4
Philip Morris	Consumer	13	9.1

a. Prepare a crosstabulation for the variables industry type and price–earnings ratio. Use industry types as the row labels.

b. Compute the row percentages for your crosstabulation in part (a).

c. What relationship, if any, do you notice between industry type and price–earnings ratio?

51. Refer to the data set in Exercise 50 containing financial data for 20 companies in the banking and consumer products industries.

a. Prepare a scatter diagram to show the relationship between the variables price–earnings ratio and profit margin.

b. Comment on any relationship that is apparent between the variables.

52. A survey of commercial buildings served by the Cincinnati Gas & Electric Company was concluded in 1992 (CG&E Commercial Building Characteristics Survey, November 25, 1992). One question asked what main heating fuel was used and another asked the year the commercial building was constructed. A partial crosstabulation of the findings follows.

Year Constructed	Fuel Type				
	Electricity	Natural Gas	Oil	Propane	Other
1973 or before	40	183	12	5	7
1974–1979	24	26	2	2	0
1980–1986	37	38	1	0	6
1987–1991	48	70	2	0	1

a. Complete the crosstabulation by showing the row totals and column totals.

b. Show the frequency distributions for year constructed and for fuel type.

c. Prepare a crosstabulation showing column percentages.

d. Prepare a crosstabulation showing row percentages.

e. Comment on the relationship between year constructed and fuel type.

COMPUTER CASE

CONSOLIDATED FOODS, INC.

Consolidated Foods, Inc. operates a chain of supermarkets in New Mexico, Arizona, and California. A recent promotional campaign has advertised the chain's offering of a new credit-card policy whereby Consolidated Foods' customers have the option of paying for their purchases with credit cards such as Visa and MasterCard in addition to the usual options of cash or personal check. The new policy is being implemented on a trial basis with the hope that the credit-card option will encourage customers to make larger purchases.

After the first month of operation, a random sample of 100 customers was selected over a one-week period. Data were collected on the method of payment and how much was spent by each of the 100 customers. The sample data are shown in Table 2.20. Prior to the new credit-card policy, approximately 50% of Consolidated Foods' customers paid in cash and approximately 50% paid by personal check.

Managerial Report

Use the tabular and graphical methods of descriptive statistics to summarize the sample data in Table 2.20. Your report should contain summaries such as the following.

1. A frequency and relative frequency distribution for the method of payment.
2. A bar graph or pie chart for the method of payment.
3. Frequency and relative frequency distributions for the amount spent in each method of payment.
4. Histograms and/or stem-and-leaf plots for the amount spent in each method of payment.

CONSOLID

TABLE 2.20 Purchase Amount and Method of Payment* for a Random Sample of 100 Consolidated Foods Customers

Cash	Personal Check	Credit Card	Cash	Personal Check	Credit Card
$ 7.40	$27.60	$50.30	$ 5.08	$52.87	$69.77
5.15	30.60	33.76	20.48	78.16	48.11
4.75	41.58	25.57	16.28	25.96	
15.10	36.09	46.24	15.57	31.07	
8.81	2.67	46.13	6.93	35.38	
1.85	34.67	14.44	7.17	58.11	
7.41	58.64	43.79	11.54	49.21	
11.77	57.59	19.78	13.09	31.74	
12.07	43.14	52.35	16.69	50.58	
9.00	21.11	52.63	7.02	59.78	
5.98	52.04	57.55	18.09	72.46	
7.88	18.77	27.66	2.44	37.94	
5.91	42.83	44.53	1.09	42.69	
3.65	55.40	26.91	2.96	41.10	
14.28	48.95	55.21	11.17	40.51	
1.27	36.48	54.19	16.38	37.20	
2.87	51.66	22.59	8.85	54.84	
4.34	28.58	53.32	7.22	58.75	
3.31	35.89	26.57		17.87	
15.07	39.55	27.89		69.22	

*The data are based on actual bills and types of payments reported for grocery purchases (*The Wall Street Journal,* April 9, 1992).

What preliminary insights do you have about the amounts spent and method of payment at Consolidated Foods? The data set for this computer case is available in the data file CONSOLID (see Appendix D).

APPENDIX 2.1

Dot Plots and Histograms with Minitab

● In this appendix we describe the steps necessary to use Minitab to generate a dot plot, a frequency distribution, and a histogram for the audit-time data in Table 2.7. We first enter the audit-time data into column C1 of a Minitab worksheet. The following steps generate the computer output shown in Figure 2.6.

Step 1.   Select the **Graph** pull-down menu
Step 2.   Select **Character Graphs**
Step 3.   Select **Dotplot**
Step 4.   When the dialog box appears:
             Enter C1 in the **Variables** box
             Select **OK**

The dot plot in panel A of Figure 2.6 will then appear.

To obtain the histogram shown in panel B of Figure 2.6, the following steps are necessary.

Step 1.   Select the **Graph** pull-down menu
Step 2.   Select **Histogram**
Step 3.   When the **Histogram** dialog box appears:
             Enter C1 in the **Graph variables** box
             Select **Bar** under **Display** and **Graph** under **For each** in the **Data display** box
             Select **Options**
Step 4.   When the **Histogram Options** dialog box appears:
             Select **Frequency** under **Type of Histogram**
             Select **Cutpoint** under **Type of Intervals**
             Select **Midpoint/cutpoint positions** under **Definition of Intervals** and enter **10:35/5** in the box
             Select **OK**
Step 5.   When the Histogram dialog box appears:
             Select **OK**

APPENDIX 2.2

Frequency Distributions and Histograms with Spreadsheets

● Spreadsheet software packages such as Microsoft Excel, Lotus 1-2-3, and Quattro Pro have the capability of performing many of the statistical methods presented in this text. Generally, the user of the spreadsheet enters data directly into the spreadsheet. Built-in statistical routines, or user-provided formulas, are used to generate the desired statistical information. In this appendix, we show how Excel can be used to construct a frequency distribution and a histogram for the audit-time data in Table 2.7.

Excel provides a worksheet of rows and columns that can be used to enter and store the data. Suppose we enter the 20 observations for the audit-time data set in rows 1 to 20 of column A (see Figure 2.11) and want to develop a frequency distribution and a histogram with five classes: 10–14, 15–19, 20–24, 25–29, and 30–34.

To develop a frequency distribution and histogram, Excel requires the user to identify what are called *bins* for the data. A bin must be identified for each class and its upper limit must be specified. Hence, five bins with upper limits of 14, 19, 24, 29, and 34 are needed for the audit-time data. In constructing the frequency distribution and histogram, Excel provides a count of the number of items with data values *less than or equal* to the upper limit of the first bin (14), a count of the number of items with data values *greater than* the first bin upper limit and *less than or equal to* the second bin upper limit (19), and so on. With the bin upper limits being equal to the upper class limits, the counts provided by Excel are the class frequencies for the frequency distribution.

Prior to implementing the Excel frequency distribution and/or histogram procedure, we must enter the bin upper limits in *ascending order* in a column or row of the worksheet. Let us select column C as a convenient location and enter the title Bin in row 2. The bin upper limits are then entered in ascending order in rows 3 through 7 of column C. Figure 2.11 is the worksheet with the audit-time data in column A and the bin upper limits in column C.

The following steps describe how to use Excel to produce a frequency distribution and a histogram for the data and worksheet in Figure 2.11.

	A	B	C	D
1	12			
2	15		Bin	
3	20		14	
4	22		19	
5	14		24	
6	14		29	
7	15		34	
8	27			
9	21			
10	18			
11	19			
12	18			
13	22			
14	33			
15	16			
16	18			
17	17			
18	23			
19	28			
20	13			

FIGURE 2.11   Data and Bin Values for the Spreadsheet Summary of the Audit-Time Data

	A	B	C	D
1	12			
2	15		Bin	
3	20		14	
4	22		19	
5	14		24	
6	14		29	
7	15		34	
8	27			
9	21			
10	18		*Bin*	*Frequency*
11	19		14	4
12	18		19	8
13	22		24	5
14	33		29	2
15	16		34	1
16	18		More	0
17	17			
18	23			
19	28			
20	13			

FIGURE 2.12 Frequency Distribution of the Audit-Time Data Constructed by Excel

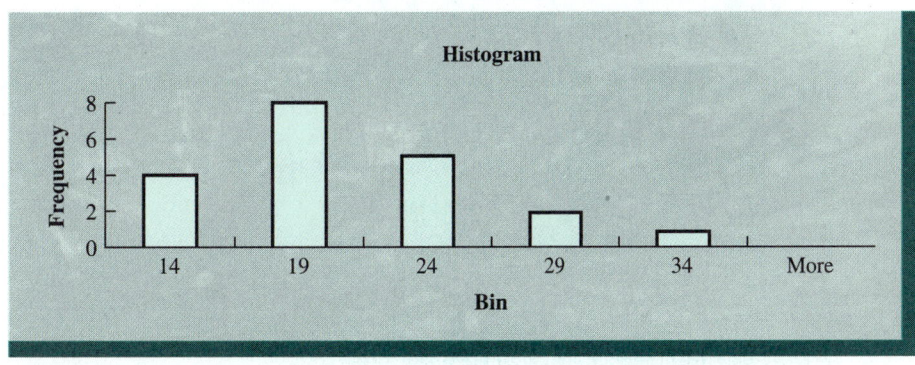

FIGURE 2.13 A Histogram of the Audit-Time Data Constructed by Excel

Step 1. Select the **Tools** pull-down menu
Step 2. Choose the **Data Analysis** option
Step 3. Choose **Histogram** from the list of Analysis Tools
Step 4. When the dialog box appears:
Enter A1:A20 in the **Input Range** box
Enter C3:C7 in the **Bin Range** box
Select **Output Range**
Enter C10 in the **Output Range** box (this identifies the upper left corner of the
section of the worksheet where the frequency distribution will appear)

Select **Chart Output** (this requests a histogram)
Select **OK**

Figure 2.12 is the frequency distribution provided by Excel. The title Bin and the upper limits are shown in cells C10 through C15. The frequencies appear in the corresponding cells of column D. Note that Excel includes a last bin labeled More in case the data set contains data values greater than the upper limit of the last bin specified by the user. When interpreting the output, the user must remember that the bin values are the upper limits of the corresponding classes.

To convert the Excel frequency distribution into an easier-to-read format, the user can replace the title Bin in cell C10 with a descriptive title such as Audit Times. The upper limits in cells C11 through C15 can be replaced by the class limits of 10–14, 15–19, 20–24, 25–29, and 30–34. Finally, the title Total and the sum of the frequencies (50) can be entered in cells C17 and D17 to complete the frequency distribution.

Figure 2.13 is the histogram generated as a result of the preceding steps. We caution that the values shown on the horizontal axis are the upper limits and not class midpoints. Finally, the axis label Bin can be replaced by a descriptive title such as Audit Times.

3

DESCRIPTIVE STATISTICS II: NUMERICAL METHODS

CONTENTS

STATISTICS IN PRACTICE ●

Barnes Hospital*
St. Louis, Missouri

Barnes Hospital at the Washington University Medical Center, established in 1914, is the leading provider of health care for the people of St. Louis and neighboring areas. The hospital is nationally recognized as one of the best in the United States. The Hospice Program at Barnes Hospital improves the quality of life for terminally ill patients and their families. The hospice team consists of a medical director, coordinator, RN supervisor, home and inpatient RNs, home health aids, social workers, chaplains, dietitians, trained volunteers, and professionals from other ancillary services as needed. Through the coordinated efforts of the hospice team, patients and families are given the guidance and support necessary to cope with the strains created by serious illness, separation, and death.

In the coordination and administration of the hospice program, monthly reports and quarterly summaries help team members review the ongoing services. Statistical summaries of performance data are used as a basis for planning and implementing policy changes.

For example, data are collected on the length of time patients stay in the hospice program. A sample of 67 patient records showed that the time in the program ranged from one day to 185 days. A frequency distribution was helpful in summarizing and communicating the length-of-stay data. In addition, the following numerical measures of descriptive statistics were used to provide valuable information about the patient time in the program.

Mean:	35.7 days
Median:	17 days
Mode:	1 day

---

*Ms. Paula H. Gianino, Hospice Coordinator at Barnes Hospital, provided this Statistics in Practice.

Interpretation of these statistics shows that the mean, or average, time a patient stays in the program is 35.7 days, or slightly over a month. However, the median shows that half of the patients are in the program 17 days or less and half are in the program 17 days or more. The mode of one day is the most frequent data value and indicates that many patients have a short stay in the program.

Other statistical summaries about the hospice program include the number of admissions, the number of days spent at home versus the number of days in the inpatient unit, the number of discharges from the inpatient unit, and the number of patient deaths at home and in the inpatient unit. These summaries are analyzed according to patient age and Medicare coverage. Overall, descriptive statistics provide valuable information about the hospice services.

In this chapter you will learn how to compute and interpret the statistical measures used by Barnes Hospital. In addition to the mean, median, and mode, you will learn about other descriptive statistics such as range, variance, standard deviation, percentiles, and correlation. These numerical measures will assist in the understanding and interpretation of data.

Barnes Hospital is a leader in health care for all ages.

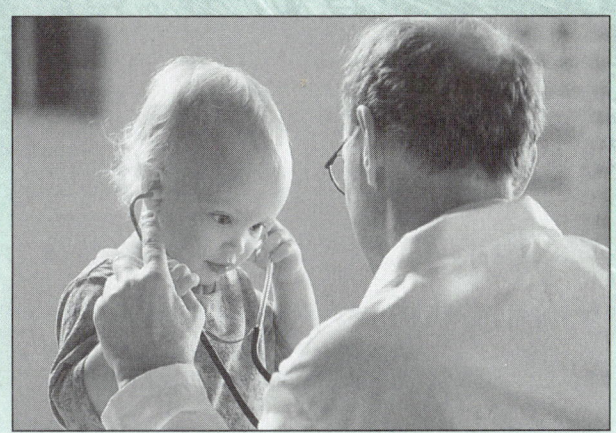

● In Chapter 2 we discussed tabular and graphical methods used to summarize data. These procedures are effective in written reports and as visual aids for presentations to individuals or groups. In this chapter, we present several numerical methods of descriptive statistics that provide additional alternatives for summarizing data.

We start by considering data sets consisting of a single variable. Whenever the data for a single variable, such as age, salary, or the like, have been obtained from a sample of n elements, the data set will contain n items, or data values. The numerical measures of location and dispersion are computed by using the n data values. If there is more than one variable, such numerical measures can be computed separately for each variable. In the two-variable case, we will develop measures of the strength of the relationship between the variables.

Several numerical measures of location, dispersion, and association are introduced. If the measures are computed for data from a sample, they are called *sample statistics*. If the measures are computed for data from a population, they are called *population parameters*.

3.1 MEASURES OF LOCATION

MEAN

Perhaps the most important numerical measure of location is the *mean,* or average value, for a variable. The mean provides a measure of central location. It is obtained by adding all the data values and dividing by the number of items. If the data are from a sample, the mean is denoted by $\bar{x}$; if the data are from a population, the mean is denoted by the Greek letter μ.

In specifying statistical formulas, it is customary to denote the value of the first data item by x_1, the value of the second data item by x_2, and so on. In general, the ith data value is denoted by x_i. Stated in this notation, the formula for the sample mean follows.

SAMPLE MEAN

$$\bar{x} = \frac{\Sigma x_i}{n} \qquad\qquad (3.1)$$

The number of items in the sample is denoted by n. In this formula, the numerator is the sum of the n data values. That is,

$$\Sigma x_i = x_1 + x_2 + \cdots + x_n$$

The Greek letter Σ is the summation sign.

To illustrate the computation of a sample mean, let us consider the following class-size data for a sample of five college classes.

$$46 \quad 54 \quad 42 \quad 46 \quad 32$$

We use the notation x_1, x_2, x_3, x_4, x_5 to represent the number of students in each of the five classes.

$$x_1 = 46 \quad x_2 = 54 \quad x_3 = 42 \quad x_4 = 46 \quad x_5 = 32$$

Hence, to compute the sample mean, we can write

$$\bar{x} = \frac{\Sigma x_i}{n} = \frac{x_1 + x_2 + x_3 + x_4 + x_5}{5} = \frac{46 + 54 + 42 + 46 + 32}{5} = 44$$

For the five classes sampled, the mean class size is 44 students.

TABLE 3.1 Monthly Starting Salaries for a Sample of 12 Business School Graduates

Graduate	Monthly Salary ($)	Graduate	Monthly Salary ($)
1	2350	7	2390
2	2450	8	2630
3	2550	9	2440
4	2380	10	2825
5	2255	11	2420
6	2210	12	2380

Another illustration of the computation of a sample mean is given in the following situation. Suppose that a college placement office sent a questionnaire to a sample of business school graduates requesting information on starting salaries. Table 3.1 shows the data that have been collected. The mean monthly starting salary for the sample of 12 business college graduates is computed as

$$\bar{x} = \frac{\Sigma x_i}{n} = \frac{x_1 + x_2 + \cdots + x_{12}}{12}$$

$$= \frac{2350 + 2450 + \cdots + 2380}{12}$$

$$= \frac{29{,}280}{12} = 2440$$

Equation (3.1) shows how the mean is computed for a sample with n items. The formula for computing the mean of a population is the same, but we use different notation to indicate that we are working with the entire population. The number of elements in the population is denoted by N and the symbol for the population mean is μ.

POPULATION MEAN

$$\mu = \frac{\Sigma x_i}{N} \tag{3.2}$$

TRIMMED MEAN

Occasionally, a variable will have one or more unusually small and/or unusually large data values that significantly influence the value of the mean. With this influence, the mean may provide a poor description of the central location of the data. To remove the effect of the unusually small and/or large data values, we can eliminate, or trim, a percentage of small and large data values from the data set. The mean of the remaining data is called the *trimmed mean*. The intent is for the trimmed mean to be a better indicator of the central location of the data. For example, to obtain a 5% trimmed mean we remove the smallest 5% of the data values *and* the largest 5% of the data values, then compute the mean of the middle 90% of the data. In general, an α percent trimmed mean is obtained by trimming α percent of the items from each end of the data and computing the mean for the remaining items.

Consider the 5% trimmed mean for the monthly starting salaries of 12 business school graduates. The smallest 5% and the largest 5% of the data values are to be trimmed from the data set. Here, 5% of 12 is .05(12) = .60 data values. In computing the trimmed mean, we simply round the number of data values trimmed to its nearest integer value; in this case .60 is rounded to 1, indicating that one item will be removed from each end of the data set. After elimination of the smallest data value (2210) and the largest data value (2825), the 5% trimmed mean based on the 10 remaining data values can be shown to be 24,245/10 = 2424.50.

MEDIAN

The *median* is another measure of central location for data. The median is the value in the middle when the data items are arranged in ascending order (rank ordered from smallest to largest). If there is an odd number of items, the median is the value of the middle item. If there is an even number of items, there is no single middle item. In this case, we follow the convention of defining the median to be the average of the values for the middle two items. For convenience the definition of the median is restated as follows.

> **MEDIAN**
>
> If there is an odd number of items, the median is the value of the middle item when all items are arranged in ascending order.
>
> If there is an even number of items, the median is the average value of the two middle items when all items are arranged in ascending order.

Let us apply this definition to compute the median class size for the sample of five college classes. Arranging the five data values in ascending order provides the following rank-ordered list.

$$32 \quad 42 \quad 46 \quad 46 \quad 54$$

Since $n = 5$ is odd, the median is the middle item in the rank-ordered list. Thus the median class size is 46 students. Even though there are two values of 46, each value is treated as a separate item when we arrange the data in ascending order and determine the median.

Suppose we also compute the median starting salary for the business college graduates. We arrange the 12 items in Table 3.1 in ascending order.

$$2210 \quad 2255 \quad 2350 \quad 2380 \quad 2380 \quad \underbrace{2390 \quad 2420}_{\text{Middle Two Values}} \quad 2440 \quad 2450 \quad 2550 \quad 2630 \quad 2825$$

Since $n = 12$ is even, we identify the middle two items. The median is the average of these two values.

$$\text{Median} = \frac{2390 + 2420}{2} = 2405$$

Although the mean is the more commonly used measure of central location, there are some situations in which the median is preferred. As we stated previously, the mean is influenced by extremely small and large data values. For instance, suppose that one of the graduates had a starting salary of $10,000 per month (maybe the individual's family owns the company). If we change the highest monthly starting salary in Table 3.1 from $2825 to $10,000 and recompute the mean, the sample mean changes from 2440 to 3038. The median of 2405, however, is unchanged, since 2390 and 2420 are still the middle two items. With the extremely high starting salary included, the median provides a better measure of central location than the mean. We can generalize to say that whenever there are extreme data values, the median is often the preferred measure of central location.

MODE

A third measure of location is the *mode*. The mode is defined as follows.

> **MODE**
> The mode is the data value that occurs with greatest frequency.

To illustrate the identification of the mode, consider the sample of five class sizes. The only value that occurs more than once is 46. Since this value, occurring with a frequency of 2, has the greatest frequency, it is the mode. As another illustration, consider the sample of starting salaries for the business school graduates. The only monthly starting salary that occurs more than once is 2380. Since this value has the greatest frequency, it is the mode.

Situations can arise for which the greatest frequency occurs at two or more different values. In these instances more than one mode exists. If the data have exactly two modes, we say that the data are *bimodal*. If data have more than two modes, we say that the data are *multimodal*. In multimodal cases the mode is almost never reported, since listing three or more modes would not be very helpful in describing a location for the data.

The mode is an important measure of location for qualitative data. For example, the qualitative data set in Table 2.1 resulted in the following frequency distribution for personal computer purchases.

Company	Frequency
Apple	13
Compaq	12
Gateway 2000	5
IBM	9
Packard Bell	11
Total	50

The mode, or most frequently purchased personal computer, is Apple. For this type of data it obviously makes no sense to speak of the mean or median. The mode provides the information of interest, the most frequently purchased brand of personal computer.

PERCENTILES

A *percentile* is a measure that locates values in the data set that are not necessarily central locations. A percentile provides information about how the data items are spread over the interval from the smallest value to the largest value. For data that do not have numerous repeated values, the pth percentile divides the data into two parts. Approximately p percent of the items have values less than the pth percentile; approximately $(100 - p)$ percent of the items have values greater than the pth percentile. The pth percentile is formally defined as follows.

PERCENTILE

The pth percentile is a value such that *at least* p percent of the items take this value or less and *at least* $(100 - p)$ percent of the items take this value or more.

Admission test scores for colleges and universities are frequently reported in terms of percentiles. For instance, suppose an applicant obtains a raw score of 54 on the verbal portion of an admission test. How this student performed in relation to other students taking the same test may not be readily apparent. However, if the raw score of 54 corresponds to the 70th percentile, we know that approximately 70% of the students had scores lower than this individual's and approximately 30% of the students had scores higher than this individual's.

The following procedure can be used to compute the pth percentile.

CALCULATING THE pTH PERCENTILE

Step 1. Arrange the data in ascending order (rank order from smallest value to largest value).

Step 2. Compute an index i

$$i = \left(\frac{p}{100} \right) n$$

where p is the percentile of interest and n is the number of items.

Step 3. (a) If i *is not an integer, round up.* The next integer value *greater* than i denotes the position of the pth percentile.

(b) If i *is an integer,* the pth percentile is the average of the data values in positions i and $i + 1$.

As an illustration of this procedure, let us determine the 85th percentile for the starting salary data in Table 3.1.

Step 1. Arrange the 12 data values in ascending order.

2210   2255   2350   2380   2380   2390   2420   2440   2450   2550   2630   2825

Step 2 .

$$i = \left(\frac{p}{100} \right) n = \left(\frac{85}{100} \right) 12 = 10.2$$

Step 3. Since i is not an integer, *round up.* The position of the 85th percentile is the next integer greater than 10.2, the 11th position.

Returning to the data, we see that the 85th percentile corresponds to the 11th data position, or 2630.

As another illustration of this procedure, let us consider the calculation of the 50th percentile. Applying step 2, we obtain

$$i = \left(\frac{50}{100} \right) 12 = 6$$

Since i is an integer, step 3(b) states that the 50th percentile is the average of the sixth and seventh data values; thus the 50th percentile is $(2390 + 2420)/2 = 2405$. Note that the *50th percentile is also the median.*

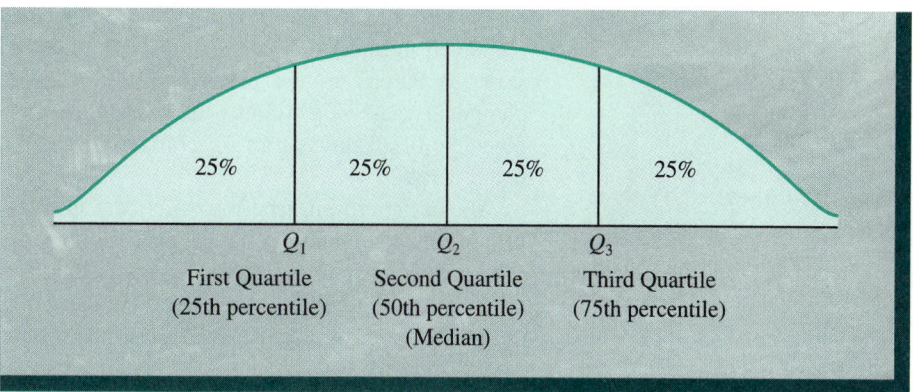

FIGURE 3.1 Location of the Quartiles

QUARTILES AND HINGES

It is often desirable to divide data into four parts, with each part containing approximately one-fourth, or 25%, of the items. Figure 3.1 shows a data set divided into four parts. The division points are referred to as the *quartiles* and are defined as

Q_1 = first quartile, or 25th percentile,

Q_2 = second quartile, or 50th percentile (also the median), and

Q_3 = third quartile, or 75th percentile.

The monthly starting salary data are again arranged in ascending order. Q_2, the second quartile (median), has already been identified as 2405.

2210   2255   2350   2380   2380   2390   2420   2440   2450   2550   2630   2825

The computations of Q_1 and Q_3 require the use of the rule for finding the 25th and 75th percentiles. Those calculations follow.

For Q_1,

$$i = \left(\frac{p}{100}\right)n = \left(\frac{25}{100}\right)12 = 3$$

Since i is an integer, step 3(b) indicates that the first quartile, or 25th percentile, is the average of the third and fourth data values; thus, $Q_1 = (2350 + 2380)/2 = 2365$.

For Q_3,

$$i = \left(\frac{p}{100}\right)n = \left(\frac{75}{100}\right)12 = 9$$

Again, since i is an integer, step 3(b) indicates that the third quartile, or 75th percentile, is the average of the ninth and tenth data values; thus, $Q_3 = (2450 + 2550)/2 = 2500$.

As shown below, the quartiles have divided the 12 data values into four parts, with each part consisting of 25% of the items.

2210   2255   2350 | 2380   2380   2390 | 2420   2440   2450 | 2550   2630   2825

$Q_1 = 2365$ $Q_2 = 2405$ $Q_3 = 2500$
                     (Median)

We have defined the quartiles as the 25th, 50th, and 75th percentiles. Thus, we have computed the quartiles in the same way as the other percentiles. However, there are some variations in the conventions used to compute quartiles; the actual values computed may vary slightly depending on the convention used. Nevertheless, the objective of all procedures for computing quartiles is to divide data into roughly four equal parts.

Another approach used to divide data into four equal parts has been developed by proponents of exploratory data analysis. A *lower hinge* (lower 25%) and an *upper hinge* (upper 25%) are computed. To find these hinges, we first arrange the items in ascending order. Then we divide the data into two equal parts: data in positions less than or equal to the median position and data in positions greater than or equal to the median position. The median for the data in positions *less than or equal to the median position* is the lower hinge. The median for the data in positions *greater than or equal to the median position* is the upper hinge.

Referring to the sample of 12 monthly starting salaries for business school graduates, we know that the median is 2405. From the listing of the data in ascending order, we know that the median position is halfway between the sixth and seventh data values. The data in positions less than or equal to the median position are the data in positions 1 to 6.

$$2210 \quad 2255 \quad 2350 \quad 2380 \quad 2380 \quad 2390$$

Following the rule for determining a median, we see that the median of these six values is $(2350 + 2380)/2 = 2365$. Thus, the *lower hinge* of the data is 2365.

The data in positions greater than or equal to the median position are the data in positions 7 to 12:

$$2420 \quad 2440 \quad 2450 \quad 2550 \quad 2630 \quad 2825$$

The median of these six values is $(2450 + 2550)/2 = 2500$. Thus, the *upper hinge* of the data is 2500. The lower hinge, the median, and the upper hinge can be used to divide the data into four parts.

For the salary data, the lower hinge is equal to the first quartile and the upper hinge is equal to the third quartile. However, this may not be true for every data set. In some cases, the hinges and the quartiles take slightly different values because they are based on slightly different computational procedures.

NOTES AND COMMENTS

In computing the hinges for data with an odd number of items, the median position is included in the computation of the lower hinge *and* in the computation of the upper hinge. For example, with nine elements, the median position is 5. The median of the data in positions 1 through 5, the data value in position 3, is the lower hinge, and the median of the data in positions 5 through 9, the data value in position 7, is the upper hinge. The median position 5 is used in both computations.

EXERCISES

METHODS

1. Consider the sample of size 5 with data values of 10, 20, 12, 17, and 16. Compute the mean and median.

2. Consider the sample of size 6 with data values of 10, 20, 21, 17, 16, and 12. Compute the mean and median.

Self-Test

3. Consider the sample of size 8 with data values of 27, 25, 20, 15, 30, 34, 28, and 25. Compute the 20th, 25th, 65th, and 75th percentiles.

4. Given a sample of 36 items, how many items should be trimmed from each end of the data set to compute the 5% trimmed mean?

APPLICATIONS

ENTRYSAL

5. According to *U.S. News & World Report,* entry-level jobs in accounting paid from $27,000 to $31,000 annually (October 31, 1994). A sample of entry-level salaries follows. Data are in thousands of dollars.

29.6	28.5	28.6	29.4	28.6
31.0	29.2	30.8	28.4	27.5
30.4	29.7	27.2	30.3	29.6
28.0	26.7	28.7	28.6	29.1
28.8	28.5	29.0	27.4	29.9

a. What is the mean entry-level salary?
b. What is the median entry-level salary?
c. What is the mode?
d. What is the first quartile?
e. What is the third quartile?

6. The American Association of Individual Investors conducts an annual survey of discount brokers. Shown below are the commissions charged for a trade of 500 shares at $50 per share for a sample of 20 discount brokers. (*AAII Journal,* January, 1994).

Broker	Commission ($)	Broker	Commission ($)
Peck	100	Pace	75
Aufhauser	32	People's	131
Broker's Ex	160	Pro Value	173
Burke	120	Royal Grimm	75
Schwab	155	Seaport	50
Downstate	90	St. Louis	64
Freeman	145	T. Rowe	134
Kennedy	33	Unified	154
Max Ule	195	White	42
Mongerson	95	Your	55

a. Compute the mean, median, and mode for the commission charged.
b. Compute and interpret the first and third quartiles.

7. A quality control inspector found the following numbers of defective parts on 16 different days.

11   14   18   14   21   17   13   21   25   19   17   13   28   13   17   18

Compute the mean, median, mode, and 90th percentile.

Self-Test

8. *American Demographics* (December 1988) reported that 25 million Americans get up each morning and go to work in their offices at home. The growing use of personal computers is suggested to be one of the reasons more people can operate at-home businesses. The article presented data on the ages of individuals who work at home. Following is a sample of age data for these individuals.

22	58	24	50	29	52	57	31	30	41
44	40	46	29	31	37	32	44	49	29

    a. Compute the mean and mode.

    b. Compute a 5% and a 10% trimmed mean.

    c. The median age of the population of all adults is 40.5 years. Use the median age of the preceding data to comment on whether the at-home workers tend to be younger or older than the population of all adults.

    d. Compute the first and third quartiles.

    e. Compute and interpret the 32nd percentile.

9. The American Association of Advertising Agencies records data on nonprogramming minutes per half-hour of prime-time television programming (*U.S. News & World Report,* April 13, 1992). Representative data follow for a sample of prime-time programs on major networks at 8:30 P.M.

6.0	6.6	5.8	7.0	6.3	6.2	7.2	5.7	6.4	7.0
6.5	6.2	6.0	6.5	7.2	7.3	7.6	6.8	6.0	6.2

    a. Compute the mean and median.

    b. Compute the first and third quartiles.

    c. Using the sample mean, find the percentage of viewing time spent on prime-time advertisements, promotions, and credits. What percentage of viewing time is spent on the programs themselves?

10. A bowler's scores for six games are 182, 168, 184, 190, 170, and 174. Using these data as a sample, compute the following descriptive statistics.

    a. Mean   **b.** Median   **c.** Mode   **d.** 75th percentile

11. Monthly sales data for car telephone units for the RC Radio Corporation follow.

80	115	82	102	94	90	88	91	89	95	105	108

Compute the mean, median, and mode for monthly sales.

12. The *Los Angeles Times* regularly reports the air quality index for various areas of Southern California. Index ratings of 0–50 are considered good, 51–100 moderate, 101–200 unhealthy, 201–275 very unhealthy, and over 275 hazardous. Recent air quality indexes for Pomona were 28, 42, 58, 48, 45, 55, 60, 49, and 50.

    a. Compute the mean, median, and mode for the data. Should the Pomona air quality index be considered good?

    b. Compute the 25th percentile and 75th percentile for the Pomona air quality data.

    c. Compute the lower and upper hinges. Compare your result with the answers to (b).

13. The following data represent the number of automobiles arriving at a toll booth during 20 intervals, each of 10-minute duration. Compute the mean, median, mode, first quartile, and third quartile for the data.

26	26	58	24	22	22	15	33	19	27
21	18	16	20	34	24	27	30	31	33

14. In automobile mileage and gasoline-consumption testing, 13 automobiles were road tested for 300 miles in both city and country driving conditions. The following data were recorded for miles-per-gallon performance.

City: 16.2 16.7 15.9 14.4 13.2 15.3 16.8 16.0 16.1 15.3 15.2 15.3 16.2
Country: 19.4 20.6 18.3 18.6 19.2 17.4 17.2 18.6 19.0 21.1 19.4 18.5 18.7

Use the mean, median, and mode to make a statement about the difference in performance for city and country driving.

15. A sample of 15 college seniors showed the following credit hours taken during the final term of the senior year:

15	21	18	16	18	21	19	15	14	18	17	20	18	15	16

a. What are the mean, median, and mode for credit hours taken? Compute and interpret.
b. Compute the first and third quartiles.
c. Compute the lower and upper hinges. Compare your answers to (b).
d. Compute and interpret the 70th percentile.

16. Pennsylvania is the nation's fifth largest producer of Christmas trees, with a projected crop of 1.5 million trees for 1994. Tree prices range from $3.50 to $5.50 per foot (*The Philadelphia Inquirer,* December 3, 1994). Suppose the following data represent the price per foot for 16 trees sold in the Philadelphia area.

3.90	4.20	3.90	5.10
4.20	4.50	4.10	5.10
4.30	4.20	4.00	5.20
4.50	4.20	4.50	5.10

a. Compute the mean, median, and mode.
b. Compute the 20th and 90th percentiles.
c. Compute the quartiles and hinges.

3.2   MEASURES OF DISPERSION

In addition to measures of location, it is often desirable to consider measures of dispersion, or variability, in the data values. For example, assume that you are a purchasing agent for a large manufacturing firm and that you regularly place orders with two different suppliers. Both suppliers indicate that approximately 10 working days are required to fill your orders. After several months of operation you find that the mean number of days required to fill orders is indeed around 10 days for both of the suppliers. The histograms summarizing the number of working days required to fill orders from the suppliers are shown in Figure 3.2. Although the mean number of days is roughly 10 for both suppliers, do the two suppliers have the same degree of reliability in terms of making deliveries on schedule? Note the dispersion, or variability, in the histograms. Which supplier would you prefer?

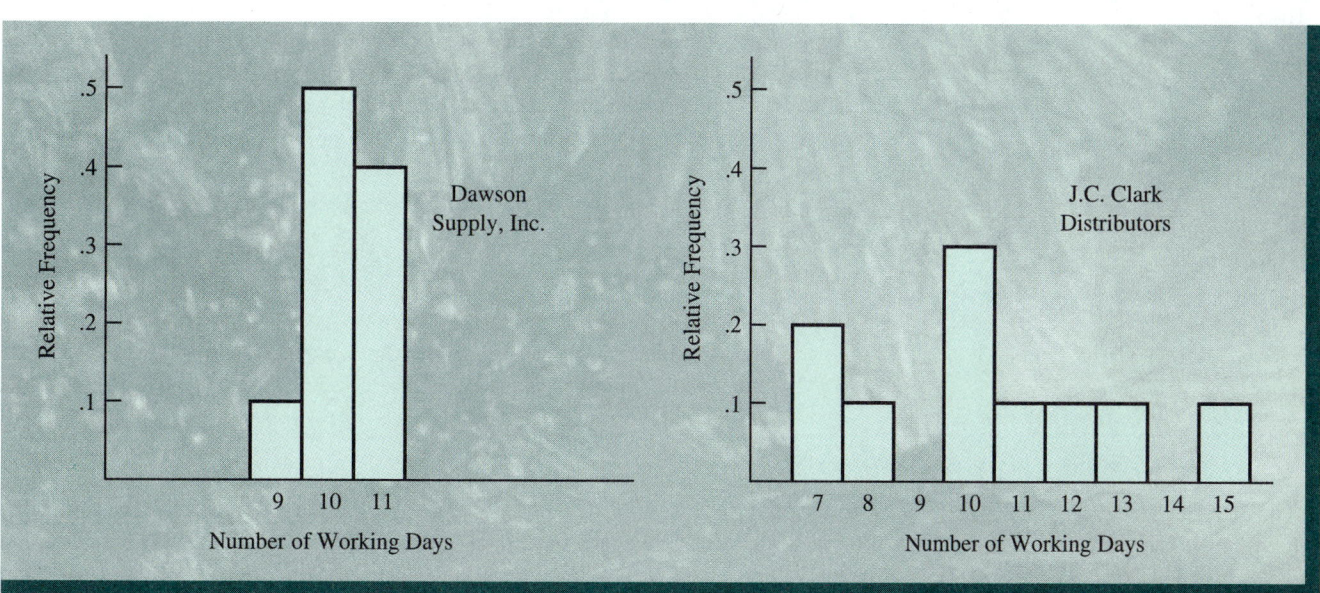

FIGURE 3.2   Historical Data Showing the Number of Days Required to Fill Orders

For most firms, receiving materials and supplies on schedule is important. The seven- or eight-day deliveries shown for J. C. Clark Distributors might be viewed favorably; however, a few of the slow 13- to 15-day deliveries could be disastrous in terms of keeping a workforce busy and production on schedule. This example illustrates a situation in which the dispersion, or variability, in the delivery times may be an overriding consideration in selecting a supplier. For most purchasing agents, the lower dispersion shown for Dawson Supply, Inc. would make Dawson the more consistent and preferred supplier.

We turn now to a discussion of some commonly used numerical measures of the dispersion, or variability, in data.

RANGE

Perhaps the simplest measure of dispersion for a data set is the *range*.

> **RANGE**
>
> $$\text{Range} = \text{Largest Value} - \text{Smallest Value}$$

Let us refer to the data on monthly starting salaries for business school graduates in Table 3.1. The largest starting salary is 2825 and the smallest is 2210. The range is $2825 - 2210 = 615$.

Although the range is the easiest of the measures of dispersion to compute, it is seldom used as the only measure of dispersion. The reason is that the range is based on only two of the items and thus is highly influenced by extreme data values. Suppose one of the graduates had a starting salary of $10,000. In this case the range would be $10,000 - 2210 = 7790$ rather than 615. This large value for the range would not be very descriptive of the variability in the data, since 11 of the 12 starting salaries are closely grouped between 2210 and 2630.

INTERQUARTILE RANGE

A measure of dispersion that overcomes the dependency on extreme data values is the *interquartile range* (IQR). This measure of dispersion is simply the difference between the third quartile, Q_3, and the first quartile, Q_1. In other words, the interquartile range is the range for the middle 50% of the data.

> **INTERQUARTILE RANGE**
>
> $$\text{IQR} = Q_3 - Q_1 \tag{3.3}$$

For the data on monthly starting salaries, the quartiles are $Q_3 = 2500$ and $Q_1 = 2365$. Thus the interquartile range is $2500 - 2365 = 135$.

VARIANCE

The *variance* is a measure of dispersion that utilizes all the data values. The variance is based on the difference between each data value and the mean. The difference between each data value x_i and the mean ($\bar{x}$ for a sample, μ for a population) is called a *deviation about the mean*. For a sample, a deviation is written $(x_i - \bar{x})$; for a population, it is written $(x_i - \mu)$. In the computation of the variance, the deviations about the mean are *squared*.

If the data set is a population, the average of the squared deviations is called the *population variance*. The population variance is denoted by the Greek symbol σ^2. For population of N items and with μ denoting the population mean, the definition of the population variance is as follows.

POPULATION VARIANCE

$$\sigma^2 = \frac{\Sigma\, (x_i - \mu)^2}{N} \qquad \text{(3.4)}$$

In most statistical applications, the data set being analyzed is a sample. When we compute a sample variance, we are often interested in using it to estimate the population variance σ^2. Although a detailed explanation is beyond the scope of this text, it can be shown that if the sum of the squared deviations about the sample mean is divided by $n - 1$, and not n, the resulting sample variance provides an unbiased estimate of the population variance. For this reason, the *sample variance,* denoted by s^2, is defined as follows.

SAMPLE VARIANCE

$$s^2 = \frac{\Sigma\, (x_i - \bar{x})^2}{n - 1} \qquad \text{(3.5)}$$

To illustrate the computation of the variance for a sample, we use the data on class size for the sample of five college classes. A summary of the data, including the computation of the deviations about the mean and the squared deviations about the mean, is given in Table 3.2. The sum of squared deviations about the mean is $\Sigma\, (x_i - \bar{x})^2 = 256$. Hence, with $n - 1 = 4$, the sample variance is

$$s^2 = \frac{\Sigma\, (x_i - \bar{x})^2}{n - 1} = \frac{256}{4} = 64$$

Before moving on, let us note that the units associated with the sample variance often cause confusion. Since the values being summed in the variance calculation,

TABLE 3.2 Computation of Deviations and Squared Deviations About the Mean for the Class-Size Data

Number of Students in Class (x_i)	Mean Class Size $\bar{x}$	Deviation About the Mean $(x_i - \bar{x})$	Squared Deviation About the Mean $(x_i - \bar{x})^2$
46	44	2	4
54	44	10	100
42	44	−2	4
46	44	2	4
32	44	−12	144
		0	256
		$\Sigma\, (x_i - \bar{x})$	$\Sigma\, (x_i - \bar{x})^2$

TABLE 3.3 Computation of the Sample Variance for the Starting Salary Data

Monthly Salary (x_i)	Sample Mean $(\bar{x})$	Deviation About the Mean $(x_i - \bar{x})$	Squared Deviation About the Mean $(x_i - \bar{x})^2$
2350	2440	−90	8,100
2450	2440	10	100
2550	2440	110	12,100
2380	2440	−60	3,600
2255	2440	−185	34,225
2210	2440	−230	52,900
2390	2440	−50	2,500
2630	2440	190	36,100
2440	2440	0	0
2825	2440	385	148,225
2420	2440	−20	400
2380	2440	−60	3,600
		0	301,850
		$\Sigma (x_i - \bar{x})$	$\Sigma (x_i - \bar{x})^2$

By (3.5),

$$s^2 = \frac{\Sigma (x_i - \bar{x})^2}{n - 1} = \frac{301,850}{11} = 27,440.91$$

$(x_i - \bar{x})^2$, are squared, the units associated with the sample variance are also *squared*. For instance, the sample variance for the class-size data is $s^2 = 64$ (student)^2. The squared units associated with variance make it difficult to obtain an intuitive understanding and interpretation of the numerical value of the variance. We recommend that you think of the variance as a measure useful in comparing the amount of dispersion in two or more data sets. In a comparison of data sets, the one with the larger variance has the most dispersion. Further interpretation of the value of the variance may not be necessary.

As another illustration of computing a sample variance, consider the starting salaries listed in Table 3.1 for the 12 business school graduates. In Section 3.1, we showed that the sample mean starting salary was 2440. The computation of the sample variance ($s^2 = 27,440.91$) is shown in Table 3.3.

Note that in Tables 3.2 and 3.3 we show both the sum of the deviations about the mean and the sum of the squared deviations about the mean. For any data set, the sum of the deviations about the mean will *always equal zero*. Hence, as shown in Tables 3.2 and 3.3, $\Sigma (x_i - \bar{x}) = 0$. This is true because the positive deviations and negative deviations always cancel each other, causing the sum of the deviations about the mean to equal zero.

STANDARD DEVIATION

The *standard deviation* is defined to be the positive square root of the variance. Following the notation we adopted for a sample variance and a population variance, we use s to denote the sample standard deviation and σ to denote the population standard deviation. The standard deviation is derived from the variance in the following way.

STANDARD DEVIATION

$$\text{Sample Standard Deviation} = s = \sqrt{s^2} \tag{3.6}$$

$$\text{Population Standard Deviation} = \sigma = \sqrt{\sigma^2} \tag{3.7}$$

Recall that the sample variance for the sample of class sizes in five college classes is $s^2 = 64$. Thus the sample standard deviation is $s = \sqrt{64} = 8$. For the data set consisting of starting salaries, the sample standard deviation is $s = \sqrt{27{,}440.91} = 165.65$.

What is gained by converting the variance to its corresponding standard deviation? Recall that the units associated with the variance are squared. For example, the sample variance for the starting salary data of business school graduates is $s^2 = 27{,}440.91$ (dollars)^2. Since the standard deviation is simply the square root of the variance, the units of the variance, dollars squared, are converted to dollars in the standard deviation. Thus, the standard deviation of the starting salary data is $165.65. In other words, the standard deviation is measured in the same units as the original data. For this reason the standard deviation is more easily compared to the mean and other statistics that are measured in the same units as the original data.

COEFFICIENT OF VARIATION

In some situations we may be interested in a descriptive statistic that indicates how large the standard deviation is in relation to the mean. This measure is called the *coefficient of variation* and is computed as follows.

COEFFICIENT OF VARIATION

$$\frac{\text{Standard Deviation}}{\text{Mean}} \times 100 \tag{3.8}$$

For the class-size data, we found a sample mean of 44 and a sample standard deviation of 8. The coefficient of variation is $(8/44) \times 100 = 18.2$. In words, the coefficient of variation tells us that the standard deviation of the sample is 18.2% of the value of the sample mean. For the starting-salary data with a sample mean of 2440 and a sample standard deviation of 165.65, the coefficient of variation, $(165.65/2440) \times 100 = 6.8$, tells us the standard deviation for this sample is only 6.8% of the value of the sample mean. In general, the coefficient of variation is a useful statistic for comparing the dispersion in data sets having different standard deviations and different means.

NOTES AND COMMENTS

1. Rounding the value of the sample mean $\bar{x}$ and the values of the squared deviations $(x_i - \bar{x})^2$ may introduce rounding errors in the computation of the variance and standard deviation. To reduce rounding errors, we recommend carrying at least six significant digits during intermediate calculations. The resulting variance or standard deviation can then be rounded to fewer digits.

2. An alternative formula for the computation of the sample variance is

$$s^2 = \frac{\sum x_i^2 - n\bar{x}^2}{n - 1}$$

where $\sum x_i^2 = x_1^2 + x_2^2 + \cdots + x_n^2$. Using this formula eases the computational burden slightly and helps reduce rounding errors. Exercise 23 requires use of this alternative formula to compute the sample variance.

EXERCISES

METHODS

17. Consider the sample of size 5 with data values of 10, 20, 12, 17, and 16. Compute the range and interquartile range.

18. Consider the sample of size 5 with data values of 10, 20, 12, 17, and 16. Compute the variance and standard deviation.

Self-Test
..........▶ **19.** Consider the sample of size 8 with data values of 27, 25, 20, 15, 30, 34, 28, and 25. Compute the range, interquartile range, variance, and standard deviation.

APPLICATIONS

20. The Hawaii Visitors Bureau collects data on the number of visitors to the islands. The following data are a representative sample of visitors (in thousands) for several days in November 1994 (*The Honolulu Advertiser,* December 28, 1994).

From the mainland, Canada, and Europe:

| 108.70 | 112.25 | 94.01 | 144.03 | 162.44 | 161.61 | 76.20 |
| 102.11 | 110.87 | 79.36 | 129.04 | 95.16 | 114.16 | 121.88 |

From Asia and the Pacific:

| 29.89 | 41.13 | 40.67 | 40.41 | 43.07 | 24.86 |
| 31.61 | 21.60 | 27.34 | 64.57 | 32.98 | 41.31 |

a. Compute the mean and median number of daily visitors from the two sources.
b. Compute the range, the standard deviation, and the coefficient of variation for the two sources of visitors.
c. What comparisons can you make between the numbers of visitors from the two sources?

21. The prices for the population of the 15 basic models of drip coffeemakers follow (*Consumer Reports 1995 Buying Guide*).

Model	Price ($)	Model	Price ($)	Model	Price ($)
Mr. Coffee PR12A	27	Mr. Coffee PR16	25	Braun	60
Krups	50	Mr. Coffee BL110	22	Proctor 42401	35
Proctor 42301	20	Braun	35	Krups	40
Black & Decker 901	22	Bunn	40	Melitta	30
Black & Decker 900	20	West Bend	35	Betty Crocker	19

Compute the range, variance, and standard deviation for this population.

22. The *Los Angeles Times* regularly reports the air quality index for various areas of Southern California. A sample of air quality index values for Pomona provided the following data: 28, 42, 58, 48, 45, 55, 60, 49, and 50.
a. Compute the range and interquartile range.
b. Compute the sample variance and sample standard deviation.
c. A sample of air quality index readings for Anaheim provided a sample mean of 48.5, a sample variance of 136, and a sample standard deviation of 11.66. What comparisons can you make between the air quality in Pomona and that in Anaheim on the basis of these descriptive statistics?

23. The Davis Manufacturing Company has just completed five weeks of operation using a new process that is supposed to increase productivity. The numbers of parts produced each week are 410, 420, 390, 400, and 380. Compute the sample variance and sample standard deviation by using the definition of sample variance (3.5) as well as the alternative formula provided in the Notes and Comments.

24. Assume that the following data are used to construct the histograms of the number of days required to fill orders for Dawson Supply, Inc. and J. C. Clark Distributors (see Figure 3.2).

Dawson Supply Days for Delivery: 11   10   9   10   11   11   10   11   10   10
Clark Distributors Days for Delivery: 8   10   13   7   10   11   10   7   15   12

Use the range and standard deviation to support the previous observation that Dawson Supply provides the more consistent and reliable delivery times.

Self-Test

25. A bowler's scores for six games were 182, 168, 184, 190, 170, and 174. Using these data as a sample, compute the following descriptive statistics.
    a. Range   b. Variance
    c. Standard deviation   d. Coefficient of variation

 LAWAGES

26. The Union Bank of Switzerland conducted a survey to obtain data on the hourly wages of blue- and white-collar workers throughout the world (*Newsweek*, February 17, 1992). Assume that a sample of 25 workers in the Los Angeles area provided the following data.

11.50	8.40	11.75	10.05	10.25	8.00	13.65	7.05	9.05
11.90	9.90	6.85	15.35	11.10	14.70	13.15	13.10	6.65
13.10	9.20	9.15	12.05	8.45	5.85	9.80		

Provide the following descriptive statistics.
    a. Mean   b. Median
    c. Range   d. Interquartile range
    e. Variance   f. Standard deviation

27. A production department uses a sampling procedure to test the quality of newly produced items. The department employs the following decision rule at an inspection station: If a sample of 14 items has a variance of more than .005, the production line must be shut down for repairs. Suppose the following data have just been collected:

3.43	3.45	3.43	3.48	3.52	3.50	3.39
3.48	3.41	3.38	3.49	3.45	3.51	3.50

Should the production line be shut down? Why or why not?

28. The following times were recorded by the quarter-mile and mile runners of a university track team (times are in minutes).

Quarter-mile Times: .92   .98   1.04   .90   .99
Mile Times: 4.52   4.35   4.60   4.70   4.50

After viewing this sample of running times, one of the coaches commented that the quarter-milers turned in the more consistent times. Use the standard deviation and the coefficient of variation to summarize the variability in the data. Does the use of the coefficient of variation indicate that the coach's statement should be qualified?

3.3   SOME USES OF THE MEAN AND THE STANDARD DEVIATION

We have described several measures of location and dispersion for data. The mean is the most widely used measure of location, whereas the standard deviation and variance are the most widely used measures of dispersion. Using only the mean and the standard deviation, we can learn much about a data set.

z-SCORES

By using the mean and standard deviation, we can determine the relative location of any data value. Suppose we have a sample of n items, with the values denoted by $x_1, x_2, \ldots, x_n$. In addition, assume that the sample mean, $\bar{x}$, and the sample stand

TABLE 3.4 z-Scores for the Class-Size Data

Number of Students in Class (x_i)	Deviation About the Mean ($x_i - \bar{x}$)	z-Score $\left(\dfrac{x_i - \bar{x}}{s}\right)$
46	2	2/8 = .25
54	10	10/8 = 1.25
42	−2	−2/8 = −.25
46	2	2/8 = .25
32	−12	−12/8 = −1.50

deviation, *s*, have been computed. Associated with each data value, x_i, is another value called its *z-score*. Equation (3.9) shows how the z-score is computed for data value x_i.

z-SCORE

$$z_i = \frac{x_i - \bar{x}}{s} \qquad (3.9)$$

where

z_i = the z-score for item *i*

$\bar{x}$ = the sample mean

s = the sample standard deviation

The z-score is often called the *standardized value*. The standardized value or z-score, z_i, can be interpreted as the *number of standard deviations x_i is from the mean $\bar{x}$*. For example, $z_1 = 1.2$ would indicate x_1 is 1.2 standard deviations greater than the sample mean. Similarly, $z_2 = -.5$ would indicate x_2 is .5, or 1/2, standard deviation less than the sample mean. As can be seen from (3.9), z-scores greater than zero occur for items with values greater than the mean, and z-scores less than zero occur for items with values less than the mean. A z-score of zero indicates that the value of the item is equal to the mean.

The z-score for any item can be interpreted as a measure of the relative location of the item in a data set. Items in two different data sets with the same z-score can be said to have the same relative location in terms of being the same number of standard deviations from the mean.

The z-scores for the class-size data are listed in Table 3.4. Recall that the sample mean $\bar{x} = 44$ and sample standard deviation $s = 8$ have been computed previously. The z-score of −1.50 for the fifth item shows it is farthest from the mean; it is 1.50 standard deviations below the mean.

CHEBYSHEV'S THEOREM

Chebyshev's theorem enables us to make statements about the percentage of items that must be within a specified number of standard deviations from the mean.

CHEBYSHEV'S THEOREM
At least $(1 - 1/k^2)$ of the items in any data set must be within *k* standard deviations of the mean, where *k* is any value greater than 1.

Some of the implications of this theorem, with $k = 2$, 3, and 4 standard deviations, follow.

- At least .75, or 75%, of the items must be within $k = 2$ standard deviations of the mean.
- At least .89, or 89%, of the items must be within $k = 3$ standard deviations of the mean.
- At least .94, or 94%, of the items must be within $k = 4$ standard deviations of the mean.

For an example using Chebyshev's theorem, assume that the midterm test scores for 100 students in a college business statistics course had a mean of 70 and a standard deviation of 5. How many students had test scores between 60 and 80? How many students had test scores between 58 and 82?

For the test scores between 60 and 80, we note that the value 60 is two standard deviations below the mean and the value 80 is two standard deviations above the mean. Using Chebyshev's theorem, we see that at least .75 or at least 75% of the items must have values within two standard deviations of the mean. Thus, at least 75 of the 100 students must have scored between 60 and 80.

For the test scores between 58 and 82, we see that $(58 - 70)/5 = -2.4$ indicates 58 is 2.4 standard deviations below the mean and that $(82 - 70)/5 = +2.4$ indicates 82 is 2.4 standard deviations above the mean. Applying Chebyshev's theorem with $k = 2.4$, we have

$$\left(1 - \frac{1}{k^2}\right) = \left[1 - \frac{1}{(2.4)^2}\right] = .826$$

At least 82.6% of the students must have test scores between 58 and 82.

THE EMPIRICAL RULE

One of the advantages of Chebyshev's theorem is that it applies to any data set regardless of the shape of the distribution of the data. In practical applications, however, it has been found that many data sets have a mound-shaped or bell-shaped distribution like the one shown in Figure 3.3. When the data are believed to approximate this distribution, the *empirical rule* can be used to determine the percentage of items that must be within a specified number of standard deviations of the mean.*

EMPIRICAL RULE
For data having a bell-shaped distribution:

- Approximately 68% of the items will be within one standard deviation of the mean.
- Approximately 95% of the items will be within two standard deviations of the mean.
- Almost all of the items will be within three standard deviations of the mean.

For example, liquid-detergent cartons are filled automatically on a production line. Filling weights frequently have a bell-shaped distribution. If the mean filling weight is

---

*The empirical rule is based on the normal probability distribution, which is covered in Chapter 6.

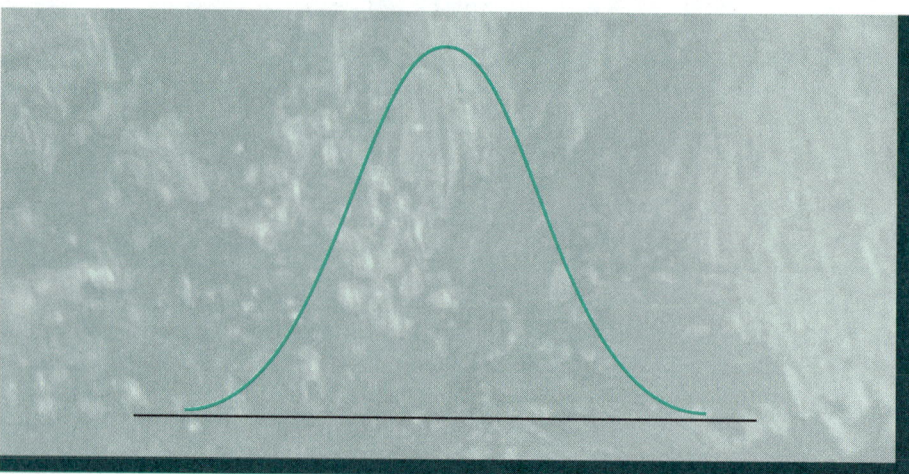

FIGURE 3.3 A Mound-Shaped or Bell-Shaped Distribution

16 ounces and the standard deviation is .25 ounces, we can use the empirical rule to draw the following conclusions.

• Approximately 68% of the filled cartons will have weights between 15.75 and 16.25 ounces (that is, within one standard deviation of the mean).
• Approximately 95% of the filled cartons will have weights between 15.50 and 16.50 ounces (that is, within two standard deviations of the mean).
• Almost all filled cartons will have weights between 15.25 and 16.75 ounces (that is, within three standard deviations of the mean).

DETECTING OUTLIERS

Sometimes a set of data will have one or more items with unusually large or unusually small values. Extreme values such as these are called *outliers*. Experienced statisticians take steps to identify outliers and then review each one carefully. An outlier may be an item for which the data has been incorrectly recorded. If so, it can be corrected before further analysis. An outlier may also be an item that was incorrectly included in the data set; if so, it can be removed. Finally, an outlier may just be an unusual item that has been recorded correctly and does belong in the data set. In such cases the item should remain.

NOTES AND COMMENTS

1. Before analyzing a data set, statisticians usually make a variety of checks to ensure the validity of data. In a large study it is not uncommon for errors to be made in recording data values or in entering the values at a computer. Identifying outliers is one tool used to check the validity of data.
2. Chebyshev's theorem is applicable for any data set and can be used to state the minimum number of items that will be within a certain number of standard deviations of the mean. If the data set is known to be approximately bell-shaped, more can be said. For instance, the empirical rule allows us to say that *approximately* 95% of the items will be within two standard deviations of the mean; Chebyshev's theorem allows us to conclude only that at least 75% of the items will be in that interval.

Standardized values (z-scores) can be used to help identify outliers. Recall that the empirical rule allows us to conclude that for data with a bell-shaped distribution, almost all the items will be within three standard deviations of the mean. Hence, in using z-scores to identify outliers, we recommend treating any item with a z-score less than −3 or greater than +3 as an outlier. Such items can then be reviewed for accuracy and to determine whether or not they belong in the data set.

Refer to the z-scores for the class-size data in Table 3.4. The z-score of −1.50 shows the fifth item is farthest from the mean. However, this standardized value is well within the −3 to +3 guideline for outliers. Thus, the z-scores show that outliers are not present in the class-size data.

EXERCISES

METHODS

29. Consider the sample of size 5 with data values of 10, 20, 12, 17, and 16. Compute the z-score for each of the five data values.

30. Consider a sample with a mean of 500 and a standard deviation of 100. What is the z-score for each of the data values 520, 650, 500, 450, and 280?

Self-Test

31. Consider a sample with a mean of 30 and a standard deviation of 5. Use Chebyshev's theorem to determine the proportion, or percentage, of the data within each of the following ranges.
  a. 20 to 40   **b.** 15 to 45   **c.** 22 to 38   **d.** 18 to 42   **e.** 12 to 48

32. Data that have a bell-shaped distribution have a mean of 30 and a standard deviation of 5. Use the empirical rule to determine the proportion, or percentage, of data within each of the following ranges.
  a. 20 to 40   **b.** 15 to 45   **c.** 25 to 35

APPLICATIONS

33. The Bureau of Economic Analysis at the Department of Commerce reported that 1993 per capita income in California was $21,884 (*USA Today*, August 24, 1994). If the standard deviation is $6,000, what is the z-score for an individual with an annual income of $12,500? What is the z-score of an individual with an annual income of $50,000? Interpret these scores and comment on whether or not either of these annual incomes should be considered an outlier.

Self-Test

34. A sample of 10 men's college basketball scores provided the following winning teams and the numbers of points scored (*USA Today*, January 11, 1995).

Winner	Score	Winner	Score
Boston U.	55	Emory	56
Northeastern	87	Queens College	77
Flagler	89	Millsaps	89
Marquette	70	Wartburg	64
Pepperdine	61	San Francisco	84

  a. Compute the mean and standard deviation for the data.
  b. In another game, York beat CCNY 108 to 75. Use the z-scores to determine whether the York score should be considered an outlier. Explain.
  c. Assume that the distribution of the points scored by winning teams is mound-shaped. Estimate the percentage of all men's college basketball games in which the winning team will score 87 or more points. Estimate the percentage of games in which the winning team will score 46 or less points.

35. According to the Roth Young Personnel Service, salaries for chain store managers range from $30,000 to $62,000 (*National Business Employment Weekly,* October 16–22, 1994). Assume that the following data are the annual salaries for a sample of chain store managers. Data are in $1000s.

CHAINSAL

33.7	45.4	44.0	47.5	59.6
45.1	37.7	43.9	48.3	53.0
39.5	42.9	51.0	35.6	41.5
49.5	45.4	58.2	55.4	62.3
32.2	45.9	47.6	56.2	56.8
48.8	31.3	51.2	43.2	54.4

a. Compute the mean and standard deviation.

b. A chain store manager in Memphis, Tennessee, earns $28,500 a year. Compute the z-score for this manager and state whether you believe the manager's salary should be considered an outlier.

c. Compute the z-scores for salaries of $30,000, $45,000, $60,000, and $75,000. Should any of them be considered an outlier?

36. Use the salary data in Exercise 35 and Chebyshev's theorem to find the percentage of chain store managers having salaries in the following ranges.
a. $30,700 to $63,100
b. $28,200 to $65,600

37. IQ scores and birth rates were discussed in an article in the *Atlantic Monthly* (May 1989). IQ scores have a bell-shaped distribution with a mean of 100 and a standard deviation of 15.
a. What percentage of the population should have an IQ score between 85 and 115?
b. What percentage of the population should have an IQ score between 70 and 130?
c. What percentage of the population should have an IQ score of more than 130?
d. A person with an IQ score of more than 145 is considered a genius. Does the empirical rule support this statement? Explain.

38. The average fuel economy of new cars sold in the United States is 27.5 miles per gallon (*The Wall Street Journal,* April 8, 1992). Assume that the standard deviation is 3.5 miles per gallon.
a. Use Chebyshev's theorem to calculate the percentage of new cars sold with miles-per-gallon ratings between 20.5 and 34.5, between 18.75 and 36.25, and between 17 and 38.
b. If it were reasonable to assume that miles-per-gallon ratings for new cars followed a bell-shaped distribution, what can be said about the percentage of new cars sold with miles-per-gallon ratings between 20.5 and 34.5? Between 17 and 38?

39. Cruise ship inspections (*St. Petersburg Times,* December 16, 1990) are performed by the (federal) Center for Environmental Health and Injury Control. General areas of inspection include potable water, food preparation and holding, general cleanliness, and storage. Ships scoring 85 or less are reinspected sooner than those with higher ratings. Inspection scores for 20 cruise ships follow.

Ship	Score	Ship	Score
Americana	98	Regent Sun	91
Costa Riviera	89	Royal Princess	87
Crown Princess	87	Seaward	94
Daphne	78	Song of America	96
Dolphin IV	95	Song of Norway	91
Fair Princess	76	Starship Atlantic	93
Jubilee	93	Starship Oceanic	97
Meridian	92	Sun Viking	88
Nordic Prince	93	Tropicana	91
Pegasus	62	Viking Princess	86

a. Compute the mean and median.
b. Compute the first and third quartiles.
c. Compute the standard deviation.
d. What are the z-scores associated with the Fair Princess and Pegasus? What is your interpretation of these values?
e. Are there any outliers? Explain.

3.4   EXPLORATORY DATA ANALYSIS

In Chapter 2 we introduced exploratory data analysis. Recall that exploratory data analysis enables us to use simple arithmetic and easy-to-draw pictures to summarize data. In this section we continue exploratory data analysis by considering five-number summaries and box plots.

FIVE-NUMBER SUMMARY

In a five-number summary, the following five numbers are used to summarize the data.

1. Smallest value
2. First quartile (Q_1)
3. Median
4. Third quartile (Q_3)
5. Largest value

The monthly starting salaries shown in Table 3.1 for a sample of 12 business school graduates follow.

2350	2450	2550	2380	2255	2210
2390	2630	2440	2825	2420	2380

The median of 2405 and the quartiles $Q_1 = 2365$ and $Q_3 = 2500$ were computed in Section 3.1. Reviewing the preceding data shows a smallest value of 2210 and a largest value of 2825. Thus the five-number summary for the salary data is 2210, 2365, 2405, 2500, 2825. Approximately one-fourth, or 25%, of the data values are between adjacent numbers in a five-number summary.

BOX PLOT

The *box plot* is a relatively recent development in the graphical summarization of data. Key to the development of a box plot is the computation of the median and the quartiles, Q_1 and Q_3. The interquartile range, IQR = $Q_3 - Q_1$, is also used. Figure 3.4 is the box plot for the monthly starting salary data. The steps used to construct the box plot follow.

1. A box is drawn with the ends of the box located at the first and third quartiles. For the salary data, $Q_1 = 2365$ and $Q_3 = 2500$. This box contains the middle 50% of the data.
2. A vertical line is drawn in the box at the location of the median (2405 for the salary data). Thus the median line divides the data into two equal parts.
3. By using the interquartile range, IQR = $Q_3 - Q_1$, fences are located. The *inner fences* are located 1.5(IQR) below Q_1 and 1.5(IQR) above Q_3. The *outer fences* are located 3(IQR) below Q_1 and 3(IQR) above Q_3. For the salary data, IQR = $Q_3 - Q_1 = 2500 - 2365 = 135$. Thus, the inner fences are $2365 - 1.5(135) =$

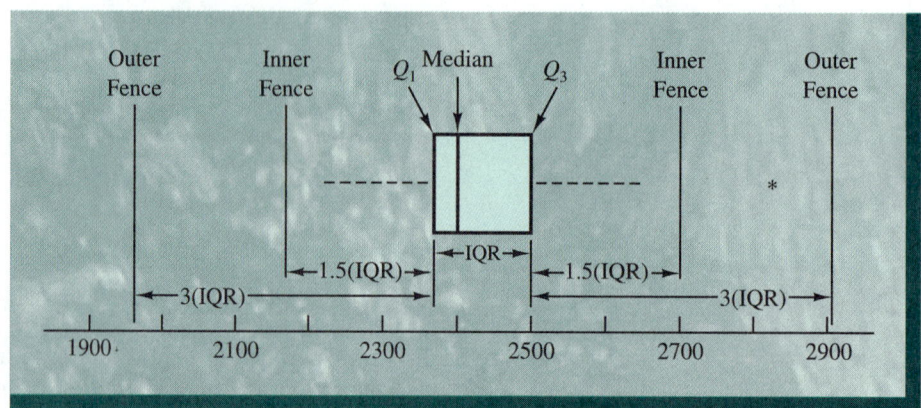

FIGURE 3.4 Box Plot of the Monthly Starting Salaries of Business School Graduates, with Lines Showing the Inner and Outer Fences

2162.5 and 2500 + 1.5(135) = 2702.5. The outer fences are 2365 − 3(135) = 1960 and 2500 + 3(135) = 2905. The fences are important aids in identifying outliers. Data between the inner and outer fences are considered *mild outliers*. Data outside the outer fences are considered *extreme outliers*.

4. The dashed lines in Figure 3.4 are called *whiskers*. The whiskers are drawn from the ends of the box to the smallest and largest data values *inside the inner fences*. Thus the whiskers end at salary data values of 2210 and 2630.

5. Finally, the locations of mild outliers are shown with the symbol * and those of extreme outliers are shown with the symbol °. In Figure 3.4 we see one mild outlier—the data value 2825. There are no extreme outliers in the salary data.

In Figure 3.4 we have included lines showing the location of the fences. These lines were drawn to show how fences are computed and where they are located for the salary data. Although the fences are always computed, generally they are not drawn on the box plots. Figure 3.5 shows the usual appearance of a box plot for the salary data.

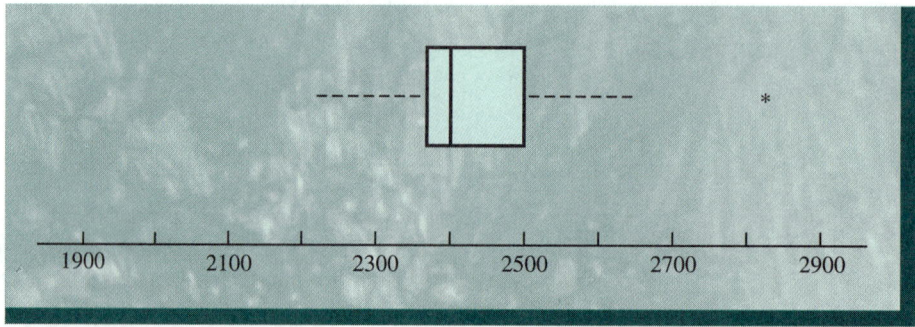

FIGURE 3.5 Box Plot of the Monthly Starting Salaries of Business School Graduates

1. When using fences to identify outliers, we may or may not select the same items as the ones we select when using z-scores less than -3 and greater than $+3$ to identify outliers. However, the objective of both approaches is simply to identify items that should be reviewed to ensure the validity of the data. Outliers identified by either procedure should be reviewed.

2. An advantage of the exploratory data analysis procedures is that they are easy to use; few numerical calculations are necessary. We simply sort the items into ascending order and identify the median and quartiles Q_1 and Q_3 to obtain the five-number summary. The fences and the box plot can then easily be determined. It is not necessary to compute the mean and the standard deviation for the data.

EXERCISES

METHODS

40. Consider the sample of size 8 with data values of 27, 25, 20, 15, 30, 34, 28, and 25. Provide the five-number summary for the data.

41. Show the box plot for the data in Exercise 40.

Self-Test
∙∙∙∙∙∙∙∙∙▶

42. Show the five-number summary and the box plot for the following data: 5, 15, 18, 10, 8, 12, 16, 10, 6.

43. A data set has a first quartile of 42 and a third quartile of 50. Compute the inner and outer fences. Should a data value of 65 be considered an outlier?

APPLICATIONS

44. *Fortune* (April 20, 1992) published its annual report on the 500 largest U.S. industrial corporations. Data on the percentage growth in sales for the past 12 months for a sample of 26 companies follow.

GROWTH

16.1	49.9	23.7	15.6	1.9	10.8	20.4
12.2	22.4	4.9	13.4	6.8	15.8	12.1
19.3	10.0	46.1	27.0	7.0	12.5	6.1
15.6	6.3	16.7	10.1	55.9		

a. Provide a five-number summary.
b. Compute the inner and outer fences.
c. Do there appear to be outliers? How would this information be helpful to a financial analyst?
d. Show a box plot.

Self-Test
∙∙∙∙∙∙∙∙∙▶

45. Annual sales, in millions of dollars, for 21 pharmaceutical companies follow (*Business Week* April 25, 1994).

8408	1374	1872	8879	2459	11413
608	14138	6452	1850	2818	1356
10498	7478	4019	4341	739	2127
3653	5794	8305			

a. Provide a five-number summary.
b. Compute the inner and outer fences.
c. Do there appear to be outliers?

d. Johnson & Johnson's sales are the largest in the list at $14,138 million. Suppose a data entry error had been made and the sales had been entered as $41,138 million. Would the method of detecting outliers in part (c) have identified the problem and allowed correction of the data entry error?

e. Show a box plot.

46. *Consumer Reports* provides performance and quality ratings for numerous consumer products. The overall ratings were provided for a sample of 16 midpriced VCRs in the *Consumer Reports 1992 Buying Guide*. The manufacturer brands and overall scores are listed in Table 3.5.

   a. Provide the mean and median overall rating.

   b. Compute the first and third quartiles.

   c. Provide the five-number summary.

   d. Similar ratings for camcorders showed a mean of 82.56, a standard deviation of 6.39, and a five-number summary of 75, 77, 82, 86, 93. Compare the *Consumer Reports* ratings data for VCRs and camcorders. Show the box plots for both.

   e. Are there any outliers in the VCR data? Explain.

INJURY

47. The Highway Loss Data Institute's Injury and Collision Loss Experience report (September 1988) rates car models on the basis of the number of insurance claims filed after accidents. Index ratings near 100 are considered average. Lower ratings are better, indicating a safer car model. Shown are ratings for 20 midsize cars and 20 small cars

TABLE 3.5 Exercise 46

Manufacturer	Score
Fisher	77
General Electric	81
Hitachi	89
J. C. Penney	78
JVC	79
Magnavox	80
Montgomery Ward	78
Mitsubishi	90
Panasonic	77
Phillips	73
Quasar	72
Radio Shack	76
RCA	79
Sanyo	75
Sony	86
Toshiba	79

Midsize cars:	81	91	93	127	68	81	60	51	58	75
	100	103	119	82	128	76	68	81	91	82
Small cars:	73	100	127	100	124	103	119	108	109	113
	108	118	103	120	102	122	96	133	80	140

Summarize the data for the midsize and small cars separately.

a. Provide a five-number summary for midsize cars and for small cars.

b. Show the box plots.

c. Make a statement about what your summaries indicate about the safety of midsize cars in comparison to small cars.

48. Morgan Stanley Capital International in Geneva, Switzerland, provided percentage changes in stock markets around the world (*Barrons*, March 30, 1992). Data shown are percentage changes over the preceding one-year period.

Country	Percent Change	Country	Percent Change
Australia	29.1	Japan	8.3
Austria	−13.4	Luxembourg	6.7
Belgium	9.3	Netherlands	13.9
Canada	8.3	New Zealand	−12.6
Denmark	15.3	Norway	−15.4
Europe	10.0	Pacific	10.3
Finland	−16.7	Portugal	−7.2
France	15.8	Singapore	22.7
Germany	6.3	Spain	11.6
Hong Kong	42.8	Sweden	9.1
Italy	−4.1	United Kingdom	11.6
Ireland	9.6	United States	27.2

a. What are the mean and median percentage changes among these world markets?

b. What are the first and third quartiles?

c. Are there any outliers? Show a box plot.

d. What percentile would you report for the United States?

TABLE 3.6 Sample Data for the Stereo and Sound Equipment Store

Week	Number of Commercials	Sales Volume ($100s)
	x	y
1	2	50
2	5	57
3	1	41
4	3	54
5	4	54
6	1	38
7	5	63
8	3	48
9	4	59
10	2	46

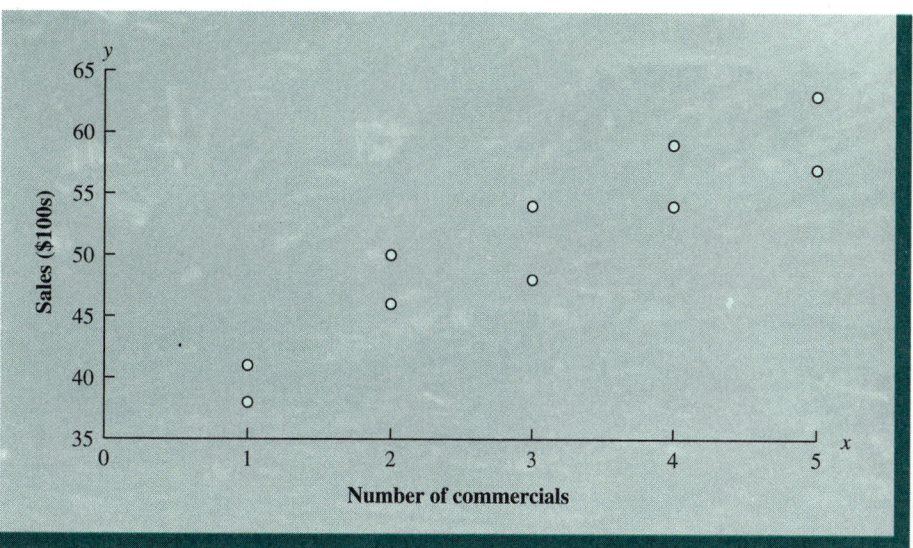

FIGURE 3.6 Scatter Diagram for the Stereo and Sound Equipment Store

3.5 MEASURES OF ASSOCIATION BETWEEN TWO VARIABLES

Thus far we have examined numerical methods that are used to summarize the data for *one variable at a time*. Often a manager or decision maker is interested in the *relationship between two variables*. In this section we present covariance and correlation as descriptive measures of the relationship between two variables.

We begin by reconsidering the application by a stereo and sound equipment store in San Francisco as presented in Section 2.5. The store's manager is interested in investigating the relationship between the number of weekend television commercials shown and the sales at the store during the following week. Sample data with sales expressed in hundreds of dollars are provided in Table 3.6. The scatter diagram in Figure 3.6 shows a positive relationship, with higher sales (y) associated with a greater number of commercials (x). In fact, the scatter diagram suggests that a straight line could be used as a linear approximation of the relationship. In the following discussion, we introduce covariance as a descriptive measure of the linear association between two variables.

COVARIANCE

For a sample of n elements with the corresponding pairs of data values $x_1 y_1, x_2 y_2,$ and so on, the *sample covariance* is defined by the following equation.

SAMPLE COVARIANCE

$$s_{xy} = \frac{\Sigma(x_i - \bar{x})(y_i - \bar{y})}{n - 1}$$

(3.10)

TABLE 3.7 Calculations for the Sample Covariance

x_i	y_i	$x_i - \bar{x}$	$y_i - \bar{y}$	$(x_i - \bar{x})(y_i - \bar{y})$
2	50	−1	−1	1
5	57	2	6	12
1	41	−2	−10	20
3	54	0	3	0
4	54	1	3	3
1	38	−2	−13	26
5	63	2	12	24
3	48	0	−3	0
4	59	1	8	8
2	46	−1	−5	5
Totals 30	510	0	0	99

$$s_{xy} = \frac{\Sigma (x_i - \bar{x})(y_i - \bar{y})}{n - 1} = \frac{99}{10 - 1} = 11$$

In this formula each x_i value is paired with a y_i value. We then sum the products obtained by multiplying the deviation of each x_i from its sample mean $\bar{x}$ by the deviation of the corresponding y_i from its sample mean $\bar{y}$; this sum is then divided by $n - 1$.

To measure the strength of the linear relationship between the number of commercials x and the sales volume y in the stereo and sound equipment store problem, we use (3.10) to compute the sample covariance. The calculations in Table 3.7 show the computation of $\Sigma(x_i - \bar{x})(y_i - \bar{y})$. Note that $\bar{x} = 30/10 = 3$ and $\bar{y} = 510/10 = 51$. Using (3.10), we obtain a sample covariance of

$$s_{xy} = \frac{\Sigma(x_i - \bar{x})(y_i - \bar{y})}{n - 1} = \frac{99}{9} = 11$$

The formula for computing the covariance of a population of size N is similar to (3.10), but we use different notation to indicate that we are working with the entire population.

POPULATION COVARIANCE

$$\sigma_{xy} = \frac{\Sigma(x_i - \mu_x)(y_i - \mu_y)}{N} \tag{3.11}$$

In (3.11) we use the notation μ_x for the population mean of the variable x and μ_y for the population mean of the variable y. The population covariance σ_{xy} is defined for a population of size N.

INTERPRETATION OF THE COVARIANCE

To aid in the interpretation of the *sample covariance,* consider Figure 3.7. It is the same as the scatter diagram of Figure 3.6 with a vertical line at $x = 3$ (the value of $\bar{x}$) and a horizontal line at $y = 51$ (the value of $\bar{y}$). Four quadrants have been identified on the graph. Points in quadrant I correspond to x_i values greater than $\bar{x}$ and y_i values greater than $\bar{y}$, points in quadrant II correspond to x_i values less than $\bar{x}$ and y_i values greater than $\bar{y}$, and so on. Thus, the value of $(x_i - \bar{x})(y_i - \bar{y})$ must be positive for points in quadrant I, negative for points in quadrant II, positive for points in quadrant III, and negative for points in quadrant IV.

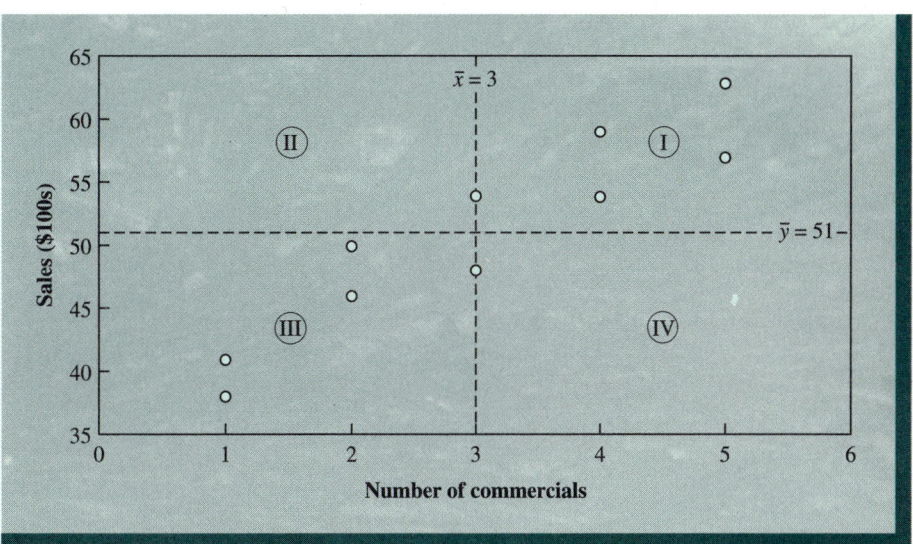

FIGURE 3.7 Partitioned Scatter Diagram for the Stereo and Sound Equipment Store

If the value of s_{xy} is positive, the points that have had the greatest influence on s_{xy} must be in quadrants I and III. Hence, a positive value for s_{xy} is indicative of a positive linear association between x and y; that is, as the value of x increases, the value of y increases. If the value of s_{xy} is negative, however, the points that have had the greatest influence on s_{xy} are in quadrants II and IV. Hence, a negative value for s_{xy} is indicative of a negative linear association between x and y; that is, as the value of x increases, the value of y decreases. Finally, if the points are evenly distributed across all four quadrants, the value of s_{xy} will be close to zero, indicating no linear association between x and y. Figure 3.8 shows the values of s_{xy} that can be expected with three different types of scatter diagrams.

Referring again to Figure 3.7, we see that the scatter diagram for the stereo and sound equipment store follows the pattern in the top panel of Figure 3.8. As we should expect, the value of the sample covariance is positive with $s_{xy} = 11$.

From the preceding discussion, it might appear that a large positive value for the covariance is indicative of a strong positive linear relationship and that a large negative value is indicative of a strong negative linear relationship. However, one problem with using covariance as a measure of the strength of the linear relationship is that the value we obtain for the covariance depends on the units of measurement for x and y. For example, suppose we are interested in the relationship between height x and weight y for individuals. Clearly the strength of the relationship should be the same whether we measure height in feet or inches. When height is measured in inches, however, we get much larger numerical values for $(x_i - \bar{x})$ than we get when it is measured in feet. Thus, with height measured in inches, we would obtain a larger value for the numerator $\Sigma(x_i - \bar{x})(y_i - \bar{y})$—and hence a larger covariance—when in fact there is no difference in the relationship. A measure of the relationship between two variables that avoids this difficulty is the *correlation coefficient*.

CORRELATION COEFFICIENT

For sample data, the Pearson product moment correlation coefficient is defined as follows.

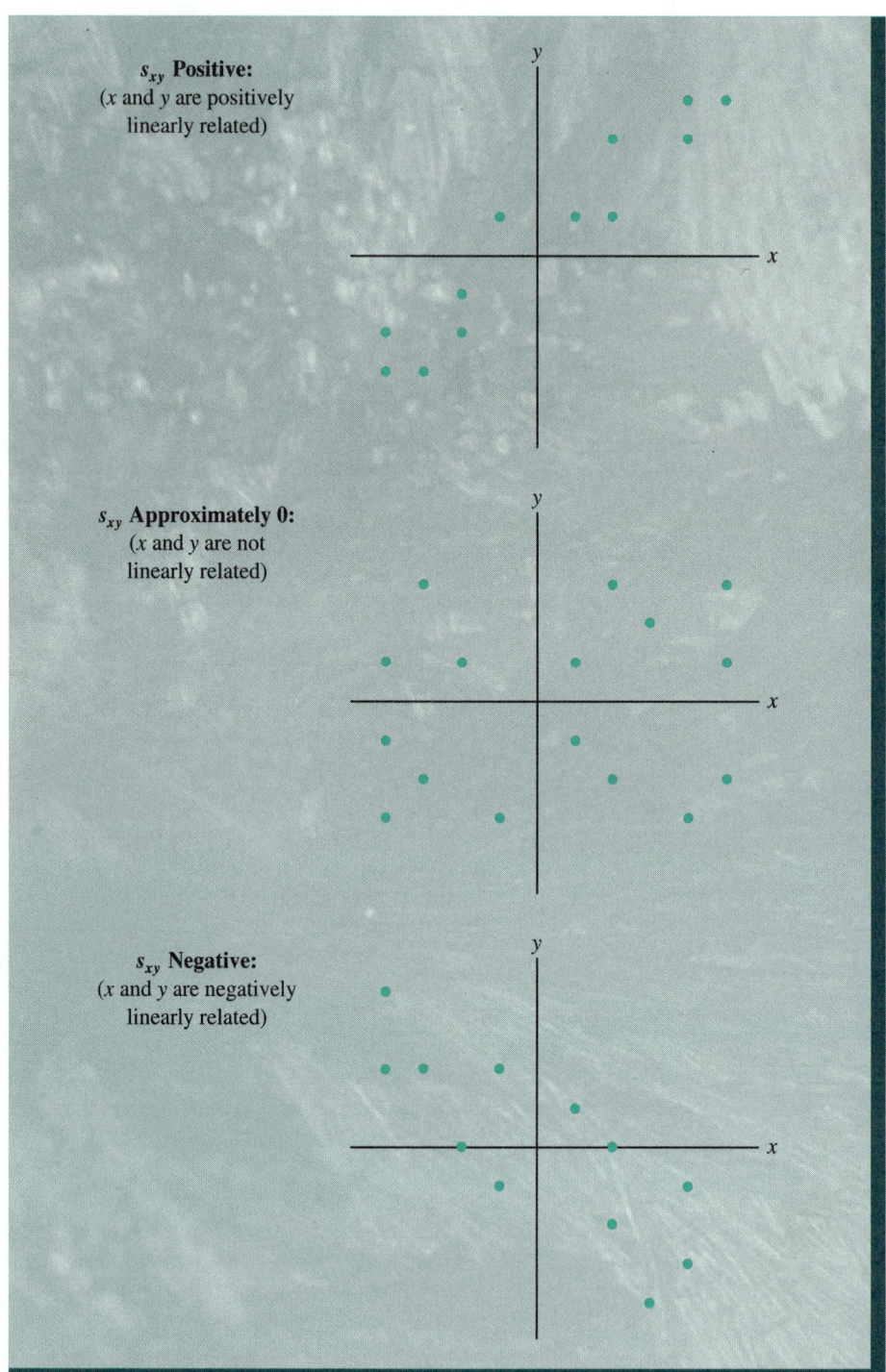

FIGURE 3.8   Interpretation of Sample Covariance

PEARSON PRODUCT MOMENT CORRELATION COEFFICIENT: SAMPLE DATA

$$r_{xy} = \frac{s_{xy}}{s_x s_y} \qquad (3.12)$$

where

r_{xy} = sample correlation coefficient

s_{xy} = sample covariance

s_x = sample standard deviation of x

s_y = sample standard deviation of y

Equation (3.12) shows that the Pearson product moment correlation coefficient for sample data (commonly referred to more simply as the *sample correlation coefficient*) is computed by dividing the sample covariance by the product of the standard deviation of x and the standard deviation of y.

Let us now compute the sample correlation coefficient for the stereo and sound equipment store. Using the data in Table 3.6, we can compute the sample standard deviations for the two variables.

$$s_x = \sqrt{\frac{\Sigma(x_i - \bar{x})^2}{n - 1}} = \sqrt{\frac{20}{9}} = 1.4907$$

$$s_y = \sqrt{\frac{\Sigma(y_i - \bar{y})^2}{n - 1}} = \sqrt{\frac{566}{9}} = 7.9303$$

Now, since $s_{xy} = 11$, we have a sample correlation coefficient of

$$r_{xy} = \frac{s_{xy}}{s_x s_y} = \frac{11}{(1.4907)(7.9303)} = +.93$$

When a calculator is used to compute the sample correlation coefficient, the formula given by (3.13) is preferred because the computation of each deviation $x_i - \bar{x}$ and $y_i - \bar{y}$ is not necessary, and thus less round-off error is introduced.

PEARSON PRODUCT MOMENT CORRELATION COEFFICIENT: SAMPLE DATA, ALTERNATE FORMULA

$$r_{xy} = \frac{\Sigma x_i y_i - (\Sigma x_i \Sigma y_i)/n}{\sqrt{\Sigma x_i^2 - (\Sigma x_i)^2/n}\sqrt{\Sigma y_i^2 - (\Sigma y_i)^2/n}} \qquad (3.13)$$

Algebraically, (3.12) and (3.13) are equivalent. In Table 3.8 we provide the calculations needed for (3.13). Using these results, we obtain

$$r_{xy} = \frac{1629 - (30)(510)/10}{\sqrt{110 - (30)^2/10}\sqrt{26576 - (510)^2/10}} = \frac{99}{\sqrt{20}\sqrt{566}} = +.93$$

Thus we see that the value for r_{xy} is the same whether we use (3.12) or (3.13).

The formula for computing the correlation coefficient for a population, denoted by the Greek letter ρ_{xy} (rho, pronounced "row"), follows.

TABLE 3.8   Computations for Using the Alternate Formula to Compute r_{xy}

x_i	y_i	$x_i y_i$	x_i^2	y_i^2
2	50	100	4	2500
5	57	285	25	3249
1	41	41	1	1681
3	54	162	9	2916
4	54	216	16	2916
1	38	38	1	1444
5	63	315	25	3969
3	48	144	9	2304
4	59	236	16	3481
2	46	92	4	2116
Totals 30	510	1629	110	26576

PEARSON PRODUCT MOMENT CORRELATION COEFFICIENT: POPULATION DATA

$$\rho_{xy} = \frac{\sigma_{xy}}{\sigma_x \sigma_y} \tag{3.14}$$

where

ρ_{xy} = population correlation coefficient

σ_{xy} = population covariance

σ_x = population standard deviation for x

σ_y = population standard deviation for y

The sample correlation coefficient r_{xy} is an estimate of the population correlation coefficient ρ_{xy}.

INTERPRETATION OF THE CORRELATION COEFFICIENT

First let us consider a simple example that illustrates the concept of a perfect positive linear relationship. The scatter diagram in Figure 3.9 depicts the relationship between the following $n = 3$ pairs of points.

x_i	1	2	3
y_i	10	30	50

The straight line drawn through each of the three points shows that there is a perfect linear relationship between the two variables x and y. The calculations needed to compute r_{xy} are shown in Table 3.9. Using (3.13), we obtain

$$r_{xy} = \frac{\Sigma x_i y_i - (\Sigma x_i \Sigma y_i)/n}{\sqrt{\Sigma x_i^2 - (\Sigma x_i)^2/n}\sqrt{\Sigma y_i^2 - (\Sigma y_i)^2/n}} = \frac{220 - 6(90)/3}{\sqrt{14 - (6)^2/3}\sqrt{3500 - (90)^2/3}}$$

$$= \frac{40}{\sqrt{2}\sqrt{800}} = 1$$

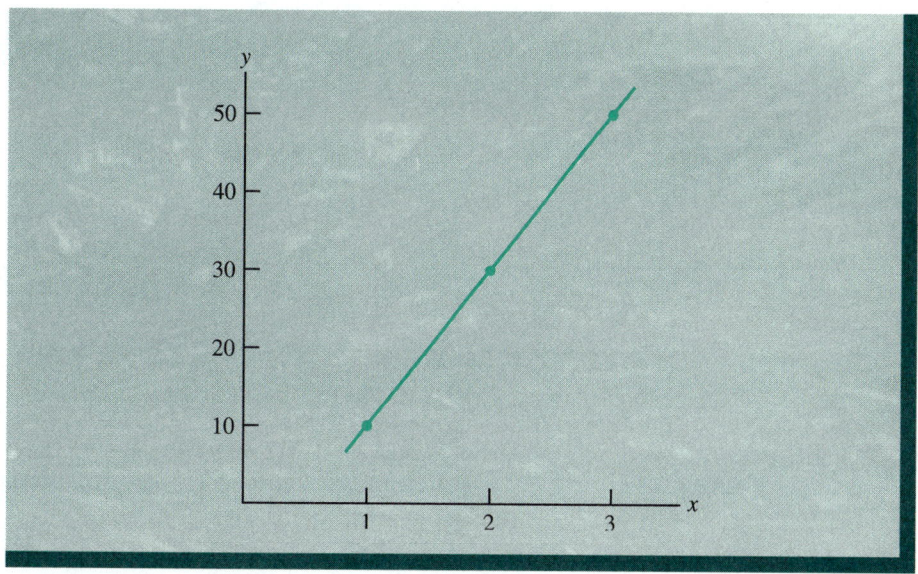

FIGURE 3.9 Scatter Diagram Depicting a Perfect Positive Linear Relationship

Thus, we see that the value of the sample correlation coefficient for this data set is 1.

In general, it can be shown that if all the points in a data set are on a straight line having positive slope, the value of the sample correlation coefficients is +1; that is, a sample correlation coefficient of +1 corresponds to a perfect positive linear relationship between x and y. Moreover, if the points in the data set are on a straight line having negative slope, the value of the sample correlation coefficient is −1; that is, a sample correlation coefficient of −1 corresponds to a perfect negative linear relationship between x and y.

Let us now suppose that for a certain data set there is a positive linear relationship between x and y but that the relationship is not perfect. The value of r_{xy} will be less than 1, indicating that the points in the scatter diagram are not all on a straight line. As the points in a data set deviate more and more from a perfect positive linear relationship, the value of r_{xy} becomes smaller and smaller. A value of r_{xy} equal to zero indicates no linear relationship between x and y and values of r_{xy} near zero indicate a weak linear relationship.

For the data set involving the stereo and sound equipment store, recall that $r_{xy} = +.93$. Therefore, we conclude that there is a positive linear relationship between the number of commercials and sales. More specifically, an increase in the number of commercials is associated with an increase in sales.

TABLE 3.9 Calculations for Computing r_{xy} for the Relationship in Figure 3.9

x_i	y_i	$x_i y_i$	x_i^2	y_i^2
1	10	10	1	100
2	30	60	4	900
3	50	150	9	2500
Totals 6	90	220	14	3500

EXERCISES

METHODS

Self-Test

49. Five observations taken for two variables follow.

x_i	4	6	11	3	16
y_i	50	50	40	60	30

  a. Develop a scatter diagram with x on the horizontal axis.
  b. What does the scatter diagram developed in (a) indicate about the relationship between the two variables?
  c. Compute and interpret the sample covariance for the data.
  d. Compute and interpret the sample correlation coefficient for the data.

50. Five observations taken for two variables follow.

x_i	6	11	15	21	27
y_i	6	9	6	17	12

  a. Develop a scatter diagram for these data.
  b. What does the scatter diagram indicate about a possible relationship between x and y?
  c. Compute and interpret the sample covariance for the data.
  d. Compute and interpret the sample correlation coefficient for the data.

APPLICATIONS

51. A high-school guidance counselor collected the following data about the grade point averages (GPA) and the SAT mathematics test scores for six seniors.

GPA	2.7	3.5	3.7	3.3	3.6	3.0
SAT	450	560	700	620	640	570

  a. Develop a scatter diagram for the data with GPA on the horizontal axis.
  b. Does there appear to be any relationship between the GPA and the SAT mathematics test score? Explain.
  c. Compute and interpret the sample covariance for the data.
  d. Compute the sample correlation coefficient for the data. What does this value tell us about the relationship between the two variables?

52. A department of transportation's study on driving speed and mileage for midsize automobiles resulted in the following data.

Driving Speed	30	50	40	55	30	25	60	25	50	55
Mileage	28	25	25	23	30	32	21	35	26	25

Compute and interpret the sample correlation coefficient for these data.

53. A sociologist collected data on the ages of wives and husbands when they married.

Wife's Age	22	27	25	32	34	25
Husband's Age	24	33	28	30	40	25

a. Develop a scatter diagram for these data with the wife's age on the horizontal axis.
b. Does there appear to be a linear association? Explain.
c. Compute and interpret the sample correlation coefficient for these data.

54. Table 3.10 gives the book value per share and the annual dividend for 15 utility stocks (*Barrons,* January 2, 1995).
    a. Develop a scatter diagram with book value on the horizontal axis.
    b. Compute and interpret the sample correlation coefficient.

CITIES

55. The daily high and low temperatures for 24 cities follow (*USA Today,* January 9, 1995).

City	High	Low	City	High	Low
Tampa	68	45	Birmingham	58	34
Kansas City	37	28	Minneapolis	17	10
Boise	52	41	Portland	51	48
Los Angeles	66	59	Memphis	54	34
Philadelphia	42	26	Buffalo	26	10
Milwaukee	25	12	Cincinnati	37	24
Chicago	27	16	Charlotte	52	33
Albany	31	9	Boston	38	19
Houston	72	49	Tulsa	54	35
Salt Lake City	51	39	Washington, D.C.	43	28
Miami	75	57	Las Vegas	58	48
Cheyenne	49	35	Detroit	27	13

What is the correlation between the high and low temperatures?

3.6 THE ROLE OF THE COMPUTER

Computer software packages can provide the descriptive statistics presented in this chapter. After the data have been entered into the computer, a few simple commands can be used to generate the desired output. In this section, we examine the descriptive statistics provided by the Minitab statistical software package; the instructions necessary to generate the output are given in Appendix 3.1. Appendix 3.2 shows how an Excel spreadsheet package can be used to provide similar information.

TABLE 3.10 Book Value and Dividends per Share for 15 Utility Stocks

UTILITY

Company	Book Value ($)	Annual Dividend ($)	Company	Book Value ($)	Annual Dividend ($)
Am Elec	22.44	2.40	Centerior	12.14	.80
Con Ed	20.89	2.98	Cons N Gas	23.31	1.94
Detroit Ed	22.09	2.06	Houston Ind	16.23	3.00
Niag Moh	14.48	1.09	NorAm Enrgy	.56	.28
Pac G&E	20.73	1.96	Panh East	.84	.84
Peco	19.25	1.55	Peoples En	18.05	1.80
Pub Sv Ent	20.37	2.16	SCEcorp	12.45	1.21
UnicomCp	26.43	1.60			

SOURCE: *Barrons,* January 2, 1995.

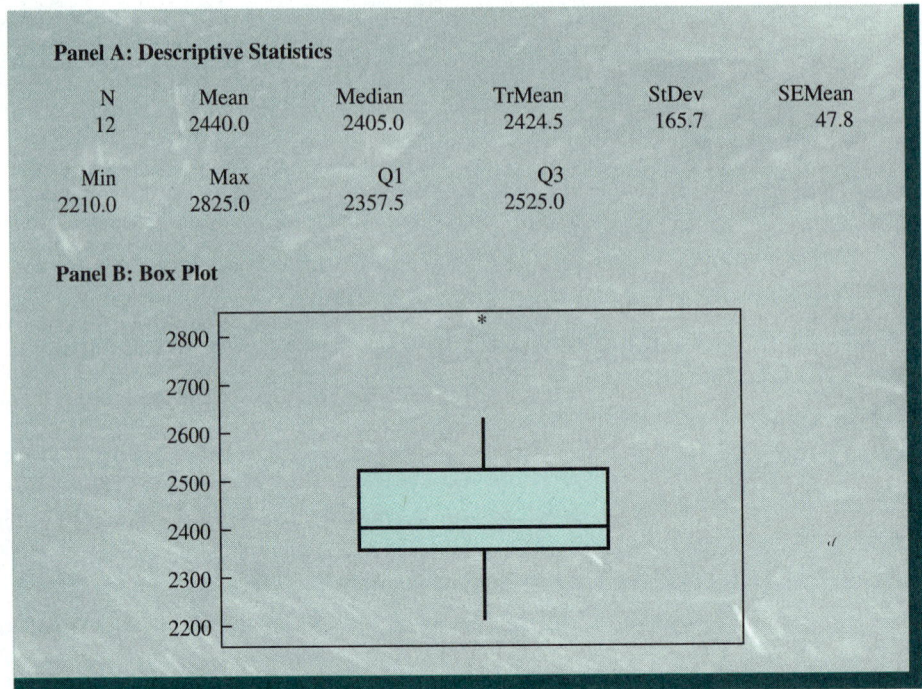

Panel A: Descriptive Statistics

N	Mean	Median	TrMean	StDev	SEMean
12	2440.0	2405.0	2424.5	165.7	47.8

Min	Max	Q1	Q3
2210.0	2825.0	2357.5	2525.0

Panel B: Box Plot

FIGURE 3.10 Descriptive Statistics and Box Plot Provided by Minitab

Table 3.1 lists the starting salaries for 12 business school graduates. Panel A of Figure 3.10 shows the descriptive statistics obtained by using Minitab to summarize these data. Definitions of the headings in panel A follow.

N	number of data values		Min	minimum data value
Mean	mean		Max	maximum data value
Median	median		Q1	first quartile
TrMean	5% trimmed mean		Q3	third quartile
StDev	standard deviation			

We have not discussed the numerical measure labelled SEMean, which is the standard error of the mean. This measure is computed by dividing the standard deviation by the square root of N. The interpretation and use of this measure are discussed in Chapter 7 when we introduce the topics of sampling and sampling distributions.

Although the numerical measures of range, interquartile range, variance, and coefficient of variation do not appear on the Minitab output, these values can be easily computed if desired from the results in Figure 3.10 by the following formulas.

$$\text{Range} = \text{Max} - \text{Min}$$
$$\text{IQR} = \text{Q3} - \text{Q1}$$
$$\text{Variance} = (\text{StDev})^2$$
$$\text{Coefficient of Variation} = (\text{StDev/Mean}) \times 100$$

Finally, note that Minitab's quartiles $Q_1 = 2357.5$ and $Q_3 = 2525$ provide slightly different values than the quartiles $Q_1 = 2365$ and $Q_3 = 2500$ that we computed in Section 3.1. The reason is that different conventions* are used to identify the quartiles

---

*With the n data values rank ordered from smallest to largest, Minitab uses the positions given by $(n + 1)/4$ and $3(n + 1)/4$ to locate Q_1 and Q_3, respectively. When a position is fractional, Minitab interpolates between the two adjacent rank-ordered data values to determine the corresponding quartile.

	x	y
x	2.22222	
y	11.00000	62.88889

Correlation of x and y = 0.930

FIGURE 3.11   Covariance and Correlation Provided by Minitab for the Number of Commercials (x) and Sales (y) Data

of a data set. Hence, the values of Q_1 and Q_3 provided by one convention may not be identical to the values of Q_1 and Q_3 provided by another convention. Any differences tend to be negligible, however, and the results provided should not mislead the user in making the usual interpretations associated with quartiles.

Panel B of Figure 3.10 is a box plot provided by Minitab. The box drawn from the first to the third quartiles contains the middle 50% of the data. The horizontal line within the box locates the median. The asterisk indicates an outlier at 2825.

Figure 3.11 shows the covariance and correlation output that Minitab provided for the stereo and sound equipment store data in Table 3.6. The variable x denotes the number of weekend television commercials and the variable y denotes the sales during the following week. The value in column x and row y is the sample covariance $s_{xy}=11$ as computed in Section 3.5. The value in column x and row x is the sample variance for the number of commercials and the value in column y and row y is the sample variance for sales. The sample correlation coefficient $r_{xy} = +.93$ is shown at the bottom of the output.

3.7   COMPUTING MEASURES OF LOCATION AND DISPERSION FOR GROUPED DATA

In most cases, measures of location and dispersion are computed by using the individual data values. Sometimes, however, we have data in only a grouped or frequency distribution form. This section describes how approximations of the mean, variance, and standard deviation can be obtained directly from a frequency distribution.

MEAN

Recall that to compute the sample mean by using the individual data values, we sum all the values and divide by $n,$ the sample size. If the data are available only in frequency distribution form, we must approximate the sum of the data values.

To do this, we treat the midpoint of each class as though it were the mean of the items in the class. With M_i denoting the midpoint for class i and f_i denoting the frequency of class i, the sum of the items in class i is approximated by $f_i M_i$. Summing these values over all classes, we obtain $\Sigma f_i M_i$, which approximates the sum of all the data values.

Once this sum is obtained, an approximation of the sample mean is computed by dividing the sum by n. The following formula can be used.

SAMPLE MEAN FOR GROUPED DATA

$$\bar{x} = \frac{\Sigma f_i M_i}{n}$$ (3.15)

TABLE 3.11 Frequency Distribution of Audit Times

Audit Time (Days)	Frequency
10–14	4
15–19	8
20–24	5
25–29	2
30–34	1
Total	20

In Section 2.2 we provided a frequency distribution of the time in days required to complete year-end audits for the public accounting firm of Sanderson and Clifford. The frequency distribution of audit times based on a sample of 20 clients was developed. This frequency distribution is shown again in Table 3.11.

What is the sample mean audit time based on the grouped data in Table 3.11? Recall that the class midpoints, M_i, are halfway between the class limits. Thus, the first class of 10–14 has a midpoint at $(10 + 14)/2 = 12$. Since this class has a frequency $f_1 = 4$, the value of $f_1M_1 = 4 \times 12 = 48$. The five class midpoints and the computations necessary to determine the sample mean with (3.15) are shown in Table 3.12. As can be seen, the sample mean audit time is 19 days.

VARIANCE

To compute the variance for grouped data, we use a slightly altered version of the formula for the variance provided in (3.5). In (3.5), the squared deviations of the data values about the sample mean $\bar{x}$ were written $(x_i - \bar{x})^2$. However, with grouped data, the individual data values, x_i, are not known. In this case, we treat the class midpoint, M_i, as being a representative value for the x_i values in the corresponding class. Thus the squared deviations about the sample mean, $(x_i - \bar{x})^2$, are replaced by $(M_i - \bar{x})^2$. Then, just as we did with the sample mean calculations for grouped data, we weight each value by the frequency of the class, f_i, and sum for all classes. The sum of the squared deviations about the mean for all the data is approximated by $\Sigma f_i(M_i - \bar{x})^2$. In this approach, the following formula is used to obtain the sample variance for grouped data.

TABLE 3.12 Computation of the Sample Mean Audit Time for Grouped Data

Audit Time (Days)	Frequency f_i	Class Midpoint M_i	$f_i M_i$
10–14	4	12	48
15–19	8	17	136
20–24	5	22	110
25–29	2	27	54
30–34	1	32	32
	20		380
			$\Sigma f_i M_i$

Sample mean $\bar{x} = \dfrac{\Sigma f_i M_i}{n} = \dfrac{380}{20} = 19$ days

TABLE 3.13 Computation of the Sample Variance of Audit Times for Grouped Data (Sample Mean $\bar{x} = 19$)

Audit Time (Days)	Frequency f_i	Class Midpoint M_i	Deviation $(M_i - \bar{x})$	Squared Deviation $(M_i - \bar{x})^2$	$f_i(M_i - \bar{x})^2$
10–14	4	12	−7	49	196
15–19	8	17	−2	4	32
20–24	5	22	3	9	45
25–29	2	27	8	64	128
30–34	1	32	13	169	169
	20				570

$$\Sigma f_i (M_i - \bar{x})^2$$

$$\text{Sample variance } s^2 = \frac{\Sigma f_i (M_i - \bar{x})^2}{n - 1} = \frac{570}{19} = 30$$

SAMPLE VARIANCE FOR GROUPED DATA

$$s^2 = \frac{\Sigma f_i(M_i - \bar{x})^2}{n - 1} \tag{3.16}$$

The calculation of the sample variance for audit times based on the grouped data from Table 3.11 is shown in Table 3.13.

STANDARD DEVIATION

The standard deviation for grouped data is simply the square root of the variance for grouped data. For the audit-time data, the sample standard deviation is $s = \sqrt{30} = 5.48$.

POPULATION SUMMARIES FOR GROUPED DATA

Before closing this section on computing measures of location and dispersion for grouped data, we note that the formulas in this section are for only data sets constituting a sample. Population summary measures are computed similarly. The grouped data formulas for a population mean and variance follow.

POPULATION MEAN FOR GROUPED DATA

$$\mu = \frac{\Sigma f_i M_i}{N} \tag{3.17}$$

POPULATION VARIANCE FOR GROUPED DATA

$$\sigma^2 = \frac{\Sigma f_i(M_i - \mu)^2}{N} \tag{3.18}$$

NOTES AND COMMENTS

1. An alternative formula for the computation of the sample variance for grouped data is

$$s^2 = \frac{\sum f_i M_i^2 - n\bar{x}^2}{n-1}$$

where $\sum f_i M_i^2 = f_1 M_1^2 + f_2 M_2^2 + \cdots + f_k M_k^2$ and k is the number of classes used to group the data. Using this formula may ease the computations slightly.

2. In computing descriptive statistics for grouped data, the class midpoints are used to approximate the data values in each class. As a result, the descriptive statistics for grouped data are approximations of the descriptive statistics that would result from using the original data directly. We therefore recommend computing descriptive statistics from the original data rather than from grouped data whenever possible.

EXERCISES

METHODS

Self-Test

56. Consider the sample data in the following frequency distribution.

Class	Midpoint	Frequency
3–7	5	4
8–12	10	7
13–17	15	9
18–22	20	5

Compute the sample mean.

Self-Test

57. Compute the sample variance and sample standard deviation for the grouped data in Exercise 56.

APPLICATIONS

58. The following frequency distribution for grades on the first examination in operations management was posted on the department bulletin board.

Examination Grade	Frequency
40–49	3
50–59	5
60–69	11
70–79	22
80–89	15
90–99	6
	Total 62

Treating these data as a sample, compute the mean, variance, and standard deviation.

59. In a survey of subscribers to *Fortune* magazine, the following question was asked: "How many of the last four issues have you read or looked through?" The following frequency distribution summarizes 500 responses (*Fortune* National Subscriber Portrait, 1994).

Number Read	Frequency
0	15
1	10
2	40
3	85
4	350
	Total 500

a. What is the mean number of issues read by a *Fortune* subscriber?

b. What is the standard deviation of the number of issues read?

60. A service station has recorded the following frequency distribution for the number of gallons of gasoline sold per car in a sample of 680 cars.

Gasoline (gallons)	Frequency
0–4	74
5–9	192
10–14	280
15–19	105
20–24	23
25–29	6
	Total 680

Compute the mean, variance, and standard deviation for these grouped data. If the service station expects to service about 120 cars on a given day, what is an estimate of the total number of gallons of gasoline that will be sold?

61. Scores obtained from a sample of patients on a depression-level test are summarized in the frequency distribution in Table 3.14. Using the given grouped data, compute the mean, variance, and standard deviation.

TABLE 3.14 Exercise 61

Depression Level Score	Frequency
25–34	3
35–44	1
45–54	2
55–64	6
65–74	4
75–84	6
85–94	2
95–104	1
Total	25

SUMMARY

In this chapter we introduced several descriptive statistics that can be used to summarize the location and dispersion of data. Unlike the tabular and graphical procedures, the measures introduced in this chapter summarize the data in terms of numerical values. When the numerical values obtained are for a sample, they are called sample statistics. When the numerical values obtained are for a population, they are called population parameters. Some of the notation used for sample statistics and population parameters follow.

	Sample Statistic	Population Parameter
Mean	$\bar{x}$	μ
Variance	s^2	σ^2
Standard deviation	s	σ

As measures of central location, we defined the mean, median, and mode. Then the concept of percentiles was used to describe the location of other values in the data set. Next, we presented the range, interquartile range, variance, standard deviation, and coefficient of variation as measures of variability or dispersion. We then described how the mean and standard deviation could be used together, applying the empirical rule and Chebyshev's theorem, to provide more information about the distribution of data.

A discussion of two exploratory data analysis techniques that can be used to summarize data more effectively was included in Section 3.4. Specifically, we showed how to develop a five-number summary and a box plot to provide simultaneous information about the location, dispersion, and shape of the distribution. In Section 3.5 we introduced covariance and the correlation coefficient as measures of association between two variables.

Output from the software package Minitab was used to illustrate how statistical computing systems can support the analysis and summarization of data. Finally, we described how the mean, variance, and standard deviation could be computed for grouped data. However, we recommend using the measures based on the individual data values unless the grouped format is the only one in which the data are available.

GLOSSARY

Population parameter   A numerical value used as a summary measure for a population of data (e.g., the population mean, μ, the population variance, σ^2, and the population standard deviation, σ).

Sample statistic   A numerical value used as a summary measure for a sample (e.g., the sample mean, $\bar{x}$, the sample variance, s^2, and the sample standard deviation, s).

Mean   A measure of central location for a data set. It is computed by summing all the data values and dividing by the number of items.

Trimmed mean   The mean of the data remaining after α percent of the smallest and α percent of the largest items have been removed. The purpose of a trimmed mean is to provide a measure of central location after elimination of the effect of extremely large and extremely small data values.

Median   A measure of central location. It is the value that splits the data into two equal groups, one with values greater than or equal to the median and one with values less than or equal to the median.

Mode   A measure of location, defined as the most frequently occurring data value.

Percentile   A value such that at least p percent of the items are less than or equal to this value and at least $(100 - p)$ percent of the items are greater than or equal to this value. The 50th percentile is the median.

Quartiles   The 25th, 50th, and 75th percentiles referred to as the first quartile, the second quartile (median), and third quartile, respectively. The quartiles can be used to divide the data set into four parts, with each part containing approximately 25% of the data.

Hinges   The value of the lower hinge is approximately the first quartile, or 25th percentile. The value of the upper hinge is approximately the third quartile, or 75th percentile. The values of the hinges and quartiles may differ slightly because of differing computational conventions.

Range   A measure of dispersion, defined to be the largest value minus the smallest value.

Interquartile range (IQR)   A measure of dispersion, defined to be the difference between the third and first quartiles.

Variance   A measure of dispersion for a data set, based on the squared deviations of the data values about the mean.

Standard deviation   A measure of dispersion for a data set, found by taking the positive square root of the variance.

Coefficient of variation A measure of relative dispersion for a data set, found by dividing the standard deviation by the mean and multiplying by 100.

z-Score A value found by dividing the deviation about the mean $(x_i - \bar{x})$ by the the standard deviation s. A z-score is referred to as a standardized value and denotes the number of standard deviations a data value x_i is from the mean.

Chebyshev's theorem A theorem applying to any data set that can be used to make statements about the percentage of items that must be within a specified number of standard deviations of the mean.

Empirical rule A rule that states the percentages of items that are within one, two, and three standard deviations from the mean for mound-shaped, or bell-shaped, distributions.

Outlier An unusually small or unusually large data value.

Five-number summary An exploratory data analysis technique that uses the following five numbers to summarize the data set: smallest value, first quartile, median, third quartile, and largest value.

Box plot A graphical summary of data. A box, drawn from the first to the third quartiles, shows the location of the middle 50% of the data. Dashed lines, called whiskers, extending from the ends of the box show the location of data greater than the third quartile and data less than the first quartile. The locations of any outliers are also noted.

Fences Values used to identify outliers. Inner fences are located 1.5(IQR) below the first quartile and 1.5(IQR) above the third quartile. Outer fences are located 3(IQR) below the first quartile and 3(IQR) above the third quartile. Data between the inner and outer fences are considered mild outliers. Data outside the outer fences are considered extreme outliers.

Covariance A numerical measure of linear association between two variables. Positive values indicate a positive relationship; negative values indicate a negative relationship.

Correlation coefficient A numerical measure of linear association between two variables that takes values between -1 and $+1$. Values near $+1$ indicate a strong positive linear relationship, values near -1 indicate a strong negative linear relationship, and values near zero indicate lack of a linear relationship.

Grouped data Data available in class intervals as summarized by a frequency distribution. Individual values of the original data are not recorded.

KEY FORMULAS

Sample Mean

$$\bar{x} = \frac{\Sigma x_i}{n} \tag{3.1}$$

Population Mean

$$\mu = \frac{\Sigma x_i}{N} \tag{3.2}$$

Interquartile Range

$$IQR = Q_3 - Q_1 \tag{3.3}$$

Population Variance

$$\sigma^2 = \frac{\Sigma(x_i - \mu)^2}{N} \tag{3.4}$$

Sample Variance

$$s^2 = \frac{\Sigma(x_i - \bar{x})^2}{n - 1} \tag{3.5}$$

Standard Deviation

$$\text{Sample Standard Deviation} = s = \sqrt{s^2} \tag{3.6}$$

$$\text{Population Standard Deviation} = \sigma = \sqrt{\sigma^2} \tag{3.7}$$

Coefficient of Variation

$$\left(\frac{\text{Standard Deviation}}{\text{Mean}}\right) \times 100 \tag{3.8}$$

z-Score

$$z_i = \frac{x_i - \bar{x}}{s} \tag{3.9}$$

Sample Covariance

$$s_{xy} = \frac{\Sigma(x_i - \bar{x})(y_i - \bar{y})}{n - 1} \tag{3.10}$$

Pearson Product Moment Correlation Coefficient: Sample Data

$$r_{xy} = \frac{s_{xy}}{s_x s_y} \tag{3.12}$$

Pearson Product Moment Correlation Coefficient: Sample Data, Alternate Formula

$$r_{xy} = \frac{\Sigma x_i y_i - (\Sigma x_i \Sigma y_i)/n}{\sqrt{\Sigma x_i^2 - (\Sigma x_i)^2/n} \sqrt{\Sigma y_i^2 - (\Sigma y_i)^2/n}} \tag{3.13}$$

Sample Mean for Grouped Data

$$\bar{x} = \frac{\Sigma f_i M_i}{n} \tag{3.15}$$

Sample Variance for Grouped Data

$$s^2 = \frac{\Sigma f_i (M_i - \bar{x})^2}{n - 1} \tag{3.16}$$

Population Mean for Grouped Data

$$\mu = \frac{\Sigma f_i M_i}{N} \tag{3.17}$$

Population Variance for Grouped Data

$$\sigma^2 = \frac{\Sigma f_i (M_i - \mu)^2}{N} \tag{3.18}$$

SUPPLEMENTARY EXERCISES

 **PRICES**

62. A sample of economists predicted what would happen to consumer prices during 1992 (*Business Week,* December 30, 1991). Their predictions about the percentage increase in consumer prices follow.

4.6	3.4	2.3	2.9	2.7	3.2	2.9
3.7	3.7	3.3	3.7	2.9	3.3	2.9
3.6	3.7	3.3	3.5	3.4	2.7	3.3
2.9	3.0	3.0	1.8			

a. Compute the mean, median, and mode.
b. Compute the first and third quartiles.
c. Compute the range and interquartile range.
d. Compute the variance and standard deviation.
e. Are there any outliers?

63. Following is a sample of yields for 10 bonds provided by Lehman Brothers (*Barron's,* January 23, 1995).

Issuer	Yield (%)	Issuer	Yield (%)
American Standard	10.59	Comcast	10.78
Inland Steel	9.92	Kroger A	9.54
Owens Illinois	10.64	Northwest Steel & Wire	11.29
Rogers Cantel	10.74	Stone Container	11.37
Westpoint Stevens	10.24	Unisys	10.58

Compute the following descriptive statistics for the data.
a. Mean　　**b.** Median　　**c.** Mode
d. 25th percentile　**e.** Range　　**f.** Interquartile range
g. Variance　　**h.** Standard deviation　**i.** Coefficient of variation

64. *Time* (January 9, 1989) published an article on the academic ability of college athletes. The article noted that some of the most successful athletic programs (citing the University of Notre Dame and Duke University) have athletes with very good college board scores. Assume that the following sample data are typical of college board scores for Notre Dame football players.

1100	970	1000	1250	880	790	1300	1050	900	950	1120

a. Compute the mean, median, and mode.
b. Compute the range and interquartile range.
c. Compute the variance and standard deviation.
d. Using z-scores, state whether or not there are any outliers in this data set.

 MORTGAGE

65. The following data show home mortgage loan amounts handled by one loan officer at the Westwood Savings and Loan Association. Data are in thousands of dollars.

52.0	68.5	63.0	57.5	64.0	42.5	55.9	73.2	67.5	66.2
55.2	60.9	53.8	58.4	43.0	61.0	63.5	55.4	63.5	50.2
69.0	68.1	60.5	75.5	60.5	82.0	70.5	81.6	72.5	74.8

a. Find the mean, median, and mode.
b. Find the first and third quartiles.

66. A sample of 10 stocks on the New York Stock Exchange (*The Wall Street Journal,* April 28, 1995) has the following price-earnings ratios: 9, 4, 6, 7, 3, 11, 4, 6, 4, 7. Using these data, compute the mean, median, mode, range, variance, and standard deviation.

67. According to the U.S. Bureau of the Census *Current Construction Report,* the average price of a new mobile home in the western part of the United States during 1993 was $40,500. Assume the standard deviation was $8,500.
   a. Should a mobile home selling for $75,000 be considered an outlier?
   b. Use Chebyshev's theorem to determine the percentage of mobile homes selling between $30,000 and $51,000.

68. Public transportation and the automobile are two methods an employee can use to get to work each day. Samples of times recorded for each method are shown. Times are in minutes.

Public Transportation:	28	29	32	37	33	25	29	32	41	34
Automobile:	29	31	33	32	34	30	31	32	35	33

   a. Compute the sample mean time to get to work for each method.
   b. Compute the sample standard deviation for each method.
   c. On the basis of your results from (a) and (b), which method of transportation should be preferred? Explain.
   d. Develop a box plot for each method. Does a comparison of the box plots support your conclusion in (c)?

EXAM

69. Final examination scores for 25 statistics students follow.

56	77	84	82	42	61	44	95	98	84
93	62	96	78	88	58	62	79	85	89
89	97	53	76	75					

   a. Provide a five-number summary.
   b. Provide a box plot.

70. The following data show the total yardage accumulated during the NCAA college football season for a sample of 20 receivers.

744	652	576	1112	971	451	1023	852	809	596
941	975	400	711	1174	1278	820	511	907	1251

   a. Provide a five-number summary.
   b. Provide a box plot.
   c. Identify any outliers.

71. The median income and the median home price for a sample of six cities follow (*Who's Buying Homes in America,* Chicago Title and Trust Company, 1994). Data are in thousands of dollars.

City	Median Income	Median Home Price
Atlanta, Georgia	$65.2	$120.2
Cleveland, Ohio	49.8	92.7
Denver, Colorado	53.8	111.7
Dallas, Texas	62.7	104.7
Orlando, Florida	50.9	98.5
Minneapolis, Minnesota	53.1	105.8

   a. What is the value of the sample covariance? Does it indicate a positive or negative relationship?
   b. What is the sample correlation coefficient?

72. *Road & Track,* October 1994 provided the following sample of the tire ratings and load-carrying capacity of automobiles tires.
   a. Develop a scatter diagram for the data with tire rating on the *x* axis.
   b. What is the sample correlation coefficient and what does it tell you about the relationship between tire rating and load-carrying capacity?

Tire Rating	Load-carrying Capacity
75	853
82	1047
85	1135
87	1201
88	1235
91	1356
92	1389
93	1433
105	2039

TABLE 3.15 Exercise 73

Call Duration	Frequency
4–7	4
8–11	5
12–15	7
16–19	2
20–23	1
24–27	1
Total	20

73. Table 3.15 is a frequency distribution for the duration of 20 long-distance telephone calls in minutes. Compute the mean, variance, and standard deviation for the data.

74. Dinner check amounts at La Maison French Restaurant have the frequency distribution shown in Table 3.16. Compute the mean, variance, and standard deviation for the data.

75. Automobiles traveling on the New York State Thruway are checked for speed by a state police radar system. Table 3.17 is a frequency distribution of speeds.
   a. What is the mean speed of the automobiles traveling on the New York State Thruway?
   b. Compute the variance and the standard deviation.

 DUKE

76. In the 1992 NCAA Division I Basketball Championships, the Duke Blue Devils became the first team since the 1973 UCLA Bruins to win back-to-back national championships. Duke's season record was 34–2, with its only losses coming at North Carolina and Wake Forest. The scores of the 36 games, with Duke's score listed first, follow (*NCAA Final Four Program,* April 1992).

TABLE 3.16 Exercise 74

Dinner Check ($)	Frequency
25–34	2
35–44	6
45–54	4
55–64	4
65–74	2
75–84	2
Total	20

TABLE 3.17 Exercise 75

Speed (Miles per Hour)	Frequency
45–49	10
50–54	40
55–59	150
60–64	175
65–69	75
70–74	15
75–79	10
Total	475

Opponent	Score	Opponent	Score
East Carolina	103–75	Louisiana State	77–67
Harvard	118–65	Georgia Tech	71–62
St. John's	91–81	North Carolina State	71–63
Canisius	96–60	Maryland	91–89
Michigan	88–85	Wake Forest	68–72
William & Mary	97–61	Virginia	76–67
Virginia	68–62	UCLA	75–65
Florida State	86–70	Clemson	98–97
Maryland	83–66	North Carolina	89–77
Georgia Tech	97–84	Maryland	94–87
North Carolina State	110–75	Georgia Tech	89–76
N.C.—Charlotte	104–82	North Carolina	94–74
Boston University	95–85	Campbell	82–56
Wake Forest	84–68	Iowa	75–62
Clemson	112–73	Seton Hall	81–69
Florida State	75–62	Kentucky	104–103
Notre Dame	100–71	Indiana	81–78
North Carolina	73–75	Michigan	71–51

   a. Compute the mean and median scores for Duke and its opponents.
   b. Compute the range and interquartile range for Duke and its opponents.
   c. Provide box plots for Duke and its opponents.
   d. Comment on what you learned.

COMPUTER CASE 1

CONSOLIDATED FOODS, INC.

Consolidated Foods, Inc., operates a chain of supermarkets in New Mexico, Arizona, and California. (See Computer Case, Chapter 2). Data in Table 3.18 show the dollar amounts and method of payment for a sample of 100 customers. Consolidated's managers requested the sample be taken to learn about payment practices of the store's customers. In particular, managers were interested in learning about how a new credit-card payment option was related to the customers' purchase amounts.

Managerial Report

Use the methods of descriptive statistics presented in Chapter 3 to summarize the sample data. Provide summaries of the dollar purchase amounts for cash customers, personal-check customers, and credit-card customers separately. Your report should contain the following summaries and discussions.

1. A comparison and interpretation of means and medians.
2. A comparison and interpretation of measures of dispersion such as the range and standard deviation.
3. The identification and interpretation of the five-number summaries for each method of payment.
4. Box plots for each method of payment.

   Use the summary section of your report to provide a discussion of what you have learned about the method of payment and the amounts of payments for Consolidated Foods' customers. The data set for this computer case are in the data file CONSOLID.

 CONSOLID

TABLE 3.18   Purchase Amount and Method of Payment for a Random Sample of 100 Consolidated Foods Customers

Cash	Personal Check	Credit Card	Cash	Personal Check	Credit Card
$ 7.40	$27.60	$50.30	$ 5.08	$52.87	$69.77
5.15	30.60	33.76	20.48	78.16	48.11
4.75	41.58	25.57	16.28	25.96	
15.10	36.09	46.24	15.57	31.07	
8.81	2.67	46.13	6.93	35.38	
1.85	34.67	14.44	7.17	58.11	
7.41	58.64	43.79	11.54	49.21	
11.77	57.59	19.78	13.09	31.74	
12.07	43.14	52.35	16.69	50.58	
9.00	21.11	52.63	7.02	59.78	
5.98	52.04	57.55	18.09	72.46	
7.88	18.77	27.66	2.44	37.94	
5.91	42.83	44.53	1.09	42.69	
3.65	55.40	26.91	2.96	41.10	
14.28	48.95	55.21	11.17	40.51	
1.27	36.48	54.19	16.38	37.20	
2.87	51.66	22.59	8.85	54.84	
4.34	28.58	53.32	7.22	58.75	
3.31	35.89	26.57		17.87	
15.07	39.55	27.89		69.22	

COMPUTER CASE 2

NATIONAL HEALTH CARE ASSOCIATION

The National Health Care Association is concerned about the shortage of nurses the health care profession is projecting for the future. To learn the current degree of job satisfaction among nurses, the association has sponsored a study of hospital nurses throughout the country. As part of this study, a sample of 50 nurses were asked to indicate their degree of satisfaction in their work, their pay, and their opportunities for promotion. Each of the three aspects of satisfaction was measured on a scale from 0 to 100, with larger values indicating higher degrees of satisfaction. The data in Table 3.19 were collected and are available in the data set HEALTH1.

In addition, the sample data in Table 3.19 were broken down by the types of hospitals employing the nurses. The types of hospitals considered were private (P), Veterans Administration (VA), and university (U). The data in Table 3.20 are available in the data set HEALTH2.

Managerial Report

Use methods of descriptive statistics to summarize the data. Present the summaries that will be beneficial in communicating the results to others. Discuss your findings. Specifically, comment on the following questions.

1. On the basis of the entire data set and the three job-satisfaction variables, what aspect of the job is most satisfying for the nurses? What appears to be the least satisfying? In what area(s), if any, do you feel improvements should be made? Discuss.
2. On the basis of descriptive measures of dispersion, what measure of job satisfaction appears to generate the greatest difference of opinion among the nurses? Explain.

TABLE 3.19 Work, Pay, and Promotion Job-Satisfaction Scores for a Sample of 50 Nurses

HEALTH1

Work	Pay	Promotion	Work	Pay	Promotion
71	49	58	72	76	37
84	53	63	71	25	74
84	74	37	69	47	16
87	66	49	90	56	23
72	59	79	84	28	62
72	37	86	86	37	59
72	57	40	70	38	54
63	48	78	86	72	72
84	60	29	87	51	57
90	62	66	77	90	51
73	56	55	71	36	55
94	60	52	75	53	92
84	42	66	74	59	82
85	56	64	76	51	54
88	55	52	95	66	52
74	70	51	89	66	62
71	45	68	85	57	67
88	49	42	65	42	68
90	27	67	82	37	54
85	89	46	82	60	56
79	59	41	89	80	64
72	60	45	74	47	63
88	36	47	82	49	91
77	60	75	90	76	70
64	43	61	78	52	72

TABLE 3.20 Work, Pay, and Promotion Job-Satisfaction Scores for Nurses in Private, VA, and University Hospitals

Private Hospitals			VA Hospitals			University Hospitals		
Work	Pay	Promotion	Work	Pay	Promotion	Work	Pay	Promotion
72	57	40	71	49	58	84	53	63
90	62	66	84	74	37	87	66	49
84	42	66	72	37	86	72	59	79
85	56	64	63	48	78	88	55	52
71	45	68	84	60	29	74	70	51
88	49	42	73	56	55	85	89	46
72	60	45	94	60	52	79	59	41
88	36	47	90	27	67	69	47	16
77	60	75	72	76	37	90	56	23
64	43	61	86	37	59	77	90	51
71	25	74	86	72	72	71	36	55
84	28	62	95	66	52	75	53	92
70	38	54	65	42	68	76	51	54
87	51	57	82	37	54	89	80	64
74	59	82	82	60	56			
89	66	62	90	76	70			
85	57	67	78	52	72			
74	47	63						
82	49	91						

HEALTH2

3. What can be learned about the types of hospitals? Does any particular type of hospital seem to have better levels of job satisfaction than the other types? Do your results suggest any recommendations for learning about and/or improving job satisfaction? Discuss.

4. What additional descriptive statistics and insights can you use to learn about and possibly improve job satisfaction?

APPENDIX 3.1

Descriptive Statistics with Minitab

● In this appendix, we describe the steps necessary to use Minitab to generate the descriptive statistics in Figures 3.10 and 3.11 of Section 3.6. The descriptive statistics in Figure 3.10 are for the data on starting salaries of 12 business school graduates (see Table 3.1). After the data are entered into column C1 of a Minitab worksheet, the following steps generate the computer output shown in panel A of Figure 3.10.

Step 1: Select the **Stat** pull-down menu
Step 2: Select the **Basic Statistics** pull-down menu
Step 3: Select the **Descriptive Statistics** option
Step 4: When the dialog box appears:
　　　　Enter C1 in the **Variables** box
　　　　Select **OK**

The following steps generate the box plot shown in panel B of Figure 3.10.

Step 1: Select the **Graph** pull-down menu
Step 2: Select **Boxplot**

Step 3:   When the dialog box appears:
            Enter C1 under **Y** in the **Graph variables** box
            Select **OK**

The covariance and correlation output in Figure 3.11 are for the advertising and sales data at the stereo and sound equipment store (see Table 3.6). After entering the data for the number of commercials into column C1 and the data for sales into column C2 of the Minitab worksheet, we named the columns *x* and *y,* respectively. The steps necessary to generate the covariance output in the first three rows of Figure 3.11 follow.

Step 1:   Select the **Stat** pull-down menu
Step 2:   Select the **Basic Statistics** pull-down menu
Step 3:   Select the **Covariance** option
Step 4:   When the dialog box appears:
            Enter C1 C2 in the **Variables** box
            Select **OK**

After selection of **OK,** the variances and covariance appear as shown in the figure.

To obtain the correlation coefficient in the last line of Figure 3.11, only one change is necessary in the steps for obtaining the covariance. In step 3, the **Correlation** option is selected.

APPENDIX 3.2 •

Descriptive Statistics with Spreadsheets

● Spreadsheet software packages can be used to generate the descriptive statistics discussed in this chapter. In this appendix, we show how Excel can be used to generate several of the measures of location and dispersion for a single variable and to generate the covariance and correlation coefficient as measures of association between two variables.

The starting-salary data from Table 3.1 have been entered into cells A1 through A12 of the spreadsheet in Figure 3.12. The following steps describe how to use Excel to generate descriptive statistics for these data.

Step 1:   Select the **Tools** pull-down menu
Step 2:   Choose the **Data Analysis** option
Step 3:   Choose **Descriptive Statistics** from the list of Analysis Tools
Step 4:   When the dialog box appears:
            Enter A1:A12 in the **Input Range** box
            Select **Output Range**
            Enter C1 in the **Output Range** box (This identifies the upper left corner of the section of the worksheet where the descriptive statistics will appear)
            Select **Summary Statistics**
            Select **OK**

Figure 3.13 shows the descriptive statistics provided by Excel. The screened areas contain the descriptive statistics covered in this chapter. The other items are either covered subsequently in the text or covered in more advanced texts.

We next illustrate the computation of the covariance and correlation coefficient, using the advertising and sales data for the stereo and sound equipment store (see Table 3.6). Figure 3.14 is an Excel spreadsheet with the data on the number of commercials in column A and the data on sales in column B. The steps necessary to generate the covariance for these data follow.

FIGURE 3.12 Monthly Starting Salary Data in Column A of Spreadsheet

	A	B	C	D	E
1	2350				
2	2450				
3	2550				
4	2380				
5	2255				
6	2210				
7	2390				
8	2630				
9	2440				
10	2825				
11	2420				
12	2380				

FIGURE 3.13 Descriptive Statistics for Monthly Starting Salaries Provided by Excel

	A	B	C	D
1	2350		Column 1	
2	2450			
3	2550		Mean	2440
4	2380		Standard Error	47.8198957
5	2255		Median	2405
6	2210		Mode	2380
7	2390		Standard Deviation	165.652978
8	2630		Sample Variance	27440.9091
9	2440		Kurtosis	1.71888364
10	2825		Skewness	1.09110869
11	2420		Range	615
12	2380		Minimum	2210
13			Maximum	2825
14			Sum	29280
15			Count	12
16			Confidence Level (95.0%)	105.250934

Step 1:   Select the **Tools** pull-down menu

Step 2:   Choose the **Data Analysis** option

Step 3:   Choose **Covariance** from the list of Analysis Tools

Step 4:   When the dialog box appears:

       Enter A1:B10 in the **Input Range** box

       Select **Output Range**

       Enter D1 in the **Output Range** box

       Select **OK**

Figure 3.15 shows the output of the covariance procedure in columns D, E, and F. The entry in cell E3 is the covariance between the two variables, $s_{xy} = 11$. The entry in cell E2 is the variance for the number of commercials and the entry in cell F3 is the variance for sales.

FIGURE 3.14 Advertising and Sales Data for Stereo and Sound Equipment Store

	A	B			
	A	**B**	**C**	**D**	**E**
1	2	50			
2	5	57			
3	1	41			
4	3	54			
5	4	54			
6	1	38			
7	5	63			
8	3	48			
9	4	59			
10	2	46			

	A	**B**	**C**	**D**	**E**	**F**
1	2	50			*Column 1*	*Column 2*
2	5	57		Column 1	2.22222222	
3	1	41		Column 2	11	62.8888889
4	3	54				
5	4	54				
6	1	38			*Column 1*	*Column 2*
7	5	63		Column 1	1	
8	3	48		Column 2	0.93049058	1
9	4	59				
10	2	46				

FIGURE 3.15 Covariance and Correlation Coefficient for Advertising and Sales Data as Computed by Excel

The steps necessary to compute the correlation coefficient from the spreadsheet in Figure 3.14 follow.

Step 1: Select the **Tools** pull-down menu
Step 2: Choose the **Data Analysis** option
Step 3: Choose **Correlation** from the list of Analysis Tools
Step 4: When the dialog box appears:
 Enter A1:B10 in the **Input Range** box
 Select **Output Range**
 Enter D6 in the **Output Range** box
 Select **OK**

The output generated by Excel begins in cell D6 of Figure 3.15. The entry in cell E8 is the correlation coefficient, $r_{xy} = +.93$; note that it is the same value we computed in Section 3.5. The entry in cell E7 is the correlation coefficient of the first variable (number of commercials) with itself and the entry in cell F8 is the correlation coefficient of the second variable (sales) with itself. Since a variable is always perfectly correlated with itself, these values are always equal to 1.

4

INTRODUCTION TO PROBABILITY

CONTENTS

STATISTICS IN PRACTICE ●

MORTON

Morton International*
Chicago, Illinois

Morton International is a company with businesses in salt, household products, rocket motors, and specialty chemicals. Carstab Corporation, a subsidiary of Morton International, produces specialty chemicals and offers a variety of chemicals designed to meet the unique specifications of its customers. For one particular customer, Carstab produced an expensive catalyst used in chemical processing. Some, but not all, of the lots produced by Carstab met the customer's specifications for the product.

Carstab's customer agreed to test each lot after receiving it and determine whether or not the catalyst would perform the desired function. Lots that did not pass the customer's test would be returned to Carstab. Over time, Carstab found that the customer was accepting 60% of the lots and returning 40%. In probability terms, this meant that each Carstab shipment to the customer had a .60 probability of being accepted and a .40 probability of being returned.

Neither Carstab nor its customer was pleased with these results. In an effort to improve service, Carstab explored the possibility of duplicating the customer's test prior to shipment. However, the high cost of the special testing equipment made that alternative infeasible.

Carstab's chemists then proposed a new, relatively low cost test that would indicate whether or not a lot would pass the customer's test. The probability question of interest was: What is the probability that a lot will pass the customer's test if it has passed the new Carstab test prior to shipment?

A sample of lots was produced and subjected to the new Carstab test. Only lots that passed the new test were sent to the customer. Probability analysis of the data indicated that if a lot passed the Carstab test, it had a .909 probability of passing the customer's test and being accepted. Alternatively, if a lot passed the Carstab test, it had only a .091 probability of being returned. The probability analysis provided key supporting evidence for the adoption and implementation of the new testing procedure at Carstab. The new test resulted in an immediate improvement in customer service and a substantial reduction in shipping and handling costs for returned lots.

The probability of a lot being accepted by the customer after passing the new Carstab test is called a conditional probability. In this chapter, you will learn how to compute this and other probabilities that are helpful in decision making.

Morton Salt and the "When It Rains It Pours" slogan.

*The authors are indebted to Michael Haskell of Morton International for providing this Statistics in Practice.

● Throughout our lives we are faced with decision-making situations that involve uncertainty. Perhaps you will be asked for an analysis of one of the following situations.

1. What is the "chance" that sales will decrease if the price of the product is increased?
2. What is the "likelihood" that the new assembly method will increase productivity?
3. How "likely" is it that the project will be completed on time?
4. What are the "odds" that the new investment will be profitable?

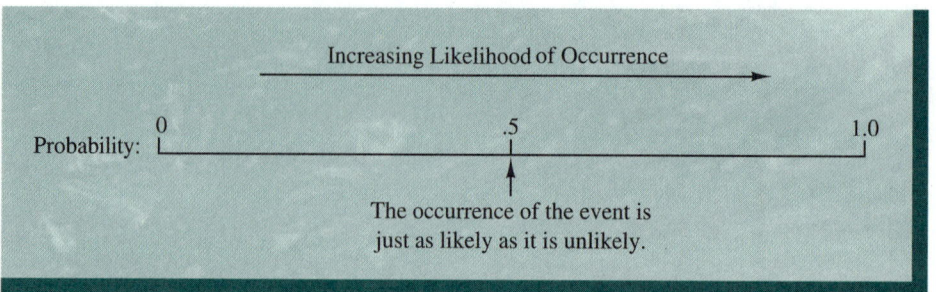

FIGURE 4.1   Probability as a Numerical Measure of the Likelihood of Occurrence

The approaches most useful in effectively dealing with such uncertainties are based on the concept of probability. In everyday terminology, *probability* can be thought of as a numerical measure of the chance or likelihood that a particular event will occur. For example, if we consider the event "rain tomorrow," we understand that, when the television weather report indicates "a near-zero probability of rain," there is almost no chance of rain. However, if a 90% probability of rain is reported, we know that rain is very likely or almost certain to occur. A 50% probability indicates that rain is just as likely to occur as not.

Probability values are always assigned on a scale from 0 to 1. A probability near 0 indicates that the event is very unlikely to occur; a probability near 1 indicates that the event is almost certain to occur. Other probabilities between 0 and 1 represent degrees of likelihood that the event will occur. Figure 4.1 depicts this view of probability.

Probability is important in decision making because it provides a mechanism for measuring, expressing, and analyzing the uncertainties associated with future events. In this chapter we introduce the fundamental concepts of probability and begin to illustrate their use as decision-making tools. In subsequent chapters we will extend these basic notions of probability and demonstrate the important role that probability plays in statistical inference.

4.1   EXPERIMENTS, THE SAMPLE SPACE, AND COUNTING RULES

Using the terminology of probability, we define an *experiment* to be any process which generates well-defined outcomes. By this we mean that, on any single repetition of the experiment, *one and only one* of the possible experimental outcomes will occur. Several examples of experiments and their associated outcomes follow.

Experiment	Experimental Outcomes
Toss a coin	Head, tail
Select a part for inspection	Defective, nondefective
Conduct a sales call	Purchase, no purchase
Roll a die	1, 2, 3, 4, 5, 6
Play a football game	Win, lose, tie

The first step in analyzing a particular experiment is to carefully define the experimental outcomes. When we have defined *all* possible experimental outcomes, we have identified the *sample space* for the experiment. That is, the sample space is defined

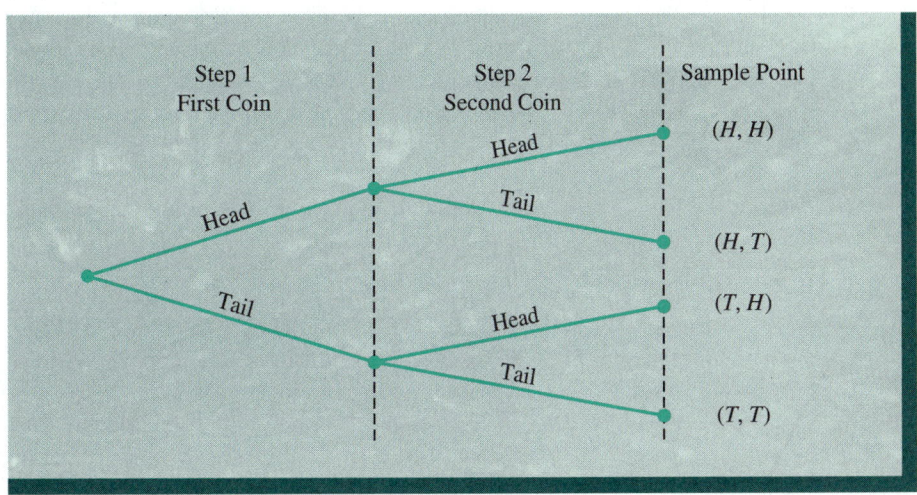

FIGURE 4.2   Tree Diagram for the Experiment of Tossing Two Coins

as the set of all possible experimental outcomes. Any one particular experimental outcome is referred to as a *sample point* and is an element of the sample space.

Let us consider the experiment of tossing a coin. The experimental outcome is defined by the upward face of the coin—a head or a tail. If we let S denote the sample space, we can use the following notation to describe the sample space and sample points for the experiment.

$$S = \{\text{Head, Tail}\}$$

With this notation, the experiment of selecting a part for inspection would have the following sample space and sample points.

$$S = \{\text{Defective, Nondefective}\}$$

Finally, suppose we consider the experiment of rolling a die, where the experimental outcome is defined as the number of dots appearing on the upward face of the die. In this experiment, the numerical values 1, 2, 3, 4, 5, and 6 represent the possible experimental outcomes or sample points. Hence, the sample space is denoted by

$$S = \{1, 2, 3, 4, 5, 6\}$$

COUNTING RULES

The ability to identify and count the sample points of an experiment is an important step in understanding what may happen when an experiment occurs. Consider an experiment of tossing two coins, with the experimental outcomes defined in terms of the pattern of heads and tails appearing on the upward faces of the two coins. How many experimental outcomes (sample points) are possible for this experiment?

We can view the experiment of tossing two coins as a two-step experiment: step 1 corresponds to tossing the first coin and step 2 corresponds to tossing the second coin. The *tree diagram* is a graphical device that is helpful in visualizing a multiple-step experiment and enumerating the experimental outcomes. Figure 4.2 is a tree diagram for the coin-tossing experiment with branches of either a head or a tail shown for the first coin (step 1) followed by the branches of either a head or a tail shown for the second coin (step 2). The notation (H, H) is used to denote the outcome corresponding to a head on the first coin and a head on the second coin. Similarly, (H, T) is used to denote the outcome of a head on the first coin and a tail on the second coin. Thus, each of the points on the right side of the tree corresponds to a sample point—an experimental outcome. We see that there are four experimental outcomes for the coin-tossing experiment, and the sample space for the experiment can be written as

$$S = \{(H, H), (H, T), (T, H), (T, T)\}$$

A rule that is helpful in determining the number of sample points for a multiple-step experiment follows.

A COUNTING RULE FOR MULTIPLE-STEP EXPERIMENTS

If an experiment can be described as a sequence of k steps in which there are n_1 possible outcomes on the first step, n_2 possible outcomes on the second step, and so on, then the total number of experimental outcomes is given by $(n_1)(n_2) \ldots (n_k)$. That is, the number of outcomes for the overall experiment is the product of the number of outcomes on each step.

Referring again to the experiment of tossing two coins, we have stated that it can be viewed as a two-step experiment. With two outcomes possible on the first toss of the coin ($n_1 = 2$) and two outcomes possible on the second toss of the coin ($n_2 = 2$), the counting rule states that there are $(n_1)(n_2) = (2)(2) = 4$ experimental outcomes.

Let us now see how the counting rule for multiple-step experiments can be used in the analysis of a capacity expansion project faced by the Kentucky Power & Light Company (KP&L). The project is designed to increase the generating capacity of one of KP&L's plants in northern Kentucky. The project is divided into two sequential stages or steps: stage 1 (design) and stage 2 (construction). While each stage will be scheduled and controlled as closely as possible, management cannot predict beforehand the exact time required to complete each stage of the project. An analysis of similar construction projects has shown completion times for the design stage of 2, 3, or 4 months and completion times for the construction stage of 6, 7, or 8 months. Because of the critical need for additional electrical power, management has set a goal of 10 months for the completion of the entire project.

Since there are three possible completion times for the design stage (step 1) and three possible completion times for the construction stage (step 2), the counting rule for multiple-step experiments can be applied here to determine that there is a total of $(3)(3) = 9$ experimental outcomes. To describe the experimental outcomes, we will use a two-number notation; for instance, $(2, 6)$ will indicate that the design stage is completed in 2 months and the construction stage is completed in 6 months. This experimental outcome results in a total of $2 + 6 = 8$ months to complete the entire project. Table 4.1 summarizes the nine experimental outcomes for the KP&L project. The tree diagram in Figure 4.3 shows how the nine outcomes (sample points) occur.

The counting rule and tree diagram have been used to help the project manager identify the experimental outcomes and determine the possible project completion times. From the information in Figure 4.3, we see that the project will be completed in from 8 to 12 months, with six of the nine experimental outcomes providing the desired completion time of 10 months or less. While it has been helpful to identify the experimental outcomes, we will need to consider how probability values can be assigned to the experimental outcomes before making a final assessment of the probability that the project will be completed within the desired 10 months. Probability assignments for experimental outcomes will be discussed in Section 4.2.

TABLE 4.1 Listing of Experimental Outcomes (Sample Points) for the KP&L Problem

Completion Time (months)			
Stage 1 (Design)	Stage 2 (Construction)	Notation for Experimental Outcome	Total Project Completion Time (months)
2	6	(2, 6)	8
2	7	(2, 7)	9
2	8	(2, 8)	10
3	6	(3, 6)	9
3	7	(3, 7)	10
3	8	(3, 8)	11
4	6	(4, 6)	10
4	7	(4, 7)	11
4	8	(4, 8)	12

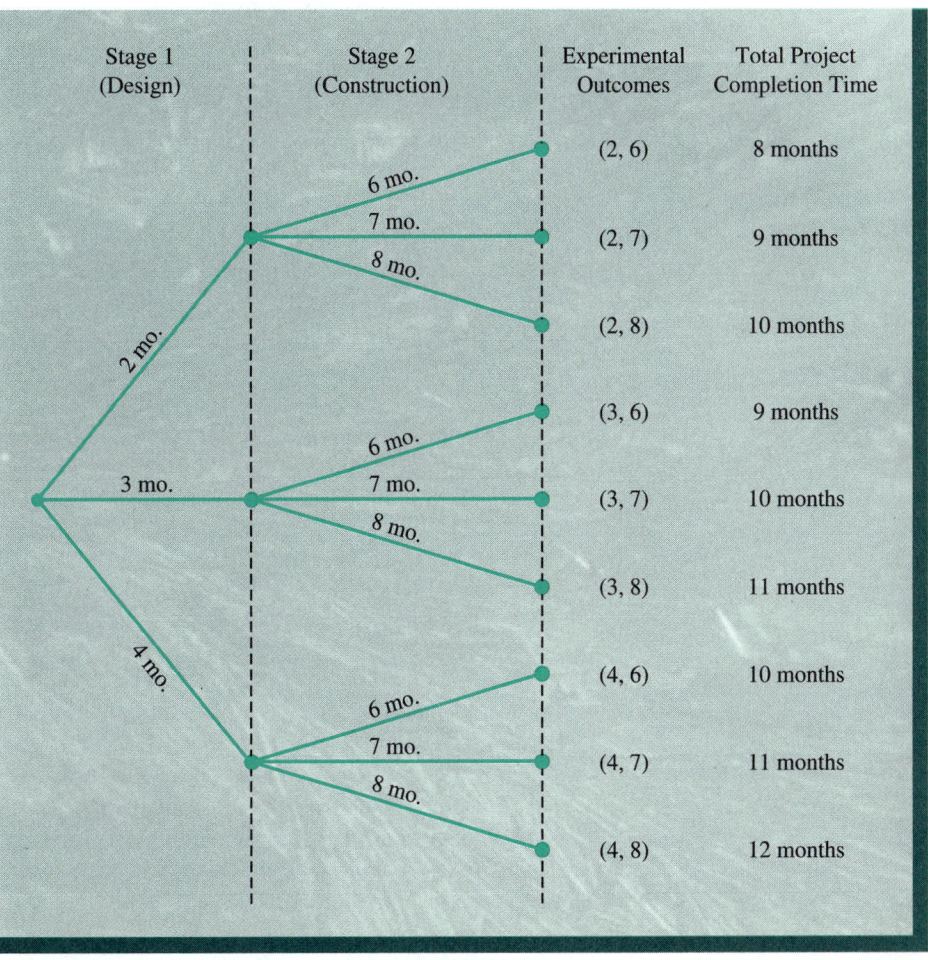

FIGURE 4.3 Tree Diagram for the KP&L Project

Another counting rule that is often useful enables one to count the number of experimental outcomes when n objects are to be selected from a set of N objects. It is called the counting rule for combinations.

COUNTING RULE FOR COMBINATIONS

The number of combinations of N objects taken n at a time is

$$\binom{N}{n} = \frac{N!}{n!(N-n)!} \tag{4.1}$$

where

$$N! = N(N-1)(N-2)\ldots(2)(1)$$
$$n! = n(n-1)(n-2)\ldots(2)(1)$$

and

$$0! = 1.$$

The notation ! means *factorial;* for example, 5 factorial is $5! = (5)(4)(3)(2)(1) = 120$. By definition, 0! is equal to 1.

As an illustration of the counting rule for combinations, consider a quality control procedure where an inspector randomly selects two of five parts to test for defects. In a group of five parts, how many combinations of two parts can be selected? The counting rule in (4.1) shows that with $N = 5$ and $n = 2$, we have

$$\binom{5}{2} = \frac{5!}{2!(5-2)!} = \frac{(5)(4)(3)(2)(1)}{(2)(1)(3)(2)(1)} = \frac{120}{12} = 10$$

Thus, there are 10 outcomes for the experiment of randomly selecting two parts from a group of five. If we label the five parts as A, B, C, D, and E, the 10 combinations or experimental outcomes can be identified as AB, AC, AD, AE, BC, BD, BE, CD, CE, and DE.

As another example, consider that the Ohio lottery system uses the random selection of six numbers from a group of 47 numbers to determine the weekly lottery winner. The counting rule for combinations (4.1) can be used to determine the number of ways six different numbers can be selected from a group of 47 numbers.

$$\binom{47}{6} = \frac{47!}{6!(47-6)!} = \frac{47!}{6!41!} = \frac{(47)(46)(45)(44)(43)(42)}{(6)(5)(4)(3)(2)(1)} = 10{,}737{,}573$$

The counting rule for combinations has told us that there are over 10 million experimental outcomes in the lottery drawing. If an individual buys a lottery ticket and selects six of the 47 numbers, there is one chance in 10,737,573 that the individual will win.

Counting rules such as the one for multiple-step experiments and the one for combinations are helpful in determining the number of outcomes in a statistical experiment. In the next section we will study ways in which probabilities are assigned to experimental outcomes. The probabilities assigned will enable the manager or decision maker to assess the risks or chances of obtaining favorable, as well as unfavorable, outcomes.

NOTES AND COMMENTS

In statistics, the notion of an experiment is somewhat different from the notion of an experiment in the physical sciences. In the physical sciences, an experiment is usually conducted in a laboratory or a controlled environment in order to learn about a scientific occurrence. When physical science experiments are repeated under identical conditions, the same outcome is expected to occur. In statistical experiments, the outcomes are determined by chance. Even though the experiment is repeated in exactly the same way, an entirely different outcome may occur. Because of this difference in outcomes, the experiments of statistics are sometimes called random experiments.

EXERCISES

METHODS

Self-Test

1. An experiment has three steps with three outcomes possible for the first step, two outcomes possible for the second step, and four outcomes possible for the third step. How many experimental outcomes exist for the entire experiment?

2. How many ways can three items be selected from a group of six items? Use the letters A, B, C, D, E, and F to identify the items, and list each of the different combinations of three items.

APPLICATIONS

3. Consider the experiment of conducting three sales calls. On each of the calls there will be either a purchase or no purchase.
   a. Construct a tree diagram for this three-step experiment.
   b. Identify each sample point and the sample space. How many sample points are there?
   c. How many sample points would there be if the experiment consisted of four sales calls?

4. A major resort in Florida is concerned about weather conditions in the Northeast as well as in Florida. In characterizing the temperature in both areas, the following three categories are used: below average, average, or above average. A combination of below-average temperatures in the Northeast with above-average temperatures in Florida means an increased volume of business for the resort. The experiment is observing the weather conditions on a particular day.
   a. How many experimental outcomes are possible?
   b. Develop a tree diagram for this experiment.

5. In the city of Milford, applications for zoning changes go through a two-step process: a review by the planning commission and a final decision by the city council. At step 1 the planning commission will review the zoning change request and make a positive or negative recommendation concerning the change. At step 2 the city council will review the planning commission's recommendation and then vote to approve or to disapprove the zoning change. In some instances, the city council vote has agreed with the planning commission's recommendation. However, in other instances, the council vote has been the opposite of the planning commission's recommendation. An application for a zoning change has just been submitted by the developer of an apartment complex. Consider the application process as an experiment.
   a. How many sample points are there for this experiment? List the sample points.
   b. Construct a tree diagram for the experiment.

6. An investor has two stocks: stock A and stock B. Each stock may increase in value, decrease in value, or remain unchanged. Consider the experiment of investing in the two stocks and observing the change (if any) in value.

    a. How many experimental outcomes are possible?

    b. Show a tree diagram for the experiment.

    c. How many of the experimental outcomes result in an increase in value for at least one of the two stocks?

    d. How many of the experimental outcomes result in an increase in value for both of the stocks?

7. An investor is reviewing the performance of six stocks and will select two for investment. How many alternative combinations of two stocks does the investor have to consider?

8. How many five-card poker hands are possible with a deck of 52 cards?

Self-Test

9. Simple random sampling uses a sample of size *n* from a population of size *N* to obtain data that can be used to make inferences about the characteristics of a population. Suppose we have a population of 50 bank accounts and want to take a random sample of four accounts in order to learn about the population. How many different random samples of four accounts are possible?

10. Williams, Inc. will be forming a three-member long-range planning committee that will be charged with developing a strategic five-year plan for the company's entry into a new product market. The president has identified seven experienced managers as candidates for the committee. How many ways can the three-member committee be formed?

11. A company is planning to expand its operation by building two plants in the western region of the country. Eight possible locations have been identified and are being evaluated. How many combinations of two locations are possible from the eight locations?

12. Many states design their automobile license plates with space for up to six letters or numerals.

    a. If a state decides to use only numerals on the license plates, how many different license plate numbers are possible? Assume that 000000 is an acceptable license plate number, although it will be used only for display purposes at the license bureau.

    b. If the state decides to use two letters followed by four numerals, how many different letter-numeral combinations are possible? Assume that the letters I and O will not be used because of their similarity to numbers 1 and 0.

    c. Would larger states, such as New York and California, tend to use more or fewer letters in license plates? Explain.

4.2   ASSIGNING PROBABILITIES TO EXPERIMENTAL OUTCOMES

Let us now see how probabilities for the experimental outcomes (sample points) can be determined. Recall the discussion at the beginning of this chapter which stated that the probability of an experimental outcome is a numerical measure of the likelihood that the experimental outcome will occur. In the assignment of probabilities to the experimental outcomes, various approaches are acceptable; however, regardless of the approach taken, the following two basic requirements must be satisfied.

1. The probability values assigned to each experimental outcome (sample point) must be between 0 and 1. That is, if we let E_i indicate experimental outcome i and $P(E_i)$ indicate the probability of this experimental outcome, we must have

$$0 \leq P(E_i) \leq 1 \qquad \text{for all } i \qquad \textbf{(4.2)}$$

2. The sum of *all* of the experimental outcome probabilities must be 1. If a sample space has k experimental outcomes, we must have

$$P(E_1) + P(E_2) + \cdots + P(E_k) = \Sigma P(E_i) = 1 \qquad \textbf{(4.3)}$$

Any method of assigning probability values to the experimental outcomes which satisfies these two requirements and results in reasonable numerical measures of the likelihood of the outcomes is acceptable. In practice, one of the following three methods can be used.

1. Classical method
2. Relative frequency method
3. Subjective method

CLASSICAL METHOD

To illustrate the classical method of assigning probabilities, let us again consider the experiment of flipping a coin. On any one flip, we will observe one of two experimental outcomes: head or tail. It would seem reasonable to assume that the two outcomes are equally likely. Therefore, since one of the two equally likely outcomes is a head, we should logically conclude that the probability of observing a head is ½, or .50. Similarly, the probability of observing a tail is also .50. When the assumption of equally likely outcomes is used as a basis for assigning probabilities, the approach is referred to as the *classical method*. If an experiment has n possible outcomes, the classical method would assign a probability of $1/n$ to each experimental outcome.

As another illustration of the classical method, consider again the experiment of rolling a die. In Section 4.1 we described the sample space and sample points for this experiment with the following notation.

$$S = \{1, 2, 3, 4, 5, 6\}$$

It would seem reasonable to conclude that the six experimental outcomes are equally likely, and hence each outcome is assigned a probability of ⅙. Thus, if $P(1)$ denotes the probability that one dot appears on the upward face of the die, then $P(1) = ⅙$. Similarly, $P(2) = ⅙$, $P(3) = ⅙$, $P(4) = ⅙$, $P(5) = ⅙$, and $P(6) = ⅙$. Note that this probability assignment satisfies the two basic requirements for assigning probabilities. In fact, requirements (4.2) and (4.3) are always satisfied when the classical method is used, since each of the n sample points is assigned a probability of $1/n$.

The classical method was developed originally in the analysis of gambling problems, where the assumption of equally likely outcomes is often reasonable. In many business problems, however, this assumption is not valid. Hence, alternative methods of assigning probabilities are required.

RELATIVE FREQUENCY METHOD

As an illustration of the relative frequency method, consider a firm that is preparing to market a new product. In order to estimate the probability that a customer will purchase the product, a test market evaluation has been set up wherein salespeople will call on potential customers. For each sales call conducted, there are two possible outcomes: the customer purchases the product or the customer does not purchase the product. Since there is no reason to assume that the two experimental outcomes are equally likely, the classical method of assigning probabilities is inappropriate.

Suppose that, in the test market evaluation of the product, 400 potential customers were contacted; 100 actually purchased the product, but 300 did not. In effect, then, we have repeated the experiment of contacting one customer 400 times and have found that the product was purchased 100 times. Hence, we might decide to use the relative frequency as an estimate of the probability of a customer making a purchase. We could assign a probability of 100/400 = .25 to the experimental outcome of purchasing the product. Similarly, 300/400 = .75 could be assigned to the experimental outcome of not purchasing the product. This approach to assigning probabilities is referred to as the *relative frequency method*.

SUBJECTIVE METHOD

The classical and relative frequency methods cannot be applied to all situations where probability assessments are desired. For example, there are situations where the experimental outcomes are not equally likely and where relative frequency data are unavailable. For example, consider the next football game that the Pittsburgh Steelers will play. What is the probability that the Steelers will win? The experimental outcomes of a win, a loss, or a tie are not necessarily equally likely. Also, since the teams involved have not played several times previously this year, no relative frequency data will be available that are relevant to the upcoming game. Thus, if we want an estimate of the probability of the Steelers winning, we must use a subjective opinion of its value.

With the subjective method of assigning probabilities to the experimental outcomes, we can use any data available as well as our experience and intuition. However, after we consider all available information, a probability value that expresses the *degree of belief* that the experimental outcome will occur must be specified. This method of assigning probability is referred to as the *subjective method.* Since subjective probability expresses a person's degree of belief, it is personal. Different people can be expected to assign different probabilities to the same event. Nonetheless, care must be taken when using the subjective method to ensure that requirements (4.2) and (4.3) are satisfied. That is, regardless of a person's degree of belief, the probability value assigned to each experimental outcome must be between 0 and 1 and the sum of all the experimental outcome probabilities must equal 1.

Even in situations where either the classical or the relative frequency approach can be applied, management may want to provide subjective probability estimates. In such cases, the best probability estimates often are obtained by combining the estimates from the classical or relative frequency approach with the subjective probability estimates.

PROBABILITIES FOR THE KP&L PROBLEM

To perform further analysis on the KP&L problem, we must develop probabilities for each of the nine experimental outcomes listed in Table 4.1. On the basis of experience and judgment, management concluded that the experimental outcomes were not equally likely. Hence, the classical method of assigning probabilities could not be used. Management then decided to conduct a study of the completion times for similar projects undertaken by KP&L over the past three years. The results of a study of 40 similar projects are summarized in Table 4.2.

After reviewing the results of the study, management decided to employ the relative frequency method of assigning probabilities. Management could have provided subjective probability estimates, but felt that the current project was quite similar to the 40 previous projects. Thus, the relative frequency method was judged best.

In using the data in Table 4.2 to compute probabilities, we note that outcome (2, 6)—stage 1 completed in 2 months and stage 2 completed in 6 months—occurred six times in the 40 projects. We can use the relative frequency method to assign a probability of 6/40 = .15 to this outcome. Similarly, outcome (2, 7) also occurred in six of the 40 projects, providing a 6/40 = .15 probability. Continuing in this manner, we obtain the probability assignments for the sample points of the KP&L project shown in Table 4.3. Note that $P(2, 6)$ represents the probability of the sample point (2, 6), $P(2, 7)$ represents the probability of the sample point (2, 7), and so on.

TABLE 4.2 Completion Results for 40 KP&L Projects

Completion Time (months)		Sample Point	Number of Past Projects Having These Completion Times
Stage 1	Stage 2		
2	6	(2, 6)	6
2	7	(2, 7)	6
2	8	(2, 8)	2
3	6	(3, 6)	4
3	7	(3, 7)	8
3	8	(3, 8)	2
4	6	(4, 6)	2
4	7	(4, 7)	4
4	8	(4, 8)	6
		Total	40

TABLE 4.3 Probability Assignments for the KP&L Problem Based on the Relative Frequency Method

Sample Point	Project Completion Time	Probability of Sample Point
(2, 6)	8 months	$P(2, 6) = 6/40 = .15$
(2, 7)	9 months	$P(2, 7) = 6/40 = .15$
(2, 8)	10 months	$P(2, 8) = 2/40 = .05$
(3, 6)	9 months	$P(3, 6) = 4/40 = .10$
(3, 7)	10 months	$P(3, 7) = 8/40 = .20$
(3, 8)	11 months	$P(3, 8) = 2/40 = .05$
(4, 6)	10 months	$P(4, 6) = 2/40 = .05$
(4, 7)	11 months	$P(4, 7) = 4/40 = .10$
(4, 8)	12 months	$P(4, 8) = 6/40 = .15$
		Total 1.00

EXERCISES

METHODS

13. Suppose an experiment has five equally likely outcomes: E_1, E_2, E_3, E_4, E_5. Assign probabilities to each outcome and show that conditions (4.2) and (4.3) are satisfied. What method did you use?

Self-Test

14. An experiment with three outcomes has been repeated 50 times and it was learned that E_1 occurred 20 times, E_2 occurred 13 times, and E_3 occurred 17 times. Assign probabilities to the outcomes. What method did you use?

15. A decision maker has subjectively assigned the following probabilities to the four outcomes of an experiment: $P(E_1) = .10$, $P(E_2) = .15$, $P(E_3) = .40$, and $P(E_4) = .20$. Are these valid probability assignments? Check to see if (4.2) and (4.3) are satisfied.

16. Consider the experiment of selecting a card from a deck of 52 cards.
   a. How many sample points are possible?
   b. Which method (classical, relative frequency, or subjective) would you recommend for assigning probabilities to the sample points?

c. What is the probability assignment for each card?

d. Show that your probability assignments satisfy the two basic requirements for assigning probabilities.

APPLICATIONS

Self-Test
⋅⋅⋅⋅⋅⋅⋅⋅⋅⋅▶

17. In a survey of new matriculants to MBA programs ("School Selection by Students," *GMAC Occasional Papers,* Stolzenberg and Giarrusso, March 1988), the following data were obtained on the marital status of the students.

Marital Status	Frequency
Never married	1106
Married	826
Other (separated, widowed, divorced)	106
Total	2038

Consider the experiment of interviewing a new MBA student and recording her or his marital status. Show your probability assignments.

TABLE 4.4   Exercise 18

Number of Refrigerators Sold	Number of Weeks
0	6
1	12
2	15
3	10
4	5
5	2
Total	50

18. A small-appliance store in Madeira has collected data on refrigerator sales for the last 50 weeks. The data are shown in Table 4.4. Suppose that we are interested in the experiment of observing the number of refrigerators sold in one week of store operations.

a. How many experimental outcomes are there?

b. Which approach would you recommend for assigning probabilities to the experimental outcomes?

c. Assign probabilities and verify that your assignments satisfy the two basic requirements.

19. Strom Construction has made bids on two contracts. The owner has identified the possible outcomes and subjectively assigned the following probabilities.

Experimental Outcome	Obtain Contract 1	Obtain Contract 2	Probability
1	Yes	Yes	.15
2	Yes	No	.15
3	No	Yes	.30
4	No	No	.25

a. Are these valid probability assignments? Why or why not?

b. What would have to be done to make the probability assignments valid?

20. An investor forecasts that the probabilities that a certain stock will either go down, remain the same, or go up are .20, .60, and .30, respectively. Does this seem reasonable? Explain.

21. Faced with the question of determining the probability of obtaining either 0 heads, 1 head, or 2 heads when flipping a coin twice, an individual argued that, since it seems reasonable to treat the outcomes as equally likely, the probability of each event is ⅓. Do you agree? Explain.

TABLE 4.5   Exercise 22

Design	Number of Times Preferred
1	5
2	15
3	30
4	40
5	10

22. A company that manufactures toothpaste is studying five different package designs. Assuming that one design is just as likely to be selected by a consumer as any other design, what selection probability would you assign to each of the package designs? In an actual experiment, 100 consumers were asked to pick the design they preferred. The data in Table 4.5 were obtained. Do the data appear to confirm the belief that one design is just as likely to be selected as another? Explain.

4.3   EVENTS AND THEIR PROBABILITIES

Until now we have used the term *event* much as it would be used in everyday language. We must now introduce the formal definition of an *event* as it relates to probability.

EVENT
An *event* is a collection of sample points.

For an example, let us return to the KP&L problem and assume that the project manager is interested in the event that the entire project can be completed in 10 months or less. Referring to Table 4.3, we see that six sample points—(2, 6), (2, 7), (2, 8), (3, 6), (3, 7), and (4, 6)—provide a project completion time of 10 months or less. Let C denote the event that the project is completed in 10 months or less; we write

$$C = \{(2, 6), (2, 7), (2, 8), (3, 6), (3, 7), (4, 6)\}$$

Event C is said to occur if *any one* of the six sample points shown above appears as the experimental outcome.

Other events that might be of interest to KP&L management include the following.

L = the event that the project is completed in *less* than 10 months

M = the event that the project is completed in *more* than 10 months

Using the information in Table 4.3, we see that these events consist of the following sample points.

$$L = \{(2, 6), (2, 7), (3, 6)\}$$
$$M = \{(3, 8), (4, 7), (4, 8)\}$$

A variety of additional events can be defined for the KP&L problem, but in each case the event must be identified as a collection of sample points for the experiment.

Given the probabilities of the sample points shown in Table 4.3, we can use the following definition to compute the probability of any event that KP&L management might want to consider.

PROBABILITY OF AN EVENT
The probability of any event is equal to the sum of the probabilities of the sample points in the event.

Using this definition, we calculate the probability of a particular event by adding the probabilities of the experimental outcomes that make up the event. We can now compute the probability that the project will take 10 months or less to complete. Since this event is given by $C = \{(2, 6), (2, 7), (2, 8), (3, 6), (3, 7), (4, 6)\}$, the probability ($P$) of event C is shown by

$$P(C) = P(2, 6) + P(2, 7) + P(2, 8) + P(3, 6) + P(3, 7) + P(4, 6)$$

Refer to the sample point probabilities in Table 4.3; we have

$$P(C) = .15 + .15 + .05 + .10 + .20 + .05 = .70$$

Similarly, since the event that the project is completed in less than 10 months is given by $L = \{(2, 6), (2, 7), (3, 6)\}$, the probability of this event is given by

$$P(L) = P(2, 6) + P(2, 7) + P(3, 6)$$

$$= .15 + .15 + .10 = .40$$

Finally, for the event that the project is completed in more than 10 months, we have $M = \{(3, 8), (4, 7), (4, 8)\}$ and thus

$$P(M) = P(3, 8) + P(4, 7) + P(4, 8)$$

$$= .05 + .10 + .15 = .30$$

Using the above probability results, we can now tell KP&L management that there is a .70 probability that the project will be completed in 10 months or less, a .40 probability that the project will be completed in less than 10 months, and a .30 probability that the project will be completed in more than 10 months. This procedure of computing event probabilities can be repeated for any event of interest to the KP&L management.

Any time that we can identify all the sample points of an experiment and assign the corresponding sample point probabilities, we can use the definition to compute the probability of an event. However, in many experiments the number of sample points is large and the identification of the sample points, as well as the determination of their associated probabilities, is extremely cumbersome, if not impossible. In the remaining sections of this chapter, we present some basic probability relationships that can be used to compute the probability of an event without knowledge of all sample point probabilities.

NOTES AND COMMENTS

1. The sample space, S, is an event. Since it contains all the experimental outcomes, it has a probability of 1; that is, $P(S) = 1$.
2. When the classical method is used to assign probabilities, the assumption is that the experimental outcomes are equally likely. In such cases, the probability of an event can be computed by counting the number of experimental outcomes in the event and dividing the result by the total number of experimental outcomes.

EXERCISES

METHODS

23. An experiment has three outcomes with $P(E_1) = .35$, $P(E_2) = .40$, $P(E_3) = .25$.
    a. What is the probability that E_1 or E_2 occurs?
    b. What is the probability that E_1 or E_3 occurs?
    c. What is the probability that E_1, E_2, or E_3 occurs?

24. An experiment has four equally likely outcomes.
    a. What is the probability that E_2 occurs?
    b. What is the probability that any two of the outcomes occur (e.g. E_1 or E_3)?
    c. What is the probability that any three of the outcomes occur (e.g. E_1 or E_2 or E_4)?

Self-Test

25. In Exercise 16 we considered the experiment of selecting a card from a deck of 52 cards. Each card corresponded to a sample point with a 1/52 probability.
   a. List the sample points in the event an ace is selected.
   b. List the sample points in the event a club is selected.
   c. List the sample points in the event a face card (jack, queen, or king) is selected.
   d. Find the probabilities associated with each of the events in (a), (b), and (c).

26. Consider the experiment of rolling a pair of dice. Suppose that we are interested in the sum of the face values showing on the dice.
   a. How many sample points are possible? (Hint: Use the counting rule for multiple-step experiments.)
   b. List the sample points.
   c. What is the probability of obtaining a value of 7?
   d. What is the probability of obtaining a value of 9 or greater?
   e. Since there are six possible even values (2, 4, 6, 8, 10, and 12) and only five possible odd values (3, 5, 7, 9, and 11), the dice should show even values more often than odd values. Do you agree with this statement? Explain.
   f. What method did you use to assign the probabilities requested above?

APPLICATIONS

Self-Test

27. Refer to the KP&L sample points and sample point probabilities in Table 4.3.
   a. The design stage (stage 1) will run over budget if it takes 4 months to complete. List the sample points in the event the design stage is over budget.
   b. What is the probability that the design stage is over budget?
   c. The construction stage (stage 2) will run over budget if it takes 8 months to complete. List the sample points in the event the construction stage is over budget.
   d. What is the probability that the construction stage is over budget?
   e. What is the probability that both stages are over budget?

28. Suppose that a manager of a large apartment complex provides the subjective probability estimates listed in Table 4.6 about the number of vacancies that will exist next month. List the sample points in each of the following events and provide the probability of the event.
   a. No vacancies.   **b.** At least four vacancies.   **c.** Two or fewer vacancies.

29. The manager of a furniture store sells from 0 to 4 china hutches each week. On the basis of past experience, the following probabilities are assigned to sales of 0, 1, 2, 3, or 4 hutches: $P(0) = .08$; $P(1) = .18$; $P(2) = .32$; $P(3) = .30$; and $P(4) = .12$.
   a. Are these valid probability assignments? Why or why not?
   b. Let A be the event that 2 or fewer are sold in one week. Find $P(A)$.
   c. Let B be the event that 4 or more are sold in one week. Find $P(B)$.

30. The 1992 *Wall Street Journal* Subscriber Study revealed characteristics of the *Journal*'s subscribers, including business responsibilities, investment activities, life-style characteristics, and personal affluence. Table 4.7 shows the total value of stock owned by the 1317 respondents. Suppose a subscriber is selected at random. What are the probabilities of the following events?
   a. Let A be the event that the total value of stock owned is at least $50,000 but less than $100,000. Find $P(A)$.
   b. Let B be the event that the total value of stock owned is less than $50,000. Find $P(B)$.
   c. Let C be the event that the total value of stock owned is $100,000 or more. Find $P(C)$.

31. A survey of 50 students at Tarpon Springs College about the number of extracurricular activities resulted in the data in Table 4.8.
   a. Let A be the event that a student participates in at least 1 activity. Find $P(A)$.
   b. Let B be the event that a student participates in 3 or more activities. Find $P(B)$.
   c. What is the probability that a student participates in exactly 2 activities?

TABLE 4.6 Exercise 28

Vacancies	Probability
0	.05
1	.15
2	.35
3	.25
4	.10
5	.10

TABLE 4.7 Exercise 30

Amount ($)	Number
Less than $15,000	216
$15,000–49,999	232
$50,000–99,999	200
$100,000–299,999	316
$300,000 or more	353

TABLE 4.8 Exercise 31

Number of Activities	Frequency
0	8
1	20
2	12
3	6
4	3
5	1

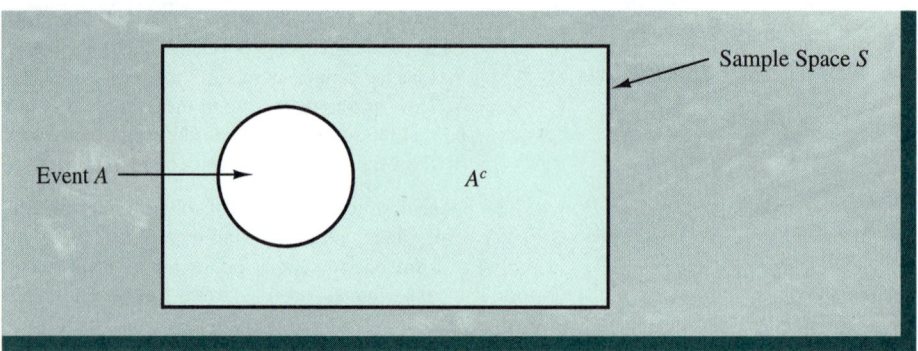

FIGURE 4.4   Complement of Event *A*

4.4 SOME BASIC RELATIONSHIPS OF PROBABILITY

COMPLEMENT OF AN EVENT

Given an event *A,* the *complement* of *A* is defined to be the event consisting of all sample points that are *not* in *A*. The complement of *A* is denoted by A^c. Figure 4.4 is a diagram, known as a *Venn diagram,* which illustrates the concept of a complement. The rectangular area represents the sample space for the experiment and as such contains all possible sample points. The circle represents event *A* and contains only the sample points that belong to *A*. The shaded region of the rectangle contains all sample points not in event *A,* and is by definition the complement of *A*.

In any probability application, either event *A* or its complement A^c must occur. Therefore, we have

$$P(A) + P(A^c) = 1$$

Solving for *P*(*A*), we obtain the following result.

> **COMPUTING PROBABILITY USING THE COMPLEMENT**
>
> $$P(A) = 1 - P(A^c) \tag{4.4}$$

Equation (4.4) shows that the probability of an event *A* can be computed easily if the probability of its complement, $P(A^c)$, is known.

As an example, consider the case of a sales manager who, after reviewing sales reports, states that 80% of new customer contacts result in no sale. By allowing *A* to denote the event of a sale and A^c to denote the event of no sale, the manager is stating that $P(A^c) = .80$. Using (4.4), we see that

$$P(A) = 1 - P(A^c) = 1 - .80 = .20$$

We can conclude that there is a .20 probability that a sale will be made on a new customer contact.

In another example, a purchasing agent states that there is a .90 probability that a supplier will send a shipment that is free of defective parts. Using the complement, we

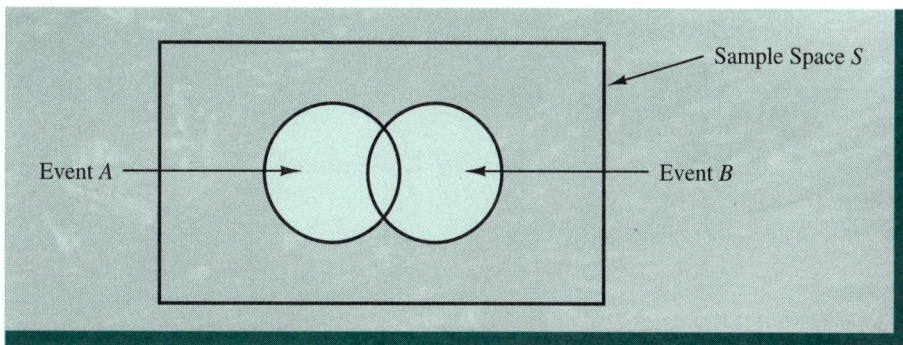

FIGURE 4.5 Union of Events *A* and *B*

can conclude that there is a $1 - .90 = .10$ probability that the shipment will contain defective parts.

ADDITION LAW

The addition law is helpful when we have two events and are interested in knowing the probability that at least one of the events occurs. That is, with events *A* and *B* we are interested in knowing the probability that event *A* or event *B* or both occur.

Before we present the addition law, we need to discuss two concepts related to the combination of events: the *union* of events and the *intersection* of events. Given two events *A* and *B,* the union of *A* and *B* is defined as follows.

> **UNION OF TWO EVENTS**
> The *union* of *A* and *B* is the event containing *all* sample points belonging to *A or B or both.* The union is denoted by $A \cup B$.

The Venn diagram in Figure 4.5 depicts the union of events *A* and *B*. Note that the two circles contain all the sample points in event *A* as well as all the sample points in event *B*. The fact that the circles overlap indicates that some sample points are contained in both *A* and *B*.

The definition of the intersection of two events *A* and *B* follows.

> **INTERSECTION OF TWO EVENTS**
> Given two events *A* and *B*, the *intersection* of *A* and *B* is the event containing the sample points belonging to *both A and B.* The intersection is denoted by $A \cap B$.

The Venn diagram depicting the intersection of the two events is shown in Figure 4.6. The area where the two circles overlap is the intersection; it contains the sample points that are in both *A* and *B*.

Let us now continue with a discussion of the addition law. The addition law provides a way to compute the probability of event *A* or *B* or both *A* and *B* occurring. In other words, the addition law is used to compute the probability of the union of two events, $A \cup B$. The addition law is written as follows.

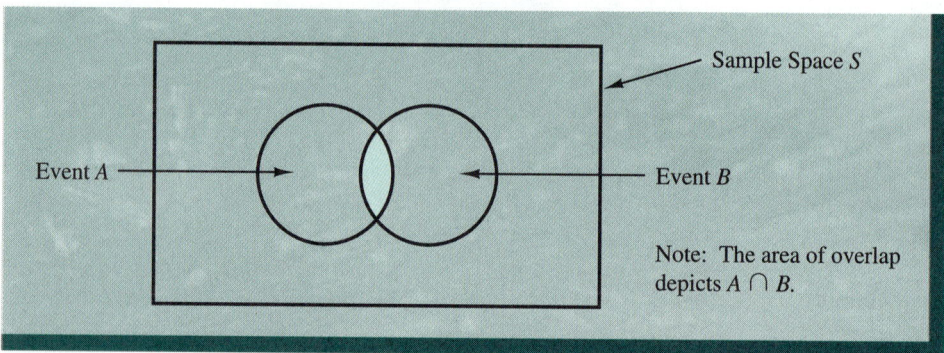

FIGURE 4.6   Intersection of Events *A* and *B*

ADDITION LAW

$$P(A \cup B) = P(A) + P(B) - P(A \cap B) \tag{4.5}$$

To grasp the addition law intuitively, note that the first two terms in the addition law, $P(A) + P(B)$, account for all the sample points in $A \cup B$. However, since the sample points in the intersection $A \cap B$ are in both A and B, when we compute $P(A) + P(B)$, we are in effect counting each of the sample points in $A \cap B$ twice. We correct for this by subtracting $P(A \cap B)$.

As an example of an application of the addition law, let us consider the case of a small assembly plant with 50 employees. Each worker is expected to complete work assignments on time and in such a way that the assembled product will pass a final inspection. On occasion, some of the workers fail to meet the performance standards by completing work late and/or assembling defective products. At the end of a performance evaluation period, the production manager found that 5 of the 50 workers had completed work late, 6 of the 50 workers had assembled defective products, and 2 of the 50 workers had both completed work late *and* assembled defective products.

Let

$$L = \text{the event that the work is completed late}$$

$$D = \text{the event that the assembled product is defective}$$

The above relative frequency information leads to the following probabilities.

$$P(L) = \frac{5}{50} = .10$$

$$P(D) = \frac{6}{50} = .12$$

$$P(L \cap D) = \frac{2}{50} = .04$$

After reviewing the performance data, the production manager decided to assign a poor performance rating to any employee whose work was either late or defective; thus the event of interest is $L \cup D$. What is the probability that the production manager assigned an employee a poor performance rating?

Note that the probability question is about the union of two events. Specifically, we want to know $P(L \cup D)$. Using (4.5), we have

$$P(L \cup D) = P(L) + P(D) - P(L \cap D)$$

Knowing values for the three probabilities on the right side of this expression, we can write

$$P(L \cup D) = .10 + .12 - .04 = .18$$

This tells us that there is a .18 probability that an employee received a poor performance rating.

As another example of the addition law, consider a recent study conducted by the personnel manager of a major computer software company. It was found that 30% of the employees who left the firm within two years did so primarily because they were dissatisfied with their salary, 20% left because they were dissatisfied with their work assignments, and 12% of the former employees indicated dissatisfaction with *both* their salary and their work assignments. What is the probability that an employee who leaves within two years does so because of dissatisfaction with salary, dissatisfaction with the work assignment, or both?

Let

$S =$ the event that the employee leaves because of salary

$W =$ the event that the employee leaves because of work assignment

We have $P(S) = .30$, $P(W) = .20$, and $P(S \cap W) = .12$. Using (4.5), the addition law, we have

$$P(S \cup W) = P(S) + P(W) - P(S \cap W) = .30 + .20 - .12 = .38$$

We find that there is a .38 probability that an employee leaves for salary or work assignment reasons.

Before we conclude our discussion of the addition law, let us consider a special case that arises for *mutually exclusive events*.

MUTUALLY EXCLUSIVE EVENTS

Two events are said to be *mutually exclusive* if the events have no sample points in common.

That is, events A and B are mutually exclusive if, when one event occurs, the other cannot occur. Thus, a requirement for A and B to be mutually exclusive is that their intersection must contain no sample points. The Venn diagram depicting two mutually exclusive events A and B is shown in Figure 4.7. In this case $P(A \cap B) = 0$ and the addition law can be written as follows.

ADDITION LAW FOR MUTUALLY EXCLUSIVE EVENTS

$$P(A \cup B) = P(A) + P(B)$$

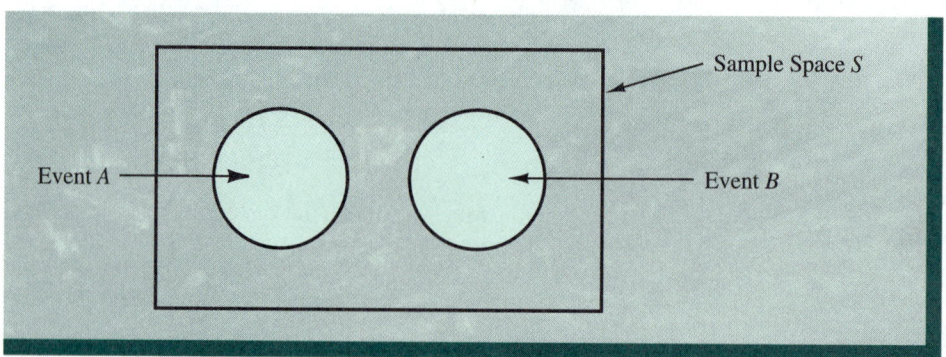

FIGURE 4.7   Mutually Exclusive Events

EXERCISES

METHODS

32. Suppose that we have a sample space with five equally likely experimental outcomes: E_1, E_2, E_3, E_4, E_5.
Let

$$A = \{E_1, E_2\}$$
$$B = \{E_3, E_4\}$$
$$C = \{E_2, E_3, E_5\}$$

a. Find $P(A)$, $P(B)$, and $P(C)$.
b. Find $P(A \cup B)$. Are A and B mutually exclusive?
c. Find A^c, C^c, $P(A^c)$, and $P(C^c)$.
d. Find $A \cup B^c$ and $P(A \cup B^c)$.
e. Find $P(B \cup C)$.

Self-Test

33. Suppose that we have a sample space $S = \{E_1, E_2, E_3, E_4, E_5, E_6, E_7\}$, where E_1, E_2, ..., E7 denote the sample points. The following probability assignments apply: $P(E_1) = .05$, $P(E_2) = .20$, $P(E_3) = .20$, $P(E_4) = .25$, $P(E_5) = .15$, $P(E_6) = .10$, and $P(E_7) = .05$.
Let

$$A = \{E_1, E_4, E_6\}$$
$$B = \{E_2, E_4, E_7\}$$
$$C = \{E_2, E_3, E_5, E_7\}$$

a. Find $P(A)$, $P(B)$, and $P(C)$.
b. Find $A \cup B$ and $P(A \cup B)$.
c. Find $A \cap B$ and $P(A \cap B)$.
d. Are events A and C mutually exclusive?
e. Find B^c and $P(B^c)$.

APPLICATIONS

34. The public accounting firm Grant Thornton conducted a survey to see how executives felt about the 1992 recession and the potential for recovery (*Journal of Accountancy,* February

1992). The probability that an executive indicated a recession existed was .74. If we were to choose one of the executives, what is the probability that she or he would indicate a recession does not exist?

35. A survey of benefits for 254 corporate executives (*Business Week,* October 24, 1994) showed that 155 executives were provided mobile phones, 152 were provided club memberships, and 110 were provided both mobile phones and club memberships as perks associated with their position.
    a. Let *M* be the event of having a mobile phone and *C* be the event of having a club membership. Find the following probabilities: $P(M)$, $P(C)$ and $P(M \cap C)$.
    b. Use the probabilities in part (a) to compute the probability that a corporate executive has at least one of the two perks.
    c. What is the probability that a corporate executive does not have either of these perks?

36. A *U.S. News/UCLA* survey of 867 entertainment leaders in Hollywood studied how the entertainment industry views itself in terms of the amount of violence on television and the general quality of television programming (*U.S. News & World Report,* May 9, 1994). Results showed that 624 leaders felt the amount of violent programming had increased in the last 10 years, 390 felt the quality of programming had decreased over the same 10 years, and 234 leaders responded both that the amount of violent programming had increased and that the quality of programming had decreased.
    a. Letting *V* be the event that the amount of violent programming has increased and *Q* be the event that the quality of programming has decreased, compute the following probabilities: $P(V)$, $P(Q)$, and $P(V \cap Q)$.
    b. Use the probabilities in part (a) to find the probability that a leader made at least one of the following two comments: the amount of violent programming has increased or the quality of programming has decreased.
    c. What is the probability that a leader did not agree with either of the two comments?

37. A survey of subscribers to *Forbes* showed that 72% have investments in money market funds and 36.4% have investments in certificates of deposit (CDs) (*Forbes* 1993 Subscriber Study). If 20% have investments in both money market funds and CDs, what is the probability that a subscriber has investments in either money market funds or CDs? What is the probability that a subscriber does not have investments in either money market funds or CDs?

Self-Test
········►

38. The survey of subscribers to *Forbes* showed that 45.8% rented a car during the past 12 months for business reasons, 54% rented a car during the past 12 months for personal reasons, and 30% rented a car during the past 12 months for both business and personal reasons (*Forbes* 1993 Subscriber Study).
    a. What is the probability that a subscriber rented a car during the past 12 months for business or personal reasons?
    b. What is the probability that a subscriber did not rent a car during the past 12 months for either business or personal reasons?

39. Let

$$A = \text{the event that a person runs five miles or more per week}$$
$$B = \text{the event that a person dies of heart disease}$$
$$C = \text{the event that a person dies of cancer}$$

Further, suppose that $P(A) = .01$, $P(B) = .25$, and $P(C) = .20$.
    a. Are events *A* and *B* mutually exclusive? Can you find $P(A \cap B)$?
    b. Are events *B* and *C* mutually exclusive? Find the probability that a person dies of heart disease or cancer.
    c. Find the probability that a person dies from causes other than cancer.

40. During winter in Cincinnati, Mr. Krebs experiences difficulty in starting his two cars. The probability that the first car starts is .80 and the probability that the second car starts is .40. There is a probability of .30 that both cars start.

    a. Define the events involved and use probability notation to show the probability information given above.

    b. What is the probability that at least one car starts?

    c. What is the probability that Mr. Krebs cannot start either of the two cars?

41. Let A be the event that a person's primary means of transportation to and from work is an automobile and B be the event that a person's primary means of transportation to and from work is a bus. Suppose that in a large city we find $P(A) = .45$ and $P(B) = .35$.

    a. Are events A and B mutually exclusive? What is the probability that a person uses an automobile or a bus in going to and from work?

    b. Find the probability that a person's primary means of transportation is something other than a bus.

4.5   CONDITIONAL PROBABILITY

Often, the probability of an event is influenced by whether or not a related event has occurred. Suppose we have an event A with probability $P(A)$. If we obtain new information and learn that a related event, denoted by B, has occurred, we will want to take advantage of this information in calculating a new probability for event A. This new probability of event A is written $P(A \mid B)$. The notation $\mid$ is used to denote the fact that we are considering the probability of event A *given* the condition that event B has occurred. Hence, the notation $P(A \mid B)$ is read "the probability of A given B."

As an illustration of the application of *conditional probability,* consider the situation of the promotion status of male and female officers of a major metropolitan police force in the eastern United States. The police force consists of 1200 officers, 960 men and 240 women. Over the past two years, 324 officers on the police force have been awarded promotions. The specific breakdown of promotions for male and female officers is shown in Table 4.9.

After reviewing the promotion record, a committee of female officers raised a discrimination case on the basis that 288 male officers had received promotions but only 36 female officers had received promotions. The police administration argued that the relatively low number of promotions for female officers was due not to discrimination, but to the fact that there are relatively few female officers on the police force. Let us show how conditional probability could be used to analyze the discrimination charge.

Let

$$M = \text{event an officer is a man}$$

$$W = \text{event an officer is a woman}$$

$$A = \text{event an officer is promoted}$$

$$A^c = \text{event an officer is not promoted}$$

TABLE 4.9   Promotion Status of Police Officers over the Past Two Years

	Men	Women	Totals
Promoted	288	36	324
Not Promoted	672	204	876
Totals	960	240	1200

TABLE 4.10 Joint Probability Table for Promotions

Joint probabilities appear in the body of the table	Men *(M)*	Women *(W)*	Totals
Promoted *(A)*	.24	.03	.27
Not Promoted *(A^c)*	.56	.17	.73
Totals	.80	.20	1.00

Marginal probabilities appear in the margins of the table

Dividing the data values in Table 4.9 by the total of 1200 officers enables us to summarize the available information in the following probability values.

$$P(M \cap A) = 288/1200 = .24 = \text{probability that a randomly selected officer is a man } and \text{ is promoted}$$

$$P(M \cap A^c) = 672/1200 = .56 = \text{probability that a randomly selected officer is a man } and \text{ is not promoted}$$

$$P(W \cap A) = 36/1200 = .03 = \text{probability that a randomly selected officer is a woman } and \text{ is promoted}$$

$$P(W \cap A^c) = 204/1200 = .17 = \text{probability that a randomly selected officer is a woman } and \text{ is not promoted}$$

Since each of these values gives the probability of the intersection of two events, the probabilities are called *joint probabilities*. Table 4.10, which provides a summary of the probability information for the police officer promotion situation, is referred to as a *joint probability table*.

The values in the margins of the joint probability table provide the probabilities of each event separately. That is, $P(M) = .80$, $P(W) = .20$, $P(A) = .27$, and $P(A^c) = .73$. These probabilities are referred to as *marginal probabilities* because of their location in the margins of the joint probability table. We note that the marginal probabilities are found by summing the joint probabilities in the corresponding row or column of the joint probability table. For instance, the marginal probability of being promoted is $P(A) = P(M \cap A) + P(W \cap A) = .24 + .03 = .27$. From the marginal probabilities, we see that 80% of the force is male, 20% of the force is female, 27% of all officers received promotions, and 73% were not promoted.

Let us begin the conditional probability analysis by computing the probability that an officer is promoted given that the officer is a man. In conditional probability notation, we are attempting to determine $P(A \mid M)$. To calculate $P(A \mid M)$, we first realize that this notation simply means that we are considering the probability of the event A (promotion) given that the condition designated as event M (the officer is a man) is known to exist. Thus $P(A \mid M)$ tells us that we are now concerned only with the promotion status of the 960 male officers. Since 288 of the 960 male officers received promotions, the probability of being promoted given that the officer is a man is 288/960 = .30. In other words, given that an officer is a man, there has been a 30% chance of receiving a promotion over the past two years.

The above procedure was easy to apply in our illustration because the data values in Table 4.9 show the number of officers in each category. We now want to demonstrate how conditional probabilities such as $P(A \mid M)$ can be computed directly from event probabilities rather than the frequency data of Table 4.9.

We have shown that $P(A \mid M) = 288/960 = .30$. Let us now divide both the numerator and denominator of this fraction by 1200, the total number of officers in the study.

$$P(A \mid M) = \frac{288}{960} = \frac{288/1200}{960/1200} = \frac{.24}{.80} = .30$$

We now see that the conditional probability $P(A \mid M)$ can be computed as .24/.80. Refer to the joint probability table (Table 4.10). Note in particular that .24 is the joint probability of A and M; that is, $P(A \cap M) = .24$. Also note that .80 is the marginal probability that a randomly selected officer is a man; that is, $P(M) = .80$. Thus, the conditional probability $P(A \mid M)$ can be computed as the ratio of the joint probability $P(A \cap M)$ to the marginal probability $P(M)$.

$$P(A \mid M) = \frac{P(A \cap M)}{P(M)} = \frac{.24}{.80} = .30$$

The fact that conditional probabilities can be computed as the ratio of a joint probability to a marginal probability provides the following general formula for conditional probability calculations for two events A and B.

CONDITIONAL PROBABILITY

$$P(A \mid B) = \frac{P(A \cap B)}{P(B)} \tag{4.6}$$

or

$$P(B \mid A) = \frac{P(A \cap B)}{P(A)} \tag{4.7}$$

The Venn diagram in Figure 4.8 is helpful in obtaining an intuitive understanding of conditional probability. The circle on the right shows that event B has occurred; the portion of the circle that overlaps with event A denotes the event $(A \cap B)$. We know that once event B has occurred, the only way that we can also observe event A is for the event $(A \cap B)$ to occur. Thus, the ratio $P(A \cap B)/P(B)$ provides the conditional probability that we will observe event A given event B has already occurred.

Let us return to the issue of discrimination against the female officers. The marginal probability in row 1 of Table 4.10 shows that the probability of promotion of an officer is $P(A) = .27$ (regardless of whether that officer is male or female). However, the critical issue in the discrimination case involves the two conditional probabilities $P(A \mid M)$ and $P(A \mid W)$. That is, what is the probability of a promotion *given* that the officer is a man, and what is the probability of a promotion *given* that the officer is a woman? If these two probabilities are equal, there is no basis for a discrimination argument because the chances of a promotion are the same for male and female officers. However, if the two conditional probabilities differ, there will be support for the position that male and female officers are treated differently in promotion decisions.

We have already determined that $P(A \mid M) = .30$. Let us now use the probability values in Table 4.10 and the basic relationship of conditional probability (4.6) to compute the probability that a randomly selected officer is promoted given that the officer is a woman; that is, $P(A \mid W)$. Using (4.6), we obtain

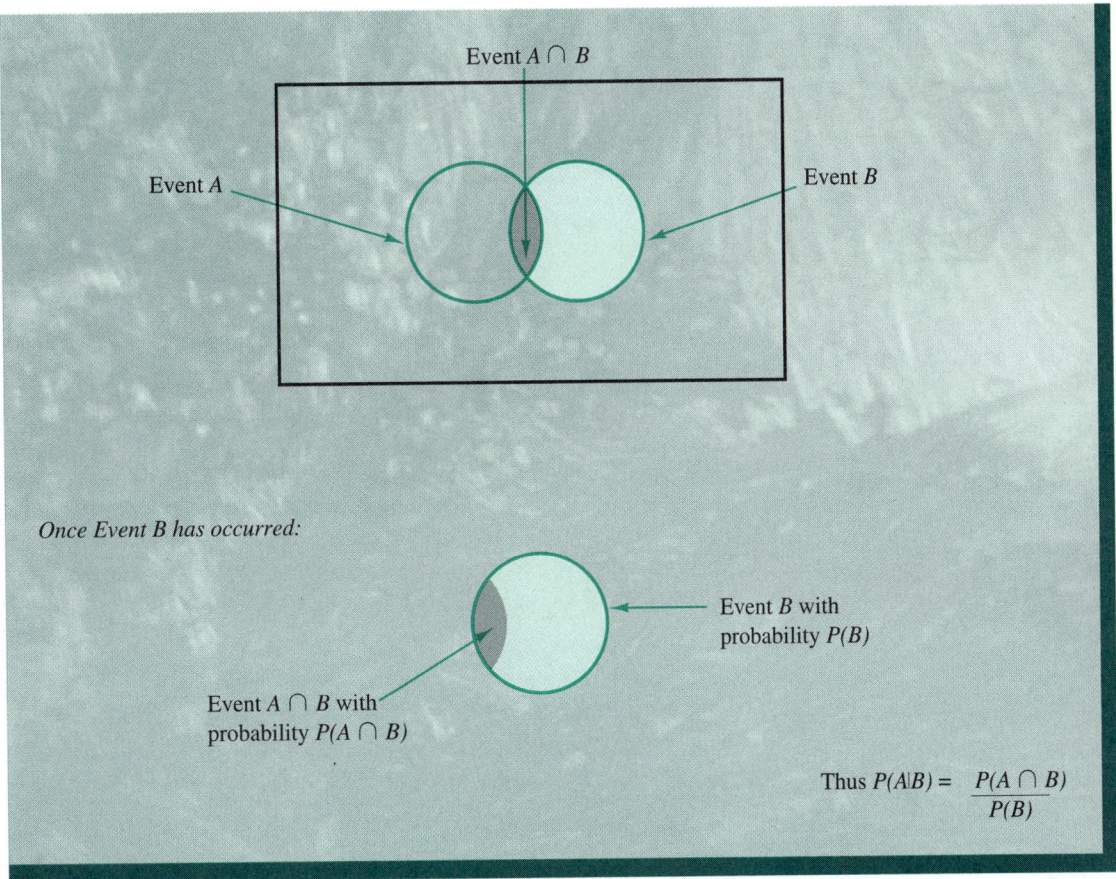

FIGURE 4.8   Conditional Probability

$$P(A \mid W) = \frac{P(A \cap W)}{P(W)} = \frac{.03}{.20} = .15$$

What conclusions do you draw? The probability of a promotion given that the officer is a man is .30, twice the .15 probability of a promotion given that the officer is a woman. While the use of conditional probability does not in itself prove that discrimination exists in this case, the conditional probability values support the argument presented by the female officers.

INDEPENDENT EVENTS

In the preceding illustration, $P(A) = .27$, $P(A \mid M) = .30$, and $P(A \mid W) = .15$. We see that the probability of a promotion (event A) is affected or influenced by whether the officer is male or female. Particularly, since $P(A \mid M) \neq P(A)$, we would say that events A and M are *dependent* events. That is, the probability of event A (promotion) is altered or affected by knowing whether or not M (the officer is a man) occurs. Similarly, with $P(A \mid W) \neq P(A)$, we would say that events A and W are *dependent* events. If the probability of event A is not changed by the existence of event M—that is, $P(A \mid M) = P(A)$—we would say that events A and M are *independent* events. This leads us to the following definition of the independence of two events.

INDEPENDENT EVENTS

Two events A and B are independent if

$$P(A \mid B) = P(A) \tag{4.8}$$

or

$$P(B \mid A) = P(B). \tag{4.9}$$

Otherwise, the events are dependent.

MULTIPLICATION LAW

Whereas the addition law of probability is used to compute the probability of a union of two events, the multiplication law is used to find the probability of an intersection of two events. The multiplication law is based on the definition of conditional probability. Using (4.6) and (4.7) and solving for $P(A \cap B)$, we obtain the *multiplication law*.

MULTIPLICATION LAW

$$P(A \cap B) = P(B)P(A \mid B) \tag{4.10}$$

or

$$P(A \cap B) = P(A)P(B \mid A) \tag{4.11}$$

To illustrate the use of the multiplication law, consider a newspaper circulation department where it is known that 84% of the households in a particular neighborhood subscribe to the daily edition of the paper. If we let D denote the event that a household subscribes to the daily edition, $P(D) = .84$. In addition, it is known that the probability that a household who already holds a daily subscription also subscribes to the Sunday edition (event S) is .75; that is, $P(S \mid D) = .75$. What is the probability that a household subscribes to both the Sunday and daily editions of the newspaper? Using the multiplication law, we compute the desired $P(S \cap D)$ as

$$P(S \cap D) = P(D)P(S \mid D) = .84(.75) = .63$$

We now know that 63% of the households subscribe to both the Sunday and daily editions.

Before concluding this section, let us consider the special case of the multiplication law when the events involved are independent. Recall that we defined independent events to exist whenever $P(A \mid B) = P(A)$ or $P(B \mid A) = P(B)$. Hence, using (4.10) and (4.11) for the special case of independent events, we obtain the following multiplication law.

MULTIPLICATION LAW FOR INDEPENDENT EVENTS

$$P(A \cap B) = P(A)P(B) \tag{4.12}$$

To compute the probability of the intersection of two independent events, we simply multiply the corresponding probabilities. Note that the multiplication law for independent events provides another way to determine whether A and B are independent. That is, if $P(A \cap B) = P(A)P(B)$, then A and B are independent; if $P(A \cap B) \neq P(A)P(B)$, then A and B are dependent.

As an application of the multiplication law for independent events, consider the situation of a service station manager who knows from past experience that 80% of the customers use a credit card when they purchase gasoline. What is the probability that the next two customers purchasing gasoline will each use a credit card? If we let

A = the event that the first customer uses a credit card

B = the event that the second customer uses a credit card

then the event of interest is $A \cap B$. Given no other information, we can reasonably assume that A and B are independent events. Thus,

$$P(A \cap B) = P(A)P(B) = (.80)(.80) = .64$$

NOTES AND COMMENTS

Do not confuse the notion of mutually exclusive events with that of independent events. Two events with nonzero probabilities cannot be both mutually exclusive and independent. If one mutually exclusive event is known to occur, the probability of the other occurring is reduced to zero. They are therefore dependent.

EXERCISES

METHODS

Self-Test

42. Suppose that we have two events, A and B, with $P(A) = .5$, $P(B) = .60$, and $P(A \cap B) = .40$.
   a. Find $P(A \mid B)$.   **b.** Find $P(B \mid A)$.
   c. Are A and B independent? Why or why not?

43. Assume that we have two events, A and B, that are mutually exclusive. Assume further that we know $P(A) = .30$ and $P(B) = .40$.
   a. What is $P(A \cap B)$?   **b.** What is $P(A \mid B)$?
   c. A student in statistics argues that the concepts of mutually exclusive events and independent events are really the same, and that if events are mutually exclusive they must be independent. Do you agree with this statement? Use the probability information in this problem to justify your answer.
   d. What general conclusion would you make about mutually exclusive and independent events given the results of this problem?

APPLICATIONS

44. A Daytona Beach nightclub has the following data on the age and marital status of 140 customers.

		Marital Status	
		Single	Married
Age	Under 30	77	14
	30 or Over	28	21

a. Develop a joint probability table for these data.

b. Use the marginal probabilities to comment on the age of customers attending the club.

c. Use the marginal probabilities to comment on the marital status of customers attending the club.

d. What is the probability of finding a customer who is single and under the age of 30?

e. If a customer is under 30, what is the probability that he or she is single?

f. Is marital status independent of age? Explain, using probabilities.

Self-Test ▸

45. In a survey of MBA students, the following data were obtained on "students' first reason for application to the school in which they matriculated" ("School Selection by Students," *GMAC Occasional Papers,* Stolzenberg and Giarrusso, March 1988).

		Reason for Application			
		School Quality	*School Cost or Convenience*	*Other*	**Totals**
Enrollment	*Full Time*	421	393	76	890
Status	*Part Time*	400	593	46	1039
	Totals	821	986	122	1929

a. Develop a joint probability table for these data.

b. Use the marginal probabilities of school quality, cost/convenience, and other to comment on the most important reason for choosing a school.

c. If a student goes full time, what is the probability that school quality is the first reason for choosing a school?

d. If a student goes part time, what is the probability that school quality is the first reason for choosing a school?

e. Let *A* be the event that a student is full time and let *B* be the event that the student lists school quality as the first reason for applying. Are events *A* and *B* independent? Justify your answer.

46. *The* 1992 *Wall Street Journal* Subscriber Study provided data on automobiles in each subscriber's household. Data for 1900 respondents follow.

		Do You Have a U.S. Car?		
		Yes	*No*	**Totals**
Do You Have	*Yes*	734	430	1164
a Foreign Car?	*No*	701	35	736
	Totals	1435	465	1900

a. Show the joint probability table for these data.

b. Use the marginal probabilities to compare U.S. and foreign car preferences among subscribers.

c. What is the probability that a household has both a U.S. and a foreign car?

d. What is the probability that a household has a car, U.S. or foreign?

e. If a household has a U.S. car, what is the probability that it also has a foreign car?

f. If a household has a foreign car, what is the probability that it also has a U.S. car?

g. Are having a U.S. car and having a foreign car independent events? Explain.

47. Some investment analysts believe the January performance of the stock market is an indicator of how the market will perform during the coming year (*USA Today,* January 10, 1995).

Historical data suggest that if the stock market rises in January, the outlook is good for stocks during the coming year. Suppose an investment analyst provides the following probability estimates.

- The probability that the stock market will be up for January is .70
- The probability that the stock market will be up for the year is .80
- The probability that the stock market will be up for January and up for the year is .63

   a. Given that the stock market is up for January, use the investment analyst's estimates to determine the probability that the stock market will be up for the year.

   b. Suppose the probability that the stock market will not be up for January but will be up for the year is .17. If the stock market is not up for January, what is the probability that it will be up for the year?

   c. Use the above conditional probabilities to comment on the use of the stock market's January performance as an indicator of its performance for the year.

   d. Do the probabilities suggest that the stock market's January performance and its annual performance are independent or dependent events? Explain.

48. The following data from a sample of 80 families in a midwestern city show the record of college attendance by fathers and their oldest sons.

		Son	
		Attended College	Did Not Attend College
Father	Attended College	18	7
	Did Not Attend College	22	33

   a. Show the joint probability table.

   b. Use the marginal probabilities to comment on the comparison between fathers and sons in terms of attending college.

   c. What is the probability that a son attended college given that his father attended college?

   d. What is the probability that a son attended college given that his father did not attend college?

   e. Is attending college by the son independent of whether or not his father attended college? Explain, using probability values.

49. The Texas Oil Company provides a limited partnership arrangement whereby small investors can pool resources in order to invest in large-scale oil exploration programs. In the exploratory drilling phase, selection of locations for new wells is based on the geologic structure of the proposed drilling sites. Experience shows that there is a .40 probability of a type A structure present at the site given a productive well. It is also known that 50% of all wells are drilled in locations with type A structure. Finally, 30% of all wells drilled are productive.

   a. What is the probability of a well being drilled in a type A structure *and* being productive?

   b. If the drilling process begins in a location with a type A structure, what is the probability of having a productive well at the location?

   c. Is finding a productive well independent of the type A geologic structure? Explain.

50. The Grant Thornton public accounting firm conducted a survey to see how executives felt about the 1992 recession and recovery potential (*Journal of Accountancy*, February 1992). Results showed that the probability of an executive indicating the existence of a recession was .74. The probability of an executive stating both that a recession existed and that a recovery would occur within six months was .41.

   a. Given that an executive indicated the existence of a recession, what is the probability that the executive felt that a recovery would occur within six months?

b. Assume that if an executive denied the existence of a recession, he or she also believed that a recovery had already begun. Construct a joint probability table for recession–no recession, and recovery–no recovery. Executives who feel a recovery is already underway and those who feel one will occur in six months should be put in the same category for this table.

c. Use the joint probability table in (b) to find the marginal probability of a recovery.

51. A purchasing agent has placed rush orders for a particular raw material with two different suppliers, *A* and *B*. If neither order arrives in four days, the production process must be shut down until at least one of the orders arrives. The probability that supplier *A* can deliver the material in four days is .55. The probability that supplier *B* can deliver the material in four days is .35.

a. What is the probability that both suppliers will deliver the material in four days? Since two separate suppliers are involved, we are willing to assume independence.

b. What is the probability that at least one supplier will deliver the material in four days?

c. What is the probability that the production process will be shut down in four days because of a shortage of raw material (that is, both orders are late)?

52. In a 1992 study of the consumer's view of the economy, the probability that a consumer would buy a house during the year was .033 and the probability that a consumer would buy a car during the year was .168 (*U.S. News & World Report,* April 13, 1992). Assume that there was only a .004 probability that a consumer would buy a house and a car during the year.

a. What is the probability that a consumer would buy either a car or a house during the year?

b. What is the probability that a consumer would buy a car during the year given that the consumer purchased a house during the year?

c. Are buying a car and buying a house independent events? Explain.

4.6   BAYES' THEOREM

In the discussion of conditional probability, we indicated that revising probabilities when new information is obtained is an important phase of probability analysis. Often, we begin our analysis with initial or *prior* probability estimates for specific events of interest. Then, from sources such as a sample, a special report, or a product test, we obtain some additional information about the events. Given this new information, we update the prior probability values by calculating revised probabilities, referred to as *posterior probabilities. Bayes' theorem* provides a means for making these probability calculations. The steps in this probability revision process are shown in Figure 4.9.

As an application of Bayes' theorem, consider a manufacturing firm that receives shipments of parts from two different suppliers. Let A_1 denote the event that a part is from supplier 1 and A_2 denote the event that a part is from supplier 2. Currently, 65% of the parts purchased by the company are from supplier 1 and the remaining 35% are from supplier 2. Hence, if a part is selected at random, we would assign the prior probabilities $P(A_1) = .65$ and $P(A_2) = .35$.

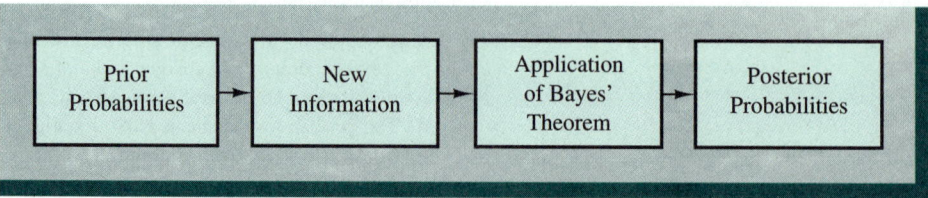

FIGURE 4.9   Probability Revision Using Bayes' Theorem

TABLE 4.11   Historical Quality Levels of Two Suppliers

	Percentage Good Parts	Percentage Bad Parts
Supplier 1	98	2
Supplier 2	95	5

The quality of the purchased parts varies with the source of supply. Historical data suggest that the quality ratings of the two suppliers are as shown in Table 4.11. If we let G denote the event that a part is good and B denote the event that a part is bad, the information in Table 4.11 provides the following conditional probability values.

$$P(G \mid A_1) = .98 \quad P(B \mid A_1) = .02$$

$$P(G \mid A_2) = .95 \quad P(B \mid A_2) = .05$$

The tree diagram in Figure 4.10 depicts the process of the firm receiving a part from one of the two suppliers and then discovering that the part is good or bad as a two-step experiment. We see that there are four experimental outcomes; two correspond to the part being good and two correspond to the part being bad.

Each of the experimental outcomes is the intersection of two events, so we can use the multiplication rule to compute the probabilities. For instance,

$$P(A_1, G) = P(A_1 \cap G) = P(A_1)P(G \mid A_1)$$

The process of computing these joint probabilities can be depicted in what is sometimes called a probability tree (see Figure 4.11). From left to right through the tree,

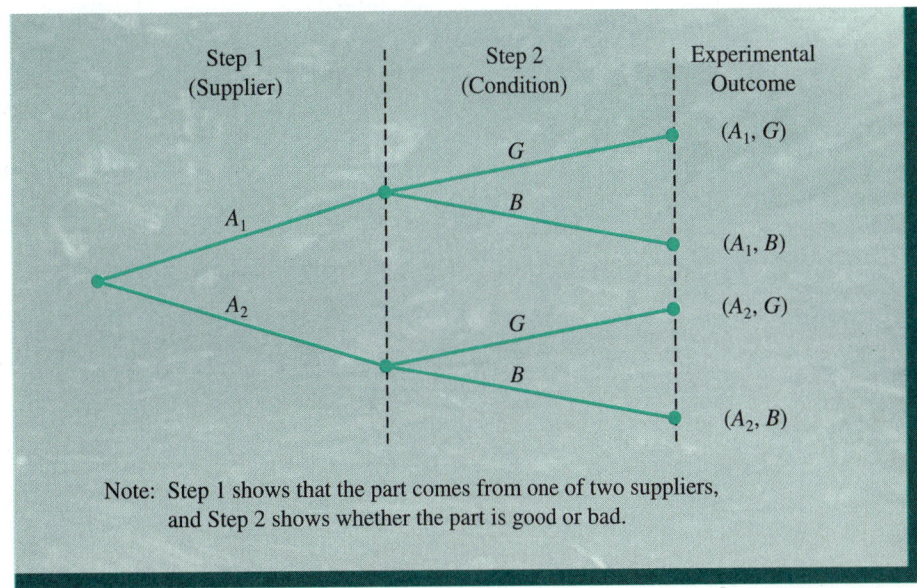

Note: Step 1 shows that the part comes from one of two suppliers, and Step 2 shows whether the part is good or bad.

FIGURE 4.10   Two-Step Tree Diagram

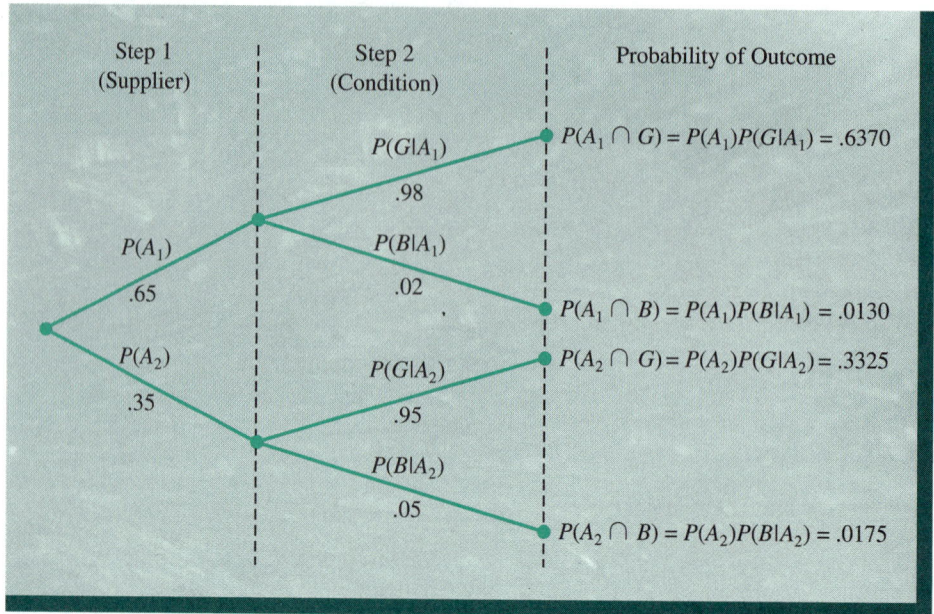

FIGURE 4.11   Probability Tree for Two-Supplier Example

the probabilities for each branch at step 1 are prior probabilities and the probabilities for each branch at step 2 are conditional probabilities. To find the probabilities of each experimental outcome, we simply multiply the probabilities on the branches leading to the outcome. Each of these joint probabilities is shown in Figure 4.11 along with the known probabilities for each branch.

Suppose now that the parts from the two suppliers are used in the firm's manufacturing process and that a machine breaks down because it attempts to process a bad part. Given the information that the part is bad, what is the probability that it came from supplier 1 and what is the probability that it came from supplier 2? With the information in the probability tree (Figure 4.11), Bayes' theorem can be used to answer these questions.

Letting B denote the event that the part is bad, we are looking for the posterior probabilities $P(A_1 \mid B)$ and $P(A_2 \mid B)$. From the law of conditional probability, we know that

$$P(A_1 \mid B) = \frac{P(A_1 \cap B)}{P(B)} \tag{4.13}$$

Referring to the probability tree, we see that

$$P(A_1 \cap B) = P(A_1)P(B \mid A_1) \tag{4.14}$$

To find $P(B)$, we note that there are only two ways event B can occur: $(A_1 \cap B)$ and $(A_2 \cap B)$. Therefore, we have

$$P(B) = P(A_1 \cap B) + P(A_2 \cap B)$$

$$= P(A_1)P(B \mid A_1) + P(A_2)P(B \mid A_2) \tag{4.15}$$

Substituting from (4.14) and (4.15) into (4.13) and writing a similar result for $P(A_2 \mid B)$, we obtain Bayes' theorem for the case of two events.

BAYES' THEOREM (TWO-EVENT CASE)

$$P(A_1 \mid B) = \frac{P(A_1)P(B \mid A_1)}{P(A_1)P(B \mid A_1) + P(A_2)P(B \mid A_2)} \qquad \text{(4.16)}$$

$$P(A_2 \mid B) = \frac{P(A_2)P(B \mid A_2)}{P(A_1)P(B \mid A_1) + P(A_2)P(B \mid A_2)} \qquad \text{(4.17)}$$

Using (4.16) and the probability values provided in our example, we have

$$P(A_1 \mid B) = \frac{P(A_1)P(B \mid A_1)}{P(A_1)P(B \mid A_1) + P(A_2)P(B \mid A_2)}$$

$$= \frac{(.65)(.02)}{(.65)(.02) + (.35)(.05)} = \frac{.0130}{.0130 + .0175}$$

$$= \frac{.0130}{.0305} = .4262$$

In addition, using (4.17), we find $P(A_2 \mid B)$.

$$P(A_2 \mid B) = \frac{(.35)(.05)}{(.65)(.02) + (.35)(.05)}$$

$$= \frac{.0175}{.0130 + .0175} = \frac{.0175}{.0305} = .5738$$

Note that in this application we started with a probability of .65 that a part selected at random was from supplier 1. However, given information that the part is bad, the probability that the part is from supplier 1 drops to .4262. In fact, if the part is bad, there is a better than 50–50 chance that the part came from supplier 2; that is, $P(A_2 \mid B) = .5738$.

Bayes' theorem is applicable when the events for which we want to compute posterior probabilities are mutually exclusive and their union is the entire sample space.* Bayes' theorem can be extended to the case where there are n mutually exclusive events $A_1, A_2, \ldots, A_n$ whose union is the entire sample space. In such a case, Bayes' theorem for the computation of any posterior probability $P(A_i \mid B)$ has the following form.

BAYES' THEOREM

$$P(A_i \mid B) = \frac{P(A_i)P(B \mid A_i)}{P(A_1)P(B \mid A_1) + P(A_2)P(B \mid A_2) + \cdots + P(A_n)P(B \mid A_n)} \qquad \text{(4.18)}$$

With prior probabilities $P(A_1), P(A_2), \ldots, P(A_n)$ and the appropriate conditional probabilities $P(B \mid A_1), P(B \mid A_2), \ldots, P(B \mid A_n)$, Equation (4.18) can be used to compute the posterior probability of the events $A_1, A_2, \ldots, A_n$.

---

*If the union of events is the entire sample space, the events are said to be *collectively exhaustive*.

TABLE 4.12 Summary of Bayes' Theorem Calculations for the Two-Supplier Problem

(1) Events A_i	(2) Prior Probabilities $P(A_i)$	(3) Conditional Probabilities $P(B \mid A_i)$	(4) Joint Probabilities $P(A_i \cap B)$	(5) Posterior Probabilities $P(A_i \mid B)$		
A_1	.65	.02	.0130	.0130/.0305	=	.4262
A_2	.35	.05	.0175	.0175/.0305	=	.5738
	1.00		$P(B) = .0305$			1.0000

THE TABULAR APPROACH

A tabular approach is helpful in conducting the Bayes' theorem calculations. Such an approach is shown in Table 4.12 for the parts supplier problem. The computations shown there are done in the following steps.

Step 1.   Prepare the following three columns:
Column 1—The mutually exclusive events for which posterior probabilities are desired.
Column 2—The prior probabilities for the events.
Column 3—The conditional probabilities of the new information *given* each event.

Step 2.   In column 4, compute the joint probabilities for each event and the new information B by using the multiplication law. These joint probabilities are found by multiplying the prior probabilities in column 2 by the corresponding conditional probabilities in column 3; that is, $P(A_i \cap B) = P(A_i)P(B \mid A_i)$.

Step 3.   Sum the joint probabilities in column 4. The sum is the probability of the new information, $P(B)$. Thus we see that in the above example there is a .0130 probability of a bad part from supplier 1 and there is a .0175 probability of a bad part from supplier 2. Since these are the only two ways in which a bad part can be obtained, the sum .0130 + .0175 shows that there is an overall probability of .0305 of finding a bad part from the combined shipments of the two suppliers.

Step 4.   In column 5, compute the posterior probabilities using the basic relationship of conditional probability,

$$P(A_i \mid B) = \frac{P(A_i \cap B)}{P(B)}$$

Note that the joint probabilities $P(A_i \cap B)$ are in column 4 and the probability $P(B)$ is the sum of column 4.

NOTES AND COMMENTS

1. Bayes' theorem is used extensively in decision analysis (Chapter 22). The prior probabilities are often subjective estimates provided by a decision maker. Sample information is obtained and posterior probabilities are computed for use in developing a decision strategy.
2. An event and its complement are mutually exclusive, and their union is the entire sample space. Thus, Bayes' theorem is always applicable for computing posterior probabilities of an event and its complement.

EXERCISES

METHODS

Self-Test ▶

53. The prior probabilities for events A_1 and A_2 are $P(A_1) = .40$ and $P(A_2) = .60$. It is also known that $P(A_1 \cap A_2) = 0$. Suppose $P(B \mid A_1) = .20$ and $P(B \mid A_2) = .05$.
    a. Are A_1 and A_2 mutually exclusive? Why or why not?
    b. Compute $P(A_1 \cap B)$ and $P(A_2 \cap B)$.
    c. Compute $P(B)$.
    d. Apply Bayes' theorem to compute $P(A_1 \mid B)$ and $P(A_2 \mid B)$.

54. The prior probabilities for events A_1, A_2, and A_3 are $P(A_1) = .20$, $P(A_2) = .50$, and $P(A_3) =. 30$. The conditional probabilities of event B given A_1, A_2, and A_3 are $P(B \mid A_1) = .50$, $P(B \mid A_2) = .40$, and $P(B \mid A_3) = .30$.
    a. Compute $P(B \cap A_1)$, $P(B \cap A_2)$, and $P(B \cap A_3)$.
    b. Apply Bayes' theorem, Equation (4.18), to compute the posterior probability $P(A_2 \mid B)$.
    c. Use the tabular approach to applying Bayes' theorem to compute $P(A_1 \mid B)$, $P(A_2 \mid B)$, and $P(A_3 \mid B)$.

APPLICATIONS

55. A consulting firm has submitted a bid for a large research project. The firm's management initially felt there was a 50–50 chance of getting the project. However, the agency to which the bid was submitted has subsequently requested additional information on the bid. Past experience indicates that on 75% of the successful bids and 40% of the unsuccessful bids the agency requested additional information.
    a. What is the prior probability of the bid being successful (that is, prior to the request for additional information)?
    b. What is the conditional probability of a request for additional information given that the bid will ultimately be successful?
    c. Compute a posterior probability that the bid will be successful given that a request for additional information has been received.

Self-Test ▶

56. A local bank is reviewing its credit-card policy with a view toward recalling some of its credit cards. In the past approximately 5% of cardholders have defaulted and the bank has been unable to collect the outstanding balance. Hence, management has established a prior probability of .05 that any particular cardholder will default. The bank has further found that the probability of missing one or more monthly payments is .20 for customers who do not default. Of course, the probability of missing one or more payments for those who default is 1.
    a. Given that a customer has missed a monthly payment, compute the posterior probability that the customer will default.
    b. The bank would like to recall its card if the probability that a customer will default is greater than .20. Should the bank recall its card if the customer misses a monthly payment? Why or why not?

57. *The Book of Risks* (1994) contains probability information about the chances people take in everyday activities. For example, the probability of a man having a motor vehicle accident during a one-year period is reported to be twice as great as the probability of a woman having a motor vehicle accident during a one-year period. Indicated probabilities are .113 for men and .057 for women. Suppose that 55% of the drivers in Lucas County are men. In filling out a driving history questionnaire, a person from Lucas County indicates involvement in a motor vehicle accident during the past year. What is the probability that the person is a woman?

58. A city has a professional basketball team playing at home and a professional hockey team playing away on the same night. According to probabilities for professional sports published in *Chance* (Fall 1992), a professional basketball team has a .641 probability of winning a

home game and a professional hockey team has a .462 probability of winning an away game. Historically, when both teams play on the same night, the chance that the next morning's leading sports story will be about the basketball game is 60% and the chance that it will be about the hockey game is 40%. Suppose that on the morning after these games the newspaper's leading sports story begins with the headline "We Win!!" What is the probability that the story is about the basketball team?

59. *M.D. Computing* (May, 1991) describes the use of Bayes' theorem and the use of conditional probability in medical diagnosis. Prior probabilities of diseases are based on the physician's assessment of such things as geographical location, seasonal influence, occurrence of epidemics, and so forth. Assume that a patient is believed to have one of two diseases, denoted D_1 and D_2, with $P(D_1) = .60$ and $P(D_2) = .40$ and that medical research has shown there is a probability associated with each symptom that may accompany the diseases. Suppose that, given diseases D_1 and D_2, the probabilities that the patient will have symptoms S_1, S_2, or S_3 are as follows.

		Symptoms		
		S_1	S_2	S_3
Disease	D_1	.15	.10	.15
	D_2	.80	.15	.03

$P(S_3|D_1)$

After a certain symptom is found to be present, the medical diagnosis may be aided by finding the revised probabilities of each particular disease. Compute the posterior probabilities of each disease given the following medical findings.

a. The patient has symptom S_1.
b. The patient has symptom S_2.
c. The patient has symptom S_3.
d. For the patient with symptom S_1 in (a), suppose we also find symptom S_2. What are the revised probabilities of D_1 and D_2?

SUMMARY

In this chapter we introduced basic probability concepts and illustrated how probability analysis can be used to provide helpful information for decision making. We described how probability can be interpreted as a numerical measure of the likelihood that an event will occur. In addition, we saw that the probability of an event can be computed either by summing the probabilities of the experimental outcomes (sample points) comprising the event or by using the relationships established by the addition, conditional probability, and multiplication laws of probability. For cases where additional information is available, we showed how Bayes' theorem can be used to obtain revised or posterior probabilities.

GLOSSARY

Probability   A numerical measure of the likelihood that an event will occur.

Experiment   Any process which generates well-defined outcomes.

Sample space   The set of all possible sample points (experimental outcomes).

Sample points   The individual outcomes of an experiment.

Tree diagram   A graphical device helpful in defining sample points of an experiment involving multiple steps.

Basic requirements of probability   Two requirements that restrict the manner in which probability assignments can be made:
 a. For each experimental outcome E_i we must have $0 \leq P(E_i) \leq 1$.
 b. If there are k experimental outcomes, then $\Sigma P(E_i) = 1$.

Classical method   A method of assigning probabilities which assumes that the experimental outcomes are equally likely.

Relative frequency method   A method of assigning probabilities on the basis of experimentation or historical data.

Subjective method   A method of assigning probabilities on the basis of judgment.

Event   A collection of sample points.

Complement of event *A*   The event containing all sample points that are not in A.

Venn diagram   A graphical device for representing symbolically the sample space and operations involving events.

Union of events *A* and *B*   The event containing all sample points that are in A, in B, or in both. The union is denoted $A \cup B$.

Intersection of *A* and *B*   The event containing all sample points that are in both A and B. The intersection is denoted $A \cap B$.

Addition law   A probability law used to compute the probability of a union, $P(A \cup B)$. It is $P(A \cup B) = P(A) + P(B) - P(A \cap B)$. For mutually exclusive events, since $P(A \cap B) = 0$, it reduces to $P(A \cup B) = P(A) + P(B)$.

Mutually exclusive events   Events that have no sample points in common; that is, $A \cap B$ is empty and $P(A \cap B) = 0$.

Conditional probability   The probability of an event given that another event has occurred. The conditional probability of A given B is $P(A \mid B) = P(A \cap B)/P(B)$.

Independent events   Two events A and B where $P(A \mid B) = P(A)$ or $P(B \mid A) = P(B)$; that is, the events have no influence on each other.

Multiplication law   A probability law used to compute the probability of an intersection, $P(A \cap B)$. It is $P(A \cap B) = P(A)P(B \mid A)$ or $P(A \cap B) = P(B)P(A \mid B)$. For independent events it reduces to $P(A \cap B) = P(A)P(B)$.

Prior probabilities   Initial estimates of the probabilities of events.

Posterior probabilities   Revised probabilities of events based on additional information.

Bayes' theorem   A method used to compute posterior probabilities.

KEY FORMULAS

Counting Rule for Combinations

$$\binom{N}{n} = \frac{N!}{n!(N-n)!} \tag{4.1}$$

Computing Probability Using the Complement

$$P(A) = 1 - P(A^c) \tag{4.4}$$

Addition Law

$$P(A \cup B) = P(A) + P(B) - P(A \cap B) \tag{4.5}$$

Conditional Probability

$$P(A \mid B) = \frac{P(A \cap B)}{P(B)} \tag{4.6}$$

$$P(B \mid A) = \frac{P(A \cap B)}{P(A)} \tag{4.7}$$

Multiplication Law

$$P(A \cap B) = P(B)P(A \mid B) \tag{4.10}$$

$$P(A \cap B) = P(A)P(B \mid A) \tag{4.11}$$

Multiplication Law for Independent Events

$$P(A \cap B) = P(A)P(B) \tag{4.12}$$

Bayes' Theorem

$$P(A_i \mid B) = \frac{P(A_i)P(B \mid A_i)}{P(A_1)P(B \mid A_1) + P(A_2)P(B \mid A_2) + \cdots + P(A_n)P(B \mid A_n)} \tag{4.18}$$

SUPPLEMENTARY EXERCISES

60. The long-distance calling market is shared by AT&T, MCI, and Sprint (*Business Week,* February 20, 1995). Suppose a survey of 200 small businesses finds 122 AT&T users, 38 MCI users, 20 Sprint users, and 20 users of other long-distance systems.

   a. Consider the experiment of observing the supplier of long-distance service for a randomly selected small business. How many experimental outcomes are possible for the categories listed above?

   b. Use the sample data to assign probabilities to the experimental outcomes.

61. A financial manager has just made two new investments—one in the oil industry and one in municipal bonds. After a one-year period, each of the investments will be classified as either successful or unsuccessful. Consider the making of the two investments as an experiment.

   a. How many sample points exist for this experiment?

   b. Show a tree diagram and list the sample points.

   c. Let $O =$ the event that the oil investment is successful and $M =$ the event that the municipal bond investment is successful. List the sample points in O and in M.

   d. List the sample points in the union of the events $(O \cup M)$.

   e. List the sample points in the intersection of the events $(O \cap M)$.

   f. Are events O and M mutually exclusive? Explain.

62. Consider an experiment with eight experimental outcomes denoted $E_1, E_2, \ldots, E_8$. Suppose the following events are identified.

$$A = \{E_1, E_2, E_3\}$$

$$B = \{E_2, E_4\}$$

$$C = \{E_1, E_7, E_8\}$$

$$D = \{E_5, E_6, E_7, E_8\}$$

Determine the sample points making up the following events.

a. $A \cup B$ b. $C \cup D$ c. $A \cap B$

d. $C \cap D$ e. $B \cap C$ f. A^c

g. D^c h. $A \cup D^c$ i. $A \cap D^c$

j. Are A and B mutually exclusive?

k. Are B and C mutually exclusive?

63. Referring to Exercise 62 and assuming that the classical method is an appropriate way of establishing probabilities, find the following probabilities.

a. $P(A)$, $P(B)$, $P(C)$, and $P(D)$

b. $P(A \cap B)$ c. $P(A \cup B)$ d. $P(A \mid B)$

e. $P(B \mid A)$ f. $P(B \cap C)$ g. $P(B \mid C)$

h. Are B and C independent events?

64. A survey of 1174 *Forbes* subscribers found the following information about corporate credit cards (*Forbes 1993 Subscriber Study*).

Type of Card	Number of Subscribers
AT&T	195
American Express	406
Diner's Club	30
MasterCard	109
Visa	157
Other	50

a. If 629 subscribers indicated they have at least one corporate credit card, what is the probability that a *Forbes* subscriber does not have a corporate credit card?

b. What is the probability that a subscriber holds a corporate American Express card?

c. Suppose it is known that 90 subscribers hold both MasterCard and Visa corporate credit cards. What is the probability that a subscriber holds one or both?

TABLE 4.13 Exercise 65

Number of Schools	Number of Students
1	1,230
2	304
3	184
4	118
5	78
6	51
7	25
8	13
9	20
10	8
11	9
12	6
Total	2,046

65. A survey of new matriculants to MBA programs was conducted by the Graduate Management Admissions Council during 1985 ("School Selection by Students," *GMAC Occasional Papers*, Stolzenberg and Giarrusso, March 1988). Table 4.13 shows the number of schools to which students applied.

a. Use these data to assign probabilities to the number of schools to which a randomly selected MBA student applied.

b. What is the probability that the student applied to only one school?

c. What is the probability that the student applied to three or more schools?

d. What is the probability that the student applied to more than six schools?

66. A telephone survey was used to determine viewer response to a new television show. The following data were obtained.

Rating	Frequency
Poor	4
Below average	8
Average	11
Above average	14
Excellent	13

TABLE 4.14   Exercise 67

Amount Owed ($)	Frequency
0–99	62
100–199	46
200–299	24
300–399	30
400–499	26
500 and over	12

a. What is the probability that a randomly selected viewer rated the new show as average or better?

b. What is the probability that a randomly selected viewer rated the new show below average or worse?

67. A bank has observed that credit-card account balances have been growing over the past year. A sample of 200 customer accounts resulted in the data in Table 4.14.

a. Let A be the event that a customer's balance is less than $200. Find $P(A)$.

b. Let B be the event that a customer's balance is $300 or more. Find $P(B)$.

68. The GMAC MBA new-matriculants survey provided the following data for 2018 students.

		Applied to More than One School	
		Yes	No
	23 and under	207	201
	24–26	299	379
Age Group	27–30	185	268
	31–35	66	193
	36 and over	51	169

a. For a randomly selected MBA student, prepare a joint probability table for the experiment consisting of observing the student's age and the number of schools to which the student applied.

b. What is the probability that an applicant was 23 or under?

c. What is the probability that an applicant was older than 26?

d. What is the probability that an applicant applied to more than one school?

69. Refer again to the data from the GMAC new-matriculants survey in Exercise 68.

a. Given that a person applied to more than one school, what is the probability that the person was 24–26 years old?

b. Given that a person is in the 36-and-over age group, what is the probability that the person applied to more than one school?

c. What is the probability that a person is 24–26 years old *or* applied to more than one school?

d. Suppose a person is known to have applied to only one school. What is the probability that the person was 31 or more years old?

e. Is the number of schools applied to independent of age? Explain.

70. A William M. Mercer Inc. survey provided the following data on salary and bonus compensation for 105 CEOs of technology and financial corporations (*The Wall Street Journal*, April 13, 1994). Total compensation is shown in millions of dollars.

		Total Compensation			
		Under $1M	$1M–$2M	Over $2M	Total
Corporation	Technology	17	21	7	45
	Financial	12	31	17	60
Total		29	52	24	105

a. Show the joint probability table for the data.

b. Use the marginal probabilities to comment on the most probable of the three compensation ranges.

c. Let T represent technology, F represent financial, and $2M$ represent total compensation over $2 million. Find P($2M$). Then compute the conditional probabilities P($2M$ | T) and P($2M$ | F). What conclusion can you draw about the compensation levels for technology and financial CEOs?

d. Is compensation independent of the type of corporation? Explain.

71. A large consumer goods company has been running a television advertisement for one of its soap products. A survey was conducted. On the basis of this survey, probabilities were assigned to the following events.

> B = individual purchased the product
>
> S = individual recalls seeing the advertisement
>
> $B \cap S$ = individual purchased the product and recalls seeing the advertisement

The probabilities assigned were P(B) = .20, P(S) = .40, and P($B \cap S$) = .12. The following problems relate to this situation.

a. What is the probability of an individual's purchasing the product given that the individual recalls seeing the advertisement? Does seeing the advertisement increase the probability that the individual will purchase the product? As a decision maker, would you recommend continuing the advertisement (assuming that the cost is reasonable)?

b. Assume that individuals who do not purchase the company's soap product buy from its competitors. What would be your estimate of the company's market share? Would you expect that continuing the advertisement will increase the company's market share? Why or why not?

c. The company has also tested another advertisement and assigned it values of P(S) = .30 and P($B \cap S$) = .10. What is P(B | S) for this other advertisement? Which advertisement seems to have had the bigger effect on customer purchases?

72. A large company has done a careful analysis of a price promotion that it is currently testing. Some 20% of the people in a large sample of individuals in the test market were both aware of the promotion and made a purchase. Further, 80% were aware of the promotion, and prior to the promotion 25% of all people in the sample were purchasers of the product.

a. What is the probability that a person will make a purchase given that he or she is aware of the price promotion?

b. Are the events "made a purchase" and "aware of the price promotion" independent? Why or why not?

c. On the basis of these results, would you recommend that the company introduce this promotion on a national scale? Why or why not?

73. Cooper Realty is a small real estate company located in Albany, New York, specializing primarily in residential listings. They have recently become interested in determining the likelihood of one of their listings being sold within a certain number of days. An analysis of company sales of 800 homes in previous years produced the following data.

| | | Days Listed Until Sold | | | |
		Under 30	31–90	Over 90	Total
Initial Asking Price	*Under $50,000*	50	40	10	100
	$50,000–99,999	20	150	80	250
	$100,000–$150,000	20	280	100	400
	Over $150,000	10	30	10	50
	Total	100	500	200	800

a. If A is defined as the event that a home is listed for over 90 days before being sold, estimate the probability of A.

b. If B is defined as the event that the initial asking price is under $50,000, estimate the probability of B.

c. What is the probability of $A \cap B$?

d. Assuming that a contract has just been signed to list a home that has an initial asking price of less than $50,000, what is the probability that the home will take Cooper Realty more than 90 days to sell?

e. Are events A and B independent?

74. In the evaluation of a sales training program, a firm found that of 50 salespersons making a bonus last year, 20 had attended a special sales training program. The firm has 200 salespersons. Let B = the event that a salesperson makes a bonus and S = the event that a salesperson attends the sales training program.

a. Find $P(B)$, $P(S \mid B)$, and $P(S \cap B)$.

b. Assume that 40% of the salespersons have attended the training program. What is the probability that a salesperson makes a bonus given that the salesperson attended the sales training program, $P(B \mid S)$?

c. If the firm evaluates the training program in terms of its effect on the probability of a salesperson's making a bonus, what is your evaluation of the training program? Comment on whether B and S are dependent or independent events.

75. A company has studied the number of lost-time accidents occurring at its Brownsville, Texas, plant. Historical records show that 6% of the employees had lost-time accidents last year. Management believes that a special safety program will reduce such accidents to 5% during the current year. In addition, it estimates that 15% of employees who had lost-time accidents last year will have a lost-time accident during the current year.

a. What percentage of the employees will have lost-time accidents in both years?

b. What percentage of the employees will have at least one lost-time accident over the two-year period?

76. In a study of television viewing habits among married couples, a researcher found that, for a popular Saturday night program, 25% of the husbands and 30% of the wives viewed the program regularly. The study showed that, for couples in which the husband watched the program regularly, 80% of the wives also watched regularly.

a. What is the probability that both the husband and wife watched the program regularly?

b. What is the probability that at least one—husband or wife—watched the program regularly?

c. What percentage of the married couples did not have at least one regular viewer of the program?

77. A statistics professor has noted from past experience that students who do the homework for the course have a .90 probability of passing the course, but students who do not do the homework have a .25 probability of passing the course. The professor estimates that 75% of the students in the course do the homework. Given that a student passes the course, what is the probability that she or he completed the homework?

78. A salesperson for Business Communication Systems, Inc. sells automatic envelope-addressing equipment to medium-size and small businesses. The probability of making a sale to a new customer is .10. During the initial contact with a customer, sometimes the salesperson is asked to call back later. Of the 30 most recent sales, 12 were made to customers who initially told the salesperson to call back later. Of 270 customers who did not make a purchase, 46 had initially asked the salesperson to call back later. If a customer asks the salesperson to call back later, should the salesperson do so? What is the probability of making a sale to a customer who has asked the salesperson to call back later?

79. Migliori Industries, Inc. manufactures a gas-saving device for use on natural gas forced-air residential furnaces. The company is currently trying to determine the probability that sales of this product will exceed 25,000 units during next year's winter sales period. The company believes that sales of the product depend to a large extent on the winter conditions. Management's best estimate of the probability that sales will exceed 25,000 units if the winter is severe is .8. This probability drops to .5 if the winter conditions are moderate. If the weather forecast gives a .7 probability of a severe winter and a .3 probability of moderate conditions, what is Migliori's best estimate that sales will exceed 25,000 units?

80. The Dallas IRS auditing staff is concerned with identifying potentially fraudulent tax returns. From past experience they believe that the probability of finding a fraudulent return given that the return contains deductions for contributions exceeding the IRS standard is .20. Given that the deductions for contributions do not exceed the IRS standard, the probability of a fraudulent return decreases to .02. If 8% of all returns exceed the IRS standard for deductions due to contributions, what is the best estimate of the percentage of fraudulent returns?

81. An oil company has purchased an option on land in Alaska. Preliminary geologic studies have assigned the following prior probabilities.

$$P(\text{high-quality oil}) = .50$$

$$P(\text{medium-quality oil}) = .20$$

$$P(\text{no oil}) = .30$$

a. What is the probability of finding oil?

b. After 200 feet of drilling on the first well, a soil test is taken. The probabilities of finding the particular type of soil identified by the test follow.

$$P(\text{soil} \mid \text{high-quality oil}) = .20$$

$$P(\text{soil} \mid \text{medium-quality oil}) = .80$$

$$P(\text{soil} \mid \text{no oil}) = .20$$

How should the firm interpret the soil test? What are the revised probabilities, and what is the new probability of finding oil?

82. In the setup of a manufacturing process, a machine is either correctly or incorrectly adjusted. The probability of a correct adjustment is .90. When correctly adjusted, the machine operates with a 5% defect rate. However, if it is incorrectly adjusted, the defect rate is 75%.

a. After the machine starts a production run, what is the probability that a defect is observed when one part is tested?

b. Suppose that the one part selected by an inspector is found to be defective. What is the probability that the machine is incorrectly adjusted? What action would you recommend?

c. Before your recommendation in (b) is followed, a second part is tested and found to be good. Using your revised probabilities from (b) as the most recent prior probabilities, compute the revised probability of an incorrect adjustment given that the second part is good. What action would you recommend now?

83. The Wayne Manufacturing Company purchases a certain part from three suppliers, A, B, and C. Supplier A supplies 60% of the parts, B 30%, and C 10%. The quality of parts is known to vary among suppliers, with A, B, and C parts having .25%, 1%, and 2% defect rates, respectively. The parts are used in one of the company's major products.

a. What is the probability that the company's major product is assembled with a defective part?

b. When a defective part is found, which supplier is the likely source?

84. A Bayesian approach can be used to revise probabilities that a prospect field will produce oil (*Oil & Gas Journal,* January 11, 1988). In one case, geological assessment indicates a 25% chance that the field will produce oil. Further, there is an 80% chance that a particular well will strike oil given that oil is present in the prospect field.

a. Suppose that one well is drilled on the field and it comes up dry. What is the probability that the prospect field will produce oil?

b. If two wells come up dry, what is the probability that the field will produce oil?

c. The oil company would like to keep looking as long as the chances of finding oil are greater than 1%. How many dry wells must be drilled before the field will be abandoned?

5

DISCRETE PROBABILITY DISTRIBUTIONS

STATISTICS IN PRACTICE ●

Xerox Corporation*
Stamford, Connecticut

Xerox Corporation is a worldwide leader in information products and services. Almost everyone is familiar with Xerox copying machines, but the company is involved in many other businesses also. For example, Xerox's Multinational Documentation and Training Services (MD&TS) group provides cost-effective, high-quality communication services including documentation, training, translation, and publishing in a variety of languages.

Professional writers and translators working for MD&TS use an online computerized publication system. Several individuals can access the system simultaneously. Occasionally, during peak demand periods, one or more individuals may be denied access to the system. In considering design alternatives for the online computerized publication system, management was interested in estimating the probability that a user would be denied access.

A computer simulation model was developed to evaluate the various designs. A key input to the simulation model was the length of time a user is on the system in each session. From observation of MD&TS users, the time per session was found to range from 10 minutes to 90 minutes. The probability distribution for the time per session, with x denoting the time per session in minutes, is shown. The column labeled $f(x)$ shows probabilities of .05 for a 10-minute session, .06 for a 20-minute session, and so on. The highest probability, .25, is for a session lasting 50 minutes.

In probability terminology, session duration is referred to as a random variable and the table below is referred to as the probability distribution for the random variable. This probability distribution and the probability distribu-

tion for the length of time between sessions were key inputs to the computer simulation model. The simulation results based on these probability distributions helped management select a computerized publication system design that ensured a near-zero probability of a user being denied access to the system.

Probability distributions such as the ones used by Xerox are the topic of this chapter. You will also learn about some special probability distributions that are widely available and the situations in which they are applicable.

Probability Distribution for Session Duration

x (minutes)	Probability $f(x)$
10	.05
20	.06
30	.08
40	.20
50	.25
60	.20
70	.08
80	.06
90	.02

The actual probability distribution used in the simulation study was modified to protect proprietary information and to simplify the discussion.

Woman using PC system.

*The authors are indebted to Soterios M. Flouris for providing this Statistics in Practice.

● In this chapter we continue the study of probability by introducing the concepts of random variables and probability distributions. The focus of this chapter is discrete probability distributions. Three special discrete probability distributions—the binomial, Poisson, and hypergeometric—are covered.

5.1 RANDOM VARIABLES

In Chapter 4 we defined the concept of an experiment and its associated experimental outcomes. A random variable provides a means for describing experimental outcomes by numerical values. The definition of a random variable follows.

> **RANDOM VARIABLE**
> A *random variable* is a numerical description of the outcome of an experiment.

In effect, a random variable associates a numerical value with each possible outcome. The particular numerical value of the random variable depends on the outcome of the experiment. A random variable can be classified as being either *discrete* or *continuous* depending on the numerical values it assumes.

DISCRETE RANDOM VARIABLES

A random variable that may assume either a finite number of values or an infinite sequence of values such as 0, 1, 2, . . . is referred to as a *discrete random variable*. For example, consider the experiment of an accountant taking the certified public accountant (CPA) examination. The examination has four parts. We can define the discrete random variable as x = the number of parts of the CPA examination passed. This discrete random variable may assume the finite number of values 0, 1, 2, 3, or 4.

As another example of a discrete random variable, consider the experiment of cars arriving at a tollbooth. The random variable of interest is x = the number of cars arriving during a one-day period. The possible values for x come from the sequence of integers 0, 1, 2, and so on. Hence, x is a discrete random variable assuming one of the values in this infinite sequence.

Although many experiments have outcomes that are naturally described by numerical values, others do not. For example, a survey question might ask an individual to recall the message in a recent television commercial. There would be two experimental outcomes: the individual cannot recall the message and the individual can recall the message. We can still describe these experimental outcomes numerically by defining the discrete random variable x as follows: let $x = 0$ if the individual cannot recall the message and $x = 1$ if the individual can recall the message. The numerical values for this random variable are arbitrary (we could have used 5 and 10), but they are acceptable in terms of the definition of a random variable—namely, x is a random variable because it provides a numerical description of the outcome of the experiment.

Table 5.1 provides some additional examples of discrete random variables. Note that in each example the discrete random variable assumes a finite number of values or an infinite sequence of values such as 0, 1, 2, ... Discrete random variables such as these are discussed in detail in this chapter.

TABLE 5.1   Examples of Discrete Random Variables

Experiment	Random Variable (x)	Possible Values for the Random Variable
Contact five customers	Number of customers who place an order	0, 1, 2, 3, 4, 5
Inspect a shipment of 50 radios	Number of defective radios	0, 1, 2, . . . 49, 50
Operate a restaurant for one day	Number of customers	0, 1, 2, 3, . . .
Sell an automobile	Gender of the customer	0 if male; 1 if female

TABLE 5.2   Examples of Continuous Random Variables

Experiment	Random Variable (x)	Possible Values for the Random Variable
Operate a bank	Time between customer arrivals in minutes	$x \geq 0$
Fill a soft drink can (max = 12.1 ounces)	Number of ounces	$0 \leq x \leq 12.1$
Work on a project to construct a new library	Percentage of project complete after six months	$0 \leq x \leq 100$
Test a new chemical process	Temperature when the desired reaction takes place (min 150 F; max 212 F)	$150 \leq x \leq 212$

CONTINUOUS RANDOM VARIABLES

A random variable that may assume any numerical value in an interval or collection of intervals is called a *continuous random variable*. Experimental outcomes that are based on measurement scales such as time, weight, distance, and temperature can be described by continuous random variables. For example, consider an experiment of monitoring incoming telephone calls to the claims office of a major insurance company. Suppose the random variable of interest is x = the time between consecutive incoming calls in minutes. This random variable may assume any value in the interval $x \geq 0$. Actually, an infinite number of values are possible for x, including values such as 1.26 minutes, 2.751 minutes, 4.3333 minutes, and so on. As another example, consider a 90-mile section of interstate highway I-75 north of Atlanta, Georgia. For an emergency ambulance service located in Atlanta, we might define the random variable as x = the location of the next traffic accident along this section of I-75. In this case, x would be a continuous random variable assuming any value in the interval $0 \leq x \leq 90$. Additional examples of continuous random variables are listed in Table 5.2. Note that each example describes a random variable that may assume any value in an interval of values. Continuous random variables and their probability distributions will be the topic of Chapter 6.

NOTES AND COMMENTS

One way to determine whether a random variable is discrete or continuous is to think of the values of the random variable as points on a line segment. Choose two points representing values of the random variable. If the entire line segment between the two points also represents possible values for the random variable, the random variable is continuous.

EXERCISES

METHODS

Self-Test

1. Consider the experiment of tossing a coin twice.
   a. List the experimental outcomes.
   b. Define a random variable that represents the number of heads occurring on the two tosses.
   c. Show what value the random variable would assume for each of the experimental outcomes.
   d. Is this random variable discrete or continuous?

2. Consider the experiment of a worker assembling a product, and record how long it takes.
   a. Define a random variable that represents the time in minutes required to assemble the product.
   b. What values may the random variable assume?
   c. Is the random variable discrete or continuous?

APPLICATIONS

Self-Test

3. Three students have interviews scheduled for summer employment at the Brookwood Institute. In each case the result of the interview will be that a position is either offered or not offered. Experimental outcomes are defined in terms of the results of the three interviews.
   a. List the experimental outcomes.
   b. Define a random variable that represents the number of offers made. Is this a discrete or continuous random variable?
   c. Show the value of the random variable for each of the experimental outcomes.

4. Home mortgage rates were listed for 12 Florida lending institutions (*The Tampa Tribune,* February 25, 1995). Assume that the random variable of interest is the number of lending institutions in this group that offer a 30-year fixed rate of 8.5% or less. What values may this random variable assume?

5. To perform a certain type of blood analysis, lab technicians must perform two procedures. The first procedure requires either 1 or 2 separate steps and the second procedure requires either 1, 2, or 3 steps.
   a. List the experimental outcomes associated with performing an analysis.
   b. If the random variable of interest is the total number of steps required to do the complete analysis, show what value the random variable will assume for each of the experimental outcomes.

6. Listed is a series of experiments and associated random variables. In each case, identify the values that the random variable can assume and state whether the random variable is discrete or continuous.

Experiment	Random Variable (x)
a. Take a 20-question examination	Number of questions answered correctly
b. Observe cars arriving at a tollbooth for one hour	Number of cars arriving at tollbooth
c. Audit 50 tax returns	Number of returns containing errors
d. Observe an employee's work	Number of nonproductive hours in an eight-hour work day
e. Weigh a shipment of goods	Number of pounds

5.2   DISCRETE PROBABILITY DISTRIBUTIONS

The *probability distribution* for a random variable describes how probabilities are distributed over the values of the random variable. For a discrete random variable *x*, the probability distribution is defined by a *probability function*, denoted by $f(x)$. The probability function provides the probability for each value of the random variable.

As an illustration of a discrete random variable and its probability distribution, consider the sales of automobiles at DiCarlo Motors in Saratoga, New York. Over the past 300 days of operation, sales data show 54 days with no automobiles sold, 117 days with 1 automobile sold, 72 days with 2 automobiles sold, 42 days with 3 automobiles sold, 12 days with 4 automobiles sold, and 3 days with 5 automobiles sold. Suppose we consider the experiment of selecting a day of operation at DiCarlo Motors. We define the random variable of interest as *x* = the number of automobiles sold during a day. From historical data, we know *x* is a discrete random variable that can assume the values 0, 1, 2, 3, 4, or 5. In probability function notation, $f(0)$ provides the probability of 0 automobiles sold, $f(1)$ provides the probability of 1 automobile sold, and so on. Since historical data show 54 of 300 days with 0 automobiles sold, we assign the value 54/300 = .18 to $f(0)$, indicating that the probability of 0 automobiles being sold during a day is .18. Similarly, since 117 of 300 days had 1 automobile sold, we assign the value 117/300 = .39 to $f(1)$, indicating that the probability of exactly 1 automobile being sold during a day is .39. Continuing in this way for the other values of the random variable, we compute the values for $f(2)$, $f(3)$, $f(4)$, and $f(5)$ as shown in Table 5.3, the probability distribution for the number of automobiles sold during a day at DiCarlo Motors.

A primary advantage of defining a random variable and its probability distribution is that once the probability distribution is known, it is relatively easy to determine the probability of a variety of events that may be of interest to a decision maker. For example, using the probability distribution for DiCarlo Motors as shown in Table 5.3, we see that the most probable number of automobiles sold during a day is 1 with a probability of $f(1)$ = .39. In addition, there is an $f(3) + f(4) + f(5)$ = .14 + .04 + .01 = .19 probability of selling 3 or more automobiles during a day. These probabilities, plus others the decision maker may ask about, provide information that can help the decision maker understand the process of selling automobiles at DiCarlo Motors.

In the development of a probability function for any discrete random variable, the following two conditions must be satisfied.

TABLE 5.3 Probability Distribution for the Number of Automobiles Sold During a Day at DiCarlo Motors

x	*f(x)*
0	.18
1	.39
2	.24
3	.14
4	.04
5	.01
Total	1.00

REQUIRED CONDITIONS FOR A DISCRETE PROBABILITY FUNCTION

$$f(x) \geq 0 \tag{5.1}$$

$$\Sigma f(x) = 1 \tag{5.2}$$

Table 5.3 shows that the probabilities for the random variable *x* satisfy condition (5.1); $f(x)$ is greater than or equal to 0 for all values of *x*. In addition, the probabilities sum to 1 so (5.2) is satisfied. Thus, the DiCarlo Motors probability function is a valid discrete probability function.

We can also present probability distributions graphically. In Figure 5.1 the values of the random variable *x* are shown on the horizontal axis and the probability associated with these values is shown on the vertical axis.

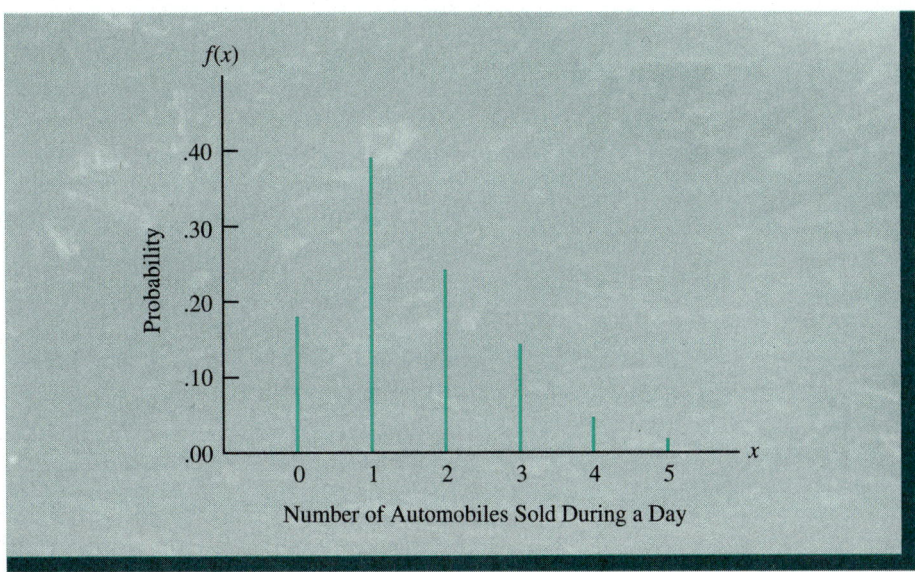

FIGURE 5.1 Graphical Representation of the Probability Distribution for Automobile Sales at DiCarlo Motors

In addition to tables and graphs, a formula that gives $f(x)$ for every value of x can provide the probability distribution for some discrete random variables. For example, consider the random variable x with the following probability distribution.

x	$f(x)$
1	1/10
2	2/10
3	3/10
4	4/10

This probability distribution can also be defined by the formula

$$f(x) = \frac{x}{10} \qquad \text{for } x = 1, 2, 3, \text{ or } 4$$

Evaluating $f(x)$ for a given value of the random variable will provide the associated probability. For example, using the above probability function, we see that $f(2) = 2/10$ provides the probability that the random variable assumes a value of 2.

The more widely used discrete probability distributions generally are specified by formulas. Three important cases are the binomial, Poisson, and hypergeometric probability distributions; they are discussed later in the chapter.

TABLE 5.4 Exercise 7

x	$f(x)$
20	.20
25	.15
30	.25
35	.40
Total	1.00

EXERCISES

METHODS

Self-Test

7. The probability distribution of the random variable x is in Table 5.4.
   a. Is this a proper probability distribution? Check to see that (5.1) and (5.2) are satisfied.
   b. What is the probability that $x = 30$?

c. What is the probability that x is less than or equal to 25?

d. What is the probability that x is greater than 30?

APPLICATIONS

Self-Test ••••••••••▶

8. The following data were collected by counting the number of operating rooms in use at Tampa General Hospital over a 20-day period: On 3 of the days only 1 operating room was used, on 5 of the days 2 were used, on 8 of the days 3 were used, and on 4 days all 4 of the hospital's operating rooms were used.

   a. Use the relative frequency approach to construct a probability distribution for the number of operating rooms in use on any given day.

   b. Draw a graph of the probability distribution.

   c. Show that your probability distribution satisfies the required conditions for a valid discrete probability distribution.

9. Information on 3731 subscribers to *The Wall Street Journal* includes the following data on household members (*The Wall Street Journal* Subscriber Study, 1992).

Number of Household Members	Frequency
1	474
2	1664
3	627
4	522
5	444

   Let x be a random variable indicating the number of household members.

   a. Use the data to develop a probability distribution for x. Specify the values for the random variable and the corresponding values for the probability function $f(x)$.

   b. Draw a graph of the probability distribution.

   c. Show that the probability distribution satisfies (5.1) and (5.2).

TABLE 5.5 Exercise 10

x	$f(x)$
$148,000	.20
$150,000	.40
$152,000	.40

10. QA Properties is considering making an offer to purchase an apartment building. Management has subjectively assessed a probability distribution for x, the purchase price, as shown in Table 5.5.

   a. Determine whether this is a proper probability distribution by checking (5.1) and (5.2).

   b. What is the probability that the apartment house can be purchased for $150,000 or less?

11. The cleaning and changeover operation for a production system requires 1, 2, 3, or 4 hours, depending on the specific product that will begin production. Let x be a random variable indicating the time in hours required to make the changeover. The following probability function can be used to compute the probability associated with any changeover time x.

$$f(x) = \frac{x}{10} \quad \text{for } x = 1, 2, 3, \text{ or } 4$$

TABLE 5.6 Exercise 12

x	$f(x)$
1000	.15
1100	.20
1200	.30
1300	.25
1400	.10

   a. Show that the probability function meets the required conditions of (5.1) and (5.2).

   b. What is the probability that the changeover will take 2 hours?

   c. What is the probability that the changeover will take more than 2 hours?

   d. Graph the probability distribution for the changeover times.

12. The director of admissions at Lakeville Community College has subjectively assessed a probability distribution for x, the number of entering students, as shown in Table 5.6.

   a. Is this a valid probability distribution?

   b. What is the probability that there will be 1200 or fewer entering students?

TABLE 5.7 Exercise 14

x	$f(x)$
-100	.10
0	.20
50	.30
100	.25
150	.10
200	

13. A psychologist has determined that the number of hours required to obtain the trust of a new patient is either 1, 2, or 3. Let x be a random variable indicating the time in hours required to gain the patient's trust. The following probability function has been proposed.

$$f(x) = \frac{x}{6} \qquad \text{for } x = 1, 2, \text{ or } 3$$

   a. Is this a valid probability function? Explain.
   b. What is the probability that it takes exactly 2 hours to gain the patient's trust?
   c. What is the probability that it takes at least 2 hours to gain the patient's trust?

14. Table 5.7 is a partial probability distribution for the MRA Company's projected profits (x = profit in \$1000s) for the first year of operation (the negative value denotes a loss).
   a. What is the proper value for $f(200)$? What is your interpretation of this value?
   b. What is the probability that MRA will be profitable?
   c. What is the probability that MRA will make at least \$100,000?

5.3 EXPECTED VALUE AND VARIANCE

EXPECTED VALUE

The *expected value,* or mean, of a random variable is a measure of the central location for the random variable. The mathematical expression for the expected value of a discrete random variable x follows.

EXPECTED VALUE OF A DISCRETE RANDOM VARIABLE

$$E(x) = \mu = \Sigma x f(x) \tag{5.3}$$

TABLE 5.8 Calculation of the Expected Value for the Number of Automobiles Sold During a Day at DiCarlo Motors

x	$f(x)$	$xf(x)$
0	.18	0(.18) = .00
1	.39	1(.39) = .39
2	.24	2(.24) = .48
3	.14	3(.14) = .42
4	.04	4(.04) = .16
5	.01	5(.01) = .05
		1.50

$$E(x) = \mu = \Sigma \, xf(x)$$

Both the notations $E(x)$ and μ can be used to denote the expected value of a random variable.

Equation (5.3) shows that to compute the expected value of a discrete random variable, we must multiply each value of the random variable by the corresponding probability $f(x)$ and then add the resulting products. Using the DiCarlo Motors automobile sales example from Section 5.2, we show the calculation of the expected value for the number of automobiles sold during a day in Table 5.8. The sum of the entries in the $xf(x)$ column shows that the expected value is 1.50 automobiles per day. We therefore know that although sales of 0, 1, 2, 3, 4, or 5 automobiles are possible on any one day, over time DiCarlo can anticipate selling an average of 1.50 automobiles per day. Assuming 30 days of operation during a month, we can use the expected value of 1.50 to anticipate average monthly sales of 30(1.50) = 45 automobiles.

VARIANCE

While the expected value provides the mean value for the random variable, we often need a measure of dispersion, or variability. Just as we used the variance in Chapter 3 to summarize the dispersion in a data set, we now use variance to summarize the variability in the values of a random variable. The mathematical expression for the variance of a discrete random variable follows.

TABLE 5.9 Calculation of the Variance for the Number of Automobiles Sold During a Day at DiCarlo Motors

x	$x-\mu$	$(x-\mu)^2$	$f(x)$	$(x-\mu)^2 f(x)$
0	$0-1.50 = -1.50$	2.25	.18	$2.25(.18) = .4050$
1	$1-1.50 = -.50$	.25	.39	$.25(.39) = .0975$
2	$2-1.50 = .50$	.25	.24	$.25(.24) = .0600$
3	$3-1.50 = 1.50$	2.25	.14	$2.25(.14) = .3150$
4	$4-1.50 = 2.50$	6.25	.04	$6.25(.04) = .2500$
5	$5-1.50 = 3.50$	12.25	.01	$12.25(.01) = \underline{.1225}$
				1.2500

$$\sigma^2 = \Sigma(x-\mu)^2 f(x)$$

VARIANCE OF A DISCRETE RANDOM VARIABLE

$$\text{Var}(x) = \sigma^2 = \Sigma(x - \mu)^2 f(x) \qquad (5.4)$$

As (5.4) shows, an essential part of the variance formula is the deviation, $x - \mu$, which measures how far a particular value of the random variable is from the expected value or mean, μ. In computing the variance of a random variable, the deviations are squared and then weighted by the corresponding value of the probability function. The sum of these weighted squared deviations for all values of the random variable is referred to as the *variance*. The notations Var(x) and σ^2 are both used to denote the variance of a random variable.

The calculation of the variance for the probability distribution of the number of automobiles sold during a day at DiCarlo Motors is summarized in Table 5.9. We see that the variance is 1.25. The *standard deviation, σ,* is defined as the positive square root of the variance. Thus, the standard deviation for the number of automobiles sold during a day is

$$\sigma = \sqrt{1.25} = 1.118$$

The standard deviation is measured in the same units as the random variable ($\sigma = 1.118$ automobiles) and therefore is often preferred in describing the variability of a random variable. The variance σ^2 is measured in squared units and is thus more difficult to interpret.

TABLE 5.10 Exercise 15

x	$f(x)$
3	.25
6	.50
9	.25
Total	1.00

TABLE 5.11 Exercise 16

y	$f(y)$
2	.20
4	.30
7	.40
8	.10
Total	1.00

EXERCISES

METHODS

15. Table 5.10 is a probability distribution for the random variable x.
    a. Compute $E(x)$, the expected value of x.
    b. Compute σ^2, the variance of x.
    c. Compute σ, the standard deviation of x.

Self-Test
▸

16. Table 5.11 is a probability distribution for the random variable y.
    a. Compute $E(y)$.
    b. Compute Var(y) and σ.

APPLICATIONS

17. A volunteer ambulance service handles from 0 to 5 service calls on any given day. The probability distribution for the number of service calls is shown in Table 5.12.
a. What is the expected number of service calls?
b. What is the variance in the number of service calls? What is the standard deviation?

Self-Test
· · · · · · · · · · ▶

TABLE 5.12 Exercise 17

Number of Service Calls	Probability
0	.10
1	.15
2	.30
3	.20
4	.15
5	.10

TABLE 5.13
Exercise 18

x	f(x)
0	.02
1	.24
2	.42
3	.20
4	.08
5	.04

TABLE 5.14 Exercise 20

Payment ($)	Probability
0	.90
400	.04
1000	.03
2000	.01
4000	.01
6000	.01

TABLE 5.15 Exercise 22

Unit Demand	Probability
300	.20
400	.30
500	.35
600	.15

18. *The 1994 Statistical Abstract of the United States* shows that the average number of television sets per household is 2.2. Assume that the probability distribution for the number of television sets per household is as shown in Table 5.13.
a. Compute the expected value of the number of television sets per household and compare it with the average reported in the *Statistical Abstract*.
b. What are the variance and standard deviation of the number of television sets per household?

19. The actual shooting records of the 1992 NCAA championship final four teams (*NCAA Final Four Program,* April 1992) showed the probability of making a 2-point basket was .50 and the probability of making a 3-point basket was .39.
a. What is the expected value of a 2-point shot for these teams?
b. What is the expected value of a 3-point shot for these teams?
c. Since the probability of making a 2-point basket is greater than the probability of making a 3-point basket, why do coaches allow some players to shoot the 3-point shot if they have the opportunity? Use expected value to explain your answer.

20. The probability distribution for damage claims paid by the Newton Automobile Insurance Company on collision insurance is shown in Table 5.14.
a. Use the expected collision payment to determine the collision insurance premium that would enable the company to break even.
b. The insurance company charges an annual rate of $260 for the collision coverage. What is the expected value of the collision policy for a policyholder? (Hint: It is the expected payments from the company minus the cost of coverage.) Why does the policyholder purchase a collision policy with this expected value?

21. The number of dots observed on the upward face of a die has the following probability function.

$$f(x) = \frac{1}{6} \quad \text{for } x = 1, 2, 3, 4, 5, 6$$

a. Show that this probability function has the properties necessary for probability distributions.
b. Draw a graph of the probability distribution.
c. What is the expected value? What is the interpretation of this value?
d. What are the variance and the standard deviation for the number of dots?

22. The demand for a product of Carolina Industries varies greatly from month to month. The probability distribution in Table 5.15, based on the past two years of data, shows the company's monthly demand.
a. If the company bases monthly orders on the expected value of the monthly demand, what should Carolina's monthly order quantity be for this product?
b. Assume that each unit demanded generates $70 in revenue and that each unit ordered costs $50. How much will the company gain or lose in a month if it places an order based on your answer to part (a) and the actual demand for the item is 300 units?

23 The *Forbes* 1993 Subscriber Study and the *Fortune* 1994 National Subscriber Portrait reported the following probability distributions for the number of vehicles per subscriber household

x	Forbes f(x)	Fortune f(x)
0	.045	.028
1	.230	.165
2	.449	.489
3	.169	.185
4	.107	.133

a. What is the expected value of the number of vehicles per household for each subscriber group?
b. What is the variance of the number of vehicles per household for each subscriber group?
c. Using your answers to parts (a) and (b), what comparisons can you make about the number of vehicles per household for *Forbes* and *Fortune* subscribers?

24. The J. R. Ryland Computer Company is considering a plant expansion that will enable the company to begin production of a new computer product. The company's president must determine whether to make the expansion a medium- or large-scale project. An uncertainty is the demand for the new product, which for planning purposes may be low demand, medium demand, or high demand. The probability estimates for demand are .20, .50, and .30, respectively. Letting x indicate the annual profit in $1000s, the firm's planners have developed the following profit forecasts for the medium- and large-scale expansion projects.

		Medium-Scale Expansion Profits		Large-Scale Expansion Profits	
		x	$f(x)$	y	$f(y)$
	Low	50	.20	0	.20
Demand	Medium	150	.50	100	.50
	High	200	.30	300	.30

a. Compute the expected value for the profit associated with the two expansion alternatives. Which decision is preferred for the objective of maximizing the expected profit?
b. Compute the variance for the profit associated with the two expansion alternatives. Which decision is preferred for the objective of minimizing the risk or uncertainty?

5.4   THE BINOMIAL PROBABILITY DISTRIBUTION

The *binomial probability distribution* is a discrete probability distribution that has many applications. It is associated with a multiple-step experiment that we call the binomial experiment.

A BINOMIAL EXPERIMENT

A *binomial experiment* has the following four properties.

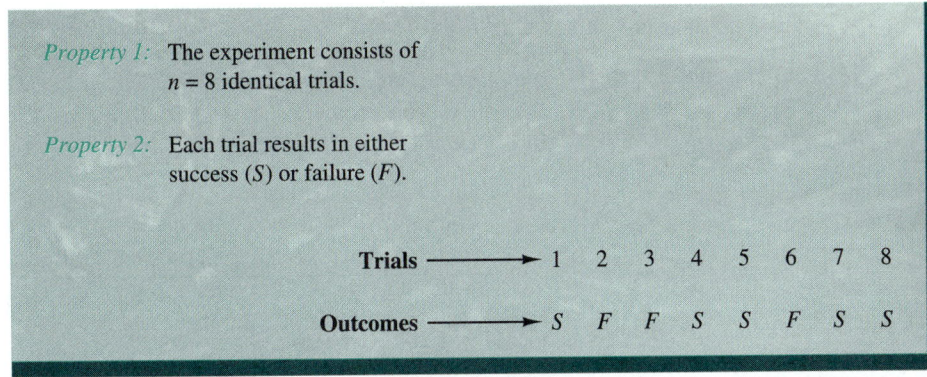

Property 1:   The experiment consists of
               $n = 8$ identical trials.

Property 2:   Each trial results in either
               success (S) or failure (F).

Trials ⟶	1	2	3	4	5	6	7	8
Outcomes ⟶	S	F	F	S	S	F	S	S

FIGURE 5.2   Diagram of an Eight-Trial Binomial Experiment

PROPERTIES OF A BINOMIAL EXPERIMENT

1. The experiment consists of a sequence of n identical trials.
2. Two outcomes are possible on each trial. We refer to one as a *success* and the other as a *failure.*
3. The probability of a success, denoted by p, does not change from trial to trial. Consequently, the probability of a failure, denoted by $1 - p$, does not change from trial to trial.
4. The trials are independent.

If properties 2, 3, and 4 are present, we say the trials are generated by a Bernoulli process. If, in addition, property 1 is present, we say we have a *binomial experiment.* Figure 5.2 depicts one possible sequence of outcomes of a binomial experiment involving eight trials.

In a binomial experiment, our interest is in the *number of successes occurring in the n trials.* If we let x denote the number of successes occurring in the n trials, we see that x can assume the values of 0, 1, 2, 3, ..., n. Since the number of values is finite, x is a *discrete* random variable. The probability distribution associated with this random variable is called the *binomial probability distribution.* For example, consider the experiment of tossing a coin five times and on each toss observing whether the coin lands with a head or a tail on its upward face. Suppose we are interested in counting the number of heads appearing over the five tosses. Does this experiment have the properties of a binomial experiment? What is the random variable of interest? Note that:

1. The experiment consists of five identical trials, where each trial involves the tossing of one coin.
2. Two outcomes are possible for each trial: a head and a tail. We can designate head a success and tail a failure.
3. The probability of a head and the probability of a tail are the same for each trial, with $p = .5$ and $1 - p = .5$.
4. The trials or tosses are independent, since the outcome on any one trial is not affected by what happens on other trials or tosses.

Thus, the properties of a binomial experiment are satisfied. The random variable of interest is $x =$ the number of heads appearing in the five trials. In this case, x can assume the values of 0, 1, 2, 3, 4, or 5.

As another example, consider an insurance salesperson who visits 10 randomly selected families. The outcome associated with each visit is classified as a success if the family purchases an insurance policy and a failure if the family does not. From past experience, the salesperson knows the probability that a randomly selected family will purchase an insurance policy is .10. Checking the properties of a binomial experiment, we observe that:

1. The experiment consists of 10 identical trials, where each trial involves contacting one family.
2. Two outcomes are possible on each trial: the family purchases a policy (success) or the family does not purchase a policy (failure).
3. The probabilities of a purchase and a nonpurchase are assumed to be the same for each sales call, with $p = .10$ and $1 - p = .90$.
4. The trials are independent since the families are randomly selected.

Since the four assumptions are satisfied, this is a binomial experiment. The random variable of interest is the number of sales obtained in contacting the 10 families. In this case, x can assume the values of 0, 1, 2, 3, 4, 5, 6, 7, 8, 9, and 10.

Property 3 of the binomial experiment is called the *stationarity assumption* and is sometimes confused with property 4, independence of trials. To see how they differ, consider again the case of the salesperson calling on families to sell insurance policies. If, as the day wore on, the salesperson got tired and lost enthusiasm, the probability of success (selling a policy) might drop to .05, for example, by the tenth call. In such a case, property 3 (stationarity) would not be satisfied, and we would not have a binomial experiment. This would be true even if property 4 held—that is, the purchase decisions of each family were made independently.

In applications involving binomial experiments, a special mathematical formula, called the *binomial probability function,* can be used to compute the probability of x successes in the n trials. Using probability concepts introduced in Chapter 4, we will show in the context of an illustrative problem how the formula can be developed.

THE MARTIN CLOTHING STORE PROBLEM

Let us consider the purchase decisions of the next three customers who enter the Martin Clothing Store. On the basis of past experience, the store manager estimates the probability that any one customer will make a purchase is .30. What is the probability that two of the next three customers will make a purchase?

Using a tree diagram (Figure 5.3), we can see that the experiment of observing the three customers each making a purchase decision has eight possible outcomes. Using S to denote success (a purchase) and F to denote failure (no purchase), we are interested in experimental outcomes involving two successes in the three trials (purchase decisions). Next, let us verify that the experiment involving the sequence of three purchase decisions can be viewed as a binomial experiment. Checking the four requirements for a binomial experiment, we note that:

1. The experiment can be described as a sequence of three identical trials, one trial for each of the three customers who will enter the store.
2. Two outcomes—the customer makes a purchase (success) or the customer does not make a purchase (failure)—are possible for each trial.
3. The probability that the customer will make a purchase (.30) or will not make a purchase (.70) is assumed to be the same for all customers.
4. The purchase decision of each customer is independent of the decisions of the other customers.

Hence, the properties of a binomial experiment are present.

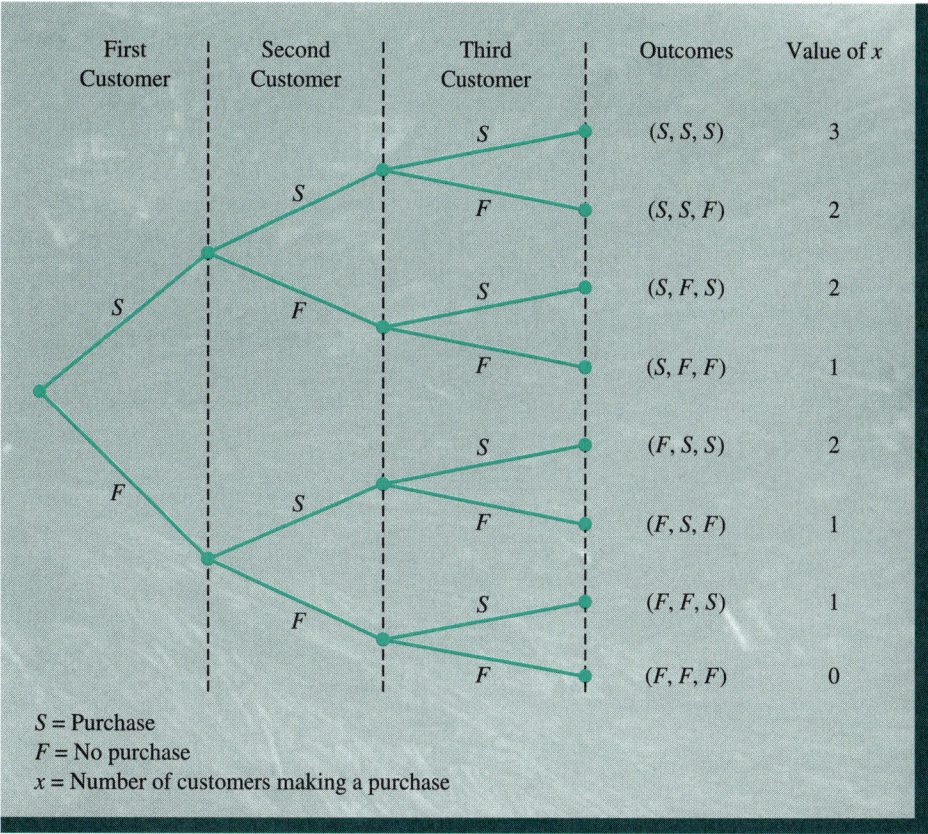

First Customer	Second Customer	Third Customer	Outcomes	Value of x
		S	(S, S, S)	3
	S	F	(S, S, F)	2
S	F	S	(S, F, S)	2
		F	(S, F, F)	1
	S	S	(F, S, S)	2
F		F	(F, S, F)	1
	F	S	(F, F, S)	1
		F	(F, F, F)	0

S = Purchase
F = No purchase
x = Number of customers making a purchase

FIGURE 5.3   Tree Diagram for the Martin Clothing Store Problem

The number of experimental outcomes resulting in exactly x successes in n trials can be computed from the following formula.*

NUMBER OF EXPERIMENTAL OUTCOMES PROVIDING EXACTLY x SUCCESSES IN n TRIALS

$$\binom{n}{x} = \frac{n!}{x!(n-x)!} \qquad (5.5)$$

where

$$n! = n(n-1)(n-2)\ldots(2)(1) \qquad (5.6)$$

and

$$0! = 1$$

Now let us return to the Martin Clothing Store experiment involving three customer purchase decisions. Equation (5.5) can be used to determine the number of experimental

---

*This is the formula introduced in Chapter 4 to determine the number of combinations of n objects selected x at a time. For the binomial experiment, this combinatorial formula provides the number of experimental outcomes (sequences of n trials) resulting in x successes.

outcomes involving two purchases; that is, the number of ways of obtaining $x = 2$ successes in the $n = 3$ trials. From (5.5) we have

$$\binom{n}{x} = \binom{3}{2} = \frac{3!}{2!(3-2)!} = \frac{(3)(2)(1)}{(2)(1)(1)} = \frac{6}{2} = 3$$

Formula (5.5) shows that three of the outcomes yield two successes. From Figure 5.3 we see these three outcomes are denoted by *SSF, SFS,* and *FSS.*

Using (5.5) to determine how many experimental outcomes have three successes (purchases) in the three trials, we obtain

$$\binom{n}{x} = \binom{3}{3} = \frac{3!}{3!(3-3)!} = \frac{3!}{3!0!} = \frac{(3)(2)(1)}{(3)(2)(1)(1)} = \frac{6}{6} = 1$$

From Figure 5.3 we see that the one experimental outcome with three successes is identified by *SSS.*

We know that (5.5) can be used to determine the number of experimental outcomes that result in x successes. But, if we are to determine the probability of x successes in n trials, we must also know the probability associated with each of these experimental outcomes. Since the trials of a binomial experiment are independent, we can simply multiply the probabilities associated with each trial outcome to find the probability of a particular sequence of outcomes.

The probability of purchases by the first two customers and no purchase by the third customer is given by

$$pp(1 - p)$$

With a .30 probability of a purchase on any one trial, the probability of a purchase on the first two trials and no purchase on the third is given by

$$(.30)(.30)(.70) = (.30)^2(.70) = .063$$

Two other sequences of outcomes result in two successes and one failure. The probabilities for all three sequences involving two successes are shown below.

Trial Outcomes				
1st Customer	2nd Customer	3rd Customer	Success-Failure Notation	Probability of Experimental Outcome
Purchase	Purchase	No purchase	SSF	$pp(1 - p) = p^2(1-p)$ $= (.30)^2(.70) = .063$
Purchase	No purchase	Purchase	SFS	$p(1 - p)p = p^2(1 - p)$ $= (.30)^2(.70) = .063$
No purchase	Purchase	Purchase	FSS	$(1 - p)pp = p^2(1 - p)$ $= (.30)^2(.70) = .063$

Observe that all three outcomes with two successes have exactly the same probability. This observation holds in general. In any binomial experiment, all sequences of trial outcomes yielding x successes in n trials have the *same probability* of occurrence. The probability of each sequence of trials yielding x successes in n trials follows.

Probability of a Particular Sequence of Trial Outcomes $= p^x(1 - p)^{(n - x)}$ **(5.7)**
with x Successes in n Trials

For the Martin Clothing Store, this formula shows that any outcome with two successes has a probability of $p^2(1 - p)^{(3 - 2)} = p^2(1 - p)^1 = (.30)^2(.70)^1 = .063$, as shown.

Since (5.5) shows the number of outcomes in a binomial experiment with x successes and (5.7) gives the probability for each sequence involving x successes, we combine (5.5) and (5.7) to obtain the following *binomial probability function*.

BINOMIAL PROBABILITY FUNCTION

$$f(x) = \binom{n}{x} p^x (1 - p)^{(n - x)} \qquad (5.8)$$

where

$f(x) =$ the probability of x successes in n trials

$n =$ the number of trials

$$\binom{n}{x} = \frac{n!}{x!(n-x)!}$$

$p =$ the probability of a success on any one trial

$(1 - p) =$ the probability of a failure on any one trial

TABLE 5.16 Probability Distribution for the Number of Customers Making a Purchase

x	$f(x)$
0	$\frac{3!}{0!3!}(.30)^0(.70)^3 = .343$
1	$\frac{3!}{1!2!}(.30)^1(.70)^2 = .441$
2	$\frac{3!}{2!1!}(.30)^2(.70)^1 = .189$
3	$\frac{3!}{3!0!}(.30)^3(.70)^0 = \underline{.027}$
	1.000

In the Martin Clothing Store example, let us compute the probability that no customer makes a purchase, exactly one customer makes a purchase, exactly two customers make a purchase, and all three customers make a purchase. The calculations are summarized in Table 5.16, which gives the probability distribution of number of customers purchasing. Figure 5.4 is a graph of this probability distribution.

The binomial probability function can be applied to *any* binomial experiment. If we are satisfied that a situation has the properties of a binomial experiment and if we know the values of n, p, and $(1 - p)$, we can use (5.8) to compute the probability of x successes in the n trials.

If we consider variations of the Martin experiment, such as 10 customers rather than three entering the store, the binomial probability function given by (5.8) is still applicable. For example, the probability of making exactly four sales to 10 potential customers entering the store is

$$f(4) = \frac{10!}{4!6!}(.30)^4(.70)^6 = .2001$$

This is a binomial experiment with $n = 10$, $x = 4$, and $p = .30$.

USING TABLES OF BINOMIAL PROBABILITIES

Tables have been developed that give the probability of x successes in n trials for a binomial experiment. The tables are generally easy to use and quicker than (5.8). A table of binomial probabilities is provided as Table 5 of Appendix B. A portion of this table is given in Table 5.17. To use this table, we must specify the values of n, p, and x for the binomial experiment of interest. In the example at the top of Table 5.17, we see that the probability of $x = 3$ successes in a binomial experiment with $n = 10$ and $p = .40$ is .2150. You can use (5.8) to verify that you would obtain the same answer if you used the binomial probability function directly.

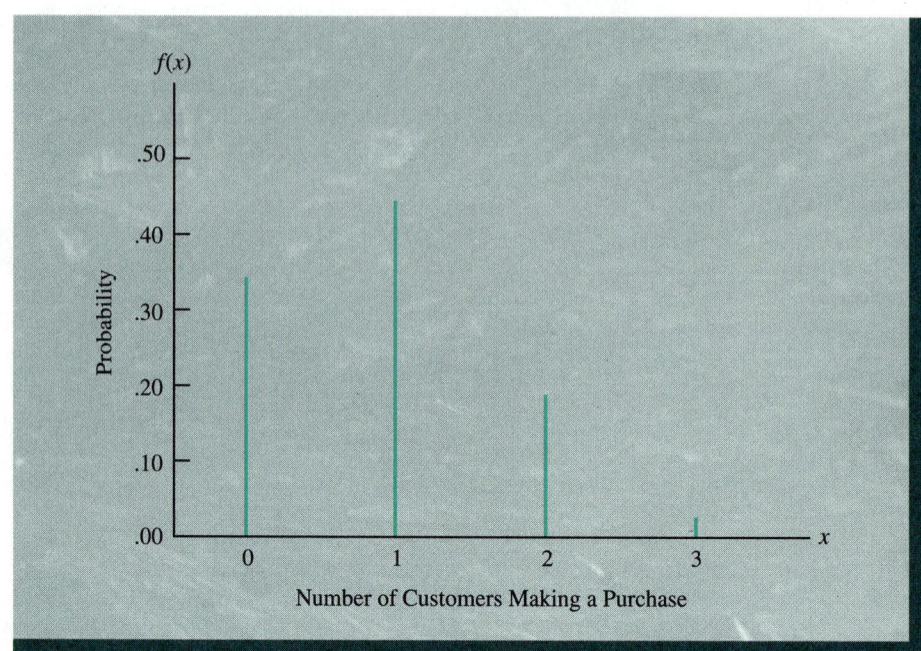

FIGURE 5.4   Graphical Representation of the Probability Distribution for the Martin Clothing Store Problem

TABLE 5.17   Selected Values from the Binomial Probability Table Example: $n = 10$, $x = 3$, $p = .40$; $f(3) = .2150$

						p					
n	x	.05	.10	.15	.20	.25	.30	.35	.40	.45	.50
9	0	.6302	.3874	.2316	.1342	.0751	.0404	.0207	.0101	.0046	.0020
	1	.2985	.3874	.3679	.3020	.2253	.1556	.1004	.0605	.0339	.0176
	2	.0629	.1722	.2597	.3020	.3003	.2668	.2162	.1612	.1110	.0703
	3	.0077	.0446	.1069	.1762	.2336	.2668	.2716	.2508	.2119	.1641
	4	.0006	.0074	.0283	.0661	.1168	.1715	.2194	.2508	.2600	.2461
	5	.0000	.0008	.0050	.0165	.0389	.0735	.1181	.1672	.2128	.2461
	6	.0000	.0001	.0006	.0028	.0087	.0210	.0424	.0743	.1160	.1641
	7	.0000	.0000	.0000	.0003	.0012	.0039	.0098	.0212	.0407	.0703
	8	.0000	.0000	.0000	.0000	.0001	.0004	.0013	.0035	.0083	.0176
	9	.0000	.0000	.0000	.0000	.0000	.0000	.0001	.0003	.0008	.0020
10	0	.5987	.3487	.1969	.1074	.0563	.0282	.0135	.0060	.0025	.0010
	1	.3151	.3874	.3474	.2684	.1877	.1211	.0725	.0403	.0207	.0098
	2	.0746	.1937	.2759	.3020	.2816	.2335	.1757	.1209	.0763	.0439
	3	.0105	.0574	.1298	.2013	.2503	.2668	.2522	**.2150**	.1665	.1172
	4	.0010	.0112	.0401	.0881	.1460	.2001	.2377	.2508	.2384	.2051
	5	.0001	.0015	.0085	.0264	.0584	.1029	.1536	.2007	.2340	.2461
	6	.0000	.0001	.0012	.0055	.0162	.0368	.0689	.1115	.1596	.2051
	7	.0000	.0000	.0001	.0008	.0031	.0090	.0212	.0425	.0746	.1172
	8	.0000	.0000	.0000	.0001	.0004	.0014	.0043	.0106	.0229	.0439
	9	.0000	.0000	.0000	.0000	.0000	.0001	.0005	.0016	.0042	.0098
	10	.0000	.0000	.0000	.0000	.0000	.0000	.0000	.0001	.0003	.0010

x	P(X = x)
0.00	0.0282
1.00	0.1211
2.00	0.2335
3.00	0.2668
4.00	0.2001
5.00	0.1029
6.00	0.0368
7.00	0.0090
8.00	0.0014
9.00	0.0001
10.00	0.0000

FIGURE 5.5 Minitab Output Showing Binomial Probabilities for the Martin Clothing Store Problem

Now let us use this table to verify the probability of four successes in 10 trials for the Martin Clothing Store problem. Note that the value of $f(4) = .2001$ can be read directly from the table of binomial probabilities, with $n = 10$, $x = 4$, and $p = .30$.

While the tables of binomial probabilities are relatively easy to use, it is impossible to have tables that show all possible values of n and p that might be encountered in a binomial experiment. However, with today's calculators, using (5.8) to calculate the desired probability is not difficult, especially if the number of trials is not large. In the exercises, you should practice using (5.8) to compute the binomial probabilities unless the problem specifically requests that you use the binomial probability table.

USING THE COMPUTER TO OBTAIN BINOMIAL PROBABILITIES

Statistical software packages such as Minitab provide a capability for computing binomial probabilities. Consider the Martin Clothing Store example with $n = 10$ and $p = .30$. To generate probabilities, the user first must enter the values of the random variable x for which probabilities are desired into a column of the worksheet. We entered the values 0, 1, 2, . . . , 10 into column 1 of a Minitab worksheet to generate the entire binomial probability distribution for the Martin Clothing Store example.

Selecting the binomial probability distribution option of Minitab provided the output shown in Figure 5.5. The first column contains the values of the random variable and the second column contains the associated probabilities. Note that the probability of four successes is .2001, as we found previously using (5.8) and Table 5.17. Computer packages can easily generate binomial probabilities for problems with any values for n and p. The appendices at the end of this chapter show how spreadsheet packages can be used to generate probabilities. Appendix 5.1 gives the step-by-step procedure for using Minitab to determine the binomial probabilities for the Martin Clothing Store problem. Appendix 5.2 describes how Excel can be used to compute the probabilities for any binomial probability distribution.

THE EXPECTED VALUE AND VARIANCE FOR THE BINOMIAL PROBABILITY DISTRIBUTION

In Section 5.3 we provided formulas for computing the expected value and variance of a discrete random variable. In the special case where the random variable has a binomial probability distribution with a known number of trials n and a known probability of success p, the general formulas for the expected value and variance can be simplified. The results follow.

EXPECTED VALUE AND VARIANCE FOR THE BINOMIAL PROBABILITY DISTRIBUTION

$$E(x) = \mu = np \tag{5.9}$$

$$\text{Var}(x) = \sigma^2 = np(1 - p) \tag{5.10}$$

For the Martin Clothing Store problem with three customers, we can use (5.9) to compute the expected number of customers making a purchase.

$$E(x) = np = 3(.30) = .9$$

Suppose that for the next month the Martin Clothing Store forecasts 1000 customers will enter the store. What is the expected number of customers who will make a purchase? The answer is $\mu = np = (1000)(.3) = 300$. Thus, to increase the expected number of sales, Martin's must induce more customers to enter the store and/or somehow increase the probability that any individual customer will make a purchase after entering.

For the Martin Clothing Store problem with three customers, we see that the variance and standard deviation for the number of customers making a purchase are

$$\sigma^2 = np(1 - p) = 3(.3)(.7) = .63$$

$$\sigma = \sqrt{.63} = .79$$

For the next 1000 customers entering the store, the variance and standard deviation for the number of customers making a purchase are

$$\sigma^2 = np(1 - p) = 1000(.3)(.7) = 210$$

$$\sigma = \sqrt{210} = 14.49$$

NOTES AND COMMENTS

1. Some binomial tables show values of p only up to and including $p = .50$. It would appear that such tables cannot be used when the probability of success exceeds $p = .50$. However, they can be used by noting that the probability of $n-x$ failures is also the probability of x successes. When the probability of success is greater than $p = .50$, one can compute the probability of $n - x$ failures instead. The probability of failure, $1 - p$, will be less than .50 when $p > .50$.

2. Some sources present binomial tables in a cumulative form. In using such tables, one must subtract to find the probability of x successes in n trials. For example, $f(2) = P(x \leq 2) - P(x \leq 1)$. Our tables provide these probabilities directly. To compute cumulative probabilities using our tables, one simply sums the individual probabilities. For example, to compute $P(x \leq 2)$ using our tables, we sum $f(0) + f(1) + f(2)$.

EXERCISES

METHODS

Self-Test

25. Consider a binomial experiment with two trials and $p = .4$.
- **a.** Draw a tree diagram showing this as a two-trial experiment (see Figure 5.3).
- **b.** Compute the probability of one success, $f(1)$.
- **c.** Compute $f(0)$.
- **d.** Compute $f(2)$.
- **e.** Find the probability of at least one success.
- **f.** Find the expected value, variance, and standard deviation.

26. Consider a binomial experiment with $n = 10$ and $p = .10$. Use the binomial tables (Table 5 of Appendix B) to answer (a) through (d).
- **a.** Find $f(0)$. **b.** Find $f(2)$. **c.** Find $P(x \leq 2)$.
- **d.** Find $P(x \geq 1)$. **e.** Find $E(x)$. **f.** Find Var(x) and σ.

27. Consider a binomial experiment with $n = 20$ and $p = .70$. Use the binomial tables (Table 5 of Appendix B) to answer (a) through (d).
- **a.** Find $f(12)$. **b.** Find $f(16)$. **c.** Find $P(x \geq 16)$.
- **d.** Find $P(x \leq 15)$. **e.** Find $E(x)$. **f.** Find Var(x) and σ.

APPLICATIONS

28. The greatest number of complaints by owners of two-year-old automobiles pertain to electrical system performance (*Consumer Reports 1995 Buyer's Guide*). Assume that an annual questionnaire sent to owners of over 300 makes and models of automobiles reveals that 10% of the owners of two-year-old automobiles found trouble spots in the electrical system that included the starter, alternator, battery, switch controls, instruments, wiring, lights, and radio.
- **a.** What is the probability that a sample of 12 owners of two-year-old automobiles will find exactly two owners with electrical system problems?
- **b.** What is the probability that a sample of 12 owners of two-year-old automobiles will find at least two owners with electrical system problems?
- **c.** What is the probability that a sample of 20 owners of two-year-old automobiles will find at least one owner with an electrical system problem?

29. *The American Almanac of Jobs and Salaries,* 1994–95, reported that 25% of accountants are employed in public accounting. Assume that this percentage applies to a group of 15 college graduates just entering the accounting profession. What is the probability that at least three graduates will be employed in public accounting?

Self-Test

30. When a new machine is functioning properly, only 3% of the items produced are defective. Assume that we will randomly select two parts produced on the machine and that we are interested in the number of defective parts found.
- **a.** Describe the conditions under which this situation would be a binomial experiment.
- **b.** Draw a tree diagram similar to Figure 5.3 showing this as a two-trial experiment.
- **c.** How many experimental outcomes result in exactly one defect being found?
- **d.** Compute the probabilities associated with finding no defects, exactly one defect, and two defects.

31. Five percent of American truck drivers are women (*Statistical Abstract of the United States,* 1994). Suppose 10 truck drivers are selected randomly to be interviewed about quality of work conditions.
- **a.** Is the selection of the 10 drivers a binomial experiment? Explain.
- **b.** What is the probability that two of the drivers will be women?
- **c.** What is the probability that none will be women?
- **d.** What is the probability that at least one will be a woman?

32. The book *100% American* by Daniel Evan Weiss reports more than 1000 statistical facts about the United States and its people. One fact reported is that 64% of the people live in the state where they were born.

    a. What is the probability that a random sample of 10 people will find at least eight people living in the state where they were born?

    b. What is the probability that a random sample of three people will find exactly one person living in the state where she or he was born?

33. National Oil Company conducts exploratory oil drilling operations in the southwestern United States. To fund the operation, investors form partnerships, which provide the financial support necessary to drill a fixed number of oil wells. Each well drilled is classified as a producer well or a dry well. Past experience in this type of exploratory operation shows that 15% of all wells drilled are producer wells. A newly formed partnership has provided the financial support for drilling at 12 exploratory locations.

    a. What is the probability that all 12 wells will be producer wells?

    b. What is the probability that all 12 wells will be dry wells?

    c. What is the probability that exactly one well will be a producer well?

    d. To make the partnership venture profitable, at least three of the exploratory wells must be producer wells. What is the probability that the venture will be profitable?

34. Military radar and missile detection systems are designed to warn a country against enemy attacks. A reliability question is whether a detection system will be able to identify an attack and issue a warning. Assume that a particular detection system has a .90 probability of detecting a missile attack. Use the binomial probability distribution to answer the following questions.

    a. What is the probability that a single detection system will detect an attack?

    b. If two detection systems are installed in the same area and operate independently, what is the probability that at least one of the systems will detect the attack?

    c. If three systems are installed, what is the probability that at least one of the systems will detect the attack?

    d. Would you recommend that multiple detection systems be used? Explain.

35. Assume that the binomial experiment applies for the case of a college basketball player shooting free throws. Late in a basketball game, a team will sometimes foul intentionally in the hope that the player shooting the free throw will miss and the team committing the foul will get the ball. Assume that the best player on the opposing team has a .82 probability of making a free throw and that the worst player has a .56 probability of making a free throw.

    a. What are the probabilities that the best player will make 0, 1, and 2 points if fouled and given two free throws?

    b. What are the probabilities that the worst player will make 0, 1, and 2 points if fouled and given two free throws?

    c. Does it make sense for a coach to have a preset plan about which player to intentionally foul late in a basketball game? Explain.

36. An American Association of Individual Investors survey found that 23% of AAII members had purchased shares of stock directly through an initial public offering (IPO) (*AAII Journal,* July 1994). In a sample of 12 AAII members,

    a. What is the probability exactly three members have purchased IPOs?

    b. What is the probability at least one member has purchased IPOs?

    c. What is the probability that two or more members have purchased IPOs?

37. A university has found that 20% of its students withdraw without completing the introductory statistics course. Assume that 20 students have registered for the course this quarter.

    a. What is the probability that two or fewer will withdraw?

    b. What is the probability that exactly four will withdraw?

    c. What is the probability that more than three will withdraw?

    d. What is the expected number of withdrawals?

38. For the special case of a binomial random variable, we stated that the variance measure could be computed from the formula $\sigma^2 = np(1 - p)$. For the Martin Clothing Store problem data in Table 5.16, we found $\sigma^2 = np(1 - p) = .63$. Use the general definition of variance for a discrete random variable, Equation (5.4), and the data in Table 5.16 to verify that the variance is in fact .63.

39. Suppose a salesperson makes a sale on 20% of customer contacts. A normal work week will enable the salesperson to contact 25 customers. What is the expected number of sales for the week? What is the variance for the number of sales for the week? What is the standard deviation for the number of sales for the week?

40. Of the next-day express mailings handled by the U.S. Postal Service, 85% are actually received by the addressee one day after the mailing. What is the expected value and variance for the number of one-day deliveries in a group of 250 express mailings?

41. Betting on the color red in the game of roulette has a $^{18}/_{38}$ chance of winning. What is the expected value and variance for the number of wins in a series of 100 bets on red?

5.5 THE POISSON PROBABILITY DISTRIBUTION

In this section we consider a discrete random variable that is often useful in estimating the number of occurrences over a specified interval of time or space. For example, the random variable of interest might be the number of arrivals at a car wash in one hour, the number of repairs needed in 10 miles of highway, or the number of leaks in 100 miles of pipeline. If the following two properties are satisfied, the number of occurrences is a random variable described by the *Poisson probability function.*

PROPERTIES OF A POISSON EXPERIMENT

1. The probability of an occurrence is the same for any two intervals of equal length.
2. The occurrence or nonoccurrence in any interval is independent of the occurrence or nonoccurrence in any other interval.

The Poisson probability function is given by (5.11).

POISSON PROBABILITY FUNCTION

$$f(x) = \frac{\mu^x e^{-\mu}}{x!} \tag{5.11}$$

where

$f(x)$ = the probability of x occurrences in an interval

μ = expected value or mean number of occurrences in an interval

$e = 2.71828$

Before we consider a specific example to see how the Poisson distribution can be applied, note that there is no upper limit on x, the number of occurrences. It is a discrete random variable that may assume an infinite sequence of values ($x = 0, 1, 2, \ldots$). The Poisson random variable has no upper limit.

AN EXAMPLE INVOLVING TIME INTERVALS

Suppose that we are interested in the number of arrivals at the drive-in teller window of a bank during a 15-minute period on weekday mornings. If we can assume that the probability of a car arriving is the same for any two time periods of equal length and that the arrival or nonarrival of a car in any time period is independent of the arrival or nonarrival in any other time period, the Poisson probability function is applicable. Suppose these assumptions are satisfied and an analysis of historical data shows that the average number of cars arriving in a 15-minute period of time is 10; then the following probability function applies.

$$f(x) = \frac{10^x e^{-10}}{x!}$$

The random variable here is x = number of cars arriving in any 15-minute period.

If management wanted to know the probability of exactly five arrivals in 15 minutes, we would set $x = 5$ and thus obtain*

$$\begin{array}{c}\text{Probability of Exactly} \\ \text{5 Arrivals in 15 Minutes}\end{array} = f(5) = \frac{10^5 e^{-10}}{5!} = .0378$$

Although the above probability was determined by evaluating the probability function with $\mu = 10$ and $x = 5$, it is often easier to refer to tables for the Poisson probability distribution. These tables provide probabilities for specific values of x and μ. We have included such a table as Table 7 of Appendix B. For convenience we have reproduced a portion of this table as Table 5.18. Note that to use the table of Poisson probabilities, we need know only the values of x and μ. From Table 5.18 we see that the probability of five arrivals in a 15-minute period is found by locating the value in the row of the table corresponding to $x = 5$ and the column of the table corresponding to $\mu = 10$. Hence, we obtain $f(5) = .0378$.

Our illustration involves computing the probability of five arrivals in a 15-minute period, but other time periods can be used. Suppose we want to compute the probability of one arrival in a three-minute period. Since 10 is the expected number of arrivals in a 15-minute period, we see that $^{10}/_{15} = ^{2}/_3$ is the expected number of arrivals in a one-minute period and that $(2/3)$ (3 minutes) = 2 is the expected number of arrivals in a three-minute period. Thus, the probability of x arrivals in a three-minute time period with $\mu = 2$ is given by the following Poisson probability function.

$$f(x) = \frac{2^x e^{-2}}{x!}$$

To find the probability of one arrival in a three-minute period, we can either use Table 7 in Appendix B or compute the probability directly.

$$\begin{array}{c}\text{Probability of Exactly} \\ \text{1 Arrival in 3 Minutes}\end{array} = f(1) = \frac{2^1 e^{-2}}{1!} = .2707$$

---

*Values of $e^{-\mu}$ can be found in Table 6 of Appendix B. Most calculators also provide these values.

TABLE 5.18 Selected Values from the Poisson Probability Tables Example: $\mu = 10$, $x = 5$; $f(5) = .0378$

x	9.1	9.2	9.3	9.4	9.5	9.6	9.7	9.8	9.9	10
					μ					
0	.0001	.0001	.0001	.0001	.0001	.0001	.0001	.0001	.0001	.0000
1	.0010	.0009	.0009	.0008	.0007	.0007	.0006	.0005	.0005	.0005
2	.0046	.0043	.0040	.0037	.0034	.0031	.0029	.0027	.0025	.0023
3	.0140	.0131	.0123	.0115	.0107	.0100	.0093	.0087	.0081	.0076
4	.0319	.0302	.0285	.0269	.0254	.0240	.0226	.0213	.0201	.0189
5	.0581	.0555	.0530	.0506	.0483	.0460	.0439	.0418	.0398	**.0378**
6	.0881	.0851	.0822	.0793	.0764	.0736	.0709	.0682	.0656	.0631
7	.1145	.1118	.1091	.1064	.1037	.1010	.0982	.0955	.0928	.0901
8	.1302	.1286	.1269	.1251	.1232	.1212	.1191	.1170	.1148	.1126
9	.1317	.1315	.1311	.1306	.1300	.1293	.1284	.1274	.1263	.1251
10	.1198	.1210	.1219	.1228	.1235	.1241	.1245	.1249	.1250	.1251
11	.0991	.1012	.1031	.1049	.1067	.1083	.1098	.1112	.1125	.1137
12	.0752	.0776	.0799	.0822	.0844	.0866	.0888	.0908	.0928	.0948
13	.0526	.0549	.0572	.0594	.0617	.0640	.0662	.0685	.0707	.0729
14	.0342	.0361	.0380	.0399	.0419	.0439	.0459	.0479	.0500	.0521
15	.0208	.0221	.0235	.0250	.0265	.0281	.0297	.0313	.0330	.0347
16	.0118	.0127	.0137	.0147	.0157	.0168	.0180	.0192	.0204	.0217
17	.0063	.0069	.0075	.0081	.0088	.0095	.0103	.0111	.0119	.0128
18	.0032	.0035	.0039	.0042	.0046	.0051	.0055	.0060	.0065	.0071
19	.0015	.0017	.0019	.0021	.0023	.0026	.0028	.0031	.0034	.0037
20	.0007	.0008	.0009	.0010	.0011	.0012	.0014	.0015	.0017	.0019
21	.0003	.0003	.0004	.0004	.0005	.0006	.0006	.0007	.0008	.0009
22	.0001	.0001	.0002	.0002	.0002	.0002	.0003	.0003	.0004	.0004
23	.0000	.0001	.0001	.0001	.0001	.0001	.0001	.0001	.0002	.0002
24	.0000	.0000	.0000	.0000	.0000	.0000	.0000	.0001	.0001	.0001

AN EXAMPLE INVOLVING LENGTH OR DISTANCE INTERVALS

Let us illustrate an application not involving time intervals where the Poisson probability distribution is useful. Suppose we are concerned with the occurrence of major defects in a section of highway one month after resurfacing. We will assume that the probability of a defect in this section of highway is the same for any two intervals of equal length and that the occurrence or nonoccurrence of a defect in any one interval is independent of the occurrence or nonoccurrence of a defect in any other interval. Hence, the Poisson probability distribution can be applied.

Suppose we learn that major defects one month after resurfacing occur at the average rate of two per mile. Let us find the probability that there will be no major defects in a particular three-mile section of the highway. Since we are interested in an interval with a length of three miles, $\mu = (2 \text{ defects/mile})(3 \text{ miles}) = 6$ represents the expected number of major defects over the three-mile section of highway. By using (5.11) or Table 7 in Appendix B, we see that the probability of no major defects is .0025. Thus, it is very unlikely that there will be no major defects in the three-mile section. In fact, there is a $1 - .0025 = .9975$ probability of at least one major defect in the highway section.

POISSON APPROXIMATION OF THE BINOMIAL PROBABILITY DISTRIBUTION

The Poisson probability distribution can be used as an approximation of the binomial probability distribution when p, the probability of success, is small and n, the number of trials, is large. Simply set $\mu = np$ and use the Poisson tables. As a rule of thumb, the approximation will be good whenever $p \leq .05$ and $n \geq 20$.

As an example, suppose we want to compute the binomial probability of $x = 3$ successes in $n = 250$ trials with $p = .01$. To use the Poisson approximation, we set $\mu = np = 250(.01) = 2.5$. Referring to the Poisson probability tables (Table 7 in Appendix B), we find $f(3) = .2138$. So, we would approximate the binomial probability of three successes as $f(3) = .2138$.

EXERCISES

METHODS

42. Consider a Poisson probability distribution with $\mu = 3$.
    a. Write the appropriate Poisson probability function.
    b. Find $f(2)$.   c. Find $f(1)$.   d. Find $P(x \geq 2)$.

Self-Test

43. Consider a Poisson probability distribution with an average number of occurrences per time period of two.
    a. Write the appropriate Poisson probability function.
    b. What is the average number of occurrences in three time periods?
    c. Write the appropriate Poisson probability function to determine the probability of x occurrences in three time periods.
    d. Find the probability of two occurrences in one time period.
    e. Find the probability of six occurrences in three time periods.
    f. Find the probability of five occurrences in two time periods.

APPLICATIONS

Self-Test

44. Phone calls arrive at the rate of 48 per hour at the reservation desk for Regional Airways.
    a. Find the probability of receiving three calls in a five-minute interval of time.
    b. Find the probability of receiving exactly 10 calls in 15 minutes.
    c. Suppose no calls are currently on hold. If the agent takes five minutes to complete the current call, how many callers do you expect to be waiting by that time? What is the probability that none will be waiting?
    d. If no calls are currently being processed, what is the probability that the agent can take three minutes for personal time without being interrupted?

45. During the period of time phone-in reservations are being taken at a local university, calls come in at the rate of one every two minutes.
    a. What is the expected number of calls in one hour?
    b. What is the probability of three calls in five minutes?
    c. What is the probability of no calls in a five-minute period?

46. The mean number of times per month that *Forbes* magazine subscribers entertain for business reasons is 3.9 (*Forbes* 1993 Subscriber Study). Assume that the number of times a subscriber entertains for business reasons follows the assumptions of a Poisson experiment and answer the following questions.
    a. What is the probability that a subscriber entertains for business reasons exactly three times during a one-month period?

b. What is the mean number of times a subscriber entertains for business reasons over a two-month period?

c. What is the probability that a subscriber entertains for business reasons at least once during a two-month period?

47. During rush periods, accidents occur in a particular metropolitan area at the rate of two per hour. The morning rush period lasts for one hour and 30 minutes and the evening rush period lasts for two hours.

a. On a particular day, what is the probability that there will be no accidents during the morning rush period?

b. What is the probability of two accidents during the evening rush period?

c. What is the probability of four or more accidents during the morning rush period?

d. On a particular day, what is the probability that there will be no accidents during both the morning and evening rush periods?

48. Airline passengers arrive randomly and independently at the passenger-screening facility at a major international airport. The mean arrival rate is 10 passengers per minute.

a. What is the probability of no arrivals in a one-minute period?

b. What is the probability that three or fewer passengers arrive in a one-minute period?

c. What is the probability of no arrivals in a 15-second period?

d. What is the probability of at least one arrival in a 15-second period?

49. Williams Company has observed that calculators fail and need to be replaced at the rate of three every 25 days.

a. What is the expected number of calculators that will fail in 30 days?

b. What is the probability that at least two will fail in 50 days?

c. What is the probability that exactly three will fail in 10 days?

50. Investment activities for subscribers to *The Wall Street Journal* show that the average number of stock transactions per year is 12 (*The Wall Street Journal* Subscriber Study, 1992). Assume that a particular investor makes transactions at this rate. Furthermore, assume that the probability of a transaction for this investor is the same for any two months and transactions in one month are independent of transactions in any other month. Answer the following questions.

a. What is the mean number of transactions per month?

b. What is the probability of no stock transactions during a month?

c. What is the probability of exactly one stock transaction during a month?

d. What is the probability of more than one stock transaction during a month?

51. A survey found that only 2% of investors believed money-market funds are not safe investments (*Business Week*, August 15, 1994). In a sample of 100 investors, what is the probability that

a. exactly two investors indicate money-market funds are not safe investments.

b. at least two investors indicate money-market funds are not safe investments.

5.6   THE HYPERGEOMETRIC PROBABILITY DISTRIBUTION

The hypergeometric probability distribution is closely related to the binomial probability distribution. The key difference between the two probability distributions is that with the hypergeometric distribution, the trials are not independent; and the probability of success changes from trial to trial.

The usual notation in applications of the hypergeometric probability distribution is to let r denote the number of items in the population of size N that are labeled success and $N - r$ denote the number of items in the population that are labeled failure. The hypergeometric probability function is used to compute the probability that in a random sample of n items, selected without replacement, we will obtain x items labeled success and $n - x$ items labeled failure. For this to occur, we must obtain x successes from the r successes in the population and $n - x$ failures from the $N - r$ failures. The following hypergeometric probability function provides $f(x)$, the probability of obtaining x successes in a sample of size n.

HYPERGEOMETRIC PROBABILITY FUNCTION

$$f(x) = \frac{\binom{r}{x}\binom{N-r}{n-x}}{\binom{N}{n}} \qquad \text{for } 0 \le x \le r \qquad \text{(5.12)}$$

where

$f(x)$ = the probability of x successes in n trials

n = the number of trials

N = number of elements in the population

r = number of elements in the population labeled success

Note that $\binom{N}{n}$ represents the number of ways a sample of size n can be selected from a population of size N; $\binom{r}{x}$ represents the number of ways x successes can be selected from a total of r successes in the population; and $\binom{N-r}{n-x}$ represents the number of ways $n-x$ failures can be selected from a total of $N - r$ failures in the population.

To illustrate the computations involved in using (5.12), let us consider the problem of selecting two of five committee members to send to a Las Vegas convention. Assume that the five-member committee consists of three women and two men. To determine the probability of randomly selecting two women, we can use (5.12) with $n = 2$, $N = 5$, $r = 3$, and $x = 2$.

$$f(2) = \frac{\binom{3}{2}\binom{2}{0}}{\binom{5}{2}} = \frac{\left(\frac{3!}{2!1!}\right)\left(\frac{2!}{2!0!}\right)}{\left(\frac{5!}{2!3!}\right)} = \frac{3}{10} = .30$$

Suppose we learn later that three committee members will be allowed to make the trip. If we use $n = 3$, $N = 5$, $r = 3$, and $x = 2$, the probability that exactly two of the three members will be women is

$$f(2) = \frac{\binom{3}{2}\binom{2}{1}}{\binom{5}{2}} = \frac{\left(\frac{3!}{2!1!}\right)\left(\frac{2!}{1!1!}\right)}{\left(\frac{5!}{2!3!}\right)} = \frac{6}{10} = .60$$

As another illustration, suppose a population consists of 10 items, four of which are classified as defective and six of which are classified as nondefective. What is the probability that a random sample of size three will contain two defective items? For this problem we can think of obtaining a defective item as a "success." Using (5.12) with $n = 3$, $N = 10$, $r = 4$, and $x = 2$, we can compute $f(2)$ as follows.

$$f(2) = \frac{\binom{4}{2}\binom{6}{1}}{\binom{10}{3}} = \frac{\left(\frac{4!}{2!2!}\right)\left(\frac{6!}{1!5!}\right)}{\left(\frac{10!}{3!7!}\right)} = \frac{36}{120} = .30$$

EXERCISES

METHODS

Self-Test

52. Suppose $N = 10$ and $r = 3$. Compute the hypergeometric probabilities for the following values of n and x.
    a. $n = 4$, $x = 1$ b. $n = 2$, $x = 2$ c. $n = 2$, $x = 0$ d. $n = 4$, $x = 2$

53. Suppose $N = 15$ and $r = 4$. What is the probability of $x = 3$ for $n = 10$?

APPLICATIONS

54. According to *Beverage Digest,* February 1993, Coke Classic and Pepsi rank number one and number two in user preference. Assume that in a group of 10 individuals six prefer Coke Classic and four prefer Pepsi. A random sample of three of these individuals is selected.
    a. What is the probability that exactly two prefer Coke Classic?
    b. What is the probability that the majority (either two or three) prefer Pepsi?

55. Blackjack, or twenty-one as it is frequently called, is a popular gambling game played in Las Vegas casinos. A player is dealt two cards. Face cards (jacks, queens, and kings) and tens have a point value of 10. Aces have a point value of 1 or 11. A 52-card deck has 16 cards with a point value of 10 (jacks, queens, kings, and tens) and four aces.
    a. What is the probability that both cards dealt are from the 20 ace and 10-point cards?
    b. What is the probability that both of the cards are aces?
    c. What is the probability that both of the cards have a point value of 10?
    d. A blackjack is a 10-point card and an ace for a value of 21. Use your answers to parts (a), (b), and (c) to determine the probability that a player is dealt blackjack. (Hint: Part (d) is not a hypergeometric problem. Develop your own logical relationship as to how the hypergeometric probabilities from parts (a), (b), and (c) can be combined to answer this question.)

Self-Test

56. Axline Computers manufactures personal computers at two plants, one in Texas and the other in Hawaii. There are 40 employees at the Texas plant and 20 in Hawaii. A random sample of 10 employees is to be asked to fill out a benefits questionnaire.
    a. What is the probability that none are at the plant in Hawaii?
    b. What is the probability that one is at the plant in Hawaii?
    c. What is the probability that two or more are at the plant in Hawaii?
    d. What is the probability that nine are at the plant in Texas?

57. There are 25 students (14 boys and 11 girls) in the sixth-grade class at St. Andrew School. Five students were absent Thursday.
    a. What is the probability that two of the absent students were girls?
    b. What is the probability that two of the absent students were boys?
    c. What is the probability that all were boys?
    d. What is the probability that none were boys?

58. A shipment of 10 items has two defective and eight nondefective units. In the inspection of the shipment, a sample of units will be selected and tested. If a defective unit is found, the shipment of 10 units will be rejected.

    a. If a sample of three items is selected, what is the probability that the shipment will be rejected?

    b. If a sample of four items is selected, what is the probability that the shipment will be rejected?

    c. If a sample of five items is selected, what is the probability that the shipment will be rejected?

    d. If management would like a .90 probability of rejecting a shipment with two defective and eight nondefective units, how large a sample would you recommend?

SUMMARY

The concept of a random variable was introduced to provide a numerical description of the outcome of an experiment. We saw that the probability distribution for a random variable describes how the probabilities are distributed over the values the random variable can assume. For any discrete random variable x, the probability distribution is defined by a probability function, denoted by $f(x)$, which provides the probability associated with each value of the random variable. Once the probability function has been defined, we can compute the expected value and the variance for the random variable.

The binomial probability distribution can be used to determine the probability of x successes in n trials whenever the experiment has the following properties:

    1. The experiment consists of a sequence of n identical trials.

    2. Two outcomes are possible on each trial, one called success and the other failure.

    3. The probability of a success p does not change from trial to trial. Consequently, the probability of failure, $1-p$, does not change from trial to trial.

    4. The trials are independent.

When the four conditions hold, a binomial probability function, or a table of binomial probabilities, can be used to determine the probability of x successes in n trials. Formulas were also presented for the mean and variance of the binomial probability distribution.

The Poisson probability distribution is used when it is desirable to determine the probability of obtaining x occurrences over an interval of time or space. The following assumptions are necessary for the Poisson distribution to be applicable.

    1. The probability of an occurrence of the event is the same for any two intervals of equal length.

    2. The occurrence or nonoccurrence of the event in any interval is independent of the occurrence or nonoccurrence of the event in any other interval.

A third discrete probability distribution, the hypergeometric, was introduced in Section 5.6. Like the binomial, it is used to compute the probability of x successes in n trials. But, in contrast to the binomial, the probability of success changes from trial to trial.

GLOSSARY

Random variable   A numerical description of the outcome of an experiment.

Discrete random variable   A random variable that can assume only a finite or infinite sequence of values.

Continuous random variable   A random variable that may assume any value in an interval or collection of intervals.

Probability distribution   A description of how the probabilities are distributed over the values the random variable can assume.

Probability function   A function, denoted by $f(x)$, that provides the probability that x takes a particular value for a discrete random variable.

Expected value   A measure of the mean, or central location, of a random variable.

Variance   A measure of the dispersion, or variability, of a random variable.

Standard deviation   The positive square root of the variance.

Binomial experiment   A probability experiment having the four properties stated in Section 5.4.

Binomial probability distribution   A probability distribution showing the probability of x successes in n trials of a binomial experiment.

Binomial probability function   The function used to compute probabilities in a binomial experiment.

Poisson probability distribution   A probability distribution showing the probability of x occurrences of an event over a specified interval of time or space.

Poisson probability function   The function used to compute Poisson probabilities.

Hypergeometric probability function   The function used to compute the probability of x successes in n trials when the trials are dependent.

KEY FORMULAS

Expected Value of a Discrete Random Variable

$$E(x) = \mu = \Sigma x f(x) \tag{5.3}$$

Variance of a Discrete Random Variable

$$\text{Var}(x) = \sigma^2 = \Sigma(x - \mu)^2 f(x) \tag{5.4}$$

Number of Experimental Outcomes Providing Exactly x Successes in n Trials

$$\binom{n}{x} = \frac{n!}{x!(n-x)!} \tag{5.5}$$

Binomial Probability Function

$$f(x) = \binom{n}{x} p^x (1 - p)^{(n-x)} \tag{5.8}$$

Expected Value for the Binomial Probability Distribution

$$E(x) = \mu = np \tag{5.9}$$

Variance for the Binomial Probability Distribution

$$\text{Var}(x) = \sigma^2 = np(1 - p) \tag{5.10}$$

Poisson Probability Function

$$f(x) = \frac{\mu^x e^{-\mu}}{x!}$$ (5.11)

Hypergeometric Probability Function

$$f(x) = \frac{\binom{r}{x}\binom{N-r}{n-x}}{\binom{N}{n}} \qquad \text{for } 0 \leq x \leq r$$ (5.12)

SUPPLEMENTARY EXERCISES

59. Which of the following are, and which are not, probability distributions? Explain.

x	f(x)
0	.20
1	.30
2	.25
3	.35

y	f(y)
0	.25
2	.05
4	.10
6	.60

z	f(z)
−1	.20
0	.50
1	−.10
2	.40

TABLE 5.19
Exercise 60

x	f(x)
0	.15
1	.30
2	.40
3	.10
4	.05

60. An automobile agency in Beverly Hills specializes in the rental of luxury automobiles. Assume that the probability distribution of daily demand at the agency is as shown in Table 5.19.
   a. Compute the expected value of daily demand.
   b. If the daily rental cost for an automobile is $75, what is the expected value of daily automobile rental?

61. At a large university, the number of student problems handled by the dean for student affairs varies from semester to semester. Assume that the number of student problems (x) handled by the dean has the probability distribution shown in Table 5.20. What are the mean and variance of the number of student problems handled by the dean each semester?

TABLE 5.20
Exercise 61

x	f(x)
0	.10
1	.15
2	.30
3	.25
4	.10
5	.10

62. The number of weekly lost-time injuries at a particular plant (x) has the probability distribution shown in Table 5.21.
   a. Compute the expected value.
   b. Compute the variance.

63. Assume that the plant in Exercise 62 initiated a safety training program and that the following numbers of lost-time injuries occurred during the 20 weeks after the training program.

TABLE 5.21
Exercise 62

x	f(x)
0	.05
1	.20
2	.40
3	.20
4	.15

Number of Injuries	Number of Weeks
0	2
1	8
2	6
3	3
4	1
Total	20

   a. Construct a probability distribution for weekly lost-time injuries based on these data.
   b. Compute the expected value and the variance and use both to evaluate the effectiveness of the safety training program.

TABLE 5.22 Exercise 64

Price of Stock (x)	$f(x)$
16	.35
17	.25
18	.25
19	.10
20	.05

64. Hub Real Estate Investment stock is currently selling for $16 per share. An investor plans to buy shares and hold the stock for one year. Let x be the random variable indicating the price of the stock after one year. The probability distribution for x is shown in Table 5.22.
   a. Show that the probability distribution in Table 5.22 has the properties of all probability distributions.
   b. What is the expected price of the stock after one year?
   c. What is the expected gain per share of the stock over the one-year period? What percentage return on the investment is reflected by this expected value?
   d. What is the variance in the price of the stock over the one-year period?
   e. Another stock with a similar expected return has a variance of 3. Which stock appears to be the better investment in terms of minimizing risk or uncertainty associated with the investment? Explain.

65. The budgeting process for a midwestern college resulted in expense forecasts for the coming year (in 1,000,000s) of $9, $10, $11, $12, and $13. Since the actual expenses are unknown, the following respective probabilities are assigned: .3, .2, .25, .05, and .2.
   a. Show the probability distribution for the expense forecast.
   b. What is the expected value of the expenses for the coming year?
   c. What is the variance in the expenses for the coming year?
   d. If income projections for the year are estimated at $12 million, comment on the financial position of the college.

66. The probability function for x, the hours needed to change over a production system, follows.

$$f(x) = \frac{x}{10} \qquad \text{for } x = 1, 2, 3, \text{ or } 4$$

   a. What is the expected value of the changeover time?
   b. What is the variance of the changeover time?

67. A study conducted at the University of Southern California investigated the use of music in television commercial messages (*New York,* March 23, 1992). The study found 42% of commercials include music. Consider a sample of 12 commercials.
   a. What is the probability that exactly six of the commercials include music?
   b. What is the probability that exactly three of the commercials include music?
   c. What is the probability that at least three of the commercials include music?

68. A Louis Harris & Associates survey of senior executives revealed that 89% were optimistic about the outlook for the U.S. economy in 1995 (*Business Week,* January 9, 1995). Answer the following questions for a sample of 15 senior executives.
   a. What is the probability that exactly 13 of the senior executives were optimistic about the U.S. economy?
   b. What is the probability that at least 13 of the senior executives were optimistic about the U.S. economy?
   c. What is the probability that exactly three of the senior executives were *not optimistic* about the U.S. economy?

69. On the basis of 1992–1993 regular season NBA basketball games, the probability of a game going into overtime is .06 (*Elias Sports Bureau,* 1993).
   a. For a weekend with 10 games, what is the probability that exactly one game will go into overtime?
   b. For a weekend with 10 games, what is the probability that two or more games will go into overtime?
   c. For 500 games during the season, what is the expected number of games that will go into overtime?

70. A new clothes-washing compound is found to remove excess dirt and stains satisfactorily on 88% of the items washed. Assume that 10 items are to be washed with the new compound.
   a. What is the probability of satisfactory results on all 10 items?
   b. What is the probability of at least two items being found with unsatisfactory results?

71. According to the *1994 Statistical Abstract of the United States,* 42% of all households have guns. Assume a random selection of 10 households. What is the probability that:
  a. Exactly four households have guns.
  b. No households have guns.
  c. Eight or more households have guns.

72. Many companies use a quality-control technique called *acceptance sampling* to monitor incoming shipments of parts, raw materials, and so on. In the electronics industry, component parts are commonly shipped from suppliers in large lots. Inspection of a sample of *n* components can be viewed as the *n* trials of a binomial experiment. The outcome for each component tested (trial) will be that the component is good or defective. Reynolds Electronics accepts a lot from a particular supplier if the defective components in the lot do not exceed 1%. Suppose a random sample of five items from a recent shipment has been tested.
  a. Assume that 1% of the shipment is defective. Compute the probability that no items in the sample are defective.
  b. Assume that 1% of the shipment is defective. Compute the probability that exactly one item in the sample is defective.
  c. What is the probability of observing one or more defective items in the sample if 1% of the shipment is defective?
  d. Would you feel comfortable accepting the shipment if one item were found to be defective? Why or why not?

73. Cars arrive at a car wash randomly and independently; the probability of an arrival is the same for any two time intervals of equal length. The mean arrival rate is 15 cars per hour. What is the probability that 20 or more cars will arrive during any given hour of operation?

74. A new automated production process has had an average of 1.5 breakdowns per day. Because of the cost associated with a breakdown, management is concerned about the possibility of having three or more breakdowns during a day. Assume that breakdowns occur randomly, that the probability of a breakdown is the same for any two time intervals of equal length, and that breakdowns in one period are independent of breakdowns in other periods. What is the probability of having three or more breakdowns during a day?

75. A regional director responsible for business development in the state of Pennsylvania is concerned about the number of small business failures. If the mean number of small business failures per month is 10, what is the probability that exactly four small businesses will fail during a given month? Assume that the probability of a failure is the same for any two months and that the occurrence or nonoccurrence of a failure in any month is independent of failures in any other month.

76. Customer arrivals at a bank are random and independent; the probability of an arrival in any one-minute period is the same as the probability of an arrival in any other one-minute period. Answer the following questions, assuming a mean arrival rate of three customers per minute.
  a. What is the probability of exactly three arrivals in a one-minute period?
  b. What is the probability of at least three arrivals in a one-minute period?

77. Most people are familiar with the game of five-card draw poker. With 52 cards and four aces, what is the probability that the deal of the five cards provides:
  a. A pair of aces?
  b. Exactly one ace?
  c. No aces?
  d. At least one ace?

78. According to the WTA Tour and ATP Tour, four of the top 10 women tennis players use Wilson rackets (*USA Today,* March 2, 1995). Suppose two of these players have reached the finals of a tournament.
  a. What is the probability that exactly one uses a Wilson racket?
  b. What is the probability that both use Wilson rackets?
  c. What is the probability that neither uses a Wilson racket?

APPENDIX 5.1

Discrete Probability Distributions with Minitab

● Statistical packages such as Minitab offer a relatively easy and efficient procedure for computing binomial probabilities. In this appendix, we show the step-by-step procedure for determining the binomial probabilities for the Martin Clothing Store problem in Section 5.4. Recall that the desired binomial probability is based on $n = 10$, $x = 4$, and $p = .30$. Before beginning the Minitab routine, the user must enter the desired values of the random variable x into a column of the worksheet. We entered the values 0, 1, 2, . . . 10 in column 1 (see Figure 5.5) to generate the entire binomial probability distribution. The Minitab steps to obtain the desired binomial probabilities follow.

Step 1. Select the **Calc** pull-down menu.
Step 2. Select the **Probability Distributions** pull-down menu.
Step 3. Select the **Binomial** option.
Step 4. When the dialog box appears:
Enter 10 in the **Number of trials** box,
Enter .3 in the **Probability of success** box, and
Enter C1 in the **Input column** box.
Select **OK** to produce the binomial probabilities.

The Minitab output with the binomial probabilities is shown in Figure 5.5.

Minitab provides Poisson probabilities in a very similar manner. The only differences are in Step 3, where the Poisson option would be selected, and step 4, where the **Mean** would be entered rather than the number of trials and the probability of success.

APPENDIX 5.2

Discrete Probability Distributions with Spreadsheets

● Excel has the capability of computing probabilities for several discrete probability distributions including the binomial, Poisson, and hypergeometric. In this appendix, we describe how Excel can be used to compute the probabilities for any binomial probability distribution. The procedures for the Poisson and hypergeometric probability distributions are similar to the one we describe for the binomial probability distribution.

Let us return to the Martin Clothing Store problem, where the binomial probabilities of interest are based on a binomial experiment with $n = 10$ and $p = .30$. Let us assume that the user is interested in the probability of $x = 4$ successes in the 10 trials. The following steps describe how to use Excel to produce the desired binomial probability.

Step 1. Select a cell in the worksheet where you want the binomial probability to appear.
Step 2. Select the **Insert** pull-down menu.
Step 3. Choose the **Function** option.

Step 4. When the Function Wizard–Step 1 of 2 dialog box appears:
Choose **Statistical** from the **Function Category** box,
Choose **BINOMDIST** from the **Function Name** box,
Select **Next>**.

Step 5. When the Function Wizard–Step 2 of 2 dialog box appears:
Enter 4 in the **numbers** box (the value of x),
Enter 10 in the **trials** box (the value of n),
Enter .30 in the **probability** box (the value of p), and
Enter false in the **cumulative** box.[1]

Note: At this point the desired binomial probability of .2001 is automatically computed and appears in the **Value** box in the upper right corner of the dialog box.

Select **Finish** and the binomial probability will appear in the worksheet cell requested in Step 1.

If the user wants other binomial probabilities, there are ways of obtaining the information without repeating the steps for each probability desired. Perhaps the easiest alternative is to stay in step 5. After the four entries have been made and the first probability appears in the value box, simply return to the numbers box and insert a new value of x. The new probability will appear in the value box. Repeated changes can be made in the dialog box, including changes to the trials, probability, and/or cumulative boxes. For each change, the desired probability will appear in the value box. When Finish is selected, only the last binomial probability will be placed in the worksheet.

If the user wants to insert multiple binomial probabilities into the worksheet, the desired values of x should be entered into the worksheet first. Then, in step 5, the user must enter the cell location of one of the values of x in the numbers box. After completing the steps for one binomial probability, individuals experienced with Excel can use Excel's Copy command to copy the binomial function into the cells where the other binomial probabilities are to appear.

The Excel procedure for generating Poisson and hypergeometric probabilities is similar to the procedure described above. Step 4 can be used to select either the POISSON or HYPGEOMDIST function name. The dialog box in step 5 will guide the user through the input values required to compute the desired probabilities.

---

[1]Placing false in the cumulative box provides the probability of exactly four successes. Placing true in this box provides the cumulative probability of four *or fewer* successes.

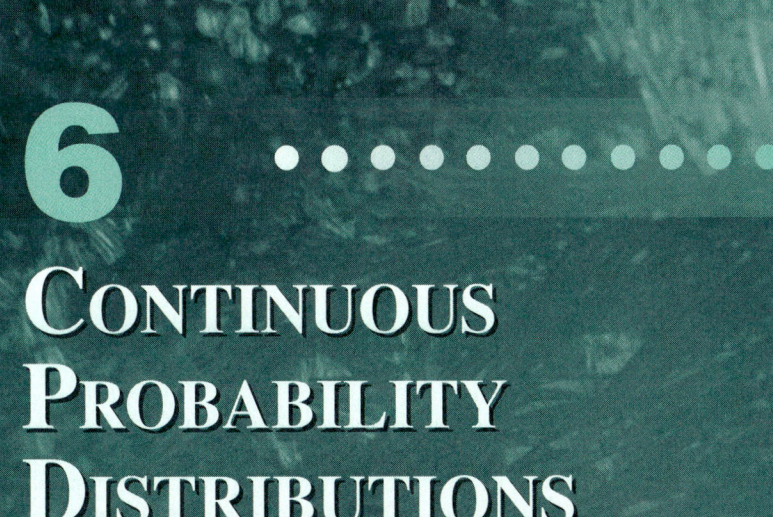

6

CONTINUOUS PROBABILITY DISTRIBUTIONS

CONTENTS

STATISTICS IN PRACTICE

P&G

Procter & Gamble*

Cincinnati, Ohio

Procter & Gamble (P&G) is in the consumer-products business worldwide. P&G produces and markets such products as detergents, disposable diapers, over-the-counter pharmaceuticals, dentifrices, bar soaps, mouthwashes, and paper towels. It has the leading brand in more categories than any other consumer products company.

As a leader in the application of statistical methods to decision making, P&G employs people with diverse academic backgrounds: engineering, statistics, operations research, and business. The major quantitative technologies for which these people provide support are probabilistic decision and risk analysis, advanced simulation, quality improvement, and quantitative methods (e.g., linear programming, regression analysis, probability analysis).

The Industrial Chemicals Division of P&G is a major supplier of fatty alcohols derived from natural substances such as coconut oil and from petroleum-based derivatives. The division wanted to know the economic risks and opportunities of expanding its fatty-alcohol production facilities, and P&G's experts in probabilistic decision and risk analysis were called in to help. After structuring and modeling the problem, they determined that the key to profitability was the cost difference between the petroleum- and coconut-based raw materials. Future costs were unknown, but the analysts were able to represent them with the following continuous random variables.

x = the coconut oil price per pound of fatty alcohol

and

y = the petroleum raw material price per pound of fatty alcohol

Since the key to profitability was the difference between these two random variables, a third random variable, $d = x - y$, was used in the analysis. Experts were interviewed to determine the probability distribution for x and y. In turn, this information was used to develop a continuous probability distribution for the difference d. The continuous probability distribution showed that there was a .90 probability that the price difference would be $.0655 or less and that there was a .50 probability that the price difference would be $.035 or less. In addition, there was only a .10 probability that the price difference would be $.0045 or less.[†]

The Industrial Chemicals Division thought that being able to quantify the impact of raw material price differences was key to reaching a consensus. The probabilities obtained were used in a sensitivity analysis of the raw material price difference. The analysis yielded sufficient insight to form the basis for a recommendation to management.

The use of continuous random variables and their probability distributions was helpful to P&G in analyzing the economic risks associated with its fatty-alcohol production. In this chapter, you will gain an understanding of continuous random variables and their probability distributions including one of the most important probability distributions in statistics, the normal distribution.

Two of Procter & Gamble's many well-known products.

---

*The authors are indebted to Mr. Joel Kahn of Procter & Gamble for providing this Statistics in Practice.

[†] The price differences stated here have been modified to protect proprietary data.

● In the preceding chapter we discussed discrete random variables and their probability distributions. In this chapter we turn to the study of continuous random variables. Specifically, we discuss three continuous probability distributions: the uniform, the normal, and the exponential.

To understand the difference between discrete and continuous random variables, first recall that for a discrete random variable we can compute the probability of the random variable assuming a particular value. For continuous random variables, the situation is much different. A continuous random variable may assume any value in an interval on the real line or in a collection of intervals. Since any interval contains an infinite number of values, it is not possible to talk about the probability that the random variable will assume a specific value; instead, we must think in terms of the probability that a continuous random variable will assume a value within a given interval.

In the discussion of discrete probability distributions, we introduced the concept of a probability function $f(x)$. Recall that this function provides the probability that the random variable x assumes some specific value. In the continuous case, the counterpart of the probability function is the *probability density function,* also denoted by $f(x)$. For a continuous random variable, the probability density function provides the value of the function at any particular value of x; it does not directly provide the probability of the random variable assuming some specific value. However, the area under the graph of $f(x)$ corresponding to a given interval provides the probability that the continuous random variable will assume a value in that interval. In Section 6.1 we demonstrate these concepts for a continuous random variable that has a uniform probability distribution.

Much of the chapter is devoted to describing and showing applications of the normal probability distribution. The normal probability distribution is of major importance; it is used extensively in statistical inference. The normal distribution can also be used as an approximation to the discrete binomial distribution, as we show in Section 6.3. The chapter closes with a discussion of the exponential probability distribution.

6.1   THE UNIFORM PROBABILITY DISTRIBUTION

Consider the random variable x that represents the flight time of an airplane traveling from Chicago to New York. Suppose the flight time can be any value in the interval from 120 minutes to 140 minutes. Since the random variable x can assume any value in that interval, x is a continuous rather than a discrete random variable. Let us assume that sufficient actual flight data are available to conclude that the probability of a flight time within any one-minute interval is the same as the probability of a flight time within any other one-minute interval from 120 to 140 minutes. With every one-minute interval being equally likely, the random variable x is said to have a *uniform probability distribution.* The *probability density function,* which defines the uniform probability distribution for the flight time random variable, is

$$f(x) = \begin{cases} \frac{1}{20} & \text{for } 120 \leq x \leq 140 \\ \\ 0 & \text{elsewhere} \end{cases}$$

Figure 6.1 is a graph of this probability density function. In general, the uniform probability density function for a random variable x is found by using the following formula.

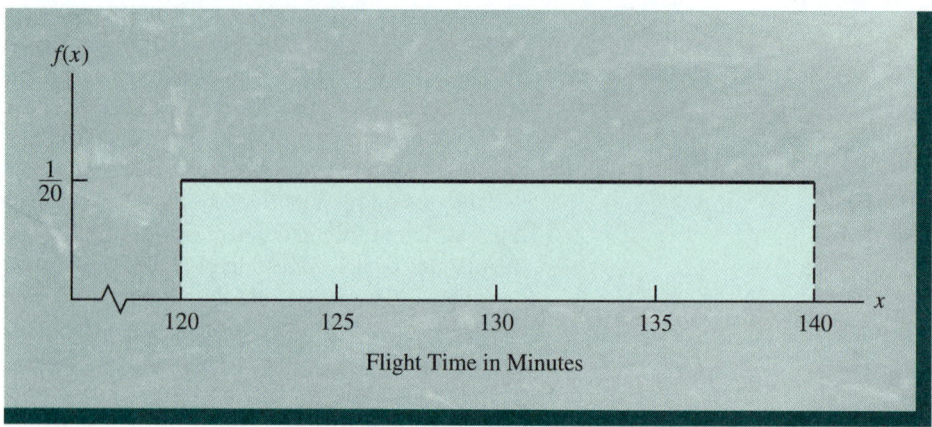

FIGURE 6.1   Uniform Probability Density Function for Flight Time

UNIFORM PROBABILITY DENSITY FUNCTION

$$f(x) = \begin{cases} \dfrac{1}{b-a} & \text{for } a \le x \le b \\\\ 0 & \text{elsewhere} \end{cases}$$ (6.1)

In the flight-time example, $a = 120$ and $b = 140$.

The graph of the probability density function $f(x)$ provides the height or value of the function at any particular value of x. Note that for a *uniform* probability density function, the height of the function is the same for each value of x. For example, in the flight-time example, $f(x) = \frac{1}{20}$ for all values of x between 120 and 140. In general, the probability density function $f(x)$, unlike the probability function for a discrete random variable, *does not represent probability*. Rather, it simply provides *the height of the function at any particular value of x.*

For a continuous random variable, we consider probability only in terms of the likelihood that a random variable has a value within a *specified interval.* In the flight-time example, an acceptable probability question is: What is the probability that the flight time is between 120 and 130 minutes? That is, what is $P(120 \le x \le 130)$? Since the flight time must be between 120 and 140 minutes and since the probability is described as being uniform over this interval, we feel comfortable saying $P(120 \le x \le 130) = .50$. In the following subsection we show that this probability can be computed as the area under the graph of $f(x)$ from 120 to 130.

AREA AS A MEASURE OF PROBABILITY

Let us make an observation about the graph in Figure 6.2. Consider the *area* under the graph of $f(x)$ in the interval from 120 to 130. The region is rectangular, and the area of a rectangle is simply the width multiplied by the height. With the width of the interval equal to $130 - 120 = 10$ and the height equal to the value of the probability density function $f(x) = \frac{1}{20}$, we have area = width × height = $10(\frac{1}{20}) = \frac{10}{20} = .50$.

What observation can you make about the area under the graph of $f(x)$ and probability? They are identical! Indeed, this is true for all continuous random variables. Once a probability density function $f(x)$ has been identified, the probability that x takes

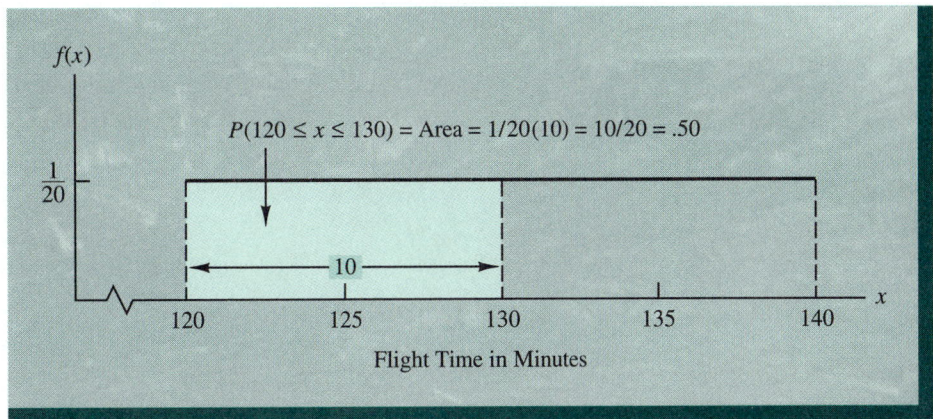

$$P(120 \leq x \leq 130) = \text{Area} = 1/20(10) = 10/20 = .50$$

Flight Time in Minutes

FIGURE 6.2 Area Provides Probability of Flight Time between 120 and 130 Minutes

a value between some lower value x_1 and some higher value x_2 can be found by computing the *area* under the graph of $f(x)$ over the interval x_1 to x_2.

Once we have the appropriate probability distribution and accept the interpretation of area as probability, we can answer any number of probability questions. For example, what is the probability of a flight time between 128 and 136 minutes? The width of the interval is $136 - 128 = 8$. With the uniform height of $1/20$, we see that $P(128 \leq x \leq 136) = 8(1/20) = .40$.

Note that $P(120 \leq x \leq 140) = 20(1/20) = 1$. That is, the total area under the graph of $f(x)$ is equal to 1. This property holds for all continuous probability distributions and is the analog of the condition that the sum of the probabilities must equal 1 for a discrete probability function. For a continuous probability density function, we must also require that $f(x) \geq 0$ for all values of x. This is the analog of the requirement that $f(x) \geq 0$ for discrete probability functions.

Two major differences stand out between the treatment of continuous random variables and the treatment of their discrete counterparts.

1. We no longer talk about the probability of the random variable assuming a particular value. Instead, we talk about the probability of the random variable assuming a value within some given interval.

2. The probability of the random variable assuming a value within some given interval from x_1 to x_2 is defined to be the area under the graph of the probability density function between x_1 and x_2. *This implies that the probability that a continuous random variable assumes any particular value exactly is zero, since the area under the graph of $f(x)$ at a single point is zero.*

The calculation of the expected value and variance for a continuous random variable is analogous to that for a discrete random variable. However, since the computational procedure involves integral calculus, we leave the derivation of the appropriate formulas to more advanced texts.

For the uniform continuous probability distribution introduced in this section, the formulas for the expected value and variance are

$$E(x) = \frac{a + b}{2}$$

$$\text{Var}(x) = \frac{(b - a)^2}{12}$$

In these formulas, a is the smallest value and b is the largest value that the random variable may assume.

Applying these formulas to the uniform probability distribution for flight times from Chicago to New York, we obtain

$$E(x) = \frac{(120 + 140)}{2} = 130$$

$$\text{Var}(x) = \frac{(140 - 120)^2}{12} = 33.33$$

The standard deviation of flight times can be found by taking the square root of the variance. Thus, $\sigma = 5.77$ minutes.

NOTES AND COMMENTS

1. Since for a continuous random variable the probability of any particular value is zero, we have $P(a \leq x \leq b) = P(a < x < b)$. This equation shows that the probability of a random variable assuming a value in any interval is the same whether or not the endpoints are included.

2. To see more clearly why the height of a probability density function is not a probability, think about a random variable with the following uniform probability distribution.

$$f(x) = \begin{cases} 2 & \text{for } 0 \leq x \leq .5 \\ 0 & \text{elsewhere} \end{cases}$$

The height of the probability density function is 2 for values of x between 0 and .5. However, we know probabilities can never be greater than 1.

EXERCISES

METHODS

Self-Test

1. The random variable x is known to be uniformly distributed between 1.0 and 1.5.
   a. Show the graph of the probability density function.
   b. Find $P(x = 1.25)$.
   c. Find $P(1.0 \leq x \leq 1.25)$.
   d. Find $P(1.20 < x < 1.5)$.

2. The random variable x is known to be uniformly distributed between 10 and 20.
   a. Show the graph of the probability density function.
   b. Find $P(x < 15)$.
   c. Find $P(12 \leq x \leq 18)$.
   d. Find $E(x)$.
   e. Find $\text{Var}(x)$.

APPLICATIONS

3. Delta Airlines quotes a flight time of 1 hour, 52 minutes for its flights from Cincinnati to Tampa. Suppose we believe that actual flight times are uniformly distributed between the quoted time and 2 hours, 10 minutes.

a. Show the graph of the probability density function for flight times.
b. What is the probability that the flight will be no more than five minutes late?
c. What is the probability that the flight will be more than 10 minutes late?
d. What is the expected flight time?

Self-Test ....▶

4. Most computer languages have a function that can be used to generate random numbers. In Microsoft's QuickBASIC, the RND function can be used to generate random numbers between 0 and 1. If we let x denote the random number generated, then x is a continuous random variable with the following probability density function.

$$f(x) = \begin{cases} 1 & \text{for } 0 \le x \le 1 \\ 0 & \text{elsewhere} \end{cases}$$

a. Graph the probability density function.
b. What is the probability of generating a random number between .25 and .75?
c. What is the probability of generating a random number with a value less than or equal to .30?
d. What is the probability of generating a random number with a value greater than .60?

5. The driving distance for the top golfers on the PGA tour is between 270 and 280 yards (*Golf World*, March 25, 1994). Assume a particular golfer routinely hits drives in this range and that the distance is uniform over the interval from 270 to 280 yards.
a. Give a mathematical expression for the probability density function.
b. What is the probability that the driving distance will be less than 274 yards?
c. What is the probability that the driving distance will be between 272 and 277 yards?

6. The label on a bottle of liquid detergent shows contents to be 12 ounces per bottle. The production operation fills the bottle uniformly according to the following probability density function.

$$f(x) = \begin{cases} 8 & \text{for } 11.975 \le x \le 12.10 \\ 0 & \text{elsewhere} \end{cases}$$

a. What is the probability that a bottle will be filled with between 12 and 12.05 ounces?
b. What is the probability that a bottle will be filled with 12.02 or more ounces?
c. Quality control accepts production that is within .02 ounces of the number of ounces shown on the container label. What is the probability that a bottle of this liquid detergent will fail to meet the quality control standard?

7. Suppose we are interested in bidding on a piece of land and we know there is one other bidder.* The seller has announced that the highest bid in excess of $10,000 will be accepted. Assume that the competitor's bid x is a random variable that is uniformly distributed between $10,000 and $15,000.
a. Suppose you bid $12,000. What is the probability that your bid will be accepted?
b. Suppose you bid $14,000. What is the probability that your bid will be accepted?
c. What amount should you bid to maximize the probability that you get the property?
d. Suppose you know someone who is willing to pay you $16,000 for the property. Would you consider bidding less than the amount in (c)? Why or why not?

---

*This exercise is based on a problem suggested to us by Professor Roger Myerson of Northwestern University.

6.2   THE NORMAL PROBABILITY DISTRIBUTION

Perhaps the most important probability distribution for describing a continuous random variable is the *normal probability distribution.* The normal probability distribution has been used in a wide variety of practical applications in which the random variables are heights and weights of people, IQ scores, scientific measurements, amounts of rainfall, and so on. Use of this probability distribution requires that the random variable be continuous. However, as we shall see in Section 6.3, a continuous normal random variable can be used as an approximation in situations involving discrete random variables.

THE NORMAL CURVE

The form, or shape, of the normal probability distribution is illustrated by the bell-shaped curve in Figure 6.3. The probability density function that defines the bell-shaped curve of the normal probability distribution follows.

NORMAL PROBABILITY DENSITY FUNCTION

$$f(x) = \frac{1}{\sqrt{2\pi}\,\sigma}\, e^{-(x-\mu)^2/2\sigma^2} \tag{6.2}$$

where

$$\mu = \text{mean}$$
$$\sigma = \text{standard deviation}$$
$$\pi = 3.14159$$
$$e = 2.71828$$

We make some observations about the characteristics of the normal probability distribution.

1. There is an entire family of normal probability distributions, with each specific normal distribution being differentiated by its mean μ and its standard deviation σ.

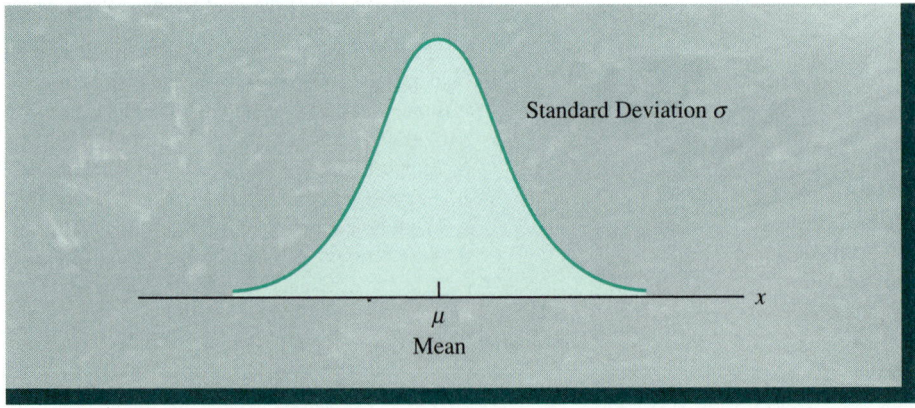

FIGURE 6.3   Bell-Shaped Curve for the Normal Probability Distribution

2. The highest point on the normal curve is at the mean, which is also the median and mode of the distribution.

3. The mean of the distribution can be any numerical value: negative, zero, or positive. Three normal curves with the same standard deviation but three different means (−10, 0, and 20) are shown below.

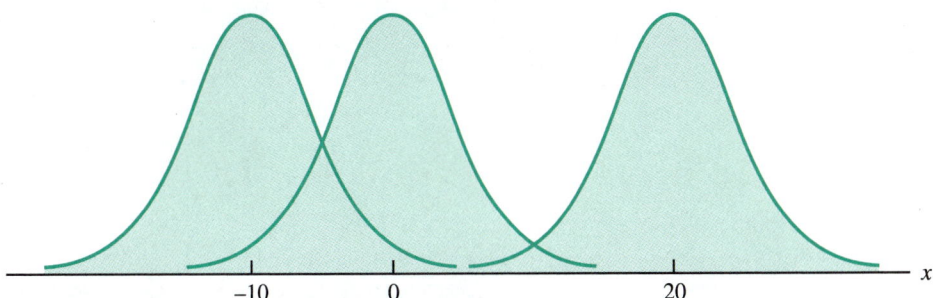

4. The normal probability distribution is symmetric, with the shape of the curve to the left of the mean a mirror image of the shape of the curve to the right of the mean. The tails of the curve extend to infinity in both directions and theoretically never touch the horizontal axis.

5. The standard deviation determines the width of the curve. Larger values of the standard deviation result in wider, flatter curves, showing more dispersion in the data. Two normal distributions with the same mean but with different standard deviations are shown below.

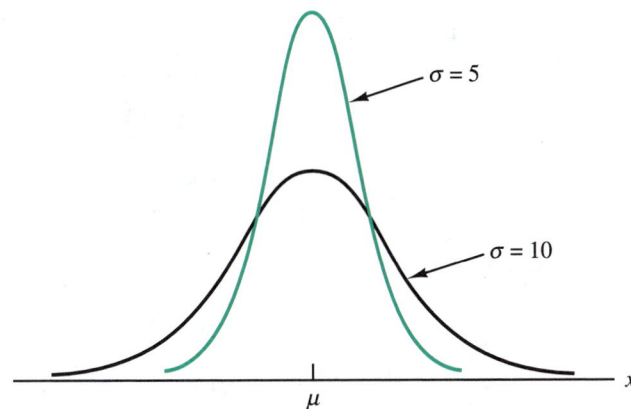

6. The total area under the curve for the normal probability distribution is 1. (This is true for all continuous probability distributions.)

7. Probabilities for the normal random variable are given by areas under the curve. Probabilities for some commonly used intervals are:

   a. 68.26% of the time, a normal random variable assumes a value within plus or minus one standard deviation of its mean.

   b. 95.44% of the time, a normal random variable assumes a value within plus or minus two standard deviations of its mean.

   c. 99.72% of the time, a normal random variable assumes a value within plus or minus three standard deviations of its mean. Figure 6.4 shows properties (a), (b), and (c) graphically.

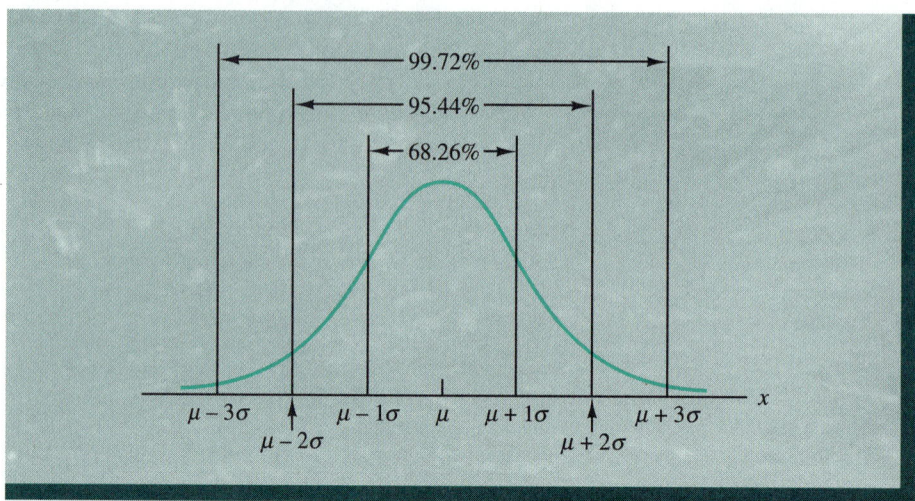

FIGURE 6.4   Areas under the Curve for Any Normal Probability Distribution

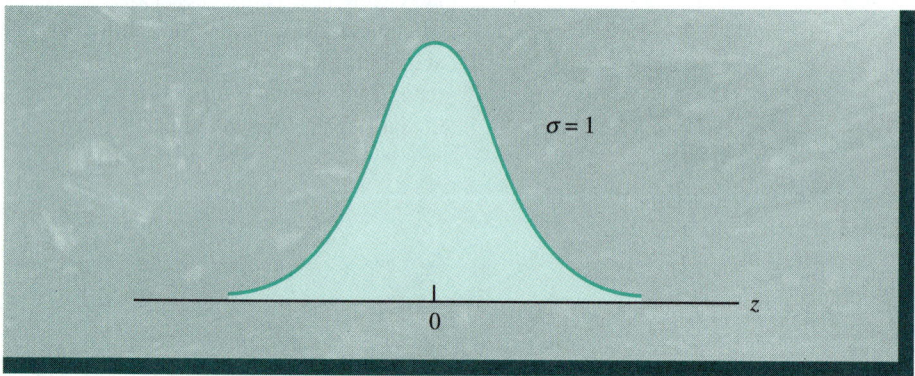

FIGURE 6.5   The Standard Normal Probability Distribution

THE STANDARD NORMAL PROBABILITY DISTRIBUTION

A random variable that has a normal distribution with a mean of zero and a standard deviation of one is said to have a *standard normal probability distribution*. The letter z is commonly used to designate this particular normal random variable. Figure 6.5 is the graph of the standard normal probability distribution. It has the same general appearance as other normal distributions, but with the special properties of $\mu = 0$ and $\sigma = 1$.

As with other continuous random variables, probability calculations with any normal probability distribution are made by computing areas under the graph of the probability density function. Thus, to find the probability that a normal random variable is within any specific interval, we must compute the area under the normal curve over that interval. For the standard normal probability distribution, areas under the normal curve have been computed and are available in tables that can be used in computing probabilities. Table 6.1 on p. 208 is such a table; it is also available as Table 1 of Appendix B and inside the front cover of this text.

To see how the table of areas under the curve for the standard normal probability distribution (Table 6.1) can be used to find probabilities, let us consider some examples. Later, we will see how this same table can be used to compute probabilities for any normal distribution. To begin, let us see how we can compute the probability that the z value for the standard normal random variable will be between .00 and 1.00, that is, $P(.00 \leq z \leq 1.00)$. The shaded region in the following graph shows this area or probability.

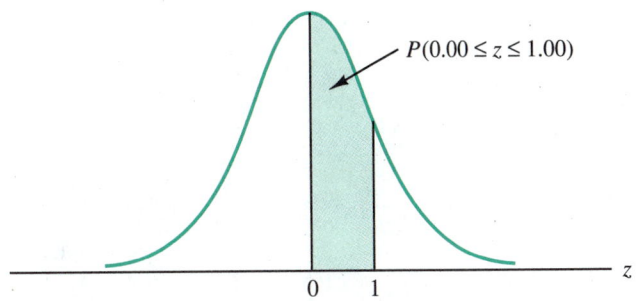

$P(0.00 \leq z \leq 1.00)$

The entries in Table 6.1 give the area under the standard normal curve between the mean, $z = 0$, and a specified positive value of z (see the graph at the top of the table). In this case we are interested in the area between $z = 0$ and $z = 1.00$. Thus, we must find the entry in the table corresponding to $z = 1.00$. To do this, we first find 1.0 in the left column of the table and then find .00 in the top row of the table. By looking in the body of the table, we find that the 1.0 row and the .00 column intersect at the value of .3413. We have found the desired probability: $P(.00 \leq z \leq 1.00) = .3413$. A portion of Table 6.1 showing these steps follows.

z	.00	.01	.02
.			
.			
.			
.9	.3159	.3186	.3212
1.0	.3413	.3438	.3461
1.1	.3643	.3665	.3686
1.2	.3849	.3869	.3888
.			
.			
.			

$P(.00 \leq z \leq 1.00)$

Using the same approach, we can find $P(.00 \leq z \leq 1.25)$. By first locating the 1.2 row and then moving across to the .05 column, we find $P(.00 \leq z \leq 1.25) = .3944$.

As another example of the use of the table of areas for the standard normal distribution, we compute the probability of obtaining a z value between $z = -1.00$ and $z = 1.00$; that is, $P(-1.00 \leq z \leq 1.00)$.

Note that we have already used Table 6.1 to show that the probability of a z value between $z = .00$ and $z = 1.00$ is .3413, and recall that the normal probability distribution

TABLE 6.1   Areas, or Probabilities, for the Standard Normal Distribution

z	.00	.01	.02	.03	.04	.05	.06	.07	.08	.09
.0	.0000	.0040	.0080	.0120	.0160	.0199	.0239	.0279	.0319	.0359
.1	.0398	.0438	.0478	.0517	.0557	.0596	.0636	.0675	.0714	.0753
.2	.0793	.0832	.0871	.0910	.0948	.0987	.1026	.1064	.1103	.1141
.3	.1179	.1217	.1255	.1293	.1331	.1368	.1406	.1443	.1480	.1517
.4	.1554	.1591	.1628	.1664	.1700	.1736	.1772	.1808	.1844	.1879
.5	.1915	.1950	.1985	.2019	.2054	.2088	.2123	.2157	.2190	.2224
.6	.2257	.2291	.2324	.2357	.2389	.2422	.2454	.2486	.2518	.2549
.7	.2580	.2612	.2642	.2673	.2704	.2734	.2764	.2794	.2823	.2852
.8	.2881	.2910	.2939	.2967	.2995	.3023	.3051	.3078	.3106	.3133
.9	.3159	.3186	.3212	.3238	.3264	.3289	.3315	.3340	.3365	.3389
1.0	.3413	.3438	.3461	.3485	.3508	.3531	.3554	.3577	.3599	.3621
1.1	.3643	.3665	.3686	.3708	.3729	.3749	.3770	.3790	.3810	.3830
1.2	.3849	.3869	.3888	.3907	.3925	.3944	.3962	.3980	.3997	.4015
1.3	.4032	.4049	.4066	.4082	.4099	.4115	.4131	.4147	.4162	.4177
1.4	.4192	.4207	.4222	.4236	.4251	.4265	.4279	.4292	.4306	.4319
1.5	.4332	.4345	.4357	.4370	.4382	.4394	.4406	.4418	.4429	.4441
1.6	.4452	.4463	.4474	.4484	.4495	.4505	.4515	.4525	.4535	.4545
1.7	.4554	.4564	.4573	.4582	.4591	.4599	.4608	.4616	.4625	.4633
1.8	.4641	.4649	.4656	.4664	.4671	.4678	.4686	.4693	.4699	.4706
1.9	.4713	.4719	.4726	.4732	.4738	.4744	.4750	.4756	.4761	.4767
2.0	.4772	.4778	.4783	.4788	.4793	.4798	.4803	.4808	.4812	.4817
2.1	.4821	.4826	.4830	.4834	.4838	.4842	.4846	.4850	.4854	.4857
2.2	.4861	.4864	.4868	.4871	.4875	.4878	.4881	.4884	.4887	.4890
2.3	.4893	.4896	.4898	.4901	.4904	.4906	.4909	.4911	.4913	.4916
2.4	.4918	.4920	.4922	.4925	.4927	.4929	.4931	.4932	.4934	.4936
2.5	.4938	.4940	.4941	.4943	.4945	.4946	.4948	.4949	.4951	.4952
2.6	.4953	.4955	.4956	.4957	.4959	.4960	.4961	.4962	.4963	.4964
2.7	.4965	.4966	.4967	.4968	.4969	.4970	.4971	.4972	.4973	.4974
2.8	.4974	.4975	.4976	.4977	.4977	.4978	.4979	.4979	.4980	.4981
2.9	.4981	.4982	.4982	.4983	.4984	.4984	.4985	.4985	.4986	.4986
3.0	.4986	.4987	.4987	.4988	.4988	.4989	.4989	.4989	.4990	.4990

is *symmetric*. Thus, the probability of a z value between $z = .00$ and $z = -1.00$ is the *same* as the probability of a z value between $z = .00$ and $z = +1.00$. Hence, the probability of a z value between $z = -1.00$ and $z = +1.00$ is

$$P(-1.00 \leq z \leq .00) + P(.00 \leq z \leq 1.00) = .3413 + .3413 = .6826.$$

This area is shown graphically in the following figure.

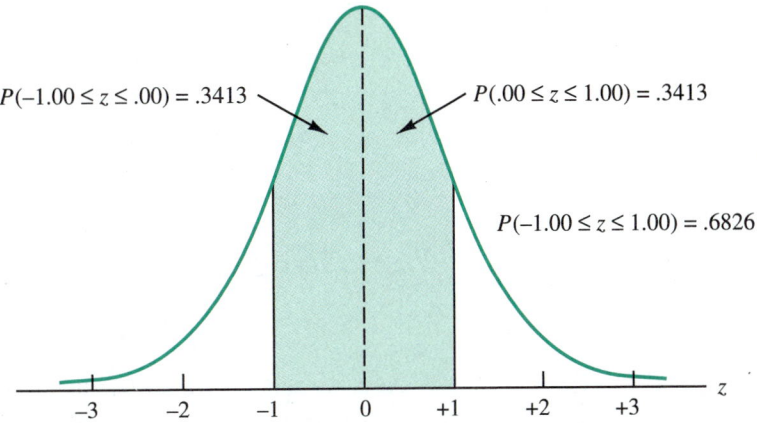

In a similar manner, we ca n use the values in Table 6.1 to show that the probability of a z value between -2.00 and $+2.00$ is $.4772 + .4772 = .9544$ and that the probability of a z value between -3.00 and $+3.00$ is $.4986 + .4986 = .9972$. Since we know that the total probability or total area under the curve for any continuous random variable must be 1.0000, the probability $.9972$ tells us that the value of z will almost always be between -3.00 and $+3.00$.

Next, we compute the probability of obtaining a z value of at least 1.58; that is, $P(z \geq 1.58)$. First, we use the $z = 1.5$ row and the $.08$ column of Table 6.1 to find that $P(.00 \leq z \leq 1.58) = .4429$. Now, since the normal probability distribution is symmetric and the total area under the curve equals 1, we know that 50% of the area must be above the mean (i.e., $z = 0$) and 50% of the area must be below the mean. Since $.4429$ is the area between the mean and $z = 1.58$, the area or probability corresponding to $z \geq 1.58$ must be $.5000 - .4429 = .0571$. This probability is shown in the following figure.

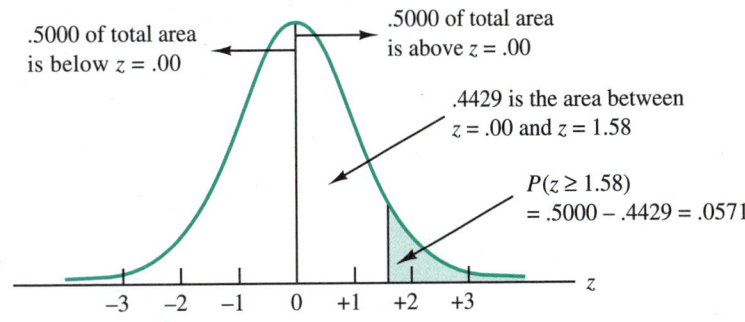

As another illustration, consider the probability that the random variable z assumes a value of $-.50$ or larger; that is, $P(z \geq -.50)$. To make this computation, we note that the probability we are seeking can be written as the sum of two probabilities: $P(z \geq -.50) = P(-.50 \leq z \leq .00) + P(z \geq 0.00)$. We have previously seen that $P(z \geq .00) = .50$. Also, we know that, since the normal distribution is symmetric, $P(-.50 \leq z \leq .00) = P(.00 \leq z \leq .50)$. Referring to Table 6.1, we find that $P(.00 \leq z \leq .50) = .1915$. Therefore $P(z \geq -.50) = .1915 + .5000 = .6915$. The following graph shows this area.

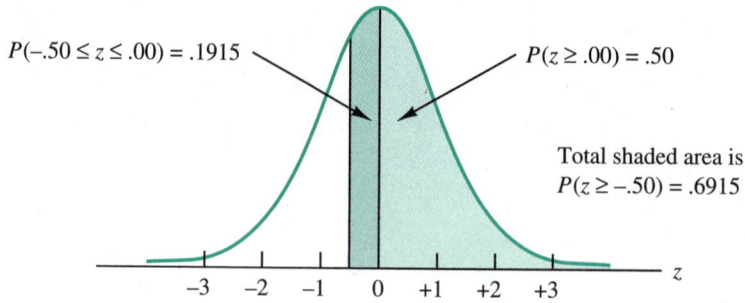

Next, we compute the probability of obtaining a z value between 1.00 and 1.58; that is, $P(1.00 \leq z \leq 1.58)$. From our previous examples, we know that there is a .3413 probability of a z value between $z = 0.00$ and $z = 1.00$ and that there is a .4429 probability of a z value between $z = 0.00$ and $z = 1.58$. Hence, there must be a .4429 − .3413 = .1016 probability of a z value between $z = 1.00$ and $z = 1.58$. Thus, $P(1.00 \leq z \leq 1.58) = .1016$. This situation is shown graphically in the following figure.

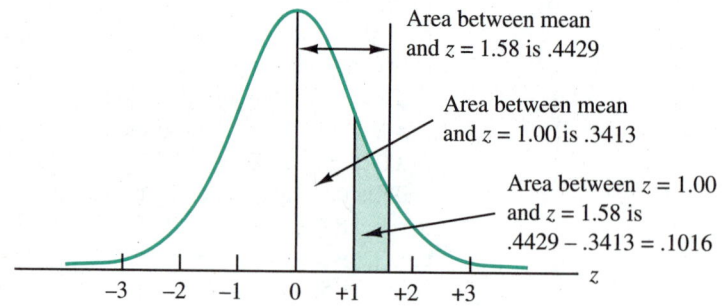

As a final illustration, let us find a z value such that the probability of obtaining a larger z value is only .10. The following figure shows this situation graphically.

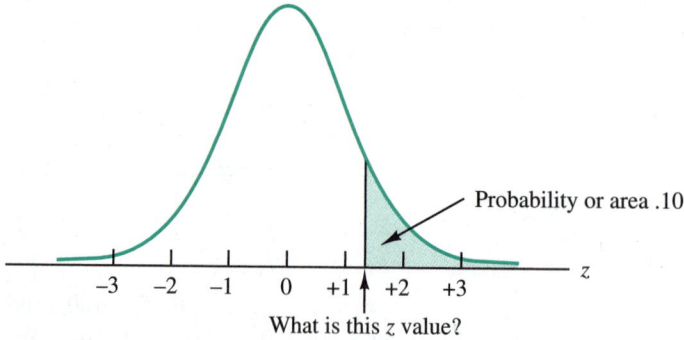

This problem is the reverse of the preceding examples. Previously we specified the z value of interest and then found the corresponding probability, or area. In this example, we are given the probability, or area, and asked to find the corresponding z value. To do so we use the table of areas for the standard normal probability distribution (Table 6.1) somewhat differently.

Recall that the body of Table 6.1 gives the area under the curve between the mean and a particular z value. We have been given the information that the area in the upper tail of the curve is .10. Hence, we must determine how much of the area is between the mean and the z value of interest. Since we know .5000 of the area is above the mean, .5000 − .1000 = .4000 must be the area under the curve *between* the mean and the desired z value. Scanning the body of the table, we find .3997 as the probability value closest to .4000. The section of the table providing this result follows.

z	.06	.07	.08	.09
.				
.				
.				
1.0	.3554	.3577	.3599	.3621
1.1	.3770	.3790	3810	.3830
1.2	.3962	.3980	.3997	.4015
1.3	.4131	.4147	.4162	.4177
1.4	.4279	.4292	.4306	.4319
.				
.	Area value in body			
	of table closest to .4000			

Reading the z value from the left column and the top row of the table, we find that the corresponding z value is 1.28. Thus, there will be an area of approximately .4000 (actually .3997) between the mean and $z = 1.28$.* In terms of the question originally asked, there is an approximately .10 probability of a z value larger than 1.28.

The examples illustrate that the table of areas for the standard normal probability distribution can be used to find probabilities associated with values of the standard normal random variable z. Two types of questions can be asked. The first type of question specifies a value, or values, for z and asks us to use the table to determine the corresponding areas, or probabilities. The second type of question provides an area, or probability, and asks us to use the table to determine the corresponding z value. Thus, we need to be flexible in using the standard normal probability table to answer the desired probability question. In most cases, sketching a graph of the standard normal probability distribution and shading the appropriate area or probability helps to visualize the situation and aids in determining the correct answer.

COMPUTING PROBABILITIES FOR ANY NORMAL PROBABILITY DISTRIBUTION

The reason for discussing the standard normal distribution so extensively is that probabilities for all normal distributions are computed by using the standard normal distribution. That is, when we have a normal distribution with any mean μ and any standard deviation σ, we answer probability questions about the distribution by first converting to the standard normal distribution. Then we can use Table 6.1 and the appropriate z values to find the desired probabilities. The formula used to convert any normal random variable x with mean μ and standard deviation σ to the standard normal distribution follows.

---

*We could use interpolation in the body of the table to get a better approximation of the z value that corresponds to an area of .4000. Doing so to provide one more decimal place of accuracy would yield a z value of 1.282. However, in most practical situations, sufficient accuracy is obtained by simply using the table value closest to the desired probability.

CONVERTING TO THE STANDARD NORMAL DISTRIBUTION

$$z = \frac{x - \mu}{\sigma} \qquad \qquad \text{(6.3)}$$

A value of x equal to its mean μ results in $z = (\mu - \mu)/\sigma = 0$. Thus, we see that a value of x equal to its mean μ corresponds to a value of z at its mean 0. Now suppose that x is one standard deviation above its mean; that is, $x = \mu + \sigma$. Applying (6.3), we see that the corresponding z value is $z = [(\mu + \sigma) - \mu]/\sigma = \sigma/\sigma = 1$. Thus, a value that is one standard deviation above its mean yields $z = 1$. In other words, we can interpret z as *the number of standard deviations that the normal random variable x is from its mean μ.*

To see how this conversion enables us to compute probabilities for any normal distribution, suppose we have a normal distribution with $\mu = 10$ and $\sigma = 2$. What is the probability that the random variable x is between 10 and 14? Using (6.3) we see that at $x = 10$, $z = (x - \mu)/\sigma = (10 - 10)/2 = 0$ and that at $x = 14$, $z = (14 - 10)/2 = 4/2 = 2$. Thus, the answer to our question about the probability of x being between 10 and 14 is given by the equivalent probability that z is between 0 and 2 for the standard normal distribution. In other words, the probability that we are seeking is the probability that the random variable x is between its mean and two standard deviations above the mean. Using $z = 2.00$ and Table 6.1, we see that the probability is .4772. Hence the probability that x is between 10 and 14 is .4772.

THE GREAR TIRE COMPANY PROBLEM

Let us look at an application of the use of the normal probability distribution. Suppose the Grear Tire Company has just developed a new steel-belted radial tire that will be sold through a national chain of discount stores. Since the tire is a new product, Grear's managers believe that the mileage guarantee offered with the tire will be an important factor in the acceptance of the product. Before finalizing the tire mileage guarantee policy, Grear's managers want probability information about the number of miles the tires will last.

From actual road tests with the tires, Grear's engineering group has estimated the mean tire mileage at $\mu = 36,500$ miles and the standard deviation at $\sigma = 5000$. In addition, the data collected indicate that a normal distribution is a reasonable assumption. What percentage of the tires can be expected to last more than 40,000 miles? In other words, what is the probability that the tire mileage will exceed 40,000? This question can be answered by finding the area of the lightly shaded region in Figure 6.6.

At $x = 40,000$, we have

$$z = \frac{x - \mu}{\sigma} = \frac{40,000 - 36,500}{5000} = \frac{3500}{5000} = .70$$

Refer now to the bottom of Figure 6.6. We see that a value of $x = 40,000$ on the Grear Tire normal distribution corresponds to a value of $z = .70$ on the standard normal distribution. Using Table 6.1, we see that the area between the mean and $z = .70$ is .2580. Referring again to Figure 6.6, we see that the area between $x = 36,500$ and $x = 40,000$ on the Grear Tire normal distribution is also .2580. Thus, .5000 - .2580 = .2420 is the probability that x will exceed 40,000. We can conclude that about 24.2% of the tires will exceed 40,000 in mileage.

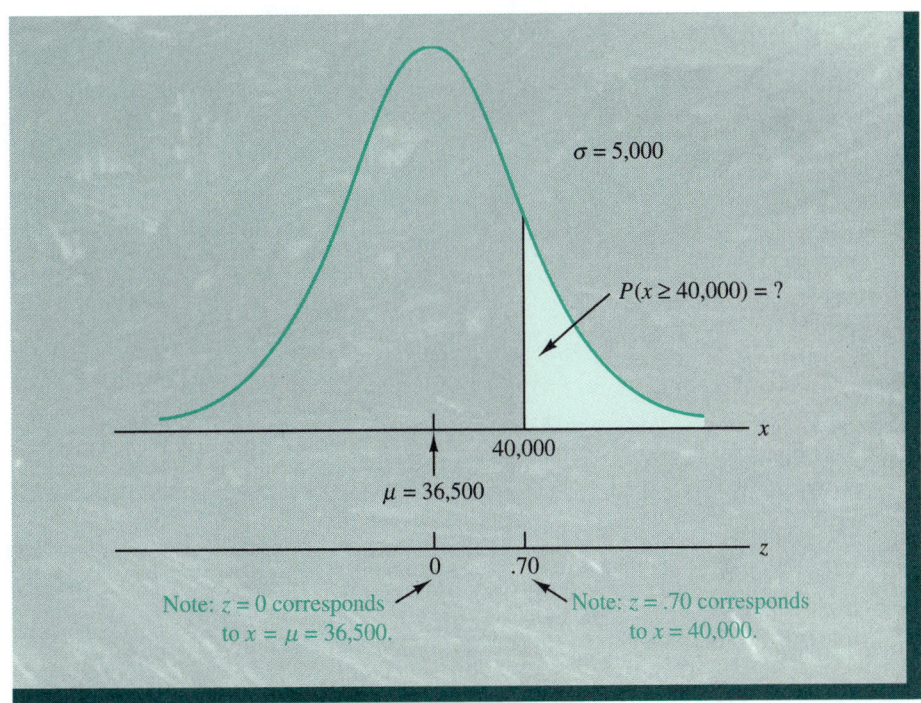

$\sigma = 5,000$

$P(x \geq 40,000) = ?$

40,000

$\mu = 36,500$

0   .70

Note: $z = 0$ corresponds to $x = \mu = 36,500$.

Note: $z = .70$ corresponds to $x = 40,000$.

FIGURE 6.6   Grear Tire Company Mileage Distribution

Let us now assume that Grear is considering a guarantee that will provide a discount on replacement tires if the original tires do not exceed the mileage stated in the guarantee. What should the guarantee mileage be if Grear wants no more than 10% of the tires to be eligible for the discount guarantee? This question is interpreted graphically in Figure 6.7.

According to Figure 6.7, 40% of the area must be between the mean and the unknown guarantee mileage. We look up .4000 in the body of Table 6.1 and see that this area is at approximately 1.28 standard deviations *below the mean*. That is, $z = -1.28$ is the value of the standard normal random variable corresponding to the desired mileage guarantee on the Grear Tire normal distribution. To find the mileage x corresponding to $z = -1.28$, we have

$$z = \frac{x - \mu}{\sigma} = -1.28$$

$$x - \mu = -1.28\sigma$$

$$x = \mu - 1.28\sigma$$

or, with $\mu = 36,500$ and $\sigma = 5000$,

$$x = 36,500 - 1.28(5000) = 30,100$$

Thus, a guarantee of 30,100 miles will meet the requirement that approximately 10% of the tires will be eligible for the guarantee. Perhaps, with this information, the firm will set its tire mileage guarantee at 30,000 miles.

Again, we see the important role that probability distributions play in providing decision-making information. Namely, once a probability distribution is established for a particular application, it can be used quickly and easily to obtain probability information about the problem. Probability does not make a decision recommendation

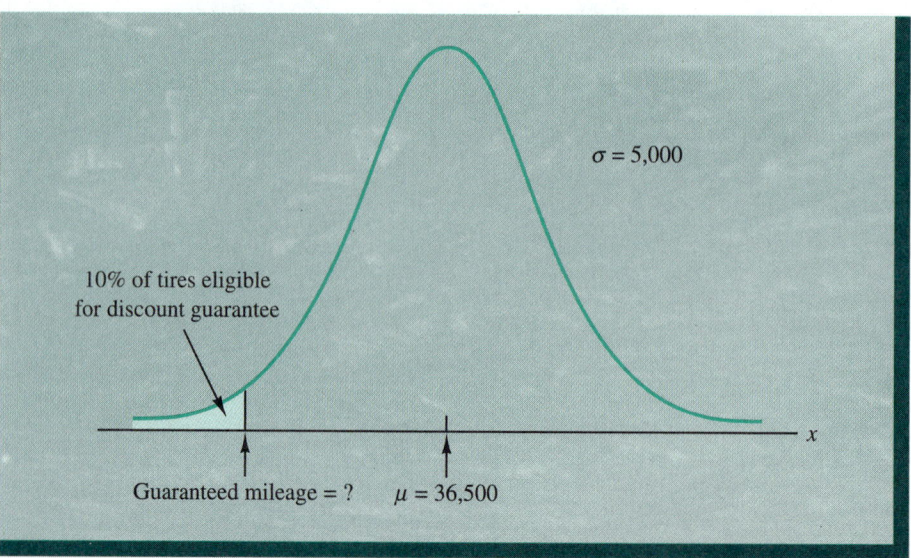

FIGURE 6.7   Grear's Discount Guarantee

directly, but it provides information that helps the decision maker better understand the risks and uncertainties associated with the problem. Ultimately, this information may assist the decision maker in reaching a good decision.

EXERCISES

METHODS

8. Using Figure 6.4 as a guide, sketch a normal curve for a random variable x that has a mean of $\mu = 100$ and a standard deviation of $\sigma = 10$. Label the horizontal axis with values of 70, 80, 90, 100, 110, 120, and 130.

9. The length of time required to complete a college examination is normally distributed with a mean of $\mu = 50$ minutes and a standard deviation of $\sigma = 5$ minutes.
   a. Sketch a normal curve for the length of the examination. Label the horizontal axis with values of 35, 40, 45, 50, 55, 60, and 65 minutes. Figure 6.4 shows that the normal curve almost touches the horizontal axis at three standard deviations below and at three standard deviations above the mean (in this case at 35 and 65).
   b. What is the probability that a student will take between 45 and 55 minutes to complete the exam?
   c. What is the probability that a student will take between 40 and 60 minutes to complete the exam?

10. Given that z is a standard normal random variable, sketch the standard normal curve. Label the horizontal axis at values of -3, -2, -1, 0, 1, 2, and 3. Then use the table of probabilities for the standard normal distribution to compute the following probabilities.
    a. $P(0 \leq z \leq 1)$ b. $P(0 \leq z \leq 1.5)$ c. $P(0 < z < 2)$ d. $P(0 < z < 2.5)$

11. Given that z is a standard normal random variable, compute the following probabilities.
    a. $P(-1 \leq z \leq 0)$ b. $P(-1.5 \leq z \leq 0)$ c. $P(-2 < z < 0)$
    d. $P(-2.5 \leq z \leq 0)$ e. $P(-3 < z \leq 0)$

12. Given that z is a standard normal random variable, compute the following probabilities.
    a. $P(0 \leq z \leq .83)$ **b.** $P(-1.57 \leq z \leq 0)$ **c.** $P(z > .44)$
    d. $P(z \geq -.23)$ **e.** $P(z < 1.20)$ **f.** $P(z \leq -.71)$

Self-Test

13. Given that z is a standard normal random variable, compute the following probabilities.
    a. $P(-1.98 \leq z \leq .49)$ **b.** $P(.52 \leq z \leq 1.22)$ **c.** $P(-1.75 \leq z \leq -1.04)$

14. Given that z is a standard normal random variable, find z for each situation.
    a. The area between 0 and z is .4750.
    b. The area between 0 and z is .2291.
    c. The area to the right of z is .1314.
    d. The area to the left of z is .6700.

Self-Test

15. Given that z is a standard normal random variable, find z for each situation.
    a. The area to the left of z is .2119.
    b. The area between $-z$ and z is .9030.
    c. The area between $-z$ and z is .2052.
    d. The area to the left of z is .9948.
    e. The area to the right of z is .6915.

16. Given that z is a standard normal random variable, find z for each situation.
    a. The area to the right of z is .01.
    b. The area to the right of z is .025.
    c. The area to the right of z is .05.
    d. The area to the right of z is .10.

APPLICATIONS

17. The demand for a new product is assumed to be normally distributed with $\mu = 200$ and $\sigma = 40$. Letting x be the number of units demanded, find the following probabilities.
    a. $P(180 \leq x \leq 220)$ **b.** $P(x \geq 250)$ **c.** $P(x \leq 100)$ **d.** $P(225 \leq x \leq 250)$

Self-Test

18. The mean cost for employee alcohol rehabilitation programs involving hospitalization is $10,000 (*USA Today*, September 12, 1991). Assume the rehabilitation program cost has a normal probability distribution with a standard deviation of $2200. Answer the following questions.
    a. What is the probability that a rehabilitation program will cost at least $12,000?
    b. What is the probability that a rehabilitation program will cost at least $6000?
    c. What is the cost range for the most expensive 10% of the rehabilitation programs?

19. College presidents receive a housing provision that averages $26,234 annually (*USA Today*, April 18, 1994). Assume that a normal distribution applies and that the standard deviation is $5,000.
    a. What percentage of college presidents receive an annual housing provision exceeding $35,000 per year?
    b. What percentage of college presidents receive an annual housing provision less than $20,000 per year?
    c. What is the annual housing provision for the 10% of the college presidents receiving the largest provision?

20. Miami University reported admission statistics for 3339 students who were admitted as freshmen for the fall semester of 1991. Of these students, 1590 had taken the Scholastic Aptitude Test (SAT). Assume the SAT verbal test scores were normally distributed with a mean of 530 and a standard deviation of 70.
    a. What percentage of students were admitted with SAT verbal scores between 500 and 600?
    b. What percentage of students were admitted with SAT verbal scores of 600 or more?
    c. What percentage of students were admitted with SAT verbal scores of 480 or less?

21. Mensa is the international high-IQ society. To be a Mensa member, a person must have an IQ of 132 or higher (*USA Today*, February 13, 1992). If IQ scores are normally distributed with

a mean of 100 and a standard deviation of 15, what percentage of the population qualifies for membership in Mensa?

22. Drivers who are members of the Teamsters Union earn an average of $17.15 per hour (*U.S. News & World Report,* April 11, 1994). Assume that available data indicate wages are normally distributed with a standard deviation of $2.25.
   a. What is the probability that wages are between $15.00 and $20.00 per hour?
   b. What is the hourly wage of the highest paid 15% of the Teamster drivers?
   c. What is the probability that wages are less than $12.00 per hour?

23. The time needed to complete a final examination in a particular college course is normally distributed with a mean of 80 minutes and a standard deviation of 10 minutes. Answer the following questions.
   a. What is the probability of completing the exam in one hour or less?
   b. What is the probability that a student will complete the exam in more than 60 minutes but less than 75 minutes?
   c. Assume that the class has 60 students and that the examination period is 90 minutes in length. How many students do you expect will be unable to complete the exam in the allotted time?

24. The average age for a person getting married for the first time is 26 years (*U.S. News & World Report,* June 6, 1994). Assume the ages for first marriages have a normal distribution with a standard deviation of four years.
   a. What is the probability that a person getting married for the first time is younger than 23 years of age?
   b. What is the probability that a person getting married for the first time is in his or her twenties?
   c. 90% of people getting married for the first time get married before what age?

25. *Team Marketing Report,* a sports-business newsletter, estimates that the average total cost for a family of four to attend a 1994 major league baseball game was $95.80 (*The Wall Street Journal,* April 5, 1994). Assume that a normal distribution applies and that the standard deviation is $10.00.
   a. What is the probability that the cost will exceed $100.00?
   b. What is the probability that a family of four will spend $75.00 or less?
   c. What is the probability that the cost will be between $85.00 and $100.00?

6.3   NORMAL APPROXIMATION OF BINOMIAL PROBABILITIES

In Section 5.4 we presented the binomial probability distribution. Recall that a binomial experiment consists of a sequence of *n* identical independent trials with each trial having two possible outcomes, a success or a failure. The probability of a success on a trial is the same for all trials and is denoted by *p*. The binomial random variable is the number of successes in the *n* trials, and probability questions pertain to the probability of *x* success in the *n* trials.

When the number of trials becomes large, evaluating the binomial probability function by hand or with a calculator is difficult. In addition, the binomial tables in Appendix B do not include values of *n* greater than 20. Hence, when we encounter a binomial probability distribution problem with a large number of trials, we may want to approximate the binomial probability distribution. In cases where the number of trials is greater than 20, $np \geq 5$, and $n(1 - p) \geq 5$, the normal probability distribution provides an easy-to-use approximation of binomial probabilities.

When using the normal approximation to the binomial, we set $\mu = np$ and $\sigma = \sqrt{np(1-p)}$ in the definition of the normal curve. Let us illustrate the normal approximation to the binomial by supposing that a particular company has a history of making errors in 10% of its invoices. A sample of 100 invoices has been taken, and we want to compute the probability that 12 invoices contain errors. That is, we want to find the binomial probability of 12 successes in 100 trials.

In applying the normal approximation to the binomial, we set $\mu = np = (100)(.1) = 10$ and $\sigma = \sqrt{np(1-p)} = \sqrt{(100)(.1)(.9)} = 3$. A normal distribution with $\mu = 10$ and $\sigma = 3$ is shown in Figure 6.8.

Recall that, with a continuous probability distribution, probabilities are computed as areas under the probability density function. As a result, the probability of any single value for the random variable is zero. To approximate the binomial probability of 12 successes, we must compute the area under the corresponding normal curve between 11.5 and 12.5. The .5 that we add and subtract from 12 is called a *continuity correction factor*. It is introduced because a continuous distribution is being used to approximate a discrete distribution. Thus, $P(x = 12)$ for the *discrete* binomial distribution is approximated by $P(11.5 \leq x \leq 12.5)$ for the *continuous* normal distribution.

Converting to the standard normal distribution to compute $P(11.5 \leq x \leq 12.5)$, we have

$$z = \frac{x - \mu}{\sigma} = \frac{12.5 - 10.0}{3} = .83 \qquad \text{at } x = 12.5$$

and

$$z = \frac{x - \mu}{\sigma} = \frac{11.5 - 10.0}{3} = .50 \qquad \text{at } x = 11.5$$

From Table 6.1 we find that the area under the curve (in Figure 6.8) between 10 and 12.5 is .2967. Similarly, the area under the curve between 10 and 11.5 is .1915. Therefore, the area between 11.5 and 12.5 is .2967 − .1915 = .1052. The normal approximation to the probability of 12 successes in 100 trials is .1052.

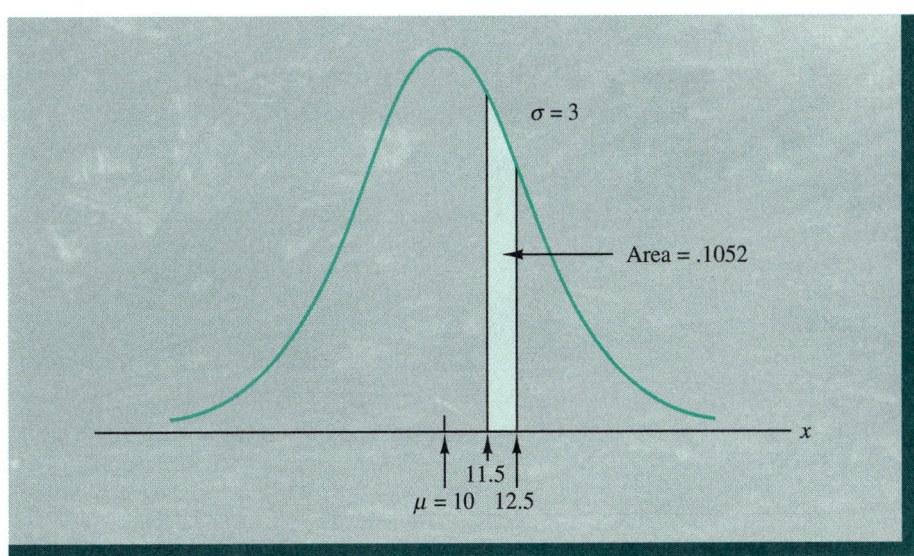

FIGURE 6.8 Normal Approximation to a Binomial Probability Distribution with $n = 100$ and $p = .10$ Showing the Probability of 12 Errors

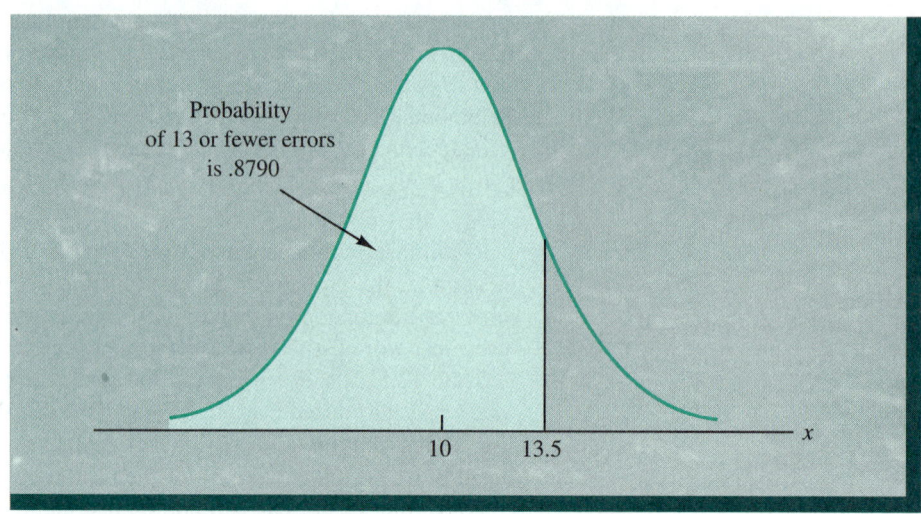

FIGURE 6.9   Normal Approximation to a Binomial Probability Distribution with $n = 100$ and $p = .10$ Showing the Probability of 13 or Fewer Errors

For another illustration, suppose we want to compute the probability of 13 or fewer errors in the sample of 100 invoices. Figure 6.9 shows the area under the normal curve that approximates this probability. Note that the use of the continuity correction factor results in the value of 13.5 being used to compute the desired probability. The z value corresponding to $x = 13.5$ is

$$z = \frac{13.5 - 10.0}{3.0} = 1.17$$

Table 6.1 shows that the area under the standard normal curve between 0 and 1.17 is .3790. The area under the normal curve approximating the probability of 13 or fewer errors is given by the lightly shaded portion of the graph in Figure 6.9. The probability is .3790 + .5000 = .8790.

EXERCISES

METHODS

Self-Test

26. A binomial probability distribution has $p = .20$ and $n = 100$.
    a. What is the mean and standard deviation?
    b. Is this a situation in which binomial probabilities can be approximated by the normal probability distribution? Explain.
    c. What is the probability of exactly 24 successes?
    d. What is the probability of 18 to 22 successes?
    e. What is the probability of 15 or fewer successes?

27. Assume a binomial probability distribution has $p = .60$ and $n = 200$.
    a. What is the mean and standard deviation?
    b. Is this a situation in which binomial probabilities can be approximated by the normal probability distribution? Explain.
    c. What is the probability of between 100 and 110 successes?
    d. What is the probability of 130 or more successes?

e. What is the advantage of using the normal probability distribution to approximate the binomial probabilities? Use part (d) to explain the advantage.

APPLICATIONS

Self-Test ▶

28. A *Consumer Reports* survey listed Saturn, Infiniti, and Lexus automobile dealers as the top three in customer service (*Consumer Reports,* April 1994). Saturn ranked number one, with only 4% of the Saturn customers citing some form of dissatisfaction with the dealer. Answer the following questions about a group of 250 Saturn customers.
   a. What is the probability that 12 or fewer customers will have some form of dissatisfaction with the dealer?
   b. What is the probability that five or more customers will have some form of dissatisfaction with the dealer?
   c. What is the probability that eight customers will have some form of dissatisfaction with the dealer?

29. The true unemployment rate is 7% (*Business Week,* November 7, 1994). Assume that 100 employable people are selected randomly.
   a. What is the expected number who are unemployed?
   b. What is the variance and standard deviation of the number who are unemployed?
   c. What is the probability that exactly nine are unemployed?
   d. What is the probability that at least five are unemployed?

30. Homes in Chicago, Illinois, in the price range $95,000–$130,000 are on the market an average of 70 days prior to sale (*U.S. News & World Report,* April 6, 1992). Assume the distribution of days on the market is normal with a standard deviation of 25 days.
   a. What is the probability that a house will be on the market 100 days or more?
   b. What is the probability that a house will sell during the second month it is on the market? That is, $P(31 \leq x \leq 60)$?
   c. For how many days are the fastest selling 20% on the market?

31. A Myrtle Beach resort hotel has 120 rooms. In the spring months, hotel room occupancy is approximately 75%. Use the normal approximation to the binomial distribution to answer the following questions.
   a. What is the probability that at least half of the rooms are occupied on a given day?
   b. What is the probability that 100 or more rooms are occupied on a given day?
   c. What is the probability that 80 or fewer rooms are occupied on a given day?

32. It is known that 30% of all customers of a major national charge card pay their bills in full before any interest charges are incurred. Use the normal approximation to the binomial distribution to answer the following questions for a group of 150 credit-card holders.
   a. What is the probability that between 40 and 60 customers pay their account balances before any interest charges are incurred? That is, find $P(40 \leq x \leq 60)$.
   b. What is the probability that 30 or fewer customers pay their account balances before any interest charges are incurred?

6.4   THE EXPONENTIAL PROBABILITY DISTRIBUTION

A continuous probability distribution that is useful in describing the time it takes to complete a task is the *exponential probability distribution.* The exponential random variable can be used to describe such things as the time between arrivals at a car wash, the time required to load a truck, the distance between major defects in a highway, and so on. The exponential probability density function follows.

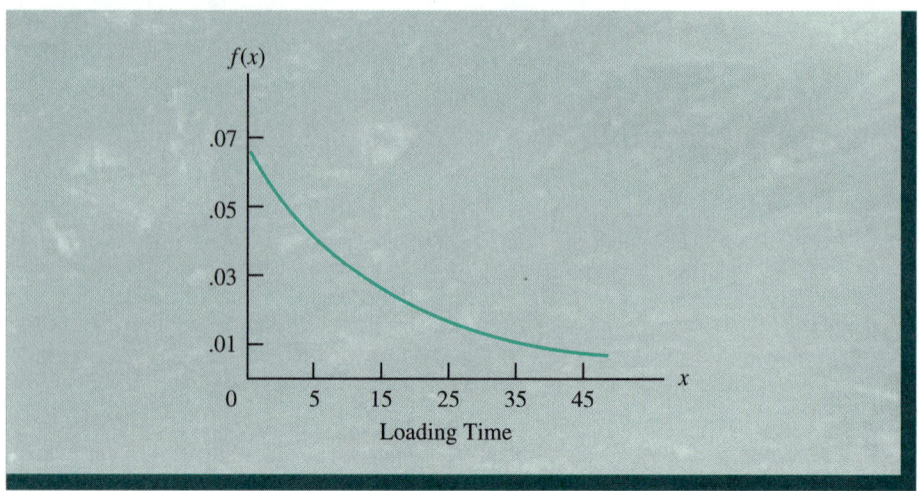

FIGURE 6.10   Exponential Probability Distribution for the Schips Loading Dock Example

EXPONENTIAL PROBABILITY DENSITY FUNCTION

$$f(x) = \frac{1}{\mu} e^{-x/\mu} \qquad \text{for } x \geq 0, \mu > 0 \tag{6.4}$$

As an example of the exponential probability distribution, assume that the time it takes to load a truck at the Schips loading dock follows such a distribution. If the mean, or average, time to load a truck is 15 minutes ($\mu = 15$), the appropriate probability density function is

$$f(x) = \frac{1}{15} e^{-x/15}$$

Figure 6.10 is the graph of this density function.

COMPUTING PROBABILITIES FOR THE EXPONENTIAL DISTRIBUTION

As with any continuous probability distribution, the area under the curve corresponding to some interval provides the probability that the random variable assumes a value in that interval. In the Schips loading dock example, the probability that loading a truck will take six minutes or less ($x \leq 6$) is defined to be the area under the curve from $x = 0$ to $x = 6$. Similarly, the probability that loading a truck will take 18 minutes or less ($x \leq 18$) is the area under the curve from $x = 0$ to $x = 18$. Note also that the probability that loading a truck will take between six minutes and 18 minutes ($6 \leq x \leq 18$) is given by the area under the curve from $x = 6$ to $x = 18$.

To compute exponential probabilities such as those just described, we use the following formula. It provides the probability of obtaining a value for the exponential random variable of less than or equal to some specific value of x, denoted by x_0.

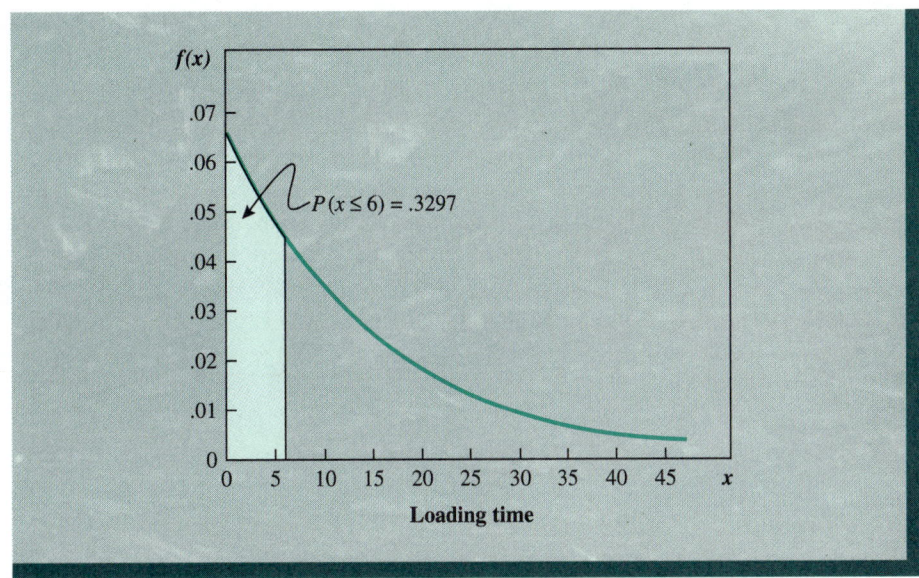

FIGURE 6.11   Probability of a Loading Time of Six Minutes or Less

EXPONENTIAL DISTRIBUTION PROBABILITIES

$$P(x \le x_0) = 1 - e^{-x_0/\mu} \qquad (6.5)$$

For the Schips loading dock example, (6.5) can be written as

$$P(\text{loading time} \le x_0) = 1 - e^{-x_0/15}$$

Hence, the probability that loading a truck will take six minutes or less ($x \le 6$) is

$$P(\text{loading time} \le 6) = 1 - e^{-6/15} = .3297.$$

Figure 6.11 shows the area or probability for a loading time of six minutes or less. Note also that the probability of loading a truck in 18 minutes or less ($x \le 18$) is

$$P(\text{loading time} \le 18) = 1 - e^{-18/15} = .6988$$

Thus, the probability that loading a truck will take between six minutes and 18 minutes is equal to .6988 − .3297 = .3691. Probabilities for any other interval can be computed similarly.

RELATIONSHIP BETWEEN THE POISSON AND EXPONENTIAL DISTRIBUTIONS

In Section 5.5 we introduced the Poisson distribution as a discrete probability distribution that is often useful in examining the number of occurrences of an event over a specified interval of time or space. Recall that the Poisson probability function is

$$f(x) = \frac{\mu^x e^{-\mu}}{x!}$$

where

$$\mu = \text{expected value or mean number of}$$
$$\text{occurrences in an interval.}$$

The continuous exponential probability distribution is related to the discrete Poisson distribution in that, if the Poisson distribution provides an appropriate description of the number of occurrences per interval, the exponential distribution provides a description of the length of the interval between occurrences.

   To illustrate this relationship, suppose the number of cars that arrive at a car wash during one hour is described by a Poisson probability distribution with a mean of 10 cars per hour. The Poisson probability function that gives the probability of x arrivals per hour is

$$f(x) = \frac{10^x e^{-10}}{x!}$$

Since the average number of arrivals is 10 cars per hour, the average time between cars arriving is

$$\frac{1 \text{ hour}}{10 \text{ cars}} = .1 \text{ hour/car}$$

Thus, the corresponding exponential distribution that describes the time between the arrivals has a mean of $\mu = .1$ hour per car; the appropriate exponential probability density function is

$$f(x) = \frac{1}{.1} e^{-x/.1} = 10 e^{-10x}$$

EXERCISES

METHODS

33. Consider the following exponential probability density function.

$$f(x) = \frac{1}{8} e^{-x/8} \qquad \text{for } x \geq 0$$

   a. Find $P(x \leq 6)$.   b. Find $P(x \leq 4)$.
   c. Find $P(x \geq 6)$.   d. Find $P(4 \leq x \leq 6)$.

Self-Test
··········▶

34. Consider the following exponential probability density function.

$$f(x) = \frac{1}{3} e^{-x/3} \qquad \text{for } x \geq 0$$

   a. Write the formula for $P(x \leq x_0)$.   b. Find $P(x \leq 2)$.
   c. Find $P(x \geq 3)$.   d. Find $P(x \leq 5)$.
   e. Find $P(2 \leq x \leq 5)$.

APPLICATIONS

35. The average life of a television set is 12 years (*Money*, April 1994). Product lifetimes often follow an exponential probability distribution. Assume that this is the case for the lifetime of a television set.
   a. What is the probability that the lifetime will be six years or less?
   b. What is the probability that the lifetime will be 15 years or more?
   c. What is the probability that the lifetime will be between five and 10 years?

36. The time between arrivals of vehicles at a particular intersection follows an exponential probability distribution with a mean of 12 seconds.
  a. Sketch this exponential probability distribution.
  b. What is the probability that the arrival time between vehicles is 12 seconds or less?
  c. What is the probability that the arrival time between vehicles is six seconds or less?
  d. What is the probability that there will be 30 or more seconds between vehicle arrivals?

37. The lifetime (hours) of an electronic device is a random variable with the following exponential probability density function.

$$f(x) = \frac{1}{50} e^{-x/50} \qquad \text{for } x \geq 0$$

  a. What is the mean lifetime of the device?
  b. What is the probability that the device will fail in the first 25 hours of operation?
  c. What is the probability that the device will operate 100 or more hours before failure?

38. Waiting times are frequently assumed to follow an exponential probability distribution. A study of waiting times at fast-food restaurants conducted by *The Orlando Sentinel* in October 1993 showed that the average waiting time to get food after placing an order at McDonald's, Burger King, and Wendy's was 60 seconds. Assume that an exponential probability distribution applies to the waiting times.
  a. What is the probability that a customer will wait 30 seconds or less?
  b. What is the probability that a customer will wait 45 seconds or less?
  c. What is the probability that a customer will wait more than two minutes?

39. For subscribers to *The Wall Street Journal,* the average number of stock transactions per year is 12 (*The Wall Street Journal* Subscriber Study, 1992). Assume that the time between transactions follows an exponential probability distribution.
  a. What is the mean number of months between stock transactions?
  b. What is the probability of a stock transaction within one month of a previous stock transaction?
  c. What is the probability that the time between successive stock transactions is three or more months?
  d. What is the probability that the time between successive stock transactions is at least one month but not more than two months?

SUMMARY

This chapter extended the discussion of probability distributions to the case of continuous random variables. The major conceptual difference between discrete and continuous probability distributions is in the method of computing probabilities. With discrete distributions, the probability function $f(x)$ provides the probability that the random variable x assumes various values. With continuous probability distributions, we associate a probability density function, denoted by $f(x)$. The probability density function does not provide probability values for a continuous random variable directly. Probabilities are given by areas under the curve or graph of the probability density function $f(x)$. Since the area under the curve above a single point is zero, we observe that the probability of any particular value is zero for a continuous random variable.

Three continuous probability distributions—the uniform, normal, and exponential distributions—were treated in detail. The normal probability distribution is used widely in statistical inference and will be used extensively in the remainder of the text.

GLOSSARY

Uniform probability distribution　A continuous probability distribution where the probability that the random variable will assume a value in any interval is the same for each interval of equal length.

Probability density function　The function that defines the probability distribution of a continuous random variable.

Normal probability distribution　A continuous probability distribution. Its probability density function is bell shaped and determined by the mean μ and standard deviation σ.

Standard normal probability distribution　A normal distribution with a mean of zero and a standard deviation of one.

Continuity correction factor　A value of .5 that is added and/or subtracted from a value of x when the continuous normal probability distribution is used to approximate the discrete binomial probability distribution.

Exponential probability distribution　A continuous probability distribution that is useful in computing probabilities for the time or space between occurrences of an event.

KEY FORMULAS

Uniform Probability Density Function

$$f(x) = \begin{cases} \dfrac{1}{b-a} & \text{for } a \leq x \leq b \\[2ex] 0 & \text{elsewhere} \end{cases}$$

(6.1)

Normal Probability Density Function

$$f(x) = \frac{1}{\sqrt{2\pi}\,\sigma}\, e^{-(x-\mu)^2/2\sigma^2}$$

(6.2)

Converting to the Standard Normal Distribution

$$z = \frac{x-\mu}{\sigma}$$

(6.3)

Exponential Probability Density Function

$$f(x) = \frac{1}{\mu} e^{-x/\mu} \qquad \text{for } x \geq 0,\, \mu > 0$$

(6.4)

Exponential Distribution Probabilities

$$P(x \leq x_0) = 1 - e^{-x_0/\mu}$$

(6.5)

SUPPLEMENTARY EXERCISES

40. In an office building the waiting time for an elevator is found to be uniformly distributed between zero and five minutes.
   a. What is the probability density function $f(x)$ for this uniform distribution?
   b. What is the probability of waiting longer than 3.5 minutes?
   c. What is the probability that the elevator arrives in the first 45 seconds?
   d. What is the probability of a waiting time between one and three minutes?
   e. What is the expected waiting time?

41. The time required to complete a particular assembly operation is uniformly distributed between 30 and 40 minutes.
   a. What is the mathematical expression for the probability density function?
   b. Compute the probability that the assembly operation will require more than 38 minutes to complete.
   c. If management wants to set a time standard for this operation, what time should be selected such that 70% of the time the operation will be completed within the time specified?
   d. Find the expected value and standard deviation for the assembly time.

42. A particular make of automobile is listed as weighing 4000 pounds. Because of weight differences due to the options ordered with the car, the actual weight varies uniformly between 3900 and 4100 pounds.
   a. What is the mathematical expression for the probability density function?
   b. What is the probability that the car will weigh less than 3950 pounds?

43. Given that z is a standard normal random variable, compute the following probabilities.
   a. $P(-.72 \leq z \leq 0)$ **b.** $P(-.35 \leq z \leq .35)$
   c. $P(.22 \leq z \leq .87)$ **d.** $P(z \leq -1.02)$

44. Given that z is a standard normal random variable, compute the following probabilities.
   a. $P(z \geq -.88)$ **b.** $P(z \geq 1.38)$
   c. $P(-.54 \leq z \leq 2.33)$ **d.** $P(-1.96 \leq z \leq 1.96)$

45. Given that z is a standard normal random variable, find z when the following information is known.
   a. The area between $-z$ and z is .90.
   b. The area to the right of z is .20.
   c. The area between -1.66 and z is .25.
   d. The area to the left of z is .40.
   e. The area between z and 1.80 is .20.

46. Motorola used the normal distribution to determine the probability of defects and the number of defects expected in a production process (*APICS—The Performance Advantage,* July 1991). Assume a production process is designed to produce items with a weight of 10 ounces and that the process mean is 10. Calculate the probability of a defect and the expected number of defects for a 1000-unit production run in the following situations.
   a. The process standard deviation is .15 and the process control is set at plus or minus one standard deviation. Units with weights less than 9.85 or greater than 10.15 ounces will be classified as defects.
   b. Through process design improvements, the process standard deviation can be reduced to .05. Assume the process control remains the same, with weights less than 9.85 or greater than 10.15 ounces being classified as defects.
   c. What is the advantage of reducing process variation and setting process control limits at a greater number of standard deviations from the mean?

47. The mean hourly operating cost of a USAir 737 airplane is $2071 (*The Tampa Tribune,* February 17, 1995). Assume that the hourly operating cost for the airplane is normally distributed.

a. If 11% of the hourly operating costs are $1800 or less, what is the standard deviation of hourly operating cost?

b. What is the probability that the hourly operating cost of a USAir 737 airplane is between $2000 and $2500?

c. What is the hourly operating cost of the 3% of the airplanes that have the lowest operating cost?

48. A soup company markets eight varieties of homemade soup throughout the eastern United States. The standard-size soup can holds a maximum of 11 ounces, whereas the label on each can advertises contents of 10¾ ounces. The extra quarter-ounce of space allows for the possibility of the automatic filling machine placing more soup than the company actually wants in a can. Experience shows that the number of ounces placed in a can is approximately normally distributed, with a mean of 10¾ ounces and a standard deviation of .1 ounce. What is the probability that the machine will attempt to place more than 11 ounces in a can, causing an overflow to occur?

49. The sales of High-Brite Toothpaste are believed to be approximately normally distributed, with a mean of 10,000 tubes per week and a standard deviation of 1500 tubes per week.

a. What is the probability that more than 12,000 tubes will be sold in any given week?

b. To have a .95 probability that the company will have sufficient stock to cover the weekly demand, how many tubes should be produced?

50. Points scored by the winning team in NCAA college football games are approximately normally distributed, with a mean of 24 and a standard deviation of 6.

a. What is the probability that a winning team in a football game scores between 20 and 30 points; that is, $P(20 \leq x \leq 30)$?

b. How many points does a winning team have to score to be in the highest 20% of scores for college football games?

51. Ward Doering Auto Sales is considering offering a special service contract that will cover the total cost of any service work required on leased vehicles. From experience, the company manager estimates that yearly service costs are approximately normally distributed, with a mean of $150 and a standard deviation of $25.

a. If the company offers the service contract to customers for a yearly charge of $200, what is the probability that any one customer's service costs will exceed the contract price of $200?

b. What is Ward's expected profit per service contract?

52. The attendance at football games at a certain stadium is normally distributed, with a mean of 45,000 and a standard deviation of 3000.

a. What percentage of the time should attendance be between 44,000 and 48,000?

b. What is the probability of the attendance exceeding 50,000?

c. For 80% of the time the attendance should be at least how many?

53. Assume that the test scores from a college admissions test are normally distributed, with a mean of 450 and a standard deviation of 100.

a. What percentage of the people taking the test score between 400 and 500?

b. Suppose someone receives a score of 630. What percentage of the people taking the test score better? What percentage score worse?

c. If a particular university will not admit anyone scoring below 480, what percentage of the persons taking the test would be acceptable to the university?

54. A survey of salaries paid to accounting graduates showed that the mean salary for public accounting managers with six to nine years of experience was $47,000 (*Student Newsbriefs, The Ohio Society of CPAs, Fall 1992*). Assume salaries are normally distributed with a standard deviation of $5500.

a. What is the probability that a manager earns between $40,000 and $50,000?

b. What is the probability that a manager earns less than $35,000?

    c. What is the probability that a manager earns $55,000 or more?

    d. How much do the top 1% of public accounting managers with six to nine years of experience earn?

55. A machine fills containers with a particular product. The standard deviation of filling weights is known from past data to be .6 ounce. If only 2% of the containers hold less than 18 ounces, what is the mean filling weight for the machine? That is, what must μ equal? Assume the filling weights have a normal distribution.

56. Consider a multiple-choice examination with 50 questions. Each question has four possible answers. Assume that a student who has done the homework and attended lectures has a .75 probability of answering any question correctly.

    a. A student must answer 43 or more questions correctly to obtain a grade of A. What percentage of the students who have done their homework and attended lectures will obtain a grade of A on this multiple-choice examination?

    b. A student who answers 35 to 39 questions correctly will receive a grade of C. What percentage of students who have done their homework and attended lectures will obtain a grade of C on this multiple-choice examination?

    c. A student must answer 30 or more questions correctly to pass the examination. What percentage of the students who have done their homework and attended lectures will pass the examination?

    d. Assume that a student has not attended class and has not done the homework for the course. Furthermore, assume that the student will simply guess at the answer to each question. What is the probability that this student will answer 30 or more questions correctly and pass the examination?

57. The book *100% American* by Daniel Evan Weiss reports that 64% of Americans live in the state where they were born. What is the probability that a random sample of 100 people will find between 60 and 70 people living in the state where they were born? That is, find $P(60 \leq x \leq 70)$.

58. A Labor Department survey asked working women what worries them most. Concern about low wages, job stress, and health benefits were mentioned most often, with 60% of working women concerned about low wages (*Business Week,* October 24, 1994). Consider a random sample of 500 working women from this population.

    a. What is the expected number of women in this group who will express a concern about low wages?

    b. What is the variance and standard deviation of the number who will express a concern about low wages?

    c. What is the probability that 290 to 320 women will express a concern about low wages?

    d. What is the probability that 325 or more women will express a concern about low wages?

59. The time in minutes for which a student uses a computer terminal at the computer center of a major university follows an exponential probability distribution with a mean of 36 minutes. Assume a student arrives at the terminal just as another student is beginning to work on the terminal.

    a. What is the probability that the wait for the second student will be 15 minutes or less?

    b. What is the probability that the wait for the second student will be between 15 and 45 minutes?

    c. What is the probability that the second student will have to wait an hour or more?

60. A new automated production process has been averaging two breakdowns per day, and the number of breakdowns per day follows a Poisson probability distribution.

    a. What is the mean time between breakdowns, assuming eight hours of operation per day?

    b. Show the exponential probability density function that can be used for the time between breakdowns.

    c. What is the probability that the process will run one hour or more before another breakdown?

d. What is the probability that the process can run a full eight-hour shift without a breakdown?

61. The time (in minutes) a checkout lane is idle between customers at a supermarket follows an exponential probability distribution with a mean of 1.2 minutes.
   a. Show the probability density function for this distribution.
   b. What is the probability that the next customer will arrive between .5 and 1.0 minutes after a customer is served?
   c. What is the probability of the checkout lane being idle for more than a minute between customers?

62. The time (in minutes) between telephone calls at an insurance claims office has the following exponential probability distribution.

$$f(x) = .50e^{-.50x} \qquad \text{for } x \geq 0$$

   a. What is the mean time between telephone calls?
   b. What is the probability of having 30 seconds or less between telephone calls?
   c. What is the probability of having one minute or less between telephone calls?
   d. What is the probability of having five or more minutes without a telephone call?

APPENDIX 6.1

Continuous Probability Distributions with Minitab

● Let us demonstrate the Minitab procedure for computing continuous probabilities by referring to the Grear Tire Company problem where tire mileage was described by a normal probability distribution with $\mu = 36{,}500$ and $\sigma = 5000$. One question asked was: What is the probability that the tire mileage will exceed 40,000 miles?

For continuous probability distributions, Minitab gives a cumulative probability; that is, Minitab gives the probability that the random variable will assume a value less than or equal to a specified constant. For the Grear tire mileage question, Minitab can be used to determine the cumulative probability that the tire mileage will be less than or equal to 40,000 miles. (The specified constant in this case is 40,000.) After obtaining the cumulative probability from Minitab, we must subtract it from one to determine the probability that the tire mileage will exceed 40,000 miles.

Prior to using Minitab to compute a probability, one must enter the specified constant into a column of the worksheet. For the Grear tire mileage question we entered the specified constant of 40,000 into column 1 of the Minitab worksheet. The steps in using Minitab to compute the cumulative probability of the normal random variable assuming a value less than or equal to 40,000 follow.

Step 1.   Select the **Calc** pull-down menu
Step 2.   Select the **Probability Distributions** pull-down menu
Step 3.   Select the **Normal** option
Step 4.   When the dialog box appears:
       Select **Cumulative probability**
       Enter 36500 in the **Mean** box
       Enter 5000 in the **Standard deviation** box
       Enter C1 in the **Input column** box (the column containing 40,000)
       Select **OK** to produce the cumulative normal probability

After the user selects **OK,** Minitab will print the cumulative probability that the normal random variable assumes a value less than or equal to 40,000. Minitab will show that this probability is .7580. Since we are interested in the probability that the tire mileage will be greater than 40,000, the desired probability is 1 − .7580 = .2420.

A second question in the Grear Tire Company problem was: What mileage guarantee should Grear set to ensure that no more than 10% of the tires qualify for the guarantee? Here we are given a probability and want to find the corresponding value for the random variable. Minitab uses an inverse calculation routine to find the value of the random variable associated with a given cumulative probability. First, we must enter the cumulative probability into a column of the Minitab worksheet (say C1). In this case, the desired cumulative probability is .10. Then, the first three steps of the Minitab procedure are as shown above. In step 4, we select **Inverse cumulative probability** instead of **Cumulative probability** and complete the step as shown above. Minitab then displays the mileage guarantee of 30,100 miles.

Minitab is capable of computing probabilities for other continuous probability distributions, including the exponential probability distribution. To compute exponential probabilities, follow the procedure shown previously for the normal probability distribution and select the **Exponential** option in step 3. Step 4 is as shown, with the exception that entering the standard deviation is not required. Output for cumulative probabilities and inverse cumulative probabilities is identical to that described for the normal probability distribution.

APPENDIX 6.2

Continuous Probability Distributions with Spreadsheets

● Excel has the capability of computing probabilities for several continuous probability distributions, including the normal and exponential probability distributions. In this appendix, we describe how Excel can be used to compute probabilities for any normal probability distribution. The procedures for the exponential and other continuous probability distributions are similar to the one we describe for the normal probability distribution.

Let us return to the Grear Tire Company problem where the tire mileage was described by a normal probability distribution with $\mu = 36,500$ and $\sigma = 5000$. Assume we are interested in the probability that tire mileage will exceed 40,000 miles. The following steps describe how to use Excel to produce the desired normal probability.

Step 1. Select a cell in the worksheet where you want the normal probability to appear
Step 2. Select the **Insert** pull-down menu
Step 3. Choose the **Function** option
Step 4. When the Function Wizard—Step 1 of 2 dialog box appears:
    Choose **Statistical** from the **Function Category** box
    Choose **NORMDIST** from the **Function Name** box
    Select **Next**>
Step 5. When the Function Wizard—Step 2 of 2 dialog box appears:
    Enter 40000 in the **x** box

Enter 36500 in the **mean** box
Enter 5000 in the **standard deviation** box
Enter true in the **cumulative** box
Select **Finish**

At this point, .7580 will appear in the cell selected in step 1, indicating that the probability of tire mileage being less than or equal to 40,000 miles is .7580. The probability that tire mileage will exceed 40,000 miles is $1 - .7580 = .2420$.

Excel uses an inverse computation to convert a given cumulative normal probability into a value for the random variable. For example, what mileage guarantee should Grear offer if the company wants no more than 10% of the tires to be eligible for the guarantee? To compute the mileage guarantee by using Excel, follow the procedure described above. However, two changes are necessary: in step 4, choose **NORMINV** from the **Function Name** box; in step 5, enter the cumulative probability of .10 in the **probability** box and then enter the mean and the standard deviation. When **Finish** is selected in step 5, the tire mileage guarantee of 30,092 or approximately 30,100 miles appears in the worksheet.

The Excel procedure for generating exponential probabilities is similar to the procedure described above. Step 4 can be used to choose the **EXPONDIST** function name. The dialog box in step 5 will guide the user through the input values required to compute the desired probability. Note that the mean is entered in the lambda box. When **Finish** is selected in step 5, the cumulative exponential probability appears in the worksheet.

7

SAMPLING AND SAMPLING DISTRIBUTIONS

CONTENTS

STATISTICS IN PRACTICE ● ● ● ● ● ● ● ● ● ● ● ● ● ● ● ● ● ●

Mead Corporation*
Dayton, Ohio

Mead Corporation, located in Dayton, Ohio, is a diversified paper and forest products company that manufactures paper, pulp, and lumber and converts paperboard into shipping containers and beverage carriers. The company's distribution capability is used to market many of its own products, including paper, school supplies, and stationery. The company's internal consulting group uses sampling for decision analysis to provide a variety of information that enables Mead to obtain significant productivity benefits and remain competitive in its industry.

For example, Mead maintains large woodland holdings, which provide the trees that are the raw material for many of the company's products. Managers need reliable and accurate information about the timberlands and forests to evaluate the company's ability to meet its future raw material needs. What is the present volume in the forests? What is the past growth of the forests? What is the projected future growth of the forests? With answers to these important questions, Mead's managers can develop plans for the future including long-term planting and harvesting schedules for the trees.

How does Mead obtain the information it needs about its vast forest holdings? Data collected from sample plots throughout the forests are the basis for learning about the population of trees owned by the company. To identify the sample plots, the timberland holdings are first divided into three sections based on location and types of trees. Using maps and tables of random numbers, Mead analysts

identify random samples of 1/5- to 1/7-acre plots in each section of the forest. The sample plots are where Mead foresters collect data and learn about the forest population.

Foresters throughout the organization participate in the field data collection process. Periodically, two-person teams gather information on each tree in every sample plot. The sample data are entered into the company's continuous forest inventory (CFI) computer system. Reports from the CFI system include a number of frequency distribution summaries containing statistics on types of trees, present forest volume, past forest growth rates, and projected future forest growth and volume. Sampling and the associated statistical summaries of the sample data provide the reports that are essential for the effective management of Mead's forests and timberland assets.

In this chapter you will learn about simple random sampling and the sample selection process. In addition, you will learn how statistics such as the sample mean and sample proportion are used to estimate the population mean and population proportion. The important concept of a sampling distribution is also introduced.

Mead's paper machine known as the "Spirit of Escanaba" is one of the largest and most modern paper machines in the world.

---

*Dr. Edward P. Winkofsky, Mead Corporation, provided this Statistics in Practice.

● In Chapter 1, we defined a *population* and a *sample* as two important aspects of a statistical study. The definitions are restated here.

1. A *population* is the set of all the elements of interest in a study.
2. A *sample* is a subset of the population.

The purpose of *statistical inference* is to obtain information about a population from information contained in a sample. Let us begin by citing two situations in which sampling is conducted to give a manager or decision maker information about a population.

1. A tire manufacturer has developed a new tire which it believes will provide an increase in mileage over the firm's current line of tires. To evaluate the new tire, managers need an estimate of the mean number of miles provided by the new tires. The manufacturer selects a sample of 120 new tires for testing. The test results in a sample mean of 36,500 miles. Hence, 36,500 miles is used as an estimate of the mean tire life for the population of new tires.

2. Members of a political party are considering supporting a particular candidate for election to the United States Senate. To decide whether or not to enter the candidate in the upcoming primary election, party leaders need an estimate of the proportion of registered voters favoring the candidate. The time and cost associated with contacting every individual in the population of registered voters are prohibitive. Hence, a sample of 400 registered voters is selected. If 160 of the 400 voters indicate a preference for the candidate, an estimate of the proportion of the population of registered voters favoring the candidate is $160/400 = .40$.

The preceding examples show how sampling and the sample results can be used to develop estimates of population characteristics. Note that in the tire mileage example, collecting the data on tire life involves wearing out each tire tested. Clearly it is not feasible to test every tire in the population; a sample is the only realistic way to obtain the desired tire mileage data. In the example involving the primary election, contacting every registered voter in the population is theoretically possible, but the time and cost in doing so are prohibitive; thus, a sample of registered voters is preferred.

The examples illustrate some of the reasons for using samples. However, it is important to realize that sample results provide only *estimates* of the values of the population characteristics. That is, we do not expect the sample mean of 36,500 miles to *exactly equal* the mean mileage for all tires in the population; neither do we expect *exactly* 40% of the population of registered voters to favor the candidate. The reason is simply that the sample contains only a portion of the population. With proper sampling methods, the sample results will provide "good" estimates of the population characteristics. But how good can we expect the sample results to be? Fortunately, statistical procedures are available for answering that question.

In this chapter we show how simple random sampling can be used to select a sample from a population. We then show how data obtained from a simple random sample can be used to compute estimates of a population mean, a population standard deviation, and a population proportion. In addition, we introduce the important concept of a sampling distribution. As we show, knowledge of the appropriate sampling distribution is what enables us to make statements about the goodness of the sample results. The last section discusses some alternatives to simple random sampling that are often employed in practice.

7.1 THE ELECTRONICS ASSOCIATES SAMPLING PROBLEM

The director of personnel for Electronics Associates, Inc. (EAI) has been assigned the task of developing a profile of the company's 2500 managers. The characteristics to be identified include the mean annual salary for the managers and the proportion of managers having completed the company's management training program.

Using the 2500 managers as the population for this study, we can find the annual salary and the training program status for each individual in the population by referring to the firm's personnel records. Let us assume that this has been done and that we have obtained the information for all 2500 managers in the population.

Using the formulas for a population mean and a population standard deviation that were presented in Chapter 3, we can compute the mean and standard deviation of annual salary for the population. Assume that these calculations have been performed with the following results.

$$\text{Population mean:} \quad \mu = \$51,800$$
$$\text{Population standard deviation:} \quad \sigma = \$4000$$

Furthermore, assume that 1500 of the 2500 managers have completed the training program. Letting p denote the proportion of the population having completed the training program, we see that $p = 1500/2500 = .60$.

A *parameter* is a numerical characteristic of a population. For example, the population mean annual salary ($\mu = \$51,800$), the population standard deviation of annual salary ($\sigma = \$4000$), and the population proportion having completed the training program ($p = .60$) are parameters of the population of EAI managers.

The question we want to consider is how the firm's director of personnel can obtain estimates of these population parameters by using a sample of managers rather than all 2500 managers in the population. Assume that a sample of 30 managers will be used. Clearly, the time and the cost of developing a profile would be substantially less for 30 managers than for the entire population. If the personnel director could be assured that a sample of 30 managers would provide adequate information about the population of 2500 managers, working with a sample would be preferable to working with the entire population. Let us explore the possibility of using a sample for the EAI study by first considering how we could identify a sample of 30 managers.

7.2 SIMPLE RANDOM SAMPLING

Several methods can be used to select a sample from a population; one of the most common is *simple random sampling*. The definition of a simple random sample and the process of selecting a simple random sample depend on whether the population is *finite* or *infinite*. Since the EAI sampling problem involves a finite population of 2500 managers, we first consider sampling from finite populations.

SAMPLING FROM FINITE POPULATIONS

A simple random sample of size n from a finite population of size N is defined as follows.

> **SIMPLE RANDOM SAMPLE (FINITE POPULATION)**
> A simple random sample of size n from a finite population of size N is a sample selected such that each possible sample of size n has the same probability of being selected.

One procedure for identifying a simple random sample from a finite population is to select the elements for the sample *one at a time* in such a way that each of the elements remaining in the population has the *same probability* of being selected. Sampling n elements in that way will satisfy the definition of a simple random sample from a finite population.

To select a simple random sample from the finite population in the EAI problem, we first assume that the 2500 EAI managers have been numbered sequentially (i.e., 1, 2, 3, . . . , 2499, 2500) in the order that their names appear in the EAI personnel file. We could then write the numbers from 1 to 2500 on equal-size pieces of paper, place the 2500 pieces of paper in a container, and mix them thoroughly. We would begin the process of identifying managers for the sample by reaching into the container and selecting one piece of paper *randomly*. The number on the chosen piece of paper would correspond to one of the numbered managers in the file of 2500 managers; thus, that manager would be selected for the sample. The remaining 2499 pieces of paper would be thoroughly mixed again, after which another piece of paper would be selected. This second number would correspond to another EAI manager to be included in the sample. The process would continue until 30 managers have been selected from the population. The 30 managers identified in this way would form a simple random sample from the population.

In this procedure we did not place a selected (sampled) piece of paper back into the container after it was drawn. Hence, we selected a simple random sample *without replacement*. We could have followed the sampling procedure of *replacing* each sampled element before selecting subsequent elements. This form of sampling, referred to as sampling *with replacement,* would have made it possible for some elements to appear in the sample more than once. Sampling with replacement is a valid way of identifying a simple random sample, but sampling without replacement is the sampling procedure used most often. Whenever we refer to simple random sampling, we assume that the sampling is done without replacement.

Rather than labeling 2500 pieces of paper to select a simple random sample of 30 EAI managers, we can use tables of random numbers to obtain the same results much more easily. Such tables are available in a variety of handbooks* that contain page after page of random numbers. We have included one such page of random numbers as Table 8 of Appendix B. Table 7.1 is a portion of this page of random numbers. The first line of the table begins as follows.

63271   59986   71744   51102   15141   80714

Each digit shown, 6, 3, 2, . . . , is a random selection of the digits 0, 1, . . . , 9, with each digit having an equal chance of occurring. The grouping of the numbers into sets of five is simply for the convenience of making the table easy to read.

Let us see how the numbers in this random number table can be used to select a simple random sample of 30 EAI managers. Again we want to select numbers from 1 to 2500 such that every number has an equal chance of being selected. Since the largest number in the EAI population, 2500, has four digits, we select random numbers from the table in sets or groups of four digits. We could select four-digit numbers from any portion of the random number table, but suppose we start by using the first row of random numbers appearing in Table 7.1. The four-digit groupings of the first 28 random numbers in the first row follow.

6327   1599   8671   7445   1102   1514   1807

Since the numbers in the table are random, the preceding four-digit numbers are all equally probable, or equally likely.

We can now use the equally likely four-digit random numbers to give each element in the population an equal chance of being included in the sample. The first number, 6327, is greater than 2500. It does not correspond to an element in the population, and

---

*For example, The Rand Corporation, *A Million Random Digits with 100,000 Normal Deviates.* New York: The Free Press, 1983.

TABLE 7.1   Random Numbers

63271	59986	71744	51102	15141	80714	58683	93108	13554	79945
88547	09896	95436	79115	08303	01041	20030	63754	08459	28364
55957	57243	83865	09911	19761	66535	40102	26646	60147	15702
46276	87453	44790	67122	45573	84358	21625	16999	13385	22782
55363	07449	34835	15290	76616	67191	12777	21861	68689	03263
69393	92785	49902	58447	42048	30378	87618	26933	40640	16281
13186	29431	88190	04588	38733	81290	89541	70290	40113	08243
17726	28652	56836	78351	47327	18518	92222	55201	27340	10493
36520	64465	05550	30157	82242	29520	69753	72602	23756	54935
81628	36100	39254	56835	37636	02421	98063	89641	64953	99337
84649	48968	75215	75498	49539	74240	03466	49292	36401	45525
63291	11618	12613	75055	43915	26488	41116	64531	56827	30825
70502	53225	03655	05915	37140	57051	48393	91322	25653	06543
06426	24771	59935	49801	11082	66762	94477	02494	88215	27191
20711	55609	29430	70165	45406	78484	31639	52009	18873	96927
41990	70538	77191	25860	55204	73417	83920	69468	74972	38712
72452	36618	76298	26678	89334	33938	95567	29380	75906	91807
37042	40318	57099	10528	09925	89773	41335	96244	29002	46453
53766	52875	15987	46962	67342	77592	57651	95508	80033	69828
90585	58955	53122	16025	84299	53310	67380	84249	25348	04332
32001	96293	37203	64516	51530	37069	40261	61374	05815	06714
62606	64324	46354	72157	67248	20135	49804	09226	64419	29457
10078	28073	85389	50324	14500	15562	64165	06125	71353	77669
91561	46145	24177	15294	10061	98124	75732	00815	83452	97355
13091	98112	53959	79607	52244	63303	10413	63839	74762	50289

hence it is discarded. The second number, 1599, is between 1 and 2500. Thus the first individual selected for the sample is manager 1599 on the list of EAI managers. Continuing the process, we ignore 8671 and 7445 before identifying individuals 1102, 1514, and 1807 as the next managers to be included in the sample. This process of selecting managers continues until the desired simple random sample of size 30 has been obtained. We note that with this random number procedure for simple random sampling, a random number used previously to identify an element for the sample may reappear in the random number table. Since we want to select the simple random sample *without replacement,* previously used random numbers are ignored because the corresponding element is already included in the sample.

Random numbers can be selected from anywhere in the random number table. Although we used the first row of the table in the example, we could have started at any other point in the table and continued in any direction. Once the arbitrary starting point is selected, it is recommended that a predetermined systematic procedure, such as reading across rows or down columns, be used to pick the subsequent random numbers.

SAMPLING FROM INFINITE POPULATIONS

Most sampling situations in business and economics involve finite populations, but in some situations the population is either infinite or so large that for practical purposes it must be treated as infinite. In sampling from an infinite population, we must use a new definition of a simple random sample. In addition, since the elements in an infinite population cannot be numbered, we must use a different process for selecting elements for the sample.

Suppose we want to estimate the average time between placing an order and receiving food for customers at a fast-food restaurant during the 11:30 A.M. to 1:30 P.M. lunch period. If we consider the population as being all possible customer visits, we see that it would not be feasible to specify a finite limit on the number of possible visits. In fact, if we define the population as being all customer visits that could *conceivably* occur during the lunch period, we can consider the population as being infinite. Our task is to select a simple random sample of *n* customers from this population. The definition of a simple random sample from an infinite population follows.

SIMPLE RANDOM SAMPLE (INFINITE POPULATION)

A simple random sample from an infinite population is a sample selected such that the following conditions are satisfied.

1. Each element selected comes from the same population.
2. Each element is selected independently.

For the problem of selecting a simple random sample of customer visits at a fast-food restaurant, we find that the first condition defined above is satisfied by any customer visit occurring during the 11:30 A.M. to 1:30 P.M. lunch period while the restaurant is operating with its regular staff under "normal" operating conditions. The second condition is satisfied by ensuring that the selection of a particular customer does not influence the selection of any other customer. That is, the customers are selected independently.

A well-known fast-food restaurant has implemented a simple random sampling procedure for just such a situation. The sampling procedure is based on the fact that some customers will present discount coupons for special prices on sandwiches, drinks, french fries, and so on. Whenever a customer presents a discount coupon, the *next* customer served is selected for the sample. Since the customers present discount coupons randomly and independently, the firm is satisfied that the sampling plan satisfies the two conditions for a simple random sample from an infinite population.

NOTES AND COMMENTS

1. Finite populations are often defined by lists such as organization membership rosters, student enrollment records, credit-card account lists, inventory product numbers, and so on. Infinite populations are often defined by an ongoing process whereby the elements of the population consist of items generated as though the process would operate indefinitely under the same conditions; in such cases, it is impossible to obtain a list of all items in the population. For example, populations consisting of all possible parts to be manufactured, all possible customer visits, all possible bank transactions, and so on can be classified as infinite populations.

2. The number of different simple random samples of size *n* that can be selected from a finite population of size *N* is

$$\frac{N!}{n!(N-n)!}.$$

In this formula, $N!$ and $n!$ refer to the factorial computations discussed in Chapter 4. For the EAI problem with $N = 2500$ and $n = 30$, this expression can be used to show that there are approximately 2.75×10^{69} different simple random samples of 30 EAI managers.

EXERCISES

METHODS

Self-Test

1. Consider a small finite population with five items labeled A, B, C, D, and E. Ten possible simple random samples of size two can be selected.
   a. List the 10 samples beginning with AB, AC, and so on.
   b. Using simple random sampling, what is the probability that each sample of size two is selected?
   c. Assume random number 1 corresponds to A, random number 2 corresponds to B, and so on. List the simple random sample of two items that will be selected by using the random digits 8 0 5 7 5 3 2.

2. Assume a finite population has 350 items. Using the last three digits of each of the following five-digit random numbers, determine the first four units that will be selected for the simple random sample.

   98601   73022   83448   02147   34229   27553   84147   93289   14209

APPLICATIONS

Self-Test

3. *Fortune* publishes data on sales, profits, assets, stockholders' equity, market value, and earnings per share for the 500 largest U.S. industrial corporations (The *Fortune* 500, 1995). Assume that you want to select a simple random sample of 10 corporations from the *Fortune* 500 list. Use column 9 of Table 7.1 beginning with 554. Read down the column and identify the numbers of the 10 corporations that would be selected.

4. The Highway Loss Data Institute reported the number of automobiles stolen in 1991 and 1992 by model (*America by the Numbers,* 1993). The 10 most frequently stolen models follow.

1. Infinity Q45	**6.** Toyota Supra
2. Volkswagen Jetta	**7.** Ford Mustang
3. Chevrolet Camaro	**8.** Cadillac Brougham
4. Accura Legend	**9.** BMW 525/535
5. Lincoln Mark VII	**10.** BMW 318/325

   a. Beginning with the first random digit in Table 7.1 (6) and reading down the column, use single-digit random numbers to select a simple random sample of five automobiles from the list.
   b. According to the information in Notes & Comments (2), how many different simple random samples of size five can be selected from this list of 10 automobile models?

5. A student government organization is interested in estimating the proportion of students who favor a mandatory "pass-fail" grading policy for elective courses. A list of names and addresses of the 645 students enrolled during the current quarter is available from the registrar's office. Using row 10 of Table 7.1 and moving across the row from left to right, identify the first 10 students who would be selected by simple random sampling. With every digit in row 10 is used, the three-digit random numbers begin with 816, 283, and 610.

6. The *County and City Data Book,* published by the Bureau of the Census, lists information on 3139 counties throughout the United States. Assume that a national study will collect data from 30 randomly selected counties. Use four-digit random numbers from the last column of Table 7.1 to identify the numbers corresponding to the first five counties selected for the sample. Ignore the first digits and begin with the four-digit random numbers 9945, 8364, 5702, and so on.

7. Assume that we want to identify a simple random sample of 12 of the 372 doctors practicing in a particular city. The doctors' names are available from a local medical organization. Use the eighth column of five-digit random numbers in Table 7.1 to identify the 12 doctors for the sample. Ignore the first two random digits in each five-digit grouping of the random numbers.

This process begins with random number 108 and proceeds down the column of random numbers.

8. An article published in *Psychology Today* ranked 286 cities in the United States on the basis of four psychological well-being indicators: alcoholism, suicide, divorce, and crime (*America by the Numbers,* 1993). Assume that a simple random sample of 12 of the 286 cities will be selected for a follow-up in-depth study. Use the third column of five-digit random numbers in Table 7.1, beginning with 71744, to select the simple random sample of 12 cities. Begin with city number 717 and use the first three digits in each row for your selection process. What are the numbers of the 12 cities in the sample?

9. Schuster's Interior Design, Inc., specializes in a variety of home decorating services for its clients. During the previous year the firm provided major decorating consultation for 875 homes. Schuster's managers were interested in obtaining information about customer satisfaction six to 12 months after project completion. To obtain this information, they decided to sample 30 of the 875 clients and interview the group to learn about client satisfaction and ways to improve service. Using the last three digits in column 10 of Table 7.1 and moving down the column would provide the random number sequence 945, 364, 702, and so on. Use this procedure to identify the first 10 clients who would be included in the sample. Assume that the 875 clients are numbered sequentially in the order in which the decorating projects were conducted.

10. Haskell Public Opinion Poll, Inc., conducts telephone surveys about a variety of political and general public interest issues. The households included in the survey are identified by taking a simple random sample from telephone directories in selected metropolitan areas. The telephone directory for a major Midwest area contains 853 pages with 400 lines per page.
   a. Describe a two-stage random selection procedure that could be used to identify a simple random sample of 200 households. The selection process should involve first selecting a page at random (stage 1) and then selecting a line on the sampled page (stage 2). Use the random numbers in Table 7.1 to illustrate this process. Select your own arbitrary starting point in the table.
   b. What would you do if the line selected in part (a) were clearly inappropriate for the study (that is, the line provided the phone number of a business, restaurant, etc.)?

11. The research group at the Paramont's King's Island theme park in Kings Mills, Ohio, uses surveys to determine what visitors like about the park.
   a. Assume that the research group treats the population of visitors as an infinite population. Is this acceptable? Explain.
   b. Assume that immediately after completing an interview with a visitor, the interviewer returns to the entrance gate and begins counting individuals as they enter the park. The 25th individual counted is selected as the next person to be sampled for the survey. After completing this interview, the interviewer returns to the entrance and again selects the 25th individual entering the park. Does this sampling process appear to provide a simple random sample? Explain.

12. Indicate whether the following populations should be considered finite or infinite.
   a. All registered voters in the state of California.
   b. All television sets that could be produced by the Allentown, Pennsylvania, plant of the TV-M Company.
   c. All orders that could be processed by a mail-order firm.
   d. All emergency telephone calls that could come into a local police station.
   e. All components that Fibercon, Inc. produced on the second shift on May 17.

7.3 POINT ESTIMATION

Now that we have described how to select a simple random sample, let us return to the EAI problem. Assume that a simple random sample of 30 managers has been selected

TABLE 7.2   Annual Salary and Training Program Status for a Simple Random Sample of 30 EAI Managers

Annual Salary ($)	Management Training Program?	Annual Salary ($)	Management Training Program?
$x_1 = 49{,}094.30$	Yes	$x_{16} = 51{,}766.00$	Yes
$x_2 = 53{,}263.90$	Yes	$x_{17} = 52{,}541.30$	No
$x_3 = 49{,}643.50$	Yes	$x_{18} = 44{,}980.00$	Yes
$x_4 = 49{,}894.90$	Yes	$x_{19} = 51{,}932.60$	Yes
$x_5 = 47{,}621.60$	No	$x_{20} = 52{,}973.00$	Yes
$x_6 = 55{,}924.00$	Yes	$x_{21} = 45{,}120.90$	Yes
$x_7 = 49{,}092.30$	Yes	$x_{22} = 51{,}753.00$	Yes
$x_8 = 51{,}404.40$	Yes	$x_{23} = 54{,}391.80$	No
$x_9 = 50{,}957.70$	Yes	$x_{24} = 50{,}164.20$	No
$x_{10} = 55{,}109.70$	Yes	$x_{25} = 52{,}973.60$	No
$x_{11} = 45{,}922.60$	Yes	$x_{26} = 50{,}241.30$	No
$x_{12} = 57{,}268.40$	No	$x_{27} = 52{,}793.90$	No
$x_{13} = 55{,}688.80$	Yes	$x_{28} = 50{,}979.40$	Yes
$x_{14} = 51{,}564.70$	No	$x_{29} = 55{,}860.90$	Yes
$x_{15} = 56{,}188.20$	No	$x_{30} = 57{,}309.10$	No

and that the corresponding data on annual salary and management training program participation are as shown in Table 7.2. The notation x_1, x_2, and so on is used to denote the annual salary of the first manager in the sample, the annual salary of the second manager in the sample, and so on. Participation in the management training program is indicated by Yes in the management training program column.

To estimate the value of a population parameter, we compute a corresponding characteristic of the sample, referred to as a *sample statistic*. For example, to estimate the population mean μ and the population standard deviation σ for the annual salary of EAI managers, we simply use the data in Table 7.2 to calculate the corresponding sample statistics: the sample mean $\bar{x}$ and the sample standard deviation s. By the formulas for a sample mean and a sample standard deviation presented in Chapter 3, the sample mean is

$$\bar{x} = \frac{\Sigma x_i}{n} = \frac{1{,}554{,}420}{30} = \$51{,}814.00$$

and the sample standard deviation is

$$s = \sqrt{\frac{\Sigma(x_i - \bar{x})^2}{n-1}} = \sqrt{\frac{325{,}009{,}260}{29}} = \$3347.72$$

In addition, by computing the proportion of managers in the sample who have responded Yes, we can estimate the proportion of managers in the population who have completed the management training program. Table 7.2 shows that 19 of the 30 managers in the sample have completed the training program. Thus, the sample proportion, denoted by $\bar{p}$, is given by

$$\bar{p} = \frac{19}{30} = .63$$

This value is used as an estimate of the population proportion p.

By making the preceding computations, we have performed the statistical procedure called *point estimation*. In point estimation we use the data from the sample to compute a value of a sample statistic that serves as an estimate of a population parameter. Using

TABLE 7.3 Summary of Point Estimates Obtained from a Simple Random Sample of 30 EAI Managers

Population Parameter	Parameter Value	Point Estimator	Point Estimate
μ = Population mean annual salary	$51,800.00	$\bar{x}$ = Sample mean annual salary	$51,814.00
σ = Population standard deviation for annual salary	$4,000.00	s = Sample standard deviation for annual salary	$3,347.72
p = Population proportion having completed the management training program	.60	$\bar{p}$ = Sample proportion having completed the management training program	.63

the terminology of point estimation, we refer to $\bar{x}$ as the *point estimator* of the population mean μ, s as the *point estimator* of the population standard deviation σ, and $\bar{p}$ as the *point estimator* of the population proportion p. The actual numerical value obtained for $\bar{x}$, s, or $\bar{p}$ in a particular sample is called the *point estimate* of the parameter. Thus, for the sample of 30 EAI managers, $51,814.00 is the point estimate of μ, $3,347.72 is the point estimate of σ, and .63 is the point estimate of p. Table 7.3 summarizes the sample results and compares the point estimates to the actual values of the population parameters.

NOTES AND COMMENTS

In our discussion of point estimators, we use $\bar{x}$ to denote a sample mean and $\bar{p}$ to denote a sample proportion. Our use of $\bar{p}$ is based on the fact that the sample proportion is also a *sample mean*. For instance, suppose that in a sample of n items with data values $x_1, x_2, \ldots, x_n$, we let $x_i = 1$ when a characteristic of interest is present for the ith item and $x_i = 0$ when the characteristic is not present. Then the sample proportion is computed by $\Sigma x_i /n$, which is the formula for a sample mean. We also like the consistency of using the bar over the letter to remind the reader that the sample proportion $\bar{p}$ estimates the population proportion just as the sample mean $\bar{x}$ estimates the population mean. Some texts in statistics use $\hat{p}$ instead of $\bar{p}$ to denote the sample proportion.

EXERCISES

METHODS

13. The following data have been collected from a simple random sample.

5   8   10   7   10   14

   a. What is the point estimate of the population mean?
   b. What is the point estimate of the population standard deviation?

14. A survey question for a sample of 150 individuals yielded 75 Yes responses, 55 No responses, and 20 No Opinions.
   a. What is the point estimate of the proportion in the population who respond Yes?
   b. What is the point estimate of the proportion in the population who respond No?

TABLE 7.4 Exercise 16

Improve Family Life	Frequency
More flexible hours	272
Higher pay	208
More help at home	120
Better day care	56
Nothing	144

APPLICATIONS

15. A simple random sample of five months of sales data provided the following information:

Month:	1	2	3	4	5
Units Sold:	94	100	85	94	92

a. What is the point estimate of the population mean number of units sold per month?

b. What is the point estimate of the population standard deviation?

16. A 1992 survey conducted by the Foundation for Women and the Center for Policy Awareness asked married working women to identify the factors that would contribute most to improved family life. Suppose the data in Table 7.4 are for a sample of 800 respondents. Use the sample results to obtain the following estimates.

a. The proportion of the population of married women who believe more flexible work hours would contribute most to improved family life.

b. The proportion of the population of married women who believe higher paying jobs would contribute most to improved family life.

17. The California Highway Patrol maintains records showing the time between a report of an accident and the arrival of an officer at the accident scene. A simple random sample of 10 records shows the following times in minutes.

12.6   3.4   4.8   5.0   6.8   2.3   3.6   8.1   2.5   10.3

a. What is a point estimate of the population mean time between an accident report and officer arrival?

b. What is a point estimate of the population standard deviation of the time between an accident report and officer arrival?

18. A report by the U.S. Department of Transportation (March 1993) indicated that one of the major complaints against the nation's air carriers is that many flights fail to arrive on schedule. A flight is considered on time if it arrives no later than 15 minutes after the scheduled time. Suppose that of a random sample of 200 flights into Los Angeles International Airport, 182 flights were classified as being on time. On the basis of these data, what is the point estimate of the proportion of all flights into Los Angeles International Airport that should be classified as *late* arrivals?

19. A 1992 Louis Harris poll called America and the Arts was used to study taxpayers' attitudes about federal funding of the arts. Suppose a sample of 500 taxpayers were selected and asked the following two questions.

Would you support a $5 tax to fund the arts?

Would you support a $10 tax to fund the arts?

Assume that 345 answered yes to the first question and 320 answered yes to the second question. Use these results to provide point estimates for each of the following population parameters.

a. The proportion of all taxpayers who would support a $5 tax to fund the arts.

b. The proportion of all taxpayers who would support a $10 tax to fund the arts.

7.4 INTRODUCTION TO SAMPLING DISTRIBUTIONS

In the preceding section we used a simple random sample of 30 EAI managers to develop point estimates of the mean and standard deviation of annual salary for the population of all EAI managers as well as the proportion of the managers in the population who have completed the company's management training program. Suppose

TABLE 7.5 Values of $\bar{x}$, s, and $\bar{p}$ from 500 Simple Random Samples of 30 EAI Managers

Sample Number	Sample Mean $\bar{x}$	Sample Standard Deviation s	Sample Proportion $\bar{p}$
1	$51,814.00	$3,347.72	.63
2	$52,669.70	$4,239.07	.70
3	$51,780.30	$4,433.43	.67
4	$51,587.90	$3,985.32	.53
.	.	.	.
.	.	.	.
500	$51,752.00	$3,857.82	.50

TABLE 7.6 Frequency Distribution of $\bar{x}$ from 500 Simple Random Samples of 30 EAI Managers

Mean Annual Salary ($)	Frequency	Relative Frequency
49,500.00–49,999.99	2	.004
50,000.00–50,499.99	16	.032
50,500.00–50,999.99	52	.104
51,000.00–51,499.99	101	.202
51,500.00–51,999.99	133	.266
52,000.00–52,499.99	110	.220
52,500.00–52,999.99	54	.108
53,000.00–53,499.99	26	.052
53,500.00–53,999.99	6	.012
Totals	500	1.000

we select another simple random sample of 30 EAI managers, and an analysis of the data from the second sample provides the following information.

Sample Mean $\bar{x} = \$52,669.70$

Sample Standard Deviation $s = \$4,239.07$

Sample Proportion $\bar{p} = .70$

These results show that different values of $\bar{x}$, s, and $\bar{p}$ have been obtained with the second sample. In general, this is to be expected because the second simple random sample is not likely to contain the same elements as the first. Let us imagine carrying out the same process of selecting a new simple random sample of 30 managers over and over again, each time computing values of $\bar{x}$, s, and $\bar{p}$. In this way we could begin to identify the variety of values that these point estimators can have. To illustrate, we repeated the simple random sampling process for the EAI problem until we obtained 500 samples of 30 managers each and their corresponding $\bar{x}$, s, and $\bar{p}$ values. A portion of the results is shown in Table 7.5. Table 7.6 gives the frequency and relative frequency distributions for the 500 $\bar{x}$ values. Figure 7.1 is the relative frequency histogram for the $\bar{x}$ results.

Recall that in Chapter 5 we defined a random variable as a numerical description of the outcome of an experiment. If we consider the process of selecting a simple random sample as an experiment, the sample mean $\bar{x}$ is the numerical description of the outcome

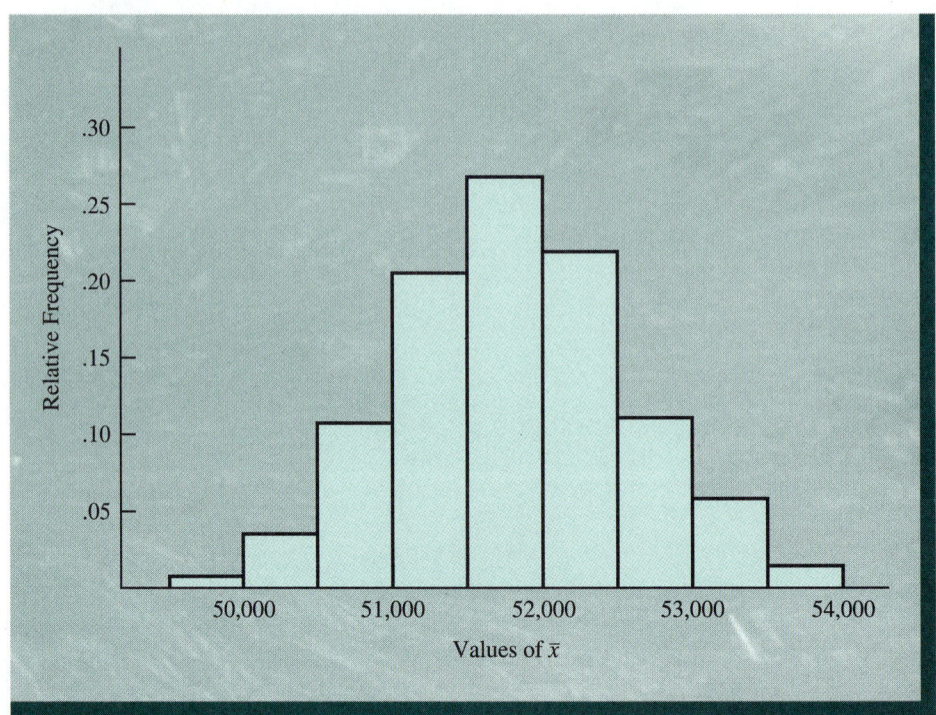

FIGURE 7.1   Relative Frequency Histogram of $\bar{x}$ Values from 500 Simple Random
Samples of Size 30 Each

of the experiment. Thus, the sample mean $\bar{x}$ is a random variable. As a result, just like
other random variables, $\bar{x}$ has a mean or expected value, a variance, and a probability
distribution. Since the various possible values of $\bar{x}$ are the result of different simple
random *samples,* the probability distribution of $\bar{x}$ is called the *sampling distribution* of
$\bar{x}$. Knowledge of this sampling distribution and its properties will enable us to make
probability statements about how close the sample mean $\bar{x}$ is to the population mean μ.

Let us return to Figure 7.1. We would need to enumerate every possible sample of 30
managers and compute each sample mean to completely determine the sampling
distribution of $\bar{x}$. However, the histogram of 500 $\bar{x}$ values gives an approximation of this
sampling distribution. From the approximation we observe the bell-shaped appearance
of the distribution. We also note that the mean of the 500 $\bar{x}$ values is near the population
mean $\mu = \$51,800$. We will describe the properties of the sampling distribution of $\bar{x}$
more fully in the next section.

The 500 values of the sample standard deviation s and the 500 values of the sample
proportion $\bar{p}$ are summarized by the relative frequency histograms in Figures 7.2 and
7.3. As in the case of $\bar{x}$, both s and $\bar{p}$ are random variables that provide numerical
descriptions of the outcome of a simple random sample. If every possible sample of size
30 were selected from the population and if a value of s and a value of $\bar{p}$ were computed
for each sample, the resulting probability distributions would be called the sampling
distribution of s and the sampling distribution of $\bar{p}$, respectively. The relative frequency
histograms of the 500 sample values, Figures 7.2 and 7.3, provide a general idea of the
appearance of these two sampling distributions.

In practice, we select *only one simple random sample* from the population. We
repeated the sampling process 500 times in this section simply to illustrate that many
different samples are possible and that the different samples generate a variety of values
for the sample statistics $\bar{x}$, s, and $\bar{p}$. The probability distribution of any particular sample

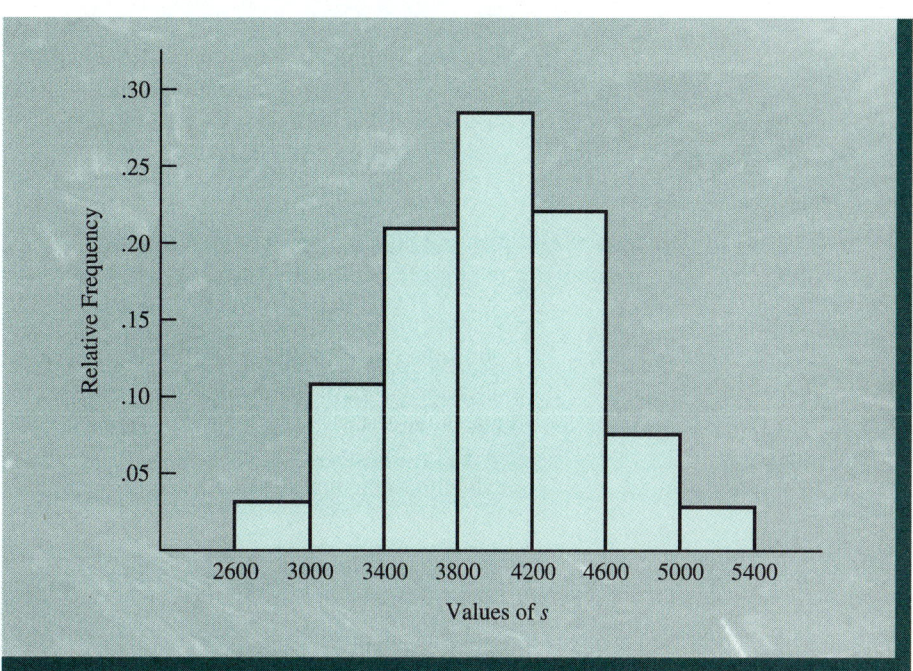

FIGURE 7.2   Relative Frequency Histogram of s Values from 500 Simple Random Samples of Size 30 Each

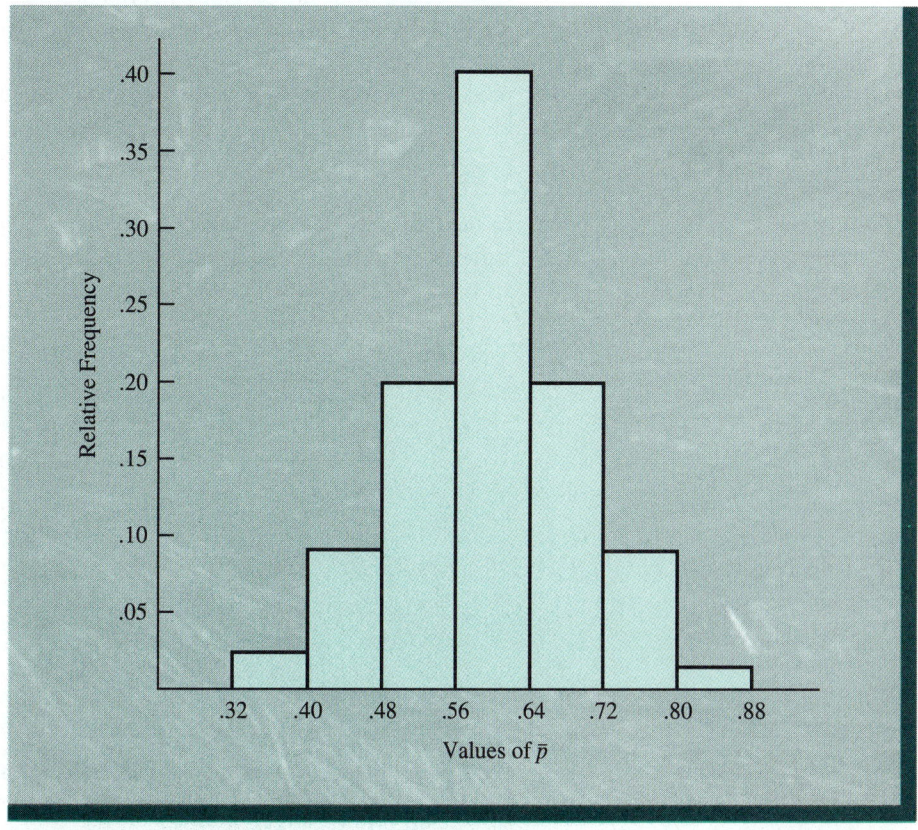

FIGURE 7.3   Relative Frequency Histogram of $\bar{p}$ Values from 500 Simple Random Samples of Size 30 Each

statistic is called the sampling distribution of the statistic. In Section 7.5 we show the characteristics of the sampling distribution of $\bar{x}$. In Section 7.6 we show the characteristics of the sampling distribution of $\bar{p}$. We defer further discussion of the sampling distribution of s until we consider sampling distributions pertaining to sample variances, which are covered in Chapter 11.

7.5   SAMPLING DISTRIBUTION OF $\bar{x}$

One of the most common statistical procedures is the use of a sample mean $\bar{x}$ to make inferences about a population mean μ. This process is shown in Figure 7.4. On each repetition of the process, we can anticipate obtaining a different value for the sample mean $\bar{x}$. The probability distribution for all possible values of the sample mean $\bar{x}$ is called the sampling distribution of the sample mean $\bar{x}$.

> **SAMPLING DISTRIBUTION OF $\bar{x}$**
> The sampling distribution of $\bar{x}$ is the probability distribution of all possible values of the sample mean $\bar{x}$.

The purpose of this section is to describe the properties of the sampling distribution of $\bar{x}$, including the expected value or mean of $\bar{x}$, the standard deviation of $\bar{x}$, and the shape or form of the sampling distribution itself. As we shall see, knowledge of the sampling distribution of $\bar{x}$ will enable us to make probability statements about the error involved when $\bar{x}$ is used to estimate μ. Let us begin by considering the mean of all possible $\bar{x}$ values or, simply, the expected value of $\bar{x}$.

EXPECTED VALUE OF $\bar{x}$

In the EAI sampling problem we saw that different simple random samples result in a variety of values for the sample mean $\bar{x}$. Since many different values of the random

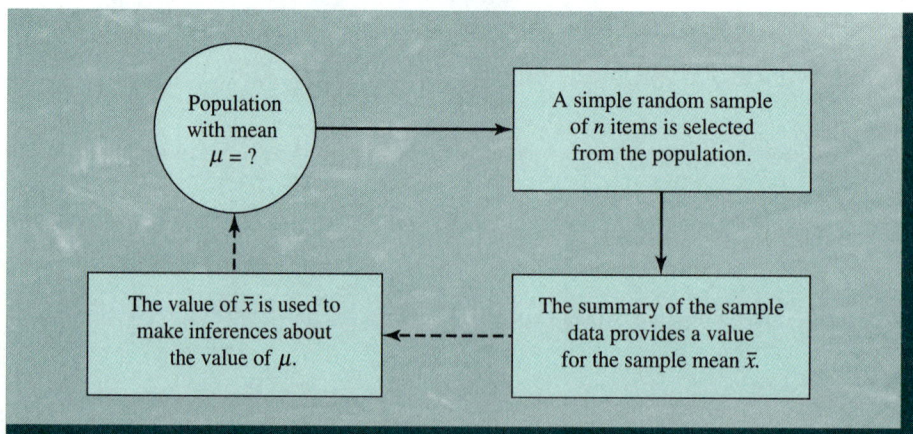

FIGURE 7.4   The Statistical Process of Using a Sample Mean to Make Inferences About a Population Mean

variable $\bar{x}$ are possible, we are often interested in the mean of all possible values of $\bar{x}$ that can be generated by the various simple random samples. The mean of the $\bar{x}$ random variable is the expected value of $\bar{x}$. Let $E(\bar{x})$ represent the expected value of $\bar{x}$ and μ represent the mean of the population from which the sample is drawn. It can be shown that with simple random sampling, these two values are equal.

EXPECTED VALUE OF $\bar{x}$

$$E(\bar{x}) = \mu \qquad (7.1)$$

where

$$E(\bar{x}) = \text{the expected value of the random variable } \bar{x}$$

$$\mu = \text{the population mean}$$

This result is derived in the chapter appendix. It shows that with simple random sampling, the expected value or mean for $\bar{x}$ is equal to the mean of the population. In Section 7.1 we saw that the mean annual salary for the population of EAI managers is $\mu = \$51,800$. Thus, according to (7.1), the mean of all possible sample means for the EAI study is also $\$51,800$.

STANDARD DEVIATION OF $\bar{x}$

Let us define the standard deviation of the sampling distribution of $\bar{x}$. We will use the following notation.

$\sigma_{\bar{x}} = $ the standard deviation of the sampling distribution of $\bar{x}$

$\sigma = $ the standard deviation of the population

$n = $ the sample size

$N = $ the population size

It can be shown that with simple random sampling, the standard deviation of $\bar{x}$ depends on whether the population is finite or infinite. The two expressions for the standard deviation of $\bar{x}$ follow.

STANDARD DEVIATION OF $\bar{x}$

Finite Population   *Infinite Population*

$$\sigma_{\bar{x}} = \sqrt{\frac{N-n}{N-1}}\left(\frac{\sigma}{\sqrt{n}}\right) \qquad\qquad \sigma_{\bar{x}} = \frac{\sigma}{\sqrt{n}} \qquad (7.2)$$

A derivation of the formulas for $\sigma_{\bar{x}}$ is discussed in the appendix to this chapter. In comparing the two expressions in (7.2), we see that the factor $\sqrt{(N-n)/(N-1)}$ is required for the finite population but not for the infinite population. This factor is commonly referred to as the *finite population correction factor*. In many practical sampling situations, we find that the population involved, although finite, is "large," whereas the sample size is relatively "small." In such cases the finite population correction factor $\sqrt{(N-n)/(N-1)}$ is close to 1. As a result, the difference between the values of the standard deviation of $\bar{x}$ for the finite and infinite population cases becomes negligible. When this occurs, $\sigma_{\bar{x}} = \sigma/\sqrt{n}$ becomes a very good approximation to the standard deviation of $\bar{x}$ even though the population is finite. A general guideline or rule of thumb for computing the standard deviation of $\bar{x}$ follows.

USE THE FOLLOWING EXPRESSION TO CALCULATE THE STANDARD DEVIATION OF $\bar{x}$

$$\sigma_{\bar{x}} = \frac{\sigma}{\sqrt{n}} \qquad (7.3)$$

whenever

1. The population is infinite; or
2. The population is finite, *and* the sample size is less than or equal to 5% of the population size—that is, $n/N \leq .05$.

In cases where $n/N > .05$, the finite population version of (7.2) should be used in the computation of $\sigma_{\bar{x}}$. Unless otherwise noted, throughout the text we will assume that the population size is "large," the finite population correction factor is unnecessary, and (7.3) can be used to compute $\sigma_{\bar{x}}$.

Now let us return to the EAI study and determine the standard deviation of all possible sample means that can be generated with samples of 30 EAI managers. In Section 7.1 we saw that the population standard deviation for the annual salary data is $\sigma = 4000$. In this case the population is finite, with $N = 2500$. However, with a sample size of 30, we have $n/N = 30/2500 = .012$. Following the rule of thumb given in (7.3), we can ignore the finite population correction factor and use (7.3) to compute the standard deviation of $\bar{x}$.

$$\sigma_{\bar{x}} = \frac{\sigma}{\sqrt{n}} = \frac{4000}{\sqrt{30}} = 730.30$$

Later we will see that the value of $\sigma_{\bar{x}}$ is helpful in determining how far the sample mean may be from the population mean. Because of the role that $\sigma_{\bar{x}}$ plays in computing possible errors, $\sigma_{\bar{x}}$ is referred to as the *standard error of the mean*.

CENTRAL LIMIT THEOREM

The final step in identifying the characteristics of the sampling distribution of $\bar{x}$ is to determine the form of the probability distribution of $\bar{x}$. We consider two cases: one in which the population distribution is unknown and one in which the population distribution is known to be normal.

When the population distribution is unknown, we rely on one of the most important theorems in statistics—the *central limit theorem*. A statement of the central limit theorem as it applies to the sampling distribution of $\bar{x}$ follows.

CENTRAL LIMIT THEOREM
In selecting simple random samples of size n from a population, the sampling distribution of the sample mean $\bar{x}$ can be approximated by a *normal probability distribution* as the sample size becomes large.

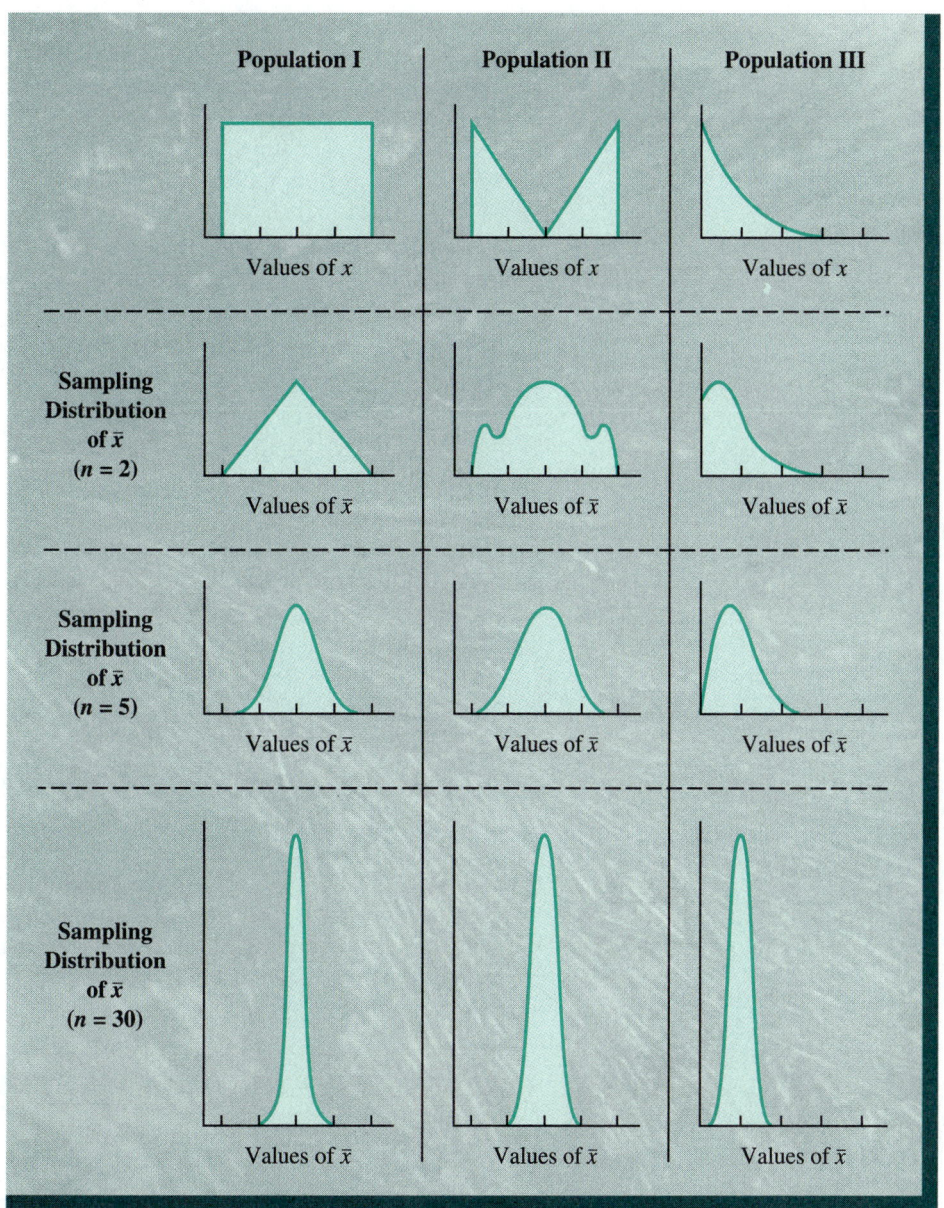

FIGURE 7.5 Illustration of the Central Limit Theorem for Three Populations

Figure 7.5 shows how the central limit theorem works for three different populations; in each case the population clearly is not normal. However, note what begins to happen to the sampling distribution of $\bar{x}$ as the sample size is increased. When the samples are of size two, we see that the sampling distribution of $\bar{x}$ begins to take on an appearance different from that of the population distribution. For samples of size five, we see all three sampling distributions beginning to take on a bell-shaped appearance. Finally, the samples of size 30 show all three sampling distributions to be approximately normal. Thus, for sufficiently large samples, the sampling distribution of $\bar{x}$ can be approximated by a normal probability distribution. However, how large must the sample size be before we can assume that the central limit theorem applies? Statistical researchers have investigated this question by studying the sampling distribution of $\bar{x}$ for a variety of populations and a variety of sample sizes. Whenever the population distribution is mound-shaped and symmetrical, sample sizes as small as five to 10 can be enough for the central limit theorem to apply. However, if the population distribution is highly skewed and clearly nonnormal, larger sample sizes are needed. General statistical practice is to assume that for most applications, the sampling distribution of $\bar{x}$ can be approximated by a normal probability distribution whenever the *sample size is 30 or more*. In effect, a sample size of 30 or more is assumed to satisfy the large-sample condition of the central limit theorem. This observation is so important that we restate it.

> The sampling distribution of $\bar{x}$ can be approximated by a normal probability distribution whenever the sample size is large. The large-sample-size condition can be assumed for simple random samples of size 30 or more.

The central limit theorem is the key to identifying the form of the sampling distribution of $\bar{x}$ whenever the population distribution is unknown. However, we may encounter some sampling situations in which the population is assumed or believed to have a normal distribution. When this condition occurs, the following result identifies the form of the sampling distribution of $\bar{x}$.

> Whenever the population has a normal probability distribution, the sampling distribution of $\bar{x}$ is a normal probability distribution for any sample size.

In summary, if we use a large ($n \geq 30$) simple random sample, the central limit theorem enables us to conclude that the sampling distribution of $\bar{x}$ can be approximated by a normal probability distribution. When the simple random sample is small ($n < 30$), the sampling distribution of $\bar{x}$ can be considered normal only if we assume that the population has a normal probability distribution.

SAMPLING DISTRIBUTION OF $\bar{x}$ FOR THE EAI PROBLEM

For the EAI study we have shown that $E(\bar{x}) = 51,800$ and $\sigma_{\bar{x}} = 730.30$. Since we are using a simple random sample of 30 managers, the central limit theorem enables us to conclude that the sampling distribution of $\bar{x}$ is approximately normal as shown in Figure 7.6.

PRACTICAL VALUE OF THE SAMPLING DISTRIBUTION OF $\bar{x}$

Whenever a simple random sample is selected and the value of the sample mean $\bar{x}$ is to *exactly equal* the population mean. The absolute value of the difference between the value of the sample mean $\bar{x}$ and the value of the population mean μ, $|\bar{x} - \mu|$, is called the *sampling error*. The practical reason we are interested in the sampling distribution of $\bar{x}$ is that it can be used to provide probability information about the size of the sampling error. To demonstrate this use, let us return to the EAI problem.

Suppose the personnel director believes the sample mean will be an acceptable estimate of the population mean if the sample mean is within $500 of the population

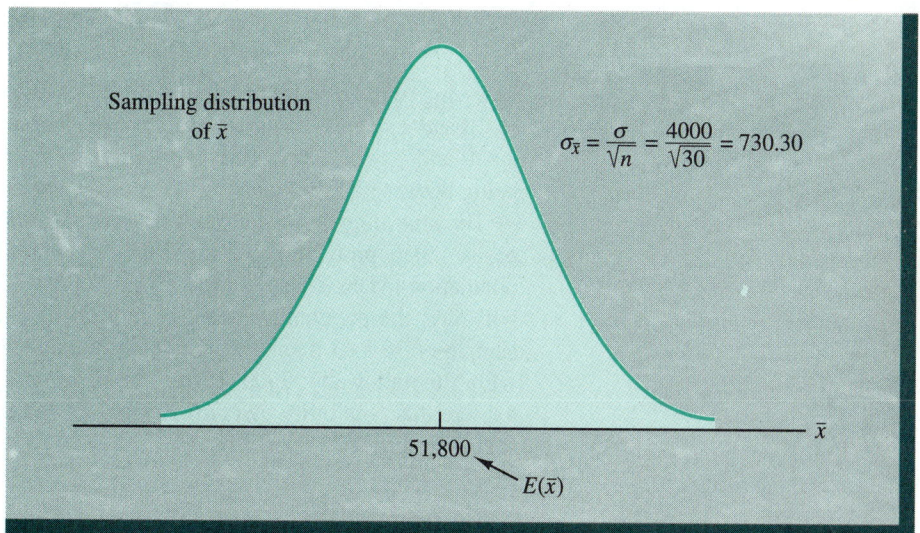

FIGURE 7.6 Sampling Distribution of $\bar{x}$ for the Mean Annual Salary of a Simple Random Sample of 30 EAI Managers

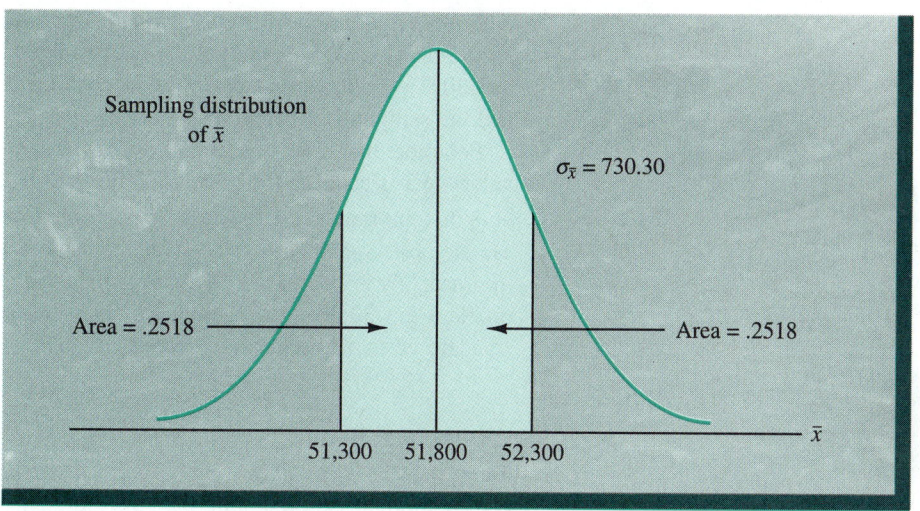

FIGURE 7.7 The Probability of a Sample Mean Being within $500 of the Population Mean

mean. In probability terms, the personnel director is really concerned with the following question: What is the probability that the sample mean we obtain from a simple random sample of 30 EAI managers will be within $500 of the population mean?

Since we have identified the properties of the sampling distribution of $\bar{x}$ (see Figure 7.6), we will use this distribution to answer the probability question. Refer to the sampling distribution of $\bar{x}$ shown again in Figure 7.7. The personnel director is asking about the probability that the sample mean is between $51,300 and $52,300. If the value of the sample mean $\bar{x}$ is in this interval, the value of $\bar{x}$ will be within $500 of the population mean. The appropriate probability is given by the area of the sampling distribution shown in Figure 7.7. Since the sampling distribution is normal, with mean 51,800 and standard deviation 730.30, we can use the standard normal probability distribution table to find the area or probability. At $\bar{x} = 51,300$, we have

$$z = \frac{51,300 - 51,800}{730.30} = -.68$$

Referring to the standard normal probability distribution table, we find an area between $z = 0$ and $z = -.68$ of .2518. Similar calculations for $\bar{x} = 52,300$ show an area between $z = 0$ and $z = +.68$ of .2518. Thus, the probability of the value of the sample mean being between 51,300 and 52,300 is .2518 + .2518 = .5036.

The preceding computations show that a simple random sample of 30 EAI managers has a .5036 probability of providing a sample mean $\bar{x}$ that is within $500 of the population mean. Thus, there is a $1 - .5036 = .4964$ probability that the sample mean will miss the population mean by more than $500. In other words, a simple random sample of 30 EAI managers has roughly a 50–50 chance of providing a sample mean within the allowable $500. Perhaps a larger sample size should be considered. Let us explore this possibility by considering the relationship between the sample size and the sampling distribution of $\bar{x}$.

THE RELATIONSHIP BETWEEN THE SAMPLE SIZE AND THE SAMPLING DISTRIBUTION OF $\bar{x}$

Suppose that in the EAI sampling problem we select a simple random sample of 100 EAI managers instead of the 30 originally considered. Intuitively, it would seem that with more data provided by the larger sample size, the sample mean based on $n = 100$ should provide a better estimate of the population mean than the sample mean based on $n = 30$. To see how much better, let us consider the relationship between the sample size and the sampling distribution of $\bar{x}$.

First note that $E(\bar{x}) = \mu$ regardless of the sample size. Thus, the mean of all possible values of $\bar{x}$ is equal to the population mean μ regardless of the sample size n. However, note that the standard error of the mean, $\sigma_{\bar{x}} = \sigma/\sqrt{n}$, is related to the square root of the sample size. Specifically, whenever the sample size is increased, the standard error of the mean $\sigma_{\bar{x}}$ is decreased. With $n = 30$, the standard error of the mean for the EAI problem is 730.30. However, with the increase in the sample size to $n = 100$, the standard error of the mean is decreased to

$$\sigma_{\bar{x}} = \frac{\sigma}{\sqrt{n}} = \frac{4000}{\sqrt{100}} = 400$$

The sampling distributions of $\bar{x}$ with $n = 30$ and $n = 100$ are shown in Figure 7.8. Since the sampling distribution with $n = 100$ has a smaller standard error, the values of $\bar{x}$ have less variation and tend to be closer to the population mean than the values of $\bar{x}$ with $n = 30$.

We can use the sampling distribution of $\bar{x}$ for the case with $n = 100$ to compute the probability that a simple random sample of 100 EAI managers will provide a sample mean that is within $500 of the population mean. Since the sampling distribution is normal, with mean 51,800 and standard deviation 400, we can use the standard normal probability distribution table to find the area or probability. At $\bar{x} = 51,300$ (Figure 7.9), we have

$$z = \frac{51,300 - 51,800}{400} = -1.25$$

Referring to the standard normal probability distribution table, we find an area between $z = 0$ and $z = -1.25$ of .3944. With a similar calculation for $\bar{x} = 52,300$, we see that the probability of the value of the sample mean being between 51,300 and 52,300 is .3944

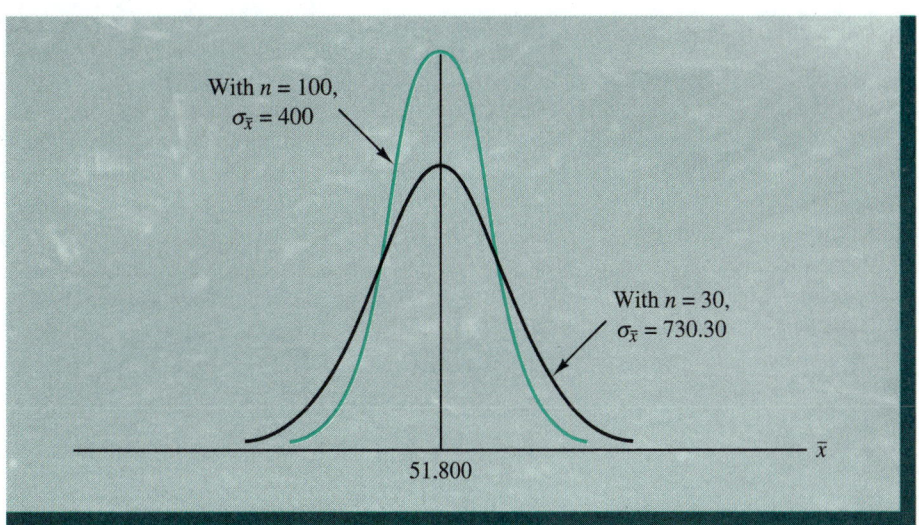

FIGURE 7.8 A Comparison of the Sampling Distributions of $\bar{x}$ for Simple Random Samples of $n = 30$ and $n = 100$ EAI Managers

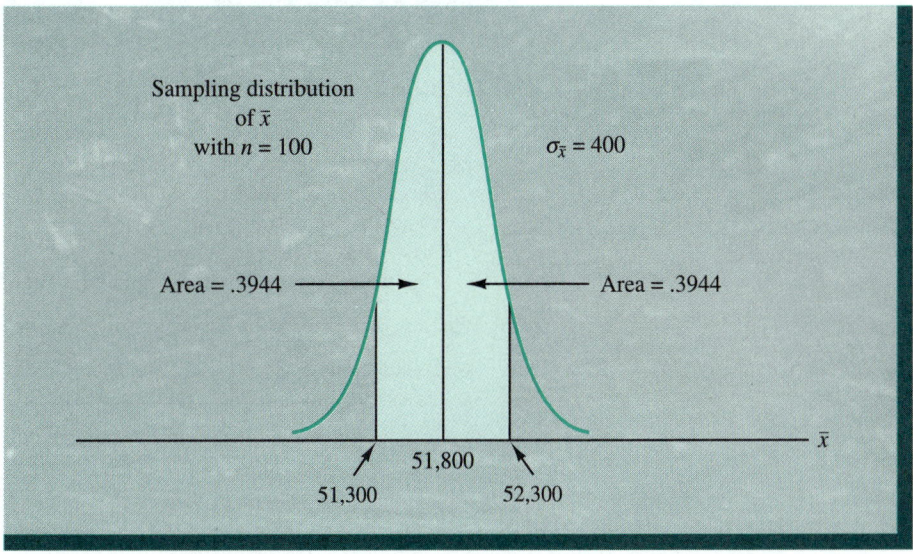

FIGURE 7.9 The Probability of a Sample Mean Being within $500 of the Population Mean when a Simple Random Sample of 100 EAI Managers Is Used

+ .3944 = .7888. Thus, by increasing the sample size from 30 to 100 EAI managers, we have increased the probability of obtaining a sample mean within $500 of the population mean from .5036 to .7888.

Perhaps an even larger sample size should be considered. However, the important point in this discussion is that as the sample size is increased, the standard error of the mean is decreased. As a result, the sampling distribution of $\bar{x}$ will have less variation. In effect, the larger sample size will provide a higher probability that the value of the sample mean is within a specified distance of the population mean.

NOTES AND COMMENTS

• • • • • • • • • • • • • • • • • •

1. In presenting the sampling distribution of $\bar{x}$ for the EAI problem, we took advantage of the fact that the population mean $\mu = 51,800$ and the population standard deviation $\sigma = 4000$ were known. However, in general, the values of the population mean μ and the population standard deviation σ that are needed to determine the sampling distribution of $\bar{x}$ will be unknown. In Chapter 8 we will show how the sample mean $\bar{x}$ and the sample standard deviation s from a simple random sample are used when μ and σ are unknown.

2. The theoretical proof of the central limit theorem requires independent observations or items in the sample. This condition is met for infinite populations and for finite populations where sampling is done with replacement. Although the central limit theorem does not directly address sampling without replacement from finite populations, general statistical practice has been to apply the findings of the central limit theorem in this situation when the population size is large.

EXERCISES

METHODS

20. A population has a mean of 200 and a standard deviation of 50. A simple random sample of size 100 will be taken and the sample mean $\bar{x}$ will be used to estimate the population mean.
    a. What is the expected value of $\bar{x}$?
    b. What is the standard deviation of $\bar{x}$?
    c. Show the sampling distribution of $\bar{x}$.
    d. What does the sampling distribution of $\bar{x}$ show?

21. What important role does the central limit theorem serve whenever $\bar{x}$ is used to estimate μ?

Self-Test
• • • • • • • • • ▶

22. A population has a mean of 200 and a standard deviation of 50. Suppose a simple random sample of size 100 is selected and $\bar{x}$ is used to estimate μ.
    a. What is the probability that the sample mean will be within ± 5 of the population mean?
    b. What is the probability that the sample mean will be within ± 10 of the population mean?

23. Assume that $\mu = 32$ and standard deviation $\sigma = 5$. Furthermore, assume that the population has 1000 items and that a simple random sample of 30 items is used to obtain information about this population.
    a. What is the expected value of $\bar{x}$?
    b. What is the standard deviation of $\bar{x}$?

24. Assume the population standard deviation is $\sigma = 25$. Compute the standard error of the mean, $\sigma_{\bar{x}}$, for sample sizes of 50, 100, 150, and 200. What can you say about the size of the standard error of the mean as the sample size is increased?

25. Suppose a simple random sample of size 50 is selected from a population with $\sigma = 10$. Find the value of the standard error of the mean in each of the following cases (use the finite population correction factor if appropriate).
    a. The population size is infinite.
    b. The population size is $N = 50,000$.
    c. The population size is $N = 5000$.
    d. The population size is $N = 500$.

26. A population has a mean of 400 and a standard deviation of 50. The probability distribution of the population is unknown.
  a. A researcher will use simple random samples of either 10, 20, 30, or 40 items to collect data about the population. With which of these sample-size alternatives will we be able to use a normal probability distribution to describe the sampling distribution of $\bar{x}$? Explain.
  b. Show the sampling distribution of $\bar{x}$ for the instances in which the normal probability distribution is appropriate.

27. A population has a mean of 100 and a standard deviation of 16. What is the probability that a sample mean will be within ± 2 of the population mean for each of the following sample sizes?
  a. $n = 50$ **b.** $n = 100$ **c.** $n = 200$ **d.** $n = 400$
  e. What is the advantage of a larger sample size?

APPLICATIONS

28. Refer to the EAI sampling problem. Suppose the simple random sample had contained 60 managers.
  a. Sketch the sampling distribution of $\bar{x}$ when simple random samples of size 60 are used.
  b. What happens to the sampling distribution of $\bar{x}$ if simple random samples of size 120 are used?
  c. What general statement can you make about what happens to the sampling distribution of $\bar{x}$ as the sample size is increased? Does this seem logical? Explain.

Self-Test
· · · · · · · · · · ►

29. In the EAI sampling problem, we showed that for $n = 30$, there was .5036 probability of obtaining a sample mean within ± $500 of the population mean.
  a. What is the probability that $\bar{x}$ is within $500 of the population mean if a sample of size 60 is used?
  b. Answer part (a) for a sample of size 120.

30. A 1993 survey conducted by the American Automobile Association showed that a family of four spends an average of $215.60 per day when on vacation. Assume that $215.60 is the population mean expenditure per day for a family of four and that $85.00 is the population standard deviation. Assume that a random sample of 40 families will be selected for further study.
  a. Show the sampling distribution of the sample mean $\bar{x}$ where $\bar{x}$ is the mean expenditure per day for a family of four; assume a random sample of 40 families.
  b. What is the probability that the simple random sample for the 40 families will provide a sample mean that is within $20 of the population mean?
  c. What is the probability that the simple random sample for the 40 families will provide a sample mean that is within $10 of the population mean?

31. A statistics class has 80 students. The mean score on the midterm exam was $\mu = 72$ and the standard deviation was $\sigma = 12$. Assume that a simple random sample of 20 students will be selected and the sample mean exam score $\bar{x}$ will be computed. Find the expected value and standard deviation of $\bar{x}$.

32. Weights for men between the ages of 20 and 30 have a mean $\mu = 170$ pounds with a standard deviation of $\sigma = 28$ pounds. If a simple random sample of 40 men in this age group is to be selected and the sample mean weight $\bar{x}$ computed, what are the values of $E(\bar{x})$ and $\sigma_{\bar{x}}$?

33. Annual surveys of starting salaries for college graduates are conducted by the College Placement Council. The mean annual starting salary for accounting majors is $26,542 (*USA Today,* September 9, 1991). Assume that for the population of graduates with accounting majors the mean annual starting salary is $26,542 and the standard deviation is $2000.
  a. What is the probability that a simple random sample of accounting graduates will have a sample mean within ± $250 of the population mean for each of the following sample sizes: 30, 50, 100, 200, and 400?
  b. What is the advantage of a larger sample size when one is attempting to estimate a population mean?

34. In 1993, women took an average of 8.5 weeks of unpaid leave from their jobs after the birth of a child (*U.S. News & World Report,* December 27, 1993). Assume that 8.5 weeks is the population mean and 2.2 weeks is the population standard deviation.

    a. What is the probability that a simple random sample of 50 women provides a sample mean leave after the birth of a child of between 7.5 and 9.5 weeks?

    b. What is the probability that a simple random sample of 50 women provides a sample mean leave after the birth of a child of between eight and nine weeks?

35. In a study of the growth rate of a certain plant, a botanist is planning to use a simple random sample of 25 plants for data-collection purposes. After analyzing the data on plant growth rate, the botanist believes that the standard error of the mean is too large. What size simple random sample should the botanist use to reduce the standard error to one-half its current value?

36. The population mean price for a new automobile is $16,012 (*U.S. News & World Report,* September 9, 1991). Assume that the population standard deviation is $4200 and that a sample of 100 new automobile purchases will be selected.

    a. Show the sampling distribution of the sample mean price for new automobiles based on the sample of 100.

    b. What is the probability that the sample mean for the 100 purchases will be within $1000 of the population mean?

    c. Repeat part (b) for values of $500, $250, and $100.

    d. To estimate the population mean price to within ± $250 or ± $100, what would you recommend?

37. An automatic machine used to fill cans of soup has the following characteristics: $\mu = 15.9$ ounces and $\sigma = .5$ ounces.

    a. Show the sampling distribution of $\bar{x}$, where $\bar{x}$ is the sample mean for 40 cans selected randomly by a quality control inspector.

    b. What is the probability of finding a sample of 40 cans with a mean $\bar{x}$ greater than 16 ounces?

38. In 1992, the National Fisheries Institute reported that tuna was the favorite seafood consumed in the United States, with a population mean annual consumption of 3.6 pounds per person. Assume that the population standard deviation is 1.5 pounds.

    a. Show the sampling distribution of the sample mean $\bar{x}$ where $\bar{x}$ is the mean number of pounds of tuna consumed per year for a sample of 100 individuals.

    b. What is the probability that the sample mean consumption is four or more pounds?

    c. What is the probability that the sample mean consumption is between 3.2 and four pounds?

39. To estimate the mean age for a population of 4000 employees, a simple random sample of 40 employees is selected.

    a. Would you use the finite population correction factor in calculating the standard error of the mean? Explain.

    b. If the population standard deviation is $\sigma = 8.2$ years, compute the standard error both with and without using the finite population correction factor. What is the rationale for ignoring the finite population correction factor whenever $n / N \le .05$?

    c. What is the probability that the sample mean age of the employees will be within ± 2 years of the population mean age?

40. A library checks out an average of $\mu = 320$ books per day, with a standard deviation of $\sigma = 75$ books. Consider a sample of 30 days of operation, with $\bar{x}$ being the sample mean number of books checked out per day.

    a. Show the sampling distribution of $\bar{x}$.

    b. What is the standard deviation of $\bar{x}$?

    c. What is the probability that the sample mean for the 30 days will be between 300 and 340 books?

    d. What is the probability that the sample mean will show 325 or more books checked out?

7.6   SAMPLING DISTRIBUTION OF $\bar{p}$

In many situations in business and economics, we use the sample proportion $\bar{p}$ to make statistical inferences about the population proportion p. This process is depicted in Figure 7.10. On each repitition of the process, we can anticipate obtaining a different value for the sample proportion $\bar{p}$. The probability distribution for all possible values of the sample proportion $\bar{p}$ is called the sampling distribution of the sample proportion $\bar{p}$.

> **SAMPLING DISTRIBUTION OF $\bar{p}$**
> The sampling distribution of $\bar{p}$ is the probability distribution of all possible values of the sample proportion $\bar{p}$.

To determine how close the sample proportion $\bar{p}$ is to the population proportion p, we need to understand the properties of the sampling distribution of $\bar{p}$: the expected value of $\bar{p}$, the standard deviation of $\bar{p}$, and the shape of the sampling distribution of $\bar{p}$.

EXPECTED VALUE OF $\bar{p}$

The expected value of $\bar{p}$ (i.e., the mean of all possible values of $\bar{p}$) can be expressed as follows.

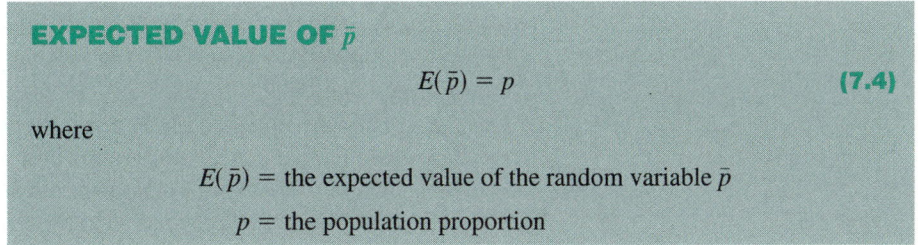

> **EXPECTED VALUE OF $\bar{p}$**
>
> $$E(\bar{p}) = p \qquad \text{(7.4)}$$
>
> where
>
> $E(\bar{p}) =$ the expected value of the random variable $\bar{p}$
>
> $p =$ the population proportion

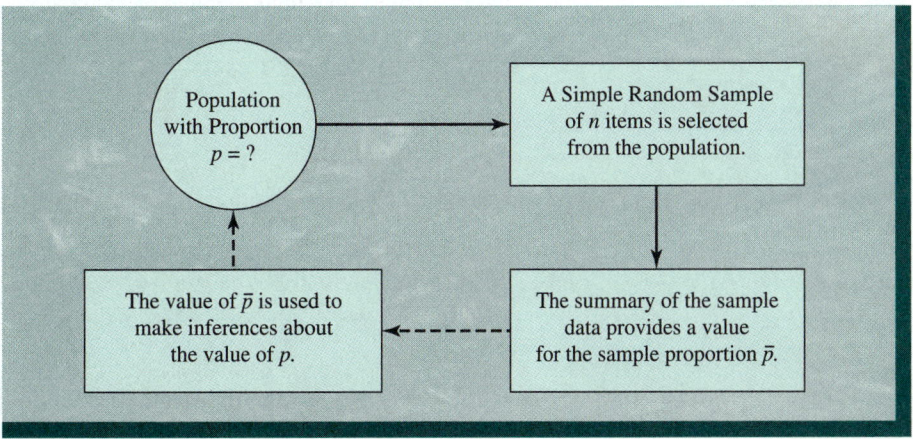

FIGURE 7.10   The Statistical Process of Using a Sample Proportion to Make Inferences about a Population Proportion

Equation (7.4) shows that the mean of all possible $\bar{p}$ values is equal to the population proportion p. Recall that in Section 7.1 we showed that $p = .60$ for the EAI population, where p was the proportion of the population of managers who had participated in the company's management training program. Thus, the expected value of $\bar{p}$ for the EAI sampling problem is .60.

STANDARD DEVIATION OF $\bar{p}$

Different simple random samples generate a variety of values for $\bar{p}$. We now are interested in determining the standard deviation of $\bar{p}$, which is referred to as the *standard error of the proportion*. Just as we found for the sample mean $\bar{x}$ the standard deviation of $\bar{p}$ depends on whether the population is finite or infinite. The two expressions for the standard deviation of $\bar{p}$ follow.

STANDARD DEVIATION OF $\bar{p}$

Finite Population	Infinite Population	
$\sigma_{\bar{p}} = \sqrt{\dfrac{N-n}{N-1}} \sqrt{\dfrac{p(1-p)}{n}}$	$\sigma_{\bar{p}} = \sqrt{\dfrac{p(1-p)}{n}}$	(7.5)

Comparing the two expressions in (7.5), we see that the only difference is the use of the finite population correction factor $\sqrt{(N-n)/(N-1)}$.

As was the case with the sample mean $\bar{x}$, we find that the difference between the expressions for the finite population and the infinite population becomes negligible if the size of the finite population is large in comparison to the sample size. We follow the same rule of thumb that we recommended for the sample mean. That is, if the population is finite with $n/N \le .05$, we will use $\sigma_{\bar{p}} = \sqrt{p(1-p)/n}$. However, if the population is finite and if $n/N > .05$, the finite population correction factor should be used, as shown in (7.5). Again, unless specifically noted, throughout the text we will assume that the population size is large in relation to the sample size and that the finite population correction factor is unnecessary.

For the EAI study we know that the population proportion of managers who have participated in the management training program is $p = .60$. With $n/N = 30/2500 = .012$, we can ignore the finite population correction factor when we compute the standard deviation of $\bar{p}$. For the simple random sample of 30 managers, $\sigma_{\bar{p}}$ is

$$\sigma_{\bar{p}} = \sqrt{\frac{p(1-p)}{n}} = \sqrt{\frac{.60(1-.60)}{30}} = \sqrt{.008} = .0894$$

FORM OF THE SAMPLING DISTRIBUTION OF $\bar{p}$

Now that we know the mean and standard deviation of $\bar{p}$, we want to consider the form of the sampling distribution of $\bar{p}$. Applying the central limit theorem as it relates to $\bar{p}$ produces the following result.

The sampling distribution of $\bar{p}$ can be approximated by a normal probability distribution whenever the sample size is large.

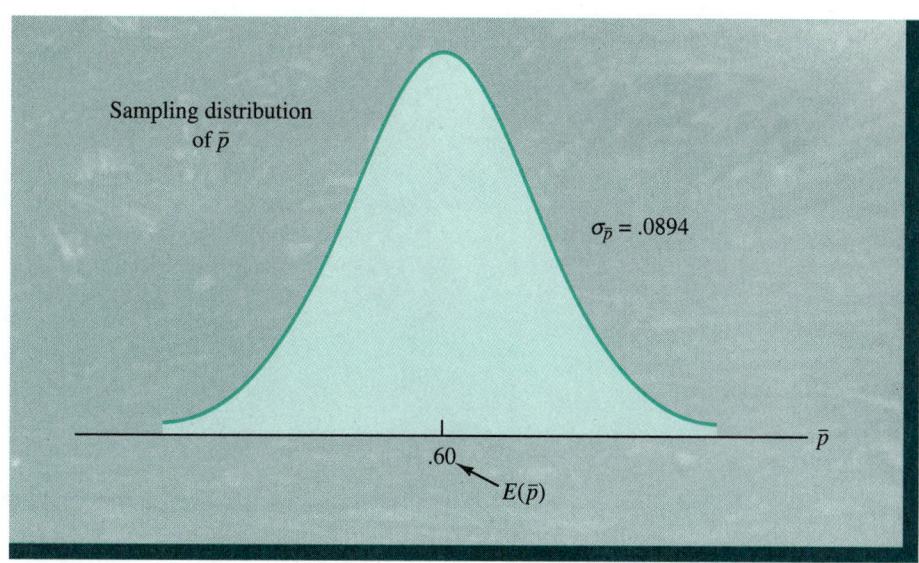

FIGURE 7.11 Sampling Distribution of $\bar{p}$ for the Proportion of EAI Managers Who Have Participated in the Management Training Program

With $\bar{p}$, the sample size can be considered large whenever the following two conditions are satisfied.

$$np \geq 5$$

$$n(1 - p) \geq 5$$

Recall that for the EAI sampling problem we know that the population proportion of managers who have participated in the training program is $p = .60$. With a simple random sample of size 30, we have $np = 30(.60) = 18$ and $n(1 - p) = 30(.40) = 12$. Thus, the sampling distribution of $\bar{p}$ can be approximated by a normal probability distribution as shown in Figure 7.11.

PRACTICAL VALUE OF THE SAMPLING DISTRIBUTION OF $\bar{p}$

Whenever a simple random sample is selected and the value of the sample proportion $\bar{p}$ is used to estimate the value of the population proportion p, we anticipate some sampling error. In this case, the sampling error is the absolute value of the difference between the value of the sample proportion $\bar{p}$ and the value of the population proportion p. The practical value of the sampling distribution of $\bar{p}$ is that it can be used to provide probability information about the sampling error.

Suppose, in the EAI problem, the personnel director wants to know the probability of obtaining a value of $\bar{p}$ that is within .05 of the population proportion of EAI managers who have participated in the training program. That is, what is the probability of obtaining a sample with a sample proportion $\bar{p}$ between .55 and .65? The area in Figure 7.12 shows this probability. Using the fact that the sampling distribution of $\bar{p}$ can be approximated by a normal probability distribution with mean .60 and standard deviation $\sigma_{\bar{p}} = .0894$, we find that the standard normal random variable corresponding to $\bar{p} = .55$ has a value of $z = (.55 - .60)/.0894 = -.56$. Referring to the standard

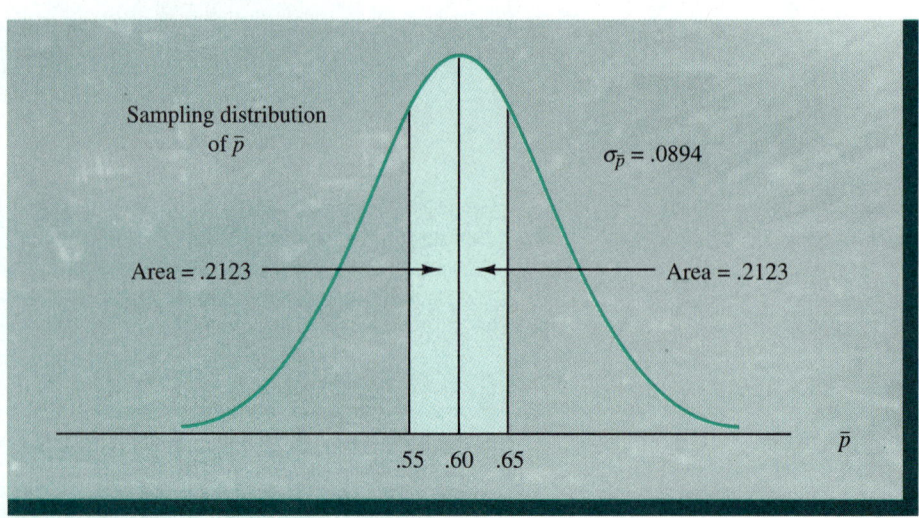

FIGURE 7.12 Sampling Distribution of $\bar{p}$ for the EAI Sampling Problem

normal probability distribution table, we see that the area between $z = -.56$ and $z = 0$ is .2123. Similarly, at $\bar{p} = .65$ we find an area between $z = 0$ and $z = .56$ of .2123. Thus, the probability of selecting a sample that provides a sample proportion $\bar{p}$ within .05 of the population proportion p is $.2123 + .2123 = .4246$.

If we consider increasing the sample size to $n = 100$, the standard error of the proportion becomes

$$\sigma_{\bar{p}} = \sqrt{\frac{.60(1 - .60)}{100}} = \sqrt{.0024} = .0490$$

With a sample size of 100 EAI managers, the probability of the sample proportion having a value within .05 of the population proportion can now be computed. Since the sampling distribution is approximately normal, with mean .60 and standard deviation .0490, we can use the standard normal probability distribution table to find the area or probability. At $\bar{p} = .55$, we have $z = (.55 - .60)/.0490 = -1.02$. Referring to the standard normal probability distribution table, we see that the area between $z = -1.02$ and $z = 0$ is .3461. Similarly, at .65 the area between $z = 0$ and $z = 1.02$ is .3461. Thus, if the sample size is increased from 30 to 100, the probability that the sample proportion $\bar{p}$ is within .05 of the population proportion p will increase from .4246 to $.3461 + .3461 = .6922$.

EXERCISES

METHODS

41. A simple random sample of size 100 is selected from a population with $p = .40$.
   a. What is the expected value of $\bar{p}$?
   b. What is the standard deviation of $\bar{p}$?
   c. Show the sampling distribution of $\bar{p}$.
   d. What does the sampling distribution of $\bar{p}$ show?

Self-Test

42. A population proportion is .40. A simple random sample of size 200 will be taken and the sample proportion $\bar{p}$ will be used to estimate the population proportion.
   a. What is the probability that the sample proportion will be within $\pm .03$ of the population proportion?

b. What is the probability that the sample proportion will be within ± .05 of the population proportion?

43. Assume that the population proportion is .55. Compute the standard error of the proportion, $\sigma_{\bar{p}}$, for sample sizes of 100, 200, 500, and 1000. What can you say about the size of the standard error of the proportion as the sample size is increased?

44. The population proportion is .30. What is the probability that a sample proportion will be within ± .04 of the population proportion for each of the following sample sizes?
    a. $n = 100$ **b.** $n = 200$ **c.** $n = 500$ **d.** $n = 1000$
    e. What is the advantage of a larger sample size?

APPLICATIONS

Self-Test

45. The president of Doerman Distributors, Inc., believes that 30% of the firm's orders come from new or first-time customers. A simple random sample of 100 orders will be used to estimate the proportion of new or first-time customers. The results of the sample will be used to verify the president's claim of $p = .30$.
    a. Assume that the president is correct and $p = .30$. What is the sampling distribution of $\bar{p}$ for this study?
    b. What is the probability that the sample proportion $\bar{p}$ will be between .20 and .40?
    c. What is the probability that the sample proportion will be within ± .05 of the population proportion $p = .30$?

46. The Grocery Manufacturers of America reported that 76% of consumers read the ingredients listed on a product's label (*America by the Numbers*, 1993). Assume the population proportion is $p = .76$ and a sample of 400 consumers is selected from the population.
    a. Show the sampling distribution of the sample proportion $\bar{p}$ where $\bar{p}$ is the proportion of the sampled consumers who read the ingredients listed on a product's label.
    b. What is the probability that the sample proportion will be within ± .03 of the population proportion?
    c. Answer part (b) for a sample of 750 consumers.

47. Louis Harris & Associates, Inc. conducted a survey of 1253 adults to learn how individuals feel about the United States' position in the global economy (*Business Week,* April 6, 1992). One question asked how concerned the individual was about U.S. industry becoming less competitive in the global economy. Assume that for the entire population, 55% of the adults are very concerned about U.S. industry becoming less competitive. Let $\bar{p}$ be the sample proportion of the polled adults who are very concerned about this issue.
    a. Show the sampling distribution of $\bar{p}$ if the population proportion is $p = .55$.
    b. What is the probability that the Harris poll sample proportion will have a sampling error of ± .02 or less?
    c. What is the probability that the Harris poll sample proportion will have a sampling error of ± .03 or less?
    d. Comment on why the Harris poll stated, "Results should be accurate to within 3 percentage points."

48. The American Association of Individual Investors reported results from a survey on a range of investment-related topics (*AAII Journal,* April 1992). One question was: Do you favor relaxed SEC rules for financial reporting by foreign corporations to allow more foreign stocks to be traded in the United States? Assume that the population proportion is .42 and that the sample size is 300.
    a. What is the probability that the sample proportion will be within ± .03 of the population proportion?
    b. What is the probability that the sample proportion will be .45 or greater?
    c. What is the probability that the sample proportion will show 50% or more favoring relaxed SEC rules for foreign corporations?

49. A particular county in West Virginia has a 9% unemployment rate. A monthly survey of 800 individuals is conducted by a state agency to monitor the unemployment rate of the county.

    a. Assume that $p = .09$. What is the sampling distribution of $\bar{p}$ when a sample of size 800 is used?

    b. What is the probability that a sample proportion $\bar{p}$ of at least .08 will be observed?

50. The Institute for Women's Policy Research reported that women now constitute 37% of all union members, an all-time high percentage (*The Wall Street Journal,* July 26, 1994). Suppose the population proportion of women who are union members is $p = .37$ and a simple random sample of 1000 union members is selected.

    a. Show the sampling distribution of $\bar{p}$, the proportion of women in the sample.

    b. What is the probability that the sample proportion will be within $\pm .03$ of the population proportion?

    c. Answer part (b) for a simple random sample of 500.

51. For the EAI sampling problem, what is the probability that the proportion of managers who have completed the firm's training program, $\bar{p}$, is within $\pm .05$ of the population proportion $p = .60$? Use samples of size 60 and 120.

52. Assume that 15% of the items produced in an assembly line operation are defective, but that the firm's production manager is not aware of this situation. Assume further that 50 parts are tested by the quality assurance department to determine the quality of the assembly operation. Let $\bar{p}$ be the sample proportion defective found by the quality assurance test.

    a. Show the sampling distribution for $\bar{p}$.

    b. What is the probability that the sample proportion will be within $\pm .03$ of the population proportion defective?

    c. If the test shows $\bar{p} = .10$ or more, the assembly line operation will be shut down to check for the cause of the defects. What is the probability that the sample of 50 parts will lead to the conclusion that the assembly line should be shut down?

53. The Food Marketing Institute shows that 17% of households spend more than $100 per week on groceries (*USA Today,* June 21, 1994). Assume the population proportion is $p = .17$ and a simple random sample of 800 households will be selected from the population.

    a. Show the sampling distribution of $\bar{p}$, the sample proportion of households spending more than $100 per week on groceries.

    b. What is the probability that the sample proportion will be within $\pm .02$ of the population proportion?

    c. Answer part (b) for a sample of 1600 households.

7.7   PROPERTIES OF POINT ESTIMATORS

In this chapter we have shown how sample statistics such as a sample mean $\bar{x}$, a sample standard deviation s, and a sample proportion $\bar{p}$ can be used as point estimators of their corresponding population parameters μ, σ, and p. It is intuitively appealing that each of these sample statistics is the point estimator of its corresponding population parameter. However, before using a sample statistic as a point estimator, statisticians check to see whether the sample statistic has certain properties associated with good point estimators. In this section we discuss the properties of good point estimators: unbiasedness, efficiency, and consistency.

Since several different sample statistics can be used as point estimators of different population parameters, we will use the following general notation in this section.

$$\theta = \text{the population parameter of interest}$$

$$\hat{\theta} = \text{the sample statistic or point estimator of } \theta$$

The notation θ is the Greek letter theta, and the notation $\hat{\theta}$ is pronounced "theta-hat." In general, θ represents any population parameter such as a population mean, population

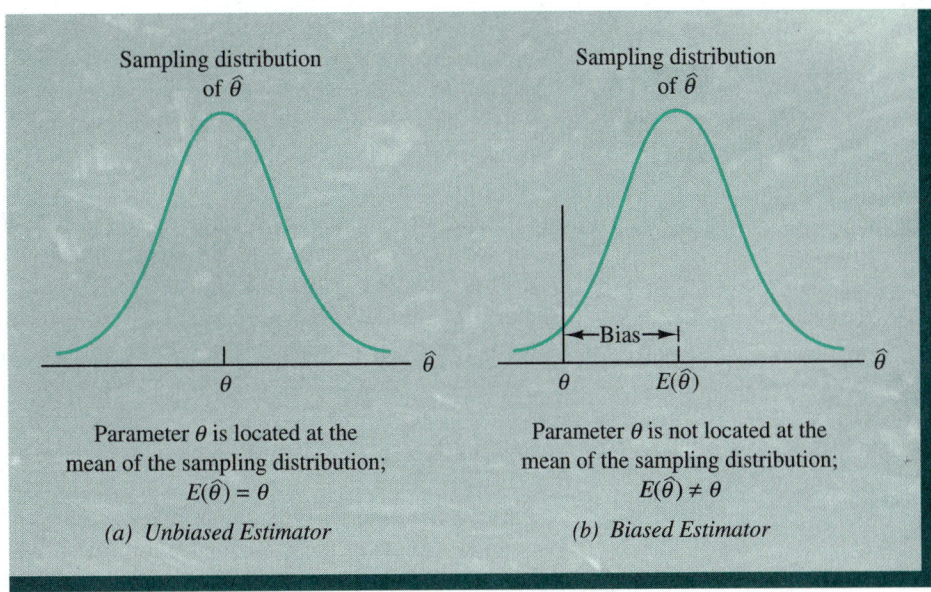

FIGURE 7.13   Examples of Unbiased and Biased Point Estimators

standard deviation, population proportion, and so on; $\hat{\theta}$ represents the corresponding sample statistic such as the sample mean, sample standard deviation, and sample proportion.

UNBIASEDNESS

If the expected value of the sample statistic is equal to the population parameter being estimated, the sample statistic is said to be an *unbiased* estimator of the population parameter. The property of unbiasedness is defined as follows.

UNBIASEDNESS

The sample statistic $\hat{\theta}$ is an unbiased estimator of the population parameter θ if

$$E(\hat{\theta}) = \theta \qquad\qquad (7.6)$$

where

$$E(\hat{\theta}) = \text{expected value of the sample statistic } \hat{\theta}.$$

Hence, the expected value, or mean, of all possible values of an unbiased sample statistic is equal to the population parameter being estimated.

Figure 7.13 shows the cases of unbiased and biased point estimators. In the illustration showing the unbiased estimator, the mean of the sampling distribution is equal to the value of the population parameter. The sampling errors balance out in this case, since sometimes the value of the point estimator $\hat{\theta}$ may be less than θ and other times it may be greater than θ. In the case of a biased estimator, the mean of the sampling distribution is less than or greater than the value of the population parameter. In the illustration in Figure 7.13(b), $E(\hat{\theta}) > \theta$; thus, the sample statistic has a high probability of overestimating the value of the population parameter. The amount of the bias is shown in the figure.

In discussing the sampling distributions of the sample mean and the sample proportion, we stated that $E(\bar{x}) = \mu$ and $E(\bar{p}) = p$. Thus, both $\bar{x}$ and $\bar{p}$ are unbiased estimators of their corresponding population parameters μ and p.

We defer a more detailed discussion of the sampling distribution of the sample standard deviation s and the sample variance s^2 until Chapter 11. However, it can be shown that $E(s^2) = \sigma^2$. Thus, we conclude that the sample variance s^2 is an unbiased estimator of the population variance σ^2. In fact, when we first presented the formulas for the sample variance and the sample standard deviation in Chapter 3, $n - 1$ rather than n was used in the denominators. The reason for using $n - 1$ rather than n is to make the sample variance an unbiased estimator of the population variance. If we had used n in the denominator, the sample variance would have been a biased estimator, tending to slightly underestimate the population variance.

EFFICIENCY

Assume that a simple random sample of n elements can be used to provide two unbiased point estimators of the same population parameter. In this situation, we would prefer to use the point estimator with the smaller standard deviation, since it tends to provide estimates closer to the population parameter. The point estimator with the smaller standard deviation is said to have greater *relative efficiency* than the other.

Figure 7.14 shows the sampling distributions of two unbiased point estimators, $\hat{\theta}_1$ and $\hat{\theta}_2$. Note that the standard deviation of $\hat{\theta}_1$ is less than the standard deviation of $\hat{\theta}_2$; thus, values of $\hat{\theta}_1$ have a greater chance of being close to the parameter θ than do values of $\hat{\theta}_2$. Since the standard deviation of point estimator $\hat{\theta}_1$ is less than the standard deviation of point estimator $\hat{\theta}_2$, $\hat{\theta}_1$ is relatively more efficient than $\hat{\theta}_2$ and is the preferred point estimator.

CONSISTENCY

A third property associated with good point estimators is *consistency*. Loosely speaking, a point estimator is consistent if the values of the point estimator tend to become closer to the population parameter as the sample size becomes larger. In other words, a large

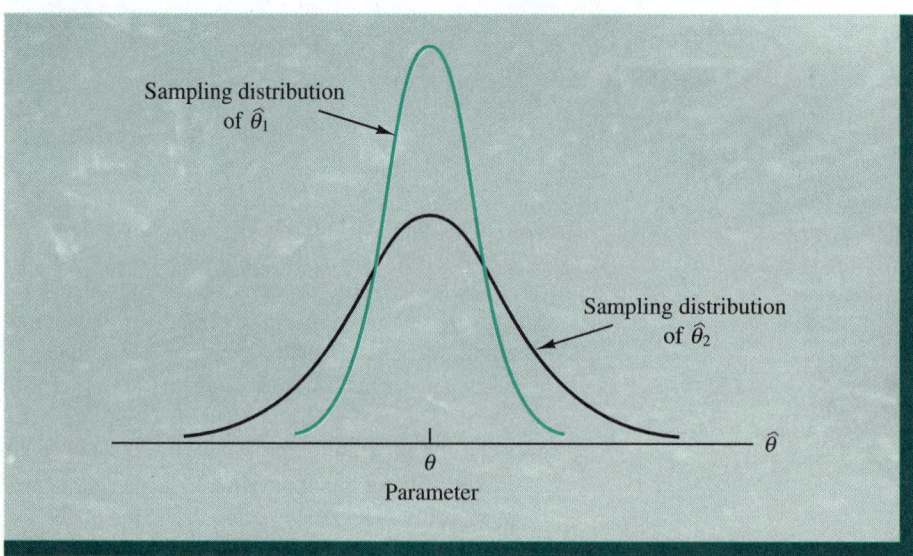

FIGURE 7.14   Sampling Distributions of Two Unbiased Point Estimators

sample size tends to provide a better point estimate than a small sample size. Note that for the sample mean $\bar{x}$, we showed that the standard deviation of $\bar{x}$ is given by $\sigma_{\bar{x}} = \sigma/\sqrt{n}$. Since $\sigma_{\bar{x}}$ is related to the sample size such that larger sample sizes provide smaller values for $\sigma_{\bar{x}}$, we conclude that a larger sample size tends to provide point estimates closer to the population mean μ. In this sense, we can say that the sample mean $\bar{x}$ is a consistent estimator of the population mean μ. Using a similar rationale, we can also conclude that the sample proportion $\bar{p}$ is a consistent estimator of the population proportion p.

NOTES AND COMMENTS

In Chapter 3 we stated that the mean and the median are two measures of central location. In this chapter we discussed only the mean. The reason is that in sampling from a normal population, where the population mean and population median are identical, the standard error of the median is approximately 25% larger than the standard error of the mean. Recall that in the EAI problem where $n = 30$, the standard error of the mean is $\sigma_{\bar{x}} = 730.30$. The standard error of the median for this problem would be approximately $1.25 \times (730.30) = 913$. As a result, the sample mean will have a higher probability of being within a specified distance of the population mean.

7.8 OTHER SAMPLING METHODS

We have described the simple random sampling procedure and discussed the properties of the sampling distributions of $\bar{x}$ and $\bar{p}$ when simple random sampling is used. However, simple random sampling is not the only sampling method available. Such methods as stratified random sampling, cluster sampling, and systematic sampling are alternatives that in some situations have advantages over simple random sampling. In this section we briefly describe some of these alternative sampling methods. A more detailed discussion of these methods is presented in Chapter 21.

STRATIFIED RANDOM SAMPLING

In *stratified random sampling,* the population is first divided into groups of elements called *strata,* such that each item in the population belongs to one and only one stratum. The basis for forming the strata, such as department, location, age, industry type, and so on, is at the discretion of the designer of the sample. However, best results are obtained when the elements within each stratum are as much alike as possible. Figure 7.15 is a diagram of a population divided into H strata.

After the strata are formed, a simple random sample is taken from each stratum. Formulas are available for combining the results for the individual stratum samples into one estimate of the population parameter of interest. The value of stratified random sampling depends on how homogeneous the elements are within the strata. If units within strata are alike (homogeneity), the strata will have low variances. Thus relatively small sample sizes can be used to obtain good estimates of the strata characteristics. If strata are homogeneous, the stratified random sampling procedure will provide results just as precise as those of simple random sampling but with a smaller total sample size.

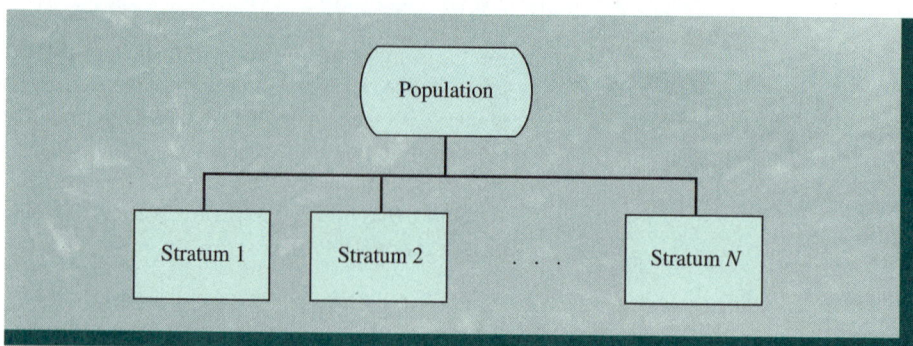

FIGURE 7.15   Diagram for Stratified Simple Random Sampling

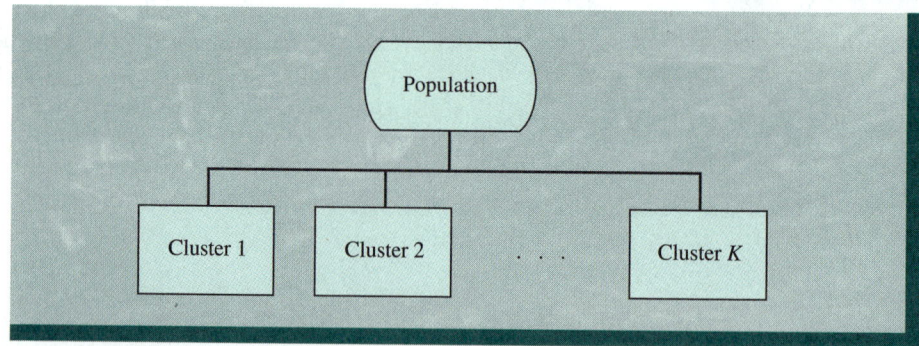

FIGURE 7.16   Diagram for Cluster Sampling

CLUSTER SAMPLING

In *cluster sampling,* the population is first divided into separate groups of elements called *clusters.* Each element of the population belongs to one and only one cluster (see Figure 7.16). A simple random sample of the clusters is then taken. All elements within each sampled cluster form the sample. Cluster sampling tends to provide best results when the elements within the clusters are heterogeneous (not alike). In the ideal case, each cluster is a representative small-scale version of the entire population. The value of cluster sampling depends on how representative each cluster is of the entire population. If all clusters are alike in this regard, sampling a small number of clusters will provide good estimates of the population parameters.

One of the primary applications of cluster sampling is area sampling, where clusters are city blocks or other well-defined areas. Cluster sampling generally requires a larger total sample size than either simple random sampling or stratified random sampling. However, it can result in cost savings because of the fact that when an interviewer is sent to a sampled cluster (say a city-block location), many sample observations can be obtained in a relatively short time. Hence, a larger sample size may be obtainable with a significantly lower cost per element and thus possibly a lower total cost.

SYSTEMATIC SAMPLING

In some sampling situations, especially those with large populations, it is time-consuming to select a simple random sample by first finding a random number and then counting or searching through the list of population items until the corresponding element is found. An alternative to simple random sampling is *systematic sampling*. For example, if a sample size of 50 is desired from a population containing 5000 elements, we might sample one element for every 5000/50 = 100 elements in the population. A systematic sample for this case involves selecting randomly one of the first 100 elements from the population list. Other sample elements are identified by starting with the first sampled element and then selecting every 100th element that follows in the population list. In effect, the sample of 50 is identified by moving systematically through the population and identifying every 100th element after the first randomly selected element. The sample of 50 usually will be easier to identify in this way than it would be if simple random sampling were used. Since the first element selected is a random choice, a systematic sample is usually assumed to have the properties of a simple random sample. This assumption is especially applicable when the list of the population elements is a random ordering of the elements in the population.

CONVENIENCE SAMPLING

The sampling methods discussed thus far are referred to as *probability sampling* techniques. Elements selected from the population have a known probability of being included in the sample. The advantage of probability sampling is that the sampling distribution of the appropriate sample statistic generally can be identified. Formulas such as the ones for simple random sampling presented in this chapter can be used to determine the properties of the sampling distribution. Then the sampling distribution can be used to make probability statements about possible sampling errors associated with the sample results.

Convenience sampling is a *nonprobability sampling* technique. As the name implies, the sample is identified primarily by convenience. Items are included in the sample without prespecified or known probabilities of being selected. For example, a professor conducting research at a university may use student volunteers to constitute a sample simply because they are readily available and will participate as subjects for little or no cost. Similarly, an inspector may sample a shipment of oranges by selecting oranges haphazardly from among several crates. Labeling each orange and using a probability method of sampling would be impractical. Samples such as wildlife captures and volunteer panels for consumer research are also convenience samples.

Convenience samples have the advantage of relatively easy sample selection and data collection; however, it is impossible to evaluate the "goodness" of the sample in terms of its representativeness of the population. A convenience sample may provide good results or it may not. There is no statistically justified procedure that will allow a probability analysis and inference about the quality of the sample results. Sometimes researchers apply statistical methods designed for probability samples to a convenience sample, arguing that the convenience sample can be treated as though it were a random sample. However, this argument cannot be supported, and we should be very cautious in interpreting the results of convenience samples that are used to make inferences about populations.

JUDGMENT SAMPLING

One additional nonprobability sampling technique is *judgment sampling*. In this approach, the person most knowledgeable on the subject of the study selects individuals or other elements of the population that he or she feels are most representative of the population. Often this is a relatively easy way of selecting a sample. For example, a reporter may sample two or three senators, judging that those senators reflect the general opinion of all senators. However, the quality of the sample results depends on the judgment of the person selecting the sample. Again, great caution is warranted in drawing conclusions based on judgment samples used to make inferences about populations.

NOTES AND COMMENTS

We recommend sampling by one of the probability sampling methods: simple random sampling, stratified simple random sampling, cluster sampling, or systematic sampling. For these methods, formulas are available for evaluating the "goodness" of the sample results in terms of the closeness of the results to the population characteristics being estimated. An evaluation of the goodness cannot be made with convenience or judgment sampling. Thus, great care should be used in interpreting the results when nonprobability sampling methods have been used to obtain statistical information.

SUMMARY

In this chapter we presented the concepts of simple random sampling and sampling distributions. We demonstrated how a simple random sample can be selected and how the data collected for the sample can be used to develop point estimates of population parameters. Since different simple random samples provided a variety of different values for the point estimators, point estimators such as $\bar{x}$ and $\bar{p}$ are random variables. The probability distribution of such a random variable is called a sampling distribution. In particular, we described the sampling distributions of the sample mean x and the sample proportion $\bar{p}$.

In considering the characteristics of the sampling distributions of $\bar{x}$ and $\bar{p}$, we stated that $E(\bar{x}) = \mu$ and $E(\bar{p}) = p$. After developing the standard deviation or standard error formulas for these estimators, we showed how the central limit theorem provided the basis for using a normal probability distribution to approximate these sampling distributions in the large-sample case. Rules of thumb were given for determining when large-sample-size conditions were satisfied. We then discussed three properties of point estimators: unbiasedness, efficiency, and consistency. Other sampling methods such as stratified random sampling, cluster sampling, and convenience sampling were discussed briefly.

GLOSSARY

Parameter   A numerical characteristic of a population, such as a population mean μ, a population standard deviation σ, a population proportion p, and so on.

Simple random sampling   Finite population: a sample selected such that each possible sample of size n has the same probability of being selected. Infinite population: a sample selected such that each element comes from the same population and the successive elements are selected independently.

Sampling without replacement   Once an element from the population has been included in the sample, it is removed from the population and cannot be selected a second time.

Sampling with replacement As each element is selected for the sample, it is returned to the population. A previously selected element can be selected again and therefore may appear in the sample more than once.

Sample statistic A sample characteristic, such as a sample mean $\bar{x}$, a sample standard deviation s, a sample proportion $\bar{p}$, and so on. The value of the sample statistic is used to estimate the value of the population parameter.

Sampling distribution A probability distribution consisting of all possible values of a sample statistic.

Point estimate A single numerical value used as an estimate of a population parameter.

Point estimator The sample statistic, such as $\bar{x}$, s, and $\bar{p}$, that provides the point estimate of the population parameter.

Finite population correction factor The term $\sqrt{(N-n)/(N-1)}$ that is used in the formulas for $\sigma_{\bar{x}}$ and $\sigma_{\bar{p}}$ whenever a finite population, rather than an infinite population, is being sampled. The generally accepted rule of thumb is to ignore the finite population correction factor whenever $n/N \le .05$.

Standard error The standard deviation of a point estimator.

Central limit theorem A theorem that enables one to use the normal probability distribution to approximate the sampling distribution of $\bar{x}$ and $\bar{p}$ whenever the sample size is large.

Unbiasedness A property of a point estimator that is present whenever the expected value of the point estimator is equal to the population parameter it estimates.

Relative efficiency Given two unbiased point estimators of the same population parameter, the point estimator with the smaller variance is said to have greater efficiency than the other.

Consistency A property of a point estimator that is present whenever larger sample sizes tend to provide point estimates closer to the population parameter.

Stratified simple random sampling A method of selecting a sample in which the population is first divided into strata and a simple random sample is then taken from each stratum.

Cluster sampling A probabilistic method of sampling in which the population is first divided into clusters and then one or more clusters is selected for sampling.

Systematic sampling A method of choosing a sample by randomly selecting one of the first k elements and then selecting every kth element thereafter.

Convenience sampling A nonprobabilistic method of sampling whereby elements are selected for the sample on the basis of convenience.

Judgment sampling A nonprobabilistic method of sampling whereby elements are selected for the sample based on the judgment of the person doing the study.

KEY FORMULAS

Expected Value of $\bar{x}$

$$E(\bar{x}) = \mu \qquad (7.1)$$

Standard Deviation of $\bar{x}$

Finite Population	Infinite Population

$$\sigma_{\bar{x}} = \sqrt{\frac{N-n}{N-1}}\left(\frac{\sigma}{\sqrt{n}}\right) \qquad \sigma_{\bar{x}} = \frac{\sigma}{\sqrt{n}} \tag{7.2}$$

Expected Value of $\bar{p}$

$$E(\bar{p}) = p \tag{7.4}$$

Standard Deviation of $\bar{p}$

Finite Population	Infinite Population

$$\sigma_{\bar{p}} = \sqrt{\frac{N-n}{N-1}}\sqrt{\frac{p(1-p)}{n}} \qquad \sigma_{\bar{p}} = \sqrt{\frac{p(1-p)}{n}} \tag{7.5}$$

SUPPLEMENTARY EXERCISES

54. Nationwide Supermarkets has 4800 retail stores in 32 states. At the end of each year, a sample of 35 stores is selected for physical inventories. Results from the inventory samples are used in annual tax reports. Assume that the retail stores are listed sequentially on a computer printout. Begin at the bottom of the second column of random numbers in Table 7.1. Ignoring the first digit in each group and using four-digit random numbers beginning with 8112, read *up* the column to identify the first five stores to be included in the simple random sample.

55. A 1993 study conducted by *The Orlando Sentinel* provided data on how much time customers wait for service at Burger King, McDonald's, and Wendy's restaurants. Assume that the population mean waiting time for a drive-through order is four minutes and that the population standard deviation is 1.5 minutes.
  a. Suppose a sample of 60 drive-through customers will be selected and the sample mean waiting time computed. Show the sampling distribution of the sample mean.
  b. What is the probability that the sample mean waiting time will be within $\pm .25$ minutes of the population mean waiting time?

56. The U.S. Department of Transportation reported the number of car miles traveled per day for residents of the 75 largest metropolitan areas in the United States (*1994 Information Please Environmental Almanac*). Tulsa, Oklahoma, provided the largest value, with residents driving 30 miles per day. Assume that this is the population mean and that the population standard deviation is 12 miles per day. A sample of 50 Tulsa residents is selected.
  a. Show the sampling distribution of $\bar{x}$ where $\bar{x}$ is the sample mean number of miles Tulsa residents travel per day in a car.
  b. What is the probability that the sample mean is within ± 2 miles of the population mean?

57. An electrical component is designed to provide a mean service life of 3000 hours, with a standard deviation of 800 hours. A customer purchases a batch of 50 components; assume that this batch can be considered a simple random sample of the population of components. What is the probability that the mean life for the group of 50 components will be at least 2750 hours? At least 3200 hours?

58. The population mean household income in Pittsburgh, Pennsylvania, is $49,000 (*U.S. News & World Report,* April 6, 1992). Assume that the population standard deviation is $12,000. Furthermore, assume that a simple random sample of households in the Pittsburgh area will be selected and the sample mean will be used to estimate the population mean.

   a. Show the sampling distribution of the sample mean if a sample of 100 households is used.

   b. What is the probability that a sample of 100 will provide a sampling error of $1000 or less?

   c. What is the probability that a sample of 200 will provide a sampling error of $1000 or less?

   d. What is the probability that a sample of 400 will provide a sampling error of $1000 or less?

   e. How large of a sample would be required if we wanted a .95 probability of having a sampling error of $1000 or less?

59. The time a fire department takes to respond to a request for emergency aid has a mean of $\mu = 14$ minutes with a standard deviation of $\sigma = 4$ minutes. Suppose we randomly sample 50 emergency requests over a two-month period. Records of aid-request times and arrival times will be used to compute a sample mean response time for the 50 requests.

   a. Show the sampling distribution of $\bar{x}$.

   b. What role does the central limit theorem play in identifying this sampling distribution?

   c. What is the probability that the sample mean will be 15 minutes or less?

   d. What is the probability that the sample mean will be within $\pm .5$ minutes of the mean time for the population?

60. The speed of automobiles on a section of I-75 in northern Florida has a mean of $\mu = 67$ miles per hour with a standard deviation of $\sigma = 6$ miles per hour. Assume the population has a *normal distribution* and a sample of 16 automobiles will be selected to compute a sample mean automobile speed.

   a. What is the expected value of $\bar{x}$?

   b. What is the standard deviation of $\bar{x}$?

   c. Show the sampling distribution of $\bar{x}$.

   d. What is the probability that the sample mean will be 65 miles per hour or more?

   e. What is the probability that the sample mean will be between 66 and 68 miles per hour?

61. According to *USA Today* (April 11, 1995), the mean number of days per year that business travelers are on the road for business is 115. The standard deviation is 60 days per year. Assume that these results apply to the population of business travelers and that a sample of 50 business travelers will be selected from the population.

   a. What is the value of the standard error of the mean?

   b. What is the probability that the sample mean will be more than 115 days per year?

   c. What is the probability that the sample mean will be within ± 5 days of the population mean?

   d. How would the probability change in part (c) if the sample size were increased to 100?

62. In a population of 5000 students, a simple random sample of 50 students is selected to estimate the mean grade point average for the population.

   a. Would you use the finite population correction factor in calculating the standard error of the mean? Explain.

   b. If the population standard deviation is $\sigma = .4$, compute the standard error of the mean, first with and then without the finite population correction factor. What is the rationale for ignoring the finite population correction factor whenever $n/N \le .05$?

   c. What is the probability that the sample mean grade point average for 50 students will be within $\pm .10$ of the population mean grade point average?

63. During a complete review of two months of billings, an accountant found the following values for the mean and standard deviation of the dollar amounts per billing: $\mu = \$22.00$ and $\sigma = \$7.00$. The company's controller believes that the accountant could have obtained very good estimates of the mean billing amount by taking a simple random sample of 50 billings. Assume that a simple random sampling procedure was conducted.

   a. Explain how the sample mean billing $\bar{x}$ would have a sampling distribution.

   b. Show the sampling distribution of $\bar{x}$.

c. What is the standard error of the mean?

d. What would happen to the sampling distribution of $\bar{x}$ if a sample size of 100 were considered?

64. In the EAI study the population of managers had annual salaries with $\mu = \$51,800$ and $\sigma = \$4000$. Samples of size 30 provided a .5036 probability of selecting a sample with $\bar{x}$ within $\pm \$500$ of the population mean. How large a sample should be selected if the personnel director wanted a .95 probability of a sample mean $\bar{x}$ being within $\pm \$500$ of μ?

65. Three firms have inventories that differ in size. Firm A has a population of 2000 items, firm B has a population of 5000 items, and firm C has a population of 10,000 items. The population standard deviation for the cost of the items is $\sigma = 144$. A statistical consultant recommends that each firm take a sample of 50 items from its population to provide statistically valid estimates of the average cost per item. Managers of the small firm state that since it has the smallest population, it should be able to obtain the data from a much smaller sample than that required by the larger firms. However, the consultant states that to obtain the same standard error and thus the same precision in the sample results, all firms should use the same sample size regardless of population size.

a. Using the finite population correction factor, compute the standard error for each of the three firms given a sample of size 50.

b. What is the probability that for each firm the sample mean $\bar{x}$ will be within ± 25 of the population mean μ?

66. A researcher reports survey results by stating that the standard error of the mean is 20. The population standard deviation is 500.

a. How large was the sample used in this survey?

b. What is the probability that the estimate would be within ± 25 of the population mean?

67. A production process is checked periodically by a quality control inspector. The inspector selects simple random samples of 30 finished products and computes the sample mean product weights $\bar{x}$. If test results over a long period of time show that 5% of the $\bar{x}$ values are over 2.1 pounds and 5% are under 1.9 pounds, what are the mean and the standard deviation for the population produced with this process?

68. The grade point average for all juniors at Strausser College has a standard deviation of .50.

a. A random sample of 20 students is to be used to estimate the population mean grade point average. What assumption is necessary to compute the probability of obtaining a sample mean within $\pm .2$ of the population mean?

b. Provided that the assumption in (a) can be made, what is the probability of $\bar{x}$ being within $\pm .2$ of the population mean?

c. If the assumption in (a) cannot be made, what would you recommend doing?

69. Assume that the proportion of persons having a college degree is $p = .35$.

a. Explain how the sampling distribution of $\bar{p}$ results from random samples of size 80 being used to estimate the proportion of individuals having a college degree.

b. Show the sampling distribution for $\bar{p}$ in this case.

c. If the sample size is increased to 200, what happens to the sampling distribution of $\bar{p}$? Compare the standard error for the $n = 80$ and $n = 200$ alternatives.

70. What is the most important factor for business travelers when they are staying in a hotel? According to *USA Today*, 74% of business travelers state that having a smoke-free room is the most important factor (*USA Today*, April 11, 1995). Assume that the population proportion is $p = .74$ and that a sample of 200 business travelers will be selected.

a. Show the sampling distribution of $\bar{p}$ the sample proportion of business travelers stating that a smoke-free room is the most important factor when staying in a hotel.

b. What is the probability that the sample proportion will be within $\pm .04$ of the population proportion?

c. What is the probability that the sample proportion will be within $\pm .02$ of the population proportion?

71. A market research firm conducts telephone surveys with a 40% historical response rate. What is the probability that in a new sample of 400 telephone numbers, at least 150 individuals will cooperate and respond to the questions? In other words, what is the probability that the sample proportion will be at least 150/400 = .375?

72. A production run is not acceptable for shipment to customers if a sample of 100 items contains 5% or more defective items. If a production run has a population proportion defective of $p = .10$, what is the probability that $\bar{p}$ will be at least .05?

73. The proportion of individuals insured by the All-Driver Automobile Insurance Company who have received at least one traffic ticket during a five-year period is .15.
    a. Show the sampling distribution of $\bar{p}$ if a random sample of 150 insured individuals is used to estimate the proportion having received at least one ticket.
    b. What is the probability that the sample proportion will be within ± .03 of the population proportion?

74. Historical records show that .50 of all orders placed at Big Burger fast-food restaurants include a soft drink. With a simple random sample of 40 orders, what is the probability that between .45 and .55 of the sampled orders will include a soft drink?

75. Lori Jeffrey is a successful sales representative for a major publisher of college textbooks. Historically, Lori obtains a book adoption on 25% of her sales calls. Viewing her sales calls for one month as a sample of all possible sales calls, assume that a statistical analysis of the data yields a standard error of the proportion of .0625.
    a. How large was the sample used in this analysis? That is, how many sales calls did Lori make during the month?
    b. Let $\bar{p}$ indicate the sample proportion of book adoptions obtained during the month. Show the sampling distribution $\bar{p}$.
    c. Using the sampling distribution of $\bar{p}$, compute the probability that Lori will obtain book adoptions on 30% or more of her sales calls during a one-month period.

APPENDIX 7.1 ●

The Expected Value and Standard Deviation of $\bar{x}$

● In this appendix we present the mathematical basis for the expressions for $E(\bar{x})$, the expected value of $\bar{x}$ as given by (7.1), and $\sigma_{\bar{x}}$, the standard deviation of $\bar{x}$ as given by (7.2).

EXPECTED VALUE OF $\bar{x}$

Assume a population with mean μ and variance σ^2. A simple random sample of size n is selected with individual observations denoted $x_1, x_2, \ldots, x_n$. A sample mean $\bar{x}$ is computed as follows.

$$\bar{x} = \frac{\Sigma x_i}{n}$$

With repeated simple random samples of size n, $\bar{x}$ is a random variable that takes different numerical values depending on the specific n items selected. The expected value of the random variable $\bar{x}$, or the mean of all possible $\bar{x}$ values, follows.

$$\text{Mean of } \bar{x} = E(\bar{x}) = E\left(\frac{\Sigma x_i}{n}\right)$$

$$= \frac{1}{n}[E(x_1 + x_2 + \cdots + x_n)]$$

$$= \frac{1}{n}[E(x_1) + E(x_2) + \cdots + E(x_n)]$$

Since for any x_i we have $E(x_i) = \mu$, we can write

$$E(\bar{x}) = \frac{1}{n}(\mu + \mu + \cdots + \mu)$$

$$= \frac{1}{n}(n\mu) = \mu.$$

The expression shows that the mean of all possible $\bar{x}$ values is the same as the population mean μ. That is, $E(\bar{x}) = \mu$.

STANDARD DEVIATION OF $\bar{x}$

Again assume a population with mean μ, variance σ^2, and a sample mean given by

$$\bar{x} = \frac{\Sigma x_i}{n}.$$

With repeated simple random samples of size n, we know that $\bar{x}$ is a random variable that takes different numerical values depending on the specific n items selected. Shown below is the derivation of the expression for the standard deviation of the $\bar{x}$ values, $\sigma_{\bar{x}}$, for the case of an infinite population. The derivation of the expression for $\sigma_{\bar{x}}$ for a finite population when sampling is done without replacement is more difficult and is beyond the scope of this text.

Returning to the infinite population case, recall that a simple random sample from an infinite population consists of observations $x_1, x_2, \ldots, x_n$ that are independent. The following two expressions are general formulas for the variance of random variables.

$$\text{Var}(ax) = a^2 \text{Var}(x) \tag{A.1}$$

where a is a constant and x is a random variable, and

$$\text{Var}(x + y) = \text{Var}(x) + \text{Var}(y) \tag{A.2}$$

where x and y are *independent* random variables. Using (A.1) and (A.2), we can develop the expression for the variance of the random variable $\bar{x}$ as follows.

$$\text{Var}(\bar{x}) = \text{Var}\left(\frac{\Sigma x_i}{n}\right) = \text{Var}\left(\frac{1}{n}\Sigma x_i\right)$$

Using (A.1) with $1/n$ viewed as the constant, we have

$$\text{Var}(\bar{x}) = \left(\frac{1}{n}\right)^2 \text{Var}(\Sigma x_i)$$

$$= \left(\frac{1}{n}\right)^2 \text{Var}(x_1 + x_2 + \cdots + x_n).$$

In the infinite population case, the random variables $x_1, x_2, \ldots, x_n$ are independent. Thus, (A.2) enables us to write

$$\text{Var}(\bar{x}) = \left(\frac{1}{n}\right)^2 \left[\text{Var}(x_1) + \text{Var}(x_2) + \cdots + \text{Var}(x_n)\right].$$

Since for any x_i, we have $\text{Var}(x_i) = \sigma^2$, we have

$$\text{Var}(\bar{x}) = \left(\frac{1}{n}\right)^2 (\underbrace{\sigma^2 + \sigma^2 + \cdots + \sigma^2}_{n \text{ items}}).$$

With n values of σ^2 in this expression, we have

$$\text{Var}(\bar{x}) = \left(\frac{1}{n}\right)^2 (n\sigma^2) = \frac{\sigma^2}{n}.$$

Taking the square root provides the formula for the standard deviation of $\bar{x}$.

$$\sigma_{\bar{x}} = \sqrt{\text{Var}(\bar{x})} = \frac{\sigma}{\sqrt{n}}$$

This expression, which appeared as (7.2), shows that as the sample size n is increased, the standard deviation of $\bar{x}$ will decrease.

8

INTERVAL ESTIMATION

$\overline{x}$

STATISTICS IN PRACTICE ● ● ● ● ● ● ● ● ● ● ● ● ● ● ● ● ●

Dollar General Corporation*

Nashville, Tennessee

Dollar General Corporation was founded in 1939 as a drygoods wholesale company. After World War II, the company began opening retail locations in rural south-central Kentucky. Today Dollar General Corporation operates more than 2000 neighborhood stores in 23 states. Serving predominantly low- and middle-income customers, Dollar General markets soft goods, and health, beauty, and cleaning supplies at low everyday prices.

Being in an inventory-intense business with approximately 17,000 different products, Dollar General made the decision to adopt the LIFO (last-in-first-out) method of inventory valuation. This method matches current costs against current revenues, which minimizes the effect of radical price changes on profit and loss results. In addition, the LIFO method reduces net income and thereby income taxes during periods of inflation. This in turn brings disposable cash generated from sales in line with income and allows for the replacement of inventory at current costs.

Accounting practices require that a LIFO index be established for inventory under the LIFO method of valuation. For example, a LIFO index of 1.048 indicates that the company's inventory value at current costs reflects a 4.8% increase due to inflation over the most recent one-year period.

The establishment of a LIFO index requires that the year-end inventory count for each product be valued at the current year-end cost and at the preceding year-end cost. To avoid counting the inventory of every product in more than 2000 retail locations, a random sample of 800 products is selected from 100 retail locations and three warehouses. Physical inventories for the 800 sampled products are taken at the end of the year. Accounting

personnel then provide the current-year and preceding-year costs needed to construct the LIFO index.

For a recent year, the LIFO index was 1.070. However, since this index is only a sample estimate of the population's LIFO index, a statement about the precision of the estimate was required. On the basis of the sample results and a 95% confidence level, the margin of error was computed to be .006. Thus, the interval from 1.064 to 1.076 provides the 95% confidence interval estimate of the population LIFO index. This precision was judged to be very good.

In this chapter you will learn how to make a probability statement about the sampling error associated with the sample mean and sample proportion. Then, you will learn how to use this information to construct and interpret confidence interval estimates of a population mean and a population proportion. You will also learn how to determine the sample size needed to ensure that the sampling error will be within acceptable limits.

This store in Bedford, Indiana, is one of more than 2000 Dollar General Stores.

---

*Mr. Robert S. Knaul, Controller, Dollar General Corporation, provided this Statistics in Practice.

● In Chapter 7 we showed that the value of the sample mean $\bar{x}$ and the sample proportion $\bar{p}$ provide point estimates of the population mean μ and the population proportion p, respectively. Since point estimates are based on a sample of the population, they cannot be expected to equal the value of the corresponding population parameter. In this chapter we will show how interval estimates of the population mean and the population proportion can be developed to provide information about the precision of an estimate. As we will show, the sampling distributions of $\bar{x}$ and $\bar{p}$ presented in Chapter 7 play an important role in the development of interval estimates of μ and p.

8.1   INTERVAL ESTIMATION OF A POPULATION MEAN: LARGE-SAMPLE CASE

In this section we show how the sampling distribution of $\bar{x}$ can be used to develop an interval estimate of a population mean μ. We begin with the large-sample case ($n \geq 30$) in which the population standard deviation σ is *known*. Once we show how to develop an interval estimate of μ for this case, we will show how to do so for the large-sample case in which σ is unknown.

Let us begin by considering a sampling study conducted by CJW, Inc., a mail-order firm that specializes in sporting equipment and accessories. The company works hard to provide the best possible customer service. To monitor the quality of its service, CJW selects a simple random sample of mail-order customers each month; each customer sampled is contacted and asked a series of questions pertaining to the level of customer service. The answers to the questions are used to compute a satisfaction score for each customer sampled; these scores range from 0 (worst possible rating) to 100 (best possible rating). A sample mean satisfaction score is then computed and used as a point estimate of the mean satisfaction score for the population of all CJW customers.

Previous monthly surveys have shown that although the sample mean satisfaction score changes from month to month, the standard deviation of satisfaction scores has tended to stabilize at a value of 20. Hence, we will assume that the population standard deviation is $\sigma = 20$. The most recent CJW customer satisfaction survey provided data on the satisfaction scores of 100 customers ($n = 100$); the sample mean satisfaction score was $\bar{x} = 82$. In the discussion that follows, we will use the sample results to develop an interval estimate of the population mean satisfaction score μ.

SAMPLING ERROR

Anytime a sample mean is used to provide a point estimate of a population mean, someone may ask: How good is the estimate? The "how good" question is a way of asking about the error involved when the value of $\bar{x}$ is used as the point estimate of μ. In general, the absolute value of the difference between an unbiased point estimator and the population parameter it estimates is called the *sampling error*. For the case of a sample mean estimating a population mean, the sampling error is

$$\text{Sampling Error} = |\bar{x} - \mu| \tag{8.1}$$

In practice, the value of the sampling error cannot be determined because the population mean μ is unknown. However, the sampling distribution of $\bar{x}$ can be used to make probability statements about the size of the sampling error. We will illustrate how this is done for the CJW sampling study.

With a sample size $n = 100$ and a population standard deviation $\sigma = 20$, the central limit theorem, introduced in Chapter 7, enables us to conclude that the sampling

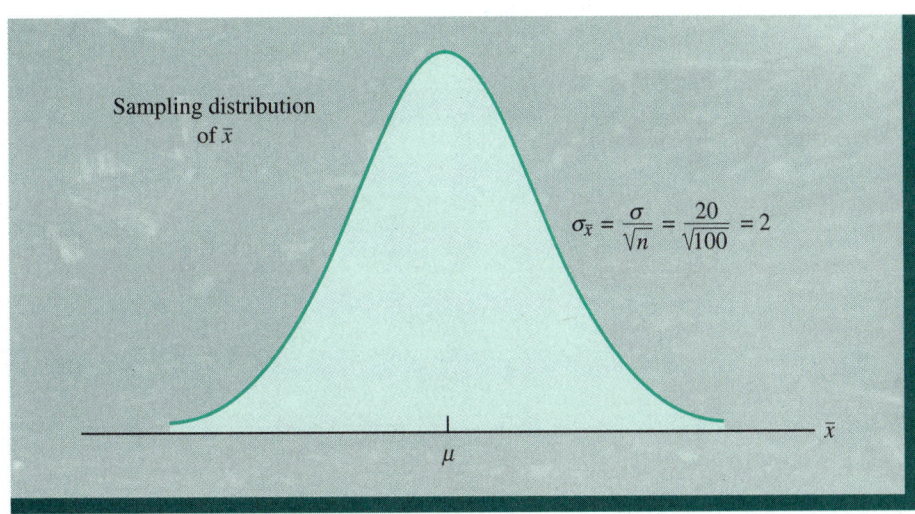

FIGURE 8.1   Sampling Distribution of the Sample Mean Satisfaction Score from Simple Random Samples of 100 Customers

distribution of $\bar{x}$ can be approximated by a normal probability distribution with a mean μ and a standard deviation $\sigma_{\bar{x}} = \sigma/\sqrt{n} = 20/\sqrt{100} = 2$. This sampling distribution is shown in Figure 8.1. Since the sampling distribution of $\bar{x}$ shows how values of $\bar{x}$ are distributed around μ, it provides information about the possible differences between $\bar{x}$ and μ. We can use this information to develop probability statements about the sampling error.

PROBABILITY STATEMENTS ABOUT THE SAMPLING ERROR

Using the table of areas for the standard normal probability distribution, we find that 95% of the values of any normally distributed random variable are within ± 1.96 standard deviations of the mean. Hence, for the sampling distribution in Figure 8.1, 95% of all $\bar{x}$ values must be within ± 1.96 standard deviations of μ. Since $1.96\sigma_{\bar{x}} = 1.96(2) = 3.92$, 95% of the sample means must be within ± 3.92 of the population mean.

The location of the sample means that provide a sampling error of 3.92 or less is shown in Figure 8.2. Note that if a sample mean is in the region denoted "95% of all $\bar{x}$ values," it provides a sampling error of 3.92 or less. However, if a sample mean is in either the lower tail or the upper tail of the distribution, the sampling error will be greater than 3.92. We therefore can make the following probability statement about the sampling error for the CJW problem.

There is a .95 probability that the sample mean will provide a sampling error of 3.92 or less.

This probability statement about the sampling error is a *precision statement* telling CJW about the error that can expected if a simple random sample of 100 customers is used to estimate the population mean. Although a .95 probability is frequently used in making precision statements, other probability values such as .90 and .99 can be used. For instance, Figure 8.3 shows the location of 99% of the sample means for the CJW problem. Using the standard normal probability distribution table, we find that 99% of the $\bar{x}$ values are within ± 2.576 standard deviations of μ. Since $2.576\sigma_{\bar{x}} = 2.576(2) = 5.15$, there is a .99 probability that the sample mean will provide a sampling error

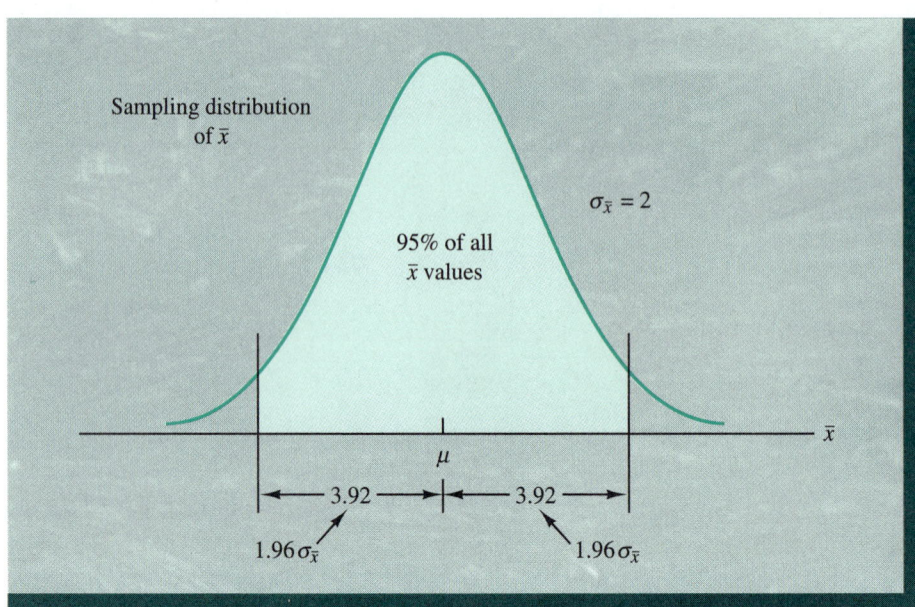

FIGURE 8.2   Sampling Distribution of $\bar{x}$ Showing the Location of Sample Means that Provide a Sampling Error of 3.92 or Less

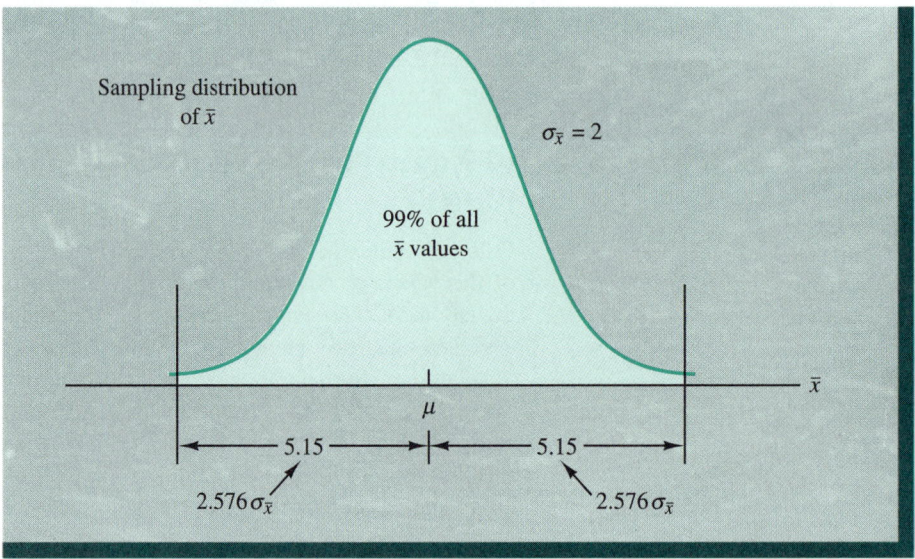

FIGURE 8.3   Sampling Distribution of $\bar{x}$ Showing the Location of 99% of the $\bar{x}$ Values

of 5.15 or less. Similarly, there is a .90 probability that the sample mean will provide a sampling error of $1.645\sigma_{\bar{x}} = 1.645(2) = 3.29$ or less.

Let us generalize the procedure we use to make precision statements about the sampling error whenever the value of a sample mean is used to estimate a population mean. We will use the Greek letter α to indicate the probability that the sampling error is *larger* than the sampling error in the precision statement. In Figure 8.4, $\alpha/2$ denotes the area, or probability, in each tail of the sampling distribution and $1 - \alpha$ denotes the area, or probability, that a sample mean will provide a sampling error less than or equal to the sampling error in the precision statement. For example, the statement that there is

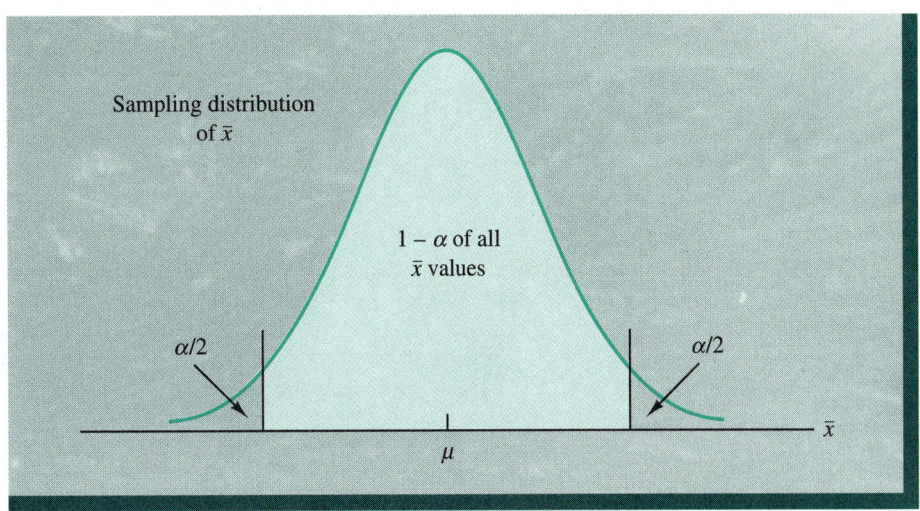

FIGURE 8.4   Areas of a Sampling Distribution of $\bar{x}$ Used to Make Probability Statements about the Sampling Error

a .95 probability that the value of a sample mean will provide a sampling error of 3.92 or less is based on $\alpha = .05$ and $1 - \alpha = .95$. The area in each tail of the sampling distribution is $\alpha/2 = .025$.

Using z to denote the standard normal random variable, we place a subscript on z to denote the *area in the upper tail* of the distribution. In general, $z_{\alpha/2}$ is the value of the standard normal random variable corresponding to an area of $\alpha/2$ in the upper tail of the distribution. With this notation, the following precision statement defines the size of the sampling error whenever $\bar{x}$ is used to estimate μ.

PRECISION STATEMENT
There is a $1 - \alpha$ probability that the value of a sample mean will provide a sampling error of $z_{\alpha/2}\sigma_{\bar{x}}$ or less.

CALCULATING AN INTERVAL ESTIMATE: LARGE-SAMPLE CASE WITH σ KNOWN

In the CJW example, we stated that there is a .95 probability that the value of the sample mean will provide a sampling error of 3.92 or less. We can construct an interval estimate for μ by subtracting 3.92 from $\bar{x}$ and adding 3.92 to $\bar{x}$; that is, $\bar{x} \pm 3.92$. To interpret interval estimate of μ, let us consider possible values of $\bar{x}$ that could be obtained from three different simple random samples, each consisting of 100 customers.

Suppose the first sample mean turns out to have the value shown in Figure 8.5 as $\bar{x}_1$. In this case, Figure 8.5 shows that the interval formed by subtracting 3.92 from $\bar{x}_1$ and adding 3.92 to $\bar{x}_1$ includes the population mean μ. Now consider what happens if the sample mean turns out to have the value shown in Figure 8.5 as $\bar{x}_2$. Although this sample mean is different from the first sample mean, we see that the interval based on $\bar{x}_2$ also includes the population mean μ. However, the interval based on the third sample mean, denoted by $\bar{x}_3$, does not include the population mean; the reason is that $\bar{x}_3$ is in a tail of the distribution at a distance farther than 3.92 from μ. Hence, subtracting and adding 3.92 to $\bar{x}_3$ forms an interval that does not include μ.

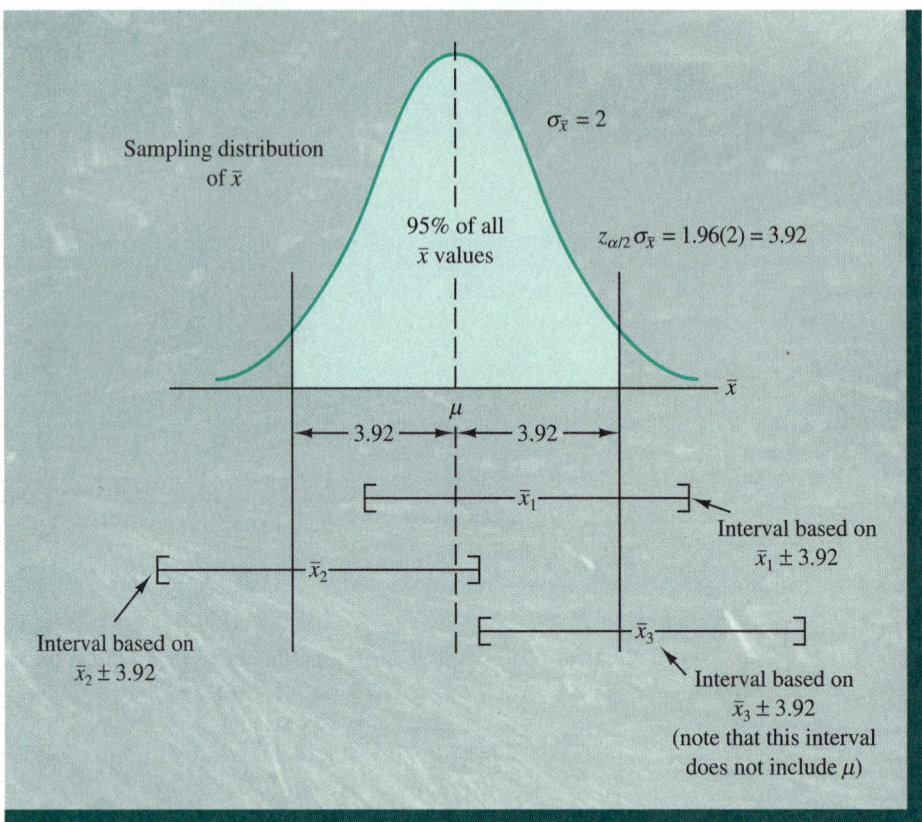

FIGURE 8.5 Intervals Formed from Selected Sample Means at Locations $\bar{x}_1$, $\bar{x}_2$, and $\bar{x}_3$

In general, any sample mean $\bar{x}$ that is within the unshaded region of Figure 8.5 will provide an interval that contains the population mean μ. Since 95% of the possible sample means will be in this region, 95% of all intervals formed by subtracting 3.92 from $\bar{x}$ and adding 3.92 to $\bar{x}$ will include μ. We therefore say that we are 95% confident that an interval constructed from $\bar{x} - 3.92$ to $\bar{x} + 3.92$ will include the population mean. Using common statistical terminology, we refer to the interval as a *confidence interval*. Since 95% of the sample means will result in an a confidence interval that includes the population mean μ, we say that the confidence interval is established at the 95% *confidence level*. The value .95 is referred to as the *confidence coefficient*.

Recall that CJW's sample of 100 customers provided a sample mean satisfaction score of $\bar{x} = 82$. Using the interval $\bar{x} \pm 3.92$, we find that the 95% confidence interval estimate of the population mean is 82 ± 3.92, or 78.08 to 85.92. Hence, at the 95% confidence level, CJW can conclude that the mean satisfaction score for the population of all mail-order customers is between 78.08 and 85.92.

Let us now state the general procedure for computing an interval estimate of a population mean for the large-sample case with σ known. As previously noted, there is a $1 - \alpha$ probability that the value of the sample mean will provide a sampling error of $z_{\alpha/2}\sigma_{\bar{x}}$ or less. Using the fact that $\sigma_{\bar{x}} = \sigma/\sqrt{n}$, we can write the procedure for calculating the *interval estimate* of a population mean as follows.

TABLE 8.1 Values of $z_{\alpha/2}$ for the Most Commonly Used Confidence Levels

Confidence Level	α	$\alpha/2$	$z_{\alpha/2}$
90%	.10	.05	1.645
95%	.05	.025	1.96
99%	.01	.005	2.576

INTERVAL ESTIMATE OF A POPULATION MEAN: LARGE-SAMPLE CASE ($n \geq 30$) WITH σ KNOWN

$$\bar{x} \pm z_{\alpha/2} \frac{\sigma}{\sqrt{n}} \tag{8.2}$$

where $1 - \alpha$ is the confidence coefficient and $z_{\alpha/2}$ is the z value providing an area of $\alpha/2$ in the upper tail of the standard normal probability distribution.

The values of $z_{\alpha/2}$ for the most commonly used confidence levels are given in Table 8.1.

CALCULATING AN INTERVAL ESTIMATE: LARGE-SAMPLE CASE WITH σ UNKNOWN

A difficulty in using (8.2) is that in most sampling situations the value of the population standard deviation σ is unknown. In the large-sample case ($n \geq 30$), we simply use the value of the sample standard deviation, s, as the point estimate of the population standard deviation σ to obtain the following interval estimate.

INTERVAL ESTIMATE OF A POPULATION MEAN: LARGE-SAMPLE CASE ($n \geq 30$) WITH σ UNKNOWN

$$\bar{x} \pm z_{\alpha/2} \frac{s}{\sqrt{n}} \tag{8.3}$$

where s is the sample standard deviation, $1 - \alpha$ is the confidence coefficient, and $z_{\alpha/2}$ is the z value providing an area of $\alpha/2$ in the upper tail of the standard normal probability distribution.

As an illustration of the interval estimation procedure, let us consider a sampling study conducted by the Statewide Insurance Company. Suppose that as part of an annual review of life insurance policies, Statewide selects a simple random sample of 36 Statewide life insurance policyholders. The corresponding life insurance policies are reviewed in terms of the amount of coverage, the cash value of the policy, disability options, and so on. For the current study, a manager has asked for a 90% confidence interval estimate of the mean age for the population of life insurance policyholders.

Table 8.2 reports the age data collected from a simple random sample of 36 policyholders. The sample mean age of $\bar{x} = 39.5$ years is the point estimate of the population mean age. In addition, the sample standard deviation for the data in Table 8.2 is $s = 7.77$. At 90% confidence, $z_{.05} = 1.645$. Using (8.3), we obtain

$$39.5 \pm 1.645 \frac{7.77}{\sqrt{36}}$$

$$39.5 \pm 2.13$$

Hence, the 90% confidence interval estimate of the population mean is 37.37 to 41.63. The manager therefore can be 90% confident that the mean age for the population of Statewide life insurance policyholders is between 37.37 years and 41.63 years.

TABLE 8.2 Ages of Life Insurance Policyholders from a Simple Random Sample of 36 Statewide Policyholders

LIFEINS

Policyholder	Age	Policyholder	Age	Policyholder	Age
1	32	13	39	25	23
2	50	14	46	26	36
3	40	15	45	27	42
4	24	16	39	28	34
5	33	17	38	29	39
6	44	18	45	30	34
7	45	19	27	31	35
8	48	20	43	32	42
9	44	21	54	33	53
10	47	22	36	34	28
11	31	23	34	35	49
12	36	24	48	36	39

COMPUTER-GENERATED CONFIDENCE INTERVALS

To illustrate the use of computer software packages in developing interval estimates of a population mean, we used Minitab to develop a 90% confidence interval estimate of the population mean age for the Statewide Insurance policyholders. The Minitab output is shown in panel A of Figure 8.6. The sample standard deviation $s = 7.77$ is shown to be the assumed value for the population standard deviation σ. Additional output shows that the sample of 36 policyholders provides a sample mean of 39.50 years, a sample standard deviation of 7.77 years, and a standard error of the mean of 1.29 years. The 90% confidence interval estimate is 37.37 years to 41.63 years as previously computed.

To compute an interval estimate of the population mean with a different confidence coefficient, we simply change the value for the confidence level in the Minitab procedure. Panel B of Figure 8.6 shows that the 95% confidence interval is 36.96 years to 42.04 years; note that, as is expected, the 95% confidence interval estimate is wider than the 90% confidence interval estimate.

NOTES AND COMMENTS

1. In developing an interval estimate of the population mean, we specify the desired confidence coefficient $(1 - \alpha)$ before selecting the sample. Thus, prior to selecting the sample, we conclude that there is a $1 - \alpha$ probability that the confidence interval we eventually compute will contain the population mean μ. However, once the sample is taken, the sample mean $\bar{x}$ is computed, and the particular interval estimate is determined, the resulting interval *may or may not* contain μ. If $1 - \alpha$ is reasonably large, we can be confident that the resulting interval will contain μ because we know that if we use this procedure repeatedly, $100(1 - \alpha)$ percent of all possible intervals developed in this way will contain μ.

2. Note that the sample size n appears in the denominator of the interval estimation expressions (8.2) and (8.3). Thus, if a particular sample size provides too wide an interval to be of any practical use, we may want to consider increasing the sample size. With n in the denominator, a larger sample size will provide a narrower interval and a greater precision. The procedure for determining the size of a simple random sample necessary to obtain a desired precision is discussed in Section 8.3.

Panel A: 90% Confidence Interval

The assumed sigma =7.77

N	Mean	StDev	SE Mean	90.0 % C.I.
36	39.50	7.77	1.29	(37.37, 41.63)

Panel B: 95% Confidence Interval

The assumed sigma =7.77

N	Mean	StDev	SE Mean	95.0 % C.I.
36	39.50	7.77	1.29	(36.96, 42.04)

FIGURE 8.6 Computer-Generated Confidence Intervals for the Statewide Insurance Company Sampling Problem

EXERCISES

METHODS

1. A simple random sample of 40 items resulted in a sample mean of 25. The population standard deviation is $\sigma = 5$.
   a. What is the standard error of the mean, $\sigma_{\bar{x}}$?
   b. At a 95% probability, what can be said about the size of the sampling error?

2. A simple random sample of 50 items resulted in a sample mean of 32 and a sample standard deviation of 6.
   a. Provide a 90% confidence interval for the population mean.
   b. Provide a 95% confidence interval for the population mean.
   c. Provide a 99% confidence interval for the population mean.

3. A sample of 60 items resulted in a sample mean of 80 and a sample standard deviation of 15.
   a. Compute the 95% confidence interval for the population mean.
   b. Assume that the same sample mean and sample standard deviation were obtained from a sample of 120 items. Provide a 95% confidence interval for the population mean.
   c. What is the effect of a larger sample size on the interval estimate of a population mean?

4. A 95% confidence interval for a population mean is reported to be 122 to 130. If the sample mean is 126 and the sample standard deviation is 16.07, what sample size was used in this study?

APPLICATIONS

5. In an effort to estimate the mean amount spent per customer for dinner at a major Atlanta restaurant, data were collected for a sample of 49 customers over a three-week period.
   a. Assume a population standard deviation of $2.50. What is the standard error of the mean?

b. With a .95 probability, what statement can be made about the sampling error?

c. If the sample mean is $22.60, what is the 95% confidence interval for the population mean?

6. Data on the automotive industry and automobile purchasing characteristics were presented in *Financial World* (April 14, 1992). The mean car payment per month was reported to be $310. Assume that this result was based on a sample of 250 car payment records and that the sample standard deviation was $100. Compute the 95% confidence interval for the mean monthly car payment.

7. The results of an annual survey of 1404 mutual funds were reported in *Forbes* (September 2, 1991). A sample of 75 funds showed a mean return over the previous 12 months of 10.2%. The sample standard deviation was 3%. Provide a 95% confidence interval for the mean return for the population of mutual funds.

8. In a study of student loan subsidies, the Department of Education reported that four-year Stafford Loan borrowers will owe an average of $12,168 upon graduation (*USA Today,* April 5, 1995). Assume that this average or mean amount owed is based on a sample of 480 student loans and that the population standard deviation for the amount owed upon graduation is $2200.

   a. Develop a 90% confidence interval estimate of the population mean amount owed.

   b. Develop a 95% confidence interval estimate of the population mean amount owed.

   c. Develop a 99% confidence interval estimate of the population mean amount owed.

   d. Discuss what happens to the width of the confidence interval as the confidence level is increased. Does this seem reasonable? Explain.

9. A container-filling operation has a historical standard deviation of 5.5 ounces. A quality control inspector periodically selects 36 containers at random and uses the sample mean filling weight to estimate the population mean filling weight for the production process.

   a. What is the standard error of the mean, $\sigma_{\bar{x}}$?

   b. With .75, .90, and .99 probabilities, what statements can be made about the sampling error? What happens to the statement about the sampling error when the probability is increased? Why does this happen?

   c. What is the 99% confidence interval for the population mean filling weight for the process if the sample mean is 48.6 ounces?

10. A subscriber survey conducted by Pulse On America, Inc. for *Fortune* magazine showed that the sample mean personal income of subscribers was $175,000 (1994 *Fortune* National Subscriber Portrait). Suppose the standard deviation of personal income for the sample of $n = 1992$ respondents is $275,000. Develop a 95% confidence interval estimate of the mean personal income for the population of all subscribers.

11. E. Lynn and Associates is an energy research firm that provides estimates of monthly heating costs for new homes based on style of house, square footage, insulation, and so on. The firm's service is used by both builders and potential buyers of new homes who want advance information on heating costs. For winter months the standard deviation in the home heating bills for residences in a certain area is $100. Assume that a sample of 36 homes in a particular subdivision will be used to estimate the mean monthly heating bill for the population of all homes in that type of subdivision.

   a. What is the standard error of the mean, $\sigma_{\bar{x}}$?

   b. Show the sampling distribution for the sample mean heating bill.

   c. With a .80 probability, what can be said about the sampling error? Show this probability on the graph of the sampling distribution in part (b).

   d. What is the 98% confidence interval for the population mean monthly heating bill if the sample mean is $196.50?

12. The profitability of used car sales was determined in a study conducted by the National Automobile Dealers Association (*USA Today,* April 12, 1995). Assume that a sample of 200 used car sales provided a sample mean profit of $300 per car and a sample standard deviation of $150. Use this information to develop a 95% confidence interval estimate of the mean profit for the population of used car sales.

13. J. D. Power & Associates' annual quality survey for automobiles found that the industry average number of defects per new car is 1.07 (*The Wall Street Journal*, January 27, 1994). Suppose a sample of 30 new automobiles taken by a particular manufacturer provides the following data on number of defects per car.

0	1	1	2	1	0	2	3	2	1	0	4	3	1	1
0	2	0	0	2	3	0	2	0	2	0	3	1	0	2

  a. Using these data, what is the sample mean number of defects per car?
  b. What is the sample standard deviation?
  c. Provide a 95% confidence interval estimate of the mean number of defects per car for the population of cars produced by this manufacturer.
  d. After viewing the confidence interval estimate in part (c), a statistical analyst suggested that the manufacturer test a larger number of new cars before drawing a conclusion about how the quality of its cars compares to the J. D. Powers & Associates industry average of 1.07 defects per car. Do you support this idea? Why or why not?

14. The International Air Transport Association surveys business travelers to develop quality ratings for transatlantic gateway airports. The maximum possible rating is 10. The highest rated airport is Amsterdam with an average rating of 7.93, followed by Toronto with a rating of 7.17 (*Newsweek*, June 13, 1994). Suppose a simple random sample of 50 business travelers is selected and each traveler is asked to provide a rating for the Miami International Airport. The ratings obtained from the sample of 50 follow.

MIAMI

6	4	6	8	7	7	6	3	3	8	10	4	8
7	8	7	5	9	5	8	4	3	8	5	5	4
4	4	8	4	5	6	2	5	9	9	8	4	8
9	9	5	9	7	8	3	10	8	9	6		

Develop a 95% confidence interval estimate of the population mean rating for Miami.

8.2   INTERVAL ESTIMATION OF A POPULATION MEAN: SMALL-SAMPLE CASE

In the small-sample case ($n < 30$), the sampling distribution of $\bar{x}$ depends on the probability distribution of the population. *If the population has a normal probability distribution,* the methodology presented in this section can be used to develop a confidence interval for a population mean. However, if the assumption of a normal probability distribution for the population is not appropriate, the only alternative is to increase the sample size to $n \geq 30$ and rely on the large-sample interval-estimation procedures given by (8.2) and (8.3).

If the population has a normal probability distribution, the sampling distribution of $\bar{x}$ will be normal regardless of the sample size. In this case, if the population standard deviation σ is *known*, (8.2) can be used to compute an interval estimate of a population mean even with a small sample. However, if the population standard deviation σ is *unknown*, the sample standard deviation s is used to estimate σ, and the appropriate confidence interval is based on a probability distribution known as the *t distribution.*

The *t* distribution is a family of similar probability distributions, with a specific *t* distribution depending on a parameter known as the *degrees of freedom.* That is, there is a unique *t* distribution with one degree of freedom, with two degrees of freedom, with three degrees of freedom, and so on. As the number of degrees of freedom increases, the difference between the *t* distribution and the standard normal probability distribution becomes smaller and smaller. Figure 8.7 shows *t* distributions with 10 and 20 degrees of

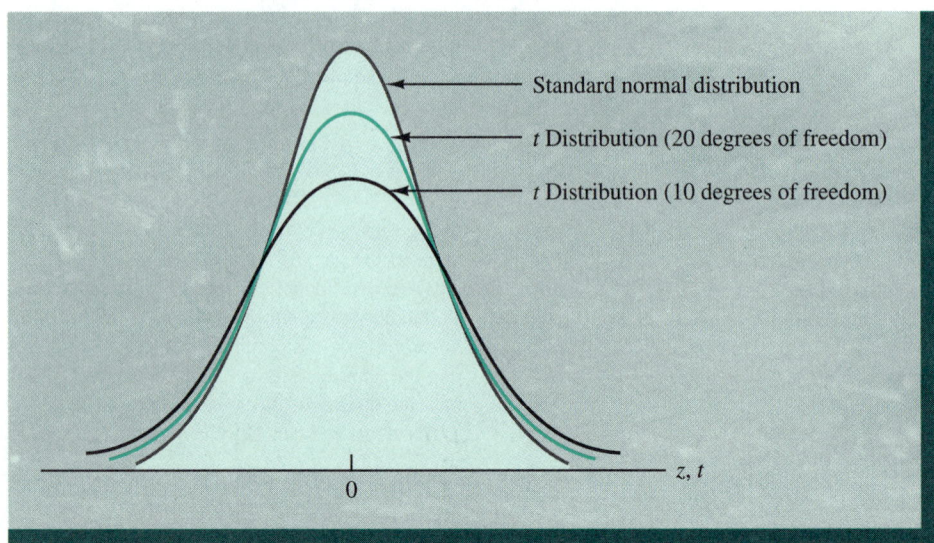

FIGURE 8.7 Comparison of the Standard Normal Distribution with *t* Distributions Having 10 and 20 Degrees of Freedom

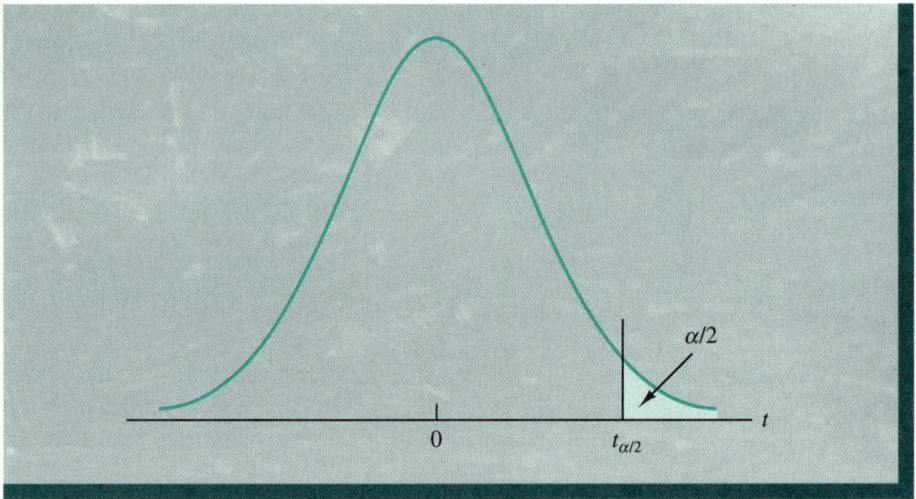

FIGURE 8.8 *t* Distribution with $\alpha/2$ Area or Probability in the Upper Tail

freedom and their relationship to the standard normal probability distribution. Note that a *t* distribution with more degrees of freedom has less dispersion and more closely resembles the standard normal probability distribution. Note also that the mean of the *t* distribution is zero.

We will use a subscript for *t* to indicate the area in the upper tail of the *t* distribution. For example, just as we used $z_{.025}$ to indicate the *z* value providing a .025 area in the upper tail of a standard normal probability distribution, we will use $t_{.025}$ to indicate a .025 area in the upper tail of the *t* distribution. In general, we will use the notation $t_{\alpha/2}$ to represent a *t* value with an area of $\alpha/2$ in the upper tail of the *t* distribution. See Figure 8.8.

Table 8.3 is a table for the *t* distribution. This table is also shown inside the front cover of the text. Note, for example, that for a *t* distribution with 10 degrees of freedom,

TABLE 8.3 t Distribution Table for Areas in the Upper Tail. Example: with 10 Degrees of Freedom, $t_{.025} = 2.228$

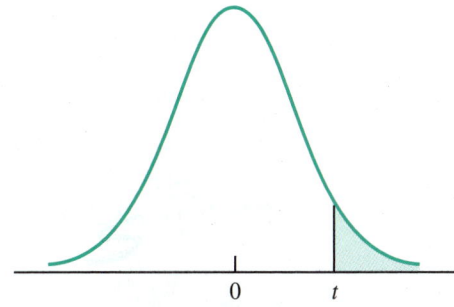

Degrees of Freedom	Upper-Tail Area (Shaded)				
	.10	.05	.025	.01	.005
1	3.078	6.314	12.706	31.821	63.657
2	1.886	2.920	4.303	6.965	9.925
3	1.638	2.353	3.182	4.541	5.841
4	1.533	2.132	2.776	3.747	4.604
5	1.476	2.015	2.571	3.365	4.032
6	1.440	1.943	2.447	3.143	3.707
7	1.415	1.895	2.365	2.998	3.499
8	1.397	1.860	2.306	2.896	3.355
9	1.383	1.833	2.262	2.821	3.250
10	1.372	1.812	2.228	2.764	3.169
11	1.363	1.796	2.201	2.718	3.106
12	1.356	1.782	2.179	2.681	3.055
13	1.350	1.771	2.160	2.650	3.012
14	1.345	1.761	2.145	2.624	2.977
15	1.341	1.753	2.131	2.602	2.947
16	1.337	1.746	2.120	2.583	2.921
17	1.333	1.740	2.110	2.567	2.898
18	1.330	1.734	2.101	2.552	2.878
19	1.328	1.729	2.093	2.539	2.861
20	1.325	1.725	2.086	2.528	2.845
21	1.323	1.721	2.080	2.518	2.831
22	1.321	1.717	2.074	2.508	2.819
23	1.319	1.714	2.069	2.500	2.807
24	1.318	1.711	2.064	2.492	2.797
25	1.316	1.708	2.060	2.485	2.787
26	1.315	1.706	2.056	2.479	2.779
27	1.314	1.703	2.052	2.473	2.771
28	1.313	1.701	2.048	2.467	2.763
29	1.311	1.699	2.045	2.462	2.756
30	1.310	1.697	2.042	2.457	2.750
40	1.303	1.684	2.021	2.423	2.704
60	1.296	1.671	2.000	2.390	2.660
120	1.289	1.658	1.980	2.358	2.617
∞	1.282	1.645	1.960	2.326	2.576

$t_{.025} = 2.228$. Similarly, for a t distribution with 20 degrees of freedom, $t_{.025} = 2.086$. As the degrees of freedom continue to increase, $t_{.025}$ approaches $z_{.025} = 1.96$.

Now that we have an idea of what the t distribution is, let us see how it is used to develop an interval estimate of a population mean. Assume that the population has a normal probability distribution and that the sample standard deviation s is used to estimate the population standard deviation σ. The following interval-estimation procedure is applicable.

INTERVAL ESTIMATE OF A POPULATION MEAN: SMALL-SAMPLE CASE ($n < 30$) WITH σ UNKNOWN

$$\bar{x} \pm t_{\alpha/2} \frac{s}{\sqrt{n}} \tag{8.4}$$

where $1 - \alpha$ is the confidence coefficient, $t_{\alpha/2}$ is the t value providing an area of $\alpha/2$ in the upper tail of a t distribution with $n - 1$ *degrees of freedom*, and s is the sample standard deviation. The population is assumed to have a normal probability distribution.

The reason the number of degrees of freedom associated with the t value in (8.4) is $n - 1$ has to do with the use of s as an estimate of the population standard deviation σ. The expression for the sample standard deviation is

$$s = \sqrt{\frac{\Sigma(x_i - \bar{x})^2}{n - 1}}$$

Degrees of freedom refers to the number of independent pieces of information that go into the computation of $\Sigma(x_i - \bar{x})^2$. The n pieces of information involved in computing $\Sigma(x_i - \bar{x})^2$ are as follows: $x_1 - \bar{x}, x_2 - \bar{x}, \ldots, x_n - \bar{x}$. In Section 3.2 we indicated that $\Sigma(x_i - \bar{x}) = 0$ for any data set. Thus, only $n - 1$ of the $x_i - \bar{x}$ values are independent; that is, if we know $n - 1$ of the values, the remaining value can be determined exactly by using the condition that the sum of the $x_i - \bar{x}$ values must be 0. Thus, $n - 1$ is the number of degrees of freedom associated with $\Sigma(x_i - \bar{x})^2$ and hence the t distribution used in (8.4).

Let us demonstrate the small-sample interval-estimation procedure by considering the training program evaluation conducted by Scheer Industries. Scheer's director of manufacturing is interested in a computer-assisted program that can be used to train the firm's maintenance employees for machine-repair operations. The expectation is that the computer-assisted method will reduce the time needed to train employees. To evaluate the training method, the director of manufacturing has requested an estimate of the mean training time required for the computer-assisted program.

Suppose management has agreed to train 15 employees with the new approach. The data on training days required for each employee in the sample are listed in Table 8.4. The sample mean and sample standard deviation for these data follow.

$$\bar{x} = \frac{\Sigma x_i}{n} = \frac{808}{15} = 53.87 \text{ days}$$

$$s = \sqrt{\frac{\Sigma(x_i - \bar{x})^2}{n - 1}} = \sqrt{\frac{651.73}{14}} = 6.82 \text{ days}$$

The point estimate of the mean training time for the population of employees is 53.87 days. We can obtain information about the precision of this estimate by developing an interval estimate of the population mean. Since the population standard deviation is

TABLE 8.4 Training Time in Days for the Computer-Assisted Training Program at Scheer Industries

Employee	Time	Employee	Time	Employee	Time
1	52	6	59	11	54
2	44	7	50	12	58
3	55	8	54	13	60
4	44	9	62	14	62
5	45	10	46	15	63

unknown, we will use the sample standard deviation $s = 6.82$ days as the point estimate of σ. With the small sample size, $n = 15$, we will use (8.4) to develop an interval estimate of the population mean at 95% confidence. If we assume that the population of training times has a normal probability distribution, the t distribution with $n - 1 = 14$ degrees of freedom is the appropriate probability distribution for the interval-estimation procedure. We see from Table 8.3 that with 14 degrees of freedom, $t_{\alpha/2} = t_{.025} = 2.145$. Using (8.4), we have

$$\bar{x} \pm t_{.025} \frac{s}{\sqrt{n}}$$

$$53.87 \pm 2.145\left(\frac{6.82}{\sqrt{15}}\right)$$

$$53.87 \pm 3.78$$

Thus, the 95% confidence interval estimate of the population mean training time is 50.09 days to 57.65 days.

The preceding approach, in which the t distribution is used to develop an interval estimate of μ, is applicable whenever the population standard deviation is unknown and the population being sampled has a normal probability distribution. However, statistical research has shown that (8.4) is applicable even if the population being sampled is not quite normal. That is, confidence intervals based on the t distribution can be used as long as the population distribution does not differ extensively from a normal probability distribution.

COMPUTER-GENERATED CONFIDENCE INTERVALS

To illustrate the use of computer software packages in developing interval estimates of a population mean for the small-sample case, we used Minitab to develop a 95% confidence interval estimate of the population mean training time for Scheer Industries. Figure 8.9 is the Minitab output. For the sample of 15 employees, the output shows a sample mean of 53.87 days, a sample standard deviation of 6.82 days, and a standard error of the mean of 1.76 days. The 95% confidence interval estimate is 50.09 days to 57.65 days as previously computed.

N	Mean	StDev	SE Mean	95.0 % C.I.	
15	53.87	6.82	1.76	(50.09,	57.65)

FIGURE 8.9 Computer-Generated Confidence Intervals for the Scheer Industries Sampling Problem

NOTES AND
COMMENTS

• • • • • • • • • • • • • • • • • •

The *t* distribution is not restricted to the small-sample situation. Actually, the *t* distribution is applicable whenever the population is normal or near normal and whenever the sample standard deviation is used to estimate the population standard deviation. If these conditions are met, the *t* distribution can be used for any sample size. However, (8.3) shows that with a large sample ($n \geq 30$), interval estimation of a population mean can be based on the standard normal probability distribution and the value $z_{\alpha/2}$. Thus, with (8.3) available for the large-sample case, we generally do not consider the use of the *t* distribution until we encounter a small-sample case.

EXERCISES

METHODS

15. For a *t* distribution with 12 degrees of freedom, find the area, or probability, that is in each region.
   a. To the left of 1.782   **b.** To the right of −1.356
   c. To the right of 2.681   **d.** To the left of −1.782
   e. Between −2.179 and +2.179   **f.** Between −1.356 and +1.782

16. Find the *t* value(s) for each of the following examples.
   a. Upper tail area of .05 with 18 degrees of freedom
   b. Lower tail area of .10 with 22 degrees of freedom
   c. Upper tail area of .01 with 5 degrees of freedom
   d. 90% of the area is between these two *t* values with 14 degrees of freedom
   e. 95% of the area is between these two *t* values with 28 degrees of freedom

Self-Test
• • • • • • • • • • ▶

17. The following data have been collected from a sample of eight items from a normal population: 10, 8, 12, 15, 13, 11, 6, 5.
   a. What is the point estimate of the population mean?
   b. What is the point estimate of the population standard deviation?
   c. What is the 95% confidence interval for the population mean?

18. A simple random sample of 20 items from a normal population resulted in a sample mean of 17.25 and a sample standard deviation of 3.3.
   a. Develop a 90% confidence interval for the population mean.
   b. Develop a 95% confidence interval for the population mean.
   c. Develop a 99% confidence interval for the population mean.

APPLICATIONS

Self-Test
• • • • • • • • • • ▶

19. In the testing of a new production method, 18 employees were selected randomly and asked to try the new method. The sample mean production rate for the 18 employees was 80 parts per hour and the sample standard deviation was 10 parts per hour. Provide 90% and 95% confidence intervals for the population mean production rate for the new method, assuming the population has a normal probability distribution.

20. The Money & Investing section of the *The Wall Street Journal* contains a summary of daily investment performance for the New York Stock Exchange, the American Stock Exchange, overseas markets, options, commodities, futures, and so on. In the New York Stock Exchange section, information is provided on each stock's 52-week high price per share, 52-week low price per share, dividend rate, yield, P/E ratio, daily volume, daily high price per share, daily low price per share, closing price per share, and daily net change. The P/E (price–earnings) ratio for each stock is determined by dividing the price of a share of stock by the earnings per share reported by the company for the most recent four quarters. A sample of 10 stocks taken from *The Wall Street Journal* (May 19, 1995) provided the following data on P/E ratios: 5, 7, 9, 10, 14, 23, 20, 15, 3, 26.

a. What is the point estimate of the mean P/E ratio for the population of all stocks listed on the New York Stock Exchange?

b. What is the point estimate of the standard deviation of the P/E ratios for the population of all stocks listed on the New York Stock Exchange?

c. With a .95 confidence coefficient, what is the interval estimate of the mean P/E ratio for the population of all stocks listed on the New York Stock Exchange? Assume the population has a normal distribution.

d. Comment on the precision of the results.

21. The following data are family sizes from a simple random sample of households in a new test market area.

Household	Family Size	Household	Family Size
1	4	7	3
2	3	8	2
3	2	9	3
4	2	10	6
5	4	11	3
6	5	12	2

Provide a 95% confidence interval for the mean family size for the population.

TABLE 8.5 Exercise 22

6.0	6.6	5.8
7.0	6.3	6.2
7.2	5.7	6.4
7.0	6.5	6.2
6.0	6.5	7.2
7.3	7.6	6.8
6.0	6.2	

22. The American Association of Advertising Agencies records data on nonprogramming minutes per half hour of prime-time television programming (*U.S. News & World Report,* April 13, 1992). Representative data for a sample of prime-time programs on major networks at 8:30 P.M. are listed in Table 8.5. Provide a point estimate and a 95% confidence interval for the mean number of nonprogramming minutes on half-hour prime-time television shows at 8:30 P.M.

23. Hertz, the nation's largest car rental company, announced that it was reviewing the rental rates for residents of Queens, Brooklyn, and the Bronx who rent cars in the New York metropolitan area (*The New York Times,* January 3, 1992). Assume Hertz obtained the following sample of 12 daily rates: 65, 58, 40, 48, 52, 60, 75, 38, 50, 51, 59, 40.

a. What is the point estimate of the mean daily car rental cost in the New York area?

b. What is a 95% confidence interval for the mean daily car rental cost in the New York area?

24. Sales personnel for Skillings Distributors are required to submit weekly reports listing the customer contacts made during the week. A sample of 61 weekly contact reports showed a mean of 22.4 customer contacts per week for the sales personnel. The sample standard deviation was five contacts.

a. Use the large-sample case (8.3) to develop a 95% confidence interval for the mean number of weekly customer contacts for the population of sales personnel.

b. Assume that the population of weekly contact data has a normal distribution. Use the *t* distribution with 60 degrees of freedom to develop a 95% confidence interval for the mean number of weekly customer contacts.

c. Compare your answers for parts (a) and (b). Comment on why in the large-sample case it is permissible to base interval estimates on the procedure used in part (a) even though the *t* distribution may also be applicable.

25. The U.S. Department of Transportation reported the number of miles that residents of metropolitan areas travel per day in a car (*1994 Information Please Environmental Almanac*).

Suppose a simple random sample of 15 residents of Cleveland provided the following data on car miles per day.

20   20   28   16   11   17   23   16   22   18   10   22   29   19   32

a. Compute a 95% confidence interval estimate of the population mean number of miles residents of Cleveland travel per day in a car.

b. What assumption about the population was necessary to obtain an answer to part (a)?

c. Suppose it is desirable to estimate the population mean number of miles to within ±2 miles at 95% confidence. Do the data provide this desired level of precision? What action, if any, would you recommend be taken?

TABLE 8.6   Exercise 26

2.1	4.8	5.5
10.4	3.3	3.5
4.8	5.8	5.3
5.5	2.8	3.6
5.9	6.6	7.8
10.5	7.5	6.0
4.5	4.8	

26. The duration (in minutes) for a sample of 20 flight-reservation telephone calls is shown in Table 8.6.

a. What is the point estimate of the population mean time for flight-reservation phone calls?

b. Assuming that the population has a normal distribution, develop a 95% confidence interval for the population mean time.

8.3   DETERMINING THE SAMPLE SIZE

In Section 8.1 we were able to make the following statement about the sampling error whenever a sample mean was used to provide a point estimate of a population mean:

> There is a $1 - \alpha$ probability that the value of the sample mean will provide a sampling error of $z_{\alpha/2}\sigma_{\bar{x}}$ or less.

Since $\sigma_{\bar{x}} = \sigma/\sqrt{n}$, we can rewrite this statement to read:

> There is a $1 - \alpha$ probability that the value of the sample mean will provide a sampling error of $z_{\alpha/2}(\sigma/\sqrt{n})$ or less.

From this statement we see that the values of $z_{\alpha/2}$, σ, and the sample size n combine to determine the sampling error mentioned in the precision statement. Once we select a confidence coefficient or probability of $1 - \alpha$, $z_{\alpha/2}$ can be determined. Given values for $z_{\alpha/2}$ and σ, we can determine the sample size n needed to provide any sampling error. Development of the formula used to compute the required sample size n follows.

Let $E =$ the maximum sampling error mentioned in the precision statement. We have

$$E = z_{\alpha/2}\frac{\sigma}{\sqrt{n}}$$

Solving for $\sqrt{n}$, we have

$$\sqrt{n} = \frac{z_{\alpha/2}\sigma}{E}$$

Squaring both sides of this equation, we obtain the following expression for the sample size.

SAMPLE SIZE FOR AN INTERVAL ESTIMATE OF A POPULATION MEAN

$$n = \frac{(z_{\alpha/2})^2\sigma^2}{E^2} \tag{8.5}$$

This sample size will provide a precision statement with a $1 - \alpha$ probability that the sampling error will be *E or less*.

In (8.5) the value E is the maximum sampling error that the user is willing to accept at the given confidence level, and the value of $z_{\alpha/2}$ follows directly from the confidence level to be used in developing the interval estimate. Although user preference must be considered, 95% confidence is the most frequently chosen value ($z_{.025} = 1.96$).

Finally, use of (8.5) requires a value for the population standard deviation σ. In most cases, σ will be unknown. However, we can use (8.5) if we have a preliminary or *planning value* for σ. In practice, one of the following procedures can be chosen.

1. Use the sample standard deviation from a previous sample of the same or similar units.
2. Use a pilot study to select a preliminary sample of units. The sample standard deviation from the preliminary sample can be used as the planning value for σ.
3. Use judgment or a "best guess" for the value of σ. For example, we might begin by estimating the largest and smallest data values in the population. The difference between the largest and smallest values provides an estimate of the range for the data. Finally, the range divided by four is often suggested as a rough approximation of the standard deviation and thus an acceptable planning value for σ.

Let us return to the Scheer Industries example in Section 8.2 to see how (8.5) can be used to determine the sample size for the study. Previously we showed that with a 95% level of confidence, a sample of 15 Scheer employees generated a population mean training time estimate of 53.87 ± 3.78 days. Assume that after viewing these results, Scheer's director of manufacturing is not satisfied with the degree of precision, feeling that a sampling error of ± 3.78 days is too large. Furthermore, suppose the director makes the following statement about the desired precision: "I would like a .95 probability that the value of the sample mean will provide a sampling error of two days or less." We can see that the director is specifying a maximum sampling error of $E = 2$ days. In addition, the .95 probability indicates that a 95% confidence level is to be used; thus, $z_{\alpha/2} = z_{.025} = 1.96$. We need a planning value for σ to use in (8.5) to determine the sample size. Do we have a planning value for σ in the Scheer Industries example? Although σ is unknown, let us take advantage of the data provided for the 15 employees in Section 8.2. We can view these data as being from a pilot study, with the sample standard deviation $s = 6.82$ days providing the planning value for σ. Thus, using (8.5), we have

$$n = \frac{(z_{\alpha/2})^2 \sigma^2}{E^2} = \frac{(1.96)^2(6.82)^2}{2^2} = 44.67$$

In cases where the computed n is a fraction, we round up to the next integer value; hence, the recommended sample size for the Scheer Industries example is 45 employees.

Finally, note that in the Scheer Industries example, $z_{.025}$ was used to determine the sample size even though the original computations for 15 employees had employed the t distribution. The reason for the use of $z_{.025}$ is that since the sample size is yet to be determined, we are anticipating that n will be larger than 30, making $z_{.025}$ the appropriate value. In addition, if n is yet to be determined, we do not know the $(n - 1)$ degrees of freedom necessary to use the t distribution. Hence, the use of (8.5) to determine the sample size will always be based on a z value rather than a t value.

EXERCISES

METHODS

27. How large a sample should one select to be 95% confident that the sampling error is 5 or less? Assume that the population standard deviation is 25.

Self-Test ▶

28. The range for a set of data is estimated to be 36.
    a. What is the planning value for the population standard deviation?
    b. How large a sample should one take to be 95% confident that the sampling error is 3 or less?
    c. How large a sample should one take to be 95% confident that the sampling error is 2 or less?

APPLICATIONS

Self-Test ▶

29. What sample size would have been recommended for the Scheer Industries example if the director of manufacturing had specified a .95 probability for a sampling error of 1.5 days or less? How large a sample would have been necessary if the precision statement had specified a .90 probability for a sampling error of two days or less? Use $\sigma = 6.82$ days.

30. In Section 8.1 the Statewide Insurance Company used a simple random sample of 36 policyholders to estimate the mean age of the population of policyholders. The resulting precision statement reported a .95 probability that the value of the sample mean provided a sampling error of 2.35 years or less. This statement was based on a sample standard deviation of 7.2 years.
    a. How large a simple random sample would have been necessary to reduce the sampling error to two years or less? To 1.5 years or less? To one year or less?
    b. Would you recommend that Statewide attempt to estimate the population mean age of the policyholders with $E = 1$ year? Explain.

31. Annual starting salaries for college graduates with business administration degrees are believed to have a standard deviation of approximately $2000. Assume that a 95% confidence interval estimate of the mean annual starting salary is desired. How large a sample should be taken if the size of the sampling error in the precision statement is
    a. $500? b. $200? c. $100?

32. The mean number of days a house is on the market prior to selling was reported for 100 different cities (*U.S. News & World Report,* April 6, 1992). In a particular city the standard deviation of the number of days a house is on the market prior to selling is 20. How many house sales records would have to be collected to estimate the population mean to within ± 2 days? Use a 95% level of confidence.

33. The U.S. Department of Transportation reported the number of miles that residents of metropolitan areas travel per day in a car (*1994 Information Please Environmental Almanac*). Suppose a preliminary simple random sample of residents of Cleveland is used to develop a planning value of 6.17 for the population standard deviation.
    a. If we want to estimate the mean number of miles that Cleveland residents travel per day in a car to within ± 2 miles, what sample size should be selected? Assume 95% confidence.
    b. If we want to estimate the mean number of miles that Cleveland residents travel per day in a car to within ±1 mile, what sample size should be selected? Assume 95% confidence.

34. From Exercise 20, the sample standard deviation of P/E ratios for stocks listed on the New York Stock Exchange is $s = 7.8$ (*The Wall Street Journal,* May 19, 1995). Assume that we are interested in estimating the population mean P/E ratio for all stocks listed on the New York Stock Exchange. How many stocks should be included in the sample if we want a .95 probability that the sampling error is 2 or less?

35. A gasoline service station shows a standard deviation of $6.25 for the charges made by credit-card customers. Assume that the station's managers want to estimate the population mean gasoline bill for credit-card customers to within ± $1.00. For a 95% confidence level, how large a sample would be necessary?

36. A national survey research firm has data indicating that the interview time for a consumer opinion study has a standard deviation of six minutes.
  a. How large a sample should be taken if the firm wants a .98 probability of estimating the population mean interview time to within two minutes or less?
  b. Assume that the simple random sample you recommended in part (a) is taken and that the mean interview time for the sample is 32 minutes. What is the 98% confidence interval estimate for the population mean interview time?

8.4 INTERVAL ESTIMATION OF A POPULATION PROPORTION

In Section 8.2 we presented the Scheer Industries example, which involved estimating the mean employee training time for a new machine-repair training program. To evaluate the program from a different perspective, management has requested that some measure of program quality be developed. The degree of success of the training program has previously been measured by the scores the employees obtain on a standard examination given at the end of the training program. From experience, the company has found that an individual passing the examination has an excellent chance of high performance on the job. After some discussion, management has agreed to base the quality evaluation of the new training method on the proportion of employees who pass the examination. Let us assume that Scheer has implemented the sample-size recommendation of the preceding section. Thus, we now have a sample of 45 employees that can be used to develop an interval estimate for the proportion of the population who will pass the examination.

In Chapter 7 we showed that a sample proportion $\bar{p}$ is an unbiased estimator of a population proportion p and that for large samples the sampling probability distribution of $\bar{p}$ can be approximated by a normal probability distribution, as shown in Figure 8.10. Recall that the use of the normal distribution as an approximation of the sampling distribution of $\bar{p}$ is based on the condition that both np and $n(1 - p)$ are 5 or more. We will be using the sampling distribution of $\bar{p}$ to make probability statements about the sampling error whenever a sample proportion $\bar{p}$ is used to estimate a population proportion p. In this case, the sampling error is defined as the absolute value of the difference between $\bar{p}$ and p, written $|\bar{p} - p|$.

The probability statements that can be made about the sampling error for the proportion take the following form.

> There is a $1 - \alpha$ probability that the value of the sample proportion will provide a sampling error of $z_{\alpha/2}\sigma_{\bar{p}}$ or less.

The rationale for the preceding statement is the same one we gave when the value of a sample mean was used as an estimate of a population mean. Namely, since we know that the sampling distribution of $\bar{p}$ can be approximated by a normal probability distribution, we can use the value of $z_{\alpha/2}$ and the value of the standard error of the proportion $\sigma_{\bar{p}}$ to make the probability statement about the sampling error.

Once we see that the probability statement about the sampling error is based on $z_{\alpha/2}\sigma_{\bar{p}}$, we can subtract and add this value to $\bar{p}$ to obtain an interval estimate of the population proportion. Such an interval estimate is given by

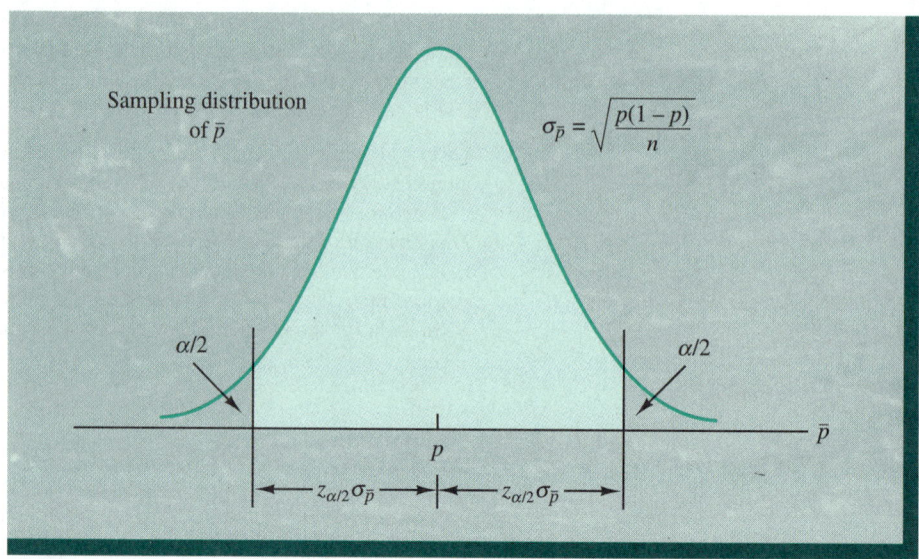

FIGURE 8.10   Normal Approximation of the Sampling Distribution of $\bar{p}$ When $np \geq 5$ and $n(1 - p) \geq 5$

$$\bar{p} \pm z_{\alpha/2}\sigma_{\bar{p}}, \tag{8.6}$$

where $1 - \alpha$ is the confidence coefficient. Since $\sigma_{\bar{p}} = \sqrt{p(1-p)/n}$, we can rewrite (8.6) as

$$\bar{p} \pm z_{\alpha/2}\sqrt{\frac{p(1 - p)}{n}} \tag{8.7}$$

However, to use (8.7) to develop an interval estimate of a population proportion p, the value of p would have to be *known*. Since the value of p is *unknown*, we simply substitute the sample proportion $\bar{p}$ for p. The resulting general expression for a confidence interval estimate of a population proportion follows.*

INTERVAL ESTIMATE OF A POPULATION PROPORTION

$$\bar{p} \pm z_{\alpha/2}\sqrt{\frac{\bar{p}(1 - \bar{p})}{n}} \tag{8.8}$$

where $1 - \alpha$ is the confidence coefficient and $z_{\alpha/2}$ is the z value providing an area of $\alpha/2$ in the upper tail of the standard normal probability distribution.

Let us return to the Scheer Industries example. Assume that in the sample of 45 employees who completed the new training program, 36 passed the examination. Thus, the point estimate of the proportion in the population who pass the examination is

---

*An unbiased estimate of $\sigma_{\bar{p}}^2$ is $\bar{p}(1 - \bar{p})/(n - 1)$, which suggests that $\sqrt{\bar{p}(1-\bar{p})/(n-1)}$ should be used in place of $\sqrt{\bar{p}(1-\bar{p})/n}$ in (8.8). However, the bias introduced by using n in the denominator does not cause any difficulty because large samples are generally used in making estimates about population proportions. In such cases the numerical difference between the results obtained by using n and those obtained by using $n - 1$ is negligible.

$\bar{p} = 36/45 = .80$. Using (8.8) and a .95 confidence coefficient, we see that the interval estimate for the population proportion is given by

$$\bar{p} \pm z_{.025} \sqrt{\frac{\bar{p}(1 - \bar{p})}{n}}$$

$$.80 \pm 1.96 \sqrt{\frac{.80(1 - .80)}{45}}$$

$$.80 \pm .12$$

Thus, at the 95% confidence level, the interval estimate of the population proportion is .68 to .92.

DETERMINING THE SAMPLE SIZE

Let us consider the question of how large the sample size should be to obtain an estimate of a population proportion at a specified level of precision. The rationale for the sample-size determination in developing interval estimates of p is very similar to the rationale used in Section 8.3 to determine the sample size for estimating a population mean.

   Previously in this section we provided the following probability statement about the sampling error.

   There is a $1 - \alpha$ probability that the value of the sample proportion will provide a sampling error of $z_{\alpha/2}\sigma_{\bar{p}}$ or less.

With $\sigma_{\bar{p}} = \sqrt{p(1-p)/n}$, the sampling error in this statement is based on the values of $z_{\alpha/2}$, the population proportion p, and the sample size n. For a given confidence coefficient $1 - \alpha$, $z_{\alpha/2}$ can be determined. Then, since the value of the population proportion is fixed, the sampling error mentioned in the precision statement is determined by the sample size n. Larger sample sizes provide better precision.

   Let E = the maximum sampling error in the precision statement; thus

$$E = z_{\alpha/2} \sqrt{\frac{p(1 - p)}{n}}$$

Solving the equation for n provides the following formula for the sample size.

SAMPLE SIZE FOR AN INTERVAL ESTIMATE OF A POPULATION PROPORTION

$$n = \frac{(z_{\alpha/2})^2 p(1 - p)}{E^2} \tag{8.9}$$

In (8.9), the value of the sampling error E must be specified by the user; in most cases, E is .10 or less. User preference also specifies the confidence level and thus the corresponding value of $z_{\alpha/2}$. Finally, use of (8.9) requires a planning value for the population proportion p. In practice, this planning value can be chosen by one of the following procedures.

TABLE 8.7   Some Possible Values for $p(1 - p)$

p	$p(1 - p)$	
.10	$(.10)(.90) = .09$	
.30	$(.30)(.70) = .21$	
.40	$(.40)(.60) = .24$	
.50	$(.50)(.50) = .25$	$\leftarrow$ Largest value for $p(1 - p)$
.60	$(.60)(.40) = .24$	
.70	$(.70)(.30) = .21$	
.90	$(.90)(.10) = .09$	

1. Use the sample proportion from a previous sample of the same or similar units.
2. Use a pilot study to select a preliminary sample of units. The sample proportion from this sample can be used as the planning value for p.
3. Use judgment or a "best guess" for the value of p.
4. If none of the preceding alternatives apply, use $p = .50$.

Let us return to the Scheer Industries example where we were interested in estimating the proportion of employees who pass the training program examination. How large a sample of employees should be used if Scheer's director of manufacturing wants to estimate the population proportion with a sampling error of .10 or less at a 95% confidence level? With $E = .10$ and $z_{.025} = 1.96$, we need a planning value for p to answer the sample-size question. Previously in this section we reported that 36 of the 45 employees who took the examination passed. Therefore, $\bar{p} = 36/45 = .80$ can be used as the planning value for p. Using (8.9), we obtain

$$n = \frac{(1.96)^2 .80(1 - .80)}{(.10)^2} = 61.47$$

Hence, a sample size of 62 employees is recommended.

The fourth alternative suggested for selecting a planning value for p is to use $p = .50$. This value of p is frequently used when no other information is available. To understand why, note that the numerator of (8.9) shows the sample size is proportional to the quantity $p(1 - p)$. A larger value for the quantity $p(1 - p)$ will result in a larger sample size. Table 8.7 gives some possible values of $p(1 - p)$. Note that the largest value of $p(1 - p)$ occurs when $p = .50$. Thus, if there is uncertainty about an appropriate planning value for p, we know that $p = .50$ will provide the largest sample-size recommendation. In effect, we are being on the safe or conservative side in recommending the largest possible sample size. If the proportion turns out to be different from the .50 planning value, the precision statement will be better than anticipated. In any case, in using $p = .50$, we are guaranteeing that the sample size will be sufficient to obtain the desired level of precision.

In the Scheer Industries example, a planning value of $p = .50$ would have provided the following recommended sample size.

$$n = \frac{(1.96)^2 .50(1 - .50)}{(.10)^2} = 96$$

This larger recommended sample size reflects the caution inherent in using the conservative planning value for the population proportion.

NOTES AND COMMENTS	The desired maximum sampling error or margin of error for estimating a population proportion is almost always .10 or less. In national public opinion polls conducted by organizations such as Gallup and Harris, a .03 or .04 margin of error is generally reported. The use of these margins of error (E in Equation 8.9) will generally provide a sample size that is large enough to satisfy the central limit theorem requirements of $np \geq 5$ and $n(1 - p) \geq 5$.

EXERCISES

METHODS

Self-Test

37. A simple random sample of 400 items provides 100 Yes responses.
    a. What is the point estimate of the proportion of the population who would provide Yes responses?
    b. What is the standard error of the proportion, $\sigma_{\bar{p}}$?
    c. Compute the 95% confidence interval for the population proportion.

38. A simple random sample of 800 units generates a sample proportion $\bar{p} = .70$.
    a. Provide a 90% confidence interval for the population proportion.
    b. Provide a 95% confidence interval for the population proportion.

39. In a survey, the planning value for the population proportion p is given as .35. How large a sample should be taken to be 95% confident that the sample proportion is within ± .05 of the population proportion?

40. How large a sample should be taken to be 95% confident that the sampling error for the estimation of a population proportion is .03 or less? Assume past data are not available for developing a planning value for p.

APPLICATIONS

Self-Test

41. In a Louis Harris survey of 400 senior executives, 248 of the executives stated that the U.S. legal system significantly hampers the ability of U.S. companies to compete with Japanese and European companies (*Business Week,* April 13, 1992).
    a. What is the point estimate of the population proportion of executives who believe the legal system hampers the ability to compete?
    b. What is the 90% confidence interval for the population proportion?

42. The Bureau of National Affairs, Inc. selected a sample of 617 companies and found that 56 companies required their employees to surrender airline frequent-flier mileage awards for business-related travel (*The Wall Street Journal,* March 28, 1994).
    a. What is the point estimate of the proportion of all companies that require their employees to surrender airline frequent-flier mileage awards?
    b. Develop a 95% confidence interval estimate of the population proportion.

43. According to a *USA Today* poll (January 11, 1990), 79% of Americans say that, if they had evidence, they would turn in a relative who killed someone. Experts were not surprised by the poll results, saying the poll reflects a "socially desirable response" rather than real-life action. The telephone poll of 305 adults was conducted by the Gordon S. Black Corporation. What is the 95% confidence interval for the population proportion?

44. A *Time*/CNN survey of 600 adults was conducted to elicit public opinion about a variety of welfare-reform proposals (*Time,* May 23, 1994). When asked whether money should be withheld from the paychecks of fathers who refuse to make child-support payments, 570 of

the respondents said yes. Develop a 95% confidence interval estimate of the proportion of all adults who believe money should be withheld from the paychecks of fathers who refuse to make child-support payments.

45. In an election campaign, a campaign manager requests that a sample of voters be polled to determine public support for the candidate. In a sample of 120 voters, 64 express plans to support the candidate.
    a. What is the point estimate of the proportion of voters in the population who will support the candidate?
    b. Develop and interpret the 95% confidence interval for the proportion of voters in the population who will support the candidate.
    c. Given the result from part (b), is the campaign manager justified in feeling confident that the candidate has the support of at least 50% of the voters? Explain.
    d. How many voters should be sampled if we want to estimate the population proportion with a sampling error of 5% or less? Continue to use the 95% confidence level.

46. A *Fortune* subscriber survey conducted by Pulse On America, Inc. showed that 665 of 831 subscribers use a personal computer at work (1994 *Fortune* National Subscriber Portrait).
    a. Develop a 95% confidence interval estimate of the proportion of *Fortune* subscribers who use a personal computer at work.
    b. How large a sample should be taken to estimate the proportion of *Fortune* subscribers who use a personal computer at work to within ± .02 of the actual value?

Self-Test ▶

47. The Tourism Institute for the State of Florida plans to sample visitors at major beaches throughout the state to estimate the proportion of beach visitors who are not residents of Florida. Preliminary estimates are that 55% of the beach visitors are not Florida residents.
    a. How large a sample should be taken to estimate the proportion of out-of-state visitors to within ± 3% of the actual value? Use a 95% confidence level.
    b. How large a sample should be taken if the error is increased to ± 6%?

48. A 1994 survey conducted by Louis Harris & Associates Inc. of 529 mutual-fund investors showed that 497 investors were confident that their investments were safe and only 127 investors planned to reduce their holdings (*Business Week,* August 15, 1994).
    a. Develop a 95% confidence interval estimate of the proportion of mutual-fund investors who are confident that their investments are safe.
    b. Develop a 95% confidence interval estimate of the proportion of mutual-fund investors who plan to reduce their holdings.

49. A firm provides national survey and interview services designed to estimate the proportion of the population who have certain beliefs or preferences. Typical questions seek to find the proportion favoring gun control, abortion, a particular political candidate, and so on. Assume that all interval estimates of population proportions are conducted at the 95% confidence level. How large a sample size would you recommend if the firm wants the sampling error to be
    a. 3% or less? b. 2% or less? c. 1% or less?

50. A survey of female executives conducted by Louis Harris & Associates showed that 33% of those surveyed rated their own company as an excellent place for women executives to work (*Working Woman,* November 1994). Suppose *Working Woman* wants to conduct an annual survey to monitor this proportion. With $p = .33$ as a planning value for the population proportion, how many female executives should be sampled for each of the following margins of error? Assume that all interval estimates are conducted at the 95% confidence level.
    a. 10%
    b. 5%
    c. 2%
    d. 1%
    e. In general, what happens to the sample size as the margin of error decreases?

51. The National Automobile Dealers Association collects data on sales numbers, prices, and usage of both new and used automobiles. One statistic of interest is the percentage of automobiles that are still on the road after 10 years (*U.S. News & World Report,* September 9, 1991).

   a. How large a sample should be taken if we want to be 95% confident that the sample percentage is within ± 2.5% of the actual percentage of automobiles that are still on the road after 10 years? Use $p = .25$ as a planning value for the population proportion.

   b. Using your sample size in part (a), assume that 357 of the automobiles sampled in 1991 were still on the road after 10 years. Provide the point estimate and a 95% confidence interval for the population proportion.

   c. In 1980, only 21% of automobiles were still on the road after 10 years. What conclusion can you make after viewing the confidence interval results for 1991 in part (b)?

SUMMARY

In this chapter we presented methods for developing a confidence interval for a population mean μ and a population proportion p. The purpose of developing a confidence interval is to give the user a better understanding of the sampling error that may be present. A wide confidence interval indicates poor precision; in such cases, the sample size can be increased to reduce the width of the confidence interval and improve the precision of the estimate.

Figure 8.11 summarizes the interval-estimation procedures for a population mean and provides a practical guide for computing the interval estimate. The figure shows that the expression used to compute an interval estimate depends on whether the sample size is large ($n \geq 30$) or small ($n < 30$), whether the population standard deviation is known, and in some cases whether or not the population has a normal or approximately normal probability distribution. If the sample size is large, no assumption is required about the distribution of the population and $z_{\alpha/2}$ is used in the computation of the interval estimate. If the sample size is small, the population must have a normal or approximately normal probability distribution in order to develop an interval estimate of μ. If this is the case, $z_{\alpha/2}$ is used in the computation of the interval estimate when σ is known, whereas $t_{\alpha/2}$ is used when σ is estimated by the sample standard deviation s. Finally, if the sample size is small and the assumption of a normally distributed population is inappropriate, we recommend increasing the sample size to $n \geq 30$ to develop a large-sample interval estimate of the population mean.

In addition, we showed how to determine the sample size so that interval estimates of μ and p would have a specified level of precision. In practice, the sample sizes required for interval estimates of a population proportion are generally large. Hence, we provided the large-sample interval-estimation formulas for a population proportion where both $np \geq 5$ and $n(1 - p) \geq 5$.

GLOSSARY

Interval estimate   An estimate of a population parameter that provides an interval believed to contain the value of the parameter.

Sampling error   The absolute value of the difference between the value of an unbiased point estimator, such as the sample mean $\bar{x}$, and the value of the population parameter it estimates, such as the population mean μ; in this case the sampling error is $| \bar{x} - \mu |$. In the case of the population proportion, the sampling error is $| \bar{p} - p |$.

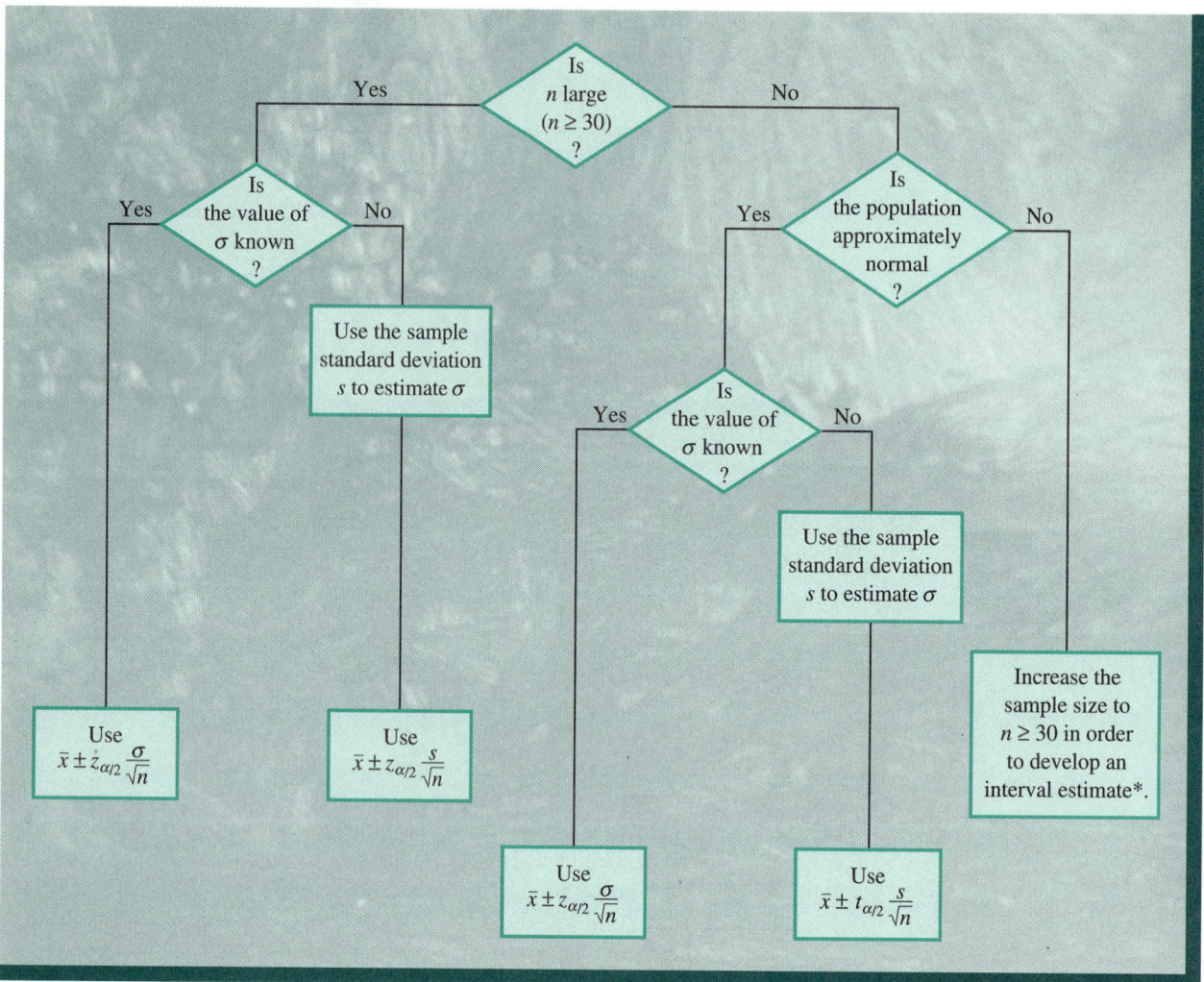

FIGURE 8.11   Summary of Interval Estimation Procedures for a Population Mean
*Sometimes methods from nonparametric statistics can be used in the small-sample case to develop confidence intervals for location parameters of a population.

Precision   A probability statement about the sampling error.

Confidence level   The confidence associated with an interval estimate. For example, if an interval-estimation procedure provides intervals such that 95% of the intervals formed using the procedure will include the population parameter, the interval estimate is said to be constructed at the 95% confidence level; note that .95 is referred to as the *confidence coefficient*.

t Distribution   A family of probability distributions that can be used to develop interval estimates of a population mean whenever the population standard deviation is unknown and the population has a normal or near-normal probability distribution.

Degrees of freedom   A parameter of the *t* distribution. When the *t* distribution is used in the computation of an interval estimate of a population mean, the appropriate *t* distribution has $n - 1$ degrees of freedom, where *n* is the size of the simple random sample.

KEY FORMULAS

Sampling Error When Estimating μ

$$|\bar{x} - \mu| \qquad\qquad (8.1)$$

Interval Estimate of a Population Mean: Large-Sample Case With σ Known

$$\bar{x} \pm z_{\alpha/2}\frac{\sigma}{\sqrt{n}} \qquad\qquad (8.2)$$

Interval Estimate of a Population Mean: Large-Sample Case With σ Unknown

$$\bar{x} \pm z_{\alpha/2}\frac{s}{\sqrt{n}} \qquad\qquad (8.3)$$

Interval Estimate of a Population Mean: Small-Sample Case With σ Unknown

$$\bar{x} \pm t_{\alpha/2}\frac{s}{\sqrt{n}} \qquad\qquad (8.4)$$

Sample Size for an Interval Estimate of a Population Mean

$$n = \frac{(z_{\alpha/2})^2\sigma^2}{E^2} \qquad\qquad (8.5)$$

Interval Estimate of a Population Proportion

$$\bar{p} \pm z_{\alpha/2}\sqrt{\frac{\bar{p}(1-\bar{p})}{n}} \qquad\qquad (8.8)$$

Sample Size for an Interval Estimate of a Population Proportion

$$n = \frac{(z_{\alpha/2})^2 p(1-p)}{E^2} \qquad\qquad (8.9)$$

SUPPLEMENTARY EXERCISES

52. A study showed that 99% of U.S. households have at least one television set and 98% of Americans watch some television every day (*In Health,* January 1992). Part of the study indicated a mean of 2.25 television sets per household. Assume that the mean number of sets per household was based on a sample of 300 households and that the sample standard deviation was 1.2 television sets per household. Provide a 95% confidence interval estimate of the population mean number of television sets per household.

53. The North Carolina Savings and Loan Association wants to develop an estimate of the mean size of home improvement loans granted by its member institutions. A sample of 100 loans granted by member institutions resulted in a sample mean of $3400 and a sample standard deviation of $650. With these data, develop a 98% confidence interval for the population mean dollar amount of home improvement loans.

54. A 1993 survey conducted by the American Automobile Association showed that a family of four spends an average of $215.60 per day while on vacation. Suppose a sample of 64 families of four vacationing at Niagara Falls resulted in a sample mean of $252.45 per day and a sample standard deviation of $74.50.

   a. Develop a 95% confidence interval estimate of the mean amount spent per day by a family of four visiting Niagara Falls.

   b. With the confidence interval from part (a), does it appear that the population mean amount spent per day by families visiting Niagara Falls is different from the mean reported by the American Automobile Association? Explain.

55. Dailey Paints, Inc., implemented a long-term test study designed to check the wear resistance of its major brand of paint. The test consisted of painting eight houses in various parts of the United States and observing the number of months until signs of peeling were observed. The following data were obtained from a normal population.

House	1	2	3	4	5	6	7	8
Months until Signs of Peeling	60	51	64	45	48	62	54	56

   a. What is a point estimate of the mean number of months until signs of peeling are observed?

   b. Develop a 95% confidence interval to estimate the population mean number of months until signs of peeling are observed.

   c. Develop a 99% confidence interval for the population mean.

56. What is the mean annual compensation paid to the chief executive officers of the largest firms in the United States? A sample of eight firms provided the annual salary/bonus data (*Business Week*, April 25, 1994) in Table 8.8.

   a. What is the point estimate of the population mean annual salary/bonus for chief executives?

   b. What is the point estimate of the population standard deviation?

   c. What is the 95% confidence interval estimate of the population mean annual compensation for chief executives?

TABLE 8.8 Exercise 56

Firm	Annual Salary/ Bonus ($1000s)
Coca-Cola	3654
General Motors	1375
Intel	2184
Motorola	1736
Readers Digest	1708
Sears	3095
Sprint	1692
Wells Fargo	2125

57. The Atlantic Fishing and Tackle Company has developed a new synthetic fishing line. To estimate the breaking strength of this line (pounds), testers subjected six lengths of line to breakage testing. The following data were obtained from a normal population.

Line	1	2	3	4	5	6
Breaking Strength (pounds)	18	24	19	21	20	18

Develop a 95% confidence interval for the mean breaking strength of the new line.

58. Sample assembly times for a particular manufactured part were 8, 10, 10, 12, 15, and 17 minutes. If the mean of the sample is used to estimate the mean of the population of assembly times, provide a point estimate and a 90% confidence interval for the population mean. Assume that the population has a normal distribution.

59. A utility company finds that a sample of 100 delinquent accounts yields an average amount owed of $131.44, with a sample standard deviation of $16.19. Develop a 90% confidence interval for the population mean amount owed.

60. In Exercise 59 the utility company sampled 100 delinquent accounts to estimate the mean amount owed by those accounts. The sample standard deviation was $16.19. How large a sample should be taken if the company wants to be 90% confident that the estimate of the population mean will have a sampling error of $1 or less?

61. Consider the Atlantic Fishing and Tackle Company problem presented in Exercise 57. How large a sample would be necessary to estimate the mean breaking strength of the new line with a .99 probability of a sampling error of one pound or less?

62. Mileage tests are conducted for a particular model of automobile. If the desired precision is stated such that there is a .98 probability of a sampling error of one mile per gallon or less, how many automobiles should be used in the test? Assume that preliminary mileage tests indicate the standard deviation to be 2.6 miles per gallon.

63. In developing patient appointment schedules, a medical center wants an estimate of the mean time that a staff member spends with each patient. How large a sample should be taken if the precision of the estimate is to be ± 2 minutes at a 95% level of confidence? How large a sample should be taken for a 99% level of confidence? Use a planning value for the population standard deviation of eight minutes.

64. Exercise 56 provides annual salary/bonus data for chief executives of firms in the United States (*Business Week,* April 25, 1994). The sample standard deviation is $656.64, with data provided in thousands of dollars. How many chief executives should be in the sample if we want to estimate the population mean annual salary/bonus with a margin of error of $100,000? Note that the margin of error is $100 in thousands of dollars. Use a 95% confidence level.

65. The New Orleans Beverage Company has been having problems with the automatic machine that places labels on bottles. The company wants an estimate of the percentage of bottles that have improperly applied labels. A simple random sample of 400 bottles revealed 18 bottles with improperly applied labels. Using these data, develop a 90% confidence interval for the population proportion of bottles with improperly applied labels.

66. H. G. Forester and Company is a distributor of lumber supplies throughout the southwestern United States. Managers at H. G. Forester want to check a shipment of more than one million pine boards to determine whether excessive warpage is present. A sample of 50 boards resulted in the identification of seven boards with excessive warpage. With these data, develop a 95% confidence interval for the proportion of boards defective in the whole shipment.

67. A University of Michigan study (January 1992) found that drug use among college students had continued its decade-long decline. However, the survey showed that alcohol consumption remained steady. Among the 1400 college students surveyed, 602 indicated they had consumed five or more drinks within the two weeks prior to the survey. Compute a 95% confidence interval for the proportion of all college students who had five or more drinks within the two-week period.

68. Towers Perrin, a compensation consultant, asked 500 U.S. companies whether they encouraged quality by giving top performers recognition and/or rewards such as cash and stock (*Business Week,* December 1991). Results showed that 56% of the companies used recognition to encourage quality, whereas 26% of the companies used cash and stock rewards. Develop 95% confidence intervals for the population in terms of both the proportion of companies that use recognition and the proportion that use cash and stock rewards to encourage quality.

69. A *Time*/CNN telephone poll of 1400 American adults asked, "Where would you rather go in your spare time?" (*Time,* April 6, 1992.) The top response by 504 adults was a shopping mall.
   a. What is the point estimate of the proportion of adults who would prefer going to a shopping mall in their spare time?
   b. At 95% confidence, what is the sampling error associated with this estimate?

70. A well-known bank credit-card firm is interested in estimating the proportion of credit-card holders who carry a nonzero balance at the end of the month and incur an interest charge. Assume that the desired precision for the proportion estimate is $\pm 3\%$ at a 98% confidence level.

a. How large a sample should be selected if it is anticipated that roughly 70% of the firm's cardholders carry a nonzero balance at the end of the month?

b. How large a sample should be selected if no planning value for the population proportion could be specified?

71. A sample of 200 people were asked to identify their major source of news information; 110 stated that their major source was television news coverage.

   a. Construct a 95% confidence interval for the proportion of people in the population who consider television their major source of news information.

   b. How large a sample would be necessary to estimate the population proportion with a sampling error of .05 or less at a 95% confidence level?

72. A survey of 502 female executives conducted by Louis Harris & Associates showed that 166 of the executives surveyed rated their own company as an excellent place for women executives to work (*Working Woman,* November 1994). Develop a 95% confidence interval of the proportion of all female executives who rate their own company as an excellent place for women executives to work.

73. *Newsweek* (April 6, 1992) reported data on the percentage of adults who smoke in the United States. Assume that the study designed to collect the data for this report had a preliminary estimate that 30% of the population smoke.

   a. How large a sample should be taken to estimate the current proportion of smokers in the population to within ± 2% at 95% confidence?

   b. Assume that the study uses your sample-size recommendation in part (a) and finds 555 smokers. What is the point estimate of the proportion of smokers in the population, and what is the 95% confidence interval?

74. Although airline schedules and cost are important factors for business travelers when choosing an airline carrier, a *USA Today* survey found that business travelers list an airline's frequent-flyer program as the most important factor (*USA Today,* April 11, 1995). From a sample of business travelers who responded to the survey, 618 of 1993 listed a frequent-flyer program as the most important factor.

   a. What is the point estimate of the proportion of the population of business travelers who believe a frequent-flyer program is the most important factor when choosing an airline carrier?

   b. Develop a 95% confidence interval estimate of the population proportion.

   c. How large a sample would be required to report the precision of the estimate as ± .01 at 95% confidence? Would you recommend that *USA Today* attempt to provide this degree of precision? Why or why not?

COMPUTER CASE

BOCK INVESTMENT SERVICES

Lisa Rae Bock started Bock Investment Services (BIS) in 1994 with the goal of making BIS the leading money market advisory service in South Carolina. To provide better service for her present clients and to attract new clients, she has developed a weekly newsletter. Lisa has been considering adding a new feature to the newsletter that will report the results of a weekly telephone survey of fund managers. To investigate the feasibility of offering this service, and to determine what type of information to include in the newsletter, Lisa selected a simple random sample of 45 money market funds. A portion of the data obtained is shown in Table 8.9, which reports fund assets and yields for the past seven and 30 days (*Barrons,* October 3, 1994). Before calling the money market fund managers to obtain additional data, Lisa decided to do some preliminary analysis of the data already collected (see Table 8.9). The data are available in the data set BOCK.

TABLE 8.9 Data for Bock Investment Services Computer Case

BOCK

Money Market Fund	Assets (Mil $)	7-day Yield (%)	30-day Yield (%)
Amcore	103.9	4.10	4.08
Alger	156.7	4.79	4.73
Arch MM/Trust	496.5	4.17	4.13
BT Instit Treas	197.8	4.37	4.32
Benchmark Div	2755.4	4.54	4.47
Bradford	707.6	3.88	3.83
Capital Cash	1.7	4.29	4.22
Cash Mgt Trust	2707.8	4.14	4.04
Composite	122.8	4.03	3.91
Cowen Standby	694.7	4.25	4.19
Cortland	217.3	3.57	3.51
Declaration	38.4	2.67	2.61
Dreyfus	4832.8	4.01	3.89
Elfun	81.7	4.51	4.41
FFB Cash	506.2	4.17	4.11
Federated Master	738.7	4.41	4.34
Fidelity Cash	13272.8	4.51	4.42
Flex-fund	172.8	4.60	4.48
Fortis	105.6	3.87	3.85
Franklin Money	996.8	3.97	3.92
Freedom Cash	1079.0	4.07	4.01
Galaxy Money	801.4	4.11	3.96
Government Cash	409.4	3.83	3.82
Hanover Cash	794.3	4.32	4.23
Heritage Cash	1008.3	4.08	4.00
Infinity/Alpha	53.6	3.99	3.91
John Hancock	226.4	3.93	3.87
Landmark Funds	481.3	4.28	4.26
Liquid Cash	388.9	4.61	4.64
MarketWatch	10.6	4.13	4.05
Merrill Lynch Money	27005.6	4.24	4.18
NCC Funds	113.4	4.22	4.20
Nationwide	517.3	4.22	4.14
Overland	291.5	4.26	4.17
Pierpont Money	1991.7	4.50	4.40
Portico Money	161.6	4.28	4.20
Prudential MoneyMart	6835.1	4.20	4.16
Reserve Primary	1408.8	3.91	3.86
Schwab Money	10531.0	4.16	4.07
Smith Barney Cash	2947.6	4.16	4.12
Stagecoach	1502.2	4.18	4.13
Strong Money	470.2	4.37	4.29
Transamerica Cash	175.5	4.20	4.19
United Cash	323.7	3.96	3.89
Woodward Money	1330.0	4.24	4.21

SOURCE: *Barron's,* October 3, 1994.

Managerial Report

1. Use appropriate descriptive statistics to summarize the data on assets and yields for the money market funds.
2. Develop a 95% confidence interval estimate of the mean assets, mean seven-day yield, and mean 30-day yield for the population of money market funds. Provide a managerial interpretation of each interval estimate.

3. Discuss the implication of your findings in terms of how Lisa could use this type of information in preparing her weekly newsletter.
4. What other information would you recommend that Lisa gather to provide the most useful information to her clients?

COMPUTER CASE

METROPOLITAN RESEARCH, INC.

Metropolitan Research, Inc., is a consumer research organization that takes surveys designed to evaluate a wide variety of products and services available to consumers. In one particular study, Metropolitan was interested in learning about consumer satisfaction with the performance of automobiles produced by a major Detroit manufacturer. A questionnaire sent to owners of one of the manufacturer's full-sized cars revealed several complaints about early transmission problems. To learn more about the transmission failures, Metropolitan used a sample of actual transmission repairs provided by a transmission repair firm in the Detroit area. The following data show the actual number of miles that 50 vehicles had been driven at the time of transmission failure. The data are available in the data set AUTO.

85,092	32,609	59,465	77,437	32,534	64,090	32,464	59,902
39,323	89,641	94,219	116,803	92,857	63,436	65,605	85,861
64,342	61,978	67,998	59,817	101,769	95,774	121,352	69,568
74,276	66,998	40,001	72,069	25,066	77,098	69,922	35,662
74,425	67,202	118,444	53,500	79,294	64,544	86,813	116,269
37,831	89,341	73,341	85,288	138,114	53,402	85,586	82,256
77,539	88,798						

Managerial Report

1. Use appropriate descriptive statistics to summarize the transmission failure data.
2. Develop a 95% confidence interval for the mean number of miles driven until transmission failure for the population of automobiles that have had transmission failure. Provide a managerial interpretation of the interval estimate.
3. Discuss the implication of your statistical finding in terms of the belief that some owners of the automobiles have experienced early transmission failures.
4. How many repair records should be sampled if the research firm wants the population mean number of miles driven until transmission failure to be estimated to within ± 5000 miles at 95% confidence?
5. What other information would you like to gather to evaluate the transmission failure problem more fully?

APPENDIX 8.1

Confidence Interval Estimation with Minitab

LARGE-SAMPLE CASE

● In Section 8.1 we discussed the use of computer-generated confidence interval estimates by showing how Minitab can be used to obtain interval estimates for the mean age in the Statewide Insurance Company study. The data are in Table 8.2. With the sample standard deviation, $s = 7.77$, as an estimate of the population standard deviation

σ, the following steps can be used to produce the 90% confidence-interval output shown in panel A of Figure 8.6 (assume the age data have been entered in column C1 of the Minitab worksheet).

Step 1.   Select the **Stat** pull-down menu
Step 2.   Select the **Basic Statistics** pull-down menu
Step 3.   Select the **1-Sample Z** option
Step 4.   When the dialog box appears:
            Enter C1 in the **Variables** box
            Enter 90 in the **Confidence interval Level** box
            Enter 7.77 in the **Sigma** box
            Select **OK** to produce the 90% confidence interval

The output in panel B of Figure 8.6 was obtained by simply changing the value of 90 to 95 in the **Confidence interval Level** box (step 4). If the user does not specify a value in the **Confidence interval Level** box, Minitab will use a default value of 95.

SMALL-SAMPLE CASE

In Section 8.2 we discussed the use of computer-generated confidence interval estimates for the small-sample case by showing how Minitab can be used to develop interval estimates for the Scheer Industries problem. With the data from Table 8.4 entered in column C1, the following steps can be used to produce a 95% confidence interval as shown in Figure 8.9.

Step 1.   Select the **Stat** pull-down menu
Step 2.   Select the **Basic Statistics** pull-down menu
Step 3.   Select the **1-Sample t** option
Step 4.   When the dialog box appears:
            Enter C1 in the **Variables** box
            Enter 95 in the **Confidence interval Level** box
            Select **OK** to produce the 95% confidence interval

A 90% confidence interval can be obtained by simply changing the value of 95 to 90 in the **Confidence interval Level** box (step 4). If the user does not specify a value in the **Confidence interval Level** box, Minitab will use a default value of 95.

APPENDIX 8.2   ●

Confidence Interval Estimation with Spreadsheets

LARGE-SAMPLE CASE

● We will show how Excel can be used to develop confidence intervals for a population mean in the large-sample case by describing how to develop a 90% confidence interval for the population mean age in the Statewide Insurance Company study introduced in Section 8.1. We assume the user has already used the Data Analysis Tools described in Appendix 3.2 to compute the sample mean of 39.5 and the sample standard deviation of 7.77.

Step 1. Select an empty cell in the Excel worksheet
Step 2. Select the **Insert** pull-down menu
Step 3. Choose the **Function** option
Step 4. When The Function Wizard—Step 1 of 2 dialog box appears:
Choose **Statistical** in the Function Category box
Choose **Confidence** in the Function Name box
Select **Next** >
Step 5. When The Function Wizard—Step 2 of 2 dialog box appears:
Enter .10 in the **alpha** box*
Enter 7.77 in the **standard_dev** box
Enter 36 in the **size** box
Choose **Finish**

The ± limit on the sampling error will appear in the cell selected in step 1. With the sample mean of 39.5 and the limit of 2.13, the 90% confidence interval obtained by subtracting 2.13 from 39.5 and adding 2.13 to 39.5 is 37.37 to 41.63.

SMALL-SAMPLE CASE

To illustrate how to develop a confidence interval for the small-sample case, we will compute a 95% confidence interval for the Scheer Industries study introduced in Section 8.2. We assume that the user has entered the training-time data from Table 8.4 into worksheet rows 1 to 15 of column A. The following steps can be used to produce a 95% confidence interval.

Step 1. Select the **Tools** pull-down menu
Step 2. Choose the **Data Analysis** option
Step 3. When the Data Analysis dialog box appears:
Choose **Descriptive Statistics**
Select **OK**
Step 4. When the **Descriptive Statistics** dialog box appears:
Enter A1:A15 in the **Input Range** box
Select **Confidence Level for Mean** and enter 95 in the box
Select **Output Range** and enter B1 in the box
Select **OK**

The value of the sample mean, 53.87, appears in cell C3 and the value of the ± limit on the sampling error, 3.78, appears in cell C16; note that the Excel label for the ± limit is Confidence Level (95.0%). With the sample mean of 53.87, the 95% confidence interval estimate obtained by subtracting 3.78 from 53.87 and adding 3.78 to 53.87 is 50.09 to 57.65.

---

*Alpha is 1 minus the confidence coefficient. For a .90 confidence coefficient the value of alpha is 1 − .90 = .10.

9

HYPOTHESIS TESTING

CONTENTS

STATISTICS IN PRACTICE •

Harris Corporation*
Melbourne, Florida

Harris Corporation's RF Communications Division, in Melbourne, Florida, is a major manufacturer of point-to-point radio communications equipment. It is a horizontally integrated manufacturing company with a multiplant facility. Most of the Harris products require medium- to high-volume production operations, including printed circuit assembly, final product assembly, and testing.

One of the company's high-volume products has an assembly called an RF deck. Each RF deck consists of 16 electronic components soldered to a machined casting that forms the plated surface of the deck. During a manufacturing run, a problem developed in the soldering process; the flow of solder onto the deck did not meet the quality criteria established for the product. After considering a variety of factors that might affect the soldering process, an engineer made the preliminary determination that the soldering problem was most likely due to defective platings.

The engineer wondered whether the proportion of defective platings in the Harris inventory exceeded that set by the supplier's design specifications. With p indicating the proportion of defective platings in the Harris inventory and p_0 indicating the proportion of defective platings set by the supplier's design specifications, the following hypotheses were formulated.

$$H_0: p \leq p_0$$

$$H_a: p > p_0$$

H_0 indicates that the Harris inventory has a defective plating proportion less than or equal to that set by the design specifications. Such a proportion would be judged acceptable, and the engineer would need to look for other causes of the soldering problem. However, H_a indicates that the Harris inventory has a defective plating proportion greater than that set by the design specifications. In that case, excessive defective platings may well be the cause of the soldering problem and action should be taken to determine why the defective proportion in inventory is so high.

Tests made on a sample of platings from the Harris inventory resulted in the rejection of H_0. The conclusion was that H_a was true and that the proportion of defective platings in inventory exceeded that set by the supplier's design specifications. Further investigation of the inventory area led to the conclusion that the underlying problem was shelf contamination during storage. By altering the storage environment, the engineer was able to solve the problem.

In this chapter you will learn how to formulate hypotheses about a population mean and a population proportion. Through the analysis of sample data, you will be able to determine whether a hypothesis should or should not be rejected. Appropriate conclusions and actions will be demonstrated for testing research hypotheses, testing the validity of assumptions, and decision making.

Maintaining quality of electronic components has a high priority at Harris Corporation.

*The authors are indebted to Richard A. Marshall of the Harris Corporation for providing this Statistics in Practice.

● In Chapters 7 and 8 we showed how a sample could be used to develop point and interval estimates of population parameters. In this chapter we continue the discussion of statistical inference by showing how *hypothesis testing* can be used to determine whether a statement about the value of a population parameter should or should not be rejected.

In hypothesis testing we begin by making a tentative assumption about a population parameter. This tentative assumption is called the *null hypothesis* and is denoted by

H_0. We then define another hypothesis, called the *alternative hypothesis,* which is the opposite of what is stated in the null hypothesis. The alternative hypothesis is denoted by H_a. The hypothesis-testing procedure involves using data from a sample to test the two competing statements indicated by H_0 and H_a.

Hypothesis testing is similar to a criminal trial. In a criminal trial the assumption is that the defendant is innocent. The null hypothesis expresses an assumption of innocence. The opposite of the null hypothesis is the alternative hypothesis—it expresses an assumption of guilt. Hence, the hypotheses for a criminal trial would be written:

$$H_0: \text{The defendant is innocent}$$

$$H_a: \text{The defendant is guilty}$$

To test these competing statements, or hypotheses, a trial is held. The testimony and evidence obtained during the trial provide the sample information. If the sample information is not inconsistent with the assumption of innocence, the null hypothesis that the defendant is innocent cannot be rejected. However, if the sample information is inconsistent with the assumption of innocence, the null hypothesis will be rejected. In that case, action will be based on the alternative hypothesis that the defendant is guilty.

The purpose of this chapter is to show how hypothesis tests can be conducted about a population mean and a population proportion. We begin by providing examples that illustrate approaches to developing null and alternative hypotheses.

9.1   DEVELOPING NULL AND ALTERNATIVE HYPOTHESES

In some applications it may not be obvious how the null and alternative hypotheses should be formulated. Care must be taken to be sure the hypotheses are structured appropriately and that the hypothesis-testing conclusion provides the information the researcher or decision maker wants. Guidelines for establishing the null and alternative hypotheses will be given for three types of situations in which hypothesis-testing procedures are commonly employed.

TESTING RESEARCH HYPOTHESES

Consider a particular automobile model that currently attains an average fuel efficiency of 24 miles per gallon. A product-research group has developed a new carburetor specifically designed to increase the miles-per-gallon rating. To evaluate the new carburetor, several will be manufactured, installed in automobiles, and subjected to research-controlled driving tests. Note that the product-research group is looking for evidence to conclude that the new design *increases* the mean miles-per-gallon rating. In this case, the research hypothesis is that the new carburetor will provide a mean miles-per-gallon rating exceeding 24; that is, $\mu > 24$. As a general guideline, a research hypothesis such as this should be formulated as the *alternative hypothesis*. Hence, the appropriate null and alternative hypotheses for the study are:

$$H_0: \mu \leq 24$$

$$H_a: \mu > 24$$

If the sample results indicate that H_0 cannot be rejected, researchers cannot conclude that the new carburetor is better. Perhaps more research and subsequent testing should be conducted. However, if the sample results indicate that H_0 can be rejected, researchers can make the inference that $H_a: \mu > 24$ is true. With this conclusion, the researchers have the statistical support necessary to state that the new carburetor increases the mean number of miles per gallon. Action to begin production with the new carburetor may be undertaken.

In research studies such as these, the null and alternative hypotheses should be formulated so that the rejection of H_0 supports the conclusion and action being sought. The research hypothesis therefore should be expressed as the alternative hypothesis.

TESTING THE VALIDITY OF A CLAIM

As an illustration of testing the validity of a claim, consider the situation of a manufacturer of soft drinks who states that two-liter containers of its products have an average of at least 67.6 fluid ounces. A sample of two-liter containers will be selected, and the contents will be measured to test the manufacturer's claim. In this type of hypothesis-testing situation, we generally assume that the manufacturer's claim is true unless the sample evidence proves otherwise. Using this approach for the soft-drink example, we would state the null and alternative hypotheses as follows.

$$H_0: \mu \geq 67.6$$

$$H_a: \mu < 67.6$$

If the sample results indicate H_0 cannot be rejected, the manufacturer's claim cannot be challenged. However, if the sample results indicate H_0 can be rejected, the inference will be made that $H_a: \mu < 67.6$ is true. With this conclusion, statistical evidence indicates that the manufacturer's claim is incorrect and that the soft-drink containers are being filled with a mean less than the claimed 67.6 ounces. Appropriate action against the manufacturer may be considered.

In any situation that involves testing the validity of a product claim, the null hypothesis is generally based on the assumption that the claim is true. The alternative hypothesis is then formulated so that rejection of H_0 will provide statistical evidence that the stated assumption is incorrect. Action to correct the claim should be considered whenever H_0 is rejected.

TESTING IN DECISION-MAKING SITUATIONS

In testing research hypotheses or testing the validity of a claim, action is taken if H_0 is rejected. In many instances, however, action must be taken both when H_0 cannot be rejected and when H_0 can be rejected. In general, this type of situation occurs when a decision maker must choose between two courses of action, one associated with the null hypothesis and another associated with the alternative hypothesis. For example, on the basis of a sample of parts from a shipment that has just been received, a quality-control inspector must decide whether to accept the entire shipment or to return the shipment to the supplier because it does not meet specifications. Assume that specifications for a particular part require a mean length of two inches per part. If the average length of the parts is greater or less than the two-inch standard, the parts will cause quality problems in the assembly operation. In this case, the null and alternative hypotheses would be formulated as follows.

$$H_0: \mu = 2$$

$$H_a: \mu \neq 2$$

If the sample results indicate H_0 cannot be rejected, the quality-control inspector will have no reason to doubt that the shipment meets specifications, and the shipment will be accepted. However, if the sample results indicate H_0 should be rejected, the conclusion will be that the parts do not meet specifications. In this case, the quality-control inspector will have sufficient evidence to return the shipment to the supplier. Thus, we see that for these types of situations, action is taken both when H_0 cannot be rejected and when H_0 can be rejected.

A SUMMARY OF FORMS FOR NULL AND ALTERNATIVE HYPOTHESES

Let μ_0 denote the specific numerical value being considered in the null and alternative hypotheses. In general, a hypothesis test about the values of a population mean μ must take one of the following three forms.

$$H_0: \mu \geq \mu_0 \qquad H_0: \mu \leq \mu_0 \qquad H_0: \mu = \mu_0$$
$$H_a: \mu < \mu_0 \qquad H_a: \mu > \mu_0 \qquad H_a: \mu \neq \mu_0$$

In many situations, the choice of H_0 and H_a is not obvious and judgment is necessary select the proper form. However, as the preceding forms show, the equality part of the expression (either $\geq$, $\leq$,or $=$) *always* appears in the null hypothesis. In selecting the proper form of H_0 and H_a, keep in mind that the alternative hypothesis is what the test is attempting to establish. Hence, asking whether the user is looking for evidence to support $\mu < \mu_0, \mu > \mu_0$, or $\mu \neq \mu_0$ will help determine H_a. The following exercises are designed to provide practice in choosing the proper form for a hypothesis test.

EXERCISES

1. The manager of the Danvers-Hilton Resort Hotel has stated that the mean guest bill for a weekend is $400 or less. A member of the hotel's accounting staff has noticed that the total charges for guest bills have been increasing in recent months. The accountant will use a sample of weekend guest bills to test the manager's claim.
   a. Which form of the hypotheses should be used to test the manager's claim? Explain.

$$H_0: \mu \geq 400 \qquad H_0: \mu \leq 400 \qquad H_0: \mu = 400$$
$$H_a: \mu < 400 \qquad H_a: \mu > 400 \qquad H_a: \mu \neq 400$$

   b. What conclusion is appropriate when H_0 cannot be rejected?
   c. What conclusion is appropriate when H_0 can be rejected?

Self-Test ··········▶

2. The manager of an automobile dealership is considering a new bonus plan that is designed to increase sales volume. Currently, the mean sales volume is 14 automobiles per month. The manager wants to conduct a research study to see whether the new bonus plan increases sales volume. To collect data on the plan, a sample of sales personnel will be allowed to sell under the new bonus plan for a one-month period.
   a. Develop the null and alternative hypotheses that are most appropriate for this research situation.
   b. Comment on the conclusion when H_0 cannot be rejected.
   c. Comment on the conclusion when H_0 can be rejected.

3. A production-line operation is designed to fill cartons with laundry detergent to a mean weight of 32 ounces. A sample of cartons is periodically selected and weighed to determine whether underfilling or overfilling is occurring. If the sample data lead to a conclusion of underfilling or overfilling, the production line will be shut down and adjusted to obtain proper filling.
   a. Formulate the null and alternative hypotheses that will help in deciding whether or not to shut down and adjust the production line.
   b. Comment on the conclusion and the decision when H_0 cannot be rejected.
   c. Comment on the conclusion and the decision when H_0 can be rejected.

TABLE 9.1   Errors and Correct Conclusions in Hypothesis Testing

		Population Condition	
		H_0 *True*	H_a *True*
Conclusion	*Accept H_0*	Correct Conclusion	Type II Error
	Reject H_0	Type I Error	Correct Conclusion

4. Because of high production-changeover time and costs, a director of manufacturing must convince management that a proposed manufacturing-method reduces costs before the new method can be implemented. The current production method operates with a mean cost of $220 per hour. A research study is to be conducted in which the cost of the new method will be measured over a sample production period.
   a. Develop the null and alternative hypotheses that are most appropriate for this study.
   b. Comment on the conclusion when H_0 cannot be rejected.
   c. Comment on the conclusion when H_0 can be rejected.

9.2 TYPE I AND TYPE II ERRORS

The null and alternative hypotheses are competing statements about the population. Either the null hypothesis H_0 is true or the alternative hypothesis H_a is true, but not both. Ideally the hypothesis testing procedure should lead to the acceptance of H_0 when H_0 is true and the rejection of H_0 when H_a is true. Unfortunately, this is not always possible. Since hypothesis tests are based on sample information, we must allow for the possibility of errors. Table 9.1 illustrates the two kinds of errors that can be made in hypothesis testing.

The first row of Table 9.1 shows what can happen when the conclusion is to accept H_0. If H_0 is true, this conclusion is correct. However, if H_a is true, we have made a *Type II error;* that is, we have accepted H_0 when it is false. The second row of Table 9.1 shows what can happen when the conclusion is to reject H_0. If H_0 is true, we have made a *Type I error;* that is, we have rejected H_0 when it is true. However, if H_a is true, rejecting H_0 is correct.

Although we cannot eliminate the possibility of errors in hypothesis testing, we can consider the probability of their occurrence. Using common statistical notation, we denote the probabilities of making the two errors as follows.

α = the probability of making a Type I error

β = the probability of making a Type II error

Recall the hypothesis-testing illustration discussed in Section 9.1 in which an automobile product-research group had developed a new carburetor designed to increase the miles-per-gallon rating of a particular automobile. With the current model obtaining an average of 24 miles per gallon, the hypothesis test was formulated as follows.

$$H_0: \mu \leq 24$$

$$H_a: \mu > 24$$

The alternative hypothesis, H_a: $\mu > 24$, indicates that the researchers are looking for sample evidence that will support the conclusion that the mean miles per gallon is greater than 24.

In this application, the Type I error of rejecting H_0 when it is true corresponds to the researchers claiming that the new carburetor improves the miles per gallon rating ($\mu > 24$) when in fact the new carburetor is not any better than the current carburetor. In contrast, the Type II error of accepting H_0 when it is false corresponds to the researchers concluding that the new carburetor is not any better than the current carburetor ($\mu \leq 24$) when in fact the new carburetor improves miles-per-gallon performance.

In practice, the person conducting the hypothesis test specifies the maximum allowable probability of making a Type I error, called the *level of significance* for the test. Common choices for the level of significance are .05 and .01. Referring to the second row of Table 9.1, note that the conclusion to *reject H_0* indicates that either a Type I error or a correct conclusion has been made. Thus, if the probability of making a Type I error is controlled for by selecting a small value for the level of significance, we have a high degree of confidence that the conclusion to reject H_0 is correct. In such cases, we have statistical support for concluding that H_0 is false and H_a is true. Any action suggested by the alternative hypothesis H_a is appropriate.

Although most applications of hypothesis testing control for the probability of making a Type I error, they do not always control for the probability of making a Type II error. Hence, if we decide to accept H_0, we cannot determine how confident we can be with that decision. Because of the uncertainty associated with making a Type II error, statisticians often recommend that we use the statement "do not reject H_0" instead of "accept H_0." Using the statement "do not reject H_0" carries the recommendation to withhold both judgment and action. In effect, by never directly accepting H_0, the statistician avoids the risk of making a Type II error. Whenever the probability of making a Type II error has not been determined and controlled, we will not make the conclusion to accept H_0. In such cases, only two conclusions are possible: *do not reject H_0* or *reject H_0*.

Although controlling for a Type II error in hypothesis testing is not common, it can be done. In fact, in Sections 9.7 and 9.8, we will illustrate procedures for determining and controlling the probability of making a Type II error. If proper controls have been established for this error, action based on the do not reject H_0 conclusion can be appropriate.

Notes and Comments

Many applications of hypothesis testing have a decision-making goal. The conclusion *reject H_0* provides the statistical support to conclude that H_a is true and take whatever action is appropriate. The statement "do not reject H_0," although inconclusive, often forces managers to behave as though H_0 is true. In this case, managers need to be aware of the fact that such behavior may be the result of a Type II error.

Exercises

Self-Test

5. Americans spend an average of 8.6 minutes per day reading newspapers (*USA Today,* April 10, 1995). A researcher believes that individuals in management positions spend more than the

national average time per day reading newspapers. A sample of individuals in management positions will be selected by the researcher. Data on newspaper-reading times will be used to test the following null and alternative hypotheses.

$$H_0: \mu \leq 8.6$$

$$H_a: \mu > 8.6$$

  a. What is the Type I error in this situation? What are the consequences of making this error?
  b. What is the Type II error in this situation? What are the consequences of making this error?

6. The label on a three-quart container of orange juice claims that the orange juice contains an average of one gram of fat or less. Answer the following questions for a hypothesis test that could be used to test the claim on the label.
  a. Develop the appropriate null and alternative hypotheses.
  b. What is the Type I error in this situation? What are the consequences of making this error?
  c. What is the Type II error in this situation? What are the consequences of making this error?

7. Carpetland salespersons have had sales averaging $8000 per week. Steve Contois, the firm's vice president, has proposed a compensation plan with new selling incentives. Steve hopes that the results of a trial selling period will enable him to conclude that the compensation plan increases the average sales per salesperson.
  a. Develop the appropriate null and alternative hypotheses.
  b. What is the Type I error in this situation? What are the consequences of making this error?
  c. What is the Type II error in this situation? What are the consequences of making this error?

8. Suppose a new production method will be implemented if a hypothesis test supports the conclusion that the new method reduces the mean operating cost per hour.
  a. State the appropriate null and alternative hypotheses if the mean cost for the current production method is $220 per hour.
  b. What is the Type I error in this situation? What are the consequences of making this error?
  c. What is the Type II error in this situation? What are the consequences of making this error?

9.3   ONE-TAILED TESTS ABOUT A POPULATION MEAN: LARGE-SAMPLE CASE

The Federal Trade Commission (FTC) periodically conducts studies designed to test the claims manufacturers make about their products. For example, the label on a large can of Hilltop Coffee states that the can contains at least three pounds of coffee. Suppose we want to check this claim by using hypothesis testing.

The first step is to develop the null and alternative hypotheses. We begin by tentatively assuming that the manufacturer's claim is correct. If the population of coffee cans has a mean weight of three or more pounds per can, Hilltop's claim about its product is correct. However, if the population of coffee cans has a mean weight less than three pounds per can, Hilltop's claim is incorrect.

With μ denoting the mean weight of cans for the population, the null and the alternative hypotheses have the following form.

$$H_0: \mu \geq 3$$

$$H_a: \mu < 3$$

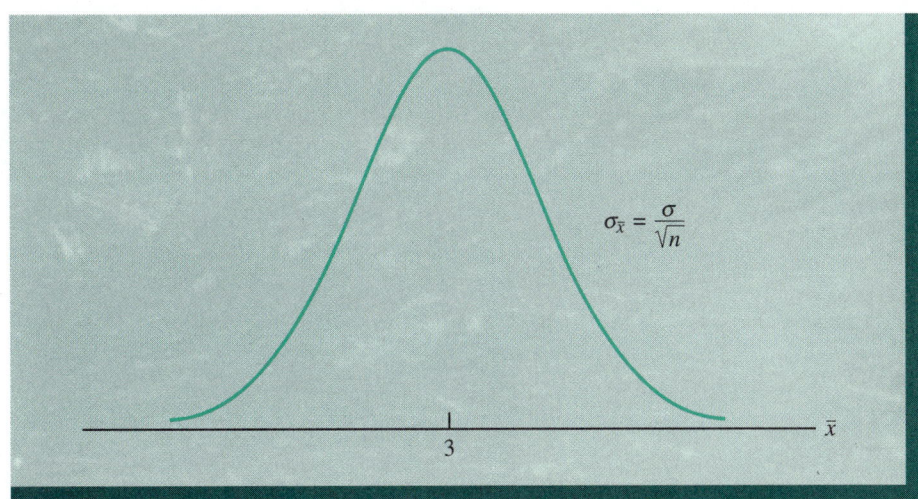

$$\sigma_{\bar{x}} = \frac{\sigma}{\sqrt{n}}$$

FIGURE 9.1 Sampling Distribution of $\bar{x}$ for the Hilltop Coffee Study When the Null Hypothesis Is True ($\mu = 3$)

If the sample data indicate that H_0 cannot be rejected, the statistical evidence does not support the conclusion that a label violation has occurred. Hence, no action would be taken against Hilltop. However, if sample data indicate that H_0 can be rejected, we will conclude that the alternative hypothesis, H_a: $\mu < 3$, is true. In that case, a conclusion of underfilling and a charge of a label violation would be appropriate.

Suppose a random sample of 36 cans of coffee is selected. Note that if the mean filling weight for the sample of 36 cans is less than three pounds, the sample results will begin to cast doubt on the null hypothesis H_0: $\mu \geq 3$. But how much less than three pounds must $\bar{x}$ be before we would be willing to risk making a Type I error and falsely accuse the company of a label violation?

To answer this question, let us tentatively assume that the null hypothesis is true with $\mu = 3$. From the study of sampling distributions in Chapter 7, we know that whenever the sample size is large ($n \geq 30$), the sampling distribution of $\bar{x}$ can be approximated by a normal probability distribution. Figure 9.1 shows the sampling distribution of $\bar{x}$ when the null hypothesis is true at $\mu = 3$.

The value of $z = (\bar{x} - 3)/\sigma_{\bar{x}}$ gives the number of standard deviations $\bar{x}$ is from $\mu = 3$. For hypothesis tests about a population mean, we will use z as a *test statistic* to determine whether $\bar{x}$ deviates enough from $\mu = 3$ to justify rejecting the null hypothesis. Note that a value of $z = -1$ means that $\bar{x}$ is 1 standard deviation below $\mu = 3$, a value of $z = -2$ means that $\bar{x}$ is 2 standard deviations below $\mu = 3$, and so on. Obtaining a value of $z < -3$ is very unlikely if the null hypothesis is true. The key question is: How small must the test statistic z be before we have enough evidence to reject the null hypothesis?

Figure 9.2 shows that the probability of observing a value of $\bar{x}$ more than 1.645 standard deviations below the mean of $\mu = 3$ is .05. Hence, if we were to reject the null hypothesis whenever the value of the test statistic $z = (\bar{x} - 3)/\sigma_{\bar{x}}$ is less than −1.645, the probability of making a Type I error would be .05. If the FTC considered .05 to be an acceptable level for the probability of making a Type I error, we would reject the null hypothesis whenever the test statistic indicates that the sample mean is more than 1.645 standard deviations below $\mu = 3$. Thus, we would reject H_0 if $z < -1.645$.

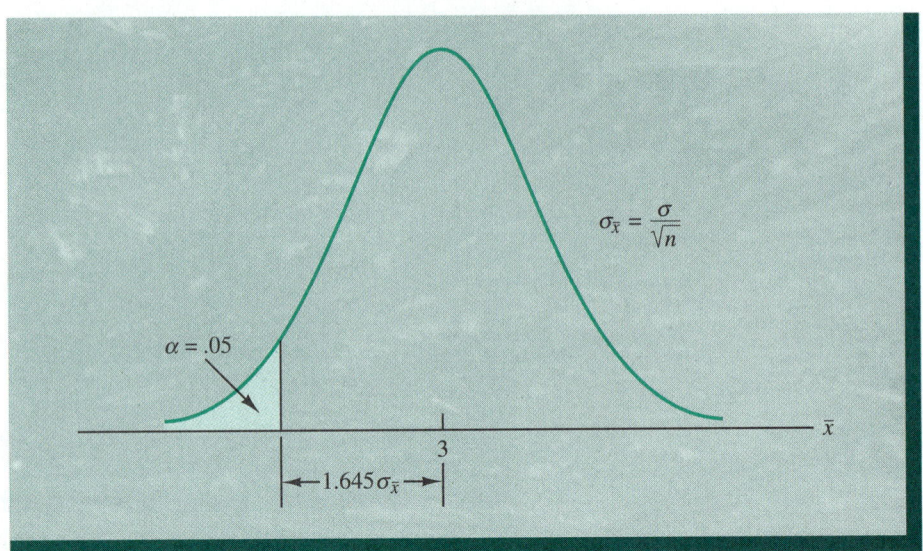

FIGURE 9.2 The Probability that $\bar{x}$ Is More than 1.645 Standard Deviations below the Mean of $\mu = 3$

The methodology of hypothesis testing requires that we specify the maximum allowable probability of a Type I error. As noted in the preceding section, this maximum probability is called the level of significance for the test; it is denoted by α, and it represents the probability of making a Type I error when the null hypothesis is true as an equality. The manager must specify the level of significance. If the cost of making a Type I error is high, a small value should be chosen for the level of significance. If the cost is not high, a larger value may be appropriate.

In the Hilltop Coffee study, the director of the FTC's testing program has made the following statement: "If the company is meeting its weight specifications exactly ($\mu = 3$), I would like a 99% chance of not taking any action against the company. While I do not want to accuse the company wrongly of underfilling its product, I am willing to live with a 1% chance of making this error."

From the director's statement, the maximum probability of a Type I error is .01. Hence, the level of significance for the hypothesis test is $\alpha = .01$. Figure 9.3 shows the sampling distributions of both $\bar{x}$ and $z = (\bar{x} - \mu)/\sigma_{\bar{x}}$ for the Hilltop Coffee example. Note that when the null hypothesis is true at $\mu = 3$, the probability is .01 that $\bar{x}$ is more than 2.33 standard deviations below the mean of 3. Therefore, we establish the following rejection rule.

$$\text{Reject } H_0 \text{ if } z = \frac{\bar{x} - \mu}{\sigma_{\bar{x}}} < -2.33$$

If the value of $\bar{x}$ is such that the test statistic z is in the rejection region, we reject H_0 and conclude that H_a is true. If the value of $\bar{x}$ is such that the test statistic z is not in the rejection region, we cannot reject H_0. Note that the rejection region in Figure 9.3 is in only one tail of the sampling distribution. In such cases, we say the test is a *one-tailed* hypothesis test.

Suppose a sample of 36 cans provides a mean of $\bar{x} = 2.92$ pounds and we know from previous studies that the population standard deviation is $\sigma = .18$. With $\sigma_{\bar{x}} = \sigma/\sqrt{n}$, the value of the test statistic is given by

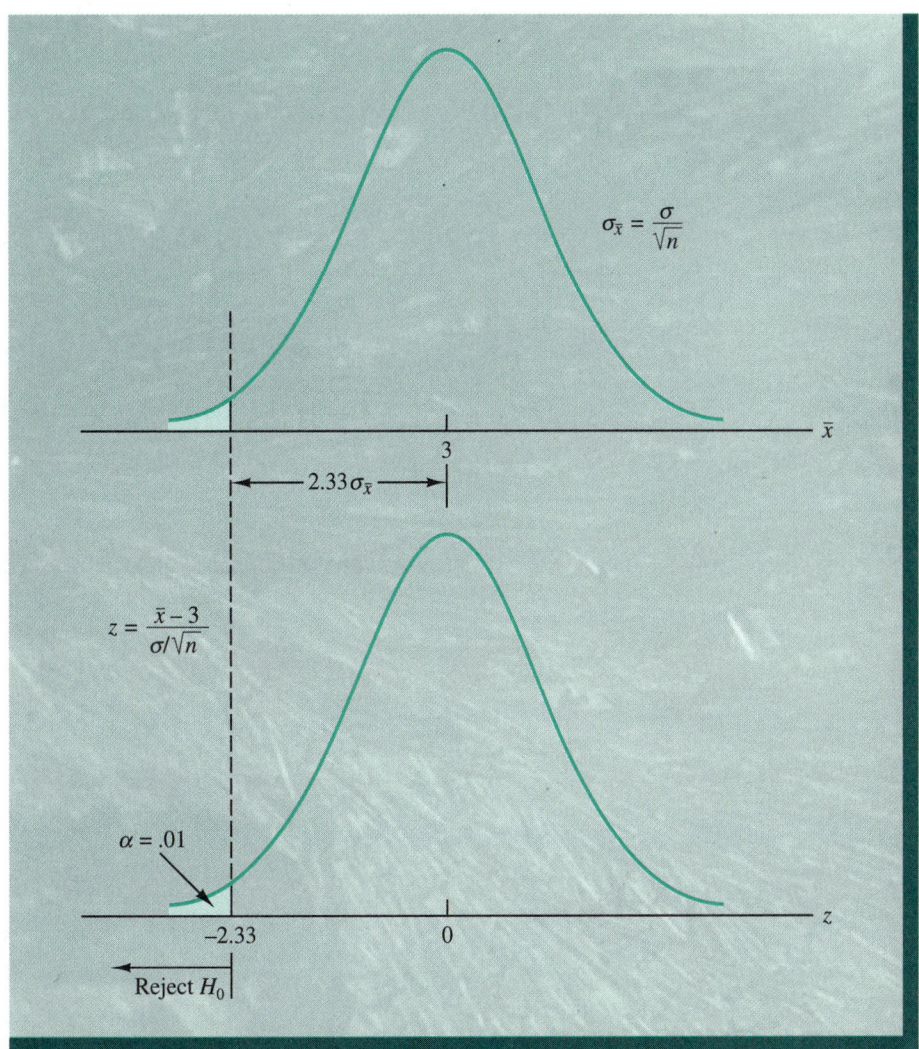

FIGURE 9.3   Hilltop Coffee Rejection Rule Has a Level of Significance of $\alpha = .01$

$$z = \frac{\bar{x} - 3}{\sigma / \sqrt{n}} = \frac{2.92 - 3}{.18 / \sqrt{36}} = -2.67$$

Figure 9.4 shows that the value of the test statistic is in the rejection region. We are now justified in concluding that $\mu < 3$ at a .01 level of significance. The director has statistical justification for taking action against Hilltop Coffee for underfilling its product.

Suppose the sample of 36 cans had provided a sample mean of $\bar{x} = 2.97$. In that case, the value of the test statistic would be

$$z = \frac{\bar{x} - 3}{\sigma / \sqrt{n}} = \frac{2.97 - 3}{.18 / \sqrt{36}} = -1.00$$

Since $z = -1.00$ is greater than -2.33, the value of the test statistic is not in the rejection region (see Figure 9.5). Hence we cannot reject the null hypothesis. No further inference can be made, and no statistical justification is provided for taking action against Hilltop Coffee.

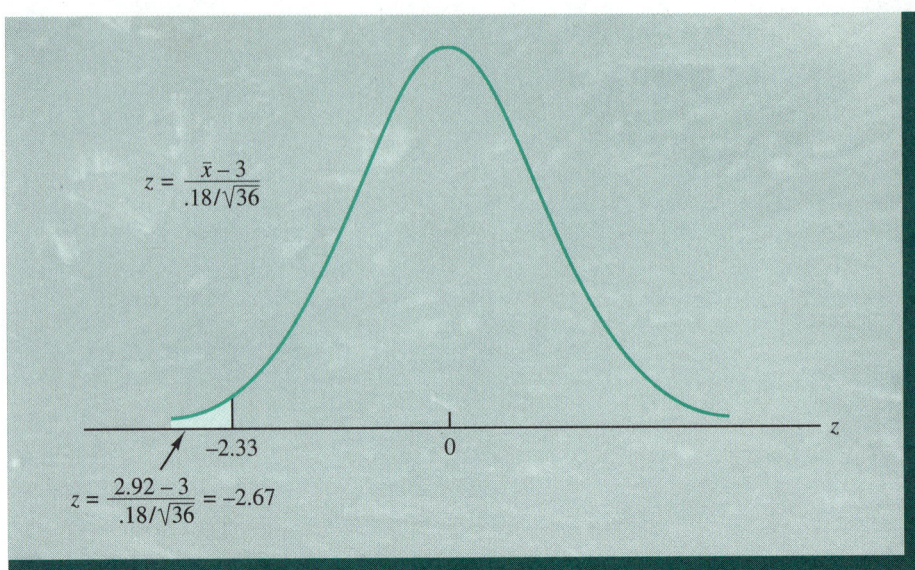

FIGURE 9.4   Value of the Test Statistic for $\bar{x} = 2.92$ Is in the Rejection Region

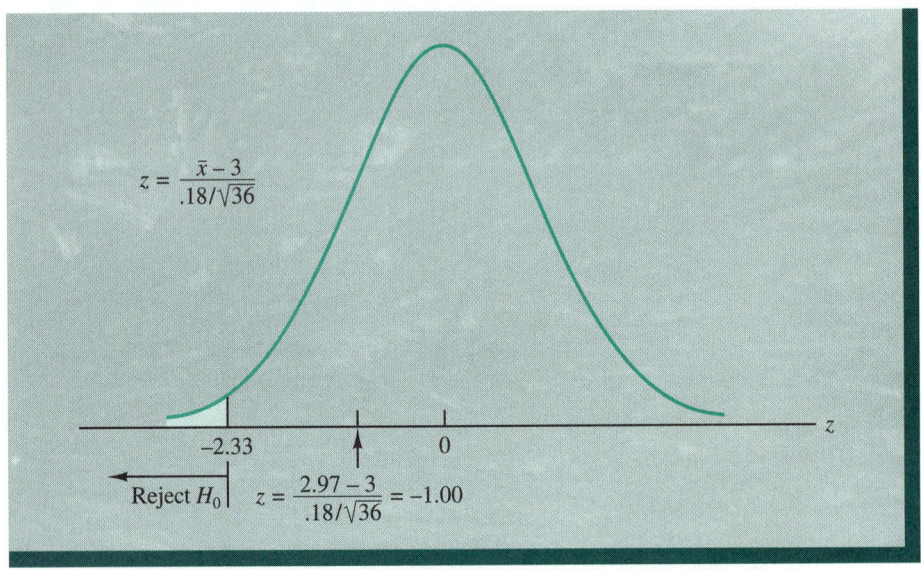

FIGURE 9.5   Value of the Test Statistic for $\bar{x} = 2.97$ Is Not in the Rejection Region

The value of z that establishes the boundary of the rejection region is called the *critical value*. In establishing the critical value, we tentatively assume the null hypothesis is true. For Hilltop Coffee, the null hypothesis is true whenever $\mu \geq 3$, and we considered only the case when $\mu = 3$. What about the case when $\mu > 3$? If $\mu > 3$, the probability of making a Type I error will be less than it is when $\mu = 3$; that is, we are even less likely to find a value of the test statistic that is in the rejection region. Since the objective of the hypothesis-testing procedure is to limit the maximum probability of making a Type I error, the critical value for the test is established by assuming $\mu = 3$.

SUMMARY: ONE-TAILED TESTS ABOUT A POPULATION MEAN

Let us generalize the hypothesis-testing procedure for one-tailed tests about a population mean. We consider the large-sample case ($n \geq 30$) in which the central limit theorem enables us to assume that the sampling distribution $\bar{x}$ can be approximated by a normal probability distribution. In this large-sample case when σ is unknown, we simply substitute the sample standard deviation s for σ in computing the test statistic. The general form of a lower-tail test, where μ_0 is a stated value for the population mean, follows.

Large-Sample ($n \geq 30$) Hypothesis Test About a Population Mean for a One-Tailed Test of the Form

$$H_0: \mu \geq \mu_0$$
$$H_a: \mu < \mu_0$$

Test Statistic: σ Known

$$z = \frac{\bar{x} - \mu_0}{\sigma/\sqrt{n}} \qquad (9.1)$$

Test Statistic: σ Unknown

$$z = \frac{\bar{x} - \mu_0}{s/\sqrt{n}}$$

Rejection Rule at a Level of Significance of α

Reject H_0 if $z < -z_\alpha$

A second form of the one-tailed test rejects the null hypothesis when the test statistic is in the upper tail of the sampling distribution. This one-tailed test and rejection rule are summarized next (see Figure 9.6). Again, we are considering the large-sample case; when σ is unknown, s can be substituted for σ in the computation of the test statistic z.

Large-Sample ($n \geq 30$) Hypothesis Test About a Population Mean for a One-Tailed Test of the Form

$$H_0: \mu \leq \mu_0$$
$$H_a: \mu > \mu_0$$

Test Statistic: σ Known

$$z = \frac{\bar{x} - \mu_0}{\sigma/\sqrt{n}} \qquad (9.2)$$

Test Statistic: σ Unknown

$$z = \frac{\bar{x} - \mu_0}{s/\sqrt{n}}$$

Rejection Rule at a Level of Significance of α

Reject H_0 if $z > z_\alpha$

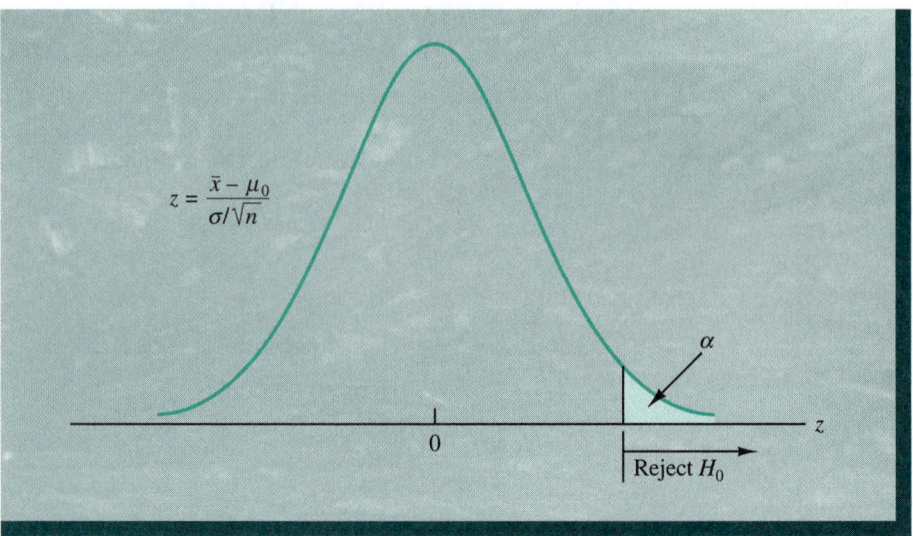

FIGURE 9.6 Rejection Region for an Upper-Tail Hypothesis Test About a Population Mean

THE USE OF *p*-VALUES

Another approach that can be used to decide whether or not to reject H_0 is based on a probability called a *p-value*. If we assume that the null hypothesis is true, the *p*-value is the probability of obtaining a sample result that is at least as unlikely as what is observed. In the Hilltop Coffee example, the rejection region is in the lower tail; therefore the *p*-value is the probability of observing a sample mean less than or equal to what is observed. The *p*-value is often called the observed level of significance.

Let us compute the *p*-value associated with the sample mean $\bar{x} = 2.92$ in the Hilltop Coffee example. The *p*-value in this case is the probability of obtaining a value for the sample mean that is less than or equal to the observed value of $\bar{x} = 2.92$, given the hypothesized value for the population mean of $\mu = 3$. Previously we showed that the test statistic $z = -2.67$ corresponded to $\bar{x} = 2.92$. Thus, as shown in Figure 9.7, the *p*-value is the area in the tail of the standard normal probability distribution for $z = -2.67$. Using the standard normal probability distribution table, we find that the area between the mean and $z = -2.67$ is .4962. Hence, there is a $.5000 - .4962 = .0038$ probability of obtaining a sample mean that is less than or equal to the observed $\bar{x} = 2.92$. The *p*-value is therefore .0038. This *p*-value shows that there is a very small probability of obtaining a sample mean as small as $\bar{x} = 2.92$ when sampling from a population with $\mu = 3$.

The *p*-value can be used to make the decision in a hypothesis test by noting that if the *p*-value is *less than the level of significance* α, the value of the test statistic is in the rejection region. Similarly, if the *p*-value is *greater than or equal to* α, the value of the test statistic is not in the rejection region. For the Hilltop Coffee example, the fact that the *p*-value of .0038 is less than the level of significance, $\alpha = .01$, indicates that the null hypothesis should be rejected. Given the level of significance α, the decision of whether or not to reject H_0 can be made as follows.

p-VALUE CRITERION FOR HYPOTHESIS TESTING

Reject H_0 if the *p*-value $< \alpha$

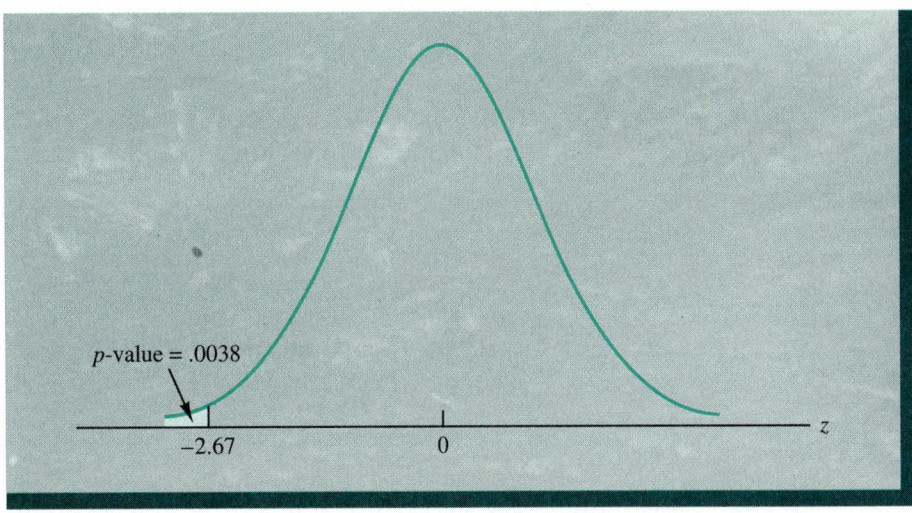

FIGURE 9.7 *p*-Value for the Hilltop Coffee Study When $\bar{x}$=2.92 and z = −2.67

The *p*-value and the corresponding test statistic will always provide the same hypothesis-testing conclusion. When the rejection region is in the lower tail of the sampling distribution, the *p*-value is the area under the curve less than or equal to the test statistic. When the rejection region is in the upper tail of the sampling distribution, the *p*-value is the area under the curve greater than or equal to the test statistic. A small *p*-value indicates a sample result that is unusual given the assumption that H_0 is true. Small *p*-values lead to rejection of H_0, whereas large *p*-values indicate that the null hypothesis cannot be rejected.

THE STEPS OF HYPOTHESIS TESTING

In conducting the Hilltop Coffee hypothesis test, we carried out the steps that are required for any hypothesis-testing procedure. A summary of the steps that can be applied to any hypothesis test follows.

STEPS OF HYPOTHESIS TESTING

1. Determine the null and alternative hypotheses that are appropriate for the application.
2. Select the test statistic that will be used to decide whether or not to reject the null hypothesis.
3. Specify the level of significance α for the test.
4. Use the level of significance to develop the rejection rule that indicates the values of the test statistic that will lead to the rejection of H_0.
5. Collect the sample data and compute the value of the test statistic.
6. a. Compare the value of the test statistic to the critical value(s) specified in the rejection rule to determine whether or not H_0 should be rejected.
   or
   b. Compute the *p*-value based on the test statistic in step 5. Use the *p*-value to determine whether or not H_0 should be rejected.

For Hilltop Coffee, the following null and alternative hypotheses were selected (step 1).

$$H_0: \mu \geq 3$$
$$H_a: \mu < 3$$

With the large sample ($n \geq 30$) and the population standard deviation given as $\sigma = .18$, the test statistic (step 2) was

$$z = \frac{\bar{x} - \mu}{\sigma/\sqrt{n}}.$$

The level of significance (step 3) was given as $\alpha = .01$. At $\alpha = .01$, the corresponding rejection rule for the test statistic (step 4) was to reject H_0 if $z < -2.33$.

With a simple random sample of $n = 36$ cans of coffee and a sample mean of $\bar{x} = 2.92$ pounds, the value of the test statistic (step 5) was computed to be

$$z = \frac{2.92 - 3.00}{.18/\sqrt{36}} = -2.67.$$

A comparison of $z = -2.67$ to the critical value specified in the rejection rule, showed that H_0 should be rejected (step 6a). Alternatively, the p-value (step 6b) associated with $z = -2.67$ was shown to be .0038. Since $.0038 < .01$, H_0 should be rejected.

NOTES AND COMMENTS

The p-value, the observed level of significance, is a measure of the likelihood of the sample results when the null hypothesis is assumed to be true. The smaller the p-value, the less likely it is that the sample results came from a situation where the null hypothesis is true. Most statistical software packages print the p-value associated with a hypothesis test. The user can then draw a hypothesis test conclusion without referring to statistical tables.

EXERCISES

METHODS

9. Consider the following hypothesis test.

$$H_0: \mu \geq 10$$
$$H_a: \mu < 10$$

A sample of 50 provides a sample mean of 9.46 and sample standard deviation of 2.
   a. At $\alpha = .05$, what is the critical value for z? What is the rejection rule?
   b. Compute the value of the test statistic z. What is your conclusion?

Self-Test

10. Consider the following hypothesis test.

$$H_0: \mu \leq 15$$
$$H_a: \mu > 15$$

A sample of 40 provides a sample mean of 16.5 and sample standard deviation of 7.
   a. At $\alpha = .02$, what is the critical value for z, and what is the rejection rule?
   b. Compute the value of the test statistic z.
   c. What is the p-value?
   d. What is your conclusion?

11. Consider the following hypothesis test.

$$H_0: \mu \geq 25$$

$$H_a: \mu < 25$$

A sample of 100 is used and the population standard deviation is 12. Use $\alpha = .05$. Provide the value of the test statistic z and your conclusion for each of the following sample results.
a. $\bar{x} = 22.0$ b. $\bar{x} = 24.0$ c. $\bar{x} = 23.5$ d. $\bar{x} = 22.8$

12. Consider the following hypothesis test.

$$H_0: \mu \leq 5$$

$$H_a: \mu > 5$$

Assume the following test statistics. Compute the corresponding p-values and make the appropriate conclusions based on $\alpha = .05$.
a. $z = 1.82$ b. $z = .45$ c. $z = 1.50$ d. $z = 3.30$ e. $z = -1.00$

APPLICATIONS

Self-Test

13. Individuals filing 1994 federal income tax returns prior to March 31, 1995, had an average refund of $1056 (*USA Today,* April 5, 1995). Consider the population of "last-minute" filers who mail their returns during the last five days of the income tax period (typically April 10 to April 15).
    a. A researcher suggests that one of the reasons individuals wait until the last five days to file their returns is that on average those individuals have a lower refund than early filers. Develop appropriate hypotheses such that rejection of H_0 will support the researcher's contention.
    b. For a sample of 400 individuals who filed a return between April 10 and April 15, the sample mean refund was $910 and the sample standard deviation was $1600. At $\alpha = .05$, what is your conclusion?
    c. What is the p-value for the test?

14. In 1990, The Motor Vehicle Manufacturers Association, Detroit, Michigan, reported statistics on the average number of years passenger cars were being used. The 1980 population mean was reported to be 6.5 years. Assume that the 1990 data were obtained from a sample of 100 passenger cars and showed a sample mean of 7.8 years and a sample standard deviation of 2.2 years.
    a. Formulate the null and alternative hypotheses for a researcher who is looking for evidence to show that individuals were driving cars longer in 1990.
    b. Do the data support the conclusion that individuals were driving cars longer? Use a .01 level of significance.
    c. What implications does this finding have for vehicle manufacturers?

15. According to the National Automobile Dealers Association, the mean price for used cars is $10,192 (*USA Today,* April 12, 1995). A manager of a Kansas City used car dealership reviewed a sample of 100 recent used car sales at the dealership. The sample mean price was $9300 and the sample standard deviation was $4500. Letting μ denote the population mean price for used cars at the Kansas City dealership, test $H_0: \mu \geq 10,192$ and $H_a: \mu < 10,192$ at a .05 level of significance.
    a. What is the hypothesis-testing conclusion?
    b. What is the p-value?
    c. What information does the hypothesis test result provide for the manager of the Kansas City dealership? What follow-up action might the manager want to consider?

16. Fightmaster and Associates Real Estate, Inc., advertises that the mean selling time of a residential home is 40 days or less. A sample of 50 recently sold residential homes shows a

sample mean selling time of 45 days and a sample standard deviation of 20 days. Using a .02 level of significance, test the validity of the company's claim.

17. Fowle Marketing Research, Inc., bases charges to a client on the assumption that telephone surveys can be completed in a mean time of 15 minutes or less. If a longer mean survey time is necessary, a premium rate is charged. Suppose a sample of 35 surveys shows a sample mean of 17 minutes and a sample standard deviation of 4 minutes. Is the premium rate justified? Test at the $\alpha = .01$ level of significance.

18. New tires manufactured by a company in Findlay, Ohio, are designed to provide a mean of at least 28,000 miles. Tests with 30 tires show a sample mean of 27,500 miles and a sample standard deviation of 1000 miles. Using a .05 level of significance, test whether or not there is sufficient evidence to reject the claim of a mean of at least 28,000 miles. What is the p-value?

19. A company currently pays its production employees a mean wage of $15.00 per hour. The company is planning to build a new factory and is considering several locations. The availability of labor at a rate less than $15.00 per hour is a major factor in the location decision. For one location, a sample of 40 workers showed a current mean hourly wage of $\bar{x} = \$14.00$ and a sample standard deviation of $s = \$2.40$.
    a. At a .10 level of significance, do the sample data indicate that the location has a mean wage rate significantly below the $15.00 per hour rate?
    b. What is the p-value?

20. A new diet program claims that participants will lose on average at least eight pounds during the first week of the program. A random sample of 40 people participating in the program showed a sample mean weight loss of seven pounds. The sample standard deviation was 3.2 pounds.
    a. What is the rejection rule with $\alpha = .05$?
    b. What is your conclusion about the claim made by the diet program?
    c. What is the p-value?

9.4 TWO-TAILED TESTS ABOUT A POPULATION MEAN: LARGE-SAMPLE CASE

Two-tailed hypothesis tests differ from one-tailed tests in that the rejection region is placed in both the lower and the upper tails of the sampling distribution. Let us introduce an example to show how and why two-tailed tests are conducted.

The United States Golf Association (USGA) has established rules that manufacturers of golf equipment must meet if their products are to be acceptable for use in USGA events. One of the rules for the manufacture of golf balls states: "A brand of golf ball, when tested on apparatus approved by the USGA on the outdoor range at the USGA Headquarters . . . shall not cover an average distance in carry and roll exceeding 280 yards. . . ." Suppose Superflight, Inc., has recently developed a high-technology manufacturing method that can produce golf balls having an average distance in carry and roll of 280 yards.

Superflight realizes, however, that if the new manufacturing process goes out of adjustment, the process may produce balls for which the average distance is less than or more than 280 yards. In the former case, sales may decline as a result of marketing an inferior product, and in the latter case the golf balls may be rejected by the USGA. Superflight's managers therefore have instituted a quality-control program to monitor the new manufacturing process.

As part of the quality-control program, an inspector periodically selects a sample of balls from the production line and subjects them to tests that are equivalent to those

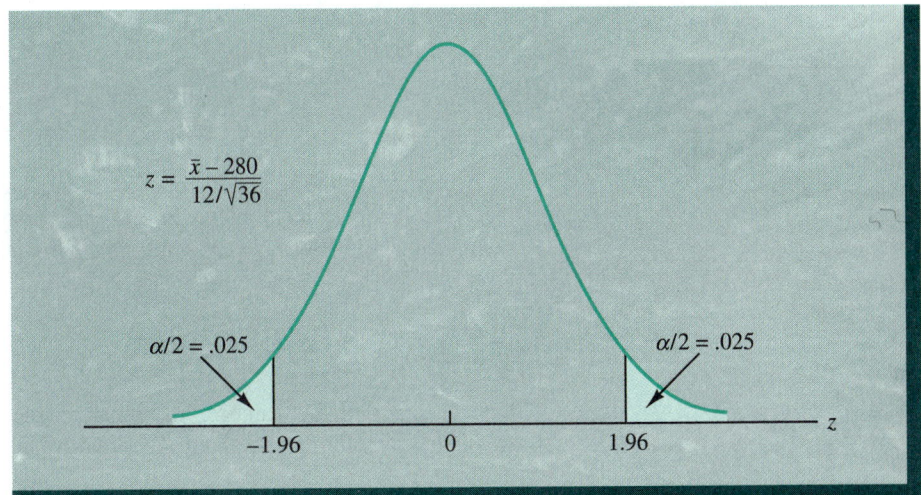

FIGURE 9.8   Rejection Region for the Two-Tailed Hypothesis Test for Superflight, Inc.

DISTANCE

TABLE 9.2 Distance Data for a Simple Random Sample of 36 Superflight Golf Balls

Ball	Yards
1	269
2	300
3	268
4	278
5	282
6	263
7	301
8	295
9	288
10	278
11	276
12	286
13	296
14	265
15	271
16	279
17	284
18	260
19	275
20	282
21	260
22	266
23	270
24	293
25	272
26	285
27	293
28	281
29	269
30	299
31	263
32	264
33	273
34	291
35	274
36	277

performed by the USGA. Having no reason to doubt that the manufacturing process is functioning correctly, we establish the following null and alternative hypotheses.

$$H_0: \mu = 280$$

$$H_a: \mu \neq 280$$

As usual, we make the tentative assumption that the null hypothesis is true. A rejection region must be established for the test statistic z. We want to reject the claim that $\mu = 280$ when the z value indicates that the sample mean $\bar{x}$ is significantly less than 280 yards or significantly more than 280 yards. Thus, H_0 should be rejected for values of the test statistic in either the lower tail or the upper tail of the sampling distribution. The test therefore is called a *two-tailed* hypothesis test.

Following the hypothesis-testing procedure developed in the previous sections, we specify a level of significance by determining a maximum allowable probability of making a Type I error. Suppose we choose $\alpha = .05$. This means that there will be a .05 probability of concluding that the mean distance is not 280 yards when in fact it is. The test statistic is

$$z = \frac{\bar{x} - \mu}{\sigma/\sqrt{n}}$$

Figure 9.8 shows the sampling distribution of z with the two-tailed rejection region for $\alpha = .05$. With two-tailed hypothesis tests, we will always determine the rejection region by placing an area or probability of $\alpha/2$ in each tail of the distribution. The values of z that provide an area of .025 in each tail can be found from the standard normal probability distribution table. We see in Figure 9.8 that $-z_{.025} = -1.96$ identifies an area of .025 in the lower tail and $z_{.025} = +1.96$ identifies an area of .025 in the upper tail. Referring to Figure 9.8, we can establish the following rejection rule.

Reject H_0 if $z < -1.96$ or if $z > 1.96$

Suppose that a simple random sample of 36 golf balls provided the data in Table 9.2. For these data we obtained a sample mean of $\bar{x} = 278.5$ yards and a sample standard deviation of $s = 12$ yards. With the value of μ from the null hypothesis and the sample standard deviation of $s = 12$ as an estimate of the population standard deviation σ, the value of the test statistic is

$$z = \frac{\bar{x} - \mu}{\sigma/\sqrt{n}} = \frac{278.5 - 280}{12/\sqrt{36}} = -.75$$

According to the rejection rule, H_0 cannot be rejected. The sample results indicate that the quality-control manager has no reason to doubt the assumption that the manufacturing process is producing golf balls with a mean distance of 280 yards.

SUMMARY: TWO-TAILED TESTS ABOUT A POPULATION MEAN

Let μ_0 represent the value of the mean in the hypotheses. The general form of the two-tailed hypothesis test about a population mean follows.

Large-Sample ($n \geq 30$) Hypothesis Test About a Population Mean for a Two-Tailed Test of the Form

$$H_0: \mu = \mu_0$$
$$H_a: \mu \neq \mu_0$$

Test Statistic: σ Known

$$z = \frac{\bar{x} - \mu_0}{\sigma/\sqrt{n}} \tag{9.3}$$

Test Statistic: σ Unknown

$$z = \frac{\bar{x} - \mu_0}{s/\sqrt{n}}$$

Rejection Rule at a Level of Significance of α

Reject H_0 if $z < -z_{\alpha/2}$ or if $z > z_{\alpha/2}$

p-VALUES FOR TWO-TAILED TESTS

If we assume the null hypothesis is true, the p-value is the probability of obtaining a sample result that is at least as unlikely as what is observed. A small p-value indicates that the sample result is unusual given the assumption that H_0 is true. Hence, as with the one-tailed hypothesis tests, a small p-value leads to the rejection of H_0.

Let us compute the p-value for the Superflight golf ball example. The sample mean of $\bar{x} = 278.5$ has a corresponding z value of $-.75$. The table for the standard normal probability distribution shows that the area between the mean and $z = -.75$ is .2734. Thus, the area in the lower tail is $.5000 - .2734 = .2266$. Looking at Figure 9.8, we see that the lower-tail portion of the rejection region has an area or probability of $\alpha/2 = .05/2 = .025$. Thus, with $.2266 > .025$, the test statistic is not in the rejection region, and the null hypothesis cannot be rejected.

One question remains: What value should we report as the p-value for the two-tailed test? At first glance, you may be inclined to say the p-value is .2266. If that is your choice, you will have to remember two different rules: one for the one-tailed test, which is to reject H_0 if p-value $< \alpha$, and another for the two-tailed test, which is to reject

```
Test of mu = 280.00 vs mu not = 280.00

The assumed sigma = 12.0


       N       Mean    StDev   SE Mean        Z   P value
      36     278.50    12.00      2.00    -0.75      0.45
```

FIGURE 9.9 Minitab Output for the Superflight Golf Ball Hypothesis Test

H_0 if p-value $< \alpha/2$. Alternatively, suppose we define the p-value for a two-tailed test as *double* the area found in the tail of the distribution. Thus, for the Superflight example, we would define the p-value to be $2(.2266) = .4532$. The advantage of this definition of the p-value for a two-tailed test is that the p-value can be compared directly to the level of significance α. Hence, with $.4532 > .05$, we see that the null hypothesis cannot be rejected. By remembering that the p-value for a two-tailed test is simply double the area found in the tail of the distribution, the previous rule to reject H_0 if p-value $< \alpha$ can be used for all hypothesis tests.

THE ROLE OF THE COMPUTER

We illustrate how computer software packages can be applied in hypothesis testing by using Minitab to perform the analysis for the Superflight golf ball study. After entering the distance data for the sample of 36 golf balls into a Minitab worksheet, we obtained the hypothesis testing output in Figure 9.9. The first line of output shows that the hypothesis test is $\mu = 280$ versus $\mu \neq 280$. The assumed sigma of 12 indicates that the sample standard deviation $s = 12$ has been used to estimate the population standard deviation σ. The sample size 36, the sample mean 278.5, the sample standard deviation 12, and the standard error of the mean 2 are shown. The value of the test statistic $z = -.75$ and the p-value $= .45$ can be used to draw the hypothesis testing conclusion. Thus, at a .05 level of significance, the null hypothesis $H_0: \mu = 280$ cannot be rejected.

THE RELATIONSHIP BETWEEN INTERVAL ESTIMATION AND HYPOTHESIS TESTING

In Chapter 8 we showed how to develop a confidence interval estimate of a population mean. In the large-sample case, the confidence interval estimate of a population mean corresponding to a $1 - \alpha$ confidence coefficient is given by

$$\bar{x} \pm z_{\alpha/2} \frac{\sigma}{\sqrt{n}} \tag{9.4}$$

when σ is known and

$$\bar{x} \pm z_{\alpha/2} \frac{s}{\sqrt{n}} \tag{9.5}$$

when σ is unknown.

Conducting a hypothesis test requires us first to make an assumption about the value of a population parameter. In the case of the population mean, the two-tailed hypothesis test has the form

$$H_0: \mu = \mu_0$$

$$H_a: \mu \neq \mu_0$$

where μ_0 is the hypothesized value for the population mean. Using the rejection rule provided by (9.3), we see that the region over which we do not reject H_0 includes all values of the sample mean $\bar{x}$ that are within $-z_{\alpha/2}$ and $+z_{\alpha/2}$ standard errors of μ_0. Thus, the do-not-reject region for the sample mean $\bar{x}$ in a two-tailed hypothesis test with a level of significance of α is given by

$$\mu_0 \pm z_{\alpha/2} \frac{\sigma}{\sqrt{n}} \qquad (9.6)$$

when σ is known and

$$\mu_0 \pm z_{\alpha/2} \frac{s}{\sqrt{n}} \qquad (9.7)$$

when σ is unknown.

A close look at (9.4) and (9.6) provides insight about the relationship between the estimation and hypothesis-testing approaches to statistical inference. Note in particular that both procedures require the computation of the values $z_{\alpha/2}$ and $\sigma/\sqrt{n}$. Focusing on α, we see that a confidence coefficient of $(1 - \alpha)$ for interval estimation corresponds to a level of significance of α in hypothesis testing. For example, a 95% confidence interval corresponds to a .05 level of significance for hypothesis testing. Furthermore, (9.4) and (9.6) show that since $z_{\alpha/2} (\sigma/\sqrt{n})$ is the plus or minus value for both expressions, if $\bar{x}$ is in the do-not-reject region defined by (9.6), the hypothesized value μ_0 will be in the confidence interval defined by (9.4). Conversely, if the hypothesized value μ_0 is in the confidence interval defined by (9.4), the sample mean $\bar{x}$ will be in the do-not-reject region for the hypothesis $H_0: \mu = \mu_0$ as defined by (9.6). These observations lead to the following procedure for using confidence interval results to draw hypothesis-testing conclusions.

A CONFIDENCE INTERVAL APPROACH TO TESTING A HYPOTHESIS OF THE FORM

$$H_0: \mu = \mu_0$$

$$H_a: \mu \neq \mu_0$$

1. Select a simple random sample from the population and use the value of the sample mean $\bar{x}$ to develop the confidence interval for the population mean μ. If σ is known, compute the interval estimate by using

$$\bar{x} \pm z_{\alpha/2} \frac{\sigma}{\sqrt{n}}$$

If σ is unknown, compute the interval estimate by using

$$\bar{x} \pm z_{\alpha/2} \frac{s}{\sqrt{n}}$$

2. If the confidence interval contains the hypothesized value μ_0, do not reject H_0. Otherwise, reject H_0.

Let us return to the Superflight golf ball study, which resulted in the following two-tailed test.

$$H_0: \mu = 280$$

$$H_a: \mu \neq 280$$

To test this hypothesis with a level of significance of $\alpha = .05$, we sampled 36 golf balls and found a sample mean distance of $\bar{x} = 278.5$ yards and a sample standard deviation of $s = 12$ yards. Using these results with $z_{.025} = 1.96$, we find that the 95% confidence interval estimate of the population mean becomes

$$\bar{x} \pm z_{.025} \frac{s}{\sqrt{n}}$$

$$278.5 \pm 1.96 \frac{12}{\sqrt{36}}$$

$$278.5 \pm 3.92$$

or

$$274.58 \text{ to } 282.42$$

This finding enables the quality-control manager to conclude with 95% confidence that the mean distance for the population of golf balls is between 274.58 and 282.42 yards. Since the hypothesized value for the population mean, $\mu_0 = 280$, is in this interval, the hypothesis-testing conclusion is that the null hypothesis, $H_0: \mu = 280$, cannot be rejected.

Note that this discussion and example pertain to two-tailed hypothesis tests about a population mean. However, the same confidence interval and hypothesis-testing relationship exists for other population parameters. In addition, the relationship can be extended to make one-tailed tests about population parameters. Doing so, however, requires the development of one-sided confidence intervals.

NOTES AND COMMENTS

1. The p-value depends only on the sample outcome. However, it is necessary to know whether the hypothesis test being investigated is one-tailed or two-tailed. Given the value of $\bar{x}$ in a sample, the p-value for a two-tailed test will always be *twice* the area in the tail of the sampling distribution at the value of $\bar{x}$.

2. The interval-estimation approach to hypothesis testing helps to highlight the role of the sample size. From (9.4) we can see that larger sample sizes n lead to narrower confidence intervals. Thus, for a given level of significance α, a larger sample is less likely to lead to an interval containing μ_0 when the null hypothesis is false. That is, the larger sample size will provide a higher probability of rejecting H_0 when H_0 is false.

EXERCISES

METHODS

21. Consider the following hypothesis test.

$$H_0: \mu = 10$$

$$H_a: \mu \neq 10$$

A sample of 36 provides a sample mean of 11 and sample standard deviation of 2.5.
a. At $\alpha = .05$, what is the rejection rule?
b. Compute the value of the test statistic z. What is your conclusion?

Self-Test
▸ 22. Consider the following hypothesis test.

$$H_0: \mu = 15$$
$$H_a: \mu \neq 15$$

A sample of 50 gives a sample mean of 14.2 and sample standard deviation of 5.
a. At $\alpha = .02$, what is the rejection rule?
b. Compute the value of the test statistic z.
c. What is the p-value?
d. What is your conclusion?

23. Consider the following hypothesis test.

$$H_0: \mu = 25$$
$$H_a: \mu \neq 25$$

A sample of 80 is used and the population standard deviation is 10. Use $\alpha = .05$. Compute the value of the test statistic z and specify your conclusion for each of the following sample results.
a. $\bar{x} = 22.0$ b. $\bar{x} = 27.0$ c. $\bar{x} = 23.5$ d. $\bar{x} = 28.0$

24. Consider the following hypothesis test.

$$H_0: \mu = 5$$
$$H_a: \mu \neq 5$$

Assume the following test statistics. Compute the corresponding p-values and specify your conclusions based on $\alpha = .05$.
a. $z = 1.80$ b. $z = -.45$ c. $z = 2.05$ d. $z = -3.50$ e. $z = -1.00$

APPLICATIONS

Self-Test
▸ 25. The Bureau of Economic Analysis in the U.S. Department of Commerce reported that the mean annual income for a resident of North Carolina is $18,688 (*USA Today,* August 24, 1995). A researcher for the state of South Carolina wants to test $H_0: \mu = 18,688$ and $H_a: \mu \neq 18,688$ where μ is the mean annual income for a resident of South Carolina.
a. What is the hypothesis test conclusion if a sample of 400 residents of South Carolina shows a sample mean annual income of $16,860 and a sample standard deviation of $14,624? Use a .05 level of significance.
b. What is the p-value for this test?

26. A study of the operation of a city-owned parking garage shows a historical mean parking time of 220 minutes per car. The garage area has recently been remodeled and the parking charges have been increased. The city manager would like to know whether these changes have had any effect on the mean parking time. Test $H_0: \mu = 220$ and $H_a: \mu \neq 220$ at a .05 level of significance.
a. What is your conclusion if a sample of 50 cars showed $\bar{x} = 208$ and $s = 80$?
b. What is the p-value?

27. A production line operates with a filling mean weight of 16 ounces per container. Overfilling or underfilling is a serious problem, and the production line should be shut down if either occurs. From past data, σ is known to be .8 ounces. A quality-control inspector samples 30 items every two hours and at that time makes the decision of whether or not to shut the line down for adjustment.

a. With a .05 level of significance, what is the rejection rule for the hypothesis-testing procedure?

b. If a sample mean of $\bar{x} = 16.32$ ounces were found, what action would you recommend?

c. If $\bar{x} = 15.82$ ounces, what action would you recommend?

d. What is the p-value for parts (b) and (c)?

28. An automobile assembly-line operation has a scheduled mean completion time of 2.2 minutes. Because of the effect of completion time on both preceding and subsequent assembly operations, it is important to maintain the 2.2-minute standard. A random sample of 45 times shows a sample mean completion time of 2.39 minutes, with a sample standard deviation of .20 minutes. Use a .02 level of significance and test whether or not the operation is meeting its 2.2-minute standard.

29. Historically, evening long-distance phone calls from a particular city have averaged 15.20 minutes per call. In a random sample of 35 calls, the sample mean time was 14.30 minutes per call, with a sample standard deviation of five minutes. Use this sample information to test whether or not there has been a change in the mean duration of long distance phone calls. Use a .05 level of significance. What is the p-value?

30. The mean salary for full professors in the United States is $61,650 (*The American Almanac of Jobs and Salaries,* 1994–1995 Edition). A sample of 36 full professors at business colleges showed $\bar{x} = \$72,800$ and $s=\$5,000$.

a. Develop a 95% confidence interval for the population mean salary of business college professors.

b. Use the confidence interval to conduct the hypothesis test: $H_0: \mu = 61,650$ and $H_a: \mu \neq 61,650$. What is your conclusion?

31. At Western University the historical mean scholarship examination score of entering students has been 900, with a standard deviation of 180. Each year a sample of applications is taken to see whether the examination scores are at the same level as in previous years. The null hypothesis tested is $H_0: \mu = 900$. A sample of 200 students in this year's class shows a sample mean score of 935. Use a .05 level of significance.

a. Use a confidence interval approach to conduct a hypothesis test.

b. Use a test statistic to test this hypothesis.

c. What is the p-value for this test?

32. An industry pays an average wage rate of $9.00 per hour. A sample of 36 workers from one company showed a mean wage of $\bar{x} = \$8.50$ and a sample standard deviation of $s= \$0.60$.

a. A one-sided confidence interval uses the sample results to establish either an upper limit or a lower limit for the value of the population parameter. For this exercise establish an upper 95% confidence limit for the hourly wage rate paid by the company. The form of this one-sided confidence interval requires that we be 95% confident that the population mean is this value or less. What is the 95% confidence statement for this one-sided confidence interval?

b. Use the one-sided confidence interval result to test $H_0: \mu \geq 9$. What is your conclusion? Explain.

9.5 TESTS ABOUT A POPULATION MEAN: SMALL-SAMPLE CASE

Assume that the sample size is small ($n < 30$) and that the sample standard deviation s is used to estimate the population standard deviation σ.* If it is also reasonable to assume that the population has a normal probability distribution, the t distribution can

---

*If $n < 30$, if the population has a normal probability distribution, and if the population standard deviation σ is *known*, $z = (\bar{x} - \mu_0)(\sigma/\sqrt{n})$ can be used as the test statistic for the small-sample hypothesis test.

be used to make inferences about the value of the population mean. In using the t distribution for hypothesis tests about a population mean, the test statistic is

$$t = \frac{\bar{x} - \mu_0}{s/\sqrt{n}}$$ (9.8)

This test statistic has a t distribution with $n - 1$ degrees of freedom.

Let us consider an example of a one-tailed hypothesis test about a population mean for the small-sample case. The International Air Transport Association surveys business travelers to develop ratings of transatlantic gateway airports. The maximum possible score is 10. A magazine devoted to business travel has decided to classify airports according to the rating they receive. Airports that have a population mean rating of 7 or more will be designated as providing superior service. Suppose a simple random sample of 12 business travelers have been asked to rate London's Heathrow airport, and that the 12 ratings obtained are 7, 8, 10, 8, 6, 9, 6, 7, 7, 8, 9, and 8. The sample mean for these data is $\bar{x} = 7.75$ and the sample standard deviation is $s = 1.215$. Assuming that the population of ratings can be approximated by a normal probability distribution, should Heathrow be designated as providing superior service?

Using a .05 level of significance, we need a test to determine whether the population mean rating for the Heathrow airport is greater than 7. The null and alternative hypotheses follows.

$$H_0: \mu \leq 7$$

$$H_a: \mu > 7$$

The Heathrow airport will be designated as providing superior service if H_0 can be rejected.

The rejection region is in the upper tail of the sampling distribution. With $n - 1 = 12 - 1 = 11$ degrees of freedom, Table 2 of Appendix B shows that $t_{.05} = 1.796$. Thus, the rejection rule is

Reject H_0 if $t > 1.796$

Using (9.8) with $\bar{x} = 7.75$ and $s = 1.215$, we have the following value for the test statistic.

$$t = \frac{\bar{x} - \mu_0}{s/\sqrt{n}} = \frac{7.75 - 7}{1.215/\sqrt{12}} = 2.14$$

Since 2.14 is greater than 1.796, the null hypothesis is rejected. At the .05 level of significance, we can conclude that the population mean rating for the Heathrow airport is greater than 7. Thus, Heathrow can be designated as providing superior service. Figure 9.10 shows that the value of the test statistic is in the rejection region.

p-VALUES AND THE t DISTRIBUTION

Let us consider the p-value for the Heathrow airport hypothesis test. As discussed in Sections 9.3 and 9.4, the p-value can be interpreted as the observed level of significance for the test. The usual rule applies: If the p-value is less than the level of significance α, the null hypothesis can be rejected. Unfortunately, the format of the t distribution table provided in most statistics textbooks does not have sufficient detail to determine the exact p-value for the test. However, we can still use the t distribution table to identify a range for the p-value. For example, the t distribution used in the Heathrow airport hypothesis test has 11 degrees of freedom. Referring to Table 2 of Appendix B,

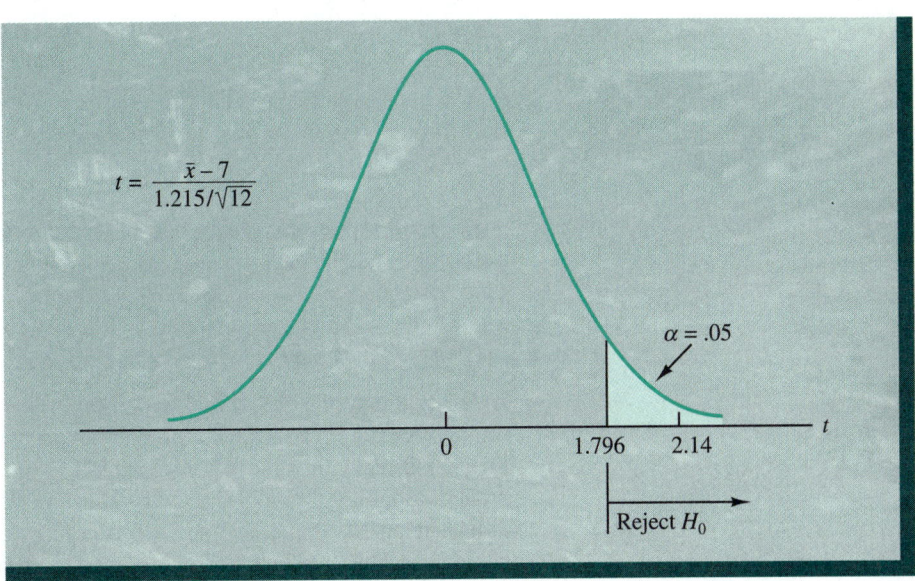

$$t = \frac{\bar{x} - 7}{1.215/\sqrt{12}}$$

FIGURE 9.10 Value of the Test Statistic ($t = 2.14$) for the Heathrow Airport Hypothesis Test

we see that row 11 provides the following information about a t distribution with 11 degrees of freedom.

Area in Upper Tail	.10	.05	.025	.01	.005
t Value	1.363	1.796	2.201	2.718	3.106

The computed t value for the hypothesis test was $t = 2.14$. The p-value is the area in the tail corresponding to $t = 2.14$. From the information above, we see 2.14 is between 1.796 and 2.201. Thus, although we cannot determine the exact p-value associated with $t = 2.14$, we do know that the p-value must be between .05 and .025. With a level of significance of $\alpha = .05$, we know that the p-value must be less than .05; thus, the null hypothesis is rejected.

THE ROLE OF THE COMPUTER

An advantage of computer software packages in testing hypotheses in the small-sample case is that the computer output will provide the p-value for the t distribution. To illustrate how computer software packages can be used to perform hypothesis testing with small samples, we used Minitab for the Heathrow airport rating study. With the ratings data for the sample of 12 business travelers entered into a Minitab worksheet, we obtained the hypothesis-testing output in Figure 9.11. The first line of output shows that the hypothesis test is being performed with the alternative hypothesis $\mu > 7$. The sample size 12, the sample mean 7.75, the sample standard deviation 1.215, and the standard error of the mean .351 are shown. The value of the test statistic $t = 2.14$ and the p-value $= .028$ can be used to draw the hypothesis-testing conclusion. Thus, at a .05 level of significance, the null hypothesis $H_0: \mu \leq 7$ is rejected. The conclusion that $\mu > 7$ and that Heathrow provides superior service is supported.

```
Test of mu = 7.000 vs mu > 7.000

    N      Mean     StDev    SE Mean       T    P Value
   12     7.750     1.215      0.351    2.14      0.028
```

FIGURE 9.11 Minitab Output for the Heathrow Airport Rating Hypothesis Test

A TWO-TAILED TEST

As an example of a two-tailed hypothesis test about a population mean using a small sample, consider the following production problem. A production process is designed to fill containers with a mean filling weight of $\mu = 16$ ounces. It is undesirable for the process to underfill containers as the consumer does not receive the amount of product indicated on the container label. It is equally undesirable for the process to overfill containers; in that case, the firm loses money since the process is placing more product in the container than is required. Quality-assurance personnel periodically select a simple random sample of eight containers and test the following two-tailed hypotheses.

$$H_0: \mu = 16$$
$$H_a: \mu \neq 16$$

If H_0 is rejected, the production manager will request that the production process be stopped and that the mechanism for regulating filling weights be readjusted to ensure a mean filling weight of 16 ounces. If the sample yields data values of 16.02, 16.22, 15.82, 15.92, 16.22, 16.32, 16.12, and 15.92 ounces and the level of significance is .05, what action should be taken? Assume that the population of filling weights is normally distributed.

Since the data have not been summarized, we must first compute the sample mean and sample standard deviation. Doing so provides the following results.

$$\bar{x} = \frac{\Sigma x_i}{n} = \frac{128.56}{8} = 16.07 \text{ ounces}$$

and

$$s = \sqrt{\frac{\Sigma(x_i - \bar{x})^2}{n-1}} = \sqrt{\frac{.22}{7}} = .18 \text{ ounces}$$

With a two-tailed test and a level of significance of $\alpha = .05$, $-t_{.025}$ and $t_{.025}$ determine the rejection region for the test. Using the table for the t distribution, we find that with $n - 1 = 8 - 1 = 7$ degrees of freedom, $-t_{.025} = -2.365$ and $t_{.025} = +2.365$. Thus, the rejection rule is written

Reject H_0 if $t < -2.365$ or if $t > 2.365$

Using $\bar{x} = 16.07$ and $s = .18$, we have

$$t = \frac{\bar{x} - \mu_0}{s/\sqrt{n}} = \frac{16.07 - 16.00}{.18/\sqrt{8}} = 1.10$$

Since $t = 1.10$ is not in the rejection region, the null hypothesis cannot be rejected. There is not enough evidence to stop the production process.

Using Table 2 of Appendix B and the row for seven degrees of freedom, we see that the computed t value of 1.10 has an upper tail area of *more than* .10. Although the format of the t distribution table prevents us from being more specific, we can at least conclude that the two-tailed p-value is greater than 2(.10) = .20. Since this value is greater than the .05 level of significance, we see that the p-value leads to the same conclusion; that is, do not reject H_0. The computer solution for this hypothesis test shows $t = 1.10$ and the exact p-value = .31.

EXERCISES

METHODS

33. Consider the following hypothesis test.

$$H_0: \mu \leq 10$$
$$H_a: \mu > 10$$

A sample of 16 provides a sample mean of 11 and sample standard deviation of 3.
a. With $\alpha = .05$, what is the rejection rule?
b. Compute the value of the test statistic t. What is your conclusion?

Self-Test

34. Consider the following hypothesis test.

$$H_0: \mu = 20$$
$$H_a: \mu \neq 20$$

Data from a sample of six items are: 18, 20, 16, 19, 17, 18.
a. Compute the sample mean.
b. Compute the sample standard deviation.
c. With $\alpha = .05$, what is the rejection rule?
d. Compute the value of the test statistic t.
e. What is your conclusion?

35. Consider the following hypothesis test.

$$H_0: \mu \geq 15$$
$$H_a: \mu < 15$$

A sample of 22 is used and the sample standard deviation is 8. Use $\alpha = .05$. Provide the value of the test statistic t and your conclusion for each of the following sample results.
a. $\bar{x} = 13.0$ **b.** $\bar{x} = 11.5$ **c.** $\bar{x} = 15.0$ **d.** $\bar{x} = 19.0$

36. Consider the following hypothesis test.

$$H_0: \mu \leq 50$$
$$H_a: \mu > 50$$

Assume a sample of 16 items provides the following test statistics. What can you say about the p-values in each case? What are your conclusions based on $\alpha = .05$?
a. $t = 2.602$ **b.** $t = 1.341$ **c.** $t = 1.960$ **d.** $t = 1.055$ **e.** $t = 3.261$

APPLICATIONS

Self-Test

37. In February 1995, the mean cost for an airline round trip with a discount fare was $258 (*USA Today,* March 30, 1995). A random sample of 15 round-trip discount fares during the month of March provided the following data.

310   260   265   255   300   310   230   250   265   280   290   240   285   250   260

a. What is the sample mean round trip discount fare in March?
b. What is the sample standard deviation?
c. Using $\alpha = .05$, test to see whether the mean round-trip discount fare has increased in March. What is your conclusion?
d. What is the p-value?

38. The average hourly wage in the United States is $10.05 (*The Tampa Tribune,* December 15, 1991). Assume that a sample of 25 individuals in Phoenix, Arizona, showed a sample mean wage of $10.83 per hour with a sample standard deviation of $3.25 per hour. Test H_0: $\mu = 10.05$ and H_a: $\mu \neq 10.05$ to see whether the population mean in Phoenix differs from the mean throughout the United States. At a .05 level of significance, what is your conclusion?

39. On the average, a housewife with a husband and two children is estimated to work 55 hours or less per week on household-related activities. The hours worked during a week for a sample of eight housewives are: 58, 52, 64, 63, 59, 62, 62, and 55.
a. Use $\alpha = .05$ to test H_0: $\mu \leq 55$, H_a: $\mu > 55$. What is your conclusion about the mean number of hours worked per week?
b. What can you say about the p-value?

40. A study of a drug designed to reduce blood pressure used a sample of 25 men between the ages of 45 and 55. With μ indicating the mean change in blood pressure for the population of men receiving the drug, the hypotheses in the study were written: H_0: $\mu \geq 0$ and H_a: $\mu < 0$. Rejection of H_0 shows that the mean change is negative, indicating that the drug is effective in lowering blood pressure.
a. At a .05 level of significance, what conclusion should be drawn if $\bar{x} = -10$ and $s = 15$?
b. What can you say about the p-value?

41. Last year the number of lunches served at an elementary-school cafeteria was normally distributed with a mean of 300 lunches per day. At the beginning of the current year, the price of a lunch was raised by 25¢. A sample of six days during the months of September, October, and November provided the following numbers of children being served lunches: 290, 275, 310, 260, 270, and 275. Do these data indicate that the mean number of lunches per day has dropped since last year? Test H_0: $\mu \geq 300$ against the alternative H_a: $\mu < 300$ at a .05 level of significance.

42. Joan's Nursery specializes in custom-designed landscaping for residential areas. The estimated labor cost associated with a particular landscaping proposal is based on the number of plantings of trees, shrubs, and so on to be used for the project. For cost-estimating purposes, managers use two hours of labor time for the planting of a medium-size tree. Actual times from a sample of 10 plantings during the past month follow (times in hours).

1.9   1.7   2.8   2.4   2.6   2.5   2.8   3.2   1.6   2.5

Using a .05 level of significance, test to see whether the mean tree-planting time exceeds two hours. What is your conclusion, and what recommendations would you consider making to the managers?

9.6   TESTS ABOUT A POPULATION PROPORTION

With the symbol p denoting the population proportion and p_0 denoting a particular hypothesized value for the population proportion, the three forms for a hypothesis test about a population proportion are as follows.

$$H_0: p \geq p_0 \qquad H_0: p \leq p_0 \qquad H_0: p = p_0$$
$$H_a: p < p_0 \qquad H_a: p > p_0 \qquad H_a: p \neq p_0$$

The first two forms are one-tailed tests, whereas the third form is a two-tailed test. The specific form used depends on the application.

Hypothesis tests about a population proportion are based on the difference between the sample proportion $\bar{p}$ and the hypothesized population proportion p_0. The methods used to conduct the tests are very similar to the procedures used for hypothesis tests about a population mean. The only difference is that we use the sample proportion $\bar{p}$ and its standard deviation $\sigma_{\bar{p}}$ in developing the test statistic. We begin by formulating null and alternative hypotheses about the value of the population proportion. Then, using the value of the sample proportion $\bar{p}$ and its standard deviation $\sigma_{\bar{p}}$, we compute a value for the test statistic z. Comparing the value of the test statistic to the critical value enables us to determine whether or not the null hypothesis should be rejected.

Let us illustrate hypothesis testing for a population proportion by considering the situation faced by Pine Creek golf course. Over the past few months, 20% of the players at Pine Creek have been women. In an effort to increase the proportion of women playing, Pine Creek used a special promotion to attract women golfers. After one week, a random sample of 400 players showed 300 men and 100 women. Course managers would like to determine whether the data support the conclusion that the proportion of women playing at Pine Creek has increased.

To determine whether the effect of the promotion has been to increase the proportion of women golfers, we state the following null and alternative hypotheses.

$$H_0: p \leq .20$$
$$H_a: p > .20$$

As usual, we begin the hypothesis-testing procedure by assuming that H_0 is true with $p = .20$. Using the sample proportion $\bar{p}$ to estimate p, we next consider the sampling distribution of $\bar{p}$. Since $\bar{p}$ is an unbiased estimator of p, we know that if $p = .20$, the mean of the sampling distribution of $\bar{p}$ is .20. In addition, we know from Chapter 7 that the standard deviation of $\bar{p}$ is given by

$$\sigma_{\bar{p}} = \sqrt{\frac{p(1-p)}{n}}$$

With the assumed value of $p = .20$ and a sample size of $n = 400$, the standard deviation of $\bar{p}$ is

$$\sigma_{\bar{p}} = \sqrt{\frac{.20(1-.20)}{400}} = .02$$

In Chapter 7 we saw that the sampling distribution of $\bar{p}$ can be approximated by a normal probability distribution if both np and $n(1-p)$ are greater than or equal to 5. In the Pine Creek case, $np = 400(.20) = 80$ and $n(1-p) = 400(.80) = 320$; thus, the normal probability distribution approximation is appropriate. The sampling distribution of $\bar{p}$ is shown in Figure 9.12.

Since the sampling distribution of $\bar{p}$ is approximately normal, the following test statistic can be used.

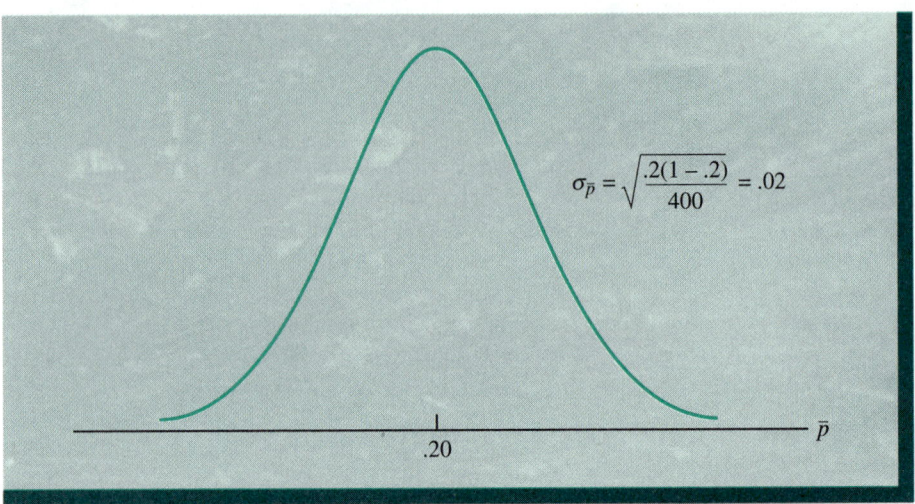

$$\sigma_{\bar{p}} = \sqrt{\frac{.2(1 - .2)}{400}} = .02$$

FIGURE 9.12 Sampling Distribution of $\bar{p}$ for the Proportion of Women Golfers at Pine Creek Golf Course

TEST STATISTIC FOR TESTS ABOUT A POPULATION PROPORTION

$$z = \frac{\bar{p} - p_0}{\sigma_{\bar{p}}} \qquad (9.9)$$

where

$$\sigma_{\bar{p}} = \sqrt{\frac{p_0(1 - p_0)}{n}} \qquad (9.10)$$

Let us assume that $\alpha = .05$ has been selected as the level of significance for the test. With $z_{.05} = 1.645$, the upper-tail rejection region for the hypothesis test (see Figure 9.13) provides the following rejection rule.

$$\text{Reject } H_0 \text{ if } z > 1.645$$

Once the rejection rule has been determined, we collect the data, compute the value of the point estimate $\bar{p}$, and compute the corresponding value of the test statistic z. By comparing the value of z to the critical value ($z_{.05} = 1.645$), we can decide whether or not to reject the null hypothesis.

Since 100 of the 400 players during the promotion were women, we obtain $\bar{p} = 100/400 = .25$. With $\sigma_{\bar{p}} = .02$, the value of the test statistic is

$$z = \frac{\bar{p} - p_0}{\sigma_{\bar{p}}} = \frac{.25 - .20}{.02} = 2.5$$

Thus, since $z = 2.5 > 1.645$, we can reject H_0. The Pine Creek managers can conclude that there has been an increase in the proportion of women players.

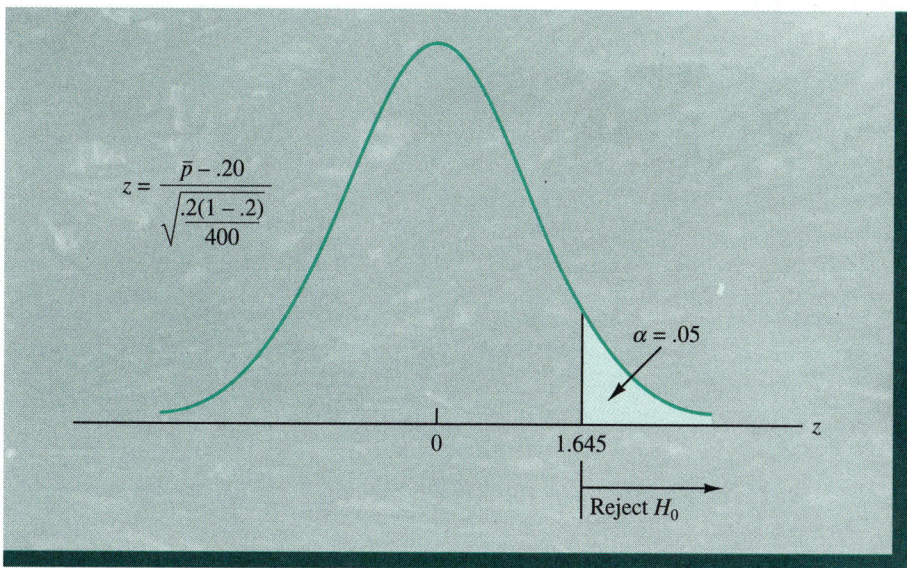

FIGURE 9.13   Rejection Region for the Pine Creek Golf Course Hypothesis Test

Using the table of areas for the standard normal probability distribution, we find that the p-value for the test can also be computed. For example, with $z = 2.50$, the table of areas shows a .4938 area or probability between the mean and $z = 2.50$. Thus, the p-value for the test is $.5000 - .4938 = .0062$. Since the p-value is less than α, the null hypothesis can be rejected.

We see that hypothesis tests about a population proportion and a population mean are similar; the primary difference is that the test statistic is based on the sampling distribution of $\bar{x}$ when the hypothesis test involves a population mean and on the sampling distribution of $\bar{p}$ when the hypothesis test involves a population proportion. The tentative assumption that the null hypothesis is true, the use of the level of significance to establish the critical value, and the comparison of the test statistic to the critical value are identical in the two testing procedures. Figure 9.14 summarizes the decision rules for hypothesis tests about a population proportion. We assume the large-sample case ($np \geq 5$ and $n(1 - p) \geq 5$) where the normal probability distribution can be used to approximate the sampling distribution of $\bar{p}$.

NOTES AND COMMENTS

We have not shown the procedure for small-sample hypothesis tests involving population proportions. In the small-sample case, the sampling distribution of $\bar{p}$ follows the binomial distribution and hence the normal approximation is not applicable. More advanced texts show how hypothesis tests are conducted for this situation. However, in practice small-sample tests are rarely conducted for a population proportion.

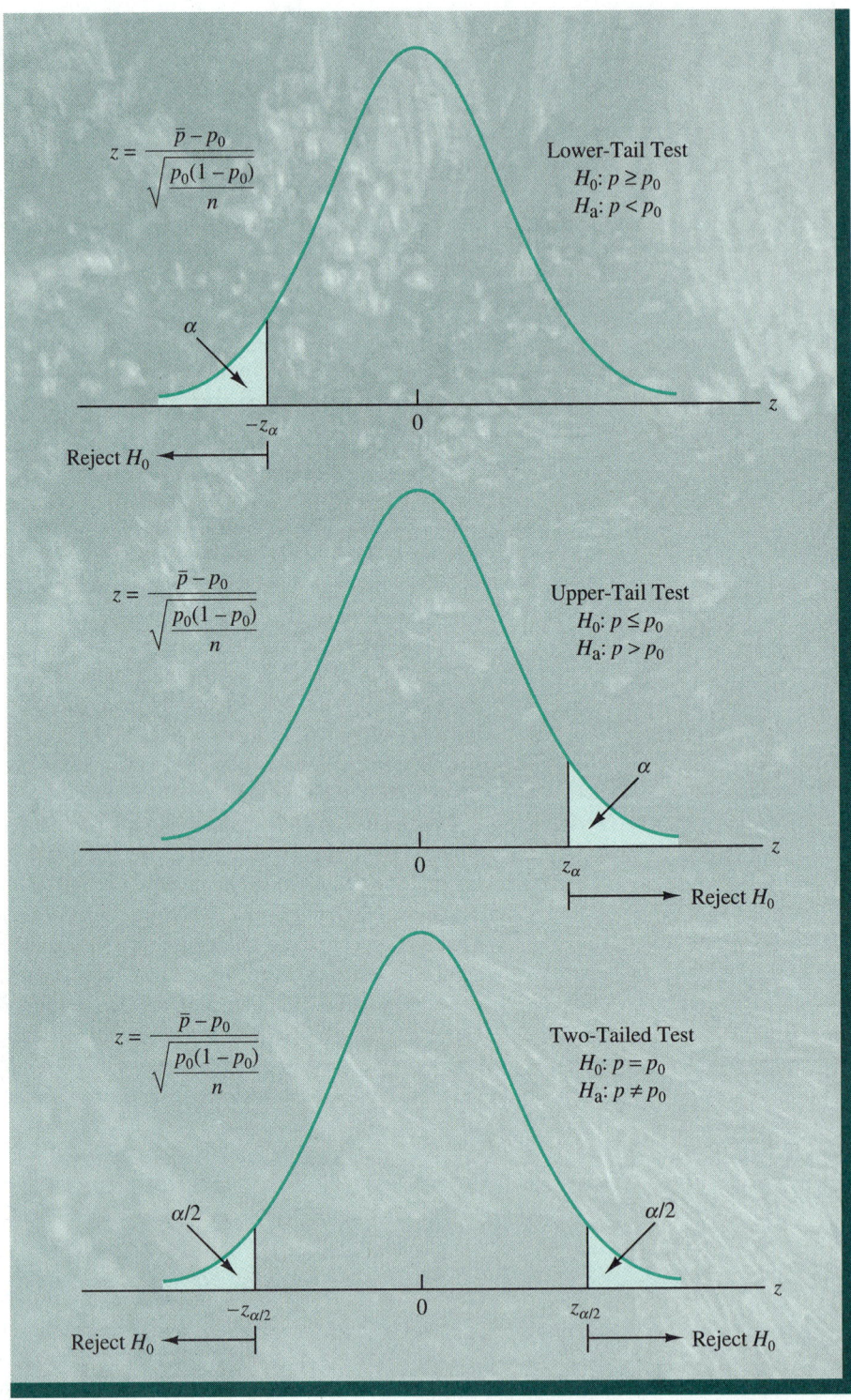

FIGURE 9.14 Summary of Rejection Rules for Hypothesis Tests About a Population Proportion

EXERCISES

METHODS

43. Consider the following hypothesis test.

$$H_0: p \le .50$$
$$H_a: p > .50$$

A sample of 200 provided a sample proportion $\bar{p} = .57$.
   a. At $\alpha = .05$, what is the rejection rule?
   b. Compute the value of the test statistic z. What is your conclusion?

Self-Test ▸ **44.** Consider the following hypothesis test.

$$H_0: p = .20$$
$$H_a: p \ne .20$$

A sample of 400 provided a sample proportion of $\bar{p} = .175$.
   a. At $\alpha = .05$, what is the rejection rule?
   b. Compute the value of the test statistic z.
   c. What is the p-value?
   d. What is your conclusion?

45. Consider the following hypothesis test.

$$H_0: p \ge .75$$
$$H_a: p < .75$$

A sample of 300 is selected. Use $\alpha = .05$. Provide the value of the test statistic z, the p-value, and your conclusion for each of the following sample results.
   a. $\bar{p} = .68$ **b.** $\bar{p} = .72$ **c.** $\bar{p} = .70$ **d.** $\bar{p} = .77$

APPLICATIONS

46. The Honolulu Board of Water Supply suggested the water-by-request rule be adopted at restaurants on the island of Oahu to conserve water. A restaurateur stated that 30% of the patrons do not drink their water (*The Honolulu Advertiser*, December 28, 1991). Hence, the conservation of water would come not only from the unused water in each glass, but also the water saved in washing the glasses. Test $H_0: p = .30$ versus $H_a: p \ne .30$. Assume a sample of 480 patrons at restaurants showed that 128 patrons did not drink their water. Test the restaurateur's claim at a .05 level of significance. What is the p-value and what is your conclusion?

Self-Test ▸ **47.** A study by *Consumer Reports* (September 1993) showed that 64% of supermarket shoppers believed supermarket brands to be as good as national name brands in terms of product quality. To investigate whether or not this result applies to its own product, the manufacturer of a national name-brand ketchup product asked 100 supermarket shoppers whether they believed the supermarket brand of ketchup was as good as the national name-brand ketchup. Use the fact that 52 of the shoppers in the sample indicated that the supermarket brand was as good as the national name brand to test $H_0: p \ge .64$ and $H_a: p < .64$. Use a .05 level of significance. What is your conclusion?

48. The director of a college placement office claims that at least 80% of graduating seniors have made employment commitments one month prior to graduation. At a .05 level of significance, what is your conclusion if a sample of 100 seniors shows that 75 made employment commitments one month prior to graduation? Should the director's claim be rejected? What is the p-value?

49. A magazine claims that 25% of its readers are college students. Of a random sample of 200 readers, 42 are college students. Use a .10 level of significance to test $H_0: p = .25$ and $H_a: p \neq .25$. What is the p-value?

50. A new television series must prove that it has more than 25% of the viewing audience after its initial 13-week run if it is to be judged successful. Assume that in a sample of 400 households, 112 were watching the series.
   a. At a .10 level of significance, can the series be judged successful on the basis of the sample information?
   b. What is the p-value for the sample results? What is your hypothesis-testing conclusion?

51. An accountant believes that a company's cash-flow problems are a direct result of the slow collection of accounts receivable. The accountant claims that at least 70% of the current accounts receivable are more than two months old. A sample of 120 accounts receivable shows 78 that are more than two months old. Test the accountant's claim at the .05 level of significance.

52. In a 1992 study of the contamination of fish in the nation's rivers and lakes, the Environmental Protection Agency found that 91% of water quality test sites showed the presence of PCB, a cancer-causing agent (*America by the Numbers,* 1993). Suppose a follow-up study of 200 rivers and lakes in 1995 shows the presence of PCB in 160 cases. Does the statistical evidence support the conclusion that as of 1995 water clean-up programs have reduced the proportion of locations with PCB? Use a .05 level of significance.

53. A television station predicts election winners on the basis of the following hypothesis test, where p is the proportion of voters selecting the leading candidate.

$$H_0: p \leq .50$$
$$H_a: p > .50$$

If H_0 can be rejected, the station will predict that the leading candidate is the winner.
   a. What is the Type I error? What are the consequences of making this error?
   b. What is the Type II error? What are the consequences of making this error?
   c. Which value, $\alpha = .05$ or $\alpha = .01$, makes more sense as the level of significance?

54. A fast-food restaurant plans a special offer that will enable customers to purchase specially designed drink glasses featuring well-known cartoon characters. If more than 15% of the customers will purchase the glasses, the special offer will be implemented. A preliminary test has been set up at several locations, and 88 of 500 customers have purchased the glasses. Should the special glass offer be implemented? Conduct a hypothesis test that will support your decision. Use a .01 level of significance. What is your recommendation?

55. At least 20% of all workers are believed to be willing to work fewer hours for less pay to obtain more time for personal and leisure activities. A *USA Today*/CNN/Gallup poll with a sample of 596 respondents found 83 willing to work fewer hours for less pay to obtain more personal and leisure time (*USA Today,* April 10, 1995). Test $H_0: p \geq .20$ and $H_a: p < .20$ using a .05 level of significance. What is your conclusion?

9.7   HYPOTHESIS TESTING AND DECISION MAKING

In Section 9.1 we noted three types of situations where hypothesis testing is used:

1. Testing research hypotheses.
2. Testing the validity of a claim.
3. Testing in decision-making situations.

In the first two situations, action is taken only when the null hypothesis H_0 is rejected and hence the alternative hypothesis H_a is concluded to be true. In the third situation—decision making—it is necessary to take action when the null hypothesis is not rejected as well as when it is rejected.

The hypothesis-testing procedures presented thus far have limited applicability in a decision-making situation because it is not considered appropriate to accept H_0 and take action based on the conclusion that H_0 is true. The reason for not taking action when the test results indicate *do not reject H_0* is that the decision to accept H_0 exposes the decision maker to the risk of making a Type II error, that is, accepting H_0 when it is false. With the hypothesis-testing procedures described in the preceding sections, the probability of a Type I error is controlled by establishing a level of significance for the test. However, the probability of making the Type II error is not controlled.

Clearly, in certain decision-making situations the decision maker may want—and in some cases may be forced—to take action with both the conclusion *do not reject H_0* and the conclusion *reject H_0*. A good illustration of this situation is lot-acceptance sampling, a topic we will discuss in more depth in Chapter 20. For example, a quality-control manager must decide to accept a shipment of batteries from a supplier or to return the shipment because of poor quality. Assume that design specifications require batteries from the supplier to have a mean useful life of at least 120 hours. To evaluate the quality of an incoming shipment, a sample of 36 batteries will be selected and tested. On the basis of the sample, a decision must be made to accept the shipment of batteries or to return it to the supplier because of poor quality. Let μ denote the mean number of hours of useful life for batteries in the shipment. The null and alternative hypotheses about the population mean follow.

$$H_0: \mu \geq 120$$

$$H_a: \mu < 120$$

If H_0 is rejected, the alternative hypothesis is concluded to be true. This conclusion indicates that the appropriate decision is to return the shipment to the supplier. However, if H_0 is not rejected, the decision maker must still determine what action should be taken. Thus, without directly concluding that H_0 is true but merely by not rejecting it, the decision maker will have made the decision to accept the shipment as being of satisfactory quality.

In such decision-making situations, it is recommended that the hypothesis-testing procedure be extended to include consideration of the probability of making a Type II error. Since a decision will be made and action taken when we do not reject H_0, knowledge of the probability of making a Type II error will be helpful. In Sections 9.8 and 9.9 we explain how to compute the probability of making a Type II error and how the sample size can be adjusted to help control the probability of making a Type II error.

9.8   CALCULATING THE PROBABILITY OF TYPE II ERRORS

In this section we show how to calculate the probability of making a Type II error for a hypothesis test about a population mean. We illustrate the procedure by using the lot-acceptance example described in Section 9.7. The null and alternative hypotheses about the mean number of hours of useful life for a shipment of batteries are $H_0: \mu \geq 120$ and $H_a: \mu < 120$. If H_0 is rejected, the decision will be to return the shipment to the supplier because the mean hours of useful life are less than the specified 120 hours. If H_0 is not rejected, the decision will be to accept the shipment.

Suppose a level of significance of $\alpha = .05$ is used to conduct the hypothesis test. The test statistic is

$$z = \frac{\bar{x} - \mu}{\sigma / \sqrt{n}} = \frac{\bar{x} - 120}{\sigma / \sqrt{n}}$$

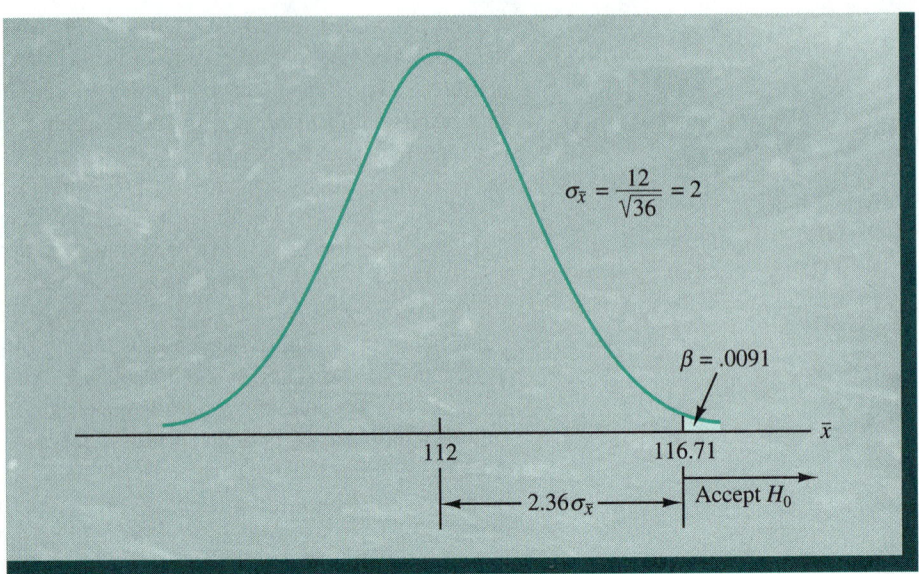

FIGURE 9.15   Probability of a Type II Error When $\mu = 112$

With $z_{.05} = 1.645$, the rejection rule for the lower-tail test becomes

$$\text{Reject } H_0 \text{ if } z < -1.645$$

Suppose a sample of 36 batteries will be selected and we know from previous testing that the standard deviation for the population is $\sigma = 12$ hours. The rejection rule indicates that we will reject H_0 when

$$z = \frac{\bar{x} - 120}{12 /\sqrt{36}} < -1.645$$

Solving for $\bar{x}$ in the preceding expression indicates that we will reject H_0 whenever

$$\bar{x} < 120 - 1.645\left(\frac{12}{\sqrt{36}}\right) = 116.71$$

Rejecting H_0 when $\bar{x} < 116.71$ means that we will make the decision to accept the shipment whenever

$$\bar{x} \geq 116.71$$

With this information, we are ready to compute probabilities associated with making a Type II error. First, recall that we make a Type II error whenever the true shipment mean is less than 120 hours and we make the decision to accept H_0: $\mu \geq 120$. Hence, to compute the probability of making a Type II error, we must select a value of μ less than 120 hours. For example, suppose the shipment is considered to be of poor quality if the batteries have a mean life of $\mu = 112$ hours. If $\mu = 112$ is really true, what is the probability of accepting H_0: $\mu \geq 120$ and hence committing a Type II error? Note that this is the probability that the sample mean $\bar{x}$ is greater than or equal to 116.71 when $\mu = 112$.

Figure 9.15 shows the sampling distribution of $\bar{x}$ when the mean is $\mu = 112$. The unshaded area in the upper tail gives the probability of obtaining $\bar{x} \geq 116.71$. Using the standard normal probability distribution calculation based on Figure 9.15, we see that

$$z = \frac{\bar{x} - \mu}{\sigma/\sqrt{n}} = \frac{116.71 - 112}{12/\sqrt{36}} = 2.36$$

TABLE 9.3 Probability of Making a Type II Error for the Lot-Acceptance Hypothesis Test

Value of μ	$z = \dfrac{116.71 - \mu}{12/\sqrt{36}}$	Probability of Making a Type II Error (β)	Power ($1 - \beta$)
112	2.36	.0091	.9909
114	1.36	.0869	.9131
115	.86	.1949	.8051
116.71	.00	.5000	.5000
117	−.15	.5596	.4404
118	−.65	.7422	.2578
119.999	−1.645	.9500	.0500

The standard normal probability distribution table shows that with $z = 2.36$, the area in the upper tail is $.5000 - .4909 = .0091$. This is the probability of making a Type II error when $\mu = 112$. Denoting the probability of making a Type II error as β, we see that when $\mu = 112$, $\beta = .0091$. Therefore, we can conclude that if the mean of the population is 112 hours, the probability of making a Type II error is only .0091.

We can repeat these calculations for other values of μ less than 120. Doing so will show a different probability of making a Type II error for each value of μ less than 120. For example, suppose the shipment of batteries has a mean useful life of $\mu = 115$ hours. Since we will accept H_0 whenever $\bar{x} \geq 116.71$, the z value for $\mu = 115$ is given by

$$z = \frac{\bar{x} - \mu}{\sigma/\sqrt{n}} = \frac{116.71 - 115}{12/\sqrt{36}} = .86$$

From the standard normal probability distribution table, we find that the area in the upper tail of the standard normal probability distribution for $z = .86$ is $.5000 - .3051 = .1949$. Thus, the probability of making a Type II error is $\beta = .1949$ when the true mean is $\mu = 115$.

In Table 9.3 we show the probability of making a Type II error for a variety of values of μ less than 120. Note that as μ increases toward 120, the probability of making a Type II error increases toward an upper bound of .95. However, as μ decreases to values farther below 120, the probability of making a Type II error diminishes. This pattern is what we should expect. When the true population mean μ is close to the null hypothesis value of $\mu = 120$, there is a high probability that we will make a Type II error. However, when the true population mean μ is far below the null hypothesis value of $\mu = 120$, there is a low probability that we will make a Type II error.

The probability of correctly rejecting H_0 when it is false is called the *power* of the test. For any particular value of μ, the power is $1 - \beta$. That is, the probability of correctly rejecting the null hypothesis is one minus the probability of making a Type II error. Values of power are listed in Table 9.3. On the basis of these values, the power associated with each value of μ is shown graphically in Figure 9.16. Such a graph is called a *power curve*. Note that the power curve extends over the values of μ for which the null hypothesis is false. The height of the power curve at any value of μ indicates the probability of correctly rejecting H_0 when H_0 is false.*

---

*Another graph, called the *operating characteristic curve,* is sometimes used to provide information about the probability of making a Type II error. The operating characteristic curve shows the probability of accepting H_0 and thus provides β for the values of μ where the null hypothesis is false. The probability of making a Type II error can be read directly from this graph. The power curve and operating characteristic curve are discussed further in Chapter 20.

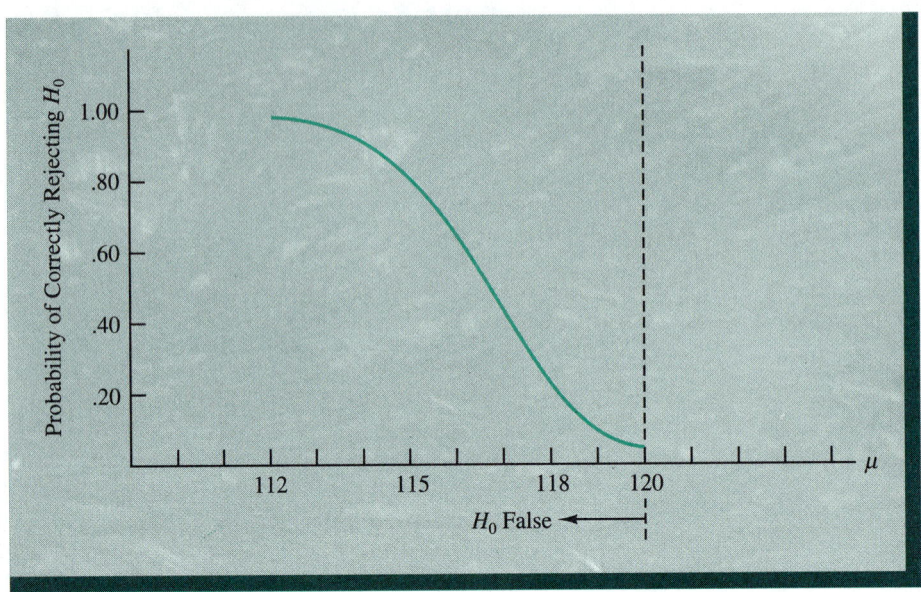

FIGURE 9.16   Power Curve for the Lot-Acceptance Hypothesis Test

In summary, the following step-by-step procedure can be used to compute the probability of making a Type II error in hypothesis tests about a population mean.

1. Formulate the null and alternative hypotheses.
2. Use the level of significance α to establish a rejection rule based on the test statistic.
3. Using the rejection rule, solve for the value of the sample mean that identifies the rejection region for the test.
4. Use the results from step 3 to state the values of the sample mean that lead to the acceptance of H_0; this defines the acceptance region for the test.
5. Using the sampling distribution of $\bar{x}$ for any value of μ from the alternative hypothesis, and the acceptance region from step 4, compute the probability that the sample mean will be in the acceptance region. This probability is the probability of making a Type II error at the chosen value of μ.

EXERCISES

METHODS

Self-Test

56. Consider the following hypothesis test.

$$H_0: \mu \geq 10$$
$$H_a: \mu < 10$$

The sample size is 120 and the population standard deviation is 5. Use $\alpha = .05$.

a. If the population mean is 9, what is the probability that the sample mean leads to the conclusion *do not reject* H_0?
b. What type of error would be made if the actual population mean is 9 and we conclude that $H_0: \mu \geq 10$ is true?
c. What is the probability of making a Type II error if the actual population mean is 8?

57. Consider the following hypothesis test.

$$H_0: \mu = 20$$

$$H_a: \mu \neq 20$$

A sample of 200 items will be taken and the population standard deviation is 10. Use $\alpha = .05$. Compute the probability of making a Type II error if the population mean is:
   a. $\mu = 18.0$.   **b.** $\mu = 22.5$.   **c.** $\mu = 21.0$.

APPLICATIONS

58. Fowle Marketing Research, Inc., bases charges to a client on the assumption that telephone surveys can be completed within 15 minutes or less. If more time is required, a premium rate is charged. With a sample of 35 surveys, a standard deviation of four minutes, and a level of significance of .01, the sample mean will be used to test the null hypothesis $H_0: \mu \leq 15$.
   a. What is your interpretation of the Type II error for this problem? What is its impact on the firm?
   b. What is the probability of making a Type II error when the actual mean time is $\mu = 17$ minutes?
   c. What is the probability of making a Type II error when the actual mean time is $\mu = 18$ minutes?
   d. Sketch the general shape of the power curve for this test.

Self-Test

59. A consumer-research group is interested in testing an automobile manufacturer's claim that a new economy model will travel at least 25 miles per gallon of gasoline ($H_0: \mu \geq 25$).
   a. With a .02 level of significance and a sample of 30 cars, what is the rejection rule based on the value of $\bar{x}$ for the test to determine whether the manufacturer's claim should be rejected? Assume that σ is three miles per gallon.
   b. What is the probability of committing a Type II error if the actual mileage is 23 miles per gallon?
   c. What is the probability of committing a Type II error if the actual mileage is 24 miles per gallon?
   d. What is the probability of committing a Type II error if the actual mileage is 25.5 miles per gallon?

60. *Young Adult* magazine states the following hypotheses about the mean age of its subscribers.

$$H_0: \mu = 28$$

$$H_a: \mu \neq 28$$

   a. What would it mean to make a Type II error in this situation?
   b. The population standard deviation is known at $\sigma = 6$ years and the sample size is 100. With $\alpha = .05$, what is the probability of accepting H_0 for μ equal to 26, 27, 29, and 30?
   c. What is the power at $\mu = 26$? What does this tell you?

61. A production line operation is tested for filling-weight accuracy with the following hypotheses.

Hypothesis	Conclusion and Action
$H_0: \mu = 16$	Filling okay; keep running
$H_a: \mu \neq 16$	Filling off standard; stop and adjust machine

The sample size is 30 and the population standard deviation is $\sigma = .8$. Use $\alpha = .05$.

  a. What would a Type II error mean in this situation?

  b. What is the probability of making a Type II error when the machine is overfilling by .5 ounces?

  c. What is the power of the statistical test when the machine is overfilling by .5 ounces?

  d. Show the power curve for this hypothesis test. What information does it contain for the production manager?

62. Refer to Exercise 58. Assume the firm selects a sample of 50 surveys and repeat parts (b) and (c). What observation can you make about how increasing the sample size affects the probability of making a Type II error?

63. Sparr Investments, Inc., specializes in tax-deferred investment opportunities for its clients. Recently Sparr has offered a payroll deduction investment program for the employees of a particular company. Sparr estimates that the employees are currently averaging $100 or less per month in tax-deferred investments. A sample of 40 employees will be used to test Sparr's hypothesis about the current level of investment activity among the population of employees. Assume the employee monthly tax-deferred investment amounts have a standard deviation of $75 and that a .05 level of significance will be used in the hypothesis test.

  a. What is the Type II error in this situation?

  b. What is the probability of the Type II error if the actual mean employee monthly investment is $120?

  c. What is the probability of the Type II error if the actual mean employee monthly investment is $130?

  d. Assume a sample size of 80 employees is used and repeat parts (b) and (c).

9.9   DETERMINING THE SAMPLE SIZE FOR A HYPOTHESIS TEST ABOUT A POPULATION MEAN

Assume that a hypothesis test is to be conducted about the value of a population mean. The user's specified level of significance determines the probability of making a Type I error for the test. By controlling the sample size, the user can also control the probability of making a Type II error. Let us show how a sample size can be determined for the following one-tailed test about a population mean.

$$H_0: \mu \geq \mu_0$$

$$H_a: \mu < \mu_0$$

where μ_0 is the hypothesized value for the population mean.

The upper part of Figure 9.17 is the sampling distribution of $\bar{x}$ when H_0 is true and $\mu = \mu_0$. Note that the user's specified level of significance α determines the rejection region for the test. Let c denote the critical value such that $\bar{x} < c$ determines the rejection region for the test. Using the upper part of Figure 9.17 with z_α indicating the z value corresponding to an area of α in the tail of the standard normal probability distribution, we compute c by the following formula.

$$c = \mu_0 - z_\alpha \frac{\sigma}{\sqrt{n}} \tag{9.11}$$

Now consider the sampling distribution in the lower part of Figure 9.17. Specifically, we have selected a value of the population mean, denoted by μ_a, that corresponds to the case when H_0 is false and H_a is true with $\mu_a < \mu_0$. Let us assume that the user specifies the probability of a Type II error that can be tolerated if the true population mean is μ_a. This probability is shown as β in Figure 9.17. Using the lower part of Figure 9.17 with z_β indicating the z value corresponding to an area of β in the tail of the standard

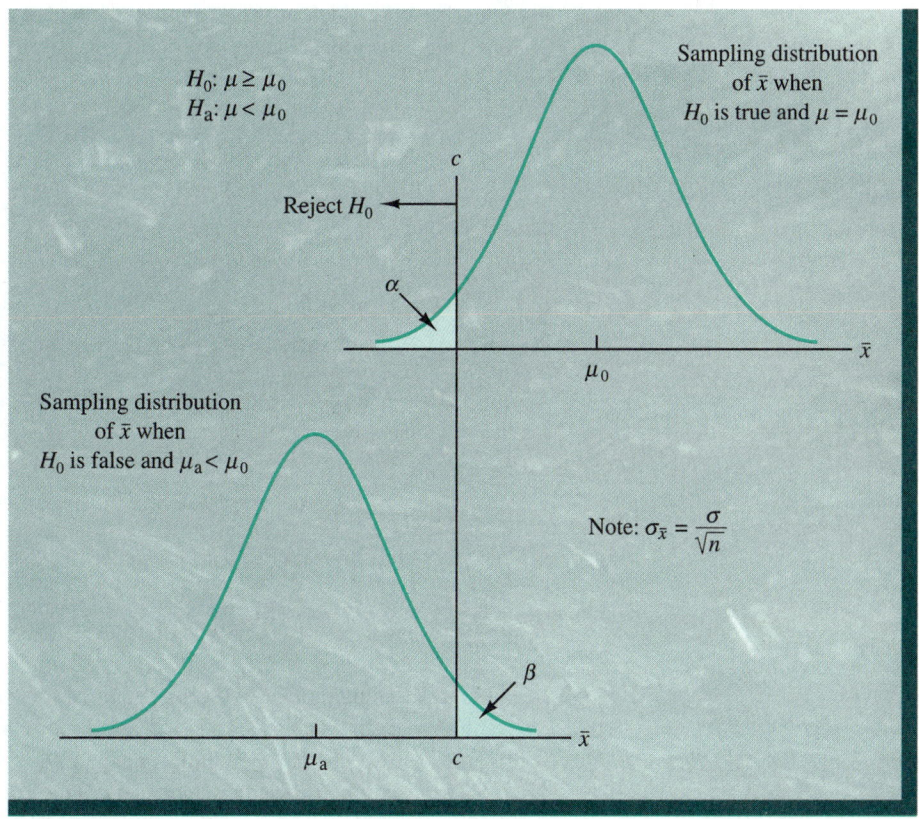

$H_0: \mu \geq \mu_0$
$H_a: \mu < \mu_0$

Sampling distribution
of $\bar{x}$ when
H_0 is true and $\mu = \mu_0$

c

Reject H_0 ←

α

μ_0

$\bar{x}$

Sampling distribution
of $\bar{x}$ when
H_0 is false and $\mu_a < \mu_0$

Note: $\sigma_{\bar{x}} = \dfrac{\sigma}{\sqrt{n}}$

β

μ_a

c

$\bar{x}$

FIGURE 9.17 Determining the Sample Size for Specified Levels of the Type I (α) and Type II (β) Errors.

normal probability distribution, we compute the critical value c by the following formula.

$$c = \mu_a + z_\beta \frac{\sigma}{\sqrt{n}} \qquad\qquad \textbf{(9.12)}$$

Since (9.11) and (9.12) are both expressions for c, we know they must be equal and thus the following expression must be true.

$$\mu_0 - z_\alpha \frac{\sigma}{\sqrt{n}} = \mu_a + z_\beta \frac{\sigma}{\sqrt{n}}$$

To determine the expression that will provide the desired sample size, we first solve for the $\sqrt{n}$ as follows.

$$\mu_0 - \mu_a = z_\alpha \frac{\sigma}{\sqrt{n}} + z_\beta \frac{\sigma}{\sqrt{n}}$$

$$\mu_0 - \mu_a = \frac{(z_\alpha + z_\beta)\sigma}{\sqrt{n}}$$

and

$$\sqrt{n} = \frac{(z_\alpha + z_\beta)\sigma}{(\mu_0 - \mu_a)}$$

Squaring both sides of the expression provides the following sample-size formula for a one-tailed hypothesis test about a population mean.

RECOMMENDED SAMPLE SIZE FOR A ONE-TAILED HYPOTHESIS TEST ABOUT A POPULATION MEAN

$$n = \frac{(z_\alpha + z_\beta)^2 \sigma^2}{(\mu_0 - \mu_a)^2} \tag{9.13}$$

where

z_α = z value providing an area of α in the tail of a standard normal distribution

z_β = z value providing an area of β in the tail of a standard normal distribution

σ = the population standard deviation

μ_0 = the value of the population mean in the null hypothesis

μ_a = the value of the population mean used for the Type II error

Note: In a two-tailed hypothesis test, use (9.13) with $z_{\alpha/2}$ replacing z_α.

Although the logic of (9.13) was developed for the hypothesis test shown in Figure 9.17, it holds for any one-tailed test about a population mean. Note that in a two-tailed hypothesis test about a population mean, $z_{\alpha/2}$ is used instead of z_α in (9.13).

Let us return to the lot-acceptance example from Sections 9.7 and 9.8. The design specification for the shipment of batteries indicated a mean useful life of at least 120 hours for the batteries. Shipments were rejected if H_0: $\mu \geq 120$ was rejected. Let us assume that the quality-control manager makes the following statements about the allowable probabilities for the Type I and Type II errors.

Type I error statement: If the mean life of the batteries in the shipment is $\mu = 120$, I am willing to risk an $\alpha = .05$ probability of rejecting the shipment.

Type II error statement: If the mean life of the batteries in the shipment is five hours under the specification (i.e., $\mu = 115$), I am willing to risk a $\beta = .10$ probability of accepting the shipment.

These statements are based on the judgment of the manager. Someone else might specify different restrictions on the probabilities. However, statements about the allowable probabilities of both errors must be made before the sample size can be determined.

In the example, $\alpha = .05$ and $\beta = .10$. Using the standard normal probability distribution, we have $z_{.05} = 1.645$ and $z_{.10} = 1.28$. From the statements about the error probabilities, we note that $\mu_0 = 120$ and $\mu_a = 115$. Finally, the population standard deviation was assumed known at a value of $\sigma = 12$. By using (9.13), we find that the recommended sample size for the lot-acceptance example is

$$n = \frac{(1.645 + 1.28)^2 (12)^2}{(120 - 115)^2} = 49.3$$

Rounding up, the recommended sample size is 50.

Since both the Type I and Type II error probabilities have been controlled at allowable levels with $n = 50$, the quality-control manager is now justified in using the accept H_0 and reject H_0 statements for the hypothesis test. The accompanying inferences of H_0 true or H_a true are made with known and allowable probabilities of error.

We can make three observations about the relationship among α, β, and the sample size n.

1. Once two of the three values are known, the other can be computed.
2. For a given level of significance α, increasing the sample size will reduce β.
3. For a given sample size, decreasing α will increase β, whereas increasing α will decrease β.

The third observation should be kept in mind when the probability of a Type II error is not being controlled. It suggests that one should not choose unnecessarily small values for the level of significance. For a given sample size, choosing a smaller level of significance α means more exposure to a Type II error. Inexperienced users of hypothesis testing often think that smaller values of α are always better. They are better if we are concerned only about the Type I error. However, smaller values of α have the disadvantage of increasing the risk of making a Type II error.

EXERCISES

METHODS

Self-Test

64. Consider the following hypothesis test.

$$H_0: \mu \geq 10$$
$$H_a: \mu < 10$$

The sample size is 120 and the population standard deviation is 5. Use $\alpha = .05$. If the actual population mean is 9, the probability of a Type II error is .2912. Suppose the researcher wants to reduce the probability of a Type II error to .10 when the actual population mean is 9. What sample size is recommended?

65. Consider the following hypothesis test.

$$H_0: \mu = 20$$
$$H_a: \mu \neq 20$$

The population standard deviation is 10. Use $\alpha = .05$. How large a sample should be taken researcher is willing to accept a .05 probability of making a Type II error when the actual population mean is 22?

APPLICATIONS

66. Suppose the project director for the Hilltop Coffee study (see Section 9.3) had asked for a .10 probability of claiming that Hilltop was not in violation when it really was underfilling by one ounce ($\mu = 2.9375$ pounds). What sample size would have been recommended?

Self-Test

67. A special industrial battery must have a life of at least 400 hours. A hypothesis test is to be conducted with a .02 level of significance. If the batteries from a particular production run have an actual mean use life of 385 hours, the production manager wants a sampling procedure that only 10% of the time would show erroneously that the batch is acceptable. What sample size is recommended for the hypothesis test? Use 30 hours as an estimate of the population standard deviation.

68. *Young Adult* magazine states the following hypotheses about the mean age of its subscribers.

$$H_0: \mu = 28$$
$$H_a: \mu \neq 28$$

If the manager conducting the test will permit a .15 probability of making a Type II error when the true mean age is 29, what sample size should be selected? Assume $\sigma = 6$ and a .05 level of significance.

69. An automobile mileage study tested the following hypotheses.

Hypothesis	Conclusion
$H_0: \mu \geq 25$ mpg	Manufacturer's claim supported
$H_a: \mu < 25$ mpg	Manufacturer's claim rejected; average mileage per gallon less than stated

For $\sigma = 3$ and a .02 level of significance, what sample size would be recommended if the reasearcher wants an 80% chance of detecting that μ is less than 25 miles per gallon when it is actually 24?

SUMMARY

Hypothesis testing is a statistical procedure that uses sample data to determine whether or not a statement about the value of a population parameter should be rejected. The hypotheses, which come from a variety of sources, must be two competing statements: a null hypothesis H_0 and an alternative hypothesis H_a. In some applications it is not obvious how the null and alternative hypotheses should be formulated. We suggested guidelines for developing hypotheses in three types of situations most frequently encountered.

1. Testing research hypotheses: The research hypothesis should be formulated as the alternative hypothesis. The null hypothesis is based on an established theory or the statement that the research treatment will have no effect. Whenever the sample data contradict the null hypothesis, the null hypothesis is rejected. In this case, the alternative or research hypothesis is supported and can be claimed true.

2. Testing the validity of a claim: Generally, this situation corresponds to the "innocent until proven guilty" analogy. The claim made is chosen as the null hypothesis; the challenge to the claim is chosen as the alternative hypothesis. Action against the claim will be taken whenever the sample data contradict the null hypothesis. When that occurs, the challenge implied by the alternative hypothesis is concluded to be true.

3. Testing in decision-making situations: Often a decision maker must choose between two courses of action, one associated with the null hypothesis and one associated with the alternative hypothesis. In those situations it is often suggested that the hypotheses be formulated such that the Type I error is the more serious error. However, whenever an action must be based on the decision to accept H_0, the hypothesis-testing procedure should be extended to control the probability of making a Type II error. The procedures were discussed in Sections 9.8 and 9.9.

Figure 9.18 summarizes the test statistics used in hypothesis tests about a population mean and provides a practical guide for selecting the hypothesis-testing procedure. The figure shows that the test statistic depends on whether the sample size is large, whether the population standard deviation is known, and in some cases whether the population has a normal or approximately normal probability distribution. If the sample size is large ($n \geq 30$), the z test statistic is used to conduct the hypothesis test. If the sample size is small ($n < 30$), the population must have a normal or approximately normal

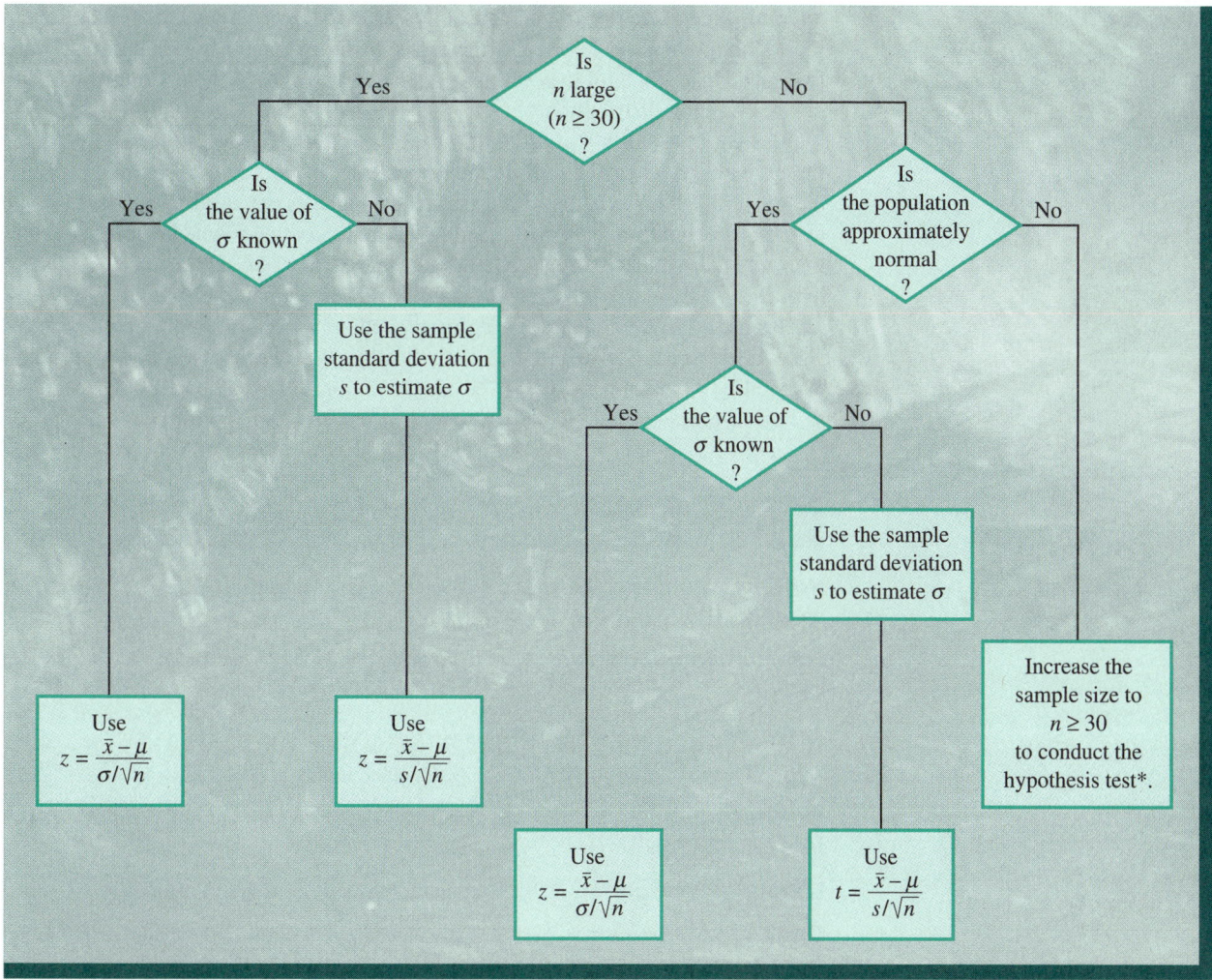

FIGURE 9.18 Summary of the Test Statistics to Be Used in a Hypothesis Test About a Population Mean*

distribution to conduct a hypothesis test about the value of μ. If that is the case, the z test statistic is used if σ is known, whereas the t test statistic is used if σ is estimated by the sample standard deviation s. Finally, note that if the sample size is small and the assumption of a normally distributed population is inappropriate, we recommend increasing the sample size to $n \geq 30$ to test a hypothesis about a population mean.

Hypothesis tests about a population proportion were developed for the large-sample case ($np \geq 5$ and $n(1 - p) \geq 5$). The test statistic used is

$$z = \frac{\bar{p} - p_0}{\sqrt{\dfrac{p_0(1 - p_0)}{n}}}$$

The rejection rule for all the hypothesis-testing procedures involves comparing the value of the test statistic with a critical value. For lower-tail tests, the null hypothesis is

---

*In some cases, nonparametric statistical methods can be used to conduct a hypothesis. These methods are discussed in Chapter 19.

rejected if the value of the test statistic is less than the critical value. For upper-tail tests, the null hypothesis is rejected if the test statistic is greater than the critical value. For two-tailed tests, the null hypothesis is rejected for values of the test statistic in either tail of the sampling distribution.

We also saw that p-values could be used for hypothesis testing. The p-value yields the probability, when the null hypothesis is true, of obtaining a sample result that is at least as unlikely as what is observed. When p-values are used to conduct a hypothesis test, the rejection rule calls for rejecting the null hypothesis whenever the p-value is less than α. The p-value is often called the observed level of significance because the null hypothesis will be rejected for any value of α larger than the p-value.

Extensions of the hypothesis-testing procedure to control the probability of making a Type II error were also presented. In Section 9.8, we showed how to compute the probability of making a Type II error. In Section 9.9 we showed how to determine a sample size that would enable us to control the probability of making a Type II error.

GLOSSARY

Null hypothesis   The hypothesis tentatively assumed true in the hypothesis-testing procedure.

Alternative hypothesis   The hypothesis concluded to be true if the null hypothesis is rejected.

Type I error   The error of rejecting H_0 when it is true.

Type II error   The error of accepting H_0 when it is false.

Critical value   A value that is compared with the test statistic to determine whether or not H_0 should be rejected.

Level of significance   The maximum probability of a Type I error.

One-tailed test   A hypothesis test in which rejection of the null hypothesis occurs for values of the test statistic in one tail of the sampling distribution.

Two-tailed test   A hypothesis test in which rejection of the null hypothesis occurs for values of the test statistic in either tail of the sampling distribution.

p-**Value**   The probability, when the null hypothesis is true, of obtaining a sample result that is at least as unlikely as what is observed. It is often called the observed level of significance.

Power   The probability of correctly rejecting H_0 when it is false.

Power curve   A graph of the probability of rejecting H_0 for all possible values of the population parameter not satisfying the null hypothesis. The power curve provides the probability of correctly rejecting the null hypothesis.

KEY FORMULAS

Test Statistics for a Large-Sample ($n \geq 30$) Hypothesis Test About a Population Mean

σ *Known* σ *Unknown*

$$z = \frac{\bar{x} - \mu_0}{\sigma/\sqrt{n}} \qquad z = \frac{\bar{x} - \mu_0}{s/\sqrt{n}} \tag{9.1}$$

Test Statistic for a Small-Sample ($n < 30$) Hypothesis Test About a Population Mean

$$t = \frac{\bar{x} - \mu_0}{s/\sqrt{n}} \qquad (9.8)$$

Test Statistic for Hypothesis Tests About a Population Proportion

$$z = \frac{\bar{p} - p_0}{\sigma_{\bar{p}}} \qquad (9.9)$$

where

$$\sigma_{\bar{p}} = \sqrt{\frac{p_0(1 - p_0)}{n}} \qquad (9.10)$$

Sample Size for a One-Tailed Hypothesis Test About a Population Mean

$$n = \frac{(z_\alpha + z_\beta)^2 \sigma^2}{(\mu_0 - \mu_a)^2}$$

In a two-tailed test, replace z_α with $z_{\alpha/2}$ (9.13)

SUPPLEMENTARY EXERCISES

70. The Ford Taurus is listed as having a highway fuel efficiency average of 30 miles per gallon (1995 *Motor Trend* New Car Buyer's Guide). A consumer interest group conducts automobile mileage tests seeking statistical evidence to show that automobile manufacturers overstate the miles per gallon ratings for particular models. In the case of the Ford Taurus, hypotheses for the test would be stated H_0: $\mu \geq 30$ and H_a: $\mu < 30$. In a sample of 50 mileage tests with Ford Taurus, the consumer interest group finds a sample mean highway milage rating of 29.5 miles per gallon and a sample standard deviation of 1.8 miles per gallon. What conclusion should be drawn from the sample results? Use a .01 level of significance.

71. The manager of the Keeton Department Store has assumed that the mean annual income of the store's credit-card customers is at least $28,000 per year. A sample of 58 credit-card customers shows a sample mean of $27,200 and a sample standard deviation of $3000. At the .05 level of significance, should this assumption be rejected? What is the *p*-value?

72. The chamber of commerce of a Florida Gulf Coast community advertises that area residential property is available at a mean cost of $25,000 or less per lot. Using a .05 level of significance, test the validity of this claim. Suppose a sample of 32 properties provided a sample mean of $26,000 per lot and a sample standard deviation of $2500. What is the *p*-value?

73. A bath soap manufacturing process is designed to produce a mean of 120 bars of soap per batch. Quantities over or under the standard are undesirable. A sample of ten batches shows the following numbers of bars of soap.

    108   118   120   122   119   113   124   122   120   123

    Using a .05 level of significance, test to see whether the sample results indicate that the manufacturing process is functioning properly.

74. The monthly rent for a two-bedroom apartment in a particular city is reported to average $550. Suppose we want to test H_0: $\mu = 550$ versus H_a: $\mu \neq 550$. A sample of 36 two-bedroom apartments is selected. The sample mean turns out to be $\bar{x} = \$562$, with a sample standard deviation of $s = \$40$.

a. Conduct this hypothesis test with a .05 level of significance.

b. Compute the *p*-value.

c. Use the sample results to construct a 95% confidence interval for the population mean. What hypothesis-testing conclusion would you draw from the confidence interval result?

75. Stout Electric Company operates a fleet of trucks that provide electrical service to the construction industry. Monthly mean maintenance cost has been $75 per truck. A random sample of 40 trucks shows a sample mean maintenance cost of $82.50 per month, with a sample standard deviation of $30. Managers want a test to determine whether or not the mean monthly maintenance cost has increased.

a. With a .05 level of significance, what is the rejection rule for this test?

b. What is your conclusion based on the sample mean of $82.50?

c. What is the *p*-value associated with this sample result? What is your conclusion based on the *p*-value?

76. In making bids on building projects, Sonneborn Builders, Inc. assumes construction workers are idle no more than 15% of the time. Hence, for a normal eight-hour shift, the mean idle time per worker should be 72 minutes or less per day. A sample of 30 construction workers had a mean idle time of 80 minutes per day. The sample standard deviation was 20 minutes. Suppose a hypothesis test is to be designed to test the validity of the company's assumption.

a. What is the *p*-value associated with the sample result?

b. Using a .05 level of significance and the *p*-value, test $H_0: \mu \leq 72$. What is your conclusion?

77. Sixty percent of Americans believe that business profits are distributed unfairly (General Social Surveys, National Opinion Research Center, University of Chicago). Suppose a sample of 40 Midwesterners showed that 27 believe business profits are distributed unfairly.

a. Do these results justify the inference that a larger proportion of Midwesterners believe that business profits are distributed unfairly? Use $\alpha = .05$.

b. What is the *p*-value?

78. The Immigration and Naturalization service reported that 79% of foreign travelers visiting the United States in 1992 stated that the primary purpose of their visit was to enjoy a vacation (*America by the Numbers,* 1993). As a follow-up study conducted in 1995, suppose a sample of 500 foreign visitors is selected and that 360 say that their primary reason for visiting the U.S. is to enjoy a vacation. Is the proportion of foreign travelers vacationing in the United States in 1995 less than the proportion reported in 1992? Support your conclusion with a statistical test using a .05 level of significance.

79. In 1991, the proportion of individuals trying to follow expert guidelines on eating right was .44 (*Time,* October 11, 1993). In a 1993 survey of 1000 individuals conducted by the American Dietetic Association, 390 individuals were trying to follow expert guidelines on eating right. Conduct a statistical test to determine whether the proportion of individuals trying to follow expert guidelines on eating right decreased over the two-year period. Use a .05 level of significance.

80. The Gallup Organization conducted a survey of 1350 people for the National Occupational Information Coordinating Committee, a panel Congress created to improve the use of job information (*The Arizona Republic,* January 12, 1990). A research question related to the study was: Do individuals hold jobs that they planned to hold or do they hold jobs for such reasons as chance or lack of choice? Let *p* indicate the population proportion of individuals who hold jobs that they planned to hold.

a. If the hypotheses are stated $H_0: p \geq .50$ and $H_a: p < .50$, discuss the research hypothesis H_a in terms of what the researcher is investigating.

b. The Gallup poll found that 41% of the respondents hold jobs they planned to hold. What is your conclusion at a .01 level of significance? Discuss.

81. A well-known doctor hypothesized that 75% of women wear shoes that are too small. A 1991 study of 356 women by the American Orthopedic Foot and Ankle Society found 313 women

who wore shoes that were at least one size too small (*New York Times,* March 10, 1991). Test $H_0: p = .70$ and $H_a: p \neq .70$ at $\alpha = .01$. What is your conclusion?

82. The filling machine for a production operation must be adjusted if more than 8% of the items being produced are underfilled. A random sample of 80 items from the day's production contained nine underfilled items. Does the sample evidence indicate that the filling machine should be adjusted? Use $\alpha = .02$. What is the *p*-value?

83. A radio station in a major resort area announced that at least 90% of the hotels and motels would be full for the Memorial Day weekend. The station advised listeners to make reservations in advance if they planned to be in the resort over the weekend. On Saturday night a sample of 58 hotels and motels showed 49 with a no-vacancy sign and nine with vacancies. What is your reaction to the radio station's claim after seeing the sample evidence? Use $\alpha = .05$ in making the statistical test. What is the *p*-value for the sample results?

84. In 1984 the percentage of individuals who reported having reduced their consumption of alcoholic beverages during the previous five years was 29% (*The Gallup Poll Monthly,* June 1994). In a 1994 Gallup study of trends in alcoholic beverage consumption, a sample of 663 individuals found that 272 individuals reported having reduced their consumption of alcoholic beverages during the previous five years. Do the results for the 1994 study indicate an increase in the proportion of individuals who are reducing their consumption of alcoholic beverages? Support your conclusion with a statistical testing using a .05 level of significance.

85. Refer again to Exercise 76.
    a. What is the probability of making a Type II error when the population mean idle time is 80 minutes?
    b. What is the probability of making a Type II error when the population mean idle time is 75 minutes?
    c. What is the probability of making a Type II error when the population mean idle time is 70 minutes?
    d. Sketch the power curve for this problem.

86. A federal funding program is available to low-income neighborhoods. To qualify for the funding a neighborhood must have a mean household income of less than $7000 per year. Neighborhoods with mean annual household income of $7000 or more do not qualify. Funding decisions are based on a sample of residents in the neighborhood. A hypothesis test with a .02 level of significance is conducted. If the funding guidelines call for a maximum probability of .05 of not funding a neighborhood with a mean annual household income of $6500, what sample size should be used in the funding decision study? Use $\sigma = \$2000$ as a planning value.

87. $H_0: \mu = 120$ and $H_a: \mu \neq 120$ are used to test whether or not a bath soap production process is meeting the standard output of 120 bars per batch. Use a .05 level of significance for the test and a planning value of 5 for the standard deviation.
    a. If the mean output drops to 117 bars per batch, the firm wants to have a 98% chance of concluding that the standard production output is not being met. How large a sample should be selected?
    b. With your sample size from part (a), what is the probability of concluding that the process is operating satisfactorily for each of the following actual mean outputs: 117, 118, 119, 121, 122, and 123 bars per batch? That is, what is the probability of a Type II error in each case?

COMPUTER CASE

QUALITY ASSOCIATES, INC.

Quality Associates, Inc., is a consulting firm that advises its clients about sampling and statistical procedures that can be used to control their manufacturing processes. In one particular application, a client gave Quality Associates a sample of 800 observations taken during a time in which that client's process was operating satisfactorily. The sample standard deviation for these data was .21; hence, the population standard deviation was assumed to be .21. Quality Associates then suggested that random samples of size 30 be taken periodically to monitor the process on an ongoing basis. By analyzing the new samples, the client could quickly learn whether the process was operating satisfactorily. When the process was not operating satisfactorily, corrective action could be taken to eliminate the problem. The design specification indicated the mean for the process should be 12. The hypotheses test suggested by Quality Associates follows.

$$H_0: \mu = 12$$
$$H_a: \mu \neq 12$$

Corrective action will be taken any time H_0 is rejected.

The following samples were collected at hourly intervals during the first day of operation of the new statistical process-control procedure. These data are available in the QUALITY data set.

QUALITY

Sample 1	Sample 2	Sample 3	Sample 4
11.55	11.62	11.91	12.02
11.62	11.69	11.36	12.02
11.52	11.59	11.75	12.05
11.75	11.82	11.95	12.18
11.90	11.97	12.14	12.11
11.64	11.71	11.72	12.07
11.80	11.87	11.61	12.05
12.03	12.10	11.85	11.64
11.94	12.01	12.16	12.39
11.92	11.99	11.91	11.65
12.13	12.20	12.12	12.11
12.09	12.16	11.61	11.90
11.93	12.00	12.21	12.22
12.21	12.28	11.56	11.88
12.32	12.39	11.95	12.03
11.93	12.00	12.01	12.35
11.85	11.92	12.06	12.09
11.76	11.83	11.76	11.77
12.16	12.23	11.82	12.20
11.77	11.84	12.12	11.79
12.00	12.07	11.60	12.30
12.04	12.11	11.95	12.27
11.98	12.05	11.96	12.29
12.30	12.37	12.22	12.47
12.18	12.25	11.75	12.03
11.97	12.04	11.96	12.17
12.17	12.24	11.95	11.94
11.85	11.92	11.89	11.97
12.30	12.37	11.88	12.23
12.15	12.22	11.93	12.25

Managerial Report

1. Conduct the hypothesis test for each sample at the .01 level of significance and determine what action, if any, should be taken. Provide the test statistic and p-value for each test.
2. Consider the standard deviation for each of the four samples. Does the assumption of .21 for the population standard deviation appear reasonable?
3. Compute limits for the sample mean $\bar{x}$ around $\mu = 12$ such that, as long as a new sample mean is within those limits, the process will be considered to be operating satisfactorily. If $\bar{x}$ exceeds

the upper limit or if $\bar{x}$ is below the lower limit, corrective action will be taken. These limits are referred to as upper and lower control limits for quality-control purposes.

4. Discuss the implications of changing the level of significance to a larger value. What mistake or error could increase if that were done?

APPENDIX 9.1

Hypothesis Testing with Minitab

LARGE-SAMPLE CASE

● In Section 9.4 we showed how Minitab could be used to perform a hypothesis test for the Superflight golf ball study. Assume that the user has entered the distance data for the 36 golf balls from Table 9.2 into column 1 of a Minitab worksheet. With the sample standard deviation $s = 12$ as an estimate of the population standard deviation σ, the following steps can be used to produce the computer output in Figure 9.9.

Step 1. Select the **Stat** pull-down menu
Step 2. Select the **Basic Statistics** pull-down menu
Step 3. Select the **1-Sample Z** option
Step 4. When the dialog box appears,
  Enter C1 in the **Variables** box
  Select the **Test mean** option and enter 280 in the box
  Select **not equal** in the **Alternative** box
  Enter 7.77 in the **Sigma** box
  Select **OK**

Although the Superflight golf ball study involved a two-tailed hypothesis test, the procedure described can be easily modified for one-tailed hypothesis tests. In Step 4 we simply select the less than or greater than option in the **Alternative** box.

SMALL-SAMPLE CASE

In Section 9.5 we showed how Minitab could be used to perform a hypothesis test for the Heathrow airport rating study. Assume that the user has entered the ratings for the 12 business travelers into column 1 of a Minitab worksheet. The following steps can be used to produce the computer output in Figure 9.11.

Step 1. Select the **Stat** pull-down menu
Step 2. Select the **Basic Statistics** pull-down menu
Step 3. Select the **1-Sample t** option
Step 4. When the dialog box appears,
  Enter C1 in the **Variables** box
  Select the **Test mean** option and enter 7 in the box
  Select the **greater than** option in the **Alternative** box
  Select **OK**

10

STATISTICAL INFERENCE ABOUT MEANS AND PROPORTIONS WITH TWO POPULATIONS

CONTENTS

μ

$\bar{x}$

STATISTICS IN PRACTICE ● ● ● ● ● ● ● ● ● ● ● ● ● ● ●

FISONS

Fisons Corporation

Rochester, New York

Fisons Corporation, Rochester, New York, is a unit of Fisons Plc., UK. Fisons opened its United States operations in 1966.

Fisons' Pharmaceutical Division uses extensive statistical procedures to test and develop new drugs. The testing process in the pharmaceutical industry usually consists of three stages: (1) preclinical testing, (2) testing for long-term usage and safety, and (3) clinical efficacy testing. At each successive stage, the chance that a drug will pass the rigorous tests decreases; however, the cost of further testing increases dramatically. Industry surveys indicate that on average the research and development for one new drug costs $250 million and takes 12 years. Hence, it is important to eliminate unsuccessful new drugs in the early stages of the testing process, as well as identify promising ones for further testing.

Statistics plays a major role in pharmaceutical research, where government regulations are very stringent and rigorously enforced. In preclinical testing, a two- or three-population statistical study typically is used to determine whether or not a new drug should continue to be studied in the long-term usage and safety program. The populations may consist of the new drug, a control, and a standard drug. The preclinical testing process begins when a new drug is sent to the pharmacology group for evaluation of efficacy—the capacity of the drug to produce the desired effects. As part of the process, a statistician is asked to design an experiment that can be used to test the new drug. The design must specify the sample size and the statistical methods of analysis. In a two-population study, one sample is used to obtain data on the efficacy of the new drug (population 1) and a second sample is used to obtain data on the efficacy of a standard drug (population 2). Depending on the intended use, the new and standard drugs are tested in such disciplines as neurology, cardiology, and immunology. In most studies, the statistical method involves hypothesis testing for the difference between the means of the new drug population and the standard drug population. If a new drug lacks efficacy or produces undesirable effects in comparison with the standard drug, the new drug is rejected and withdrawn from further testing. Only new drugs that show promising comparisons with the standard drugs are forwarded to the long-term usage and safety testing program.

Further data collection and multipopulation studies are conducted in the long-term usage and safety testing program and in the clinical testing programs. The Food and Drug Administration (FDA) requires that statistical methods be defined prior to such testing to avoid data-related biases. In addition, to avoid human biases, some of the clinical trials are double or triple blind. That is, neither the subject nor the investigator knows what drug is administered to whom. If the new drug meets all requirements in relation to the standard drug, a new drug application (NDA) is filed with the FDA. The application is rigorously scrutinized by statisticians and scientists at the agency.

In this chapter you will learn how to construct interval estimates and make hypothesis tests about means and proportions with two populations. Techniques will be presented for analyzing independent random samples as well as matched samples.

Some of the drug products manufactured by the pharmaceutical division of Fisons Corporation.

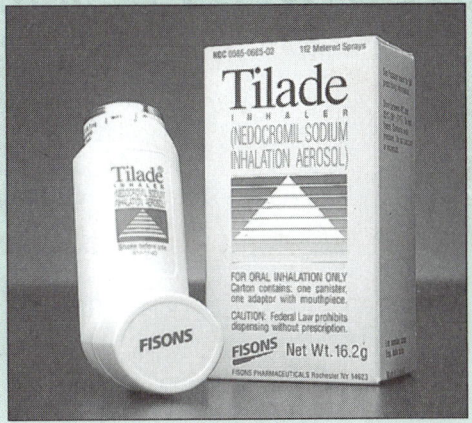

● In Chapters 8 and 9 we showed how to develop interval estimates and conduct hypothesis tests for situations involving one population mean and one population proportion. In this chapter we continue our discussion of statistical inference by showing how interval estimates and hypothesis tests can be developed for situations involving two populations, when the difference between the two population means or the two population proportions is of prime importance. For example, we may want to develop an interval estimate of the difference between the mean starting salary for a population of men and the mean starting salary for a population of women or conduct a hypothesis test to determine whether there is any difference between the proportion of defective parts in a population of parts produced by supplier A and the proportion of defective parts in a population of parts produced by supplier B. We will begin our discussion of statistical inference about means and proportions with two populations by showing how an interval estimate of the difference between the means of two populations can be developed for a sampling study conducted by Greystone Department Stores, Inc.

10.1 ESTIMATION OF THE DIFFERENCE BETWEEN THE MEANS OF TWO POPULATIONS: INDEPENDENT SAMPLES

Greystone Department Stores, Inc., operates two stores in Buffalo, New York; one is in the inner city and the other is in a suburban shopping center. The regional manager has noticed that products that sell well in one store do not always sell well in the other. She believes this situation may be attributable to differences in customer demographics at the two locations. Customers may differ in age, education, income, and so on. Suppose the regional manager has asked us to investigate the difference between the mean ages of the customers who shop at the two stores.

Let us define population 1 as all customers who shop at the inner-city store and population 2 as all customers who shop at the suburban store. Let

μ_1 = mean of population 1 (i.e., the mean age of all customers who shop at the inner-city store) and

μ_2 = mean of population 2 (i.e., the mean age of all customers who shop at the suburban store).

The difference between the two population means is $\mu_1 - \mu_2$.

To estimate $\mu_1 - \mu_2$, we will select a simple random sample of n_1 customers from population 1 and a simple random sample of n_2 customers from population 2. Since the simple random sample of n_1 customers is selected independently of the simple random sample of n_2 customers, we have the case of *independent simple random samples*. Let

$\bar{x}_1$ = sample mean age for the simple random sample of n_1 inner-city customers and

$\bar{x}_2$ = sample mean age for the simple random sample of n_2 suburban customers.

Since $\bar{x}_1$ is a point estimator of μ_1 and $\bar{x}_2$ is a point estimator of μ_2, the point estimator of the difference in the two population means is expressed as follows.

POINT ESTIMATOR OF THE DIFFERENCE BETWEEN THE MEANS OF TWO POPULATIONS

$$\bar{x}_1 - \bar{x}_2 \qquad (10.1)$$

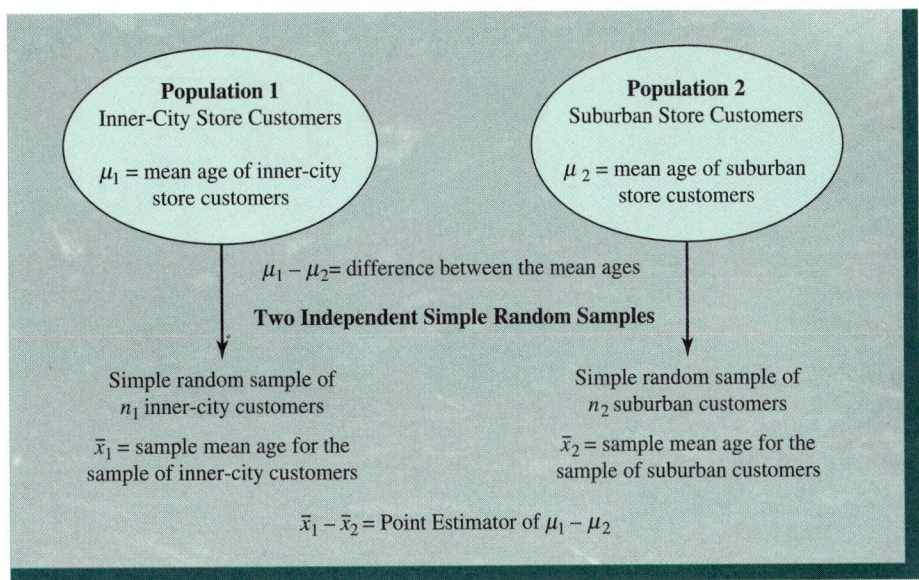

FIGURE 10.1   Estimating the Difference Between the Means of Two Populations

Thus, we see that the point estimator of the difference between the two population means is the difference between the sample means of the two independent simple random samples. Figure 10.1 provides an overview of the process used to estimate the difference between two sample means based on two independent simple random samples.

Assume the customer age data collected from the two independent simple random samples of Greystone customers provide the following results.

Store	Number of Customers Sampled	Sample Mean Age	Sample Standard Deviation
Inner City	36	$\bar{x}_1 = 40$ years	$s_1 = 9$ years
Suburban	49	$\bar{x}_2 = 35$ years	$s_2 = 10$ years

Using (10.1), we find that a point estimate of the difference between the mean ages of the two populations is $\bar{x}_1 - \bar{x}_2 = 40 - 35 = 5$ years. Thus, we are led to believe that the customers at the inner-city store have a mean age five years greater than the mean age of the suburban store customers. However, as with all point estimates, we know that five years is only one of many possible estimates of the difference between the mean ages of the two populations. If Greystone selected another simple random sample of 36 inner-city customers and another simple random sample of 49 suburban customers, the difference between the two new sample means would probably not equal five years. The sampling distribution of $\bar{x}_1 - \bar{x}_2$ is the probability distribution of the difference in sample means for all possible sets of two samples.

SAMPLING DISTRIBUTION $\bar{x}_1 - \bar{x}_2$

We can use the sampling distribution of $\bar{x}_1 - \bar{x}_2$ to develop an interval estimate of the difference between the two population means in much the same way as we used the sampling distribution of $\bar{x}$ for interval estimation with a single population mean. The sampling distribution of $\bar{x}_1 - \bar{x}_2$ has the following properties.

SAMPLING DISTRIBUTION OF $\bar{x}_1 - \bar{x}_2$

$$\text{Expected Value: } E(\bar{x}_1 - \bar{x}_2) = \mu_1 - \mu_2 \tag{10.2}$$

$$\text{Standard Deviation: } \sigma_{\bar{x}_1 - \bar{x}_2} = \sqrt{\frac{\sigma_1^2}{n_1} + \frac{\sigma_2^2}{n_2}} \tag{10.3}$$

where

σ_1 = standard deviation of population 1

σ_2 = standard deviation of population 2

n_1 = sample size for the simple random sample
from population 1

n_2 = sample size for the simple random sample
from population 2

Distribution form: If the sample sizes are both *large* ($n_1 \geq 30$ and $n_2 \geq 30$), the sampling distribution of $\bar{x}_1 - \bar{x}_2$ can be approximated by a normal probability distribution.

Figure 10.2 shows the sampling distribution of $\bar{x}_1 - \bar{x}_2$ and its relationship to the individual sampling distributions of $\bar{x}_1$ and $\bar{x}_2$.

Let us now develop an interval estimate of the difference between the means of two populations. We consider two cases, one in which the sample sizes are large ($n_1 \geq 30$ and $n_2 \geq 30$) and another in which one or both sample sizes are small ($n_1 < 30$ and/or $n_2 < 30$). We consider the large-sample case first.

INTERVAL ESTIMATE OF $\mu_1 - \mu_2$: LARGE-SAMPLE CASE

In the large-sample case, the sampling distribution of $\bar{x}_1 - \bar{x}_2$ can be approximated by a normal probability distribution. With this approximation we can use the following expression to develop an interval estimate of the difference between the means of the two populations.

INTERVAL ESTIMATE OF THE DIFFERENCE BETWEEN THE MEANS OF TWO POPULATIONS: LARGE-SAMPLE CASE ($n_1 \geq 30$ AND $n_2 \geq 30$) WITH σ_1 AND σ_2 KNOWN

$$\bar{x}_1 - \bar{x}_2 \pm z_{\alpha/2}\sigma_{\bar{x}_1 - \bar{x}_2} \tag{10.4}$$

where $1 - \alpha$ is the confidence coefficient

Note that to use (10.4) to develop an interval estimate of the difference between the means of two populations, we must know the value of $\sigma_{\bar{x}_1 - \bar{x}_2}$, the standard deviation of the sampling distribution of $\bar{x}_1 - \bar{x}_2$. However, (10.3) shows that the value of $\sigma_{\bar{x}_1 - \bar{x}_2}$ depends on the values of σ_1 and σ_2, the standard deviations of each of the populations. When the population standard deviations are unknown, we can use the sample standard deviations as estimates of the population standard deviations and estimate $\sigma_{\bar{x}_1 - \bar{x}_2}$ as follows.

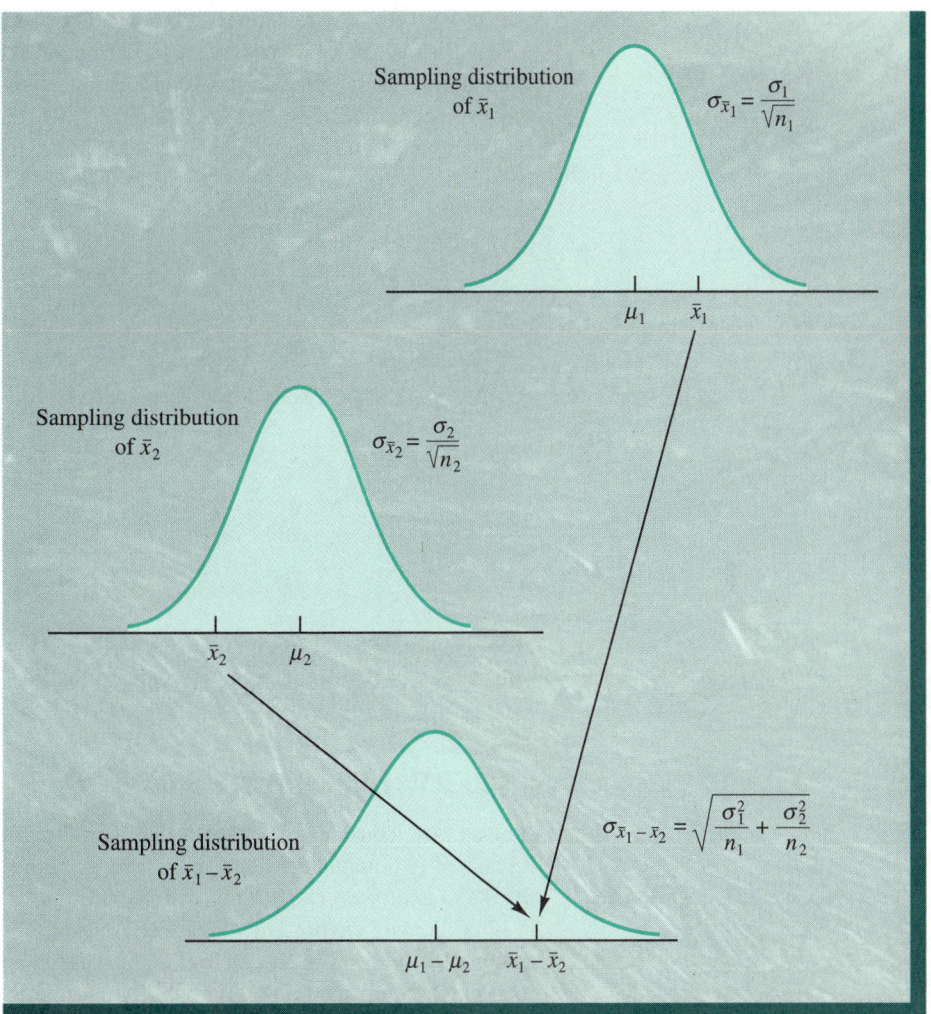

FIGURE 10.2 Sampling Distribution of $\bar{x}_1 - \bar{x}_2$ and Its Relationship to the Individual Sampling Distributions of $\bar{x}_1$ and $\bar{x}_2$

POINT ESTIMATOR OF $\sigma_{\bar{x}_1 - \bar{x}_2}$

$$s_{\bar{x}_1 - \bar{x}_2} = \sqrt{\frac{s_1^2}{n_1} + \frac{s_2^2}{n_2}} \qquad (10.5)$$

In the large-sample case, we can use this point estimator of $\sigma_{\bar{x}_1 - \bar{x}_2}$ to develop an approximate confidence interval estimate of the difference between the two population means.

INTERVAL ESTIMATE OF THE DIFFERENCE BETWEEN THE MEANS OF TWO POPULATIONS: LARGE-SAMPLE CASE ($n_1 \geq 30$ AND $n_2 \geq 30$) with σ_1 AND σ_2 UNKNOWN

$$\bar{x}_1 - \bar{x}_2 \pm z_{\alpha/2} s_{\bar{x}_1 - \bar{x}_2} \qquad (10.6)$$

where $1 - \alpha$ is the confidence coefficient.

Let us use (10.6) to develop a confidence interval estimate of the difference between the mean ages of the two customer populations in the Greystone Department Store study. Recall that the sample mean age and sample standard deviation for the simple random sample of 36 inner-city customers are $\bar{x}_1 = 40$ years and $s_1 = 9$ years, respectively; the sample mean and sample standard deviation for the simple random sample of 49 suburban customers are $\bar{x}_2 = 35$ years and $s_2 = 10$ years, respectively. Using (10.5) to estimate $\sigma_{\bar{x}_1 - \bar{x}_2}$, we have

$$s_{\bar{x}_1 - \bar{x}_2} = \sqrt{\frac{(9)^2}{36} + \frac{(10)^2}{49}} = \sqrt{4.29} = 2.07$$

With $z_{\alpha/2} = z_{.025} = 1.96$, (10.6) provides the following 95% confidence interval.

$$5 \pm (1.96)(2.07)$$

or

$$5 \pm 4.06$$

Thus, at a 95% level of confidence, the interval estimate for the difference between the mean ages of the two Greystone populations is .94 years to 9.06 years.

INTERVAL ESTIMATE OF $\mu_1 - \mu_2$: SMALL-SAMPLE CASE

Let us now consider the interval-estimation procedure for the difference between the means of two populations whenever one or both sample sizes are less than 30—that is, $n_1 < 30$ and/or $n_2 < 30$. This will be referred to as the small-sample case.

In Chapter 8 we presented a procedure for interval estimation of the mean for a single population with a small sample. Recall that the procedure required the assumption that the population had a normal probability distribution. With the sample standard deviation s used as an estimate of the population standard deviation σ, the t distribution was used to develop an interval estimate of the population mean.

To develop interval estimates for the two-population small-sample case, we will make two assumptions about the two populations and the samples selected from the two populations.

1. Both populations have normal probability distributions.
2. The variances of the populations are equal ($\sigma_1^2 = \sigma_2^2 = \sigma^2$).

Given these assumptions, the sampling distribution of $\bar{x}_1 - \bar{x}_2$ is normally distributed regardless of the sample sizes. The expected value of $\bar{x}_1 - \bar{x}_2$ is $\mu_1 - \mu_2$. Because of the equal variances assumption, (10.3) can be written

$$\sigma_{\bar{x}_1 - \bar{x}_2} = \sqrt{\frac{\sigma^2}{n_1} + \frac{\sigma^2}{n_2}} = \sqrt{\sigma^2 \left(\frac{1}{n_1} + \frac{1}{n_2} \right)} \qquad \textbf{(10.7)}$$

The sampling distribution of $\bar{x}_1 - \bar{x}_2$ is shown in Figure 10.3.

If the variance σ^2 of the populations is known, (10.4) can be used to develop the interval estimate of the difference between the two population means. However, in most

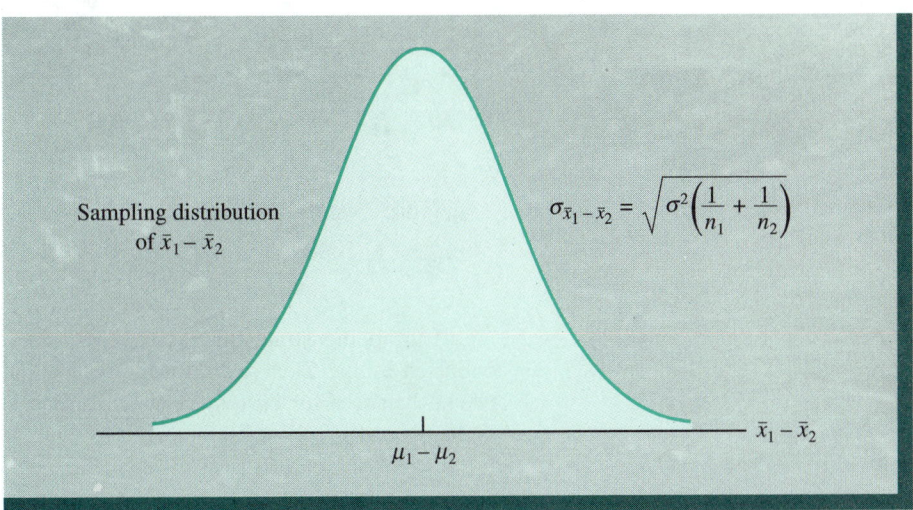

FIGURE 10.3 Sampling Distribution of $\bar{x}_1 - \bar{x}_2$ when the Populations Have Normal Distributions with Equal Variances

cases, σ^2 is unknown; thus, the two sample variances s_1^2 and s_2^2 must be used to develop the estimate of σ^2 in (10.7). Since (10.7) is based on the assumption that $\sigma_1^2 = \sigma_2^2 = \sigma^2$, we do not need separate estimates of σ_1^2 and σ_2^2. In fact, we can combine the data from the two samples to provide the best single estimate of σ^2. The process of combining the results of two independent simple random samples to provide one estimate of σ^2 is referred to as *pooling*. The *pooled estimator* of σ^2, denoted by s^2, is a weighted average of the two sample variances s_1^2 and s_2^2. The formula for the pooled estimator of σ^2 follows.

POOLED ESTIMATOR OF σ^2

$$s^2 = \frac{(n_1 - 1)s_1^2 + (n_2 - 1)s_2^2}{n_1 + n_2 - 2} \tag{10.8}$$

With s^2 as the pooled estimator of σ^2 and using (10.7), we can obtain the following estimator of the standard deviation of $\bar{x}_1 - \bar{x}_2$.

POINT ESTIMATOR OF $\sigma_{\bar{x}_1 - \bar{x}_2}$ WHEN $\sigma_1^2 = \sigma_2^2 = \sigma^2$

$$s_{\bar{x}_1 - \bar{x}_2} = \sqrt{s^2\left(\frac{1}{n_1} + \frac{1}{n_2}\right)} \tag{10.9}$$

The t distribution can now be used to compute an interval estimate of the difference between the means of the two populations. Since there are $n_1 - 1$ degrees of freedom associated with the random sample from population 1 and $n_2 - 1$ degrees of freedom associated with the random sample from population 2, the t distribution will have $n_1 + n_2 - 2$ degrees of freedom. The interval-estimation procedure follows.

INTERVAL ESTIMATE OF THE DIFFERENCE BETWEEN THE MEANS OF TWO POPULATIONS: SMALL-SAMPLE CASE ($n_1 < 30$ AND/OR $n_2 < 30$)

$$\bar{x}_1 - \bar{x}_2 \pm t_{\alpha/2} s_{\bar{x}_1 - \bar{x}_2} \qquad (10.10)$$

where the t value is based on a t distribution with $n_1 + n_2 - 2$ degrees of freedom and where $1 - \alpha$ is the confidence coefficient.

Let us demonstrate the interval-estimation procedure for a sampling study conducted by the Clearview National Bank. Independent random samples of checking account balances for customers at two Clearview branch banks yielded the following results.

Branch Bank	Number of Checking Accounts	Sample Mean Balance	Sample Standard Deviation
Cherry Grove	12	$\bar{x}_1 = \$1000$	$s_1 = \$150$
Beechmont	10	$\bar{x}_2 = \$920$	$s_2 = \$120$

Let us use these data to develop a 90% confidence interval for the difference between the mean checking account balances at the two branch banks. Suppose that checking account balances are normally distributed at both branches and that the variances of checking account balances at both branches are equal. Using (10.8), we see that the pooled estimate of the population variance becomes

$$s^2 = \frac{(n_1 - 1)s_1^2 + (n_2 - 1)s_2^2}{n_1 + n_2 - 2} = \frac{(11)(150)^2 + (9)(120)^2}{12 + 10 - 2} = 18{,}855$$

The corresponding estimate of the standard deviation of $\bar{x}_1 - \bar{x}_2$ is

$$s_{\bar{x}_1 - \bar{x}_2} = \sqrt{s^2\left(\frac{1}{n_1} + \frac{1}{n_2}\right)} = \sqrt{18{,}855\left(\frac{1}{12} + \frac{1}{10}\right)} = 58.79$$

The appropriate t distribution for the interval-estimation procedure has $n_1 + n_2 - 2 = 12 + 10 - 2 = 20$ degrees of freedom. With $\alpha = .10$, $t_{\alpha/2} = t_{.05} = 1.725$. Thus, using (10.10), we see that the interval estimate becomes

$$\bar{x}_1 - \bar{x}_2 \pm t_{.05}\, s_{\bar{x}_1 - \bar{x}_2}$$

$$1000 - 920 \pm (1.725)(58.79)$$

$$80 \pm 101.41$$

At a 90% level of confidence, the interval estimate of the difference between the mean account balances at the two branch banks is −$21.41 to $181.41. The fact that the interval includes a negative range of values indicates that the actual difference between the two means, $\mu_1 - \mu_2$, may be negative. Thus, μ_2 could actually be larger than μ_1, indicating that the population mean balance could be greater for the Beechmont branch even though the results show a greater sample mean balance at the Cherry Grove branch. The fact that the confidence interval contains the value 0 can be interpreted as indicating that we do not have sufficient evidence to conclude that the population mean account balances differ between the two branches.

NOTES AND COMMENTS

· · · · · · · · · · · · · · · · ·

1. The use of the t distribution in the small-sample procedure presented in this section is based on the assumptions that both populations have a normal probability distribution and that $\sigma_1^2 = \sigma_2^2$. Fortunately, this procedure is a *robust* statistical procedure, meaning that it is relatively insensitive to these assumptions. For instance, if $\sigma_1^2 \neq \sigma_2^2$, the procedure provides acceptable results if n_1 and n_2 are approximately equal.

2. The t distribution is not restricted to the small-sample situation; it is applicable whenever both populations are normally distributed and the variances of the populations are equal. However, (10.4) and (10.6) show how to determine an interval estimate of the difference between the means of two populations when the sample sizes are large. Thus, in the large-sample case, use of the t distribution and its corresponding assumptions is not required. We therefore do not need to refer to the t distribution until we have a small-sample case.

EXERCISES

METHODS

Self-Test ▶

1. Consider the results in Table 10.1 for two independent random samples taken from two populations.
   a. What is the point estimate of the difference between the two population means?
   b. Provide a 90% confidence interval for the difference between the two population means.
   c. Provide a 95% confidence interval for the difference between the two population means.

TABLE 10.1   Exercise 1

Sample 1	Sample 2
$n_1 = 50$	$n_2 = 35$
$\bar{x}_1 = 13.6$	$\bar{x}_2 = 11.6$
$s_1 = 2.2$	$s_2 = 3.0$

2. Consider the following results for two independent random samples taken from two populations.

Sample 1	Sample 2
$n_1 = 10$	$n_2 = 8$
$\bar{x}_1 = 22.5$	$\bar{x}_2 = 20.1$
$s_1 = 2.5$	$s_2 = 2.0$

a. What is the point estimate of the difference between the two population means?
b. What is the pooled estimate of the population variance?
c. Develop a 95% confidence interval for the difference between the two population means.

TABLE 10.2   Exercise 3

Sample 1	Sample 2
10	8
12	8
9	6
7	7
7	4
9	9

3. Consider the data in Table 10.2 for two independent random samples taken from two populations.
   a. Compute the two sample means.
   b. Compute the two sample standard deviations.
   c. What is the point estimate of the difference between the two population means?
   d. What is the pooled estimate of the population variance?
   e. Develop a 95% confidence interval for the difference between the two population means.

APPLICATIONS

4. Data gathered by the U.S. Department of Transportation (*1994 Information Please Environmental Almanac*) show the number of miles that residents of the 75 largest metropolitan areas travel per day in a car. Suppose that for a simple random sample of 50 Buffalo residents the mean is 22.5 miles a day and the standard deviation is 8.4 miles a day, and for an independent simple random sample of 100 Boston residents the mean is 18.6 miles a day and the standard deviation is 7.4 miles a day.
   a. What is the point estimate of the difference between the mean number of miles that Buffalo residents travel per day and the mean number of miles that Boston residents travel per day?
   b. What is the 95% confidence interval for the difference between the two population means?

5. A college admissions board is interested in estimating the difference between the mean grade point averages of students from two high schools. Independent simple random samples of students at the two high schools provided the results in Table 10.3.
   a. What is the point estimate of the difference between the means of the two populations?
   b. Develop a 90% confidence interval for the difference between the two population means.
   c. Develop a 95% confidence interval for the difference between the two population means.

TABLE 10.3   Exercise 5

Mt. Washington	Country Day
$n_1 = 46$	$n_2 = 33$
$\bar{x}_1 = 3.02$	$\bar{x}_2 = 2.72$
$s_1 = .38$	$s_2 = .45$

6. The International Air Transport Association surveyed business travelers to determine ratings of transatlantic gateway airports. The maximum possible score was 10, the highest rated airport was Amsterdam with an average rating of 7.93, followed by Toronto with a rating of 7.17 (*Newsweek,* June 13, 1994). Suppose a simple random sample of 50 business travelers were asked to rate the Miami airport and an independent simple random sample of 50 business travelers were asked to rate the Los Angeles airport. The rating scores follow.

Miami

6	4	6	8	7	7	6	3	3	8	10	4	8
7	8	7	5	9	5	8	4	3	8	5	5	4
4	4	8	4	5	6	2	5	9	9	8	4	8
9	9	5	9	7	8	3	10	8	9	6		

Los Angeles

10	9	6	7	8	7	9	8	10	7	6	5	7
3	5	6	8	7	10	8	4	7	8	6	9	9
5	3	1	8	9	6	8	5	4	6	10	9	8
3	2	7	9	5	3	10	3	5	10	8		

AIRPORT

Develop a 95% confidence interval estimate of the difference between the mean ratings of the Miami and Los Angeles airports.

TABLE 10.4   Exercise 7

Branch 1	Branch 2
$n_1 = 32$	$n_2 = 36$
$\bar{x}_1 = \$500$	$\bar{x}_2 = \$375$
$s_1 = \$150$	$s_2 = \$130$

7. The Butler County Bank and Trust Company wants to estimate the difference between the mean credit-card balances at two of its branch banks. Independent random samples of credit-card customers generated the results in Table 10.4.
   a. Develop a point estimate of the difference between the mean balances at the two branches.
   b. Develop a 99% confidence interval for the difference between the mean balances.

Self-Test

TABLE 10.5   Exercise 8

Neighborhood 1	Neighborhood 2
$n_1 = 8$	$n_2 = 12$
$\bar{x}_1 = \$15,700$	$\bar{x}_2 = \$14,500$
$s_1 = \$700$	$s_2 = \$850$

8. An urban-planning group is interested in estimating the difference between the mean household incomes for two neighborhoods in a large metropolitan area. Independent random samples of households in the neighborhoods provided the results in Table 10.5.
   a. Develop a point estimate of the difference between the mean incomes in the two neighborhoods.
   b. Develop a 95% confidence interval for the difference between the mean incomes in the two neighborhoods.
   c. What assumptions were made to compute the interval estimates in part (b)?

9. Production quantities for two assembly-line workers are listed in Table 10.6. Each data value indicates the amount produced during a randomly selected one-hour period.

TABLE 10.6 Exercise 9

Worker 1	Worker 2
20	22
18	18
21	20
22	23
20	24

a. Develop a point estimate of the difference between the mean hourly production rates of the two workers. Which worker appears to have the higher mean production rate?

b. Develop a 90% confidence interval for the difference between the mean production rates of the two workers. Does the confidence interval support the conclusion that the worker having the higher sample mean production rate is actually the worker with the overall higher production rate? Explain.

10. Women who are union members earn $2.50 per hour more than women who are not union members (*The Wall Street Journal*, July 26, 1994). Suppose independent random samples of 15 unionized women and 20 nonunionized women in manufacturing have been selected and the following hourly wage rates are found.

 **UNION**

Union Workers

22.40 18.90 16.70 14.05 16.20 20.00 16.10 16.30 19.10
16.50 18.50 19.80 17.00 14.30 17.20

Nonunion Workers

17.60 14.40 16.60 15.00 17.65 15.00 17.55 13.30 11.20
15.90 19.20 11.85 16.65 15.20 15.30 17.00 15.10 14.30
13.90 14.50

a. Suppose we want to develop an interval estimate of the difference in the mean wage rates between unionized and nonunionized women working in manufacturing. What assumptions must be made about the two populations?

b. What is the pooled estimate of the population variance?

c. Develop a 95% confidence interval estimate of the difference between the two population means.

d. Does there appear to be any difference in the mean wage rate between these two groups? Explain.

10.2 HYPOTHESIS TESTS ABOUT THE DIFFERENCE BETWEEN THE MEANS OF TWO POPULATIONS: INDEPENDENT SAMPLES

In this section we present procedures that can be used to test hypotheses about the difference between the means of two populations. The methodology is again divided into large-sample ($n_1 \geq 30$, $n_2 \geq 30$) and small-sample ($n_1 < 30$ and / or $n_2 < 30$) cases.

LARGE-SAMPLE CASE

As part of a study to evaluate differences in educational quality between two training centers, a standardized examination is given to individuals who are trained at the two centers. The examination scores are a major factor in assessing any quality differences between the centers.

Let

$$\mu_1 = \text{the mean examination score for the population of individuals trained at center A and}$$

$$\mu_2 = \text{the mean examination score for the population of individuals trained at center B.}$$

We begin with the tentative assumption that there is no difference in the training quality provided at the two centers. Hence, in terms of the mean examination scores, the null hypothesis is that $\mu_1 - \mu_2 = 0$. If sample evidence leads to the rejection of this hypothesis, we will conclude that the mean examination scores differ for the two populations. This conclusion indicates a quality differential between the two centers and

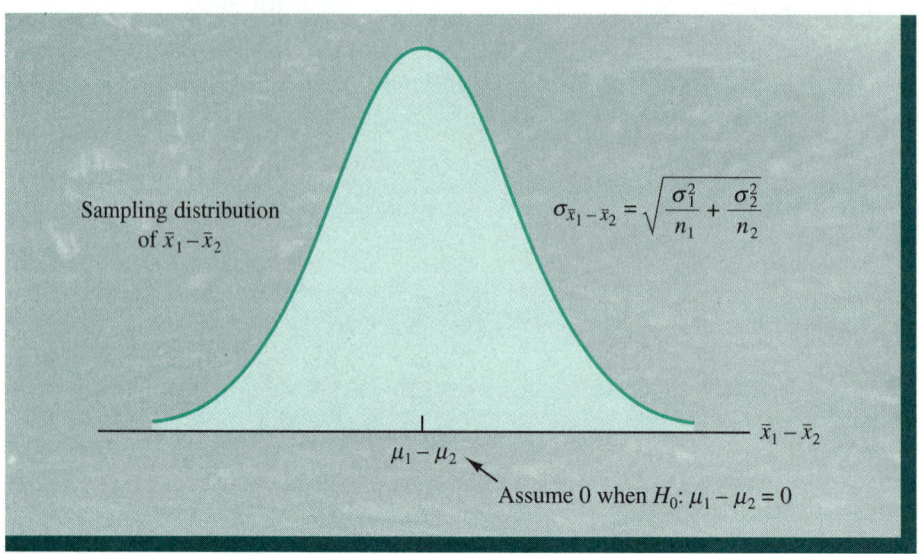

FIGURE 10.4   Sampling Distribution of $\bar{x}_1 - \bar{x}_2$ with $H_0: \mu_1 - \mu_2 = 0$

that a follow-up study investigating the reasons for the differential may be warranted. The null and alternative hypotheses are written as follows.

$$H_0: \mu_1 - \mu_2 = 0$$

$$H_a: \mu_1 - \mu_2 \neq 0$$

Following the hypothesis-testing procedure from Chapter 9, we make the tentative assumption that H_0 is true. Using the difference between the sample means as the point estimator of the difference between the population means, we consider the sampling distribution of $\bar{x}_1 - \bar{x}_2$ when H_0 is true. For the large-sample case, this distribution is as shown in Figure 10.4. Since the sampling distribution of $\bar{x}_1 - \bar{x}_2$ can be approximated by a normal probability distribution, the following test statistic is used.

$$z = \frac{(\bar{x}_1 - \bar{x}_2) - (\mu_1 - \mu_2)}{\sqrt{\sigma_1^2/n_1 + \sigma_2^2/n_2}} \tag{10.11}$$

Whenever $n_1 \geq 30$ and $n_2 \geq 30$, we will use s_1^2 and s_2^2 as estimates of σ_1^2 and σ_2^2 to compute the test statistic.

The value of z given by (10.11) can be interpreted as the number of standard deviations $\bar{x}_1 - \bar{x}_2$ is from the value of $\mu_1 - \mu_2$ specified in H_0. For $\alpha = .05$ and thus $z_{\alpha/2} = z_{.025} = 1.96$, the rejection region for the two-tailed hypothesis test is shown in Figure 10.5. The rejection rule is

Reject H_0 if $z < -1.96$ or if $z > +1.96$.

Let us assume that independent random samples of individuals trained at the two centers provide the examination scores in Table 10.7; summary statistics are given in Table 10.8. Using s_1^2 and s_2^2 to estimate σ_1^2 and σ_2^2, we find that the test statistic z given by (10.11) for the null hypothesis $H_0: \mu_1 - \mu_2 = 0$ becomes

$$z = \frac{(82.5 - 78) - 0}{\sqrt{(8)^2/30 + (10)^2/40}} = 2.09$$

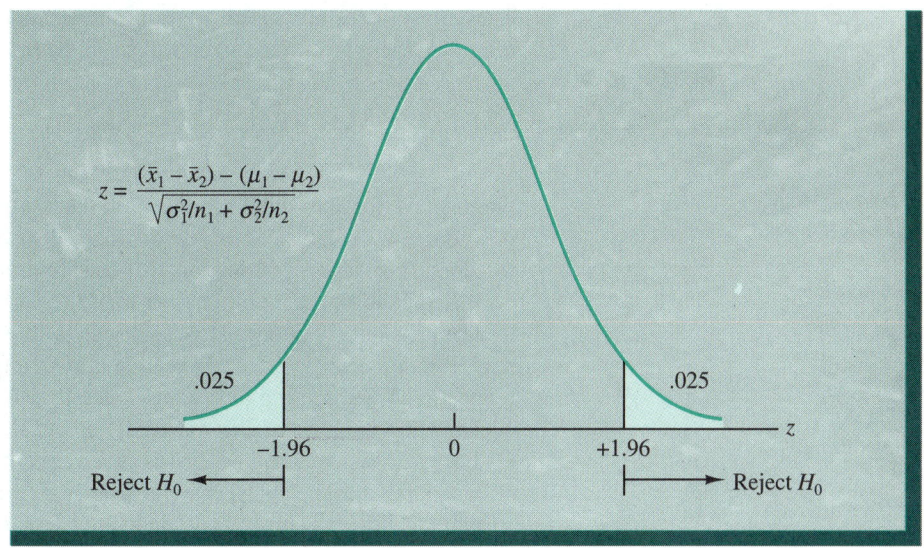

$$z = \frac{(\bar{x}_1 - \bar{x}_2) - (\mu_1 - \mu_2)}{\sqrt{\sigma_1^2/n_1 + \sigma_2^2/n_2}}$$

.025

.025

−1.96   0   +1.96 z

Reject H_0 Reject H_0

FIGURE 10.5   Rejection Region for the Two-Tailed Hypothesis Test with $\alpha = .05$

TABLE 10.7 Examination Score Data

Training Center A				Training Center B		
97	83	91	64	66	91	84
90	84	87	85	83	78	85
94	76	73	72	74	87	85
79	82	92	64	70	93	84
78	85	64	74	82	89	59
87	85	74	93	82	79	62
83	91	88	70	75	84	91
89	72	88	79	78	65	83
76	86	74	79	99	78	80
84	70	73	75	57	66	76

EXAMDATA

TABLE 10.8 Examination Score Results

Training Center A	Training Center B
$n_1 = 30$	$n_2 = 40$
$\bar{x}_1 = 82.5$	$\bar{x}_2 = 78$
$s_1 = 8$	$s_2 = 10$

Since $z = 2.09 > 1.96$, the conclusion is to reject H_0. Thus, the sample scores lead the firm to conclude that the two centers differ in educational quality.

With $z = 2.09$, the standard normal probability distribution table can be used to compute the p-value for this two-tailed test. With an area of .4817 between the mean and $z = 2.09$, the p-value is $2(.5000 - .4817) = .0366$; since the p-value is less than $\alpha = .05$, the p-value approach also results in the rejection of H_0.

In this hypothesis test, we were interested in determining whether the means of the two populations differ. Since we did not have a prior belief that one mean might be greater than or less than the other, the hypotheses $H_0: \mu_1 - \mu_2 = 0$ and $H_a: \mu_1 - \mu_2 \neq 0$ were appropriate. In other hypothesis tests about the difference between the means of two populations, we may want to find out whether one of the means is greater than or perhaps less than the other mean. In these cases, a one-tailed hypothesis test would be appropriate. The two forms of a one-tailed test about the difference between two population means follow.

$$H_0: \mu_1 - \mu_2 \leq 0 \qquad H_0: \mu_1 - \mu_2 \geq 0$$

$$H_a: \mu_1 - \mu_2 > 0 \qquad H_a: \mu_1 - \mu_2 < 0$$

These hypotheses are tested by using the test statistic z given by (10.11). The rejection region is determined in the same way as in the one-tailed approach presented in Chapter 9.

SMALL-SAMPLE CASE

Let us now consider hypothesis tests about the difference between the means of two populations for the small-sample case; that is, where $n_1 < 30$ and/or $n_2 < 30$. The procedure we will use is based on the t distribution with $n_1 + n_2 - 2$ degrees of freedom. As discussed in Section 10.1, assumptions are made that both populations have normal probability distributions and that the variances of the populations are equal.

The problem situation that we will use to illustrate the small-sample case involves a new computer software package that has been developed to help systems analysts reduce the time required to design, develop, and implement an information system. To evaluate the benefits of the new software package, a random sample of 24 systems analysts is selected. Each analyst is given specifications for a hypothetical information system, and 12 of the analysts are instructed to produce the information system by using current technology. The other 12 analysts are first trained in the use of the new software package and then instructed to use it to produce the information system.

In this study, there are two populations: a population of systems analysts using the current technology and a population of systems analysts using the new software package. In terms of the time required to complete the information-system design project, the population means are

$$\mu_1 = \text{the mean project-completion time for systems analysts using the current technology}$$

and

$$\mu_2 = \text{the mean project-completion time for systems analysts using the new software package.}$$

The researcher in charge of the new software-evaluation project hopes to show that the new software package will provide a shorter mean project-completion time. Thus, the researcher is looking for evidence to conclude that μ_2 is less than μ_1; in this case, the difference between the two population means, $\mu_1 - \mu_2$, will be greater than zero. The research hypothesis $\mu_1 - \mu_2 > 0$ is stated as the alternative hypothesis.

$$H_0: \mu_1 - \mu_2 \leq 0$$
$$H_a: \mu_1 - \mu_2 > 0$$

In tentatively assuming H_0 is true, we are taking the position that using the new software package takes as much time or perhaps even more than the current technology. The researcher is looking for evidence to reject H_0 and conclude that the new software package ensures a shorter mean completion time.

Suppose that the 24 analysts complete the study with the results shown in Table 10.9. Under the assumption that the variances of the populations are equal, (10.8) is used to compute the pooled estimate of σ^2.

TABLE 10.9 Results of Study

Current Technology	New Software Package
$n_1 = 12$	$n_2 = 12$
$\bar{x}_1 = 325$ hours	$\bar{x}_2 = 288$ hours
$s_1 = 40$ hours	$s_2 = 44$ hours

$$s^2 = \frac{(n_1 - 1)s_1^2 + (n_2 - 1)s_2^2}{n_1 + n_2 - 2} = \frac{11(40)^2 + 11(44)^2}{12 + 12 - 2} = 1768$$

The test statistic for the small-sample case is

$$t = \frac{(\bar{x}_1 - \bar{x}_2) - (\mu_1 - \mu_2)}{\sqrt{s^2\left(\frac{1}{n_1} + \frac{1}{n_2}\right)}}$$

(10.12)

In the case of two independent random samples of sizes n_1 and n_2, the t distribution will have $n_1 + n_2 - 2$ degrees of freedom. For $\alpha = .05$, the t distribution table shows that with $12 + 12 - 2 = 22$ degrees of freedom, $t_{.05} = 1.717$. Thus, the rejection region for the one-tailed test is

$$\text{Reject } H_0 \text{ if } t > 1.717.$$

The sample data and (10.12) provide the following value for the test statistic.

$$t = \frac{(325 - 288) - 0}{\sqrt{1768\left(\frac{1}{12} + \frac{1}{12}\right)}} = 2.16$$

Checking the rejection region, we see that $t = 2.16$ allows the rejection of H_0 at the .05 level of significance. Thus, the sample results enable the researcher to conclude that the new software package provides a shorter mean completion time.

THE ROLE OF THE COMPUTER

Computer software packages can be used for testing hypotheses about the difference between the means of two populations. We will illustrate the use of Minitab to perform the t-test for the case involving the use of the new software package to produce an information system (see Table 10.9). Assume the user has entered the completion times for the 12 systems analysts who used the current technology into column 1 of a Minitab worksheet and those of the 12 systems analysts who used the new software package into column 2; column 1 is labeled CURRENT and column 2 is labeled NEW. Using the Minitab 2-Sample t option, we obtained the hypothesis-testing output shown in Figure 10.6. The first part of the output gives the mean completion time, the standard deviation, and the standard error of the mean for the two samples. The row beginning with TTEST provides the hypothesis-testing results. The output TTEST MU CURRENT = MU NEW (VS GT) indicates that we have elected to perform a one-tailed test with a greater-than alternative hypothesis. With a p-value of .021, we can reject the null hypothesis at the .05 level of significance; thus, the conclusion is that the new software package provides a shorter mean completion time.

Note that the computer solution also provides the 95% confidence interval for the difference between the two population means. Although the hypothesis test enables us to conclude that the new software is better, the 95% confidence interval shows that on average the improvement that can be expected with the new software may be as little as one hour or as much as 73 hours. The wide confidence interval suggests that further

```
Twosample T for CURRENT vs NEW
              N       Mean      StDev    SE Mean
CURRENT     12       325.0      40.0        12
NEW         12       288.0      44.0        13


95% C.I. for mu CURRENT - mu NEW: (1, 73)


T-Test mu CURRENT = mu NEW (vs >): T= 2.16   P=0
```

FIGURE 10.6   Minitab Output for the Hypothesis Test About the Current and New Software Technology

study may be desirable to obtain a more precise estimate of how much improvement can be anticipated with the new software package.

NOTES AND COMMENTS

1. In the preceding section we stated that using the t distribution for inferences about the means of two populations is fairly insensitive to the assumptions of normal populations and equal variances. However, if a user feels strongly that these assumptions are not appropriate for a particular application, one of the following actions should be taken:

   a. Consider the nonparametric Wilcoxon rank sum test presented in Chapter 19.

   b. If the populations are approximately normally distributed but the variances may not be equal ($\sigma_1^2 \neq \sigma_2^2$), use (10.5) to estimate $\sigma_{\bar{x}_1 - \bar{x}_2}$. The t distribution can still be used, with the degrees of freedom given by

$$df = \frac{[1/n_1 + (s_2^2/s_1^2)/n_2]^2}{[1/n_1^2(n_1 - 1)] + [(s_2^2/s_1^2)^2/n_2^2(n_2 - 1)]}.$$

   c. Increase both sample sizes to the large-sample case with $n_1 \geq 30$ and $n_2 \geq 30$.

2. In hypothesis tests about the difference between the means of two populations, the null hypothesis almost always contains the condition that there is no difference between the means. Hence, the following null hypotheses are possible choices.

$$H_0: \mu_1 - \mu_2 = 0 \qquad H_0: \mu_1 - \mu_2 \leq 0 \qquad H_0: \mu_1 - \mu_2 \geq 0$$

   In some instances, we may want to determine whether there is a nonzero difference D_0 between the population means. The specific value chosen for D_0 depends on the application under study. However, in this case, the null hypothesis may be of the following forms.

$$H_0: \mu_1 - \mu_2 = D_0 \qquad H_0: \mu_1 - \mu_2 \leq D_0 \qquad H_0: \mu_1 - \mu_2 \geq D_0$$

   The hypothesis-testing computations remain the same with the exception that D_0 is used for the value of $\mu_1 - \mu_2$ in (10.11) and (10.12).

EXERCISES

METHODS

Self-Test

11. Consider the following hypothesis test.

$$H_0: \mu_1 - \mu_2 \leq 0$$
$$H_a: \mu_1 - \mu_2 > 0$$

The results in Table 10.10 are for two independent samples taken from the two populations.
   a. With $\alpha = .05$, what is your hypothesis-testing conclusion?
   b. What is the p-value?

TABLE 10.10 Exercise 11

Sample 1	Sample 2
$n_1 = 40$	$n_2 = 50$
$\bar{x}_1 = 25.2$	$\bar{x}_2 = 22.8$
$s_1 = 5.2$	$s_2 = 6.0$

12. Consider the following hypothesis test.

$$H_0: \mu_1 - \mu_2 = 0$$
$$H_a: \mu_1 - \mu_2 \neq 0$$

The following results are for two independent samples taken from the two populations.

Sample 1	Sample 2
$n_1 = 80$	$n_2 = 70$
$\bar{x}_1 = 104$	$\bar{x}_2 = 106$
$s_1 = 8.4$	$s_2 = 7.6$

a. With $\alpha = .05$, what is your hypothesis-testing conclusion?

b. What is the p-value?

13. Consider the following hypothesis test.

$$H_0: \mu_1 - \mu_2 = 0$$

$$H_a: \mu_1 - \mu_2 \neq 0$$

TABLE 10.11 Exercise 13

Sample 1	Sample 2
$n_1 = 8$	$n_2 = 7$
$\bar{x}_1 = 1.4$	$\bar{x}_2 = 1.0$
$s_1 = 0.4$	$s_2 = 0.6$

The results in Table 10.11 are for two independent samples taken from the two populations. With $\alpha = .05$, what is your hypothesis-testing conclusion?

APPLICATIONS

14. Refer to Exercise 6, in which two independent random samples of business travelers rated the Miami and Los Angeles airports. Summary statistics follow.

Airport	Sample Size	Sample Mean	Sample Standard Deviation
Miami	50	6.34	2.163
Los Angeles	50	6.72	2.374

Is the mean rating for the Los Angeles airport greater than the mean rating for the Miami airport? Support your conclusion with a statistical test using a .05 level of significance.

Self-Test

15. The Greystone Department Store study in Section 10.1 supplied the following data on customer ages from independent random samples taken at two store locations.

Inner-City Store	Suburban Store
$n_1 = 36$	$n_2 = 49$
$\bar{x}_1 = 40$ years	$\bar{x}_2 = 35$ years
$s_1 = 9$ years	$s_2 = 10$ years

For $\alpha = .05$, test $H_0: \mu_1 - \mu_2 = 0$ against the alternative $H_a: \mu_1 - \mu_2 \neq 0$. What is your conclusion about the mean ages of the populations of customers at the two stores?

16. The Educational Testing Service conducted a study to investigate differences between the scores of male and female students on the Scholastic Aptitude Test (*Journal of Educational Measurement,* Spring 1987). The study identified a random sample of 562 female and 852 male students who had achieved the same high score on the mathematics portion of the test. That is, the female and male students were viewed as having similarly high abilities in

TABLE 10.12 Exercise 16

Female Students	Male Students
$\bar{x}_1 = 547$	$\bar{x}_2 = 525$
$s_1 = 83$	$s_2 = 78$

mathematics. The SAT verbal scores for the two samples are summarized in Table 10.12. Do the data support the conclusion that given a population of female students and a population of male students with similarly high mathematical abilities, that the female students will have a significantly higher verbal ability? Test at a .02 level of significance. What is your conclusion?

17. A firm is studying the delivery times of two raw material suppliers. The firm is basically satisfied with supplier A and is prepared to stay with that supplier if the mean delivery time is the same as or less than that of supplier B. However, if the firm finds that the mean delivery time of supplier B is less than that of supplier A, it will begin making raw material purchases from supplier B.
   a. What are the null and alternative hypotheses for this situation?
   b. Assume that independent samples show the following delivery time characteristics for the two suppliers.

Supplier A	Supplier B
$n_1 = 50$	$n_2 = 30$
$\bar{x}_1 = 14$ days	$\bar{x}_2 = 12.5$ days
$s_1 = 3$ days	$s_2 = 2$ days

With $\alpha = .05$, what is your conclusion for the hypotheses from part (a)? What action do you recommend in terms of supplier selection?

TABLE 10.13 Exercise 18

Male Employees	Female Employees
$n_1 = 44$	$n_2 = 32$
$\bar{x}_1 = \$9.25$	$\bar{x}_2 = \$8.70$
$s_1 = \$1.00$	$s_2 = \$.80$

18. In a wage discrimination case involving male and female employees, independent samples of male and female employees with five years' experience or more provided the hourly wage results shown in Table 10.13. The null hypothesis is that male employees have a mean hourly wage less than or equal to that of the female employees. Rejection of H_0 leads to the conclusion that male employees have a mean hourly wage exceeding that of the female employees. Test the hypothesis with $\alpha = .01$. Does wage discrimination appear to be present in this case?

19. A production line is designed on the assumption that the difference between mean assembly times for two operations is five minutes. Independent tests for the two assembly operations yield the following results.

Operation A	Operation B
$n_1 = 100$	$n_2 = 50$
$\bar{x}_1 = 14.8$ minutes	$\bar{x}_2 = 10.4$ minutes
$s_1 = .8$ minutes	$s_2 = .6$ minutes

TABLE 10.14 Exercise 20

Accounting	Finance
28.8	26.3
25.3	23.6
26.2	25.0
27.9	23.0
27.0	27.9
26.2	24.5
28.1	29.0
24.7	27.4
25.2	23.5
29.2	26.9
29.7	26.2
29.3	24.0

Using $\alpha = .02$, test the hypothesis that the difference between the mean assembly times is $\mu_1 - \mu_2 = 5$ minutes.

20. Starting salary data for college graduates is reported by the College Placement Council (*USA Today,* April 6, 1992). Annual salaries in thousands of dollars for a sample of accounting majors and a sample of finance majors are listed in Table 10.14.
   a. Use a .05 level of significance to test the hypothesis that there is no difference between the mean annual starting salary of accounting majors and the mean annual starting salary of finance majors. What is your conclusion?
   b. Provide the point estimate and the 95% confidence interval for the difference between the mean starting salaries for the two majors.

10.3 INFERENCES ABOUT THE DIFFERENCE BETWEEN THE MEANS OF TWO POPULATIONS: MATCHED SAMPLES

Suppose a manufacturing company has two methods by which employees can perform a production task. To maximize production output, the company wants to identify the method with the shortest mean completion time per unit. Let μ_1 denote the mean completion time for production method 1 and μ_2 denote the mean completion time for production method 2. With no preliminary indication of the preferred production method, we begin by tentatively assuming that the two production methods have the same mean completion time. Thus, the null hypothesis is $H_0: \mu_1 - \mu_2 = 0$. If this hypothesis is rejected, we can conclude that the mean completion times differ. In this case, the method providing the shorter mean completion time would be recommended. The null and alternative hypotheses are written as follows.

$$H_0: \mu_1 - \mu_2 = 0$$
$$H_a: \mu_1 - \mu_2 \neq 0$$

In choosing the sampling procedure that will be used to collect production time data and test the hypotheses, we consider two alternative designs. One is based on *independent samples* and the other is based on *matched samples*.

1. *Independent-sample design:* A simple random sample of workers is selected and each worker uses method 1. A second independent simple random sample of workers is selected and each worker uses method 2. The test of the difference between means is based on the procedures in Section 10.2.

2. *Matched-sample design:* One simple random sample of workers is selected. Each worker first uses one method and then uses the other method. The order of the two methods is assigned randomly to the workers, with some workers performing method 1 first and others performing method 2 first. Each worker provides a pair of data values, one value for method 1 and another value for method 2.

In the matched-sample design the two production methods are tested under similar conditions (i.e., with the same workers); hence this design often leads to a smaller sampling error than the independent sample design. The primary reason is that in a matched-sample design, variation between workers is eliminated as a source of sampling error.

Let us demonstrate the analysis of a matched-sample design by assuming that it is the method used to test the difference between the two production methods. A random sample of six workers is used. The data on completion times for the six workers are given in Table 10.15. Note that each worker provides a pair of data values, one for each production method. Also note that the last column contains the difference in completion times d_i for each worker in the sample.

The key to the analysis of the matched-sample design is to realize that we consider only the column of differences. We therefore have six data values (.6, −.2, .5, .3, .0, and .6) that will be used to analyze the difference between the means of the two production methods.

Let $\mu_d = $ the mean of the *difference* values for the population of workers. With this notation, the null and alternative hypotheses are rewritten as follows.

$$H_0: \mu_d = 0$$
$$H_a: \mu_d \neq 0$$

If H_0 can be rejected, we can conclude that the mean completion times differ.

The d notation is a reminder that the matched sample provides *difference* data. The sample mean and sample standard deviation for the six difference values in Table 10.15 follow.

$$\bar{d} = \frac{\Sigma d_i}{n} = \frac{1.8}{6} = .30$$

$$s_d = \sqrt{\frac{\Sigma(d_i - \bar{d})^2}{n-1}} = \sqrt{\frac{.56}{5}} = .335$$

In Chapter 9 we stated that if the population can be assumed to be normally distributed, the t distribution with $n - 1$ degrees of freedom can be used to test the null hypothesis about a population mean. With difference data, the test statistic becomes

$$t = \frac{\bar{d} - \mu_d}{s_d/\sqrt{n}} \qquad\qquad \textbf{(10.13)}$$

With $\alpha = .05$ and $n - 1 = 5$ degrees of freedom ($t_{.025} = 2.571$), the rejection rule for the two-tailed test becomes

Reject H_0 if $t < -2.571$ or if $t > 2.571$.

With $\bar{d} = .30$, $s_d = .335$, and $n = 6$, the value of the test statistic for the null hypothesis H_0: $\mu_d = 0$ is

$$t = \frac{\bar{d} - \mu_d}{s_d/\sqrt{n}} = \frac{.30 - 0}{.335/\sqrt{6}} = 2.19$$

Since $t = 2.19$ is not in the rejection region, the sample data do not provide sufficient evidence to reject H_0.

Using the sample results, we can obtain an interval estimate of the difference between the two population means by using the single-population methodology of Chapter 8. The calculation follows.

$$0.3 \pm t_{\alpha/2}\frac{s_d}{\sqrt{n}}$$

$$0.3 \pm 2.571\frac{.335}{\sqrt{6}}$$

$$0.3 \pm .35$$

TABLE 10.15   Task-Completion Times for a Matched-Sample Design

Worker	Completion Time for Method 1 (minutes)	Completion Time for Method 2 (minutes)	Difference in Completion Times (d_i)
1	6.0	5.4	.6
2	5.0	5.2	−.2
3	7.0	6.5	.5
4	6.2	5.9	.3
5	6.0	6.0	.0
6	6.4	5.8	.6

Thus, the 95% confidence interval for the difference between the means of the two production methods is −.05 minutes to .65 minutes. Note that since the confidence interval includes the value of zero, the sample data do not provide sufficient evidence to reject H_0.

NOTES AND COMMENTS

1. In the example presented in this section, workers performed the production task with first one method and then the other method. This example illustrates a matched-sample design in which each sampled item (worker) provides a pair of data values. It is also possible to use different but "similar" items to provide the pair of data values. For example, a worker at one location could be matched with a similar worker at another location (similarity based on age, education, sex, experience, etc.). The pairs of workers would provide the difference data that could be used in the matched-sample analysis.

2. Since a matched-sample procedure for inferences about two population means generally provides better precision than the independent-sample approach, it is the recommended design. However, in some applications the matching cannot be achieved, or perhaps the time and cost associated with matching are excessive. In such cases, the independent-sample design should be used.

3. The example presented in this section had a sample size of six workers and thus was a small-sample case. The t distribution was used in both the hypothesis-test and interval-estimation computations. If the sample size is large $(n \geq 30)$, use of the t distribution is unnecessary; in such cases, statistical inferences can be based on the z values of the standard normal probability distribution.

EXERCISES

METHODS

21. Consider the following hypothesis test.

$$H_0: \mu_d \leq 0$$

$$H_a: \mu_d > 0$$

The following data are from matched samples taken from two populations.

	Population	
Element	1	2
1	21	20
2	28	26
3	18	18
4	20	20
5	26	24

TABLE 10.16 Exercise 22

	Population	
Element	1	2
1	11	8
2	7	8
3	9	6
4	12	7
5	13	10
.6	15	15
7	15	14

Self-Test

a. Compute the difference value for each element.
b. Compute $\bar{d}$.
c. Compute the standard deviation s_d.
d. Test the hypothesis using $\alpha = .05$. What is your conclusion?

22. The data in Table 10.16 are from matched samples taken from two populations.
   a. Compute the difference value for each element.
   b. Compute $\bar{d}$.
   c. Compute the standard deviation s_d.
   d. What is the point estimate of the difference between the two population means?
   e. Provide a 95% confidence interval for the difference between the two population means.

APPLICATIONS

23. A market research firm used a sample of individuals to rate the purchase potential of a particular product before and after the individuals saw a new television commercial about the product. The purchase-potential ratings were based on a 0 to 10 scale, with higher values indicating a higher purchase potential. The null hypothesis stated that the mean rating "after" would be less than or equal to the mean rating "before." Rejection of this hypothesis would show that the commercial improved the mean purchase-potential rating. Use $\alpha = .05$ and the following data to test the hypothesis and comment on the value of the commercial.

	Purchase Rating			Purchase Rating	
Individual	After	Before	Individual	After	Before
1	6	5	5	3	5
2	6	4	6	9	8
3	7	7	7	7	5
4	4	3	8	6	6

24. To investigate the amount of savings due to purchasing store brands versus name brand products, *Consumer Reports* shopped for a list of items at an A&P grocery store. One cart was filled with national brand products and the other cart was filled with the store brands of the same products (*Consumer Reports,* September 1993). A portion of the data obtained follows.

Product, Size	Name Brand Price ($)	Store Brand Price ($)
Ketchup, 2 lb.	1.69	0.79
Coffee, 12 oz.	2.79	1.59
Soda, 6-pack	2.79	1.64
Paper towels, 90 sheets	1.39	0.50
Ice cream, 1/2 gal.	3.99	2.39
American cheese, 1 lb.	3.99	2.99
Thin spaghetti, 1 lb.	0.89	0.53
Butter, 1 lb.	2.39	1.69
White rice, 5 lb.	3.99	1.59
Vegetable oil, qt.	2.19	1.69

   a. Does the sampling procedure used by *Consumer Reports* represent an independent-sample design or a matched-sample design? Explain.
   b. Develop a 95% confidence interval for the difference in price between name brand products and store brand products. What assumption was necessary to develop your interval estimate?

25. The cost of transportation from the airport to the downtown area depends on the method of transportation. One-way costs ($) for taxi and shuttle bus transportation for a sample of 10 major cities follow (*USA Today*, February 13, 1992). Provide a 95% confidence interval for the mean cost increase associated with taxi transportation.

City	Taxi	Shuttle Bus	City	Taxi	Shuttle Bus
Atlanta	15	7	Minneapolis	16.5	7.5
Chicago	22	12.5	New Orleans	18	7
Denver	11	5	New York (LaGuardia)	16	8.5
Houston	15	4.5	Philadelphia	20	8
Los Angeles	26	11	Washington, D.C.	10	5

TABLE 10.17 Exercise 26

Respondent	Television	Reading
1	10	6
2	14	16
3	16	8
4	18	10
5	15	10
6	14	8
7	10	14
8	12	14
9	4	7
10	8	8
11	16	5
12	5	10
13	8	3
14	19	10
15	11	6

26. A survey was made of Book-of-the-Month-Club members to ascertain whether members spend more time watching television than they do reading (*The Cincinnati Enquirer*, November 21, 1991). Assume a small sample of respondents in this survey provided the weekly hours of television watching and weekly hours of reading listed in Table 10.17. Using a .05 level of significance, can you conclude that Book-of-the-Month-Club members spend more time per week, on average, watching television than reading?

27. A manufacturer produces both a deluxe and a standard model of an automatic sander designed for home use. Selling prices obtained from a sample of retail outlets follow.

Retail Outlet	Model Price ($) Deluxe	Model Price ($) Standard	Retail Outlet	Model Price ($) Deluxe	Model Price ($) Standard
1	39	27	5	40	30
2	39	28	6	39	34
3	45	35	7	35	29
4	38	30			

a. The manufacturer's suggested retail prices for the two models show a $10 price differential. Using a .05 level of significance, test that the mean difference between the prices of the two models is $10.

b. What is the 95% confidence interval for the difference between the mean prices of the two models?

TABLE 10.18 Exercise 28

Salesperson	Weekly Sales Before	Weekly Sales After
1	15	18
2	12	14
3	18	19
4	15	18
5	16	18

28. A company attempts to evaluate the potential for a new bonus plan by selecting a random sample of five salespersons to use the bonus plan for a trial period. The weekly sales volumes before and after implementation of the bonus plan are shown in Table 10.18.

a. Use $\alpha = .05$ and test to see whether the bonus plan will result in an increase in the mean weekly sales.

b. Provide a 90% confidence interval for the mean increase in weekly sales that can be expected if a new bonus plan is implemented.

29. Word-processing systems are often justified on the basis of improved efficiency for a secretarial staff. The following typing rates in words per minute are for seven secretaries who previously used electronic typewriters and who are now using computer-based word processors. Test at the .05 level of significance to see whether the mean typing rate has increased with the word-processing system.

Secretary	Electronic Typewriter	Word Processor	Secretary	Electronic Typewriter	Word Processor
1	72	75	5	52	55
2	68	66	6	55	57
3	55	60	7	64	64
4	58	64			

10.4   INFERENCES ABOUT THE DIFFERENCE BETWEEN THE PROPORTIONS OF TWO POPULATIONS

A tax preparation firm is interested in comparing the quality of work at two of its regional offices. By randomly selecting samples of tax returns prepared at each office and having the sample returns verified for accuracy, the firm will be able to estimate the proportion of erroneous returns prepared at each office. Of particular interest is the difference between these proportions.

Let

p_1 = proportion of erroneous returns for population 1 (office 1),

p_2 = proportion of erroneous returns for population 2 (office 2),

$\bar{p}_1$ = sample proportion for a simple random sample from population 1, and

$\bar{p}_2$ = sample proportion for a simple random sample from population 2

The difference between the two population proportions is given by $p_1 - p_2$. The point estimator of $p_1 - p_2$ follows.

POINT ESTIMATOR OF THE DIFFERENCE BETWEEN THE PROPORTIONS OF TWO POPULATIONS

$$\bar{p}_1 - \bar{p}_2 \qquad (10.14)$$

Thus, the point estimator of the difference between two population proportions is the difference between the sample proportions of two independent simple random samples.

SAMPLING DISTRIBUTION OF $\bar{p}_1 - \bar{p}_2$

In the study of the difference between two population proportions, $\bar{p}_1 - \bar{p}_2$ is the point estimator of interest. As we have seen in several preceding cases, the sampling distribution of the point estimator is a key factor in developing interval estimates and in testing hypotheses about the parameters of interest. The properties of the sampling distribution of $\bar{p}_1 - \bar{p}_2$ follow.

> ### SAMPLING DISTRIBUTION OF $\bar{p}_1 - \bar{p}_2$
>
> $$\text{Expected Value: } E(\bar{p}_1 - \bar{p}_2) = p_1 - p_2 \tag{10.15}$$
>
> $$\text{Standard Deviation: } \sigma_{\bar{p}_1 - \bar{p}_2} = \sqrt{\frac{p_1(1 - p_1)}{n_1} + \frac{p_2(1 - p_2)}{n_2}} \tag{10.16}$$
>
> where
>
> n_1 = sample size for the simple random sample from population 1
>
> n_2 = sample size for the simple random sample from population 2
>
> Distribution form: If the sample sizes are large (i.e., $n_1 p_1$, $n_1(1 - p_1)$, $n_2 p_2$, and $n_2(1 - p_2)$ are all greater than or equal to 5), the sampling distribution of $\bar{p}_1 - \bar{p}_2$ can be approximated by a normal probability distribution.

Figure 10.7 shows the sampling distribution of $\bar{p}_1 - \bar{p}_2$.

INTERVAL ESTIMATION OF $p_1 - p_2$

Let us assume that independent simple random samples of tax returns from the two offices provide the following information.

Office 1	Office 2
$n_1 = 250$	$n_2 = 300$
Number of returns with errors = 35	Number of returns with errors = 27

The sample proportions for the two offices follow.

$$\bar{p}_1 = \frac{35}{250} = .14$$

$$\bar{p}_2 = \frac{27}{300} = .09$$

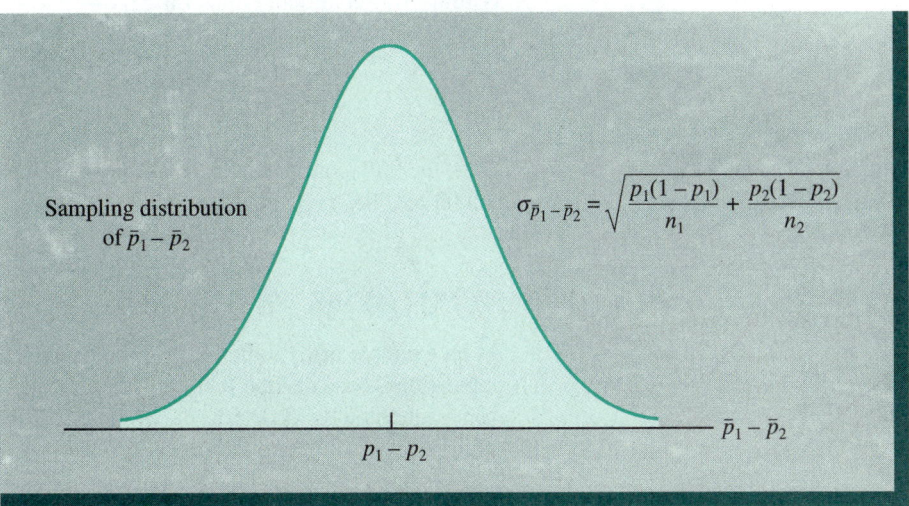

FIGURE 10.7 Sampling Distribution of $\bar{p}_1 - \bar{p}_2$

The point estimate of the difference between the proportions of erroneous tax returns for the two populations is $\bar{p}_1 - \bar{p}_2 = .14 - .09 = .05$. Specifically, we are led to believe that office 1 has a 5% greater error rate than office 2. However, as with all point estimates, we know that the .05 difference is only one of many possible sample values for the difference between the two population proportions. The following expression can be used to develop an interval estimate of the difference between the proportions of the two populations.

> **INTERVAL ESTIMATE OF THE DIFFERENCE BETWEEN THE PROPORTIONS OF TWO POPULATIONS: LARGE-SAMPLE CASE WITH** $n_1 p_1, n_1(1 - p_1), n_2 p_2,$ **and** $n_2(1 - p_2) \geq 5$
>
> $$\bar{p}_1 - \bar{p}_2 \pm z_{\alpha/2} \sigma_{\bar{p}_1 - \bar{p}_2} \tag{10.17}$$
>
> where $1 - \alpha$ is the confidence coefficient.

Let us use (10.17) to develop an interval estimate of the difference between the population proportions of erroneous tax returns at the two offices. Since p_1 and p_2 are unknown, we cannot use (10.16) to calculate $\sigma_{\bar{p}_1 - \bar{p}_2}$. However, using $\bar{p}_1$, the point estimator of p_1, and $\bar{p}_2$, the point estimator of p_2, we can estimate $\sigma_{\bar{p}_1 - \bar{p}_2}$ as follows.

> **POINT ESTIMATOR OF** $\sigma_{\bar{p}_1 - \bar{p}_2}$
>
> $$s_{\bar{p}_1 - \bar{p}_2} = \sqrt{\frac{\bar{p}_1(1 - \bar{p}_1)}{n_1} + \frac{\bar{p}_2(1 - \bar{p}_2)}{n_2}} \tag{10.18}$$

This expression provides an estimate of $\sigma_{\bar{p}_1 - \bar{p}_2}$ and can be used in (10.17) to obtain an interval estimate of $p_1 - p_2$.

Using (10.18), we have

$$s_{\bar{p}_1 - \bar{p}_2} = \sqrt{\frac{.14(.86)}{250} + \frac{.09(.91)}{300}} = .0275$$

With a 90% confidence interval $z_{\alpha/2} = z_{.05} = 1.645$; (10.17) provides the following interval estimate.

$$(.14 - .09) \pm 1.645(.0275)$$
$$.05 \pm .045$$

Thus, the 90% confidence interval for the difference between the two offices' error rates is .005 to .095.

HYPOTHESIS TESTS ABOUT $p_1 - p_2$

As an example of hypothesis tests about the difference between the proportions of two populations, consider the data collected in the preceding example and assume that the firm is attempting to determine whether the error proportions differ between the two offices. Let us illustrate the procedure we can use to test the following hypotheses.

$$H_0: p_1 - p_2 = 0$$
$$H_a: p_1 - p_2 \neq 0$$

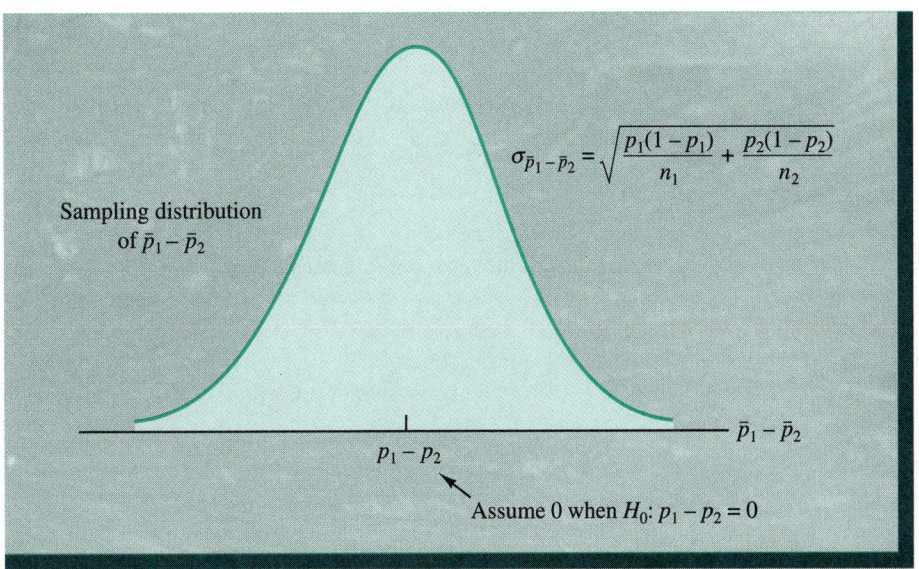

FIGURE 10.8 Sampling Distribution of $\bar{p}_1 - \bar{p}_2$ with $H_0: p_1 - p_2 = 0$

Figure 10.8 shows the sampling distribution of $\bar{p}_1 - \bar{p}_2$ based on the assumption that there is no difference between the two population proportions. That is, $p_1 - p_2 = 0$. With the sampling distribution approximately normal, the test statistic for the difference between two population proportions can be written

$$z = \frac{(\bar{p}_1 - \bar{p}_2) - (p_1 - p_2)}{\sigma_{\bar{p}_1 - \bar{p}_2}} \tag{10.19}$$

With $\alpha = .10$ and $z_{\alpha/2} = z_{.05} = 1.645$, the rejection rule is

Reject H_0 if $z < -1.645$ or if $z > 1.645$

The computation of z in (10.19) requires a value for the standard error of the difference between proportions $\sigma_{\bar{p}_1 - \bar{p}_2}$. Since this standard error is unknown, it must be estimated from the sample data. We may be tempted to use $\bar{p}_1$ and $\bar{p}_2$ in (10.18) as we did with the interval-estimation procedure, but in hypothesis testing we often adjust (10.18) to a slightly different form. For the *special case* in which the hypotheses involve no difference between the population proportions (i.e., either $H_0: p_1 - p_2 = 0$, $H_0: p_1 - p_2 \leq 0$, or $H_0: p_1 - p_2 \geq 0$), (10.18) is modified to reflect the fact that when we assume H_0 to be true at the equality, we are assuming $p_1 = p_2$. When this occurs, we combine or *pool* the two sample proportions to provide one estimate. This pooled estimator, denoted by $\bar{p}$, follows.

$$\bar{p} = \frac{n_1 \bar{p}_1 + n_2 \bar{p}_2}{n_1 + n_2} \tag{10.20}$$

With $\bar{p}$ used in place of both $\bar{p}_1$ and $\bar{p}_2$, (10.18) is revised to

$$s_{\bar{p}_1 - \bar{p}_2} = \sqrt{\bar{p}(1 - \bar{p})\left(\frac{1}{n_1} + \frac{1}{n_2}\right)} \tag{10.21}$$

Using (10.20) and (10.21), we can now proceed with the calculations.

$$\bar{p} = \frac{250(.14) + 300(.09)}{550} = \frac{62}{550} = .113$$

$$s_{\bar{p}_1-\bar{p}_2} = \sqrt{(.113)(.887)\left(\frac{1}{250} + \frac{1}{300}\right)} = .0271$$

Using (10.19), the value of the test statistic becomes

$$z = \frac{(\bar{p}_1 - \bar{p}_2) - (p_1 - p_2)}{s_{\bar{p}_1-\bar{p}_2}} = \frac{(.14 - .09) - 0}{.0271} = 1.85$$

Since $1.85 > 1.645$, at the .10 level of significance the null hypothesis is rejected. The sample evidence indicates a significant difference between the two offices' error proportions.

As we saw with the hypothesis tests about differences between two population means, one-tailed tests can be developed for the difference between two population proportions. The one-tailed rejection regions are established as in the one-tailed hypothesis-testing procedures for a single-population proportion.

EXERCISES

METHODS

TABLE 10.19 Exercise 30

Sample 1	Sample 2
$n_1 = 400$	$n_2 = 300$
$\bar{p}_1 = .48$	$\bar{p}_2 = .36$

30. Consider the results in Table 10.19 for two independent samples taken from two populations.
   a. What is the point estimate of the difference between the two population proportions?
   b. Develop a 90% confidence interval for the difference between the two population proportions.
   c. Develop a 95% confidence interval for the difference between the two population proportions.

Self-Test ••••••••••▶

31. Consider the following hypothesis test.

TABLE 10.20 Exercise 31

Sample 1	Sample 2
$n_1 = 200$	$n_2 = 300$
$\bar{p}_1 = .22$	$\bar{p}_2 = .16$

$$H_0: p_1 - p_2 \geq 0$$
$$H_a: p_1 - p_2 < 0$$

The results in Table 10.20 are for two independent samples taken from the two populations.
   a. With $\alpha = .05$, what is your hypothesis-testing conclusion?
   b. What is the p-value?

APPLICATIONS

32. *Business Week*/Harris polls (*Business Week,* April 6, 1992) compared the views adults held about their children's future in 1989 with those held in 1992. In a 1989 poll, 59% of the adults sampled felt their children would have a better life than they had. In a 1992 poll, 34% of the adults sampled felt their children would have a better life. Assume that 1250 adults were used in both polls. Provide a 95% confidence interval estimate of the difference between the proportions in 1989 and 1992. What is your interpretation of the interval estimate and the difference shown?

33. A 1994 Gallup poll found that 16% of 505 men and 25% of 496 women surveyed favored a law forbidding the sale of all beer, wine, and liquor throughout the nation (*The Gallup Poll Monthly,* June 1994). Develop a 95% confidence interval for the difference between the proportion of women who favor such a ban and the proportion of men who favor such a ban.

34. In December 1993, the women and family issues committee of the American Institute of Certified Public Accountants (AICPA) mailed surveys asking about family-friendly policies and women's upward mobility to 5300 firms of all sizes (excluding sole practitioners). Of the 1710 responses, 57% were from firms with five or fewer AICPA members, 26% were from firms with six to 10 members, 9% were from firms with 11 to 20 members, and 8% were from firms with more than 20 members. For the firms with fewer than five AICPA members, 58% of the hires within the previous three years were women and 42% were men. In contrast, firms with more than 20 AICPA members hired 43% women and 57% men (*Journal of Accountancy,* October 1994). Develop a 95% confidence interval estimate of the difference between the proportion of women hired by firms with fewer than five AICPA members and the proportion of women hired by firms with more than 20 AICPA members.

35. Two loan officers at the North Ridge National Bank show the following data for defaults on loans that they have approved (the data are based on samples of loans granted over the past five years).

Loan Officer	Loans Reviewed in the Sample	Defaulted Loans
A	60	9
B	80	6

Using $\alpha = .05$, test the hypothesis that the default rates are the same for the two loan officers.

36. A sample of 1545 men and an independent sample of 1691 women were used to compare the amount of housework done by women and men in dual-earner marriages. The study showed that 67.5% of the men felt the division of housework was fair and 60.8% of the women felt the division of housework was fair (*American Journal of Sociology,* September 1994). Is the proportion of men who felt the division of housework was fair greater than the proportion of women who felt the division of housework was fair? Support your conclusion with a statistical test using a .05 level of significance.

37. A survey firm conducts door-to-door surveys on a variety of issues. Some individuals cooperate with the interviewer and complete the interview questionnaire and others do not. The sample data in Table 10.21 are available.
   a. Using $\alpha = .05$, test the hypothesis that the response rate is the same for both men and women.
   b. Compute the 95% confidence interval for the difference between the proportions of men and women who cooperate with the survey.

TABLE 10.21　Exercise 37

Respondents	Sample Size	Number Cooperating
Men	200	110
Women	300	210

38. In a test of the quality of two television commercials, each commercial was shown in a separate test area six times over a one-week period. The following week a telephone survey was conducted to identify individuals who had seen the commercials. The individuals who had seen the commercials were asked to state the primary message in the commercials. The following results were recorded.

Commercial	Number Who Saw Commercial	Number Who Recalled Primary Message
A	150	63
B	200	60

   a. Using $\alpha = .05$, test the hypothesis that there is no difference in the recall proportions for the two commercials.
   b. Compute a 95% confidence interval for the difference between the recall proportions for the two populations.

39. In a study designed to test the effectiveness of a new drug for treating rheumatoid arthritis, investigators divided 73 rheumatoid arthritis patients between the ages of 18 and 75 into three groups. Patients in one group were given a high dose of the drug, patients in another group were given a low dose, and patients in the third group were given a placebo. After four weeks, 19 of 24 patients in the high-dosage group indicated that they felt better, whereas 11 of the 25 patients in the low-dosage group and two of the 24 patients in the placebo group felt better (*The Lancet,* October 1994).
   a. Is the proportion of patients who felt better in the high-dosage group greater than the proportion of patients who felt better in the low-dosage group? What is your conclusion? Use $\alpha = .05$ for any statistical test.

    b. Suppose the researcher wanted to compare the new drug to the placebo. Can such a test be conducted with the data available in this study? Explain.

SUMMARY

In this chapter we discussed procedures for developing interval estimates and conducting hypothesis tests involving two populations. First, we showed how to make inferences about the difference between the means of two populations when independent simple random samples are selected. We considered both the large- and small-sample cases. The z values from the standard normal probability distribution are used for inferences about the difference between two population means when the sample sizes are large. In the small-sample case, if the populations are normally distributed with equal variances, the t distribution is used for inferences.

Inferences about the difference between the means of two populations were then discussed for the matched-sample design. In the matched-sample design each element provides a pair of data values, one from each population. The difference between the paired data values is then used in the statistical analysis. The matched-sample design is generally preferred to the independent-sample design because the matched-sample procedure often reduces the sampling error and improves the precision of the estimate.

Finally, interval estimation and hypothesis testing about the difference between two population proportions were discussed. Statistical procedures for analyzing the difference between proportions for two populations are similar to the procedures for analyzing the difference between two population means.

GLOSSARY

Pooled variance   An estimate of the variance of a population based on the combination of two (or more) sample results. The pooled variance estimate is appropriate whenever the variances of two (or more) populations are assumed equal.

Independent samples   Samples selected from two (or more) populations in such a way that the elements making up one sample are chosen independently of the elements making up the other sample(s).

Matched samples   Samples in which each data value of one sample is matched with a corresponding data value of the other sample.

KEY FORMULAS

Point Estimator of the Difference between the Means of Two Populations

$$\bar{x}_1 - \bar{x}_2 \tag{10.1}$$

Expected Value of $\bar{x}_1 - \bar{x}_2$

$$E(\bar{x}_1 - \bar{x}_2) = \mu_1 - \mu_2 \tag{10.2}$$

Standard Deviation of $\bar{x}_1 - \bar{x}_2$

$$\sigma_{\bar{x}_1 - \bar{x}_2} = \sqrt{\frac{\sigma_1^2}{n_1} + \frac{\sigma_2^2}{n_2}} \tag{10.3}$$

Interval Estimate of the Difference between the Means of Two Populations: Large-Sample Case ($n_1 \geq 30$ and $n_2 \geq 30$) with σ_1 and σ_2 Known

$$\bar{x}_1 - \bar{x}_2 \pm z_{\alpha/2}\, \sigma_{\bar{x}_1 - \bar{x}_2} \tag{10.4}$$

Point Estimator of $\sigma_{\bar{x}_1 - \bar{x}_2}$

$$s_{\bar{x}_1 - \bar{x}_2} = \sqrt{\frac{s_1^2}{n_1} + \frac{s_2^2}{n_2}} \tag{10.5}$$

Interval Estimate of the Difference between the Means of Two Populations: Large-Sample Case ($n_1 \geq 30$ and $n_2 \geq 30$) with σ_1 and σ_2 Unknown

$$\bar{x}_1 - \bar{x}_2 \pm z_{\alpha/2}\, s_{\bar{x}_1 - \bar{x}_2} \tag{10.6}$$

Standard Deviation of $\bar{x}_1 - \bar{x}_2$ when $\sigma_1^2 = \sigma_2^2$

$$\sigma_{\bar{x}_1 - \bar{x}_2} = \sqrt{\frac{\sigma^2}{n_1} + \frac{\sigma^2}{n_2}} = \sqrt{\sigma^2 \left(\frac{1}{n_1} + \frac{1}{n_2} \right)} \tag{10.7}$$

Pooled Estimator of σ^2

$$s^2 = \frac{(n_1 - 1)s_1^2 + (n_2 - 1)s_2^2}{n_1 + n_2 - 2} \tag{10.8}$$

Point Estimator of $\sigma_{\bar{x}_1 - \bar{x}_2}$ when $\sigma_1^2 = \sigma_2^2 = \sigma^2$

$$s_{\bar{x}_1 - \bar{x}_2} = \sqrt{s^2 \left(\frac{1}{n_1} + \frac{1}{n_2} \right)} \tag{10.9}$$

Interval Estimate of the Difference between the Means of Two Populations: Small-Sample Case ($n_1 < 30$ and/or $n_2 < 30$)

$$\bar{x}_1 - \bar{x}_2 \pm t_{\alpha/2} s_{\bar{x}_1 - \bar{x}_2} \tag{10.10}$$

Test Statistic for Hypothesis Tests about the Difference between the Means of Two Populations (Large-Sample Case)

$$z = \frac{(\bar{x}_1 - \bar{x}_2) - (\mu_1 - \mu_2)}{\sqrt{\sigma_1^2/n_1 + \sigma_2^2/n_2}} \tag{10.11}$$

Test Statistic for Hypothesis Tests about the Difference between the Means of Two Populations (Small-Sample Case)

$$t = \frac{(\bar{x}_1 - \bar{x}_2) - (\mu_1 - \mu_2)}{\sqrt{s^2 \left(\frac{1}{n_1} + \frac{1}{n_2} \right)}} \tag{10.12}$$

Sample Mean for Matched Samples

$$\bar{d} = \frac{\Sigma d_i}{n}$$

Sample Standard Deviation for Matched Samples

$$s_d = \sqrt{\frac{\Sigma(d_i - \bar{d})^2}{n - 1}}$$

Test Statistic for Matched Samples

$$t = \frac{\bar{d} - \mu_d}{s_d/\sqrt{n}} \qquad (10.13)$$

Point Estimator of the Difference between the Proportions of Two Populations

$$\bar{p}_1 - \bar{p}_2 \qquad (10.14)$$

Expected Value of $\bar{p}_1 - \bar{p}_2$

$$E(\bar{p}_1 - \bar{p}_2) = p_1 - p_2 \qquad (10.15)$$

Standard Deviation of $\bar{p}_1 - \bar{p}_2$

$$\sigma_{\bar{p}_1 - \bar{p}_2} = \sqrt{\frac{p_1(1 - p_1)}{n_1} + \frac{p_2(1 - p_2)}{n_2}} \qquad (10.16)$$

Interval Estimate of the Difference between the Proportions of Two Populations: Large-Sample Case with $n_1 p_1$, $n_1(1 - p_1)$, $n_2 p_2$, and $n_2(1 - p_2) \geq 5$

$$\bar{p}_1 - \bar{p}_2 \pm z_{\alpha/2}\sigma_{\bar{p}_1 - \bar{p}_2} \qquad (10.17)$$

Point Estimator of $\sigma_{\bar{p}_1 - \bar{p}_2}$

$$s_{\bar{p}_1 - \bar{p}_2} = \sqrt{\frac{\bar{p}_1(1 - \bar{p}_1)}{n_1} + \frac{\bar{p}_2(1 - \bar{p}_2)}{n_2}} \qquad (10.18)$$

Test Statistic for Hypothesis Tests about the Difference between the Proportions of Two Populations

$$z = \frac{(\bar{p}_1 - \bar{p}_2) - (p_1 - p_2)}{\sigma_{\bar{p}_1 - \bar{p}_2}} \qquad (10.19)$$

Pooled Estimator of the Population Proportion

$$\bar{p} = \frac{n_1\bar{p}_1 + n_2\bar{p}_2}{n_1 + n_2} \qquad (10.20)$$

Point Estimator of $\sigma_{\bar{p}_1 - \bar{p}_2}$ when $p_1 = p_2$

$$s_{\bar{p}_1 - \bar{p}_2} = \sqrt{\bar{p}(1 - \bar{p})\left(\frac{1}{n_1} + \frac{1}{n_2}\right)} \qquad (10.21)$$

TABLE 10.22 Exercise 40

Master's Degree	Bachelor's Degree
$n_1 = 60$	$n_2 = 80$
$\bar{x}_1 = \$30,000$	$\bar{x}_2 = \$26,000$
$s_1 = \$2,500$	$s_2 = \$2,000$

SUPPLEMENTARY EXERCISES

40. Starting annual salaries for individuals with master's and bachelor's degrees in business were collected in two independent random samples. Use the data in Table 10.22 to develop a 90% confidence interval estimate of the increase in starting salary that can be expected upon completion of a master's program.

41. Safegate Foods, Inc., is redesigning the checkout lanes in its supermarkets throughout the country. Two designs have been suggested. Tests on customer checkout times have been conducted at two stores where the two new systems have been installed. A summary of the sample data follows.

System A	System B
$n_1 = 120$	$n_2 = 100$
$\bar{x}_1 = 4.1$ minutes	$\bar{x}_2 = 3.3$ minutes
$s_1 = 2.2$ minutes	$s_2 = 1.5$ minutes

Test at the .05 level of significance to determine whether there is a difference between the mean checkout times of the two systems. Which system is preferred?

42. Samples of final examination scores for two statistics classes with different instructors provided the results in Table 10.23. With $\alpha = .05$, test whether these data are sufficient to conclude that the mean grades for the two classes differ.

TABLE 10.23 Exercise 42

Instructor A	Instructor B
$n_1 = 12$	$n_2 = 15$
$\bar{x}_1 = 72$	$\bar{x}_2 = 78$
$s_1 = 8$	$s_2 = 10$

43. In a study of job attitudes and job satisfaction, a sample of 50 men and 50 women were asked to rate their overall job satisfaction on a 1 to 10 scale. High ratings indicate a high degree of job satisfaction. From the following sample results, do you find a significant difference between the levels of job satisfaction for men and women? Use $\alpha = .05$.

Men	Women
$\bar{x}_1 = 7.2$	$\bar{x}_2 = 6.4$
$s_1 = 1.7$	$s_2 = 1.4$

44. Figure Perfect, Inc., is a women's figure salon that specializes in weight-reduction programs. Weights for a sample of clients before and after a six-week introductory program are listed in Table 10.24. Using $\alpha = .05$, test to determine whether the introductory program provides a statistically significant weight loss.

TABLE 10.24 Exercise 43

	Weight	
Client	Before	After
1	140	132
2	160	158
3	210	195
4	148	152
5	190	180
6	170	164

45. A cable television firm is considering submitting bids for rights to operate in two regions of the state of Florida. Surveys of the two regions provided the following data on customer acceptance of the cable television service.

Region I	Region II
$n_1 = 500$	$n_2 = 800$
Number indicating an intent to purchase $= 175$	Number indicating an intent to purchase $= 360$

Develop a 99% confidence interval for the difference between population proportions of customer acceptance in the two regions.

46. A group of physicians in Denmark conducted a year-long study on the effectiveness of nicotine chewing gum in helping people to stop smoking (*New England Journal of Medicine,* 1988). The 113 people who participated in the study were all smokers. Sixty were given chewing gum with 2 milligrams of nicotine and 53 were given a placebo chewing gum with no nicotine content. No one in the study knew which type of gum he or she had been given. All were told to use the gum and refrain from smoking.

   a. State the null and alternative hypotheses that would be appropriate if the researchers hoped to show that the group given nicotine chewing gum had a higher proportion of nonsmokers one year after the study began.

   b. Results showed that 23 of the smokers given nicotine chewing gum had remained nonsmokers for the one-year period and 12 of the smokers given the placebo had remained nonsmokers during the same period. Do these results support the conclusion that nicotine gum can help a person to stop smoking? Test using $\alpha = .05$. What is the *p*-value?

47. A large automobile-insurance company selected samples of single and married male policyholders and recorded the number who had made an insurance claim over the preceding three-year period.

Single Policyholders	Married Policyholders
$n_1 = 400$	$n_2 = 900$
Number making claims = 76	Number making claims = 90

   a. Using $\alpha = .05$, test to determine whether the claim rates differ between single and married male policyholders.

   b. Provide a 95% confidence interval for the difference between the proportions for the two populations.

48. Medical tests were conducted to learn about drug-resistant tuberculosis (*The New York Times,* January 24, 1992). Of 142 cases tested in New Jersey, nine were found to be drug-resistant. Of 268 cases tested in Texas, five were found to be drug-resistant. Do these data suggest a statistically significant difference between the proportions of drug-resistant cases in the two states? Test $H_0: p_1 - p_2 = 0$ at the .02 level of significance. What is the *p*-value and what is your conclusion?

COMPUTER CASE

PAR, INC.

Par, Inc., is a major manufacturer of golf equipment. Management believes that Par's market share could be increased with the introduction of a cut-resistant, longer-lasting golf ball. Therefore, the research group at Par has been investigating a new golf ball coating that is designed to resist cuts and provide a more durable ball. The tests with the coating have been very promising.

One of the researchers voiced concern about the effect of the new coating on driving distances. Par would like the new cut-resistant ball to offer driving distances comparable to those of the current-model golf ball. To compare the driving distances for the two balls, 40 balls of both the new and current models were subjected to distance tests. The testing was performed with a mechanical hitting machine so that any difference between the mean distances for the two models could be attributed to a difference in the design. The results of the tests, with distances measured to the nearest yard, follow. These data are available on the data disk in the file named GOLF.

GOLF

Model		Model		Model		Model	
Current	**New**	**Current**	**New**	**Current**	**New**	**Current**	**New**
264	277	270	272	263	274	281	283
261	269	287	259	264	266	274	250
267	263	289	264	284	262	273	253
272	266	280	280	263	271	263	260
258	262	272	274	260	260	275	270
283	251	275	281	283	281	267	263
258	262	265	276	255	250	279	261
266	289	260	269	272	263	274	255
259	286	278	268	266	278	276	263
270	264	275	262	268	264	262	279

Managerial Report

1. Formulate and present the rationale for a hypothesis test that Par could use to compare the driving distances of the current and new golf balls.
2. Analyze the data to provide the hypothesis-testing conclusion. What is the p-value for your test? What is your recommendation for Par, Inc.?
3. Provide descriptive statistical summaries of the data for each model.
4. What is the 95% confidence interval for the population mean of each model and what is the 95% confidence interval for the difference between the means of the two populations?
5. Do you see a need for larger sample sizes and more testing with the golf balls? Discuss.

11

INFERENCES ABOUT POPULATION VARIANCES

CONTENTS

STATISTICS IN PRACTICE

U.S. General Accounting Office*

Washington, D.C.

The U.S. General Accounting Office (GAO) is an independent, nonpolitical audit organization in the legislative branch of the federal government. The GAO evaluators determine the effectiveness of current and proposed federal programs. To carry out their duties, evaluators must be proficient in records review, legislative research, and statistical analysis techniques.

In one case, the GAO evaluators studied a Department of Interior program established to help clean up the nation's rivers and lakes. As part of this program, federal grants were made to small cities throughout the United States. Congress asked the GAO to determine how effectively the program was operating. To do so, the GAO examined records and visited the sites of several waste treatment plants.

One objective of the GAO audit was to ensure that the effluent (treated sewage) at the plants met certain standards. Among other things the audits reviewed sample data on the oxygen content, the pH level, and the amount of suspended solids in the effluent. A requirement of the program was that a variety of tests be taken daily at each plant and that the collected data be sent periodically to the state engineering department. The GAO's investigation of the data showed whether various characteristics of the effluent were within acceptable limits.

For example, the mean or average pH level of the effluent was examined carefully. In addition, the variance in the reported pH levels was reviewed. The following hypothesis test was conducted about the variance in pH level for the population of effluent.

$$H_0: \sigma^2 = \sigma_0^2$$

$$H_a: \sigma^2 \neq \sigma_0^2$$

*The authors thank Mr. Art Foreman and Mr. Dale Ledman of the U.S. General Accounting Office for providing this Statistics in Practice.

In this test, σ_0^2 is the population variance in pH level expected at a properly functioning plant. In one particular plant, the null hypothesis was rejected. Further analysis showed that this plant had a variance in pH level that was significantly less than normal.

The auditors visited the plant to examine the measuring equipment and to discuss their statistical findings with the plant manager. The auditors found that the measuring equipment was not being used because the operator did not know how to work it. Instead, the operator had been told by an engineer what level of pH was acceptable and had simply recorded similar values without actually conducting the test. The unusually low variance in this plant's data had resulted in rejection of H_0. The GAO suspected that other plants might have similar problems and recommended an operator training program to improve the data-collection aspect of the pollution-control program.

In this chapter you will learn how to conduct statistical inferences about the variances of one and two populations. Two new distributions, the chi-square distribution and the F distribution, will be introduced and used to make interval estimates and hypothesis tests about population variances.

Analyst records data during a water quality test.

● In the preceding four chapters we examined methods of statistical inference involving population means and population proportions. In this chapter we expand the discussion to situations involving inferences about population variances. As an example of a case in which a variance can provide important decision-making information, consider the production process of filling containers with a liquid detergent product. The filling mechanism for the process is adjusted so that the mean filling quantity is 16 ounces per container. Although a mean of 16 ounces is desired, the variance of the fillings is also critical. That is, even with the filling mechanism properly adjusted for the mean of 16 ounces, we cannot expect every container to have exactly 16 ounces. By selecting a sample of containers, we can compute a sample variance for the number of ounces placed in a container. This value will serve as an estimate of the variance for the population of containers being filled by the production process. If the sample variance is modest, the production process will be continued. However, if the sample variance is excessive, overfilling and underfilling may be occurring even though the mean may be correct at 16 ounces. In this case, the filling mechanism will be readjusted in an attempt to reduce the filling variance for the containers.

In the following section we consider inferences about the variance of a single population. Subsequently, we will discuss procedures that can be used to make inferences about the variances of two populations.

11.1   INFERENCES ABOUT A POPULATION VARIANCE

In preceding chapters we used the sample variance

$$s^2 = \frac{\Sigma(x_i - \bar{x})^2}{n-1} \tag{11.1}$$

as the point estimator of the population variance σ^2. In using the sample variance as a basis for making inferences about a population variance, the sampling distribution of the quantity $(n-1)s^2/\sigma^2$ is very helpful. This sampling distribution is described as follows.

> **SAMPLING DISTRIBUTION OF** $(n-1)s^2/\sigma^2$
> Whenever a simple random sample of size n is selected from a *normal population*, the sampling distribution of
>
> $$\frac{(n-1)s^2}{\sigma^2} \tag{11.2}$$
>
> has a *chi-square distribution* with $n-1$ degrees of freedom.

Figure 11.1 shows some possible forms of the sampling distribution of $(n-1)s^2/\sigma^2$.

Tables of areas or probabilities are readily available for the chi-square distribution. Since the sampling distribution of $(n-1)s^2/\sigma^2$ is known to have a chi-square distribution whenever a simple random sample of size n is selected from a normal population, we can use the chi-square distribution to develop interval estimates and conduct hypothesis tests about a population variance.

INTERVAL ESTIMATION OF σ^2

To show how the chi-square distribution can be used to develop a confidence interval estimate of a population variance σ^2, suppose that we are interested in estimating the

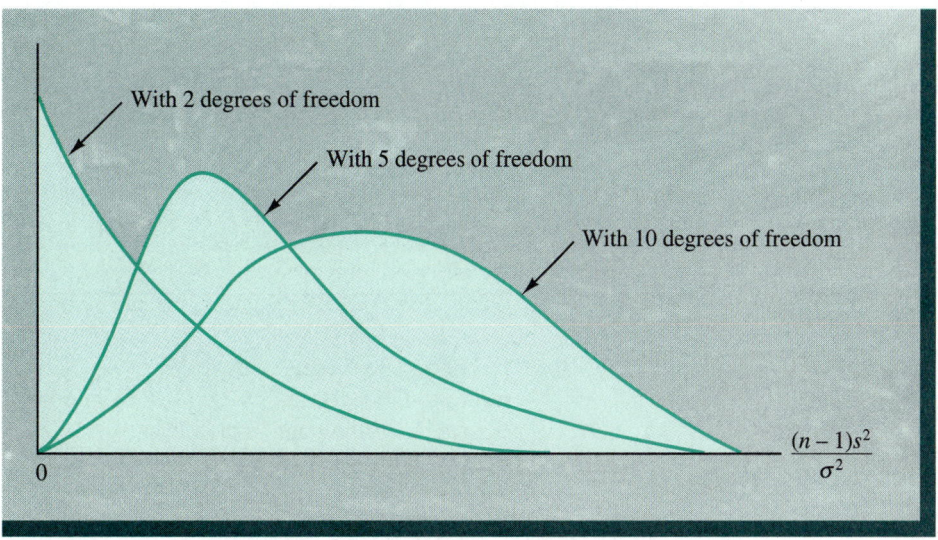

FIGURE 11.1 Examples of the Sampling Distribution of $(n-1)s^2/\sigma^2$ (a Chi-Square Distribution)

population variance for the production filling process mentioned at the beginning of this chapter. A sample of 20 containers is taken, and the sample variance for the filling quantities is found to be $s^2 = .0025$. However, we know we cannot expect the variance of a sample of 20 containers to provide the exact value of the variance for the population of containers filled by the production process. Hence, our interest will be in developing an interval estimate for the population variance.

We will use the notation χ_α^2 to denote the value for the chi-square distribution that provides an area or probability of α to the *right* of the stated χ_α^2 value. For example, in Figure 11.2 the chi-square distribution with 19 degrees of freedom is shown with $\chi_{.025}^2 = 32.8523$ indicating that 2.5% of the chi-square values are to the right of 32.8523, and $\chi_{.975}^2 = 8.90655$ indicating that 97.5% of the chi-square values are to the right of 8.90655. Refer to Table 11.1 and verify that these chi-square values with 19 degrees of freedom (19th row of the table) are correct. Table 3 of Appendix B is a more extensive table of chi-square distribution values.

From the graph in Figure 11.2 we see that .95, or 95%, of the chi-square values are between $\chi_{.975}^2$ and $\chi_{.025}^2$. That is, there is a .95 probability of obtaining a χ^2 value such that

$$\chi_{.975}^2 \leq \chi^2 \leq \chi_{.025}^2$$

However, since we stated in (11.2) that $(n - 1)s^2/\sigma^2$ follows a chi-square distribution, we can substitute $(n - 1)s^2/\sigma^2$ for the χ^2 and write

$$\chi_{.975}^2 \leq \frac{(n - 1)s^2}{\sigma^2} \leq \chi_{.025}^2 \qquad \text{(11.3)}$$

In effect, (11.3) provides an interval estimate in that .95, or 95%, of all possible values for $(n - 1)s^2/\sigma^2$ will be in the interval $\chi_{.975}^2$ to $\chi_{.025}^2$. We now need to do some algebraic manipulations with (11.3) to develop an interval estimate for the population variance σ^2. Working with the leftmost inequality in (11.3), we have

$$\chi_{.975}^2 \leq \frac{(n - 1)s^2}{\sigma^2}$$

TABLE 11.1   Selected Values from the Chi-Square Distribution Table*

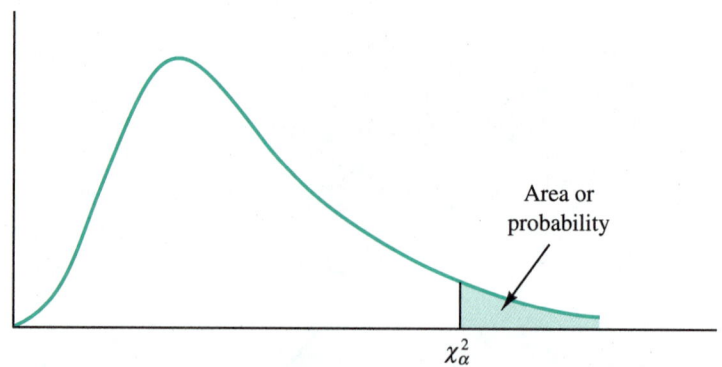

Degrees of Freedom	Area in Upper Tail					
	.99	.975	.95	.05	.025	.01
1	$157{,}088 \times 10^{-9}$	$982{,}069 \times 10^{-9}$	$393{,}214 \times 10^{-8}$	3.84146	5.02389	6.63490
2	.0201007	.0506356	.102587	5.99147	7.37776	9.21034
3	.114832	.215795	.351846	7.81473	9.34840	11.3449
4	.297110	.484419	.710721	9.48773	11.1433	13.2767
5	.554300	.831211	1.145476	11.0705	12.8325	15.0863
6	.872085	1.237347	1.63539	12.5916	14.4494	16.8119
7	1.239043	1.68987	2.16735	14.0671	16.0128	18.4753
8	1.646482	2.17973	2.73264	15.5073	17.5346	20.0902
9	2.087912	2.70039	3.32511	16.9190	19.0228	21.6660
10	2.55821	3.24697	3.94030	18.3070	20.4831	23.2093
11	3.05347	3.81575	4.57481	19.6751	21.9200	24.7250
12	3.57056	4.40379	5.22603	21.0261	23.3367	26.2170
13	4.10691	5.00874	5.89186	22.3621	24.7356	27.6883
14	4.66043	5.62872	6.57063	23.6848	26.1190	29.1413
15	5.22935	6.26214	7.26094	24.9958	27.4884	30.5779
16	5.81221	6.90766	7.96164	26.2962	28.8454	31.9999
17	6.40776	7.56418	8.67176	27.5871	30.1910	33.4087
18	7.01491	8.23075	9.39046	28.8693	31.5264	34.8053
19	7.63273	8.90655	10.1170	30.1435	32.8523	36.1908
20	8.26040	9.59083	10.8508	31.4104	34.1696	37.5662
21	8.89720	10.28293	11.5913	32.6705	35.4789	38.9321
22	9.54249	10.9823	12.3380	33.9244	36.7807	40.2894
23	10.19567	11.6885	13.0905	35.1725	38.0757	41.6384
24	10.8564	12.4011	13.8484	36.4151	39.3641	42.9798
25	11.5240	13.1197	14.6114	37.6525	40.6465	44.3141
26	12.1981	13.8439	15.3791	38.8852	41.9232	45.6417
27	12.8786	14.5733	16.1513	40.1133	43.1944	46.9630
28	13.5648	15.3079	16.9279	41.3372	44.4607	48.2782
29	14.2565	16.0471	17.7083	42.5569	45.7222	49.5879
30	14.9535	16.7908	18.4926	43.7729	46.9792	50.8922
40	22.1643	24.4331	26.5093	55.7585	59.3417	63.6907
50	29.7067	32.3574	34.7642	67.5048	71.4202	76.1539
60	37.4848	40.4817	43.1879	79.0819	83.2976	88.3794

*For additional χ^2 distribution values, see Table 3 of Appendix B.

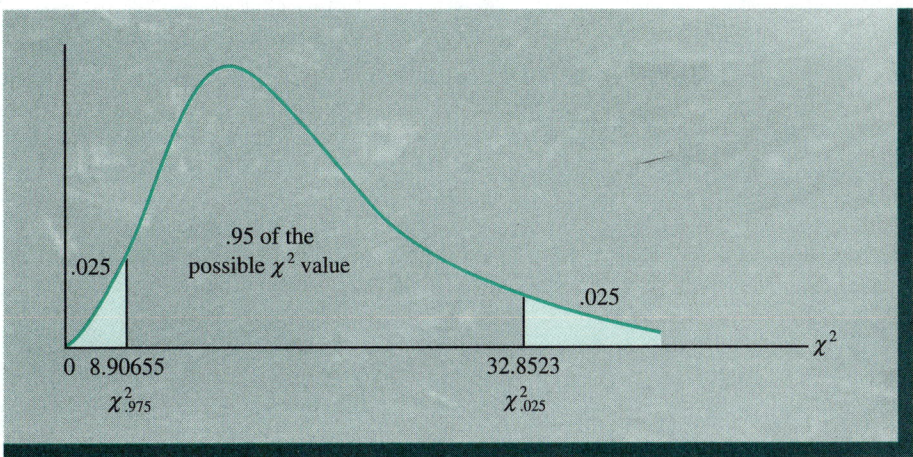

FIGURE 11.2 A Chi-Square Distribution with 19 Degrees of Freedom

Thus

$$\sigma^2 \chi^2_{.975} \leq (n - 1)s^2$$

or

$$\sigma^2 \leq \frac{(n - 1)s^2}{\chi^2_{.975}} \qquad \text{(11.4)}$$

Performing similar algebraic manipulations with the rightmost inequality in (11.3) gives

$$\frac{(n - 1)s^2}{\chi^2_{.025}} \leq \sigma^2 \qquad \text{(11.5)}$$

Finally, the results of (11.4) and (11.5) can be combined to provide

$$\frac{(n - 1)s^2}{\chi^2_{.025}} \leq \sigma^2 \leq \frac{(n - 1)s^2}{\chi^2_{.975}} \qquad \text{(11.6)}$$

Since (11.3) is true for 95% of the $(n - 1)s^2/\sigma^2$ values, (11.6) provides a 95% confidence interval estimate of the population variance σ^2.

Let us return to the problem of providing an interval estimate of the population variance of filling quantities. Recall that the sample of 20 containers provided a sample variance of $s^2 = .0025$. With a sample size of 20, we have 19 degrees of freedom. As shown in Figure 11.2, we have already determined that $\chi^2_{.975} = 8.90655$ and $\chi^2_{.025} = 32.8523$. Using these values in (11.6) provides the following interval estimate for the population variance.

$$\frac{(19)(.0025)}{32.8523} \leq \sigma^2 \leq \frac{(19)(.0025)}{8.90655}$$

or

$$.0014 \leq \sigma^2 \leq .0053$$

Taking the square root of those values gives the following 95% confidence interval for the population standard deviation.

$$.0374 \leq \sigma \leq .0728$$

Thus, we have illustrated the process of using the chi-square distribution to establish interval estimates of a population variance and a population standard deviation. Note specifically that since $\chi^2_{.975}$ and $\chi^2_{.025}$ were used, the interval estimate has a .95 confidence coefficient. Extending (11.6) to the general case of any confidence coefficient, we have the following interval estimate of a population variance.

INTERVAL ESTIMATE OF A POPULATION VARIANCE

$$\frac{(n-1)s^2}{\chi^2_{\alpha/2}} \leq \sigma^2 \leq \frac{(n-1)s^2}{\chi^2_{(1-\alpha/2)}} \tag{11.7}$$

where the χ^2 values are based on a chi-square distribution with $n-1$ degrees of freedom and where $1-\alpha$ is the confidence coefficient.

HYPOTHESIS TESTING

Let us now consider an example and the statistical methodology necessary to test hypotheses about the value of a population variance. The St. Louis Metro Bus Company has recently made a concerted effort to promote an image of reliability by encouraging its drivers to maintain consistent schedules. As a standard policy the company expects arrival times at various bus stops to have low variability. In terms of the variance of arrival times, the company standard specifies an arrival time variance of 4 or less with arrival times measured in minutes. Periodically, the company collects arrival-time data at various bus stops to determine whether the variability guideline is being maintained. The sample results are used to test the following hypotheses.

$$H_0: \sigma^2 \leq 4$$

$$H_a: \sigma^2 > 4$$

In tentatively assuming H_0 to be true, we are assuming that the variance of arrival times is within the company guidelines. We will reject H_0 only if the sample evidence indicates that the guidelines are not being maintained. In this sense, rejection of H_0 suggests that follow-up steps are necessary to reduce the arrival time variance.

Assume that a random sample of 10 bus arrivals will be taken at a particular downtown intersection. If the population of arrival times has a normal probability distribution, we know from (11.2) that the quantity $(n-1)s^2/\sigma^2$ has a chi-square distribution with $n-1$ degrees of freedom. With the null hypothesis assumed true at $\sigma^2 = 4$ and with a sample size of $n = 10$, we can conclude that

$$\frac{(n-1)s^2}{\sigma^2} = \frac{9s^2}{4}$$

has a chi-square distribution with $n-1 = 9$ degrees of freedom. Thus, once the sample data are obtained and the sample variance s^2 is computed, the following equation will provide an observed chi-square (χ^2) value.

$$\chi^2 = \frac{9s^2}{4} \tag{11.8}$$

Figure 11.3 is the chi-square distribution showing the rejection region for this one-tailed test. Note that we will reject H_0 only if the sample variance s^2 leads to a large χ^2 value.

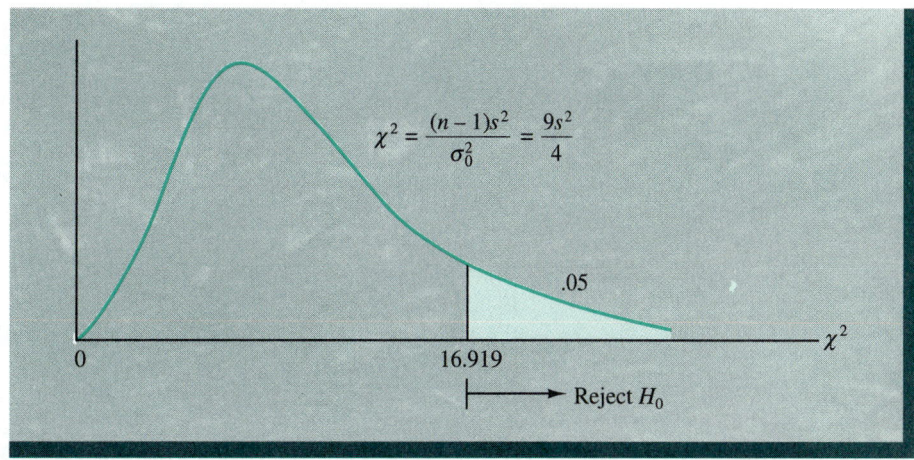

FIGURE 11.3 Rejection Region for the St. Louis Metro Bus Test with $\alpha = .05$

With $\alpha = .05$, Table 11.1 shows that with 9 degrees of freedom $\chi^2_{.05} = 16.919$. With this critical value for the test, the rejection rule is:

$$\text{Reject } H_0 \text{ if } \chi^2 > 16.919$$

Let us assume that the sample of arrival times for 10 buses shows a sample variance of $s^2 = 4.8$. Is this sample evidence sufficient to reject H_0 and conclude that the buses are not meeting the company's arrival-time variance guideline? With $s^2 = 4.8$ and (11.8) we obtain the following χ^2 value.

$$\chi^2 = \frac{9(4.8)}{4} = 10.8$$

Since $\chi^2 = 10.8$ is less than 16.919, we cannot reject H_0. Hence, the sample variance of $s^2 = 4.8$ is insufficient evidence to conclude that the arrival-time variance is not meeting the company standard.

In practice, one-tailed tests are the most frequently encountered tests about population variances. That is, in situations involving arrival times, production times, filling weights, part dimensions, and so on, low variances are generally desired, whereas large variances tend to be unacceptable. With a statement about the maximum allowable variance, we can test the null hypothesis that the variance is less than or equal to the maximum allowable value against the alternative hypothesis that the variance is greater than the maximum allowable value. We now outline the decision rule for making this one-tailed test about a population variance.

One-Tailed Test About A Population Variance

$$H_0: \sigma^2 \leq \sigma_0^2$$
$$H_a: \sigma^2 > \sigma_0^2$$

Test Statistic

$$\chi^2 = \frac{(n-1)s^2}{\sigma_0^2}$$

Rejection Rule

Reject H_0 if $\chi^2 > \chi_\alpha^2$

where σ_0^2 is the hypothesized value for the population variance and χ_α^2 is based on a chi-square distribution with $n - 1$ degrees of freedom.

However, just as we saw with population means and proportions, other forms of the hypotheses can be developed. The one-tailed test for H_0: $\sigma^2 \geq \sigma_0^2$ is similar to the preceding test. The procedure for this test follows. Note that the rejection region is in the lower tail of the chi-square distribution at the critical value of $\chi_{(1-\alpha)}^2$.

One-Tailed Test About a Population Variance

$$H_0: \sigma^2 \geq \sigma_0^2$$
$$H_a: \sigma^2 < \sigma_0^2$$

Test Statistic

$$\chi^2 = \frac{(n-1)s^2}{\sigma_0^2}$$

Rejection Rule

Reject H_0 if $\chi^2 < \chi_{(1-\alpha)}^2$

where σ_0^2 is the hypothesized value for the population variance and $\chi_{(1-\alpha)}^2$ is based on a chi-square distribution with $n - 1$ degrees of freedom.

The two-tailed test with H_0: $\sigma^2 = \sigma_0^2$, like other two-tailed tests, places an area of $\alpha/2$ in each tail of the distribution to establish the two critical values for the test. The decision rule for conducting a two-tailed test about a population variance follows.

Two-Tailed Test About a Population Variance

$$H_0: \sigma^2 = \sigma_0^2$$
$$H_a: \sigma^2 \neq \sigma_0^2$$

Test Statistic

$$\chi^2 = \frac{(n-1)s^2}{\sigma_0^2}$$

Rejection Rule

Reject H_0 if $\chi^2 < \chi_{(1-\alpha/2)}^2$ or if $\chi^2 > \chi_{\alpha/2}^2$

where σ_0^2 is the hypothesized value for the population variance and $\chi_{(1-\alpha/2)}^2$ and $\chi_{\alpha/2}^2$ are based on a chi-square distribution with $n - 1$ degrees of freedom.

Let us demonstrate the use of the chi-square distribution in conducting a two-tailed test about a population variance by considering a situation faced by a bureau of motor vehicles. Historically, the variance in test scores for individuals applying for driver's licenses has been $\sigma^2 = 100$. A new examination with new test questions has been developed. Administrators of the bureau of motor vehicles would like the variance in the test scores for the new examination to remain at the historical level. To evaluate the variance in the new-examination test scores, the following two-tailed hypothesis test has been proposed.

$$H_0: \sigma^2 = 100$$
$$H_a: \sigma^2 \neq 100$$

Rejection of H_0 will indicate that a change in the variance has occurred and suggest that some questions in the new examination may need revision to make the variance of the new test scores similar to the variance of the old test scores. A sample of 30 applicants for driver's licenses will be given the new version of the examination.

The chi-square distribution can be used to conduct this two-tailed test. With a .05 level of significance, the critical values will be $\chi^2_{.975}$ and $\chi^2_{.025}$. With $n - 1 = 29$ degrees of freedom, Table 11.1 shows that $\chi^2_{.975} = 16.0471$ and $\chi^2_{.025} = 45.7222$. The rejection rule for the two-tailed test becomes

$$\text{Reject } H_0 \text{ if } \chi^2 < 16.0471 \text{ or if } \chi^2 > 45.7222$$

What is the appropriate conclusion if the sample of 30 new-examination scores provides a sample variance of $s^2 = 64$? With $H_0: \sigma^2 = 100$, the value of the χ^2 statistic is computed to be

$$\chi^2 = \frac{(n-1)s^2}{\sigma_0^2} = \frac{29(64)}{100} = 18.56$$

Since 18.56 is not in the rejection region, we are not able to reject H_0. There is no statistical evidence that the variance in the new-examination scores differs from the historical variance in examination scores.

EXERCISES

METHODS

1. Find the following chi-square distribution values from Table 11.1 or Table 3 of Appendix B.
   a. $\chi^2_{.05}$ with df=12   **b.** $\chi^2_{.025}$ with df=15
   c. $\chi^2_{.975}$ with df=20   **d.** $\chi^2_{.01}$ with df=10
   e. $\chi^2_{.95}$ with df=18

Self-Test

2. A sample of 20 items provides a sample standard deviation of 5.
   a. Compute the 90% confidence interval estimate of the population variance.
   b. Compute the 95% confidence interval estimate of the population variance.
   c. Compute the 95% confidence interval estimate of the population standard deviation.

3. A sample of 16 items provides a sample standard deviation of 8. Test the following hypotheses using $\alpha = .05$. What is your conclusion?

$$H_0: \sigma^2 \leq 50$$
$$H_a: \sigma^2 > 50$$

TABLE 11.2 Exercise 5

Company	Earnings per Share
Applebee's	0.48
Bob Evans	1.14
Cracker Barrel	0.89
First Alert	0.79
Food Lion	0.26
Microsoft	1.97
Novell	0.97
Tyson Foods	1.22
Zenith Labs	0.84

APPLICATIONS

4. The variance in drug weights is critical in the pharmaceutical industry. For a specific drug, with weights measured in grams, a sample of 18 units provided a sample variance of $s^2 = .36$.
   a. Construct a 90% confidence interval estimate of the population variance for the weights of this drug.
   b. Construct a 90% confidence interval estimate of the population standard deviation.

5. The earnings per share for a sample of stocks traded over the counter is shown in Table 11.2 (*Financial World,* September 1, 1994).
   a. Compute the variance and the standard deviation for these data.
   b. What is the 95% confidence interval estimate of the variance of earnings per share for the population of stocks traded over the counter?
   c. What is the 95% confidence interval estimate of the standard deviation of earnings per share for the population of stocks traded over the counter?

6. A study of worker attitudes about their jobs was conducted for the airline industry (*Industrial Relations,* Winter 1988). A sample of airline employees provided a sample mean age of 40 years and a sample standard deviation of 9.5 years. Compute the 95% confidence interval estimate of the population standard deviation for the following sample sizes.
   a. $n = 30$ b. $n = 51$ c. $n = 101$
   d. What happens to the interval estimate of the population standard deviation as the sample size increases?

7. In the St. Louis Metro Bus Company example, the sample of 10 bus arrivals showed a sample variance of $s^2 = 4.8$.
   a. Provide a 95% confidence interval estimate of the population variance of arrival times.
   b. Assume that the sample variance of $s^2 = 4.8$ had been obtained from a sample of 25 bus arrivals. Provide a 95% confidence interval estimate of the population variance of arrival times.
   c. What effect does a larger sample size have on the interval estimate of a population variance? Does this seem reasonable?

8. *Barron's* (March 30, 1992) reported the percentage changes in major investment markets around the world. On the basis of market performance during 1991, which ranged from + 42.8% in Hong Kong to −16.7% in Finland, the variance in the percentage returns over a three-month period was 48. A sample of 24 markets during the first three months of 1992 showed a sample variance in the percentage returns to be 67.6.
   a. Using a .05 level of significance, test whether the variance in percentage returns for the investment markets appears to have increased in the first three months of 1992. What is your conclusion?
   b. Compute the 95% confidence interval estimate of the variance in percentage returns over a three-month period based on the 1992 sample.
   c. Compute the 95% confidence interval estimate of the standard deviation in the percentage returns.

 **Self-Test**

9. A certain part must be machined to very close tolerances to be acceptable to customers. Production specifications call for a maximum variance in the lengths of the parts of .0004. Suppose the sample variance for 30 parts turns out to be $s^2 = .0005$. Using $\alpha = .05$, test to see whether the population variance specification is being violated.

10. The average useful life of a VCR is six years with a standard deviation of .75 years (*Consumer Reports 1995 Buying Guide*). A sample of the useful life of 30 television sets provided a sample standard deviation of two years. Construct a hypothesis test that can be used to determine whether the standard deviation of the useful life of television sets is significantly greater than the standard deviation of the useful life of VCRs. With a .05 level of significance, what is your conclusion?

11. The variance in the filling amounts of cups of soft drink from an automatic drink machine is an important consideration to the owner of the soft-drink service. If the variance is too large,

overfilling and underfilling of cups will cause customer dissatisfaction with the service. An acceptable variance in filling amounts is $\sigma^2 \leq .25$ where filling amounts are measured in ounces. In a test of filling amounts for a particular machine, a sample of 18 cups showed a sample variance of .40.

a. Do the sample results indicate that the filling mechanism on the machine should be adjusted because of a large variance in filling amounts? Use a .05 level of significance.

b. Provide a 90% confidence interval estimate of the variance in the filling amounts for this machine.

12. The variance in the number of vehicles owned or leased by subscribers to *Fortune* magazine is .94 (*Fortune Subscriber Portrait 1994*). Assume a sample of 12 subscribers to another magazine provided the following data on the number of vehicles owned or leased: 2, 1, 2, 0, 3, 2, 2, 1, 2, 1, 0, and 1.

a. Compute the sample variance in the number of vehicles owned or leased by the 12 subscribers.

b. Test the hypothesis that the variance in the number of vehicles owned or leased is the same for both magazines. With a .05 level of significance, what is your conclusion?

11.2 INFERENCES ABOUT THE VARIANCES OF TWO POPULATIONS

In some statistical applications we might want to compare the variances in product quality resulting from two different production processes, the variances in assembly times for two assembly methods, or the variances in temperatures for two heating devices. In making comparisons about the variances of two populations, we will be using data collected from two independent random samples, one from population 1 and another from population 2. The two sample variances s_1^2 and s_2^2 will be the basis for making inferences about the two population variances σ_1^2 and σ_2^2. Whenever the two population variances are equal ($\sigma_1^2 = \sigma_2^2$), the sampling distribution of the ratio of the two sample variances s_1^2 / s_2^2 is as follows.

SAMPLING DISTRIBUTION OF s_1^2 / s_2^2 **WHEN** $\sigma_1^2 = \sigma_2^2$

Whenever independent simple random samples of sizes n_1 and n_2 are selected from normal populations with equal variances, the sampling distribution of

$$\frac{s_1^2}{s_2^2} \tag{11.9}$$

has an F distribution with $n_1 - 1$ degrees of freedom for the numerator and $n_2 - 1$ degrees of freedom for the denominator; s_1^2 is the sample variance for the random sample of n_1 items from population 1 and s_2^2 is the sample variance for the random sample of n_2 items from population 2.

Figure 11.4 is a graph of the F distribution with 20 degrees of freedom for both the numerator and denominator. As can be seen from this graph, the F distribution is not symmetric and the F values can never be negative. The shape of any particular F distribution depends on its numerator and denominator degrees of freedom.

We will use F_α to denote the value for the F distribution that provides an area or probability of α to the *right* of the stated F_α value. For example, as noted in Figure 11.4, $F_{.05}$ denotes the upper 5% of the F values for an F distribution with 20 degrees of

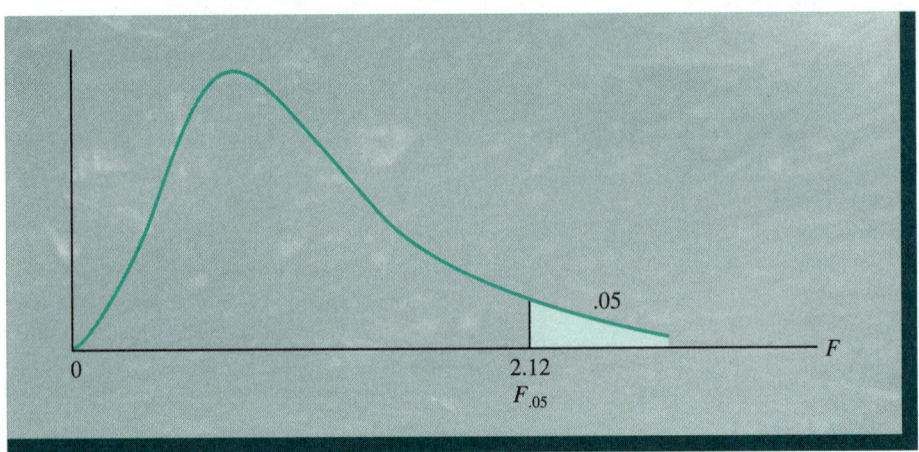

FIGURE 11.4 *F* Distribution with 20 Degrees of Freedom for the Numerator and 20 Degrees of Freedom for the Denominator

freedom for the numerator and 20 degrees of freedom for the denominator. Table 11.3 shows that for this particular F distribution, $F_{.05} = 2.12$. Table 4 of Appendix B is a more extensive table of F distribution values. Let us show how the F distribution can be used for a hypothesis test about the variances of two populations.

Dullus County Schools is renewing its school bus service contract for the coming year and must select one of two bus companies, the Milbank Company or the Gulf Park Company. We will use the variance of the arrival or pickup/delivery times as a primary measure of the quality of the bus service. Low variance values indicate the more consistent and higher quality service. If the variances of arrival times associated with the two services are equal, Dullus School administrators will select the company offering the better financial terms. However, if the sample data on bus arrival times for the two companies indicate a significant difference between the variances, the administrators may want to give special consideration to the company with the better or lower variance service. The appropriate hypotheses follow.

$$H_0: \sigma_1^2 = \sigma_2^2$$

$$H_a: \sigma_1^2 \neq \sigma_2^2$$

If H_0 can be rejected, the conclusion of unequal service quality is appropriate. In that case, the company with the lower sample variance would be preferred.

Assume that the hypothesis test will be conducted with $\alpha = .10$. Furthermore, assume that we obtain samples of arrival times from school systems currently using the two school bus services. A sample of 25 arrival times is available for the Milbank service (population 1) and a sample of 16 arrival times is available for the Gulf Park service (population 2). Figure 11.5 is the graph of the F distribution with $n_1 - 1 = 24$ degrees of freedom for the numerator and $n_2 - 1 = 15$ degrees of freedom for the denominator. Note that the two-tailed rejection region is indicated by the critical values at $F_{.95}$ and $F_{.05}$.

Let us assume that the two samples of bus arrival times resulted in sample variances of $s_1^2 = 48$ for the Milbank service and $s_2^2 = 20$ for the Gulf Park service. What conclusion is appropriate? Assume that the two populations of arrival times have normal probability distributions, and assume that H_0 is true with $\sigma_1^2 = \sigma_2^2$. The F distribution can be used to reach a conclusion. Specifically, we compute $F = s_1^2/s_2^2$ and use the rejection region shown in Figure 11.5. Thus, we find

TABLE 11.3   Selected Values from the *F* Distribution Table*

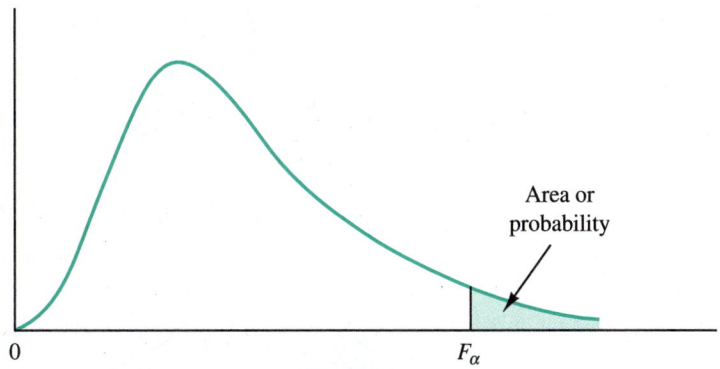

Area or probability

0 F_α

		Table of $F_{.05}$ Values					
Denominator Degrees of Freedom	**Numerator Degrees of Freedom**						
	6	**7**	**8**	**9**	**10**	**12**	**15**	**20**
1	234.0	236.8	238.9	240.5	241.9	243.9	245.9	248.0
2	19.33	19.35	19.37	19.38	19.40	19.41	19.43	19.45
3	8.94	8.89	8.85	8.81	8.79	8.74	8.70	8.66
4	6.16	6.09	6.04	6.00	5.96	5.91	5.86	5.80
5	4.95	4.88	4.82	4.77	4.74	4.68	4.62	4.56
6	4.28	4.21	4.15	4.10	4.06	4.00	3.94	3.87
7	3.87	3.79	3.73	3.68	3.64	3.57	3.51	3.44
8	3.58	3.50	3.44	3.39	3.35	3.28	3.22	3.15
9	3.37	3.29	3.23	3.18	3.14	3.07	3.01	2.94
10	3.22	3.14	3.07	3.02	2.98	2.91	2.85	2.77
11	3.09	3.01	2.95	2.90	2.85	2.79	2.72	2.65
12	3.00	2.91	2.85	2.80	2.75	2.69	2.62	2.54
13	2.92	2.83	2.77	2.71	2.67	2.60	2.53	2.46
14	2.85	2.76	2.70	2.65	2.60	2.53	2.46	2.39
15	2.79	2.71	2.64	2.59	2.54	2.48	2.40	2.33
16	2.74	2.66	2.59	2.54	2.49	2.42	2.35	2.28
17	2.70	2.61	2.55	2.49	2.45	2.38	2.31	2.23
18	2.66	2.58	2.51	2.46	2.41	2.34	2.27	2.19
19	2.63	2.54	2.48	2.42	2.38	2.31	2.23	2.16
20	2.60	2.51	2.45	2.39	2.35	2.28	2.20	2.12
21	2.57	2.49	2.42	2.37	2.32	2.25	2.18	2.10
22	2.55	2.46	2.40	2.34	2.30	2.23	2.15	2.07
23	2.53	2.44	2.37	2.32	2.27	2.20	2.13	2.05
24	2.51	2.42	2.36	2.30	2.25	2.18	2.11	2.03

*For additional *F* distribution values, see Table 4 of Appendix B.

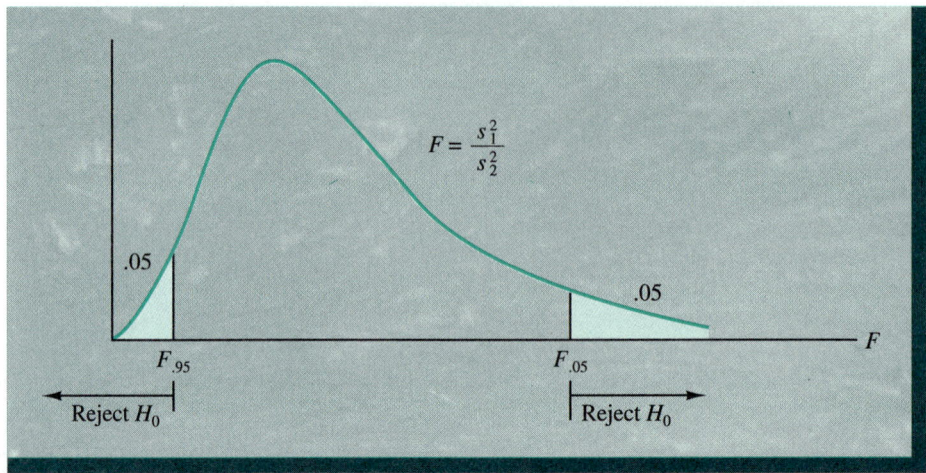

FIGURE 11.5   Rejection Region for the Dullus County School Bus Example with $\alpha = .10$

$$F = \frac{s_1^2}{s_2^2} = \frac{48}{20} = 2.40$$

Using Table 4 of Appendix B, we find that the upper-tail critical value with 24 numerator degrees of freedom and 15 denominator degrees of freedom is $F_{.05} = 2.29$. Although Table 4 does not provide $F_{.95}$ values, note that the determination of this lower-tail critical value is not necessary. We can already observe that $F = 2.40$ exceeds $F_{.05} = 2.29$. Thus, at the .10 level of significance, H_0 is rejected. This finding leads us to the conclusion that the two bus services differ in terms of pickup/delivery time variances. The recommendation is that the Dullus School administrators give special consideration to the better or lower variance service offered by the Gulf Park Company.

In the Dullus School example, you might feel that we were lucky in carrying out the test because the lower-tail critical value $F_{.95}$, which is not provided in the F distribution table, was not necessary. We were able to draw the appropriate hypothesis-testing conclusion without knowing the value of $F_{.95}$. If you ever need to know a lower-tail F value, $F_{(1-\alpha)}$, it can be determined by using an upper-tail F_α value and the following relationship.

$$F_{(1-\alpha),\text{df}_1,\text{df}_2} = \frac{1}{F_{\alpha,\text{df}_2,\text{df}_1}} \qquad \textbf{(11.10)}$$

Thus, with 24 degrees of freedom in the numerator ($\text{df}_1 = 24$) and 15 degrees of freedom in the denominator ($\text{df}_2 = 15$), $F_{.95}$ is the reciprocal of the $F_{.05}$ value with 15 degrees of freedom in the numerator and 24 degrees of freedom in the denominator. In the F distribution table, we find that $F_{.05}$ with 15 numerator and 24 denominator degrees of freedom is 2.11. Hence, the value of $F_{.95}$ with 24 degrees of freedom in the numerator and 15 degrees of freedom in the denominator is

$$F_{.95} = \frac{1}{2.11} = .47$$

Although (11.10) can be used to compute a lower-tail F value, common practice is to conduct the hypothesis test computations so that only upper-tail F values are needed. In hypothesis tests with H_0: $\sigma_1^2 = \sigma_2^2$, we simply denote the population with the *larger sample variance* as population 1. That is, deciding which population to denote as either population 1 or 2 is arbitrary. By labeling the population with the larger sample variance as population 1, we guarantee that a rejection of H_0 can occur only in the *upper tail.*

Although the lower-tail critical value still exists, we do not need to know its value because the convention of using the population with the largest sample variance as population 1 always places the ratio s_1^2/s_2^2 in the upper-tail direction. In the Dullus School example, population 1, the Milbank bus service, had the largest sample variance. Hence, we proceeded directly with the test. If the Gulf Park bus service had provided the largest sample variance, we would have denoted Gulf Park as population 1 and followed the same statistical testing procedure. A summary of the two-tailed test for the equality of two population variances with this procedure follows.

Two-Tailed Test About the Variances of Two Populations

$$H_0: \sigma_1^2 = \sigma_2^2$$

$$H_a: \sigma_1^2 \neq \sigma_2^2$$

Denote the population providing the *largest sample variance* as population 1.

Test Statistic

$$F = \frac{s_1^2}{s_2^2}$$

Rejection Rule

Reject H_0 if $F > F_{\alpha/2}$

where the value of $F_{\alpha/2}$ is based on an F distribution with $n_1 - 1$ degrees of freedom for the numerator and $n_2 - 1$ degrees of freedom for the denominator.

One-tailed tests involving two population variances are also possible. Again the F distribution is used, with the one-tailed rejection region enabling us to conclude whether one population variance is significantly greater or significantly less than the other. Only upper-tail F values are needed. For any one-tailed test we set up the null hypothesis so that the rejection region is in the upper tail. This can be accomplished by labeling the population with the larger variance in H_a as population 1. The general procedure follows.

One-Tailed Test About the Variances of Two Populations

$$H_0: \sigma_1^2 \leq \sigma_2^2$$
$$H_a: \sigma_1^2 > \sigma_2^2$$

Test Statistic

$$F = \frac{s_1^2}{s_2^2}$$

Rejection Rule

Reject H_0 if $F > F_{\alpha}$

where the value of F_{α} is based on an F distribution with $n_1 - 1$ degrees of freedom for the numerator and $n_2 - 1$ degrees of freedom for the denominator.

Let us demonstrate the use of the F distribution to conduct a one-tailed test about the variances of two populations by considering a public opinion survey. Samples of 31 men and 41 women will be used to study attitudes about current political issues. The researcher conducting the study wants to test to see whether the sample data indicate that women have a greater variation in attitude on political issues than men. In the form of the one-tailed hypothesis test given previously, women will be denoted as population 1 and men will be denoted as population 2. The hypothesis test will be stated as follows.

$$H_0: \sigma^2_{\text{women}} \leq \sigma^2_{\text{men}}$$
$$H_a: \sigma^2_{\text{women}} > \sigma^2_{\text{men}}$$

If H_0 is rejected, the researcher will have the statistical support necessary to conclude that women have a greater variation in attitude on political issues.

With the sample variance for women in the numerator and the sample variance for men in the denominator, the F distribution with $41 - 1 = 40$ degrees of freedom in the numerator and $31 - 1 = 30$ degrees of freedom in the denominator will be used to conduct the one-tailed test. With a .05 level of significance, the rejection region is based on $F_{.05}$. Using Table 4 of Appendix B, we find that $F_{.05} = 1.79$. Thus, the rejection rule becomes

$$\text{Reject } H_0 \text{ if } F > 1.79$$

where F is computed from the ratio of the two sample variances s_1^2/s_2^2.

Assume that the survey shows a sample variance of $s_1^2 = 120$ for the 41 women and a sample variance of $s_2^2 = 80$ for the 31 men. What is the appropriate statistical conclusion? The F statistic becomes

$$F = \frac{s_1^2}{s_2^2} = \frac{120}{80} = 1.50$$

Since 1.50 is less than 1.79, H_0 cannot be rejected. Hence, the sample results do not support the conclusion that women have a greater variation than men in their attitudes on political issues.

NOTES AND COMMENTS

Researchers have confirmed the fact that the F distribution is sensitive to the assumption of normal populations. The F distribution should not be used unless it is reasonable to assume that both populations are at least approximately normally distributed.

EXERCISES

METHODS

13. Find the following F distribution values from Table 4 of Appendix B.
    a. $F_{.05}$ with degrees of freedom 12 and 10
    b. $F_{.025}$ with degrees of freedom 20 and 15
    c. $F_{.01}$ with degrees of freedom 8 and 12
    d. $F_{.975}$ with degrees of freedom 10 and 20

14. A sample of 16 items from population 1 has a sample variance $s_1^2 = 5.8$ and a sample of 20 items from population 2 has a sample variance $s_2^2 = 2.4$. Test the following hypotheses at the .05 level of significance.

$$H_0: \sigma_1^2 \leq \sigma_2^2$$
$$H_a: \sigma_1^2 > \sigma_2^2$$

What is your conclusion?

Self-Test ▶ 15. Consider the following hypothesis test.

$$H_0: \sigma_1^2 = \sigma_2^2$$
$$H_a: \sigma_1^2 \neq \sigma_2^2$$

What is your conclusion if $n_1 = 25$, $s_1^2 = 4.0$, $n_2 = 21$, and $s_2^2 = 8.2$? Use $\alpha = .05$.

APPLICATIONS

16. The average price of a new automobile in 1991 was $16,700, an increase of 4.3% over the 1990 average price of $16,012 (*U.S. News & World Report,* September 9, 1991). Assume that samples of 121 new 1991 automobiles have a sample standard deviation in price of $4200 and 121 new 1990 automobiles have a sample standard deviation in price of $3850. Using a .05 level of significance, can you conclude that the variance in prices of new automobiles also increased in 1991?

Self-Test ▶ 17. Most individuals are aware of the fact that the average annual repair cost for an automobile depends on the age of the automobile. For example, the average annual repair cost for automobiles four years old ($400) is almost twice as large as the average annual repair cost for automobiles two years old ($220) (*Consumer Reports 1992 Buyer's Guide*). A researcher is interested in finding out whether the variance of the annual repair costs also increases with the age of the automobile. A sample of 25 automobiles four years old showed a sample standard deviation for annual repair costs of $170 and a sample of 25 automobiles two years old showed a sample standard deviation for annual repair costs of $100.
    a. State the null and alternative versions of the research hypothesis that the variance in annual repair costs is larger for the older automobiles.
    b. For a .01 level of significance, what is your conclusion? Discuss the reasonableness of your findings.

18. The Educational Testing Service has conducted studies designed to identify differences between the scores of male and female students on the Scholastic Aptitude Test (*Journal of Educational Measurement,* Spring 1987). For a sample of female students, the standard deviation of test scores was 83 on the verbal portion of the SAT. For a sample of male students, the standard deviation was 78 on the same test. Assume the standard deviations were based on random samples of 121 female and 121 male students. Do the data indicate a difference between the variances of female and male students' scores on the verbal portion of the SAT? Use $\alpha = .05$.

BAGS 19. The variance in a production process is an important measure of the quality of the process. A large variance often signals an opportunity for improvement in the process by finding ways to reduce the process variance. Data showing the weight of tea bags in grams for two machines were presented in *Quality Progress* (February 1995). Conduct a statistical test to determine whether there is a significant difference between the variances in the bag weights for the two machines. Use a .05 level of significance. What is your conclusion? Which machine, if either, provides the greater opportunity for quality improvements?

Machine 1	2.95	3.45	3.50	3.75	3.48	3.26	3.33	3.20
	3.16	3.20	3.22	3.38	3.90	3.36	3.25	3.28
	3.20	3.22	2.98	3.45	3.70	3.34	3.18	3.35
	3.12							
Machine 2	3.22	3.30	3.34	3.28	3.29	3.25	3.30	3.27
	3.38	3.34	3.35	3.19	3.35	3.05	3.36	3.28
	3.30	3.28	3.30	3.20	3.16	3.33		

20. On the basis of data provided by the Romac 1994 Salary Survey (*National Business Employment Weekly,* October 16, 1994), the variance in annual salaries for seniors in public accounting firms is approximately 2.1 and the variance in annual salaries for managers in public accounting firms is approximately 11.1. The salary data were provided in thousands of dollars. Assuming that the salary data were based on samples of 25 seniors and 25 managers, test the hypothesis that the population variances in the salaries are equal. With a .05 level of significance, what is your conclusion?

 DOWJONES

21. The Dow Jones Industrial Average varies throughout the day as investors make stock transactions. A sample of the Dow Jones Industrial Average taken at different times during two days in September 1994 follows (*Barron's,* September 26, 1994).

Sept 19	Sept 20
3947	3919
3952	3908
3948	3904
3947	3903
3950	3901
3944	3900
3946	3894
3945	3893
3937	3898
3930	3897
3939	3899

   a. Compute the variances of the Dow Jones Industrial Average for the two days.

   b. Using a .05 level of significance, test to determine whether the variances for the two days are equal. What is your conclusion?

22. A research hypothesis is that the variance of stopping distances of automobiles on wet pavement is substantially greater than the variance of stopping distances of automobiles on dry pavement. In the research study, 16 automobiles traveling at the same speeds are tested for stopping distances on wet pavement and then tested for stopping distances on dry pavement. On wet pavement, the standard deviation of stopping distances is 32 feet. On dry pavement, the standard deviation is 16 feet.

   a. At a .05 level of significance, do the sample data justify the conclusion that the variance in stopping distances on wet pavement is greater than the variance in stopping distances on dry pavement?

   b. What are the implications of your statistical conclusions in terms of driving safety recommendations?

SUMMARY

In this chapter we have presented statistical procedures that can be used to make inferences about population variances. In the process we have introduced two new probability distributions; the chi-square distribution and the F distribution. The chi-square distribution can be used as the basis for interval estimation and hypothesis tests about the variance of a normal population.

We illustrated the use of the F distribution in hypothesis tests about the variances of two normal populations. In particular, we showed that with independent simple random samples of sizes n_1 and n_2 selected from two normal populations with equal variances $\sigma_1^2 = \sigma_2^2$, the sampling distribution of the ratio of the two sample variances s_1^2 / s_2^2 has an F distribution with $n_1 - 1$ degrees of freedom for the numerator and $n_2 - 1$ degrees of freedom for the denominator.

KEY FORMULAS

Interval Estimate of a Population Variance

$$\frac{(n-1)s^2}{\chi^2_{\alpha/2}} \leq \sigma^2 \leq \frac{(n-1)s^2}{\chi^2_{(1-\alpha/2)}}$$

(11.7)

Sampling Distribution of s_1^2/s_2^2 when $\sigma_1^2 = \sigma_2^2$

$$F = \frac{s_1^2}{s_2^2}$$

(11.9)

SUPPLEMENTARY EXERCISES

23. Because of staffing decisions, managers of the Gibson-Marimont Hotel are interested in the variability in the number of rooms occupied per day during a particular season of the year. A sample of 20 days of operation shows a sample mean of 290 rooms occupied per day and a sample standard deviation of 30 rooms.
    a. What is the point estimate of the population variance?
    b. Provide a 90% confidence interval estimate of the population variance.
    c. Provide a 90% confidence interval estimate of the population standard deviation.

24. Initial public offerings (IPOs) of stocks are on average underpriced. However, in some cases, the IPOs are actually overpriced (*Financial Analysts Journal,* December 1987). The standard deviation measures the dispersion or variation in the underpricing-overpricing indicator. A sample of 13 Canadian IPOs that were subsequently traded on the Toronto Stock Exchange had a standard deviation of 14.95. Develop a 95% confidence interval estimate of the population standard deviation for the underpricing-overpricing indicator.

25. Historical delivery times for Buffalo Trucking, Inc., have had a mean of three hours and a standard deviation of .5 hours. A sample of 22 deliveries over the past month provides a sample mean of 3.1 hours and a sample standard deviation of .75 hours.
    a. Use a hypothesis test to determine whether the sample results lead to rejection of the hypothesis that the historical delivery variance is $\sigma^2 = (.5)^2 = .25$. Use $\alpha = .05$.
    b. Compute the 95% confidence intervals for the population variance and the population standard deviation.

26. Part variability is critical in the manufacturing of ball bearings. Large variances in the size of the ball bearings cause bearing failure and rapid wearout. Production standards call for a maximum variance of .0001 when the bearing sizes are measured in inches. A sample of 15 bearings shows a sample standard deviation of .014 inches.
    a. Using $\alpha = .10$, determine whether the sample indicates that the maximum acceptable variance is being exceeded.
    b. Compute the 90% confidence interval estimate of the variance of the ball bearings in the population.

27. The filling variance for boxes of cereal is designed to be .02 or less. A sample of 41 boxes of cereal shows a sample standard deviation of .16 ounces. Using $\alpha = .05$, determine whether the variance in the cereal box fillings is exceeding the design specification.

28. City Trucking, Inc., claims consistent delivery times for its routine customer deliveries. A sample of 22 truck deliveries shows a sample variance of 1.5. Test to determine whether $H_0: \sigma^2 \leq 1$ can be rejected. Use $\alpha = .10$.

29. Using a sample of nine days over the past six months, a dentist has seen the following numbers of patients: 22, 25, 20, 18, 15, 22, 24, 19, and 26. If the number of patients seen per day is normally distributed, would an analysis of these sample data reject the hypothesis that the variance in the number of patients seen per day is equal to 10? Use a .10 level of significance. What is your conclusion?

30. A sample standard deviation for the number of passengers taking a particular airline flight is 8. A 95% confidence interval estimate of the population standard deviation is 5.86 passengers to 12.62 passengers.
    a. Was a sample size of 10 or 15 used in the statistical analysis?
    b. If the sample standard deviation of $s = 8$ had been based on a sample of 25 flights, what change would you expect in the confidence interval for the population standard deviation? Compute a 95% confidence interval estimate of σ with a sample of size 25.

31. A firm gives a mechanical aptitude test to all job applicants. A sample of 20 male applicants shows a sample variance of 80 for the test scores. A sample of 16 female applicants shows a sample variance of 220. Using $\alpha = .05$, determine whether the test score variances differ for male and female job applicants. If you find a difference in variances, which group has the higher variance in mechanical aptitude?

32. The grade point averages of 352 students who completed a college course in financial accounting have a standard deviation of .940 (*The Accounting Review*, January 1988). The grade point averages of 73 students who dropped out of the same course have a standard deviation of .797. Do the data indicate a difference between the variances of grade point averages for students who completed a financial accounting course and students who dropped out? Use a .05 level of significance. Note: $F_{.025}$ with 351 and 72 degrees of freedom is 1.466.

TABLE 11.4   Exercise 34

Method	Sample Size	Sample Variance
A	31	25
B	25	12

33. The accounting department analyzes the variance of the weekly unit costs reported by two production departments. A sample of 16 cost reports for each of the two departments shows cost variances of 2.3 and 5.4, respectively. Is this sample sufficient to conclude that the two production departments differ in terms of unit cost variance? Use $\alpha = .10$.

34. Two new assembly methods are tested and the variances in assembly times are reported in Table 11.4. Using $\alpha = .10$, test for equality of the two population variances.

35. Two secretaries are each given eight typing assignments of equal difficulty. The sample standard deviations of the completion times are 3.8 minutes and 5.2 minutes, respectively. Do the data suggest a difference in the variability of completion times for the two secretaries? Test the hypothesis at a .10 level of significance.

COMPUTER CASE

AIR FORCE TRAINING PROGRAM

An Air Force introductory course in electronics uses a personalized system of instruction whereby each student views a videotaped lecture and then is given a programmed instruction text. The students work independently with the text until they have completed the training and passed a test. Of concern is the varying pace at which the students complete this portion of their training program. Some students are able to cover the programmed instruction text relatively quickly, whereas other students work much longer with the text and require additional time to complete the course. The fast students wait until the slow students complete the introductory course before the entire group proceeds together with other aspects of their training.

A proposed alternative system involves use of computer-assisted instruction. In this method, all students view the same videotaped lecture and then each is assigned to a computer terminal for further instruction. The computer guides the student, working independently, through the self-training portion of the course.

To compare the proposed and current methods of instruction, an entering class of 122 students was assigned randomly to one of the two methods. One group of 61 students used the current programmed-text method and the other group of 61 students used the proposed computer-assisted method. The time in hours was recorded for each student in the study. The following data are provided on the data disk in the file named TRAINING.

TRAINING

Course-Completion Times (hours) for Current Training Method

76	76	77	74	76	74	74	77	72	78	73
78	75	80	79	72	69	79	72	70	70	81
76	78	72	82	72	73	71	70	77	78	73
79	82	65	77	79	73	76	81	69	75	75
77	79	76	78	76	76	73	77	84	74	74
69	79	66	70	74	72					

Course-Completion Times (hours) for Proposed Computer-Assisted Method

74	75	77	78	74	80	73	73	78	76	76
74	77	69	76	75	72	75	72	76	72	77
73	77	69	77	75	76	74	77	75	78	72
77	78	78	76	75	76	76	75	76	80	77
76	75	73	77	77	77	79	75	75	72	82
76	76	74	72	78	71					

Managerial Report

1. Use appropriate descriptive statistics to summarize the training-time data for each method. What similarities and/or differences do you observe from the sample data?
2. Use the methods of Chapter 10 to comment on any difference between the population means for the two methods. Discuss your findings.
3. Compute the standard deviation and variance for each training method. Conduct a hypothesis test about the equality of population variances for the two training methods. Discuss your findings.
4. What conclusion can you reach about any differences between the two methods? What is your recommendation? Explain.
5. Can you suggest other data or testing that might be desirable before making a final decision on the training program to be used in the future?

12

TESTS OF GOODNESS OF FIT AND INDEPENDENCE

CONTENTS

STATISTICS IN PRACTICE ● ● ● ● ● ● ● ● ● ● ● ● ● ● ● ● ● ●

United Way*

Rochester, New York

The United Way of Greater Rochester is a nonprofit fund-raising and social planning organization dedicated to improving the quality of life of residents in the six counties it serves. The annual United Way/Red Cross campaign, conducted each spring, helps support more than 140 human service agencies. These agencies meet a wide variety of human needs—physical, mental, and social—and serve people of all ages, backgrounds, and economic means. Because of widespread volunteer involvement, United Way is able to hold its operating costs to less than nine cents of every dollar raised.

The United Way of Greater Rochester decided to conduct a survey to learn more about community perceptions of charities. Focus-group interviews were held with professional, service, and general worker groups to get preliminary information on perceptions. The information obtained was then used to help develop the questionnaire for the survey. The questionnaire was pretested, modified, and distributed to 440 individuals; 323 completed questionnaires were obtained.

A variety of descriptive statistics, including frequency distributions and crosstabulations, were provided from the data collected. An important part of the analysis involved the use of contingency tables and chi-square tests of independence. One use of such statistical tests was to determine whether perceptions of administrative expenses were independent of occupation.

The hypotheses for the test of independence were:

H_0: Perception of United Way administrative expenses is independent of the occupation of the respondent.

H_a: Perception of United Way administrative expenses is not independent of the occupation of the respondent.

Two questions in the survey provided the data for the statistical test. One question obtained data on perceptions of the percentage of funds going to administrative expenses (up to 10%, 11–20%, and 21% or more). The other question asked for the occupation of the respondent.

The chi-square test at a 5% level of significance led to rejection of the null hypothesis of independence and to the conclusion that perceptions of United Way's administrative expenses did vary by occupation. Actual administrative expenses were less than 9%, but 35% of the respondents perceived that administrative expenses were 21% or more. Hence, many had very inaccurate perceptions of administrative costs. In this group, production-line, clerical, sales, and professional-technical employees had more inaccurate perceptions than other groups.

In this chapter, you will learn how a statistical test of independence, such as that described here, is conducted. The community perceptions study helped United Way of Rochester to develop adjustments to its program and fund-raising activities.

A poster child for the annual United Way campaign.

*The authors are indebted to Dr. Philip R. Tyler, Marketing Consultant to the United Way, for providing this Statistics in Practice.

● In Chapter 11 we showed how the chi-square distribution could be used in estimation and in hypothesis tests about a population variance. Here, we introduce two additional hypothesis-testing procedures, both based on the use of the chi-square distribution. Like other hypothesis-testing procedures, these tests compare sample results with those that are expected when the null hypothesis is true. The conclusion of the hypothesis test is based on how "close" the sample results are to the expected results.

In the following section we introduce a goodness of fit test for a multinomial population. Later we discuss the test for independence using contingency tables and then show goodness of fit tests for Poisson and normal probability distributions.

12.1 GOODNESS OF FIT TEST: A MULTINOMIAL POPULATION

In this section we consider the case in which each element of a population is assigned to one and only one of several classes or categories. Such a population is a *multinomial population*. The multinomial probability distribution can be thought of as an extension of the binomial distribution to the case of three or more categories of outcomes. On each trial of a multinomial experiment, one and only one of the outcomes occurs. Each trial of the experiment is assumed to be independent, and the probabilities must stay the same for each trial.

As an example, consider the market analysis being conducted by the J. Scott and Associates market research firm. The study involves a market-share evaluation. Over the past year market shares have stabilized, with 30% for company A, 50% for company B, and 20% for company C. Recently company C has developed a "new and improved" product that will replace its current entry in the market. Managers of company C have asked J. Scott and Associates to determine whether the new product will cause a shift in the market shares of the three competitors.

In this case, the population of interest is a multinomial population; each customer is classified as buying from company A, company B, or company C. Thus, we have a multinomial population with three classifications or categories. Let us use the following notation.

$$p_A = \text{market share for company A}$$

$$p_B = \text{market share for company B}$$

$$p_C = \text{market share for company C}$$

J. Scott and Associates will conduct a sample survey and compute the proportion preferring each company's product. A hypothesis test will then be conducted to see whether the new product has caused a change in market shares. On the assumption that company C's new product will not alter the market shares, the null and alternative hypotheses are stated as follows.

$$H_0: p_A = .30, p_B = .50, \text{ and } p_C = .20$$

$$H_a: \text{The population proportions are not} \\ p_A = .30, p_B = .50, \text{ and } p_C = .20$$

If the sample results lead to the rejection of H_0, J. Scott and Associates will have evidence that the introduction of the new product has had an impact on the market shares.

Let us assume that the market research firm has used a consumer panel of 200 customers for the study. Each individual has been asked to specify a purchase preference among the three alternatives: company A's product, company B's product, and company C's new product. The 200 responses are summarized below.

Company A's Product	Company B's Product	Company C's New Product
48	98	54

We now can perform a *goodness of fit test* that will determine whether the sample of 200 customer purchase preferences is consistent with the null hypothesis. The goodness of fit test is based on a comparison of the sample of *observed* results, such as those shown above, with the *expected* results under the assumption that the null hypothesis is true. Hence, the next step in our example is to compute expected purchase preferences for the 200 customers under the assumption that $p_A = .30$, $p_B = .50$, and $p_C = .20$. Doing so provides the expected results.

Company A's Product	Company B's Product	Company C's New Product
200(.30) = 60	200(.50) = 100	200(.20) = 40

Thus, we see that the expected frequency for each category is found by multiplying the sample size of 200 by the hypothesized proportion for the category.

The goodness of fit test now focuses on the differences between the observed frequencies and the expected frequencies. Large differences between observed and expected frequencies cast doubt on the assumption that the hypothesized proportions or market shares are correct. Whether the differences between the observed and expected frequencies are "large" or "small" is a question answered with the aid of the following test statistic.

TEST STATISTIC FOR GOODNESS OF FIT

$$\chi^2 = \sum_{i=1}^{k} \frac{(f_i - e_i)^2}{e_i} \qquad (12.1)$$

where

f_i = observed frequency for category i

e_i = expected frequency for category i based on the assumption that H_0 is true

k = the number of categories

Note: The test statistic has a chi-square distribution with $k - 1$ degrees of freedom provided that the expected frequencies are 5 *or more* for all categories.

Let us return to the market-share data for the three companies. Since the expected frequencies are all 5 or more, we can proceed with the computation of the chi-square test statistic.

$$\chi^2 = \frac{(48 - 60)^2}{60} + \frac{(98 - 100)^2}{100} + \frac{(54 - 40)^2}{40} = 2.40 + .04 + 4.90 = 7.34$$

Suppose we test the null hypothesis that the multinomial population has the proportions of $p_A = .30$, $p_B = .50$, and $p_C = .20$ at the $\alpha = .05$ level of significance. Since we will reject the null hypothesis if the differences between the observed and expected frequencies are *large*, we will place a rejection area of .05 in the upper tail of the chi-square distribution. Checking the chi-square distribution table (Table 3 of Appendix B), we find that with $k - 1 = 3 - 1 = 2$ degrees of freedom, $\chi^2_{.05} = 5.99$. Since $7.34 > 5.99$, we reject H_0. In rejecting H_0 we are concluding that the introduction of the new product by company C will alter the current market-share structure. The goodness of fit test itself allows no further conclusions, but we can compare the observed and expected frequencies informally to obtain an idea of how the market-share structure has changed.

Considering company C, we find that the observed frequency of 54 is larger than the expected frequency of 40. Since the expected frequency was based on current market shares, the larger observed frequency suggests that the new product will have a positive effect on company C's market share. Comparisons of the observed and expected frequencies for the other two companies indicate that company C's gain in market share will hurt company A more than company B.

As illustrated in the example, the goodness of fit test uses the chi-square distribution to determine whether a hypothesized multinomial probability distribution for a population provides a good fit. The hypothesis test is based on differences between the observed frequencies in a sample and the expected frequencies based on the assumed population distribution. Let us outline the general steps that can be used to conduct a goodness of fit test for any hypothesized multinomial population distribution.

MULTINOMIAL DISTRIBUTION GOODNESS OF FIT TEST: A SUMMARY

1. Set up the null and alternative hypotheses.

   H_0: The population follows a multinomial probability distribution with specified probabilities for each of k categories.

   H_a: The population does not follow a multinomial probability distribution with the specified probabilities for each of the k categories.

2. Select a random sample and record the observed frequencies, f_i, for each category.

3. Assuming the null hypothesis is true, determine the expected frequency, e_i, in each category by multiplying the category probability by the sample size.

4. Compute the value of the test statistic.

$$\chi^2 = \sum_{i=1}^{k} \frac{(f_i - e_i)^2}{e_i}$$

5. Rejection rule:

$$\text{Reject } H_0 \text{ if } \chi^2 > \chi^2_\alpha$$

where α is the level of significance for the test and there are $k - 1$ degrees of freedom.

NOTES AND COMMENTS

• • • • • • • • • • • • • • •

1. For χ^2 goodness of fit tests the rejection region is always in the upper tail. The differences between observed and expected frequencies are squared, and larger differences lead to larger values for χ^2.
2. Many applications of the goodness of fit test involve choosing a sample and observing the category to which each sampled item belongs. In such cases one must take care to choose a random sample. Otherwise, the independence assumption will not be satisfied.

EXERCISES

METHODS

Self-Test

1. Test the following hypotheses by using the χ^2 goodness of fit test.

$$H_0: p_A = .40, p_B = .40, \text{ and } p_C = .20$$

$$H_a: \text{The population proportions are not}$$
$$p_A = .40, p_B = .40, \text{ and } p_C = .20$$

   A sample of size 200 yielded 60 in category A, 120 in category B, and 20 in category C. Use $\alpha = .01$ and test to see whether the proportions are as stated in H_0.

2. Suppose we have a multinomial population with four categories: A, B, C, and D. The null hypothesis is that the proportion of items is the same in every category. The null hypothesis is

$$H_0: p_A = p_B = p_C = p_D = .25.$$

   A sample of size 300 yielded the following numbers in each category.

$$A: 85 \qquad B: 95 \qquad C: 50 \qquad D: 70$$

   Use $\alpha = .05$ and the χ^2 test to determine whether H_0 should be rejected.

APPLICATIONS

Self-Test

3. During the first 13 weeks of the television season, the Saturday evening 8:00 P.M. to 9:00 P.M. audience proportions were recorded as ABC 29%, CBS 28%, NBC 25%, and independents 18%. A sample of 300 homes two weeks after a Saturday night schedule revision yielded the following viewing audience data: ABC 95 homes, CBS 70 homes, NBC 89 homes, and independents 46 homes. Test with $\alpha = .05$ to determine whether the viewing audience proportions have changed.

4. In November 1993, 17% of American manufacturers felt we were "well on our way to a national recovery," 29% felt we had "just entered a recovery from a recession," 46% were "uncertain whether we were heading back into a recession or into a recovery," 7% felt we were still in a recession, and 1% were not sure. A survey of 500 manufacturers in May 1994 elicited the following responses (Grant Thornton Survey of American Manufacturers, 1994).

Opinion Category	Number of Respondents
Well on our way to recovery	165
Just entering a recovery	105
Uncertain state	210
Still in a recession	15
Not sure	5

Perform a goodness of fit test to see whether opinions have changed. Use $\alpha = .01$.

5. The four major competitors in the computer-workstation market were reported to be Sun Microsystems (29%), Hewlett-Packard (18.8%), IBM (16%), and Digital Equipment (11.6%), with other manufacturers holding 24.6% of the market (*USA Today*, February 13, 1992). Assume that one year later a survey of 400 computer workstations finds 106 Sun, 72 Hewlett-Packard, 80 IBM, 48 Digital, and 94 other systems in use. Do the data suggest any changes have occurred during the one-year period? Test at a .05 level of significance.

6. A new container design has been adopted by a manufacturer. Color preferences indicated in a sample of 150 individuals follow.

Red	Blue	Green
40	64	46

Use $\alpha = .10$ and test for a difference in preference among the three colors. Hint: Formulate the null hypothesis as $H_0: p_1 = p_2 = p_3 = \frac{1}{3}$.

7. Consumer panel preferences for three proposed store displays follow.

Display A	Display B	Display C
43	53	39

Use $\alpha = .05$ and test to see whether there is a difference in preference among the three display designs.

8. Grade-distribution guidelines for a statistics course at a major university are: 10% A, 30% B, 40% C, 15% D, and 5% F. A sample of 120 statistics grades at the end of a semester showed 18 As, 30 Bs, 40 Cs, 22 Ds, and 10 Fs. Use $\alpha = .05$ and test whether the actual grades deviate significantly from the grade-distribution guidelines.

12.2   TEST OF INDEPENDENCE: CONTINGENCY TABLES

Another important application of the chi-square distribution involves using sample data to test for the independence of two variables. Let us illustrate the test of independence by considering the study conducted by the Alber's Brewery of Tucson, Arizona. Alber's manufactures and distributes three types of beer: light, regular, and dark. In an analysis of the market segments for the three beers, the firm's market research group has raised the question of whether or not preferences for the three beers differ among male and female beer drinkers. If beer preference is independent of the sex of the beer drinker, one advertising campaign will be initiated for all of Alber's beers. However, if beer preference depends on the sex of the beer drinker, the firm will tailor its promotions to different target markets.

A test of independence addresses the question of whether or not the beer preference (light, regular, or dark) is independent of the sex of the beer drinker (male, female). The hypotheses for this test of independence are:

H_0: Beer preference is independent of the sex of the beer drinker.

H_a: Beer preference is not independent of the sex of the beer drinker.

Table 12.1 can be used to describe the situation being studied. After identification of the population as all male and female beer drinkers, a sample can be selected and each

TABLE 12.1   Contingency Table for Beer Preference and Sex of Beer Drinker

		Beer Preference		
		Light	Regular	Dark
Sex	Male	cell(1,1)	cell(1,2)	cell(1,3)
	Female	cell(2,1)	cell(2,2)	cell(2,3)

individual asked to state his or her preference for the three Alber's beers. Every individual in the sample will be classified in one of the six cells in the table. For example, an individual may be a male preferring regular beer (cell (1,2)), a female preferring light beer (cell (2,1)), a female preferring dark beer (cell (2,3)), and so on. Since we have listed all possible combinations of beer preference and sex or, in other words, listed all possible contingencies, Table 12.1 is called a *contingency table.* The test of independence takes the contingency table format and for that reason is sometimes referred to as a *contingency table test.*

Suppose a simple random sample of 150 beer drinkers has been selected. After tasting each beer, the individuals in the sample are asked to state their preference or first choice. The crosstabulation in Table 12.2 summarizes the responses for the study. As we see, the data for the test of independence are collected in terms of counts or frequencies for each cell or category. Of the 150 individuals in the sample, 20 were men who favored light beer, 40 were men who favored regular beer, 20 were men who favored dark beer, and so on.

Note that the data in Table 12.2 are the sample or observed frequencies for each of six classes or categories. If we can determine the expected frequencies under the assumption of independence between beer preference and sex of the beer drinker, we can use the chi-square distribution, just as we did in the preceding section, to determine whether or not there is a significant difference between observed and expected frequencies.

Expected frequencies for the cells of the contingency table are based on the following rationale. First we assume that the null hypothesis of independence between beer preference and sex of the beer drinker is true. Then we note that in the entire sample of 150 beer drinkers, a total of 50 prefer light beer, 70 prefer regular beer, and 30 prefer dark beer. In terms of fractions we conclude that $50/150 = 1/3$ of the beer drinkers prefer light beer, $70/150 = 7/15$ prefer regular beer, and $30/150 = 1/5$ prefer dark beer. If the *independence* assumption is valid, we argue that these fractions must be

TABLE 12.2   Sample Results for Beer Preferences of Male and Female Beer Drinkers (Observed Frequencies)

		Beer Preference			Total
		Light	Regular	Dark	
Sex	Male	20	40	20	80
	Female	30	30	10	70
	Total	50	70	30	150

applicable to both male and female beer drinkers. Thus, under the assumption of independence, we would expect the sample of 80 male beer drinkers to show that $(\frac{1}{3})80 = 26.67$ prefer light beer, $(\frac{7}{15})80 = 37.33$ prefer regular beer, and $(\frac{1}{5})80 = 16$ prefer dark beer. Application of the same fractions to the 70 female beer drinkers provides the expected frequencies shown in Table 12.3.

Let e_{ij} denote the expected frequency for the contingency table category in row i and column j. With this notation, let us reconsider the expected frequency calculation for males (row $i = 1$) who prefer regular beer (column $j = 2$)—that is, expected frequency e_{12}. Following the preceding argument for the computation of expected frequencies, we can show that

$$e_{12} = (\tfrac{7}{15})80 = 37.33$$

This expression can be written slightly differently as

$$e_{12} = (\tfrac{7}{15})80 = (\tfrac{70}{150})80 = \frac{(80)(70)}{150} = 37.33$$

Note that 80 in the expression is the total number of males (row 1 total), 70 is the total number of individuals preferring regular beer (column 2 total), and 150 is the total sample size. Hence, we see that

$$e_{12} = \frac{(\text{Row 1 Total})(\text{Column 2 Total})}{\text{Sample Size}}$$

Generalization of the expression shows that the following formula provides the expected frequencies for a contingency table in the test of independence.

EXPECTED FREQUENCIES FOR CONTINGENCY TABLES UNDER THE ASSUMPTION OF INDEPENDENCE

$$e_{ij} = \frac{(\text{Row } i \text{ Total})(\text{Column } j \text{ Total})}{\text{Sample Size}} \tag{12.2}$$

Using the formula for male beer drinkers who prefer dark beer, we find an expected frequency of $e_{13} = (80)(30)/150 = 16.00$, as shown in Table 12.3. Use (12.2) to verify the other expected frequencies shown in Table 12.3.

The test procedure for comparing the observed frequencies of Table 12.2 with the expected frequencies of Table 12.3 is similar to the goodness of fit calculations made in

TABLE 12.3 Expected Frequencies if Beer Preference Is Independent of the Sex of the Beer Drinker

		Beer Preference			
		Light	Regular	Dark	Total
Sex	Male	26.67	37.33	16.00	80
	Female	23.33	32.67	14.00	70
	Total	50.00	70.00	30.00	150

the preceding section. Specifically, the χ^2 value based on the observed and expected frequencies is computed as follows.

TEST STATISTIC FOR INDEPENDENCE

$$\chi^2 = \sum_i \sum_j \frac{(f_{ij} - e_{ij})^2}{e_{ij}} \tag{12.3}$$

where

f_{ij} = observed frequency for contingency table category in row i and column j

e_{ij} = expected frequency for contingency table category in row i and column j based on the assumption of independence

Note: With n rows and m columns in the contingency table, the test statistic has a chi-square distribution with $(n - 1)(m - 1)$ degrees of freedom provided that the expected frequencies are 5 *or more* for all categories.

The double summation in (12.3) is used to indicate that the calculation must be made for all the cells in the contingency table.

By reviewing the expected frequencies in Table 12.3, we see that the expected frequencies are 5 or more for each category. We therefore proceed with the computation of the chi-square test statistic. Using Tables 12.2 and 12.3, we obtain

$$\chi^2 = \frac{(20 - 26.67)^2}{26.67} + \frac{(40 - 37.33)^2}{37.33} + \cdots + \frac{(10 - 14.00)^2}{14.00}$$

$$= 1.67 + .19 + \cdots + 1.14 = 6.13.$$

The number of degrees of freedom for the appropriate chi-square distribution is computed by multiplying the number of rows minus 1 by the number of columns minus 1. With two rows and three columns, we have $(2 - 1)(3 - 1) = (1)(2) = 2$ degrees of freedom for the test of independence of beer preference and sex of the beer drinker. With $\alpha = .05$ for the level of significance of the test, Table 3 of Appendix B shows an upper-tail χ^2 value of $\chi^2_{.05} = 5.99$. Note that we are again using the upper-tail value because we will reject the null hypothesis only if the differences between observed and expected frequencies provide a large χ^2 value. In our example, $\chi^2 = 6.13$ is greater than the critical value of $\chi^2_{.05} = 5.99$. Thus, we reject the null hypothesis of independence and conclude that beer preference is not independent of the sex of the beer drinker.

Although the test for independence allows no further conclusions, again we can compare the observed and expected frequencies informally to obtain an idea of how the dependence between beer preference and sex of the beer drinker comes about. Refer to Tables 12.2 and 12.3. We see that male beer drinkers have higher observed than expected frequencies for both regular and dark beers, whereas female beer drinkers have a higher observed than expected frequency only for light beer. These observations give us insight about the beer preference differences between male and female beer drinkers.

Let us summarize the steps in a contingency table test of independence.

CONTINGENCY TABLE TEST: A SUMMARY

1. Set up the null and alternative hypotheses.

H_0: The column variable is independent of the row variable

H_a: The column variable is not independent of the row variable

2. Select a random sample and record the observed frequencies for each cell of the contingency table.
3. Use (12.2) to compute the expected frequency for each cell.
4. Use (12.3) to compute a χ^2 value as a test statistic.
5. Rejection rule:

$$\text{Reject } H_0 \text{ if } \chi^2 > \chi_\alpha^2$$

where α is the level of significance for the test and with n rows and m columns there are $(n - 1)(m - 1)$ degrees of freedom.

NOTES AND COMMENTS

The test statistic for the chi-square tests in this chapter requires an expected frequency of 5 for each category. When a category has fewer than 5, it is often appropriate to combine two adjacent categories to obtain an expected frequency of 5 or more in each category. Problem 20 provides an example in which adjacent categories must be combined.

EXERCISES

METHODS

Self-Test

9. Table 12.4 is a 2×3 contingency table with observed frequencies for a sample of 200. Test for independence of the row and column factors by using the χ^2 test with $\alpha = .025$.

10. Below is a 3×3 contingency table with observed frequencies for a sample of 240. Test for independence of the row and column factors by using the χ^2 test with $\alpha = .05$.

TABLE 12.4 Exercise 9

Row Factor	Column Factor		
	A	B	C
P	20	44	50
Q	30	26	30

Row Factor	Column Factor		
	A	B	C
P	20	30	20
Q	30	60	25
R	10	15	30

APPLICATIONS

Self-Test

11. The 1992 NCAA basketball championship final four teams were Duke, Michigan, Indiana, and Cincinnati. The following data are the season three-point shooting records (*NCAA Final Four Program,* April 1992) for the four teams. At the .05 level of significance, is there a difference in three-point shooting abilities among the four teams? What is your conclusion?

3-Point Shooting	Duke	Michigan	Indiana	Cincinnati
Made	160	113	154	202
Missed	214	228	215	331

TABLE 12.5 Exercise 12

		Product	
Salesperson	**A**	**B**	**C**
Troutman	14	12	4
Kempton	21	16	8
McChristian	15	5	10

12. The numbers of units sold by three salespersons over a three-month period are reported in Table 12.5. Use $\alpha = .05$ and test for the independence of salesperson and type of product. What is your conclusion?

13. Starting positions for business and engineering graduates are classified by industry as shown in the following table.

	Industry			
Degree Major	Oil	Chemical	Electrical	Computer
Business	30	15	15	40
Engineering	30	30	20	20

Use $\alpha = .01$ and test for independence of degree major and industry type.

TABLE 12.6 Exercise 14

Response	**Men**	**Women**
Right thing	243	207
Wait longer	48	66
Not sure	9	27

14. A CBS News/*New York Times* poll (February 24, 1991) asked a sample of individuals a series of questions about the involvement of the United States in the Persian Gulf war. One question asked men and women: "Do you think the United States did the right thing in starting the ground war against Iraq, or should the United States have waited longer to see if bombing from the air worked?" Assume the responses for men and women were summarized in the contingency table shown in Table 12.6. Use the chi-square test of independence to analyze the data. What is your conclusion at a .05 level of significance?

15. Medical researchers at Harvard and Boston University randomly assigned 227 General Electric employees with alcohol problems to one of three alcohol-treatment groups: a 28-day hospitalization followed by Alcoholics Anonymous (AA) meetings, AA meetings only with no hospitalization, or a choice of the two programs (*USA Today*, September 12, 1991). Two years later, the researchers identified the patients who had remained sober after completing a program. Assume the data are as shown in the following contingency table.

	Program		
Status	Hospitalization	AA Only	Choice
Remained sober	28	13	12
Did not remain sober	48	63	63

Use the chi-square test of independence with a .01 level of significance to analyze the data. What is your conclusion and recommendation?

16. A research study (*GMAC Occasional Papers*, March 1988) provided data on the primary reason for application to an MBA program by full-time and part-time students. Do the data suggest full-time and part-time students differ in their reasons for applying to MBA programs? Explain. Use $\alpha = .01$.

Student Status	Primary Reason for Application		
	Program Quality	Convenience/Cost	Other
Full-time	421	393	76
Part-time	400	593	46

17. A sport preference poll yielded the following data for men and women:

Sex	Favorite Sport		
	Baseball	Basketball	Football
Men	19	15	24
Women	16	18	16

Use $\alpha = .05$ and test for similar sport preferences by men and women. What is your conclusion?

18. Three suppliers provide the following data on defective parts.

Supplier	Part Quality		
	Good	Minor Defect	Major Defect
A	90	3	7
B	170	18	7
C	135	6	9

Use $\alpha = .05$ and test for independence between supplier and part quality. What does the result of your analysis tell the purchasing department?

19. A study of educational levels of voters and their political party affiliations yielded the following results.

Educational Level	Party Affiliation		
	Democratic	Republican	Independent
Did not complete high school	40	20	10
High school degree	30	35	15
College degree	30	45	25

Use $\alpha = .01$ and determine whether party affiliation is independent of the educational level of the voters.

20. In a *Business Week*/Harris executive poll, senior executives were asked: "Compared with the last 12 months, do you think the rate of growth of the gross domestic product will go up, go down, or stay the same over the next 12 months?" The poll was repeated at three successive points in time. The results are summarized below (*Business Week,* January 9, 1995).

		Date of Survey			
		12/94	*6/94*	*12/93*	**Total**
Outlook	*Go Up*	152	177	101	430
	Go Down	104	72	36	212
	Stay the Same	144	152	261	557
	Not Sure	0	0	4	4
	Total	400	401	402	1203

Have the executives changed their outlook over time? Use $\alpha = .01$ to test. (Hint: Combine the "not sure" category with the "stay the same" category to obtain 5 or more for each expected frequency.)

12.3   GOODNESS OF FIT TEST: POISSON AND NORMAL DISTRIBUTIONS

In Section 12.1 we introduced the goodness of fit test for a multinomial population. In general, the goodness of fit test can be used with any hypothesized probability distribution. In this section we illustrate the goodness of fit test procedure for cases in which the population is hypothesized to have a Poisson or a normal probability distribution. As we shall see, the goodness of fit test and the use of the chi-square distribution for the test follow the same general procedure used for the goodness of fit test in Section 12.1.

A POISSON DISTRIBUTION

Let us illustrate the goodness of fit test for the case in which the hypothesized population distribution is a Poisson distribution. As an example, consider the arrival of customers at Dubek's Food Market in Tallahassee, Florida. Dubek's managers base staffing decisions about the number of clerks and the number of checkout lanes on the anticipated arrivals of customers at the store. Because of some recent staffing problems, Dubek's managers have asked a local consulting firm to assist with the scheduling of clerks for the checkout lanes. The general objective of the consulting firm's work is to provide enough clerks to achieve a good level of service while maintaining a reasonable total payroll cost.

After reviewing the checkout lane operation, the consulting firm makes a recommendation for a clerk-scheduling procedure. The procedure, based on a mathematical analysis of waiting lines, is applicable only if the number of customers arriving during a specified time period follows the Poisson probability distribution. Therefore, before the scheduling process is implemented, data on customer arrivals must be collected and a statistical test conducted to see whether an assumption of a Poisson distribution for arrivals is reasonable.

We define the arrivals at the store in terms of the *number of customers* entering the store during five-minute intervals. Hence, the following null and alternative hypotheses are appropriate for the Dubek's Food Market study.

H_0: The number of customers entering the store during five-minute intervals has a Poisson probability distribution

H_a: The number of customers entering the store during five-minute intervals does not have a Poisson distribution

If a sample of customer arrivals indicates H_0 cannot be rejected, Dubek's will proceed with the implementation of the consulting firm's scheduling procedure. However, if the sample leads to the rejection of H_0, the assumption of the Poisson distribution for the arrivals cannot be made, and other scheduling procedures will have to be considered.

To test the assumption of a Poisson distribution for the number of arrivals during weekday morning hours, a store employee randomly selects a sample of 128 five-minute intervals during weekday mornings over a three-week period. For each five-minute interval in the sample, the store employee records the number of customer arrivals. In summarizing the data, the employee determines the number of five-minute intervals having no arrivals, the number of five-minute intervals having one arrival, the number of five-minute intervals having two arrivals, and so on. These data are summarized in Table 12.7. The number of customers arriving is the category description, and the observed frequencies are recorded in the column showing the number of five-minute intervals having the corresponding number of customer arrivals.

Table 12.7 gives the observed frequency for the 10 categories. We now want to use a goodness of fit test to determine whether or not the sample of 128 time periods supports the hypothesized Poisson probability distribution. To conduct the goodness of fit test, we need to consider the expected frequency for each of the 10 categories under the assumption that the Poisson distribution of arrivals is true. That is, we need to compute the expected number of time periods in which no customers, one customer, two customers, and so on would arrive if, in fact, the customer arrivals have a Poisson distribution.

The Poisson probability function, which was first introduced in Chapter 5, is

$$f(x) = \frac{\mu^x e^{-\mu}}{x!}$$ (12.4)

In this function, μ represents the mean or expected number of customers arriving per five-minute period and x is the random variable indicating the number of customers arriving during a five-minute period. In this case, x may be equal to 0, 1, 2, and so on. Finally, $f(x)$ is the probability that x customers will arrive in a five-minute interval.

Before we use (12.4) to compute Poisson probabilities, we must obtain an estimate of μ, the mean number of customer arrivals during a five-minute time period. The sample mean for the data in Table 12.7 provides this estimate. With no customers arriving in two five-minute time periods, one customer arriving in eight five-minute time periods, and so on, the total number of customers who arrived during the sample of 128 five-minute time periods is given by $0(2) + 1(8) + 2(10) + \cdots + 9(6) = 640$. The 640 customer arrivals over the sample of 128 periods provides a mean arrival rate of $\mu = 640/128 = 5$ customers per five-minute period. With this value for the mean of the Poisson probability distribution, an estimate of the Poisson probability function for Dubek's Food Market is

$$f(x) = \frac{5^x e^{-5}}{x!}$$ (12.5)

Assume that the Poisson probability distribution, with $\mu = 5$, is appropriate for Dubek's customer arrivals. The probability function then can be evaluated for different values of x to determine the probability associated with each category of arrivals. These probabilities, which can also be found in Table 7 of Appendix B, are given in Table 12.8. For example, the probability of zero customers arriving during a five-minute interval is $f(0) = .0067$, the probability of one customer arriving during a five-minute interval is $f(1) = .0337$, and so on. As we saw in Section 12.1, the expected frequencies for the categories are found by multiplying the probabilities by the sample size. For example,

TABLE 12.7 Observed Frequency of Dubek's Customer Arrivals for a Sample of 128 Five-Minute Time Periods

Category Description: Number of Customers Arriving	Observed Frequency
0	2
1	8
2	10
3	12
4	18
5	22
6	22
7	16
8	12
9	6
Total	128

TABLE 12.8 Expected Frequency of Dubek's Customer Arrivals, Assuming a Poisson Probability Distribution with $\mu = 5$

Category Description: Number of Customers Arriving (x)	Poisson Probability $f(x)$	Expected Number of Five-Minute Time Periods with x Arrivals, $128\,f(x)$
0	.0067	.8576
1	.0337	4.3136
2	.0842	10.7776
3	.1404	17.9712
4	.1755	22.4640
5	.1755	22.4640
6	.1462	18.7136
7	.1044	13.3632
8	.0653	8.3584
9	.0363	4.6464
10 or more	.0318	4.0704
	Total	128.0000

the expected number of periods with zero arrivals is given by $(.0067)(128) = .8576$, the expected number of periods with one arrival is given by $(.0337)(128) = 4.3136$, and so on.

Before we make the usual chi-square calculations to compare the observed and expected frequencies, note that in Table 12.8, four of the categories have an expected frequency less than 5. This condition violates the requirements for use of the chi-square distribution. However, expected category frequencies less than 5 cause no difficulty, since adjacent categories can be combined to satisfy the "at least 5" expected frequency requirement. In particular, we will combine 0 and 1 into a single category and then combine 9 with "10 or more" into another single category. Thus, the rule of a minimum expected frequency of 5 in each category is satisfied.

Having combined the categories for the observed results in Table 12.7 accordingly, we can compare the observed frequencies with the expected frequencies. This comparison is summarized in Table 12.9.

As in Section 12.1, the goodness of fit test focuses on the differences between observed and expected frequencies, $f_i - e_i$. Obviously, large differences cast doubt on the assumption that the customer arrivals have a Poisson distribution.

Using the observed and expected frequencies shown in Table 12.9, we again compute the chi-square test statistic,

$$\chi^2 = \sum_{i=1}^{k} \frac{(f_i - e_i)^2}{e_i}$$

Doing so, we have

$$\chi^2 = \frac{(4.8288)^2}{5.1712} + \frac{(-.7776)^2}{10.7776} + \cdots + \frac{(-2.7168)^2}{8.7168}$$

$$= 4.5091 + .0561 + \cdots + .8468 = 10.98$$

We need to determine the appropriate degrees of freedom associated with this goodness of fit test. In general, the chi-square distribution for a goodness of fit test has $k - p - 1$ degrees of freedom, where k is the number of categories and p is the number of population parameters estimated from the sample data. For the Poisson distribution goodness of fit test we are considering, Table 12.9 shows $k = 9$ categories. Since the sample data were used to estimate the mean of the Poisson distribution, $p = 1$. Thus,

TABLE 12.9 Comparison of the Observed and Expected Frequencies for Dubek's Customer Arrivals

Category Description: Number of Customers Arriving	Observed Frequency (f_i)	Expected Frequency (e_i)	Difference $(f_i - e_i)$
0 or 1	10	5.1712	4.8288
2	10	10.7776	−.7776
3	12	17.9712	−5.9712
4	18	22.4640	−4.4640
5	22	22.4640	−.4640
6	22	18.7136	3.2864
7	16	13.3632	2.6368
8	12	8.3584	3.6416
9 or more	6	8.7168	−2.7168
Total	128	128.0000	

there are $k - p - 1 = k - 2 = 9 - 2 = 7$ degrees of freedom for the chi-square distribution in the Dubek's Food Market study.

Suppose we test the null hypothesis that the probability distribution for the customer arrivals is Poisson with a .05 level of significance ($\alpha = .05$). This is an upper-tail test, since we will reject the null hypothesis only if the difference between the observed and expected frequencies—and thus the χ^2 value—becomes large. We check the χ^2 values in Table 3 of Appendix B and find that with seven degrees of freedom, $\chi^2_{.05} = 14.07$. As in similar one-tailed tests, we will reject the null hypothesis only if the computed value of χ^2 exceeds the value of χ^2_α.

Checking the preceding calculations for the Dubek's Food Market study, we find a computed $\chi^2 = 10.98$. Since this value is less than the critical value of 14.07, we cannot reject the null hypothesis. Hence, for this analysis, the assumption of a Poisson probability distribution for weekday morning customer arrivals cannot be rejected. With this statistical finding, Dubek's managers will proceed with the consulting firm's scheduling procedure for weekday mornings.

A summary of the steps involved in conducting a Poisson distribution goodness of fit test is now given.

POISSON DISTRIBUTION GOODNESS OF FIT TEST: A SUMMARY

1. Set up the null and alternative hypotheses.

   H_0: The population has a Poisson probability distribution

   H_a: The population does not have a Poisson probability distribution

2. Select a random sample and
   a. Record the observed frequency, f_i, for each value of the Poisson random variable.
   b. Compute the mean number of occurrences, μ.

3. Compute the expected frequency of occurrences, e_i, for each value of the Poisson random variable. Multiply the sample size by the Poisson probability of occurrence for each value of the Poisson random variable (if there are fewer than five expected occurrences for some values, combine adjacent values and reduce the number of categories as necessary).

> **4.** Compute the value of the test statistic,
>
> $$\chi^2 = \sum_{i=1}^{k} \frac{(f_i - e_i)^2}{e_i}.$$
>
> **5.** Rejection rule:
>
> $$\text{Reject } H_0 \text{ if } \chi^2 > \chi_\alpha^2$$
>
> where α is the level of significance for the test and there are $k - 2$ degrees of freedom.

A NORMAL DISTRIBUTION

The goodness of fit test for a normal probability distribution is also based on the use of the chi-square distribution. It is similar to the procedure we have just discussed for the Poisson distribution. In particular, observed frequencies for several categories of sample data are compared to expected frequencies under the assumption that the population has a normal distribution. Since the normal probability distribution is continuous, we must modify the way the categories are defined and how the expected frequencies are computed. Let us demonstrate the goodness of fit test for a normal probability distribution by considering the job applicant test data for Chemline, Inc., listed in Table 12.10.

TABLE 12.10 Chemline Employee Aptitude Test Scores for 50 Randomly Chosen Job Applicants

71	66	61	65	54	93
60	86	70	70	73	73
55	63	56	62	76	54
82	79	76	68	53	58
85	80	56	61	61	64
65	62	90	69	76	79
77	54	64	74	65	65
61	56	63	80	56	71
79	84				

Chemline hires approximately 400 new employees annually for its four plants located throughout the United States. Standardized tests are given by the personnel department, and performance on the test is a major factor in the employee-hiring decision. With numerous tests being given annually, the personnel director has asked whether a normal distribution could be applied to the population of test scores. If such a distribution can be applied, use of the distribution would be helpful in evaluating specific test scores. That is, scores in the upper 20%, lower 40%, and so on, could be identified quickly. Hence, we want to test the null hypothesis that the population of aptitude test scores follows a normal probability distribution.

Let us first use the data in Table 12.10 to develop estimates of the mean and standard deviation of the normal distribution that will be considered in the null hypothesis. We use the sample mean $\bar{x}$ and the sample standard deviation s as point estimators of the mean and standard deviation of the normal distribution. The calculations follow.

$$\bar{x} = \frac{\Sigma x_i}{n} = \frac{3421}{50} = 68.42$$

$$s = \sqrt{\frac{\Sigma(x_i - \bar{x})^2}{n - 1}} = \sqrt{\frac{5310.0369}{49}} = 10.41$$

Using these values, we state the following hypotheses about the distribution of the job-applicant test scores.

H_0: The population of test scores has a normal distribution with mean 68.42 and standard deviation 10.41

H_a: The population of test scores does not have a normal distribution with mean 68.42 and standard deviation 10.41

The hypothesized normal distribution is shown in Figure 12.1.

Now let us consider a way of defining the categories for a goodness of fit test involving a normal distribution. For the discrete probability distribution in the Poisson

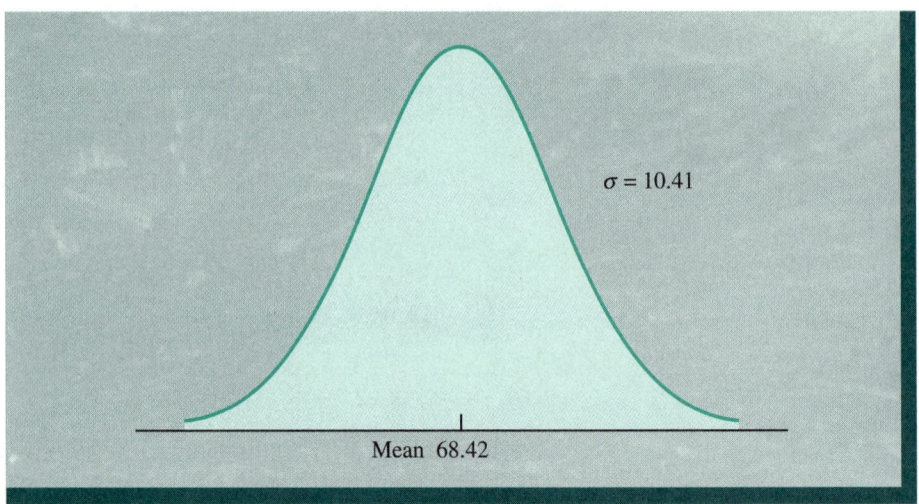

FIGURE 12.1   Hypothesized Normal Distribution of Test Scores for the Chemline Job Applicants

distribution test, the categories were readily defined in terms of the number of customers arriving, such as 0, 1, 2, and so on. However, with a continuous probability distribution such as the normal, we must use a different procedure for defining the categories. We need to define the categories in terms of *intervals* of test scores.

Recall the rule of thumb for an expected frequency of at least 5 in each interval or category. We have to define the categories of test scores such that the expected frequencies will be at least 5 for each category. With a sample size of 50, one way of doing this is to divide the normal distribution into 10 equal-probability intervals (see Figure 12.2). With a sample size of 50, we would expect five outcomes in each interval

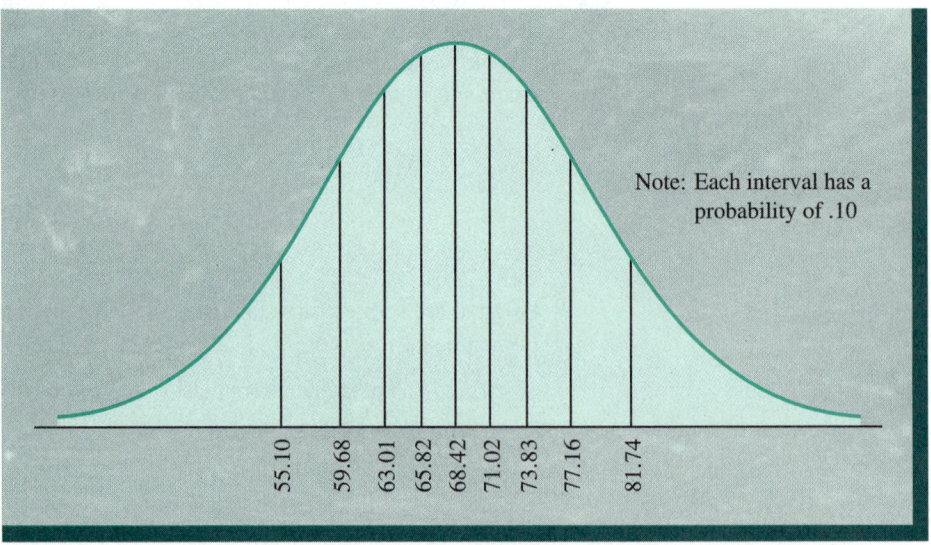

FIGURE 12.2   Normal Probability Distribution for the Chemline Example with 10 Equal-Probability Intervals

or category, and the rule of thumb for expected frequencies would be satisfied. This is the procedure we follow for determining the number of categories for the goodness of fit test whenever a continuous probability distribution is being considered. Namely, we break the assumed population distribution into equal-probability intervals such that at least five observations are expected in each.

Let us look more closely at the procedure for calculating the category boundaries. Since the normal probability distribution is being assumed, the standard normal probability tables can be used to determine these boundaries. First consider the test score cutting off the lowest 10% of the test scores. From Table 1 of Appendix B we find that the z value for this test score is -1.28. Therefore, the test score of $x = 68.42 - 1.28(10.41) = 55.10$ provides this cutoff value for the lowest 10% of the scores. For the lowest 20%, we find $z = -.84$, and thus $x = 68.42 - .84(10.41) = 59.68$. Working through the normal distribution in that way provides the following test score values.

$$
\begin{array}{lll}
\text{Lower 10\%:} & 68.42 - 1.28(10.41) = 55.10 \\
\text{Lower 20\%:} & 68.42 - .84(10.41) = 59.68 \\
\text{Lower 30\%:} & 68.42 - .52(10.41) = 63.01 \\
\text{Lower 40\%:} & 68.42 - .25(10.41) = 65.82 \\
\text{Mid-score:} & 68.42 + 0(10.41) = 68.42 \\
\text{Upper 40\%:} & 68.42 + .25(10.41) = 71.02 \\
\text{Upper 30\%:} & 68.42 + .52(10.41) = 73.83 \\
\text{Upper 20\%:} & 68.42 + .84(10.41) = 77.16 \\
\text{Upper 10\%:} & 68.42 + 1.28(10.41) = 81.74 \\
\end{array}
$$

These cutoff or interval boundary points are identified on the graph in Figure 12.2.

With the categories or intervals of test scores now defined and with the known expected frequency of 5 per category, we can return to the sample data of Table 12.10 and determine the observed frequencies for the categories. Doing so provides the results in Table 12.11. Also note that Table 12.11 contains a column of differences between the observed and expected frequencies.

With the results in Table 12.11, the goodness of fit calculations proceed exactly as before. Namely, we compare the observed and expected results by computing a χ^2 value.

TABLE 12.11 Observed and Expected Frequencies for Chemline Job-Applicant Test Scores

Test Score Interval	Observed Frequency (f_i)	Expected Frequency (e_i)	Difference ($f_i - e_i$)
Less than 55.10	5	5	0
55.10 to 59.68	5	5	0
59.68 to 63.01	9	5	4
63.01 to 65.82	6	5	1
65.82 to 68.42	2	5	−3
68.42 to 71.02	5	5	0
71.02 to 73.83	2	5	−3
73.83 to 77.16	5	5	0
77.16 to 81.74	5	5	0
81.74 and Over	6	5	1
Total	50	50	

$$\chi^2 = \sum_{i=1}^{k} \frac{(f_i - e_i)^2}{e_i} = \frac{0^2}{5} + \frac{0^2}{5} + \frac{4^2}{5} + \cdots + \frac{1^2}{5} = 7.20$$

To determine whether the computed χ^2 value of 7.20 is large enough to reject H_0, we need to refer to the appropriate chi-square probability distribution tables. Using the rule for computing the number of degrees of freedom for the goodness of fit test, we have $k - p - 1 = 10 - 2 - 1 = 7$ degrees of freedom, where there are $k = 10$ categories and $p = 2$ parameters (mean and standard deviation) estimated from the sample data. Using a .10 level of significance for this hypothesis test, we have $\chi^2_{.10} = 12.017$ for the upper-tail rejection region. With $7.20 < 12.017$, we conclude that the null hypothesis cannot be rejected. Hence, the hypothesis that the probability distribution for the Chemline job applicant test scores is a normal probability distribution cannot be rejected.

A summary of the steps for the normal distribution goodness of fit test follows.

NORMAL DISTRIBUTION GOODNESS OF FIT TEST: A SUMMARY

1. Set up the null and alternative hypotheses.

H_0: The population has a normal probability distribution

H_a: The population does not have a normal probability distribution

2. Select a random sample and
   a. Compute the mean and standard deviation.
   b. Define intervals of values so that the expected frequency is at least 5 for each interval. Using equal probability intervals is a good approach.
   c. Record the observed frequency of data values, f_i, in each interval defined.
3. Compute the expected number of occurrences, e_i, for each interval of values defined in 2(b). Multiply the sample size by the probability of a normal random variable being in the interval.
4. Compute the value of the test statistic,

$$\chi^2 = \sum_{i=1}^{k} \frac{(f_i - e_i)^2}{e_i}.$$

5. Rejection rule:

Reject H_0 if $\chi^2 > \chi^2_\alpha$

where α is the level of significance for the test and there are $k - 3$ degrees of freedom.

TABLE 12.12   Exercise 21

Number of Occurrences	Observed Frequency
0	39
1	30
2	30
3	18
4	3

EXERCISES

METHODS

Self-Test

21. Shown in Table 12.12 are data on the number of occurrences per time period and observed frequencies. Use $\alpha = .05$ and the goodness of fit test to see whether the data fit a Poisson distribution.

22. The following data are believed to have come from a normal probability distribution. Use the goodness of fit test and $\alpha = .025$ to test this claim.

17	23	22	24	19	23	18	22	20	13	11	21	18	20	21
21	18	15	24	23	23	43	29	27	26	30	28	33	23	29

TABLE 12.13 Exercise 23

Number of Accidents	Observed Frequency (days)
0	34
1	25
2	11
3	7
4	3

APPLICATIONS

23. The number of automobile accidents per day in a particular city is believed to have a Poisson distribution. A sample of 80 days during the past year gives the data listed in Table 12.13. Do these data support the belief that the number of accidents per day has a Poisson distribution? Use $\alpha = .05$.

24. The number of incoming phone calls at a company switchboard during one-minute intervals is believed to have a Poisson distribution. Use $\alpha = .10$ and the following data to test the assumption that the incoming phone calls have a Poisson distribution:

Number of Incoming Phone Calls During a One-Minute Interval	Observed Frequency
0	15
1	31
2	20
3	15
4	13
5	4
6	2
Total	100

TABLE 12.14 Exercise 25

18	20	22	27	22
25	22	27	25	24
26	23	20	24	26
27	25	19	21	25
26	25	31	29	25
25	28	26	28	24

25. The weekly demand for a product is believed to be normally distributed. Use a goodness of fit test and the data in Table 12.14 to test this assumption. Use $\alpha = .10$. The sample mean is 24.5 and the sample standard deviation is 3.

26. Use $\alpha = .01$ and conduct a goodness of fit test to see whether the following sample appears to have been selected from a normal distribution.

55	86	94	58	55	95	55	52	69	95	90	65	87	50	56
55	57	98	58	79	92	62	59	88	65					

After you complete the goodness of fit calculations, construct a histogram of the data. Does the histogram representation support the conclusion reached with the goodness of fit test? (Note: $\bar{x} = 71$ and $s = 17$.)

SUMMARY

In this chapter we introduced the goodness of fit test and the test of independence, both of which are based on the use of the chi-square distribution. The purpose of the goodness of fit test is to determine whether a hypothesized probability distribution can be used as a model for a particular population of interest. The computations for conducting the goodness of fit test involve comparing observed frequencies from a sample with expected frequencies when the hypothesized probability distribution is assumed true. A chi-square distribution is used to determine whether the differences between observed and expected frequencies are sufficient to reject the hypothesized probability distribution. We illustrated the goodness of fit test for multinomial, Poisson, and normal probability distributions.

A test of independence for two variables is a straightforward extension of the methodology employed in the goodness of fit test for a multinomial population. A contingency table is used to determine the observed and expected frequencies. Then a chi-square value is computed. Large chi-square values, caused by large differences between observed and expected frequencies, lead to the rejection of the null hypothesis of independence.

GLOSSARY

Multinomial population   A population in which each element is assigned to one and only one of several categories. The multinomial probability distribution extends the binomial probability distribution from two to three or more categories.

Goodness of fit test   A statistical test conducted to determine whether or not to reject a hypothesized probability distribution for a population.

Contingency table   A table used to summarize observed and expected frequencies for a test of independence.

KEY FORMULAS

Test Statistic for Goodness of Fit

$$\chi^2 = \sum_{i=1}^{k} \frac{(f_i - e_i)^2}{e_i} \tag{12.1}$$

Expected Frequencies for Contingency Tables under the Assumption of Independence

$$e_{ij} = \frac{(\text{Row } i \text{ Total})(\text{Column } j \text{ Total})}{\text{Sample Size}} \tag{12.2}$$

Test Statistic for Independence

$$\chi^2 = \sum_i \sum_j \frac{(f_{ij} - e_{ij})^2}{e_{ij}} \tag{12.3}$$

TABLE 12.15   Exercise 27

Sales Territories			
I	II	III	IV
60	45	59	36

SUPPLEMENTARY EXERCISES

27. In setting sales quotas, the marketing manager makes the assumption that order potentials are the same for each of four sales territories. A sample of 200 sales in Table 12.15 shows the numbers of orders from the territories. Should the manager's assumption be rejected? Use $\alpha = .05$.

28. Seven percent of mutual fund investors rate corporate stocks "very safe," 58% rate them "somewhat safe," 24% rate them "not very safe," 4% rate them "not at all safe," and 7% are "not sure." A *Business Week*/Harris poll asked 529 mutual fund investors how they would

TABLE 12.16 Exercise 28

Safety Rating	Frequency
Very safe	48
Somewhat safe	323
Not very safe	79
Not at all safe	16
Not sure	63
Total	529

rate corporate bonds on safety (*Business Week,* August 15, 1994). The responses shown in Table 12.16 were obtained.

Do mutual fund investors' attitudes toward corporate bonds differ from their attitudes toward corporate stock? Support your conclusion with a statistical test using $\alpha = .01$.

29. A community park is to be opened soon. A sample of 140 individuals has been asked to state their preference for when they would most like to visit the park. The sample results follow.

Week Day	Saturday	Sunday	Holiday
20	20	40	60

In developing a staffing plan, should the park manager plan on the same number visiting the park each day? Support your conclusion with a statistical test using $\alpha = .05$.

30. A regional transit authority was concerned about the number of riders on one of its bus routes. In setting up the route, the assumption was that the number of riders was the same on every day from Monday through Friday. Using the data shown in Table 12.17, test with $\alpha = .05$ to determine whether the transit authority's assumption is correct.

31. A sample of parts provided the following contingency table data on part quality by production shift.

Shift	Number Good	Number Defective
First	368	32
Second	285	15
Third	176	24

TABLE 12.17 Exercise 30

Day	Number of Riders
Monday	13
Tuesday	16
Wednesday	28
Thursday	17
Friday	16

Use $\alpha = .05$ and test the hypothesis that part quality is independent of the production shift. What is your conclusion?

32. The Graduate Management Admission Council (GMAC) sponsored a survey of MBA students to learn about characteristics of the population of students interested in graduate education in business administration. The following table was published in the *GMAC Occasional Papers* (March 1988). Do the data suggest male and female students differ in their reasons for application to MBA programs? Explain. Use $\alpha = .05$.

MBA Students	Primary Reason for Application		
	Program Quality	Convenience/Cost	Other
Male	519	599	86
Female	298	390	36

TABLE 12.18 Exercise 33

Loan Officer	Loan Approval Decision	
	Approved	Rejected
Miller	24	16
McMahon	17	13
Games	35	15
Runk	11	9

33. A lending institution supplied the data in Table 12.18 on loan approvals by four loan officers. Use $\alpha = .05$ and test to determine whether the loan approval decision is independent of the loan officer reviewing the loan application.

34. A survey of commercial buildings served by the Cincinnati Gas & Electric Company was concluded in 1992 (CG&E Commercial Building Characteristics Survey, November 25,

1992). One question asked the main type of heating fuel used and another asked the year of construction. A crosstabulation of the findings follows.

		Electricity	Natural Gas	Oil	Propane	Other	Total
		Fuel Type					**Total**
Year Constructed	1973 or before	40	183	12	5	7	247
	1974–1979	24	26	2	2	0	54
	1980–1986	37	38	1	0	6	82
	1987–1991	48	70	2	0	1	121
	Total	149	317	17	7	14	504

Do fuel type and year constructed appear to be related? Conduct a statistical test with $\alpha = .025$ to support your conclusion.

35. Below is a crosstabulation of industry type and P/E ratio for 20 companies in the consumer products and banking industries (*Business Week,* August 15, 1994).

		5–9	10–14	15–19	20–24	25–29	Total
		P/E Ratio					**Total**
Industry	Consumer	0	3	5	1	1	10
	Banking	4	4	2	0	0	10
	Total	4	7	7	1	1	20

Does there appear to be a relationship between industry type and P/E ratio? Support your conclusion with a statistical test using $\alpha = .05$.

36. The following data were collected on the number of emergency ambulance calls for an urban county and a rural county in Virginia (*Journal of the Operational Research Society,* November 1986).

		Sun	Mon	Tue	Wed	Thur	Fri	Sat	Total
		Day of Week							**Total**
County	Urban	61	48	50	55	63	73	43	393
	Rural	7	9	16	13	9	14	10	78
	Total	68	57	66	68	72	87	53	471

Conduct a test for independence using $\alpha = .05$. What is your conclusion?

37. A random sample of final examination grades for a college course follows.

```
55   85   72   99   48   71   88   70   59   98   80   74   93   85   74
82   90   71   83   60   95   77   84   73   63   72   95   79   51   85
76   81   78   65   75   87   86   70   80   64
```

Use $\alpha = .05$ and test to determine whether a normal distribution should be rejected as being representative of the population's distribution of grades.

TABLE 12.19   Exercise 39

Number of Sales	Observed Frequency (days)
0	30
1	32
2	25
3	10
4	3
Total	100

38. The 1991 office occupancy rates were reported for four California metropolitan areas (*Business Week,* 1991). Do the following data suggest that the office vacancies were independent of metropolitan area? Use a .05 level of significance. What is your conclusion?

Occupancy Status	Los Angeles	San Diego	San Francisco	San Jose
Occupied	160	116	192	174
Vacant	40	34	33	26

39. A salesperson makes four calls per day. A sample of 100 days gives the frequencies of sales volumes listed in Table 12.19. Assume the population is a binomial distribution with a probability of purchase equal to $p = .30$. Recall that in Chapter 5 binomial probabilities were given by

$$f(x) = \frac{n!}{x!(n-x)!} p^x(1-p)^{n-x}.$$

For this exercise $n = 4$, $p = .30$, and $x = 0, 1, 2, 3,$ and 4.

a. Compute the expected frequencies for $x = 0, 1, 2, 3,$ and 4 by using the binomial probability function. Combine categories if necessary to satisfy the requirement that the expected frequency is 5 or more for all categories.

b. Should the assumption of a binomial distribution be rejected? Use $\alpha = .05$.

13

ANALYSIS OF VARIANCE AND EXPERIMENTAL DESIGN

$\bar{x}$

STATISTICS IN PRACTICE ●

Burke Marketing Services, Inc.*

Cincinnati, Ohio

Burke Marketing Services, Inc., is one of the most experienced market research firms in the industry. Burke writes more proposals, on more projects, every day than any other market research company in the world. Supported by state-of-the-art technology, Burke offers a wide variety of research capabilities, providing answers to nearly any marketing question.

In one study, Burke was retained by a firm to evaluate potential new versions of a children's dry cereal. To maintain confidentiality, we refer to the cereal manufacturer as the Anon Company. The four key factors that Anon's product developers thought would enhance the taste of the cereal were:

1. Ratio of wheat to corn in the cereal flake.
2. Type of sweetener: sugar, honey, or artificial.
3. Presence or absence of flavor bits with a fruit taste.
4. Short or long cooking time.

An experiment was designed to determine what effects these four factors had on cereal taste. For example, one test cereal was made with a specified ratio of wheat to corn, sugar as the sweetener, flavor bits, and a short cooking time; another test cereal was made with a different ratio of wheat to corn and the other three factors the same, and so on. Groups of children then taste-tested the cereals and stated what they thought about the taste of each.

Analysis of variance was the statistical method used to study the data obtained from the taste tests. The results of the analysis showed that:

- The flake composition and sweetener type were very influential in taste evaluation.
- The flavor bits actually detracted from the taste of the cereal.
- The cooking time had no effect on the taste.

This information helped Anon identify the factors that would lead to the best-tasting cereal.

The experimental design employed by Burke and the subsequent analysis of variance were helpful in making a product design recommendation. In this chapter, we will see how such procedures are carried out.

Burke's in-store research provides valuable statistical information for clients.

*The authors are indebted to Dr. Ronald Tatham of Burke Marketing Services for providing this Statistics in Practice.

● In this chapter we introduce a statistical procedure called *analysis of variance* (ANOVA). First, we show how ANOVA can be used to test for the equality of three or more population means using data obtained from an observational study. Then, we discuss the use of ANOVA for the analysis of data obtained through experimental studies. We describe the completely randomized, the randomized block, and the factorial experimental designs, and show how ANOVA can be used to analyze the experimental data corresponding to each design. In the following chapters we will see that ANOVA plays a key role in analyzing the results of regression analysis involving both experimental and observational data.

13.1   AN INTRODUCTION TO ANALYSIS OF VARIANCE

National Computer Products, Inc. (NCP), manufactures printers and fax machines at plants in Charlotte, Houston, and San Diego. To measure how much employees at these plants know about total quality management, a random sample of six employees was selected from each plant and given a quality-awareness examination. The examination scores obtained for these 18 employees are listed in Table 13.1. The sample means, sample variances, and sample standard deviations for each group are also provided. Managers want to use these data to test the hypothesis that the mean examination score is the same for all three plants.

We will define population 1 as all employees at the Charlotte plant, population 2 as all employees at the Houston plant, and population 3 as all employees at the San Diego plant. Let

$$\mu_1 = \text{mean examination score for population 1,}$$

$$\mu_2 = \text{mean examination score for population 2, and}$$

$$\mu_3 = \text{mean examination score for population 3}$$

Although we will never know the actual values of μ_1, μ_2, and μ_3, we want to use the sample results to test the following hypotheses.

$$H_0: \mu_1 = \mu_2 = \mu_3$$

$$H_a: \text{Not all population means are equal}$$

As we will demonstrate shortly, analysis of variance is a statistical procedure for testing whether the observed differences are significant.

ASSUMPTIONS FOR ANALYSIS OF VARIANCE

To test the preceding hypotheses by using analysis of variance, we must make the following three assumptions.

1. **For each population, the response variable is normally distributed.** Implication: In the NCP example, the examination scores (response variable) must be normally distributed at each plant.

TABLE 13.1   Examination Scores for 18 Employees

| | Plant 1 | Plant 2 | Plant 3 |
Observation	Charlotte	Houston	San Diego
1	85	71	59
2	75	75	64
3	82	73	62
4	76	74	69
5	71	69	75
6	85	82	67
Sample mean	79	74	66
Sample variance	34	20	32
Sample standard deviation	5.83	4.47	5.66

2. **The variance of the response variable, denoted σ^2, is the same for all of the populations.** Implication: In the NCP example, the variance of examination scores must be the same for all three plants.
3. **The observations must be independent.** Implication: In the NCP example, the examination score for each employee must be independent of the examination score for any other employee.

A CONCEPTUAL OVERVIEW

Suppose the assumptions for analysis of variance are satisfied in the NCP example. If the null hypothesis is true ($\mu_1 = \mu_2 = \mu_3 = \mu$), each sample observation would have been drawn from the same normal probability distribution with mean μ and variance σ^2. For a visual perspective, consider the Minitab dotplots for the NCP data shown in Figure 13.1. Does it appear that the observations in each sample have been drawn from populations with the same mean? Although this is purely a subjective observation, you might agree that the employees at the Charlotte plant appear to have higher examination scores, whereas the employees at the San Diego plant appear to have lower examination scores.

If the means for the three populations are equal, we would expect the three sample means to be close together. In fact, the closer the three sample means are to one another, the more evidence we have for the conclusion that the population means are equal. Alternatively, the more the sample means differ, the more evidence we have for the conclusion that the population means are not equal. In other words, if the variability among the sample means is "small," it supports H_0; if the variability among the sample means is "large," it supports H_a.

If the null hypothesis, $H_0: \mu_1 = \mu_2 = \mu_3$, is true, we can use the variability among the sample means to develop an estimate of σ^2. And, if the assumptions for analysis of variance are satisfied, each sample will have come from the same normal probability distribution with mean μ and variance σ^2. Recall from Chapter 7 that the sampling distribution of the sample mean $\bar{x}$ for a simple random sample of size n from a normal population will be normally distributed with mean μ and variance σ^2/n. Figure 13.2 illustrates such a sampling distribution.

If the null hypothesis is true, we can think of each of the three sample means, $\bar{x}_1 = 79$, $\bar{x}_2 = 74$, and $\bar{x}_3 = 66$, from Table 13.1 as values drawn at random from the sampling distribution shown in Figure 13.2. In this case, the mean and variance of the three $\bar{x}$ values can be used to estimate the mean and variance of the sampling distribution. In the NCP example, the best estimate of the mean of the sampling distribution of $\bar{x}$ is the mean or average of the three sample means. That is, $(79 + 74 + 66)/3 = 73$. We refer

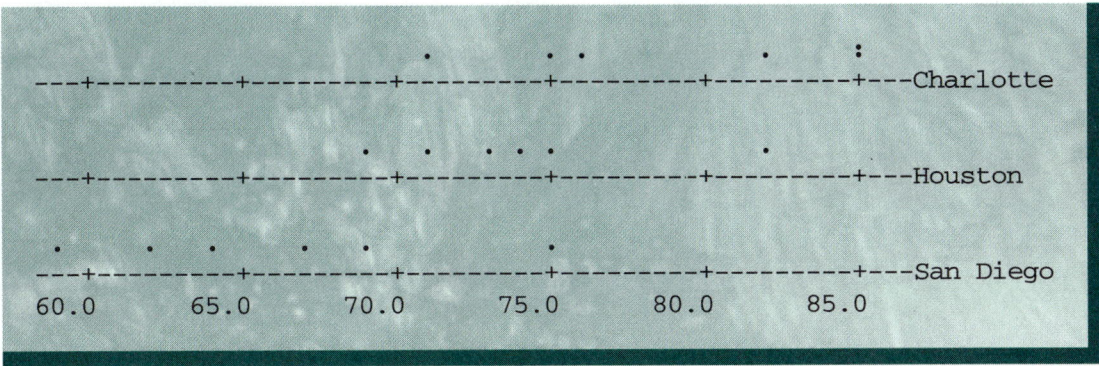

FIGURE 13.1 Minitab Dotplot for Examination Scores

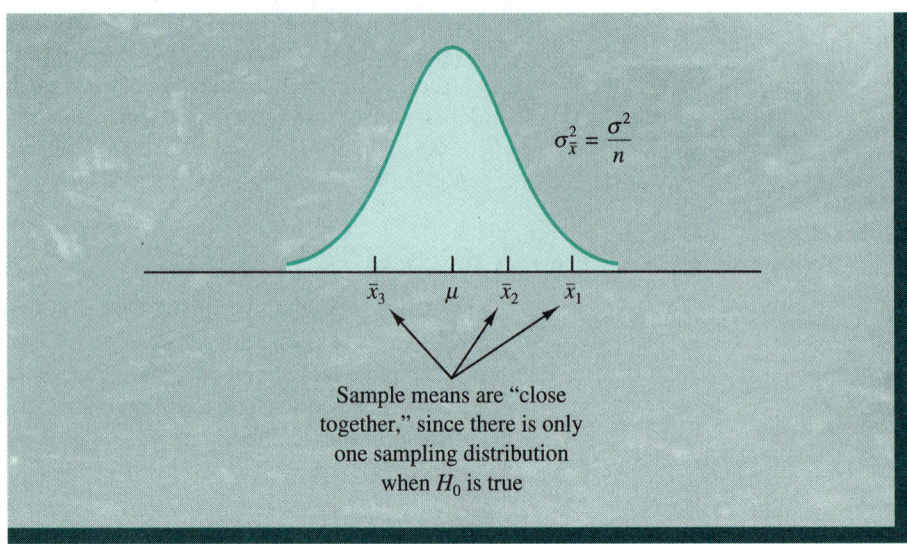

FIGURE 13.2 Sampling Distribution of $\bar{x}$ Given H_0 Is True

to this estimate as the *overall sample mean*. To estimate the variance of the sampling distribution of $\bar{x}$, we compute the variance by using the three sample means.

$$s_{\bar{x}}^2 = \frac{(79 - 73)^2 + (74 - 73)^2 + (66 - 73)^2}{3 - 1} = \frac{86}{2} = 43$$

Since $\sigma_{\bar{x}}^2 = \sigma^2/n$, solving for σ^2 gives

$$\sigma^2 = n\sigma_{\bar{x}}^2$$

Hence,

$$\text{Estimate of } \sigma^2 = n \text{ (Estimate of } \sigma_{\bar{x}}^2) = ns_{\bar{x}}^2 = 6(43) = 258$$

The result, $ns_{\bar{x}}^2 = 258$, is referred to as the *between-samples* estimate of σ^2.

The between-samples estimate of σ^2 is based on the assumption that the null hypothesis is true. In this case, each sample comes from the same population, and there is only one sampling distribution of $\bar{x}$. To illustrate what happens when H_0 is false, suppose the population means *all differ*. Note that since the three samples are from normal populations with different means, there will be three different sampling distributions. Figure 13.3 shows that in this case, the sample means are not as close together as they were when H_0 was true. Thus, $s_{\bar{x}}^2$ will be larger, causing the between-samples estimate of σ^2 to be larger. In general, when the population means are not equal, the between-samples estimate will overestimate the population variance σ^2.

The variation within each of the samples also has an effect on the conclusion we reach in analysis of variance. When a simple random sample is selected from each population, each of the sample variances provides an unbiased estimate of σ^2. Hence, we can combine or pool the individual estimates of σ^2 into one overall estimate. The estimate of σ^2 obtained in this way is called the *pooled* or *within-samples* estimate of σ^2. Because each sample variance provides an estimate of σ^2 based only on the variation within each sample, the within-samples estimate of σ^2 is not affected by whether or not the population means are equal. When the sample sizes are equal, the

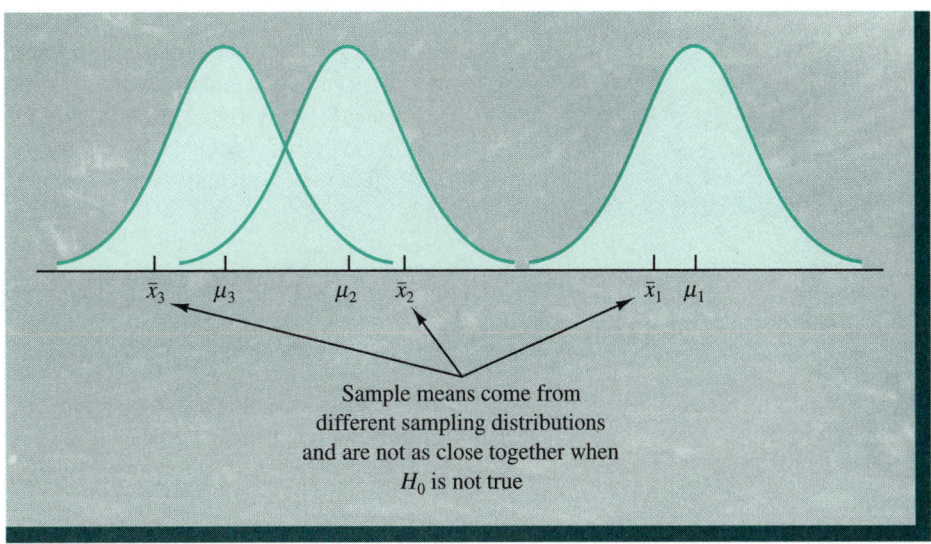

FIGURE 13.3   Sampling Distribution for $\bar{x}$ Given H_0 Is False

within-samples estimate of σ^2 can be obtained by computing the average of the individual sample variances. For the NCP example we obtain

$$\text{Within-Samples Estimate of } \sigma^2 = \frac{34 + 20 + 32}{3} = \frac{86}{3} = 28.67$$

In the NCP example, the between-samples estimate of σ^2 (258) is much larger than the within-samples estimate of σ^2 (28.67). In fact, the ratio of these two estimates is $258/28.67 = 9.00$. Recall, however, that the between-samples approach provides a good estimate of σ^2 only if the null hypothesis is true; if the null hypothesis is false, the between-samples approach *overestimates* σ^2. The within-samples approach provides a good estimate of σ^2 in either case. Thus, if the null hypothesis is true, the two estimates will be similar and their ratio will be close to 1. If the null hypothesis is false, the between-samples estimate will be larger than the within-samples estimate, and their ratio will be large. In the next section we will show how large this ratio must be to reject H_0.

In summary, the logic behind ANOVA is based on the development of two independent estimates of the common population variance σ^2. One estimate of σ^2 is based on the variability among the sample means themselves, and the other estimate of σ^2 is based on the variability of the data within each sample. By comparing these two estimates of σ^2, we will be able to determine whether the population means are equal. Since the methodology involves a comparison of variances, it is referred to as analysis of variance.

NOTES AND COMMENTS

1. In Chapter 10 we presented statistical methods for testing the hypothesis that the means of two populations are equal. ANOVA can also be used to test the hypothesis that the means of two populations are equal. In practice, however, analysis of variance is usually not used unless there are three or more population means.
2. In Chapter 10 we discussed how to test for the equality of two population means whenever one or both sample sizes are less than 30. As part of that discussion we illustrated the process of combining the results of two indenpendent random

samples to provide one estimate of σ^2; that process was referred to as pooling, and the resulting sample variance was referred to as the pooled estimator of σ^2. In analysis of variance, the within-samples estimate of σ^2 is simply the generalization of that concept to the case of more than two samples; that is why we also referred to the within-samples estimator as the pooled estimator of σ^2.

13.2 ANALYSIS OF VARIANCE: TESTING FOR THE EQUALITY OF k POPULATION MEANS

Analysis of variance can be used to test for the equality of k population means. The general form of the hypotheses tested is

$$H_0: \mu_1 = \mu_2 = \cdots = \mu_k$$

$$H_a: \text{Not all population means are equal}$$

where

$$\mu_j = \text{mean of the } j\text{th population.}$$

We assume that a simple random sample of size n_j has been selected from each of the k populations. Let

$$x_{ij} = \text{the } i\text{th observation in the } j\text{th sample,}$$

$$n_j = \text{the number of observations in the } j\text{th sample,}$$

$$\bar{x}_j = \text{the mean of the } j\text{th sample,}$$

$$s_j^2 = \text{the variance of the } j\text{th sample, and}$$

$$s_j = \text{the standard deviation of the } j\text{th sample.}$$

The formulas for the jth sample mean and variance follow.

$$\bar{x}_j = \frac{\sum\limits_{i=1}^{n_j} x_{ij}}{n_j} \tag{13.1}$$

$$s_j^2 = \frac{\sum\limits_{i=1}^{n_j} (x_{ij} - \bar{x}_j)^2}{n_j - 1} \tag{13.2}$$

The overall sample mean, denoted $\bar{\bar{x}}$, is the sum of all the observations divided by the total number of observations. That is,

$$\bar{\bar{x}} = \frac{\sum\limits_{j=1}^{k} \sum\limits_{i=1}^{n_j} x_{ij}}{n_T} \tag{13.3}$$

where

$$n_T = n_1 + n_2 + \cdots + n_k \tag{13.4}$$

If the size of each sample is n, $n_T = kn$; in this case (13.3) reduces to

$$\bar{\bar{x}} = \frac{\sum\limits_{j=1}^{k}\sum\limits_{i=1}^{n_j} x_{ij}}{nk} = \frac{\sum\limits_{j=1}^{k}\sum\limits_{i=1}^{n_j} x_{ij}/n}{k} = \frac{\sum\limits_{j=1}^{k} \bar{x}_j}{k} \qquad \textbf{(13.5)}$$

In other words, whenever the sample sizes are the same, the overall sample mean is just the average of the k sample means.

Since each sample in the NCP example consists of $n = 6$ observations, the overall sample mean can be computed by using (13.5). For the data in Table 13.1 we obtained the following result.

$$\bar{\bar{x}} = \frac{79 + 74 + 66}{3} = 73$$

Thus, if the null hypothesis is true, the overall sample mean of 73 is the best estimate of the population mean μ.

BETWEEN-SAMPLES ESTIMATE OF POPULATION VARIANCE

In the preceding section we introduced the concept of a between-samples estimate of σ^2. This estimate of σ^2 is called the *mean square between* and is denoted MSB. The formula for computing MSB is

$$\text{MSB} = \frac{\sum\limits_{j=1}^{k} n_j (\bar{x}_j - \bar{\bar{x}})^2}{k - 1} \qquad \textbf{(13.6)}$$

The numerator in (13.6) is called the *sum of squares between* and is denoted SSB. The denominator, $k - 1$, represents the degrees of freedom associated with SSB. Hence, the mean square between can be computed by the following formula.

MEAN SQUARE BETWEEN

$$\text{MSB} = \frac{\text{SSB}}{k - 1} \qquad \textbf{(13.7)}$$

where

$$\text{SSB} = \sum_{j=1}^{k} n_j (\bar{x}_j - \bar{\bar{x}})^2 \qquad \textbf{(13.8)}$$

If H_0 is true, MSB provides an unbiased estimate of σ^2. However, if the means of the k populations are not equal, MSB is not an unbiased estimate of σ^2; in fact, in that case, MSB should overestimate σ^2.

For the NCP data in Table 13.1, we obtain the following results.

$$\text{SSB} = \sum_{j=1}^{k} n_j (\bar{x}_j - \bar{\bar{x}})^2 = 6(79 - 73)^2 + 6(74 - 73)^2 + 6(66 - 73)^2 = 516$$

$$\text{MSB} = \frac{\text{SSB}}{k - 1} = \frac{516}{2} = 258$$

WITHIN-SAMPLES ESTIMATE OF POPULATION VARIANCE

The second estimate of σ^2 is based on the variation of the sample observations within each sample. This estimate of σ^2 is called the *mean square within* and is denoted MSW. The formula for computing MSW is

$$\text{MSW} = \frac{\sum_{j=1}^{k} (n_j - 1)s_j^2}{n_T - k} \tag{13.9}$$

The numerator in (13.9) is called the *sum of squares within* and is denoted SSW. The denominator of MSW is referred to as the degrees of freedom associated with SSW. Hence, the formula for MSW can also be stated as follows.

MEAN SQUARE WITHIN

$$\text{MSW} = \frac{\text{SSW}}{n_T - k} \tag{13.10}$$

where

$$\text{SSW} = \sum_{j=1}^{k} (n_j - 1)s_j^2 \tag{13.11}$$

Note that MSW is based on the variation within each of the samples; it is not influenced by whether or not the null hypothesis is true. Thus, MSW always provides an unbiased estimate of σ^2.

For the NCP data in Table 13.1 we obtain the following results.

$$\text{SSW} = \sum_{j=1}^{k} (n_j - 1)s_j^2 = (6 - 1)34 + (6 - 1)20 + (6 - 1)32 = 430$$

$$\text{MSW} = \frac{\text{SSW}}{n_T - k} = \frac{430}{18 - 3} = \frac{430}{15} = 28.67$$

COMPARING THE VARIANCE ESTIMATES: THE *F* TEST

Let us assume that the null hypothesis is true. In that case, MSB and MSW provide two independent, unbiased estimates of σ^2. Recall from Chapter 11 that for normal populations, the sampling distribution of the ratio of two independent estimates of σ^2 follows an *F* distribution. Hence, if the null hypothesis is true and the ANOVA assumptions are valid, the sampling distribution of MSB/MSW is an *F* distribution with numerator degrees of freedom equal to $k - 1$ and denominator degrees of freedom equal to $n_T - k$.

If the means of the k populations are not equal, the value of MSB/MSW will be inflated because MSB overestimates σ^2. Hence, we will reject H_0 if the resulting value of MSB/MSW appears to be too large to have been selected at random from an *F* distribution with degrees of freedom $k - 1$ in the numerator and $n_T - k$ in the denominator. The value of MSB/MSW that will cause us to reject H_0 depends on α, the level of significance. Once α is selected, a critical value can be determined. Figure 13.4

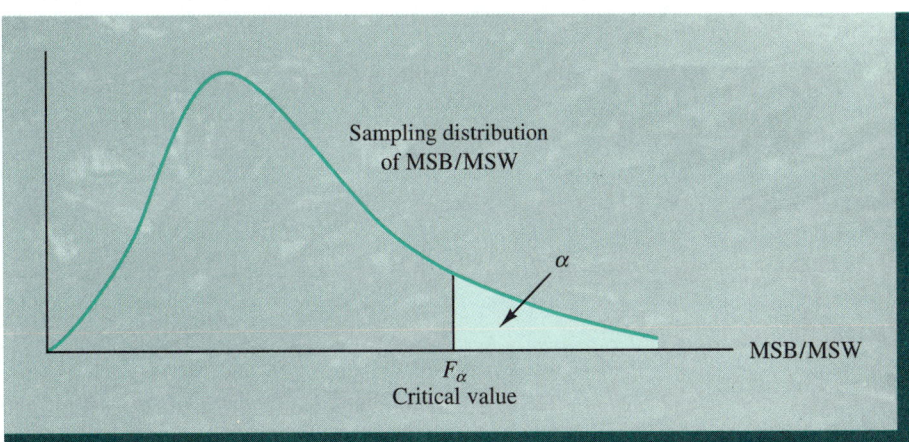

FIGURE 13.4 Sampling Distribution of MSB/MSW; the Critical Value for Rejecting the Null Hypothesis of Equality of Means Is F_α

shows the sampling distribution of MSB/MSW and the rejection region associated with a level of significance equal to α where F_α denotes the critical value. A summary of the overall procedure follows.

Test for the Equality of k Population Means

$$H_0: \mu_1 = \mu_2 \cdots \mu_k$$

H_a: Not all population means are equal

Test Statistic

$$F = \frac{\text{MSB}}{\text{MSW}} \qquad \text{(13.12)}$$

Rejection Rule at a Level of Significance α

Reject H_0 if $F > F_\alpha$

where the value of F_α is based on an F distribution with $k - 1$ numerator degrees of freedom and $n_T - k$ denominator degrees of freedom.

Suppose the manager responsible for making the decision in the National Computer Products example was willing to accept a probability of a Type I error of $\alpha = .05$. From Table 4 of Appendix B we can determine the critical F value by locating the value corresponding to numerator degrees of freedom equal to $k - 1 = 3 - 1 = 2$ and denominator degrees of freedom equal to $n_T - k = 18 - 3 = 15$. Thus, we obtain the value $F_{.05} = 3.68$. Note that this tells us that if we were to select a value at random from an F distribution with two numerator degrees of freedom and 15 denominator degrees of freedom, only 5% of the time would we observe a value greater than 3.68. Moreover, the theory behind the analysis of variance tells us that if the null hypothesis is true, the ratio of MSB/MSW would be a value from this F distribution. Hence, the appropriate rejection rule for the NCP example is written

TABLE 13.2   Analysis of Variance Table for the NCP Example

Source of Variation	Sum of Squares	Degrees of Freedom	Mean Square	F
Between	516	2	258.00	9.00
Within	430	15	28.67	
Total	946	17		

Reject H_0 if MSB/MSW > 3.68.

Recall that MSB = 258 and MSW = 28.67. Since MSB/MSW = 258/28.67 = 9.00 is greater than the critical value, $F_{.05}$ = 3.68, we have sufficient evidence to reject the null hypothesis that the means of the three populations are equal. In other words, analysis of variance supports the conclusion that the population mean examination scores at the three NCP plants are not equal.

THE ANOVA TABLE

The results of the preceding calculations can be displayed conveniently in a table referred to as the *analysis of variance table*. Table 13.2 is the analysis of variance table for the National Computer Products example. The sum of squares associated with the source of variation referred to as "Total" is called the total sum of squares (SST). Note that the results for the NCP example suggest that SST = SSB + SSW, and that the degrees of freedom associated with this total sum of squares is the sum of the degrees of freedom associated with the between-samples estimate of σ^2 and the within-samples estimate of σ^2.

We point out that SST divided by its degrees of freedom $n_T - 1$ is nothing more than the overall sample variance that would be obtained if we treated the entire set of 18 observations as one data set. With the entire data set as one sample, the formula for computing the total sum of squares, SST, is

$$SST = \sum_{j=1}^{k} \sum_{i=1}^{nj} (x_{ij} - \bar{\bar{x}})^2 \qquad \text{(13.13)}$$

It can be shown that the results we observed for the analysis of variance table for the NCP example also apply to other problems. That is,

$$SST = SSB + SSW \qquad \text{(13.14)}$$

In other words, SST can be partitioned into two sums of squares: the sum of squares between and the sum of squares within. Note also that the degrees of freedom corresponding to SST, $n_T - 1$, can be partitioned into the degrees of freedom corresponding to SSB, $k - 1$, and the degrees of freedom corresponding to SSW, $n_T - k$. The analysis of variance can be viewed as the process of partitioning the total sum of squares and the degrees of freedom into their corresponding sources: between and within. Dividing the sum of squares by the appropriate degrees of freedom provides the variance estimates and the F value used to test the hypothesis of equal population means.

COMPUTER RESULTS FOR ANALYSIS OF VARIANCE

Because of the widespread availability of statistical computer packages, analysis of variance computations with large sample sizes and/or a large number of populations can be performed easily. In Figure 13.5 we show output for the NCP example obtained from the Minitab computer package. The first part of the computer output contains the familiar ANOVA table format. Comparing Figure 13.5 with Table 13.2, we see that the same information is available, although some of the headings are slightly different. The heading SOURCE is used for the source of variation column, FACTOR identifies the between-samples row, and ERROR identifies the within-samples row. The sum of squares and degrees of freedom columns are interchanged, and a p-value is provided for the F test.

Note that below the ANOVA table the computer output contains the respective sample sizes, the sample means, and the standard deviations. In addition, Minitab provides a figure that shows individual 95% confidence interval estimates of each population mean. In developing these confidence interval estimates, Minitab uses MSW as the estimate of σ^2. Thus, the square root of MSW provides the best estimate of the population standard deviation σ. This estimate of σ on the computer output is Pooled StDev; it is equal to 5.354. To provide an illustration of how these interval estimates are developed, we will compute a 95% confidence interval estimate of the population mean for the Charlotte plant, identified as PLANT 1 in the computer output.

From our study of interval estimation in Chapter 8, we know that the general form of an interval estimate of a population mean is

$$\bar{x} \pm t_{\alpha/2}\frac{s}{\sqrt{n}} \tag{13.15}$$

where s is the estimate of the population standard deviation σ. Since in the analysis of variance the best estimate of σ is provided by the square root of MSW or the Pooled StDev, we use a value of 5.354 for s in (13.15). The degrees of freedom for the t value is 15, the degrees of freedom associated with the within-samples estimate of σ^2. Hence, with $t_{.025} = 2.131$ we obtain

$$79 \pm 2.131\frac{5.354}{\sqrt{6}} = 79 \pm 4.66$$

From this calculation, we see that the figure shown on the Minitab output for Plant 1 depicts an interval from 74.34 to 83.66. Since the sample sizes are equal for the NCP example, the confidence intervals for Plants 2 and 3 are also constructed by adding and

```
Analysis of Variance
Source      DF          SS          MS          F          p
Factor       2       516.0       258.0       9.00      0.003
Error       15       430.0        28.7
Total       17       946.0
                                        Individual 95% CIs For Mean
                                        Based on Pooled StDev
   Level     N        Mean       StDev   ---+---------+---------+---------+---
PLANT 1      6      79.000       5.831                          (------*------)
PLANT 2      6      74.000       4.472                   (------*-----)
PLANT 3      6      66.000       5.657      (-----*------)
                                        ---+---------+---------+---------+---
Pooled StDev =       5.354              63.0      70.0      77.0      84.0
```

FIGURE 13.5 Minitab Output for the NCP Analysis of Variance

subtracting 4.66 from each sample mean. Thus, in the figure provided by Minitab we see that the widths of the confidence intervals are the same.

NOTES AND COMMENTS

1. The overall sample mean can also be computed as a weighted average of the k sample means.

$$\bar{\bar{x}} = \frac{n_1\bar{x}_1 + n_2\bar{x}_2 + \cdots + n_k\bar{x}_k}{n_T}$$

In problems where the sample means are provided, this formula is simpler than (13.3) for computing the overall mean.

2. If each sample consists of n observations, (13.6) can be written as

$$\text{MSB} = \frac{n\sum_{j=1}^{k}(\bar{x}_j - \bar{\bar{x}})^2}{k-1} = n\left[\frac{\sum_{j=1}^{k}(\bar{x}_j - \bar{\bar{x}})^2}{k-1}\right] = ns_{\bar{x}}^2$$

Note that this is the same result we presented in Section 13.1 when we introduced the concept of the between-samples estimate of σ^2. Equation (13.6) is simply a generalization of this result to the unequal sample-size case.

3. If each sample has n observations, $n_T = kn$; thus, $n_T - k = k(n-1)$, and (13.9) can be rewritten as

$$\text{MSW} = \frac{\sum_{j=1}^{k}(n-1)s_j^2}{k(n-1)} = \frac{(n-1)\sum_{j=1}^{k}s_j^2}{k(n-1)} = \frac{\sum_{j=1}^{k}s_j^2}{k}$$

In other words, if the sample sizes are the same, the within-samples estimate of σ^2 is just the average of the k sample variances. Note that this is the result we used in Section 13.1 when we introduced the concept of the within-samples estimate of σ^2.

EXERCISES

METHODS

Self-Test

1. Samples of five observations were selected from each of three populations. The data obtained follow.

Observation	Sample 1	Sample 2	Sample 3
1	32	44	33
2	30	43	36
3	30	44	35
4	26	46	36
5	32	48	40
Sample mean	30	45	36
Sample variance	6.00	4.00	6.50

a. Develop the dotplots for these data. From your subjective evaluation of the dotplots, do the observations in each sample appear to have been drawn from the same population?

b. Compute the between-samples estimate of σ^2.

c. Compute the within-samples estimate of σ^2.

d. At the $\alpha = .05$ level of significance, can we reject the null hypothesis that the means of the three populations are equal?

e. Set up the ANOVA table for this problem.

2. Four observations were selected from each of three populations. The data obtained follow.

Observation	Sample 1	Sample 2	Sample 3
1	165	174	169
2	149	164	154
3	156	180	161
4	142	158	148
Sample mean	153	169	158
Sample variance	96.67	97.33	82.00

a. Compute the between-samples estimate of σ^2.

b. Compute the within-samples estimate of σ^2.

c. At the $\alpha = .05$ level of significance, can we reject the null hypothesis that the three population means are equal? Explain.

d. Set up the ANOVA table for this problem.

3. Samples were selected from three populations. The data obtained are shown in Table 13.3.

a. Compute the between-samples estimate of σ^2.

b. Compute the within-samples estimate of σ^2.

c. At the $\alpha = .05$ level of significance, can we reject the null hypothesis that the three population means are equal? Explain.

d. Set up the ANOVA table for this problem.

TABLE 13.3 Exercise 3

Sample 1	Sample 2	Sample 3
93	77	88
98	87	75
107	84	73
102	95	84
	85	75
	82	
$\bar{x}_j$ 100	85	79
s_j^2 35.33	35.60	43.50

4. A random sample of 16 observations was selected from each of four populations. A portion of the ANOVA table follows.

Source of Variation	Sum of Squares	Degrees of Freedom	Mean Square	F
Between			400	
Within				
Total	1500			

a. Provide the missing entries for the ANOVA table.

b. At the $\alpha = .05$ level of significance, can we reject the null hypothesis that the means of the four populations are equal?

5. Random samples of 25 observations were selected from each of three populations. For these data, SSB = 120 and SSW = 216.

a. Set up the ANOVA table for this problem.

b. At the $\alpha = .05$ level of significance, what is the critical *F* value?

c. At the $\alpha = .05$ level of significance, can we reject the null hypothesis that the three population means are equal?

APPLICATIONS

Self-Test

6. To test whether the mean time needed to mix a batch of material is the same for machines produced by three manufacturers, the Jacobs Chemical Company obtained the data in

TABLE 13.4 Exercise 6

	Manufacturer		
	1	**2**	**3**
	20	28	20
	26	26	19
	24	31	23
	22	27	22
$\bar{x}_j$	23	28	21
s_j^2	6.67	4.67	3.33

TABLE 13.5 Exercise 7

	Superior	Peer	Subordinate
	8	6	6
	5	6	5
	4	7	7
	6	5	4
	6	3	3
	7	4	5
	5	7	7
	5	6	5
$\bar{x}_j$	5.75	5.5	5.25
s_j^2	1.64	2.00	1.93

Table 13.4 on the time (in minutes) needed to mix the material. Use these data to test whether the population mean times for mixing a batch of material differ for the three manufacturers. Use $\alpha = .05$.

7. Managers at all levels of an organization need adequate information to perform their respective tasks. A recent study investigated the effect the source has on the dissemination of the information (*Journal of Management Information Systems,* Fall 1988). In this particular study the sources of information were a superior, a peer, and a subordinate. In each case, a measure of dissemination was obtained, with higher values indicating greater dissemination of information. Using $\alpha = .05$ and the data in Table 13.5, test whether or not the source of information significantly affects dissemination. What is your conclusion, and what does it suggest about the use and dissemination of information?

8. A study investigated the perception of corporate ethical values among individuals specializing in marketing (*Journal of Marketing Research,* July 1989). Suppose the following data were obtained in a similar study (higher scores indicate higher ethical values). Using $\alpha = .05$, test for significant differences in perception among the three groups of specialists.

	Marketing Managers	Marketing Research	Advertising
	6	5	6
	5	5	7
	4	4	6
	5	4	5
	6	5	6
	4	4	6
$\bar{x}_j$	5	4.5	6
s_j^2	.8	.3	.4

9. To test for any significant difference in the number of hours between breakdowns for four machines, the following data were obtained.

MACHINES

	Machine			
	1	**2**	**3**	**4**
	6.4	8.7	11.1	9.9
	7.8	7.4	10.3	12.8
	5.3	9.4	9.7	12.1
	7.4	10.1	10.3	10.8
	8.4	9.2	9.2	11.3
	7.3	9.8	8.8	11.5
$\bar{x}_j$	7.1	9.1	9.9	11.4
s_j^2	1.21	.93	.70	1.02

At the $\alpha = .05$ level of significance, is there any difference in the population mean times among the four machines?

10. The *Business Week* Global 1000 ranks companies on the basis of their market value (*Business Week,* July 11, 1994). The following table shows the P/E ratios for 30 companies classified as being in the finance economic sector. An industry code of 1 indicates a banking firm, a code of 2 a financial services firm, and a code of 3 an insurance firm. At the .05 level of significance, test whether the mean price/earnings ratio is the same for these three groups of financial firms.

Company	Industry Code	P/E	Company	Industry Code	P/E
Citicorp	1	8.0	Dean Witter, Discover	2	10.0
NationsBank	1	10.0	MBNA	2	18.0
Wells Fargo	1	13.0	Cincinnati Financial	2	14.0
First Union	1	3.4	Franklin Resources	2	14.0
KeyCorp	1	11.0	Fannie Mae	2	11.0
Chase Manhattan	1	6.0	American International	3	15.0
Fifth Third Bancorp	1	16.0	Group		
Bank of New York	1	9.0	Allstate	3	16.0
First Chicago	1	6.0	Marsh & McLennan	3	18.0
Mellon Bank	1	10.0	American General	3	10.0
Fleet Financial	1	12.0	Cigna	3	11.0
Group			Lincoln National	3	9.0
First Bank System	1	15.0	AFLAC	3	14.0
American Express	2	12.0	Equitable	3	15.0
Travelers	2	22.0	Chubb	3	11.0
Merrill Lynch	2	17.0	General Re	3	16.0

MKTVALUE

13.3 MULTIPLE COMPARISON PROCEDURES

When we use analysis of variance to test whether the means of k populations are equal, rejection of the null hypothesis allows us to conclude only that the population means are *not all equal*. In some cases we will want to go a step further and determine where the differences among means occur. The purpose of this section is to introduce two methods that can be used to conduct statistical comparisons between pairs of population means.[xi]

FISHER'S LSD

Suppose that analysis of variance has provided statistical evidence to reject the null hypothesis of equal population means. In this case, Fisher's least significance difference (LSD) procedure can be used to determine where the differences occur. To illustrate the use of Fisher's LSD procedure in making pairwise comparisons of population means, recall the NCP example introduced in Section 13.1. Using analysis of variance, we concluded that the population mean examination scores are not the same at the three plants. In this case, the follow-up question is: We believe the plants differ, but where do the differences occur? That is, do the means of populations 1 and 2 differ? Or those of populations 1 and 3? Or those of populations 2 and 3?

In Chapter 10 we presented a statistical procedure for testing the hypothesis that the means of two populations are equal. With a slight modification in how we estimate the population variance, Fisher's LSD procedure is based on the t test statistic presented for the two-population case. The following table provides a summary of Fisher's LSD procedure.

Fisher's LSD Procedure

$$H_0: \mu_i = \mu_j$$

$$H_a: \mu_i \neq \mu_j$$

Test Statistic

$$t = \frac{\bar{x}_i - \bar{x}_j}{\sqrt{MSW\left(\frac{1}{n_i} + \frac{1}{n_j}\right)}} \tag{13.16}$$

Rejection Rule

Reject H_0 if $t < -t_{\alpha/2}$ or $t > t_{\alpha/2}$

where the value of $t_{\alpha/2}$ is based on a t distribution with $n_T - k$ degrees of freedom.

Let us now apply this procedure to determine whether there is a significant difference between the means of population 1 (Charlotte) and population 2 (Houston). Table 13.1 shows that the sample mean is 79 for the Charlotte plant and 74 for the Houston plant. Table 13.2 shows that the value of MSW is 28.67; this is the estimate of σ^2 and is based on 15 degrees of freedom. At the .05 level of significance, the t distribution table shows that with $n_T - k = 18 - 3 = 15$ degrees of freedom, $t_{.025} = 2.131$. Thus, if $t < -2.131$ or $t > 2.131$, we reject H_0: $\mu_1 = \mu_2$. For the NCP data we obtain the following t value.

$$t = \frac{79 - 74}{\sqrt{28.67\left(\frac{1}{6} + \frac{1}{6}\right)}} = 1.62$$

Since $t = 1.62$, we do not have sufficient statistical evidence to reject the null hypothesis; hence, we cannot conclude that the population mean score at the Charlotte plant is different from the population mean score at the Houston plant.

Many practitioners find it easier to determine how large the difference between the sample means must be to reject H_0. In this case the test statistic is $\bar{x}_i - \bar{x}_j$, and the test is conducted by the following procedure.

Fisher's LSD Procedure Based on the Test Statistic $\bar{x}_i - \bar{x}_j$

$$H_0: \mu_i = \mu_j$$
$$H_a: \mu_i \neq \mu_j$$

Test Statistic

$$\bar{x}_i - \bar{x}_j$$

Rejection Rule at a Level of Significance α

Reject H_0 if $|\bar{x}_i - \bar{x}_j| > LSD$

where

$$LSD = t_{\alpha/2}\sqrt{MSW\left(\frac{1}{n_i} + \frac{1}{n_j}\right)} \tag{13.17}$$

For the NCP example the value of LSD is

$$\text{LSD} = 2.131 \sqrt{28.67\left(\frac{1}{6} + \frac{1}{6}\right)} = 6.59$$

Note that when the sample sizes are equal, only one value for LSD is computed. In such cases we can simply compare the magnitude of the difference between any two means with the value of LSD. For example, the difference between the sample means for population 1 (Charlotte) and population 3 (San Diego) is $79 - 66 = 13$. Since this difference is greater than 6.59, we can reject the null hypothesis that the population mean examination score for the Charlotte plant is equal to the population mean score for the San Diego plant. Similarly, since the difference between the sample means for populations 2 and 3 is $74 - 66 = 8 > 6.59$, we can also reject the hypothesis that the population mean examination score for the Houston plant is equal to the population mean examination score for the San Diego plant. In effect, our conclusion is that the Charlotte and Houston plants both differ from the San Diego plant.

Fisher's LSD can also be used to develop a confidence interval estimate of the difference between the means of two populations. The general procedure follows.

CONFIDENCE INTERVAL ESTIMATE OF THE DIFFERENCE BETWEEN TWO POPULATION MEANS USING FISHER'S LSD PROCEDURE

$$\bar{x}_i - \bar{x}_j \pm \text{LSD} \tag{13.18}$$

where

$$\text{LSD} = t_{\alpha/2} \sqrt{\text{MSW}\left(\frac{1}{n_i} + \frac{1}{n_j}\right)} \tag{13.19}$$

and $t_{\alpha/2}$ is based on a t distribution with $n_T - k$ degrees of freedom.

If the confidence interval in (13.19) includes the value zero, we cannot reject the hypothesis that the two population means are equal. However, if the confidence interval does not include the value zero, we conclude that there is a difference between the population means. For the NCP example, recall that $\text{LSD} = 6.59$ (corresponding to $t_{.025} = 2.131$). Thus, a 95% confidence interval estimate of the difference between the means of populations 1 and 2 is $79 - 74 \pm 6.59 = 5 \pm 6.59 = -1.59$ to 11.59; since this interval includes zero, we cannot reject the hypothesis that the two population means are equal.

TYPE I ERROR RATES

We began the discussion of Fisher's LSD procedure with the premise that analysis of variance had given us statistical evidence to reject the null hypothesis of equal population means. We showed how Fisher's LSD procedure can be used in such cases to determine where the differences occur. Technically, this is referred to as a *protected* or *restricted* LSD test since it is employed only if we first find a significant F value by using analysis of variance. To see why this is important in multiple comparison tests, we need to explain the difference between a *comparisonwise* Type I error rate and an *experimentwise* Type I error rate.

In the NCP example we used Fisher's LSD procedure to make three pairwise comparisons.

Test 1	Test 2	Test 3
H_0: $\mu_1 = \mu_2$	H_0: $\mu_1 = \mu_3$	H_0: $\mu_2 = \mu_3$
H_a: $\mu_1 \neq \mu_2$	H_a: $\mu_1 \neq \mu_3$	H_a: $\mu_2 \neq \mu_3$

In each case, we used a level of significance of $\alpha = .05$. Therefore, for each test, if the null hypothesis is true, the probability that we will make a Type I error is $\alpha = .05$; hence, the probability that we will not make a Type I error is $1 - .05 = .95$. In discussing multiple comparison procedures we refer to this probability of a Type I error ($\alpha = .05$) as the *comparisonwise Type I error rate;* comparisonwise Type I error rates indicate the level of significance associated with a single pairwise comparison.

Let us now consider a slightly different question. What is the probability that in making three pairwise comparisons, we will commit a Type I error on at least one of the three tests? To answer this question, note that the probability that we will not make a Type I error on any of the three tests is $(.95)(.95)(.95) = .8574$.* Therefore, the probability of making at least one Type I error is $1 - .8574 = .1426$. Thus, when we use Fisher's LSD procedure to make all three pairwise comparisons, the Type I error rate associated with this approach is not .05, but actually .1426; we refer to this error rate as the *overall* or *experimentwise Type I error rate.* To avoid confusion, we denote the experimentwise Type I error rate as α_{EW}.

The experimentwise Type I error rate gets larger for problems with more populations. For example, for a problem with five populations, there are 10 possible pairwise comparisons. If we tested all possible pairwise comparisons by using Fisher's LSD with a comparisonwise error rate of $\alpha = .05$, the experimentwise Type I error rate would be $1 - (1 - .05)^{10} = .40$. In such cases, practitioners look to alternatives that provide better control over the experimentwise error rate.

One alternative for controlling the overall experimentwise error rate, referred to as the Bonferroni adjustment, involves using a smaller comparisonwise error rate for each test. For example, if we want to test C pairwise comparisons and want the maximum probability of making a Type I error for the overall experiment to be α_{EW}, we simply use a comparisonwise error rate equal to α_{EW}/C. In the NCP example, if we want to use Fisher's LSD procedure to test all three pairwise comparisons with a maximum experimentwise error rate of $\alpha_{EW} = .05$, we set the comparisonwise error rate to be $\alpha = .05/3 = .017$. For a problem with five populations and 10 possible pairwise comparisons, the Bonferroni adjustment would suggest a comparisonwise error rate of $.05/10 = .005$. Recall from our discussion of hypothesis testing in Chapter 9 that for a fixed sample size, any decrease in the probability of making a Type I error will result in an increase in the probability of making a Type II error, which corresponds to accepting the hypothesis that the two population means are equal when in fact they are not equal. As a result, many practitioners are reluctant to perform individual tests with a very low comparisonwise Type I error rate because of the increased risk of making a Type II error.

Several other procedures, such as Tukey's procedure and Duncan's multiple range test, have been developed to help in such situations. However, there is considerable controversy in the statistical community as to which procedure is "best." The truth is that no one procedure is best for all types of problems.

---

*The assumption is that the three tests are independent, and hence the joint probability of the three events can be obtained by simply multiplying the individual probabilities. In fact, the three tests are not independent since MSW is used in each test; therefore, the error involved is even greater than that shown.

EXERCISES

METHODS

11. In Exercise 1, five observations were selected from each of three populations. For these data, $\bar{x}_1 = 30$, $\bar{x}_2 = 45$, $\bar{x}_3 = 36$, and MSW = 5.5. At the $\alpha = .05$ level of significance, the null hypothesis of equal population means was rejected. In the following calculations, use $\alpha = .05$.

TABLE 13.6 Exercise 12

	Sample 1	Sample 2	Sample 3
	63	82	69
	47	72	54
	54	88	61
	40	66	48
$\bar{x}_j$	51	77	58
s_j^2	96.67	97.34	81.99

   a. Using Fisher's LSD procedure, test to see whether there is a significant difference between the means of populations 1 and 2, populations 1 and 3, and populations 2 and 3.

   b. Use Fisher's LSD procedure to develop a 95% confidence interval estimate of the difference between the means of populations 1 and 2.

12. Four observations were selected from each of three populations. The data obtained are listed in Table 13.6. In the following calculations, use $\alpha = .05$.

   a. Using analysis of variance, test for a significant difference among the means of the three populations.

   b. Use Fisher's LSD procedure to see which means are different.

APPLICATIONS

13. Refer to Exercise 6. For these data $\bar{x}_1 = 23$, $\bar{x}_2 = 28$, $\bar{x}_3 = 21$, and MSW = 4.89. At the $\alpha = .05$ level of significance, use Fisher's LSD procedure to test for the equality of the means for manufacturers 1 and 3. What conclusion can you draw after carrying out this test?

14. Refer to Exercise 13. Use Fisher's LSD procedure to develop a 95% confidence interval estimate of the difference between the means of population 1 and population 2.

15. Refer to Exercise 8. At the $\alpha = .05$ level of significance, we can conclude that there are differences in the perceptions for marketing managers ($\bar{x}_1 = 5$), marketing research specialists ($\bar{x}_2 = 4.5$), and advertising specialists ($\bar{x}_3 = 6$); for these data MSW = .5. Use the procedures in this section to determine where the differences occur. Use $\alpha = .05$.

16. In Exercise 9, data showing the number of hours between breakdowns for four machines are provided; the sample means are 7.1, 9.1, 9.9, and 11.4, and MSW = .97. Use Fisher's LSD procedure to test for the equality of the means for machines 2 and 4. Use a .05 level of significance.

17. Refer to Exercise 16. Use the Bonferroni adjustment to test for a significant difference between all pairs of means. Assume that a maximum overall experimentwise error rate of .05 is desired.

18. Refer to Exercise 10. At the .05 level of significance, we can conclude that there are differences between the mean price/earnings ratios of banking firms ($\bar{x}_1 = 9.95$), financial services firms ($\bar{x}_2 = 14.75$), and insurance firms ($\bar{x}_3 = 13.5$); for these data MSW = 13.0. Use the procedures in this section to determine where the differences occur. Use $\alpha = .05$.

13.4 AN INTRODUCTION TO EXPERIMENTAL DESIGN

Statistical studies can be classified as being either experimental or observational. In an *experimental study,* variables of interest are identified. Then, one or more factors in the study are controlled so that data can be obtained about how the factors influence the variables. In *observational* or *nonexperimental* studies, no attempt is made to control the factors. A survey (see Chapter 21) is perhaps the most common type of observational study.

The NCP example that we used to introduce analysis of variance is an illustration of an observational statistical study. To measure how much NCP employees knew about total quality management, a random sample of six employees was selected from each of NCP's three plants and given a quality-awareness examination. The examination scores for these employees were then analyzed by analysis of variance to test the hypothesis that the population mean examination scores were equal for the three plants.

As an example of an experimental statistical study, let us consider the problem facing Chemitech, Inc. Chemitech has developed a new filtration system for municipal water supplies. The components for the new filtration system will be purchased from several suppliers, and Chemitech will assemble the components at its plant in Columbia, South Carolina. The industrial engineering group has been given the responsibility of determining the best assembly method for the new filtration system. After considering a variety of possible approaches, the group has narrowed the alternatives to three: method A, method B, and method C. These methods differ in the sequence of steps used to assemble the product. Managers at Chemitech want to determine which assembly method can produce the greatest number of filtration systems per week.

In the Chemitech experiment, assembly method is referred to as a *factor*. Since there are three assembly methods corresponding to this factor, we say that there are three *treatments* associated with this experiment: one treatment corresponds to method A, another to method B, and the third to method C. In general, a factor is just a variable that the experimenter has selected for investigation, and a treatment is a level of a factor. The Chemitech problem is an example of a single-factor experiment involving a qualitative factor (method of assembly). Other experiments may consist of multiple factors; some may be qualitative and some may be quantitative.

The three assembly methods or treatments define the three populations of interest for the Chemitech experiment. One population is all Chemitech employees who use assembly method A, another is those who use method B, and the third is those who use method C. Note that for each population the random variable of interest (the response variable) is the number of filtration systems assembled per week, and the primary statistical objective of the experiment is to determine whether the mean number of units produced per week is the same for all three populations. In experimental design terminology, the random variable of interest is called the *dependent variable,* the *response variable,* or simply the *response.*

Suppose a random sample of three employees is selected from all assembly workers at the Chemitech production facility. In experimental design terminology, the three randomly selected workers are the *experimental units.* The experimental design that we will use for the Chemitech problem is called a *completely randomized design.* This type of design requires that each of the three assembly methods or treatments be assigned randomly to one of the experimental units or workers. For example, method A might be assigned to the second worker, method B to the first worker, and method C to the third worker. The concept of *randomization,* as illustrated in this example, is an important principle of all experimental designs.

Note that the experiment would result in only one measurement or number of units assembled for each treatment. In other words, we have a sample size of one corresponding to each treatment. To obtain additional data for each assembly method, we must repeat or replicate the basic experimental process. Suppose, for example, that instead of selecting just three workers at random we had selected 15 workers and then randomly assigned each of the three treatments to five of the workers. Since each method of assembly is assigned to five workers, we say that five replicates have been obtained. The process of *replication* is another important principle of experimental design. Figure 13.6 shows the completely randomized design for the Chemitech experiment.

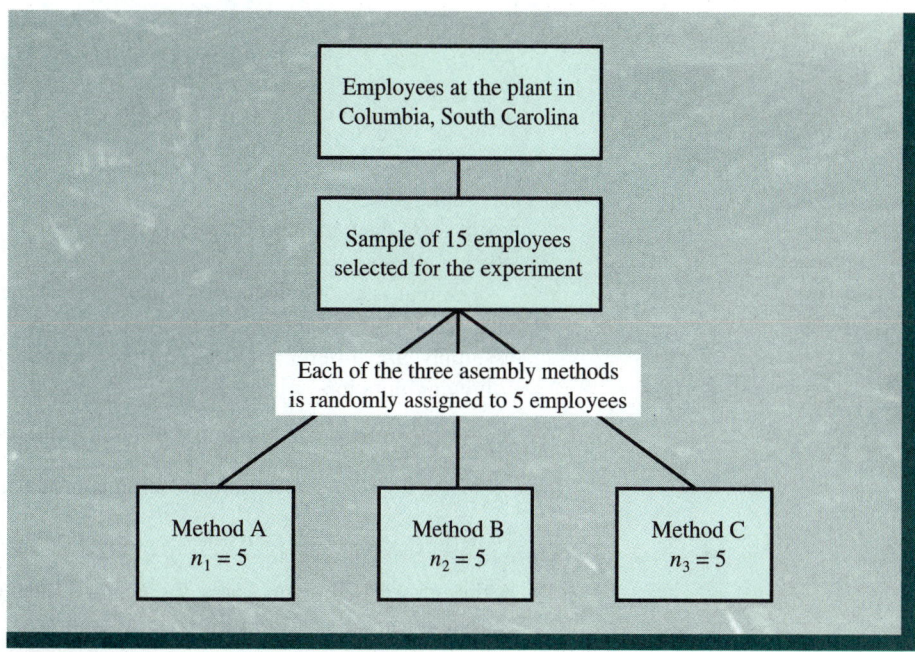

FIGURE 13.6 Completely Randomized Design for Evaluating the Chemitech Assembly Method Experiment

DATA COLLECTION

Once we are satisfied with the experimental design, we proceed by collecting and analyzing the data. In the Chemitech case, the employees would be instructed in how to perform the assembly method that they have been assigned and then would begin assembling the new filtration systems by that method. Suppose this has been done and the number of units assembled by each employee during one week is as shown in Table 13.7. The sample mean number of units produced with each of the three assembly methods is reported in the following table.

TABLE 13.7 Number of Units Produced by 15 Workers

| | | Method | |
Observation	A	B	C
1	58	58	48
2	64	69	57
3	55	71	59
4	66	64	47
5	67	68	49
Sample mean	62	66	52
Sample variance	27.5	26.5	31.0
Sample standard deviation	5.24	5.15	5.57

Assembly Method	Mean Number Produced
A	62
B	66
C	52

From these data, method B appears to result in higher production rates than either of the other methods.

The real issue is whether the three sample means observed are different enough for us to conclude that the means of the populations corresponding to the three methods of assembly are different. To write this question in statistical terms, we introduce the following notation.

μ_1 = mean number of units produced per week for method A

μ_2 = mean number of units produced per week for method B

μ_3 = mean number of units produced per week for method C

Although we will never know the actual values of μ_1, μ_2, and μ_3, we want to use the sample means to test the following hypotheses.

$$H_0: \mu_1 = \mu_2 = \mu_3$$
$$H_a: \text{Not all population means are equal}$$

The problem we face in analyzing data from a completely randomized experimental design is the same problem we faced when we first introduced analysis of variance as a method for testing whether the means of more than two populations are equal. In the next section we will show how analysis of variance is applied in problem situations such as this.

NOTES AND COMMENTS

1. Randomization in experimental design is the analog of probability sampling in an observational study.
2. In many medical experiments, potential bias is eliminated by using a double-blind study. In such studies neither the physician applying the treatment nor the subject knows which treatment is being applied. Many other types of experiments could benefit from this type of study.

13.5 COMPLETELY RANDOMIZED DESIGNS

The hypotheses we want to test when analyzing the data from a completely randomized design are exactly the same as the general form of the hypotheses we presented in Section 13.2.

$$H_0: \mu_1 = \mu_2 = \cdots = \mu_k$$
$$H_a: \text{Not all population means are equal}$$

Hence, to test for the equality of means in situations where the data have been collected in a completely randomized experimental design, we can use analysis of variance as introduced in Sections 13.1 and 13.2. Recall that analysis of variance requires the calculation of two independent estimates of the population variance σ^2.

BETWEEN-TREATMENTS ESTIMATE OF POPULATION VARIANCE

In the context of experimental design the between-samples estimate of σ^2 is referred to as the *mean square due to treatments* and is denoted MSTR. It is the same as what we called mean square between, MSB, in Section 13.2. It is also referred to as the *mean square between treatments*. The formula for computing MSTR follows:

$$\text{MSTR} = \frac{\sum_{j=1}^{k} n_j(\bar{x}_j - \bar{\bar{x}})^2}{k - 1} \qquad \text{(13.20)}$$

The numerator in (13.20) is called the *sum of squares between* or *sum of squares due to treatments* and is denoted SSTR. The denominator $k - 1$ represents the degrees of freedom associated with SSTR.

For the Chemitech data in Table 13.7, we obtain the following results (note: $\bar{\bar{x}} = 60$).

$$\text{SSTR} = \sum_{j=1}^{k} n_j(\bar{x}_j - \bar{\bar{x}})^2 = 5(62 - 60)^2 + 5(66 - 60)^2 + 5(52 - 60)^2 = 520$$

$$\text{MSTR} = \frac{\text{SSTR}}{k - 1} = \frac{520}{3 - 1} = 260$$

WITHIN-TREATMENTS ESTIMATE OF POPULATION VARIANCE

The second estimate of σ^2 is based on the variation of the sample observations within each sample or treatment. In our discussion of analysis of variance, we referred to this estimate of σ^2 as the within-samples estimate of population variance. This estimate is referred to as the *mean square due to error* and is denoted MSE. It is the same as what we called mean square within, MSW, in Section 13.2. It is also referred to as the *mean square within treatments*. The formula for computing MSE follows.

$$\text{MSE} = \frac{\sum_{j=1}^{k} (n_j - 1)s_j^2}{n_T - k} \qquad \text{(13.21)}$$

The numerator in (13.21) is given the name *sum of squares within* or *sum of squares due to error* and is denoted SSE. The denominator of MSE is referred to as the degrees of freedom associated with the within-treatment variance estimate.

For the Chemitech data in Table 13.7, we obtain the following results.

$$\text{SSE} = \sum_{j=1}^{k} (n_j - 1)s_j^2 = 4(27.5) + 4(26.5) + 4(31) = 340$$

$$\text{MSE} = \frac{\text{SSE}}{n_T - k} = \frac{340}{15 - 3} = 28.33$$

COMPARING THE VARIANCE ESTIMATES: THE F TEST

If the null hypothesis is true and the ANOVA assumptions are valid, the sampling distribution of MSTR/MSE is an F distribution with numerator degrees of freedom equal to $k - 1$ and denominator degrees of freedom equal to $n_T - k$. Recall also that if the means of the k populations are not equal, the value of MSTR/MSE will be inflated because MSTR overestimates σ^2. Hence we will reject H_0 if the resulting value of MSTR/MSE appears to be too large to have been selected at random from an F distribution with degrees of freedom $k - 1$ in the numerator and $n_T - k$ in the denominator.

For the Chemitech problem the value of $F = $ MSTR/MSE $= 260/28.33 = 9.18$. The critical F value is based on two numerator degrees of freedom and 12 denominator degrees of freedom. For a .05 level of significance, Table 4 of Appendix B shows a value of $F_{.05} = 3.89$. Since the observed value of F is greater than the critical value, we reject the null hypothesis and conclude that not all of the population means are equal.

THE ANOVA TABLE

Using the terminology we have introduced for the completely randomized experimental design, we can now write the result that shows how the total sum of squares, SST, is partitioned.

$$\text{SST} = \text{SSTR} + \text{SSE} \qquad \text{(13.22)}$$

This result also holds true for the degrees of freedom associated with each of these sums of squares; that is, the total degrees of freedom is the sum of the degrees of freedom associated with SSTR and SSE. The general form of the ANOVA table for a completely randomized design is shown in Table 13.8; Table 13.9 is the corresponding ANOVA table for the Chemitech problem.

PAIRWISE COMPARISONS

We can use Fisher's LSD procedure to test all possible pairwise comparisons for the Chemitech problem. At the 5% level of significance, the t distribution table shows that with $n_T - k = 15 - 3 = 12$ degrees of freedom, $t_{.025} = 2.179$. Using MSE $= 28.33$ in place of MSW in (13.17), we obtain Fisher's least significant difference.

$$\text{LSD} = t_{\alpha/2}\sqrt{\text{MSE}\left(\frac{1}{n_1} + \frac{1}{n_2}\right)} = 2.179\sqrt{28.33\left(\frac{1}{5} + \frac{1}{5}\right)} = 7.34$$

TABLE 13.8 ANOVA Table for a Completely Randomized Design

Source of Variation	Sum of Squares	Degrees of Freedom	Mean Square	F
Treatments	SSTR	$k - 1$	$\text{MSTR} = \dfrac{\text{SSTR}}{k-1}$	$\dfrac{\text{MSTR}}{\text{MSE}}$
Error	SSE	$n_T - k$	$\text{MSE} = \dfrac{\text{SSE}}{n_T-k}$	
Total	SST	$n_T - 1$		

TABLE 13.9 ANOVA Table for the Chemitech Problem

Source of Variation	Sum of Squares	Degrees of Freedom	Mean Square	F
Treatments	520	2	260.00	9.18
Error	340	12	28.33	
Total	860	14		

If the magnitude of the difference between any two sample means exceeds 7.34, we can reject the hypothesis that the corresponding population means are equal. For the Chemitech data in Table 13.7, we obtain the following results.

TABLE 13.10 Exercise 19

	Treatment		
Observation	A	B	C
1	162	142	126
2	142	156	122
3	165	124	138
4	145	142	140
5	148	136	150
6	174	152	128
$\bar{x}_j$	156	142	134
s_j^2	164.4	131.2	110.4

Sample Differences	Significant?
Method A − Method B = 62 − 66 = − 4	No
Method A − Method C = 62 − 52 = 10	Yes
Method B − Method C = 66 − 52 = 14	Yes

Thus, the difference in the population means is attributable to the difference between the means for method A and method C and the difference between the means for method B and method C. Methods A and B therefore are preferred to method C. However, more testing should be done to compare method A with method B. The current study does not provide sufficient evidence to conclude that these two methods differ.

NOTES AND COMMENTS

The computational aspect of the analysis of variance procedure is devoted primarily to computing the appropriate sums of squares. When a hand calculator is used to compute the sums of squares, some computational help can be obtained by using alternate forms of the sums-of-squares formulas. In Appendix 13.1 we provide a step-by-step procedure for using these revised formulas to compute the sums of squares for a completely randomized design.

EXERCISES

METHODS

Self-Test ▶

19. The data in Table 13.10 are from a completely randomized design.
   a. Compute the sum of squares between treatments.
   b. Compute the mean square between treatments.
   c. Compute the sum of squares due to error.
   d. Compute the mean square due to error.
   e. At the $\alpha = .05$ level of significance, test whether the means for the three treatments are equal.

20. Refer to exercise 19.
   a. Set up the ANOVA table.
   b. At the $\alpha = .05$ level of significance, use Fisher's least significant difference procedure to test all possible pairwise comparisons. What conclusion can you draw after carrying out this procedure?

21. In a completely randomized experimental design, seven experimental units were used for each of the five levels of the factor. Complete the following ANOVA table.

Source of Variation	Sum of Squares	Degrees of Freedom	Mean Square	F
Treatments	300			
Error				
Total	460			

22. Refer to Exercise 21.
    a. What hypotheses are implied in this problem?
    b. At the $\alpha = .05$ level of significance, can we reject the null hypothesis in (a)? Explain.

23. In an experiment designed to test the output levels of three different treatments, the following results were obtained: SST = 400, SSTR = 150, $n_T = 19$. Set up the ANOVA table and test for any significant difference between the mean output levels of the three treatments. Use $\alpha = .05$.

24. In a completely randomized experimental design, 12 experimental units were used for the first treatment, 15 for the second treatment, and 20 for the third treatment. Complete the following analysis of variance. At a .05 level of significance, is there a significant difference between the treatments?

Source of Variation	Sum of Squares	Degrees of Freedom	Mean Square	F
Treatments	1200			
Error				
Total	1800			

TABLE 13.11   Exercise 25

	Treatment		
	A	B	C
	136	107	92
	120	114	82
	113	125	85
	107	104	101
	131	107	89
	114	109	117
	129	97	110
	102	114	120
		104	98
		89	106
$\bar{x}_j$	119	107	100
s_j^2	146.86	96.44	173.78

25. Develop the analysis of variance computations for the experimental design in Table 13.11. At $\alpha = .05$, is there a significant difference between the treatment means?

APPLICATIONS

26. Three different methods for assembling a product were proposed by an industrial engineer. To investigate the number of units assembled correctly with each method, 30 employees were randomly selected and randomly assigned to the three proposed methods in such a way that each method was used by 10 workers. The number of units assembled correctly was recorded, and the analysis of variance procedure was applied to the resulting data set. The following results were obtained: SST = 10,800, SSTR = 4560.
    a. Set up the ANOVA table for this problem.
    b. Using $\alpha = .05$, test for any significant difference in the means for the three assembly methods.

27. In an experiment designed to test the breaking strength of four types of cables, the following results were obtained: SST = 85.05, SSTR = 61.64, $n_T = 24$. Set up the ANOVA table and test for any significant difference in the mean breaking strength of the four cables. Use $\alpha = .05$.

28. To study the effect of temperature on yield in a chemical process, five batches were produced at each of three temperature levels. The results follow. Construct an analysis of variance table. Using a .05 level of significance, test to see whether the temperature level appears to have an effect on the mean yield of the process.

	Temperature		
	50°C	60°C	70°C
	34	30	23
	24	31	28
	36	34	28
	39	23	30
	32	27	31
$\bar{x}_j$	33	29	28
s_j^2	32	17.5	9.5

TABLE 13.12 Exercise 29

Direct	Indirect	Combination
17.0	16.6	25.2
18.5	22.2	24.0
15.8	20.5	21.5
18.2	18.3	26.8
20.2	24.2	27.5
16.0	19.8	25.8
13.3	21.2	24.2
x_j 17.0	20.4	25.0
s_j^2 5.01	6.26	4.01

29. Auditors must make judgments about various aspects of an audit on the basis of their own direct experience, indirect experience, or a combination of the two. In a study, auditors were asked to make judgments about the frequency of errors to be found in an audit (*Journal of Accounting Research,* Autumn 1988). The judgments by the auditors were then compared to the actual results. Suppose the data in Table 13.12 were obtained from a similar study; lower scores indicate better judgments. Using $\alpha = .05$, test to see whether the basis for the judgment affects the quality of the judgment. What is your conclusion?

30. Four different paints are advertised as having the same drying time. To check the manufacturer's claims, five samples were tested for each of the paints. The time in minutes until the paint was dry enough for a second coat to be applied was recorded. The following data were obtained.

	Paint 1	Paint 2	Paint 3	Paint 4
	128	144	133	150
	137	133	143	142
	135	142	137	135
	124	146	136	140
	141	130	131	153
$\bar{x}_j$	133	139	136	144
s_j^2	47.5	50	21	54.5

At the $\alpha = .05$ level of significance, test to see whether the mean drying time is the same for each type of paint.

TABLE 13.13 Exercise 31

	Automobile		
	A	B	C
	19	19	24
	21	20	26
	20	22	23
	19	21	25
	21	23	27
$\bar{x}_j$	20	21	25
s_j^2	1	2.5	2.5

31. Three top-of-the-line intermediate-size automobiles manufactured in the United States have been test-driven and compared on a variety of criteria by a well-known automotive magazine. In the area of gasoline mileage performance, five automobiles of each brand were each test-driven 500 miles; the miles per gallon data obtained are reported in Table 13.13. Use the analysis of variance procedure with $\alpha = .05$ to determine whether there is a significant difference in the mean number of miles per gallon for the three types of automobiles.

32. Refer to Exercise 29. Use Fisher's least significant difference procedure to test all possible pairwise comparisons. What conclusion can you draw after carrying out this procedure? Use $\alpha = .05$.

33. Refer to Exercise 31. Use Fisher's least significant difference procedure to test all possible pairwise comparisons. What conclusion can you draw after carrying out this procedure? Use $\alpha = .05$.

13.6   RANDOMIZED BLOCK DESIGN

Thus far we have considered the completely randomized experimental design. Recall that to test for a difference among treatment means, we computed an F value by using the ratio

$$F = \frac{\text{MSTR}}{\text{MSE}} \qquad\qquad \textbf{(13.23)}$$

A problem can arise whenever differences due to extraneous factors (ones not considered in the experiment) cause the MSE term in this ratio to become large. In such cases, the F value in (13.28) can become small, signaling no difference among treatment means when in fact such a difference exists.

In this section we present an experimental design known as a *randomized block design*. Its purpose is to control some of the extraneous sources of variation by removing such variation from the MSE term. This design tends to provide a better estimate of the true error variance and leads to a more powerful hypothesis test in terms of the ability to detect differences among treatment means. To illustrate, let us consider a stress study for air traffic controllers.

AIR TRAFFIC CONTROLLER STRESS TEST

A study measuring the fatigue and stress of air traffic controllers has resulted in proposals for modification and redesign of the controller's work station. After consideration of several designs for the work station, three specific alternatives have been selected as having the best potential for reducing controller stress. The key question is: To what extent do the three alternatives differ in terms of their effect on controller stress? To answer this question we need to design an experiment that will provide measurements of air traffic controller stress under each alternative.

In a completely randomized design, a random sample of controllers would be assigned to each work station alternative. However, controllers are believed to differ substantially in their ability to handle stressful situations. What is high stress to one controller might be only moderate or even low stress to another. Hence, when considering the within-group source of variation (MSE), we must realize that this variation includes both random error and error due to individual controller differences. In fact, managers expected controller variability to be a major contributor to the MSE term.

One way to separate the effect of the individual differences is to use a randomized block design. Such a design will identify the variability stemming from individual controller differences and remove it from the MSE term. The randomized block design calls for a single sample of controllers. Each controller in the sample is tested with each of the three work station alternatives. In experimental design terminology, the work station is the *factor of interest* and the controllers are the *blocks*. The three treatments or populations associated with the work station factor correspond to the three work station alternatives. For simplicity, we refer to the work station alternatives as system A, system B, and system C.

The *randomized* aspect of the randomized block design is the random order in which the treatments (systems) are assigned to the controllers. If every controller were to test the three systems in the same order, any observed difference in systems might be due to the order of the test rather than to true differences in the systems.

To provide the necessary data, the three types of work station were installed at the Cleveland Control Center in Oberlin, Ohio. Six controllers were selected at random and assigned to operate each of the systems. A follow-up interview and a medical

TABLE 13.14 A Randomized Block Design for the Air Traffic Controller Stress Test

		Treatments		
		System A	System B	System C
	Controller 1	15	15	18
	Controller 2	14	14	14
Blocks	Controller 3	10	11	15
	Controller 4	13	12	17
	Controller 5	16	13	16
	Controller 6	13	13	13

examination of each controller participating in the study provided a measure of the stress for each controller on each system. The data are reported in Table 13.14.

Table 13.15 is a summary of the stress data collected. In this table we have included column totals (treatments) and row totals (blocks) as well as some sample means that will be helpful in making the sum of squares computations for the ANOVA procedure. Since lower stress values are viewed as better, the sample data available seem to favor system B with its mean stress rating of 13. However, the usual question remains: Do the sample results justify the conclusion that the mean stress levels for the three systems differ? That is, are the differences statistically significant? An analysis of variance computation similar to the one performed for the completely randomized design can be used to answer this statistical question.

THE ANOVA PROCEDURE

The ANOVA procedure for the randomized block design requires us to partition the sum of squares total (SST) into three groups: sum of squares due to treatments, sum of squares due to blocks, and sum of squares due to error. The formula for this partitioning follows.

TABLE 13.15 Summary of Stress Data for the Air Traffic Controller Stress Test

		Treatments			Row or Block Totals	Block Means
		System A	System B	System C		
	Controller 1	15	15	18	48	$\bar{x}_{1\cdot} = 48/3 = 16.0$
	Controller 2	14	14	14	42	$\bar{x}_{2\cdot} = 42/3 = 14.0$
Blocks	Controller 3	10	11	15	36	$\bar{x}_{3\cdot} = 36/3 = 12.0$
	Controller 4	13	12	17	42	$\bar{x}_{4\cdot} = 42/3 = 14.0$
	Controller 5	16	13	16	45	$\bar{x}_{5\cdot} = 45/3 = 15.0$
	Controller 6	13	13	13	39	$\bar{x}_{6\cdot} = 39/3 = 13.0$
Column or Treatment Totals		81	78	93	252	$\bar{\bar{x}} = \dfrac{252}{18} = 14.0$
Treatment Means		$\bar{x}_{\cdot 1} = \dfrac{81}{6}$ $= 13.5$	$\bar{x}_{\cdot 2} = \dfrac{78}{6}$ $= 13.0$	$\bar{x}_{\cdot 3} = \dfrac{93}{6}$ $= 15.5$		

$$\text{SST} = \text{SSTR} + \text{SSBL} + \text{SSE} \qquad \textbf{(13.24)}$$

This sum of squares partition is summarized in the ANOVA table for the randomized block design as shown in Table 13.16. The notation used in the table is

$$k = \text{the number of treatments,}$$

$$b = \text{the number of blocks, and}$$

$$n_T = \text{the total sample size } (n_T = kb)$$

Note that the ANOVA table also shows how the $n_T - 1$ total degrees of freedom are partitioned such that $k - 1$ degrees of freedom go to treatments, $b - 1$ go to blocks, and $(k - 1)(b - 1)$ go to the error term. The mean square column shows the sum of squares divided by the degrees of freedom, and $F = \text{MSTR/MSE}$ is the F ratio used to test for a significant difference among the treatment means. The primary contribution of the randomized block design is that, by including blocks, we have removed the individual controller differences from the MSE term and obtained a more powerful test for the stress differences in the three work station alternatives.

COMPUTATIONS AND CONCLUSIONS

To compute the F statistic needed to test for a difference among treatment means with a randomized block design, we need to compute MSTR and MSE. To calculate these two mean squares, we must first compute SSTR and SSE; in doing so, we will also compute SSBL and SST. To simplify the presentation, we perform the calculations in four steps. In addition to k, b, and n_T as previously defined, the following notation is used.

$$x_{ij} = \text{value of the observation corresponding to treatment } j \text{ in block } i$$

$$\bar{x}_{\cdot j} = \text{sample mean of the } j\text{th treatment}$$

$$\bar{x}_{i\cdot} = \text{sample mean for the } i\text{th block}$$

$$\bar{\bar{x}} = \text{overall sample mean}$$

Step 1.   Compute the total sum of squares (SST).

$$\text{SST} = \sum_{i=1}^{b} \sum_{j=1}^{k} (x_{ij} - \bar{\bar{x}})^2 \qquad \textbf{(13.25)}$$

Step 2.   Compute the sum of squares due to treatments (SSTR).

TABLE 13.16   ANOVA Table for the Randomized Block Design with k Treatments and b Blocks

Source of Variation	Sum of Squares	Degrees of Freedom	Mean Square	F
Treatments	SSTR	$k-1$	$\text{MSTR} = \dfrac{\text{SSTR}}{k-1}$	$\dfrac{\text{MSTR}}{\text{MSE}}$
Blocks	SSBL	$b-1$	$\text{MSBL} = \dfrac{\text{SSBL}}{b-1}$	
Error	SSE	$(k-1)(b-1)$	$\text{MSE} = \dfrac{\text{SSE}}{(k-1)(b-1)}$	
Total	SST	n_T-1		

$$\text{SSTR} = b \sum_{j=1}^{k} (\bar{x}_{.j} - \bar{\bar{x}})^2 \tag{13.26}$$

Step 3. Compute the sum of squares due to blocks (SSBL).

$$\text{SSBL} = k \sum_{i=1}^{b} (\bar{x}_{i.} - \bar{\bar{x}})^2 \tag{13.27}$$

Step 4. Compute the sum of squares due to error (SSE).

$$\text{SSE} = \text{SST} - \text{SSTR} - \text{SSBL} \tag{13.28}$$

For the air traffic controller data in Table 13.15, these steps lead to the following sums of squares.

Step 1. $\text{SST} = (15 - 14)^2 + (15 - 14)^2 + (18 - 14)^2 + \cdots + (13 - 14)^2 = 70$

Step 2. $\text{SSTR} = 6[(13.5 - 14)^2 + (13.0 - 14)^2 + (15.5 - 14)^2] = 21$

Step 3. $\text{SSBL} = 3[(16 - 14)^2 + (14 - 14)^2 + (12 - 14)^2 + (14 - 14)^2 +$
$(15 - 14)^2 + (13 - 14)^2] = 30$

Step 4. $\text{SSE} = 70 - 21 - 30 = 19$

These sums of squares divided by their degrees of freedom provide the corresponding mean square values shown in Table 13.17. The *F* ratio used to test for differences between treatment means is MSTR/MSE = 10.5/1.9 = 5.53. Checking the *F* values in Table 4 of Appendix B, we find that the critical *F* value at $\alpha = .05$ (two numerator degrees of freedom and 10 denominator degrees of freedom) is 4.10. With $F = 5.53$, we reject the null hypothesis $H_0: \mu_1 = \mu_2 = \mu_3$ and conclude that the work station designs differ in terms of the mean stress effects on air traffic controllers.

Some general comments can be made about the randomized block design. The experimental design described in this section is a *complete* block design; the word "complete" indicates that each block is subjected to all *k* treatments. That is, all controllers (blocks) were tested with all three systems (treatments). Experimental designs in which some but not all treatments are applied to each block are referred to as *incomplete* block designs. A discussion of incomplete block designs is beyond the scope of this text.

In addition, note that in the air traffic controller stress test, each controller in the study was required to use all three systems. This approach guarantees a complete block design, but in some cases blocking is carried out with "similar" experimental units in each block. For example, assume that in a pretest of air traffic controllers, the population of controllers was divided into groups ranging from extremely high stress individuals to extremely low stress individuals. The blocking could still be accomplished by having three controllers from each of the stress classifications participate in the study. Each

TABLE 13.17 ANOVA Table for the Air Traffic Controller Stress Test

Source of Variation	Sum of Squares	Degrees of Freedom	Mean Square	F
Treatments	21	2	10.5	10.5/1.9 = 5.53
Blocks	30	5	6.0	
Error	19	10	1.9	
Total	70	17		

block would then consist of three controllers in the same stress class. The randomized aspect of the block design would be the random assignment of the three controllers in each block to the three systems.

Finally, note that the ANOVA table shown in Table 13.16 provides an F value to test for treatment effects but *not* for blocks. The reason is that the experiment was designed to test a single factor—work station design. The blocking based on individual stress differences was conducted to remove such variation from the MSE term. However, the study was not designed to test specifically for individual differences in stress.

Some analysts compute $F = $ MSB/MSE and use that statistic to test for significance of the blocks. Then they use the result as a guide to whether the same type of blocking would be desired in future experiments. However, if individual stress difference is to be a factor in the study, a different experimental design should be used. A test of significance on blocks should not be performed as a basis for a conclusion about a second factor.

NOTES AND COMMENTS

1. The matched-samples t test introduced in Chapter 10 is an example of a randomized block design with two blocks.
2. Alternate formulas for SST, SSTR, and SSBL can be developed that can ease the computational burden of hand calculation. In Appendix 13.2 we have included a step-by-step procedure that illustrates the use of these alternate formulas.

EXERCISES

METHODS

Self-Test ▸

34. Consider the experimental results of a randomized block design reported in Table 13.18. Make the calculations necessary to set up the analysis of variance table. Using $\alpha = .05$, test for any significant differences.

TABLE 13.18   Exercise 34

		Treatments		
		A	*B*	*C*
Blocks	*1*	10	9	8
	2	12	6	5
	3	18	15	14
	4	20	18	18
	5	8	7	8

35. The following data were obtained for a randomized block design involving five treatments and three blocks: SST = 430, SSTR = 310, SSBL = 85. Set up the ANOVA table and test for any significant differences. Use $\alpha = .05$.

36. An experiment has been conducted for four treatments with eight blocks. Complete the following analysis of variance table.

Source of Variation	Sum of Squares	Degrees of Freedom	Mean Square	F
Treatments	900			
Blocks	400			
Error				
Total	1800			

Using $\alpha = .05$, test for any significant differences.

APPLICATIONS

37. An automobile dealer conducted a test to determine if the time in minutes needed to complete a minor engine tuneup depends on whether a computerized engine analyzer or an electronic analyzer is used. Because tuneup time varies among compact, intermediate, and full-size cars, the three types of cars were used as blocks in the experiment. The data obtained follow.

		Analyzer	
		Computerized	Electronic
Car	Compact	50	42
	Intermediate	55	44
	Full-size	63	46

Using $\alpha = .05$, test for any significant differences.

38. Five different auditing procedures were compared in terms of total audit time. To control for possible variation due to the person conducting the audit, four accountants were selected randomly and treated as blocks in the experiment. The following values were obtained by the ANOVA procedure: SST = 100, SSTR = 45, SSBL = 36. Using $\alpha = .05$, test to see whether there is any significant difference in the mean total audit time for the five auditing procedures.

39. An important factor in selecting software for word-processing and database management systems is the time required to learn how to use the system. To evaluate three file management systems, a firm designed a test involving five word-processing operators. Since operator variability was believed to be a significant factor, each of the five operators was trained on each of the three file management systems. The data obtained follow.

		System		
		A	B	C
Operator	1	16	16	24
	2	19	17	22
	3	14	13	19
	4	13	12	18
	5	18	17	22

Using $\alpha = .05$, test to see whether there is any difference in the mean training time (in hours) for the three systems.

40. A study reported in the *Journal of the American Medical Association* investigated the cardiac demands of heavy snow shoveling. Ten healthy men underwent exercise testing with a treadmill and a cycle ergometer modified for arm cranking. The men then cleared two 15-mile-long tracts of heavy, wet snow by using a lightweight plastic snow shovel and an electric snow thrower. Each subject's heart rate, blood pressure, oxygen uptake, and perceived exertion during snow removal were compared with the values obtained during treadmill and arm-ergometer testing. Suppose the following table gives the heart rates in beats per minute for each of the 10 subjects.

Subject	Treadmill	Arm-Crank Ergometer	Snow Shovel	Snow Thrower
1	177	205	180	98
2	151	177	164	120
3	184	166	167	111
4	161	152	173	122
5	192	142	179	151
6	193	172	205	158
7	164	191	156	117
8	207	170	160	123
9	177	181	175	127
10	174	154	191	109

SNOW

At the .05 level of significance, test for any significant differences.

13.7 FACTORIAL EXPERIMENTS

The experimental designs we have considered thus far enable us to draw statistical conclusions about one factor. However, in some experiments we want to draw conclusions about more than one variable or factor. *Factorial experiments* and their corresponding ANOVA computations are valuable designs when simultaneous conclusions about two or more factors are required. The term "factorial" is used because the experimental conditions include all possible combinations of the factors. For example, if there are a levels of factor A and b levels of factor B, the experiment will involve collecting data on ab treatment combinations. In this section we will show the analysis for a two-factor factorial experiment. The basic approach can be extended to experiments involving more than two factors.

As an illustration of a two-factor factorial experiment, we will consider a study involving the Graduate Management Admissions Test (GMAT), a standardized test used by graduate schools of business to evaluate an applicant's ability to pursue a graduate program in that field. Scores on the GMAT range from 200 to 800, with higher scores implying higher aptitude.

In an attempt to improve students' performance on the GMAT exam, a major Texas university is considering offering the following three GMAT preparation programs.

1. A three-hour review session covering the types of questions generally asked on the GMAT.
2. A one-day program covering relevant exam material, along with the taking and grading of a sample exam.
3. An intensive 10-week course involving the identification of each student's weaknesses and the setting up of individualized programs for improvement.

Hence, one factor in this study is the GMAT preparation program, which has three treatments: three-hour review, one-day program, and 10-week course. Before selecting the preparation program to adopt, further study will be conducted to determine how the proposed programs affect GMAT scores.

The GMAT is usually taken by students from three colleges: the College of Business, the College of Engineering, and the College of Arts and Sciences. Therefore, a second factor of interest in the experiment is whether or not a student's undergraduate college affects the GMAT score. This second factor, undergraduate college, also has three treatments: business, engineering, and arts and sciences. The factorial design for this

TABLE 13.19 Nine Treatment Combinations for the Two-Factor GMAT Experiment

		Factor B: College		
		Business	*Engineering*	*Arts and Sciences*
Factor A:	*3-hour review*	1	2	3
Preparation	*1-day program*	4	5	6
Program	*10-week course*	7	8	9

experiment with three treatments corresponding to factor A, the preparation program, and three treatments corresponding to factor B, the undergraduate college, will have a total of $3 \times 3 = 9$ treatment combinations. These treatment combinations or experimental conditions are summarized in Table 13.19.

Assume that a sample of two students will be selected corresponding to each of the nine treatment combinations shown in Table 13.19: two business students will take the three-hour review, two will take the one-day program, and two will take the 10-week course. In addition, two engineering students and two arts and sciences students will take each of the three preparation programs. In experimental design terminology, the sample size of two for each treatment combination indicates that we have two replications. Additional replications and a larger sample size could easily have been used, but we elected to minimize the computational aspects for this illustration.

This experimental design requires that six students who plan to attend graduate school be randomly selected from *each* of the three undergraduate colleges. Then two students from each college should be assigned randomly to each preparation program, resulting in a total of 18 students being used in the study.

Let us assume that the students have been randomly selected, have participated in the preparation program, and have taken the GMAT. The scores obtained are reported in Table 13.20.

The analysis of variance computations with the data in Table 13.20 will provide answers to the following questions.

- **Main effect (factor A):** Do the preparation programs differ in terms of effect on GMAT scores?
- **Main effect (factor B):** Do the undergraduate colleges differ in terms of student ability to perform on the GMAT?

TABLE 13.20 GMAT Scores for the Two-Factor Experiment

		Factor B: College		
		Business	*Engineering*	*Arts and Sciences*
	3-hour review	500	540	480
		580	460	400
Factor A:				
Preparation	*1-day program*	460	560	420
Program		540	620	480
	10-week course	560	600	480
		600	580	410

TABLE 13.21   ANOVA Table for the Two-Factor Factorial Experiment with r Replications

Source of Variation	Sum of Squares	Degrees of Freedom	Mean Square	F
Factor A	SSA	$a - 1$	$MSA = \dfrac{SSA}{a - 1}$	$\dfrac{MSA}{MSE}$
Factor B	SSB	$b - 1$	$MSB = \dfrac{SSB}{b - 1}$	$\dfrac{MSB}{MSE}$
Interaction	SSAB	$(a - 1)(b - 1)$	$MSAB = \dfrac{SSAB}{(a - 1)(b - 1)}$	$\dfrac{MSAB}{MSE}$
Error	SSE	$ab(r - 1)$	$MSE = \dfrac{SSE}{ab(r - 1)}$	
Total	SST	$n_T - 1$		

- **Interaction effect (factors A and B):** Do students in some colleges do better on one type of preparation program whereas others do better on a different type of preparation program?

The term *interaction* refers to a new effect that we can now study because we have used a factorial experiment. If the interaction effect has a significant impact on the GMAT scores, we can conclude that the effect of the type of preparation program depends on the undergraduate college.

THE ANOVA PROCEDURE

The ANOVA procedure for the two-factor factorial experiment is similar to the completely randomized experiment and the randomized block experiment in that we again partition the sum of squares and the degrees of freedom into their respective sources. The formula for partitioning the sum of squares for the two-factor factorial experiments follows.

$$SST = SSA + SSB + SSAB + SSE \tag{13.29}$$

The partitioning of the sum of squares and degrees of freedom is summarized in Table 13.21. The following notation is used.

a = number of levels of factor A

b = number of levels of factor B

r = number of replications

n_T = total number of observations taken in the experiment; $n_T = abr$

COMPUTATIONS AND CONCLUSIONS

To compute the F statistics needed to test for the significance of factor A, factor B, and the interaction, we need to compute MSA, MSB, MSAB, and MSE. To calculate these four mean squares, we must first compute SSA, SSB, SSAB, and SSE; in doing so we will also compute SST. To simplify the presentation, we perform the calculations in five steps. In addition to a, b, r, and n_T as previously defined, the following notation is used.

x_{ijk} = observation corresponding to the kth replicate taken from treatment i of factor A and treatment j of factor B

$\bar{x}_{i\cdot}$ = sample mean for the observations in treatment i (factor A)

$\bar{x}_{\cdot j}$ = sample mean for the observations in treatment j (factor B)

$\bar{x}_{ij}$ = sample mean for the observations corresponding to the combination of treatment i (factor A) and treatment j (factor B)

$\bar{\bar{x}}$ = overall sample mean of all n_T observations

Step 1. Compute the total sum of squares.

$$\text{SST} = \sum_{i=1}^{a} \sum_{j=1}^{b} \sum_{k=1}^{r} (x_{ijk} - \bar{\bar{x}})^2 \qquad \textbf{(13.30)}$$

Step 2. Compute the sum of squares for factor A.

$$\text{SSA} = br \sum_{i=1}^{a} (\bar{x}_{i\cdot} - \bar{\bar{x}})^2 \qquad \textbf{(13.31)}$$

Step 3. Compute the sum of squares for factor B.

$$\text{SSB} = ar \sum_{j=1}^{b} (\bar{x}_{\cdot j} - \bar{\bar{x}})^2 \qquad \textbf{(13.32)}$$

Step 4. Compute the sum of squares for interaction.

$$\text{SSAB} = r \sum_{i=1}^{a} \sum_{j=1}^{b} (\bar{x}_{ij} - \bar{x}_{i\cdot} - \bar{x}_{\cdot j} + \bar{\bar{x}})^2 \qquad \textbf{(13.33)}$$

Step 5. Compute the sum of squares due to error.

$$\text{SSE} = \text{SST} - \text{SSA} - \text{SSB} - \text{SSAB} \qquad \textbf{(13.34)}$$

Table 13.22 reports the data collected in the experiment and the various sums that will help us with the sum of squares computations. Using (13.30) to (13.34), we have the following sums of squares for the GMAT two-factor factorial experiment.

Step 1. $\text{SST} = (500 - 515)^2 + (580 - 515)^2 + (540 - 515)^2 + \cdots +$
$(410 - 515)^2 = 82{,}450$

Step 2. $\text{SSA} = (3)(2)[(493.33 - 515)^2 + (513.33 - 515)^2 +$
$(538.33 - 515)^2] = 6100$

Step 3. $\text{SSB} = (3)(2)[(540 - 515)^2 + (560 - 515)^2 + (445 - 515)^2] = 45{,}300$

Step 4. $\text{SSAB} = 2[(540 - 493.33 - 540 + 515)^2 + (500 - 493.33 -$
$560 + 515)^2 + \cdots + (445 - 538.33 - 445 + 515)^2] = 11{,}200$

Step 5. $\text{SSE} = 82{,}450 - 6100 - 45{,}300 - 11{,}200 = 19{,}850$

These sums of squares divided by their corresponding degrees of freedom, as shown in Table 13.23, provide the appropriate mean square values for testing the two main effects (preparation program and undergraduate college) and the interaction effect. The F ratio used to test for differences among preparation programs is 1.38. The critical F value at $\alpha = .05$ (with two numerator degrees of freedom and nine denominator degrees of freedom) is 4.26. With $F = 1.38$, we cannot reject the null hypothesis and must conclude that there is no significant difference among the three preparation programs. However, for the undergraduate college effect, $F = 10.27$ exceeds the critical F value of 4.26. Hence, the analysis of variance results enable us to conclude that there is a

TABLE 13.22   GMAT Summary Data for the Two-Factor Experiment

Factor A: Preparation Program	Factor B: College — Business	Factor B: College — Engineering	Factor B: College — Arts and Sciences	Row Totals	Factor A Means
3-hour review	500 580 1080 $\bar{x}_{11} = \frac{1080}{2} = 540$	540 460 1000 $\bar{x}_{12} = \frac{1000}{2} = 500$	480 400 880 $\bar{x}_{13} = \frac{880}{2} = 440$	2960	$\bar{x}_{1.} = \frac{2960}{6} = 493.33$
1-day program	460 540 1000 $\bar{x}_{21} = \frac{1000}{2} = 500$	560 620 1180 $\bar{x}_{22} = \frac{1180}{2} = 590$	420 480 900 $\bar{x}_{23} = \frac{900}{2} = 450$	3080	$\bar{x}_{2.} = \frac{3080}{6} = 513.33$
10-week course	560 600 1160 $\bar{x}_{31} = \frac{1160}{2} = 580$	600 580 1180 $\bar{x}_{32} = \frac{1180}{2} = 590$	480 410 890 $\bar{x}_{33} = \frac{890}{2} = 445$	3230	$\bar{x}_{3.} = \frac{3230}{6} = 538.33$
Column Totals	3240	3360	2670	9270 ⟵ Overall total	
Factor B Means	$\bar{x}_{.1} = \frac{3240}{6} = 540$	$\bar{x}_{.2} = \frac{3360}{6} = 560$	$\bar{x}_{.3} = \frac{2670}{6} = 445$	$\bar{\bar{x}} = \frac{9270}{18} = 515$	

Treatment combination totals (→ 1080)

TABLE 13.23 ANOVA Table for the Two-Factor GMAT Study

Source of Variation	Sum of Squares	Degrees of Freedom	Mean Square	F
Factor A	6,100	2	3,050	3050/2206 = 1.38
Factor B	45,300	2	22,650	22,650/2206 = 10.27
Interaction	11,200	4	2,800	2800/2206 = 1.27
Error	19,850	9	2,206	
Total	82,450	17		

```
             Analysis of Variance for GMAT

       SOURCE        DF         SS
       Factor A       2        6100
       Factor B       2       45300
       Interaction    4       11200
       Error          9       19850
       Total         17       82450
```

FIGURE 13.7 Computer Output for the GMAT Two-Factor Design

difference in GMAT test scores among the three undergraduate colleges; that is, the three undergraduate colleges do not provide the same preparation for performance on the GMAT. Finally, the interaction F value of $F = 1.27$ (critical F value = 3.63 at $\alpha = .05$) means that we cannot identify a significant interaction effect. Therefore, we have no reason to believe that the three preparation programs differ in their ability to prepare students from the different colleges for the GMAT.

Undergraduate college was found to be a significant factor. Checking the calculations in Table 13.23, we see that the sample means are: business students $\bar{x}_{.1} = 540$, engineering students $\bar{x}_{.2} = 560$, and arts and sciences students $\bar{x}_{.3} = 445$. Tests on individual treatment means can be conducted; yet after reviewing the three sample means we would anticipate no difference in preparation for business and engineering graduates. However, the arts and sciences students appear to be significantly less prepared for the GMAT than students in the other colleges. Perhaps this observation will lead the university to consider other options for assisting these students in preparing for graduate management admission tests.

Because of the computational effort involved in any modest- to large-size factorial experiment, the computer usually plays an important role in performing and summarizing the analysis of variance computations. Figure 13.7 is the computer printout for the analysis of variance of the GMAT two-factor factorial experiment.

NOTES AND COMMENTS

Alternate formulas for SST, SSA, SSB, SSAB, and SSE can be developed that can ease the computational burden of hand calculation. In Appendix 13.3 we have included a step-by-step procedure that illustrates the use of these alternate formulas.

EXERCISES

METHODS

Self-Test ▶

41. A factorial experiment involving three levels of factor A and two levels of factor B resulted in the following data.

		Factor B		
		Level 1	Level 2	Level 3
Factor A	Level 1	135	90	75
		165	66	93
	Level 2	125	127	120
		95	105	136

Test for any significant main effect and any interaction. Use $\alpha = .05$.

42. The calculations for a factorial experiment involving four levels of factor A, three levels of factor B, and three replications resulted in the following data: SST = 280, SSA = 26, SSB = 23, SSAB = 175. Set up the ANOVA table and test for any significant main effects and any interaction effect. Use $\alpha = .05$.

APPLICATIONS

43. A mail-order catalog firm designed a factorial experiment to test the effect of the size of a magazine advertisement and the advertisement design on the number of catalog requests received (1000s). Three advertising designs and two different-size advertisements were considered. The data obtained are reported in Table 13.24. Use the ANOVA procedure for factorial designs to test for any significant effects due to type of design, size of advertisement, or interaction. Use $\alpha = .05$.

44. An amusement park has been studying methods for decreasing the waiting time (minutes) for rides by loading and unloading riders more efficiently. Two alternative loading/unloading methods have been proposed. To account for potential differences due to the type of ride and the possible interaction between the method of loading and unloading and the type of ride, a factorial experiment was designed. Using the following data, test for any significant effect due to the loading and unloading method, the type of ride, and interaction. Use $\alpha = .05$.

TABLE 13.24   Exercise 43

		Size of Advertisement	
		Small	Large
Design	A	8	12
		12	8
	B	22	26
		14	30
	C	10	18
		18	14

TABLE 13.25   Exercise 45

		Price		
		$1.49	$1.79	$1.99
Size	1/4 pound	955	845	820
		985	860	845
	1/3 pound	945	910	860
		875	905	935

	Type of Ride		
	Roller Coaster	Screaming Demon	Log Flume
Method 1	41	52	50
	43	44	46
Method 2	49	50	48
	51	46	44

45. Jack's Restaurant is considering a new specialty sandwich. To determine the effect of sandwich price and sandwich size on sales, the new sandwich was test-marketed in selected company restaurants. The data in terms of the number of sandwiches sold per day are reported in Table 13.25. Test for any significant differences due to price, size, and interaction. Use $\alpha = .05$.

46. A recent study reported in *The Accounting Review* examined the separate and joint effects of two levels of time pressure (low and moderate) and three levels of knowledge (naive, declarative, and procedural) on key word selection behavior in tax research. Subjects were given a tax case containing a set of facts, a tax issue, and a key word index consisting of 1336 key words. They were asked to select the key words they believed would refer them to tax authority relevant to resolving the tax case. Prior to the experiment, a group of tax experts had determined that there were 19 relevant key words in the index. Subjects in the naive group had little or no declarative or procedural knowledge, subjects in the declarative group had significant declarative knowledge but little or no procedural knowledge, and subjects in the procedural group had significant declarative knowledge and procedural knowledge. Declarative knowledge consists of knowledge of both the applicable tax rules and the technical terms used to describe such rules. Procedural knowledge is knowledge of the rules that guide the tax researcher's search for relevant key words. Subjects in the low time pressure situation were told they had 25 minutes to complete the problem, an amount of time which should be "more than adequate" to complete the case; subjects in moderate time pressure situation were told they would have "only" 11 minutes to complete the case (*The Accounting Review,* January 1995). Suppose 25 subjects were selected for each of the six treatment combinations and the sample means for each treatment combination are as follows (standard deviations are in parentheses).

		Knowledge		
		Naive	*Declarative*	*Procedural*
Time Pressure	*Low*	1.13 (1.12)	1.56 (1.33)	2.00 (1.54)
	Moderate	0.48 (0.80)	1.68 (1.36)	2.86 (1.80)

Use the ANOVA procedure to test for any significant differences due to time pressure, knowledge, and interaction. Use a .05 level of significance. Assume that the total sum of squares for this experiment is 327.50.

SUMMARY

In this chapter we have shown how analysis of variance can be used to test for differences among means of several populations or treatments. In addition, we introduced the completely randomized, the randomized block, and the two-factor factorial experimental designs. The completely randomized design and the randomized block design are used to draw conclusions about differences in the means of a single factor. The primary purpose of blocking in the randomized block design is to remove extraneous sources of variation from the error term. Such blocking provides a better estimate of the true error variance and a better test to determine whether the population or treatment means of the factor differ significantly.

We showed that the basis for the statistical tests used in analysis of variance and experimental design is the development of two independent estimates of the population variance σ^2. In the single-factor case, one estimator is based on the variation between the treatments; this estimator provides an unbiased estimate of σ^2 only if the means

$\mu_1, \mu_2, \ldots, \mu_k$ are all equal. A second estimator of σ^2 is based on the variation of the observations within each sample; this estimator will always provide an unbiased estimate of σ^2. By computing the ratio of these two estimators (the F statistic) we developed a rejection rule for determining whether or not to reject the null hypothesis that the population or treatment means are equal. In all the experimental designs considered, the partitioning of the sum of squares and degrees of freedom into their various sources enabled us to compute the appropriate values for the analysis of variance calculations and tests. We also showed how Fisher's LSD procedure and the Bonferroni adjustment can be used to perform pairwise comparisons to determine which means are different.

GLOSSARY

ANOVA table   A table used to summarize the analysis of variance computations and results. It contains columns showing the source of variation, the degrees of freedom, the sum of squares, the mean square, and the F values.

Partitioning   The process of allocating the total sum of squares and degrees of freedom to the various components.

Multiple comparison procedures   Statistical procedures used to conduct statistical comparisons between pairs of the population means or treatments.

Comparisonwise Type I error rate   The probability of a Type I error associated with a single pairwise comparison.

Experimentwise Type I error rate   The probability of making a Type I error on at least one of several pairwise comparisons.

Factor   Another word for the variable of interest in an experiment.

Treatment   Different levels of a factor.

Single-factor experiment   An experiment involving only one factor with k populations or treatments.

Experimental units   The objects of interest in the experiment.

Completely randomized design   An experimental design in which the treatments are randomly assigned to the experimental units.

Mean square   The sum of squares divided by its corresponding degrees of freedom. This quantity is used in the F ratio to determine whether significant differences among means are present.

Blocking   The process of using the same or similar experimental units for all treatments. The purpose of blocking is to remove a source of variation from the error term and hence provide a more powerful test for a difference in population or treatment means.

Randomized block design   An experimental design employing blocking.

Factorial experiment   An experimental design that allows statistical conclusions about two or more factors.

Replication   The number of times each experimental condition is repeated in an experiment.

Interaction   The effect produced when the levels of one factor interact with the levels of another factor in influencing the response variable.

KEY FORMULAS

Analysis of Variance

jth Sample Mean

$$\bar{x}_j = \frac{\sum_{i=1}^{n_j} x_{ij}}{n_j} \tag{13.1}$$

jth Sample Variance

$$s_j^2 = \frac{\sum_{i=1}^{n_j} (x_{ij} - \bar{x}_j)^2}{n_j - 1} \tag{13.2}$$

Overall Sample Mean

$$\bar{\bar{x}} = \frac{\sum_{j=1}^{k} \sum_{i=1}^{n_j} x_{ij}}{n_T} \tag{13.3}$$

$$n_T = n_1 + n_2 + \cdots + n_k \tag{13.4}$$

Mean Square Between

$$\text{MSB} = \frac{\text{SSB}}{k - 1} \tag{13.7}$$

Sum of Squares Between

$$\text{SSB} = \sum_{j=1}^{k} n_j (\bar{x}_j - \bar{\bar{x}})^2 \tag{13.8}$$

Mean Square Within

$$\text{MSW} = \frac{\text{SSW}}{n_T - k} \tag{13.10}$$

Sum of Squares Within

$$\text{SSW} = \sum_{j=1}^{k} (n_j - 1) s_j^2 \tag{13.11}$$

Test for the Equality of k Population Means

$$F = \frac{\text{MSB}}{\text{MSW}} \tag{13.12}$$

Total Sum of Squares

$$\text{SST} = \sum_{j=1}^{k} \sum_{i=1}^{n_j} (x_{ij} - \bar{\bar{x}})^2 \tag{13.13}$$

Partition of Sum of Squares

$$\text{SST} = \text{SSB} + \text{SSW} \tag{13.14}$$

Multiple Comparison Procedures

Test Statistic for Fisher's LSD

$$t = \frac{\bar{x}_i - \bar{x}_j}{\sqrt{\text{MSW}\left(\dfrac{1}{n_i} + \dfrac{1}{n_j}\right)}} \tag{13.16}$$

Fisher's LSD

$$\text{LSD} = t_{\alpha/2}\sqrt{\text{MSW}\left(\frac{1}{n_i} + \frac{1}{n_j}\right)} \tag{13.17}$$

Completely Randomized Designs

Mean Square Due to Treatments

$$\text{MSTR} = \frac{\displaystyle\sum_{j=1}^{k} n_j(\bar{x}_j - \bar{\bar{x}})^2}{k - 1} \tag{13.20}$$

Mean Square Due to Error

$$\text{MSE} = \frac{\displaystyle\sum_{j=1}^{k} (n_j - 1)s_j^2}{n_T - k} \tag{13.21}$$

The F Value

$$F = \frac{\text{MSTR}}{\text{MSE}} \tag{13.23}$$

Randomized Block Designs

Total Sum of Squares

$$\text{SST} = \sum_{i=1}^{b} \sum_{j=1}^{k} (x_{ij} - \bar{\bar{x}})^2 \tag{13.25}$$

Sum of Squares Due to Treatments

$$\text{SSTR} = b \sum_{j=1}^{k} (\bar{x}_{\cdot j} - \bar{\bar{x}})^2 \tag{13.26}$$

Sum of Squares Due to Blocks

$$\text{SSBL} = k \sum_{i=1}^{b} (\bar{x}_{i\cdot} - \bar{\bar{x}})^2 \tag{13.27}$$

Sum of Squares Due to Error

$$\text{SSE} = \text{SST} - \text{SSTR} - \text{SSBL} \tag{13.28}$$

Factorial Experiments

Total Sum of Squares

$$SST = \sum_{i=1}^{a} \sum_{j=1}^{b} \sum_{k=1}^{r} (x_{ijk} - \bar{\bar{x}})^2 \qquad (13.30)$$

Sum of Squares for Factor A

$$SSA = br \sum_{i=1}^{a} (\bar{x}_{i\cdot} - \bar{\bar{x}})^2 \qquad (13.31)$$

Sum of Squares for Factor B

$$SSB = ar \sum_{j=1}^{b} (\bar{x}_{\cdot j} - \bar{\bar{x}})^2 \qquad (13.32)$$

Sum of Squares for Interaction

$$SSAB = r \sum_{i=1}^{a} \sum_{j=1}^{b} (\bar{x}_{ij} - \bar{x}_{i\cdot} - \bar{x}_{\cdot j} + \bar{\bar{x}})^2 \qquad (13.33)$$

Sum of Squares for Error

$$SSE = SST - SSA - SSB - SSAB \qquad (13.34)$$

SUPPLEMENTARY EXERCISES

TABLE 13.26 Exercise 47

	Area 1	Area 2
	92	90
	89	102
	98	96
	105	88
$\bar{x}_j$	96	94
s_j^s	50	40

47. A simple random sample of the asking prices ($1000s) of four houses currently for sale in each of two residential areas resulted in the data in Table 13.26.
   a. Use the procedure developed in Chapter 10 to test whether the mean asking price is the same in both areas. Use $\alpha = .05$.
   b. Use the ANOVA procedure to test whether the mean asking price is the same. Compare your analysis with part (a). Use $\alpha = .05$.

48. Suppose that in exercise 47 data were collected for another residential area. The asking prices for the simple random sample from the third area were $81,000, $86,000, $75,000, and $90,000; the sample mean and sample variance for these data are 83 and 42, respectively. Is the mean asking price the same for all three areas? Use $\alpha = .05$.

49. An analysis of the number of units sold by 10 salespersons in each of four sales territories resulted in the following data.

	Sales Territory			
Category	1	2	3	4
Number of salespersons	10	10	10	10
Mean number sold ($\bar{x}_j$)	130	120	132	114
Sample variance (s_j^2)	72	64	69	67

Test at the $\alpha = .05$ level to see whether there is any significant difference in the mean number of units sold in the four sales territories.

50. Suppose that in Exercise 49 the number of salespersons in each territory was $n_1 = 10, n_2 = 12, n_3 = 10,$ and $n_4 = 15$. Using the same data for $\bar{x}$ and s^2 as given in Exercise 49,

test at the $\alpha = .05$ level to see whether there is any significant difference in the population mean number of units sold in the four sales territories.

51. Executives rated service quality in each of several American industries (*Journal of Accountancy,* February 1992). Assume the following sample of ratings for the airline, retail, hotel, and automotive industries was obtained; higher scores indicate a higher service quality rating. At the $\alpha = .05$ level of significance, test for a significant difference in the population mean quality ratings for the four industries. What is your conclusion?

	Airlines	Retail	Hotel	Automotive
	59	63	70	49
	56	49	68	55
	47	60	62	48
	46	54	69	49
	55	56	59	50
	54	55		
	48			
$\bar{x}_j$	52.14	56.17	65.6	50.20
s_j^2	25.81	23.77	23.20	7.70

52. Three different assembly methods have been proposed for a new product. A completely randomized experimental design was chosen to determine which assembly method results in the greatest number of parts produced per hour, and 30 workers were randomly selected and assigned to use one of the proposed methods. The number of units produced by each worker follows.

ASSEMBLY

	Method		
	A	B	C
	97	93	99
	73	100	94
	93	93	87
	100	55	66
	73	77	59
	91	91	75
	100	85	84
	86	73	72
	92	90	88
	95	83	86
$\bar{x}_j$	90	84	81
s_j^2	98.00	168.44	159.78

Use these data and test to see whether the mean number of parts produced is the same with each method. Use $\alpha = .05$.

MKTCAP

53. Table 13.27 shows stocks with high earnings growth divided into groups based on market capitalization: large cap (above $1.5 billion), medium cap ($250 million to $1.5 billion), and shadow stocks (small firms with low institutional interest). Since the price–earnings ratios for stocks with high growth potential tend to be above the market average, many analysts look at the ratio of the market price per share to the forecasted earnings per share; such ratios are provided in the columns labeled P/E Est. (*AAII Journal,* June 1994). At the .05 level of significance, test whether the mean ratio of the market price per share to the forecasted earnings per share is the same for the three groups.

TABLE 13.27   Exercise 53

Large Cap	P/E Est.	Medium Cap	P/E Est.	Shadow Stocks	P/E Est.
U.S. Healthcare	16.7	Vencor Inc.	20.4	Ashworth Inc.	23.4
Cisco Systems	24.8	Westcott Communications	22.3	Homecare Management Inc.	30.8
Parametric Technology	25.4	CML Group	10.4	Methode Electric B	20.6
United Healthcare	25.2	Snyder Oil	33.1	Marten Transport	10.5
EMC Corp.	18.6	Owens & Minor	22.1	Gates/F.A. Distribution	15.6
American Power Conversion	29.7	Xilinx Inc.	24.1	Rotech Medical Corp.	20.2
Cabletron Systems	19.4	Invacare Corp.	15.3	Cosmetic Center B	16.5
CUC International	30.0	Tech Data Corp.	17.0	Volunteer Capital	26.1
Intel Corp.	10.3	Briggs & Stratton	13.5	BGS Systems	8.1
BMC Software	15.0	KCS Energy Inc.	10.1		
Microsoft Corp.	23.6	Applebee's International	35.8		
Blockbuster Entertainment	20.1	Bowne & Co.	10.6		
Linear Technology	31.9	Horizon Healthcare	26.0		
Sysco Corp	21.5	Oakwood Homes	14.7		
Home Depot	31.8	Progress Software	18.5		

54. In a completely randomized experimental design, three brands of paper towels were tested for their ability to absorb water. Equal-size towels were used, with four sections of towels tested per brand. The absorbency rating data follow. At a .05 level of significance, does there appear to be a difference in the ability of the brands to absorb water?

	Brand		
	x	y	z
	91	99	83
	100	96	88
	88	94	89
	89	99	76
$\bar{x}_j$	92	97	84
s_j^2	30	6	35.33

TABLE 13.28   Exercise 55

	Method 1	Method 2	Method 3
	58	52	48
	64	63	57
	55	65	59
	66	58	47
	67	62	49
$\bar{x}_j$	62	60	52
s_j^2	27.5	26.5	31

55. To find out whether there is any significant difference in the mean number of units produced per week by each of three production methods, a completely randomized experimental design was used to obtain the data in Table 13.28. At the $\alpha = .05$ level of significance, is there any difference in the means for the three methods?

56. Following are the percentage changes in the Dow Jones Industrial Average in each of the four years of six presidential terms (*The Beacon Street Financial,* February 1992). Does there appear to be any significant effect due to the year of the presidential term on stock market performance? Use $\alpha = .05$.

MKTPERF

	First Year	Second Year	Third Year	Fourth Year
	10.9	−18.9	15.2	4.3
	−15.2	4.8	6.1	14.6
	−16.7	−27.6	38.3	17.9
	−17.3	−3.1	4.2	14.9
	−9.2	19.6	20.3	−3.7
	27.7	22.6	2.3	11.9
	27.0	−4.3	20.3	8.8
$\bar{x}_j$	1.03	−0.99	15.24	9.81
s_j^2	416.93	343.04	159.31	55.43

57. Hargreaves Automotive Parts, Inc., wanted to compare the mileage for four different types of brake linings. Thirty linings of each type were produced and placed on a fleet of rental cars. The number of miles that each brake lining lasted until it no longer met the required federal safety standard was recorded, and an average value was computed for each type of lining. The following data were obtained.

Type	Sample Size	Sample Mean	Standard Deviation
A	30	32,000	1450
B	30	27,500	1525
C	30	34,200	1650
D	30	30,300	1400

Test to see whether the corresponding population means are equal. Use $\alpha = .05$.

58. A manufacturer of batteries for electronic toys and calculators is considering three new battery designs. An attempt was made to determine whether the mean lifetime in hours is the same for each of the three designs.

	Design A	Design B	Design C
	78	112	115
	98	99	101
	88	101	100
	96	116	120
$\bar{x}_j$	90	107	109
s_j^2	82.67	68.67	100.67

Test to see whether the population means are equal. Use $\alpha = .05$.

TABLE 13.29   Exercise 59

	Light	Heavy
Nonbrowser	Browser	Browser
4	5	5
5	6	7
6	5	5
3	4	7
3	7	4
4	4	6
5	6	5
4	5	7
$\bar{x}_j$ 4.25	5.25	5.75
s_j^2 1.07	1.07	1.36

59. A study was conducted to investigate browsing activity by shoppers (*Journal of the Academy of Marketing Science,* Winter 1989). Each shopper was initially classified as a nonbrowser, light browser, or heavy browser. For each shopper in the study a measure was obtained to determine how comfortable the shopper was in a store. Higher scores indicated greater comfort. Suppose the data in Table 13.29 is from a related study.

a. Using $\alpha = .05$, test for differences among comfort levels for the three types of browsers.

b. Use Fisher's LSD procedure to compare the comfort levels of nonbrowsers and light browsers. Use $\alpha = .05$. What is your conclusion?

60. A research firm tests the miles per gallon characteristics of three brands of gasoline. Because of different gasoline performance characteristics in different brands of automobiles, five brands of automobiles are selected and treated as blocks in the experiment. That is, each brand of automobile is tested with each type of gasoline. The results of the experiment (in miles per gallon) follow.

		Gasoline Brands		
		I	II	III
	A	18	21	20
	B	24	26	27
Automobiles	C	30	29	34
	D	22	25	24
	E	20	23	24

At $\alpha = .05$, is there a significant difference in the mean miles per gallon characteristics of the three brands of gasoline?

61. Analyze the experimental data provided in Exercise 60 using the ANOVA procedure for completely randomized designs. Compare your findings with those obtained in Exercise 60. What is the advantage of attempting to remove the block effect?

TABLE 13.30 Exercise 62

		Location		
	1	*2*	*3*	*4*
Compound A	99	73	85	103
Compound B	82	72	85	97
Compound C	81	79	82	86

62. Three different road-repair compounds were tested at four different highway locations. At each location, three sections of the road were repaired, each section with one of the three compounds. Data were then collected on the number of days of traffic usage before additional repair was required. These data are reported in Table 13.30. Using $\alpha = .01$, test for significant differences in the compounds.

63. A factorial experiment was designed to test for any significant differences in the time needed to perform English to foreign language translations with two computerized language translators. Since the type of language translated was also considered a significant factor, translations were made with both systems for three different languages: Spanish, French, and German. Use the following data for translation time in hours.

	Language		
	Spanish	*French*	*German*
System 1	8	10	12
	12	14	16
System 2	6	14	16
	10	16	22

Test for any significant differences due to language translator, type of language, and interaction. Use $\alpha = .05$.

TABLE 13.31 Exercise 64

	Loading System	
	Manual	*Automatic*
Machine 1	30	30
	34	26
Machine 2	20	24
	22	28

64. A manufacturing company designed a factorial experiment to determine whether the number of defective parts produced by two machines differed and if the number of defective parts produced also depended on whether raw material needed by each machine was loaded manually or by an automatic feed system. The data in Table 13.31 gives the numbers of defective parts produced. Using $\alpha = .05$, test for any significant effect due to machine, loading system, and interaction.

COMPUTER CASE

WENTWORTH MEDICAL CENTER

As part of a long-term study of individuals 65 years of age or older, sociologists and physicians at the Wentworth Medical Center in upstate New York conducted a study to investigate the relationship between geographic location and depression. A sample of 60 individuals, all in reasonably good health, was selected; 20 individuals were residents of Florida, 20 were residents of New York, and 20 were residents of North Carolina. Each of the individuals sampled was given a standardized test to measure depression. The data collected follow; higher test scores indicate higher levels of depression. These data are available on the data disk in the file MEDICAL1.

A second part of the study considered the relationship between geographic location and depression for individuals 65 years of age or older who had a chronic health condition such as arthritis, hypertension, and/or heart ailment. A sample of 60 individuals with such conditions was identified. Again, 20 were residents of Florida, 20 were residents of New York, and 20 were residents of North Carolina. The levels of depression recorded for this study follow. These data are available on the data disk in the file MEDICAL2.

Data from MEDICAL1			Data from MEDICAL2		
Florida	New York	North Carolina	Florida	New York	North Carolina
3	8	10	13	14	10
7	11	7	12	9	12
7	9	3	17	15	15
3	7	5	17	12	18
8	8	11	20	16	12
8	7	8	21	24	14
8	8	4	16	18	17
5	4	3	14	14	8
5	13	7	13	15	14
2	10	8	17	17	16
6	6	8	12	20	18
2	8	7	9	11	17
6	12	3	12	23	19
6	8	9	15	19	15
9	6	8	16	17	13
7	8	12	15	14	14
5	5	6	13	9	11
4	7	3	10	14	12
7	7	8	11	13	13
3	8	11	17	11	11

MEDICAL1

MEDICAL2

Managerial Report

1. Use descriptive statistics to summarize the data from the two studies. What are your preliminary observations about the depression scores?
2. Use analysis of variance on both data sets. State the hypotheses being tested in each case. What are your conclusions?
3. Use inferences about individual treatment means where appropriate. What are your conclusions?
4. Discuss extensions of this study or other analyses that you feel might be helpful.

APPENDIX 13.1 ●

Computational Procedure for a Completely Randomized Design

● The following step-by-step procedure is designed to ease the burden of computing the appropriate sums of squares for completely randomized designs. The formulas can be applied to both balanced and unbalanced designs.

NOTATION

$$x_{ij} = \text{value of the } i\text{th observation for treatment } j$$

$$T_j = \text{sum of all observations for treatment } j$$

$$T = \text{sum of all observations}$$

$$n_j = \text{sample size for the } j\text{th treatment}$$

$$n_T = \text{total sample size for the experiment}$$

$$k = \text{number of treatments}$$

PROCEDURE

Step 1. Compute the total sum of squares.

$$\text{SST} = \sum_{j=1}^{k} \sum_{i=1}^{n_j} x_{ij}^2 - \frac{T^2}{n_T}$$

Step 2. Compute the sum of squares due to treatments.

$$\text{SSTR} = \sum_{j=1}^{k} \frac{T_j^2}{n_j} - \frac{T^2}{n_T}$$

Step 3. Compute the sum of squares due to error.

$$\text{SSE} = \text{SST} - \text{SSTR}$$

EXAMPLE

Using this computational procedure with the Chemitech data in Table 13.7, we obtain the following results.

Step 1. SST = 54,860 − 810,000/15 = 860
Step 2. SSTR = (310)²/5 + (330)²/5 + (260)²/5 − 810,000/15 = 520
Step 3. SSE = SST − SSTR = 860 − 520 = 340

APPENDIX 13.2 ●

Computational Procedure for a Randomized Block Design

● The following step-by-step procedure is designed to help in computing the appropriate sums of squares for randomized block designs.

NOTATION

$x_{ij} = \text{value of the observation corresponding to treatment } j \text{ in block } i$

$T_{i.} = \text{the total of all observations in block } i$

$T_{.j} = \text{the total of all observations in treatment } j$

$T = \text{the total of all observations}$

$k = \text{the number of treatments}$

$b = \text{the number of blocks}$

$n_T = \text{the total sample size } (n_T = kb)$

PROCEDURE

Step 1. Compute the total sum of squares.

$$\text{SST} = \sum_{i=1}^{b} \sum_{j=1}^{k} x_{ij}^2 - \frac{T^2}{n_T}$$

Step 2. Compute the sum of squares due to treatments.

$$\text{SSTR} = \frac{\sum_{j=1}^{k} T_{\cdot j}^2}{b} - \frac{T^2}{n_T}$$

Step 3. Compute the sum of squares due to blocks (SSBL).

$$\text{SSBL} = \frac{\sum_{i=1}^{b} T_{i\cdot}^2}{k} - \frac{T^2}{n_T}$$

Step 4. Compute the sum of squares due to error (SSE).

$$\text{SSE} = \text{SST} - \text{SSTR} - \text{SSBL}$$

EXAMPLE

For the air traffic controller data in Table 13.14, we obtain the following results.

Step 1. $\text{SST} = 3598 - \dfrac{(252)^2}{18} = 70$

Step 2. $\text{SSTR} = \dfrac{(81)^2 + (78)^2 + (93)^2}{6} - \dfrac{(252)^2}{18} = 21$

Step 3. $\text{SSBL} = \dfrac{(48)^2 + (42)^2 + \cdots + (39)^2}{3} - \dfrac{(252)^2}{18} = 30$

Step 4. $\text{SSE} = 70 - 21 - 30 = 19$

APPENDIX 13.3

Computational Procedure for a Two-Factor Factorial Design

NOTATION

x_{ijk} = observation corresponding to the kth replicate taken from treatment i of factor A and treatment j of factor B

$T_{i\cdot}$ = total of all observations in treatment i (factor A)

$T_{\cdot j}$ = total of all observations in treatment j (factor B)

T_{ij} = total of all observations in the combination of treatment i (factor A) and treatment j (factor B)

T = total of all observations

a = number of levels of factor A

b = number of levels of factor B

r = number of replications

n_T = total number of observations; $n_T = abr$

PROCEDURE

Step 1. Compute the total sum of squares.

$$\text{SST} = \sum_{i=1}^{a} \sum_{j=1}^{b} \sum_{k=1}^{r} x_{ijk}^2 - \frac{T^2}{n_T}$$

Step 2. Compute the sum of squares due to factor A.

$$\text{SSA} = \frac{\sum_{i=1}^{a} T_{i\cdot}^2}{br} - \frac{T^2}{n_T}$$

Step 3. Compute the sum of squares due to factor B.

$$\text{SSB} = \frac{\sum_{j=1}^{b} T_{\cdot j}^2}{ar} - \frac{T^2}{n_T}$$

Step 4. Compute the sum of squares due to interaction.

$$\text{SSAB} = \frac{\sum_{i=1}^{a} \sum_{j=1}^{b} T_{ij}^2}{r} - \frac{T^2}{n_T} - \text{SSA} - \text{SSB}$$

Step 5. Compute the sum of squares due to error.

$$\text{SSE} = \text{SST} - \text{SSA} - \text{SSB} - \text{SSAB}$$

EXAMPLE

For the GMAT data in Table 13.20, these steps lead to the following sums of squares.

Step 1. $\text{SST} = 4,856,500 - \dfrac{(9270)^2}{18} = 82,450$

Step 2. $\text{SSA} = \dfrac{(2960)^2 + (3080)^2 + (3230)^2}{6} - \dfrac{(9270)^2}{18} = 6100$

Step 3. $\text{SSB} = \dfrac{(3240)^2 + (3360)^2 + (2670)^2}{6} - \dfrac{(9270)^2}{18} = 45,300$

Step 4. $SSAB = \dfrac{(1080)^2 + (1000)^2 + \cdots + (890)^2}{2} - \dfrac{(9270)^2}{18}$
$-6100 - 45{,}300 = 11{,}200$

Step 5. $SSE = 82{,}450 - 6100 - 45{,}300 - 11{,}200 = 19{,}850$

APPENDIX 13.4 ●

Analysis of Variance with Minitab

●   To illustrate how Minitab can be used to test for the equality of k population means, we show how to test whether the mean examination score is the same at each plant in the National Computer Products example introduced in Section 13.1. We assume that the user has entered the examination score data into the first three columns of a Minitab worksheet, and that column 1 is labeled Plant 1, column 2 is labeled Plant 2, and column 3 is labeled Plant 3. The following steps produce the Minitab output in Figure 13.5.

Step 1.   Select the **Stat** pull-down menu
Step 2.   Select the **ANOVA** pull-down menu

	A	B	C	D	E	F	G
1	Charlotte	Houston	San Diego				
2	85	71	59				
3	75	75	64				
4	82	73	62				
5	76	74	69				
6	71	69	75				
7	85	82	67				
8							
9							
10	Anova: Single Factor						
11							
12	SUMMARY						
13	*Groups*	*Count*	*Sum*	*Average*	*Variance*		
14	Charlotte	6	474	79	34		
15	Houston	6	444	74	20		
16	San Diego	6	396	66	32		
17							
18							
19	ANOVA						
20	*Source of Variation*	*SS*	*df*	*MS*	*F*	*P-value*	*F crit*
21	Between Groups	516	2	258	9	0.003	3.6823
22	Within Groups	430	15	28.67			
23							
24	Total	946	17				

FIGURE 13.8   Excel Solution for the NCP Analysis of Variance Example

Step 3. Select the **Oneway (Unstacked)** option
Step 4. When the dialog box appears:
          Enter C1–C3 in the **Responses (in separate columns) box**
          Select **OK**

APPENDIX 13.5 ●

Analysis of Variance with Spreadsheets

● To illustrate how Excel can be used to test for the equality of k population means, we show how to test whether the mean examination score is the same at each plant in the National Computer Products example introduced in Section 13.1. We assume that the user has entered the examination score data into worksheet rows 2 to 7 of columns A, B, and C as shown in Figure 13.8; note that the cells in row 1 for columns A, B, and C are labeled Plant 1, Plant 2, and Plant 3. The following steps are used to test whether the mean examination scores are equal.

Step 1. Select the **Tools** pull-down menu
Step 2. Select the **Data Analysis** option
Step 3. When the Data Analysis dialog box appears:
          Choose **Anova: Single Factor**
          Select **OK**
Step 4. When the Anova: Single Factor dialog box appears:
          Enter A1:C7 in the **Input Range** box
          Select **Columns**
          Select **Labels in First Row**
          Select **Output Range** and enter C10 in the box
          Select **OK**

14

SIMPLE LINEAR REGRESSION

CONTENTS

STATISTICS IN PRACTICE ●●●●●●●●●●●●●●●●●●●●●●●

Polaroid Corporation*

Cambridge, Massachusetts

Polaroid's consumer photography business began in 1947 when the company's founder, Dr. Edwin Land, announced a one-step dry process for producing a finished photograph within one minute after taking the picture. The first Polaroid Land camera and Polaroid Land film went on sale in 1949. Since then, Polaroid's continuous experimentation and development in chemistry, optics, and electronics have produced photographic systems of ever higher quality, reliability, and convenience.

Polaroid's other major business segment, technical and industrial photography, focuses on making Polaroid's instant photography a key component of the growing number of imaging systems used in today's visual communications environment. To this end, Polaroid markets a wide variety of instant photographic systems, cameras, components, and films for professional, industrial, scientific, and medical uses. Other businesses include magnetics, sunglasses, industrial polarizers, chemicals, custom coating, and holography.

Sensitometry, the measurement of the sensitivity of photographic materials, provides information on many characteristics of film, such as its useful exposure range. Within Polaroid's central sensitometry laboratory, scientists systematically sample and analyze instant films that have been stored at temperature and humidity levels approximating those to which the films will be subjected after they have been purchased by consumers. To investigate the relationship between film speed and the age of a Polaroid extended range, color professional print film, Polaroid's central sensitometry lab selected film samples ranging in age (time since manufacture) from one to 13 months. The data showed that film speed decreases with age, and that a straight-line or linear relationship could be used to approximate the relationship between change in film speed and age of the film.

Using regression analysis, Polaroid was able to develop the following equation relating the change in the film speed to the film's age.

$$\hat{y} = -19.8 - 7.6x$$

where

$$\hat{y} = \text{change in film speed}$$

$$x = \text{film age in months}$$

This equation shows that the average decrease in film speed is 7.6 units per month. The information provided by this analysis, when coupled with consumer purchase and use patterns, enables Polaroid to make manufacturing adjustments that help the company produce films with the performance levels its customers require.

In this chapter you will learn how regression analysis can be used to develop an equation relating two variables, such as the change in film speed to the age of the film in the Polaroid example. In subsequent chapters we will extend this concept to cases involving more than two variables.

Polaroid is the leader in quality instant photography products.

*The authors are indebted to Mr. Lawrence Friedman, Manager, Photographic Quality, for providing this Statistics in Practice.

● Managerial decisions often are based on the relationship between two or more variables. For example, after considering the relationship between advertising expenditures and sales, a marketing manager might attempt to predict sales for a given level of advertising expenditures. In another case, a public utility might use the relationship between the daily high temperature and the demand for electricity to predict electricity usage on the basis of next month's anticipated daily high temperatures. Sometimes a manager will rely on intuition to judge how two variables are related. However, if data can be obtained, a statistical procedure called *regression analysis* can be used to develop an equation showing how the variables are related.

In regression terminology, the variable that is being predicted is called the *dependent* variable. The variable or variables being used to predict the value of the dependent variable are called the *independent* variables. For example, in analyzing the effect of advertising expenditures on sales, a marketing manager's desire to predict sales would suggest making sales the dependent variable. Advertising expenditure would be the independent variable used to help predict sales. In statistical notation, y denotes the dependent variable and x denotes the independent variable.

In this chapter we consider the simplest type of regression analysis involving one independent variable and one dependent variable in which the relationship between the variables is approximated by a straight line. This is called *simple linear regression.* Regression analysis involving two or more independent variables is called multiple regression analysis; multiple regression and cases involving curvilinear relationships are covered in Chapters 15 and 16.

14.1   THE SIMPLE LINEAR REGRESSION MODEL

As an illustration of regression analysis, let us consider the situation of Armand's Pizza Parlors, a chain of Italian-food restaurants located in a five-state area. The most successful locations for Armand's have been near college campuses. The managers believe that sales for these restaurants (denoted by y) are related positively to the size of the student population (denoted by x); that is, restaurants near campuses with a large population tend to generate more sales than those located near campuses with a small population. Using regression analysis, we can develop an equation showing how the dependent variable y is related to the independent variable x.

THE REGRESSION MODEL AND THE REGRESSION EQUATION

In the Armand's Pizza Parlors example, every restaurant has associated with it a value of x (student population) and a corresponding value of y (quarterly sales). The equation that describes how y is related to x and an error term is called the *regression model*. The regression model used in *simple linear regression* follows.

> **SIMPLE LINEAR REGRESSION MODEL**
> $$y = \beta_0 + \beta_1 x + \epsilon \tag{14.1}$$

In the simple linear regression model, β_0 and β_1 are the parameters and ϵ (the Greek letter epsilon) is a random variable. A close examination of the simple linear regression model reveals that y is a linear function of x (the $\beta_0 + \beta_1 x$ part) plus ϵ. The random variable ϵ is an error term that accounts for the variability in y that cannot be explained by the linear relationship between x and y.

In Section 14.4 we will discuss all of the assumptions for the simple linear regression model and ϵ. One of the assumptions is that the mean or expected value of ϵ is zero. A consequence of this assumption is that the mean or expected value of y, denoted $E(y)$, is equal to $\beta_0 + \beta_1 x$; in other words, the mean value of y is a linear function of x. The equation that describes how the mean value of y is related to x is called the *regression equation*. The regression equation for *simple linear regression* follows.

SIMPLE LINEAR REGRESSION EQUATION

$$E(y) = \beta_0 + \beta_1 x \qquad (14.2)$$

In simple linear regression, the graph of the regression equation is a straight line; β_0 is the y intercept of the regression line, β_1 is the slope, and $E(y)$ is the mean or expected value of y for a given value of x. Examples of possible regression lines for simple linear regression are shown in Figure 14.1. The regression line in panel A of the figure shows that the mean value of y is related positively to x, with larger values of $E(y)$ associated with larger values of x. The regression line in panel B shows that the mean value of y is related negatively to x, with smaller values of $E(y)$ associated with larger values of x. The regression line in panel C shows the case in which y is not related to x; that is, the mean value of y is the same for every value of x.

THE ESTIMATED REGRESSION EQUATION

If the values of the parameters β_0 and β_1 were known, we could use (14.2) to compute the mean value of y for a known value of x. Unfortunately, the parameter values are not known in practice and must be estimated by using sample data. Sample statistics (denoted b_0 and b_1) are computed as estimates of the parameters β_0 and β_1. Substituting the values of the sample statistics b_0 and b_1 for β_0 and β_1 in the regression equation, we obtain the *estimated regression equation*. In simple linear regression, the estimated regression equation is written in the following form.

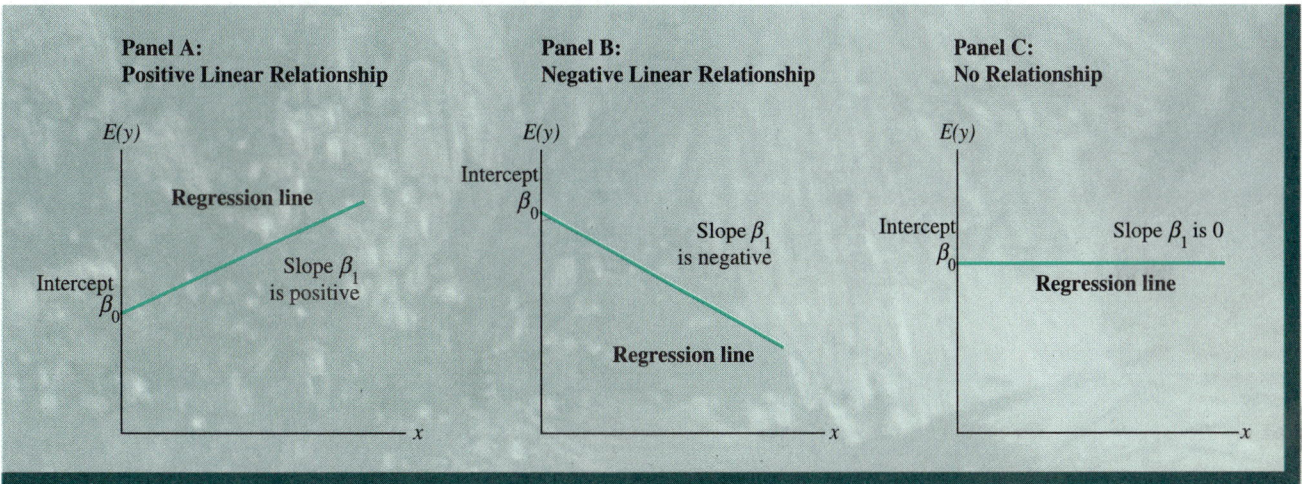

FIGURE 14.1   Possible Regression Lines in Simple Linear Regression

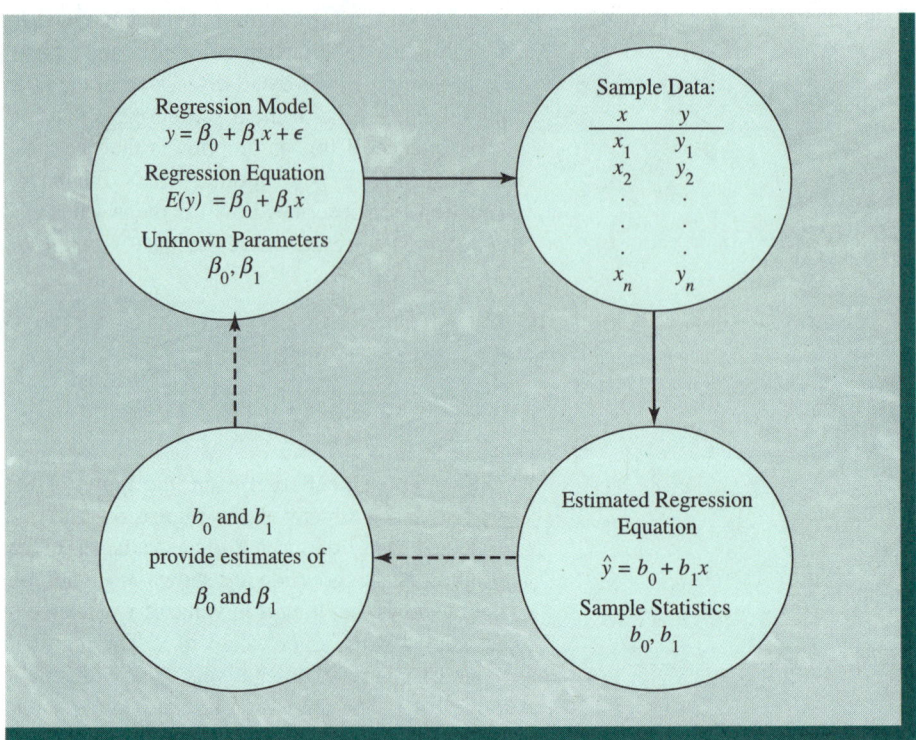

FIGURE 14.2 The Estimation Process in Simple Linear Regression

ESTIMATED SIMPLE LINEAR REGRESSION EQUATION

$$\hat{y} = b_0 + b_1 x \qquad \qquad (14.3)$$

In simple linear regression, the graph of the estimated regression equation is called the *estimated regression line;* b_0 is the y intercept, b_1 is the slope, and $\hat{y}$ is the estimated value of y for a given value of x. In the next section, we show how the least squares method can be used to compute the values of b_0 and b_1 in the estimated regression equation. Figure 14.2 is a summary of the estimation process for simple linear regression.

NOTES AND COMMENTS

We caution the reader that regression analysis *cannot* be interpreted as a procedure for establishing a *cause-and-effect* relationship between variables. It can only indicate how or to what extent variables are *associated* with each other. Any conclusions about cause and effect must be based on the *judgment* of the individual or individuals most knowledgeable about the application.

14.2 THE LEAST SQUARES METHOD

The *least squares method* is a procedure for finding the estimated regression equation. To illustrate the least squares method for the Armand's Pizza Parlors example, suppose data were collected from a sample of 10 Armand's restaurants located near college campuses. For the ith restaurant in the sample, x_i is the size of the student population (in thousands) and y_i is the quarterly sales (in thousands of dollars). The values of x_i and y_i for the 10 restaurants in the sample are summarized in Table 14.1. We see that restaurant 1, with $x_1 = 2$ and $y_1 = 58$, is near a campus with 2000 students and has quarterly sales of \$58,000. Restaurant 2, with $x_2 = 6$ and $y_2 = 105$, is near a campus with 6000 students and has quarterly sales of \$105,000. The largest sales value is for restaurant 10, which is near a campus with 26,000 students and has quarterly sales of \$202,000.

Figure 14.3 is a scatter diagram of the data in Table 14.1. The size of the student population is shown on the horizontal axis and the value of quarterly sales is shown on the vertical axis. Scatter diagrams for regression analysis are constructed with values of the independent variable x on the horizontal axis and values of the dependent variable y on the vertical axis. The scatter diagram enables us to observe the data graphically and to draw preliminary conclusions about the possible relationship between the variables.

What preliminary conclusions can be drawn from Figure 14.3? Sales appear to be higher at campuses with larger student populations. In addition, for these data the relationship between the size of the student population and sales appears to be approximated by a straight line; indeed, there seems to be a positive linear relationship between x and y. We therefore choose the simple linear regression model to represent the relationship between quarterly sales and student population. Given that choice, our next task is to use the sample data in Table 14.1 to determine the values of b_0 and b_1 in the estimated simple linear regression equation. For the ith restaurant, the estimated regression equation provides

$$\hat{y}_i = b_0 + b_1 x_i \tag{14.4}$$

where

$\qquad x_i =$ size of the student population (1000s) for the ith restaurant,

$\qquad b_0 =$ the y intercept of the estimated regression line,

$\qquad b_1 =$ the slope of the estimated regression line, and

$\qquad \hat{y}_i =$ estimated value of quarterly sales (\$1000s) for the ith restaurant

With y_i denoting the observed (actual) sales for restaurant i and $\hat{y}_i$ in (14.4) representing the estimated value of sales for restaurant i, every restaurant in the sample will have an

TABLE 14.1   Student Population and Quarterly Sales Data for 10 Armand's Pizza Parlors

Restaurant i	Student Population (1000s) x_i	Quarterly Sales (\$1000s) y_i
1	2	58
2	6	105
3	8	88
4	8	118
5	12	117
6	16	137
7	20	157
8	20	169
9	22	149
10	26	202

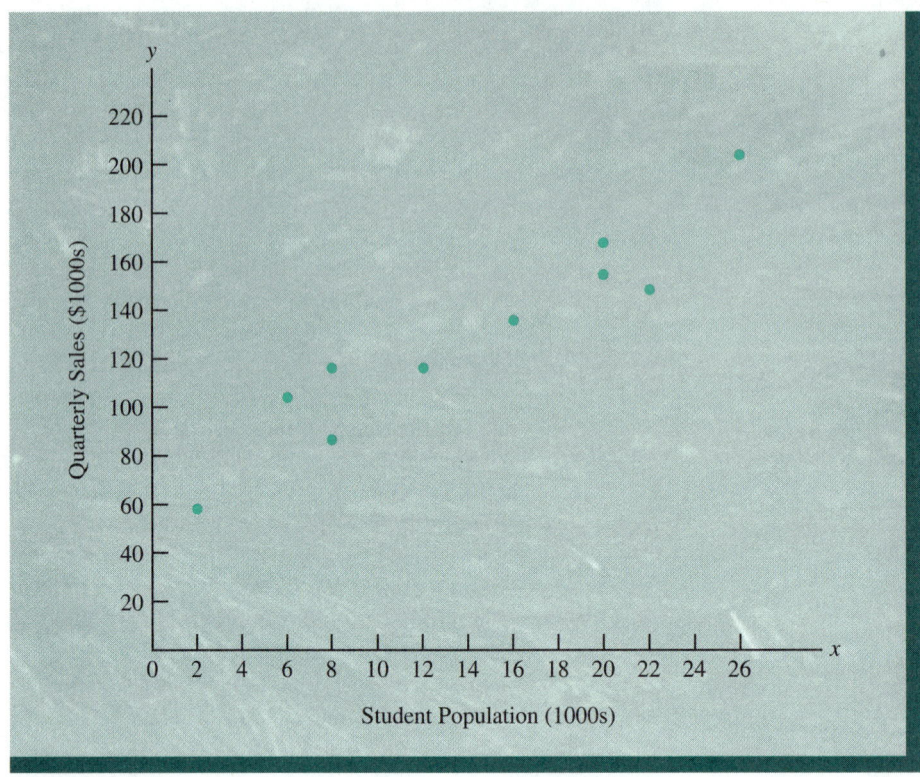

FIGURE 14.3   Scatter Diagram of Student Population and Quarterly Sales for Armand's Pizza Parlors

observed value of sales y_i and an estimated value of sales $\hat{y}_i$. For the estimated regression line to provide a good fit to the data, we want the differences between the observed sales values and the estimated sales values to be small.

The least squares method uses the sample data to provide the values of b_0 and b_1 that minimize the *sum of the squares of the deviations* between the observed values of the dependent variable y_i and the estimated values of the dependent variable $\hat{y}_i$. The criterion for the least squares method is given by (14.5).

LEAST SQUARES CRITERION

$$\min \Sigma(y_i - \hat{y}_i)^2 \tag{14.5}$$

where

y_i = observed value of the dependent variable for the ith observation

$\hat{y}_i$ = estimated value of the dependent variable for the ith observation

Differential calculus can be used to show (see the appendix to this chapter) that the values of b_0 and b_1 that minimize (14.5) can be found by using (14.6) and (14.7).

SLOPE AND y-INTERCEPT FOR THE ESTIMATED REGRESSION EQUATION

$$b_1 = \frac{\Sigma x_i y_i - (\Sigma x_i \, \Sigma y_i)/n}{\Sigma x_i^2 - (\Sigma x_i)^2/n} \qquad \textbf{(14.6)}$$

$$b_0 = \bar{y} - b_1 \bar{x} \qquad \textbf{(14.7)}$$

where

$\quad x_i$ = value of the independent variable for the ith observation

$\quad y_i$ = value of the dependent variable for the ith observation

$\quad \bar{x}$ = mean value for the independent variable

$\quad \bar{y}$ = mean value for the dependent variable

$\quad n$ = total number of observations

In computing b_1 with a calculator, it is best to carry as many significant digits as possible in the intermediate calculations; we recommend carrying at least four significant digits.

Some of the calculations necessary to develop the least squares estimated regression equation for Armand's Pizza Parlors are shown in Table 14.2. In this example there are 10 restaurants, or observations; hence $n = 10$. Using (14.6), (14.7), and the information in Table 14.2, we can compute the slope and intercept of the estimated regression equation for Armand's Pizza Parlors. The calculation of the slope (b_1) proceeds as follows.

$$b_1 = \frac{\Sigma x_i y_i - (\Sigma x_i \Sigma y_i)/n}{\Sigma x_i^2 - (\Sigma x_i)^2/n}$$

$$= \frac{21{,}040 - (140)(1300)/10}{2528 - (140)^2/10}$$

TABLE 14.2 Calculations for the Least Squares Estimated Regression Equation for Armand's Pizza Parlors

Restaurant i	x_i	y_i	$x_i y_i$	x_i^2
1	2	58	116	4
2	6	105	630	36
3	8	88	704	64
4	8	118	944	64
5	12	117	1,404	144
6	16	137	2,192	256
7	20	157	3,140	400
8	20	169	3,380	400
9	22	149	3,278	484
10	26	202	5,252	676
Totals	140	1300	21,040	2528
	Σx_i	Σy_i	$\Sigma x_i y_i$	Σx_i^2

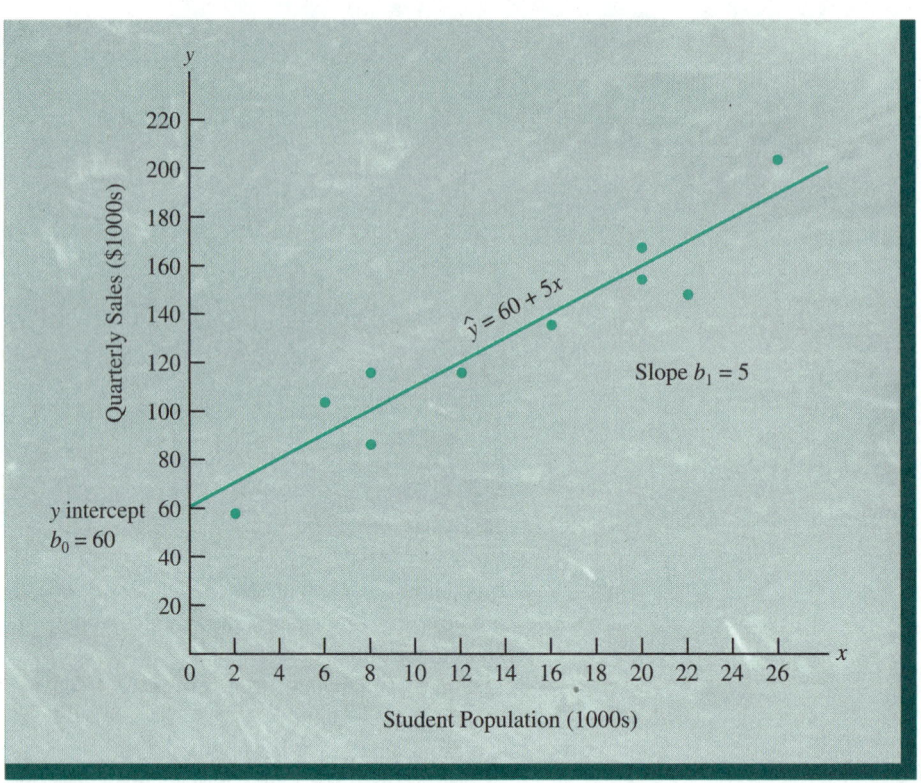

FIGURE 14.4 Graph of the Estimated Regression Equation for Armand's Pizza Parlors: $\hat{y} = 60 + 5x$

$$b_1 = \frac{2840}{568}$$

$$= 5$$

The calculation of the y intercept (b_0) follows.

$$\bar{x} = \frac{\Sigma x_i}{n} = \frac{140}{10} = 14$$

$$\bar{y} = \frac{\Sigma y_i}{n} = \frac{1300}{10} = 130$$

$$b_0 = \bar{y} - b_1\bar{x}$$

$$= 130 - 5(14)$$

$$= 60$$

Thus, the estimated regression equation found by using the least squares method is

$$\hat{y} = 60 + 5x$$

Figure 14.4 shows the graph of this equation on the scatter diagram.

The slope of the estimated regression equation ($b_1 = 5$) is positive, implying that as student population increases, sales increase. In fact, we can conclude (since sales are measured in $1000s and student population in 1000s) that an increase in the student population of 1000 is associated with an increase of $5000 in expected sales; that is, sales are expected to increase by $5.00 per student.

If we believe the least squares estimated regression equation adequately describes the relationship between x and y, it would seem reasonable to use the estimated regression equation to predict the value of y for a given value of x. For example, if we wanted to predict sales for a restaurant to be located near a campus with 16,000 students, we would compute

$$\hat{y} = 60 + 5(16)$$

$$= 140$$

Hence, we would predict quarterly sales of $140,000 for this restaurant. In the following sections we will discuss methods for assessing the appropriateness of using the estimated regression equation for estimation and prediction.

NOTES AND COMMENTS

The least squares method provides an estimated regression equation that minimizes the sum of squared deviations between the observed values of the dependent variable y_i and the estimated values of the dependent variable $\hat{y}_i$. This is the least squares criterion for choosing the equation that provides the best fit. If some other criterion were used, such as minimizing the sum of the absolute deviations between y_i and $\hat{y}_i$, a different equation would be obtained. In practice, the least squares method is the most widely used.

EXERCISES

METHODS

Self-Test

1. Given are five observations for two variables, x and y.

x_i	1	2	3	4	5
y_i	3	7	5	11	14

 a. Develop a scatter diagram for these data.
 b. What does the scatter diagram developed in (a) indicate about the relationship between the two variables?
 c. Try to approximate the relationship between x and y by drawing a straight line through the data.
 d. Develop the estimated regression equation by computing the values of b_0 and b_1 using (14.6) and (14.7).
 e. Use the estimated regression equation to predict the value of y when $x = 4$.

2. Given are five observations for two variables, x and y.

x_i	2	3	5	1	8
y_i	25	25	20	30	16

 a. Develop a scatter diagram for these data.
 b. What does the scatter diagram developed in (a) indicate about the relationship between the two variables?

c. Try to approximate the relationship between x and y by drawing a straight line through the data.
d. Develop the estimated regression equation by computing the values of b_0 and b_1 using (14.6) and (14.7).
e. Use the estimated regression equation to predict the value of y when $x = 6$.

3. Given are five observations collected in a regression study on two variables.

x_i	2	4	5	7	8
y_i	2	3	2	6	4

a. Develop a scatter diagram for these data.
b. Develop the estimated regression equation for these data.
c. Use the estimated regression equation to predict the value of y when $x = 4$.

APPLICATIONS

Self-Test
.... ▶

4. The following data were collected on the height (inches) and weight (pounds) of women swimmers.

Height	68	64	62	65	66
Weight	132	108	102	115	128

a. Develop a scatter diagram for these data with height as the independent variable.
b. What does the scatter diagram developed in (a) indicate about the relationship between the two variables?
c. Try to approximate the relationship between height and weight by drawing a straight line through the data.
d. Develop the estimated regression equation by computing the values of b_0 and b_1 using (14.6) and (14.7).
e. If a swimmer's height is 63 inches, what would you estimate her weight to be?

5. The data in Table 14.3 are the monthly starting salaries and the grade point averages (GPA) of students who have obtained a bachelor's degree in business administration.
a. Develop a scatter diagram for these data with GPA as the independent variable.
b. What does the scatter diagram developed in (a) indicate about the relationship between the two variables?
c. Draw a straight line through the data to approximate a linear relationship between GPA and salary.
d. Use the least squares method to develop the estimated regression equation.
e. Predict the monthly starting salary for a student with a 3.0 GPA and for a student with a 3.5 GPA.

TABLE 14.3   Exercise 5

GPA	Monthly Salary ($)	
2.6	1800	4680
3.4	2100	7140
3.6	2500	9000
3.2	2000	6400
3.5	2400	8400
2.9	2100	6090

(handwritten left margin: 6.76, 11.56, 12.96, 10.24, 12.25, 8.41)

6. Performance data for a Century Coronado 21 with a 310-hp MerCruiser V-8 gasoline inboard engine was reported in *Boating* (September 1991). Data on how the boat speed in miles per hour (mph) affected fuel consumption in gallons per hour (gph) follow.

Speed (mph)	Fuel Consumption (gph)
6.1	2.3
10.7	4.8
20.9	7.5
27.5	9.2
31.5	12.4

a. Develop a scatter diagram for these data.

b. What does the scatter diagram developed in (a) indicate about the relationship between the two variables?

c. Develop the estimated regression equation showing how fuel consumption is related to the boat speed.

d. What is the estimated fuel consumption if the boat speed is 25 mph?

7. Major hotels frequently provide special rates for business travelers. The lowest rates are charged when reservations are made 14 days in advance. The following table reports the business rates and the 14-day-advance super-saver rates for one night at a sample of six ITT Sheraton Hotels (*Sky Magazine*, January 1995).

Hotel Location	Business Rate	14-Day Advance Rate
Birmingham	$ 89	$ 81
Miami	130	115
Atlanta	98	89
Chicago	149	138
New Orleans	199	149
Nashville	114	94

a. Develop a scatter diagram for these data with business rates as the independent variable.

b. Develop the least squares estimated regression equation.

c. The ITT Sheraton Hotel in Tampa offers a business rate of $135 per night. Estimate the 14-day-advance super-saver rate at this hotel.

8. *Consumer Reports* uses a survey to collect data on the annual cost of repairs for more than 300 makes and models of automobiles (*Consumer Reports* 1992 Buying Guide). The following data are the average annual repair cost ($) and the age of the automobile (years).

Age	1	2	3	4	5
Repair	135	175	320	300	450

a. Develop the estimated regression equation showing how annual repair cost is related to the age of an automobile.

b. What is the estimated annual repair cost for a three-year-old automobile?

TABLE 14.4 Exercise 9

Sales person	Years of Experience	Annual Sales ($1000s)
1	1	80
2	3	97
3	4	92
4	4	102
5	6	103
6	8	111
7	10	119
8	10	123
9	11	117
10	13	136

9. Table 14.4 lists some data a sales manager has collected on annual sales and years of experience.

a. Develop a scatter diagram for these data with years of experience as the independent variable.

b. Develop an estimated regression equation that can be used to predict annual sales given the years of experience.

c. Use the estimated regression equation to predict annual sales for a salesperson with nine years of experience.

10. Tire rating and load-carrying capacity for a sample of automobile tires follow (*Road & Track*, October 1994).

Tire Rating	Load-carrying Capacity
75	853
82	1047
85	1135
87	1201
88	1235
91	1356
92	1389
93	1433
105	2039

a. Develop a scatter diagram for these data with tire rating as the independent variable.
b. Develop the least squares estimated regression equation.
c. Estimate the load-carrying capacity for a tire that has a rating of 90.

11. Reported in Table 14.5 are the number of golf courses and the number of paid rounds of golf (in millions) for the Myrtle Beach, South Carolina, area over an eight-year period (*Myrtle Beach Magazine,* October 1991).

TABLE 14.5   Exercise 11

Number of Golf Courses	Number of Paid Rounds of Golf	
26	1.0	26
30	1.1	33
31	1.2	37.2
32	1.3	41.6
33	1.4	46.2
35	1.6	56
38	1.8	68.4
43	2.0	86

a. Develop a scatter diagram for these data with number of golf courses as the independent variable.
b. Does there appear to be a linear relationship?
c. Develop the estimated regression equation relating the number of paid rounds of golf to the number of golf courses.
d. Suppose that next year 57 golf courses will be available. What is an estimate of the number of paid rounds of golf? Discuss any potential problem associated with making this estimate.

12. The following table gives the percentage of women working in each company (x) and the percentage of management jobs held by women in that company (y); the data represent companies in retailing and trade (*Louis Rukeyser's Business Almanac*).

Company	x_i	y_i
Federated Department Stores	72	61
Kroger	47	16
Marriott	51	32
McDonald's	57	46
Sears	55	36

a. Develop a scatter diagram for these data.
b. What does the scatter diagram developed in (a) indicate about the relationship between x and y?
c. Develop the estimated regression equation for these data.
d. Predict the percentage of management jobs held by women in a company that has 60% women employees.
e. Use the estimated regression equation to predict the percentage of management jobs held by women in a company where 55% of the jobs are held by women. How does this predicted value compare to the 36% value observed for Sears, a company in which 55% of the employees are women?

13. The following table reports the median income and the median home price for a sample of six cities (*Who's Buying Homes in America,* Chicago Title and Trust Company, 1994). Data are in thousands of dollars.

City	Median Income	Median Home Price
Atlanta	$65.2	$120.2
Cleveland	49.8	92.7
Denver	53.8	111.7
Dallas	62.7	104.7
Orlando	50.9	98.5
Minneapolis	53.1	105.8

a. Develop a scatter diagram for these data with median income as the independent variable.
b. Develop the least squares estimated regression equation.
c. Estimate the median home price in a city with a median income of $60,000.

14. To the Internal Revenue Service, the reasonableness of total itemized deductions depends on the taxpayer's adjusted gross income. Large deductions, which include charity and medical deductions, are more reasonable for taxpayers with large adjusted gross incomes. If a taxpayer claims larger than average itemized deductions for a given level of income, the chances of an IRS audit are increased. Data on adjusted gross income and the average or reasonable amount of itemized deductions follow (*Money,* October 1994). The data are in thousands of dollars.

Adjusted Gross Income	Total Itemized Deductions
$ 22	$ 9.6
27	9.6
32	10.1
48	11.1
65	13.5
85	17.7
120	25.5

a. Develop a scatter diagram for these data with adjusted gross income as the independent variable.
b. Use the least squares method to develop the estimated regression equation.
c. Estimate a reasonable level of total itemized deductions for a taxpayer with an adjusted gross income of $52,500. If this taxpayer has claimed total itemized deductions of $20,400, would the IRS agent's request for an audit appear justified? Explain.

14.3 THE COEFFICIENT OF DETERMINATION

For the Armand's Pizza Parlors example, we developed the estimated regression equation $\hat{y} = 60 + 5x$ to approximate the linear relationship between the size of the student population x and quarterly sales y. A question now is: How well does the estimated regression equation fit the data? In this section, we show that the *coefficient of determination* provides a measure of the goodness of fit for the estimated regression equation.

For the ith observation in the sample that we used to estimate b_0 and b_1, the deviation between the observed value of the dependent variable, y_i, and the estimated value of the dependent variable, $\hat{y}_i$, is called the *ith residual*. The ith residual represents the error in using $\hat{y}_i$ to estimate y_i. Thus, for the ith observation, the residual is $y_i - \hat{y}_i$. The sum of squares of these residuals or errors is the quantity that is minimized by the least squares method. This quantity, also known as the *sum of squares due to error*, is denoted by SSE.

SUM OF SQUARES DUE TO ERROR

$$SSE = \Sigma(y_i - \hat{y}_i)^2 \tag{14.8}$$

The value of SSE is a measure of the error in using the estimated regression equation to estimate the values of the dependent variable in the sample.

In Table 14.6 we show the calculations required to compute the sum of squares due to error for the Armand's Pizza Parlors example. For instance, for restaurant 1 the values

TABLE 14.6   Calculation of SSE for Armand's Pizza Parlors

Restaurant i	x_i = Student Population (1000s)	y_i = Quarterly Sales ($1000s)	$\hat{y}_i = 60 + 5x_i$	$y_i - \hat{y}_i$	$(y_i - \hat{y}_i)^2$
1	2	58	70	−12	144
2	6	105	90	15	225
3	8	88	100	−12	144
4	8	118	100	18	324
5	12	117	120	−3	9
6	16	137	140	−3	9
7	20	157	160	−3	9
8	20	169	160	9	81
9	22	149	170	−21	441
10	26	202	190	12	144
					SSE = 1530

TABLE 14.7   Computation of the Total Sum of Squares for Armand's Pizza Parlors

Restaurant i	x_i = Student Population (1000s)	y_i = Quarterly Sales ($1000s)	$y_i - \bar{y}$	$(y_i - \bar{y})^2$
1	2	58	−72	5,184
2	6	105	−25	625
3	8	88	−42	1,764
4	8	118	−12	144
5	12	117	−13	169
6	16	137	7	49
7	20	157	27	729
8	20	169	39	1,521
9	22	149	19	361
10	26	202	72	5,184
			SST =	15,730

of the independent and dependent variables are $x_1 = 2$ and $y_1 = 58$. Using the estimated regression equation, we find that the estimated value of sales for restaurant 1 is $\hat{y}_1 = 60 + 5(2) = 70$. Thus, the error in using $\hat{y}_1$ to estimate y_1 for restaurant 1 is $y_1 - \hat{y}_1 = 58 - = -12$. The squared error, $(-12)^2 = 144$, is shown in the last column of Table 14.6. After computing and squaring the residuals for each restaurant in the sample, we sum them to obtain SSE = 1530. Thus, SSE = 1530 measures the error in using the estimated regression equation $\hat{y} = 60 + 5x$ to predict sales.

Now suppose we are asked to develop an estimate of sales without knowledge of the size of the student population. Without knowledge of any related variables, we would use the sample mean as an estimate of sales at any given restaurant. Table 14.2 shows that for the sales data, $\Sigma y_i = 1300$. Hence, the mean value of sales for the sample of 10 Armand's restaurants is $\bar{y} = \Sigma y_i / n = 1300/10 = 130$. In Table 14.7 we show the sum of squared deviations obtained by using the sample mean $\bar{y} = 130$ to estimate the value of sales for each restaurant in the sample. For the ith restaurant in the sample, the difference $y_i - \bar{y}$ provides a measure of the error involved in using $\bar{y}$ to estimate sales. The corresponding sum of squares, called the *total sum of squares,* is denoted SST.

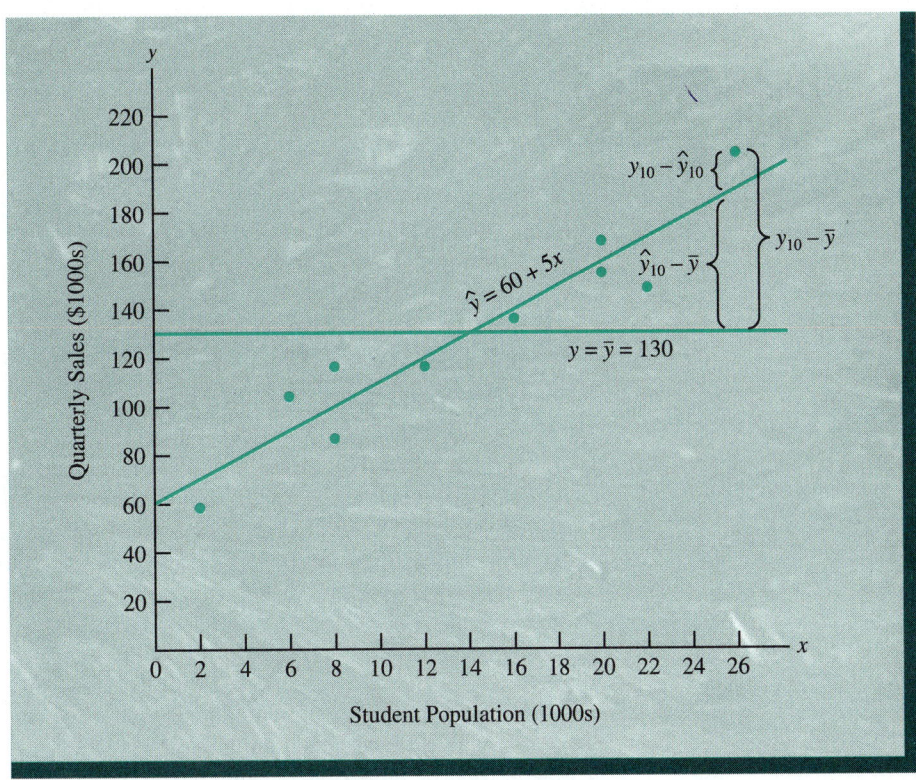

FIGURE 14.5 Deviations about the Estimated Regression Line and the Line $y = \bar{y}$ for Armand's Pizza Parlors

TOTAL SUM OF SQUARES

$$SST = \Sigma(y_i - \bar{y})^2 \qquad \text{(14.9)}$$

The sum at the bottom of the last column in Table 14.7 is the total sum of squares for Armand's Pizza Parlors; it is SST = 15,730.

In Figure 14.5 we show the estimated regression line $\hat{y} = 60 + 5x$ and the line corresponding to $\bar{y} = 130$. Note that the points cluster more closely around the estimated regression line than they do about the line $\bar{y} = 130$. For example, for the 10th restaurant in the sample we see that the error is much larger when $\bar{y} = 130$ is used as an estimate of y_{10} than when $\hat{y}_{10} = 60 + 5(26) = 190$ is used. We can think of SST as a measure of how well the observations cluster about the $\bar{y}$ line and SSE as a measure of how well the observations cluster about the $\hat{y}$ line.

To measure how much the $\hat{y}$ values on the estimated regression line deviate from $\bar{y}$, another sum of squares is computed. This sum of squares, called the *sum of squares due to regression*, is denoted SSR.

SUM OF SQUARES DUE TO REGRESSION

$$SSR = \Sigma(\hat{y}_i - \bar{y})^2 \qquad \text{(14.10)}$$

From the preceding discussion, we should expect that SST, SSR, and SSE are related. Indeed, the relationship among these three sums of squares provides one of the most important results in statistics.

RELATIONSHIP AMONG SST, SSR, AND SSE

$$SST = SSR + SSE \qquad\qquad (14.11)$$

where

$$SST = \text{total sum of squares}$$
$$SSR = \text{sum of squares due to regression}$$
$$SSE = \text{sum of squares due to error}$$

Equation (14.11) shows that the total sum of squares can be partitioned into two components, the regression sum of squares and the sum of squares due to error. Hence, if the values of any two of these sum of squares are known, the third sum of squares can be computed easily. For instance, in the Armand's Pizza Parlors example, we already know that SSE = 1530 and SST = 15,730; therefore, solving for SSR in (14.11), we find that the sum of squares due to regression is

$$SSR = SST - SSE = 15,730 - 1530 = 14,200$$

Now let us see how the three sums of squares, SST, SSR, and SSE, can be used to provide a measure of the goodness of fit for the estimated regression equation. The estimated regression equation would provide a perfect fit if every value of the dependent variable y_i happened to lie on the estimated regression line. In this case, $y_i - \hat{y}_i$ would be zero for each observation, resulting in SSE = 0. Since SST = SSR + SSE, we see that for a perfect fit SSR must equal SST, and the ratio (SSR/SST) must equal one. Poorer fits will result in larger values for SSE. Solving for SSE in (14.10), we see that SSE = SST − SSR. Hence, the largest value for SSE (and hence the poorest fit) occurs when SSR = 0 and SSE = SST.

The ratio SSR/SST, which will take values between zero and one, is used to evaluate the goodness of fit for the estimated regression equation. This ratio is called the *coefficient of determination* and is denoted by r^2.

COEFFICIENT OF DETERMINATION

$$r^2 = \frac{SSR}{SST} \qquad\qquad (14.12)$$

For the Armand's Pizza Parlors example, the value of the coefficient of determination is

$$r^2 = \frac{SSR}{SST} = \frac{14,200}{15,730} = .9027$$

When we express the coefficient of determination as a percentage, r^2 can be interpreted as the percentage of the total sum of squares that can be explained by using the estimated regression equation. For Armand's Pizza Parlors, we can conclude that 90.27% of the total sum of squares can be explained by using the estimated regression equation $\hat{y} = 60 + 5x$ to predict sales. In other words, 90.27% of the variation in sales can be explained by the linear relationship between the size of the student population and sales. We should be very pleased to find such a good fit for the estimated regression equation.

COMPUTATIONAL EFFICIENCIES

In modern applications of regression analysis, a computer software package is almost always used to perform the calculations required to determine the estimated regression equation and the value of the coefficient of determination. However, when solving a small problem with a calculator, we can realize computational efficiencies by using alternative formulas for SST and SSR. We illustrate with the Armand's Pizza Parlors example.

The total sum of squares can be computed by the following alternate formula.

COMPUTATIONAL FORMULA FOR SST

$$\text{SST} = \Sigma y_i^2 - (\Sigma y_i)^2/n \qquad (14.13)$$

Using the information in Table 14.8 and (14.13), we obtain SST $= 184{,}730 - (1300)^2/10 = 15{,}730$ (the same value as shown previously). Next, the sum of squares due to regression, SSR, can be calculated directly by the following alternate formula.

COMPUTATIONAL FORMULA FOR SSR

$$\text{SSR} = \frac{[\Sigma x_i y_i - (\Sigma x_i \Sigma y_i)/n]^2}{\Sigma x_i^2 - (\Sigma x_i)^2/n} \qquad (14.14)$$

Using the data in Table 14.8, we have

$$\text{SSR} = \frac{[21{,}040 - (140)(1300)/10]^2}{2528 - (140)^2/10} = \frac{8{,}065{,}600}{568} = 14{,}200$$

With SST and SSR known, we can compute the coefficient of determination by using (14.12).

TABLE 14.8 Computing SST and SSR for Armand's Pizza Parlors Using the Computational Formulas

Restaurant i	x_i	y_i	$x_i y_i$	x_i^2	y_i^2
1	2	58	116	4	3,364
2	6	105	630	36	11,025
3	8	88	704	64	7,744
4	8	118	944	64	13,924
5	12	117	1,404	144	13,689
6	16	137	2,192	256	18,769
7	20	157	3,140	400	24,649
8	20	169	3,380	400	28,561
9	22	149	3,278	484	22,201
10	26	202	5,252	676	40,804
Totals	140	1300	21,040	2528	184,730
	Σx_i	Σy_i	$\Sigma x_i y_i$	Σx_i^2	Σy_i^2

$$r^2 = \frac{\text{SSR}}{\text{SST}} = \frac{14{,}200}{15{,}730} = .9027$$

Finally, if SSE is also desired, we can use the relationship among SST, SSR, and SSE as follows.

$$\text{SSE} = \text{SST} - \text{SSR} = 15{,}730 - 14{,}200 = 1530$$

THE CORRELATION COEFFICIENT

In Chapter 3 we introduced the *correlation coefficient* as a descriptive measure of the strength of linear association between two variables, x and y. Values of the correlation coefficient are always between -1 and $+1$. A value of $+1$ indicates that the two variables x and y are perfectly related in a positive linear sense. That is, all data points are on a straight line that has a positive slope. A value of -1 indicates that x and y are perfectly related in a negative linear sense, with all data points on a straight line that has a negative slope. Values of the correlation coefficient close to zero indicate that x and y are not linearly related.

In Section 3.5 we presented the equation for computing the sample correlation coefficient. If a regression analysis has already been performed and the coefficient of determination r^2 has been computed, the sample correlation coefficient can be computed as follows.

SAMPLE CORRELATION COEFFICIENT

$$r_{xy} = (\text{the sign of } b_1) \sqrt{\text{Coefficient of Determination}}$$

$$= \pm \sqrt{r^2} \qquad\qquad (14.15)$$

where

$$b_1 = \text{the slope of the estimated regression equation } \hat{y} = b_0 + b_1 x$$

That is, the sample correlation coefficient is plus or minus the square root of the coefficient of determination. The sign for the sample correlation coefficient is positive if the estimated regression equation has a positive slope ($b_1 > 0$) and negative if the estimated regression equation has a negative slope ($b_1 < 0$).

For the Armand's Pizza Parlor example, the value of the coefficient of determination corresponding to the estimated regression equation $\hat{y} = 60 + 5x$ is .9027. Since the slope of the estimated regression equation is positive, (14.15) shows that the sample correlation coefficient is $+\sqrt{.9027} = +.9501$. With a sample correlation coefficient of $r_{xy} = +.9501$, we would conclude that there is a strong positive linear association between x and y.

In the case of a linear relationship between two variables, both the coefficient of determination and the sample correlation coefficient provide measures of the strength of the relationship. The coefficient of determination provides a measure between zero and one whereas the sample correlation coefficient provides a measure between -1 and $+1$. Although the sample correlation coefficient is restricted to a linear relationship between two variables, the coefficient of determination can be used for nonlinear relationships and for relationships that have two or more independent variables. In that sense, the coefficient of determination has a wider range of applicability.

NOTES AND COMMENTS

• • • • • • • • • • • • • • • •

1. In developing the least squares estimated regression equation and computing the coefficient of determination, we made no probabilistic assumptions and no statistical tests for significance of the relationship between x and y. Larger values of r^2 simply imply that the least squares line provides a better fit to the data; that is, the observations are more closely grouped about the least squares line. But, using only r^2, we can draw no conclusion about whether the relationship between x and y is statistically significant. Such a conclusion must be based on considerations that involve the sample size and the properties of the appropriate sampling distributions of the least squares estimators.

2. As a practical matter, for typical data found in the social sciences, values of r^2 as low as .25 are often considered useful. For data in the physical and life sciences, r^2 values of .60 or greater are often found; in fact, in some cases, r^2 values greater than .90 can be found. In business applications, r^2 values vary greatly, depending on the unique characteristics of each application.

EXERCISES

METHODS

Self-Test
• • • • • • • • • •▶

15. The data from Exercise 1 follow.

x_i	1	2	3	4	5
y_i	3	7	5	11	14

The estimated regression equation for these data is $\hat{y} = .20 + 2.60x$.
a. Compute SSE, SST, and SSR using (14.8), (14.9), and (14.11).
b. Compute the coefficient of determination r^2. Comment on the goodness of fit.
c. Recompute SST and SSR using (14.13) and (14.14). Do you get the same results as in (a)?
d. Compute the sample correlation coefficient.

16. The data from Exercise 2 follow.

x_i	2	3	5	1	8
y_i	25	25	20	30	16

The estimated regression equation for these data is $\hat{y} = 30.33 - 1.88x$.
a. Compute SSE, SST, and SSR.
b. Compute the coefficient of determination r^2. Comment on the goodness of fit.
c. Compute the sample correlation coefficient.

17. The data from Exercise 3 follow.

x_i	2	4	5	7	8
y_i	2	3	2	6	4

The estimated regression equation for these data is $\hat{y} = .75 + .51x$. What percentage of the total sum of squares can be accounted for by the estimated regression equation? What is the value of the sample correlation coefficient?

APPLICATIONS

Self-Test

TABLE 14.9
Exercise 18

	Monthly
GPA	Salary ($)
2.6	1800
3.4	2100
3.6	2500
3.2	2000
3.5	2400
2.9	2100

18. In Exercise 5, data were collected on the monthly salaries y and the grade point averages x for students who had obtained a bachelor's degree in business administration. The data from Exercise 5 are listed in Table 14.9. The estimated regression equation for these data is $\hat{y} = -109.46 + 581.08x$.
    a. Compute SST, SSR, and SSE.
    b. Compute the coefficient of determination r^2. Comment on the goodness of fit.
    c. What is the value of the sample correlation coefficient?

19. The data from Exercise 7 follow.

Hotel Location	Business Rate	14-Day Advance Rate
Birmingham	$ 89	$ 81
Miami	130	115
Atlanta	98	89
Chicago	149	138
New Orleans	199	149
Nashville	114	94

The estimated regression equation for these data is $\hat{y} = 25.21 + .6608x$. What percentage of the total sum of squares can be accounted for by the estimated regression equation? Comment on the goodness of fit. What is the sample correlation coefficient?

TABLE 14.10 Exercise 20

Absorbence Reading (x_i)	Milligrams of Protein (y_i)
.509	0
.756	20
1.020	40
1.400	80
1.570	100
1.790	127

20. A medical laboratory at Duke University estimates the amount of protein in liver samples through the use of a regression model. A spectrometer emitting light shines through a substance containing the sample, and the amount of light absorbed is used to estimate the amount of protein in the sample. A new estimated regression equation is developed daily because of differing amounts of dye in the solution. On one day, six samples with known protein concentrations gave the absorbence readings shown in Table 14.10.
    a. Use these data to develop an estimated regression equation relating the light absorbence reading to milligrams of protein present in the sample.
    b. Compute r^2. Would you feel comfortable using this regression model to estimate the amount of protein in a sample?
    c. In a sample just received, the light absorbence reading was .941. Estimate the amount of protein in the sample.

21. An important application of regression analysis in accounting is in the estimation of cost. By collecting data on volume and cost and using the least squares method to develop an estimated regression equation relating volume and cost, an accountant can estimate the cost associated with a particular manufacturing operation (*Managerial Accounting*, D. Ricketts, 1991). Consider the following sample of production volumes and total cost data for a manufacturing operation.

Production Volume (Units)	Total Cost ($)
400	4000
450	5000
550	5400
600	5900
700	6400
750	7000

a. Use these data to develop an estimated regression equation that could be used to predict the total cost for a given production volume.
b. What is the variable, or additional, cost per unit produced?
c. Compute the coefficient of determination. What percentage of the variation in total cost can be explained by volume?
d. The company's production schedule shows 500 units must be produced next month. What is the estimated total cost for this operation?

22. Are company presidents and chief executive officers paid according to the profit performance of the company? The following table lists corporate data on percentage change in return on equity over a two-year period and percentage change in the pay of presidents and chief executive officers immediately after the two-year period (*Business Week,* April 25, 1994).

	X	Y
Company	**Two-Year Change in Return on Equity (%)**	**Change in Executive Compensation (%)**
Dupont	−64.4	0
Monsanto	29.6	55
Morton International	−9.3	17
Union Carbide	−16.4	58
W. R. Grace	3.4	−11
International Flavors	18.8	24
Great Lakes Chemical	17.0	10

a. Develop the estimated regression equation with the two-year percentage change in return on equity as the independent variable.
b. Compute r^2. Would you feel comfortable using the percentage change in return on equity over a two-year period to predict the percentage change in the pay of presidents and chief executive officers? Discuss.
c. What is the sample correlation coefficient? Does it reflect a strong or weak relationship between return on equity and executive compensation?

14.4 MODEL ASSUMPTIONS

In conducting a regression analysis, we begin by making an assumption about the appropriate model for the relationship between the dependent and independent variable(s). For the case of simple linear regression, the assumed regression model is

$$y = \beta_0 + \beta_1 x + \epsilon$$

Then, the least squares method is used to develop values for b_0 and b_1, the estimates of the model parameters β_0 and β_1, respectively. The resulting estimated regression equation is

$$\hat{y} = b_0 + b_1 x$$

We saw that the value of the coefficient of determination (r^2) is a measure of the goodness of fit of the estimated regression equation. However, even with a large value of r^2, the estimated regression equation should not be used until further analysis of the appropriateness of the assumed model has been conducted. An important step in determining whether the assumed model is appropriate involves testing for the significance of the relationship. The tests of significance in regression analysis are based on the following assumptions about the error term ϵ.

ASSUMPTIONS ABOUT THE ERROR TERM ϵ IN THE REGRESSION MODEL

$$y = \beta_0 + \beta_1 x + \epsilon$$

1. The error term ϵ is a random variable with a mean or expected value of zero; that is, $E(\epsilon) = 0$.
   Implication: Since β_0 and β_1 are constants, $E(\beta_0) = \beta_0$ and $E(\beta_1) = \beta_1$; thus, for a given value of x, the expected value of y is

$$E(y) = \beta_0 + \beta_1 x. \tag{14.16}$$

   As we indicated previously, equation (14.16) is referred to as the regression equation.

2. The variance of ϵ, denoted by σ^2, is the same for all values of x.
   Implication: The variance of y equals σ^2 and is the same for all values of x.

3. The values of ϵ are independent.
   Implication: The value of ϵ for a particular value of x is not related to the value of ϵ for any other value of x; thus, the value of y for a particular value of x is not related to the value of y for any other value of x.

4. The error term ϵ is a normally distributed random variable.
   Implication: Since y is a linear function of ϵ, y is also a normally distributed random variable.

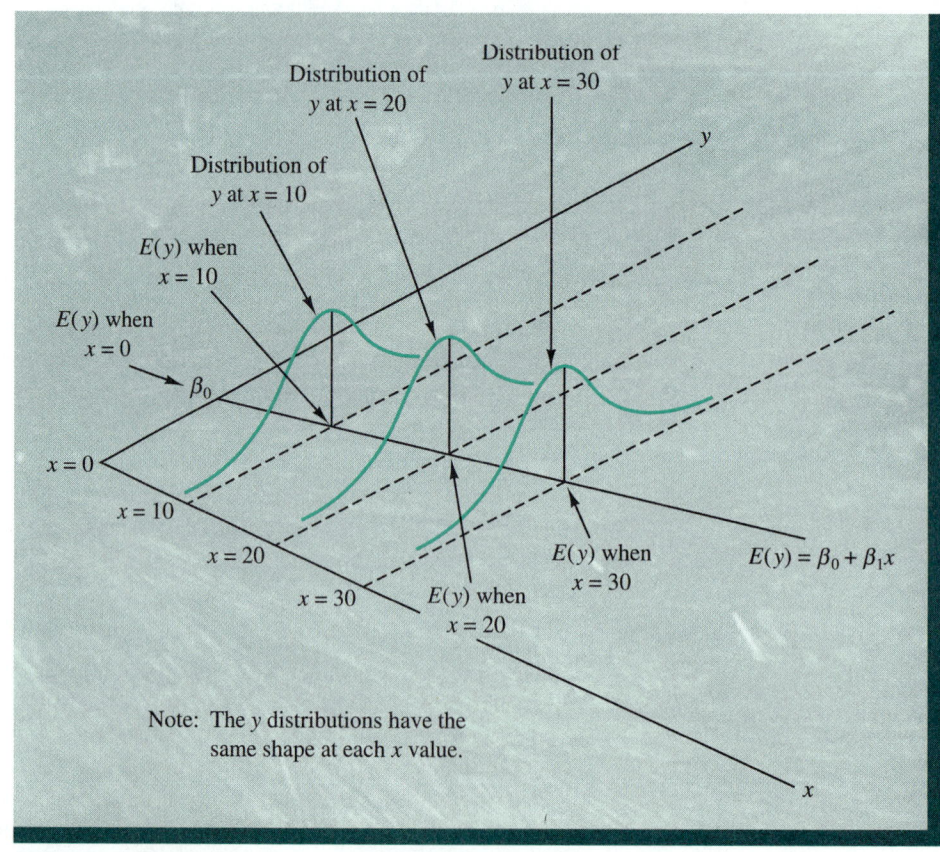

FIGURE 14.6   Assumptions for the Regression Model

Figure 14.6 is an illustration of the model assumptions and their implications; note that in this graphical interpretation, the value of $E(y)$ changes according to the specific value of x considered. However, regardless of the x value, the probability distribution of ϵ and hence the probability distributions of y are normally distributed, each with the same variance. The specific value of the error ϵ at any particular point depends on whether the actual value of y is greater than or less than $E(y)$.

At this point, we must keep in mind that we are also making an assumption or hypothesis about the form of the relationship between x and y. That is, we have assumed that a straight line represented by $\beta_0 + \beta_1 x$ is the basis for the relationship between the variables. We must not lose sight of the fact that some other model, for instance $y = \beta_0 + \beta_1 x^2 + \epsilon$, may turn out to be a better model for the underlying relationship.

14.5 TESTING FOR SIGNIFICANCE

The simple linear regression equation shows that the mean or expected value of y is a linear function of x: $E(y) = \beta_0 + \beta_1 x$. If the value of β_1 is zero, $E(y) = \beta_0 + (0)x = \beta_0$. In this case, the mean value of y does not depend on the value of x and hence we would conclude that x and y are not linearly related. Alternatively, if the value of β_1 is not equal to zero, we would conclude that the two variables are related. Thus, to test for a significant regression relationship, we must conduct a hypothesis test to determine whether the value of β_1 is zero. Two tests are commonly used. Both require an estimate of σ^2, the variance of ϵ in the regression model.

AN ESTIMATE OF σ^2

From the regression model and its assumptions we can conclude that σ^2, the variance of ϵ, also represents the variance of the y values about the regression line. Recall that the deviations of the y values about the estimated regression line are called residuals. Thus, SSE, the sum of squared residuals, is a measure of the variability of the actual observations about the estimated regression line. The mean square error (MSE) provides the estimate of σ^2; it is SSE divided by its degrees of freedom.

With $\hat{y}_i = b_0 + b_1 x_i$, SSE can be written as

$$\text{SSE} = \Sigma(y_i - \hat{y}_i)^2 = \Sigma(y_i - b_0 - b_1 x_i)^2$$

Every sum of squares has associated with it a number called its degrees of freedom. Statisticians have shown that SSE has $n - 2$ degrees of freedom since two parameters (β_0 and β_1) must be estimated to compute SSE. Thus, the mean square is computed by dividing SSE by $n - 2$. MSE provides an unbiased estimator of σ^2. Since the value of MSE provides an estimate of σ^2, the notation s^2 is also used.

MEAN SQUARE ERROR (ESTIMATE OF σ^2)

$$s^2 = \text{MSE} = \frac{\text{SSE}}{n - 2} \tag{14.17}$$

In Section 14.3 we showed that for the Armand's Pizza Parlors example, SSE = 1530; hence,

$$s^2 = \text{MSE} = \frac{1530}{8} = 191.25$$

provides an unbiased estimate of σ^2.

To estimate σ we take the square root of s^2. The resulting value, s, is referred to as the *standard error of the estimate*.

STANDARD ERROR OF THE ESTIMATE

$$s = \sqrt{\text{MSE}} = \sqrt{\frac{\text{SSE}}{n-2}} \qquad (14.18)$$

For the Armand's Pizza Parlors example, $s = \sqrt{\text{MSE}} = \sqrt{191.25} = 13.829$. In the following discussion, we use the standard error of the estimate in the tests for a significant relationship between x and y.

t TEST

The simple linear regression model is $y = \beta_0 + \beta_1 x + \epsilon$. If x and y are linearly related, we must have $\beta_1 \neq 0$. The purpose of the t test is to see whether we can conclude that $\beta_1 \neq 0$. We will use the sample data to test the following hypotheses about the parameter β_1.

$$H_0: \beta_1 = 0$$

$$H_a: \beta_1 \neq 0$$

If H_0 is rejected, we will conclude that $\beta_1 \neq 0$ and that there is a statistically significant relationship between the two variables. However, if H_0 cannot be rejected, we will have insufficient evidence to conclude that a significant relationship exists. As usual, the properties of the sampling distribution of b_1, the least squares estimator of β_1, provide the basis for the hypothesis test.

First, let us consider what would have happened if we had used a different random sample for the same regression study. For example, suppose that Armand's Pizza Parlors had used the sales records of a different sample of 10 restaurants. A regression analysis of this new sample might result in an estimated regression equation similar to our previous estimated regression equation $\hat{y} = 60 + 5x$. However, it is doubtful that we would obtain exactly the same equation (with an intercept of exactly 60 and a slope of exactly 5). Indeed, b_0 and b_1, the least squares estimators, are sample statistics that have their own sampling distributions. The properties of the sampling distribution of b_1 follow.

SAMPLING DISTRIBUTION OF b_1

Expected Value

$$E(b_1) = \beta_1$$

Standard Deviation

$$\sigma_{b_1} = \frac{\sigma}{\sqrt{\Sigma x_i^2 - (\Sigma x_i)^2/n}} \qquad (14.19)$$

Distribution Form

Normal

Note that the expected value of b_1 is equal to β_1, so b_1 is an unbiased estimator of β_1.

Since we do not know the value of σ, we develop an estimate of σ_{b_1}, denoted s_{b_1}, by estimating σ with s in (14.19). Thus, we obtain the following estimate of σ_{b_1}.

ESTIMATED STANDARD DEVIATION OF b_1

$$s_{b_1} = \frac{s}{\sqrt{\Sigma x_i^2 - (\Sigma x_i)^2/n}} \qquad (14.20)$$

For Armand's Pizza Parlors, $s = 13.829$. Hence, using $\Sigma x_i^2 = 2528$ and $\Sigma x_i = 140$ as shown in Table 14.8, we have

$$s_{b_1} = \frac{13.829}{\sqrt{2528 - (140)^2/10}} = .5803$$

as the estimated standard deviation of b_1.

The t test for a significant relationship is based on the fact that the test statistic

$$\frac{b_1 - \beta_1}{s_{b_1}}$$

follows a t distribution with $n - 2$ degrees of freedom. If the null hypothesis is true, then $\beta_1 = 0$ and $t = b_1/s_{b_1}$. With b_1/s_{b_1} as the test statistic, the steps of the t test for a significant relationship are as follows.

t TEST FOR SIGNIFICANCE IN REGRESSION

$$H_0: \beta_1 = 0$$
$$H_a: \beta_1 \neq 0$$

Test Statistic

$$t = \frac{b_1}{s_{b_1}} \qquad (14.21)$$

Rejection Rule

Reject H_0 if $t < -t_{\alpha/2}$ or if $t > t_{\alpha/2}$

where $t_{\alpha/2}$ is based on a t distribution with $n - 2$ degrees of freedom.

Let us conduct this test of significance for Armand's Pizza Parlors. The test statistic (14.21) is

$$t = \frac{b_1}{s_{b_1}} = \frac{5}{.5803} = 8.62$$

From Table 2 of Appendix B we find that the two-tailed t value corresponding to $\alpha = .01$ and $n - 2 = 10 - 2 = 8$ degrees of freedom is $t_{.005} = 3.355$. With $8.62 > 3.355$, we reject H_0 and conclude at the .01 level of significance that β_1 is not equal to zero. The statistical evidence is sufficient to conclude that we have a significant relationship between student population and sales.

F TEST

An *F* test, based on the *F* probability distribution, can also be used to test for significance in regression. With only one independent variable, the *F* test will provide the same conclusion as the *t* test; that is, if the *t* test indicates $\beta_1 \neq 0$ and hence a significant relationship, the *F* test will also indicate a significant relationship. But with more than one independent variable, only the *F* test can be used to test for an overall significant relationship.

The logic behind the use of the *F* test for determining whether the regression relationship is statistically significant is based on the development of two independent estimates of σ^2. We have just seen that MSE provides an estimate of σ^2. If the null hypothesis H_0: $\beta_1 = 0$ is true, the sum of squares due to regression, SSR, divided by its degrees of freedom provides another independent estimate of σ^2. This estimate is called the *mean square due to regression,* or simply the *mean square regression,* and is denoted MSR. In general,

$$MSR = \frac{SSR}{\text{regression degrees of freedom}}$$

For the models we consider in this text, the regression degrees of freedom is always equal to the number of independent variables; thus,

$$MSR = \frac{SSR}{\text{number of independent variables}} \tag{14.22}$$

Since we consider only regression models with one independent variable in this chapter, we have MSR = SSR/1 = SSR. Hence, for Armand's Pizza Parlors, MSR = SSR = 14,200.

If the null hypothesis (H_0: $\beta_1 = 0$) is true, MSR and MSE are two independent estimates of σ^2 and the sampling distribution of MSR/MSE follows an *F* distribution with numerator degrees of freedom equal to one and denominator degrees of freedom equal to $n - 2$. Therefore, when $\beta_1 = 0$, the value of MSR/MSE should be close to one. However, if the null hypothesis is false ($\beta_1 \neq 0$), MSR will overestimate σ^2 and the value of MSR/MSE will be inflated; thus, large values of MSR/MSE lead to the rejection of H_0 and the conclusion that the relationship between *x* and *y* is statistically significant. A summary of how the *F* test is used to test for a significant relationship follows.

F TEST FOR SIGNIFICANCE IN SIMPLE LINEAR REGRESSION

$$H_0: \beta_1 = 0$$
$$H_a: \beta_1 \neq 0$$

Test Statistic

$$F = \frac{MSR}{MSE} \tag{14.23}$$

Rejection Rule

Reject H_0 if $F > F_\alpha$

where F_α is based on an *F* distribution with 1 degree of freedom in the numerator and $n - 2$ degrees of freedom in the denominator.

TABLE 14.11 General Form of the ANOVA Table for Simple Linear Regression

Source of Variation	Sum of Squares	Degrees of Freedom	Mean Square	F
Regression	SSR	1	$MSR = \dfrac{SSR}{1}$	$F = \dfrac{MSR}{MSE}$
Error	SSE	$n - 2$	$MSE = \dfrac{SSE}{n-2}$	
Total	SST	$n - 1$		

TABLE 14.12 ANOVA Table for the Armand's Pizza Parlors Problem

Source of Variation	Sum of Squares	Degrees of Freedom	Mean Square	F
Regression	14,200	1	$\dfrac{14,200}{1} = 14,200$	$\dfrac{14,200}{191.25} = 74.25$
Error	1,530	8	$\dfrac{1530}{8} = 191.25$	
Total	15,730	9		

Let us conduct the F test for the Armand's Pizza Parlors example. The test statistic is

$$F = \frac{MSR}{MSE} = \frac{14,200}{191.25} = 74.25$$

From Table 4 of Appendix B we find that the F value corresponding to $\alpha = .01$ with one degree of freedom in the numerator and $n - 2 = 10 - 2 = 8$ degrees of freedom in the denominator is $F_{.01} = 11.26$. With $74.25 > 11.26$, we reject H_0 and conclude at the .01 level of significance that β_1 is not equal to zero. The F test has provided the statistical evidence necessary to conclude that we have a significant relationship between student population and sales.

In Chapter 13 we covered analysis of variance (ANOVA) and showed how an ANOVA table could be used to provide a convenient summary of the computational aspects of analysis of variance. A similar ANOVA table can be used to summarize the results of the F test for significance in regression. Table 14.11 is the general form of the ANOVA table for the two-variable regression studies we are covering in this chapter. Table 14.12 is the ANOVA table with the F test computations we have just performed for Armand's Pizza Parlors. Regression, error, and total are listed as the three sources of variation, with SSR, SSE, and SST appearing as the corresponding sum of squares in column two. The degrees of freedom, 1 for regression, $n - 2$ for error, and $n - 1$ for total are shown in column three. Column 4 contains the values of MSR and MSE and column 5 contains the value of $F = MSR/MSE$. Almost all computer printouts of regression analysis include an ANOVA table summary of the test for significance.

SOME CAUTIONS ABOUT THE INTERPRETATION OF SIGNIFICANCE TESTS

Rejecting the null hypothesis H_0: $\beta_1 = 0$ and concluding that the relationship between x and y is significant does not enable us to conclude that a *cause-and-effect* relationship is present between x and y. Concluding a cause-and-effect relationship is warranted only if the analyst has some type of theoretical justification that the relationship is in fact causal. In the Armand's Pizza Parlors example, we can conclude that there is a significant relationship between the size of the student population x and sales y; moreover, the estimated regression equation $\hat{y} = 60 + 5x$ provides the least squares estimate of the relationship. We cannot, however, conclude that changes in student population x *cause* changes in sales y just because we have identified a statistically significant relationship. The appropriateness of such a cause-and-effect conclusion is left to supporting theoretical justification and to good judgment on the part of the analyst. Armand's managers felt that increases in the student population were a likely cause of increased sales. Thus, the result of the significance test enabled them to conclude that a cause-and-effect relationship was present.

In addition, just because we are able to reject H_0: $\beta_1 = 0$ and demonstrate statistical significance does not enable us to conclude that the relationship between x and y is linear. We can state only that x and y are related and that a linear relationship explains a significant portion of the variability in y over the range of values for x observed in the sample. Figure 14.7 illustrates this situation. The test for significance has rejected the null hypothesis H_0: $\beta_1 = 0$ and has led to the conclusion that x and y are significantly related, but the figure shows that the actual relationship between x and y is not linear. Although the linear approximation provided by $\hat{y} = b_0 + b_1x$ is very good over the range of x values observed in the sample, it becomes very poor for x values outside that range.

Given a significant relationship, we should feel confident in using the estimated regression equation for predictions corresponding to x values within the range of the x values observed in the sample. For Armand's Pizza Parlors, this range corresponds to values of x between 2 and 26. But unless there are reasons to believe the model is valid beyond this range, predictions outside the range of the independent variable should be made with caution. For Armand's Pizza Parlors, since the regression relationship has been found significant at the .01 level, we should feel confident using it to predict sales for restaurants where the associated student population is between 2000 and 26,000.

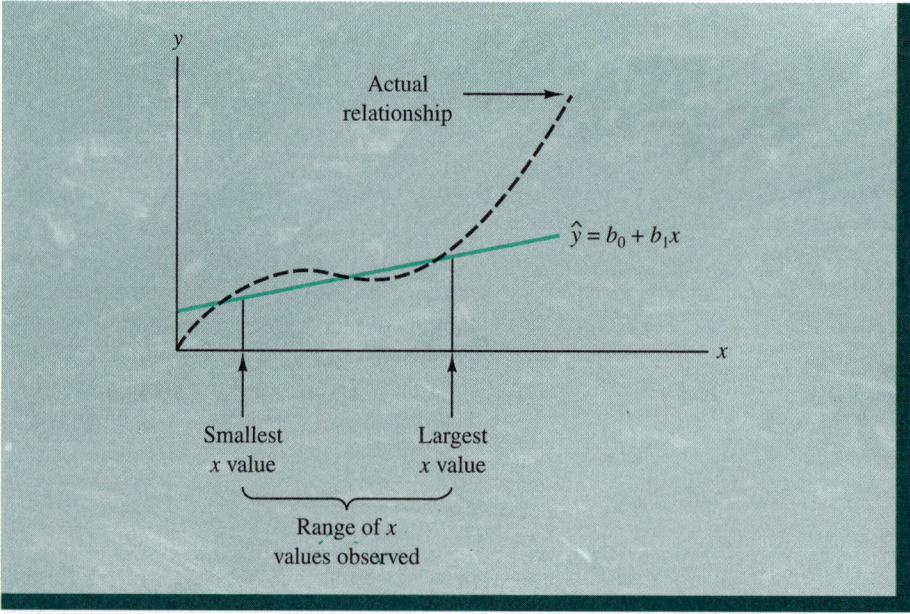

FIGURE 14.7   Example of a Linear Approximation of a Nonlinear Relationship

NOTES AND COMMENTS

1. The assumptions made about the error term (Section 14.4) are what allow the tests of statistical significance in this section. The properties of the sampling distribution of b_1 and the subsequent t and F tests follow directly from these assumptions.

2. Do not confuse statistical significance with practical significance. With very large sample sizes, statistically significant results can be obtained for small values of b_1; in such cases, one must exercise care in concluding that the relationship has practical significance.

3. A test of significance for a linear relationship between x and y can also be performed by using the sample correlation coefficient r_{xy}. With ρ_{xy} denoting the population correlation coefficient, the hypotheses are as follows.

$$H_0: \rho_{xy} = 0$$
$$H_a: \rho_{xy} \neq 0$$

A significant relationship can be concluded if H_0 is rejected. The details of this test are provided in Appendix 14.2. However, the t and F tests presented previously in this section give the *same result* as the test for significance using the correlation coefficient. Conducting a test for significance using the correlation coefficient therefore is not necessary if a t or F test has already been conducted.

EXERCISES

METHODS

Self-Test

23. The data from Exercise 1 follow.

x_i	1	2	3	4	5
y_i	3	7	5	11	14

a. Compute the mean square error using (14.17).
b. Compute the standard error of the estimate using (14.18).
c. Compute the estimated standard deviation of b_1 using (14.20).
d. Use the t test to test the following hypotheses ($\alpha = .05$):

$$H_0: \beta_1 = 0$$
$$H_a: \beta_1 \neq 0$$

e. Use the F test to test the hypotheses in (d) at a .05 level of significance. Present the results in the analysis of variance table format (see Table 14.11).

24. The data from exercise 2 follow.

x_i	2	3	5	1	8
y_i	25	25	20	30	16

a. Compute the mean square error using (14.17).
b. Compute the standard error of the estimate using (14.18).
c. Compute the estimated standard deviation of b_1 using (14.20).
d. Use the t test to test the following hypotheses ($\alpha = .05$):

$$H_0: \beta_1 = 0$$
$$H_a: \beta_1 \neq 0$$

e. Use the F test to test the hypotheses in (d) at a .05 level of significance. Present the results in the analysis of variance table format.

25. The data from Exercise 3 follow.

x_i	2	4	5	7	8
y_i	2	3	2	6	4

a. What is the value of the standard error of the estimate?
b. Test for a significant relationship by using the t test. Use $\alpha = .05$.
c. Use the F test to test for a significant relationship. Use $\alpha = .05$. What is your conclusion?

Self-Test ▸

26. In Exercise 5 the data on grade point average and monthly salary were as shown in Table 14.13.
a. Does the t test indicate a significant relationship between grade point average and monthly salary? What is your conclusion? Use $\alpha = .05$.
b. Test for a significant relationship using the F test. What is your conclusion? Use $\alpha = .05$.
c. Show the ANOVA table.

TABLE 14.13
Exercise 26

GPA	Monthly Salary ($)
2.6	1800
3.4	2100
3.6	2500
3.2	2000
3.5	2400
2.9	2100

27. Refer to Exercise 9, where an estimated regression equation relating years of experience and annual sales was developed. At a .05 level of significance, determine whether years of experience and annual sales are related.

28. Refer to Exercise 10, where an estimated regression equation relating tire rating to load carrying capacity was developed (*Road and Track*, October 1994). At a .01 level of significance, test whether these two variables are related. Show the ANOVA table. What is your conclusion?

29. Refer to Exercise 21, where data on production volume and cost were used to develop an estimated regression equation relating production volume and cost for a particular manufacturing operation. Using $\alpha = .05$, test whether the production volume is significantly related to the total cost. Show the ANOVA table. What is your conclusion?

30. Refer to Exercise 22, where the following data were used to determine whether company presidents and chief executive officers are paid on the basis of company profit performance (*Business Week*, April 25, 1994).

Company	Two-Year Change in Return on Equity (%)	Change in Executive Compensation (%)
Dupont	−64.4	0
Monsanto	29.6	55
Morton International	−9.3	17
Union Carbide	−16.4	58
W. R. Grace	3.4	−11
International Flavors	18.8	24
Great Lakes Chemical	17.0	10

Is there evidence of a significant relationship between the two variables? Conduct the appropriate statistical test and state your conclusion. Use $\alpha = .05$.

31. Refer to exercise 20, where an estimated regression equation was developed relating light absorbence readings and milligrams of protein. Test whether the absorbence readings and the amount of protein are related at the .01 level of significance.

14.6 USING THE ESTIMATED REGRESSION EQUATION FOR ESTIMATION AND PREDICTION

The simple linear regression model is an assumption about the relationship between x and y. Using the least squares method, we obtained the estimated simple linear regression equation. If the results show a statistically significant relationship between x and y, and the fit provided by the estimated regression equation appears to be good, the estimated regression equation should be useful for estimation and prediction.

POINT ESTIMATION

In the Armand's Pizza Parlors example, the estimated regression equation $\hat{y} = 60 + 5x$ provides an estimate of the relationship between the size of the student population x and quarterly sales y. We can use the estimated regression equation to develop a point estimate of the mean value of y for a particular value of x or to predict an individual value of y corresponding to a given value of x. For instance, suppose Armand's managers want a point estimate of the mean sales for all restaurants located near college campuses with 10,000 students. Using the estimated regression equation $\hat{y} = 60 + 5x$, we see that for $x = 10$ (or 10,000 students), $\hat{y} = 60 + 5(10) = 110$. Thus, a point estimate of the mean sales for all restaurants located near campuses with 10,000 students is $110,000.

Now suppose Armand's managers want to predict sales for an individual restaurant located near Talbot College, a school with 10,000 students. In this case we are not interested in the mean value for all restaurants located near campuses with 10,000 students; we are just interested in predicting sales for one individual restaurant. As it turns out, the point estimate is the same as the point estimate for the mean value of y. Hence, we would predict sales of $\hat{y} = 60 + 5(10) = 110$ or $110,000 for this one restaurant.

INTERVAL ESTIMATION

Point estimates do not provide any idea of the precision associated with the estimate. For that we must develop interval estimates much like those in Chapters 8, 10, and 11. The first type of interval estimate, a *confidence interval estimate,* is an interval estimate of the *mean value of y* for a given value of x. The second type of interval estimate, a *prediction interval estimate,* is used whenever we want an interval estimate of an *individual value of y* corresponding to a given value of x. With point estimation we obtain the same value whether we are estimating the mean value of y or predicting an individual value of y, but with interval estimates we obtain different values.

CONFIDENCE INTERVAL ESTIMATE OF THE MEAN VALUE OF y

The estimated regression equation provides a point estimate of the mean value of y for a given value of x. In describing the confidence interval estimation procedure, we will use the following notation.

x_p = the particular or given value of the independent variable x

$E(y_p)$ = the mean or expected value of the dependent variable y corresponding to the given x_p

$\hat{y}_p = b_0 + b_1 x_p$ = the estimate of $E(y_p)$ when $x = x_p$

Using this notation to estimate the mean sales for all Armand's restaurants located near a campus with 10,000 students, we have $x_p = 10$, and $E(y_p)$ denotes the unknown mean value of sales for all restaurants where $x_p = 10$. The estimate of $E(y_p)$ is provided by $\hat{y}_p = 60 + 5(10) = 110$.

In general, we cannot expect $\hat{y}_p$ to equal $E(y_p)$ exactly. If we want to make an inference about how close $\hat{y}_p$ is to the true mean value $E(y_p)$, we will have to consider the variance of the estimates based on the estimated regression equation. Statisticians have developed a formula for estimating the variance of $\hat{y}_p$ given x_p. This estimate, denoted by $s_{\hat{y}_p}^2$, is

$$s_{\hat{y}_p}^2 = s^2 \left[\frac{1}{n} + \frac{(x_p - \bar{x})^2}{\Sigma x_i^2 - (\Sigma x_i)^2/n} \right] \tag{14.24}$$

The estimate of the standard deviation of $\hat{y}_p$ is given by the square root of (14.24).

$$s_{\hat{y}_p} = s \sqrt{\frac{1}{n} + \frac{(x_p - \bar{x})^2}{\Sigma x_i^2 - (\Sigma x_i)^2/n}} \tag{14.25}$$

The computational results for Armand's Pizza Parlors in Section 14.5 provided $s = 13.829$. With $\Sigma x_i^2 = 2528$, $\Sigma x_i = 140$, $\bar{x} = \Sigma x_i/n = 140/10 = 14$, and $x_p = 10$, we can use (14.25) to obtain

$$s_{\hat{y}_p} = 13.829 \sqrt{\frac{1}{10} + \frac{(10 - 14)^2}{2528 - (140)^2/10}}$$

$$= 13.829 \sqrt{.1282} = 4.95$$

The general expression for a confidence interval estimate of $E(y_p)$ at a given x_p follows.

CONFIDENCE INTERVAL ESTIMATE OF $E(y_P)$

$$\hat{y}_p \pm t_{\alpha/2} s_{\hat{y}_p} \tag{14.26}$$

where the confidence coefficient is $1 - \alpha$ and $t_{\alpha/2}$ is based on a t distribution with $n - 2$ degrees of freedom.

Using (14.26) to develop a 95% confidence interval estimate of the mean sales for all Armand's restaurants located near campuses with 10,000 students, we need the value of t for $\alpha/2 = .025$ and $n - 2 = 10 - 2 = 8$ degrees of freedom. Using Table 2 of Appendix B, we have $t_{.025} = 2.306$. Thus, with $\hat{y}_p = 110$ and $s_{\hat{y}_p} = 4.95$, we have

$$110 \pm 2.306(4.95)$$

$$110 \pm 11.415$$

In dollars, the 95% confidence interval for the mean sales of all restaurants near campuses with 10,000 students is $110,000 \pm 11,415$. Therefore, the confidence interval estimate for the mean sales when the student population is 10,000 is $98,585 to $121,415.

Note that the estimated standard deviation of $\hat{y}_p$ given by (14.25) is smallest when $x_p = \bar{x}$ and the quantity $x_p - \bar{x} = 0$. In this case, the estimated standard deviation of $\hat{y}_p$ becomes

$$s_{\hat{y}_p} = s \sqrt{\frac{1}{n} + \frac{(x_p - \bar{x})^2}{\Sigma x_i^2 - (\Sigma x_i)^2/n}} = s \sqrt{\frac{1}{n}}$$

This result implies that we can make the best or most precise estimate of the mean value of y whenever we are using the mean value of the independent variable; that is, whenever $x_p = \bar{x}$. In fact, the further x_p is from $\bar{x}$, the larger $x_p - \bar{x}$ becomes. As a result, confidence intervals for the mean value of y will become wider as x_p deviates more from $\bar{x}$. This pattern is shown graphically in Figure 14.8.

PREDICTION INTERVAL ESTIMATE OF AN INDIVIDUAL VALUE OF y

Suppose that instead of estimating the mean value of sales for all Armand's restaurants located near campuses with 10,000 students, we want to estimate the sales for an individual restaurant located near Talbot College, a school with 10,000 students. As noted previously, the point estimate of an individual value of y given $x = x_p$ is provided by the estimated regression equation with $\hat{y}_p = b_0 + b_1 x_p$. For the restaurant at Talbot College, we have $x_p = 10$ and corresponding estimated sales of $\hat{y}_p = 60 + 5(10) =$

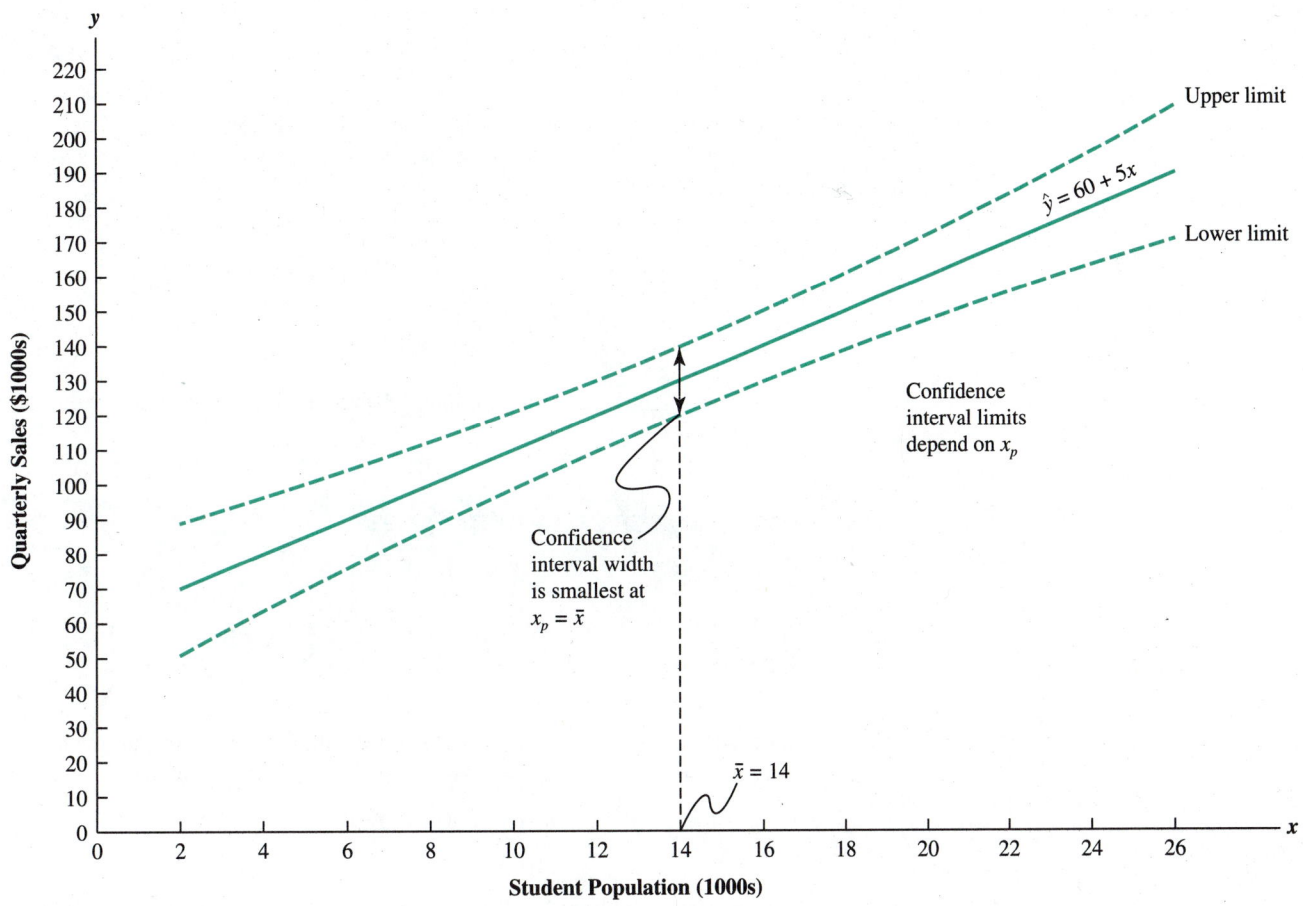

FIGURE 14.8   Confidence Intervals for the Mean Sales y at Given Values of Student Population x

110, or \$110,000. Note that this value is the same as the point estimate of the mean sales for all restaurants located near campuses with 10,000 students.

To develop a prediction interval estimate, we must first determine the variance associated with using $\hat{y}_p$ as an estimate of an individual value of y when $x = x_p$. This variance is made up of the sum of the following two components.

1. The variance of individual y values about the mean $E(y_p)$, an estimate of which is given by s^2.
2. The variance associated with using $\hat{y}_p$ to estimate $E(y_p)$, an estimate of which is given by $s_{\hat{y}_p}^2$.

Statisticians have shown that an estimate of the variance of an individual value of y_p, which we denote s_{ind}^2, is given by

$$
\begin{aligned}
s_{ind}^2 &= s^2 + s_{\hat{y}_p}^2 \\
&= s^2 + s^2\left[\frac{1}{n} + \frac{(x_p - \bar{x})^2}{\Sigma x_i^2 - (\Sigma x_i)^2/n}\right] \\
&= s^2\left[1 + \frac{1}{n} + \frac{(x_p - \bar{x})^2}{\Sigma x_i^2 - (\Sigma x_i)^2/n}\right]
\end{aligned}
\tag{14.27}
$$

Hence, an estimate of the standard deviation of an individual value of y_p is given by

$$
s_{ind} = s\sqrt{1 + \frac{1}{n} + \frac{(x_p - \bar{x})^2}{\Sigma x_i^2 - (\Sigma x_i)^2/n}}
\tag{14.28}
$$

For Armand's Pizza Parlors, the estimated standard deviation corresponding to the prediction of sales for one specific restaurant located near a campus with 10,000 students is computed as follows.

$$
\begin{aligned}
s_{ind} &= 13.829\sqrt{1 + \frac{1}{10} + \frac{(10 - 14)^2}{2528 - (140)^2/10}} \\
&= 13.829\sqrt{1.1282} \\
&= 14.69
\end{aligned}
$$

The general expression for a prediction interval estimate for an individual value of y at a given x_p follows.

> ### PREDICTION INTERVAL ESTIMATE OF y_p
>
> $$\hat{y}_p \pm t_{\alpha/2}s_{ind} \tag{14.29}$$
>
> where the confidence coefficient is $1 - \alpha$ and $t_{\alpha/2}$ is based on a t distribution with $n - 2$ degrees of freedom.

The 95% prediction interval for sales at Armand's Talbot College restaurant can be found by using $t_{.025} = 2.306$ and $s_{ind} = 14.69$. Expression (14.29) provides

$$110 \pm 2.306(14.69)$$

$$110 \pm 33.875$$

In dollars, this prediction interval is \$110,000 ± \$33,875 or \$76,125 to \$143,875. Note that this prediction interval for the individual restaurant is wider than the confidence interval for the mean sales of all restaurants located near campuses with 10,000 students

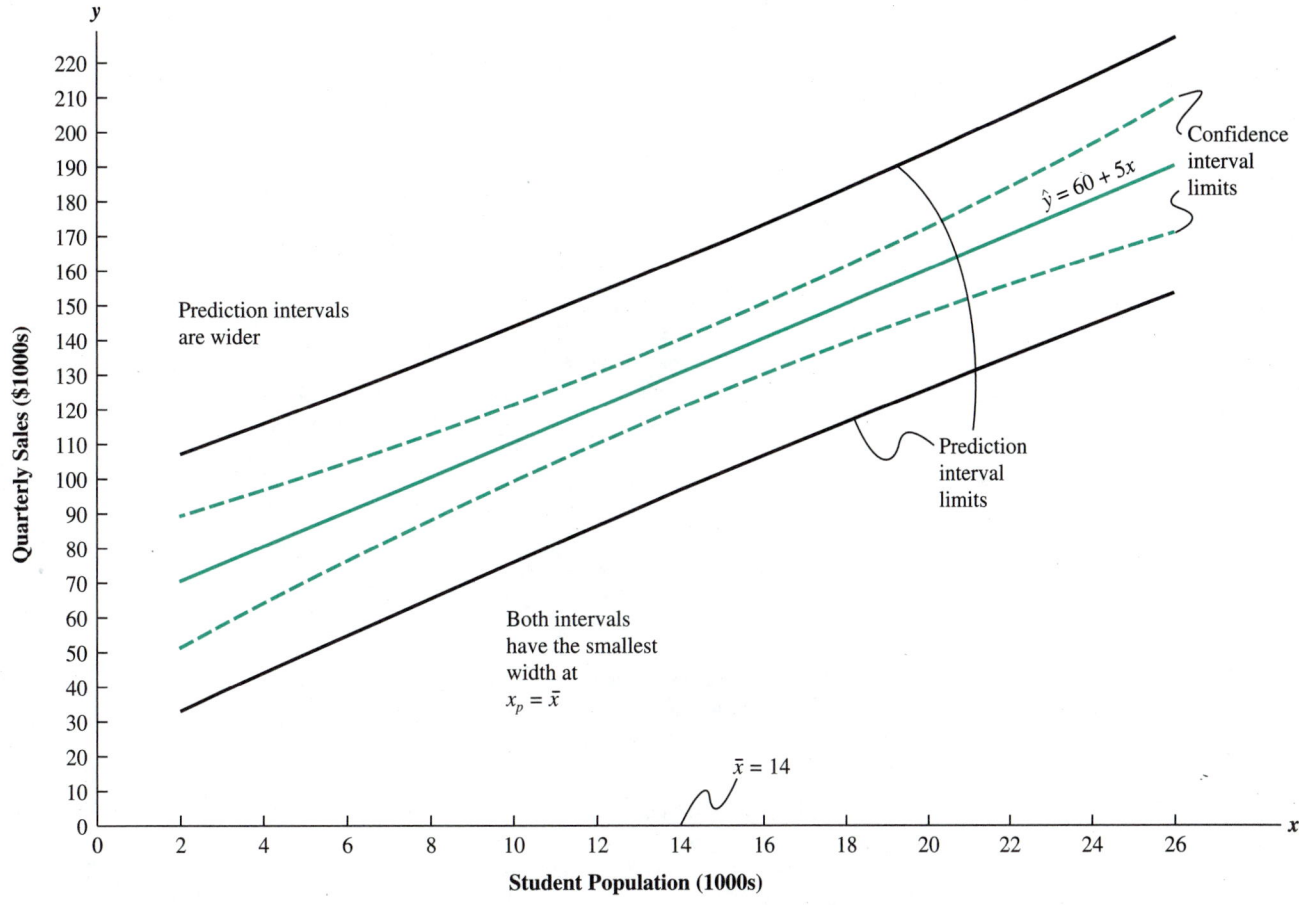

FIGURE 14.9 Confidence and Prediction Intervals for Sales y at Given Values of Student Population x

($98,585 to $121,415). The difference reflects the fact that we are able to estimate the mean value of y more precisely than we can predict any one particular or individual value of y.

Both confidence interval estimates and prediction interval estimates are most precise when the value of the independent variable is $x_p = \bar{x}$. The general shapes of confidence intervals and the wider prediction intervals are shown together in Figure 14.9.

EXERCISES

METHODS

Self-Test ▶ **32.** The data from Exercise 1 follow.

x_i	1	2	3	4	5
y_x	3	7	5	11	14

a. Use (14.25) to estimate the standard deviation of $\hat{y}_p$ when $x = 4$.

b. Use (14.26) to develop a 95% confidence interval estimate of the expected value of y when $x = 4$.

c. Use (14.28) to estimate the standard deviation of an individual value when $x = 4$.

d. Use (14.29) to develop a 95% prediction interval for $x = 4$.

33. The data from Exercise 2 follow.

x_i	2	3	5	1	8
y_i	25	25	20	30	16

a. Estimate the standard deviation of $\hat{y}_p$ when $x = 3$.

b. Develop a 95% confidence interval estimate of the expected value of y when $x = 3$.

c. Estimate the standard deviation of an individual value when $x = 3$.

d. Develop a 95% prediction interval when $x = 3$.

34. The data from Exercise 3 follow.

x_i	2	4	5	7	8
y_i	2	3	2	6	4

Develop the 95% confidence and prediction intervals when $x = 3$. Explain why these two intervals are different.

APPLICATIONS

Self-Test

35. In Exercise 5, the data on grade point average x and monthly salary y provided the estimated regression equation $\hat{y} = 290.54 + 581.08x$.

a. Develop a 95% confidence interval estimate of the mean starting salary for all students with a 3.0 GPA.

b. Develop a 95% prediction interval estimate of the starting salary for Joe Heller, a student with a GPA of 3.0.

36. In Exercise 10, data on tire ratings x and load-carrying capacities y of automobile tires provided the estimated regression equation $\hat{y} = -2196.89 + 39.42x$ (Road & Track, October 1994).

a. Verify that the point estimate of the load-carrying capacity of a tire rated 90 is 1351 pounds.

b. Develop a 95% confidence interval estimate of the mean load-carrying capacity for all tires that have a rating of 90.

c. Develop a 95% prediction interval estimate of the load-carrying capacity for one tire that has a rating of 90.

d. Discuss the differences in your answers to parts (b) and (c).

37. In Exercise 13, the following data on median income x and the median home price y for a sample of six cities were provided (Who's Buying Homes in America, Chicago Title and Trust Company, 1994). Data are in thousands of dollars.

City	Median Income		Median Home Price			
Atlanta	$65.2	55.92	$120.2	105.6	14.6	213.12
Cleveland	49.8		92.7	105.6	-12.9	166.41
Denver	53.8		111.7	105.6	6.1	37.22
Dallas	62.7		104.7	105.6	-.9	.81
Orlando	50.9		98.5	105.6	-7.1	50.41
Minneapolis	53.1		105.8	105.6	.2	.04

21.64

a. The estimated regression equation for these data is $\hat{y} = 43.4 + 1.11x$. Phoenix has a median income of $51,100 or $51.1 thousand dollars. What is the estimate of the median home price in Phoenix?

b. Develop an interval estimate of the median home price in Phoenix. Use $\alpha = .05$. Is this a confidence interval estimate or a prediction interval estimate? Explain.

c. According to *Who's Buying Homes in America* (Chicago Title and Trust Company, 1994), the median home price in Phoenix was $105,700. What was the error involved in using the estimated regression equation to predict the median home price in Phoenix?

38. In Exercise 14, data were given on the adjusted gross income x and the amount of itemized deductions taken by taxpayers (*Money,* October 1994). Data were reported in thousands of dollars. With the estimated regression equation $\hat{y} = 4.68 + .16x$, the point estimate of a reasonable level of total itemized deductions for a taxpayer with an adjusted gross income of $52,500 is $13,080.

a. Develop a 95% confidence interval estimate of the mean amount of total itemized deductions for all taxpayers with an adjusted gross income of $52,500.

b. Develop a 95% prediction interval estimate for the amount of total itemized deductions for a particular taxpayer with an adjusted gross income of $52,500.

c. If the particular taxpayer referred to in part (b) has claimed total itemized deductions of $20,400, would the IRS agent's request for an audit appear to be justified?

d. Using your answer to part (b), give the IRS agent a guideline as to the amount of total itemized deductions a taxpayer with an adjusted gross income of $52,500 should have before an audit is recommended.

39. Refer to exercise 21, where data on the production volume x and total cost y for a particular manufacturing operation were used to develop the estimated regression equation $\hat{y} = 1246.67 + 7.6x$.

a. The company's production schedule shows that 500 units must be produced next month. What is the point estimate of the total cost for next month?

b. Develop a 99% prediction interval estimate of the total cost for next month.

c. If an accounting cost report at the end of next month shows that the actual production cost during the month was $6000, should managers be concerned about incurring such a high total cost for the month? Discuss.

14.7   COMPUTER SOLUTION

Performing the regression analysis computations without the help of a computer can be quite time consuming. In this section we discuss how the computational burden can be minimized by using a computer software package such as Minitab.

We entered Armand's student population data into a Minitab worksheet. The independent variable was named POP and the dependent variable was named SALES to assist with interpretation of the computer output. Using Minitab, we obtained the printout for Armand's Pizza Parlors shown in Figure 14.10.* The interpretation of this printout follows.

1. Minitab prints the estimated regression equation as SALES = 60.0 + 5.00 POP.

2. A table is printed that shows the values of the coefficients b_0 and b_1, the standard deviation of each coefficient, the t value obtained by dividing each coefficient value by its standard deviation, and the p-value associated with the t test. Thus, to test H_0: $\beta_1 = 0$ versus H_a: $\beta_1 \neq 0$, we could compare 8.62 (located in the t-ratio column) to the appropriate critical value. This is the procedure described for the t test in Section 14.5. Alternatively, we could use the p-value provided by Minitab

---

* The Minitab steps necessary to generate the output are given in Appendix 14.3.

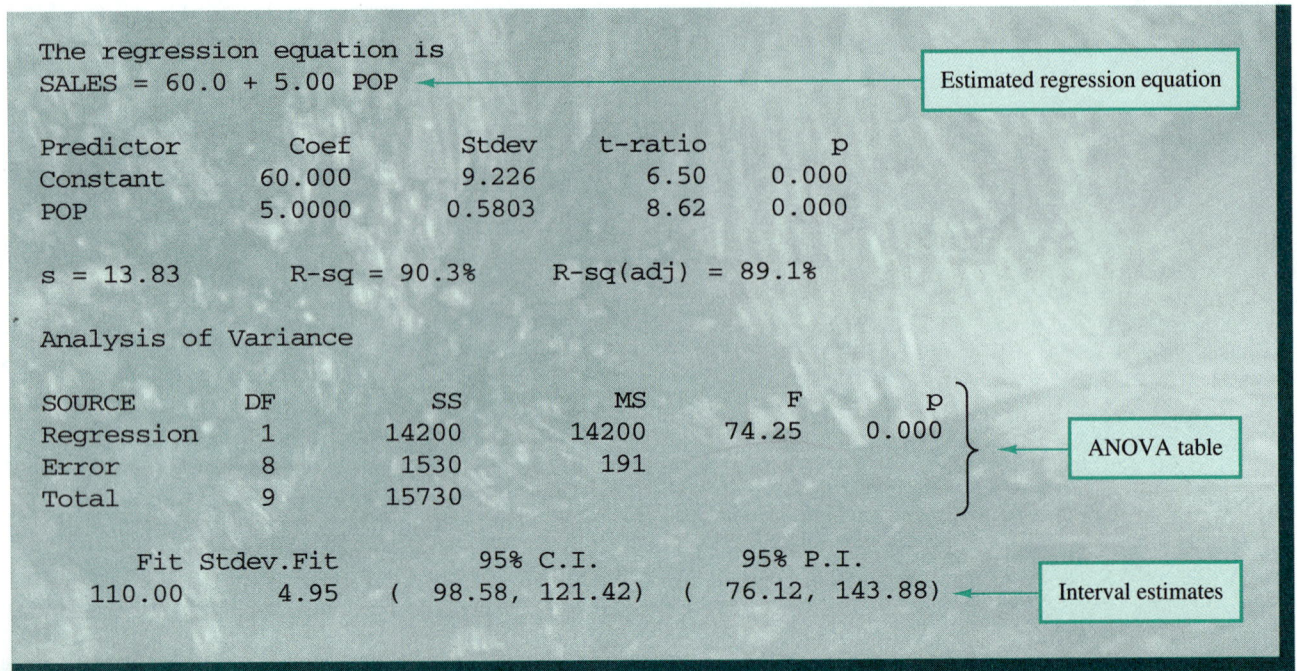

The regression equation is
SALES = 60.0 + 5.00 POP ← Estimated regression equation

Predictor	Coef	Stdev	t-ratio	p
Constant	60.000	9.226	6.50	0.000
POP	5.0000	0.5803	8.62	0.000

s = 13.83   R-sq = 90.3%   R-sq(adj) = 89.1%

Analysis of Variance

SOURCE	DF	SS	MS	F	p
Regression	1	14200	14200	74.25	0.000
Error	8	1530	191		
Total	9	15730			

← ANOVA table

Fit	Stdev.Fit	95% C.I.	95% P.I.
110.00	4.95	(98.58, 121.42)	(76.12, 143.88)

← Interval estimates

FIGURE 14.10   Minitab Output for the Armand's Pizza Parlors Problem

to perform the same test. Recall from Chapter 9 that the *p*-value is the probability of obtaining a sample result more unlikely than what is observed. Since the *p*-value in this case is zero (to three decimal places), the sample results indicate that the null hypothesis (H_0: $\beta_1 = 0$) should be rejected.

3. Minitab prints the standard error of the estimate, $s = 13.83$, as well as information about the goodness of fit. Note that "R-sq = 90.3%" is the coefficient of determination expressed as a percentage. The output "R-Sq (adj) = 89.1%" is discussed in Chapter 15.

4. The ANOVA table is printed below the heading Analysis of Variance. Note that DF is an abbreviation for degrees of freedom and that MSR is given as 14,200 and MSE as 191. The ratio of these two values provides the *F* value of 74.25; in Section 14.5 we showed how the *F* value can be used to determine whether there is a significant relationship between SALES and POP. Minitab also prints the *p*-value associated with this *F* test. Since the *p*-value is zero (to three decimal places), the relationship is judged statistically significant.

5. The 95% confidence interval estimate of the expected sales and the 95% prediction interval estimate of sales for an individual restaurant located near a campus with 10,000 students are printed below the ANOVA table. The confidence interval is (98.58, 121.42) and the prediction interval is (76.12, 143.88) as we showed in Section 14.6.

EXERCISES

APPLICATIONS

Self-Test ▶ **40.** The commercial division of a real estate firm is conducting a regression analysis of the relationship between *x*, annual gross rents ($1000s), and *y*, selling price ($1000s) for apartment buildings. Data have been collected on several properties recently sold, and the following output has been obtained in a computer run.

```
The regression equation is
Y = 20.0 + 7.21 X

Predictor        Coef      Stdev     t-ratio
Constant       20.000     3.2213       6.21
X               7.210     1.3626       5.29

Analysis of Variance

SOURCE           DF          SS
Regression        1      41587.3
Error             7
Total             8      51984.1
```

a. How many apartment buildings were in the sample?
b. Write the estimated regression equation.
c. What is the value of s_{b_1}?
d. Use the F statistic to test the significance of the relationship at a .05 level of significance.
e. Estimate the selling price of an apartment building with gross annual rents of $50,000.

41. Following is a portion of the computer output for a regression analysis relating y = maintenance expense (dollars per month) to x = usage (hours per week) of a particular brand of computer terminal.

```
The regression equation is

Y = 6.1092 + .8951 X

Predictor        Coef      Stdev
Constant       6.1092     0.9361
X              0.8951     0.1490

Analysis of Variance

SOURCE           DF          SS          MS

Regression        1      1575.76     1575.76
Error             8       349.14       43.64
Total             9      1924.90
```

a. Write the estimated regression equation.
b. Use a t test to determine whether monthly maintenance expense is related to usage at the .05 level of significance.
c. Use the estimated regression equation to predict monthly maintenance expense for any terminal that is used 25 hours per week.

42. A regression model relating x, number of salespersons at a branch office, to y, annual sales at the office ($1000s), has been developed. The computer output from a regression analysis of the data follows.

TABLE 14.14 Exercise 43

Population	Value ($1000s)
1410	61
1523	92
1354	93
822	45
746	50
1281	29
1016	56
1070	45
1694	183
1910	156
1745	120
1353	75
1016	122

```
The regression equation is
Y = 80.0 + 50.00 X

Predictor        Coef       Stdev     t-ratio
Constant         80.0       11.333      7.06
X                50.0        5.482      9.12


Analysis of Variance

SOURCE          DF           SS            MS
Regression       1        6828.6        6828.6
Error           28        2298.8          82.1
Total           29        9127.4
```

a. Write the estimated regression equation.
b. How many branch offices were involved in the study?
c. Compute the F statistic and test the significance of the relationship at a .05 level of significance.
d. Predict the annual sales at the Memphis branch office. This branch has 12 salespersons.

PRESCRIP

43. The data in Table 14.14 show the dollar value of prescriptions for 13 pharmacies in Iowa and the population of the city served by the given pharmacy ("The Use of Categorical Variables in Data Envelopment Analysis," R. Banker and R. Morey, *Management Science,* December 1986).
   a. Use a computer package to develop a scatter diagram for these data; plot population on the horizontal axis.
   b. Does there appear to be any relationship between these two variables?
   c. Use the computer package to develop the estimated regression line that could be used to predict the dollar value of prescriptions given the population of the city.
   d. Test for the significance of the relationship at a .05 level of significance.
   e. Predict the dollar value for a particular city with a population of 1500 people. Use $\alpha = .05$.

HOME1

44. The National Association of Home Builders compared the median home prices with the median household incomes in cities throughout the United States (*USA Today,* September 10, 1991). Twenty-three of the most affordable cities are listed in the following table. Both home prices and household incomes are shown in thousands of dollars.

City	Median Income	Median Home Price	City	Median Income	Median Home Price
Amarillo, Texas	$36.7	$69.0	Lorain, Ohio	$38.8	$72.5
Brazoria, Texas	42.4	80.0	Mansfield, Ohio	35.6	58.5
Canton, Ohio	34.1	66.0	Milwaukee, Wisconsin	41.8	72.0
Davenport, Iowa	38.4	59.0	Oklahoma City, Oklahoma	34.5	63.0
Daytona Beach, Florida	31.0	63.0	Omaha, Nebraska	38.8	65.0
Detroit, Michigan	44.6	77.0	Rockford, Illinois	41.6	73.5
Fort Walton Beach, Florida	34.2	65.0	Saginaw, Michigan	39.7	61.0
Grand Rapids, Michigan	40.3	73.0	Shreveport, Louisiana	34.4	66.0
Jackson, Michigan	36.8	60.0	Toledo, Ohio	39.4	65.0
Kansas City, Missouri	41.1	77.0	Tulsa, Oklahoma	36.2	68.0
Lansing, Michigan	40.0	70.0	Winter Haven, Florida	30.2	56.0
			Youngstown, Ohio	34.9	59.0

a. Use a computer package to develop a scatter diagram for these data; plot median income on the horizontal axis.

b. Does there appear to be any relationship between these two variables?

c. Use the computer package to develop the estimated regression equation that could be used to predict the median home price given the median income.

d. Test the significance of the relationship at the .05 level of significance.

e. Did the estimated regression equation provide a good fit? Explain.

f. Predict the expected median home price for cities with a median income of $35,000.

g. Predict the median home price for Elmira, New York, a city with a median income of $35,000.

14.8   RESIDUAL ANALYSIS: VALIDATING MODEL ASSUMPTIONS

As we have previously noted, the *residual* for observation i is the difference between the observed value of the dependent variable (y_i) and the estimated value of the dependent variable ($\hat{y}_i$).

> **RESIDUAL FOR OBSERVATION i**
>
> $$y_i - \hat{y}_i \tag{14.30}$$
>
> where
>
> y_i is the observed value of the dependent variable
>
> $\hat{y}_i$ is the estimated value of the dependent variable

In other words, the ith residual is the error resulting from using the estimated regression equation to predict the value of y_i. The residuals for the Armand's Pizza Parlors example are computed in Table 14.15. The observed values of the dependent variable are in the second column and the estimated values of the dependent variable, obtained using the estimated regression equation $\hat{y} = 60 + 5x$, are in the third column. The corresponding residuals are in the fourth column. An analysis of these residuals will help determine whether the assumptions that have been made about the regression model are appropriate.

Let us now review the regression assumptions for the Armand's Pizza Parlors example. A simple linear regression model was assumed.

$$y = \beta_0 + \beta_1 x + \epsilon \tag{14.31}$$

This model indicates that we assumed sales (y) to be a linear function of the size of the student population (x) plus an error term ϵ. In Section 14.4 we made the following assumptions about the error term ϵ.

1. $E(\epsilon) = 0$.

2. The variance of ϵ, denoted by σ^2, is the same for all values of x.

3. The values of ϵ are independent.

4. The error term ϵ has a normal probability distribution.

These assumptions provide the theoretical basis for the t test and the F test used to determine whether the relationship between x and y is significant, and for the confidence and prediction interval estimates presented in Section 14.6. If the assumptions about the

TABLE 14.15   Residuals for Armand's Pizza Parlors

Student Population x_i	Sales y_i	Estimated Sales $\hat{y}_i = 60 + 5x_i$	Residuals $y_i - \hat{y}_i$
2	58	70	−12
6	105	90	15
8	88	100	−12
8	118	100	18
12	117	120	−3
16	137	140	−3
20	157	160	−3
20	169	160	9
22	149	170	−21
26	202	190	12

error term ϵ appear questionable, the hypothesis tests about significance of the regression relationship and the interval estimation results may not be valid.

The residuals provide the best information about ϵ; hence an analysis of the residuals is an important step in determining whether the assumptions for ϵ are appropriate. Much of residual analysis is based on an examination of graphical plots. In this section, we discuss the following residual plots.

1. A plot of the residuals against values of the independent variable x.
2. A plot of residuals against the predicted values of the dependent variable $\hat{y}$.
3. A standardized residual plot.
4. A normal probability plot.

RESIDUAL PLOT AGAINST x

A residual plot against the independent variable x is a graph in which the values of the independent variable are represented by the horizontal axis and the corresponding residual values are represented by the vertical axis. A point is plotted for each residual. The first coordinate for each point is given by the value of x_i and the second coordinate is given by the corresponding value of the residual $y_i - \hat{y}_i$. For a residual plot against x with the Armand's Pizza Parlors data from Table 14.15, the coordinates of the first point are (2, −12), corresponding to $x_1 = 2$ and $y_1 - \hat{y}_1 = -12$; the coordinates of the second point are (6, 15), corresponding to $x_2 = 6$ and $y_2 - \hat{y}_2 = 15$, and so on. Figure 14.11 is the resulting residual plot.

Before interpreting the results for this residual plot, let us consider some general patterns that might be observed in any residual plot. Three examples are shown in Figure 14.12. If the assumption that the variance of ϵ is the same for all values of x and the assumed regression model is an adequate representation of the relationship between the variables, the residual plot should give an overall impression of a horizontal band of points such as the one in panel A of Figure 14.12. However, if the variance of ϵ is not the same for all values of x—for example, if variability about the regression line is greater for larger values of x—a pattern such as the one in panel B of Figure 14.12 could be observed. In this case, the assumption of a constant variance of ϵ is violated. Another possible residual plot is shown in panel C. In this case, we would conclude that the model is not an adequate representation of the relationship between the variables. A curvilinear regression model or multiple regression model should be considered.

Now let us return to the residual plot for Armand's Pizza Parlors shown in Figure 14.11. The residuals appear to approximate the horizontal pattern in panel A of Figure

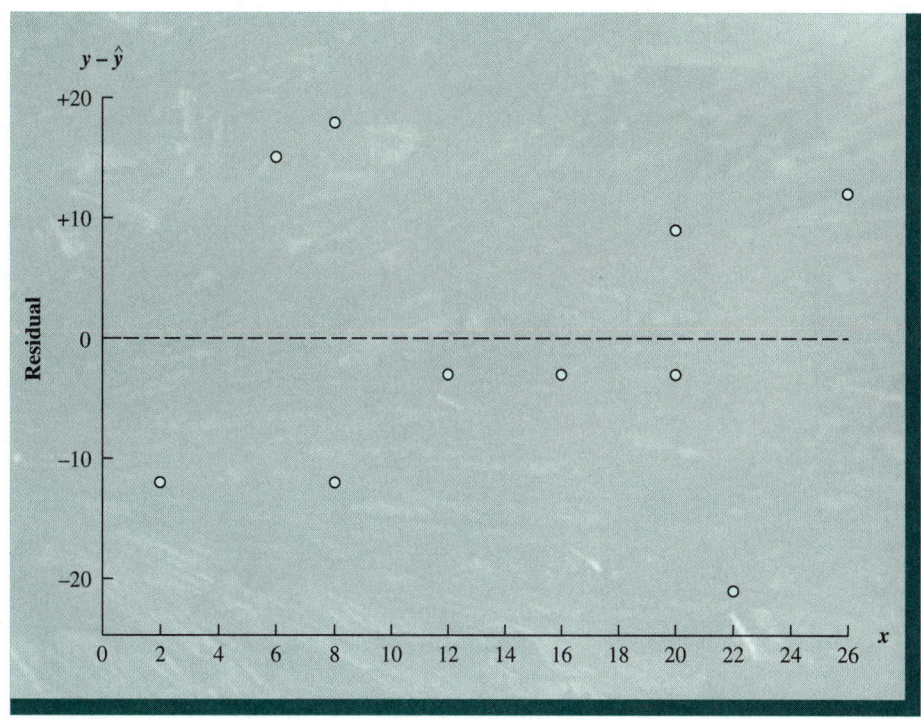

FIGURE 14.11   Plot of the Residuals Against the Independent Variable x for Armand's Pizza Parlors

14.12. Hence, we conclude that the residual plot does not provide evidence that the assumptions made for Armand's regression model should be challenged. At this point, we are confident in the conclusion that Armand's simple linear regression model is valid.

Experience and good judgment are always factors in the effective interpretation of residual plots. Seldom does a residual plot conform precisely to one of the patterns shown in Figure 14.12. Yet analysts who frequently conduct regression studies and frequently review residual plots become very good at understanding the differences between patterns that are reasonable and patterns that indicate the assumptions of the model should be questioned. A residual plot as shown here is one of the techniques that is used to assess the validity of the assumptions for a regression model.

RESIDUAL PLOT AGAINST $\hat{y}$

Another residual plot represents the predicted value of the dependent variable $\hat{y}$ on the horizontal axis and the residual values on the vertical axis. A point is plotted for each residual. The first coordinate for each point is given by $\hat{y}_i$ and the second coordinate is given by the corresponding value of the ith residual $y_i - \hat{y}_i$. With the Armand's data from Table 14.15, the coordinates of the first point are (70, −12), corresponding to $\hat{y}_1 = 70$ and $y_1 - \hat{y}_1 = -12$; the coordinates of the second point are (90, 15), and so on. Figure 14.13 is the residual plot. Note that the pattern of this residual plot is the same as the pattern of the residual plot against the independent variable x. It is not a pattern that would lead us to question the model assumptions. For simple linear regression, both the residual plot against x and the residual plot against $\hat{y}$ provide the same information. For multiple regression analysis, the residual plot against $\hat{y}$ is more widely used because of the presence of more than one independent variable.

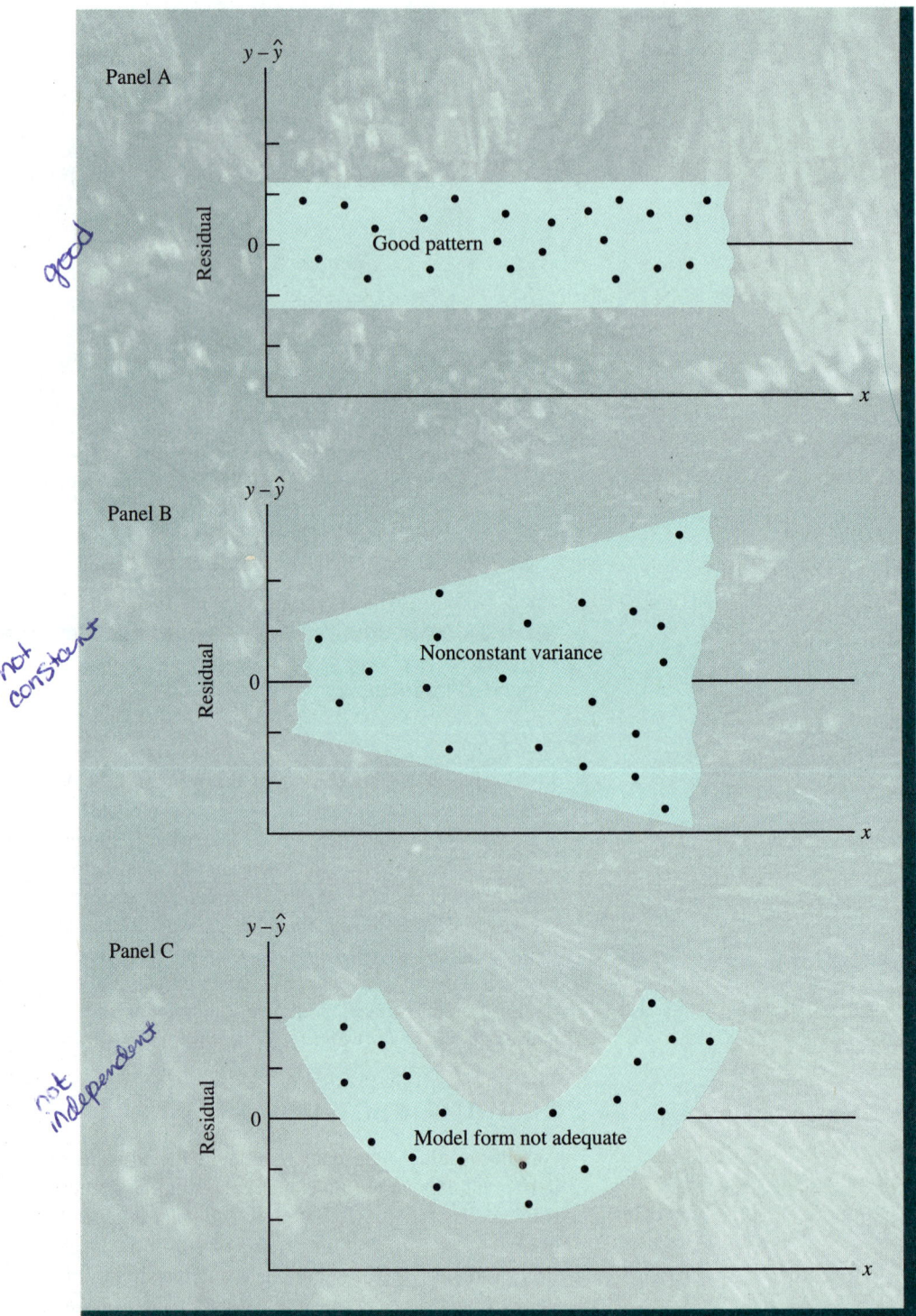

FIGURE 14.12 Residual Plots from Three Regression Studies

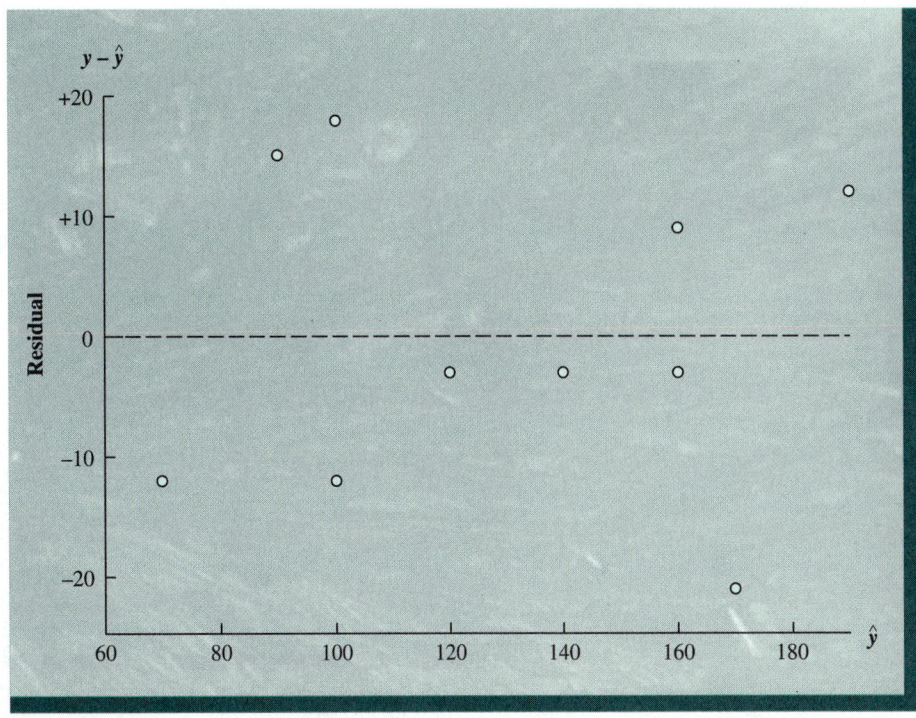

FIGURE 14.13 Plot of Residuals Against the Predicted Values $\hat{y}$ for Armand's Pizza Parlors

STANDARDIZED RESIDUALS

Many of the residual plots provided by computer software packages use a standardized version of the residuals. As we have seen in preceding chapters, a random variable is standardized by subtracting its mean and dividing the result by its standard deviation. With the least squares method, the mean of the residuals is zero. Thus, simply dividing each residual by its standard deviation provides the standardized residual.

It can be shown that the standard deviation of residual i depends on the standard error of the estimate s and the corresponding value of the independent variable x_i.

STANDARD DEVIATION OF THE *ith* RESIDUAL*

$$s_{y_i - \hat{y}_i} = s \sqrt{1 - h_i} \qquad (14.32)$$

where

$$s_{y_i - \hat{y}_i} = \text{the standard deviation of residual } i$$

$$s = \text{the standard error of the estimate}$$

$$h_i = \frac{1}{n} + \frac{(x_i - \bar{x})^2}{\Sigma(x_i - \bar{x})^2} \qquad (14.33)$$

---

*This is actually an estimate of the standard deviation of the *i*th residual, since s is used instead of σ. The value of σ is never known when working with real data and is always estimated by s.

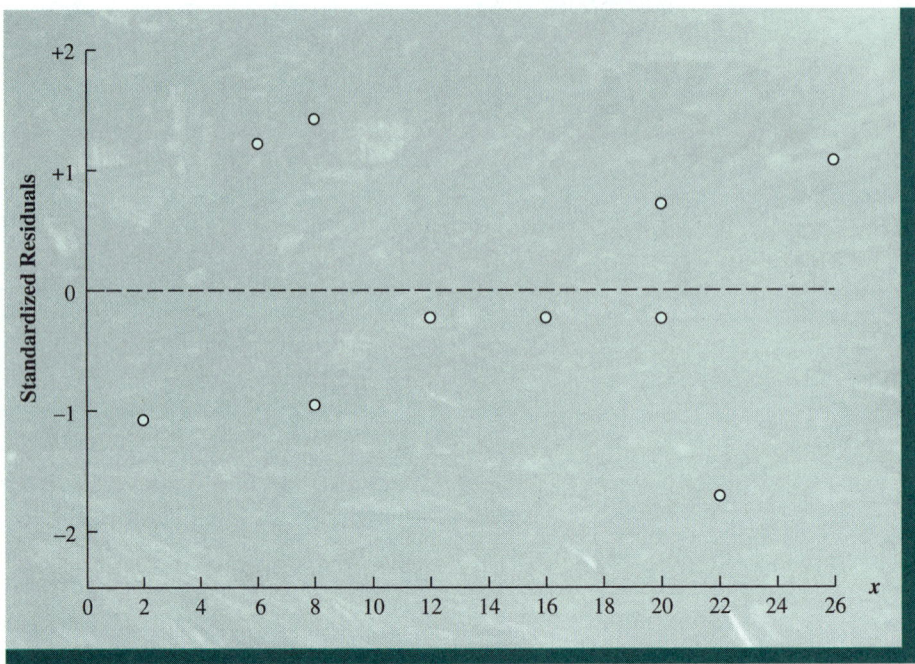

FIGURE 14.14 Plot of the Standardized Residuals Against the Independent Variable x for Armand's Pizza Parlors

Note that (14.32) shows that the ith residual standard deviation depends on x_i because of the presence of h_i in the formula.[†] Once the standard deviation of each residual has been calculated, we can compute the standardized residual by dividing each residual by its corresponding standard deviation.

STANDARDIZED RESIDUAL FOR OBSERVATION i

$$\frac{y_i - \hat{y}_i}{s_{y_i - \hat{y}_i}}$$

(14.34)

Table 14.18 shows the calculation of the standardized residuals for Armand's Pizza Parlors. Recall that previous calculations showed $s = 13.829$. Figure 14.14 is the plot of the standardized residuals against the independent variable x.

The standardized residual plot can provide insight about the assumption that the error term ϵ has a normal distribution. If this assumption is satisfied, the distribution of the standardized residuals should appear to come from a standard normal probability distribution.[*] Thus, when looking at a standardized residual plot, we should expect to see approximately 95% of the standardized residuals between −2 and +2. We see in

---

[†]h_i is referred to as the *leverage* of observation i. Leverage will be discussed further when we consider influential observations in Section 14.9.

[*]Since s is used instead of σ in (14.33), the probability distribution of the standardized residuals is not technically normal. However, in most regression studies, the sample size is large enough that a normal approximation is very good.

TABLE 14.16 Computation of Standardized Residuals for Armand's Pizza Parlors

Restaurant i	x_i	$x_i - \bar{x}$	$(x_i - \bar{x})^2$	$\dfrac{(x_i - \bar{x})^2}{\Sigma(x_i - \bar{x})^2}$	h_i	$s_{y_i - \hat{y}_i}$	$y_i - \hat{y}_i$	Standardized Residual
1	2	−12	144	.2535	.3535	11.1193	−12	−1.0792
2	6	−8	64	.1127	.2127	12.2709	15	1.2224
3	8	−6	36	.0634	.1634	12.6493	−12	−.9487
4	8	−6	36	.0634	.1634	12.6493	18	1.4230
5	12	−2	4	.0070	.1070	13.0682	−3	−.2296
6	16	2	4	.0070	.1070	13.0682	−3	−.2296
7	20	6	36	.0634	.1634	12.6493	−3	−.2372
8	20	6	36	.0634	.1634	12.6493	9	.7115
9	22	8	64	.1127	.2127	12.2709	−21	−1.7114
10	26	12	144	.2535	.3535	11.1193	12	1.0792
		Total	568					

Note: The values of the residuals were computed in Table 14.15.

TABLE 14.17 Normal Scores for $n = 10$

Order Statistic	Normal Score
1	−1.55
2	−1.00
3	−.65
4	−.37
5	−.12
6	.12
7	.37
8	.65
9	1.00
10	1.55

TABLE 14.18 Normal Scores and Ordered Standardized Residuals for Armand's Pizza Parlors

Normal Scores	Ordered Standardized Residuals
−1.55	−1.7114
−1.00	−1.0792
−.65	−.9487
−.37	−.2372
−.12	−.2296
.12	−.2296
.37	.7115
.65	1.0792
1.00	1.2224
1.55	1.4230

Figure 14.14 that for the Armand's example all standardized residuals are between −2 and +2. Therefore, on the basis of the standardized residuals, we have no reason to question the assumption that ϵ has a normal distribution.

Because of the effort required to compute the estimated values of $\hat{y}$, the residuals, and the standardized residuals, most statistical packages provide those values as optional regression output. Hence, residual plots can be easily obtained. For large problems computer packages are the only practical means for developing the residual plots we have discussed in this section.

NORMAL PROBABILITY PLOT

Another approach for determining the validity of the assumption that the error term has a normal distribution is the normal probability plot. To show how a normal probability plot is developed, we introduce the concept of *normal scores*.

Suppose 10 values are selected randomly from a normal probability distribution with a mean of zero and a standard deviation of one, and that the sampling process is repeated over and over with the values in each sample of 10 ordered from smallest to largest. For now, let us consider only the smallest value in each sample. The random variable representing the smallest value obtained in repeated sampling is called the first-order statistic.

Statisticians have shown that for samples of size 10 from a standard normal probability distribution, the expected value of the first-order statistic is −1.55. This expected value is called a normal score. For the case with a sample of size $n = 10$, there are 10 order statistics and 10 normal scores (see Table 14.17). In general, if we have a data set consisting of n observations, there are n order statistics and hence n normal scores.

Let us now show how the 10 normal scores can be used to determine whether or not the standardized residuals for Armand's Pizza Parlors appear to come from a standard normal probability distribution. We begin by ordering the 10 standardized residuals from Table 14.16. The 10 normal scores and the ordered standardized residuals are shown together in Table 14.18. If the normality assumption is satisfied, the smallest standardized residual should be close to the smallest normal score, the next smallest standardized residual should be close to the next smallest normal score, and so on. If we were to develop a plot with the normal scores on the horizontal axis and the corresponding standardized residuals on the vertical axis, the plotted points should cluster closely around a 45-degree line passing through the origin if the standardized residuals are approximately normally distributed. Such a plot is referred to as a *normal probability plot*.

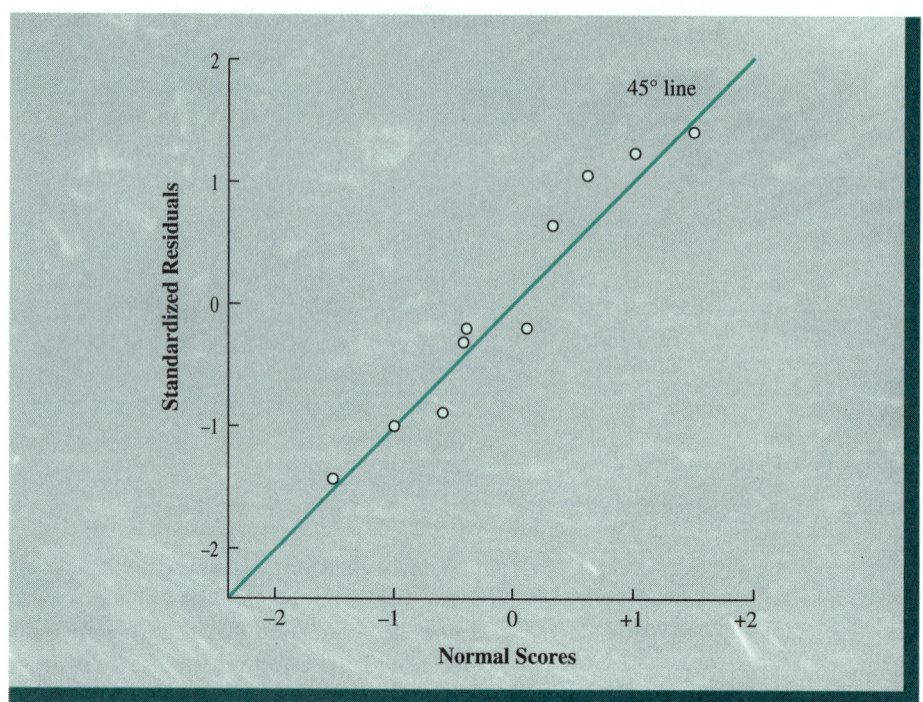

FIGURE 14.15   Normal Probability Plot for Armand's Pizza Parlors

Figure 14.15 is the normal probability plot for the Armand's Pizza Parlors example. Judgment is used to determine whether the pattern observed deviates from the line enough to conclude that the standardized residuals are not from a standard normal probability distribution. In Figure 14.15, we see that the points are grouped closely about the line. We therefore conclude that the assumption of the error term having a normal probability distribution is reasonable. In general, the more closely the points are clustered about the 45-degree line, the stronger the evidence supporting the normality assumption. Any substantial curvature in the normal probability plot is evidence that the residuals have not come from a normal distribution. Normal scores and the associated normal probability plot are routinely constructed by statistical packages such as Minitab.

NOTES AND COMMENTS

1. We use residual and normal probability plots to validate the assumptions of a regression model. If our review indicates that one or more assumptions are questionable, a different regression model and/or a transformation of the data should be considered. The appropriate corrective action when the assumptions are violated must be based on good judgment; recommendations from an experienced statistician can be valuable.

2. Analysis of residuals is the primary method statisticians use to verify that the assumptions associated with a regression model are valid. Even if no violations are found, it does not necessarily follow that the model will yield good predictions. However, if in addition statistical tests support the conclusion of significance and the coefficient of determination is large, we should be able to develop good estimates and predictions by using the estimated regression equation.

EXERCISES

METHODS

Self-Test

45. Given are data for two variables, x and y.

x_i	6	11	15	18	20
y_i	6	8	12	20	30

a. Develop an estimated regression equation for these data.
b. Compute the residuals.
c. Develop a plot of the residuals against the independent variable x. Do the assumptions about the error terms seem to be satisfied?
d. Compute the standardized residuals.
e. Develop a plot of the standardized residuals against $\hat{y}$. What conclusions can you draw from this plot?

TABLE 14.19 Exercise 46

Observation	x_i	y_i
1	2	4
2	3	5
3	4	4
4	5	6
5	7	4
6	7	6
7	7	9
8	8	5
9	9	11

46. The data in Table 14.19 were used in a regression study.
a. Develop an estimated regression equation for these data.
b. Construct a plot of the residuals. Do the assumptions about the error terms seem to be satisfied?

APPLICATIONS

Self-Test

47. Data on advertising expenditures ($) and revenue (in thousands of dollars) for the Four Seasons Restaurant follow.

Advertising Expenditures	Revenue
1	19
2	32
4	44
6	40
10	52
14	53
20	54

a. Let x equal advertising expenditures ($1000s) and y equal sales ($1000s). Use the method of least squares to develop a straight line approximation of the relationship between the two variables.
b. Test whether sales and advertising expenditures are related at a .05 level of significance.
c. Prepare a residual plot of $y - \hat{y}$ versus $\hat{y}$. Use the result of (a) to obtain the values of $\hat{y}$.
d. What conclusions can you draw from residual analysis? Should this model be used, or should we look for a better one?

48. Refer to Exercise 9, where an estimated regression equation relating years of experience and annual sales was developed.
a. Compute the residuals and construct a residual plot for this problem.
b. Do the assumptions about the error terms seem reasonable in light of the residual plot?

49. The following table lists the number of employees and the yearly revenue for the 10 largest wholesale bakers (*Louis Rukeyser's Business Almanac*).

Company	Employees	Revenues ($Millions)
Nabisco Brands USA	9,500	1,734
Continental Baking Co.	22,400	1,600
Campbell Taggart, Inc.	19,000	1,044
Keebler Company	8,943	988
Interstate Bakeries Corp.	11,200	704
Flowers Industries, Inc.	10,200	557
Sunshine Biscuits, Inc.	5,000	490
American Bakeries Co.	6,600	461
Entenmann's Inc.	3,734	450
Kitchens of Sara Lee	1,550	405

a. Use a computer package to develop an estimated regression equation relating yearly revenues y to the number of employees x.
b. Construct a residual plot of the standardized residuals against the independent variable.
c. Do the assumptions about the error terms and model form seem reasonable in light of the residual plot?

14.9   RESIDUAL ANALYSIS: OUTLIERS AND INFLUENTIAL OBSERVATIONS

In Section 14.8 we showed how residual analysis could be used to determine when violations of assumptions about the regression model have occurred. In this section, we discuss how residual analysis can be used to identify observations that can be classified as outliers or as being especially influential in determining the estimated regression equation. Some steps that should be taken when such observations have been found are discussed.

DETECTING OUTLIERS

TABLE 14.20
Data Set Illustrating the Effect of an Outlier

x_i	y_i
1	45
1	55
2	50
3	75
3	40
3	45
4	30
4	35
5	25
6	15

Figure 14.16 is a scatter diagram for a data set that has an outlier, a data point (observation) that does not fit the trend shown by the remaining data. Outliers represent observations that are suspect and warrant careful examination. They may represent erroneous data; if so, the data should be corrected. They may signal a violation of model assumptions; if so, another model should be considered. Finally, they may simply be unusual values that have occurred by chance. In this case, they should be retained.

To illustrate the process of detecting outliers, consider the data set in Table 14.20; Figure 14.17 is a scatter diagram. Except for observation 4 ($x_4 = 3$, $y_4 = 75$), a pattern suggesting a negative linear relationship is apparent. Indeed, given the pattern of the rest of the data, we would have expected y_4 to be much smaller and hence would identify the corresponding observation as an outlier. For the case of simple linear regression, one can often detect outliers by simply examining the scatter diagram.

The standardized residuals can also be used to identify outliers. If an observation deviates greatly from the pattern of the rest of the data (e.g., the outlier in Figure 14.16), the corresponding standardized residual will be large in absolute value. Many computer packages automatically identify observations with standardized residuals that are large in absolute value. In Figure 14.18 we show the Minitab output from a regression analysis of the data in Table 14.20. The next to last line of the output shows that the standardized residual for observation 4 is 2.67. Minitab identifies any observation with a standardized residual of less than −2 or greater than +2 as an outlier; in such cases, the observation is printed on a separate line with an R next to the standardized residual, as shown in Figure 14.18. With normally distributed errors, standardized residuals should be outside these limits approximately 5% of the time.

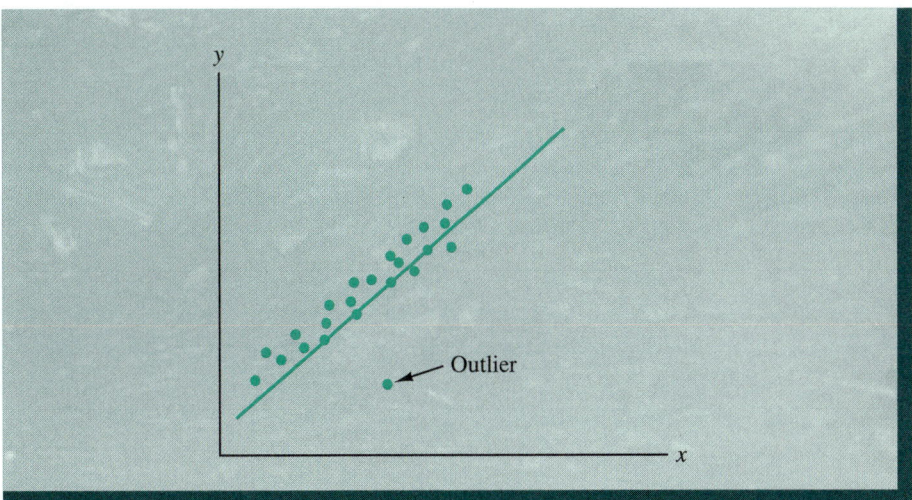

FIGURE 14.16 A Data Set with an Outlier

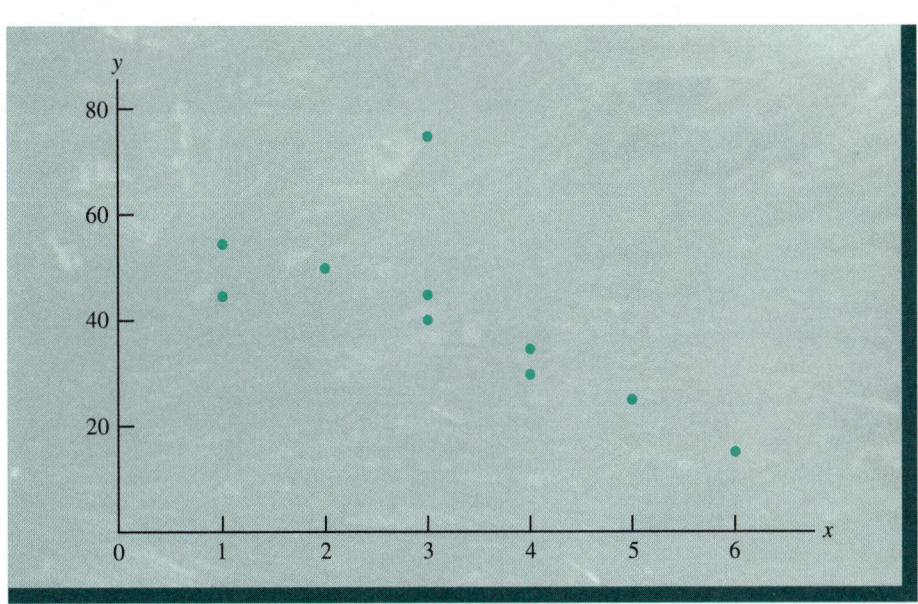

FIGURE 14.17 Scatter Diagram for Outlier Data Set

In deciding how to handle an outlier, we should first check to see if it is a valid observation. Perhaps an error has been made in initially recording the data or in entering the data into the computer file. For example, suppose that in checking the data for the outlier in Table 14.20, we find that an error has been made and that the correct value for observation 4 is $x_4 = 3$, $y_4 = 30$. Figure 14.19 is the Minitab output obtained after correction of the value of y_4. We see that using the incorrect data value had a substantial effect on the goodness of fit. With the correct data, the value of r^2 has increased from 49.7 to 83.8% and the value of b_0 has decreased from 64.958 to 59.237. The slope of the line has changed from -7.331 to -6.949. The identification of the outlier enabled us to correct the data error and improve the regression results.

```
The regression equation is
Y = 65.0 - 7.33 X

Predictor         Coef        Stdev      t-ratio          p
Constant        64.958        9.258         7.02      0.000
X               -7.331        2.608        -2.81      0.023

s = 12.67        R-sq = 49.7%      R-sq(adj) = 43.4%

Analysis of Variance

SOURCE          DF          SS          MS          F          p
Regression       1       1268.2      1268.2       7.90      0.023
Error            8       1284.3       160.5
Total            9       2552.5

Unusual Observations
Obs.      X           Y        Fit Stdev.Fit   Residual    St.Resid
  4    3.00       75.00      42.97      4.04      32.03        2.67R

R denotes an obs. with a large st. resid.
```

FIGURE 14.18　Minitab Output for Regression Analysis of the Outlier Data Set

```
The regression equation is
Y = 59.2 - 6.95 X

Predictor         Coef        Stdev      t-ratio          p
Constant        59.237        3.835        15.45      0.000
X               -6.949        1.080        -6.43      0.000

s = 5.248        R-sq = 83.8%      R-sq(adj) = 81.8%

Analysis of Variance

SOURCE          DF          SS          MS          F          p
Regression       1       1139.7      1139.7      41.38      0.000
Error            8        220.3        27.5
Total            9       1360.0
```

FIGURE 14.19　Minitab Output for the Revised Outlier Data Set

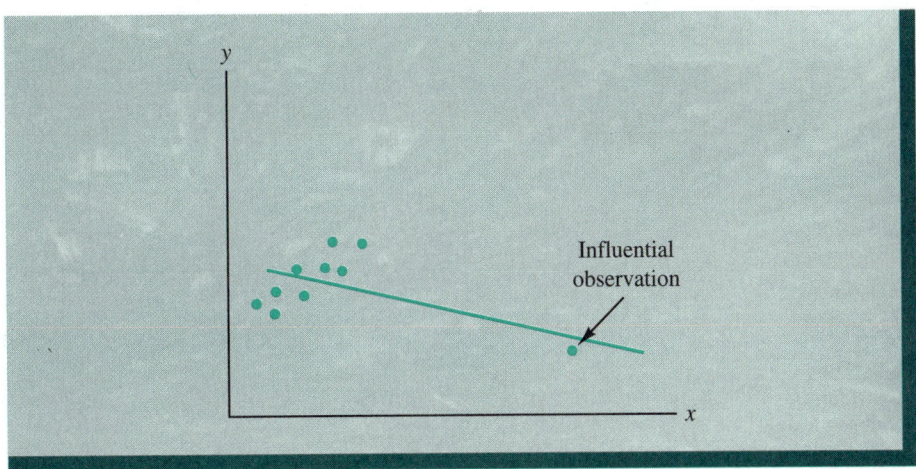

FIGURE 14.20   A Data Set with an Influential Observation

DETECTING INFLUENTIAL OBSERVATIONS

Sometimes one or more observations have a strong influence on the results obtained. Figure 14.20 shows an example of an influential observation in simple linear regression. The estimated regression line has a negative slope. However, if the influential observation were dropped from the data set, the slope of the estimated regression line would change from negative to positive and the y-intercept would be smaller. Clearly, this one observation is much more influential in determining the estimated regression line than any of the others; dropping one of the other observations from the data set would have very little effect on the estimated regression equation.

Influential observations can be identified from a scatter diagram when only one independent variable is present. An influential observation may be an outlier (an observation with a y value that deviates substantially from the trend), it may correspond to an x value far away from its mean (e.g., see Figure 14.20), or it may be caused by a combination of the two (a somewhat off-trend y value and a somewhat extreme x value).

Since influential observations may have such a dramatic effect on the estimated regression equation, they must be examined carefully. We should first check to make sure that no error has been made in collecting or recording the data. If an error has occurred, it can be corrected and a new estimated regression equation can be developed. If the observation is valid, we might consider ourselves fortunate to have it. Such a point, if valid, can contribute to a better understanding of the appropriate model and can lead to a better estimated regression equation. The presence of the influential observation in Figure 14.20, if valid, would suggest trying to obtain data on intermediate values of x to understand better the relationship between x and y.

Observations with extreme values for the independent variables are called *high leverage points*. The influential observation in Figure 14.20 is a point with high leverage. The leverage of an observation is determined by how far the values of the independent variables are from their mean values. For the single-independent-variable case, the leverage of the ith observation, denoted h_i, can be computed by using (14.35).

TABLE 14.21
Data Set with a
High Leverage
Observation

x_i	y_i
10	125
10	130
15	120
20	115
20	120
25	110
70	100

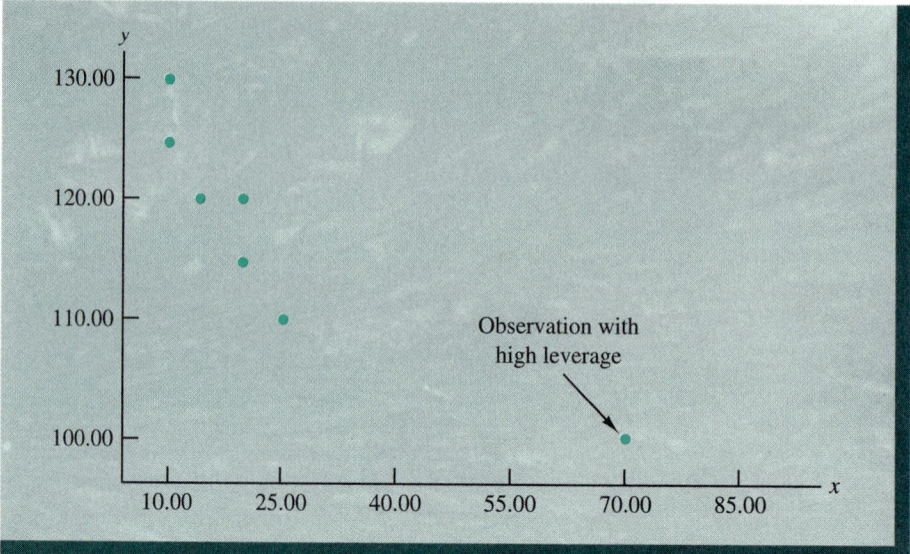

FIGURE 14.21   Scatter Diagram for the Data Set with a High Leverage Observation

LEVERAGE OF OBSERVATION i

$$h_i = \frac{1}{n} + \frac{(x_i - \bar{x})^2}{\Sigma(x_i - \bar{x})^2} \qquad (14.35)$$

From the formula, it is clear that the farther x_i is from its mean $\bar{x}$, the higher the leverage of observation i.

Many computer packages automatically identify observations with high leverage as part of the standard regression output. As an illustration of how the Minitab statistical package identifies points with high leverage, let us consider the data set in Table 14.21.

From Figure 14.21, a scatter diagram for the data set in Table 14.21, it is clear that observation 7 ($x = 70$, $y = 100$) is an observation with an extreme value of x. Hence, we would expect it to be identified as a point with high leverage. For this observation, the leverage is computed by using (14.35) as follows.

$$h_7 = \frac{1}{n} + \frac{(x_7 - \bar{x})^2}{\Sigma(x_i - \bar{x})^2} = \frac{1}{7} + \frac{(70 - 24.286)^2}{2621.43} = .94$$

For the case of simple linear regression, Minitab identifies observations as having high leverage if $h_i > 6/n$; for the data set in Table 14.21, $6/n = 6/7 = .86$. Since $h_7 = .94 >$ .86, Minitab will identify observation 7 as a high leverage point. Figure 14.22 shows the Minitab output for a regression analysis of this data set. Observation 7 ($x = 70$, $y = 100$) is identified as having large influence; it is printed on a separate line at the bottom, with an X in the right margin.

Influential observations that are caused by an interaction of large residuals and high leverage can be difficult to detect. Diagnostic procedures are available that take both into account in determining when an observation is influential. One such measure, called Cook's D statistic, will be discussed in Chapter 15.

```
The regression equation is
Y = 127 -0.425 X

Predictor          Coef        Stdev      t-ratio          p
Constant        127.466        2.961        43.04      0.000
X               -0.42507      0.09537       -4.46      0.007

s = 4.883          R-sq = 79.9%      R-sq(adj) = 75.9%

Analysis of Variance

SOURCE          DF            SS            MS          F          p
Regression       1        473.65        473.65      19.87      0.007
Error            5        119.21         23.84
Total            6        592.86

Unusual Observations
Obs.      X            Y        Fit Stdev.Fit  Residual    St.Resid
  7     70.0       100.00      97.71     4.73      2.29        1.91 X

X denotes an obs. whose X value gives it large influence
```

FIGURE 14.22   Minitab Output for the Data Set with a High Leverage Observation

NOTES AND COMMENTS

Once an observation has been identified as potentially influential because of a large residual or high leverage, its impact on the estimated regression equation should be evaluated. More advanced texts discuss diagnostics for doing so. However, if one is not familiar with the more advanced material, a simple procedure is to run the regression analysis with and without the observation. Although time-consuming, this approach will reveal the influence of the observation on the results.

EXERCISES

METHODS

Self-Test

50. Consider the following data for two variables, x and y.

x_i	135	110	130	145	175	160	120
y_i	145	100	120	120	130	130	110

a. Compute the standardized residuals for these data. Do there appear to be any outliers in the data? Explain.
b. Plot the standardized residuals against y. Does this plot reveal any outliers?

TABLE 14.22 Exercise 52

Number of Golf Courses	Number of Paid Rounds of Golf
26	1.0
30	1.1
31	1.2
32	1.3
33	1.4
35	1.6
38	1.8
43	2.0
57	2.5
67	3.0

c. Develop a scatter diagram for these data. Does the scatter diagram indicate any outliers in the data? In general, what implications does this finding have for simple linear regression?

51. Consider the following data for two variables, x and y.

x_i	4	5	7	8	10	12	12	22
y_i	12	14	16	15	18	20	24	19

a. Compute the standardized residuals for these data. Do there appear to be any outliers in the data? Explain.

b. Compute the leverage values for these data. Do there appear to be any influential observations in these data? Explain.

c. Develop a scatter diagram for these data. Does the scatter diagram indicate any influential observations? Explain.

APPLICATIONS

Self-Test ▸

52. Table 14.22 gives the number of golf courses and the number of paid rounds of golf (in millions) for the Myrtle Beach, South Carolina, area over a 10-year period (*Myrtle Beach Magazine,* October 1991).

a. Develop the estimated regression equation for these data.

b. Use residual analysis to determine whether any outliers and/or influential observations are present. Briefly summarize your findings and conclusions.

53. The National Association of Home Builders compared the median home prices with the median household incomes in cities throughout the United States (*USA Today*, September 10, 1991). The 25 most affordable cities are listed in the following table. Both home prices and household incomes are in thousands of dollars.

HOME2

City	Median Income	Median Home Price	City	Median Income	Median Home Price
Amarillo, Texas	36.7	69.0	Milwaukee, Wisconsin	41.8	72.0
Brazoria, Texas	42.4	80.0	Minneapolis, Minnesota	48.0	91.0
Canton, Ohio	34.1	66.0	Nashua, New Hampshire	52.9	111.0
Davenport, Iowa	38.4	59.0	Oklahoma City, Oklahoma	34.5	63.0
Daytona Beach, Florida	31.0	63.0	Omaha, Nebraska	38.8	65.0
Detroit, Michigan	44.6	77.0	Rockford, Illinois	41.6	73.5
Fort Walton Beach, Florida	34.2	65.0	Saginaw, Michigan	39.7	61.0
Grand Rapids, Michigan	40.3	73.0	Shreveport, Louisiana	34.4	66.0
Jackson, Michigan	36.8	60.0	Toledo, Ohio	39.4	65.0
Kansas City, Missouri	41.1	77.0	Tulsa, Oklahoma	36.2	68.0
Lansing, Michigan	40.0	70.0	Winter Haven, Florida	30.2	56.0
Lorain, Ohio	38.8	72.5	Youngstown, Ohio	34.9	59.0
Mansfield, Ohio	35.6	58.5			

a. Develop the estimated regression equation that can be used to predict the median home price given the median income.

b. Use residual analysis to determine whether any outliers and/or influential observations are present. Briefly summarize your findings and conclusions.

54. Table 14.23 lists the temperatures for air and water in the Myrtle Beach, South Carolina, area (*Myrtle Beach and South Carolina Grand Strand,* 1992).

TEMPSC

a. Develop the estimated regression equation that can be used to predict the water temperature given the air temperature.

TABLE 14.23 Exercise 54

Month	Air	Water
January	57	49
February	59	51
March	65	56
April	75	66
May	81	71
June	86	78
July	88	83
August	88	80
September	84	77
October	75	72
November	68	60
December	59	50

b. Use residual analysis to determine whether any outliers and/or influential observations are present. Briefly summarize your findings and conclusions.

SUMMARY

In this chapter we showed how regression analysis can be used to determine how a dependent variable y is related to an independent variable x. In simple linear regression, the regression model is $y = \beta_0 + \beta_1 x + \epsilon$. The simple linear regression equation $E(y) = \beta_0 + \beta_1 x$ describes how the mean or expected value of y is related to x. We used sample data and the least squares method to develop the estimated regression equation $\hat{y} = b_0 + b_1 x$. In effect, b_0 and b_1 are the sample statistics used to estimate the unknown model parameters β_0 and β_1.

The coefficient of determination was presented as a measure of the goodness of fit for the estimated regression equation; it can be interpreted as the proportion of the variation in the dependent variable y that can be explained by the estimated regression equation. We reviewed correlation as a descriptive measure of the strength of a linear relationship between two variables.

The assumptions about the regression model and its associated error term ϵ were discussed, and t and F tests, based on those assumptions, were presented as a means for determining whether the relationship between two variables is statistically significant. We showed how to use the estimated regression equation to develop confidence interval estimates of the mean value of y and prediction interval estimates of individual values of y.

The chapter concluded with a section on the computer solution of regression problems and two sections on the use of residual analysis to validate the model assumptions and to identify outliers and influential observations.

GLOSSARY

Dependent variable The variable that is being predicted or explained. It is denoted by y.

Independent variable The variable that is doing the predicting or explaining. It is denoted by x.

Simple linear regression Regression analysis involving one independent variable and one dependent variable in which the relationship between the variables is approximated by a straight line.

Regression model The probability model describing how y is related to x; in simple linear regression, the regression model is $y = \beta_0 + \beta_1 x + \epsilon$.

Regression equation The equation that describes how the mean or expected value of the dependent variable is related to the independent variable; in simple linear regression, $E(y) = \beta_0 + \beta_1 x$.

Estimated regression equation The estimate of the regression equation developed from sample data by using the least squares method. For simple linear regression, the estimated regression equation is $\hat{y} = b_0 + b_1 x$.

Scatter diagram A graph of bivariate data in which the independent variable is on the horizontal axis and the dependent variable is on the vertical axis.

Least squares method   The procedure used to develop the estimated regression equation. The objective is to minimize $\Sigma(y_i - \hat{y}_i)^2$.

Coefficient of determination   A measure of the goodness of fit of the estimated regression equation. It can be interpreted as the proportion of the variation in the dependent variable y that is explained by the estimated regression equation.

Residual   The difference between the observed value of the dependent variable and the value predicted by using the estimated regression equation; that is, for the ith observation the residual is $y_i - \hat{y}_i$.

Correlation coefficient   A measure of the strength of the linear relationship between two variables (previously discussed in Chapter 3).

Mean Square Error   The unbiased estimate of the variance of the error term, σ^2. It is denoted by MSE or s^2 .

Standard Error of the Estimate   The square root of the mean square error, denoted by s. It is the estimate of σ, the standard deviation of the error term ϵ.

ANOVA table   The analysis of variance table used to summarize the computations associated with the F test for significance.

Confidence interval estimate   The interval estimate of the mean value of y for a given value of x.

Prediction interval estimate   The interval estimate of an individual value of y for a given value of x.

Residual analysis   The analysis of the residuals used to determine whether the assumptions made about the regression model appear to be valid. Residual analysis is also used to identify unusual and influential observations.

Residual plots   Graphical representations of the residuals that can be used to determine whether the assumptions made about the regression model appear to be valid.

Standardized residual   The value obtained by dividing a residual by its standard deviation.

Normal probability plot   A graph of normal scores plotted against values of the standardized residuals. This plot helps determine whether the assumption that the error term has a normal probability distribution appears to be valid.

Outlier   A data point or observation that does not fit the trend shown by the remaining data.

Influential observation   An observation that has a strong influence or effect on the regression results.

High leverage points   Observations with extreme values for the independent variables.

KEY FORMULAS

Simple Linear Regression Model

$$y = \beta_0 + \beta_1 x + \epsilon \tag{14.1}$$

Simple Linear Regression Equation

$$E(y) = \beta_0 + \beta_1 x \tag{14.2}$$

Estimated Simple Linear Regression Equation

$$\hat{y} = b_0 + b_1 x \tag{14.3}$$

Least Squares Criterion

$$\text{Min } \Sigma(y_i - \hat{y}_i)^2 \tag{14.5}$$

Slope and y-Intercept for the Estimated Regression Equation

$$b_1 = \frac{\Sigma x_i y_i - (\Sigma x_i \, \Sigma y_i)/n}{\Sigma x_i^2 - (\Sigma x_i)^2/n} \tag{14.6}$$

$$b_0 = \bar{y} - b_1 \bar{x} \tag{14.7}$$

Sum of Squares Due to Error

$$\text{SSE} = \Sigma(y_i - \hat{y}_i)^2 \tag{14.8}$$

Total Sum of Squares

$$\text{SST} = \Sigma(y_i - \bar{y})^2 \tag{14.9}$$

Sum of Squares Due to Regression

$$\text{SSR} = \Sigma(\hat{y}_i - \bar{y})^2 \tag{14.10}$$

Relationship among SST, SSR, and SSE

$$\text{SST} = \text{SSR} + \text{SSE} \tag{14.11}$$

Coefficient of Determination

$$r^2 = \frac{\text{SSR}}{\text{SST}} \tag{14.12}$$

Computational Formula for SST

$$\text{SST} = \Sigma y_i^2 - (\Sigma y_i)^2/n \tag{14.13}$$

Computational Formula for SSR

$$\text{SSR} = \frac{[\Sigma x_i y_i - (\Sigma x_i \, \Sigma y_i)/n]^2}{\Sigma x_i^2 - (\Sigma x_i)^2/n} \tag{14.14}$$

Sample Correlation Coefficient

$$r_{xy} = (\text{sign of } b_1)\sqrt{\text{Coefficient of Determination}} = \pm \sqrt{r^2} \tag{14.15}$$

Mean Square Error (Estimate of σ^2)

$$s^2 = \text{MSE} = \frac{\text{SSE}}{n - 2} \tag{14.17}$$

Standard Error of the Estimate

$$s = \sqrt{\text{MSE}} = \sqrt{\frac{\text{SSE}}{n - 2}} \qquad (14.18)$$

Standard Deviation of b_1

$$\sigma_{b_1} = \frac{\sigma}{\sqrt{\Sigma x_i^2 - (\Sigma x_i)^2/n}} \qquad (14.19)$$

Estimated Standard Deviation of b_1

$$s_{b_1} = \frac{s}{\sqrt{\Sigma x_i^2 - (\Sigma x_i)^2/n}} \qquad (14.20)$$

t Test Statistic

$$t = \frac{b_1}{s_{b_1}} \qquad (14.21)$$

Mean Square Due to Regression

$$\text{MSR} = \frac{\text{SSR}}{\text{Number of independent variables}} \qquad (14.22)$$

The F Test Statistic

$$F = \frac{\text{MSR}}{\text{MSE}} \qquad (14.23)$$

Estimated Standard Deviation of $\hat{y}_p$

$$s_{\hat{y}_p} = s\sqrt{\frac{1}{n} + \frac{(x_p - \bar{x})^2}{\Sigma x_i^2 - (\Sigma x_i)^2/n}} \qquad (14.25)$$

Confidence Interval Estimate of $E(\hat{y}_p)$

$$\hat{y}_p \pm t_{\alpha/2} s_{\hat{y}_p} \qquad (14.26)$$

Estimated Standard Deviation when Predicting an Individual Value

$$s_{\text{ind}} = s\sqrt{1 + \frac{1}{n} + \frac{(x_p - \bar{x})^2}{\Sigma x_i^2 - (\Sigma x_i)^2/n}} \qquad (14.28)$$

Prediction Interval Estimate of y_p

$$\hat{y}_p \pm t_{\alpha/2} s_{\text{ind}} \qquad (14.29)$$

Residual for Observation i

$$y_i - \hat{y}_i \qquad (14.30)$$

Standard Deviation of the ith Residual

$$s_{y_i - \hat{y}_i} = s\sqrt{1 - h_i} \qquad (14.32)$$

Standardized Residual for Observation i

$$\frac{y_i - \hat{y}_i}{s_{y_i - \hat{y}_i}} \qquad (14.34)$$

Leverage for Observation i

$$h_i = \frac{1}{n} + \frac{(x_i - \bar{x})^2}{\Sigma(x_i - \bar{x})^2} \qquad (14.35)$$

SUPPLEMENTARY EXERCISES

55. Does a high value of r^2 imply that two variables are causally related? Explain.

56. In your own words, explain the difference between an interval estimate of the mean value of y for a given x and an interval estimate for an individual value of y for a given x.

57. What is the purpose of testing whether or not $\beta_1 = 0$? If we reject $\beta_1 = 0$, does this imply a good fit?

58. A study of how much supermarket shoppers could save by purchasing store brand products rather than name brand products was reported in *Consumer Reports* (September 1993). The following data are from a sample of commonly purchased items with brand product prices between $1.00 and $4.00.

Product and Size	Name Brand Price	Store Brand Price
Kraft mayonnaise, qt.	$2.79	$1.19
Heinz ketchup, 2 lb.	1.69	.79
Lipton tea, 100 bags	2.79	1.39
Folgers coffee, 12 oz.	2.79	1.59
Coca-Cola Classic, 6 pack	2.79	1.64
Planters peanuts, 12 oz.	3.79	2.39
Del Monte peaches, 1 lb.	1.19	.83
Kleenex, 250 count	1.59	1.29
Breyers ice cream, 1/2 gal.	3.99	2.39
Oscar Mayer bacon, 1 lb.	3.49	2.09

   a. Develop an estimated regression equation with name brand price as the independent variable and store brand price as the dependent variable.
   b. What is the coefficient of determination? Did the estimated regression equation provide a good fit?
   c. A common price for name brand items is $1.99. On average, what would you expect to pay for an equivalent store brand item? What percentage savings would be realized by purchasing the store brand item?

d. Johnson & Johnson shampoo (20 oz.) has a price of $3.29. What would you expect to pay for an equivalent store brand shampoo product?

59. The law in Hamilton County, Ohio, requires the publication of delinquent property tax information. The county publication lists the name of the property owner, the property valuation, and the amount of taxes, assessments, interest, and penalties due. The property valuation and the amount of taxes due for a sample of 10 delinquent properties are shown in Table 14.24 (*Delinquent Land Tax, Hamilton County,* November 17, 1994). The property valuation is in thousands of dollars.

a. Develop the estimated regression equation that could be used to estimate the amount of taxes due given the property valuation.

b. Use the estimated regression equation to estimate the taxes due for a property located on Red Bank Road. The valuation of the property is $42,400.

c. Do you believe the estimated regression equation would provide a good prediction of the amount of tax due? Use r^2 to support your answer.

TABLE 14.24
Exercise 59

Property Valuation	Amount Due
$18.8	$445
24.4	539
20.4	1212
35.8	2237
14.8	479
40.4	1181
49.0	4187
14.5	409
37.3	1002
54.7	2062

60. *Value Line* (February 24, 1995) reported that the market beta for Woolworth Corporation is 1.25. Market betas for individual stocks are determined by simple linear regression. For each stock, the dependent variable is its quarterly percentage return (capital appreciation plus dividends) minus the percentage return that could be obtained from a risk-free investment (the Treasury Bill rate is used as the risk-free rate). The independent variable is the quarterly percentage return (capital appreciation plus dividends) for the stock market (S&P 500) minus the percentage return from a risk-free investment. An estimated regression equation is developed with quarterly data; the market beta for the stock is the slope of the estimated regression equation (b_1). The value of the market beta is often interpreted as a measure of the risk associated with the stock. Market betas greater than 1 indicate that the stock is more volatile than the market average; market betas less than 1 indicate that the stock is less volatile than the market average. Shown in Table 14.25 are the differences between the percentage return and the risk-free return for 10 quarters for the S&P 500 and IBM.

a. Develop an estimated regression equation that can be used to determine the market beta for IBM. What is IBM's market beta?

b. Use the market betas of Woolworth and IBM to compare the risk associated with the two stocks.

c. Did the estimated regression equation provide a good fit? Explain.

TABLE 14.25
Exercise 60

S&P 500	IBM
1.2	−0.7
−2.5	−2.0
−3.0	−5.5
2.0	4.7
5.0	1.8
1.2	4.1
3.0	2.6
−1.0	2.0
.5	−1.3
2.5	5.5

61. Monsanto Company conducted a study to determine the relationship between the percentage of supplemental methionine used in feed and the body weight of poultry. With the data collected in this study, regression analysis was used to develop the following estimated regression line.

$$\hat{y} = .21 + .42x$$

where

$$\hat{y} = \text{estimated body weight in kilograms}$$

$$x = \text{percentage of supplemental methionine used in the feed}$$

The coefficient of determination r^2 was .78, indicating a reasonably good fit for the data. Suppose a sample size of 30 was used for the study and SST = 45.

a. Compute SSR and SSE.

b. Test for a significant regression relationship using $\alpha = .01$.

c. What is the value of the sample correlation coefficient?

62. The PJH&D Company is in the process of deciding whether to purchase a maintenance contract for its new word-processing system. Managers feel that maintenance expense should be related to usage and have collected the information shown in Table 14.26 on weekly usage (hours) and annual maintenance expense (hundreds of dollars).

a. Develop the estimated regression equation that relates annual maintenance expense to weekly usage.

TABLE 14.26 Exercise 62

Weekly Usage (hours)	Annual Maintenance Expense
13	17.0
10	22.0
20	30.0
28	37.0
32	47.0
17	30.5
24	32.5
31	39.0
40	51.5
38	40.0

b. Test the significance of the relationship in (a) at a .05 level of significance.

c. PJH&D expects to operate the word processor 30 hours per week. Develop a 95% prediction interval for the company's annual maintenance expense.

d. If the maintenance contract costs $3000 per year, would you recommend purchasing it? Why or why not?

TABLE 14.27 Exercise 63

Line Speed	Number of Defective Parts Found
20	21
20	19
40	15
30	16
60	14
40	17

63. In a manufacturing process the assembly line speed (feet per minute) was thought to affect the number of defective parts found during the inspection process. To test this theory, managers devised a situation in which the same batch of parts was inspected visually at a variety of line speeds. Table 14.27 lists the collected data.

a. Develop the estimated regression equation that relates line speed to the number of defective parts found.

b. At a .05 level of significance, determine whether line speed and number of defective parts found are related.

c. Did the estimated regression equation provide a good fit to the data?

d. Develop a 95% confidence interval to predict the mean number of defective parts for a line speed of 50 feet per minute.

64. Exercise 58 gives data on name brand price and store brand price for products frequently purchased in a supermarket (*Consumer Reports,* September 1993).

a. Use the t test to determine whether there is a significant relationship between name brand price and store brand price. Use $\alpha = .05$. What is your conclusion?

b. Use the F test to determine whether there is a significant relationship between name brand price and store brand price. Use $\alpha = .05$. Show the ANOVA table. What is your conclusion?

c. A common price for name brand items is $1.99. Develop a 95% confidence interval estimate of the mean store brand price for items with a name brand price of $1.99.

d. S & W olives (6 oz.) has a price of $1.99. Develop a 95% prediction interval estimate of the store brand price for olives.

65. A sociologist was hired by a large city hospital to investigate the relationship between the number of unauthorized days that employees are absent per year and the distance (miles) between home and work for the employees. A sample of 10 employees was chosen, and the following data were collected.

Distance to Work	Number of Days Absent
1	8
3	5
4	8
6	7
8	6
10	3
12	5
14	2
14	4
18	2

a. Develop a scatter diagram for these data. Does a linear relationship appear reasonable? Explain.

b. Develop the least squares estimated regression equation.

c. Is there a significant relationship between the two variables? Use $\alpha = .05$.

d. Did the estimated regression equation provide a good fit? Explain.

e. Use the estimated regression equation developed in (b) to develop a 95% confidence interval estimate of the expected number of days absent for employees living five miles from the company.

66. Exercise 60 gives data on quarterly percentage returns that can be used to compute the market beta for IBM.
   a. Use the t test to determine whether there is a significant relationship. Use $\alpha = .05$. What is your conclusion?
   b. Use the F test to determine whether there is a significant relationship. Use $\alpha = .05$. What is your conclusion?
   c. Present the results of the F test in the analysis of variance table format.

67. Performance data for a Century Coronado 21 with a 310-hp MerCruiser V-8 gasoline inboard engine were reported in *Boating* (September 1991). Data on how the engine revolutions per minute (rpm) affected boat speed in miles per hour (mph) follow.

rpm	mph
1000	6.1
1500	10.7
2000	20.9
2500	27.5
3000	31.5
3500	33.6
4000	37.9
4500	40.2
4800	40.7

   a. Develop the estimated regression equation showing how boat speed is related to engine revolutions per minute.
   b. Test the significance of the relationship at a .05 level of significance.
   c. Develop a plot of the standardized residuals against $\hat{y}$. What conclusions can you draw from this plot?

68. The 1992 U.S. Men's Olympic Marathon Trials (Columbus, Ohio, April 11, 1992) provided marathon qualifying times and ages for 109 runners. Table 14.28 reports the number of minutes by which the qualifying times exceeded two hours and the age for a sample of eight runners.
   a. Develop the estimated regression equation showing how qualifying time is related to age.
   b. Test the significance of the relationship at a .05 level of significance.
   c. Develop a plot of the standardized residuals against $\hat{y}$. What conclusion can you draw from this plot?

69. The regional transit authority for a major metropolitan area wants to determine whether there is any relationship between the age of a bus and the annual maintenance cost. A sample of 10 buses resulted in the data in Table 14.29. Compute the sample correlation coefficient for the data in the table.

70. Reconsider the regional transit authority problem presented in Exercise 69.
   a. Develop the least squares estimated regression equation.
   b. Test to see whether the two variables are significantly related with $\alpha = .05$.
   c. Did the least squares line provide a good fit to the observed data? Explain.
   d. Develop a 95% prediction interval for the maintenance cost for a specific bus that is four years old.

71. A marketing professor at Givens College is interested in the relation between hours spent studying and total points earned in a course. Data collected on 10 students who took the course last quarter are given in Table 14.30. Compute the sample correlation coefficient for these data.

72. Reconsider the Givens College data in Exercise 71.
   a. Develop an estimated regression equation showing how total points earned is related to hours spent studying.

TABLE 14.28   Exercise 68

Age	Qualifying Time
33	12.1
33	12.6
31	13.1
26	14.0
26	14.1
25	14.6
30	15.0
29	15.5

TABLE 14.29   Exercise 69

Age of Bus (years)	Maintenance Cost ($)
1	350
2	370
2	480
2	520
2	590
3	550
4	750
4	800
5	790
5	950

TABLE 14.30   Exercise 71

Hours Spent Studying	Total Points Earned
45	40
30	35
90	75
60	65
105	90
65	50
90	90
80	80
55	45
75	65

b. Test the significance of the model with $\alpha = .05$.

c. Predict the total points earned by Mark Sweeney. He spent 95 hours studying.

d. Develop a 95% prediction interval for the total points earned by Mark Sweeney.

73. Exercise 58 gives data on name brand price and store brand price for items frequently purchased in a supermarket (*Consumer Reports*, September 1993). The estimated regression equation is $\hat{y} = .042 + .564x$.

a. Compute the residuals for this data set.

b. What product has the largest residual? What is your interpretation of the value of that residual?

c. What product has the smallest residual? What is your interpretation of the value of that residual?

d. Prepare a residual plot against the name brand price x.

e. Does the residual plot provide any indication that the assumptions of the regression model should be questioned?

74. Do big-budget motion pictures bring in big money at the box office? Data for 1994 motion pictures follow (*Entertainment Weekly*, September 1994).

Motion Picture	Budget ($ Millions)	Gross Sales ($ Millions)
Forrest Gump	50	275
The Flintstones	46	130
Speed	30	120
Maverick	60	100
Color of Night	40	20
The Mask	23	105
City Slickers II	45	44
Clear and Present Danger	62	120
Beverly Hills Cop III	50	42
The Crow	23	51

A regression analysis was performed with budget as the independent variable and gross sales as the dependent variable. Using the partial computer printout in Figure 14.23, answer the following questions.

a. What is the estimated regression equation?

b. What is the coefficient of determination?

c. What is the value of the standard error of the estimate?

d. Conduct a t test at a .05 level of significance.

```
Predictor      Coef      Stdev     t-ratio
Constant       50.43     80.95
Budget         1.172     1.804     _____


s = 75.21   R-sq = _____%


Analysis of Variance

SOURCE          DF        SS        MS        F
Regression      1         2388      _____  _____
Error           8         45258     _____
Total           9         _____
```

FIGURE 14.23 Computer Printout for the Motion Picture Regression Analysis— Exercise 74

e. Conduct an F test at a .05 level of significance.

f. Discuss the relationship between budget and gross in the motion picture industry. What does the regression analysis tell the producers who favor big-budget motion pictures?

COMPUTER CASE

U.S. DEPARTMENT OF TRANSPORTATION

As part of a study on transportation safety, the U.S. Department of Transportation collected data on the number of fatal accidents per 1000 licenses and the percentage of licensed drivers under the age of 21 in a sample of 42 cities. Data collected over a one-year period follow. These data are available on the data disk in the file named SAFETY.

Percent Under 21	Fatal Accidents per 1000 Licenses	Percent Under 21	Fatal Accidents per 1000 Licenses
13	2.962	17	4.100
12	0.708	8	2.190
8	0.885	16	3.623
12	1.652	15	2.623
11	2.091	9	0.835
17	2.627	8	0.820
18	3.830	14	2.890
8	0.368	8	1.267
13	1.142	15	3.224
8	0.645	10	1.014
9	1.028	10	0.493
16	2.801	14	1.443
12	1.405	18	3.614
9	1.433	10	1.926
10	0.039	14	1.643
9	0.338	16	2.943
11	1.849	12	1.913
12	2.246	15	2.814
14	2.855	13	2.634
14	2.352	9	0.926
11	1.294	17	3.256

SAFETY

Managerial Report

1. Develop numerical and graphical summaries of the data.
2. Use regression analysis to investigate the relationship between the number of fatal accidents and the percentage of drivers under the age of 21. Discuss your findings.
3. What conclusion and/or recommendations can you derive from your analysis?

APPENDIX 14.1 ●●●●●●●●●●●●●●●●●●●●●●●●●●●

Calculus-Based Derivation of Least Squares Formulas

● As mentioned in the chapter, the least squares method is a procedure for determining the values of b_0 and b_1 that minimize the sum of squared residuals. The sum of squared residuals is given by

$$\Sigma(y_i - \hat{y}_i)^2$$

Substituting $\hat{y}_i = b_0 + b_1 x_i$, we get

$$\Sigma(y_i - b_0 - b_1 x_i)^2 \qquad \text{(14A.1)}$$

as the expression that must be minimized.

To minimize (14A.1), we must take the partial derivatives with respect to b_0 and b_1, set them equal to zero, and solve. Doing so, we get

$$\frac{\partial \Sigma(y_i - b_0 - b_1 x_i)^2}{\partial b_0} = -2\Sigma(y_i - b_0 - b_1 x_i) = 0 \qquad \text{(14A.2)}$$

$$\frac{\partial \Sigma(y_i - b_0 - b_1 x_i)^2}{\partial b_1} = -2\Sigma x_i(y_i - b_0 - b_1 x_i) = 0 \qquad \text{(14A.3)}$$

Dividing (14A.2) by two and summing each term individually yields

$$-\Sigma y_i + \Sigma b_0 + \Sigma b_1 x_i = 0$$

Bringing Σy_i to the other side of the equal sign and noting that $\Sigma b_0 = nb_0$, we obtain

$$nb_0 + (\Sigma x_i)b_1 = \Sigma y_i \qquad \text{(14A.4)}$$

Similar algebraic simplification applied to (14A.3) yields

$$(\Sigma x_i)b_0 + (\Sigma x_i^2)b_1 = \Sigma x_i y_i \qquad \text{(14A.5)}$$

Equations (14A.4) and (14A.5) are known as the *normal equations*. Solving (14A.4) for b_0 yields

$$b_0 = \frac{\Sigma y_i}{n} - b_1 \frac{\Sigma x_i}{n} \qquad \text{(14A.6)}$$

Using (14A.6) to substitute for b_0 in (14A.5) provides

$$\frac{\Sigma x_i \Sigma y_i}{n} - \frac{(\Sigma x_i)^2}{n}b_1 + (\Sigma x_i^2)b_1 = \Sigma x_i y_i \qquad \text{(14A.7)}$$

Rearranging (14A.7), we obtain

$$b_1 = \frac{\Sigma x_i y_i - (\Sigma x_i \, \Sigma y_i)/n}{\Sigma x_i^2 - (\Sigma x_i)^2/n} \qquad \text{(14A.8)}$$

Since $\bar{y} = \Sigma y_i/n$ and $\bar{x} = \Sigma x_i/n$, we can rewrite (14A.6) as

$$b_0 = \bar{y} - b_1 \bar{x} \qquad \text{(14A.9)}$$

Equations (14A.8) and (14A.9) are the formulas we used in the chapter to compute the coefficients in the estimated regression equation.

APPENDIX 14.2

A Test for Significance Using Correlation

● Using the sample correlation coefficient r_{xy}, we can determine whether or not the linear relationship between x and y is significant by testing the following hypotheses about the population correlation coefficient ρ_{xy}.

$$H_0: \rho_{xy} = 0$$
$$H_a: \rho_{xy} \neq 0$$

If H_0 is rejected, we can conclude that the population correlation coefficient is not equal to zero and that the linear relationship between the two variables is significant. This test for significance follows.

A Test For Significance Using Correlation

$$H_0: \rho_{xy} = 0$$
$$H_a: \rho_{xy} \neq 0$$

Test Statistic

$$t = r_{xy} \sqrt{\frac{n-2}{1 - r_{xy}^2}} \qquad \text{(14A.10)}$$

Rejection Rule

Reject H_0 if $t < -t_{\alpha/2}$ or if $t > t_{\alpha/2}$

where $t_{\alpha/2}$ is based on a t distribution with $n-2$ degrees of freedom.

In Section 14.4, we found that the sample with $n = 10$ provided the sample correlation coefficient for student population and sales of $r_{xy} = .9501$. The test statistic is

$$t = r_{xy} \sqrt{\frac{n-2}{1 - r_{xy}^2}} = .9501 \sqrt{\frac{10 - 2}{1 - (.9501)^2}} = 8.61$$

From Table 2 of Appendix B, we find that the t value corresponding to $\alpha = .01$ and $n - 2 = 10 - 2 = 8$ degrees of freedom is $t_{.005} = 3.355$. With $8.61 > 3.355$, we reject H_0 and conclude at the .01 level of significance that ρ_{xy} is not equal to zero. This finding provides the statistical evidence necessary to conclude that there is a significant linear relationship between student population and sales.

Note that the test statistic t and the conclusion of a significant relationship are identical to the results obtained in Section 14.5 for the t test conducted using Armand's estimated regression equation $\hat{y} = 60 + 5x$. Performing regression analysis provides the conclusion of a significant relationship between x and y and in addition provides the equation showing how the variables are related. Most analysts therefore use modern computer packages to perform regression analysis and find that using correlation as a test of significance is unnecessary.

APPENDIX 14.3

Regression Analysis with Minitab

● In Section 14.7 we discussed the computer solution of regression problems by showing Minitab's output for the Armand's Pizza Parlors problem. In this appendix, we describe the steps required to generate the Minitab computer solution. First, the data must be entered in a Minitab worksheet. Student population data were entered in column C1 and sales data were entered in column C2. The variable names POP and SALES were entered as the column headings on the worksheet. In subsequent steps, we could refer to the data by using the variable names POP and SALES or the column indicators C1 and C2. The following steps describe how to use Minitab to produce the regression results.

Step 1.   Select the **Stat** pull-down menu
Step 2.   Select the **Regression** pull-down menu
Step 3.   Choose the **Regression** option
Step 4.   When the Regression dialog box appears:
            Enter SALES in the **Response** box
            Enter POP in the **Predictors** box
            Select **OK** to obtain the regression analysis

The summary output is shown in Figure 14.9. The Minitab regression dialog box provides additional output information that can be obtained by selecting the desired options. For example, residuals, standardized residuals, high leverage data points, and the correlation matrix can be obtained in that way.

APPENDIX 14.4 ·

Regression Analysis with Spreadsheets

● Let us demonstrate regression analysis with spreadsheets by using Excel to provide the computations for the Armand's Pizza Parlors problem. Figure 14.24 shows that we have entered Armand's data in columns A and B of the spreadsheet. Student population data are in cells 2 to 11 of column A and sales data are in cells 2 to 11 of column B. The following steps describe how to use Excel to produce the regression results.

Step 1.   Select the **Tools** pull-down menu
Step 2.   Choose the **Data Analysis** option
Step 3.   When the Analysis Tools dialog box appears,
            Choose **Regression**
Step 4.   When the Regression dialog box appears:
            Enter B2:B11 in the **Input Y Range** box
            Enter A2:A11 in the **Input X Range** box
            Enter A14 in the **Output Range** box
               (Any upper-left corner cell indicating where the output is to begin may be entered here.)
            Select **OK** to begin the regression analysis

The summary output begins with row 14 in Figure 14.24. The Multiple R cell gives the sample correlation coefficient of .9501 as before. The coefficient of determination (90.27%) and the standard error of the estimate (13.829) are also shown as before. The analysis of variance table is next. The p-value under the heading Significance F shows that the null hypothesis H_0: $\beta_1 = 0$ can be rejected, indicating that the relationship between student population and sales is significant. The regression coefficients of 60 for the intercept and 5 for the independent variable population are significant. They show that the estimated regression equation is $\hat{y} = 60 + 5x$. The t statistic and the p-value for

	A	B	C	D	E	F	G
1	Population	Sales					
2	2	58					
3	6	105					
4	8	88					
5	8	118					
6	12	117					
7	16	137					
8	20	157					
9	20	169					
10	22	149					
11	26	202					
12							
13							
14	SUMMARY OUTPUT						
15							
16	*Regression Statistics*						
17	Multiple R	0.9501					
18	R Square	0.9027					
19	Adjusted R Square	0.8906					
20	Standard Error	13.829					
21	Observations	10					
22							
23	ANOVA						
24		*df*	*SS*	*MS*	*F*	*Significance F*	
25	Regression	1	14200	14200	74.25	0.000	
26	Residual	8	1530	191.25			
27	Total	9	15730				
28							
29		*Coefficients*	*Standard Error*	*t Stat*	*P-value*	*Lower 95%*	*Upper 95%*
30	Intercept	60	9.2260	6.50	0.000	38.72	81.28
31	X Variable 1	5	0.5803	8.62	0.000	3.66	6.34

FIGURE 14.24 Excel Spreadsheet Solution to the Armand's Pizza Parlors Problem

the t test show that the relationship is significant. Finally, the Lower 95% and Upper 95% cells provide the 95% confidence interval estimates for the regression model parameters β_0 and β_1. For example, we can be 95% confident that β_0 is between 38.72 and 81.28 and 95% confident that β_1 is between 3.66 and 6.34.

15

MULTIPLE REGRESSION

STATISTICS IN PRACTICE ● ● ● ● ● ● ● ● ● ● ● ● ● ● ● ● ● ●

Champion International Corporation*

Stamford, Connecticut

Champion International Corporation is one of the largest forest product companies in the world, with more than three million acres of timberlands in the United States. It produces building materials, such as lumber and plywood, white paper products, such as printing and writing grades of white paper, and brown paper products, such as liner-board and corrugated containers. To make these paper products, Champion's pulp mills process wood chips and chemicals to produce wood pulp. The wood pulp is then used at a paper mill to produce paper products.

In the production of white paper products, the pulp must be bleached to remove any discoloration. A key bleaching agent used in the process is chlorine dioxide, which, because of its combustible nature, is usually produced at Champion pulp mill facilities and then piped in solution form into the bleaching tower of the pulp mill. To improve one of the processes that Champion uses to produce chlorine dioxide, a study was undertaken to look at process control and efficiency. One of the aspects studied was the chemical-feed rate for chlorine dioxide production.

To produce the chlorine dioxide, four chemicals flow at metered rates into the chlorine dioxide generator. The chlorine dioxide produced in the generator flows to an absorber where chilled water absorbs the chlorine dioxide gas to form a chlorine dioxide solution. The solution is then piped into the paper mill. A key part of controlling the process involves the chemical-feed rates. Historically, the chemical-feed rates were simply set by experienced operators; this approach, however, led to overcontrol by

the operators. Consequently, chemical engineers at the millrequested that a set of control equations, one for each chemical feed, be developed to aid the operators in setting the rates.

Using multiple regression analysis, statistical analysts at Champion were able to develop a multiple regression equation for each of the four chemicals used in the process. Each equation related the production of chlorine dioxide to the amount of chemical used and the concentration level of the chlorine dioxide solution. The resulting set of four equations was programmed into a microcomputer at each mill. In the new system, operators enter the concentration of the chlorine dioxide solution and the desired production rate; the computer software then calculates the chemical feed needed to achieve the desired production rate. Since the operators have begun using the control equations, the chlorine dioxide generator efficiency has increased, and the number of times the concentrations have been within acceptable ranges has increased significantly.

Champion used multiple regression analysis to develop its control equations. In this chapter we will discuss how statistical computer packages such as Minitab are used for such purposes. Most of the concepts introduced in Chapter 14 for simple linear regression can be directly extended to the multiple regression case.

Logs are the raw material for Champion International's lumber, paper, and container products.

---

*The authors are indebted to Marian Williams and Bill Griggs of Champion International Corporation for providing this Statistics in Practice.

● In Chapter 14 we presented simple linear regression and demonstrated its use in developing an equation that describes the relationship between two variables. Recall that the variable being predicted or explained by the equation is called the dependent variable and the variable being used to predict or explain the dependent variable is called the independent variable. In this chapter we continue our study of regression analysis by considering situations involving two or more independent variables. This subject area is called *multiple regression analysis.* It enables us to consider more factors and thus obtain better estimates than are possible with simple linear regression.

15.1 THE MULTIPLE REGRESSION MODEL

Multiple regression analysis is the study of how a dependent variable y is related to two or more independent variables. In the general case, we will use p to denote the number of independent variables.

THE REGRESSION MODEL AND THE REGRESSION EQUATION

The concepts of a regression model and a regression equation introduced in the preceding chapter are applicable in the multiple regression case. The equation that describes how the dependent variable y is related to the independent variables $x_1, x_2, \ldots x_p$ and an error term is called the *regression model.* We begin with the assumption that the multiple regression model has the following form.

MULTIPLE REGRESSION MODEL

$$y = \beta_0 + \beta_1 x_1 + \beta_2 x_2 + \ldots + \beta_p x_p + \epsilon \qquad (15.1)$$

In the multiple regression model, β_0, β_1, $\beta_2 \ldots \beta_p$ are the parameters and ϵ (the Greek letter epsilon) is a random variable. A close examination of this model reveals that y is a linear function of $x_1, x_2, \ldots x_p$ (the $\beta_0 + \beta_1 x_1 + \beta_2 x_2 + \ldots + \beta_p x_p$ part) plus ϵ. The random variable ϵ is an error term that accounts for the variability in y which cannot be explained by the linear effect of the p independent variables.

In Section 15.4 we will discuss all of the assumptions for the multiple regression model and ϵ. One of the assumptions is that the mean or expected value of ϵ is zero. A consequence of this assumption is that the mean or expected value of y, denoted $E(y)$, is equal to $\beta_0 + \beta_1 x_1 + \beta_2 x_2 + \ldots + \beta_p x_p$. The equation that describes how the mean value of y is related to $x_1, x_2, \ldots x_p$ is called the *multiple regression equation.*

MULTIPLE REGRESSION EQUATION

$$E(y) = \beta_0 + \beta_1 x_1 + \beta_2 x_2 + \ldots + \beta_p x_p \qquad (15.2)$$

THE ESTIMATED MULTIPLE REGRESSION EQUATION

If the values of β_0, β_1, $\beta_2 \ldots \beta_p$ were known, (15.2) could be used to compute the mean value of y at given values of $x_1, x_2, \ldots x_p$. Unfortunately, these parameter values will not, in general, be known and must be estimated from sample data. A simple random sample

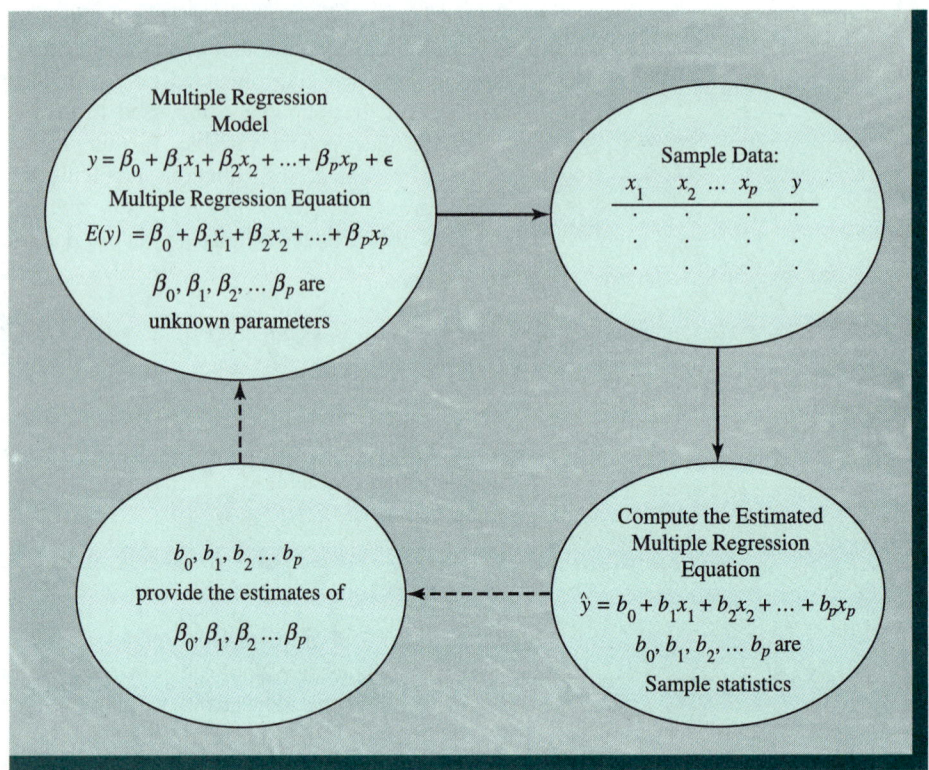

FIGURE 15.1   The Estimation Process for Multiple Regression

is used to compute sample statistics b_0, b_1, b_2, ... b_p that are used as the point estimators of the parameters β_0, β_1, β_2 ... β_p. These sample statistics provide the following estimated multiple regression equation.

ESTIMATED MULTIPLE REGRESSION EQUATION

$$\hat{y} = b_0 + b_1x_1 + b_2x_2 + ... + b_px_p \qquad \textbf{(15.3)}$$

where

$$b_0, b_1, b_2, ... b_p \text{ are the estimates of } \beta_0, \beta_1, \beta_2 ... \beta_p$$

$$\hat{y} = \text{estimated value of the dependent variable}$$

The estimation process for multiple regression is shown in Figure 15.1.

15.2   THE LEAST SQUARES METHOD

In Chapter 14, we used the least squares method to develop the estimated regression equation that best approximated the straight-line relationship between the dependent and independent variables. This same approach is used to develop the estimated multiple regression equation. The least squares criterion is restated as follows.

> ### LEAST SQUARES CRITERION
>
> $$\min \Sigma \, (y_i - \hat{y}_i)^2 \qquad\qquad \text{(15.4)}$$
>
> where
>
> y_i = observed value of the dependent variable for the ith observation
>
> $\hat{y}_i$ = estimated value of the dependent variable for the ith observation

The estimated values of the dependent variable are computed by using the estimated multiple regression equation,

$$\hat{y} = b_0 + b_1x_1 + b_2x_2 + \ldots + b_px_p$$

As (15.4) shows, the least squares method uses sample data to provide the values of b_0, $b_1, b_2, \ldots b_p$ that make the sum of squared residuals [the deviations between the observed values of the dependent variable (y_i) and the estimated values of the dependent variable ($\hat{y}_i$)] a minimum.

In Chapter 14 we presented formulas for computing the least squares estimators b_0 and b_1 for the estimated simple linear regression equation $\hat{y} = b_0 + b_1x$. With relatively small data sets, we were able to use those formulas to compute b_0 and b_1 by manual calculations. In multiple regression, however, the presentation of the formulas for the regression coefficients $b_0, b_1, b_2, \ldots b_p$ involves the use of matrix algebra and is beyond the scope of this text.* Therefore, in presenting multiple regression, we will focus on how computer software packages can be used to obtain the estimated regression equation and other information. The emphasis will be on how to interpret the computer output rather than on how to make the multiple regression computations.

AN EXAMPLE: BUTLER TRUCKING COMPANY

As an illustration of multiple regression analysis, we will consider a problem faced by the Butler Trucking Company, an independent trucking company in southern California. A major portion of Butler's business involves deliveries throughout its local area. To develop better work schedules, the managers want to estimate the total daily travel time for their drivers.

Initially the managers believed that the total daily travel time would be closely related to the number of miles traveled in making the daily deliveries. A simple random sample of 10 driving assignments provided the data shown in Table 15.1 and the scatter diagram shown in Figure 15.2. After reviewing this scatter diagram, the managers hypothesized that the simple linear regression model $y = \beta_0 + \beta_1x_1 + \epsilon$ could be used to describe the relationship between the total travel time (y) and the number of miles traveled (x_1). To estimate the parameters β_0 and β_1, the least squares method was used to develop the estimated regression equation,

$$\hat{y} = b_0 + b_1x_1 \qquad\qquad \text{(15.5)}$$

In Figure 15.3, we show the Minitab computer output from applying simple linear regression to the data in Table 15.1. The estimated regression equation is

---

*In the appendix to the chapter we show how to compute b_0, b_1, and b_2 algebraically when there are two independent variables.

TABLE 15.1 Preliminary Data for Butler Trucking

Driving Assignment	x_1 = Miles Traveled	y = Travel Time (hours)
1	100	9.3
2	50	4.8
3	100	8.9
4	100	6.5
5	50	4.2
6	80	6.2
7	75	7.4
8	65	6.0
9	90	7.6
10	90	6.1

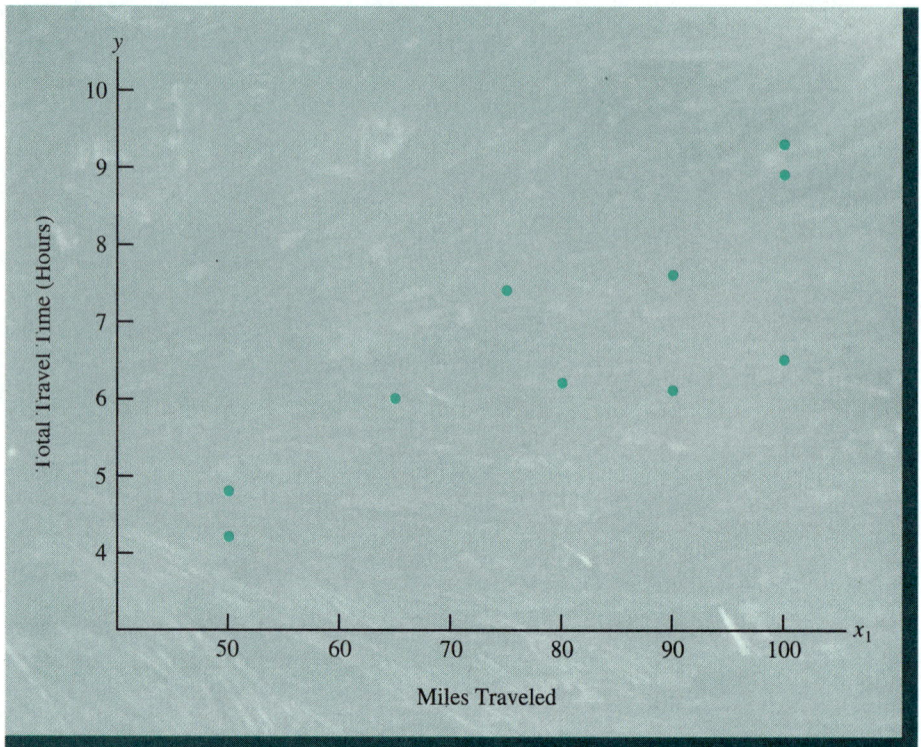

FIGURE 15.2 Scatter Diagram of Preliminary Data for Butler Trucking

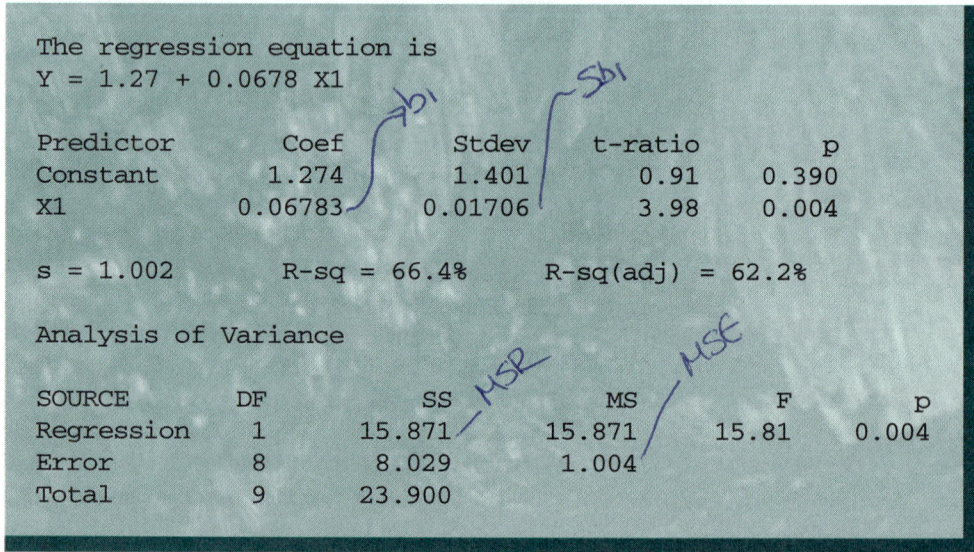

FIGURE 15.3 Minitab Output for Butler Trucking with One Independent Variable

$$\hat{y} = 1.27 + .0678x_1$$

At the .05 level of significance, the F value of 15.81 and its corresponding p-value of .004 indicate that the relationship is significant; that is, we can reject H_0: $\beta_1 = 0$ since the p-value is less than $\alpha = .05$. Note that the same conclusion is obtained from the t value of 3.98 and its associated p-value of .004. Thus, we can conclude that the

TABLE 15.2 Data for Butler Trucking with Miles Traveled (x_1) and Number of Deliveries (x_2) as the Independent Variables

Driving Assignment	x_1 = Miles Traveled	x_2 = Number of Deliveries	y = Travel Time (hours)
1	100	4	9.3
2	50	3	4.8
3	100	4	8.9
4	100	2	6.5
5	50	2	4.2
6	80	2	6.2
7	75	3	7.4
8	65	4	6.0
9	90	3	7.6
10	90	2	6.1

BUTLER

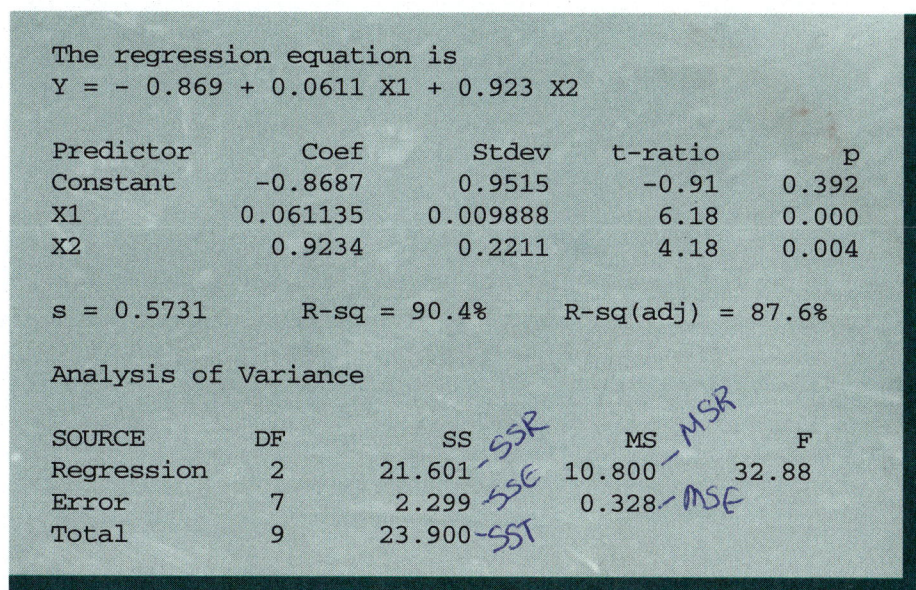

```
The regression equation is
Y = - 0.869 + 0.0611 X1 + 0.923 X2

Predictor        Coef        Stdev      t-ratio          p
Constant      -0.8687      0.9515        -0.91      0.392
X1           0.061135    0.009888         6.18      0.000
X2             0.9234      0.2211         4.18      0.004

s = 0.5731      R-sq = 90.4%      R-sq(adj) = 87.6%

Analysis of Variance

SOURCE        DF          SS              MS            F
Regression     2      21.601         10.800        32.88
Error          7       2.299          0.328
Total          9      23.900
```

FIGURE 15.4 Minitab Output for Butler Trucking with Two Independent Variables

relationship between the total travel time and the number of miles traveled is significant; longer travel times are associated with more miles traveled. With a coefficient of determination (expressed as a percentage) of R-sq = 66.4%, we see that 66.4% of the variability in travel time can be explained by the linear effect of the number of miles traveled. This finding is fairly good, but the managers might want to consider adding a second independent variable to explain some of the remaining variability in the dependent variable.

In attempting to identify another independent variable, the managers felt that the number of deliveries could also contribute to the total travel time. The Butler Trucking data, with the number of deliveries added, are shown in Table 15.2. The Minitab computer solution with both miles traveled (x_1) and number of deliveries (x_2) as independent variables is shown in Figure 15.4. The estimated regression equation is

$$\hat{y} = -.869 + .0611x_1 + .923x_2 \qquad (15.6)$$

In the next section we will discuss the use of the coefficient of multiple determination in measuring how good a fit is provided by this estimated regression equation. Before doing so, let us examine more carefully the values of $b_1 = .0611$ and $b_2 = .923$ in (15.6).

A NOTE ON INTERPRETATION OF COEFFICIENTS

One observation can be made at this point about the relationship between the estimated regression equation with only the miles traveled as an independent variable and the equation that includes the number of deliveries as a second independent variable. The value of b_1 is not the same in both cases. In simple linear regression, we interpret b_1 as the amount of change in y for a one-unit change in the independent variable. In multiple regression analysis, this interpretation must be modified somewhat. That is, in multiple regression analysis, we interpret each regression coefficient as follows: b_i represents an estimate of the change in y corresponding to a one-unit change in x_i when all other independent variables are held constant. In the Butler Trucking example involving two independent variables, $b_1 = .0611$. Thus, .0611 hours is an estimate of the expected increase in travel time corresponding to an increase of one mile in the distance traveled when the number of deliveries is held constant. Similarly, since $b_2 = .923$, an estimate of the expected increase in travel time corresponding to an increase of one delivery when the number of miles traveled is held constant is .923 hours.

EXERCISES

Note to student: The exercises involving data in this and subsequent sections were designed to be solved by means of a computer software package.

METHODS

1. The estimated regression equation for a model involving two independent variables and 10 observations follows.

$$\hat{y} = 29.1270 + .5906x_1 + .4980x_2$$

a. Interpret b_1 and b_2 in this estimated regression equation.
b. Estimate y when $x_1 = 180$ and $x_2 = 310$.

Self-Test

2. Consider the following data for a dependent variable y and two independent variables, x_1 and x_2.

x_1	x_2	y
30	12	94
47	10	108
25	17	112
51	16	178
40	5	94
51	19	175
74	7	170
36	12	117
59	13	142
76	16	211

a. Using these data, develop an estimated regression equation relating y to x_1. Estimate y if $x_1 = 45$.

b. Using these data, develop an estimated regression equation relating y to x_2. Estimate y if $x_2 = 15$.

c. Using these data, develop an estimated regression equation relating y to x_1 and x_2. Estimate y if $x_1 = 45$ and $x_2 = 15$.

3. In a regression analysis involving 30 observations, the following estimated regression equation was obtained.

$$\hat{y} = 17.6 + 3.8x_1 - 2.3x_2 + 7.6x_3 + 2.7x_4$$

a. Interpret b_1, b_2, b_3, and b_4 in this estimated regression equation.

b. Estimate y when $x_1 = 10$, $x_2 = 5$, $x_3 = 1$, and $x_4 = 2$.

APPLICATIONS

4. A shoe store has developed the following estimated regression equation relating sales to inventory investment and advertising expenditures.

$$\hat{y} = 25 + 10x_1 + 8x_2$$

where

$$x_1 = \text{inventory investment (\$1000s)}$$

$$x_2 = \text{advertising expenditures (\$1000s)}$$

$$y = \text{sales (\$1000s)}$$

a. Estimate sales if there is a \$15,000 investment in inventory and an advertising budget of \$10,000.

b. Interpret b_1 and b_2 in this estimated regression equation.

5. The owner of Showtime Movie Theaters, Inc., would like to estimate weekly gross revenue as a function of advertising expenditures. Historical data for a sample of eight weeks follow.

Weekly Gross Revenue ($1000s)	Television Advertising ($1000s)	Newspaper Advertising ($1000s)
96	5.0	1.5
90	2.0	2.0
95	4.0	1.5
92	2.5	2.5
95	3.0	3.3
94	3.5	2.3
94	2.5	4.2
94	3.0	2.5

a. Develop an estimated regression equation with the amount of television advertising as the independent variable.

b. Develop an estimated regression equation with both television advertising and newspaper advertising as the independent variables.

c. Is the estimated regression equation coefficient for television advertising expenditures the same in part (a) and in part (b)? Interpret the coefficient in each case.

d. What is the estimate of the gross revenue for a week when \$3500 is spent on television advertising and \$1800 is spent on newspaper advertising?

6. The following table reports the horsepower, time required to go from zero to 60 miles per hour, and price in thousands of dollars for 10 popular sports cars (*Road & Track*, October 1994).

AUTO1

Sports Car	Horsepower	Zero to 60 mph (Seconds)	Price ($1000s)
BMW M3	240	6.0	38.4
Corvette	300	5.7	41.4
Dodge Viper	400	4.8	54.8
Ford Mustang	240	6.9	25.8
Honda Prelude	190	7.1	25.6
Mitsubishi 3000GT	320	5.7	43.7
Toyota Supra	320	5.3	48.2
Nissan 300ZX	300	6.0	40.8
Alfa Romeo	320	7.6	38.1
Mazda RX-7	255	5.5	35.0

a. Use horsepower as the independent variable and price as the dependent variable. What is the estimated regression equation?
b. Use horsepower and zero to 60 as two independent variables and price as the dependent variable. What is the estimated regression equation?
c. If your goal is to estimate the price of a sports car, do you prefer simple linear regression in part (a) or the multiple regression in part (b)? Discuss.
d. A new sports car has been advertised as having a horsepower of 236 and being able to go from zero to 60 in 5.9 seconds. Use your regression analysis to estimate the price of this new sports car.

7. Heller Company manufactures lawnmowers and related lawn equipment. The managers believe the quantity of lawnmowers sold depends on the price of the mower and the price of a competitor's mower. Let

$$y = \text{quantity sold (1000s)},$$
$$x_1 = \text{price of competitor's mower (\$), and}$$
$$x_2 = \text{price of Heller's mower (\$)}.$$

The managers want an estimated regression equation that relates quantity sold to the prices of the Heller mower and the competitor's mower. The following table lists prices in 10 cities.

MOWER

Competitor's Price (x_1)	Heller's Price (x_2)	Quantity Sold (y)
120	100	102
140	110	100
190	90	120
130	150	77
155	210	46
175	150	93
125	250	26
145	270	69
180	300	65
150	250	85

a. Determine the estimated regression equation that can be used to predict the quantity sold given the competitor's price and Heller's price.
b. Interpret b_1 and b_2.

c. Predict the quantity sold in a city where Heller prices its mower at $160 and the competitor prices its mower at $170.

8. The following table gives the value of prescriptions sold (in $1000s) by 13 pharmacies in Iowa, the population of the city served by the given pharmacy, and the average prescription inventory value. ("The Use of Categorical Variables in Data Envelopment Analysis," R. Banker and R. Morey, *Management Science,* December 1986).

PHARMACY

Value ($1000s)	Population	Average Inventory Value ($)
61	1,410	8,000
92	1,523	9,000
93	1,354	13,694
45	822	4,250
50	746	6,500
29	1,281	7,000
56	1,016	4,500
45	1,070	5,000
183	1,694	27,000
156	1,910	21,560
120	1,745	15,000
75	1,353	8,500
122	1,016	18,000

a. Determine the estimated regression equation that can be used to predict the dollar value of prescriptions y given the population size x_1 and the average inventory value x_2.

b. What other variables do you think might be useful in predicting y?

9. Two experts provided subjective lists of school districts that they think are among the best in the country. For each school district the average class size, the combined SAT score, and the percentage of students who attended a 4-year college were provided (*The Wall Street Journal*, March 31, 1989).

SCHOOLS1

District	Average Class Size	Combined SAT Score	% Attend 4-Year College
Blue Springs, Mo.	25	1083	74
Garden City, N.Y.	18	997	77
Indianapolis, Ind.	30	716	40
Newport Beach, Calif.	26	977	51
Novi, Mich.	20	980	53
Piedmont, Calif.	28	1042	75
Pittsburg, Pa.	21	983	66
Scarsdale, N.Y.	20	1110	87
Wayne, Pa.	22	1040	85
Weston, Mass.	21	1031	89
Farmingdale, N.Y.	22	947	81
Mamaroneck, N.Y.	20	1000	69
Mayfield, Ohio	24	1003	48
Morristown, N.J.	22	972	64
New Rochelle, N.Y.	23	1039	55
Newtown Square, Pa.	17	963	79
Omaha, Neb.	23	1059	81
Shaker Heights, Ohio	23	940	82

a. Using these data, develop an estimated regression equation relating the percentage of students that attend a 4-year college to the average class size and the combined SAT score.

b. Estimate the percentage of students that attend a 4-year college if the average class size is 20 and the combined SAT score is 1000.

10. Data on housing markets were provided for 100 cities in the United States (*U.S. News & World Report,* April 6, 1992). The following table reports the median cost of a new home, the number of new housing starts during 1991–1992, and the average household income for a sample of 16 cities. All data are in 1000s.

HOUSING

City	Median Cost	Housing Starts	Household Income	City	Median Cost	Housing Starts	Household Income
Chicago	181.8	12.9	$61.0	West Palm Beach	130.4	8.9	$58.1
Dayton	107.8	3.8	48.4	San Antonio	72.5	1.5	57.0
Atlanta	100.6	24.2	54.7	Pittsburgh	79.5	4.9	49.2
Oklahoma City	68.9	3.3	53.2	Jacksonville	82.1	8.0	47.5
Columbia	90.3	3.1	57.4	Cleveland	122.9	5.4	54.0
Tacoma	96.1	4.1	51.1	Gary	98.2	3.2	45.7
Mobile	68.5	1.0	41.0	Scranton	81.6	2.5	44.8
Baltimore	121.8	11.1	62.8	Richmond	102.8	6.0	64.5

a. Using these data, develop the estimated regression equation relating cost to the number of housing starts and the household income.

b. Estimate the median cost for a city with 8000 housing starts and an average household income of $50,000.

15.3   THE MULTIPLE COEFFICIENT OF DETERMINATION

In Chapter 14, we used the coefficient of determination to measure the goodness of fit for the estimated regression equation. The same concept applies to multiple regression. The term *multiple coefficient of determination* indicates that we are measuring the goodness of fit for the estimated multiple regression equation.

In simple linear regression we showed that the total sum of squares can be partitioned into two components: the sum of squares due to regression and the sum of squares due to error. The same procedure applies to the sum of squares in multiple regression.

RELATIONSHIP AMONG SST, SSR, AND SSE

$$\text{SST} = \text{SSR} + \text{SSE} \tag{15.7}$$

where

$$\text{SST} = \text{total sum of squares} = \Sigma(y_i - \bar{y})^2$$

$$\text{SSR} = \text{sum of squares due to regression} = \Sigma(\hat{y}_i - \bar{y})^2$$

$$\text{SSE} = \text{sum of squares due to error} = \Sigma(y_i - \hat{y}_i)^2$$

Because of the computational difficulty in computing the three sums of squares, we rely on computer packages to determine those values. The analysis of variance part of the Minitab output in Figure 15.4 shows the three values for the Butler Trucking problem with two independent variables: SST = 23.900, SSR = 21.601, and SSE = 2.229. With only one independent variable (number of miles traveled), the Minitab output in Figure 15.3 shows that SST = 23.900, SSR = 15.871, and SSE = 8.029. The value of SST is the same in both cases since it does not depend on $\hat{y}$, but SSR increases and SSE decreases when a second independent variable (number of deliveries) is added. The implication is that the estimated multiple regression equation provides a better fit for the observed data.

The multiple coefficient of determination, denoted R^2, is computed by the same formula as that used for the coefficient of determination in simple linear regression.

MULTIPLE COEFFICIENT OF DETERMINATION

$$R^2 = \frac{\text{SSR}}{\text{SST}} \qquad (15.8)$$

The multiple coefficient of determination can be interpreted as the proportion of the variability in the dependent variable that can be explained by the estimated multiple regression equation. Hence, when multiplied by 100, it can be interpreted as the percentage of variation in y that can be explained by the estimated regression equation.

In the two-independent-variable Butler Trucking example, with SSR = 21.601 and SST = 23.900, we have

$$R^2 = \frac{21.601}{23.900} = .904$$

Therefore, 90.4% of the variability in travel time y is explained by the estimated multiple regression equation with miles traveled and number of deliveries as the independent variables. In Figure 15.4, we see that the multiple coefficient of determination is also provided by the Minitab output; it is denoted by R-sq = 90.4%.

Figure 15.3 shows that the R-sq value for the estimated regression equation with only one independent variable, number of miles traveled (x_1), is 66.4%. Thus, the percentage of the variability in travel times that is explained by the estimated regression equation increases from 66.4% to 90.4% when number of deliveries is added as a second independent variable. In general, R^2 always increases as independent variables are added to the model. Adding independent variables causes the prediction errors to become smaller, thus reducing the sum of squares due to error SSE. Since SSR = SST − SSE, when SSE becomes smaller, SSR becomes larger, causing R^2 = SSR/SST to increase.

Many analysts prefer adjusting R^2 for the number of independent variables to avoid overestimating the impact of adding an independent variable on the amount of variability explained by the estimated regression equation. With n denoting the number of observations and p denoting the number of independent variables, the *adjusted multiple coefficient of determination* is computed as follows.

ADJUSTED MULTIPLE COEFFICIENT OF DETERMINATION

$$R_a^2 = 1 - (1 - R^2)\frac{n - 1}{n - p - 1} \qquad (15.9)$$

For the Butler Trucking example with $n = 10$ and $p = 2$, we have

$$R_a^2 = 1 - (1 - .904)\frac{10 - 1}{10 - 2 - 1} = .88$$

Thus, after adjusting for the two independent variables, we have an adjusted multiple coefficient of determination of .88. This value is provided by the Minitab output in Figure 15.4 as R-sq(adj) = 87.6%; the value we calculated differs because we used a rounded value of R^2 in the calculation.

NOTES AND COMMENTS

If the value of R^2 is small and the model contains a large number of independent variables, the adjusted coefficient of determination can take a negative value; in such cases, Minitab sets the adjusted coefficient of determination to zero.

EXERCISES

METHODS

11. In Exercise 1, the following estimated regression equation based on 10 observations was presented.

$$\hat{y} = 29.1270 + .5906x_1 + .4980x_2$$

The values of SST and SSR are 6,724.125 and 6,216.375, respectively.
a. Find SSE.   b. Compute R^2.   c. Compute R_a^2.
d. Comment on the goodness of fit.

Self-Test

12. In Exercise 2, 10 observations were provided for a dependent variable y and two independent variables x_1 and x_2; for these data SST = 15,182.9, and SSR = 14,052.2.
a. Compute R^2.   b. Compute R_a^2.
c. Does the estimated regression equation explain a large amount of the variability in the data? Explain.

13. In Exercise 3, the following estimated regression equation based on 30 observations was presented.

$$\hat{y} = 17.6 + 3.8x_1 - 2.3x_2 + 7.6x_3 + 2.7x_4$$

The values of SST and SSR are 1805 and 1760, respectively.
a. Compute R^2.   b. Compute R_a^2.   c. Comment on the goodness of fit.

APPLICATIONS

14. In Exercise 4, the following estimated regression equation relating sales to inventory investment and advertising expenditures was given.

$$\hat{y} = 25 + 10x_1 + 8x_2$$

The data used to develop the model came from a survey of 10 stores; for those data, SST = 16,000 and SSR = 12,000.

a. For the estimated regression equation given, compute R^2.

b. Compute R_a^2.

c. Does the model appear to explain a large amount of variability in the data? Explain.

Self-Test
▶

15. In Exercise 5, the owner of Showtime Movie Theaters, Inc., used multiple regression analysis to predict gross revenue (y) as a function of television advertising (x_1) and newspaper advertising (x_2). The estimated regression equation was

$$\hat{y} = 83.2 + 2.29x_1 + 1.30x_2$$

The computer solution provided SST = 25.5 and SSR = 23.435.

a. Compute and interpret R^2 and R_a^2.

b. When television advertising was the only independent variable, $R^2 = .653$ and $R_a^2 = 59.5\%$. Do you prefer the multiple regression results? Explain.

16. In Exercise 6, data were given on horsepower (x_1), time to go from zero to 60 miles per hour (x_2), and price in thousands of dollars (y) for 10 popular sports cars (*Road & Track*, October 1994). When horsepower was the only independent variable, $R^2 = .821$ and $R_a^2 = .799$. When both independent variables were used, the estimated regression equation was

$$\hat{y} = 31 + .108x_1 - 3.8x_2$$

The computer solution provided SST = 736.02 and SSR = 674.34.

a. Compute and interpret R^2 and R_a^2.

b. Discuss the benefits of using the multiple regression results.

17. In Exercise 9, an estimated regression equation was developed relating the percentage of students that attend a 4-year college to the average class size and the combined SAT score.

a. Compute and interpret R^2 and R_a^2.

b. Does the estimated regression equation provide a good fit to the data? Explain.

18. Refer to Exercise 10, where data were reported on median cost of a new home, number of new housing starts, and average household income for a sample of 16 cities (*U.S. News & World Report,* April 6, 1992).

a. Use a computer solution for the multiple regression prediction of the median cost of a new home. What are the values of R^2 and R_a^2?

b. Does the estimated regression equation provide a good fit to the data? Explain.

15.4 MODEL ASSUMPTIONS

In Section 15.1 we introduced the following multiple regression model.

MULTIPLE REGRESSION MODEL

$$y = \beta_0 + \beta_1 x_1 + \beta_2 x_2 + \ldots + \beta_p x_p + \epsilon \tag{15.10}$$

The assumptions about the error term ϵ in the multiple regression model parallel those for the simple linear regression model.

ASSUMPTIONS ABOUT THE ERROR TERM ϵ IN THE REGRESSION MODEL $y = \beta_0 + \beta_1 x_1 + \cdots + \beta_p x_p + \epsilon$

1. The error ϵ is a random variable with mean or expected value of zero; that is, $E(\epsilon) = 0$.

   Implication: For given values of $x_1, x_2, \ldots, x_p$, the expected, or average, value of y is given by

   $$E(y) = \beta_0 + \beta_1 x_1 + \beta_2 x_2 + \cdots + \beta_p x_p. \tag{15.11}$$

   Equation (15.11) is the *multiple regression equation* we introduced in Section 15.1. In this equation, $E(y)$ represents the average of all possible values of y that might occur for the given values of $x_1, x_2, \ldots, x_p$.

2. The variance of ϵ is denoted by σ^2 and is the same for all values of the independent variables $x_1, x_2, \ldots, x_p$.

   Implication: The variance of y equals σ^2 and is the same for all values of $x_1, x_2, \ldots, x_p$.

3. The values of ϵ are independent.

   Implication: The size of the error for a particular set of values for the independent variables is not related to the size of the error for any other set of values.

4. The error ϵ is a normally distributed random variable reflecting the deviation between the y value and the expected value of y given by $\beta_0 + \beta_1 x_1 + \beta_2 x_2 + \cdots + \beta_p x_p$.

   Implication: Since $\beta_0, \beta_1, \ldots, \beta_p$ are constants, for the given values of $x_1, x_2, \ldots, x_p$, the dependent variable y is also a normally distributed random variable.

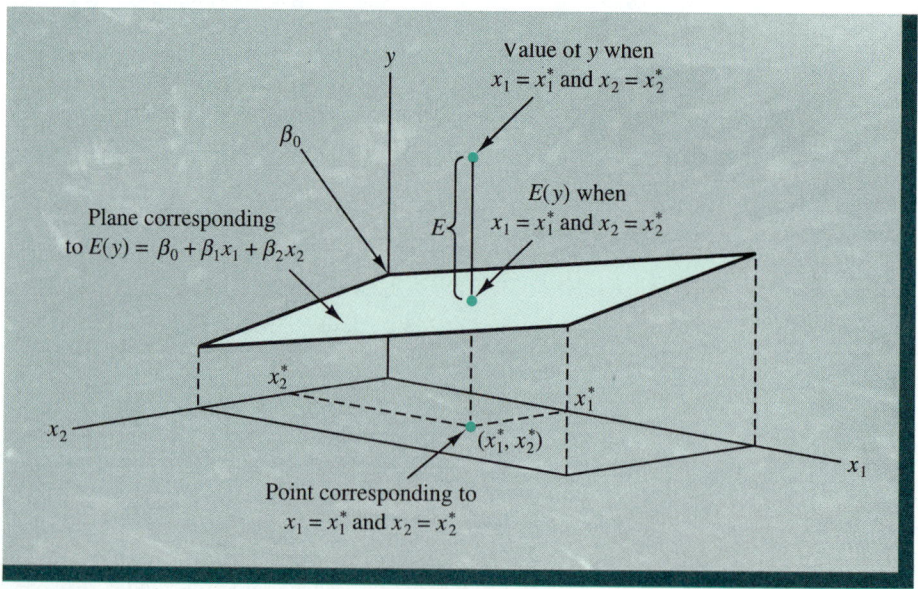

FIGURE 15.5 Graph of the Regression Equation for Multiple Regression Analysis with Two Independent Variables

To obtain more insight about the form of the relationship given by (15.11), consider the following two-independent-variable multiple regression equation.

$$E(y) = \beta_0 + \beta_1 x_1 + \beta_2 x_2$$

The graph of this equation is a plane in three-dimensional space. Figure 15.5 is such a graph with x_1 and x_2 on the horizontal axis and y on the vertical axis. Note that ϵ is shown as the difference between the actual y value and the expected value of y, $E(y)$, when $x_1 = x_1^*$ and $x_2 = x_2^*$.

In regression analysis, the term *response variable* is often used in place of the term *dependent variable*. Furthermore, since the multiple regression equation generates a plane or surface, its graph is called a response surface.

15.5 TESTING FOR SIGNIFICANCE

In this section we show how to conduct significance tests for a multiple regression relationship. The significance tests we used in simple linear regression were a t test and an F test. In simple linear regression, both tests provide the same conclusion; that is, if the null hypothesis is rejected, we conclude that $\beta_1 \neq 0$. In multiple regression, the t test and the F test have different purposes.

1. The F test is used to determine whether there is a significant relationship between the dependent variable and the set of all the independent variables; we will refer to the F test as the test for *overall significance*.
2. If the F test shows an overall significance, the t test is used to determine whether each of the individual independent variables is significant. A separate t test is conducted for each of the independent variables in the model; we refer to each of these t tests as a test for *individual significance*.

In the material that follows, we will explain the F test and the t test and apply each to the Butler Trucking Company example.

F TEST

The multiple regression model as defined in Section 15.4 is

$$y = \beta_0 + \beta_1 x_1 + \beta_2 x_2 + ... + \beta_p x_p + \epsilon$$

The hypotheses for the F test involve the parameters of the multiple regression model.

H_0: $\beta_1 = \beta_2 = ... = \beta_p = 0$

H_a: One or more of the parameters is not equal to zero

If H_0 is rejected, we have sufficient statistical evidence to conclude that one or more of the parameters is not equal to zero and that the overall relationship between y and the set of independent variables $x_1, x_2, ... x_p$ is significant. However, if H_0 cannot be rejected, we do not have sufficient evidence to conclude that a significant relationship is present.

Before describing the steps of the F test, we need to review the concept of *mean square*. A mean square is a sum of squares divided by its corresponding degrees of freedom. In the multiple regression case, the total sum of squares has $n - 1$ degrees of freedom, the sum of squares due to regression (SSR) has p degrees of freedom, and the sum of squares due to error has $n - p - 1$ degrees of freedom. Hence, the mean square due to regression (MSR) is SSR $/p$ and the mean square due to error (MSE) is SSE $/(n - p - 1)$.

$$\text{MSR} = \frac{\text{SSR}}{p} \qquad (15.12)$$

and

$$\text{MSE} = \frac{\text{SSE}}{n - p - 1} \qquad (15.13)$$

As discussed in Chapter 14, MSE provides an unbiased estimate of σ^2, the variance of the error term ϵ. If $H_0: \beta_1 = \beta_2 = \dots = \beta_p = 0$ is true, MSR also provides an unbiased estimate of σ^2, and the value of MSR/MSE should be close to one. However, if H_0 is false, MSR overestimates σ^2 and the value of MSR/MSE becomes larger. To determine how large the value of MSR/MSE must be to reject H_0, we make use of the fact that if H_0 is true and the assumptions about the multiple regression model are valid, the sampling distribution of MSR/MSE is an F distribution with p degrees of freedom in the numerator and $n - p - 1$ in the denominator. A summary of the F test for significance in multiple regression follows.

F TEST FOR OVERALL SIGNIFICANCE

$H_0: \beta_1 = \beta_2 = \dots = \beta_p = 0$

H_a: One or more of the parameters is not equal to zero

Test Statistic

$$F = \frac{\text{MSR}}{\text{MSE}} \qquad (15.14)$$

Rejection Rule

Reject H_0 if $F > F_\alpha$

where F_α is based on an F distribution with p degrees of freedom in the numerator and $n - p - 1$ degrees of freedom in the denominator.

Let us apply the F test to the Butler Trucking Company multiple regression problem. With two independent variables, the hypotheses are written as follows.

$H_0: \beta_1 = \beta_2 = 0$

$H_a: \beta_1$ and/or β_2 is not equal to zero

Figure 15.6 is the Minitab output for the multiple regression model with miles traveled (x_1) and number of deliveries (x_2) as the two independent variables. In the analysis of variance part of the output, we see that MSR = 10.8 and MSE = .328. Using (15.14), we obtain the test statistic.

$$F = \frac{10.8}{.328} = 32.9$$

```
The regression equation is
Y = 0.869 + 0.0611 X1 + 0.923 X2

Predictor          Coef        Stdev      t-ratio          p
Constant        -0.8687       0.9515       -0.91      0.392
X1             0.061135     0.009888        6.18      0.000
X2               0.9234       0.2211        4.18      0.004

s = 0.5731       R-sq = 90.4%      R-sq(adj) = 87.6%

Analysis of Variance

SOURCE          DF          SS          MS          F          P
Regression       2      21.601      10.800      32.88      0.000
Error            7       2.299       0.328
Total            9      23.900
```

FIGURE 15.6 Minitab Output for Butler Trucking with Two Independent Variables, Miles Traveled (x_1) and Number of Deliveries (x_2)

TABLE 15.3 ANOVA Table for a Multiple Regression Model with p Independent Variables

Source	Sum of Squares	Degrees of Freedom	Mean Square	F
Regression	SSR	p	$MSR = \dfrac{SSR}{p}$	$F = \dfrac{MSR}{MSE}$
Error	SSE	$n - p - 1$	$MSE = \dfrac{SSE}{n - p - 1}$	
Total	SST	$n - 1$		

Note that the F value on the Minitab output is $F = 32.88$; the value we calculated differs because we used rounded values for MSR and MSE in the calculation. With a level of significance $\alpha = .01$, Table 4 of Appendix B shows that with two degrees of freedom in the numerator and seven degrees of freedom in the denominator, $F_{.01} = 9.55$. Since $32.9 > 9.55$, we reject $H_0: \beta_1 = \beta_2 = 0$ and conclude that a significant relationship is present between travel time y and the two independent variables, miles traveled and number of deliveries. The p-value $= 0.000$ in the last column of the analysis of variance table (Figure 15.6) also indicates that we can reject $H_0: \beta_1 = \beta_2 = 0$ since the p-value is less than α.

As noted previously, the mean square error provides an unbiased estimate of σ^2, the variance of the error term ϵ. Referring to Figure 15.6, we see that the estimate of σ^2 is $MSE = .328$. The square root of MSE is the estimate of the standard deviation of the error term. As defined in Section 14.5, this standard deviation is called the standard error of the estimate and is denoted s. Hence, we have $s = \sqrt{MSE} = \sqrt{.328} = .5731$. Note that the value of the standard error of the estimate appears in the Minitab output in Figure 15.6.

Table 15.3 is the general analysis of variance (ANOVA) table that provides the F test results for a multiple regression model. The test statistic F appears in the last column and can be compared to F_α with p degrees of freedom in the numerator and $n - p - 1$ degrees of freedom in the denominator to make the hypothesis test conclusion. By reviewing the Minitab output for Butler Trucking Company in Figure 15.6, we see that Minitab's analysis of variance table contains this information.

t TEST

If the F test has shown that the multiple regression relationship is significant, a t test can be conducted to determine the significance of each of the individual parameters. The t test for individual significance follows.

---

t TEST FOR INDIVIDUAL SIGNIFICANCE

For any parameter β_i

$$H_0: \beta_i = 0$$
$$H_a: \beta_i \neq 0$$

Test Statistic

$$t = \frac{b_i}{s_{b_i}} \tag{15.15}$$

Rejection Rule

Reject H_0 if $t < -t_{\alpha/2}$ or if $t > t_{\alpha/2}$

where $t_{\alpha/2}$ is based on a t distribution with $n - p - 1$ degrees of freedom.

In the test procedure, s_{b_i} is the estimate of the standard deviation of b_i. The value of s_{b_i} will be provided by the computer software package.

Let us conduct the t test for the Butler Trucking regression problem. Refer to the section of Figure 15.6 that shows the Minitab output for the t-ratio calculations. Values of b_1, b_2, s_{b_1}, and s_{b_2} are as follows.

$$b_1 = .061135 \quad s_{b_1} = .009888$$

$$b_2 = .9234 \quad s_{b_2} = .2211$$

Using (15.15), we obtain the test statistic for the hypotheses involving parameters β_1 and β_2.

$$t = .061135/.009888 = 6.18$$

$$t = .9234/.2211 = 4.18$$

Note that both of these t-ratio values are provided by the Minitab output in Figure 15.6. Using $\alpha = .01$ and $n - p - 1 = 10 - 2 - 1 = 7$ degrees of freedom, we can use Table 2 of Appendix B to show $t_{.005} = 3.499$. With $6.18 > 3.499$, we reject $H_0: \beta_1 = 0$. Similarly, with $4.18 > 3.499$, we reject $H_0: \beta_2 = 0$. Note that the p-values of .000 and .004 on the Minitab output also indicate rejection of these hypotheses. Hence, both parameters are statistically significant.

MULTICOLLINEARITY

We have used the term *independent variable* in regression analysis to refer to any variable being used to predict or explain the value of the dependent variable. The term does not mean, however, that the independent variables themselves are independent in any statistical sense. On the contrary, most independent variables in a multiple regression problem are correlated to some degree with one another. For example, in the Butler Trucking example involving the two independent variables x_1 (miles traveled) and x_2 (number of deliveries), we could treat the miles traveled as the dependent variable and the number of deliveries as the independent variable to determine whether those two variables are themselves related. We could then compute the sample correlation coefficient $r_{x_1 x_2}$ to determine the extent to which the variables are related. Doing so yields $r_{x_1 x_2} = .28$. Thus, we find some degree of linear association between the two independent variables. In multiple regression analysis the term *multicollinearity* refers to the correlation among the independent variables.

To provide a better perspective of the potential problems of multicollinearity, let us consider a modification of the Butler Trucking example. Instead of x_2 being the number of deliveries, let x_2 denote the number of gallons of gasoline consumed. Clearly, x_1 (the miles traveled) and x_2 are related; that is, we know that the number of gallons of gasoline used depends on the number of miles traveled. Hence, we would conclude logically that x_1 and x_2 are highly correlated independent variables.

Assume that we obtain the equation $\hat{y} = b_0 + b_1 x_1 + b_2 x_2$ and find that the F test shows the relationship to be significant. Then suppose we conduct a t test on β_1 to determine whether $\beta_1 \neq 0$, and we cannot reject $H_0: \beta_1 = 0$. Does this mean that travel time is not related to miles traveled? Not necessarily. What it probably means is that with x_2 already in the model, x_1 does not make a significant contribution to determining the value of y. This interpretation makes sense in our example, since if we know the amount of gasoline consumed, we do not gain much additional information useful in predicting y by knowing the miles traveled. Similarly, a t test might lead us to conclude $\beta_2 = 0$ on the grounds that, with x_1 in the model, knowledge of the amount of gasoline consumed does not add much.

To summarize, in t tests for the significance of individual parameters, the difficulty caused by multicollinearity is that it is possible to conclude that none of the individual parameters are significantly different from zero when an F test on the overall multiple regression equation indicates a significant relationship. This problem is avoided when there is very little correlation among the independent variables.

Statisticians have developed several tests for determining whether multicollinearity is high enough to cause problems. According to the rule of thumb test, multicollinearity is a potential problem if the absolute value of the sample correlation coefficient exceeds .7 for any two of the independent variables. The other types of tests are more advanced and beyond the scope of this text.

If possible, every attempt should be made to avoid including independent variables that are highly correlated. In practice, however, strict adherence to this policy is rarely possible. The decision maker is warned that when there is reason to believe substantial multicollinearity is present, separating the effects of the individual independent variables on the dependent variable is difficult.

NOTES AND COMMENTS

Ordinarily, multicollinearity does not affect the way in which we perform our regression analysis or interpret the output from a study. However, when multicollinearity is severe—that is, when two or more of the independent variables are highly correlated with one another—we can have difficulty interpreting the results of t tests on the individual parameters. In addition to the type of problem illustrated in this section, severe cases of multicollinearity have been shown to result in least squares estimates that have the wrong sign. That is, in simulated studies where researchers created the underlying regression model and then applied the least squares technique to develop estimates of β_0, β_1, β_2, and so on, it has been shown that under conditions of high multicollinearity the least squares estimates can have a sign opposite that of the parameter being estimated. For example, β_2 might actually be +10 and b_2, its estimate, might turn out to be −2. Thus, little faith can be placed in the individual coefficients if multicollinearity is present to a high degree.

EXERCISES

METHODS

Self-Test

19. In Exercise 1, the following estimated regression equation based on 10 observations was presented.

$$\hat{y} = 29.1270 + .5906x_1 + .4980x_2$$

Here SST = 6,724.125, SSR = 6,216.375, s_{b_1} = .0813, and s_{b_2} = .0567.

a. Compute MSR and MSE.
b. Compute F and perform the appropriate F test. Use $\alpha = .05$.
c. Perform a t test for the significance of β_1. Use $\alpha = .05$.
d. Perform a t test for the significance of β_2. Use $\alpha = .05$.

20. Refer to the data presented in Exercise 2. The estimated regression equation for these data is

$$\hat{y} = -18.4 + 2.01x_1 + 4.74x_2$$

Here SST = 15182.9, SSR = 1405.2, s_{b_1} = .2471, and s_{b_2} = .9484.

a. Test for a significant relationship among x_1, x_2, and y. Use $\alpha = .05$.
b. Is β_1 significant? Use $\alpha = .05$.
c. Is β_2 significant? Use $\alpha = .05$.

21. The following estimated regression equation was developed for a model involving two independent variables.

$$\hat{y} = 40.7 + 8.63x_1 + 2.71x_2$$

After x_2 was dropped from the model, the least squares method was used to obtain an estimated regression equation involving only x_1 as an independent variable.

$$\hat{y} = 42.0 + 9.01x_1$$

a. Give an interpretation of the coefficient of x_1 in both models.
b. Could multicollinearity explain why the coefficient of x_1 differs in the two models? If so, how?

APPLICATIONS

22. In Exercise 4 the following estimated regression equation for relating sales to inventory investment and advertising expenditures was given.

$$\hat{y} = 25 + 10x_1 + 8x_2$$

The data used to develop the model came from a survey of 10 stores; for these data SST = 16,000 and SSR = 12,000.

a. Compute SSE, MSE, and MSR.
b. Use an F test and a .05 level of significance to determine whether there is a relationship among the variables.

 **Self-Test**

23. Refer to Exercise 5.
    a. Use $\alpha = .01$ to test the hypotheses

$$H_0: \beta_1 = \beta_2 = 0$$

$$H_a: \beta_1 \text{ and/or } \beta_2 \text{ is not equal to zero}$$

for the model $y = \beta_0 + \beta_1 x_1 + \beta_2 x_2 + \epsilon$, where

$$x_1 = \text{television advertising (\$1000s) and}$$

$$x_2 = \text{newspaper advertising (\$1000s).}$$

    b. Use $\alpha = .05$ to test the significance of β_1. Should x_1 be dropped from the model?
    c. Use $\alpha = .05$ to test the significance of β_2. Should x_2 be dropped from the model?

24. Refer to the data in exercise 6. With horsepower (x_1) and time to go from zero to 60 miles per hour (x_2) being used to predict the price of a sports car in thousands of dollars (y), the estimated regression equation was

$$\hat{y} = 31 + .108x_1 - 3.8x_2$$

    a. Use the F test to determine the overall significance of the relationship. What is your conclusion at the .05 level of significance?
    b. Use the t test to determine the significance of β_1 and β_2. What is your conclusion at the .05 level of significance?

25. The following data show the price-earnings (P/E) ratio, the net profit margin, and the growth rate for 19 companies listed in "The *Forbes* 500s on Wall Street" (*Forbes*, May 1, 1989).

FORBES1

Firm	P/E Ratio	Profit Margin (%)	Growth Rate (%)
Exxon	11.3	6.5	10
Chevron	10.0	7.0	5
Texaco	9.9	3.9	5
Mobil	9.7	4.3	7
Amoco	10.0	9.8	8
Pfizer	11.9	14.7	12
Bristol Meyers	16.2	13.9	14
Merck	21.0	20.3	16
American Home Products	13.3	16.9	11
Abbott Laboratories	15.5	15.2	18
Eli Lilly	18.9	18.7	11
Upjohn	14.6	12.8	10
Warner-Lambert	16.0	8.7	7
Amdahl	8.4	11.9	4
Digital	10.4	9.8	19
Hewlett-Packard	14.8	8.1	18
NCR	10.1	7.3	6
Unisys	7.0	6.9	6
IBM	11.8	9.2	6

a. Determine the estimated regression equation that can be used to predict the price-earnings ratio given the net profit margin and the growth rate.

b. Use the F test to determine the overall significance of the relationship. What is your conclusion at the .05 level of significance?

c. Use the t test to determine the significance of β_1 and β_2. What is your conclusion at the .05 level of significance?

d. Remove any independent variable that is not significant from the estimated regression equation. What is your recommended estimated regression equation? Compare the R^2 with the value of R^2 from part (a). Discuss the differences.

26. Refer to the data in Exercise 10. The estimated regression equation for these data is

$$\hat{y} = -5.7 + 1.54x_1 + 1.81x_2$$

where

$$\hat{y} = \text{estimated cost,}$$
$$x_1 = \text{number of housing starts, and}$$
$$x_2 = \text{household income.}$$

a. Test for a significant relationship among $x_1, x_2,$ and y. Use $\alpha = .05$.

b. Is β_1 significant? Use $\alpha = .05$.

c. Is β_2 significant? Use $\alpha = .05$.

d. Briefly discuss the results obtained.

15.6   USING THE ESTIMATED REGRESSION EQUATION FOR ESTIMATION AND PREDICTION

The procedures for estimating the mean value of y and predicting an individual value of y in multiple regression are similar to those in regression analysis involving one independent variable. First, recall that in Chapter 14 we showed that the point estimate of the expected value of y for a given value of x was the same as the point estimate of an individual value of y. In both cases, we used $\hat{y} = b_0 + b_1x$ as the point estimate.

In multiple regression we use the same procedure. That is, we substitute the given values of $x_1, x_2, \ldots, x_p$ into the estimated regression equation and use the corresponding value of $\hat{y}$ as the point estimate. Suppose that for the Butler Trucking example we want to use the estimated regression equation involving x_1 (miles traveled) and x_2 (number of deliveries) to develop two estimates:

1. A *confidence interval estimate* of the mean travel time for all trucks that travel 100 miles and make two deliveries.

2. A *prediction interval estimate* of the travel time for *one specific* truck that travels 100 miles and makes two deliveries.

Using the estimated regression equation $\hat{y} = -.869 + .0611x_1 + .923x_2$ with $x_1 = 100$ and $x_2 = 2$, we obtain the following value of $\hat{y}$.

$$\hat{y} = -.869 + .0611(100) + .923(2) = 7.09$$

Hence, the point estimate of travel time in both cases is approximately seven hours.

To develop interval estimates for the mean value of y and for an individual value of y, we use a procedure similar to that for regression analysis involving one independent variable. The formulas required are beyond the scope of the text, but computer packages for multiple regression analysis will often provide confidence intervals once the values

TABLE 15.4 The 95% Confidence and Prediction Interval Estimates for Butler Trucking

Value of x_1	Value of x_2	Confidence Interval		Prediction Interval	
		Lower Limit	Upper Limit	Lower Limit	Upper Limit
50	2	3.146	4.924	2.414	5.656
50	3	4.127	5.789	3.368	6.548
50	4	4.815	6.948	4.157	7.607
100	2	6.258	7.926	5.500	8.683
100	3	7.385	8.645	6.520	9.510
100	4	8.135	9.742	7.362	10.515

of $x_1, x_2 \ldots, x_p$ are specified by the user. In Table 15.4 we show 95% confidence and prediction interval estimates for the Butler Trucking example for selected values of x_1 and x_2; these values were obtained by using Minitab. Note that the interval estimate for an individual value of y is wider than the interval estimate for the expected value of y. This difference simply reflects the fact that for given values of x_1 and x_2 we can estimate the mean travel time for all trucks with more precision than we can predict the travel time for one specific truck.

EXERCISES

METHODS

27. In Exercise 1, the following estimated regression equation based on 10 observations was presented.

$$\hat{y} = 29.1270 + .5906x_1 + .4980x_2$$

   a. Develop a point estimate of the mean value of y when $x_1 = 180$ and $x_2 = 310$.
   b. Develop a point estimate for an individual value of y when $x_1 = 180$ and $x_2 = 310$.

Self-Test ▶ 28. Refer to the data in Exercise 2. The estimated regression equation for those data is

$$\hat{y} = -18.4 + 2.01x_1 + 4.74x_2$$

   a. Develop a 95% confidence interval estimate of the mean value of y when $x_1 = 45$ and $x_2 = 15$.
   b. Develop a 95% prediction interval estimate of y when $x_1 = 45$ and $x_2 = 15$.

Self-Test ▶ 29. In Exercise 5, the owner of Showtime Movie Theaters, Inc., used multiple regression analysis to predict gross revenue (y) as a function of television advertising (x_1) and newspaper advertising (x_2). The estimated regression equation was

$$\hat{y} = 83.2 + 2.29x_1 + 1.30x_2$$

   a. What is the gross revenue expected for a week when \$3500 is spent on television advertising ($x_1 = 3.5$) and \$1800 is spent on newspaper advertising ($x_2 = 1.8$)?
   b. Provide a 95% confidence interval estimate for the mean revenue of all weeks with the expenditures listed in part (a).
   c. Provide a 95% prediction interval estimate for next week's revenue, assuming that the advertising expenditures will be allocated as in part (a).

30. In Exercise 6, data were given on the horsepower (x_1), time to go from zero to 60 miles per hour (x_2), and price in thousands of dollars (y) for 10 popular sports cars (*Road & Track,* October 1994). The estimated regression equation was

$$\hat{y} = 31 + .108x_1 - 3.8x_2$$

   a. Estimate the price of a Dodge Stealth that has a horsepower of 222 and a zero to 60 miles per hour time of 6.4 seconds.
   b. Provide a 95% confidence interval estimate for the mean price of all automobiles with the characteristics listed in part (a).
   c. Provide a 95% prediction interval estimate for the Dodge Stealth described in part (a).

31. In Exercise 9, an estimated regression equation was developed relating the percentage of students that attend a 4-year college to the average class size and the combined SAT score.
   a. Develop a 95% confidence interval estimate of the mean percentage of students that attend a 4-year college for a school district that has an average class size of 25 and whose students have a combined SAT score of 1000.
   b. Suppose that a school district in Conway, South Carolina, has an average class size of 25 and a combined SAT score of 950. Develop a 95% prediction interval estimate of the percentage of students that attend a 4-year college.

15.7 QUALITATIVE INDEPENDENT VARIABLES

Thus far, the examples we have considered have involved quantitative independent variables such as student population, distance traveled, and number of deliveries. In many situations, however, we must work with qualitative independent variables such as gender (male, female), method of payment (cash, credit card, check), and so on. The purpose of this section is to show how qualitative variables are handled in regression analysis. To illustrate the use and interpretation of a qualitative independent variable, we will consider a problem facing the managers of Johnson Filtration, Inc.

AN EXAMPLE: JOHNSON FILTRATION, INC.

Johnson Filtration, Inc., provides maintenance service for water-filtration systems throughout southern Florida. Customers contact Johnson with requests for maintenance service on their water-filtration systems. To estimate the service time and the service cost, Johnson's managers want to predict the repair time necessary for each maintenance request. Hence, repair time in hours is the dependent variable. Repair time is believed to be related to two factors, the number of months since the last maintenance service and the type of repair problem (mechanical or electrical). Data for a sample of 10 service calls are reported in Table 15.5.

Let y denote the repair time in hours and x_1 denote the number of months since the last maintenance service. The regression model that uses only x_1 to predict y is

$$y = \beta_0 + \beta_1 x_1 + \epsilon$$

Using Minitab to develop the estimated regression equation, we obtained the output shown in Figure 15.7. The estimated regression equation is

$$\hat{y} = 2.15 + .304x_1 \qquad \textbf{(15.16)}$$

TABLE 15.5   Data for the Johnson Filtration Example

Service Call	Repair Time in Hours	Months Since Last Service	Type of Repair
1	2.9	2	electrical
2	3.0	6	mechanical
3	4.8	8	electrical
4	1.8	3	mechanical
5	2.9	2	electrical
6	4.9	7	electrical
7	4.2	9	mechanical
8	4.8	8	mechanical
9	4.4	4	electrical
10	4.5	6	electrical

```
The regression equation is
Y = 2.15 + 0.304 X1


Predictor        Coef         Stdev       t-ratio          p
Constant       2.1473        0.6050         3.55      0.008
X1             0.3041        0.1004         3.03      0.016


s = 0.7810      R-sq = 53.4%      R-sq(adj) = 47.6%


Analysis of Variance


SOURCE          DF            SS            MS          F        p
Regression      1         5.5960        5.5960       9.17    0.016
Error           8         4.8800        0.6100
Total           9        10.4760
```

FIGURE 15.7   Minitab Output for Johnson Filtration with Months Since Last Service (x_1) as the Independent Variable

At the .05 level of significance, the p-value of .016 for the t (or F) test indicates that the number of months since the last service is significantly related to repair time. R-sq = 53.4% indicates that x_1 alone explains 53.4% of the variability in repair time.

To incorporate the type of failure into the regression model, we define the following variable.

$$x_2 = \begin{cases} 0 \text{ if the type of repair is mechanical} \\ 1 \text{ if the type of repair is electrical} \end{cases}$$

In regression analysis x_2 is called a *dummy* or *indicator* variable. Using this dummy variable, we can write the multiple regression model as

$$y = \beta_0 + \beta_1 x_1 + \beta_2 x_2 + \epsilon$$

Table 15.6 is the revised data set that includes the values of the dummy variable. Using Minitab and the data in Table 15.6, we can develop estimates of the model parameters. The Minitab output in Figure 15.8 shows that the estimated multiple regression equation is

TABLE 15.6   Data for the Johnson Filtration Example with Type of Repair Indicated by a Dummy Variable ($x_2 = 0$ for mechanical; $x_2 = 1$ for electrical)

Customer	Repair Time in Hours (y)	Months Since Last Service (x_1)	Type of Repair (x_2)
1	2.9	2	1
2	3.0	6	0
3	4.8	8	1
4	1.8	3	0
5	2.9	2	1
6	4.9	7	1
7	4.2	9	0
8	4.8	8	0
9	4.4	4	1
10	4.5	6	1

JOHNSON

```
The regression equation is
Y = 0.930 + 0.388 X1 + 1.26 X2


Predictor        Coef         Stdev      t-ratio          p
Constant       0.9305       0.4670         1.99      0.087
X1            0.38762      0.06257         6.20      0.000
X2             1.2627       0.3141         4.02      0.005


s = 0.4590      R-sq = 85.9%      R-sq(adj) = 81.9%


Analysis of Variance


SOURCE          DF           SS            MS          F          p
Regression       2       9.0009        4.5005      21.36      0.001
Error            7       1.4751        0.2107
Total            9      10.4760
```

FIGURE 15.8   Minitab Output for Johnson Filtration with Months Since Last Service (x_1) and Type of Repair (x_2) as the Independent Variables

$$\hat{y} = .93 + .388x_1 + 1.26x_2 \qquad \text{(15.17)}$$

At the .05 level of significance, the p-value of .001 associated with the F test ($F = 21.36$) indicates that the regression relationship is significant. The t test part of the printout in Figure 15.8 shows that both months since last service (p-value = .000) and type of repair (p-value = .005) are statistically significant. In addition, R-sq = 85.9% and R-sq (adj) = 81.9% indicate that the estimated regression equation does a good job of explaining the variability in repair times. Thus, equation (15.17) should prove helpful in estimating the repair time necessary for the various service calls.

INTERPRETING THE PARAMETERS

The multiple regression equation for the Johnson Filtration example is

$$E(y) = \beta_0 + \beta_1 x_1 + \beta_2 x_2 \qquad \text{(15.18)}$$

To understand how to interpret the parameters β_0, β_1, and β_2 when a qualitative variable is present, consider the case when $x_2 = 0$ (mechanical repair). Using $E(y \mid \text{mechanical})$ to denote the mean repair time *given* a mechanical repair, we have

$$E(y \mid \text{mechanical}) = \beta_0 + \beta_1 x_1 + \beta_2(0) = \beta_0 + \beta_1 x_1 \qquad \textbf{(15.19)}$$

Similarly, for an electrical repair ($x_2 = 1$), we have

$$E(y \mid \text{electrical}) = \beta_0 + \beta_1 x_1 + \beta_2(1) = \beta_0 + \beta_1 x_1 + \beta_2 \qquad \textbf{(15.20)}$$
$$= (\beta_0 + \beta_2) + \beta_1 x_1$$

Comparing (15.19) and (15.20), we see that the expected repair time is a linear function of x_1 for both mechanical and electrical repairs. The slope of both equations is β_1, but the y-intercept differs. The y-intercept is β_0 in (15.19) for mechanical repairs and $(\beta_0 + \beta_2)$ in (15.20) for electrical repairs. The interpretation of β_2 is that it indicates the difference between the expected repair time for an electrical repair and the expected repair time for a mechanical repair.

If β_2 is positive, the expected repair time for an electrical repair will be greater than that for a mechanical repair; if β_2 is negative, the expected repair time for an electrical repair will be less than that for a mechanical repair. Finally, if $\beta_2 = 0$, there is no difference in repair time between electrical and mechanical repairs and the type of repair is not related to the repair time.

Using the estimated multiple regression equation $\hat{y} = .93 + .388x_1 + 1.26x_2$, we see that .93 is the estimate of β_0 and 1.26 is the estimate of β_2. Thus, when $x_2 = 0$ (mechanical repair)

$$\hat{y} = .93 + .388x_1 \qquad \textbf{(15.21)}$$

and when $x_2 = 1$ (electrical repair)

$$\hat{y} = .93 + .388x_1 + 1.26(1) \qquad \textbf{(15.22)}$$
$$= 2.19 + .388x_1$$

In effect, the use of a dummy variable for type of repair has provided two equations that can be used to predict the repair time, one corresponding to mechanical repairs and one corresponding to electrical repairs. In addition, with $b_2 = 1.26$, we have learned that, on average, electrical repairs require 1.26 hours longer than mechanical repairs.

Figure 15.9 is the plot of the Johnson data from Table 15.6. Repair time in hours (y) is represented by the vertical axis and months since last service (x_1) is represented by the horizontal axis. A data point for a mechanical repair is indicated by an M and a data point for an electrical repair is indicated by an E. Equations (15.21) and (15.22) are plotted on the graph to show graphically the two equations that can be used to predict the repair time, one corresponding to mechanical repairs and one corresponding to electrical repairs.

MORE COMPLEX QUALITATIVE VARIABLES

Because the qualitative variable for the Johnson Filtration example had two levels (mechanical and electrical), defining a dummy variable with zero indicating a mechanical repair and one indicating an electrical repair was easy. However, when a qualitative variable has more than two levels, care must be taken in both defining and interpreting the dummy variables. As we will show, if a qualitative variable has k levels, $k - 1$ dummy variables are required, with each dummy variable being coded as 0 or 1.

For example, suppose a manufacturer of copy machines has organized the sales territories for a particular state into three regions: A, B, and C. The managers want to use regression analysis to help predict the number of copiers sold per week. With the number of units sold as the dependent variable, they are considering several independent

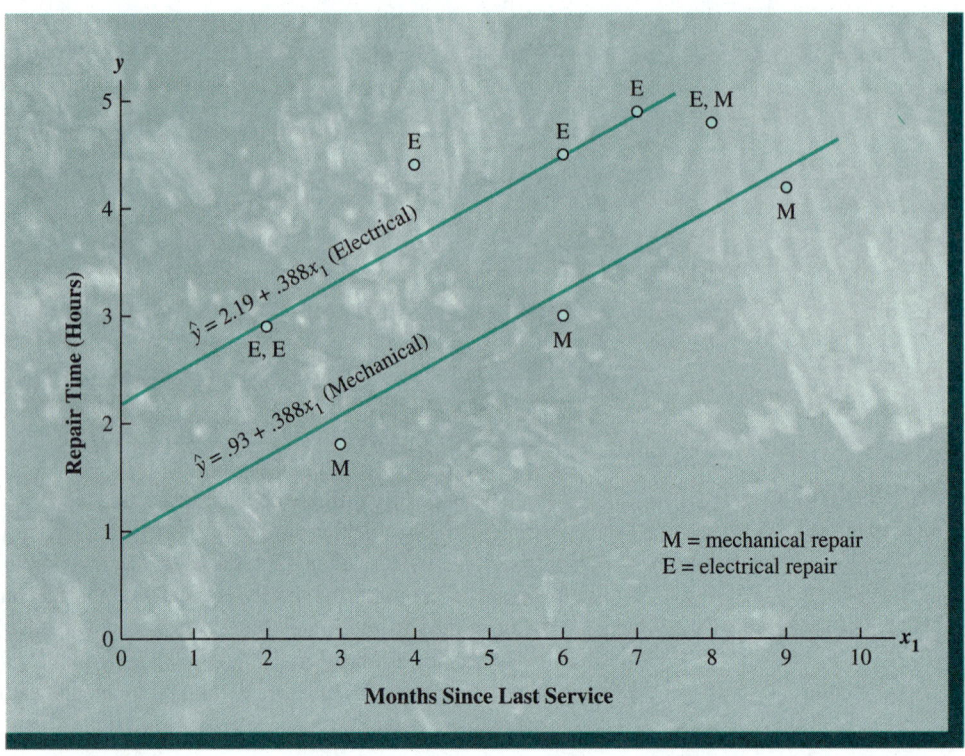

FIGURE 15.9   Scatter Diagram for the Johnson Filtration Repair Data from Table 15.6

variables (the number of sales personnel, advertising expenditures, and so on). Suppose the managers believe sales region is also an important factor in predicting the number of copiers sold. Since sales region is a qualitative variable with three levels, A, B and C, we will need $3 - 1 = 2$ dummy variables to represent the sales region. Each variable can be coded 0 or 1 as follows.

$$x_1 = \begin{cases} 1 \text{ if sales region B} \\ 0 \text{ otherwise} \end{cases}$$

$$x_2 = \begin{cases} 1 \text{ if sales region C} \\ 0 \text{ otherwise} \end{cases}$$

With this definition, we have the following values of x_1 and x_2.

Region	x_1	x_2
A	0	0
B	1	0
C	0	1

Observations corresponding to region A would be coded $x_1 = 0, x_2 = 0$, observations corresponding to region B would be coded $x_1 = 1, x_2 = 0$, and observations corresponding to region C would be coded $x_1 = 0, x_2 = 1$.

The regression equation relating the expected value of the number of units sold, $E(y)$, to the dummy variables would be written as

$$E(y) = \beta_0 + \beta_1 x_1 + \beta_2 x_2$$

To help us interpret the parameters β_0, β_1, and β_2, consider the following three variations of the regression equation.

$$E(y \mid \text{region A}) = \beta_0 + \beta_1(0) + \beta_2(0) = \beta_0$$

$$E(y \mid \text{region B}) = \beta_0 + \beta_1(1) + \beta_2(0) = \beta_0 + \beta_1$$

$$E(y \mid \text{region C}) = \beta_0 + \beta_1(0) + \beta_2(1) = \beta_0 + \beta_2$$

Thus, β_0 is the mean or expected value of sales for region A, β_1 is the difference between the mean number of units sold in region B and the mean number of units sold in region A, and β_2 is the difference between the mean number of units sold in region C and the mean number of units sold in region A.

Two dummy variables are required for a qualitative variable with three levels, but the assignment of $x_1 = 0$, $x_2 = 0$ to indicate region A, $x_1 = 1$, $x_2 = 0$ to indicate region B, and $x_1 = 0$, $x_2 = 1$ to indicate region C was arbitrary. For example, we could have chosen $x_1 = 1$, $x_2 = 0$ to indicate region A, $x_1 = 0$, $x_2 = 0$ to indicate region B, and $x_1 = 0$, $x_2 = 1$ to indicate region C. In that case, β_1 would have been interpreted as the mean difference between regions A and B and β_2 as the mean difference between regions C and B. The important point to remember is that when a qualitative variable has k levels, $k - 1$ dummy variables are required in the multiple regression analysis. If the sales region example had a fourth region, labeled D, three dummy variables would be necessary with x_3 defined as follows.

$$x_3 = \begin{cases} 1 \text{ if sales region D} \\ 0 \text{ otherwise} \end{cases}$$

EXERCISES

METHODS

Self-Test

32. Consider a regression study involving a dependent variable y, a quantitative independent variable x_1, and a qualitative variable with two levels (level 1 and level 2).
    a. Write a multiple regression equation relating x_1 and the qualitative variable to y.
    b. What is the expected value of y corresponding to level 1 of the qualitative variable?
    c. What is the expected value of y corresponding to level 2 of the qualitative variable?
    d. Interpret the parameters in your regression equation.

33. Consider a regression study involving a dependent variable y, a quantitative independent variable x_1, and a qualitative independent variable with three possible levels (level 1, level 2, and level 3).
    a. How many dummy variables are required to represent the qualitative variable?
    b. Write a multiple regression equation relating x_1 and the qualitative variable to y.
    c. Interpret the parameters in your regression equation.

APPLICATIONS

Self-Test

34. The following regression model has been proposed to predict sales at a fast-food outlet.

$$y = \beta_0 + \beta_1 x_1 + \beta_2 x_2 + \beta_3 x_3 + \epsilon$$

where

$x_1 = $ number of competitors within one mile

$x_2 = $ population within one mile (1000s)

$$x_3 = \begin{cases} 1 \text{ if drive-up window present} \\ 0 \text{ otherwise} \end{cases}$$

$y = $ sales ($1000s)

The following estimated regression equation was developed after 20 outlets were surveyed.

$$\hat{y} = 10.1 - 4.2x_1 + 6.8x_2 + 15.3x_3$$

a. What is the expected amount of sales attributable to the drive-up window?

b. Predict sales for a store with two competitors, a population of 8000 within one mile, and no drive-up window.

c. Predict sales for a store with one competitor, a population of 3000 within one mile, and a drive-up window.

35. Refer to the Johnson Filtration problem introduced in this section. Suppose that in addition to information on the number of months since the machine was serviced and whether a mechanical or an electrical failure had occurred, the managers obtained a list showing which repairperson had performed the service. The revised data follow.

 **REPAIR**

Repair Time (hours)	Months Since Previous Service Call (months)	Type of Failure	Repairperson
2.9	2	Electrical	Dave Newton
3.0	6	Mechanical	Dave Newton
4.8	8	Electrical	Bob Jones
1.8	3	Mechanical	Dave Newton
2.9	2	Electrical	Dave Newton
4.9	7	Electrical	Bob Jones
4.2	9	Mechanical	Bob Jones
4.8	8	Mechanical	Bob Jones
4.4	4	Electrical	Bob Jones
4.5	6	Electrical	Dave Newton

a. Ignore for now the months since the previous service call (x_1) and the repairperson who performed the service. Develop the estimated simple linear regression equation to predict the repair time (y) given the type of failure (x_2). Recall that $x_2 = 0$ if the failure is mechanical and 1 if the failure is electrical.

b. Does the equation that you developed in (a) provide a good fit for the observed data? Explain.

c. Ignore for now the months since the previous service call and the type of failure associated with the machine. Develop the estimated simple linear regression equation to predict the repair time given the repairperson who performed the service. Let $x_3 = 0$ if Bob Jones performed the service and $x_3 = 1$ if Dave Newton performed the service.

d. Does the equation that you developed in (c) provide a good fit for the observed data? Explain.

36. This problem is an extension of the situation described in Exercise 35.

a. Develop the estimated regression equation to predict the repair time given the number of months since the previous service call, the type of failure, and the repairperson who performed the service.

b. At the .05 level of significance, test whether the estimated regression equation developed in (a) represents a significant relationship between the independent variables and the dependent variable.

c. Is the addition of the independent variable x_3, the repairperson who performed the service, statistically significant? Use $\alpha = .05$. What explanation can you give for the results observed?

37. *MacUser* (June 1994) provided data that would help a personal computer owner select the best color monitor for his or her computer system. Price and other data for a sample of color monitors follow.

Color Monitor	Focus Rating	Monitor Size	Price ($)
Sony CPD-1730	51.5	Regular	1329
Nec 5FGe	49.5	Regular	1155
SuperMac 20 Plus	48.0	Large	1949
Ikegini CT-20D	55.0	Large	2695
Mitsubishi 17	43.0	Regular	1169
E-Machines E20	54.0	Large	2899
Sony GDM2038	57.5	Large	2859
Nano F550i	52.5	Regular	1399
SuperMac 17T	47.5	Regular	1249
Radius 20v	47.0	Large	2199

MONITOR1

a. Develop a dummy variable that will account for the monitor size. Regular monitors are 16 to 17 inches. Large monitors are 20 to 21 inches.
b. Develop an estimated multiple regression equation to show how price is related to the focus rating and the monitor size.
c. Is monitor size a significant factor in the price of color monitors? Use $\alpha = .05$. Explain.
d. A salesperson says that you can expect to pay more than $1000 extra for a large monitor. Do you agree? Given a constant focus rating, what is the average increase in price when going from a regular to a large monitor?
e. Develop a scatter diagram similar to Figure 15.9 that will show how price is related to focus rating for both regular and large color monitors.
f. IBM's 21P is a 21-inch color monitor with a focus rating of 51. Use the regression equation in part (b) to estimate the price of this color monitor.

38. The American Heart Association collects data on the risk of strokes. A 10-year study provided data on how age, blood pressure, and smoking relate to the risk of strokes (*U.S. News & World Report,* April 13, 1992). Assume that the following data are from a portion of this study. Risk is interpreted as the probability (times 100) that the patient will have a stroke over the next 10-year period. For the smoking variable, define a dummy variable with 1 indicating a smoker and 0 indicating a nonsmoker.

STROKE

Risk	Age	Pressure	Smoker
12	57	152	No
24	67	163	No
13	58	155	No
56	86	177	Yes
28	59	196	No
51	76	189	Yes
18	56	155	Yes
31	78	120	No
37	80	135	Yes
15	78	98	No
22	71	152	No
36	70	173	Yes
15	67	135	Yes
48	77	209	Yes
15	60	199	No
36	82	119	Yes
8	66	166	No
34	80	125	Yes
3	62	117	No
37	59	207	Yes

a. Using these data, develop an estimated regression equation that relates risk of a stroke to the person's age, blood pressure, and whether the person is a smoker.
b. Is smoking a significant factor in the risk of a stroke? Explain. Use $\alpha = .05$.
c. What is the probability of a stroke over the next 10 years for Art Speen, a 68-year-old smoker who has blood pressure of 175? What action might the physician recommend for this patient?

15.8   RESIDUAL ANALYSIS

In Chapter 14, we showed how residual analysis can be used to validate the assumptions for a simple linear regression model and to assist in identifying outliers and influential observations. Residual analysis serves similar purposes for a multiple regression model. In multiple regression, the residual for observation i is defined the same way as in simple linear regression.

> **RESIDUAL FOR OBSERVATION i**
>
> $$y_i - \hat{y}_i \qquad (15.23)$$
>
> where
>
> y_i is the observed value of the dependent variable for observation i
>
> $\hat{y}_i$ is the estimated value of the dependent variable for observation i

The only difference between the residuals for simple linear regression and those for multiple regression is that in using (15.23) for multiple regression, we compute $\hat{y}_i$ with the estimated multiple regression equation $\hat{y} = b_0 + b_1x_1 + b_2x_2 + \ldots + b_px_p$.

In Chapter 14 we pointed out that standardized residuals were frequently used in residuals plots and in the identification of outliers. The general formula for the standardized residual for observation i follows.

> **STANDARDIZED RESIDUAL FOR OBSERVATION i**
>
> $$\frac{y_i - \hat{y}_i}{s_{y_i - \hat{y}_i}} \qquad (15.24)$$
>
> where
>
> $s_{y_i - \hat{y}_i}$ = the standard deviation of residual i

The general formula for the standard deviation of residual i is defined as follows.

> **STANDARD DEVIATION OF RESIDUAL i**
>
> $$s_{y_i - \hat{y}_i} = s\sqrt{1 - h_i} \qquad (15.25)$$
>
> where
>
> s = standard error of the estimate
>
> h_i = leverage of observation i

TABLE 15.7 Residuals and Standardized Residuals for the Butler Trucking Regression Analysis

Miles Traveled (x_1)	Deliveries (x_2)	Travel Time (y)	Predicted Value ($\hat{y}$)	Residual ($y - \hat{y}$)	Standardized Residual
100	4	9.3	8.93846	0.361541	0.78344
50	3	4.8	4.95830	−0.158304	−0.34962
100	4	8.9	8.93846	−0.038460	−0.08334
100	2	6.5	7.09161	−0.591609	−1.30929
50	2	4.2	4.03488	0.165121	0.38167
80	2	6.2	5.86892	0.331083	0.65431
75	3	7.4	6.48667	0.913331	1.68917
65	4	6.0	6.79875	−0.798749	−1.77372
90	3	7.6	7.40369	0.196311	0.36703
90	2	6.1	6.48026	−0.380263	−0.77639

As we stated in Chapter 14, the leverage of an observation is determined by how far the values of the independent variables are from their means. The computation of $h_i\, s_{y_i - \hat{y}_i}$ and hence the standardized residual for observation i in multiple regression analysis is too complex to be done by hand. However, the standardized residuals can be easily obtained as part of the output from statistical software packages. Table 15.7 lists the predicted values, the residuals, and the standardized residuals for the Butler Trucking example presented previously in this chapter; we obtained these values by using the Minitab statistical software package. The predicted values in the table are based on the estimated regression equation $\hat{y} = -.869 + .0611x_1 + .923x_2$.

The residuals and standardized residuals can now be used to test the following assumptions about the regression model's error term ϵ.

1. $E(\epsilon) = 0$.
2. The variance of ϵ, denoted by σ^2, is the same for all values of x.
3. The values of ϵ are independent.
4. ϵ is normally distributed.

To determine whether these assumptions are valid, our preference initially is to plot the standardized residuals against the predicted values. In reviewing the subsequent standardized residual plot, we will look for the same patterns that we looked for when analyzing the residuals in simple linear regression.

Three possible residual patterns are shown in Figure 15.10. If the first three assumptions about ϵ are satisfied and the assumed regression model is an adequate representation of the relationship among the variables, the residual plot should approximate a horizontal band of points such as shown in panel A. If the variance of ϵ is not constant, a pattern such as the one shown in panel B could be observed. The residual plot pattern in panel C suggests that the model is not an adequate representation of the relationship among the variables and that a different multiple regression model should be considered.

The standardized residuals and the predicted values of y from Table 15.7 were used in Figure 15.11, the standardized residual plot for the Butler Trucking multiple regression example. This standardized residual plot does not indicate any unusual abnormalities. Also, all of the standardized residuals are between −2 and +2; hence, we have no reason to question the normality assumption (assumption 4). We conclude that the model assumptions are reasonable.

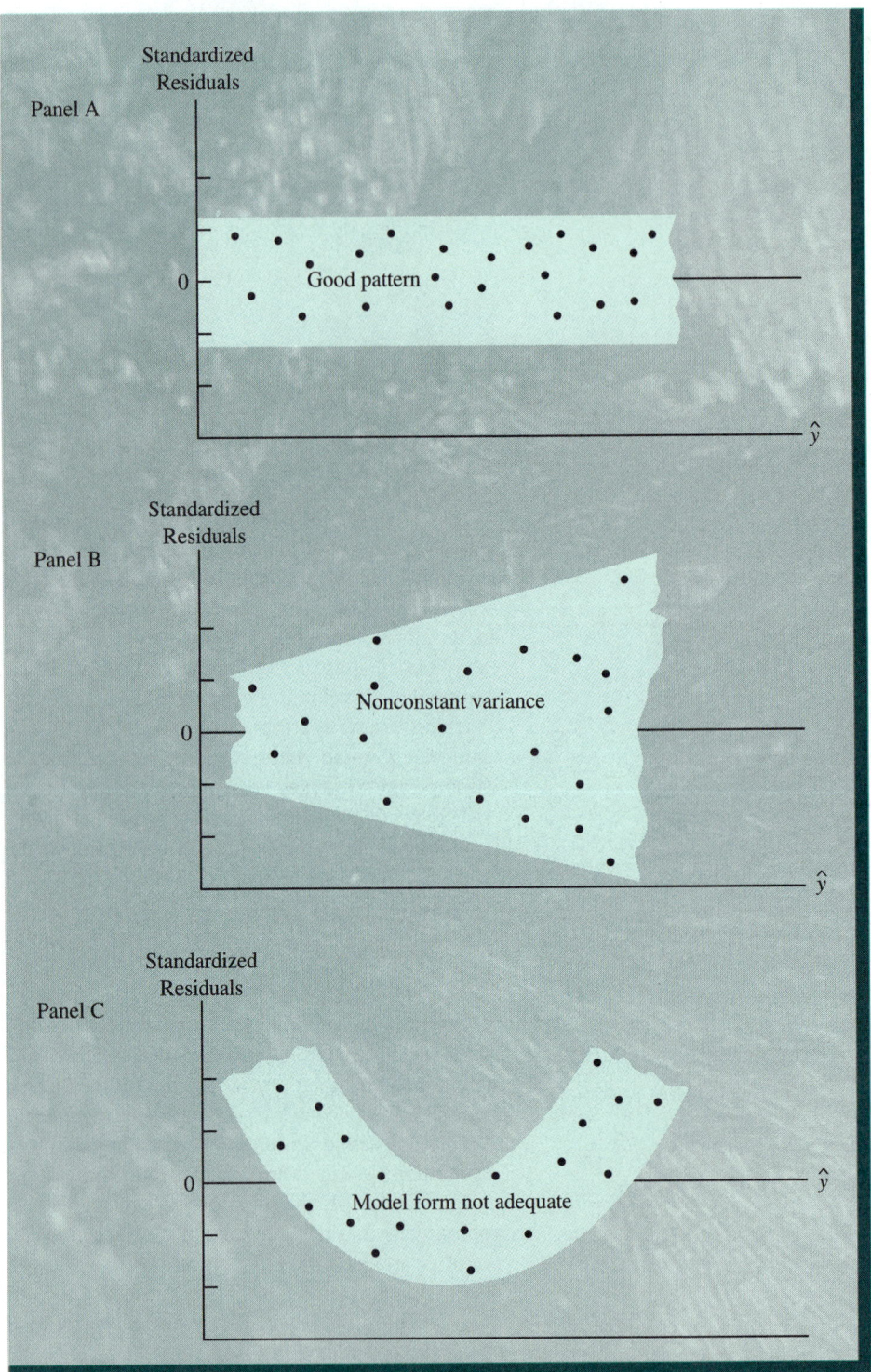

FIGURE 15.10   Possible Residual Patterns and Their Causes

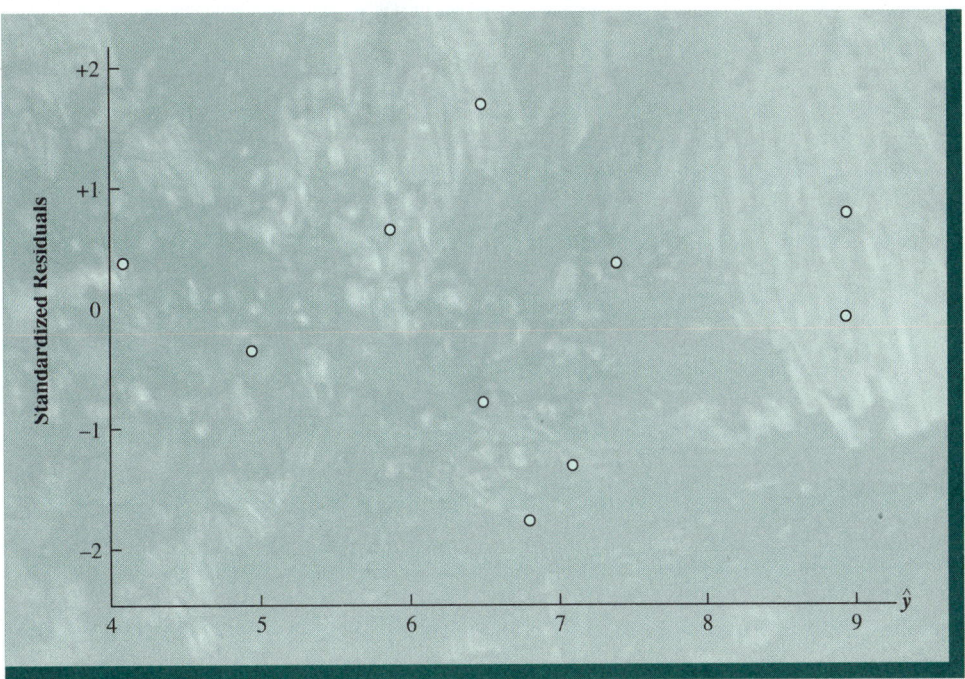

FIGURE 15.11 Standardized Residual Plot for Butler Trucking

A normal probability plot also can be used to determine whether the distribution of ϵ appears to be normal. The procedure and interpretation for a normal probability plot were discussed in Section 14.8. The same procedure is appropriate for multiple regression. Again, we would use a statistical software package to perform the computations and provide the normal probability plot.

DETECTING OUTLIERS

An outlier is an observation that is unusual in comparison with the other data; in other words, an outlier does not fit the pattern of the other data. In Chapter 14 we showed an example of an outlier and discussed how standardized residuals can be used to detect outliers. Minitab classifies an observation as an outlier if the value of its standardized residual is less than −2 or greater than +2. Applying this rule to the standardized residuals for the Butler Trucking example (see Table 15.7), we do not detect any outliers in the data set.

In general, the presence of one or more outliers in a data set tends to increase the value of the standard error of the estimate (s). Since s is used in the computation of $s_{y_i - \hat{y}_i}$, the value in the denominator of the standardized residual (15.24), the size of the standardized residual will decrease as s increases. As a result, even though a residual may be unusually large, the large denominator in (15.24) may cause the standardized residual rule to fail to identify the observation as being an outlier. We can circumvent this difficulty by using a form of the standardized residuals called *studentized deleted residuals*.

STUDENTIZED DELETED RESIDUALS AND OUTLIERS

Suppose the ith observation is deleted from the data set and a new estimated regression equation is developed with the remaining $n − 1$ observations. Let $s_{(i)}$ denote the standard

TABLE 15.8 Studentized Deleted Residuals for Butler Trucking

Miles Traveled (x_1)	Deliveries (x_2)	Travel Time (y)	Standardized Residual	Studentized Deleted Residual
100	4	9.3	0.78344	0.75939
50	3	4.8	−0.34962	−0.32654
100	4	8.9	−0.08334	−0.07720
100	2	6.5	−1.30929	−1.39494
50	2	4.2	0.38167	0.35709
80	2	6.2	0.65431	0.62519
75	3	7.4	1.68917	2.03187
65	4	6.0	−1.77372	−2.21314
90	3	7.6	0.36703	0.34312
90	2	6.1	−0.77639	−0.75190

error of the estimate based on the data set with the ith observation deleted. If we compute the standard deviation of residual i (15.25) using $s_{(i)}$ instead of s, and then compute the standardized residual for observation i (15.24) using the revised $s_{y_i - \hat{y}_i}$ value, the resulting standardized residual is called a studentized deleted residual. If the ith observation is an outlier, $s_{(i)}$ will be less than s. The absolute value of the ith studentized deleted residual therefore will be larger than the absolute value of the standardized residual. In this sense, studentized deleted residuals may detect outliers that standardized residuals do not detect.

Many statistical software packages provide an option for obtaining studentized deleted residuals. Using Minitab, we obtained the studentized deleted residuals for the Butler Trucking example; the results are reported in Table 15.8. The t distribution can be used to determine whether the studentized deleted residuals indicate the presence of outliers. Recall that p denotes the number of independent variables and n denotes the number of observations. Hence, if we delete the ith observation, the number of observations in the reduced data set is $n - 1$; in this case the error sum of squares has $(n - 1) - p - 1$ degrees of freedom. For the Butler Trucking example with $n = 10$ and $p = 2$, the degrees of freedom with the ith observation deleted is $9 - 2 - 1 = 6$. At a .05 level of significance, the t distribution (Table 2 of Appendix B) shows that with six degrees of freedom, $t_{.025} = 2.447$. If the value of the ith studentized deleted residual is less than −2.447 or greater than +2.447, we can conclude that the ith observation is an outlier. Since the studentized deleted residuals in Table 15.8 do not exceed those limits, we conclude that outliers are not present in the data set.

INFLUENTIAL OBSERVATIONS

In Section 14.9 we discussed how the leverage of an observation can be used to identify observations for which the value of the independent variable may have a strong influence on the regression results. As we indicated in the discussion of standardized residuals, the leverage of an observation, denoted h_i, measures how far the values of the independent variables are from their mean values. The leverage values are easily obtained as part of the output from statistical software packages. Minitab computes the leverage values and uses the rule of thumb $h_i > 3(p + 1)/n$ to identify influential

TABLE 15.9 Leverage and Cook's Distance Measures for Butler Trucking

Miles Traveled x_1	Deliveries x_2	Travel Time y	Leverage h_i	Cook's D D_i
100	4	9.3	.351704	.110994
50	3	4.8	.375863	.024536
100	4	8.9	.351704	.001256
100	2	6.5	.378451	.347923
50	2	4.2	.430220	.036663
80	2	6.2	.220557	.040381
75	3	7.4	.110009	.117562
65	4	6.0	.382657	.650029
90	3	7.6	.129098	.006656
90	2	6.1	.269737	.074217

observations. For the Butler Trucking example with $p = 2$ independent variables and $n = 10$ observations, the critical value for leverage is $3(2 + 1)/10 = .9$. The leverage values for the Butler Trucking example obtained by using Minitab are reported in Table 15.9. Since h_i does not exceed .9, we do not detect influential observations in the data set.

USING COOK'S DISTANCE MEASURE TO IDENTIFY INFLUENTIAL OBSERVATIONS

TABLE 15.10 Data Set Illustrating Potential Problem Using the Leverage Criterion

x_i	y_i	Leverage h_i
1	18	.204170
1	21	.204170
2	22	.164205
3	21	.138141
4	23	.125977
4	24	.125977
5	26	.127715
15	39	.909644

A problem that can arise in using leverage to identify influential observations is that an observation can be identified as having high leverage and not necessarily be influential in terms of the resulting estimated regression equation. For example, Table 15.10 is a data set consisting of eight observations and their corresponding leverage values (obtained by using Minitab). Since the leverage for the eighth observation is .91 > .75 (the critical leverage value), this observation is identified as influential. Before reaching any final conclusions, however, let us consider the situation from a different perspective.

In Figure 15.12 are the scatter diagram and the estimated regression equation corresponding to the data set in Table 15.10. We used Minitab to develop the following estimated regression equation for these data.

$$\hat{y} = 18.2 + 1.39x$$

The straight line in Figure 15.12 is the graph of this equation. Now, let us delete the observation $x = 15$, $y = 39$ from the data set and fit a new estimated regression equation to the remaining seven observations; the new estimated regression equation is

$$\hat{y} = 18.1 + 1.42x$$

We note that the y-intercept and slope of the new estimated regression equation are not very different from the values obtained by using all the data. Although the leverage criterion identified the eighth observation as influential, this observation clearly had little influence on the results obtained. Thus, in some situations using only leverage to identify influential observations can lead to wrong conclusions.

Cook's distance measure uses both the leverage of observation i, h_i, and the residual for observation i, $(y_i - \hat{y}_i)$, to determine whether the observation is influential.

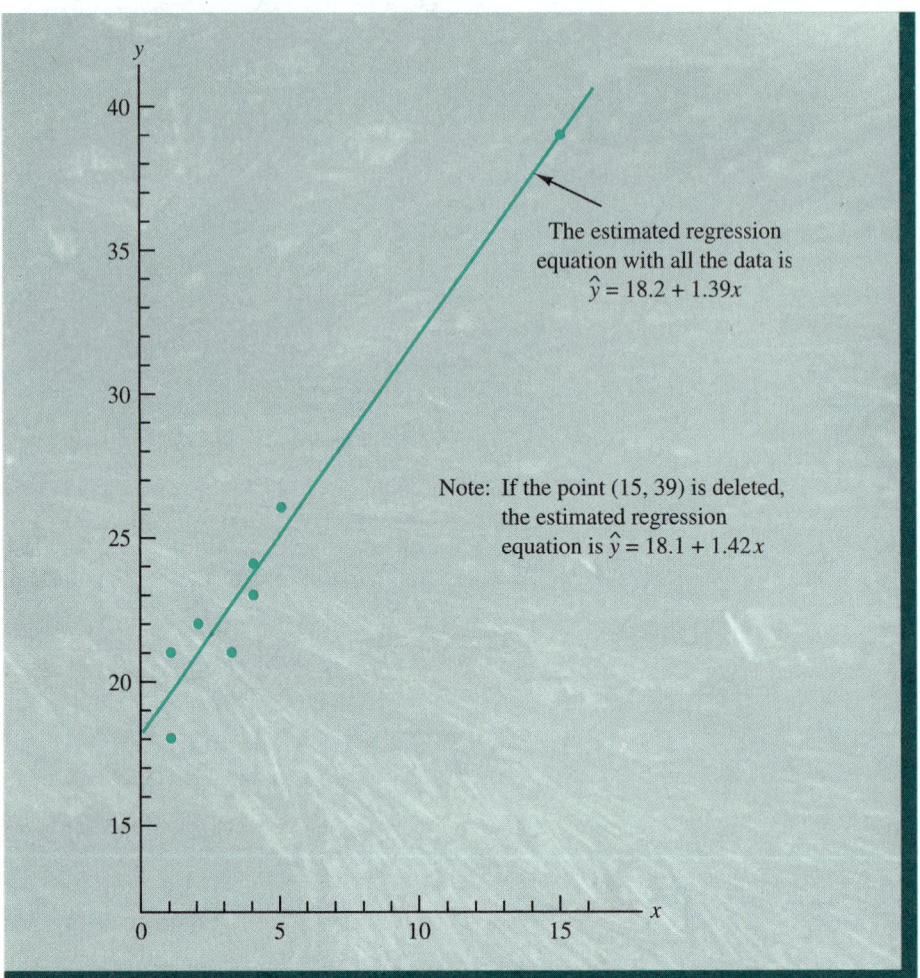

FIGURE 15.12   Scatter Diagram for the Data Set in Table 15.10

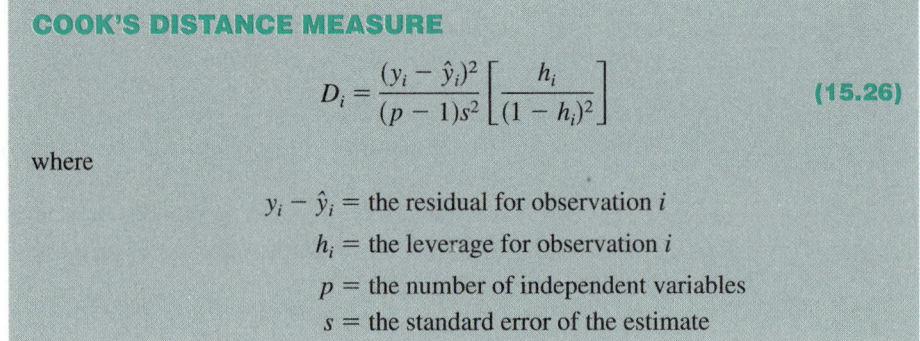

COOK'S DISTANCE MEASURE

$$D_i = \frac{(y_i - \hat{y}_i)^2}{(p - 1)s^2} \left[\frac{h_i}{(1 - h_i)^2} \right] \qquad (15.26)$$

where

$y_i - \hat{y}_i$ = the residual for observation i

h_i = the leverage for observation i

p = the number of independent variables

s = the standard error of the estimate

The value of Cook's distance measure will be large and indicate an influential observation if the residual and/or the leverage is large. As a rule of thumb, values of $D_i > 1$ indicate that the ith observation is influential and should be studied further. The last column of Table 15.9 provides Cook's distance measure for the Butler Trucking problem as given by Minitab. Observation 8 with $D_i = .650029$ has the most influence.

However, applying the rule $D_i > 1$, we should not be concerned about the presence of influential observations in the Butler Trucking data set.

NOTES AND COMMENTS

1. The procedures for identifying outliers and influential observations provide warnings about the potential effects some observations may have on the regression results. Each outlier and influential observation warrants careful examination. If data errors are found, the errors can be corrected and the regression analysis repeated. In general, outliers and influential observations should not be removed from the data set unless clear evidence shows that they are not based on elements of the population being studied and should not have been included in the original data set.

2. To determine whether the value of Cook's distance measure D_i is large enough to conclude that the ith observation is influential, we can also compare the value of D_i to the 50th percentile of an F distribution (denoted $F_{.50}$) with $p + 1$ numerator degrees of freedom and $n - p - 1$ denominator degrees of freedom. F tables corresponding to a .50 level of significance must be available to carry out the test. The rule of thumb we provided $(D_i > 1)$ is based on the fact that the table value is very close to one for a wide variety of cases.

EXERCISES

METHODS

Self-Test

39. Data for two variables, x and y, follow.

x_i	1	2	3	4	5
y_i	3	7	5	11	14

a. Develop the estimated regression equation for these data.
b. Plot the standardized residuals versus $\hat{y}$. Do there appear to be any outliers in these data? Explain.
c. Compute the studentized deleted residuals for these data. At the .05 level of significance, can any of these observations be classified as an outlier? Explain.

40. Data for two variables, x and y, follow.

x_i	22	24	26	28	40
y_i	12	21	31	35	70

a. Develop the estimated regression equation for these data.
b. Compute the studentized deleted residuals for these data. At the .05 level of significance, can any of these observations be classified as an outlier? Explain.
c. Compute the leverage values for these data. Do there appear to be any influential observations in these data? Explain.
d. Compute Cook's distance measure for these data. Are any observations influential? Explain.

APPLICATIONS

41. Exercise 5 gave the following data on weekly gross revenue ($1000s), television advertising ($1000s), and newspaper advertising ($1000s) for Showtime Movie Theaters.

SHOWTIME

Weekly Gross Revenue ($1000s)	Television Advertising ($1000s)	Newspaper Advertising ($1000s)
96	5.0	1.5
90	2.0	2.0
95	4.0	1.5
92	2.5	2.5
95	3.0	3.3
94	3.5	2.3
94	2.5	4.2
94	3.0	2.5

a. Find an estimated regression equation relating weekly gross revenue to television and newspaper advertising.
b. Plot the standardized residuals against $\hat{y}$. Does the residual plot support the assumptions about ϵ? Explain.
c. Check for any outliers in these data. What are your conclusions?
d. Are there any influential observations? Explain.

42. Exercise 6 provided data on the horsepower (x_1), time to go from zero to 60 miles per hour (x_2), and price in thousands of dollars (y) for 10 popular sports cars. The estimated regression equation was

$$\hat{y} = 31 + .108x_1 - 3.8x_2$$

a. Compute the residuals for each of the 10 sports cars.
b. Plot the standardized residuals against $\hat{y}$.
c. Check for any outliers. What are your conclusions?
d. Are there any influential observations? Explain.

43. In Exercise 9, data were provided showing the percentage of students that attend a 4-year college, the average class size, and the combined SAT score.
a. Develop an estimated regression equation that can be used to predict the percentage of students that attend a 4-year college given the combined SAT score.
b. Based on the estimated regression equation developed in (a), are there any outliers and/or influential observations in these data? Explain.
c. Develop an estimated regression equation that can be used to predict the percentage of students that attend a 4-year college given the average class size and the combined SAT score.
d. Based upon the estimated regression equation developed in (c), are there any outliers and/or influential observations in these data? Explain.

SUMMARY

In this chapter, we introduced multiple regression analysis as an extension of simple linear regression analysis presented in Chapter 14. Multiple regression analysis enables us to understand how a dependent variable is related to two or more independent variables. The regression equation $E(y) = \beta_0 + \beta_1x_1 + \beta_2x_2 + \dots + \beta_px_p$ shows that the expected value or mean value of the dependent variable y is related to the values of the independent variables $x_1, x_2, \dots x_p$. Sample data and the least squares method are used to develop the estimated regression equation $\hat{y} = b_0 + b_1x_1 + b_2x_2 + \dots + b_px_p$. In effect $b_0, b_1, b_2, \dots b_p$ are sample statistics used to estimate the unknown model parameters $\beta_0, \beta_1, \beta_2 \ldots \beta_p$. Computer printouts were used throughout the chapter to emphasize the fact that statistical software packages are the only realistic means of performing the numerous computations required in multiple regression analysis.

The multiple coefficient of determination was presented as a measure of the goodness of fit of the estimated regression equation. It determines the proportion of the variation of y that can be explained by the estimated regression equation. The adjusted multiple coefficient of determination is a similar measure of goodness of fit that adjusts for the number of independent variables and thus avoids overestimating the impact of adding more independent variables.

An F test and a t test were presented as ways to determine statistically whether the relationship among the variables is significant. The F test is used to determine whether there is a significant overall relationship between the dependent variable and the set of all independent variables. The t test is used to determine whether there is a significant relationship between the dependent variable and an individual independent variable given the other independent variables in the regression model. Correlation among the independent variables, known as multicollinearity, was discussed.

The section on qualitative independent variables showed how dummy variables can be used to incorporate qualitative data into multiple regression analysis. The chapter concluded with a section on how residual analysis can be used to validate the model assumptions, detect outliers, and identify influential observations. Standardized residuals, leverage, studentized deleted residuals, and Cook's distance measure were discussed.

GLOSSARY

Multiple regression   Regression analysis involving two or more independent variables.

Multiple regression model   The mathematical equation that describes how the dependent variable y is related to the independent variables $x_1, x_2, \ldots, x_p$ and an error term ϵ.

Multiple regression equation   The mathematical equation relating the expected value or mean value of the dependent variable to the values of the independent variables; that is $E(y) = \beta_0 + \beta_1 x_1 + \beta_2 x_2 + \ldots + \beta_p x_p$.

Estimated multiple regression equation   The estimate of the multiple regression equation based on sample data and the least squares method; it is $\hat{y} = b_0 + b_1 x_1 + b_2 x_2 + \ldots + b_p x_p$.

Least squares method   The method used to develop the estimated regression equation. It minimizes the sum of squared residuals (the deviations between the observed values of the dependent variable, y_i, and the estimated values of the dependent variable, $\hat{y}_i$).

Multiple coefficient of determination   A measure of the goodness of fit of the estimated multiple regression equation. It can be interpreted as the proportion of the variation in the dependent variable that is explained by the estimated regression equation.

Adjusted multiple coefficient of determination   A measure of the goodness of fit of the estimated multiple regression equation that adjusts for the number of independent variables in the model and thus avoids overestimating the impact of adding more independent variables.

Multicollinearity   The term used to describe the correlation among the independent variables.

Qualitative independent variable   An independent variable with qualitative data.

Dummy variable   A variable used to model the effect of qualitative independent variables. A dummy variable may take only the value zero or one.

Leverage   A measure of how far the values of the independent variables are from their mean values.

Outlier   An observation that does not fit the pattern of the other data.

Studentized deleted residuals   Standardized residuals that are based on a revised standard error of the estimate obtained by deleting observation i from the data set and then performing the regression analysis and computations.

Influential observation   An observation that has a strong influence on the regression results.

Cook's D   A measure of the influence of an observation based on the residual and leverage.

KEY FORMULAS

Multiple Regression Model

$$y = \beta_0 + \beta_1 x_1 + \beta_2 x_2 + \cdots + \beta_p x_p + \epsilon \tag{15.1}$$

Multiple Regression Equation

$$E(y) = \beta_0 + \beta_1 x_1 + \beta_2 x_2 + \cdots + \beta_p x_p \tag{15.2}$$

Estimated Multiple Regression Equation

$$\hat{y} = b_0 + b_1 x_1 + b_2 x_2 + \cdots + b_p x_p \tag{15.3}$$

Least Squares Criterion

$$\min \Sigma(y_i - \hat{y}_i)^2 \tag{15.4}$$

Relationship Among SST, SSR, and SSE

$$\text{SST} = \text{SSR} + \text{SSE} \tag{15.7}$$

Multiple Coefficient of Determination

$$R^2 = \frac{\text{SSR}}{\text{SST}} \tag{15.8}$$

Adjusted Multiple Coefficient of Determination

$$R_a^2 = 1 - (1 - R^2)\frac{n-1}{n-p-1} \tag{15.9}$$

Mean Square Regression

$$\text{MSR} = \frac{\text{SSR}}{p} \tag{15.12}$$

Mean Square Error

$$\text{MSE} = \frac{\text{SSE}}{n-p-1} \tag{15.13}$$

F Test Statistic

$$F = \frac{\text{MSR}}{\text{MSE}} \tag{15.14}$$

t Test Statistic

$$t = \frac{b_i}{s_{b_i}}$$ (15.15)

Residual for Observation i

$$y_i - \hat{y}_i$$ (15.23)

Standardized Residual for Observation i

$$\frac{y_i - \hat{y}_i}{s_{y_i - \hat{y}_i}}$$ (15.24)

Standard Deviation of Residual i

$$s_{y_i - \hat{y}_i} = s\sqrt{1 - h_i}$$ (15.25)

Cook's Distance Measure

$$D_i = \frac{(y_i - \hat{y}_i)^2}{(p - 1)s^2}\left[\frac{h_i}{(1 - h_i)^2}\right]$$ (15.26)

SUPPLEMENTARY EXERCISES

44. The admissions officer for Clearwater College developed the following estimated regression equation relating the final college GPA to the student's SAT mathematics score and high-school GPA.

$$\hat{y} = -1.41 + .0235x_1 + .00486x_2$$

where

x_1 = high-school grade point average

x_2 = SAT mathematics score

y = final college grade point average

a. Interpret the coefficients in this estimated regression equation.
b. Estimate the final college GPA for a student who has a high-school average of 84 and a score of 540 on the SAT mathematics test.

45. The personnel director for Electronics Associates developed the following estimated regression equation relating an employee's score on a job satisfaction test to his or her length of service and wage rate.

$$\hat{y} = 14.4 - 8.69x_1 + 13.5x_2$$

where

x_1 = length of service (years)

x_2 = wage rate (dollars)

y = job satisfaction test score (higher scores indicate more job satisfaction)

a. Interpret the coefficients in this estimated regression equation.
b. Develop an estimate of the job satisfaction test score for an employee who has four years of service and makes $6.50 per hour.

46. In a regression analysis involving 18 observations and four independent variables, it was determined that SSR = 18,051.63 and SSE = 1014.3.
a. Determine R^2 and R_a^2.
b. Test for the significance of the relationship at $\alpha = .01$.

47. The following estimated regression equation involving three independent variables has been developed.

$$\hat{y} = 18.31 + 8.12x_1 + 17.9x_2 - 3.6x_3$$

Computer output indicates that $s_{b_1} = 2.1$, $s_{b_2} = 9.72$, and $s_{b_3} = .71$. There were 15 observations in the study.
a. Test $H_0: \beta_1 = 0$ at $\alpha = .05$.
b. Test $H_0: \beta_2 = 0$ at $\alpha = .05$.
c. Test $H_0: \beta_3 = 0$ at $\alpha = .05$.
d. Would you recommend dropping any of the independent variables from the model?

48. A partial computer output from a regression analysis follows.

```
The regression equation is
Y = 8.103 + 7.602 X1 + 3.111 X2


Predictor           Coef          Stdev       t-ratio
Constant           _____         2.667       _____
X1                 _____         2.105       _____
X2                 _____         0.613       _____


s = 3.35       R-sq = 92.3%      R-sq(adj) = _____%


Analysis of Variance


SOURCE          DF           SS          MS          F
Regression     _____        1612        _____      _____
Error           12          _____      _____
Total          _____        _____
```

a. Compute the appropriate t-ratios.
b. Test for the significance of β_1 and β_2 at $\alpha = .05$.
c. Compute the entries in the DF, SS, and MS = SS/DF columns.
d. Compute R_a^2.

49. Recall that in exercise 44, the admissions officer for Clearwater College developed the following estimated regression equation relating final college GPA to the student's SAT mathematics score and high-school GPA.

$$\hat{y} = -1.41 + .0235x_1 + .00486x_2$$

where

$$x_1 = \text{high-school grade point average}$$

$$x_2 = \text{SAT mathematics score}$$

$$y = \text{final college grade point average}$$

A portion of the Minitab computer output follows.

```
The regression equation is
Y = -1.41 + .0235 X1 + .00486 X2


Predictor           Coef           Stdev          t-ratio
Constant          -1.4053          0.4848          _____
X1                 0.023467        0.008666        _____
X2                 _____        0.001077        _____


s = 0.1298       R-sq = _____      R-sq(adj) = _____


Analysis of Variance


SOURCE          DF              SS            MS            F
Regression      _____        1.76209        _____        _____
Error           _____        _____       _____
Total            9            1.88000
```

a. Complete the missing entries in this output.
b. Compute F and test at a .05 level of significance to see whether a significant relationship is present.
c. Did the estimated regression equation provide a good fit to the data? Explain.
d. Use the t test and $\alpha = .05$ to test $H_0: \beta_1 = 0$ and $H_0: \beta_2 = 0$.

50. Recall that in Exercise 45 the personnel director for Electronics Associates developed the following estimated regression equation relating an employee's score on a job satisfaction test to length of service and wage rate.

$$\hat{y} = 14.4 - 8.69x_1 + 13.5x_2$$

where

$$x_1 = \text{length of service (years)}$$

$$x_2 = \text{wage rate (dollars)}$$

$$y = \text{job satisfaction test score (higher} \\ \text{scores indicate more job satisfaction)}$$

A portion of the Minitab computer output follows.

```
The regression equation is
Y = 14.4 - 8.69 X1 + 13.52 X2

Predictor              Coef            Stdev         t-ratio
Constant             14.448           8.191            1.76
X1                   _____          1.555          _____
X2                   13.517           2.085          _____

s = 3.773        R-sq = _____ %   R-sq(adj) = _____ %

Analysis of Variance

SOURCE              DF              SS             MS              F
Regression           2            _____        _____        _____
Error             _____          71.17         _____
Total                7            720.0
```

a. Complete the missing entries in this output.
b. Compute F and test using $\alpha = .05$ to see whether a significant relationship is present.
c. Did the estimated regression equation provide a good fit to the data? Explain.
d. Use the t test and $\alpha = .05$ to test $H_0: \beta_1 = 0$ and $H_0: \beta_2 = 0$.

51. Bauman Construction Company makes bids on a variety of projects. In an effort to estimate the bid to be made by one of its competitors, Bauman obtained data on 15 previous bids and developed the following estimated regression equation.

$$\hat{y} = 80 + 45x_1 - 3x_2$$

where

$$\hat{y} = \text{competitor's bid (\$1000s)}$$

$$x_1 = \text{square feet (1000s)}$$

$$x_2 = \text{local index of construction activity}$$

a. Estimate the competitor's bid on a project involving 50,000 square feet and an index of construction activity of 70.
b. If $SSR = 19,780$ and $SST = 21,533$, test at $\alpha = .01$ for the significance of the relationship.

52. The following data set, reported in *Louis Rukeyser's Business Almanac* (1988), shows the percentage of management jobs held by women in various companies and the percentage of women in each company.

Industry/Company	Management Jobs Held by Women (%)	Women Employees (%)
Industrial		
DuPont	7	22
Exxon	8	27
General Motors	6	19
Goodyear Tire and Rubber	25	39
Technology		
AT&T	32	48
General Electric	6	26
IBM	16	28
Xerox	23	38
Consumer Products		
Johnson & Johnson	18	47
PepsiCo	28	46
Phillip Morris (excluding General Foods)	14	31
Procter & Gamble	17	28
Retailing and Trade		
Federated Department Stores	61	72
Kroger	16	47
Marriott	32	51
McDonald's	46	57
Sears, Roebuck	36	55
Media		
ABC (excluding Capital Cities)	36	43
Time	46	54
Times Mirror	27	37
Financial Services		
American Express	37	57
BankAmerica	64	72
Chemical Bank	34	57
Prudential Life Insurance	32	53
Wells Fargo Bank	58	71

JOBS

a. Fit a simple linear regression model that can be used to predict the percentage of management jobs held by women given the percentage of women employed by the company.

b. Did the model developed in (a) provide a good fit to the data? Explain.

c. Use dummy variables to develop a model relating the percentage of management jobs held by women to the type of industry (industrial, technology, and so on).

d. What conclusions can you reach from the model developed in (c)?

e. Develop a model that can be used to predict the percentage of management jobs held by women given the percentage of women employed by the company and the type of industry.

f. From your analyses, what final conclusions can you draw about the percentage of management jobs held by women?

53. Refer to Exercise 52.

a. Develop a standardized residual plot for the estimated regression equation developed in (a) of exercise 52. Does the pattern of the residual plot appear acceptable? Explain.

b. Are there any outliers? Explain.

c. Are there any influential observations? If so, what effect do they have on the model?

54. Following are data on horsepower, time from zero to 60 miles per hour, top speed, miles per gallon, and price in thousands of dollars for 10 popular sports cars (*Road & Track*, October 1994).

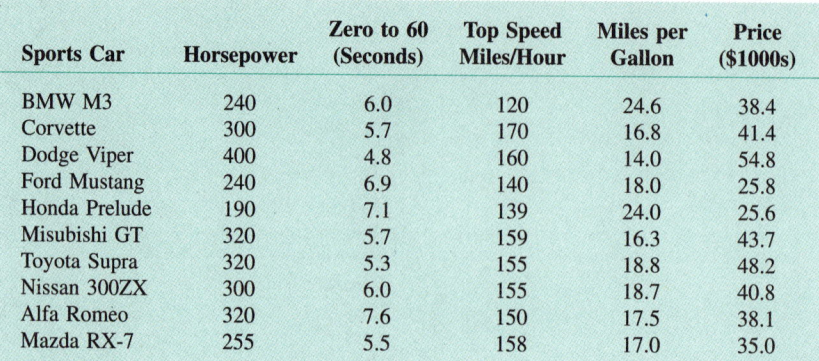

Sports Car	Horsepower	Zero to 60 (Seconds)	Top Speed Miles/Hour	Miles per Gallon	Price ($1000s)
BMW M3	240	6.0	120	24.6	38.4
Corvette	300	5.7	170	16.8	41.4
Dodge Viper	400	4.8	160	14.0	54.8
Ford Mustang	240	6.9	140	18.0	25.8
Honda Prelude	190	7.1	139	24.0	25.6
Misubishi GT	320	5.7	159	16.3	43.7
Toyota Supra	320	5.3	155	18.8	48.2
Nissan 300ZX	300	6.0	155	18.7	40.8
Alfa Romeo	320	7.6	150	17.5	38.1
Mazda RX-7	255	5.5	158	17.0	35.0

a. Develop an estimated regression equation with horsepower, time from zero to 60 miles per hour, top speed, and miles per gallon as four independent variables to predict price.
b. Use the F test to determine the significance of the regression results. At a .05 level of significance, what is your conclusion?
c. Use the t test to determine the significance of each independent variable. At a .05 level of significance, what is your conclusion?
d. Delete any independent variable that is not significant and provide your recommended estimated regression equation. What is the coefficient of determination?
e. Develop a standardized residual plot. Does the pattern of the residual plot appear reasonable? Explain.
f. Are there any outliers?
g. Are there any influential observations?

COMPUTER CASE

CONSUMER RESEARCH, INC.

Consumer Research, Inc., is an independent agency that conducts research on consumer attitudes and behaviors for a variety of firms. In one study, a client asked for an investigation of consumer characteristics that can be used to predict the amount charged by credit-card users. Data were collected on annual income, household size, and annual credit-card charges for a sample of 50 consumers. The data follow and are on the data disk in the file named CONSUMER.

Income ($1000s)	Household Size	Amount Charged ($)	Income ($1000s)	Household Size	Amount Charged ($)
54	3	4016	54	6	5573
30	2	3159	30	1	2583
32	4	5100	48	2	3866
50	5	4742	34	5	3586
31	2	1864	67	4	5037
55	2	4070	50	2	3605
37	1	2731	67	5	5345
40	2	3348	55	6	5370
66	4	4764	52	2	3890
51	3	4110	62	3	4705

continued

CONSUMER

Income ($1000s)	Household Size	Amount Charged ($)	Income ($1000s)	Household Size	Amount Charged ($)
25	3	4208	64	2	4157
48	4	4219	22	3	3579
27	1	2477	29	4	3890
33	2	2514	39	2	2972
65	3	4214	35	1	3121
63	4	4965	39	4	4183
42	6	4412	54	3	3730
21	2	2448	23	6	4127
44	1	2995	27	2	2921
37	5	4171	26	7	4603
62	6	5678	61	2	4273
21	3	3623	30	2	3067
55	7	5301	22	4	3074
42	2	3020	46	5	4820
41	7	4828	66	4	5149

Managerial Report

1. Use methods of descriptive statistics to summarize the data. Comment on the findings.
2. Develop estimated regression equations, first using annual income as the independent variable and then using household size as the independent variable. Which variable is the better predictor of annual credit-card charges? Discuss your findings.
3. Develop an estimated regression equation with annual income and household size as the independent variables. Discuss your findings.
4. What is the predicted annual credit-card charge for a three-person household with an annual income of $40,000?
5. Discuss the need for other independent variables that could be added to the model. What additional variables might be helpful?

APPENDIX 15.1 ●

Calculus-Based Derivation and Solution of Multiple Regression Problems with Two Independent Variables

● For the multiple regression analysis case involving two independent variables, the least squares criterion calls for the minimization of

$$SSE = \Sigma(y_i - b_0 - b_1 x_{1i} - b_2 x_{2i})^2 \qquad \textbf{(15A.1)}$$

To minimize (15A.1), we must take the partial derivatives of SSE with respect to b_0, b_1, and b_2. We can then set the partial derivatives equal to zero and solve for the estimated regression coefficients b_0, b_1, and b_2. Taking the partial derivatives and setting them equal to zero provides

TABLE 15A.1 Calculation of Coefficients for Normal Equations

y_i	x_{1i}	x_{2i}	x_{1i}^2	x_{2i}^2	$x_{1i}x_{2i}$	$x_{1i}y_i$	$x_{2i}y_i$
9.3	100	4	10,000	16	400	930	37.2
4.8	50	3	2,500	9	150	240	14.4
8.9	100	4	10,000	16	400	890	35.6
6.5	100	2	10,000	4	200	650	13.0
4.2	50	2	2,500	4	100	210	8.4
6.2	80	2	6,400	4	160	496	12.4
7.4	75	3	5,625	9	225	555	22.2
6.0	65	4	4,225	16	260	390	24.0
7.6	90	3	8,100	9	270	684	22.8
6.1	90	2	8,100	4	180	549	12.2
67.0	800	29	67,450	91	2,345	5,594	202.2

$$\frac{\partial \text{SSE}}{\partial b_0} = -2\Sigma(y_i - b_0 - b_1 x_{1i} - b_2 x_{2i}) = 0, \qquad \textbf{(15A.2)}$$

$$\frac{\partial \text{SSE}}{\partial b_1} = -2\Sigma x_{1i}(y_i - b_0 - b_1 x_{1i} - b_2 x_{2i}) = 0, \text{ and}$$

$$\textbf{(15A.3)}$$

$$\frac{\partial \text{SSE}}{\partial b_2} = -2\Sigma x_{2i}(y_i - b_0 - b_1 x_{1i} - b_2 x_{2i}) = 0$$

$$\textbf{(15A.4)}$$

Dividing (15A.2) by two and summing the terms individually yields

$$-\Sigma y_i + \Sigma b_0 + \Sigma b_1 x_{1i} + \Sigma b_2 x_{2i} = 0$$

Bringing Σy_i to the right side of the equation and noting that $\Sigma b_0 = nb_0$, we obtain

$$nb_0 + (\Sigma x_{1i})b_1 + (\Sigma x_{2i})b_2 = \Sigma y_i. \qquad \textbf{(15A.5)}$$

Similar algebraic simplification applied to (15A.3) and (15A.4) leads to the following equations.

$$(\Sigma x_{1i})b_0 + (\Sigma x_{1i}^2)b_1 + (\Sigma x_{1i}x_{2i})b_2 = \Sigma x_{1i}y_i \qquad \textbf{(15A.6)}$$

$$(\Sigma x_{2i})b_0 + (\Sigma x_{1i}x_{2i})b_1 + (\Sigma x_{2i}^2)b_2 = \Sigma x_{2i}y_i \qquad \textbf{(15A.7)}$$

Equations (15A.5) through (15A.7) are known as the *normal equations*. Application of these procedures to a regression model involving p independent variables would lead to $p + 1$ normal equations of this type. However, matrix algebra generally is used for that type of derivation.

SOLVING THE NORMAL EQUATIONS FOR BUTLER TRUCKING

Refer to Table 15A.1. Substituting the values in Table 15A.1 results in the following normal equations.

$$10b_0 + 800b_1 + 29b_2 = 67.0 \qquad \textbf{(15A.8)}$$

$$800b_0 + 67,450b_1 + 2345b_2 = 5594.0 \qquad \textbf{(15A.9)}$$

$$29b_0 + 2345b_1 + 91b_2 = 202.2 \qquad \textbf{(15A.10)}$$

By multiplying (15A.8) by 80 and subtracting the result from (15A.9), we can eliminate b_0 and obtain an equation involving only b_1 and b_2.

$$
\begin{array}{rl}
800b_0 + 67{,}450.0b_1 + 2345b_2 = & 5594.0 \\
-800b_0 - 64{,}000.0b_1 - 2320b_2 = & -5360 \\
\hline
3450b_1 + \quad 25b_2 = & 234.0
\end{array}
$$

(15A.11)

Now multiply (15A.8) by 2.9 and subtract the result from (15A.10). This manipulation yields a second equation involving only b_1 and b_2.

$$
\begin{array}{rl}
29b_0 + 2345b_1 + 91.0b_2 = & 202.2 \\
-29b_0 - 2320b_1 - 84.1b_2 = & -194.3 \\
\hline
25b_1 + \quad 6.9b_2 = & 7.9
\end{array}
$$

(15A.12)

With equations (15A.11) and (15A.12), we can solve simultaneously for b_1 and b_2. Multiplying (15A.12) by 25/6.9 and subtracting the result from (15A.11) gives us an equation involving only b_1.

$$
\begin{array}{rl}
3{,}450.0000b_1 + 25b_2 = & 234.0000 \\
- \quad 90.5797b_1 - 25b_2 = & -28.6232 \\
\hline
3{,}359.4203b_1 \qquad = & 205.3768
\end{array}
$$

(15A.13)

Using (15A.13) to solve for b_1 we get

$$
b_1 = \frac{205.3768}{3{,}359.4203} = .061135
$$

Using this value for b_1, we can substitute into (15A.12) to solve for b_2:

$$
25(.061135) + 6.9b_2 = 7.9
$$

$$
1.528375 + 6.9b_2 = 7.9
$$

$$
6.9b_2 = 6.371625
$$

$$
b_2 = .923424
$$

Now we can substitute the values obtained for b_1 and b_2 into (15A.8) thus obtaining b_0:

$$
10b_0 + 800(.061135) + 29(.923424) = 67.0
$$

$$
10b_0 + 48.90800 \quad + 26.779296 \ = 67.0
$$

$$
10b_0 \qquad\qquad\qquad = -8.687296
$$

$$
b_0 \qquad\qquad\qquad = -.8687296
$$

Rounding, we obtain the following estimated regression equation for Butler Trucking.

$$
\hat{y} = -.8687 + .0611x_1 + .9234x_2
$$

16

REGRESSION ANALYSIS: MODEL BUILDING

$\bar{x}$

STATISTICS IN PRACTICE ●

Monsanto Company*

Monsanto

St. Louis, Missouri

Monsanto Company traces its roots to one entrepreneur's investment of $500 and a dusty warehouse on the Mississippi riverfront, where in 1901 John F. Queeney began manufacturing saccharin. Today, Monsanto is one of the nation's largest chemical companies, producing more than a thousand products ranging from industrial chemicals to synthetic playing surfaces used in modern sports stadiums. Monsanto is a worldwide corporation with manufacturing facilities, laboratories, technical centers, and marketing operations in 65 countries.

Monsanto's Nutrition Chemical Division manufactures and markets a methionine supplement used in poultry, swine, and cattle feed products. Since poultry growers work with high volumes and low profit margins, cost-effective poultry feed products with the best possible nutrition value are needed. Optimal feed composition will result in rapid growth and high final body weight for a given level of feed intake. The chemical industry has worked closely with poultry growers to optimize poultry feed products. Ultimately, success depends on keeping the cost of poultry low in comparison with the cost of beef and other meat products.

Monsanto used regression analysis to model the relationship between body weight y and the amount of methionine x added to the poultry feed. Initially, the following simple linear estimated regression equation was developed.

$$\hat{y} = .21 + .42x$$

*The authors are indebted to James R. Ryland and Robert M. Schisla, Senior Research Specialists, Monsanto Nutrition Chemical Division, for providing this Statistics in Practice.

This estimated regression equation proved statistically significant; however, the analysis of the residuals indicated that a curvilinear relationship would be a better model of the relationship between body weight and methionine.

Further research conducted by Monsanto showed that although small amounts of methionine tended to increase body weight, at some point body weight leveled off and additional amounts of the methionine were of little or no benefit. In fact, when the amount of methionine increased beyond nutritional requirements, body weight tended to decline. The following estimated multiple regression equation was used to model the curvilinear relationship between body weight and methionine.

$$\hat{y} = -.189 + 1.32x - .506x^2$$

Use of the regression results enabled Monsanto to determine the optimal level of methionine to be used in poultry feed products.

In this chapter we will extend the discussion of regression analysis by showing how curvilinear models such as the one used by Monsanto can be developed. In addition, we will describe a variety of tools that help determine which independent variables lead to the best estimated regression equation.

Monsanto's researchers develop the latest in feed products for these baby chicks.

● Model building is the process of developing an estimated regression equation that describes the relationship between a dependent variable and one or more independent variables. The major issues in model building are finding the proper functional form of the relationship and selecting the independent variables to be included in the model. In Section 16.1 we establish the framework for model building by introducing the concept of a general linear model. Section 16.2, which provides the foundation for the more sophisticated computer-based procedures, introduces a general approach for determining when to add/or delete independent variables. In Section 16.3 we consider a larger regression problem involving eight independent variables and 25 observations; this problem is used to illustrate the variable-selection procedures presented in Section 16.4, including stepwise regression, the forward-selection procedure, the backward-elimination procedure, and best-subsets regression. In Section 16.5 we show how the Durbin-Watson test can be used to detect serial or autocorrelation, and in Section 16.6 we show how regression analysis can be used for analysis of variance and experimental design problems.

16.1   THE GENERAL LINEAR MODEL

Suppose we have collected data for one dependent variable y and k independent variables $x_1, x_2, \ldots, x_k$. Our objective is to use these data to develop an estimated regression equation that provides the best relationship between the dependent and independent variables. As a general framework for developing more complex relationships among the independent variables, we introduce the concept of a general linear model involving p independent variables.

> **GENERAL LINEAR MODEL**
>
> $$y = \beta_0 + \beta_1 z_1 + \beta_2 z_2 + \cdots + \beta_p z_p + \epsilon \qquad \text{(16.1)}$$

In (16.1), each of the independent variables z_j (where $j = 1, 2, \ldots, p$) is a function of $x_1, x_2, \ldots, x_k$ (the variables for which data have been collected). In some cases, each z_j may be a function of only one x variable. The simplest case is when we have collected data for just one variable x_1 and want to estimate y by using a straight-line relationship. In this case $z_1 = x_1$ and (16.1) becomes

$$y = \beta_0 + \beta_1 x_1 + \epsilon \qquad \text{(16.2)}$$

Note that this is just the simple linear regression model introduced in Chapter 14 with the exception that the independent variable is labeled x_1 instead of x. In the statistical literature, this model is called a *simple first-order model with one predictor variable*.

MODELING CURVILINEAR RELATIONSHIPS

More complex types of relationships can be modeled with (16.1). To illustrate how this is done, let us consider the problem facing Reynolds, Inc., a manufacturer of industrial scales and laboratory equipment. Managers at Reynolds want to investigate the relationship between length of employment of their salespeople and the number of electronic laboratory scales sold. Table 16.1 gives the number of scales sold by 15 randomly selected salespeople for the most recent sales period and the number of months each salesperson has been employed by the firm. Figure 16.1 is the scatter diagram for these data. The scatter diagram indicates a possible curvilinear relationship between the length of time employed and the number of units sold. Before considering how to develop a curvilinear relationship for Reynolds, let us consider the Minitab output in Figure 16.2 corresponding to a simple first-order model; the estimated regression is

TABLE 16.1 Data for the Reynolds Example

Scales Sold	Months Employed
275	41
296	106
317	76
376	104
162	22
150	12
367	85
308	111
189	40
235	51
83	9
112	12
67	6
325	56
189	19

 REYNOLDS

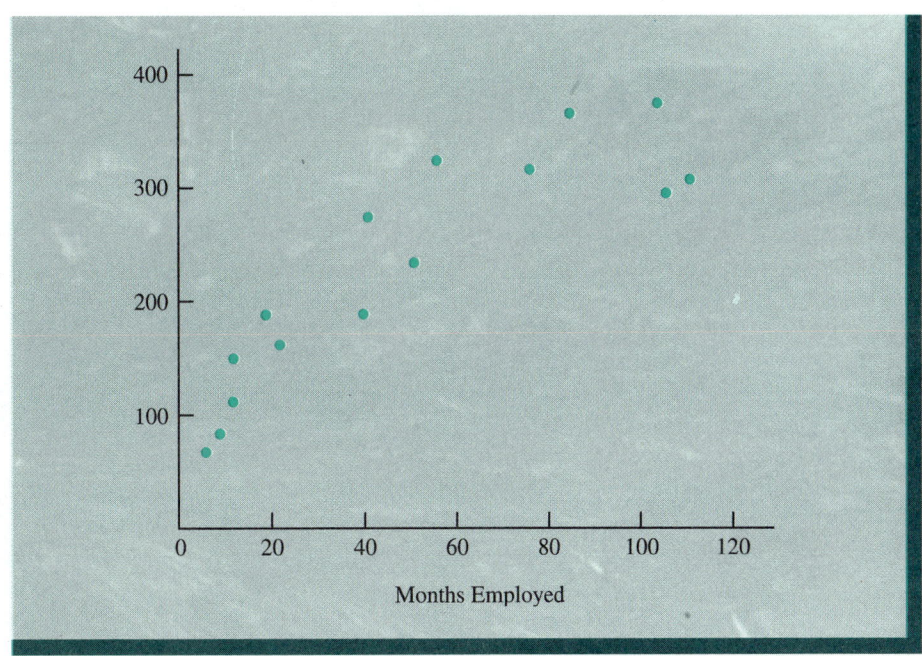

FIGURE 16.1 Scatter Diagram for the Reynolds Example

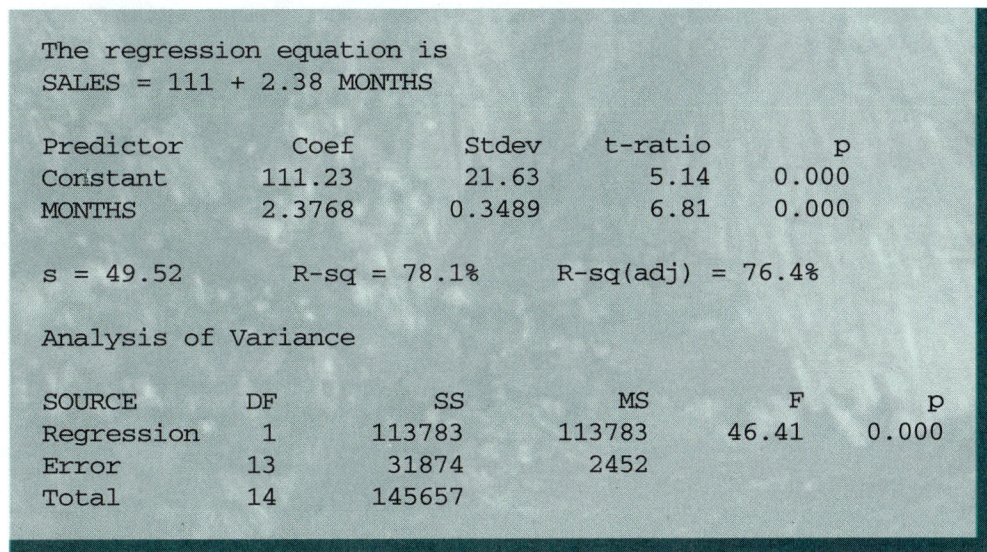

FIGURE 16.2 Minitab Output for the Reynolds Example: First-Order Model

$$\text{SALES} = 111 + 2.38 \text{ MONTHS}$$

where

SALES = number of electronic laboratory scales sold and

MONTHS = the number of months the salesperson has been employed.

Figure 16.3 is the corresponding standardized residual plot. Although the computer output shows that a linear relationship explains a high percentage of the variability in sales (R-sq=78.1%), the standardized residual plot suggests that a curvilinear relationship is needed.

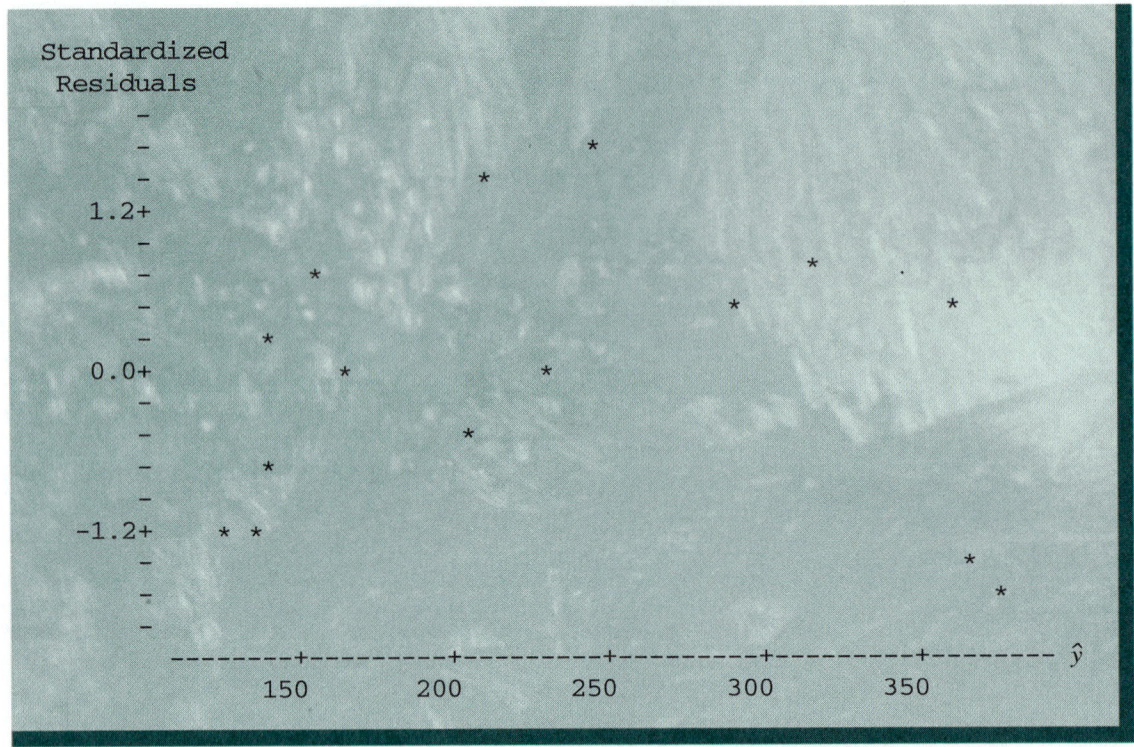

FIGURE 16.3   Standardized Residual Plot for the Reynolds Example: First-Order Model

To account for the curvilinear relationship, we set $z_1 = x_1$ and $z_2 = x_1^2$ in (16.1) to obtain the model

$$y = \beta_0 + \beta_1 x_1 + \beta_2 x_1^2 + \epsilon \qquad \textbf{(16.3)}$$

This model is called a *second-order model with one predictor variable.* To develop an estimated regression equation corresponding to this second-order model, the statistical software package we are using needs the original data in Table 16.1, as well as that data corresponding to adding a second independent variable that is the square of the number of months the employee has been with the firm. In Figure 16.4 we show the Minitab output corresponding to the second order model; the estimated regression equation is

SALES = 45.3 + 6.34 MONTHS − .0345 MONTHSQ

where

MONTHSQ = the square of the number of months the

salesperson has been employed

Figure 16.5 is the corresponding standardized residual plot. It shows that the previous curvilinear pattern has been removed. At the .05 level of significance, the computer output shows that the overall model is significant (*p*-value for the *F* test is 0.000); note also that the *p*-value corresponding to the *t*-ratio for MONTHSQ is less than .05, and hence we can conclude that adding MONTHSQ to the model involving MONTHS is significant. With an R-sq(adj) value of 88.6%, we should be pleased with the fit provided by this second-order model. More important, however, is seeing how easy it is to handle curvilinear relationships in regression analysis.

```
The regression equation is
SALES = 45.3 + 6.34 MONTHS - 0.0345 MONTHSQ

Predictor         Coef       Stdev      t-ratio        p
Constant         45.35       22.77         1.99    0.070
MONTHS           6.345       1.058         6.00    0.000
MONTHSQ      -0.034486    0.008948        -3.85    0.002


s = 34.45       R-sq = 90.2%      R-sq(adj) = 88.6%

Analysis of Variance

SOURCE          DF          SS           MS          F        p
Regression       2      131413        65707      55.36    0.000
Error           12       14244         1187
Total           14      145657
```

FIGURE 16.4 Minitab Output for the Reynolds Example: Second-Order Model

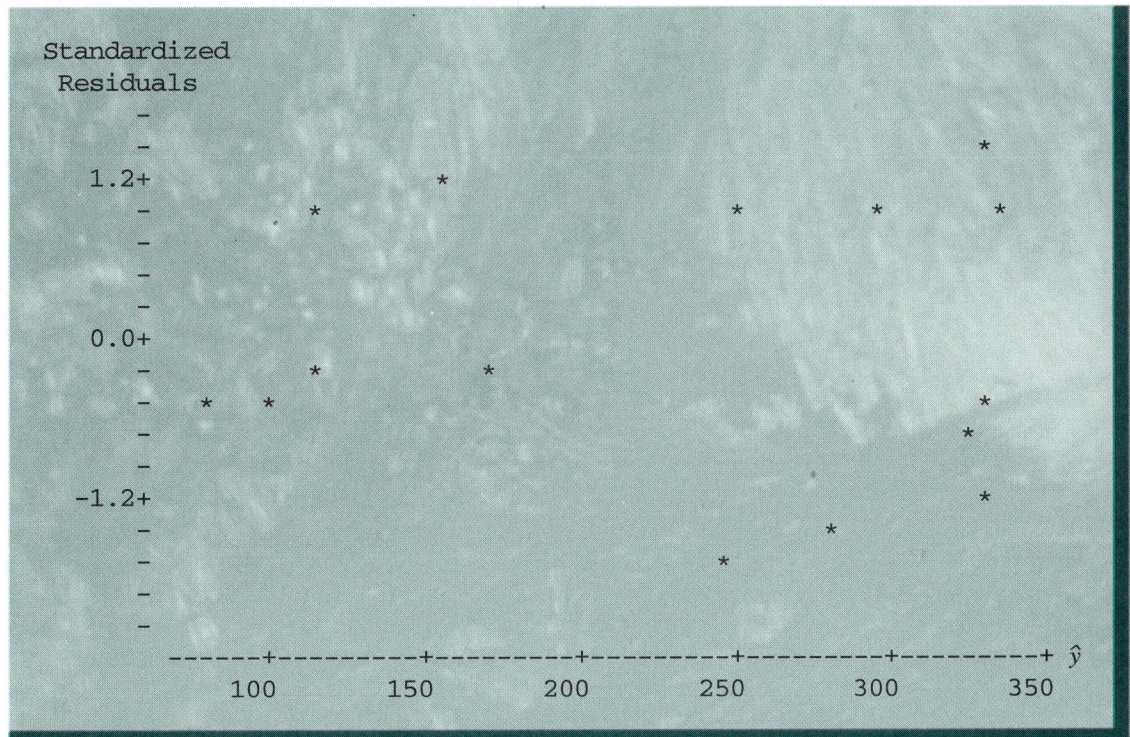

FIGURE 16.5 Standardized Residual Plot for the Reynolds Example: Second-Order Model

Clearly, many types of relationships can be modeled by using (16.1). The regression techniques with which we have been working are definitely not limited to linear, or straight-line, relationships. In multiple regression analysis the word *linear* in the term "general linear model" refers only to the fact that $\beta_0, \beta_1, \ldots, \beta_p$ all have exponents of one; it does not imply that the relationship between y and the x_i's is linear. Indeed, in this

TABLE 16.2 Data for the Tyler Personal Care Example

Price	Advertising Expenditure ($1000s)	Sales (1000s)	Price	Advertising Expenditure ($1000s)	Sales (1000s)
$2.00	50	478	$2.00	100	810
$2.50	50	373	$2.50	100	653
$3.00	50	335	$3.00	100	345
$2.00	50	473	$2.00	100	832
$2.50	50	358	$2.50	100	641
$3.00	50	329	$3.00	100	372
$2.00	50	456	$2.00	100	800
$2.50	50	360	$2.50	100	620
$3.00	50	322	$3.00	100	390
$2.00	50	437	$2.00	100	790
$2.50	50	365	$2.50	100	670
$3.00	50	342	$3.00	100	393

TYLER

TABLE 16.3 Mean Sales (1000s) for the Tyler Personal Care Example

		Price		
		$2.00	*$2.50*	*$3.00*
Advertising	*$50,000*	461	364	332
Expenditure	*$100,000*	808	646	375

Mean sales of 808,000 units
when price = $2.00 and
advertising expenditure = $100,000

section we have seen one example of (16.1) being used to model a curvilinear relationship.

INTERACTION

If the original data set consists of observations for y and two independent variables x_1 and x_2, we can develop a complete second-order model with two predictor variables by setting $z_1 = x_1, z_2 = x_2, z_3 = x_1^2, z_4 = x_2^2$, and $z_5 = x_1 x_2$ in the general linear model of (16.1). The model obtained is

$$y = \beta_0 + \beta_1 x_1 + \beta_2 x_2 + \beta_3 x_1^2 + \beta_4 x_2^2 + \beta_5 x_1 x_2 + \epsilon \qquad \text{(16.4)}$$

In this second-order model, the variable $z_5 = x_1 x_2$ is added to account for the potential effects of the two variables acting together. This type of effect is called *interaction*.

To provide an illustration of interaction and what it means, let us review the regression study conducted by Tyler Personal Care for one of its new shampoo products. Two factors believed to have the most influence on sales were unit selling price and advertising expenditure. To investigate the effects of these two variables on sales, prices of $2.00, $2.50, and $3.00 were paired with advertising expenditures of $50,000 and $100,000 in 24 test markets. The unit sales that were observed (in 1000s) are reported in Table 16.2.

Table 16.3 is a summary of these data. Note that the mean sales corresponding to a price of $2.00 and an advertising expenditure of $50,000 is 461,000, and the mean sales

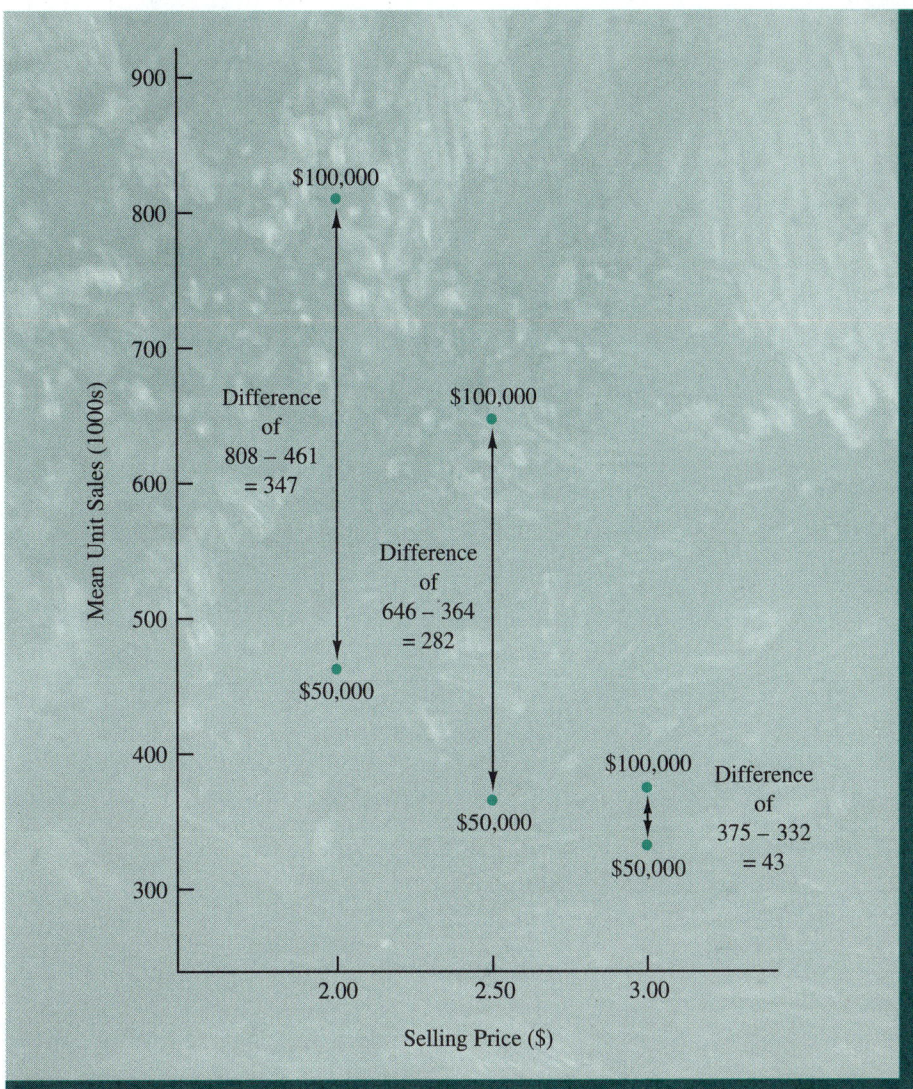

FIGURE 16.6 Mean Sales as a Function of Selling Price and Advertising Expenditure

corresponding to a price of $2.00 and an advertising expenditure of $100,000 is 808,000. Hence, with price held constant at $2.00, the difference in mean sales between advertising expenditures of $50,000 and $100,000 is 808,000 − 461,000 = 347,000 units. When the price of the product is $2.50, the difference in mean sales is 646,000 − 364,000 = 282,000 units. Finally, when the price is $3.00, the difference in mean sales is 375,000 − 332,000 = 43,000 units. Clearly, the difference in mean sales between advertising expenditures of $50,000 and $100,000 depends on the price of the product. In other words, at higher selling prices, the effect of increased advertising expenditure diminishes. These observations provide evidence of interaction between the price and advertising expenditure variables.

To provide another perspective of interaction, Figure 16.6 shows the mean sales for the six price-advertising expenditure combinations. This graph also shows that the effect of advertising expenditure on mean sales depends on the level of the price of the

```
The regression equation is
SALES = - 276 + 175 PRICE + 19.7 ADVER - 6.08 PRICEADV

Predictor        Coef        Stdev      t-ratio         p
Constant       -275.8        112.8        -2.44     0.024
PRICE          175.00        44.55         3.93     0.001
ADVER          19.680        1.427        13.79     0.000
PRICEADV       -6.0800      0.5635       -10.79     0.000

s = 28.17        R-sq = 97.8%       R-sq(adj) = 97.5%

Analysis of Variance

SOURCE         DF          SS           MS          F         p
Regression      3       709316       236439     297.87    0.000
Error          20        15875          794
Total          23       725191
```

FIGURE 16.7   Minitab Output for the Tyler Personal Care Example

product; we again see the effect of interaction. When interaction between two variables is present, we cannot study the effect of one variable on the response y independently of the other variable. In other words, meaningful conclusions can be developed only if we consider the joint effect that both variables have on the response.

To account for the effect of interaction, we will use the following regression model.

$$y = \beta_0 + \beta_1 x_1 + \beta_2 x_2 + \beta_3 x_1 x_2 + \epsilon \qquad \text{(16.5)}$$

where

$$y = \text{unit sales (1000s)}$$

$$x_1 = \text{price (\$)}$$

$$x_2 = \text{advertising expenditure (\$1000s)}$$

Note that (16.5) reflects Tyler's belief that the number of units sold depends linearly on selling price and advertising expenditure (accounted for by the $\beta_1 x_1$ and $\beta_2 x_2$ terms), and that there is interaction between the two variables (accounted for by the $\beta_3 x_1 x_2$ term).

To develop an estimated regression equation, a general linear model involving three independent variables (z_1, z_2, and z_3) was used.

$$y = \beta_0 + \beta_1 z_1 + \beta_2 z_2 + \beta_3 z_3 + \epsilon \qquad \text{(16.6)}$$

where

$$z_1 = x_1$$

$$z_2 = x_2$$

$$z_3 = x_1 x_2$$

Figure 16.7 is the Minitab output corresponding to the interaction model for the Tyler Personal Care example. The resulting estimated regression equation is

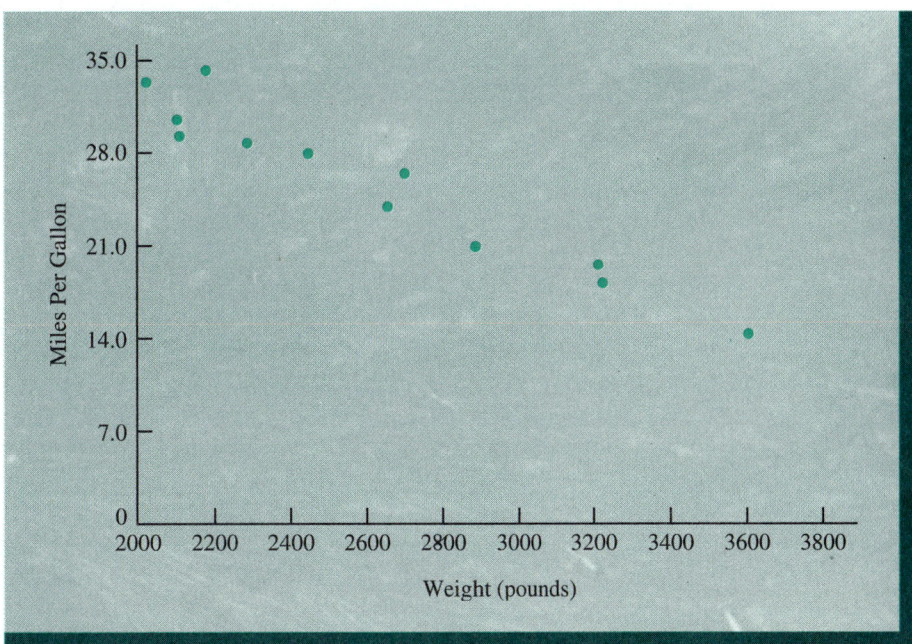

FIGURE 16.8 Scatter Diagram for the Miles per Gallon Problem

TABLE 16.4 Miles per Gallon Ratings and Weights for 12 Automobiles

Miles per Gallon	Weight
28.7	2289
29.2	2113
34.2	2180
27.9	2448
33.3	2026
26.4	2702
23.9	2657
30.5	2106
18.1	3226
19.5	3213
14.3	3607
20.9	2888

 MPG

$$\text{SALES} = -276 + 175\,\text{PRICE} + 19.7\,\text{ADVER} - 6.08\,\text{PRICEADV}$$

where

$$\text{SALES} = \text{unit sales (1000s)}$$

$$\text{PRICE} = \text{price of the product (\$)}$$

$$\text{ADVER} = \text{advertising expenditure (\$1000s)}$$

$$\text{PRICEADV} = \text{interaction term (PRICE times ADVER)}$$

Since the p-value corresponding to the t test for PRICEADV is 0.000, we conclude that interaction is significant given the linear effect of the price of the product and the advertising expenditure. Thus, the regression results show that the effect of advertising expenditure on sales depends on the price.

TRANSFORMATIONS INVOLVING THE DEPENDENT VARIABLE

In showing how the general linear model can be used to model a variety of possible relationships between the independent variables and the dependent variable, we have focused attention on transformations involving one or more of the independent variables. Often it is worthwhile to consider transformations involving the dependent variable y. As an illustration of when we might want to transform the dependent variable, consider the data in Table 16.4, the miles per gallon ratings and weights for 12 automobiles. The scatter diagram in Figure 16.8 shows a negative linear relationship between these two variables. Therefore, we use a simple first-order model to relate the two variables. The Minitab output is in Figure 16.9; the resulting estimated regression equation is

$$\text{MPG} = 56.1 - 0.0116\,\text{WEIGHT}$$

```
The regression equation is
MPG = 56.1 - 0.0116 WEIGHT


Predictor        Coef        Stdev      t-ratio          p
Constant       56.096        2.582        21.72      0.000
WEIGHT      -0.0116436    0.0009677       -12.03      0.000


s = 1.671         R-sq = 93.5%      R-sq(adj) = 92.9%


Analysis of Variance


SOURCE          DF          SS           MS           F
Regression       1        403.98       403.98     144.76       0.
Error           10         27.91         2.79
Total           11        431.88


Unusual Observations
Obs.   WEIGHT        MPG        Fit  Stdev.Fit  Residual
   3     2180      34.200     30.713      0.644      3.487


R denotes an obs. with a large st. resid.
```

FIGURE 16.9 Minitab Output for the Miles Per Gallon Problem

where

$$MPG = \text{miles per gallon rating and}$$

$$WEIGHT = \text{weight of the car in pounds}$$

The model is significant (p-value for the F test is 0.000) and the fit is very good (R-sq = 93.5%). However, we note in Figure 16.9 that observation 3 is identified as having a large standardized residual.

Figure 16.10 is the standardized residual plot corresponding to the first-order model. The pattern we observe does not look like the horizontal band we should expect to find if the assumptions about the error term are valid. Instead, the variability in the residuals appears to increase as the value of $\hat{y}$ increases. In other words, we have the wedge-shaped pattern referred to in Chapters 14 and 15 as being indicative of a nonconstant variance. We are not justified in reaching any conclusions about the statistical significance of the resulting estimated regression equation since the underlying assumptions for the tests of significance do not appear to be satisfied.

Often the problem of nonconstant variance can be corrected by transforming the dependent variable to a different scale. For instance, if we work with the logarithm of the dependent variable instead of the original dependent variable, the effect will be to compress the values of the dependent variable and thus diminish the effects of nonconstant variance. Most statistical packages provide the ability to apply logarithmic transformations using either the base 10 (common logarithm) or the base $e = 2.71828\ldots$ (natural logarithm). We applied a natural logarithmic transformation to the miles per gallon data and developed the estimated regression equation relating weight to the natural logarithm of miles per gallon. The regression results obtained by using the

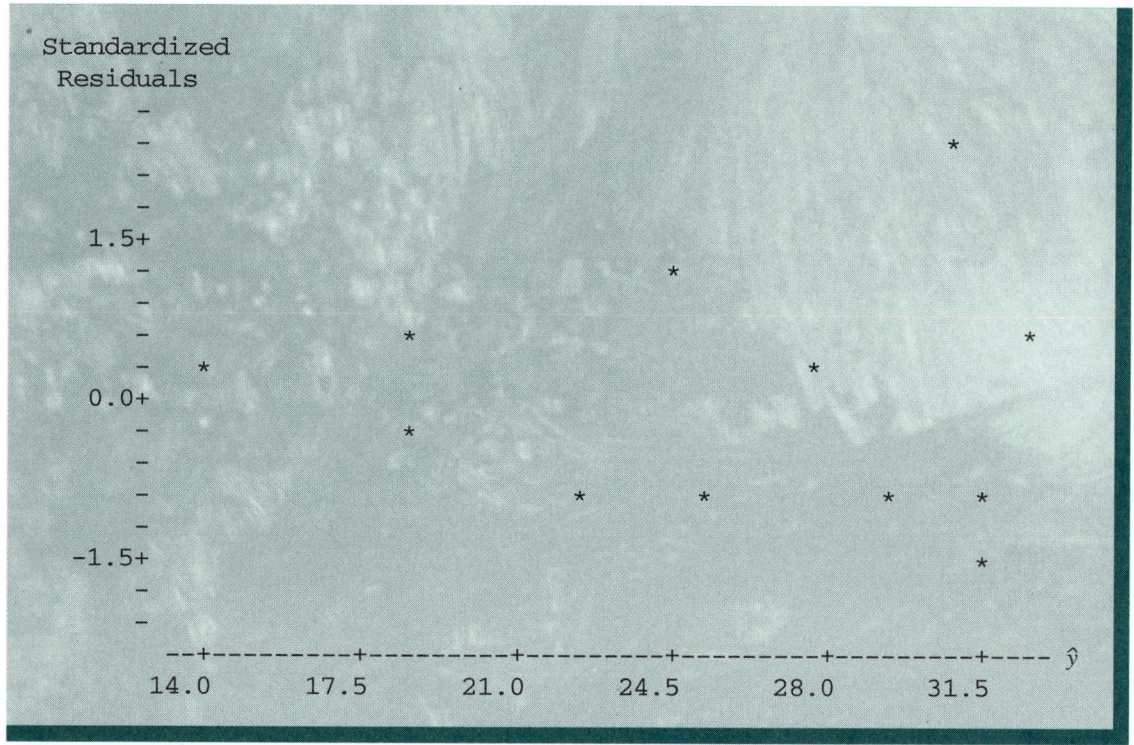

FIGURE 16.10 Standardized Residual Plot for the Miles per Gallon Problem

natural logarithm of miles per gallon as the dependent variable, labeled LOGEMPG in the output, are in Figure 16.11; Figure 16.12 is the corresponding standardized residual plot.

Looking at the residual plot in Figure 16.12, we see that the wedge-shaped pattern has now disappeared. Moreover, none of the observations are identified as having a large standardized residual. The model with the logarithm of miles per gallon as the dependent variable is statistically significant and provides an excellent fit to the observed data. Hence, we would recommend using the estimated regression equation

$$\text{LOGEMPG} = 4.52 - 0.000501 \text{ WEIGHT}$$

To estimate the miles per gallon rating for an automobile that weighs 2500 pounds, we first develop an estimate of the logarithm of the miles per gallon rating.

$$\text{LOGEMPG} = 4.52 - 0.000501(2500) = 3.2675$$

The miles per gallon estimate is obtained by finding the number whose natural logarithm is 3.2675. Using a calculator with an exponential function, or raising e to the power 3.2675, we obtain 26.2 miles per gallon.

Another approach to problems of nonconstant variance is to use $1/y$ as the dependent variable instead of y. This type of transformation is called a *reciprocal transformation.* For instance, if the dependent variable is measured in miles per gallon, the reciprocal transformation would result in a new dependent variable whose units would be 1/(miles per gallon) or gallons per mile. In general, there is no way to determine whether a logarithmic transformation or a reciprocal transformation will perform best without actually trying each of them.

```
The regression equation is
LOGEMPG = 4.52 -0.000501 WEIGHT


Predictor         Coef        Stdev      t-ratio        p
Constant       4.52423      0.09932       45.55      0.000
WEIGHT      -0.00050110   0.00003722     -13.46      0.000


s = 0.06425      R-sq = 94.8%      R-sq(adj) = 94.2%


Analysis of Variance


SOURCE         DF          SS           MS         F          p
Regression      1       0.74822      0.74822    181.22      0.000
Error          10       0.04129      0.00413
Total          11       0.78950
```

FIGURE 16.11   Minitab Output for the Miles per Gallon Problem: Logarithmic Transformation

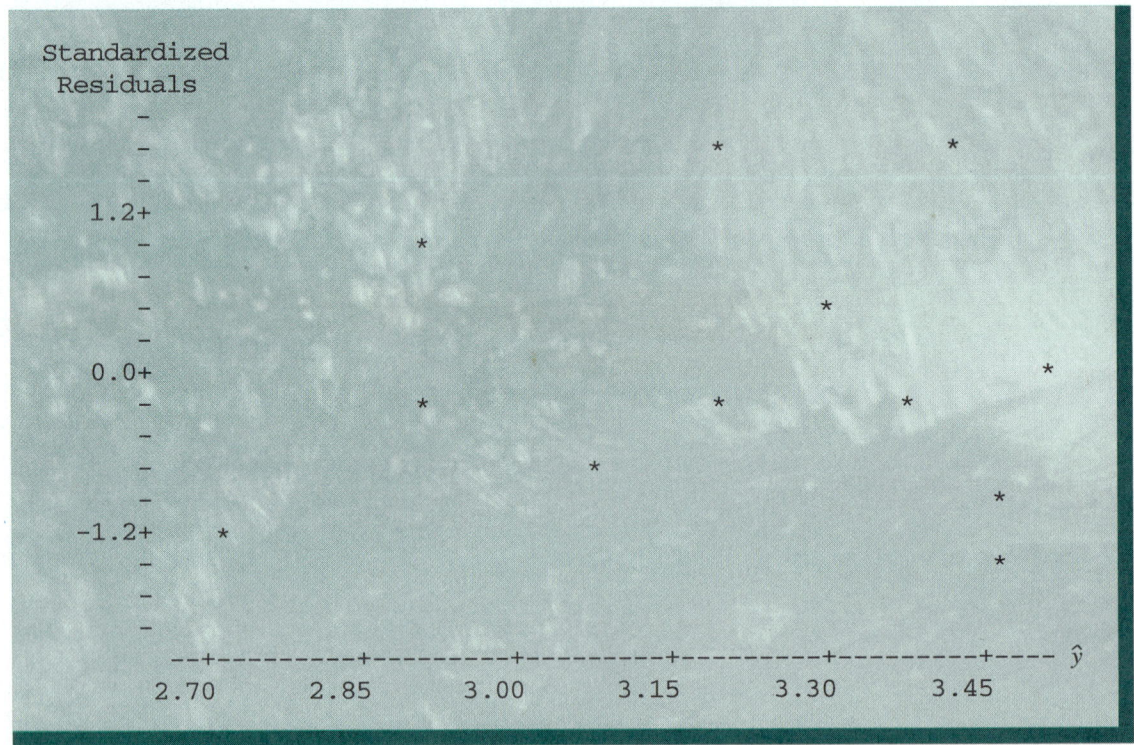

FIGURE 16.12   Standardized Residual Plot for the Miles per Gallon Problem: Logarithmic Transformation

NONLINEAR MODELS THAT ARE INTRINSICALLY LINEAR

Models in which the parameters $(\beta_0, \beta_1, \ldots, \beta_p)$ have exponents other than one are called nonlinear models. However, for the case of the exponential model, we can perform a transformation of variables that will enable us to perform regression analysis with (16.1), the general linear model. The exponential model involves the following regression equation.

$$E(y) = \beta_0 \beta_1^x \qquad \textbf{(16.7)}$$

This model is appropriate when the dependent variable y increases or decreases by a constant percentage, instead of by a fixed amount, as x increases.

As an example, suppose sales for a product y are related to advertising expenditure x (in \$1000s) according to the following exponential model.

$$E(y) = 500(1.2)^x$$

Thus, for $x = 1$, $E(y) = 500(1.2)^1 = 600$; for $x = 2$, $E(y) = 500(1.2)^2 = 720$; and for $x = 3$, $E(y) = 500(1.2)^3 = 864$. Note that $E(y)$ is not increasing by a constant amount in this case, but by a constant percentage; the percentage increase is 20%.

We can transform this nonlinear model to a linear model by taking the logarithm of both sides of (16.7).

$$\log E(y) = \log \beta_0 + x \log \beta_1 \qquad \textbf{(16.8)}$$

Now if we let $y' = \log E(y)$, $\beta_0' = \log \beta_0$, and $\beta_1' = \log \beta_1$, we can rewrite (16.8) as

$$y' = \beta_0' + \beta_1' x$$

It is clear that the formulas for simple linear regression can now be used to develop estimates of β_0' and β_1'. Denoting the estimates as b_0' and b_1' leads to the following estimated regression equation.

$$\hat{y}' = b_0' + b_1' x \qquad \textbf{(16.9)}$$

To obtain predictions of the original dependent variable y given a value of x, we would first substitute the value of x into (16.9) and compute $\hat{y}'$. The antilog of $\hat{y}'$ would be our prediction of y, or the expected value of y.

Many nonlinear models cannot be transformed into an equivalent linear model. However, such models have had limited use in business and economic applications. Furthermore, the mathematical background needed for study of such models is beyond the scope of this text.

EXERCISES

METHODS

Self-Test

1. Consider the following data for two variables, x and y.

x	22	24	26	30	35	40
y	12	21	33	35	40	36

a. Develop an estimated regression equation for the data of the form $\hat{y} = b_0 + b_1 x$.

b. Using the results from (a), test for a significant relationship between x and y; use $\alpha = .05$.

c. Develop a scatter diagram for the data. Does the scatter diagram suggest an estimated regression equation of the form $\hat{y} = b_0 + b_1 x + b_2 x^2$? Explain.

d. Develop an estimated regression equation for the data of the form $\hat{y} = b_0 + b_1 x + b_2 x^2$.

e. Refer to (d). Is the relationship between x, x^2, and y significant? Use $\alpha = .05$.

f. Predict the value of y when $x = 25$.

2. Consider the following data for two variables, x and y.

x	9	32	18	15	26
y	10	20	21	16	22

a. Develop an estimated regression equation for the data of the form $\hat{y} = b_0 + b_1 x$. Comment on the adequacy of this equation for predicting y.
b. Develop an estimated regression equation for the data of the form $\hat{y} = b_0 + b_1 x + b_2 x^2$. Comment on the adequacy of this equation for predicting y.
c. Predict the value of y when $x = 20$.

3. Consider the following data for two variables, x and y.

x	2	3	4	5	7	7	7	8	9
y	4	5	4	6	4	6	9	5	11

a. Does there appear to be a linear relationship between x and y? Explain.
b. Develop the estimated regression equation relating x and y.
c. Plot the standardized residuals versus $\hat{y}$ for the estimated regression equation developed in (b). Do the model assumptions appear to be satisfied? Explain.
d. Perform a logarithmic transformation on the dependent variable y. Develop an estimated regression equation using the transformed dependent variable. Do the model assumptions appear to be satisfied by using the transformed dependent variable? Does a reciprocal transformation work better in this case? Explain.

TABLE 16.5 Exercise 4

Traffic Flow (y)	Vehicle Speed (x)
1256	35
1329	40
1226	30
1335	45
1349	50
1124	25

APPLICATIONS

4. The highway department is doing a study on the relationship between traffic flow and speed. The following model has been hypothesized.

$$y = \beta_0 + \beta_1 x + \epsilon$$

where

$y = $ traffic flow in vehicles per hour
$x = $ vehicle speed in miles per hour

The data in Table 16.5 were collected during rush hour for six highways leading out of the city.
a. Develop an estimated regression equation for the data.
b. Using $\alpha = .01$, test for a significant relationship.

Self-Test

5. In working further with the problem of Exercise 4, statisticians suggested the use of the following curvilinear estimated regression equation.

$$\hat{y} = b_0 + b_1 x + b_2 x^2$$

a. Use the data of Exercise 4 to estimate the parameters of this estimated regression equation.
b. Using $\alpha = .01$, test for a significant relationship.
c. Estimate the traffic flow in vehicles per hour at a speed of 38 miles per hour.

TABLE 16.6 Exercise 6

Number of Facilities	Average Distance (miles)
9	1.66
11	1.12
16	.83
21	.62
27	.51
30	.47

6. A study of emergency service facilities investigated the relationship between the number of facilities and the average distance traveled to provide the emergency service (*Management Science*, July 1988). Table 16.6 gives the data collected.
a. Develop a scatter diagram for these data, treating average travel distance as the dependent variable.

b. Does a simple linear model appear to be appropriate? Explain.

c. Develop an estimated regression equation for the data that you believe will best explain the relationship between these two variables.

7. Performance data for a Century Coronado 21 with a 310-hp MerCruiser V-8 gasoline inboard engine were reported in *Boating*, September 1991. Data on how the engine speed in revolutions per minute (rpm) affected boat speed in miles per hour (mph) follow.

Engine Speed (rpm)	Boat Speed (mph)
1000	6.1
1500	10.7
2000	20.9
2500	27.5
3000	31.5
3500	33.6
4000	37.9
4500	40.2
4800	40.7

a. Develop an estimated regression equation that shows how boat speed is related to engine speed.

b. Estimate the boat speed for an engine being run at 2800 rpm.

8. An 18-year study of the smoking habits of 18- to 24-year-olds was conducted by the Institute for Social Research at the University of Michigan (*USA Today*, June 21, 1994). The following table gives the percentage who smoked daily for each year of the study.

SMOKE

Year	Percentage Smoking	Year	Percentage Smoking
1	28.0	10	19.5
2	28.5	11	19.0
3	27.5	12	19.0
4	25.0	13	18.0
5	22.5	14	19.0
6	20.5	15	19.5
7	21.0	16	18.5
8	21.5	17	17.0
9	19.0	18	19.0

a. Develop a scatter diagram of the data using percentage smoking as the dependent variable and year as the independent variable. Does a simple linear regression model appear to be appropriate? Discuss.

b. Develop an estimated multiple regression equation with time and time squared as the two independent variables.

c. Consider the nonlinear relationship shown by equation (16.7). Use logarithms to develop an estimated regression equation for this model.

d. Do you prefer the estimated regression equation developed in part (b) or that in part (c)? Discuss.

e. What general statement would you make about the trend in smoking habits over the 18-year period?

9. Data on housing markets were provided for 100 cities in the United States (*U.S. News & World Report*, April 6, 1992). Data on the median cost of a new home, the number of new housing

starts during 1991–1992, and the average household income for a sample of 16 cities follow. All data are in thousands.

City	Cost	Housing Starts	Household Income
Chicago	$181.8	12.9	$61.0
Dayton	107.8	3.8	48.4
Atlanta	100.6	24.2	54.7
Oklahoma City	68.9	3.3	53.2
Columbia	90.3	3.1	57.4
Tacoma	96.1	4.1	51.1
Mobile	68.5	1.0	41.0
Baltimore	121.8	11.1	62.8
West Palm Beach	130.4	8.9	58.1
San Antonio	72.5	1.5	57.0
Pittsburgh	79.5	4.9	49.2
Jacksonville	82.1	8.0	47.5
Cleveland	122.9	5.4	54.0
Gary	98.2	3.2	45.7
Scranton	81.6	2.5	44.8
Richmond	102.8	6.0	64.5

 HOUSING

a. Using these data, develop an estimated regression equation that can be used to predict the median cost of a new home.
b. Use the estimated regression equation developed in (a) to predict the median cost of a new home in a city with 8000 housing starts and a household income of $45,000.

16.2   DETERMINING WHEN TO ADD OR DELETE VARIABLES

In this section we will show how an F test can be used to determine whether it is advantageous to add one or more variables to a multiple regression model. This test is based on a determination of the amount of reduction in the error sum of squares resulting from adding one or more independent variables to the model. We will first illustrate how the test can be used in the context of the Butler Trucking example.

In Chapter 15, the Butler Trucking example was introduced to illustrate the use of multiple regression analysis. Recall that the managers wanted to develop an estimated regression equation to predict total daily travel time for trucks using two independent variables: miles traveled and number of deliveries. With miles traveled x_1 as the only independent variable, the least squares procedure provided the following estimated regression equation.

$$\hat{y} = 1.27 + .0678x_1$$

In Chapter 15 we showed that the error sum of squares for this model was SSE=8.029. When x_2, the number of deliveries, was added as a second independent variable, we obtained the following estimated regression equation.

$$\hat{y} = -.869 + .0611x_1 + .923x_2$$

The error sum of squares for this model was SSE=2.299. Clearly, adding x_2 resulted in a reduction of SSE. The question we want to answer is: Does adding the variable x_2 lead to a *significant* reduction in SSE?

We use the notation SSE(x_1) to denote the error sum of squares when x_1 is the only independent variable in the model, SSE(x_1, x_2) to denote the error sum of squares when

x_1 and x_2 are both in the model, and so on. Hence, the reduction in SSE resulting from adding x_2 to the model involving just x_1 is

$$\text{SSE}(x_1) - \text{SSE}(x_1, x_2) = 8.029 - 2.299 = 5.730$$

An F test is conducted to determine whether this reduction is significant.

The numerator of the F statistic is the reduction in SSE divided by the number of variables added to the original model. Here only one variable, x_2, has been added; thus, the numerator of the F statistic is

$$\frac{\text{SSE}(x_1) - \text{SSE}(x_1, x_2)}{1} = 5.730$$

The result is a measure of the reduction in SSE per variable added to the model. The denominator of the F statistic is the mean square error for the model that includes all of the independent variables. For Butler Trucking this corresponds to the model containing both x_1 and x_2; thus, $p = 2$ and

$$\text{MSE} = \frac{\text{SSE}(x_1, x_2)}{n - p - 1} = \frac{2.299}{7} = .3284$$

The following F statistic provides the basis for testing whether the addition of x_2 is statistically significant.

$$F = \frac{\dfrac{\text{SSE}(x_1) - \text{SSE}(x_1, x_2)}{1}}{\dfrac{\text{SSE}(x_1, x_2)}{n - p - 1}} \qquad \textbf{(16.10)}$$

The numerator degrees of freedom for this F test is equal to the number of variables added to the model, and the denominator degrees of freedom is equal to $n - p - 1$.

For the Butler Trucking problem, we obtain

$$F = \frac{\dfrac{5.730}{1}}{\dfrac{2.299}{7}} = \frac{5.730}{.3284} = 17.45$$

Refer to Table 4 of Appendix B. We find that for a level of significance of $\alpha = .05$, $F_{.05} = 5.59$. Since $F = 17.45 > F_{.05} = 5.59$, we reject the null hypothesis that x_2 is not statistically significant; in other words, adding x_2 to the model involving only x_1 results in a significant reduction in the error sum of squares.

When we want to test for the significance of adding only one more independent variable to a model, the result found with the F test just described could also be obtained by using the t test for the significance of an individual parameter (described in Section 15.4). Indeed, the F statistic we just computed is the square of the t statistic used to test the significance of an individual parameter.

Since the t test is equivalent to the F test when only one variable is being added to the model, we can now further clarify the proper use of the t test for testing the significance of an individual parameter. If an individual parameter is not significant, the corresponding variable can be dropped from the model. However, if the t test shows that two or more parameters are not significant, no more than one variable can ever be dropped from a model on the basis of a t test; if one variable is dropped, a second variable that was not significant initially might become significant.

We now turn to a consideration of whether the addition of more than one variable—as a set—results in a significant reduction in the error sum of squares.

THE GENERAL CASE

Consider the following multiple regression model involving q independent variables, where $q < p$.

$$y = \beta_0 + \beta_1 x_1 + \beta_2 x_2 + \cdots + \beta_q x_q + \epsilon \qquad \textbf{(16.11)}$$

If we add variables $x_{q+1}, x_{q+2}, \ldots, x_p$ to this model, we obtain a model involving p independent variables.

$$y = \beta_0 + \beta_1 x_1 + \beta_2 x_2 + \cdots + \beta_q x_q \qquad \textbf{(16.12)}$$
$$+ \beta_{q+1} x_{q+1} + \beta_{q+2} x_{q+2} + \cdots + \beta_p x_p + \epsilon$$

To test whether the addition of $x_{q+1}, x_{q+2}, \ldots, x_p$ is statistically significant, the null and alternative hypotheses can be stated as follows.

$$H_0: \beta_{q+1} = \beta_{q+2} = \cdots = \beta_p = 0$$

H_a: One or more of the parameters is not equal to zero

The following F statistic provides the basis for testing whether the additional variables are statistically significant.

$$F = \frac{\dfrac{\text{SSE}(x_1, x_2, \ldots, x_q) - \text{SSE}(x_1, x_2, \ldots, x_q, x_{q+1}, \ldots, x_p)}{p - q}}{\dfrac{\text{SSE}(x_1, x_2, \ldots, x_q, x_{q+1}, \ldots, x_p)}{n - p - 1}} \qquad \textbf{(16.13)}$$

This computed F value is then compared with F_α, the table value with $p - q$ numerator degrees of freedom and $n - p - 1$ denominator degrees of freedom. If $F > F_\alpha$, we reject H_0 and conclude that the set of additional variables is statistically significant. Note that for the special case where $q = 1$ and $p = 2$, (16.13) reduces to (16.10).

Many students find (16.13) somewhat complex. To provide a simpler description of this F ratio, we can refer to the model with the smaller number of independent variables as the reduced model and the model with the larger number of independent variables as the full model. If we let SSE(reduced) denote the error sum of squares for the reduced model and SSE(full) denote the error sum of squares for the full model, we can write the numerator of (16.13) as

$$\frac{\text{SSE(reduced)} - \text{SSE(full)}}{\text{number of extra terms}} \qquad \textbf{(16.14)}$$

Note that "number of extra terms" denotes the difference between the number of independent variables in the full model and the number of independent variables in the reduced model. The denominator of (16.13) is the error sum of squares for the full model divided by the corresponding degrees of freedom; in other words, the denominator is the mean square error for the full model. Denoting the mean square error for the full model as MSE(full) enables us to write (16.13) as

$$F = \frac{\dfrac{\text{SSE(reduced)} - \text{SSE(full)}}{\text{number of extra terms}}}{\text{MSE(full)}} \qquad \textbf{(16.15)}$$

To illustrate the use of this F statistic, suppose we have a regression problem involving 30 observations. One model with the independent variables x_1, x_2, and x_3 has an error sum of squares of 150 and a second model with the independent variables x_1, x_2, x_3, x_4, and x_5 has an error sum of squares of 100. Did the addition of the two independent variables x_4 and x_5 result in a significant reduction in the error sum of squares?

First, note that the degrees of freedom for SST is $30 - 1 = 29$ and that the degrees of freedom for the regression sum of squares for the full model is five (the number of independent variables in the full model). Thus, the degrees of freedom for the error sum of squares for the full model is $29 - 5 = 24$, and hence MSE(full) $= 100/24 = 4.17$. Therefore the F statistic is

$$F = \frac{\dfrac{150 - 100}{2}}{4.17} = 6.00$$

This computed F value is compared with the table F value with two numerator and 24 denominator degrees of freedom. At the .05 level of significance, Table 4 of Appendix B shows $F_{.05} = 3.40$. Since $F = 6.00$ is greater than 3.40, we conclude that the addition of variables x_4 and x_5 is statistically significant.

NOTES AND COMMENTS

Computation of the F statistic can also be based on the difference in the regression sums of squares. To show this form of the F statistic, we first note that

$$SSE(reduced) = SST - SSR(reduced) \text{ and}$$
$$SSE(full) = SST - SSR(full)$$

Hence

$$SSE(reduced) - SSE(full) = [SST - SSR(reduced)] - [SST - SSR(full)]$$
$$= SSR(full) - SSR(reduced)$$

Thus,

$$F = \frac{\dfrac{SSR(full) - SSR(reduced)}{\text{number of extra terms}}}{MSE(full)}$$

EXERCISES

METHODS

10. In a regression analysis involving 27 observations, the following estimated regression equation was developed.

$$\hat{y} = 25.2 + 5.5x_1$$

For this estimated regression equation SST $= 1550$ and SSE $= 520$.

a. At $\alpha = .05$, test if x_1 is significant.

Suppose that variables x_2 and x_3 are added to the model and the following regression equation is obtained.

$$\hat{y} = 16.3 + 2.3x_1 + 12.1x_2 - 5.8x_3$$

For this estimated regression equation SST = 1550 and SSE = 100.

b. Use an F test and a .05 level of significance to determine whether x_2 and x_3 contribute significantly to the model.

Self-Test

11. In a regression analysis involving 30 observations, the following estimated regression equation was obtained.

$$\hat{y} = 17.6 + 3.8x_1 - 2.3x_2 + 7.6x_3 + 2.7x_4$$

For this estimated regression equation SST = 1805 and SSR = 1760.

a. At $\alpha = .05$, test the significance of the relationship among the variables.

Suppose variables x_1 and x_4 are dropped from the model and the following estimated regression equation is obtained.

$$\hat{y} = 11.1 - 3.6x_2 + 8.1x_3$$

For this model SST = 1805 and SSR = 1705.

b. Compute SSE(x_1, x_2, x_3, x_4).
c. Compute SSE(x_2, x_3).
d. Use an F test and a .05 level of significance to determine whether x_1 and x_4 contribute significantly to the model.

APPLICATIONS

Self-Test

12. The following table gives some of the data available for 14 teams in the National Football League after 15 games.

FOOTBALL

Team	Won–Lost	Total Points	Rushing Yards	Passing Yards	Interceptions Made by Team	Interceptions Made by Opponent
Atlanta	5–10	305	1907	2473	19	23
Chicago	12–3	187	2134	2718	14	24
Dallas	3–12	358	1858	3386	24	10
Detroit	4–11	292	1184	1971	15	12
Green Bay	3–12	298	1274	3046	22	20
L.A. Rams	9–6	277	1882	3604	17	22
Minnesota	10–5	206	1744	3633	16	35
New Orleans	9–6	274	1843	2963	15	17
N.Y. Giants	10–5	277	1492	3096	14	15
Philadelphia	9–6	312	1812	3247	17	29
Phoenix	7–8	372	1909	3633	19	14
San Francisco	10–5	256	2453	3131	14	21
Tampa Bay	4–11	340	1650	3169	33	18
Washington	7–8	367	1377	3930	24	14

a. Develop an estimated regression equation that can be used to predict the total points scored given the number of interceptions made by the team.
b. Develop an estimated regression equation that can be used to predict the total points scored given the number of interceptions made by the team, the number of rushing yards, and the number of interceptions made by the opponents.
c. At a .05 level of significance, test to see whether the addition of the number of rushing yards and the number of interceptions made by the opponents contributes significantly to the estimated regression equation developed in (a). Explain.

TABLE 16.7 Exercise 14

Risk	Age	Blood Pressure	Smoker
12	57	152	0
24	67	163	0
13	58	155	0
56	86	177	1
28	59	196	0
51	76	189	1
18	56	155	1
31	78	120	0
37	80	135	1
15	78	98	0
22	71	152	0
36	70	173	1
15	67	135	1
48	77	209	1
15	60	199	0
36	82	119	1
8	66	166	0
34	80	125	1
3	62	117	0
37	59	207	1

STROKE

13. Refer to exercise 12.
    a. Develop an estimated regression equation that relates the total points scored to the number of passing yards, the number of interceptions made by the team, and the number of interceptions made by the opponents.
    b. Develop an estimated regression equation using the independent variables in (a) and the number of rushing yards.
    c. At a .05 level of significance, did the number of rushing yards contribute significantly to the estimated regression equation developed in (a)? Explain.

14. The American Heart Association collects data on the risk of strokes. A 10-year study provided data on how age, blood pressure, and smoking relate to the risk of strokes (*U.S. News & World Report,* April 13, 1992). Data from a portion of this study are listed in Table 16.7. Risk is interpreted as the probability (times 100) that a person will have a stroke over the next 10-year period. For the smoker variable, 1 indicates a smoker and 0 indicates a nonsmoker.
    a. Develop an estimated regression equation that can be used to predict the risk of stroke given the age and blood-pressure level.
    b. Consider adding two independent variables to the model developed in (a), one for the interaction between age and blood-pressure level and the other for whether the person is a smoker. Develop an estimated regression equation using these four independent variables.
    c. At a .05 level of significance, test to see whether the addition of the interaction term and the smoker variable contribute significantly to the estimated regression equation developed in (a).

16.3 FIRST STEPS IN THE ANALYSIS OF A LARGER PROBLEM

In introducing multiple regression analysis, we used the Butler Trucking example extensively. The small size of this problem was an advantage in exploring introductory concepts, but would make it difficult to illustrate some of the variable-selection issues involved in model building. To provide an illustration of the variable-selection

TABLE 16.8   The Cravens Data

SALES	TIME	POTEN	ADV	SHARE	CHANGE	ACCTS	WORK	RATING
3,669.88	43.10	74,065.1	4,582.9	2.51	0.34	74.86	15.05	4.9
3,473.95	108.13	58,117.3	5,539.8	5.51	0.15	107.32	19.97	5.1
2,295.10	13.82	21,118.5	2,950.4	10.91	−0.72	96.75	17.34	2.9
4,675.56	186.18	68,521.3	2,243.1	8.27	0.17	195.12	13.40	3.4
6,125.96	161.79	57,805.1	7,747.1	9.15	0.50	180.44	17.64	4.6
2,134.94	8.94	37,806.9	402.4	5.51	0.15	104.88	16.22	4.5
5,031.66	365.04	50,935.3	3,140.6	8.54	0.55	256.10	18.80	4.6
3,367.45	220.32	35,602.1	2,086.2	7.07	−0.49	126.83	19.86	2.3
6,519.45	127.64	46,176.8	8,846.2	12.54	1.24	203.25	17.42	4.9
4,876.37	105.69	42,053.2	5,673.1	8.85	0.31	119.51	21.41	2.8
2,468.27	57.72	36,829.7	2,761.8	5.38	0.37	116.26	16.32	3.1
2,533.31	23.58	33,612.7	1,991.8	5.43	−0.65	142.28	14.51	4.2
2,408.11	13.82	21,412.8	1,971.5	8.48	0.64	89.43	19.35	4.3
2,337.38	13.82	20,416.9	1,737.4	7.80	1.01	84.55	20.02	4.2
4,586.95	86.99	36,272.0	10,694.2	10.34	0.11	119.51	15.26	5.5
2,729.24	165.85	23,093.3	8,618.6	5.15	0.04	80.49	15.87	3.6
3,289.40	116.26	26,878.6	7,747.9	6.64	0.68	136.58	7.81	3.4
2,800.78	42.28	39,572.0	4,565.8	5.45	0.66	78.86	16.00	4.2
3,264.20	52.84	51,866.1	6,022.7	6.31	−0.10	136.58	17.44	3.6
3,453.62	165.04	58,749.8	3,721.1	6.35	−0.03	138.21	17.98	3.1
1,741.45	10.57	23,990.8	861.0	7.37	−1.63	75.61	20.99	1.6
2,035.75	13.82	25,694.9	3,571.5	8.39	−0.43	102.44	21.66	3.4
1,578.00	8.13	23,736.3	2,845.5	5.15	0.04	76.42	21.46	2.7
4,167.44	58.44	34,314.3	5,060.1	12.88	0.22	136.58	24.78	2.8
2,799.97	21.14	22,809.5	3,552.0	9.14	−0.74	88.62	24.96	3.9

CRAVENS

procedures discussed in the next section, we introduce a data set consisting of 25 observations on eight independent variables. Permission to use these data was provided by Dr. David W. Cravens of the Department of Marketing at Texas Christian University. Consequently, we refer to the data set as the Cravens data.*

The Cravens data are for a company that sells products in several sales territories, each of which is assigned to a single sales representative. A regression analysis was conducted to determine whether a variety of predictor (independent) variables could explain sales in each territory. A random sample of 25 sales territories resulted in the data in Table 16.8; the variable definitions are given in Table 16.9.

As a preliminary step, let us consider the sample correlation coefficients between each pair of variables. Figure 16.13 is the correlation matrix obtained by using the Minitab correlation command. Note that the sample correlation coefficient between SALES and TIME is .623, between SALES and POTEN is .598, and so on.

Looking at the sample correlation coefficients between the independent variables, we see that the correlation between TIME and ACCTS is .758; hence, if ACCTS were used as an independent variable, TIME would not add much more explanatory power to the model. Recall the rule-of-thumb test from the discussion of multicollinearity in Section 15.4: multicollinearity can cause problems if the absolute value of the sample correlation coefficient exceeds .7 for any two of the independent variables. If possible, then, we should avoid including both TIME and ACCTS in the same regression model. The sample correlation coefficient of .549 between CHANGE and RATING is also high and may warrant further consideration.

---

*For details see David W. Cravens, Robert B. Woodruff, and Joe C. Stamper, "An Analytical Approach for Evaluating Sales Territory Performance," *Journal of Marketing,* 36 (January 1972): 31–37.

TABLE 16.9   Minitab Variable Definitions for the Cravens Data

Variable	Definition
SALES	Total sales credited to the sales representative.
TIME	Length of time employed in months.
POTEN	Market potential; total industry sales in units for the sales territory.*
ADV	Advertising expenditure in the sales territory.
SHARE	Market share; weighted average for the past four years.
CHANGE	Change in the market share over the previous four years.
ACCTS	Number of accounts assigned to the sales representative.*
WORK	Work load; a weighted index based on annual purchases and concentrations of accounts.
RATING	Sales representative overall rating on eight performance dimensions; an aggregate rating on a 1–7 scale.

*These data were coded to preserve confidentiality.

	SALES	TIME	POTEN	ADV	SHARE	CHANGE	ACCTS	WORK
TIME	0.623							
POTEN	0.598	0.454						
ADV	0.596	0.249	0.174					
SHARE	0.484	0.106	-0.211	0.264				
CHANGE	0.489	0.251	0.268	0.377	0.085			
ACCTS	0.754	0.758	0.479	0.200	0.403	0.327		
WORK	-0.117	-0.179	-0.259	-0.272	0.349	-0.288	-0.199	
RATING	0.402	0.101	0.359	0.411	-0.024	0.549	0.229	-0.277

FIGURE 16.13   Sample Correlation Coefficients for the Cravens Data (as Printed by Minitab)

Looking at the sample correlation coefficients between SALES and each of the independent variables can give us a quick indication of which independent variables are, by themselves, good predictors. We see that the single best predictor of SALES is ACCTS, since it has the highest sample correlation coefficient (.754). Recall that for the case of one independent variable, the square of the sample correlation coefficient is the coefficient of determination. Thus, ACCTS can explain $(.754)^2(100)$, or 56.85%, of the variability in SALES. The next most important independent variables are TIME, POTEN, and ADV, each with a sample correlation coefficient of approximately .6.

Although there are potential multicollinearity problems, let us consider developing an estimated regression equation using all eight independent variables. The Minitab computer package provided the results in Figure 16.14. The eight-variable multiple regression model has an adjusted coefficient of determination of 88.3%. Note, however, that the p column (the p-values for the t tests of individual parameters) shows that only POTEN, ADV, and SHARE are significant at the $\alpha = .05$ level, given the effect of all the other variables. Hence, we might be inclined to investigate the results that would be obtained if we used just those three variables. Figure 16.15 shows the Minitab results obtained for the estimated regression equation with those three variables. We see that the estimated regression equation has an adjusted coefficient of determination of 82.7%, which, although not quite as good as that for the eight-independent-variable estimated regression equation, is very high.

```
The regression equation is
SALES = - 1508 + 2.01 TIME + 0.0372 POTEN + 0.151 ADV + 199 SHARE + 291 CHANGE
            + 5.55 ACCTS + 19.8 WORK + 8 RATING


Predictor          Coef          Stdev        t-ratio          p
Constant          1507.8         778.6         -1.94        0.071
TIME               2.010         1.931          1.04        0.313
POTEN            0.037205      0.008202         4.54        0.000
ADV              0.15099        0.04711         3.21        0.006
SHARE            199.02          67.03          2.97        0.009
CHANGE           290.9          186.8           1.56        0.139
ACCTS              5.551         4.776          1.16        0.262
WORK              19.79         33.68           0.59        0.565
RATING             8.2         128.5            0.06        0.950


s = 449.0        R-sq = 92.2%        R-sq(adj) = 88.3%


Analysis of Variance


SOURCE          DF          SS           MS            F          p
Regression       8       38153568      4769196       23.65      0.000
Error           16        3225984       201624
Total           24       41379552
```

FIGURE 16.14   Minitab Output for the Model Involving All Eight Independent Variables

```
The regression equation is
SALES = - 1604 + 0.0543 POTEN + 0.167 ADV + 283 SHARE


Predictor          Coef          Stdev        t-ratio          p
Constant         -1603.6         505.6         -3.17        0.005
POTEN            0.054286      0.007474         7.26        0.000
ADV              0.16748        0.04427         3.78        0.001
SHARE            282.75          48.76          5.80        0.000


s = 545.5        R-sq = 84.9%        R-sq(adj) = 82.7%

Analysis of Variance


SOURCE          DF          SS           MS            F          p
Regression       3       35130240     11710080      39.35      0.000
Error           21        6249310       297586
Total           24       41379552
```

FIGURE 16.15   Minitab Output for the Model Involving POTEN, ADV, and SHARE

How can we find an estimated regression equation that will do the best job given the data available? One approach is to compute all possible regressions. That is, we could develop eight one-variable estimated regression equations (each of which corresponds to one of the independent variables), 28 two-variable estimated regression equations (the number of combinations of eight variables taken two at a time), and so on. In all, for the Cravens data, 255 different estimated regression equations involving one or more independent variables would have to be fitted to the data.

With the excellent computer packages available today, it is possible to compute all possible regressions. But doing so involves a great amount of computation and requires the model builder to review a large volume of computer output, much of which is associated with obviously poor models. Statisticians prefer a more systematic approach to selecting the subset of independent variables providing the best estimated regression equation. In the next section, we introduce some of the more popular approaches.

16.4   VARIABLE-SELECTION PROCEDURES

In this section, we discuss four computer-based methods for selecting the independent variables in a regression model: stepwise regression, forward selection, backward elimination, and best-subsets regression. Given a data set with several possible independent variables, we can use these methods to identify which independent variables provide the best model. The first three methods are iterative; at each step a single variable is added or deleted and the new model is evaluated. The process continues until a stopping criterion indicates that the procedure cannot find a better model. The last method (best subsets) is not a one-variable-at-a-time method; it evaluates regression models involving different subsets of the independent variables.

The criterion for selecting an independent variable to add or delete from the model at each step is based on the F statistic introduced in Section 16.2. Suppose, for instance, that we are considering adding x_3 to a model involving x_1 or deleting x_3 from a model involving x_1 and x_3. In Section 16.2 we showed that

$$F = \frac{\dfrac{\text{SSE}(x_1) - \text{SSE}(x_1, x_3)}{1}}{\dfrac{\text{SSE}(x_1, x_3)}{n - p - 1}}$$

can be used as a criterion for determining whether the presence of x_3 in the model causes a significant reduction in the error sum of squares. The value of this F statistic is the criterion used in the first three methods to determine whether a variable should be added to or deleted from the regression model at each step. It is also used to indicate when the iterative procedure should stop. The first three procedures stop when no more significant reduction in the error sum of squares can be obtained. As also noted in Section 16.2, when only one variable is to be added or deleted at a time, the t statistic (recall that $t^2 = F$) provides the same criterion.

With the stepwise-regression procedure, a variable can be added or deleted at each step. The procedure stops when no more improvement can be obtained by adding or deleting a variable. With the forward-selection procedure, a variable is added at each step, but variables are never deleted. The procedure stops when no more improvement can be obtained by adding a variable. With the backward-elimination procedure, the procedure starts with a model involving all the possible independent variables. At each step a variable is eliminated. The procedure stops when no more improvement can be obtained by deleting a variable.

STEPWISE REGRESSION

We illustrate the stepwise-regression procedure by using the Cravens data. To see how a step of the procedure is performed, suppose that after three steps the following three independent variables have been selected: ACCTS, ADV, and POTEN. At the next step, the procedure first determines whether any of the variables *already in the model* should be deleted. It does so by first determining which of the three variables is the least significant addition in moving from a two- to three-independent-variable model. An *F* statistic is computed for each of the three variables. The *F* statistic for ACCTS enables us to test whether adding ACCTS to a model that already includes ADV and POTEN leads to a significant reduction in SSE. If not, the stepwise procedure will consider dropping ACCTS from the model. Before doing so, however, a similar *F* statistic will be computed for ADV and POTEN. The variable with the smallest *F* statistic makes the least significant addition in moving from a two- to three-independent-variable regression model and becomes a candidate for deletion. If any variable is to be deleted, that will be the one.

We will denote by FMIN the smallest of the *F* statistics for all variables in the regression model at the beginning of a new step. The variable with the smallest *F* statistic is the least significant addition to the model. If the value of FMIN is too small to be significant, the corresponding variable is deleted from the model. If FMIN is large enough to be significant, none of the variables are deleted from the model (none of the other variables can have smaller *F* statistics).

The user of a computer-based stepwise-regression procedure must specify a cutoff value for the *F* statistic so that the method can determine when FMIN is large enough to be significant. With the Minitab package, the smallest significant *F* value is denoted FREMOVE. If the user does not specify a value for FREMOVE, it is automatically set equal to four by Minitab. Whenever FMIN < FREMOVE, the stepwise procedure of Minitab will delete the corresponding variable from the model. If FMIN ≥ FREMOVE, no variable is deleted at that step of the procedure.

If no variable can be removed from the model, the stepwise procedure next checks to see whether adding a variable can improve the model. For each variable *not in the model,* an *F* statistic is computed. The largest of these *F* statistics corresponds to the variable that will cause the largest reduction in SSE. That variable then becomes a candidate for inclusion in the model. We will denote the largest *F* statistic for variables not currently in the model by FMAX. Again, a cutoff value for the *F* statistic must be used to determine whether FMAX is large enough for the corresponding variable to make a significant improvement in the model.

The cutoff value for determining when to add a variable is denoted FENTER in the Minitab computer package. If the user does not specify a cutoff value for FENTER, Minitab will automatically set FENTER equal to four. If FMAX > FENTER, the corresponding variable is added to the model and the stepwise-regression procedure goes on to the next step. The procedure stops when no variables can be deleted and no variables can be added.

In summary, at each step of the stepwise-regression procedure, the first consideration is to see whether any variable can be removed. If none of the variables can be removed, the procedure checks to see whether any variables can be added. Because of the nature of the stepwise procedure, a variable can enter the model at one step, be deleted at a subsequent step, and then reenter the model at a later step. The procedure stops when

```
STEPWISE REGRESSION OF SALES ON 8 PREDICTORS, WITH N = 25

     STEP        1        2        3        4
 CONSTANT    709.32    50.30  -327.23 -1441.93

 ACCTS         21.7     19.0     15.6      9.2
 T-RATIO       5.50     6.41     5.19     3.22

 ADV                   0.227    0.216    0.175
 T-RATIO                4.50     4.77     4.74

 POTEN                          0.0219   0.0382
 T-RATIO                          2.53     4.79

 SHARE                                     190
 T-RATIO                                  3.82

 S             881      650      583      454
 R-SQ        56.85    77.51    82.77    90.04
```

FIGURE 16.16 Minitab Stepwise Regression Output for the Cravens Data

FMIN ≥ FREMOVE (no variables can be deleted) and FMAX ≤ FENTER (no variables can be added).

Figure 16.16 shows the results obtained by using the Minitab stepwise-regression procedure for the Cravens data. As we noted in Section 16.2, when only one variable is being added, the t statistic provides the same criterion as the F statistic. (One can show that $F = t^2$.) The entries in the T-RATIO row are the t statistics. The values of FREMOVE and FENTER were both automatically set equal to four. At step 1, there are no variables to consider for deletion. The variable providing the largest value for the F statistic is ACCTS, with $F = t^2 = (5.5)^2 = 30.25$. Since $30.25 > 4$, ACCTS is added to the model. On the next three steps, ADV, POTEN, and SHARE are added to the model. After step 4, an F statistic was computed for each of the four variables in the model. The values of the F statistics were $t^2 = (3.22)^2 = 10.37$, $t^2 = 22.47$, $t^2 = 22.94$, and $t^2 = 14.59$ for ACCTS, ADV, POTEN, and SHARE, respectively. Thus, FMIN=10.37, and the corresponding variable is ACCTS. Since $10.37 > 4$, no variable is dropped from the model.

An F statistic was then computed for each of the other four variables not in the model. Since all of these F statistics were less than four, no variables were added to the model. The stepwise procedure stopped at this point; no variables could be deleted and none could be added to improve the model. The results in Figure 16.16 were printed at this point. The estimated regression equation identified by the Minitab stepwise-regression procedure is

$$\hat{y} = -1441.93 + 9.2 \text{ ACCTS} + .175 \text{ ADV} + .0382 \text{ POTEN} + 190 \text{ SHARE}$$

Note also in Figure 16.16 that, with the error sum of squares being reduced at each step, $s = \sqrt{\text{MSE}}$ has been reduced from 881 with the best one-variable model to 454 after four steps. The value of R-sq has been increased from 56.85% to 90.04%.

FORWARD SELECTION

Forward selection is another computer-based procedure for variable selection. It is similar to the stepwise-regression procedure but does not permit a variable to be deleted from the model once it has been added. The forward-selection procedure starts with no independent variables. It adds variables one at a time as long as a significant reduction in the error sum of squares (SSE) can be achieved. When no variable can be added that will cause a further significant reduction in SSE, the procedure stops and prints out the results. For the Cravens data, the stepwise-regression procedure added one variable at each step and did not delete any variables. Thus, for the Cravens data, the forward-selection procedure leads to the same model as that provided by the stepwise procedure.

BACKWARD ELIMINATION

The backward-elimination procedure begins with a model that includes all the independent variables the model builder wants considered. (Figure 16.14 shows a regression model involving all eight independent variables for the Cravens data.) It then deletes one variable at a time, using the same criterion for removing variables as that in the stepwise-regression procedure. The variable with the smallest F statistic is deleted, provided F is less than the preestablished cutoff criterion. The major difference from the stepwise procedure is that once a variable has been removed from the model, it cannot reenter at a subsequent step.

Forward selection and backward elimination are the two extremes of model building; forward selection starts with no independent variables in the model and adds variables one at a time whereas backward elimination starts with all independent variables in the model and deletes variables one at a time. The two procedures may lead to the same model, but it is possible for them to lead to two different models, especially as the number of independent variables in the data set increases.

Backward elimination for the Cravens data provided the following estimated regression equation.

$$\hat{y} = -1114 + 3.06 \text{ TIME} + .0421 \text{ POTEN} + .129 \text{ ADV} + 257 \text{ SHARE} + 325 \text{ CHANGE}$$

The value of R-sq is 91.50%. Comparing the backward-elimination model with the forward-selection model, we see that three independent variables—POTEN, ADV, and SHARE—are common to both. However, the backward-elimination model has included TIME and CHANGE instead of ACCTS as recommended by the forward-selection procedure. The R-sq values, 90.04% and 91.50% are similar for the two approaches.

Which model to use remains a topic for discussion. Ultimately, the analyst's judgment must be applied. The best-subsets regression procedure provides additional model-building information to be considered before a final decision is made.

BEST-SUBSETS REGRESSION

Stepwise regression, forward selection, and backward elimination are approaches to choosing the regression model by adding or deleting independent variables one at a time. There is no guarantee that the best model for a given number of variables will be

Vars	R-sq	Adj. R-sq	s	TIME	POTEN	ADV	SHARE	CHANGE	ACCTS	WKLOAD	RATING
1	56.8	55.0	881.09						X		
1	38.8	36.1	1049.3	X							
2	77.5	75.5	650.40			X			X		
2	74.6	72.3	691.11		X	X					
3	84.9	82.7	545.53		X	X	X				
3	82.8	80.3	582.66		X	X			X		
4	90.0	88.1	453.86		X	X	X		X		
4	89.6	87.5	463.95	X	X	X	X				
5	91.5	89.3	430.21	X	X	X	X		X		
5	91.2	88.9	436.75		X	X	X	X	X		
6	92.0	89.4	428.00	X	X	X	X	X	X		
6	91.6	88.9	438.20		X	X	X	X	X	X	
7	92.2	89.0	435.67	X	X	X	X	X	X	X	
7	92.0	88.8	440.29	X	X	X	X	X	X		X
8	92.2	88.3	449.02	X	X	X	X	X	X	X	X

FIGURE 16.17 Portion of Minitab Best-Subsets Regression Output

found. Hence, these one-variable-at-a-time methods are properly viewed as heuristics for selecting a good regression model.

Some software packages have a procedure called best-subsets regression that enables the user to find, given a specified number of independent variables, the best regression model. Minitab has such a procedure. Figure 16.17 is a portion of the computer output obtained by using the best-subsets procedure for the Cravens data set.

This output identifies the two best one-variable estimated regression equations, the two best two-variable equations, the two best three-variable equations, and so on. The criterion used in determining which estimated regression equations are best for any number of predictors is the value of the coefficient of determination (R-sq). For instance, ACCTS, with an R-sq = 56.8%, provides the best estimated regression equation using only one independent variable; ADV and ACCTS, with an R-sq = 77.5%, provides the best estimated regression equation using two independent variables; and POTEN, ADV, and SHARE, with an R-sq = 84.9%, provides the best estimated regression equation with three independent variables. For the Cravens data, the adjusted coefficient of determination (Adj. R-sq = 89.4%) is largest for the model with six independent variables: TIME, POTEN, ADV, SHARE, CHANGE, and ACCTS. However, the best model with four independent variables (POTEN, ADV, SHARE, ACCTS) has an adjusted coefficient of determination almost as high (88.1%). All other things being equal, a simpler model with fewer variables is usually preferred.

TABLE 16.10 Selected Models Involving ACCTS, ADV, POTEN, and SHARE

Model	Independent Variables	Adj. R-sq
1	ACCTS	55.0
2	ADV, ACCTS	75.5
3	POTEN, SHARE	72.3
4	POTEN, ADV, ACCTS	80.3
5	POTEN, ADV, SHARE	82.7
6	POTEN. ADV, SHARE, ACCTS	88.1

MAKING THE FINAL CHOICE

The analysis performed on the Cravens data to this point is good preparation for choosing a final model, but more analysis should be conducted before the final choice. As we have noted in Chapters 14 and 15, a careful analysis of the residuals should be done. We want the residual plot for the chosen model to resemble approximately a horizontal band. Let us assume that there is no difficulty with the residuals and that we want to use the results of the best-subsets procedure to help choose the model.

The best-subsets procedure has shown us that the best four-variable model has the independent variables POTEN, ADV, SHARE, and ACCTS. This also happens to be the four-variable model identified with the stepwise-regression procedure. Table 16.10 is helpful in making the final choice. It shows several possible models consisting of some or all of these four independent variables.

From Table 16.10, we see that the model with just ACCTS and ADV is good. The adjusted coefficient of determination is 75.5%, and the model with all four variables provides only a 12.6-percentage-point improvement. The simpler two-variable model might be preferred, for instance, if it is difficult to measure market potential (POTEN). However, if the data are readily available and highly accurate predictions of sales are needed, the model builder would clearly prefer the model with all four variables.

NOTES AND COMMENTS

1. In the stepwise procedure, FENTER cannot be set smaller than FREMOVE. To see why, suppose this condition was not satisfied. For instance, suppose a model builder set FENTER = 2 and FREMOVE = 4 and at some step of the procedure a variable with an F statistic of 3 was entered into the model. At the next step, any variable with an F statistic of 3 would be a candidate for removal from the model (since 3 < FREMOVE = 4). If the stepwise procedure deleted it, then at the very next step the variable would enter again, it would be deleted again, and so on. Thus, the procedure would cycle forever. To avoid this problem, the stepwise procedure requires that FENTER be greater than or equal to FREMOVE.

2. Functions of the independent variables can be used to create new independent variables for use with any of the procedures in this section. For instance, if we wanted $x_1 x_2$ in the model to account for interaction, we would use the data for x_1 and x_2 to create the data for $z = x_1 x_2$.

3. None of the procedures that add or delete variables one at a time can be guaranteed to identify the best regression model. But they are excellent approaches to finding good models—especially when little multicollinearity is present.

EXERCISES

APPLICATIONS

15. Two experts provided subjective lists of school districts that they think are among the best in the country. For each school district, the following data were obtained: average class size, instructional spending per student, average teacher salary, combined SAT score, percentage of students taking the SAT, and percentage of graduates attending a four-year college (*The Wall Street Journal,* March 31, 1989).

SCHOOLS2

City	Average Class Size	Instructional Spending Per Student ($)	Average Teacher Salary ($)	Combined SAT Score/ (% Taking Test)	Attend 4-Year College (%)
Blue Springs, MO	25	3,060	29,359	1083/(8)	74
Garden City, NY	18	9,700	51,000	997/(99)	77
Indianapolis, IN	30	3,222	30,482	716/(42)	40
Newport Beach, CA (Newport-Mesa)	26	4,028	37,043	977/(46)	51
Novi, MI	20	3,067	39,797	980/(15)	53
Piedmont, CA (Piedmont City)	28	4,208	37,274	1,042/(91)	75
Pittsburgh, PA (Fox Chapel area)	21	4,884	37,156	983/(80)	66
Scarsdale, NY (Edgemont)	20	9,853	31,555	1,110/(98)	87
Wayne, PA (Radnor Township)	22	5,022	40,406	1,040/(95)	85
Weston, MA	21	4,680	39,800	1,031/(99)	89
Farmingdale, NY	22	6,729	45,846	947/(75)	81
Mamaroneck, NY	20	10,405	49,625	1,000/(90)	69
Mayfield, OH	24	5,881	36,228	1,003/(25)	48
Morristown, NJ	22	6,300	37,000	972/(80)	64
New Rochelle, NY	23	8,875	41,650	1,039/(80)	55
Newton Square, PA (Marple-Newton)	17	5,313	38,000	963/(75)	79
Omaha, NB (Westside)	23	4,815	32,500	1,059/(31)	81
Shaker Heights, OH	23	4,370	38,639	940/(56)	82

Let the dependent variable be the percentage of graduates attending a four-year college.
a. Develop the best one-variable estimated regression equation.
b. Use the stepwise procedure to develop the best estimated regression equation.
c. Use the backward-elimination procedure to develop the best estimated regression equation.
d. Use the best-subsets regression procedure to develop the best estimated regression equation.

16. Financial data for a sample of 30 companies are listed in Table 16.11 (*Financial World,* September 1, 1994). Let stock price be the dependent variable and earnings per share (x_1) and book value per share (x_2) be the independent variables. To account for the possibility of curvilinear relationships, add $x_3 = x_1^2$ and $x_4 = x_2^2$ to make a total of four independent variables.
a. Use the stepwise regression procedure to develop the best estimated regression equation.
b. Use the backward-elimination procedure to develop the best estimated regression equation.
c. What is the recommended estimated regression equation?
d. What does this analysis show about the relationship of stock price to earnings per share and book value per share?

17. Refer to the data in Exercise 12. Let the dependent variable be the number of wins.
a. Develop the best one-variable estimated regression equation.
b. Use the stepwise procedure to develop the best estimated regression equation.

TABLE 16.11 Exercise 16

Company	Earnings per Share	Book Value per Share	Stock Price
Acme	$2.59	$15.00	$25.50
Aldus	1.41	9.22	29.50
Am. Fed. Bk.	1.26	7.75	11.63
Applebee's	.49	3.60	14.75
Banta Corp.	2.16	14.89	32.75
Bob Evans	1.15	7.41	21.50
Cintas Corp.	1.12	5.64	31.00
Commerce Clearing House	.72	5.76	19.00
Cracker Barrel	.89	6.09	23.13
Devon Group	2.01	8.86	19.50
Duracraft	1.69	5.41	40.00
First Alert	.79	3.18	25.75
Food Lion	.26	3.71	5.94
Gentex	.83	3.09	21.00
Gould Pumps	1.12	8.80	20.25
Haggar Corp.	2.80	15.26	29.00
Hubco Inc.	2.27	11.74	21.13
Information Resources	.74	8.59	13.75
Irwin Financial	2.82	12.08	21.75
Kelly Services	1.35	11.06	28.75
Lone Star	.62	4.44	20.00
Mark Twain	2.40	13.75	27.50
Micro Systems	1.03	4.01	28.50
Novell	.98	3.58	16.13
Pacific Phy.	.55	5.00	11.50
Proffitts Inc.	.50	13.39	18.75
Rival	1.44	6.57	20.38
Sybase	1.07	3.81	37.00
Tyson Foods	1.23	17.06	23.88
Zenith Labs	.85	3.63	15.63

STKPRICE

c. Use the backward-elimination procedure to develop the best estimated regression equation.

d. Use the best-subsets regression procedure to develop the best estimated regression equation.

18. Data on the golfing abilities of some of the Professional Golf Association's top golfers follow (*Golf Digest 1995 Record Book*). DISTANCE is the average yards per drive, ACCURACY is the percentage of drives landing in the fairway, GREENS is the percentage of greens reached in par or better, PUTTS is the average number of putts per green, SANDSAVE is the percentage saves from greenside traps, and SCORE is the average score per 18 holes of golf.

GOLFER	DISTANCE	ACCURACY	GREENS	PUTTS	SANDSAVE	SCORE
Nick Price	277.5	73.6	69.6	1.773	58.2	69.39
Greg Norman	277.1	73.3	69.0	1.747	57.3	68.81
Tom Lehman	269.3	70.8	70.8	1.766	47.9	69.46
Fuzzy Zoeller	270.7	75.5	72.8	1.784	53.2	69.89
Loren Roberts	254.3	75.6	69.0	1.737	57.8	69.61
Jose Maria Olazabal	266.8	64.4	62.3	1.762	73.7	70.17
Corey Pavin	252.3	76.9	64.5	1.749	65.4	69.63
Jeff Maggert	266.1	73.4	67.2	1.770	45.5	70.25

PGA

continued

GOLFER	DISTANCE	ACCURACY	GREENS	PUTTS	SANDSAVE	SCORE
Hale Irwin	254.7	78.0	68.5	1.759	46.4	69.72
Scott Hoch	259.9	70.8	70.0	1.791	60.3	70.10
Steve Lowery	264.9	66.2	65.5	1.768	49.5	70.90
Mike Springer	273.2	64.7	65.7	1.772	49.6	70.61
Bob Estes	263.2	73.3	70.9	1.771	60.4	69.78
Phil Mickelson	273.7	63.0	68.1	1.744	54.9	69.66
John Huston	275.0	69.3	69.2	1.757	55.2	70.17
Bill Glasson	277.1	73.4	73.0	1.787	56.5	69.93

a. If average score is the dependent variable, what is the best one-variable estimated regression equation? What does the estimated regression equation suggest for golfers on the Professional Golf Association's tour?

b. Use the methods in this section to develop the best estimated multiple regression equation for estimating a golfer's average score.

c. Does the estimated regression equation developed in (b) appear reasonable in terms of interpretation?

d. Mark McCumber has the following data: driving distance 264.6 yards, driving accuracy 75.3%, greens 71.3%, putts 1.791, and sand saves 56.6%. What is your regression estimate of the average score for this professional golfer?

19. The following table gives the price-earnings ratio, net profit margin, and growth rate for 19 companies listed in "The *Forbes* 500s on Wall Street" (*Forbes*, May 1, 1989). The data in the Industry column are simply codes used to define the industry for each company: 1 = energy-international oil; 2 = health-drugs, and 3 = electronics-computers.

FORBES2

Firm	P/E Ratio	Profit Margin	Growth Rate	Industry
Exxon	11.3	6.5	10	1
Chevron	10.0	7.0	5	1
Texaco	9.9	3.9	5	1
Mobil	9.7	4.3	7	1
Amoco	10.0	9.8	8	1
Pfizer	11.9	14.7	12	2
Bristol Meyers	16.2	13.9	14	2
Merck	21.0	20.3	16	2
American Home Products	13.3	16.9	11	2
Abbott Laboratories	15.5	15.2	18	2
Eli Lilly	18.9	18.7	11	2
Upjohn	14.6	12.8	10	2
Warner-Lambert	16.0	8.7	7	2
Amdahl	8.4	11.9	4	3
Digital	10.4	9.8	19	3
Hewlett-Packard	14.8	8.1	18	3
NCR	10.1	7.3	6	3
Unisys	7.0	6.9	6	3
IBM	11.8	9.2	6	3

Develop the best estimated regression equation that can be used to predict price-earnings ratio. Briefly describe the process you used to develop a recommended estimated regression equation for these data.

20. Refer to Exercise 14. Using age, blood pressure, whether a person is a smoker, and any interaction involving those variables, develop an estimated regression equation that can be used to predict risk. Briefly describe the process you used to develop an estimated regression equation for these data.

16.5	RESIDUAL ANALYSIS

In Chapters 14 and 15 we showed how residual plots can be used to detect violations of assumptions about the regression model. We looked for violations of assumptions about the error term ϵ and the assumed functional form of the model. Some of the actions that can be taken when such violations are detected have been discussed in this chapter. When a different functional form is needed, curvilinear and interaction terms can be included through the use of the general linear model. When several independent variables are considered, the variable-selection procedures of the preceding section may be appropriate.

In Chapters 14 and 15 we also discussed how residual analysis can be used to identify observations that can be classified as outliers or as being influential in determining the estimated regression equation. Some steps that should be taken when such observations are found were noted. In many regression studies involving data collected over time, a special type of correlation among the error terms can cause problems; it is called *serial correlation* or autocorrelation. In this section we show how the Durbin-Watson test can be used to detect significant autocorrelation.

AUTOCORRELATION AND THE DURBIN-WATSON TEST

Often, the data used for regression studies in business and economics are collected over time. It is not uncommon for the value of y at time t, denoted by y_t, to be related to the value of y at previous time periods. In such cases, we say autocorrelation (also called serial correlation) is present in the data. If the value of y in time period t is related to its value in time period $t - 1$, first-order autocorrelation is present. If the value of y in time period t is related to the value of y in time period $t - 2$, second-order autocorrelation is present, and so on.

When autocorrelation is present, one of the assumptions of the regression model is violated: the error terms are not independent. In the case of first-order autocorrelation, the error at time t, denoted ϵ_t, will be related to the error at time period $t - 1$, denoted ϵ_{t-1}. Two cases of first-order autocorrelation are illustrated in Figure 16.18. Panel A is the case of positive autocorrelation; panel B is the case of negative autocorrelation. With positive autocorrelation we expect a positive residual in one period to be followed by a positive residual in the next period, a negative residual in one period to be followed by a negative residual in the next period, and so on. With negative autocorrelation, we expect a positive residual in one period to be followed by a negative residual in the next period, then a positive residual, and so on.

When autocorrelation is present, serious errors can be made in statistical inferences about the regression model. It is therefore important to be able to detect autocorrelation and take corrective action. We will show how the Durbin-Watson statistic can be used to detect first-order autocorrelation.

Suppose the values of ϵ are not independent but are related in the following manner:

$$\epsilon_t = \rho\epsilon_{t-1} + z_t \qquad \textbf{(16.16)}$$

where ρ is a parameter with an absolute value less than one and z_t is a normally and independently distributed random variable with mean zero and variance σ^2. From (16.16) we see that if $\rho = 0$, the error terms are not related, and each has a mean of zero and a variance of σ^2. In this case, there is no autocorrelation and the regression assumptions are satisfied. If $\rho > 0$, we have positive autocorrelation; if $\rho < 0$, we have

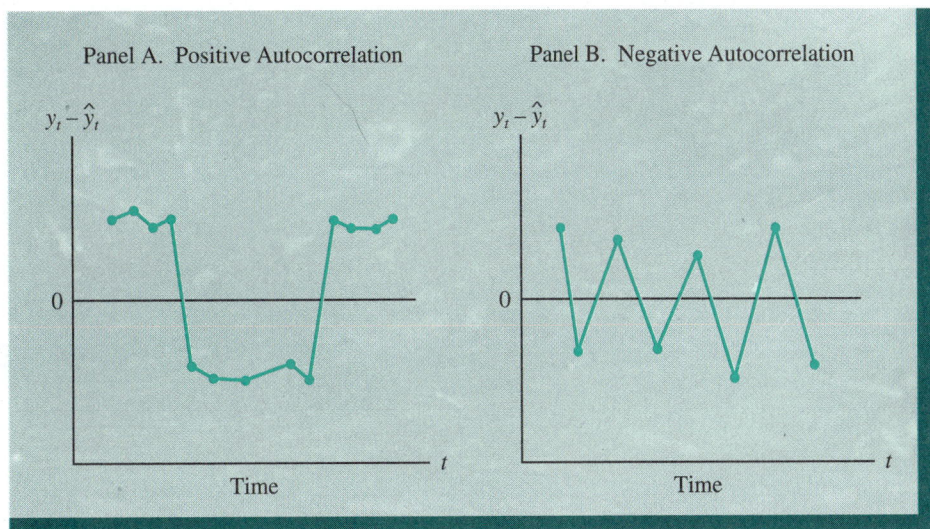

FIGURE 16.18 Two Data Sets with First-Order Autocorrelation

negative autocorrelation. In either of these cases, the regression assumptions about the error term are violated.

The Durbin-Watson test for autocorrelation uses the residuals to determine whether $\rho = 0$. To simplify the notation for the Durbin-Watson statistic, we denote the ith residual by $e_i = y_i - \hat{y}_i$. The Durbin-Watson statistic is given by the following formula.

DURBIN-WATSON STATISTIC

$$d = \frac{\sum_{t=2}^{n} (e_t - e_{t-1})^2}{\sum_{t=1}^{n} e_t^2}$$

(16.17)

If successive values of the residuals are close together (positive autocorrelation), the Durbin-Watson statistic will be small. If successive values of the residuals are far apart (negative autocorrelation), the Durbin-Watson statistic will be large.

The Durbin-Watson statistic ranges in value from zero to four, with a value of two indicating no autocorrelation is present. Durbin and Watson have developed tables that can be used to determine when their test statistic indicates the presence of autocorrelation. Table 16.12 shows lower and upper bounds (d_L and d_U) for hypothesis tests using $\alpha = .05$, $\alpha = .025$, and $\alpha = .01$; n denotes the number of observations and k is the number of independent variables in the model. The null hypothesis to be tested is always that there is no autocorrelation.

$$H_0: \rho = 0$$

The alternative hypothesis to test for positive autocorrelation is

$$H_a: \rho > 0$$

TABLE 16.12   Critical Values for the Durbin-Watson Test for Autocorrelation
NOTE: Entries in the table are the critical values for a one-tailed Durbin-Watson test for autocorrelation. For a two-tailed test, the level of significance is doubled.

	Significance Points of d_L and d_U: $\alpha = .05$ Number of Independent Variables									
k	1		2		3		4		5	
n	d_L	d_U	d_L	d_U	d_L	d_U	d_L	d_U	d_L	d_U
15	1.08	1.36	0.95	1.54	0.82	1.75	0.69	1.97	0.56	2.21
16	1.10	1.37	0.98	1.54	0.86	1.73	0.74	1.93	0.62	2.15
17	1.13	1.38	1.02	1.54	0.90	1.71	0.78	1.90	0.67	2.10
18	1.16	1.39	1.05	1.53	0.93	1.69	0.82	1.87	0.71	2.06
19	1.18	1.40	1.08	1.53	0.97	1.68	0.86	1.85	0.75	2.02
20	1.20	1.41	1.10	1.54	1.00	1.68	0.90	1.83	0.79	1.99
21	1.22	1.42	1.13	1.54	1.03	1.67	0.93	1.81	0.83	1.96
22	1.24	1.43	1.15	1.54	1.05	1.66	0.96	1.80	0.86	1.94
23	1.26	1.44	1.17	1.54	1.08	1.66	0.99	1.79	0.90	1.92
24	1.27	1.45	1.19	1.55	1.10	1.66	1.01	1.78	0.93	1.90
25	1.29	1.45	1.21	1.55	1.12	1.66	1.04	1.77	0.95	1.89
26	1.30	1.46	1.22	1.55	1.14	1.65	1.06	1.76	0.98	1.88
27	1.32	1.47	1.24	1.56	1.16	1.65	1.08	1.76	1.01	1.86
28	1.33	1.48	1.26	1.56	1.18	1.65	1.10	1.75	1.03	1.85
29	1.34	1.48	1.27	1.56	1.20	1.65	1.12	1.74	1.05	1.84
30	1.35	1.49	1.28	1.57	1.21	1.65	1.14	1.74	1.07	1.83
31	1.36	1.50	1.30	1.57	1.23	1.65	1.16	1.74	1.09	1.83
32	1.37	1.50	1.31	1.57	1.24	1.65	1.18	1.73	1.11	1.82
33	1.38	1.51	1.32	1.58	1.26	1.65	1.19	1.73	1.13	1.81
34	1.39	1.51	1.33	1.58	1.27	1.65	1.21	1.73	1.15	1.81
35	1.40	1.52	1.34	1.58	1.28	1.65	1.22	1.73	1.16	1.80
36	1.41	1.52	1.35	1.59	1.29	1.65	1.24	1.73	1.18	1.80
37	1.42	1.53	1.36	1.59	1.31	1.66	1.25	1.72	1.19	1.80
38	1.43	1.54	1.37	1.59	1.32	1.66	1.26	1.72	1.21	1.79
39	1.43	1.54	1.38	1.60	1.33	1.66	1.27	1.72	1.22	1.79
40	1.44	1.54	1.39	1.60	1.34	1.66	1.29	1.72	1.23	1.79
45	1.48	1.57	1.43	1.62	1.38	1.67	1.34	1.72	1.29	1.78
50	1.50	1.59	1.46	1.63	1.42	1.67	1.38	1.72	1.34	1.77
55	1.53	1.60	1.49	1.64	1.45	1.68	1.41	1.72	1.38	1.77
60	1.55	1.62	1.51	1.65	1.48	1.69	1.44	1.73	1.41	1.77
65	1.57	1.63	1.54	1.66	1.50	1.70	1.47	1.73	1.44	1.77
70	1.58	1.64	1.55	1.67	1.52	1.70	1.49	1.74	1.46	1.77
75	1.60	1.65	1.57	1.68	1.54	1.71	1.51	1.74	1.49	1.77
80	1.61	1.66	1.59	1.69	1.56	1.72	1.53	1.74	1.51	1.77
85	1.62	1.67	1.60	1.70	1.57	1.72	1.55	1.75	1.52	1.77
90	1.63	1.68	1.61	1.70	1.59	1.73	1.57	1.75	1.54	1.78
95	1.64	1.69	1.62	1.71	1.60	1.73	1.58	1.75	1.56	1.78
100	1.65	1.69	1.63	1.72	1.61	1.74	1.59	1.76	1.57	1.78

—*Table continues*

The alternative hypothesis to test for negative autocorrelation is

$$H_a\colon \rho < 0$$

A two-sided test is also possible. In this case the alternative hypothesis is

TABLE 16.12 (Continued)

	Significance Points of d_L and d_U: $\alpha = .025$ Number of Independent Variables									
k	**1**		**2**		**3**		**4**		**5**	
n	d_L	d_U	d_L	d_U	d_L	d_U	d_L	d_U	d_L	d_U
15	0.95	1.23	0.83	1.40	0.71	1.61	0.59	1.84	0.48	2.09
16	0.98	1.24	0.86	1.40	0.75	1.59	0.64	1.80	0.53	2.03
17	1.01	1.25	0.90	1.40	0.79	1.58	0.68	1.77	0.57	1.98
18	1.03	1.26	0.93	1.40	0.82	1.56	0.72	1.74	0.62	1.93
19	1.06	1.28	0.96	1.41	0.86	1.55	0.76	1.72	0.66	1.90
20	1.08	1.28	0.99	1.41	0.89	1.55	0.79	1.70	0.70	1.87
21	1.10	1.30	1.01	1.41	0.92	1.54	0.83	1.69	0.73	1.84
22	1.12	1.31	1.04	1.42	0.95	1.54	0.86	1.68	0.77	1.82
23	1.14	1.32	1.06	1.42	0.97	1.54	0.89	1.67	0.80	1.80
24	1.16	1.33	1.08	1.43	1.00	1.54	0.91	1.66	0.83	1.79
25	1.18	1.34	1.10	1.43	1.02	1.54	0.94	1.65	0.86	1.77
26	1.19	1.35	1.12	1.44	1.04	1.54	0.96	1.65	0.88	1.76
27	1.21	1.36	1.13	1.44	1.06	1.54	0.99	1.64	0.91	1.75
28	1.22	1.37	1.15	1.45	1.08	1.54	1.01	1.64	0.93	1.74
29	1.24	1.38	1.17	1.45	1.10	1.54	1.03	1.63	0.96	1.73
30	1.25	1.38	1.18	1.46	1.12	1.54	1.05	1.63	0.98	1.73
31	1.26	1.39	1.20	1.47	1.13	1.55	1.07	1.63	1.00	1.72
32	1.27	1.40	1.21	1.47	1.15	1.55	1.08	1.63	1.02	1.71
33	1.28	1.41	1.22	1.48	1.16	1.55	1.10	1.63	1.04	1.71
34	1.29	1.41	1.24	1.48	1.17	1.55	1.12	1.63	1.06	1.70
35	1.30	1.42	1.25	1.48	1.19	1.55	1.13	1.63	1.07	1.70
36	1.31	1.43	1.26	1.49	1.20	1.56	1.15	1.63	1.09	1.70
37	1.32	1.43	1.27	1.49	1.21	1.56	1.16	1.62	1.10	1.70
38	1.33	1.44	1.28	1.50	1.23	1.56	1.17	1.62	1.12	1.70
39	1.34	1.44	1.29	1.50	1.24	1.56	1.19	1.63	1.13	1.69
40	1.35	1.45	1.30	1.51	1.25	1.57	1.20	1.63	1.15	1.69
45	1.39	1.48	1.34	1.53	1.30	1.58	1.25	1.63	1.21	1.69
50	1.42	1.50	1.38	1.54	1.34	1.59	1.30	1.64	1.26	1.69
55	1.45	1.52	1.41	1.56	1.37	1.60	1.33	1.64	1.30	1.69
60	1.47	1.54	1.44	1.57	1.40	1.61	1.37	1.65	1.33	1.69
65	1.49	1.55	1.46	1.59	1.43	1.62	1.40	1.66	1.36	1.69
70	1.51	1.57	1.48	1.60	1.45	1.63	1.42	1.66	1.39	1.70
75	1.53	1.58	1.50	1.61	1.47	1.64	1.45	1.67	1.42	1.70
80	1.54	1.59	1.52	1.62	1.49	1.65	1.47	1.67	1.44	1.70
85	1.56	1.60	1.53	1.63	1.51	1.65	1.49	1.68	1.46	1.71
90	1.57	1.61	1.55	1.64	1.53	1.66	1.50	1.69	1.48	1.71
95	1.58	1.62	1.56	1.65	1.54	1.67	1.52	1.69	1.50	1.71
100	1.59	1.63	1.57	1.65	1.55	1.67	1.53	1.70	1.51	1.72

—Table continues

$$H_a: \rho \neq 0$$

Figure 16.19 shows how the values of d_L and d_U in Table 16.12 are to be used to test for autocorrelation. Panel A illustrates the test for positive autocorrelation. If $d < d_L$, we conclude that positive autocorrelation is present. If $d_L \leq d \leq d_U$, we say the test is inconclusive. If $d > d_U$, we conclude that there is no evidence of positive autocorrelation.

TABLE 16.12   (Continued)

					Significance Points of d_L and d_U: $\alpha = .01$					
					Number of Independent Variables					
k	**1**		**2**		**3**		**4**		**5**	
n	d_L	d_U	d_L	d_U	d_L	d_U	d_L	d_U	d_L	d_U
15	0.81	1.07	0.70	1.25	0.59	1.46	0.49	1.70	0.39	1.96
16	0.84	1.09	0.74	1.25	0.63	1.44	0.53	1.66	0.44	1.90
17	0.87	1.10	0.77	1.25	0.67	1.43	0.57	1.63	0.48	1.85
18	0.90	1.12	0.80	1.26	0.71	1.42	0.61	1.60	0.52	1.80
19	0.93	1.13	0.83	1.26	0.74	1.41	0.65	1.58	0.56	1.77
20	0.95	1.15	0.86	1.27	0.77	1.41	0.68	1.57	0.60	1.74
21	0.97	1.16	0.89	1.27	0.80	1.41	0.72	1.55	0.63	1.71
22	1.00	1.17	0.91	1.28	0.83	1.40	0.75	1.54	0.66	1.69
23	1.02	1.19	0.94	1.29	0.86	1.40	0.77	1.53	0.70	1.67
24	1.04	1.20	0.96	1.30	0.88	1.41	0.80	1.53	0.72	1.66
25	1.05	1.21	0.98	1.30	0.90	1.41	0.83	1.52	0.75	1.65
26	1.07	1.22	1.00	1.31	0.93	1.41	0.85	1.52	0.78	1.64
27	1.09	1.23	1.02	1.32	0.95	1.41	0.88	1.51	0.81	1.63
28	1.10	1.24	1.04	1.32	0.97	1.41	0.90	1.51	0.83	1.62
29	1.12	1.25	1.05	1.33	0.99	1.42	0.92	1.51	0.85	1.61
30	1.13	1.26	1.07	1.34	1.01	1.42	0.94	1.51	0.88	1.61
31	1.15	1.27	1.08	1.34	1.02	1.42	0.96	1.51	0.90	1.60
32	1.16	1.28	1.10	1.35	1.04	1.43	0.98	1.51	0.92	1.60
33	1.17	1.29	1.11	1.36	1.05	1.43	1.00	1.51	0.94	1.59
34	1.18	1.30	1.13	1.36	1.07	1.43	1.01	1.51	0.95	1.59
35	1.19	1.31	1.14	1.37	1.08	1.44	1.03	1.51	0.97	1.59
36	1.21	1.32	1.15	1.38	1.10	1.44	1.04	1.51	0.99	1.59
37	1.22	1.32	1.16	1.38	1.11	1.45	1.06	1.51	1.00	1.59
38	1.23	1.33	1.18	1.39	1.12	1.45	1.07	1.52	1.02	1.58
39	1.24	1.34	1.19	1.39	1.14	1.45	1.09	1.52	1.03	1.58
40	1.25	1.34	1.20	1.40	1.15	1.46	1.10	1.52	1.05	1.58
45	1.29	1.38	1.24	1.42	1.20	1.48	1.16	1.53	1.11	1.58
50	1.32	1.40	1.28	1.45	1.24	1.49	1.20	1.54	1.16	1.59
55	1.36	1.43	1.32	1.47	1.28	1.51	1.25	1.55	1.21	1.59
60	1.38	1.45	1.35	1.48	1.32	1.52	1.28	1.56	1.25	1.60
65	1.41	1.47	1.38	1.50	1.35	1.53	1.31	1.57	1.28	1.61
70	1.43	1.49	1.40	1.52	1.37	1.55	1.34	1.58	1.31	1.61
75	1.45	1.50	1.42	1.53	1.39	1.56	1.37	1.59	1.34	1.62
80	1.47	1.52	1.44	1.54	1.42	1.57	1.39	1.60	1.36	1.62
85	1.48	1.53	1.46	1.55	1.43	1.58	1.41	1.60	1.39	1.63
90	1.50	1.54	1.47	1.56	1.45	1.59	1.43	1.61	1.41	1.64
95	1.51	1.55	1.49	1.57	1.47	1.60	1.45	1.62	1.42	1.64
100	1.52	1.56	1.50	1.58	1.48	1.60	1.46	1.63	1.44	1.65

Source: J. Durbin and G. S. Watson, "Testing for Serial Correlation in Least Squares Regression II," *Biometrika,* 38, 1951, 159–178.

Panel B illustrates the test for negative autocorrelation. If $d > 4 - d_L$, we conclude that negative autocorrelation is present. If $4 - d_U \leq d \leq 4 - d_L$, we say the test is inconclusive. If $d < 4 - d_U$, we conclude that there is no evidence of negative autocorrelation.

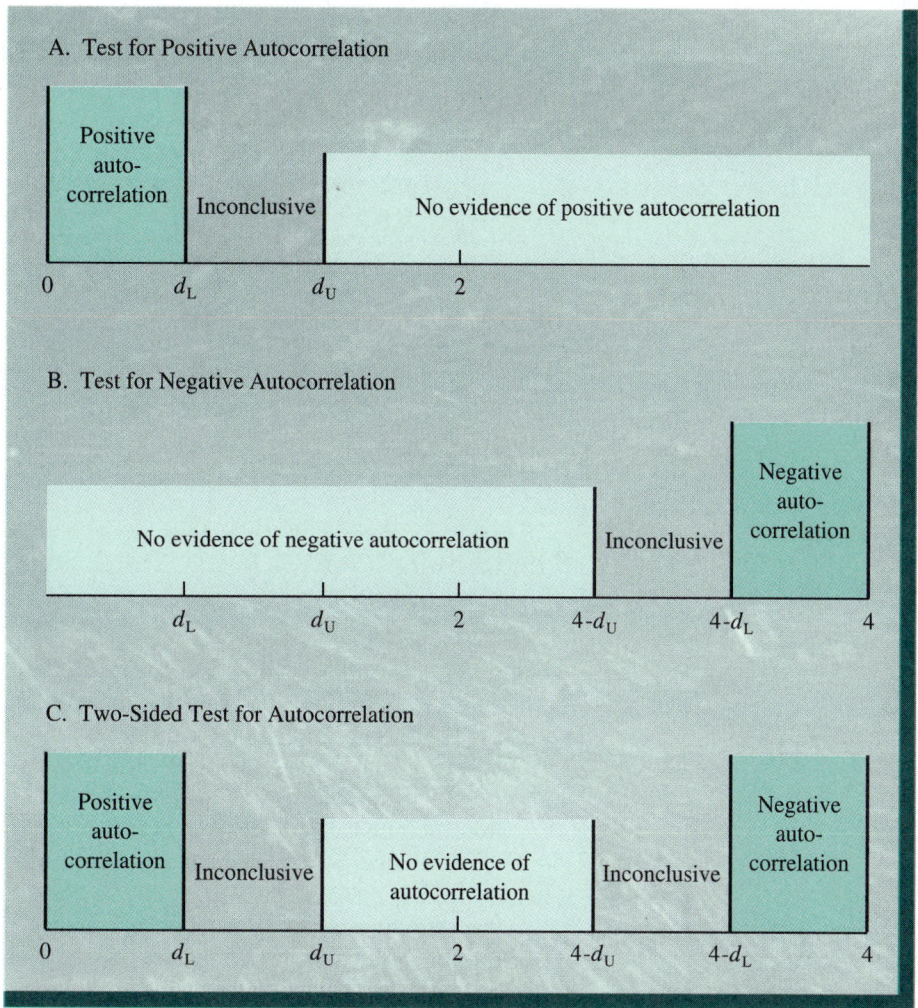

FIGURE 16.19 Hypothesis Test for Autocorrelation Using the Durbin-Watson Statistic

Panel C illustrates the two-sided test. If $d < d_L$ or $d > 4 - d_L$, we reject H_0 and conclude that autocorrelation is present. If $d_L \leq d \leq d_U$ or $4 - dU \leq d \leq 4 - dL$, we say the test is inconclusive. If $d_U < d < 4 - d_U$, we conclude that there is no evidence of autocorrelation.

If significant autocorrelation is identified, we should investigate whether we have omitted one or more key independent variables that have time-ordered effects on the dependent variable. If no such variables can be identified, including an independent variable that measures the time of the observation (for instance, the value of this variable could be one for the first observation, two for the second observation, and so on) will sometimes eliminate or reduce the autocorrelation. When these attempts to reduce or remove autocorrelation do not work, transformations on the dependent or independent variables can prove helpful; a discussion of such transformations can be found in more advanced texts on regression analysis.

Note that the Durbin-Watson tables list the smallest sample size as 15. The reason is that the test is generally inconclusive for smaller sample sizes; in fact, many statisticians believe the sample size should be at least 50 for the test to produce worthwhile results.

APPLICATIONS

Self-Test
▸▸▸▸▸▸▸▸▸▸▸▸

21. Consider the data set in Exercise 19.
   a. Develop the estimated regression equation that can be used to predict the price-earnings ratio given the profit margin.
   b. Plot the residuals obtained from the estimated regression equation developed in (a) as a function of the order in which the data are presented. Does any autocorrelation appear to be present in the data? Explain.
   c. At the .05 level of significance, test for any positive autocorrelation in the data.

22. Refer to the Cravens data set in Table 16.9. In Section 16.3 we showed that the estimated regression equation involving ACCTS, ADV, POTEN, and SHARE had an adjusted coefficient of determination of 88.1%. Use the .05 level of significance and apply the Durbin-Watson test to determine whether positive autocorrelation is present.

16.6 MULTIPLE REGRESSION APPROACH TO ANALYSIS OF VARIANCE AND EXPERIMENTAL DESIGN

In Section 15.7 we discussed the use of dummy variables in multiple regression analysis. In this section we show how the use of dummy variables in a multiple regression equation can provide another approach to solving analysis of variance and experimental design problems. We will demonstrate the multiple regression approach to analysis of variance by applying it to the National Computer Products, Inc. (NCP) problem introduced in Chapter 13.

Recall that NCP manufactures printers and fax machines at plants in Charlotte, Houston, and San Diego. To measure how much the employees know about total quality management, a random sample of six employees was selected from each plant and given a quality-awareness exam. Managers want to use the exam scores of the 18 employees to determine whether the mean examination scores are the same at each plant.

We begin the regression approach to this problem by defining two dummy variables that will be used to indicate the plant from which each sample observation was selected. Since there are three plants or populations in the NCP problem, we need two dummy variables. In general, if the factor being investigated involves k distinct levels or populations, we need to define $k - 1$ dummy variables. For the NCP problem we define x_1 and x_2 as shown in Table 16.13.

We can use the dummy variables x_1 and x_2 to relate the score on the quality-awareness examination y to the plant at which the employee works.

$E(y)$ = Expected value of the score on the quality-awareness examination

$$= \beta_0 + \beta_1 x_1 + \beta_2 x_2$$

Thus, if we are interested in the expected value of the examination score for an employee who works at the Charlotte plant, our procedure for assigning numerical values to the dummy variables x_1 and x_2 would result in setting $x_1 = x_2 = 0$. The multiple regression equation then reduces to

$$E(y) = \beta_0 + \beta_1(0) + \beta_2(0) = \beta_0$$

We can interpret β_0 as the expected value of the examination score for employees who work at the Charlotte plant.

TABLE 16.13 NCP Problem with Dummy Variables

x_1	x_2	
0	0	Observation is associated with the Charlotte plant
1	0	Observation is associated with the Houston plant
0	1	Observation is associated with the San Diego plant

TABLE 16.14   Input Data for the NCP Problem

	Charlotte			Houston			San Diego	
x_1	x_2	y	x_1	x_2	y	x_1	x_2	y
0	0	85	1	0	71	0	1	59
0	0	75	1	0	75	0	1	64
0	0	82	1	0	73	0	1	62
0	0	76	1	0	74	0	1	69
0	0	71	1	0	69	0	1	75
0	0	85	1	0	82	0	1	67

```
The regression equation is
Y = 79.0 - 5.00 X1 - 13.0 X2

Predictor        Coef        Stdev      t-ratio          p
Constant       79.000        2.186        36.14      0.000
X1             -5.000        3.091        -1.62      0.127
X2            -13.000        3.091        -4.21      0.001

s = 5.354        R-sq = 54.5%        R-sq(adj) = 48.5%

Analysis of Variance

SOURCE          DF            SS            MS          F          p
Regression       2        516.00        258.00       9.00      0.003
Error           15        430.00         28.67
Total           17        946.00
```

16.20   Multiple Regression Output for the NCP Problem

Next let us consider the forms of the multiple regression equation for each of the other plants. For the Houston plant, $x_1 = 1$ and $x_2 = 0$, and

$$E(y) = \beta_0 + \beta_1(1) + \beta_2(0) = \beta_0 + \beta_1$$

For the San Diego plant, $x_1 = 0$ and $x_2 = 1$, and

$$E(y) = \beta_0 + \beta_1(0) + \beta_2(1) = \beta_0 + \beta_2$$

We see that $\beta_0 + \beta_1$ represents the expected value of the examination score for employees at the Houston plant, and $\beta_0 + \beta_2$ represents the expected value of the examination score for employees at the San Diego plant.

We now want to estimate the coefficients $\beta_0, \beta_1,$ and β_2 and hence develop an estimate of the expected value of the examination score for each plant. The sample data consisting of 18 observations of $x_1, x_2,$ and y were entered into Minitab. The actual input data and the output from Minitab are in Table 16.14 and Figure 16.20, respectively.

In Figure 16.20, we see that the estimates of $\beta_0, \beta_1,$ and β_2 are $b_0 = 79$, $b_1 = -5$, and $b_2 = -13$. Thus, the best estimate of the expected value of the examination score for each plant is as follows.

Plant	Estimate of $E(y)$
Charlotte	$b_0 = 79$
Houston	$b_0 + b_1 = 79 - 5 = 74$
San Diego	$b_0 + b_2 = 79 - 13 = 66$

Note that the best estimate of the expected value of the examination score for each plant obtained from the regression analysis is the same as the sample mean found previously by applying the ANOVA procedure. That is, $\bar{x}_1 = 79$, $\bar{x}_2 = 74$, and $\bar{x}_3 = 66$.

Now let us see how we can use the output from the multiple regression package to perform the ANOVA test on the difference in the means for the three plants. First, we observe that if there is no difference in the means,

$$E(y) \text{ for the Houston plant} - E(y) \text{ for the Charlotte plant} = 0 \text{ and}$$

$$E(y) \text{ for the San Diego plant} - E(y) \text{ for the Charlotte plant} = 0$$

Since β_0 equals $E(y)$ for the Charlotte plant and $\beta_0 + \beta_1$ equals $E(y)$ for the Houston plant, the first difference is equal to $(\beta_0 + \beta_1) - \beta_0 = \beta_1$. Moreover, since $\beta_0 + \beta_2$ equals $E(y)$ for the San Diego plant, the second difference is equal to $(\beta_0 + \beta_2) - \beta_0 = \beta_2$. We would conclude that there is no difference in the three means if $\beta_1 = 0$ and $\beta_2 = 0$. Hence, the null hypothesis for a test for difference of means can be stated as

$$H_0: \beta_1 = \beta_2 = 0$$

Recall that to test this type of null hypothesis about the significance of the regression relationship, we must compare the value of MSR/MSE to the critical value from an F distribution with numerator and denominator degrees of freedom equal to the degrees of freedom for the regression sum of squares and the error sum of squares, respectively. In the current problem, the regression sum of squares has two degrees of freedom and the error sum of squares has 15 degrees of freedom. Thus, we obtain the following values for MSR and MSE.

$$\text{MSR} = \frac{\text{SSR}}{2} = \frac{516}{2} = 258$$

$$\text{MSE} = \frac{\text{SSE}}{15} = \frac{430}{15} = 28.67$$

Hence, the computed F value is

$$F = \frac{\text{MSR}}{\text{MSE}} = \frac{258}{28.67} = 9.00$$

At a .05 level of significance, the critical value of F with two numerator degrees of freedom and 15 denominator degrees of freedom is 3.68. Since the observed value of F is greater than the critical value of 3.68, we reject the null hypothesis $H_0: \beta_1 = \beta_2 = 0$ and conclude that the means for the three plants are different.

EXERCISES

METHODS

Self-Test

23. Consider a completely randomized design involving four treatments: A, B, C, and D. Write a multiple regression equation that can be used to analyze these data. Define all variables.

24. Write a multiple regression equation that can be used to analyze the data for a randomized block design involving three treatments and two blocks. Define all variables.

25. Write a multiple regression equation that can be used to analyze the data for a two-factorial design with two levels for factor A and three levels for factor B. Define all variables.

APPLICATIONS

Self-Test

26. The Jacobs Chemical Company wants to estimate the mean time (minutes) required to mix a batch of material on machines produced by three different manufacturers. To limit the cost of testing, four batches of material were mixed on machines produced by each of the three manufacturers. The times needed to mix the material follow.

Manufacturer 1	Manufacturer 2	Manufacturer 3
20	28	20
26	26	19
24	31	23
22	27	22

a. Write a multiple regression equation that can be used to analyze the data.
b. What are the best estimates of the coefficients in your regression equation?
c. In terms of the regression equation coefficients, what hypotheses must we test to see whether the mean time to mix a batch of material is the same for all three manufacturers?
d. For the $\alpha = .05$ level of significance, what conclusion should be drawn?

TABLE 16.15 Exercise 27

Paint 1	Paint 2	Paint 3	Paint 4
128	144	133	150
137	133	143	142
135	142	137	135
124	146	136	140
141	130	131	153

27. Four different paints are advertised as having the same drying time. To check the manufacturers' claims, five samples were tested for each of the paints. The time in minutes until the paint was dry enough for a second coat to be applied was recorded for each sample. Table 16.15 gives the data.
a. Using $\alpha = .05$, test for any significant differences in mean drying time among the paints.
b. What is your estimate of mean drying time for paint 2? How is it obtained from the computer output?

28. An automobile dealer conducted a test to determine if the time needed to complete a minor engine tuneup depends on whether a computerized engine analyzer or an electronic analyzer is used. Because tuneup time varies among compact, intermediate, and full-sized cars, the three types of cars were used as blocks in the experiment. The data (time in minutes) obtained follow.

		Car	
	Compact	Intermediate	Full Size
Analyzer Computerized	50	55	63
Electronic	42	44	46

Using $\alpha = .05$, test for any significant differences.

29. A mail-order catalog firm designed a factorial experiment to test the effect of the size of a magazine advertisement and the advertisement design on the number of catalog requests received (1000s). Three advertising designs and two sizes of advertisements were considered. The following data were obtained. Test for any significant effects due to type of design, size of advertisement, or interaction. Use $\alpha = .05$.

| | | Size of Advertisement | |
		Small	Large
Design	A	8 12	12 8
	B	22 14	26 30
	C	10 18	18 14

SUMMARY

In this chapter we discussed several concepts used by model builders in identifying the best estimated regression equation. First, we introduced the concept of a general linear model to show how the methods discussed in Chapters 14 and 15 could be extended to handle curvilinear relationships and interaction effects. Then we discussed how transformations involving the dependent variable could be used to account for problems such as nonconstant variance in the error term.

In many applications of regression analysis, a large number of independent variables are considered. We presented a general approach based on an F statistic for adding or deleting variables from a regression model. We then introduced a larger problem involving 25 observations and eight independent variables. We saw that one issue encountered in solving larger problems is finding the best subset of the independent variables. To help in that task, we discussed several variable-selection procedures: stepwise regression, forward selection, backward elimination, and best-subsets regression.

In Section 16.5, we extended the applications of residual analysis to show the Durbin-Watson test for autocorrelation. The chapter concluded with a discussion of how multiple regression models could be developed to provide another approach for solving analysis of variance and experimental design problems.

GLOSSARY

General linear model   A model of the form $y = \beta_0 + \beta_1 z_1 + \beta_2 z_2 + \cdots + \beta_p z_p + \epsilon$, where each of the independent variables $z_j, j = 1, 2, \ldots, p$, is a function of $x_1, x_2, \ldots, x_k$, the variables for which data have been collected.

Interaction   The effect of two independent variables acting together.

Variable-selection procedures   Methods for selecting a subset of the independent variables for a regression model.

Autocorrelation   Correlation in the errors that arises when the error terms at successive points in time are related.

Serial correlation   Same as autocorrelation.

Durbin-Watson test   A test to determine whether first-order autocorrelation is present.

KEY FORMULAS

General Linear Model

$$y = \beta_0 + \beta_1 z_1 + \beta_2 z_2 + \cdots + \beta_p z_p + \epsilon \qquad (16.11)$$

General F Test for Adding or Deleting $p - q$ Variables

$$F = \frac{\dfrac{\text{SSE}(x_1, x_2, \ldots, x_q) - \text{SSE}(x_1, x_2, \ldots, x_q, x_{q+1}, \ldots, x_p)}{p - q}}{\dfrac{\text{SSE}(x_1, x_2, \ldots, x_q, x_{q+1}, \ldots, x_p)}{n - p - 1}} \qquad (16.13)$$

Autocorrelated Error Terms

$$\epsilon_t = \rho\,\epsilon_{t-1} + z_t \qquad (16.16)$$

Durbin-Watson Statistic

$$d = \frac{\displaystyle\sum_{t=2}^{n} (e_t - e_{t-1})^2}{\displaystyle\sum_{t=1}^{n} e_t^2} \qquad (16.17)$$

SUPPLEMENTARY EXERCISES

30. *MacUser* (June 1994) provided the following data on the facts a user needs to select the right color monitor for a computer system. For the monitor characteristics focus and brightness, higher scores indicate better quality. For the monitor characteristics misconvergence, distortion, and uniformity, lower scores indicate better quality. Use the methods in this chapter to develop an estimated regression equation that can be used to estimate the price of the monitor on the basis of the five characteristics. What is the coefficient of determination? Discuss your results.

MONITOR2

MONITOR	FOCUS	BRIGHT	MISCONV	DISTORT	UNIFORM	PRICE
Sony CPD-1730	51.5	43.8	2.0	9.4	9.5	1100
Nanao T560i	66.0	37.5	3.6	10.9	6.4	1700
Nokia 447B	47.0	30.8	3.0	11.0	4.9	920
E-Machines T16 II	51.5	22.3	3.3	12.7	4.9	1200
Nanao F560iW	58.0	29.6	3.4	18.0	9.6	1490
NEC 5FGe	49.5	30.6	4.9	15.2	8.2	1100
Mitsubishi Pro 17	51.0	38.2	6.1	7.8	3.0	1175
Sony 17se	50.0	29.2	3.5	14.0	6.8	1195
Mirror 16″ Trinitron	43.5	30.4	3.2	20.2	4.9	999
Altima V-Scan 70	53.5	28.4	4.1	9.3	10.4	1000
ViewSonic 17	53.0	36.4	7.1	8.7	7.2	1010
Tatung CM-17MBD	42.0	30.9	4.0	17.5	6.7	875
Philips 1720	50.5	27.5	5.9	13.1	5.4	1170
Sigma ErgoView 17	46.0	25.1	4.2	21.5	6.0	1035
Sceptre P766D	49.5	20.8	4.7	15.0	8.5	880

continued

MONITOR	FOCUS	BRIGHT	MISCONV	DISTORT	UNIFORM	PRICE
Nanao F550iW	52.5	28.8	5.7	17.5	8.9	1225
Mitsubishi Scan 16	43.0	25.8	4.1	16.7	8.6	875
SuperMac 17·T	47.5	23.0	3.3	14.2	10.0	1045
Orchestra Tuba	46.0	28.7	4.4	15.6	8.8	995
Nanao F550i	53.0	27.3	4.2	16.5	8.5	1120
Relisys VividView 16	48.5	25.0	5.8	13.1	12.8	800
Mitsubishi Scan 17FS	52.5	19.6	6.4	15.9	9.4	1085

31. A study reported in the *Journal of Accounting Research* (Autumn 1987) investigated the relationship between audit delay (AUDELAY), the length of time from a company's fiscal year-end to the date of the auditor's report, and variables that describe the client and the auditor. Some of the independent variables that were included in this study follow.

INDUS   A dummy variable coded 1 if the firm was an industrial company or 0 if the firm was a bank, savings and loan, or insurance company.

PUBLIC   A dummy variable coded 1 if the company was traded on an organized exchange or over the counter; otherwise coded 0.

ICQUAL   A measure of overall quality of internal controls, as judged by the auditor, on a five-point scale ranging from "virtually none" (1) to "excellent" (5).

INTFIN   A measure ranging from 1 to 4, as judged by the auditor, where 1 indicates "all work performed subsequent to year-end" and 4 indicates "most work performed prior to year-end."

Suppose that in a similar study a sample of 40 companies provided the following data.

AUDIT

AUDELAY	INDUS	PUBLIC	ICQUAL	INTFIN
62	0	0	3	1
45	0	1	3	3
54	0	0	2	2
71	0	1	1	2
91	0	0	1	1
62	0	0	4	4
61	0	0	3	2
69	0	1	5	2
80	0	0	1	1
52	0	0	5	3
47	0	0	3	2
65	0	1	2	3
60	0	0	1	3
81	1	0	1	2
73	1	0	2	2
89	1	0	2	1
71	1	0	5	4
76	1	0	2	2
68	1	0	1	2
68	1	0	5	2
86	1	0	2	2
76	1	1	3	1
67	1	0	2	3
57	1	0	4	2
55	1	1	3	2
54	1	0	5	2
69	1	0	3	3
82	1	0	5	1
94	1	0	1	1
74	1	1	5	2

continued

AUDELAY	INDUS	PUBLIC	ICQUAL	INTFIN
75	1	1	4	3
69	1	0	2	2
71	1	0	4	4
79	1	0	5	2
80	1	0	1	4
91	1	0	4	1
92	1	0	1	4
46	1	1	4	3
72	1	0	5	2
85	1	0	5	1

a. Develop the estimated regression equation using all of the independent variables.

b. Did the estimated regression equation developed in (a) provide a good fit? Explain.

c. Develop a scatter diagram showing AUDELAY as a function of INTFIN. What does this scatter diagram indicate about the relationship between AUDELAY and INTFIN?

d. On the basis of your observations about the relationship between AUDELAY and INTFIN, develop an alternative estimated regression equation to the one developed in (a) to explain as much of the variability in AUDELAY as possible.

32. The following data set, reported in *Louis Rukeyser's Business Almanac* (1988, Simon & Schuster, p. 47), shows the percentage of management jobs held by women in various companies and the percentage of women in each company.

JOBS

Industry/Company	Management Jobs Held by Women (%)	Women Employees (%)
Industrial		
DuPont	7	22
Exxon	8	27
General Motors	6	19
Goodyear Tire and Rubber	25	39
Technology		
AT&T	32	48
General Electric	6	26
IBM	16	28
Xerox	23	38
Consumer products		
Johnson & Johnson	18	47
PepsiCo	28	46
Phillip Morris (excluding General Foods)	14	31
Procter & Gamble	17	28
Retailing and trade		
Federated Department Stores	61	72
Kroger	16	47
Marriott	32	51
McDonald's	46	57
Sears, Roebuck	36	55
Media		
ABC (excluding Capital Cities)	36	43
Time	46	54
Times Mirror	27	37
Financial services		
American Express	37	57
BankAmerica	64	72
Chemical Bank	34	57
Prudential Life Insurance	32	53
Wells Fargo Bank	58	71

In addition to the percentage of women employed in the company, create other independent variables by using dummy variables to account for the type of industry.

a. Develop the best one-variable estimated regression equation that can be used to predict the percentage of management jobs held by women.

b. Use the stepwise procedure to develop the best estimated regression equation.

c. Use the backward-elimination procedure to develop the best estimated regression equation.

33. Refer to the data in Exercise 31. Consider a model in which only INDUS is used to predict AUDELAY. At a .01 level of significance, test for any positive autocorrelation in the data.

34. Refer to the data in Exercise 31.

a. Develop an estimated regression equation that can be used to predict AUDELAY by using INDUS and ICQUAL.

b. Plot the residuals obtained from the estimated regression equation developed in (a) as a function of the order in which the data are presented. Does any autocorrelation appear to be present in the data? Explain.

c. At the .05 level of significance, test for any positive autocorrelation in the data.

35. Refer to the data in Exercise 32.

a. Develop an estimated regression equation that can be used to predict the percentage of management jobs held by women given the percentage of women employees in the company.

b. Plot the residuals obtained from the estimated regression equation developed in (a) as a function of the order in which the data are presented. Does any autocorrelation appear to be present in the data? Explain.

c. At the .05 level of significance, test for any positive autocorrelation in the data.

36. A study was conducted to investigate browsing activity by shoppers (*Journal of the Academy of Marketing Science*, Winter 1989). Shoppers were classified as nonbrowsers, light browsers, and heavy browsers. For each shopper in the study, a measure was obtained to determine how comfortable the shopper was in the store. Higher scores indicated greater comfort. Assume that the data in Table 16.16 are from this study. Use a .05 level of significance to test for differences in comfort levels among the three types of browsers.

TABLE 16.16 Exercise 36

Nonbrowser	Light Browser	Heavy Browser
4	5	5
5	6	7
6	5	5
3	4	7
3	7	4
4	4	6
5	6	5
4	5	7

COMPUTER CASE

UNEMPLOYMENT STUDY

Layoffs and unemployment have affected a substantial number of workers in recent years. A study reported in *Industrial and Labor Relations Review* (April 1988) provided data on variables that may be related to the number of weeks a manufacturing worker has been jobless. The dependent variable in the study (WEEKS) was defined as the number of weeks a worker has been jobless due to a layoff. The following independent variables were used in the study.

AGE	The age of the worker.
EDUC	The number of years of education.
MARRIED	A dummy variable; 1 if married, 0 otherwise.
HEAD	A dummy variable; 1 if the head of household, 0 otherwise.
TENURE	The number of years on the old job.
MGT	A dummy variable; 1 if management occupation, 0 otherwise.
SALES	A dummy variable; 1 if sales occupation, 0 otherwise.

Assume the following data were collected for 50 displaced workers. These data are available on the data disk in the file named LAYOFFS.

WEEKS	AGE	EDUC	MARRIED	HEAD	TENURE	MGT	SALES
37	30	14	1	1	1	0	0
62	27	14	1	0	6	0	0
49	32	10	0	1	11	0	0
73	44	11	1	0	2	0	0
8	21	14	1	1	2	0	0
15	26	13	1	0	7	1	0
52	26	15	1	0	6	0	0
72	33	13	0	1	6	0	0
11	27	12	1	1	8	0	0
13	33	12	0	1	2	0	0
39	20	11	1	0	1	0	0
59	35	7	1	1	6	0	0
39	36	17	0	1	9	1	0
44	26	12	1	1	8	0	0
56	36	15	0	1	8	0	0
31	38	16	1	1	11	0	1
62	34	13	0	1	13	0	0
25	27	19	1	0	8	0	0
72	44	13	1	0	22	0	0
65	45	15	1	1	6	0	0
44	28	17	0	1	3	0	1
49	25	10	1	1	1	0	0
80	31	15	1	0	12	0	0
7	23	15	1	0	2	0	0
14	24	13	1	1	7	0	0
94	62	13	0	1	8	0	0
48	31	16	1	0	11	0	0
82	48	18	0	1	30	0	0
50	35	18	1	1	5	0	0
37	33	14	0	1	6	0	1
62	46	15	0	1	6	0	0
37	35	8	0	1	6	0	0
40	32	9	1	1	13	0	0
16	40	17	1	0	8	1	0
34	23	12	1	1	1	0	0
4	36	16	0	1	8	0	1
55	33	12	1	0	10	0	1
39	32	16	0	1	11	0	0
80	62	15	1	0	16	0	1
19	29	14	1	1	12	0	0
98	45	12	1	0	17	0	0
30	38	15	0	1	6	0	1
22	40	8	1	1	16	0	1
57	42	13	1	0	2	1	0
64	45	16	1	1	22	0	0
22	39	11	1	1	4	0	0
27	27	15	1	0	10	0	1
20	42	14	1	1	6	1	0
30	31	10	1	1	8	0	0
23	33	13	1	1	8	0	0

LAYOFFS

Managerial Report

Use the methods presented in this and previous chapters to analyze this data set. Present a summary of your analysis, including key statistical results, conclusions, and recommendations, in a managerial report. Include any technical material that you feel is appropriate (computer output, residual plots, etc.) in an appendix.

17

INDEX NUMBERS

STATISTICS IN PRACTICE ●

BLS

U.S. Department of Labor
Bureau of Labor Statistics
Washington D.C.

The U.S. Department of Labor, through its Bureau of Labor Statistics, compiles and distributes indexes and statistics that are indicators of business and economic activity in the United States. For instance, the Bureau compiles and publishes the Consumer Price Index, the Producer Price Index, and statistics on average hours and earnings of various groups of workers. Perhaps the most widely quoted index produced by the Bureau of Labor Statistics is the Consumer Price Index. It is often used as a measure of inflation.

In February 1995, the Labor Department reported that the Consumer Price Index had increased by .3% over the January level. "The price increases were across-the-board, but higher clothing and housing costs were major contributors" (*The Wall Street Journal*, February 16, 1995). The Labor Department further noted that the core rate of inflation jumped by .4%. The core rate excludes the volatile food and energy components of the Consumer Price Index and is sometimes viewed as a better indicator of inflationary pressures. Despite strong economic growth, the Consumer Price Index rose only 2.7% for all of 1994. Federal Reserve Chairman Alan Greenspan noted that 1994 was the third consecutive year in which inflation had been less than 3%.

Despite the low inflation rates over the preceding few years, the Federal Reserve had been aggressively increasing interest rates during 1994 to combat anticipated future inflation. The reasoning was that the economy was growing at such a fast rate that higher prices were sure to follow. After reviewing the January 1995 increase in the Consumer Price Index, experts were divided on whether or not inflation was picking up. Some expressed concern about the increase in the core rate of inflation, whereas others pointed to a slowdown in the rate of growth of industrial production, reported by the Federal Reserve Board, as an indication that inflationary pressures would subside.

Another indicator that inflationary pressures would be moderate for the near-term future was given by the Producer Price Index. It measures price changes in wholesale markets and is often seen as a leading indicator of changes in the Consumer Price Index. The Producer Price Index was up .3% in Janurary 1995, but its core rate was up only .2%. For all of 1994, the Producer Price Index was up only 1.7%.

In this chapter we will see how various indexes, such as the Consumer and Producer Price Indexes, are computed and how they should be interpreted.

The U.S. government provides a large volume of business and economic data.

● Each month the U.S. government publishes a variety of indexes that are designed to help individuals understand current business and economic conditions. Perhaps the most widely known and cited of these indexes is the Consumer Price Index (CPI). As its name implies, the CPI is an indicator of what is happening to prices consumers are paying for items purchased. Specifically, the CPI measures changes in price over a period of time. With a given starting point or *base period* and its associated index of 100, the CPI can be used to compare current period consumer prices with those in the base period. For example, a CPI of 125 reflects the condition that consumer prices as a whole are running approximately 25% above the base period prices for the same items. Although relatively few individuals know exactly what this number means, they do know enough about the CPI to understand that an increase means higher prices. The CPI is widely used as a measure of inflation.

The CPI is perhaps the best known index. However, many other governmental and private-sector indexes are available to help us measure and understand how economic conditions in one period compare with economic conditions in other periods. The purpose of this chapter is to describe the most widely used types of indexes. We will begin by constructing some simple index numbers to gain a better understanding of how indexes are computed.

17.1   PRICE RELATIVES

TABLE 17.1   Unleaded Gasoline Cost

Year	Price per Gallon ($)
1982	1.30
1983	1.24
1984	1.21
1985	1.20
1986	.93
1987	.95
1988	.95
1989	1.02
1990	1.16
1991	1.14
1992	1.13
1993	1.12

Source: U.S. Energy Administration, *Monthly Energy Review.*

The simplest form of a price index shows how the current price per unit for a given item compares to a base period price per unit for the same item. For example, Table 17.1 reports the cost of one gallon of unleaded gasoline for the years 1982 through 1993. To facilitate comparisons with other years, the actual cost-per-gallon figure can be converted to a *price relative,* which expresses the unit price in each period as a percentage of the unit price in a base period.

$$\text{Price relative in period } t = \frac{\text{Price in period } t}{\text{Base period price}}(100) \qquad \textbf{(17.1)}$$

For the gasoline prices in Table 17.1 and with 1982 as the base year, the price relatives for one gallon of unleaded gasoline in the years 1982 through 1993 can be calculated. These price relatives are listed in Table 17.2. Note how easily the price in any one year can be compared with the price in the base year by knowing the price relative. For example, the price relative of 93 in 1984 shows that the gasoline cost in 1984 was 7% below the 1982 base-year cost. Similarly, the 1993 price relative of 86 shows a 14% decrease in gasoline cost in 1993 from the 1982 base-year cost. Price relatives, such as the ones for unleaded gasoline, are extremely helpful in terms of understanding and interpreting changing economic and business conditions over time.

17.2   AGGREGATE PRICE INDEXES

Although price relatives can be used to identify price changes over time for individual items, we are often more interested in the general price change for a group of items taken as a whole. For example, if we want an index that measures the change in the overall cost of living over time, we will want the index to be based on the price changes for a variety of items, including food, housing, clothing, transportation, medical care, and so on. An *aggregate price index* is developed for the specific purpose of measuring the combined change of a group of items.

Consider the development of an aggregate price index for a group of items categorized as normal automotive operating expenses. For illustration, we limit the items included in the group to gasoline, oil, tire, and insurance expenses.

Table 17.3 gives the data for the four components of our automotive operating expense index for the years 1982 and 1993. With 1982 as the base period, an aggregate price index for the four components will give us a measure of the change in normal automotive operating expenses over the 1982–1993 period.

TABLE 17.2 Price Relatives for One Gallon of Unleaded Gasoline (1982–1993)

Year	Price Relative (Base 1982)
1982	$(1.30/1.30)100 = 100$
1983	$(1.24/1.30)100 = 95$
1984	$(1.21/1.30)100 = 93$
1985	$(1.20/1.30)100 = 92$
1986	$(.93/1.30)100 = 72$
1987	$(.95/1.30)100 = 73$
1988	$(.95/1.30)100 = 73$
1989	$(1.02/1.30)100 = 78$
1990	$(1.16/1.30)100 = 89$
1991	$(1.14/1.30)100 = 88$
1992	$(1.13/1.30)100 = 87$
1993	$(1.12/1.30)100 = 86$

An unweighted aggregate index can be developed by simply summing the unit prices in the year of interest (e.g., 1993) and dividing that sum by the sum of the unit prices in the base year (1982). Let

$$P_{it} = \text{unit price for item } i \text{ in period } t \text{ and}$$

$$P_{i0} = \text{unit price for item } i \text{ in the base period.}$$

An unweighted aggregate price index in period t, denoted by I_t, is given by

$$I_t = \frac{\Sigma P_{it}}{\Sigma P_{i0}}(100) \qquad \textbf{(17.2)}$$

where the sums are over all items in the group.

An unweighted aggregate index for normal automotive operating expenses in 1993 ($t = 1993$) is given by

$$I_{1993} = \frac{1.12 + 2.00 + 130.00 + 650.00}{1.30 + 1.50 + 80.00 + 300.00}(100)$$

$$= \frac{783.12}{382.80}(100) = 205$$

From the unweighted aggregate price index, we might conclude that the price of normal automotive operating expenses increased 105% over the period from 1982 to 1993. But note that the unweighted aggregate approach to establishing a composite price index for automotive expenses is heavily influenced by the items with large per-unit prices. Consequently, items with relatively low unit prices such as gasoline and oil are dominated by the high-unit-price items such as tires and insurance. The unweighted aggregate index for automotive operating expenses is too heavily influenced by price changes in tires and insurance.

Because of the sensitivity of an unweighted index to one or more high-priced items, this form of aggregate index is not widely used. A weighted aggregate price index provides a better comparison when usage quantities differ.

The philosophy behind the *weighted aggregate index* is that each item in the group should be weighted according to its importance. In most cases, the *quantity* of usage is the best measure of importance. Hence, one must obtain a measure of the quantity of usage for the various items in the group. Table 17.4 gives annual usage information for each item of automotive operating expense based on the typical operation of a midsize automobile for approximately 15,000 miles per year. The quantity weights listed show the expected annual usage for this type of driving situation.

Let $Q_i =$ quantity for item i. The weighted aggregate price index in period t is given by

TABLE 17.3 Data for Automotive Operating Expense Index ($)

Item	1982	1993
Gallon of gas	1.30	1.12
Quart of oil	1.50	2.00
Tires	80.00	130.00
Insurance policy	300.00	650.00

$$I_t = \frac{\Sigma P_{it}Q_i}{\Sigma P_{i0}Q_i}(100) \qquad \textbf{(17.3)}$$

where the sums are over all items in the group. It is based on dividing total operating costs in 1993 by total operating costs in 1982.

Let $t = 1993$, and use the quantity weights in Table 17.4. We obtain the following weighted aggregate price index for automotive operating expenses in 1993.

$$I_{1993} = \frac{1.12(1000) + 2.00(15) + 130.00(2) + 650.00(1)}{1.30(1000) + 1.50(15) + 80.00(2) + 300.00(1)}(100)$$

$$= \frac{2060}{1782.5}(100) = 116$$

TABLE 17.4 Annual Usage Information for Automotive Operating Expense Index

Item	Quantity Weights*
Gallons of gasoline	1000
Quarts of oil	15
Tires	2
Insurance policy	1

*Based on 15,000 miles per year. Tire usage is based on a 30,000-mile tire life.

From this weighted aggregate price index, we would conclude that the price of automotive operating expenses has increased 16% over the period from 1982 through 1993.

Clearly, compared with the unweighted aggregate index, the weighted index provides a more accurate indication of the price change for automotive operating expenses over the 1982–1993 period. Taking the quantity of usage of gasoline into account helps to offset the large increase in insurance costs. The weighted index shows a more moderate increase in automotive operating expenses than the unweighted index. In general, the weighted aggregate index with quantities of usage as weights is the preferred method for establishing a price index for a group of items.

In the weighted aggregate price index formula (17.3), note that the quantity term Q_i does not have a second subscript to indicate the time period. The reason is that the quantities Q_i are considered *fixed* and do not vary with time as the prices do. The fixed weights or quantities are specified by the designer of the index at levels believed to be representative of typical usage. Once established, they are held constant or fixed for all periods of time the index is in use. Indexes for years other than 1993 require the gathering of new price data P_{it}, but the weighting quantities Q_i remain the same.

In a special case of the fixed-weight aggregate index, the quantities are determined from base-year usages. In this case we write $Q_i = Q_{i0}$, with the zero subscript indicating base-year quantity weights; (17.3) becomes

$$I_t = \frac{\Sigma P_{it}Q_{i0}}{\Sigma P_{i0}Q_{i0}}(100) \qquad \textbf{(17.4)}$$

Whenever the fixed quantity weights are determined from base-year usage, the weighted aggregate index is given the name *Laspeyres index.*

Another option for determining quantity weights is to revise the quantities each period. A quantity Q_{it} is determined for each year that the index is computed. The weighted aggregate index in period t with these quantity weights is given by

$$I_t = \frac{\Sigma P_{it}Q_{it}}{\Sigma P_{i0}Q_{it}}(100) \qquad \textbf{(17.5)}$$

Note that the same quantity weights are used for the base period (period 0) and for period t. However, the weights are based on usage in period t, not the base period. This weighted aggregate index is known as the *Paasche index.* It has the advantage of being based on current usage patterns. However, this method of computing a weighted aggregate index has two disadvantages: the normal usage quantities Q_{it} must be redetermined each year, thus adding to the time and cost of data collection, and each year the index numbers for previous years must be recomputed to reflect the effect of the new quantity weights. Because of these disadvantages, the Laspeyres index is more widely used. The automotive operating expense index was computed with base-period quantities; hence, it is a Laspeyres index. Had usage figures for 1993 been used, we would have had a Paasche index. Indeed, because of more fuel efficient cars, gasoline usage has decreased and a Paasche index would differ from a Laspeyres index.

EXERCISES

METHODS

1. The following table reports prices and usage quantities for two items in 1986 and 1995.

	Quantity		Unit Price ($)	
Item	1986	1995	1986	1995
A	1500	1800	7.50	7.75
B	2	1	630.00	1500.00

a. Compute price relatives for each item in 1995 using 1986 as the base period.
b. Compute an unweighted aggregate price index for the two items in 1995 using 1986 as the base period.
c. Compute a weighted aggregate price index for the two items using the Laspeyres method.
d. Compute a weighted aggregate price index for the two items using the Paasche method.

2. An item with a price relative of 132 cost $10.75 in 1995. Its base year was 1990.
  a. What was the percentage increase or decrease in cost of the item over the 5-year period?
  b. What did the item cost in 1990?

APPLICATIONS

Self-Test

3. A large manufacturer purchases an identical component from three independent suppliers that differ in unit price and quantity supplied. The relevant data for 1993 and 1995 are given in Table 17.5.
  a. Compute the price relatives for each of the component suppliers separately. Compare the price increases by the suppliers over the two-year period.
  b. Compute an unweighted aggregate price index for the component part in 1995.
  c. Compute a 1995 weighted aggregate price index for the component part. What is the interpretation of this index for the manufacturing firm?

TABLE 17.5 Exercise 3

	Quantity	Unit Price ($)	
Supplier	(1993)	1993	1995
A	150	5.45	6.00
B	200	5.60	5.95
C	120	5.50	6.20

4. R&B Beverages, Inc., provides a complete line of beer, wine, and soft-drink products for distribution through retail outlets in central Iowa. Unit-price data for 1994 and 1995 and quantities sold in cases for 1994 follow.

	1994 Quantity	Unit Price ($)	
Item	(cases)	1994	1995
Beer	35,000	15.00	16.25
Wine	5,000	60.00	64.00
Soft drink	60,000	9.80	10.00

Compute a weighted aggregate index for the R&B Beverage sales in 1995, with 1994 as the base period.

5. Under the LIFO inventory valuation method, a price index for inventory must be established for tax purposes. The quantity weights are based on year-ending inventory levels. Use the beginning-of-the-year price per unit as the base-period price and develop a weighted aggregate index for the total inventory value at the end of the year. What type of weighted aggregate price index must be developed for the LIFO inventory valuation?

	Ending	Unit Price ($)	
Product	Inventory	Beginning	Ending
A	500	.15	.19
B	50	1.60	1.80
C	100	4.50	4.20
D	40	12.00	13.20

TABLE 17.6 Price Relatives for Automotive Operating Expense Index

Item	Unit Price ($) 1982 (P_0)	1993 (P_t)	Price Relative $(P_t/P_0)100$	Annual Usage
Gallons of gasoline	1.30	1.12	86	1,000
Quarts of oil	1.50	2.00	133	15
Tires	80.00	130.00	163	2
Insurance policy	300.00	650.00	217	1

17.3 COMPUTING AN AGGREGATE PRICE INDEX FROM PRICE RELATIVES

In Section 17.1 we defined the concept of a price relative and showed how a price relative can be computed with knowledge of the current-period unit price and the base-period unit price. We now want to show how aggregate price indexes like the ones developed in Section 17.2 can be computed directly from information about the price relative of each item in the group. Because of the limited use of unweighted indexes, we restrict our attention to weighted aggregate price indexes. Let us return to the automotive operating expense index of the preceding section. The necessary information for the four items is given in Table 17.6.

Let w_i be the weight applied to the price relative for item i. The general expression for a weighted average of price relatives is given by

$$I_t = \frac{\sum \frac{P_{it}}{P_{i0}} w_i}{\Sigma w_i} (100) \qquad (17.6)$$

The proper choice of weights in (17.6) will enable us to compute a weighted aggregate price index from the price relatives. The proper choice of weights is given by multiplying the base-period price by the quantity of usage.

$$w_i = P_{i0} Q_i \qquad (17.7)$$

Substitution of the value for w_i shown in (17.7) into (17.6) provides the following expression for a weighted price relatives index.

$$I_t = \frac{\sum \frac{P_{it}}{P_{i0}} (P_{i0} Q_i)(100)}{\Sigma P_{i0} Q_i} \qquad (17.8)$$

With the canceling of the P_{i0} terms in the numerator, the weighted price relatives index becomes

$$I_t = \frac{\Sigma P_{it} Q_i}{\Sigma P_{i0} Q_i} (100)$$

Thus, we see that the weighted price relatives index with $w_i = P_{i0} Q_i$ provides a price index identical to the weighted aggregate index presented in Section 17.2. (See equation (17.3).) Use of base-period quantities (i.e., $Q_i = Q_{i0}$) in (17.7) leads to a Laspeyres index. Use of current-period quantities (i.e., $Q_i = Q_{it}$) in (17.7) leads to a Paasche index.

TABLE 17.7 Automotive Operating Expense Index (1982–1993) Based on Weighted Price Relatives

Item	Price Relatives	Base Price ($)	Quantity Q_i	Weight $w_i = P_{i0}Q_i$	Weighted Price Relatives $(P_{it}/P_{i0})(100)w_i$
Gasoline	86	1.30	1000	1300.00	111,800.00
Oil	133	1.50	15	22.50	2,992.50
Tires	163	80.00	2	160.00	26,080.00
Insurance	217	300.00	1	300.00	65,100.00
				Totals 1782.50	205,972.50

$$I_{1993} = \frac{205,972.50}{1782.50} = 116$$

Let us return to the automotive operating expense data. We can use the price relatives in Table 17.6 and equation (17.6) to compute a weighted average of price relatives. The results obtained by using the weights specified by (17.7) are reported in Table 17.7. The index number 116 represents a 16% increase in automotive operating expenses, which is the same as the increase identified by the weighted aggregate index computation in Section 17.2.

EXERCISES

METHODS

Self-Test

6. In Table 17.8 are price relatives for three items, along with base-period prices and usage. Compute a weighted aggregate price index for the current period.

APPLICATIONS

Self-Test

7. The Mitchell Chemical Company produces a special industrial chemical that is a blend of three chemical ingredients. The beginning-year cost per pound, the ending-year cost per pound, and the blend proportions follow.

Ingredient	Cost per Pound ($) Beginning	Ending	Quantity (pounds) per 100 Pounds of Product
A	2.50	3.95	25
B	8.75	9.90	15
C	.99	.95	60

a. Compute the price relatives for the three ingredients.
b. Compute a weighted average of the price relatives to develop a one-year cost index for raw materials used in the product. What is your interpretation of this index value?

8. An investment portfolio consists of four stocks. The purchase price, current price, and number of shares are reported in the following table.

TABLE 17.8 Exercise 6

Item	Price Relative	Base Period Price	Usage
A	150	22.00	20
B	90	5.00	50
C	120	14.00	40

Stock	Purchase Price/Share ($)	Current Price/Share ($)	Number of Shares
Holiday Trans	15.50	17.00	500
NY Electric	18.50	20.25	200
KY Gas	26.75	26.00	500
PQ Soaps	42.25	45.50	300

Construct a weighted average of price relatives as an index of the performance of the portfolio to date. Interpret this price index.

9. Compute the price relatives for the R&B Beverages products in Exercise 4. Use a weighted average of price relatives to show that this method provides the same index as the weighted aggregate method.

17.4   SOME IMPORTANT PRICE INDEXES

We have identified the procedures used to compute price indexes for single items or groups of items. Now let us consider some price indexes that are important measures of business and economic conditions. Specifically, we will consider the Consumer Price Index, the Producer Price Index, and the Dow Jones averages.

CONSUMER PRICE INDEX

Perhaps the most widely known and cited measure of change in general economic conditions is the *Consumer Price Index* (CPI). This index, published monthly by the U.S. Bureau of Labor Statistics, is the primary measure of the cost of living in the United States. The group of items used to develop the index consists of a *market basket* of 400 items including food, housing, clothing, transportation, and medical items. The CPI is a weighted aggregate price index with fixed weights.* The weight applied to each item in the market basket derives from a usage survey of urban families throughout the United States.

The January 1995 CPI, computed with a 1982–1984 base index of 100, was 150.6. This means that the cost of purchasing the market basket of goods and services had increased 50.6% since the base period 1982–1984. The 40-year time series of the CPI from 1950 to 1990 is shown in Figure 17.1. Note how the CPI measure reflects the sharp inflationary behavior of the economy in the late 1970s and early 1980s.

PRODUCER PRICE INDEX

The *Producer Price Index* (PPI), also published monthly by the U.S. Bureau of Labor Statistics, measures the monthly changes in prices in primary markets in the United States. This index replaces the old Wholesale Price Index. The PPI is based on prices for the first transaction of each product in nonretail markets. All commodities sold in commercial transactions in these markets are represented. The survey covers raw, manufactured, and processed goods at each level of processing and includes the output of industries classified as manufacturing, agriculture, forestry, fishing, mining, gas and electricity, and public utilities. One of the common uses of this index is as a leading indicator of the future trend of consumer prices and the cost of living. An increase in the PPI reflects producer price increases that will eventually be passed on to the consumer through higher retail prices.

Weights for the various items in the PPI are based on the value of shipments. The weighted average of price relatives is calculated by the Laspeyres method. The January 1995 PPI, computed with a 1982 base index of 100, was 126.9.

---

*There are actually two Consumer Price Indexes. The Bureau of Labor Statistics publishes a Consumer Price Index for all urban consumers (CPI-U) and a revised Consumer Price Index for urban wage earners and clerical workers (CPI-W). The CPI-U is the one most widely quoted, and it is published regularly in *The Wall Street Journal.*

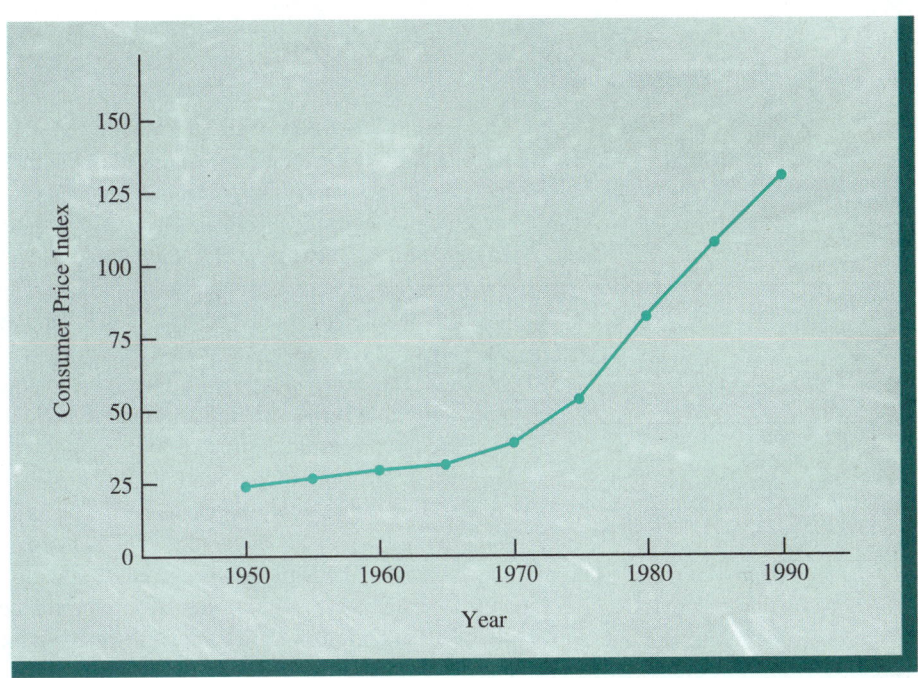

FIGURE 17.1 Consumer Price Index, 1950−1990 with Base 1982−1984 = 100

TABLE 17.9 The 30 Industrial Companies Used in the Dow Jones Industrial Average (February 1995)

AT&T	DuPont	Minnesota Mining and Manufacturing
Allied Signal	Eastman Kodak	J. P. Morgan
Alcoa	Exxon	Philip Morris
American Express	General Electric	Procter & Gamble
Bethlehem Steel	General Motors	Sears
Boeing	Goodyear	Texaco
Caterpillar	IBM	Union Carbide
Chevron	International Paper	United Technologies
Coca Cola	McDonald's	Westinghouse
Disney	Merck	Woolworth

DOW JONES AVERAGES

The *Dow Jones averages* are indexes designed to show price trends and movements on the New York Stock Exchange. The best known of the Dow Jones indexes is the Dow Jones Industrial Average (DJIA), which is based on common stock prices of 30 industrial companies. It is the sum of these stock prices divided by a divisor which is revised from time to time to adjust for stock splits and switching of companies in the index. Unlike the other price indexes that we have studied, it is not expressed as a percentage of base-year prices. The specific firms used in February 1995 to compute the DJIA are listed in Table 17.9.

Other Dow Jones averages are computed for 20 transportation stocks and for 15 utility stocks. The Dow Jones averages are computed and published daily in *The Wall Street Journal* and other financial publications.

17.5   DEFLATING A SERIES BY PRICE INDEXES

Many business and economic series reported over time, such as company sales, industry sales, and inventories, are measured in dollar amounts. These time series often show an increasing growth pattern over time, which is generally interpreted as indicating an increase in the physical volume associated with the activities. For example, a total dollar amount of inventory up by 10% might be interpreted to mean that the physical inventory is 10% larger. Such interpretations can be very misleading if a time series is measured in terms of dollars, since the total dollar amount is a combination of both price and quantity changes. Hence, in periods when price changes are significant, the changes in the dollar amounts may not be indicative of quantity changes unless we are able to adjust the time series to eliminate the price-change effect.

For example, from 1976 to 1980, the total amount of spending in the construction industry increased approximately 75%. That figure suggests excellent growth in construction activity. However, construction prices were increasing just as fast as—or sometimes even faster than—the 75% rate. In fact, while total construction spending was increasing, construction activity was staying relatively constant or, as in the case of new housing starts, decreasing. To interpret construction activity correctly for the 1976–1980 period, we must adjust the total spending series by a price index to remove the price-increase effect. Whenever we remove the price-increase effect from a time series, we say we are *deflating the series.*

In relation to personal income and wages, we often hear discussions about issues such as "real wages" or the "purchasing power" of wages. These concepts are based on the notion of deflating an hourly wage index. For example, Figure 17.2 shows the pattern of hourly wages of manufacturing workers for the period 1989–1993. We see a trend of wage increases from $10.48 per hour to $11.76 per hour. Should manufacturing workers be pleased with this growth in hourly wages? The answer depends on what has happened to the purchasing power of their wages. If we can compare the purchasing

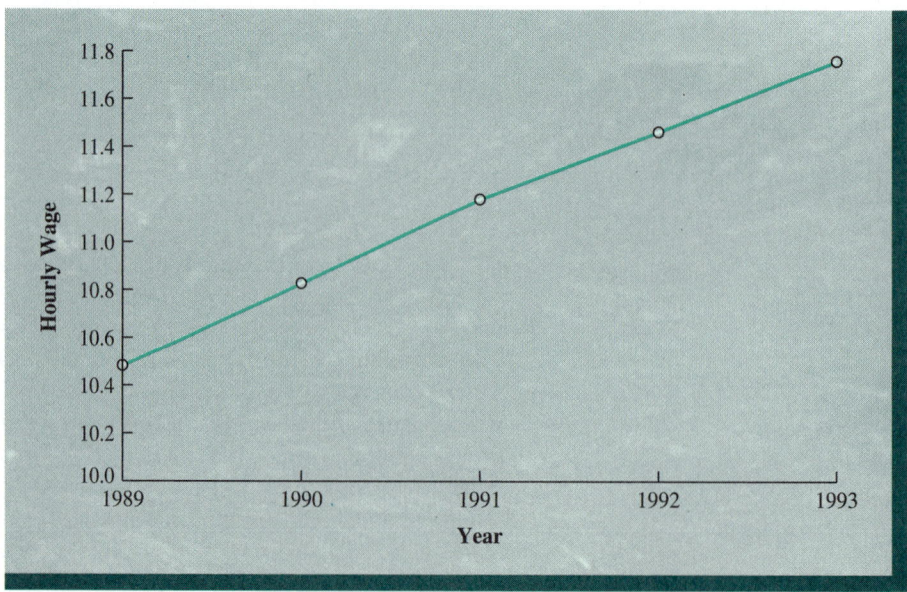

FIGURE 17.2   Actual Hourly Wages of Manufacturing Workers

TABLE 17.10 Hourly Wages of Manufacturing Workers and Consumer Price Index: 1989–1993

Year	Hourly Wage ($)	CPI (1982–1984 Base)
1989	10.48	124.0
1990	10.83	130.7
1991	11.18	136.2
1992	11.46	140.3
1993	11.76	144.5

TABLE 17.11 Deflated Series of Hourly Wages for Manufacturing Workers

Year	Deflated Hourly Wage
1989	($10.48/124.0)(100) = $8.45
1990	($10.83/130.7)(100) = $8.29
1991	($11.18/136.2)(100) = $8.21
1992	($11.46/140.3)(100) = $8.17
1993	($11.76/144.5)(100) = $8.14

power of the $10.48 hourly wage in 1989 with the purchasing power of the $11.76 hourly wage in 1993, we will be better able to judge the relative improvement in wages.

Table 17.10 reports both the hourly wage rate and the CPI for the period 1989–1993. With these data, we will show how the CPI can be used to deflate the index of hourly wages. The deflated series is found by dividing the hourly wage rate in each year by the corresponding value of the CPI and multiplying by 100. The deflated hourly wage index for manufacturing workers is given in Table 17.11; Figure 17.3 is a graph showing the deflated, or real, wages.

What does the deflated series of wages tell us about the real wages or purchasing power of workers during the 1989–1993 period? In terms of base period dollars (1982–1984 = 100), the hourly wage rate has actually declined from $8.45 to $8.14, or 3.7%. Hence, after we remove the price-increase effect, we see that manufacturing workers have lost ground to inflation; their purchasing power has declined. This effect is seen clearly in Figure 17.3. Thus, the advantage of using price indexes to deflate a series is that we have a clearer picture of the real dollar changes that are occurring.

This process of deflating a series measured over time has an important application in the computation of the Gross Domestic Product (GDP). The GDP is the total value of all goods and services produced in a given country. Obviously, over time the GDP will show gains that are in part due to price increases if the GDP is not deflated by a price index. Therefore, to adjust the total value of goods and services to reflect actual changes in the volume of goods and services produced and sold, the GDP must be computed with a price index deflator. The process is similar to that discussed in the real wages computation.

EXERCISES

APPLICATIONS

Self-Test ▸

TABLE 17.12 Exercise 11

Year	Total Personal Income ($ billions)
1989	4380.3
1990	4673.8
1991	4850.9
1992	5144.9
1993	5388.3

10. Average hourly wages for factory workers in 1980 were $7.27; in 1993, they were $11.76. The CPI in 1980 was 82.4; in 1993 it was 144.5.
   a. Deflate the hourly wage rates in 1980 and 1993 to find the real wage rates.
   b. What is the percentage change in actual hourly wages from 1980 to 1993?
   c. What is the percentage change in real wages from 1980 to 1993?

11. Total U.S. personal income for the five years from 1989 through 1993 is reported in Table 17.12. Use the Consumer Price Index information in Table 17.10 to deflate the personal income series. What has been the percentage increase in real personal income from 1991 to 1993?

12. The U.S. Bureau of the Census reported the following total inventories of all manufacturers for the five years from 1988 through 1992.

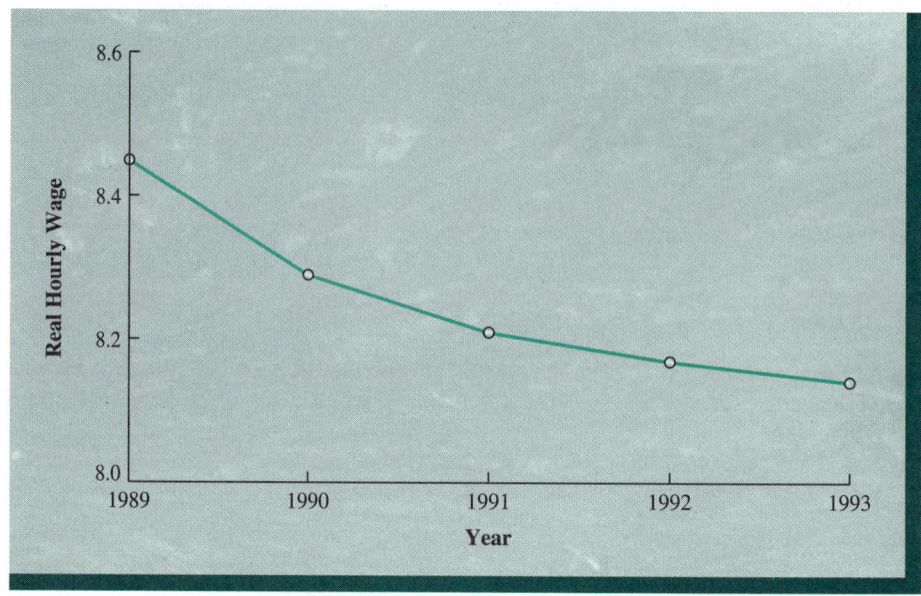

FIGURE 17.3   Real Hourly Wages of Manufacturing Workers (1982–1984 =100)

Year	Total Inventories ($ billions)
1988	361
1989	380
1990	392
1991	380
1992	373

a. The CPI in 1988 was 118.3; the CPI for 1989–1993 is given in Table 17.10. Use this information to deflate the inventory series and comment on the pattern of manufacturers' inventories in terms of constant dollars.

b. The following Producer Price Indexes (finished consumer goods, excluding food) are for 1988 through 1992, with 1982 as the base year. Use the PPI to deflate the series.

Year	PPI (1982 = 100)
1988	103.1
1989	108.9
1990	115.3
1991	118.7
1992	120.8

TABLE 17.13   Exercise 13

Year	Retail Sales ($)	CPI (1982–1984 base)
1978	380,000	65.2
1983	520,000	99.6
1988	700,000	118.3
1993	870,000	144.5

c. Do you feel that the CPI or the PPI is more appropriate to use as a deflator for inventory values?

13. Dooley Retail Outlets has had the total retail sales volumes listed in Table 17.13 for selected years since 1978. Also shown is the CPI with the index base of 1982–1984. Deflate the sales volume figures on the basis of 1982–1984 constant dollars, and comment on the firm's sales volumes in terms of deflated dollars.

17.6   PRICE INDEXES: OTHER CONSIDERATIONS

In the preceding sections we described several methods used to compute price indexes, discussed the use of some important indexes, and presented a procedure for using price indexes to deflate a time series. Several other issues must be considered to enhance our understanding of how price indexes are constructed and how they are used. Some are discussed in this section.

SELECTION OF ITEMS

The primary purpose of a price index is to measure the price change over time for a specified class of items, products, and so on. Whenever the class of items is very large, the index cannot be based on all items in the class. Rather, a sample of representative items must be used. By collecting price and quantity information for the sampled items, we hope to obtain a good idea of the price behavior of all items that the index is representing. For example, in the Consumer Price Index the total number of items that might be considered in the population of normal purchase items for a consumer could be 2000 or more. However, the index is based on the price-quantity characteristics of just 400 items. The selection of the specific items in the index is not a trivial task. Surveys of user purchase patterns as well as good judgment go into the selection process. A simple random sample is not used to select the 400 items.

After the initial selection process, the group of items in the index must be periodically reviewed and revised whenever purchase patterns change. Thus, the issue of which items to include in an index must be resolved before an index can be developed and again before it is revised.

SELECTION OF A BASE PERIOD

Most indexes are established with a base-period value of 100 at some specific time. All future values of the index are then related to the base period value. But what base period is appropriate for an index? This is not an easy question, and the answer must be based on the judgment of the developer of the index.

Many of the indexes established by the United States government as of 1995 have a 1982 base period. As a general guideline, the base period should not be too far from the current period. For example, a Consumer Price Index with a 1945 base period would be difficult for most individuals to understand because of unfamiliarity with conditions in 1945. The base period for most indexes therefore is adjusted periodically to a more recent period of time. The CPI base period was changed from 1967 to the 1982–1984 average in 1988. The PPI currently uses 1982 as its base period (i.e., 1982 = 100).

QUALITY CHANGES

The purpose of a price index is to measure changes in prices over time. Ideally, price data are collected for the same set of items at several times, and then the index is computed. A basic assumption is that the prices are identified for the same items each period. A problem is encountered when a product changes in quality from one period to the next. For example, a manufacturer may alter the quality of a product by using less expensive materials, fewer features, and so on, from year to year. The price may go up in following years, but the price is for a lower quality product. Consequently, the price may actually go up more than is represented by the list price for the item. It is very difficult, if not impossible, to adjust an index for decreases in the quality of an item.

A substantial quality improvement also may cause an increase in the price of a product. A portion of the price related to the quality improvement should be excluded from the index computation. However, adjusting an index for a price increase that is related to higher quality of an item is extremely difficult, if not impossible.

Although common practice is to ignore minor quality changes in developing a price index, major quality changes must be addressed because they can alter the product description from period to period. If a product description is changed, the index must be modified to account for it; in some cases, the product might be deleted from the index.

17.7 QUANTITY INDEXES

In addition to the price indexes described in the preceding sections, other types of indexes are useful. In particular, one other application of index numbers is to measure changes in quantity levels over time. This type of index is called a *quantity index*.

Recall that in the development of the weighted aggregate price index in Section 17.2, to compute an index number for period t we needed data on unit prices at a base period (P_0) and period t (P_t). We stated the formula for a weighted aggregate price index as

$$I_t = \frac{\sum P_{it}Q_i}{\sum P_{i0}Q_i}(100)$$

The numerator, $\sum P_{it}Q_i$, represents the total value of fixed quantities of the index items in period t. The denominator, $\sum P_{i0}Q_i$, represents the total value of the same fixed quantities of the index items in year 0.

Computation of a weighted aggregate quantity index is similar to that of a weighted aggregate price index. Quantities for each item are measured in the base period and period t, with Q_{i0} and Q_{it}, respectively, representing those quantities for item i. The quantities are then weighted by a fixed price, the value added, or some other factor. The "value added" to a product is the sales value minus the cost of purchased inputs. The formula for computing a weighted aggregate quantity index for period t is

$$I_t = \frac{\sum Q_{it}w_i}{\sum Q_{i0}w_i}(100) \tag{17.9}$$

In some quantity indexes the weight for item i is taken to be the base-period price (P_{i0}), in which case the weighted aggregate quantity index is

$$I_t = \frac{\sum Q_{it}P_{i0}}{\sum Q_{i0}P_{i0}}(100) \tag{17.10}$$

Quantity indexes can also be computed on the basis of weighted quantity relatives. One formula for this version of a quantity index follows.

$$I_t = \frac{\sum \dfrac{Q_{it}}{Q_{i0}}(Q_{i0}P_i)(100)}{\sum Q_{i0}P_i} \tag{17.11}$$

This formula is the quantity version of the weighted price relatives formula developed in Section 17.3 (see equation (17.8)).

The *Index of Industrial Production,* developed by the Federal Reserve Board, is probably the best known quantity index. It is reported monthly and the base period is 1987. The index is designed to measure changes in volume of production levels for a variety of manufacturing classifications in addition to mining and utilities. In January 1995 the index was 121.9.

EXERCISES

METHODS

Self-Test ▸

14. Data on quantities of three items sold in 1990 and 1995 are given in Table 17.14 along with the sales prices of the items in 1990. Compute a weighted aggregate quantity index for 1995.

APPLICATIONS

Self-Test ▸

15. A trucking firm handles four commodities for a particular distributor. Total shipments for the commodities in 1991 and 1995, as well as the 1991 prices, are reported in the following table.

TABLE 17.14 Exercise 14

	Quantity Sold		Price/Unit
Item	1990	1995	1990 ($)
A	350	300	18.00
B	220	400	4.90
C	730	850	15.00

	Shipments		Price/Shipment
Commodity	1991	1995	1991
A	120	95	$1200
B	86	75	$1800
C	35	50	$2000
D	60	70	$1500

Develop a weighted aggregate quantity index with a 1991 base. Comment on the growth or decline in quantities over the 1991–1995 period.

16. An automobile dealer reports the 1989 and 1995 sales for three models in Table 17.15. Compute quantity relatives and use them to develop a weighted aggregate quantity index for 1995 using the two years' data.

TABLE 17.15 Exercise 16

	Sales		Mean Price per Sale
Model	1989	1995	(1989)
Sedan	200	170	$15,200
Sport	100	80	$17,000
Wagon	75	60	$16,800

SUMMARY

Price and quantity indexes are important measures of changes in price and quantity levels within the business and economic environment. Price relatives are simply the ratio of the current unit price of an item to a base-period unit price multiplied by 100, with a value of 100 indicating no difference in the current- and base-period prices. Aggregate price indexes are created as a composite measure of the overall change in prices for a given group of items or products. Usually the items in an aggregate price index are weighted by their quantity of usage. A weighted aggregate price index can also be computed by weighting the price relatives by the usage quantities for the items in the index.

The Consumer Price Index and the Producer Price Index are both widely quoted indexes with 1982–1984 and 1982, respectively, as base years. The Dow Jones Industrial Average is another widely quoted price index. It is a weighted sum of the prices of 30 common stocks listed on the New York Stock Exchange. Unlike many other indexes, it is not stated as a percentage of some base-period value.

Often price indexes are used to deflate some other economic series reported over time. We saw how the CPI could be used to deflate hourly wages to obtain an index of real wages. Selection of the items to be included in the index, selection of a base period for the index, and adjustment for changes in quality are important additional considerations in the development of an index number. Quantity indexes were briefly discussed, and the Index of Industrial Production was mentioned as an important quantity index.

GLOSSARY

Price relative A price index for a given item that is computed by dividing a current unit price by a base-period unit price and multiplying the result by 100.

Aggregate price index A composite price index based on the prices of a group of items.

Weighted aggregate price index A composite price index where the prices of the items in the composite are weighted by their relative importance.

Laspeyres index A weighted aggregate price index where the weight for each item is its base-period quantity.

Paasche index A weighted aggregate price index where the weight for each item is its current-period quantity.

Consumer Price Index A monthly price index that uses the price changes in a market basket of consumer goods and services to measure the changes in consumer prices over time.

Producer Price Index A monthly price index that is designed to measure changes in prices of goods sold in primary markets (i.e., first purchase of a commodity in nonretail markets).

Dow Jones averages Aggregate price indexes reflecting the prices of stocks listed on the New York Stock Exchange.

Quantity index An index that is designed to measure changes in quantities over time.

Index of Industrial Production A quantity index that is designed to measure changes in the physical volume or production levels of industrial goods over time.

KEY FORMULAS

Price Relative in Period t

$$\frac{\text{Price in period } t}{\text{Base period price}}(100) \qquad (17.1)$$

Unweighted Aggregate Price Index in Period t

$$I_t = \frac{\Sigma P_{it}}{\Sigma P_{i0}}(100) \qquad (17.2)$$

Weighted Aggregate Price Index in Period t

$$I_t = \frac{\Sigma P_{it}Q_i}{\Sigma P_{i0}Q_i}(100) \qquad (17.3)$$

Weighted Average of Price Relatives

$$I_t = \frac{\Sigma \dfrac{P_{it}}{P_{i0}}w_i}{\Sigma w_i}(100) \qquad (17.6)$$

$$\text{Weighting Factor for (17.6)}$$

$$w_i = P_{i0}Q_i \qquad (17.7)$$

$$\text{Weighted Aggregate Quantity Index}$$

$$I_t = \frac{\Sigma Q_{it} w_i}{\Sigma Q_{i0} w_i}(100) \qquad (17.9)$$

SUPPLEMENTARY EXERCISES

TABLE 17.16
Exercise 17

Year	Price ($1000s)
1990	116.8
1991	131.1
1992	136.8
1993	142.0

17. The median purchase prices for existing single-family houses in Chicago, for the years 1990–1993 are listed in Table 17.16 (*Statistical Abstract of the United States, 1994*).
    a. Use 1990 as the base year and develop a price index for existing single-family homes in Chicago over this four-year period.
    b. Use 1991 as the base year and develop a price index for existing single-family homes in Chicago over this four-year period.

18. Nickerson Manufacturing Company has the following data on units shipped and quantities shipped for each of its four products:

Products	Base-Period Quantities (1991)	Mean Shipping Cost per Unit ($)	
		1991	1995
A	2000	10.50	15.90
B	5000	16.25	32.00
C	6500	12.20	17.40
D	2500	20.00	35.50

    a. Compute the price relative for each product.
    b. Compute a weighted aggregate price index that reflects the shipping cost change over the four-year period.

19. Use the price data in Exercise 18 to compute a Paasche index for the shipping cost if 1995 quantities are 4000, 3000, 7500, and 3000 for each of the four products.

20. Boran Stockbrokers, Inc., selects four stocks for the purpose of developing its own index of stock market behavior. Costs per share for a 1993 base period, January 1995, and March 1995 follow. Base-year quantities have been set on the basis of historical volumes for the four stocks.

Stock	Industry	1993 Quantity	Cost per Share ($)		
			1993 Base	January 1995	March 1995
A	Oil	100	31.50	32.75	32.50
B	Computer	150	65.00	59.00	57.50
C	Steel	75	40.00	42.00	39.50
D	Real Estate	50	18.00	16.50	13.75

Use the 1993 base period to compute the Boran index for January 1995 and March 1995. Comment on what the index tells you about what is happening in the stock market.

21. Compute the price relatives for the four stocks making up the Boran index in Exercise 20. Use the weighted aggregates of price relatives to compute the January 1995 and March 1995 Boran indexes.

22. Consider the following price relatives and quantity information for grain production in Iowa (*Statistical Abstract of the United States*, 1994).

Product	1991 Quantities (millions of bushels)	Base Price per Bushel ($)	1991–1993 Price Relatives
Corn	1427	2.30	109
Soybeans	350	5.51	118

What is the 1993 weighted aggregate price index for the Iowa grains?

23. Fresh fruit price and quantity data for the years 1988 and 1993 follow (*Statistical Abstract of the United States*, 1994). Quantity data reflect per capita consumption in pounds and prices are per pound.

Fruit	1988 per Capita Consumption (pounds)	1988 Price ($/pound)	1993 Price ($/pound)
Bananas	24.3	.41	.41
Apples	19.9	.71	.78
Oranges	13.9	.56	.56
Pears	3.2	.64	.89

a. Compute a price relative for each product.

b. Compute a weighted aggregate price index for fruit products. Comment on the change in fruit prices over the five-year period.

24. Starting faculty salaries (nine-month basis) for assistant professors of business administration at a major Midwestern university are listed in Table 17.17. Use the CPI to deflate the salary data to constant dollars. Comment on the trend in salaries in higher education as indicated by these data.

25. The five-year historical prices per share for a particular stock and the Consumer Price Index with a 1982–1984 base period follow.

Year	Price per Share ($)	CPI (1982–1984 Base)
1989	51.00	124.0
1990	54.00	130.7
1991	58.00	136.2
1992	59.50	140.3
1993	59.00	144.5

Deflate the stock price series and comment on the investment aspects of this stock.

26. A major manufacturing company has reported the quantity and product value information for 1991 and 1995 in Table 17.18. Compute a weighted aggregate quantity index for the data. Comment on what this quantity index means.

TABLE 17.17 Exercise 24

Year	Starting Salary ($)	CPI (1982–1984 Base)
1970	14,000	38.8
1975	17,500	53.8
1980	23,000	82.4
1985	37,000	107.6
1990	53,000	130.7
1993	60,000	144.5

TABLE 17.18 Exercise 26

Product	Quantities 1991	1995	Value ($)
A	800	1,200	30.00
B	600	500	20.00
C	200	500	25.00

18

FORECASTING

CONTENTS

STATISTICS IN PRACTICE

Nevada Occupational Health Clinic*

Sparks, Nevada

Nevada Occupational Health Clinic is a privately owned medical clinic in Sparks, Nevada. The clinic specializes in industrial medicine and has been in operation at the same site for more than 15 years. In the beginning of 1991, the clinic entered a rapid growth phase in which monthly billings increased from $57,000 to more than $300,000 in 26 months. The clinic was still undergoing dramatic growth when the main clinic building burned to the ground on April 6, 1993.

The clinic's insurance policy covered physical property and equipment as well as loss of income due to the interruption of regular business operations. Settling the property insurance claim was a relatively straightforward matter of determining the value of the physical property and equipment lost during the fire. However, determining the value of the income lost during the seven months that it took to rebuild the clinic was a complicated matter involving negotiations between the business owners and

*The authors are indebted to Bard Betz, Director of Operations, and Curtis Brauer, Executive Administrative Assistant, Nevada Occupational Health Clinic, for providing this Statistics in Practice.

the insurance company. There were no preestablished rules for calculating "what would have happened" to the clinic's billings if the fire had not occurred. To estimate the lost income, the clinic used a forecasting method to project the growth in business that would have been realized during the seven-month lost-business period. The actual history of billings prior to the fire provided the basis for a forecasting model with linear trend and seasonal components as discussed in this chapter. This forecasting model enabled the clinic to establish an accurate estimate of the loss, which eventually was accepted by the insurance company.

A 1993 fire closed the Nevada Occupational Health Clinic for seven months.

● A critical aspect of managing any organization is planning for the future. Indeed, the long-run success of an organization is related closely to how well managers are able to anticipate the future and develop appropriate strategies. Good judgment, intuition, and an awareness of the state of the economy may give a manager a rough idea or "feeling" of what is likely to happen in the future. However, converting that feeling into a number that can be used as next quarter's sales volume or next year's raw material cost is difficult. The purpose of this chapter is to introduce several forecasting methods that can be used to predict future aspects of a business operation.

Suppose we have been asked to provide quarterly estimates of the sales volume for a particular product during the coming one-year period. Production schedules, raw material purchasing, inventory policies, and sales quotas will all be affected by the quarterly estimates we provide. Consequently, poor estimates may result in poor planning and hence increased costs for the firm. How should we go about providing the quarterly sales volume estimates?

We will certainly want to review the actual sales data for the product in past periods. Suppose we have actual sales data for each quarter over the past three years. Using these historical data, we can identify the general level of sales and determine whether there is a trend, such as an increase or decrease in sales volume, over time. A further review of the data might reveal a seasonal pattern, such as peak sales in the third quarter of each year and lowest sales during the first quarter. By reviewing historical data over time, we can develop a better understanding of the pattern of past sales that can lead to better predictions of future sales for the product.

The historical sales data form what is called a *time series.* Specifically, a time series is a set of observations on a variable measured at successive points in time or over successive periods of time. In this chapter, we will introduce several procedures for analyzing time series. The objective of such analyses is to provide good *forecasts* or predictions of future values of the time series.

Forecasting methods can be classified as quantitative or qualitative. Quantitative forecasting methods can be used when (1) past information about the variable being forecast is available, (2) the information can be quantified, and (3) the pattern of the past can be assumed to continue into the future. In such cases, a forecast can be developed by using a time series method or a causal method.

If the historical data are restricted to past values of the variable, the forecasting procedure is called a time series method. The objective of time series methods is to discover a pattern in the historical data and then extrapolate the pattern into the future; the forecast is based solely on past values of the variable and/or on past forecast errors. In this chapter we discuss three time series methods: smoothing (moving averages, weighted moving averages, and exponential smoothing), trend projection, and trend projection adjusted for seasonal influence.

Causal forecasting methods are based on the assumption that the variable we are forecasting has a cause-effect relationship with one or more other variables. In this chapter we discuss the use of regression analysis as a causal forecasting method. For instance, the sales volume for many products is influenced by advertising expenditures; in such cases, regression analysis can often be used to develop an equation showing how the two variables are related. Then, once the advertising budget has been set for the next period, we could substitute this value into the estimated regression equation to develop a prediction or forecast of the sales volume for that period. Note that if a time series method were used to develop the forecast, advertising expenditures would not be considered; that is, a time series method would base the forecast solely on past sales.

Qualitative methods generally involve the use of expert judgment to develop forecasts. For instance, a panel of experts might develop a consensus forecast of the prime rate for a year from now. An advantage of qualitative procedures is that they can be applied when the information on the variable being forecast cannot be quantified and when historical data are either not applicable or unavailable. Figure 18.1 provides an overview of the types of forecasting methods.

18.1 THE COMPONENTS OF A TIME SERIES

To explain the pattern or behavior of the data in a time series, it is helpful to think of the time series as consisting of several components. The usual assumption is that four separate components—trend, cyclical, seasonal, and irregular—combine to provide the time series values. Let us look more closely at each of these components.

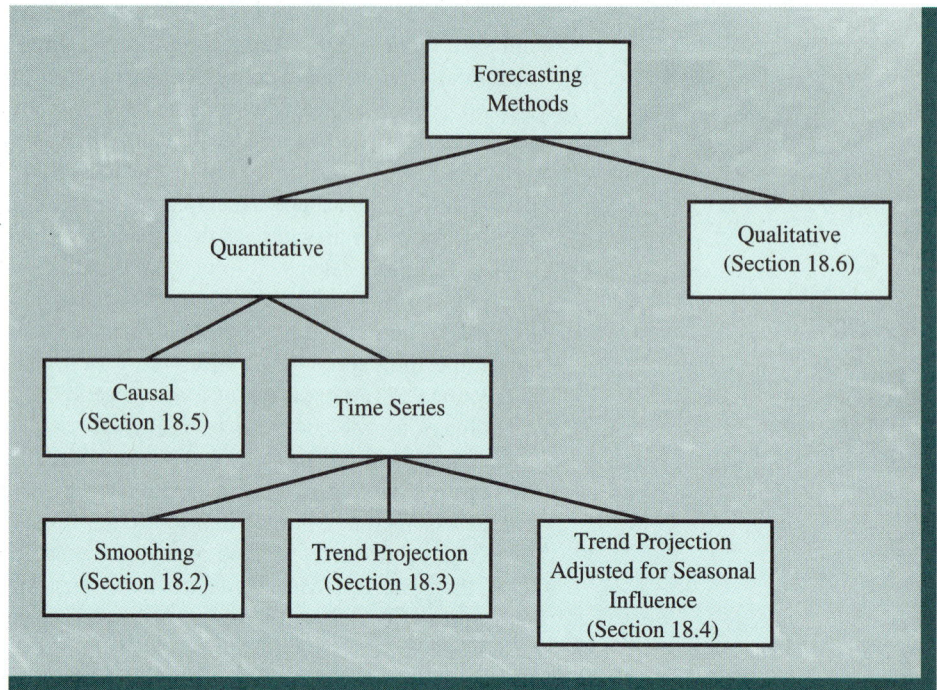

FIGURE 18.1   An Overview of Forecasting Methods

● ● ● ● ● ● ● ● ● ● ● ● ● ● ● ● ●   TREND COMPONENT

In time series analysis the measurements may be taken every hour, day, week, month, or year or at any other regular interval.* Although time series data generally exhibit random fluctuations, the time series may still show gradual shifts or movements to relatively higher or lower values over a longer period of time. The gradual shifting of the time series is called the *trend* in the time series; this shifting or trend is usually the result of long-term factors such as changes in the population, demographic characteristics of the population, technology, and/or consumer preferences.

For example, a manufacturer of photographic equipment may see substantial month-to-month variability in the number of cameras sold. However, in reviewing the sales over the past 10 to 15 years, the manufacturer may find a gradual increase in the annual sales volume. Suppose the sales volume was approximately 17000 cameras in 1985, 23000 cameras in 1990, and 25000 cameras in 1995. Although actual month-to-month sales volumes may vary substantially, this gradual growth in sales over time shows an upward trend for the time series. The straight line in Figure 18.2 may be a good approximation of the trend in the sales data. The trend for camera sales appears to be linear and increasing over time, but sometimes the trend in a time series is better described by other patterns.

Figure 18.3 shows some other possible time series trend patterns. Panel A is a nonlinear trend; in this case, the time series shows little growth initially, then a period of rapid growth, and finally a leveling off. This pattern might be a good approximation

---

*We limit our discussion to time series in which the values of the series are recorded at equal intervals. Cases in which the observations are not made at equal intervals are beyond the scope of this text.

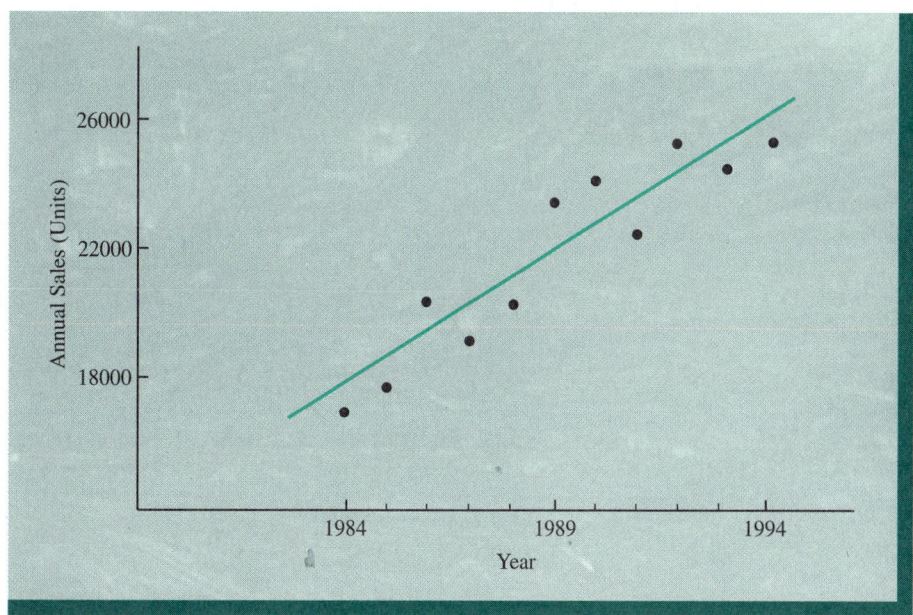

FIGURE 18.2 Linear Trend of Camera Sales

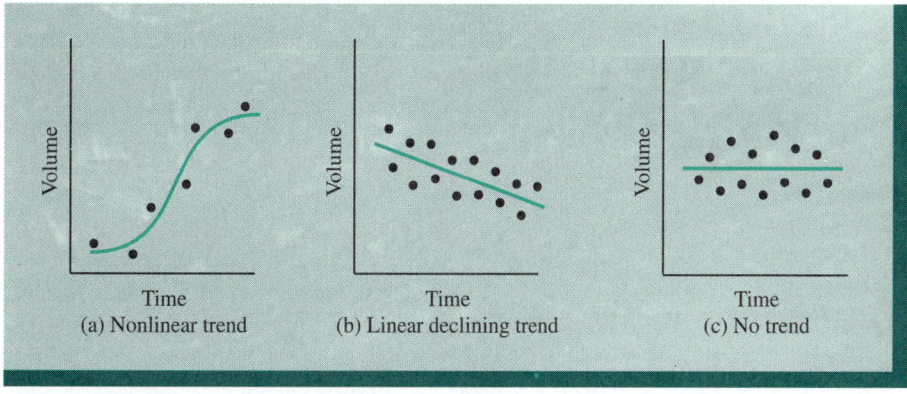

FIGURE 18.3 Examples of Some Possible Time Series Trend Patterns

of sales for a product from introduction through a growth period and into a period of market saturation. The linear decreasing trend in panel B represents a time series that has a steady decrease over time. The horizontal line in panel C represents a time series that has no consistent increase or decrease over time and hence no trend.

CYCLICAL COMPONENT

Although a time series may exhibit a trend, not all future values of the time series will be exactly on the trend line. In fact, time series often show alternating sequences of points below and above the trend line. Any recurring sequence of points above and

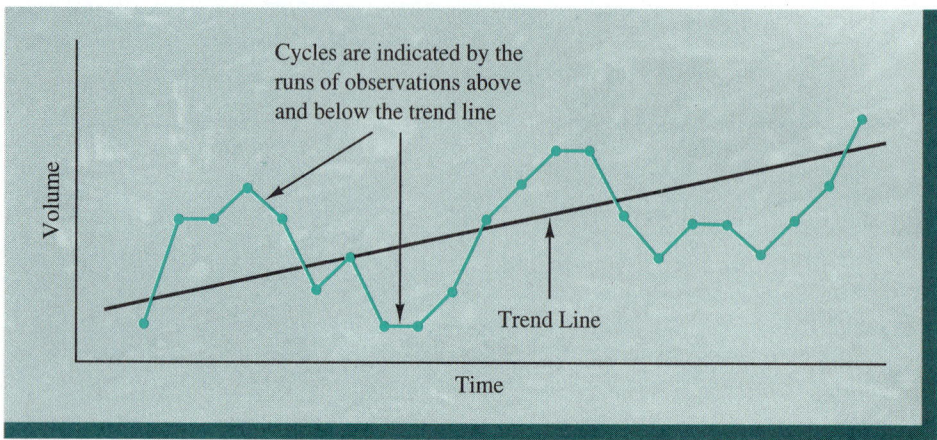

FIGURE 18.4 Trend and Cyclical Components of a Time Series with Data Points One Year Apart

below the trend line lasting more than one year can be attributed to the *cyclical component* of the time series. Figure 18.4 is the graph of a time series with an obvious cyclical component. The observations are taken at intervals one year apart.

Many time series exhibit cyclical behavior with regular runs of observations below and above the trend line. The general belief is that this component of the time series represents multiyear cyclical movements in the economy. For example, periods of moderate inflation followed by periods of rapid inflation can lead to time series that alternate below and above a generally increasing trend line (e.g., a time series for housing costs). Many time series in the early 1980s and early 1990s displayed this type of behavior.

SEASONAL COMPONENT

Time series commonly show a regular pattern of variability within one-year periods. For example, a manufacturer of swimming pools expects low sales activity in the fall and winter months, with peak sales in the spring and summer months. Manufacturers of snow removal equipment and heavy clothing expect the opposite yearly pattern. The component of the time series that represents the variability in the data due to seasonal influences is called the *seasonal component*. Although we generally think of seasonal movement in a time series as occurring within one year, the seasonal component can also be used to represent any regularly repeating pattern that is less than one year in duration. For example, daily traffic volume data show within-the-day "seasonal" behavior, with peak levels occurring during rush hours, moderate flow during the rest of the day and early evening, and light flow from midnight to early morning.

IRREGULAR COMPONENT

The *irregular component* of the time series is the residual, or "catch-all," factor that accounts for the deviation of the actual time series value from what we would expect if the trend, cyclical, and seasonal components completely explained the time series. The irregular component is caused by the short-term, unanticipated, and nonrecurring factors that affect the time series. Since this component accounts for the random variability in the time series, it is unpredictable. We cannot predict its impact on the time series in advance.

18.2 USING SMOOTHING METHODS IN FORECASTING

In this section we discuss three forecasting methods: moving averages, weighted moving averages, and exponential smoothing. Since the objective of each of these methods is to "smooth out" the random fluctuations caused by the irregular component of the time series, they are referred to as smoothing methods. Smoothing methods are appropriate for a stable time series; that is, a time series that exhibits no significant trend, cyclical, or seasonal effects. These methods adapt well to changes in the level of the time series. However, without modification, they do not work as well when a significant trend, cyclical, and seasonal components are present.

Smoothing methods are easy to use and generally provide a high level of accuracy for short-range forecasts, such as a forecast for the next time period. We begin with the moving averages method.

MOVING AVERAGES

In the *moving averages* method, we use the average of the *most recent n* data values in the time series as the forecast for the next period. Mathematically, the moving average calculation is made as follows.

> **MOVING AVERAGE**
>
> $$\text{Moving Average} = \frac{\Sigma(\text{most recent } n \text{ data values})}{n} \qquad (18.1)$$

The term "moving" is used because every time a new observation becomes available for the time series, it replaces the oldest observation in (18.1) and a new average is computed. The average changes, or moves, as new observations become available.

To illustrate the moving averages method, consider the 12 weeks of data in Table 18.1 and Figure 18.5. These data show the number of gallons of gasoline sold by a gasoline distributor in Bennington, Vermont, over the past 12 weeks. Figure 18.5 indicates that, although random variability is present, the time series appears to be stable over time. Hence, the smoothing methods of this section are applicable.

To use moving averages to forecast gasoline sales, we must first select the number of data values to be included in the moving average. As an example, let us compute forecasts using a three-week moving average. The moving average calculation for the first three weeks of the gasoline sales time series is

$$\text{Moving Average (Weeks 1–3)} = \frac{17 + 21 + 19}{3} = 19$$

We then use this moving average as the forecast for week 4. Since the actual value observed in week 4 is 23, the forecast error in week 4 is $23 - 19 = 4$. In general, the error associated with any forecast is the difference between the observed value of the time series and the forecast.

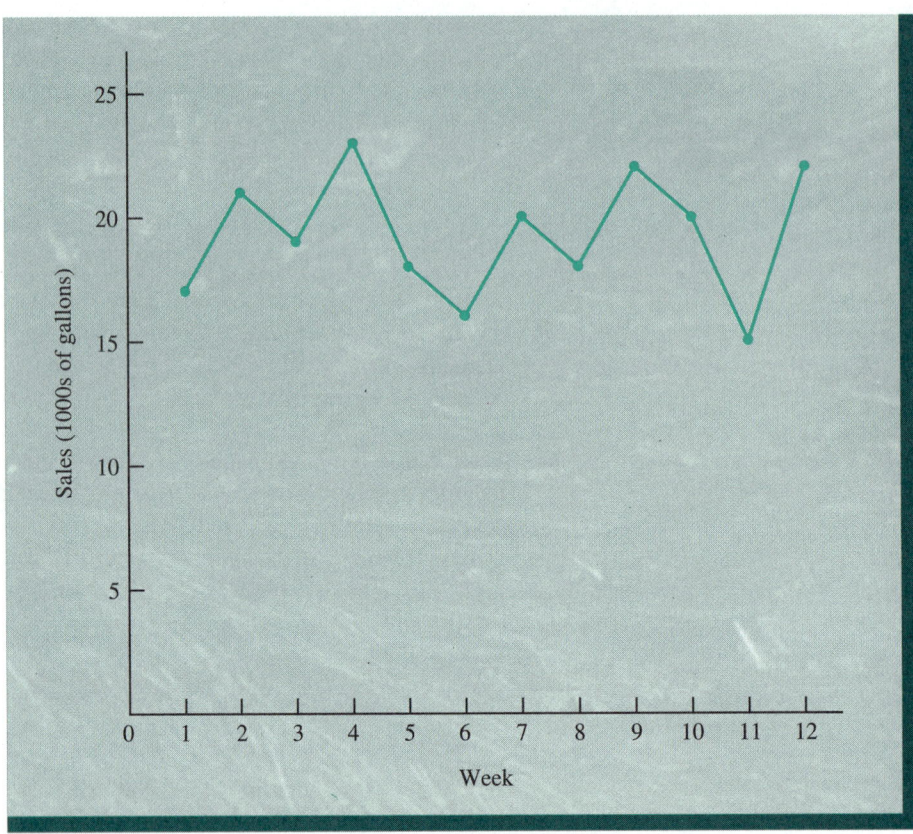

FIGURE 18.5   Graph of Gasoline Sales Time Series

TABLE 18.1   Gasoline Sales Time Series

Week	Sales (1000s of gallons)
1	17
2	21
3	19
4	23
5	18
6	16
7	20
8	18
9	22
10	20
11	15
12	22

The calculation for the second three-week moving average is

$$\text{Moving Average (Weeks 2–4)} = \frac{21 + 19 + 23}{3} = 21$$

Hence, the forecast for week 5 is 21. The error associated with this forecast is $18 - 21 = -3$. Thus, the forecast error may be positive or negative depending on whether the forecast is too low or too high. A complete summary of the three-week moving average calculations for the gasoline sales time series is provided in Table 18.2 and Figure 18.6.

Forecast Accuracy   An important consideration in selecting a forecasting method is the accuracy of the forecast. Clearly, we want forecast errors to be small. The last two columns of Table 18.2, which contain the forecast errors and the squared forecast errors, can be used to develop a measure of accuracy.

For the gasoline sales time series, we can use the last column of Table 18.2 to compute the average of the sum of the squared errors. Doing so we obtain

$$\text{Average of the Sum of Squared Errors} = \frac{92}{9} = 10.22$$

This average of the sum of squared errors is commonly referred to as the *mean squared error* (MSE). The MSE is an often-used measure of the accuracy of a forecasting method and is the one we use in this chapter.

TABLE 18.2 Summary of Three-Week Moving Average Calculations

Week	Time Series Value	Moving Average Forecast	Forecast Error	Squared Forecast Error
1	17			
2	21			
3	19			
4	23	19	4	16
5	18	21	− 3	9
6	16	20	− 4	16
7	20	19	1	1
8	18	18	0	0
9	22	18	4	16
10	20	20	0	0
11	15	20	− 5	25
12	22	19	3	9
		Totals	0	92

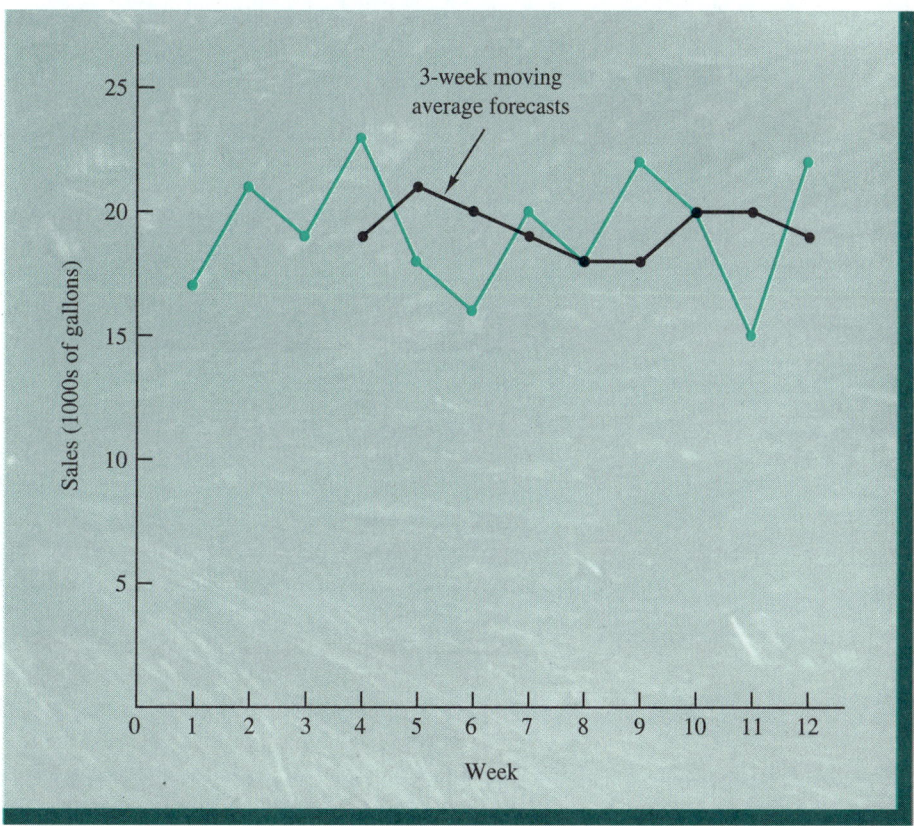

FIGURE 18.6 Graph of Gasoline Sales Time Series and Three-Week Moving Average Forecasts

As we indicated previously, to use the moving averages method, we must first select the number of data values to be included in the moving average. Not surprisingly, for a particular time series, moving averages of different lengths will differ in their ability to forecast the time series accurately. One possible approach to choosing the number of values to be included in the moving average is to use trial and error to identify the length that minimizes the MSE. Then, if we are willing to assume that the length that is best for the past will also be best for the future, we would forecast the next value in the time series by using the number of data values that minimized the MSE for the historical time series. Exercise 2 at the end of the section will ask you to consider four-week and five-week moving averages for the gasoline sales data. A comparison of the MSEs will indicate the number of weeks of data you may want to include in the moving average calculation.

WEIGHTED MOVING AVERAGES

In the moving averages method, each observation in the moving average calculation receives the same weight. One possible variation, known as *weighted moving averages,* involves selecting weights for each of the data values and then computing a weighted mean as the forecast. In most cases, the most recent observation receives the most weight, and the weight decreases for older data values. For example, using the gasoline sales time series, let us illustrate the computation of a weighted three-week moving average, where the most recent observation receives a weight three times as great as that given the oldest observation, and the next oldest observation receives a weight twice as great as the oldest. The weighted moving average forecast for week 4 would be computed as follows.

$$\text{Forecast for Week 4} = \tfrac{1}{6}(17) + \tfrac{2}{6}(21) + \tfrac{3}{6}(19) = 19.33$$

Note that for the weighted moving average, the sum of the weights is equal to one. This was also true for the simple moving average, where each weight was $\tfrac{1}{3}$. However, recall that the simple or unweighted moving average provided a forecast of 19. Exercise 3 at the end of the section will ask you to calculate the remaining values for the three-week weighted moving average and compare the forecast accuracy with that obtained for the unweighted moving average.

Forecast Accuracy   To use the weighted moving averages method we must first select the number of data values to be included in the weighted moving average and then choose weights for each of the data values. In general, if we believe that the recent past is a better predictor of the future than the distant past, larger weights should be given to the more recent observations. However, when the time series is highly variable, selecting approximately equal weights for the data values may be best. Note that the only requirement in selecting the weights is that their sum must equal one. To determine whether one particular combination of number of data values and weights provides a more accurate forecast than another combination, we will continue to use the MSE criterion as the measure of forecast accuracy. That is, if we assume that the combination that is best for the past will also be best for the future, we would use the combination of number of data values and weights that minimized MSE for the historical time series to forecast the next value in the time series.

EXPONENTIAL SMOOTHING

Exponential smoothing uses a weighted average of past time values as the forecast; it is a special case of the weighted moving averages method in which we select only one weight—the weight for the most recent observation. The weights for the other data values are computed automatically and become smaller as the observations move farther into the past. The basic exponential smoothing model follows.

EXPONENTIAL SMOOTHING MODEL

$$F_{t+1} = \alpha Y_t + (1 - \alpha)F_t \qquad (18.2)$$

where

$$F_{t+1} = \text{forecast of the time series for period } t + 1$$

$$Y_t = \text{actual value of the time series in period } t$$

$$F_t = \text{forecast of the time series for period } t$$

$$\alpha = \text{smoothing constant } (0 \leq \alpha \leq 1)$$

Equation (18.2) shows that the forecast for period $t + 1$ is a weighted average of the actual value in period t and the forecast for period t; note in particular that the weight given to the actual value in period t is α and that the weight given to the forecast in period t is $1 - \alpha$. We can demonstrate that the exponential smoothing forecast for any period is also a weighted average of *all the previous actual values* for the time series with a time series consisting of three periods of data: Y_1, Y_2, and Y_3. To start the calculations, we let F_1 equal the actual value of the time series in period 1; that is, $F_1 = Y_1$. Hence, the forecast for period 2 is

$$F_2 = \alpha Y_1 + (1 - \alpha)F_1$$

$$= \alpha Y_1 + (1 - \alpha)Y_1$$

$$= Y_1$$

Thus, the exponential smoothing forecast for period 2 is equal to the actual value of the time series in period 1.

The forecast for period 3 is

$$F_3 = \alpha Y_2 + (1 - \alpha)F_2 = \alpha Y_2 + (1 - \alpha)Y_1$$

Finally, substituting this expression for F_3 in the expression for F_4, we obtain

$$F_4 = \alpha Y_3 + (1 - \alpha)F_3$$

$$= \alpha Y_3 + (1 - \alpha)[\alpha Y_2 + (1 - \alpha)Y_1]$$

$$= \alpha Y_3 + \alpha(1 - \alpha)Y_2 + (1 - \alpha)^2 Y_1$$

Hence, F_4 is a weighted average of the first three time series values. The sum of the coefficients, or weights, for Y_1, Y_2, and Y_3 equals one. A similar argument can be made to show that, in general, any forecast F_{t+1} is a weighted average of all the previous time series values.

Despite the fact that exponential smoothing provides a forecast that is a weighted average of all past observations, all past data do not need to be saved to compute the forecast for the next period. In fact, once the *smoothing constant* α has been selected, only two pieces of information are needed to compute the forecast. Equation (18.2) shows that with a given α we can compute the forecast for period $t + 1$ simply by knowing the actual and forecast time series values for period t—that is, Y_t and F_t.

To illustrate the exponential smoothing approach to forecasting, consider the gasoline sales time series in Table 18.1 and Figure 18.5. As indicated, the exponential smoothing forecast for period 2 is equal to the actual value of the time series in period 1. Thus, with

TABLE 18.3   Summary of the Exponential Smoothing Forecasts and Forecast Errors for Gasoline Sales with Smoothing Constant $\alpha = .2$

Week (t)	Time Series Value (Y_t)	Exponential Smoothing Forecast (F_t)	Forecast Error $(Y_t - F_t)$
1	17		
2	21	17.00	4.00
3	19	17.80	1.20
4	23	18.04	4.96
5	18	19.03	-1.03
6	16	18.83	-2.83
7	20	18.26	1.74
8	18	18.61	$-.61$
9	22	18.49	3.51
10	20	19.19	.81
11	15	19.35	-4.35
12	22	18.48	3.52

$Y_1 = 17$, we will set $F_2 = 17$ to start the exponential smoothing computations. Referring to the time series data in Table 18.1, we find an actual time series value in period 2 of $Y_2 = 21$. Thus, period 2 has a forecast error of $21 - 17 = 4$.

Continuing with the exponential smoothing computations provides the following forecast for period 3.

$$F_3 = .2Y_2 + .8F_2 = .2(21) + .8(17) = 17.8$$

Once the actual time series value in period 3, $Y_3 = 19$, is known, we can generate a forecast for period 4 as follows.

$$F_4 = .2Y_3 + .8F_3 = .2(19) + .8(17.8) = 18.04$$

By continuing the exponential smoothing calculations, we are able to determine the weekly forecast values and the corresponding weekly forecast errors, as listed in Table 18.3. Note that we have not shown an exponential smoothing forecast or the forecast error for period 1, because F_1 was set equal to Y_1 to begin the smoothing computations. For week 12, we have $Y_{12} = 22$ and $F_{12} = 18.48$. Can you use this information to generate a forecast for week 13 before the actual value of week 13 becomes known? Using the exponential smoothing model, we have

$$F_{13} = .2Y_{12} + .8F_{12} = .2(22) + .8(18.48) = 19.18$$

Thus, the exponential smoothing forecast of the amount sold in week 13 is 19.18, or 19,180 gallons of gasoline. With this forecast, the firm can make plans and decisions accordingly. The accuracy of the forecast will not be known until the firm conducts its business through week 13.

Figure 18.7 is the plot of the actual and forecast time series values. Note in particular how the forecasts smooth out the irregular fluctuations in the time series.

Forecast Accuracy   In the preceding exponential smoothing calculations, we used a smoothing constant of $\alpha = .2$. Although any value of α between zero and one is acceptable, some values will yield better forecasts than others. Insight into choosing a good value for α can be obtained by rewriting the basic exponential smoothing model as follows.

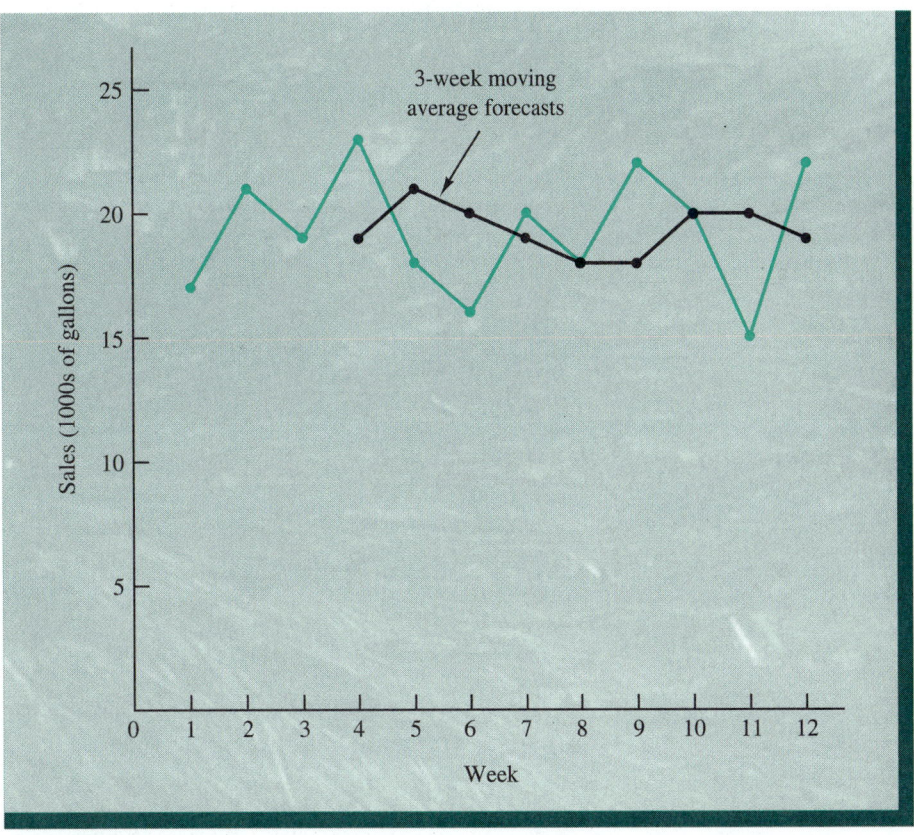

FIGURE 18.7 Graph of Actual and Forecast Gasoline Sales Time Series with Smoothing Constant $\alpha = .2$

$$F_{t+1} = \alpha Y_t + (1 - \alpha)F_t$$

$$F_{t+1} = \alpha Y_t + F_t - \alpha F_t$$

$$F_{t+1} = F_t + \alpha(Y_t - F_t) \qquad\qquad \textbf{(18.1)}$$

Forecast
in period t

Forecast error
in period t

Hence, the new forecast F_{t+1} is equal to the previous forecast F_t plus an adjustment, which is α times the most recent forecast error, $Y_t - F_t$. That is, the forecast in period $t + 1$ is obtained by adjusting the forecast in period t by a fraction of the forecast error. If the time series contains substantial random variability, a small value of the smoothing constant is preferred. The reason for this choice is that since much of the forecast error is due to random variability, we do not want to overreact and adjust the forecasts too quickly. For a time series with relatively little random variability, larger values of the smoothing constant have the advantage of quickly adjusting the forecasts when forecasting errors occur and thus allowing the forecasts to react faster to changing conditions.

The criterion we will use to determine a desirable value for the smoothing constant α is the same as the criterion we proposed for determining the number of periods of data

TABLE 18.4   MSE Computations for Forecasting Gasoline Sales with $\alpha = .2$

Week (t)	Time Series Value (Y_t)	Forecast (F_t)	Forecast Error $(Y_t - F_t)$	Squared Forecast Error $(Y_t - F_t)^2$
1	17			
2	21	17.00	4.00	16.00
3	19	17.80	1.20	1.44
4	23	18.04	4.96	24.60
5	18	19.03	− 1.03	1.06
6	16	18.83	− 2.83	8.01
7	20	18.26	1.74	3.03
8	18	18.61	− .61	.37
9	22	18.49	3.51	12.32
10	20	19.19	.81	.66
11	15	19.35	− 4.35	18.92
12	22	18.48	3.52	12.39
			Total	98.80

$$\text{MSE} = \frac{98.80}{11} = 8.98$$

TABLE 18.5   MSE Computations for Forecasting Gasoline Sales with $\alpha = .3$

Week (t)	Time Series Value (Y_t)	Forecast (F_t)	Forecast Error $(Y_t - F_t)$	Squared Forecast Error $(Y_t - F_t)^2$
1	17			
2	21	17.00	4.00	16.00
3	19	18.20	.80	.64
4	23	18.44	4.56	20.79
5	18	19.81	− 1.81	3.28
6	16	19.27	− 3.27	10.69
7	20	18.29	1.71	2.92
8	18	18.80	− .80	.64
9	22	18.56	3.44	11.83
10	20	19.59	.41	.17
11	15	19.71	− 4.71	22.18
12	22	18.30	3.70	13.69
			Total	102.83

$$\text{MSE} = \frac{102.83}{11} = 9.35$$

to include in the moving averages calculation. That is, we choose the value of α that minimizes the mean squared error (MSE). The MSE calculations for the exponential smoothing forecast of gasoline sales with $\alpha = .2$ are summarized in Table 18.4. Note that there is one less squared error term than the number of time periods, because we had no past values with which to make a forecast for period 1. Would a different value of α have provided better results in terms of a lower MSE value? Perhaps the most straightforward way to answer this question is simply to try another value for α. We will then compare its mean squared error with the MSE value of 8.98 obtained by using a smoothing constant of $\alpha = .2$.

The exponential smoothing results with $\alpha = .3$ are shown in Table 18.5. With MSE = 9.35, we see that for the current data set, a smoothing constant of $\alpha = .3$ results in less forecast accuracy than a smoothing constant of $\alpha = .2$. Hence, we would be inclined to prefer the original smoothing constant of $\alpha = .2$. Using a trial-and-error calculation with other values of α, we can find a "good" value for the smoothing constant. This value can be used in the exponential smoothing model to provide forecasts for the future. At a later date, after new time series observations have been obtained, we analyze the newly collected time series data to determine whether the smoothing constant should be revised to provide better forecasting results.

NOTES AND COMMENTS

1. Another measure of forecast accuracy is the *mean absolute deviation* (MAD). This measure is simply the average of the absolute values of all the forecast errors. Using the errors given in Table 18.2, we obtain

$$\text{MAD} = \frac{4 + 3 + 4 + 1 + 0 + 4 + 0 + 5 + 3}{9} = 2.67.$$

   One major difference between MSE and MAD is that the MSE measure is influenced much more by large forecast errors than by small errors (since for the MSE measure the errors are squared). The selection of the best measure of forecasting accuracy is not a simple matter. Indeed, forecasting experts often disagree as to which measure should be used.

2. Spreadsheet packages are an effective aid in choosing a good value of α for exponential smoothing and selecting weights for the weighted moving averages method. With the time series data and the forecasting formulas in the spreadsheets, you can experiment with different values of α (or moving average weights) and choose the value of α providing the smallest MSE. In the chapter appendix we show how Excel can be used to develop forecasts using moving averages and exponential smoothing.

EXERCISES

METHODS

Self-Test

1. Consider the following time series data.

Week	1	2	3	4	5	6
Value	8	13	15	17	16	9

   a. Develop a three-week moving average for this time series. What is the forecast for week 7?
   b. Compute the MSE for the three-week moving average.
   c. Use $\alpha = .2$ to compute the exponential smoothing values for the time series. What is the forecast for week 7?
   d. Compare the three-week moving average forecast with the exponential smoothing forecast using $\alpha = .2$. Which appears to provide the better forecast?
   e. Use a smoothing constant of .4 to compute the exponential smoothing values. Does a smoothing constant of .2 or .4 appear to provide the better forecast? Explain.

2. Refer to the gasoline sales time series data in Table 18.1.
   a. Compute four-week and five-week moving averages for the time series.
   b. Compute the MSE for the four-week and five-week moving average forecasts.

c. What appears to be the best number of weeks of past data to use in the moving average computation? Remember that the MSE for the three-week moving average is 10.22.

3. Refer again to the gasoline sales time series data in Table 18.1.
   a. Using a weight of ½ for the most recent observation, ⅓ for the second most recent, and ⅙ for third most recent, compute a three-week weighted moving average for the time series.
   b. Compute the MSE for the weighted moving average in (a). Do you prefer this weighted moving average to the unweighted moving average? Remember that the MSE for the unweighted moving average is 10.22.
   c. Suppose you are allowed to choose any weights as long as they sum to one. Could you always find a set of weights that would make the MSE smaller for a weighted moving average than for an unweighted moving average? Why or why not?

TABLE 18.6   Exercise 6

Year	Attendance
1980	2.49
1981	2.82
1982	2.72
1983	2.60
1984	2.81
1985	2.98
1986	2.86
1987	3.13
1988	2.98
1989	3.16
1990	3.20
1991	2.85

TABLE 18.7   Exercise 9

Month	Sales
1	105
2	135
3	120
4	105
5	90
6	120
7	145
8	140
9	100
10	80
11	100
12	110

4. With the gasoline time series data from Table 18.1, show the exponential smoothing forecasts using $\alpha = .1$. Applying the MSE criterion, would you prefer a smoothing constant of $\alpha = .1$ or $\alpha = .2$ for the gasoline sales time series?

5. With a smoothing constant of $\alpha = .2$, equation (18.2) shows that the forecast for the 13th week of the gasoline sales data from Table 18.1 is given by $F_{13} = .2Y_{12} + .8F_{12}$. However, the forecast for week 12 is given by $F_{12} = .2Y_{11} + .8F_{11}$. Thus, we could combine these two results to show that the forecast for the 13th week can be written

$$F_{13} = .2Y_{12} + .8(.2Y_{11} + .8F_{11}) = .2Y_{12} + .16Y_{11} + .64F_{11}$$

   a. Making use of the fact that $F_{11} = .2Y_{10} + .8F_{10}$ (and similarly for F_{10} and F_9), continue to expand the expression for F_{13} until it is written in terms of the past data values $Y_{12}, Y_{11}, Y_{10}, Y_9, Y_8$, and the forecast for period 8.
   b. Refer to the coefficients or weights for the past data $Y_{12}, Y_{11}, Y_{10}, Y_9$, and Y_8; what observation can you make about how exponential smoothing weights past data values in arriving at new forecasts? Compare this weighting pattern with the weighting pattern of the moving averages method.

APPLICATIONS

6. Paramount Kings Island Amusement Park, in Kings Island, Ohio, reported the park attendance figures (in millions) listed in Table 18.6 (*The Cincinnati Enquirer,* April 5, 1992).
   a. Use exponential smoothing with smoothing constants of .2 and .3 to forecast the attendance figures.
   b. What is the forecast of park attendance for 1992?

7. Corporate triple A bond interest rates for 12 consecutive months follow.

9.5   9.3   9.4   9.6   9.8   9.7   9.8   10.5   9.9   9.7   9.6   9.6

   a. Develop three-month and four-month moving averages for this time series. Does the three-month or four-month moving average provide the better forecasts? Explain.
   b. What is the moving average forecast for the next month?

Self-Test

8. The values of Alabama building contracts (in millions of dollars) for a 12-month period follow.

240   350   230   260   280   320   220   310   240   310   240   230

   a. Compare a three-month moving averages forecast with an exponential smoothing forecast using $\alpha = .2$. Which provides the better forecasts?
   b. What is the forecast for the next month?

9. The time series in Table 18.7 is for the sales of a particular product over the past 12 months.
   a. Use $\alpha = .3$ to compute the exponential smoothing values for the time series.
   b. Use a smoothing constant of .5 to compute the exponential smoothing values. Does a smoothing constant of .3 or .5 appear to provide the better forecasts?

10. The Dow Jones Industrial Average (DJIA) is based on common stock prices of 30 industrial companies. This average is used to describe what is happening in the stock market. The weekly closing levels of the DJIA for 12 weeks follow.

Week	DJIA	Week	DJIA
1	4480	7	4520
2	4470	8	4470
3	4475	9	4440
4	4510	10	4480
5	4500	11	4530
6	4480	12	4550

   a. Compute the exponential smoothing forecasts using $\alpha = .2$.
   b. Compute the exponential smoothing forecasts using $\alpha = .3$.
   c. Which exponential smoothing model provides the better forecasts? What is the forecast of the DJIA for week 13?

11. The following data represent 15 quarters of manufacturing capacity utilization (in percentages).

Quarter/Year	Utilization	Quarter/Year	Utilization
1/1991	82.5	1/1993	78.8
2/1991	81.3	2/1993	78.7
3/1991	81.3	3/1993	78.4
4/1991	79.0	4/1993	80.0
1/1992	76.6	1/1994	80.7
2/1992	78.0	2/1994	80.7
3/1992	78.4	3/1994	80.8
4/1992	78.0		

   a. Compute three- and four-quarter moving averages for this time series. Which moving average provides the better forecast for the fourth quarter of 1994?
   b. Use smoothing constants of $\alpha = 0.4$ and $\alpha = 0.5$ to develop forecasts for the fourth quarter of 1994. Which smoothing constant provides the better forecast?
   c. On the basis of the analyses in parts (a) and (b), which method—moving averages or exponential smoothing—provides the better forecast? Explain.

18.3 USING TREND PROJECTION IN FORECASTING

In this section we show how to forecast a time series that has a long-term linear trend. The type of time series for which the trend projection method is applicable shows a consistent increase or decrease over time; the time series is not stable so the smoothing methods described in the preceding section are not applicable. Consider the time series data for bicycle sales of a particular manufacturer over the past 10 years, as shown in Table 18.8 and Figure 18.8. Note that 21,600 bicycles were sold in year 1, 22,900 were sold in year 2, and so on. In year 10, the most recent year, 31,400 bicycles were sold. Although Figure 18.8 shows some up and down movement over the past 10 years, the time series seems to have an overall increasing or upward trend.

We do not want the trend component of a time series to follow each and every up and down movement. Rather, the trend component should reflect the gradual shifting—in this case, growth—of the time series values. After we view the time series data in Table

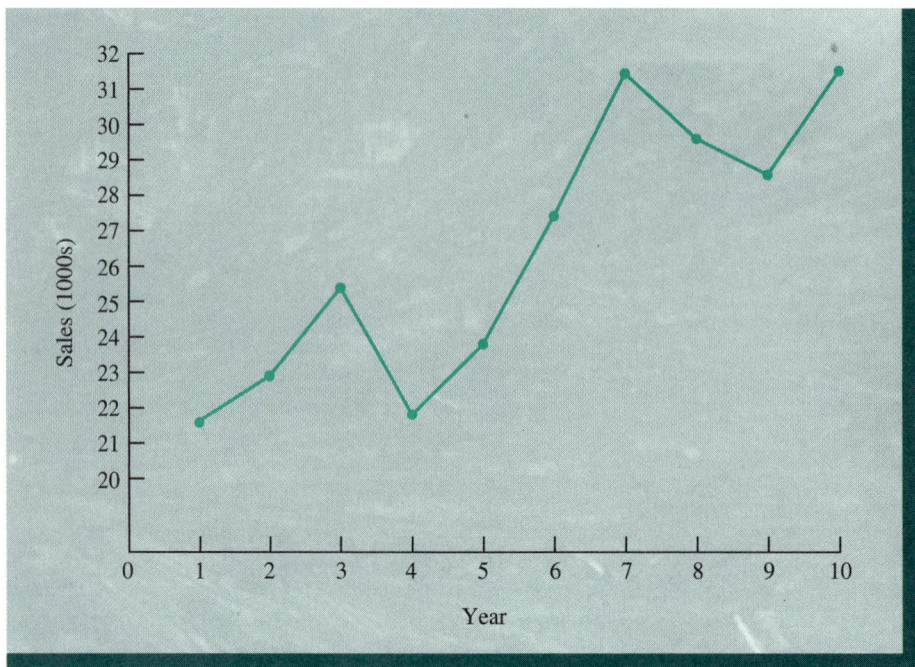

FIGURE 18.8   Graph of the Bicycle Sales Time Series

TABLE 18.8 Bicycle Sales Time Series

Year (t)	Sales (1000s) (Y_t)
1	21.6
2	22.9
3	25.5
4	21.9
5	23.9
6	27.5
7	31.5
8	29.7
9	28.6
10	31.4

18.8 and the graph in Figure 18.8, we might agree that a linear trend as shown in Figure 18.9 provides a reasonable description of the long-run movement in the series.

We use the bicycle sales data to illustrate the calculations involved in applying regression analysis to identify a linear trend. Recall that in the discussion of simple linear regression in Chapter 14, we described how the least squares method is used to find the best straight-line relationship between two variables. That is the methodology we will use to develop the trend line for the bicycle sales time series. Specifically, we will be using regression analysis to estimate the relationship between time and sales volume.

In Chapter 14 the estimated regression equation describing a straight-line relationship between an independent variable x and a dependent variable y was written

$$\hat{y} = b_0 + b_1 x \tag{18.4}$$

To emphasize the fact that in forecasting the independent variable is time, we will use t in (18.4) instead of x; in addition, we will use T_t in place of $\hat{y}$. Thus, for a linear trend, the estimated sales volume expressed as a function of time can be written as follows.

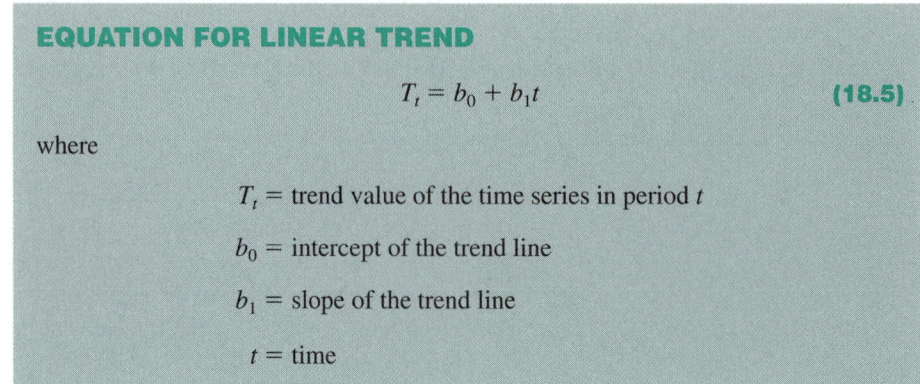

EQUATION FOR LINEAR TREND

$$T_t = b_0 + b_1 t \tag{18.5}$$

where

T_t = trend value of the time series in period t

b_0 = intercept of the trend line

b_1 = slope of the trend line

t = time

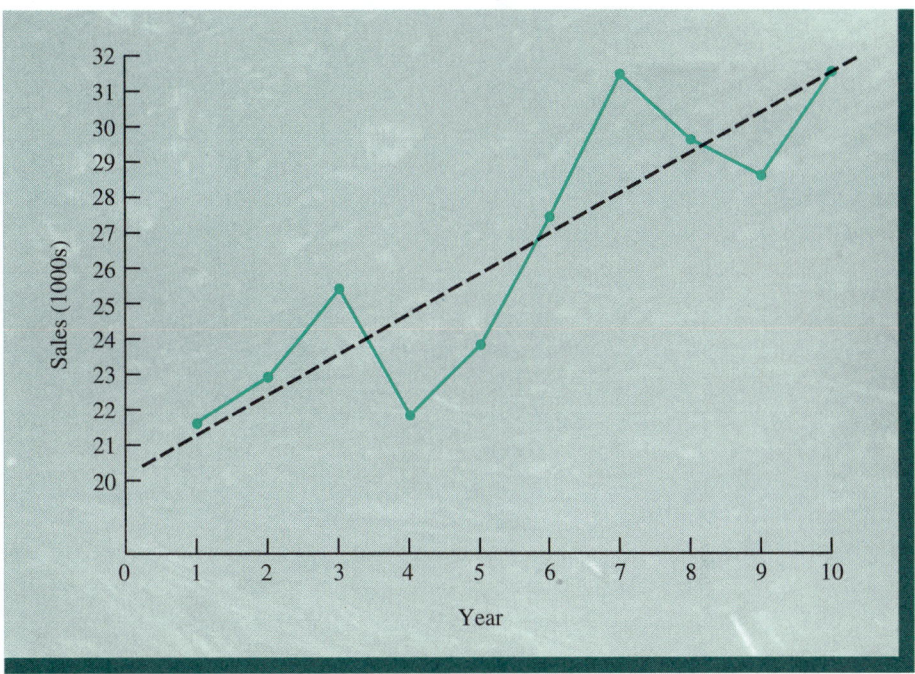

FIGURE 18.9 Trend Represented by a Linear Function for Bicycle Sales

In (18.5), we will let $t = 1$ for the time of the first observation on the time series data, $t = 2$ for the time of the second observation, and so on. Note that for the time series on bicycle sales, $t = 1$ corresponds to the oldest time series value and $t = 10$ corresponds to the most recent year's data. Formulas for computing the estimated regression coefficients (b_1 and b_0) in (18.4) were presented in Chapter 14; they are repeated here with t replacing x and Y_t replacing y_i.

COMPUTING THE SLOPE (b_1) AND INTERCEPT (b_0)

$$b_1 = \frac{\Sigma t Y_t - (\Sigma t\, \Sigma Y_t)/n}{\Sigma t^2 - (\Sigma t)^2/n} \qquad \text{(18.6)}$$

$$b_0 = \overline{Y} - b_1 \overline{t} \qquad \text{(18.7)}$$

where

Y_t = value of the time series in period t

n = number of periods

$\overline{Y}$ = average value of the time series; that is, $\overline{Y} = \Sigma Y_t / n$

$\overline{t}$ = average value of t; that is, $\overline{t} = \Sigma t/n$

Using the relationships for b_0 and b_1 and the bicycle sales data of Table 18.8, we have the following calculations.

t	Y_t	tY_t	t^2
1	21.6	21.6	1
2	22.9	45.8	4
3	25.5	76.5	9
4	21.9	87.6	16
5	23.9	119.5	25
6	27.5	165.0	36
7	31.5	220.5	49
8	29.7	237.6	64
9	28.6	257.4	81
10	31.4	314.0	100
Totals 55	264.5	1545.5	385

where

$$\bar{t} = \frac{55}{10} = 5.5$$

$$\bar{Y} = \frac{264.5}{10} = 26.45$$

$$b_1 = \frac{1545.5 - (55)(264.5)/10}{385 - (55)^2/10} = 1.10$$

$$b_0 = 26.45 - 1.10(5.5) = 20.4$$

Therefore,

$$T_t = 20.4 + 1.1t \qquad \textbf{(18.8)}$$

is the expression for the linear trend component for the bicycle sales time series.

• • • • • • • • • • • • • • • • • • • TREND PROJECTIONS

The slope of 1.1 indicates that over the past 10 years the firm has had an average growth in sales of around 1100 units per year. If we assume that the past 10-year trend in sales is a good indicator of the future, (18.8) can be used to project the trend component of the time series. For example, substituting $t = 11$ into (18.8) yields next year's trend projection, T_{11}.

$$T_{11} = 20.4 + 1.1(11) = 32.5$$

Thus, using the trend component only, we would forecast sales of 32,500 bicycles next year.

The use of a linear function to model the trend is common. However, as we discussed previously, sometimes time series have a curvilinear, or nonlinear, trend similar to those in Figure 18.10. In Chapter 16 we discussed how regression analysis can be used to model curvilinear relationships of the type shown in panel A of Figure 18.10. More advanced texts discuss in detail how to develop regression models for more complex relationships such as the one shown in panel B of Figure 18.10.

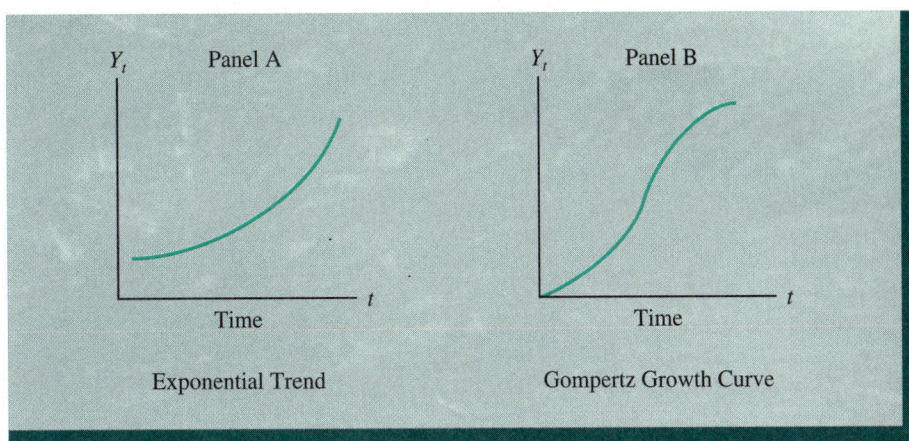

FIGURE 18.10 Some Possible Forms of Nonlinear Trend Patterns

EXERCISES

METHODS

Self-Test

12. Consider the following time series.

t	1	2	3	4	5
Y_t	6	11	9	14	15

Develop an equation for the linear trend component for this time series. What is the forecast for $t = 6$?

13. Consider the following time series.

t	1	2	3	4	5	6
Y_t	205	202	195	190	191	188

Develop an equation for the linear trend component for this time series. What is the forecast for $t = 7$?

APPLICATIONS

Self-Test

14. The trend for the future appears to be increasing numbers of two-income households for married couples (*Business Week*, April 6, 1992). With working wives, a surge in affluent two-income households is anticipated. The following data from the Department of Commerce show the number of two-income married couples earning $50,000 or more annually. The data are in millions of couples with annual income based on constant 1990 dollars.

Year	Millions of Couples
1970	9.5
1975	10.5
1980	14.0
1985	14.9
1990	18.0

Develop a linear trend equation for this time series. If the trend in two-income households continues, what is the forecast of the number of working couples who will make at least $50,000 annually in 1995?

TABLE 18.9
Exercise 15

Year	Attendance
1	28,000
2	30,000
3	31,500
4	30,400
5	30,500
6	32,200
7	30,800

15. Table 18.9 gives average attendance figures for home football games at a major university for the past seven years. Develop the equation for the linear trend component for this time series.

16. Automobile sales at B. J. Scott Motors, Inc., provided the following 10-year time series.

Year	Sales
1	400
2	390
3	320
4	340
5	270
6	260
7	300
8	320
9	340
10	370

Plot the time series and comment on the appropriateness of a linear trend. What type of functional form do you believe would be most appropriate for the trend pattern of this time series?

TABLE 18.10
Exercise 17

Year	Cost/Unit ($)
1	20.00
2	24.50
3	28.20
4	27.50
5	26.60
6	30.00
7	31.00
8	36.00

17. The president of a small manufacturing firm has been concerned about the continual increase in manufacturing costs over the past several years. Shown in Table 18.10 is a time series of the cost per unit for the firm's leading product over the past eight years.
   a. Show a graph of this time series. Does a linear trend appear to be present?
   b. Develop the equation for the linear trend component for the time series. What is the average cost increase that the firm has been realizing per year?

18. Earnings per share for the Walgreen Company for a 10-year period follow.

   .64   .73   .94   1.14   1.33   1.53   1.67   1.68   2.10   2.50

   a. Use a linear trend projection to forecast this time series for the coming year.
   b. What does this time series analysis tell you about the Walgreen Company? Do the historical data indicate that the Walgreen Company is a good investment?

19. *The Wall Street Journal* (February 3, 1992) reported the combined number of applications for admission at 10 business schools (Dartmouth, Harvard, Stanford, Pennsylvania, MIT, Columbia, Virginia, Chicago, Northwestern, and UCLA) for 1984–1991. The depressed job market of the late 1980s and early 1990s appears to have prompted an unexpected upsurge of interest in graduate programs of business administration. Eager to escape troubled businesses and also enhance their credentials, many recession-weary professionals gave up jobs and headed to business schools. The numbers of applications expressed in thousands are reported in Table 18.11.

TABLE 18.11
Exercise 19

Year	Applications
1984	25.2
1985	28.0
1986	27.5
1987	31.3
1988	33.4
1989	33.1
1990	36.0
1991	36.4

   a. Develop a linear trend equation for the time series. What is the average annual increase in the number of applications over the eight-year period?
   b. What is the forecast of the number of applications at these 10 schools for 1992?

20. Gross revenue data (in millions of dollars) for Delta Airlines for a 10-year period follow.

Year	Revenue	Year	Revenue
1	2428	6	4264
2	2951	7	4738
3	3533	8	4460
4	3618	9	5318
5	3616	10	6915

a. Develop a linear trend equation for this time series. Comment on what the equation tells about the gross revenue for Delta Airlines for the 10-year period.

b. Provide the forecasts for gross revenue for years 11 and 12.

21. The following table gives numbers of ATM terminals (in thousands) in service from 1985 to 1993 (*Bank Network News,* November 25, 1993).

Year	Number of Terminals
1987	68.0
1988	72.5
1989	75.6
1990	80.2
1991	83.5
1992	87.3
1993	94.8

a. Develop a linear trend equation for this time series.

b. Use the trend equation to estimate the increase in the number of ATM terminals per year.

c. Provide forecasts for the number of ATM terminals for 1994 and 1995.

18.4 USING TREND AND SEASONAL COMPONENTS IN FORECASTING

We have shown how to forecast a time series that has a trend component. In this section we extend the discussion by showing how to forecast a time series that has both trend and seasonal components.

Many situations in business and economics involve period-to-period comparisons. For instance, we might be interested to learn that unemployment is up 2% from last month's level, steel production rose 5% over last month's output, or the production of electric power is down 3% from that of the previous month. Care must be exercised in using such information, however, because whenever a seasonal influence is present, such comparisons may be misleading. For instance, a 3% decline in electric power consumption from August to September might represent only the seasonal effect associated with a decrease in the use of air conditioning and not a long-term decline in the use of electric power. Indeed, after adjusting for the seasonal effect, we might even find that the use of electric power has increased relative to other Septembers.

Removing the seasonal effect from a time series is known as deseasonalizing the time series. It makes period-to-period comparisons more meaningful and can help identify whether a trend is present. The approach we take in this section is appropriate when only seasonal effects are present or when both seasonal and trend components are present. The first step is to compute seasonal indexes and use them to deseasonalize the data. Then, if a trend is apparent in the deseasonalized data, we use regression analysis on the deseasonalized data to estimate the trend component.

THE MULTIPLICATIVE MODEL

In addition to a trend component (T) and a seasonal component (S), we will assume that the time series has an irregular component (I). The irregular component accounts for any random effects in the time series that cannot be explained by the trend and seasonal components. Using T_t, S_t, and I_t to identify the trend, seasonal, and irregular components at time t, we will assume that the time series value, denoted Y_t, can be described by the following *multiplicative time series model.*

$$Y_t = T_t \times S_t \times I_t \tag{18.9}$$

In this model, T_t is the trend measured in units of the item being forecast. However, the S_t and I_t components are measured in relative terms, with values above 1.00 indicating effects above the trend and values below 1.00 indicating effects below the trend.

In this section we will illustrate the use of the multiplicative model with trend, seasonal, and irregular components by working with the quarterly data in Table 18.12 and Figure 18.11. These data represent television set sales (in thousands of units) for a particular manufacturer over the past four years. We begin by showing how to identify the seasonal component of the time series.

CALCULATING THE SEASONAL INDEXES

Figure 18.11 indicates that sales are lowest in the second quarter of each year and increase in quarters 3 and 4. Hence, we conclude that television-set sales have a seasonal pattern. The computational procedure used to identify each quarter's seasonal influence begins by computing a moving average to isolate the combined seasonal and irregular components, S_t and I_t.

We use one year of data in each calculation. Since we are working with a quarterly series, we will use four data values in each moving average. The moving average calculation for the first four quarters of the television-set sales data follows.

$$\text{First Moving Average} = \frac{4.8 + 4.1 + 6.0 + 6.5}{4} = \frac{21.4}{4} = 5.35$$

Note that the moving average calculation for the first four quarters yields the average quarterly sales over the first year of the time series. Continuing the moving average calculation, we next add the 5.8 value for the first quarter of year 2 and drop the 4.8 for the first quarter of year 1. Thus, the second moving average is

TABLE 18.12 Quarterly Data for Television Set Sales

Year	Quarter	Sales (1000s)
1	1	4.8
	2	4.1
	3	6.0
	4	6.5
2	1	5.8
	2	5.2
	3	6.8
	4	7.4
3	1	6.0
	2	5.6
	3	7.5
	4	7.8
4	1	6.3
	2	5.9
	3	8.0
	4	8.4

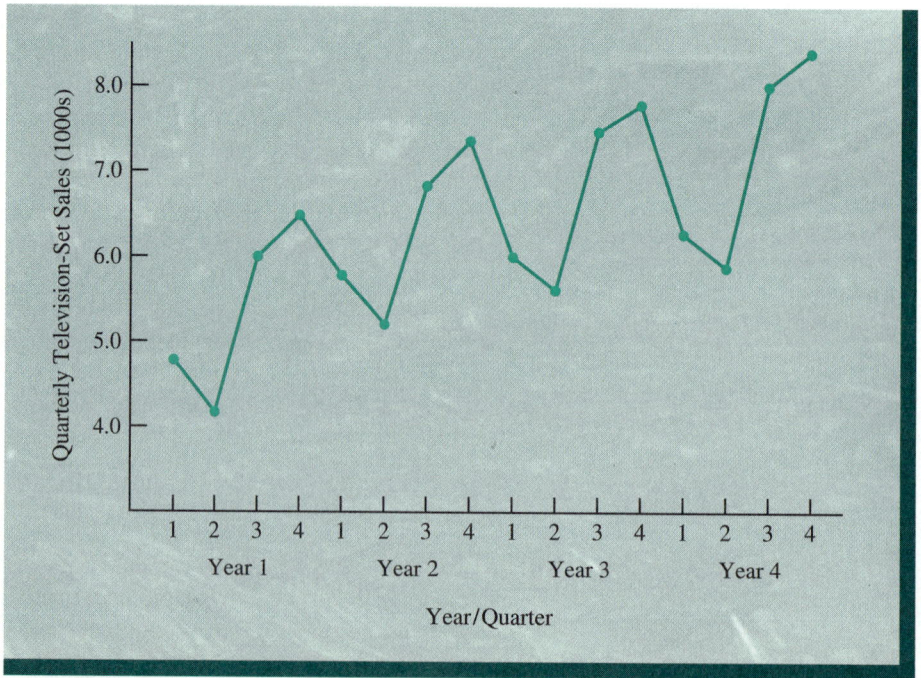

FIGURE 18.11 Graph of Quarterly Television-Set Sales Time Series

$$\text{Second Moving Average} = \frac{4.1 + 6.0 + 6.5 + 5.8}{4} = \frac{22.4}{4} = 5.60$$

Similarly, the third moving average calculation is $(6.0+6.5+5.8+5.2)/4=5.875$.

Before we proceed with the moving average calculations for the entire time series, let us return to the first moving average calculation, which resulted in a value of 5.35. The 5.35 value represents an average quarterly sales volume (across all seasons) for year 1. As we look back at the calculation of the 5.35 value, perhaps it makes sense to associate 5.35 with a "middle" quarter of the moving average group. However, with four quarters in the moving average, there is no middle quarter. The 5.35 value corresponds to the last half of quarter 2 and the first half of quarter 3. Similarly, if we go to the next moving average value of 5.60, the middle corresponds to the last half of quarter 3 and the first half of quarter 4.

Recall that the reason for computing moving averages is to isolate the combined seasonal and irregular components. However, the moving average values we have computed do not correspond directly to the original quarters of the time series. We can resolve this difficulty by using the midpoints between successive moving average values. For example, since 5.35 corresponds to the first half of quarter 3 and 5.60 corresponds to the last half of quarter 3, we will use $(5.35 + 5.60)/2 = 5.475$ as the moving average value for quarter 3. Similarly, we associate a moving average value of $(5.60 + 5.875)/2 = 5.738$ with quarter 4. The result is a *centered moving average*. Table 18.13 is a complete summary of the moving average calculations for the television-set sales data.

If the number of data points in a moving average calculation is an odd number, the middle point will correspond to one of the periods in the time series. In such cases, we would not have to center the moving average values to correspond to a particular time period as we have done in the calculations in Table 18.13.

What do the centered moving averages in Table 18.13 tell us about this time series? Figure 18.12 is a plot of the actual time series values and the centered moving average values. Note particularly how the centered moving average values tend to smooth out the fluctuations in the time series. Since the moving average values were computed for four quarters of data, they do not include the fluctuations due to seasonal influences. Each point in the centered moving average represents the value of the time series as though there were no seasonal or irregular influence.

By dividing each time series observation by the corresponding centered moving average, we can identify the seasonal-irregular effect in the time series. For example, the third quarter of year 1 shows $6.0/5.475 = 1.096$ as the combined seasonal-irregular value. The resulting seasonal-irregular values for the entire time series are summarized in Table 18.14.

Consider the third quarter. The results from years 1, 2, and 3 show third-quarter values of 1.096, 1.075, and 1.109, respectively. Thus, in all cases, the seasonal-irregular value appears to have an above-average influence in the third quarter. Since the year-to-year fluctuations in the seasonal-irregular value can be attributed primarily to the irregular component, we can average the computed values to eliminate the irregular influence and obtain an estimate of the third-quarter seasonal influence.

$$\text{Seasonal Effect of Third Quarter} = \frac{1.096 + 1.075 + 1.109}{3} = 1.09$$

We refer to 1.09 as the *seasonal index* for the third quarter. In Table 18.15 we summarize the calculations involved in computing the seasonal indexes for the television-set sales time series. We see that the seasonal indexes for the four quarters are: quarter 1, .93; quarter 2, .84; quarter 3, 1.09; and quarter 4, 1.14.

TABLE 18.13 Moving Average Calculations for the Television-Set Sales Time Series

Year	Quarter	Sales (1000s)	Four-Quarter Moving Average	Centered Moving Average
1	1	4.8		
	2	4.1		
			5.350	
	3	6.0		5.475
			5.600	
	4	6.5		5.738
			5.875	
2	1	5.8		5.975
			6.075	
	2	5.2		6.188
			6.300	
	3	6.8		6.325
			6.350	
	4	7.4		6.400
			6.450	
3	1	6.0		6.538
			6.625	
	2	5.6		6.675
			6.725	
	3	7.5		6.763
			6.800	
	4	7.8		6.838
			6.875	
4	1	6.3		6.938
			7.000	
	2	5.9		7.075
			7.150	
	3	8.0		
	4	8.4		

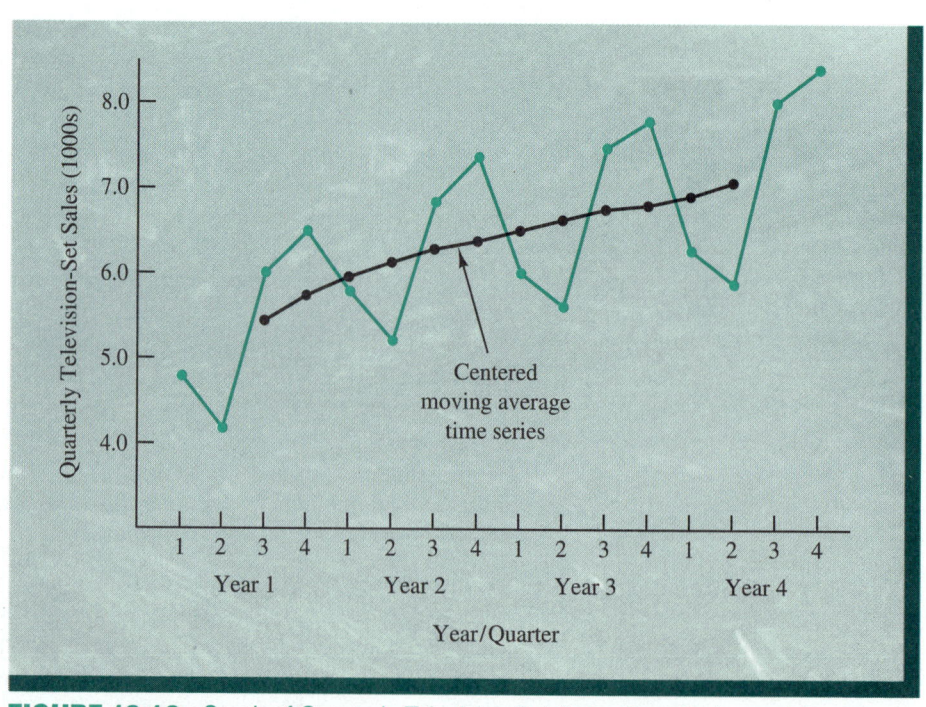

FIGURE 18.12 Graph of Quarterly Television-Set Sales Time Series and Centered Moving Average

TABLE 18.14 Seasonal-Irregular Values for the Television-Set Sales Time Series

Year	Quarter	Sales (1000s)	Centered Moving Average	Seasonal-Irregular Value
1	1	4.8		
	2	4.1		
	3	6.0	5.475	1.096
	4	6.5	5.738	1.133
2	1	5.8	5.975	.971
	2	5.2	6.188	.840
	3	6.8	6.325	1.075
	4	7.4	6.400	1.156
3	1	6.0	6.538	.918
	2	5.6	6.675	.839
	3	7.5	6.763	1.109
	4	7.8	6.838	1.141
4	1	6.3	6.938	.908
	2	5.9	7.075	.834
	3	8.0		
	4	8.4		

TABLE 18.15 Seasonal Index Calculations for the Television-Set Sales Time Series

Quarter	Seasonal-Irregular Component Values $(S_t I_t)$	Seasonal Index (S_t)
1	.971, .918, .908	.93
2	.840, .839, .834	.84
3	1.096, 1.075, 1.109	1.09
4	1.133, 1.156, 1.141	1.14

Interpretation of the values in Table 18.15 provides some observations about the seasonal component in television-set sales. The best sales quarter is the fourth quarter, with sales averaging 14% above the average quarterly value. The worst, or slowest, sales quarter is the second quarter; its seasonal index of .84 shows that the sales average is 16% below the average quarterly sales. The seasonal component corresponds clearly to the intuitive expectation that television viewing interest and thus television purchase patterns tend to peak in the fourth quarter because of the coming winter season and reduction in outdoor activities. The low second-quarter sales reflect the reduced interest in television viewing due to the spring and presummer activities of potential customers.

One final adjustment is sometimes necessary in obtaining the seasonal indexes. The multiplicative model requires that the average seasonal index equal 1.00; that is, the sum of the four seasonal indexes in Table 18.15 must equal 4.00. This is necessary if the seasonal effects are to even out over the year, as they must. The average of the seasonal indexes in our example is equal to 1.00, so no adjustment is required. In some cases, a slight adjustment is needed and can be made by simply multiplying each seasonal index by the number of seasons divided by the sum of the unadjusted seasonal indexes. For example, for quarterly data we would multiply each seasonal index by 4/(sum of the unadjusted seasonal indexes). Some of the exercises will require this adjustment to obtain the appropriate seasonal indexes.

TABLE 18.16 Deseasonalized Values for the Television-Set Sales Time Series

Year	Quarter	Sales (1000s) (Y_t)	Seasonal Index (S_t)	Deseasonalized Sales $(Y_t /S_t = T_t I_t)$
1	1	4.8	.93	5.16
	2	4.1	.84	4.88
	3	6.0	1.09	5.50
	4	6.5	1.14	5.70
2	1	5.8	.93	6.24
	2	5.2	.84	6.19
	3	6.8	1.09	6.24
	4	7.4	1.14	6.49
3	1	6.0	.93	6.45
	2	5.6	.84	6.67
	3	7.5	1.09	6.88
	4	7.8	1.14	6.84
4	1	6.3	.93	6.77
	2	5.9	.84	7.02
	3	8.0	1.09	7.34
	4	8.4	1.14	7.37

DESEASONALIZING THE TIME SERIES

The purpose of finding seasonal indexes is to remove the seasonal effects from a time series. This process is referred to as *deseasonalizing* the time series. Economic time series adjusted for seasonal variations (deseasonalized time series) are often reported in publications such as the *Survey of Current Business, The Wall Street Journal,* and *Business Week.* Using the notation of the multiplicative model, we have

$$Y_t = T_t \times S_t \times I_t$$

By dividing each time series observation by the corresponding seasonal index, we have removed the effect of season from the time series. The deseasonalized time series for television-set sales is summarized in Table 18.16. Figure 18.13 is a graph of the deseasonalized television-set sales time series.

USING THE DESEASONALIZED TIME SERIES TO IDENTIFY TREND

Although the graph in Figure 18.13 shows some up and down movement over the past 16 quarters, the time series seems to have an upward linear trend. To identify this trend, we will use the same procedure as in the preceding section; in this case, the data are quarterly deseasonalized sales values. Hence, for a linear trend, the estimated sales volume expressed as a function of time is

$$T_t = b_0 + b_1 t$$

where

T_t = trend value for television-set sales in period t,

b_0 = intercept of the trend line, and

b_1 = slope of the trend line.

As before, $t = 1$ corresponds to the time of the first observation for the time series, $t = 2$ corresponds to the time of the second observation, and so on. Thus, for the deseason-

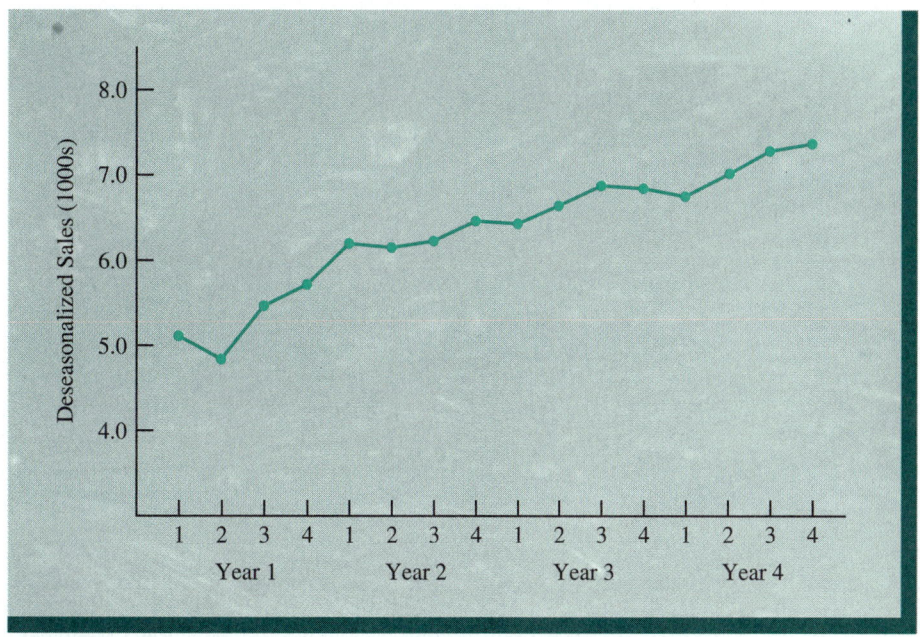

FIGURE 18.13   Deseasonalized Television-Set Sales Time Series

alized television-set sales time series, $t = 1$ corresponds to the first deseasonalized quarterly sales value and $t = 16$ corresponds to the most recent deseasonalized quarterly sales value. The formulas for computing the value of b_0 and the value of b_1 follow.

$$b_1 = \frac{\Sigma t Y_t - (\Sigma t \Sigma Y_t)/n}{\Sigma t^2 - (\Sigma t)^2/n}$$

$$b_0 = \bar{Y} - b_1 \bar{t}$$

Note that Y_t now refers to the deseasonalized time series value at time t and not to the actual value of the time series. Using the given relationships for b_0 and b_1 and the deseasonalized sales data of Table 18.16, we have the following calculations.

t	Y_t (Deseasonalized)	tY_t	t^2
1	5.16	5.16	1
2	4.88	9.76	4
3	5.50	16.50	9
4	5.70	22.80	16
5	6.24	31.20	25
6	6.19	37.14	36
7	6.24	43.68	49
8	6.49	51.92	64
9	6.45	58.05	81
10	6.67	66.70	100
11	6.88	75.68	121
12	6.84	82.08	144
13	6.77	88.01	169
14	7.02	98.28	196
15	7.34	110.10	225
16	7.37	117.92	256
Totals 136	101.74	914.98	1496

where

$$\bar{t} = \frac{136}{16} = 8.5$$

$$\bar{Y} = \frac{101.74}{16} = 6.359$$

$$b_1 = \frac{914.98 - (136)(101.74)/16}{1496 - (136)^2/16} = .148$$

$$b_0 = 6.359 - .148(8.5) = 5.101$$

Therefore,

$$T_t = 5.101 + .148t$$

is the expression for the linear trend component of the time series.

The slope of .148 indicates that over the past 16 quarters, the firm has had an average deseasonalized growth in sales of around 148 sets per quarter. If we assume that the past 16-quarter trend in sales data is a reasonably good indicator of the future, this equation can be used to project the trend component of the time series for future quarters. For example, substituting $t = 17$ into the equation yields next quarter's trend projection, T_{17}.

$$T_{17} = 5.101 + .148(17) = 7.617$$

Thus, the trend component yields a sales forecast of 7617 television sets for the next quarter. Similarly, the trend component produces sales forecasts of 7765, 7913, and 8061 television sets in quarters 18, 19, and 20, respectively.

SEASONAL ADJUSTMENTS

The final step in developing the forecast when both trend and seasonal components are present is to use the seasonal index to adjust the trend projection. Returning to the television-set sales example, we have a trend projection for the next four quarters. Now we must adjust the forecast for the seasonal effect. The seasonal index for the first quarter of year 5 ($t = 17$) is .93, so we obtain the quarterly forecast by multiplying the forecast based on trend ($T_{17} = 7617$) by the seasonal index (.93). Thus, the forecast for the next quarter is 7617(.93) = 7084. Table 18.17 gives the quarterly forecast for quarters 17 through 20. The high-volume fourth quarter has a 9190-unit forecast and the low-volume second quarter has a 6523-unit forecast.

TABLE 18.17 Quarterly Forecasts for the Television-Set Sales Time Series

Year	Quarter	Trend Forecast	Seasonal Index (see Table 18.16)	Quarterly Forecast
5	1	7617	.93	(7617)(.93) = 7084
	2	7765	.84	(7765)(.84) = 6523
	3	7913	1.09	(7913)(1.09) = 8625
	4	8061	1.14	(8061)(1.14) = 9190

MODELS BASED ON MONTHLY DATA

In the preceding television-set sales example, we used quarterly data to illustrate the computation of seasonal indexes. However, many businesses use monthly rather than quarterly forecasts. In such cases, the procedures introduced in this section can be applied with minor modifications. First, a 12-month moving average replaces the four-quarter moving average; second, 12 monthly seasonal indexes, rather than four quarterly seasonal indexes, must be computed. Otherwise the computational and forecasting procedures are identical. Exercise 24 at the end of this section asks you to develop monthly seasonal indexes for a situation requiring monthly forecasts.

CYCLICAL COMPONENT

Mathematically, the multiplicative model of (18.9) can be expanded to include a cyclical component.

$$Y_t = T_t \times C_t \times S_t \times I_t \tag{18.10}$$

The cyclical component, like the seasonal component, is expressed as a percentage of trend. As mentioned in Section 18.1, this component is attributable to multiyear cycles in the time series. It is analogous to the seasonal component, but over a longer period of time. However, because of the length of time involved, obtaining enough relevant data to estimate the cyclical component is often difficult. Another difficulty is that cycles usually vary in length. We leave further discussion of the cyclical component to texts on forecasting methods.

EXERCISES

METHODS

Self-Test

22. Consider the time series data in Table 18.18.
  a. Show the four-quarter and centered moving average values for this time series.
  b. Compute seasonal indexes for the four quarters.

TABLE 18.18 Exercise 22

Quarter	Year 1	Year 2	Year 3
1	4	6	7
2	2	3	6
3	3	5	6
4	5	7	8

APPLICATIONS

23. The quarterly sales data (number of copies sold) for a college textbook over the past three years follow.

Quarter	Year 1	Year 2	Year 3
1	1690	1800	1850
2	940	900	1100
3	2625	2900	2930
4	2500	2360	2615

  a. Show the four-quarter and centered moving average values for this time series.
  b. Compute seasonal indexes for the four quarters.
  c. When does the textbook publisher have the largest seasonal index? Does this appear reasonable? Explain.

24. Identify the monthly seasonal indexes for the three years of expenses for a six-unit apartment house in southern Florida given in Table 18.19. Use a 12-month moving average calculation.

TABLE 18.19 Exercise 24

	Expenses		
Month	Year 1	Year 2	Year 3
January	170	180	195
February	180	205	210
March	205	215	230
April	230	245	280
May	240	265	290
June	315	330	390
July	360	400	420
August	290	335	330
September	240	260	290
October	240	270	295
November	230	255	280
December	195	220	250

25. Air pollution control specialists in southern California monitor the amount of ozone, carbon dioxide, and nitrogen dioxide in the air on an hourly basis. The hourly time series data exhibit seasonality, with the levels of pollutants showing patterns over the hours in the day. On July 15, 16, and 17, the following levels of nitrogen dioxide were observed in the downtown area for the 12 hours from 6:00 A.M. to 6:00 P.M.

July 15:	25	28	35	50	60	60	40	35	30	25	25	20
July 16:	28	30	35	48	60	65	50	40	35	25	20	20
July 17:	35	42	45	70	72	75	60	45	40	25	25	25

a. Identify the hourly seasonal indexes for the 12-hour daily readings.
b. With the seasonal indexes from (a), the data were deseasonalized; the trend equation developed for the deseasonalized data was $T_t = 32.983 + .3922t$. Using the trend component only, develop forecasts for the 12 hours for July 18.
c. Use the seasonal indexes from (a) to adjust the trend forecasts developed in (b).

26. Electric power consumption is measured in kilowatt-hours (kWh). The local utility company has an interrupt program whereby commercial customers that participate receive favorable rates but must agree to cut back consumption if the utility requests them to do so. Timko Products cut back consumption at 12:00 noon Thursday. To assess the savings, the utility must estimate Timko's usage without the interrupt. The period of interrupted service was from noon to 8:00 P.M. Data on electric power consumption for the past 72 hours are available.

Time Period	Monday	Tuesday	Wednesday	Thursday
12–4 A.M.	—	19,281	31,209	27,330
4–8 A.M.	—	33,195	37,014	32,715
8–12 noon	—	99,516	119,968	152,465
12–4 P.M.	124,299	123,666	156,033	
4–8 P.M.	113,545	111,717	128,889	
8–12 midnight	41,300	48,112	73,923	

a. Is there a seasonal effect over the 24-hour period? Compute seasonal indexes for the six four-hour periods.
b. Use trend adjusted for seasonal indexes to estimate Timko's normal usage over the period of interrupted service.

18.5　USING REGRESSION ANALYSIS IN FORECASTING

In the discussion of regression analysis in Chapters 14, 15, and 16, we showed how one or more independent variables could be used to predict the value of a single dependent variable. Looking at regression analysis as a forecasting tool, we can view the time series value that we want to forecast as the dependent variable. Hence, if we can identify a good set of related independent, or predictor, variables we may be able to develop an estimated regression equation for predicting or forecasting the time series.

The approach we used in Section 18.3 to fit a linear trend line to the bicycle sales time series is a special case of regression analysis. In that example, two variables— bicycle sales and time—were shown to be linearly related.* The inherent complexity of most real-world problems necessitates the consideration of more than one variable to predict the variable of interest. The statistical technique known as multiple regression analysis can be used in such situations.

Recall that to develop an estimated multiple regression equation, we need a sample of observations for the dependent variable and all independent variables. In time series analysis the n periods of time series data provide a sample of n observations on each variable that can be used in the analysis. For a function involving k independent variables, we use the following notation.

$$Y_t = \text{ value of the time series in period } t$$

$$x_{1t} = \text{value of independent variable 1 in period } t$$

$$x_{2t} = \text{value of independent variable 2 in period } t$$

$$\cdot$$
$$\cdot$$
$$\cdot$$

$$x_{kt} = \text{value of independent variable } k \text{ in period } t$$

The n periods of data necessary to develop the estimated regression equation would appear as shown in the following table.

Period	Time Series (Y_t)	Value of Independent Variables						
		x_{1t}	x_{2t}	x_{3t}	·	·	·	x_{kt}
1	Y_1	x_{11}	x_{21}	x_{31}				x_{k1}
2	Y_2	x_{12}	x_{22}	x_{32}				x_{k2}
·	·	·	·	·	·	·	·	·
·	·	·	·	·	·	·	·	·
·	·	·	·	·	·	·	·	·
n	Y_n	x_{1n}	x_{2n}	x_{3n}				x_{kn}

As you might imagine, several choices are possible for the independent variables in a forecasting model. One possible choice for an independent variable is simply time. This is the choice we made in Section 18.3 when we estimated the trend of the time

---

*In a purely technical sense, the number of bicycles sold is not viewed as being related to time; instead, time is used as a surrogate for variables to which the number of bicycles sold is actually related but which are either unknown or too difficult or too costly to measure.

series using a linear function of the independent variable time. Letting $x_{1t} = t$, we obtain an estimated regression equation of the form

$$\hat{Y}_t = b_0 + b_1 t$$

where $\hat{Y}_t$ is the estimate of the time series value Y_t and where b_0 and b_1 are the estimated regression coefficients. In a more complex model, additional terms could be added corresponding to time raised to other powers. For example, if $x_{2t} = t^2$ and $x_{3t} = t^3$, the estimated regression equation would become

$$\hat{Y}_t = b_0 + b_1 x_{1t} + b_2 x_{2t} + b_3 x_{3t}$$
$$= b_0 + b_1 t + b_2 t^2 + b_3 t^3$$

Note that this model provides a forecast of a time series with curvilinear characteristics over time.

Other regression-based forecasting models have a mixture of economic and demographic independent variables. For example, in forecasting sales of refrigerators, we might select the following independent variables.

$$x_{1t} = \text{price in period } t$$

$$x_{2t} = \text{total industry sales in period } t - 1$$

$$x_{3t} = \text{number of building permits}$$
$$\text{for new houses in period } t - 1$$

$$x_{4t} = \text{population forecast for period } t$$

$$x_{5t} = \text{advertising budget for period } t$$

According to the usual multiple regression procedure, an estimated regression equation with five independent variables would be used to develop forecasts.

Whether or not a regression approach provides a good forecast depends largely on how well we are able to identify and obtain data for independent variables that are closely related to the time series. Generally, during the development of an estimated regression equation, we will want to consider many possible sets of independent variables. Thus, part of the regression analysis procedure should be the selection of the set of independent variables that provides the best forecasting model.

In the chapter introduction we stated that the *causal forecasting models* use time series related to the one being forecast in an effort to explain the cause of a time series' behavior. Regression analysis is the tool most often used in developing such causal models. The related time series become the independent variables, and the time series being forecast is the dependent variable.

In another type of regression-based forecasting model, the independent variables are all previous values of the same time series. For example, if the time series values are denoted $Y_1, Y_2, \ldots, Y_n$, then with a dependent variable Y_t, we might try to find an estimated regression equation relating Y_t to the most recent times series values Y_{t-1}, Y_{t-2}, and so on. With the three most recent periods as independent variables, the estimated regression equation would be

$$\hat{Y}_t = b_0 + b_1 Y_{t-1} + b_2 Y_{t-2} + b_3 Y_{t-3}$$

Regression models in which the independent variables are previous values of the time series are referred to as *autoregressive models*.

Finally, another regression-based forecasting approach incorporates a mixture of the independent variables previously discussed. For example, we might select a combination of time variables, some economic/demographic variables, and some previous values of the time series variable itself.

18.6 QUALITATIVE APPROACHES TO FORECASTING

In the preceding sections we discussed several types of quantitative forecasting methods. Most of those techniques require historical data on the variable of interest, so they cannot be applied when historical data are not available. Furthermore, even when such data are available, a significant change in environmental conditions affecting the time series may make the use of past data questionable in predicting future values of the time series. For example, a government-imposed gasoline rationing program would raise questions about the validity of a gasoline sales forecast based on historical data. Qualitative forecasting techniques afford an alternative in these and other cases.

DELPHI METHOD

One of the most commonly used qualitative forecasting techniques is the *Delphi method,* originally developed by a research group at the Rand Corporation. It is an attempt to develop forecasts through "group consensus." In its usual application, the members of a panel of experts—all of whom are physically separated from and unknown to each other—are asked to respond to a series of questionnaires. The responses from the first questionnaire are tabulated and used to prepare a second questionnaire that contains information and opinions of the entire group. Each respondent is then asked to reconsider and possibly revise his or her previous response in light of the group information provided. This process continues until the coordinator feels that some degree of consensus has been reached. The goal of the Delphi method is not to produce a single answer as output, but instead to produce a relatively narrow spread of opinions within which the majority of experts concur.

EXPERT JUDGMENT

Qualitative forecasts often are based on the judgment of a single expert or represent the consensus of a group of experts. For example, each year a group of experts at Merrill Lynch gather to forecast the level of the Dow Jones Industrial Average and the prime rate for the next year. In doing so, the experts individually consider information that they believe will influence the stock market and interest rates; then they combine their conclusions into a forecast. No formal model is used, and no two experts are likely to consider the same information in the same way.

Expert judgment is a forecasting method that is commonly recommended when conditions in the past are not likely to hold in the future. Even though no formal quantitative model is used, expert judgment has provided good forecasts in many situations.

SCENARIO WRITING

The qualitative procedure known as *scenario writing* consists of developing a conceptual scenario of the future based on a well-defined set of assumptions. Different sets of assumptions lead to different scenarios. The job of the decision maker is to decide how likely each scenario is and then to make decisions accordingly.

•••••••••••••••••• INTUITIVE APPROACHES

Subjective or *intuitive qualitative approaches* are based on the ability of the human mind to process a variety of information that, in most cases, is difficult to quantify. These techniques are often used in group work, wherein a committee or panel seeks to develop new ideas or solve complex problems through a series of "brainstorming sessions." In such sessions, individuals are freed from the usual group restrictions of peer pressure and criticism because they can present any idea or opinion without regard to its relevancy and, even more important, without fear of criticism.

SUMMARY

This chapter provided an introduction to the basic methods of time series analysis and forecasting. First, we showed that to explain the behavior of a time series, it is often helpful to think of the time series as consisting of four separate components: trend, cyclical, seasonal, and irregular. By isolating these components and measuring their apparent effect, one can forecast future values of the time series.

We discussed how smoothing methods can be used to forecast a time series that exhibits no significant trend, seasonal, or cyclical effect. The moving averages approach consists of computing an average of past data values and then using that average as the forecast for the next period. In the exponential smoothing method, a weighted average of past time series values is used to compute a forecast.

For time series that have only a long-term trend, we showed how regression analysis could be used to make trend projections. For time series in which both trend and seasonal influences are significant, we showed how to isolate the effects of the two factors and prepare better forecasts. Finally, regression analysis was described as a procedure for developing so-called causal forecasting models. A causal forecasting model is one that relates the time series value (dependent variable) to other independent variables that are believed to explain (cause) the time series behavior.

Qualitative forecasting methods were discussed as approaches that could be used when little or no historical data are available. These methods are also considered most appropriate when the past pattern of the time series is not expected to continue into the future.

GLOSSARY

Time series　A set of observations measured at successive points in time or over successive periods of time.

Forecast　A projection or prediction of future values of a time series.

Trend　The long-run shift or movement in the time series observable over several periods of time.

Cyclical component　The component of the time series model that results in periodic above-trend and below-trend behavior of the time series lasting more than one year.

Seasonal component　The component of the time series model that shows a periodic pattern over one year or less.

Irregular component　The component of the time series model that reflects the random variation of the time series values beyond what can be explained by the trend, cyclical, and seasonal components.

Moving averages A method of forecasting or smoothing a time series by averaging each successive group of data points.

Mean squared error (MSE) An approach to measuring the accuracy of a forecasting model. This measure is the average of the sum of the squared differences between the forecast values and the actual time series values.

Weighted moving averages A method of forecasting or smoothing a time series by computing a weighted average of past data values. The sum of the weights must equal one.

Exponential smoothing A forecasting technique that uses a weighted average of past time series values to arrive at smoothed time series values that can be used as forecasts.

Smoothing constant A parameter of the exponential smoothing model that provides the weight given to the most recent time series value in the calculation of the forecast value.

Multiplicative time series model A model whereby the separate components of the time series are multiplied together to identify the actual time series value. When the four components of trend, cyclical, seasonal, and irregular are assumed present, we obtain $Y_t = T_t \times C_t \times S_t \times I_t$. When the cyclical component is not modeled, we obtain $Y_t = T_t \times S_t \times I_t$.

Deseasonalized time series A time series from which the effect of season has been removed by dividing each original time series observation by the corresponding seasonal index.

Causal forecasting methods Forecasting methods that relate a time series to other variables that are believed to explain or cause its behavior.

Autoregressive model A time series model whereby a regression relationship based on past time series values is used to predict the future time series values.

Delphi approach A qualitative forecasting method that obtains forecasts through group consensus.

Scenario writing A qualitative forecasting method that consists of developing a conceptual scenario of the future based on a well-defined set of assumptions.

KEY FORMULAS

Moving Average

$$\text{Moving Average} = \frac{\Sigma(\text{most recent } n \text{ data values})}{n} \qquad (18.1)$$

Exponential Smoothing Model

$$F_{t+1} = \alpha Y_t + (1 - \alpha)F_t \qquad (18.2)$$

Equation for Linear Trend

$$T_t = b_0 + b_1 t \qquad (18.5)$$

Multiplicative Time Series Model with Trend, Seasonal, and Irregular Components

$$Y_t = T_t \times S_t \times I_t \qquad (18.9)$$

Multiplicative Time Series Model with Trend, Cyclical, Seasonal, and Irregular Components

$$Y_t = T_t \times C_t \times S_t \times I_t \qquad (18.10)$$

SUPPLEMENTARY EXERCISES

27. Moving averages often are used to identify movements in stock prices. Approximate monthly closing prices (in dollars per share) for Toys "R" Us for December 1992 through November 1993 follow.

Month	Price ($)	Month	Price ($)
December 1992	40	June 1993	34
January 1993	38	July 1993	37
February 1993	39	August 1993	35
March 1993	41	September 1993	37
April 1993	36	October 1993	40
May 1993	41	November 1993	41

a. Use a three-month moving average to smooth the time series. Forecast the closing price for December 1993.

b. Use a three-month weighted moving average to smooth the time series. Use a weight of .4 for the most recent period, .4 for the next period back, and .2 for the third period back. Forecast the closing price for December 1993.

c. Use exponential smoothing with a smoothing constant of $\alpha = .35$ to smooth the time series. Forecast the closing price for December 1993.

d. Which of the three methods do you prefer? Why?

28. The numbers of component parts used in a production process in the last 10 weeks are reported in Table 18.20. Using a smoothing constant of $\alpha = .25$, develop the exponential smoothing values for this time series. Indicate your forecast for next week.

TABLE 18.20
Exercise 28

Week	Parts
1	200
2	350
3	250
4	360
5	250
6	210
7	280
8	350
9	290
10	320

29. The percentage of individual investors' portfolios committed to stock depends on the state of the economy (*AAII Journal,* April 1992). As of February 1982, a typical portfolio consisted of stocks (32%), stock funds (26%), cash (23%), bonds (10%), and bond funds (9%). The following table reports the percentage of stocks in a typical portfolio in nine quarters from 1990 to 1992.

Quarter	Stock %
1st — 1990	27.0
2nd — 1990	26.0
3rd — 1990	26.5
4th — 1990	27.5
1st — 1991	25.5
2nd — 1991	30.0
3rd — 1991	28.0
4th — 1991	30.5
1st — 1992	32.0

a. Use exponential smoothing to forecast this time series. Consider smoothing constants of $\alpha = .2, .3,$ and .4. What value of the smoothing constant provides the best forecast?

b. What is the forecast of the percentage of assets committed to stocks for the second quarter of 1992?

TABLE 18.21
Exercise 30

Week	Demand
1	22
2	18
3	23
4	21
5	17
6	24
7	20
8	19
9	18
10	21

30. A chain of grocery stores noted the weekly demand (in cases) reported in Table 18.21 for a particular brand of automatic-dishwasher detergent. Use exponential smoothing with $\alpha = .2$ to develop a forecast for week 11.

31. United Dairies, Inc., supplies milk to several independent grocers throughout Dade County, Florida. Managers at United Dairies want to develop a forecast of the number of half-gallons of milk sold per week. Sales data for the past 12 weeks follow.

Week	Sales	Week	Sales
1	2750	7	3300
2	3100	8	3100
3	3250	9	2950
4	2800	10	3000
5	2900	11	3200
6	3050	12	3150

Using exponential smoothing with $\alpha = .4$, develop a forecast of demand for the 13th week.

32. The Garden Avenue Seven sells tapes of its musical performances. The following table reports sales (in units) for the past 18 months. The group's manager wants an accurate method for forecasting future sales.

Month	Sales	Month	Sales	Month	Sales
1	293	7	381	13	549
2	283	8	431	14	544
3	322	9	424	15	601
4	355	10	433	16	587
5	346	11	470	17	644
6	379	12	481	18	660

a. Use exponential smoothing with $\alpha = .3, .4$, and $.5$. Which value of α provides the best forecasts?
b. Use trend projection to provide a forecast. What is the value of MSE?
c. Which method of forecasting would you recommend to the manager? Why?

33. The Mayfair Department Store in Davenport, Iowa, is trying to determine the amount of sales lost while it was shut down because of the summer 1993 floods. Sales data for January–June 1993 follow.

Month	Sales ($1000s)
January	185.72
February	167.84
March	205.11
April	210.36
May	255.57
June	261.19

a. Use exponential smoothing, with $\alpha = .4$, to develop a forecast for July and August. (Hint: Use the forecast for July as the actual sales in July in developing the August forecast.) Comment on the use of exponential smoothing for forecasts more than one period into the future.
b. Use trend projection to forecast sales for July and August.
c. Mayfair's insurance company has proposed a settlement based on lost sales of $240,000 in July and August. Is this amount fair? If not, what amount would you recommend as a counteroffer?

34. Canton Supplies, Inc., is a service firm that employs approximately 100 individuals. Managers of Canton Supplies are concerned about meeting monthly cash obligations and want to develop a forecast of monthly cash requirements. Because of a recent change in operating policy, only the past seven months of data are considered to be relevant. With the following historical data, use trend projection to develop a forecast of cash requirements for each of the next two months.

TABLE 18.22
Exercise 35

Year	Number
1980	16000
1981	18300
1982	21000
1983	25000
1984	30000
1985	32000
1986	37500
1987	41100
1988	44000
1989	47500
1990	50000
1991	51000
1992	53000
1993	55000
1994	57000

Month	1	2	3	4	5	6	7
Cash Required ($1000s)	205	212	218	224	230	240	246

35. Table 18.22 reports the number of cable television subscribers (in thousands) by year from 1980 to 1994 (*Television & Cable Factbook,* 1994)
  a. Develop a linear trend equation for this time series. Comment on what the equation tells about the number of cable subscribers for the 15-year period.
  b. Provide forecasts of the number of cable subscribers for 1995 and 1996.

36. The Costello Music Company has been in business for five years. During that time, sales of electric organs have increased from 12 units in the first year to 76 units in the most recent year. Fred Costello, the firm's owner, wants to develop a forecast of organ sales for the coming year. The historical data follow.

Year	1	2	3	4	5
Sales	12	28	34	50	76

  a. Show a graph of this time series. Does a linear trend appear to be present?
  b. Develop the equation for the linear trend component for the time series. What is the average increase in sales that the firm has been realizing per year?

37. Hudson Marine has been an authorized dealer for C&D marine radios for the past seven years. The following table reports the number of radios sold each year.

Year	1	2	3	4	5	6	7
Number Sold	35	50	75	90	105	110	130

  a. Show a graph of this time series. Does a linear trend appear to be present?
  b. Develop the equation for the linear trend component for the time series.
  c. Use the linear trend developed in (b) and prepare a forecast for annual sales in year 8.

TABLE 18.23   Exercise 38

Year	PC Systems	Mainframe Systems
1990	21	147
1991	80	182
1992	175	195
1993	215	198
1994	262	210
1995	326	239

38. *Software Magazine* (March 1992) reported a study that predicted spending for data management software through 1995. The projection of software spending in millions of dollars was made for personal computer (PC) systems and mainframe systems. The data are given in Table 18.23.
  a. Fit a linear trend to both the PC systems data and the mainframe systems data.
  b. Forecast data management software sales for PC systems and mainframe computer systems in 1996.
  c. Using the trend equation, compare what is happening to data management software sales for PC systems and mainframe computer systems.

39. The following table gives the number of cellular telephone subscribers (in thousands) by year from 1986 to 1994 (*State of the Cellular Industry,* 1994)

Year	Number
1986	682
1987	1231
1988	2069
1989	3509
1990	5283
1991	7557
1992	11033
1993	16009

Plot the time series and comment on the appropriateness of a linear trend. What type of functional form do you believe would be most appropriate for the trend pattern of this time series?

40. Refer to the Hudson Marine problem in Exercise 37. Suppose the quarterly sales values for the seven years of historical data are as follows.

Year	Quarter 1	Quarter 2	Quarter 3	Quarter 4	Total Yearly Sales
1	6	15	10	4	35
2	10	18	15	7	50
3	14	26	23	12	75
4	19	28	25	18	90
5	22	34	28	21	105
6	24	36	30	20	110
7	28	40	35	27	130

  a. Show the four-quarter moving average values for this time series. Plot both the original time series and the moving average series on the same graph.
  b. Compute the seasonal indexes for the four quarters.
  c. When does Hudson Marine experience the largest seasonal effect? Does this seem reasonable? Explain.

41. Consider the Costello Music Company problem in Exercise 36. The quarterly sales data follow.

Year	Quarter 1	Quarter 2	Quarter 3	Quarter 4	Total Yearly Sales
1	4	2	1	5	12
2	6	4	4	14	28
3	10	3	5	16	34
4	12	9	7	22	50
5	18	10	13	35	76

  a. Compute the seasonal indexes for the four quarters.
  b. When does Costello Music experience the largest seasonal effect? Does this appear reasonable? Explain.

42. Refer to the Hudson Marine data in Exercise 40.
  a. Deseasonalize the data and use the deseasonalized time series to identify the trend.
  b. Use the results of (a) to develop a quarterly forecast for next year based on trend.
  c. Use the seasonal indexes developed in Exercise 40 to adjust the forecasts developed in (b) to account for the effect of season.

43. Consider the Costello Music Company time series in Exercise 41.

  a. Deseasonalize the data and use the deseasonalized time series to identify the trend.

  b. Use the results of (a) to develop a quarterly forecast for next year based on trend.

  c. Use the seasonal indexes developed in Exercise 41 to adjust the forecasts developed in (b) to account for the effect of season.

COMPUTER CASE 1

FORECASTING FOOD AND BEVERAGE SALES

The Vintage Restaurant is on Captiva Island, a resort community near Fort Myers, Florida. The restaurant, which is owned and operated by Karen Payne, has just completed its third year of operation. During that time, Karen has sought to establish a reputation for the restaurant as a high-quality dining establishment that specializes in fresh seafood. The efforts by Karen and her staff have proved successful, and her restaurant has become one of the best and fastest-growing restaurants on the island.

Karen has concluded that to plan for the growth of the restaurant in the future, she needs to develop a system that will enable her to forecast food and beverage sales by month for up to one year in advance. Karen has the following data on total food and beverage sales for the three years of operation.

Month	First Year	Second Year	Third Year
January	242	263	282
February	235	238	255
March	232	247	265
April	178	193	205
May	184	193	210
June	140	149	160
July	145	157	166
August	152	161	174
September	110	122	126
October	130	130	148
November	152	167	173
December	206	230	235

Managerial Report

Perform an analysis of the sales data for the Vintage Restaurant. Prepare a report for Karen that summarizes your findings, forecasts, and recommendations. Include:

1. A graph of the time series.

2. An analysis of the seasonality of the data. Indicate the seasonal indexes for each month, and comment on the high and low seasonal sales months. Do the seasonal indexes make intuitive sense? Discuss.

3. A forecast of sales for January through December of the fourth year.

4. Recommendations as to when the system that you have developed should be updated to account for new sales data.

5. Any detailed calculations of your analysis in the appendix of your report.

Assume that January sales for the fourth year turn out to be $295,000. What was your forecast error? If this is a large error, Karen may be puzzled about the difference between your forecast and the actual sales value. What can you do to resolve her uncertainty in the forecasting procedure?

COMPUTER CASE 2

FORECASTING LOST SALES

The Carlson Department Store suffered heavy damage when a hurricane struck on August 31, 1992. The store was closed for four months (September 1992 through December 1992), and Carlson is now involved in a dispute with its insurance company about the amount of lost sales during the time the store was closed. Two key issues must be resolved: (1) the amount of sales Carlson would have made if the hurricane had not struck and (2) whether Carlson is entitled to any compensation for excess sales due to increased business activity after the storm. More than $8 billion in federal disaster relief and insurance money came into the county, resulting in increased sales at department stores and numerous other businesses.

Table 18.24 gives Carlson's sales data for the 48 months preceding the storm. Table 18.25 reports the U.S. Department of Commerce data on total sales for the 48 months preceding the storm for all department stores in the county, as well as the total sales in the county for the four

TABLE 18.24 Sales for Carlson Department Store, September 1988 Through August 1992 (Millions of Dollars)

Month	1988	1989	1990	1991	1992
January		1.45	2.31	2.31	2.56
February		1.80	1.89	1.99	2.28
March		2.03	2.02	2.42	2.69
April		1.99	2.23	2.45	2.48
May		2.32	2.39	2.57	2.73
June		2.20	2.14	2.42	2.37
July		2.13	2.27	2.40	2.31
August		2.43	2.21	2.50	2.23
September	1.71	1.90	1.89	2.09	
October	1.90	2.13	2.29	2.54	
November	2.74	2.56	2.83	2.97	
December	4.20	4.16	4.04	4.35	

TABLE 18.25 Department Store Sales for the County, September 1988 Through December 1992 (Millions of Dollars)

Month	1988	1989	1990	1991	1992
January		46.8	46.8	43.8	48.0
February		48.0	48.6	45.6	51.6
March		60.0	59.4	57.6	57.6
April		57.6	58.2	53.4	58.2
May		61.8	60.6	56.4	60.0
June		58.2	55.2	52.8	57.0
July		56.4	51.0	54.0	57.6
August		63.0	58.8	60.6	61.8
September	55.8	57.6	49.8	47.4	69.0
October	56.4	53.4	54.6	54.6	75.0
November	71.4	71.4	65.4	67.8	85.2
December	117.6	114.0	102.0	100.2	121.8

months the Carlson Department Store was closed. Carlson's managers have asked you to analyze these data and develop estimates of the lost sales at the Carlson Department Store for the months of September through December 1992. They also have asked you to determine whether a case can be made for excess storm-related sales during the same period. If such a case can be made, Carlson is entitled to compensation for excess sales it would have earned in addition to ordinary sales.

Managerial Report

Prepare a report for the managers of the Carlson Department Store that summarizes your findings, forecasts, and recommendations. Include:

1. An estimate of sales had there been no hurricane.
2. An estimate of countywide department store sales had there been no hurricane.
3. An estimate of lost sales for the Carlson Department Store for September through December 1992.

In addition, use the countywide actual department stores sales for September through December 1992 and the estimate in part (2) to make a case for or against excess storm-related sales.

APPENDIX 18.1 ●

Forecasting with Spreadsheets

● In this Appendix we show how Excel can be used to develop forecasts using three forecasting methods: moving averages, exponential smoothing, and trend projection.

MOVING AVERAGES

To show how Excel can be used to develop forecasts using the moving averages method, we will develop a forecast for the gasoline sales time series in Table 18.1 and Figure 18.5. We assume that the user has entered the sales data for the 12 weeks into worksheet rows 1 through 12 of column A. The following steps can be used to produce a three-week moving average.

Step 1. Select the **Tools** pull-down menu
Step 2. Select the **Data Analysis** option
Step 3. When the Analysis Tools dialog box appears, choose **Moving Average**
Step 4. When the Moving Average dialog box appears:
Enter A1:A12 in the **Input Range** box
Enter 3 in the **Interval** box
Enter B1 in the Output Range box
Select **OK**

The three-week moving average forecasts will appear in column B of the worksheet. Note that forecasts for periods of other length can be computed easily by entering a different value in the Interval box.

EXPONENTIAL SMOOTHING

To show how Excel can be used for exponential smoothing, we again develop a forecast for the gasoline sales time series in Table 18.1 and Figure 18.5. We assume that the user has entered the sales data for the 12 weeks into worksheet rows 1 through 12 of column

A and that the smoothing constant is $\alpha = .2$. The following steps can be used to produce a forecast.

Step 1. Select the **Tools** pull-down menu
Step 2. Select the **Data Analysis** option
Step 3. When the Analysis Tools dialog box appears, choose **Exponential Smoothing**
Step 4. When the Exponential Smoothing dialog box appears:
    Enter A1:A12 in the **Input Range** box
    Enter .8 in the **Damping factor** box
    Enter B1 in the Output Range box
    Select **OK**

The exponential smoothing forecasts will appear in column B of the worksheet. Note that the value we entered in the Damping factor box is $1 - \alpha$; forecasts for other smoothing constants can be computed easily by entering a different value for $1 - \alpha$ in the Damping factor box.

TREND PROJECTION

To show how Excel can be used for trend projection, we develop a forecast for the bicycle sales time series in Table 18.8 and Figure 18.8. We assume that the user has entered the year (1–10) for each observation into worksheet rows 1 through 10 of column A and the sales values into worksheet rows 1 through 10 of column B. The following steps can be used to produce a forecast for year 11 by trend projection.

Step 1. Select an empty cell in the worksheet
Step 2. Select the **Insert** pull-down menu
Step 3. Choose the **Function** option
Step 4. When the Function Wizard—Step 1 of 2 dialog box appears:
    Choose **Statistical** in the Function Category box
    Choose **Forecast** in the Function Name box
    Select **Next**
Step 5. When the Function Wizard—Step 2 of 2 dialog box appears:
    Enter 11 in the **x** box
    Enter B1:B10 in the **Known y's** box
    Enter A1:A10 in the **Known x's** box
    Select **Finish**

The forecast for year 11, in this case 32.5, will appear in the cell selected in Step 1.

19

NONPARAMETRIC METHODS

STATISTICS IN PRACTICE ●

West Shell Realtors*

Cincinnati, Ohio

West Shell Realtors was founded in 1958 with one office and a sales staff of three people. The company's first-year sales were $900,000. In 1964, the company began a long-term expansion program, with new offices being added almost yearly. West Shell is now one of the largest realtors in Greater Cincinnati, with offices also in southwest Ohio, southeast Indiana, and northern Kentucky.

Statistical analysis helps real estate firms such as West Shell monitor sales performance in their effort to remain competitive. Monthly reports are generated for each of West Shell's offices as well as for the total company. Statistical summaries of total sales dollars, number of units sold, and mean selling price per unit are essential in keeping both office managers and the company's top managers informed of progress and trouble spots in the organization.

In addition to monthly summaries of ongoing operations, the company uses statistical considerations to guide corporate plans and strategies. West Shell has implemented a strategy of planned expansion in recent years. Each time an expansion plan calls for the establishment of a new sales office, the company must address the question of office location. Selling prices of homes, turnover rates, and forecast sales volumes are the types of data used in evaluating and comparing alternative locations.

In one instance during an expansion phase, West Shell identified two suburbs, Clifton and Roselawn, as prime

*The authors are indebted to Rodney Fightmaster of West Shell Realtors for providing this Statistics in Practice.

candidates for a new office. A variety of factors were considered in comparing the two areas, including local selling prices of homes. West Shell employed nonparametric statistical methods with small samples to help identify any differences in sales patterns for the two areas.

Samples of 25 sales in the Clifton area and 18 sales in the Roselawn area were taken, and the Mann-Whitney-Wilcoxon rank-sum test was chosen as an appropriate statistical test of the difference in the pattern of selling prices. At the .05 level of significance, the Mann-Whitney-Wilcoxon test did not allow rejection of the null hypothesis that the two populations of selling prices were identical. Thus, West Shell was able to focus on criteria other than selling prices of homes in the site selection process.

The real estate business continues to be extremely competitive. At West Shell, statistical considerations play a meaningful role in helping the company maintain its leadership in the industry. In this chapter we will learn how nonparametric statistical tests such as the Mann-Whitney-Wilcoxon test are applied. We will also discuss the proper interpretation of such tests.

West Shell uses statistical analysis of home sales to remain competitive.

● The statistical methods presented thus far in the text are generally known as *parametric methods*. In this chapter we introduce several *nonparametric methods*. Such methods are often applicable in situations where the parametric methods of the preceding chapters are not. Nonparametric methods typically require less restrictive assumptions about the level of data measurement and fewer assumptions about the form of the probability distributions generating the sample data.

One consideration in determining whether a parametric or a nonparametric method is appropriate is the scale of measurement used to generate the data. All data are generated by one of four scales of measurement: nominal, ordinal, interval, and ratio. Hence, all statistical analyses are conducted with either nominal, ordinal, interval, or ratio data.

Let us define and provide examples of the four scales of measurement.

1. *Nominal scale.* The scale of measurement is nominal if the data are simply labels or categories used to define an attribute of an element. Nominal data may be numeric or nonnumeric.
   Examples. The exchange where a stock is listed (NYSE, NASDAQ, or AMEX) is nonnumeric nominal data. An individual's social security number is numeric nominal data.

2. *Ordinal scale.* The scale of measurement is ordinal if the data can be used to rank, or order, the observations. Ordinal data may be numeric or nonnumeric.
   Examples. The measures small, medium, and large for the size of an item are nonnumeric ordinal data. The class ranks of individuals measured as 1, 2, 3, . . . are numeric ordinal data.

3. *Interval scale.* The scale of measurement is interval if the data have the properties of ordinal data and the interval between observations is expressed in terms of a fixed unit of measure. Interval data must be numeric.
   Examples. Measures of temperature are interval data. Suppose it is 80 degrees in one location and 40 degrees in another. We can rank the locations with respect to warmth; the first location is warmer than the second. The fixed unit of measure, a degree, enables us to say how much warmer it is at the first location: 40 degrees.

4. *Ratio scale.* The scale of measurement is ratio if the data have the properties of interval data and the ratio of measures is meaningful. Ratio data must be numeric.
   Examples. Variables such as distance, height, weight, and time are measured on a ratio scale. Temperature measures are not ratio data because there is no inherently defined zero point. For instance, the freezing point of water is 32 degrees on a Fahrenheit scale and zero degrees on a Celsius scale. Ratios are not meaningful with temperature data. For instance, it makes no sense to say that 80 degrees is twice as warm as 40 degrees.

In Chapter 1 we classified data as qualitative or quantitative. Data obtained by using a nominal or ordinal scale are considered qualitative. Data obtained by using an interval or ratio scale are quantitative.

Most of the statistical methods referred to as parametric require the use of interval- or ratio-scaled data. With these levels of measurement arithmetic operations are meaningful and means, variances, standard deviations, and so on can be computed, interpreted, and used in the analysis. With nominal or ordinal data, it is inappropriate to compute means, variances, and standard deviations; hence, parametric methods normally cannot be used. Nonparametric methods are often the only way to analyze such data and draw statistical conclusions.

Another consideration in determining whether a parametric method or a nonparametric method should be employed is the assumption about the population from which the data were obtained. For example, a parametric procedure for testing a hypothesis about the difference between the means of two populations was presented in Chapter 10. In the small-sample case, the t distribution can be used for this test if we are willing to assume that the populations are normally distributed with equal variances. If this assumption about the populations is not appropriate, the parametric method based on the use of the t distribution should not be used even if the data are interval or ratio scaled.

However, nonparametric methods, which require no assumptions about the population probability distributions, are available for testing for differences between two populations. Because no probability distribution assumptions are required in such cases, nonparametric methods are often called *distribution-free* methods.

In general, for a statistical method to be classified as nonparametric, it must satisfy at least one of the following conditions.*

1. The method can be used with nominal data.
2. The method can be used with ordinal data.
3. The method can be used with interval or ratio data when no assumption can be made about the population probability distribution.

If the level of data measurement is interval or ratio and if the necessary probability distribution assumptions for the population are appropriate, parametric methods provide more powerful or more discerning statistical procedures. In many cases where a nonparametric method as well as a parametric method can be applied, the nonparametric method is almost as good or almost as powerful as the parametric method. In cases where the data are nominal or ordinal or in cases where the assumptions required by parametric methods are inappropriate, only nonparametric methods are available. Because of the less restrictive data-measurement requirements and the fewer assumptions needed about the population distribution, nonparametric methods are regarded as more generally applicable than parametric methods. The sign test, the Wilcoxon signed-rank test, the Mann-Whitney-Wilcoxon test, the Kruskal-Wallis test, and Spearman rank correlation are the nonparametric methods presented in this chapter.

19.1　SIGN TEST

A common market research application of the *sign test* involves using a sample of n potential customers to identify a preference for one of two brands of a product such as coffee, soft drinks, and detergents. The n expressions of preference are nominal data because the consumer simply names, or labels, a preference. Given these data, our objective is to determine whether there is a difference in preference between the two items being compared. As we will see, the sign test is a nonparametric statistical procedure for answering this question.

SMALL-SAMPLE CASE

The small-sample case for the sign test should be used whenever $n \leq 20$. Let us illustrate the use of the sign test for the small-sample case by considering a study conducted for Sun Coast Farms; Sun Coast produces an orange juice product marketed under the name Citrus Valley. A competitor of Sun Coast Farms has begun producing a new orange juice product known as Tropical Orange. In a study of consumer preferences for the two brands, 12 individuals were given unmarked samples of each product. The brand each individual tasted first was selected randomly. After tasting the two products, the individuals were asked to state a preference for one of the two brands. The purpose of the study is to determine whether consumers prefer one product over the other. Letting p indicate the proportion of the population of consumers favoring Citrus Valley, we want to test the following hypotheses.

*See W. J. Conover, *Practical Nonparametric Statistics,* 2nd ed. (New York: John Wiley & Sons, 1980).

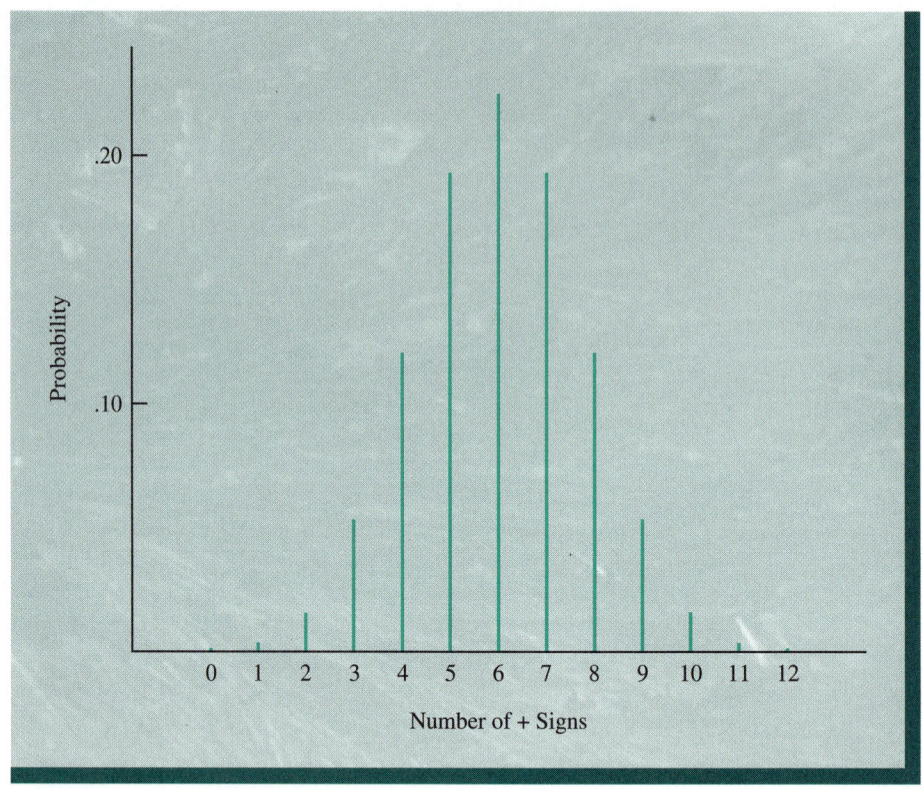

FIGURE 19.1 Binomial Probabilities for the Number of Plus Signs when $n = 12$ and $p = .50$

$$H_0: p = .50$$
$$H_a: p \neq .50$$

TABLE 19.1 Binomial Probabilities with $n = 12$, $p = .50$

Number of Plus Signs	Probability
0	.0002
1	.0029
2	.0161
3	.0537
4	.1208
5	.1934
6	.2256
7	.1934
8	.1208
9	.0537
10	.0161
11	.0029
12	.0002

If H_0 cannot be rejected, we will have no evidence indicating a difference in preference for the two brands of orange juice. However, if H_0 can be rejected, we can conclude that the consumer preferences are different for the two brands. In that case, the brand selected by the greater number of consumers can be considered the most preferred brand.

In the following discussion we will show how the small-sample version of the sign test can be used to test these hypotheses and draw a conclusion about consumer preferences. To record the preference data for the 12 individuals participating in the study, we use a plus sign if the individual expresses a preference for Citrus Valley and a minus sign if the individual expresses a preference for Tropical Orange. Because the data are recorded in terms of plus or minus signs, this nonparametric test is called the sign test.

Under the assumption that H_0 is true ($p = .50$), the number of plus values follows a binomial probability distribution with $p = .50$. With a sample size of $n = 12$, Table 5 in Appendix B shows the probabilities for the binomial probability distribution with $p = .50$ as displayed in Table 19.1. Figure 19.1 is a graphical representation of this binomial probability distribution. It shows the probability of the number of plus signs under the assumption that H_0 is true and is therefore the appropriate sampling distribution for the hypothesis test. We use this sampling distribution to determine a rule for rejecting H_0; our approach is similar to the method we used to develop rejection rules for hypothesis testing in Chapter 9. For example, using $\alpha = .05$, we would place

TABLE 19.2 Preference Data for the Sun Coast Farms Taste Test

Individual	Brand Preference	Recorded Data
1	Tropical Orange	–
2	Tropical Orange	–
3	Citrus Valley	+
4	Tropical Orange	–
5	Tropical Orange	–
6	Tropical Orange	–
7	Tropical Orange	–
8	Tropical Orange	–
9	Citrus Valley	+
10	Tropical Orange	–
11	Tropical Orange	–
12	Tropical Orange	–

a rejection region or area of approximately .025 in each tail of the distribution in Figure 19.1. Starting at the lower end of the distribution, we see that the probability of obtaining zero, one, or two plus signs is $.0002 + .0029 + .0161 = .0192$. Note that we stop at 2 plus signs because adding the probability of three plus signs would make the area in the lower tail equal to $.0192 + .0537 = .0729$, which substantially exceeds the desired area of .025. At the upper end of the distribution, we find the same probability of .0192 corresponding to 10, 11, or 12 plus signs. Thus, the closest we can come to $\alpha = .05$ without exceeding it is $.0192 + .0192 = .0384$. We therefore adopt the following rejection rule.

Reject H_0 if the number of plus signs is less than 3 or greater than nine

The preference data obtained for the Sun Coast Farms example are reported in Table 19.2. Since only two plus signs are observed, the null hypothesis is rejected. The study provides evidence that consumer preference differs for the two brands of orange juice. We would advise Sun Coast Farms that consumers indicate a preference for the competitor's Tropical Orange brand.

In the Sun Coast Farms example, all 12 individuals in the study were able to state a preference. In many situations, one or more individuals in the sample are not able to state a definite preference. In such cases, the individual's response of no preference can be dropped and the analysis conducted with a smaller sample size.

The binomial probability distribution as shown in Table 5 of Appendix B can be used to provide the decision rule for any sign test up to a sample size of $n = 20$. With the null hypothesis $p = .50$ and the sample size n, the decision rule can be established for any level of significance. In addition, by considering the probabilities in only the lower or upper tail of the binomial probability distribution, we can develop rejection rules for one-tailed tests. Appendix B does not provide binomial probability distribution tables for sample sizes greater than 20. In such cases, we can use the large-sample normal approximation of binomial probabilities to determine the appropriate rejection rule for the sign test.

LARGE-SAMPLE CASE

Using the null hypothesis $H_0: p = .50$ and a sample size of $n > 20$, the sampling distribution for the number of plus signs can be approximated by a normal probability distribution.

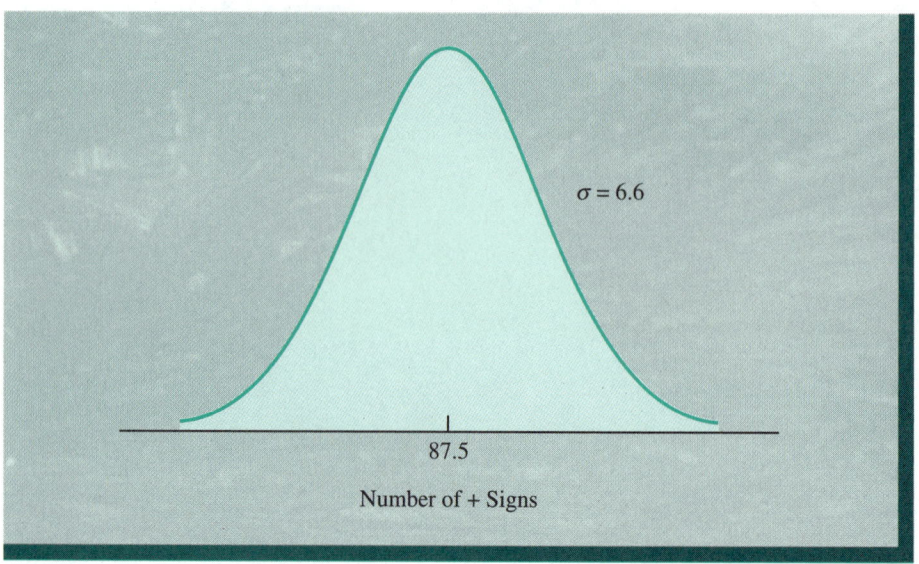

FIGURE 19.2   Probability Distribution of the Number of Plus Signs for a Sign Test with $n = 175$

NORMAL APPROXIMATION OF THE SAMPLING DISTRIBUTION OF THE NUMBER OF PLUS SIGNS WHEN NO PREFERENCE IS STATED

$$\text{Mean: } \mu = .50n \qquad \text{(19.1)}$$

$$\text{Standard Deviation: } \sigma = \sqrt{.25n} \qquad \text{(19.2)}$$

Distribution form: approximately normal provided $n > 20$.

Let us consider an application of the sign test to political polling. A poll taken during a recent presidential election campaign asked 200 registered voters to rate the Democratic and Republican candidates in terms of best overall foreign policy. Results of the poll showed 72 rated the Democratic candidate higher, 103 rated the Republican candidate higher, and 25 indicated no difference between the candidates. Does the poll indicate a significant difference between the two candidates in terms of public opinion about their foreign policies?

Using the sign test, we see that $n = 200 - 25 = 175$ individuals were able to indicate the candidate they believed had the best overall foreign policy. Using (19.1) and (19.2), we find that the sampling distribution of the number of plus signs has the following properties.

$$\mu = .50n = .50(175) = 87.5$$

$$\sigma = \sqrt{.25n} = \sqrt{.25(175)} = 6.6$$

In addition, with $n = 175$ we can assume that the sampling distribution is approximately normal. This distribution is shown in Figure 19.2. Since the distribution is approximately normal, we can use the table of areas for the standard normal probability distribution to develop the rejection rule for the test. With $\alpha = .05$, the rejection rule for this two-tailed test can be written as follows.

$$\text{Reject } H_0 \text{ if } z < -1.96 \text{ or if } z > +1.96$$

Using the number of times the Democratic candidate received the higher foreign policy rating as the number of plus signs ($x = 72$), we have the following value of the test statistic.

$$z = \frac{x - \mu}{\sigma} = \frac{72 - 87.5}{6.6} = -2.35$$

Since $z = -2.35$ is less than -1.96, the hypothesis of no difference in foreign policy for the two candidates should be rejected at the .05 level of significance. This study suggests that the Republican candidate is perceived to have the higher-rated foreign policy.

HYPOTHESIS TESTS ABOUT A MEDIAN

In Chapter 9 we described how hypothesis tests can be used to make an inference about a population mean. We now show how the sign test can be used to conduct hypothesis tests about a population median. Recall that the median splits a population in such a way that 50% of the values are at the median or above and 50% are at the median or below. We can apply the sign test to conduct a hypothesis test about the value of a median by using a plus sign whenever the data in the sample are above the median and a minus sign whenever the data in the sample are below the median. Any data exactly equal to the hypothesized value of the median should be discarded. The computations for the sign test are done in exactly the same way as before.

For example, the following hypothesis test is being conducted about the median price of new homes in St. Louis, Missouri.

$$H_0: \text{Median} = \$130,000$$

$$H_a: \text{Median} \neq \$130,000$$

In a sample of 62 new homes, 34 have prices above $130,000, 26 have prices below $130,000, and two have prices of exactly $130,000.

Using (19.1) and (19.2) for the $n = 60$ homes with prices different than $130,000, we obtain

$$\mu = .50n = .50(60) = 30$$

$$\sigma = \sqrt{.25n} = \sqrt{.25(60)} = 3.87$$

With $x = 34$ as the number of plus signs, the test statistic becomes

$$z = \frac{x - \mu}{\sigma} = \frac{34 - 30}{3.87} = 1.03$$

Using a two-tailed test and a level of significance of $\alpha = .05$, we reject H_0 if z is less than -1.96 or greater than $+1.96$. Since the test statistic is $z = 1.03$, we cannot reject H_0. On the basis of these data, we are unable to reject the null hypothesis that the median selling price of a new home in St. Louis is $130,000.

NOTES AND COMMENTS

1. The number of plus signs was used in the calculations to determine whether to reject the null hypothesis that $p = .50$. One could just as easily use the number of minus signs; the test result would be the same.

2. Just as in the small-sample case, the sampling distribution of the number of plus signs in the large-sample case follows a binomial probability distribution with $p = .5$. So, even in the large-sample case, one could use the binomial probability distribution to find the rejection region and conduct the hypothesis test. As we have pointed out previously, the normal approximation of the binomial distribution is valid whenever np and $n(1-p) \geq 5$. With $p = .5$, as it is with the sign test, this sample size requirement is satisfied with $n \geq 10$. Here, however, we have suggested using the small-sample test and the binomial distribution unless $n > 20$ because binomial tables are readily available for $n \leq 20$. There is no point in using an approximation when the exact distribution can be used just as easily.

EXERCISES

METHODS

Self-Test

1. The following table lists the preferences indicated by 10 individuals in taste tests involving two brands of a product.

Individual	Brand A Versus Brand B	Individual	Brand A Versus Brand B
1	+	6	+
2	+	7	−
3	+	8	+
4	−	9	−
5	+	10	+

With $\alpha = .05$, test for a significant difference in the preferences for the two brands. A plus indicates a preference for brand A over brand B.

Self-Test

2. The following hypothesis test is to be conducted.

$$H_0: \text{Median} \leq 150$$

$$H_a: \text{Median} > 150$$

A sample of size 30 yields 22 cases in which a value greater than 150 is obtained, three cases in which a value of exactly 150 is obtained, and five cases in which a value less than 150 is obtained. Use $\alpha = .01$ and conduct the hypothesis test.

APPLICATIONS

3. Are stock splits beneficial to stockholders? SNL Securities studied stock splits in the banking industry over the period January 1, 1993 through June 30, 1994 and found that stock splits tended to increase the value of an individual's stock holding (Barron's, October 3, 1994). Assume that of a sample of 20 recent stock splits 14 led to an increase in value, four led to a decrease in value, and two resulted in no change. Suppose a sign test is to be used to determine whether stock splits continue to be beneficial for holders of bank stocks.

a. What are the null and alternative hypotheses?

b. With $\alpha = .05$, what is the rejection rule?

c. What is your conclusion?

Self-Test

4. A Louis Harris poll asked 1253 adults a series of questions about the state of the economy and their children's future (*Business Week,* April 6, 1992). One question was, "Do you expect your children to have a better life than you have had, a worse life, or a life about as good as yours?" The responses were 34% better, 29% worse, 33% about the same, and 4% not sure. Use the sign test and a .05 level of significance to determine whether more adults feel their children will have a better future than feel their children will have a worse future. What is your conclusion?

5. In a television preference poll, a sample of 180 individuals were asked to state a preference for one of two shows aired at the same time on Friday evenings. "Big Town Detective" was favored by 100, "The Friday Variety Special" was favored by 65, and 15 were unable to state a preference for one over the other. Is there evidence of a significant difference in preference for the two shows? Use $\alpha = .05$ for the test.

6. Menu planning at the Hampshire House Restaurant involves the question of customer preferences for steak and seafood. Of a sample of 250 customers who were asked to state a preference for the two menu items, 140 stated a preference for steak and 110 stated a preference for seafood. Use $\alpha = .05$ and test for a difference in preference for the two menu items.

7. The nationwide median hourly wage for a particular labor group is $14.50. A sample of 200 individuals in this labor group was taken in one city; 134 individuals had a wage rate less than $14.50 per hour, 54 individuals had a wage rate greater than $14.50 per hour, and 12 individuals had a wage rate of $14.50. Test the null hypothesis that the median hourly wage in this city is the same as the nationwide median hourly wage. Use a .02 level of significance.

8. In a sample of 150 college basketball games, the home team won 98 games. Test to see whether the data support the claim that there is a home-team advantage in college basketball. Use a .05 level of significance. What is your conclusion?

9. The median number of part-time employees at fast-food restaurants in a particular city was known to be 15 last year. City officials think the use of part-time employees may be increasing. A sample of nine fast-food restaurants showed that more than 15 part-time employees worked at seven of the restaurants, one restaurant had exactly 15 part-time employees, and one had fewer than 15 part-time employees. Test at $\alpha = .05$ to see whether there has been an increase in the median number of part-time employees.

TABLE 19.3 Exercise 11

11.50	8.40	11.75
10.05	10.25	8.00
13.65	7.05	9.05
11.90	9.90	6.85
15.35	11.10	14.70
13.15	13.10	6.65
13.10	9.20	9.15
12.05	8.45	5.85
9.80		

10. "The median annual income adults say would make their dreams come true is $102,000, up from $50,000 seven years ago, according to a survey by Roper Starch Worldwide of New York" (*The Wall Street Journal,* October 21, 1994). Suppose that of a sample of 225 individuals in a certain Ohio county, 122 individuals report that the amount of income needed to make their dreams come true is less than $102,000 and 103 report that the amount needed is more than $102,000. Test the null hypothesis that the median amount of annual income needed to make dreams come true in the Ohio county is $102,000. Use $\alpha = .05$. What is your conclusion?

11. The median hourly wage for the population of blue- and white-collar workers nationwide is $9.00 per hour. A sample of workers was selected in the Los Angeles area (*Newsweek,* February 17, 1992). Use the sample data in Table 19.3 to test H_0: median ≤ 9, H_a: median > 9 for the population of workers in Los Angeles. Use a .05 level of significance. What is your conclusion?

19.2 WILCOXON SIGNED-RANK TEST

The Wilcoxon signed-rank test is the nonparametric alternative to the parametric matched-sample test presented in Chapter 10. In the matched-sample situation, each experimental unit generates two paired or matched observations, one from population 1 and one from population 2. The differences between the matched observations provide insight about the differences between the two populations.

The methodology of the parametric matched-sample analysis (the t test on paired differences) requires interval data and the assumption that the population of differences between the pairs of observations is *normally distributed*. With this assumption, the t distribution can be used to test the null hypothesis of no difference between population means. If the assumption of normally distributed differences is not appropriate, the nonparametric Wilcoxon signed-rank test can be used. We illustrate this nonparametric test by comparing the effectiveness of two production methods.

A manufacturing firm is attempting to determine whether two production methods differ in task-completion time. A sample of 11 workers was selected, and each worker completed a production task using each of the production methods. The production method that each worker used first was selected randomly. Thus, each worker in the sample provided a pair of observations, as shown in Table 19.4. A positive difference in task-completion times indicates that method 1 required more time, and a negative difference in times indicates that method 2 required more time. Do the data indicate that the methods are significantly different in terms of task-completion times?

In effect, we have two populations of task-completion times, one population associated with each method. The following hypotheses will be tested.

$$H_0\text{: The populations are identical}$$

$$H_a\text{: The populations are not identical}$$

If H_0 cannot be rejected, we will not have evidence to conclude that the task-completion times differ for the two methods. However, if H_0 can be rejected, we will conclude that the two methods differ in task-completion time.

The first step of the Wilcoxon signed-rank test requires a ranking of the *absolute value* of the differences between the two methods. We discard any differences of zero and then rank the remaining absolute differences from lowest to highest. Tied differences are assigned the average ranking of their positions in the combined data set. The ranking of the absolute values of differences is shown in the fourth column of Table 19.5. Note that the difference of zero for worker 8 is discarded from the rankings; then the smallest absolute difference of .1 is assigned the rank of 1. This ranking of absolute differences continues with the largest absolute difference of .9 assigned the rank of 10. The tied absolute differences for workers 3 and 5 are assigned the average rank of 3.5 and the tied absolute differences for workers 4 and 10 are assigned the average rank of 5.5.

Once the ranks of the absolute differences have been determined, the ranks are given the sign of the original difference in the data. For example, the .1 difference for worker 7, which was assigned the rank of 1, is given the value of $+1$ because the observed difference between the two methods was positive. The .2 difference, which was assigned the rank of 2, is given the value of -2 because the observed difference between the two methods was negative for worker 2. The complete list of signed ranks, as well as their sum, is shown in the last column of Table 19.5.

Let us return to the original hypothesis of identical population task-completion times for the two methods. If the populations representing task-completion times for each of the two methods are identical, we would expect the positive ranks and the negative ranks to cancel each other, so that the sum of the signed rank values would be approximately zero. Thus, the test for significance under the Wilcoxon signed-rank test involves determining whether the computed sum of signed ranks ($+44$ in our example) is significantly different from zero.

TABLE 19.4 Production Task-Completion Times (Minutes)

Worker	Method 1	Method 2	Difference
1	10.2	9.5	.7
2	9.6	9.8	−.2
3	9.2	8.8	.4
4	10.6	10.1	.5
5	9.9	10.3	−.4
6	10.2	9.3	.9
7	10.6	10.5	.1
8	10.0	10.0	.0
9	11.2	10.6	.6
10	10.7	10.2	.5
11	10.6	9.8	.8

TABLE 19.5 Ranking of Absolute Differences for the Production Task-Completion Time Example

Worker	Difference	Absolute Value of Difference	Rank	Signed Rank
1	.7	.7	8	+ 8
2	− .2	.2	2	− 2
3	.4	.4	3.5	+ 3.5
4	.5	.5	5.5	+ 5.5
5	− .4	.4	3.5	− 3.5
6	.9	.9	10	+10
7	.1	.1	1	+ 1
8	0	0	—	—
9	.6	.6	7	+ 7
10	.5	.5	5.5	+ 5.5
11	.8	.8	9	+ 9
		Sum of Signed Ranks		+44.0

Let T denote the sum of the signed-rank values in a Wilcoxon signed-rank test. It can be shown that if the two populations are identical and the number of matched pairs of data is 10 or more, the sampling distribution of T can be approximated by a normal probability distribution as follows.

SAMPLING DISTRIBUTION OF T FOR IDENTICAL POPULATIONS

$$\text{Mean: } \mu_T = 0 \tag{19.3}$$

$$\text{Standard Deviation: } \sigma_T = \sqrt{\frac{n(n+1)(2n+1)}{6}} \tag{19.4}$$

Distribution form: approximately normal provided $n \geq 10$.

For the example, we have $n = 10$, since we discarded the observation with the difference of zero (worker 8). Thus, using (19.4), we have

$$\sigma_T = \sqrt{\frac{10(11)(21)}{6}} = 19.62$$

Figure 19.3 is the sampling distribution of T under the assumption of identical populations.

The value of the test statistic z is:

$$z = \frac{T - \mu_T}{\sigma_T} = \frac{44 - 0}{19.62} = 2.24$$

Testing the null hypothesis of no difference using a level of significance of $\alpha = .05$, we reject H_0 if $z < -1.96$ or if $z > 1.96$. With the value of $z = 2.24$, we reject H_0 and conclude that the two populations are not identical and that the methods differ in

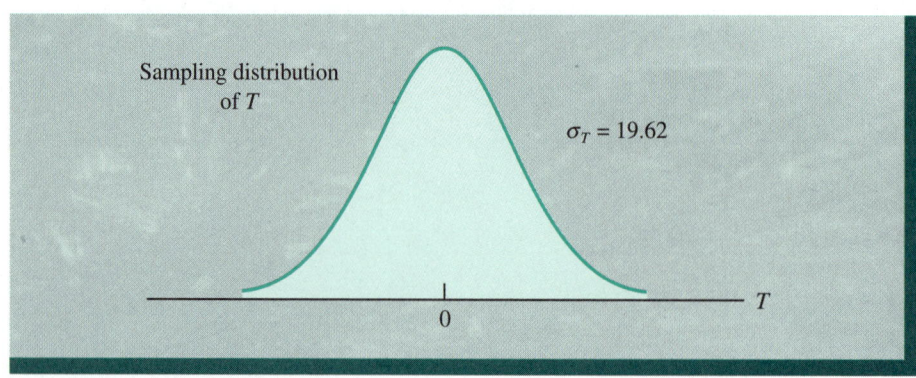

FIGURE 19.3 Sampling Distribution of the Wilcoxon T for the Production Task-Completion Time Example

task-completion time. The fact that method 2 had the shorter completion times for eight of the 11 workers leads us to conclude that differences between the two populations indicate method 2 to be the better production method.

EXERCISES

APPLICATIONS

Self-Test ▶

12. Two fuel additives are being tested to determine their effect on miles per gallon for passenger cars. Test results for 12 cars follow; each car was tested with both fuel additives. Use $\alpha = .05$ and the Wilcoxon signed-rank test to see whether there is a significant difference in the additives.

TABLE 19.6 Exercise 13

Subject	Without Relaxant	With Relaxant
1	15	10
2	12	10
3	22	12
4	8	11
5	10	9
6	7	5
7	8	10
8	10	7
9	14	11
10	9	6

Car	Additive 1	Additive 2	Car	Additive 1	Additive 2
1	20.12	18.05	7	16.16	17.20
2	23.56	21.77	8	18.55	14.98
3	22.03	22.57	9	21.87	20.03
4	19.15	17.06	10	24.23	21.15
5	21.23	21.22	11	23.21	22.78
6	24.77	23.80	12	25.02	23.70

Self-Test ▶

13. A sample of 10 men was used in a study to test the effects of a relaxant on the time required to fall asleep for male adults. Data for 10 subjects showing the number of minutes required to fall asleep with and without the relaxant are given in Table 19.6. Use a .05 level of significance to determine whether the relaxant reduces the time required to fall asleep. What is your conclusion?

14. The following table reports the net income per share during the third quarters of 1994 and 1993 for a sample of 12 companies (*The Wall Street Journal*, October 19, 1994). Use $\alpha = .05$ and the Wilcoxon signed-rank test to determine whether the data indicate that net income per share for the third quarter has increased. What is your conclusion?

Company	1994 Net Income	1993 Net Income
AK Steel	$1.56	$ .16
Adtran	.26	.12
Alex Brown	.87	.95
American Business Information	.24	.20
Apple Computer	.95	.02
Atria Software	.13	.05
Baybanks	1.51	.95
Bemis	.35	.02
Bush Industries	.42	.31
Capital Guaranty	.37	.59
Chase Manhattan	1.49	1.25
Eli Lilly	1.10	1.00

TABLE 19.7 Exercise 15

Delivery	Service 1	Service 2
1	24.5	28.0
2	26.0	25.5
3	28.0	32.0
4	21.0	20.0
5	18.0	19.5
6	36.0	28.0
7	25.0	29.0
8	21.0	22.0
9	24.0	23.5
10	26.0	29.5
11	31.0	30.0

15. A test was conducted of two overnight mail-delivery services. Two samples of identical deliveries were set up so that both delivery services were notified of the need for a delivery at the same time. The number of hours required to make each delivery is reported in Table 19.7 for each service. Do the data shown suggest a difference in the delivery times for the two services? Use a .05 level of significance for the test.

16. Elsbernd Investors, Inc., provides a six-week training program for newly hired management trainees. As part of the program-evaluation procedure, the firm gives each trainee a pretest and posttest. Use a one-tailed test with $\alpha = .05$ and analyze the following data as part of the evaluation of the firm's management training program. What is your conclusion?

Trainee	Pretest Score	Posttest Score
1	45	65
2	60	70
3	65	63
4	60	67
5	52	60
6	62	58
7	57	70
8	70	65
9	72	80
10	66	88
11	78	74

17. Ten test-market cities were selected as part of a market research study designed to evaluate the effectiveness of a particular advertising campaign. The sales dollars for each city were recorded for the week prior to the promotional program. Then the campaign was conducted for two weeks and new sales data were collected for the week immediately after the campaign. The two sets of sales data in thousands of dollars follow.

City	Precampaign Sales	Postcampaign Sales
Kansas City	130	160
Dayton	100	105
Cincinnati	120	140
Columbus	95	90
Cleveland	140	130
Indianapolis	80	82
Louisville	65	55
St. Louis	90	105
Pittsburgh	140	152
Peoria	125	140

Use $\alpha = .05$. What conclusion would you draw about the value of the advertising program?

19.3   MANN-WHITNEY-WILCOXON TEST

In this section we present another nonparametric method that can be used to determine whether there is a difference between two populations. This test, unlike the signed-rank test, is not based on a matched sample. Two independent samples, one from each population, are used. The test was developed jointly by Mann, Whitney, and Wilcoxon. It is sometimes called the *Mann-Whitney test* and sometimes the *Wilcoxon rank-sum test*. Both the Mann-Whitney and Wilcoxon versions of this test are equivalent; we refer to it as the *Mann-Whitney-Wilcoxon (MWW) test*.

The MWW test is based on independent random samples from each population. Recall that in Chapter 10 we conducted a parametric test for the difference between the means of two populations. The following hypotheses were tested.

$$H_0: \mu_1 - \mu_2 = 0$$
$$H_a: \mu_1 - \mu_2 \neq 0$$

In the small-sample case, the parametric method used was based on two assumptions.

1. Both populations are normally distributed.
2. The variances of the two populations are equal.

The nonparametric MWW test does not require either assumption. The only requirement of the MWW test is that the measurement scale for the data generated by the two independent random samples be at least ordinal. Instead of testing for the difference between the means of the two populations, the MWW test determines whether the two populations are identical. The hypotheses for the MWW test follow.

$$H_0: \text{The two populations are identical}$$

$$H_a: \text{The two populations are not identical}$$

We demonstrate how the MWW test can be applied by first showing an application for the small-sample case.

SMALL-SAMPLE CASE

The small-sample case for the MWW test should be used whenever the sample sizes for both populations are less than or equal to 10. We illustrate the use of the MWW test for

TABLE 19.8 High School Class-Standing Data

Garfield Students		Mulberry Students	
Student	Class Standing	Student	Class Standing
Fields	8	Hart	70
Clark	52	Phipps	202
Jones	112	Kirkwood	144
Tibbs	21	Abbott	175
		Guest	146

the small-sample case by considering the academic potential of students attending Johnston High School. The majority of students attending Johnston High School previously attended either Garfield Junior High School or Mulberry Junior High School. The question raised by school administrators was whether the population of students who had attended Garfield were identical to the population of students who had attended Mulberry in terms of academic potential. The following hypotheses were considered.

H_0: The two populations are identical in terms of academic potential

H_a: The two populations are not identical in terms of academic potential

Using high school records, Johnston High School administrators selected a random sample of four high school students who had attended Garfield Junior High and another random sample of five students who had attended Mulberry Junior High. The current high school class standing was recorded for each of the nine students used in the study. The ordinal class standings for the nine students are listed in Table 19.8.

The first step in the MWW procedure is to rank the *combined* data from the two samples from low to high. The lowest value (class standing 8) receives a rank of 1 and the highest value (class standing 202) receives a rank of 9. The ranking of the nine students is given in Table 19.9.

The next step is to sum the ranks for each sample separately. This calculation is shown in Table 19.10. The MWW procedure can use the sum of the ranks for either sample. In the following discussion, we use the sum of the ranks for the sample of four students from Garfield. We denote this sum by the symbol T. Thus, for our example, $T = 11$.

Let us consider the properties of the sum of the ranks for the Garfield sample. Since there are four students in the sample, Garfield could have the top four students in the study. If this were the case, $T = 1 + 2 + 3 + 4 = 10$ would be the smallest value

TABLE 19.9 Ranking of High School Students

Student	Class Standing	Combined Sample Rank
Fields	8	1
Tibbs	21	2
Clark	52	3
Hart	70	4
Jones	112	5
Kirkwood	144	6
Guest	146	7
Abbott	175	8
Phipps	202	9

TABLE 19.10 Rank Sums for High School Students from Each Junior High School

Garfield Students			Mulberry Students		
Student	Class Standing	Sample Rank	Student	Class Standing	Sample Rank
Fields	8	1	Hart	70	4
Clark	52	3	Phipps	202	9
Jones	112	5	Kirkwood	144	6
Tibbs	21	2	Abbott	175	8
			Guest	146	7
Sum of Ranks		11			34

possible for the rank sum T. Conversely, Garfield could have the bottom four students, in which case $T = 6 + 7 + 8 + 9 = 30$ would be the largest value possible for T. Hence, T for the Garfield sample must take a value between 10 and 30.

Note that values of T near 10 imply that Garfield has the significantly better, or higher ranking, students, whereas values of T near 30 imply that Garfield has the significantly weaker, or lower ranking, students. Thus, if the two populations of students were identical in terms of academic potential, we would expect the value of T to be near the average of the two values, or $(10 + 30)/2 = 20$.

Critical values of the MWW T statistic are provided in Table 10 of Appendix B for cases in which both sample sizes are less than or equal to 10.* In that table, n_1 refers to the sample size corresponding to the sample whose rank sum is being used in the test. The value of T_L is read directly from the table and the value of T_U is computed from (19.5).

$$T_U = n_1(n_1 + n_2 + 1) - T_L \qquad (19.5)$$

Neither the value of T_L nor the value of T_U is in the rejection region. The null hypothesis of identical populations should be rejected only if T is strictly less than T_L or strictly greater than T_U.

For example, using Table 10 of Appendix B with a .05 level of significance, we see that the lower-tail critical value for the MWW statistic with $n_1 = 4$ (Garfield) and $n_2 = 5$ (Mulberry) is $T_L=12$. The upper-tail critical value for the MWW statistic computed by using (19.5) is

$$T_U = 4(4 + 5 + 1) - 12 = 28$$

Thus, the MWW decision rule indicates that the null hypothesis of identical populations can be rejected if the sum of the ranks for the first sample (Garfield) is less than 12 or greater than 28. The rejection rule can be written as

Reject H_0 if $T < 12$ or if $T > 28$

Referring to Table 19.10, we see that $T = 11$. Hence, the null hypothesis H_0 is rejected, and we can conclude that the population of students at Garfield differs from the population of students at Mulberry in terms of academic potential. The higher class ranking obtained by the sample of Garfield students suggests that Garfield students are better prepared for high school than the Mulberry students.

LARGE-SAMPLE CASE

When both sample sizes are greater than or equal to 10, a normal approximation of the distribution of T can be used to conduct the analysis for the MWW test. We illustrate the large-sample case by considering a situation at Third National Bank.

Third National Bank has two branch offices. Data collected from two independent simple random samples, one from each branch, are given in Table 19.11. Do the data indicate whether the populations of checking account balances at the two branch banks are identical?

The first step in the MWW test is to rank the *combined* data from the lowest to the highest values. Using the combined set of 22 observations in Table 19.11, we find the

*A more comprehensive table of critical values for the Mann-Whitney-Wilcoxon test can be found in *Practical Nonparametric Statistics,* by W. J. Conover.

TABLE 19.11 Account Balances for Two Branches of Third National Bank

Branch 1		Branch 2	
Sampled Account	Account Balance ($)	Sampled Account	Account Balance ($)
1	1095	1	885
2	955	2	850
3	1200	3	915
4	1195	4	950
5	925	5	800
6	950	6	750
7	805	7	865
8	945	8	1000
9	875	9	1050
10	1055	10	935
11	1025		
12	975		

lowest data value of $750 (sixth item of sample 2) and assign to it a rank of 1. Continuing the ranking gives us the following list.

Account Balance ($)	Item	Assigned Rank
750	6th of sample 2	1
800	5th of sample 2	2
805	7th of sample 1	3
850	2nd of sample 2	4
.	.	.
.	.	.
.	.	.
1195	4th of sample 1	21
1200	3rd of sample 1	22

In ranking the combined data, we may find that two or more data values are the same. In that case, the tied values are given the *average* ranking of their positions in the combined data set. For example, the balance of $945 (eighth item of sample 1) will be assigned the rank of 11. However, the next two values in the data set are tied with values of $950 (see the sixth item of sample 1 and the fourth item of sample 2). Since these two values will be considered for assigned ranks of 12 and 13, they are both assigned the rank of 12.5. At the next highest data value of $955, we continue the ranking process by assigning $955 the rank of 14. Table 19.12 is the entire data set with the assigned rank of each observation.

The next step in the MWW test is to sum the ranks for each sample. The sums are given in Table 19.12. The test procedure can be based on the sum of the ranks for either sample. We use the sum of the ranks for the sample from branch 1. Thus, for this example, $T = 169.5$.

Given that the sample sizes are $n_1 = 12$ and $n_2 = 10$, we can use the normal approximation to the sampling distribution of the rank sum T. The appropriate sampling distribution is given by the following expressions.

TABLE 19.12   Combined Ranking of the Data in the Two Samples from Third National Bank

Branch 1			Branch 2		
Sampled Account	Account Balance ($)	Rank	Sampled Account	Account Balance ($)	Rank
1	1095	20	1	885	7
2	955	14	2	850	4
3	1200	22	3	915	8
4	1195	21	4	950	12.5
5	925	9	5	800	2
6	950	12.5	6	750	1
7	805	3	7	865	5
8	945	11	8	1000	16
9	875	6	9	1050	18
10	1055	19	10	935	10
11	1025	17		Sum of Ranks	83.5
12	975	15			
	Sum of Ranks	169.5			

SAMPLING DISTRIBUTION OF T FOR IDENTICAL POPULATIONS

$$\text{Mean: } \mu_T = \tfrac{1}{2} n_1(n_1 + n_2 + 1) \tag{19.6}$$

$$\text{Standard Deviation: } \sigma_T = \sqrt{\tfrac{1}{12} n_1 n_2 (n_1 + n_2 + 1)} \tag{19.7}$$

Distribution form: approximately normal provided $n_1 \geq 10$ and $n_2 \geq 10$.

For branch 1, we have

$$\mu_T = \tfrac{1}{2} 12(12 + 10 + 1) = 138$$

$$\sigma_T = \sqrt{\tfrac{1}{12} 12(10)(12 + 10 + 1)} = 15.17$$

Figure 19.4 is the sampling distribution of T. Following the usual hypothesis-testing procedure, we compute the test statistic z to determine whether the observed value of T appears to be from the sampling distribution of Figure 19.4. If T does not appear to be from that distribution, we will reject the null hypothesis and conclude that the populations are not identical. Computing the test statistic, we have

$$z = \frac{T - \mu_T}{\sigma_T} = \frac{169.5 - 138}{15.17} = 2.08$$

At a .05 level of significance, we know that, to reject H_0, z must be less than -1.96 or greater than $+1.96$. Since $z = 2.08$, we reject H_0. Thus, we conclude that the two populations are not identical. That is, the populations of account balances at the two branches are not the same.

In summary, the Mann-Whitney-Wilcoxon rank-sum test consists of the following steps to determine whether two independent random samples are selected from identical populations.

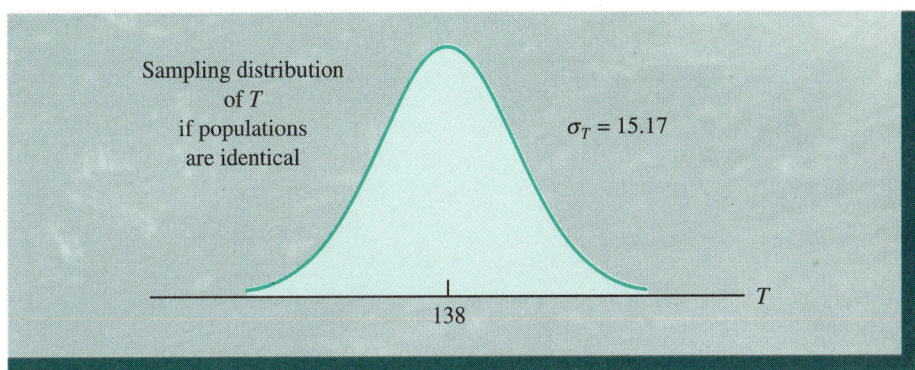

FIGURE 19.4   Sampling Distribution of T for the Third National Bank Example

1. Rank the combined sample observations from lowest to highest, with tied values being assigned the average of the tied rankings.
2. Compute T, the sum of the ranks for the first sample.
3. In the large-sample case, make the test for significant differences between the two populations by using the observed value of T and comparing it to the sampling distribution of T for identical populations (see equations 19.6 and 19.7). The value of the standardized test statistic z will provide the basis for deciding whether to reject H_0. In the small-sample case, use Table 10 in Appendix B to find the critical values for the test.

NOTES AND COMMENTS

The nonparametric test discussed in this section is used to determine whether two populations are identical. Parametric statistical tests, such as the t test described in Chapter 10, test the equality of two population means. When we reject the hypothesis that the means are equal, we conclude that the populations differ in their means. When we reject the hypothesis that the populations are identical by using the MWW test, we cannot state how they differ. The populations could have different means, different variances, and/or different forms. Nonetheless, if we believe that the populations are the same in every aspect but the means, a rejection of H_0 by the nonparametric method implies that the means differ. The major advantages of the MWW test over the parametric t test are that it does not require any assumptions about the form of the probability distribution from which the measurements come and it can be used with ordinal data.

EXERCISES

APPLICATIONS

Self-Test

18. Two fuel additives are being tested to determine their effect on gas mileage. Seven cars were tested with additive 1; another independent sample of nine cars were tested with additive 2. Table 19.13 reports the miles per gallon obtained with the two additives. Use $\alpha = .05$ and the MWW test to see whether there is a significant difference in gasoline mileage.

Self-Test

19. Starting salary data for college graduates are reported by the College Placement Council (*USA Today,* April 6, 1992). Annual salaries in thousands of dollars for a sample of accounting majors and a sample of finance majors follow.

TABLE 19.13 Exercise 18

Additive 1	Additive 2
17.3	18.7
18.4	17.8
19.1	21.3
16.7	21.0
18.2	22.1
18.6	18.7
17.5	19.8
	20.7
	20.2

Accounting	Finance
28.8	26.3
25.3	23.6
26.2	25.0
27.9	23.0
27.0	27.9
26.2	24.5
28.1	29.0
24.7	27.4
25.2	23.5
29.2	26.9
29.7	26.2
29.3	24.0

a. Use a .05 level of significance to test the null hypothesis that there is no difference between the starting salaries of accounting majors and finance majors. What is your conclusion?

b. What are the sample means for accounting majors and finance majors?

20. The Anderson Company sent two groups of employees to a privately run program providing word-processing training. One group was from the data-processing department; the other was from the typing pool. At the completion of the program, the Anderson Company received a report showing the class rank for each of its employees. Of the 70 persons finishing the program, the 13 employees of the Anderson Company had the class ranks given in Table 19.14. Use $\alpha = .10$ and test to see whether there is a performance difference between the two groups in the word-processing program.

TABLE 19.14 Exercise 20

Data-Processing Group	Typists
1	17
12	26
15	29
23	33
30	45
33	51
	62

21. Mileage performance tests were conducted for two models of automobiles. Twelve automobiles of each model were selected randomly and a miles-per-gallon rating for each model was developed on the basis of 1000 miles of highway driving. The data follow.

Model 1		Model 2	
Automobile	Miles per Gallon	Automobile	Miles per Gallon
1	20.6	1	21.3
2	19.9	2	17.6
3	18.6	3	17.4
4	18.9	4	18.5
5	18.8	5	19.7
6	20.2	6	21.1
7	21.0	7	17.3
8	20.5	8	18.8
9	19.8	9	17.8
10	19.8	10	16.9
11	19.2	11	18.0
12	20.5	12	20.1

Use $\alpha = .10$ and test for a significant difference in the populations of miles-per-gallon ratings for the two models.

TABLE 19.15 P/E Ratios for Japanese and United States Companies

Japan			United States		
Company	**P/E Ratio**		**Company**	**P/E Ratio**	
Sumitomo Corp.	153		Gannet	19	
Kinden	21		Motorola	24	
Heiwa	18		Schlumberger	24	
NCR Japan	125		Oracle Systems	43	
Suzuki Motor	31		Gap	22	
Fuji Bank	213		Winn-Dixie	14	
Sumitomo Chemical	64		Ingersoll-Rand	21	
Seibu Railway	666		American Electric Power	14	
Shiseido	33		Hercules	21	
Toho Gas	68		Times Mirror	38	
			WellPoint Health	15	
			Northern States Power	14	

Source: *Business Week,* July 11, 1994.

22. *Business Week* annually publishes statistics on the world's 1000 largest companies. A company's price/earnings (P/E) ratio is the company's current stock price divided by the latest 12 months' earnings per share. Listed in Table 19.15 are the P/E ratios for a sample of 10 Japanese and 12 United States companies (*Business Week,* July 11, 1994). Is there a significant difference in P/E ratios between the two countries? Use the MWW test and $\alpha = .01$ to support your conclusion.

23. Police records show the following numbers of daily crime reports for a sample of days during the winter months and a sample of days during the summer months. Using a .05 level of significance, determine whether there is a significant difference between the winter and summer months in terms of the number of crime reports.

Winter	Summer
18	28
20	18
15	24
16	32
21	18
20	29
12	23
16	38
19	28
20	18

TABLE 19.16 Exercise 24

Dallas	San Antonio
445	460
489	451
405	435
485	479
439	475
449	445
436	429
420	434
430	410
405	422
	425
	459
	430

24. A certain brand of microwave oven was priced at 10 stores in Dallas and 13 stores in San Antonio. The data are reported in Table 19.16. Use a .05 level of significance and test whether prices for the microwave oven are the same in the two cities.

25. Miami University reported the starting salaries by major for graduates of the Richard T. Farmer School of Business Administration (*Miami University Class Profile,* 1990). The following starting salaries are reported in thousands of dollars. Use the Mann-Whitney-Wilcoxon test to see whether there is evidence to conclude that the starting salaries of majors in management information systems differ from those of general business majors. Use a .05 level of significance.

Management Information Systems	General Business
27.2	25.6
29.0	29.1
28.0	21.7
27.0	24.0
27.5	25.2
30.5	25.0
24.3	25.0
32.5	23.8
26.0	

19.4   KRUSKAL-WALLIS TEST

The MWW test in Section 19.3 can be used to test whether two populations are identical. It has been extended to the case of three or more populations by Kruskal and Wallis. The hypotheses for the *Kruskal-Wallis test* with $k \geq 3$ populations can be written as follows.

$$H_0: \text{All populations are identical}$$

$$H_a: \text{Not all populations are identical}$$

The Kruskal-Wallis test is based on the analysis of independent random samples from each of the k populations.

In Chapter 13 we showed that analysis of variance (ANOVA) can be used to test for the equality of means among three or more populations. The ANOVA procedure requires interval or ratio data, all populations to be normally distributed, and the variances of the populations to be equal.

The nonparametric Kruskal-Wallis test can be used with ordinal data as well as with interval or ratio data. In addition, the Kruskal-Wallis test does not require the assumptions of normality and equal variances that are required by the parametric analysis of variance procedure. Hence, whenever the data from $k \geq 3$ independent random samples are ordinal, or whenever the assumptions of normality and equal variances are questionable, the Kruskal-Wallis test provides an alternate statistical procedure for testing whether the populations are identical. We demonstrate the Kruskal-Wallis test by using it in an employee-selection application.

Williams Manufacturing Company hires employees for its management staff from three local colleges. Recently, the company's personnel department has been collecting and reviewing annual performance ratings in an attempt to determine whether there are differences in performance among the managers hired from these colleges. Performance-rating data are available from independent samples of seven employees from college A, six employees from college B, and seven employees from college C. These data are summarized in Table 19.17; the overall performance rating of each manager is given on a 0–100 scale, with 100 being the highest possible performance rating.

Suppose we want to test whether the three populations are identical in terms of performance evaluations. The Kruskal-Wallis test statistic, which is based on the sum of ranks for each of the samples, can be computed as follows.

TABLE 19.17 Performance Evaluation Ratings for 20 Williams Employees

College A	College B	College C
25	60	50
70	20	70
60	30	60
85	15	80
95	40	90
90	35	70
80		75

TABLE 19.18 Combined Rankings for the 20 Williams Employees

College A	Rank	College B	Rank	College C	Rank
25	3	60	9	50	7
70	12	20	2	70	12
60	9	30	4	60	9
85	17	15	1	80	15.5
95	20	40	6	90	18.5
90	18.5	35	5	70	12
80	15.5	—		75	14
Sum of Ranks	95		27		88

KRUSKAL-WALLIS TEST STATISTIC

$$W = \left[\frac{12}{n_T(n_T + 1)} \sum_{i=1}^{k} \frac{R_i^2}{n_i} \right] - 3(n_T + 1) \qquad \text{(19.8)}$$

where

k = the number of populations

n_i = the number of items in sample i

$n_T = \Sigma n_i$ = total number of items in all samples

R_i = sum of the ranks for sample i

Kruskal and Wallis were able to show that, under the null hypothesis in which the populations are identical, the sampling distribution of W can be approximated by a chi-square distribution with $k - 1$ degrees of freedom. This approximation is generally acceptable if each of the sample sizes is greater than or equal to five.

To compute the W statistic for our example, we must first rank all 20 data items. The lowest data value of 15 from the college B sample receives a rank of 1, whereas the highest data value of 95 from the college A sample receives a rank of 20. The data values, their associated ranks, and the sum of the ranks for the three samples are given in Table 19.18. Note that we assign the average rank to tied items;* for example, the data values of 60, 70, 80, and 90 had ties.

The sample sizes are

$$n_1 = 7 \qquad n_2 = 6 \qquad n_3 = 7$$

and

$$n_T = \Sigma n_i = 7 + 6 + 7 = 20$$

---

*If numerous tied ranks are observed, (19.8) must be modified; the modified formula is given in *Practical Nonparametric Statistics* by W. J. Conover.

We compute the W statistic by using (19.8).

$$W = \frac{12}{20(21)} \left[\frac{(95)^2}{7} + \frac{(27)^2}{6} + \frac{(88)^2}{7} \right] - 3(20 + 1) = 8.92$$

The chi-square distribution table (Table 3 of Appendix B) shows that with $k - 1 = 2$ degrees of freedom and $\alpha = .05$ in the upper tail of the distribution, the critical chi-square value is $\chi^2 = 5.99147$. Since the test statistic $W = 8.92$ is greater than 5.99147, we reject the null hypothesis that the three populations are identical. As a result, we conclude that manager performance differs significantly depending on the college attended. Furthermore, since the performance ratings are lowest for college B, it would be reasonable for the company to either cut back recruiting from college B or at least evaluate its graduates more thoroughly.

NOTES AND COMMENTS

The Kruskal-Wallis procedure illustrated in the example began with the collection of interval-scaled data showing employee performance evaluation ratings. The procedure also would have worked had the data been the ordinal rankings of the 20 employees. In that case, the Kruskal-Wallis test could have been applied directly to the original data; the step of constructing the rank orderings from the performance evaluation ratings would have been omitted.

EXERCISES

METHODS

Self-Test

26. Three products received the following performance ratings by a panel of 15 consumers.

Product		
A	B	C
50	80	60
62	95	45
75	98	30
48	87	58
65	90	57

Use the Kruskal-Wallis test and $\alpha = .05$ to determine whether there is a significant difference in the performance ratings for the products.

27. Three admission-test-preparation programs are being evaluated. The scores obtained by a sample of 20 people who used the test-preparation programs yielded the results reported in Table 19.19. Use the Kruskal-Wallis test to determine whether there is a significant difference among the three test preparation programs. Use $\alpha = .01$.

TABLE 19.19
Exercise 27

Program		
A	B	C
540	450	600
400	540	630
490	400	580
530	410	490
490	480	590
610	370	620
	550	570

APPLICATIONS

Self-Test

28. An American Medical Association survey found that the average annual income for doctors is $155,000 (*St. Petersburg Times,* December 15, 1990). The following table gives the annual

income in thousands of dollars for samples of physicians specializing in surgery, radiology, and obstetrics. Do the data indicate differences in annual income for the three specialties? Use a .05 level of significance. What is your conclusion?

Surgery	Radiology	Obstetrics
240	250	200
205	180	175
275	210	185
200	225	220
195	190	188
205	215	202

TABLE 19.20
Exercise 29

Automobile

A	B	C
19	19	24
21	20	26
20	22	23
19	21	25
21	23	27

29. In Chapter 13 the ANOVA procedure was used to test for significant differences in gas mileage for three types of automobiles. The miles per gallon data obtained from tests on five automobiles of each type are reported in Table 19.20.
    a. Use the Kruskal-Wallis test with $\alpha = .05$ to determine whether there is a significant difference in the gasoline mileage for the three automobiles.
    b. What information available in the data is used by the ANOVA procedure and not the Kruskal-Wallis test?

30. A large corporation has been sending many of its first-level managers to an off-site supervisory skills course. Four different management-development centers offer this course, and the corporation wants to determine whether they differ in the quality of training provided. A sample of 20 employees who have attended these programs has been chosen and the employees ranked in terms of supervisory skills. The results follow.

Course	Supervisory Skills Rank				
1	3	14	10	12	13
2	2	7	1	5	11
3	19	16	9	18	17
4	20	4	15	6	8

TABLE 19.21 Exercise 31

M&Ms	Kit Kat	Milky Way II
230	225	200
210	205	208
240	245	202
250	235	190
230	220	180

Note that the top-ranked supervisor attended course 2 and the lowest-ranked supervisor attended course 4. Use $\alpha = .05$ and test to see whether there is a significant difference in the training provided by the four programs.

31. The better selling candies are high in calories. Hershey's Milk Chocolate bar has an average of 240 calories, Twix has an average of 280 calories, and Reese's Peanut Butter Cups have an average of 250 calories (*USA Today,* April 7, 1992). Assume that the data in Table 19.21 represent the calorie content from samples of M&Ms, Kit Kat, and Milky Way II. Test for significant differences in the calorie content of these three candies. At a .05 level of significance, what is your conclusion?

19.5 RANK CORRELATION

The correlation coefficient is a measure of the linear association between two variables for which interval or ratio data are available. In this section, we consider measures of association between two variables when only ordinal data are available. The *Spearman rank-correlation coefficient* r_s has been developed for this purpose.

SPEARMAN RANK-CORRELATION COEFFICIENT

$$r_s = 1 - \frac{6 \, \Sigma d_i^2}{n(n^2 - 1)}$$ (19.9)

where

$n =$ the number of items or individuals being ranked

$x_i =$ the rank of item i with respect to one variable

$y_i =$ the rank of item i with respect to a second variable

$d_i = x_i - y_i$

Let us illustrate the use of the Spearman rank-correlation coefficient with an example. A company wants to determine whether individuals who were expected at the time of employment to be better salespersons actually turn out to have better sales records. To investigate this question, the vice president in charge of personnel carefully reviewed the original job interview summaries, academic records, and letters of recommendation for 10 current members of the firm's salesforce. After the review, the vice president ranked the 10 individuals in terms of their potential for success, basing the assessment solely on the information available at the time of employment. Then a list was obtained of the number of units sold by each salesperson over the first two years. On the basis of actual sales performance, a second ranking of the 10 salespersons was carried out. Table 19.22 gives the relevant data and the two rankings. The statistical question is whether there is agreement between the ranking of potential at the time of employment and the ranking based on the actual sales performance over the first two years.

Let us compute the Spearman rank-correlation coefficient for the data in Table 19.22. The computations are summarized in Table 19.23. We see that the rank-correlation coefficient is a positive .73. The Spearman rank-correlation coefficient ranges from -1.0 to $+1.0$ and its interpretation is similar to that of the sample correlation coefficient in that positive values near 1.0 indicate a strong association between the rankings; as one rank increases, the other rank increases. Rank correlations near -1.0 indicate a strong negative association between the rankings; as one rank increases, the other rank

TABLE 19.22   Sales Potential and Actual Two-Year Sales Data for 10 Salespeople

Salesperson	Ranking of Potential	Two-Year Sales (units)	Ranking According to Two-Year Sales
A	2	400	1
B	4	360	3
C	7	300	5
D	1	295	6
E	6	280	7
F	3	350	4
G	10	200	10
H	9	260	8
I	8	220	9
J	5	385	2

TABLE 19.23 Computation of the Spearman Rank-Correlation Coefficient for Sales Potential and Sales Performance

Salesperson	x_i = Ranking of Potential	y_i = Ranking of Sales Performance	$d_i = x_i - y_i$	d_i^2
A	2	1	1	1
B	4	3	1	1
C	7	5	2	4
D	1	6	−5	25
E	6	7	−1	1
F	3	4	−1	1
G	10	10	0	0
H	9	8	1	1
I	8	9	−1	1
J	5	2	3	9
				$\Sigma d_i^2 = 44$

$$r_s = 1 - \frac{6\Sigma d_i^2}{n(n^2 - 1)} = 1 - \frac{6(44)}{10(100 - 1)} = .73$$

decreases. The value $r_s = .73$ indicates a positive correlation between potential and actual performance. Individuals ranked high on potential tend to rank high on performance.

A TEST FOR SIGNIFICANT RANK CORRELATION

At this point, we have seen how sample results can be used to compute the sample rank-correlation coefficient. As with many other statistical procedures, we may want to use the sample results to make an inference about the population rank correlation ρ_s between two variables. To make an inference about the population rank correlation based on the sample rank-correlation coefficient r_s, we must test the following hypotheses.

$$H_0: \rho_s = 0$$

$$H_a: \rho_s \neq 0$$

Under the null hypothesis of no rank correlation ($\rho_s = 0$), the rankings are independent, and the sampling distribution of r_s is as follows.

SAMPLING DISTRIBUTION OF r_s

$$\text{Mean: } \mu_{r_s} = 0 \tag{19.10}$$

$$\text{Standard deviation: } \sigma_{r_s} = \sqrt{\frac{1}{n-1}} \tag{19.11}$$

Distribution form: approximately normal provided $n \geq 10$.

The sample rank-correlation coefficient for sales potential and sales performance in our example is $r_s = .73$. With this value, we can test for a significant rank correlation. From (19.10) we have $\mu_{r_s} = 0$ and from (19.11) we have $\sigma_{r_s} = \sqrt{1/(10 - 1)} = .33$. Using the test statistic, we have

$$z = \frac{r_s - \mu_{r_s}}{\sigma_{r_s}} = \frac{.73 - 0}{.33} = 2.21$$

At a .05 level of significance, we see that the null hypothesis of no correlation will be rejected if $z < -1.96$ or if $z > 1.96$. Since $z = 2.21 > 1.96$, we reject the hypothesis of no rank correlation. Thus, we can conclude that there is a significant rank correlation between sales potential and sales performance.

EXERCISES

METHODS

Self-Test

32. Consider the set of rankings on a sample of 10 elements in Table 19.24.
    a. Compute the Spearman rank-correlation coefficient for the data.
    b. Test for significant rank correlation using $\alpha = .05$ and state your conclusion.

33. Consider the following two sets of rankings for six items.

TABLE 19.24
Exercise 32

Element	x_i	y_i
1	10	8
2	6	4
3	7	10
4	3	2
5	4	5
6	2	7
7	8	6
8	5	3
9	1	1
10	9	9

	Case One				Case Two		
Item	First Ranking	Second Ranking		Item	First Ranking	Second Ranking	
A	1	1		A	1	6	
B	2	2		B	2	5	
C	3	3		C	3	4	
D	4	4		D	4	3	
E	5	5		E	5	2	
F	6	6		F	6	1	

Note that in the first case the rankings are identical, whereas in the second case the rankings are exactly opposite. What value should you expect for the Spearman rank-correlation coefficient for each of these cases? Explain. Calculate the rank-correlation coefficient for each case.

APPLICATIONS

Self-Test

34. *Financial World* (May 1992) presented a comparison of several educational statistics for the states. For a sample of 11 states, the following table gives the ranks on pupil-teacher ratio (1 = lowest, 11 = highest) and expenditure per pupil (1 = highest, 11 = lowest).

	Rank				Rank	
State	Pupil-Teacher Ratio	Expenditure per Pupil	State	Pupil-Teacher Ratio	Expenditure per Pupil
Arizona	10	9	Massachusetts	1	1
Colorado	8	5	Nebraska	2	7
Florida	6	4	North Dakota	7	8
Idaho	11	2	South Dakota	5	10
Iowa	4	6	Washington	9	3
Louisiana	3	11			

At the $\alpha = .05$ level, does there appear to be a relationship between expenditure per pupil and pupil-teacher ratio?

TABLE 19.25 Exercise 35

1973–1982 Rank	1983–1992 Rank	1973–1982 Rank	1983–1992 Rank
1	128	11	222
2	34	12	5
3	148	13	118
4	220	14	228
5	16	15	205
6	2	16	78
7	199	17	209
8	15	18	237
9	177	19	119
10	245	20	242

35. A mutual fund holds a diversified portfolio of stocks. Many funds claim to provide consistent top performance, but there is considerable disagreement over whether that is possible. Lipper Analytical Services, in a study of 309 mutual funds, ranked the 20 top-performing mutual funds for the period 1973–1982 and ranked the same funds again for the period 1983–1992. The fund rankings for the two periods are reported in Table 19.25 (*AAII Journal*, February 1995).
   a. Compute the average ranks of the funds in the two time periods. Comment on your finding.
   b. Compute the rank correlation by using these 20 funds over the two time periods. (Hint: First rank the 20 funds with respect to each other for the time period 1983–1992. That is, convert the second set of rankings to a 1–20 basis.)
   c. Is the rank correlation coefficient found in part (b) significant? Use $\alpha = .05$.
   d. Interpret for a mutual fund investor the meaning of the rank correlation found here.

36. In a poll of men and women television viewers, preferences for the top 10 shows led to the following rankings. Is there a relationship between the rankings by the two groups? Use $\alpha = .10$.

TABLE 19.26 Exercise 37

Professor	Ranking by Current Students	Ranking by Recent Graduates
1	4	6
2	6	8
3	8	5
4	3	1
5	1	2
6	2	3
7	5	7
8	10	9
9	7	4
10	9	10

Television Show	Ranking by Men	Ranking by Women	Television Show	Ranking by Men	Ranking by Women
1	1	5	6	3	2
2	5	10	7	10	9
3	8	6	8	4	8
4	7	4	9	6	1
5	2	7	10	9	3

37. A student organization surveyed both recent graduates and current students to obtain information on the quality of teaching at a particular university. An analysis of the responses provided the teaching-ability rankings reported in Table 19.26 for 10 professors. Do the rankings given by the current students agree with the rankings given by the recent graduates? Use $\alpha = .10$ and test for a significant rank correlation.

SUMMARY

In this chapter we have presented several statistical procedures that are classified as nonparametric methods. The parametric methods of the preceding chapters generally require interval or ratio data and often are based on assumptions about the population (for example, the assumption that the probability distribution is normal). Since nonparametric methods can be applied to nominal and ordinal data as well as interval and ratio data and do not require population-distribution assumptions, nonparametric methods expand the class of problems that can be subjected to statistical analysis.

The sign test is a nonparametric procedure for identifying differences between two populations when the only data available are nominal data. In the small-sample case, the binominal probability distribution can be used to determine the critical values for the sign test; in the large-sample case, a normal approximation can be used. The Wilcoxon signed-rank test is a procedure for analyzing matched-sample data whenever interval- or ratio-scaled data are available for each matched pair. No assumptions are made about the population distribution. The Wilcoxon procedure tests the hypothesis that the two populations being considered are identical.

The Mann-Whitney-Wilcoxon test is a nonparametric method for testing for a difference between two populations based on two independent random samples. Tables were presented for the small-sample case, and a normal approximation was provided for the large-sample case. The Kruskal-Wallis test extends the Mann-Whitney-Wilcoxon test to the case of three or more populations. The Kruskal-Wallis test is the nonparametric analog of the parametric ANOVA test for differences among population means.

In the last section of this chapter we introduced the Spearman rank-correlation coefficient as a measure of association for two ordinal or rank-ordered sets of items.

GLOSSARY

Nonparametric methods   Statistical methods that require very few, if any, assumptions about the population probability distributions and the level of measurement. These methods can be applied when nominal or ordinal data are available.

Distribution-free methods   Another name for nonparametric statistical methods that indicates the lack of assumptions about the population probability distribution.

Sign test   A nonparametric statistical test for identifying differences between two populations based on the analysis of nominal data.

Wilcoxon signed-rank test   A nonparametric statistical test for identifying differences between two populations based on the analysis of two matched or paired samples.

Mann-Whitney-Wilcoxon (MWW) test   A nonparametric statistical test for identifying differences between two populations based on the analysis of two independent samples.

Kruskal-Wallis test   A nonparametric test for identifying differences among three or more populations.

Spearman rank-correlation coefficient   A correlation measure based on rank-ordered data for two variables.

KEY FORMULAS

Sign Test (Large-Sample Case)

$$\text{Mean: } \mu = .50n \tag{19.1}$$

$$\text{Standard Deviation: } \sigma = \sqrt{.25n} \tag{19.2}$$

Wilcoxon Signed-Rank Test

$$\text{Mean:} \quad \mu_T = 0 \tag{19.3}$$

$$\text{Standard Deviation: } \sigma_T = \sqrt{\frac{n(n+1)(2n+1)}{6}} \tag{19.4}$$

Mann-Whitney-Wilcoxon Test (Large-Sample)

$$\text{Mean: } \mu_T = \tfrac{1}{2}\, n_1(n_1 + n_2 + 1) \tag{19.6}$$

$$\text{Standard Deviation: } \sigma_T = \sqrt{\tfrac{1}{12}\, n_1 n_2 (n_1 + n_2 + 1)} \tag{19.7}$$

Kruskal-Wallis Test Statistic

$$W = \left[\frac{12}{n_T(n_T + 1)} \sum_{i=1}^{k} \frac{R_i^2}{n_i} \right] - 3(n_T + 1) \tag{19.8}$$

Spearman Rank-Correlation Coefficient

$$r_s = 1 - \frac{6 \sum d_i^2}{n(n^2 - 1)} \tag{19.9}$$

SUPPLEMENTARY EXERCISES

38. Mueller Beverage Products of Milwaukee, Wisconsin, has conducted a market research study to determine whether consumers would prefer Mueller's Old Brew Beer to their usual beer. Each individual participating in the test was given a glass of his or her usual beer and a glass of Mueller's Old Brew. The two glasses were not labeled, and the individuals had no way of knowing beforehand which of the two glasses was Mueller's Old Brew and which was their usual brand. The beer that each individual tasted first was randomly selected. After tasting the beer in each glass, the individuals were asked to indicate their preferred beer. The test results from a sample of 24 individuals follow:

Individual	Brand Preferred	Value Recorded	Individual	Brand Preferred	Value Recorded
1	Old Brew	+	13	Usual brand	−
2	Old Brew	+	14	Usual brand	−
3	Usual brand	−	15	Old Brew	+
4	Old Brew	+	16	Usual brand	−
5	Usual brand	−	17	Old Brew	+
6	Old Brew	+	18	Old Brew	+
7	Usual brand	−	19	Old Brew	+
8	Old Brew	+	20	Usual brand	−
9	Old Brew	+	21	Old Brew	+
10	Usual brand	−	22	Old Brew	+
11	Old Brew	+	23	Usual brand	−
12	Usual brand	−	24	Old Brew	+

If an individual selected Mueller's Old Brew as the preferred beer, a plus sign was recorded. If the individual stated a preference for his or her usual brand, a minus sign was recorded. Do the data for the 24 individuals indicate a significant difference in the preferences for the beers? Use $\alpha = .05$.

39. Two pilots for a prime-time television show (a western and a mystery show) are being tested. Both have been shown to a group of 12 viewers. The viewer preferences follow.

Viewer	Preference	Viewer	Preference
1	Mystery	7	Mystery
2	Mystery	8	Western
3	Mystery	9	Mystery
4	Western	10	Mystery
5	Mystery	11	Mystery
6	Western	12	Mystery

TABLE 19.27 Exercise 41

Worker	Method 1 (minutes)	Method 2 (minutes)
1	10.2	9.5
2	9.6	9.8
3	9.2	8.8
4	10.6	10.1
5	9.9	10.3
6	10.2	9.3
7	10.6	10.5
8	10.0	10.0
9	11.2	10.6
10	10.7	10.2
11	10.6	9.8

Using $\alpha = .05$, test to see whether there is a significant difference in preferences.

40. In a soft-drink taste test, 48 individuals stated a preference for one of two well-known brands. Results showed 28 favoring brand A, 16 favoring brand B, and four undecided. Use the sign test with $\alpha = .10$ and determine whether there is a significant difference in preferences for the two brands of soft drinks.

41. Use the sign test and perform the statistical analysis that will help determine whether the task-completion times for two production methods differ. The data are given in Table 19.27. Use $\alpha = .05$.

42. The national median sales price of existing one-family homes in 1993 was $106,700 (*Statistical Abstract of the United States, 1994*). Assume that the following data were obtained for sales of existing one-family homes in Houston and Philadelphia.

City	Greater than $106,700	Equal to $106,700	Less than $106,700
Houston	11	2	32
Philadelphia	27	1	13

a. Is the median resale price in Houston lower than the national median of $106,700? Use a statistical test with $\alpha = .05$ to support your conclusion.

b. Is the median resale price in Philadelphia higher than the national median of $106,700? Use a statistical test with $\alpha = .05$ to support your conclusion.

43. Mayfield Products, Inc., has collected data on 12 individuals' preferences for two brands of detergent. The individuals and their preferences are listed in the following table, where a plus sign indicates a preference for brand A.

Individual	Brand A Versus Brand B	Individual	Brand A Versus Brand B
1	−	7	−
2	+	8	+
3	+	9	+
4	+	10	−
5	−	11	+
6	+	12	+

With $\alpha = .10$, test for a significant difference in the preferences for the two brands.

44. Twelve homemakers were asked to estimate the retail selling price of two models of refrigerators. Their estimates of selling price are reported in Table 19.28. Use these data and test at the .05 level of significance to determine whether there is a difference between the two models in terms of homemakers' perceptions of selling price.

TABLE 19.28 Exercise 44

Homemaker	Model 1	Model 2
1	$650	$ 900
2	760	720
3	740	690
4	700	850
5	590	920
6	620	800
7	700	890
8	690	920
9	900	1000
10	500	690
11	610	700
12	720	700

45. A study was designed to evaluate the weight-gain potential of a new poultry feed. A sample of 12 chickens was used in a six-week study. The weight of each chicken was recorded before and after the six-week test period. The differences between the before and after weights of the 12 chickens are 1.5, 1.2, $-.2$, .0, .5, .7, .8, 1.0, .0, .6, .2, $-.01$. A negative value indicates a weight loss during the test period, whereas .0 indicates no weight change over the period. Use a .05 level of significance to determine whether the new feed appears to provide a weight gain for the chickens.

46. The data in Table 19.29 are product weights for items produced on two production lines. Test for a difference between the product weights for the two lines. Use $\alpha = .10$.

47. A client wants to determine whether there is a significant difference in the time required to complete a program evaluation with the three different methods that are in common use. The times (in hours) required for each of 18 evaluators to conduct a program evaluation follow.

TABLE 19.29 Exercise 46

Production Line 1	Production Line 2
13.6	13.7
13.8	14.1
14.0	14.2
13.9	14.0
13.4	14.6
13.2	13.5
13.3	14.4
13.6	14.8
12.9	14.5
14.4	14.3
	15.0
	14.9

Method 1	Method 2	Method 3
68	62	58
74	73	67
65	75	69
76	68	57
77	72	59
72	70	62

Use $\alpha=.05$ and test to see whether there is a significant difference in the time required by the three methods.

48. A sample of 20 engineers who have been with a company for three years has been rank-ordered with respect to managerial potential. Some of the engineers have attended the company's management-development course, others have attended an off-site management-development program at a local university, and the remainder have not attended any program. Use the rankings in Table 19.30 and $\alpha = .025$ to test for a significant difference in the managerial potential of the three groups.

49. Course evaluation ratings for four instructors follow. Use $\alpha = .05$ and the Kruskal-Wallis procedure to test for a significant difference in teaching abilities.

TABLE 19.30 Exercise 48

No Program	Company Program	Off-Site Program
16	12	7
9	20	1
10	17	4
15	19	2
11	6	3
13	18	8
	14	5

Instructor	Course-Evaluation Rating								
Black	88	80	79	68	96	69			
Jennings	87	78	82	85	99	99	85	94	
Swanson	88	76	68	82	85	82	84	83	81
Wilson	80	85	56	71	89	87			

50. In the following table, 12 *Fortune* 500 companies are ranked in terms of both sales and profits (*Fortune*, April 18, 1994).

Company	Sales Rank	Profits Rank	Company	Sales Rank	Profits Rank
Pepsico	1	1	Baxter International	2	10
Quaker Oats	3	2	Seagram	4	12
Baker Hughes	5	3	Dow Corning	6	11
Adolph Coors	7	7	Tektronix	8	8
Data General	9	9	Dexter	10	5
SPX	11	6	NCH	12	4

TABLE 19.31   Exercise 51

Soft Drink	Ranking by Individual 1	Individual 2
A	1	3
B	3	2
C	5	5
D	6	7
E	7	6
F	4	1
G	2	4

Is there a relationship between sales and profits? Using $\alpha = .05$, support your conclusion with a statistical test.

51. Two individuals provided the preference rankings of seven soft drinks listed in Table 19.31. Compute the rank correlation for the two individuals.

52. A sample of 15 students received the following rankings on midterm and final examinations in a statistics course.

Rank Midterm	Final	Rank Midterm	Final	Rank Midterm	Final
1	4	6	2	11	14
2	7	7	5	12	15
3	1	8	12	13	11
4	3	9	6	14	10
5	8	10	9	15	13

Compute the Spearman rank-correlation coefficient for the data and test for a significant correlation with $\alpha = .10$.

20

STATISTICAL METHODS FOR QUALITY CONTROL

CONTENTS

STATISTICS IN PRACTICE ●

Dow Chemical U.S.A.*

Freeport, Texas

Dow Chemical U.S.A., Texas Operations, began in 1940 when The Dow Chemical Company purchased 800 acres of Texas land on the Gulf Coast to build a magnesium production facility. That original site has expanded to cover more than 5000 acres and is now one of the largest petrochemical complexes in the world. Among the products from Texas Operations are magnesium, styrene, plastics, adhesives, solvent, glycol, and chlorine. Some products are made solely for use in other processes, but many end up as essential ingredients in products such as pharmaceuticals, toothpastes, dog food, water hoses, ice chests, milk cartons, garbage bags, shampoos, and furniture.

Dow's Texas Operations produces more than 30% of the world's magnesium, an extremely lightweight metal used in products ranging from tennis racquets to suitcases to "mag" wheels. The Magnesium Department was the first group in Texas Operations to train its technical people and managers in the use of statistical quality control. Some of the earliest successful applications of statistical quality control were in chemical processing.

In one application involving the operation of a drier, samples of the output were taken at periodic intervals; the average value for each sample was computed and recorded on a chart called an $\bar{x}$ chart. Such a chart enabled Dow

analysts to monitor trends in the output that might indicate the process was not operating correctly. In one instance, analysts began to observe values for the sample mean that were not indicative of a process operating within its design limits. On further examination of the control chart and the operation itself, the analysts found that the variation could be traced to problems involving one operator. The $\bar{x}$ chart recorded after that operator was retrained showed a significant improvement in the process quality.

Dow Chemical has achieved quality improvements everywhere statistical quality control has been used. Documented savings of several hundred thousand dollars per year have been realized, and new applications are continually being discovered.

In this chapter we will show how an $\bar{x}$ chart such as the one used by Dow Chemical can be developed. Such charts are a part of statistical quality control known as statistical process control. We will also discuss methods of quality control for situations in which a decision to accept or reject a group of items is based on a sample.

Magnesium is the primary product at Dow's Texas operations.

---

*The authors are indebted to Clifford B. Wilson, Magnesium Technical Manager, The Dow Chemical Company, for providing this Statistics in Practice.

● The American Society for Quality Control (ASQC) defines *quality* as "the totality of features and characteristics of a product or service that bears on its ability to satisfy given needs." In other words, quality measures how well a product or service meets customer needs. Organizations recognize that to be competitive in today's global economy, they must strive for high levels of quality. As a result, there has been an increased emphasis on methods for monitoring and maintaining quality.

Quality assurance refers to the entire system of policies, procedures, and guidelines established by an organization to achieve and maintain quality. Quality assurance consists of two principal functions: quality engineering and quality control. The objective of *quality engineering* is to include quality in the design of products and processes and to identify potential quality problems prior to production. *Quality control* consists of making a series of inspections and measurements to determine whether quality standards are being met. If quality standards are not being met, corrective and/or preventive action can be taken to achieve and maintain conformance. As we will show in this chapter, statistical techniques are extremely useful in quality control.

Traditional manufacturing approaches to quality control have been found to be less than satisfactory and are being replaced by improved managerial tools and techniques. Ironically, it was two U.S. consultants, Dr. W. Edwards Deming and Dr. Joseph Juran, who helped educate the Japanese in quality management. In recent years, U.S. firms have relearned those lessons from Japan.

Although quality is everybody's job, Deming stressed that quality must be led by managers. He developed a list of 14 points that he believed are the key responsibilities of managers. For instance, Deming stated that managers must cease dependence on mass inspection; must end the practice of awarding business solely on the basis of price; must seek continual improvement in all production processes and services; must foster a team-oriented environment; and must eliminate numerical goals, slogans, and work standards that prescribe numerical quotas. Perhaps most important, managers must create a work environment in which a commitment to quality and productivity is maintained at all times.

In 1987, the U.S. Congress enacted Public Law 107, the Malcolm Baldrige National Quality Improvement Act. The Baldrige Award is given annually to U.S. firms that excel in quality. This award, along with the perspectives of individuals like Dr. Deming and Dr. Juran, has helped top managers recognize that improving service quality and product quality is the most critical challenge facing their companies. Winners of the Malcolm Baldrige Award include Motorola, IBM, Xerox, and Federal Express. In this chapter we present two statistical methods used in quality control. The first method, *statistical process control,* uses graphical displays known as *control charts* to monitor a production process; the goal is to determine whether the process can be continued or whether it should be adjusted to achieve a desired quality level. The second method, *acceptance sampling,* is used in situations where a decision to accept or reject a group of items must be based on the quality found in a sample.

20.1 STATISTICAL PROCESS CONTROL

In this section we consider quality-control procedures for a production process whereby goods are manufactured continuously. On the basis of sampling and inspection of production output, a decision will be made to either continue the production process or adjust it to bring the items or goods being produced up to acceptable quality standards.

Despite high standards of quality in manufacturing and production operations, machine tools will invariably wear out, vibrations will throw machine settings out of adjustment, purchased materials will be defective, and human operators will make mistakes. Any or all of these factors can result in poor-quality output. Fortunately, procedures are available for monitoring production output so that poor quality can be detected early and the production process can be adjusted or corrected.

If the variation in the quality of the production output is due to *assignable causes* such as tools wearing out, incorrect machine settings, poor-quality raw materials, or operator error, the process should be adjusted or corrected as soon as possible. Alternatively, if the variation is due to what are called common causes—that is, randomly occurring variations in materials, temperature, humidity, and so on, which the

TABLE 20.1   The Outcomes of Statistical Process Control

| | | State of Production Process | |
		H_0 True *Process in Control*	H_0 False *Process Out of Control*
Decision	*Continue Process*	Correct decision	Type II error (allowing an out-of-control process to continue)
	Adjust Process	Type I error (adjusting an in-control process)	Correct decision

manufacturer cannot possibly control—the process does not need to be adjusted. The main objective of statistical process control is to determine whether variations in output are due to assignable causes or common causes.

Whenever assignable causes are detected, we conclude that the process is *out of control.* In that case, corrective action will be taken to bring the process back to an acceptable level of quality. However, if the variation in the output of a production process is due only to common causes, we conclude that the process is *in statistical control,* or simply *in control;* in such cases, no changes or adjustments are necessary.

The statistical procedures for process control are based on the hypothesis-testing methodology presented in Chapter 9. The null hypothesis H_0 is formulated in terms of the production process being in control. The alternative hypothesis H_a is formulated in terms of the production process being out of control. Table 20.1 shows that correct decisions to continue an in-control process and adjust an out-of-control process are possible. However, as with other hypothesis-testing procedures, both a Type I error (adjusting an in-control process) and a Type II error (allowing an out-of-control process to continue) are also possible.

CONTROL CHARTS

A *control chart* provides a basis for deciding whether the variation in the output is due to common causes (in control) or assignable causes (out of control). Whenever an out-of-control situation is detected, adjustments and/or other corrective action will be taken to bring the process back into control.

Control charts can be classified by the type of data they contain. An $\bar{x}$ chart is used if the quality of the output is measured in terms of a variable such as length, weight, temperature, and so on. In that case, the decision to continue or to adjust the production process will be based on the mean value found in a sample of the output. To introduce some of the concepts common to all control charts, let us consider some specific features of an $\bar{x}$ chart.

Figure 20.1 shows the general structure of an $\bar{x}$ chart. The center line of the chart corresponds to the mean of the process when the process is *in control.* The vertical line identifies the scale of measurement for the variable of interest. Each time a sample is taken from the production process, a value of the sample mean $\bar{x}$ is computed and a data point showing the value of $\bar{x}$ is plotted on the control chart.

The two lines labeled UCL and LCL are important in determining whether the process is in control or out of control. The lines are called the *upper control limit* and the *lower control limit,* respectively. They are chosen so that when the process is in control, there will be a high probability that the value of $\bar{x}$ will be between the two control limits. Values outside the control limits provide strong statistical evidence that the process is out of control and corrective action should be taken.

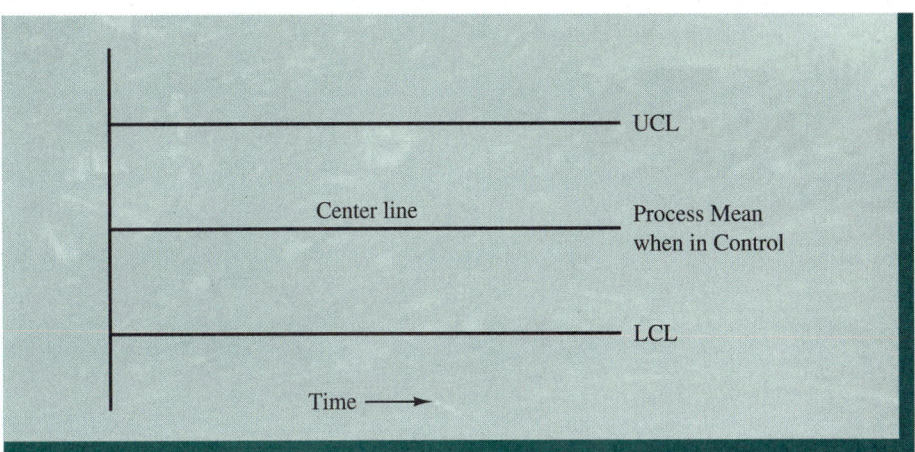

FIGURE 20.1 $\bar{x}$ Chart Structure

Over time, more and more data points will be added to the control chart. The order of the data points will be from left to right as the process is sampled. In essence, every time a point is plotted on the control chart, we are carrying out a hypothesis test to determine whether or not the process is in control.

In addition to the $\bar{x}$ chart, other control charts can be used to monitor the range of the measurements in the sample (R chart), the proportion defective in the sample (p chart), and the number of defective items in the sample (np chart). In each case, the general structure of the control chart follows the format of the $\bar{x}$ chart in Figure 20.1. The major difference among the charts is the measurement scale used; for instance, in a p chart the measurement scale denotes the proportion of defective items in the sample instead of the sample mean. In the following discussion, we will illustrate the construction and use of the $\bar{x}$ chart, R chart, p chart, and np chart.

$\bar{x}$ CHART: PROCESS MEAN AND STANDARD DEVIATION KNOWN

To illustrate the construction of an $\bar{x}$ chart, let us consider the situation at KJW Packaging. This company operates a production line where cartons of cereal are filled. Suppose KJW knows that when the process is operating correctly—and hence the system is in control—the mean filling weight is $\mu = 16.05$ ounces and the process standard deviation is $\sigma = .10$ ounces. In addition, assume the filling weights are normally distributed. This distribution is shown in Figure 20.2.

The sampling distribution of $\bar{x}$, as presented in Chapter 7, can be used to determine the variation that can be expected in $\bar{x}$ values for a process that is in control. To show how this is done, let us first briefly review the properties of the sampling distribution of $\bar{x}$. First, recall that the expected value or mean of $\bar{x}$ is equal to μ, the mean filling weight when the production line is in control. For samples of size n, the formula for the standard deviation of $\bar{x}$, called the standard error of the mean, is

$$\sigma_{\bar{x}} = \frac{\sigma}{\sqrt{n}}$$ (20.1)

In addition, since the filling weights are normally distributed, the sampling distribution of $\bar{x}$ is normal for any sample size. Thus, the sampling distribution of $\bar{x}$ is a normal

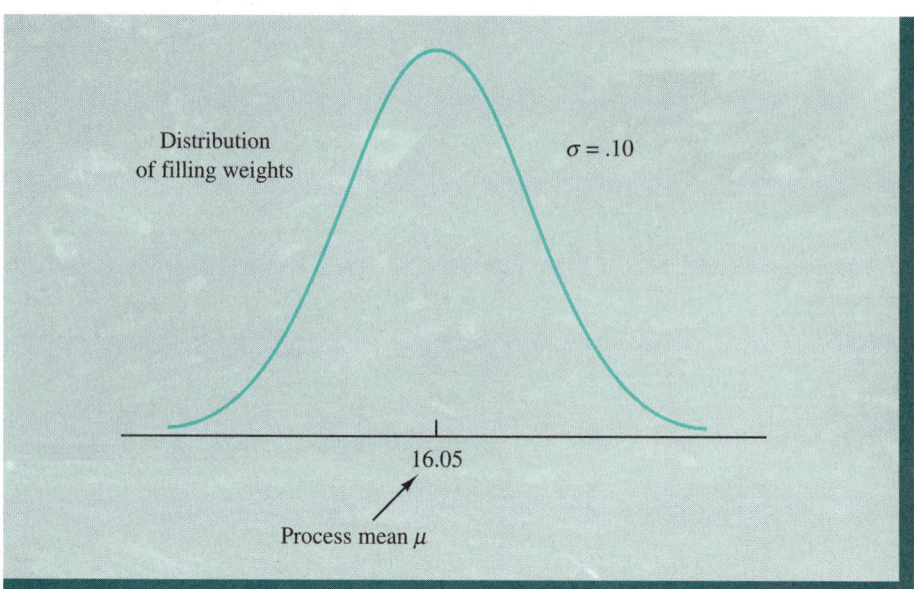

FIGURE 20.2 Distribution of Cereal-Carton Filling Weights

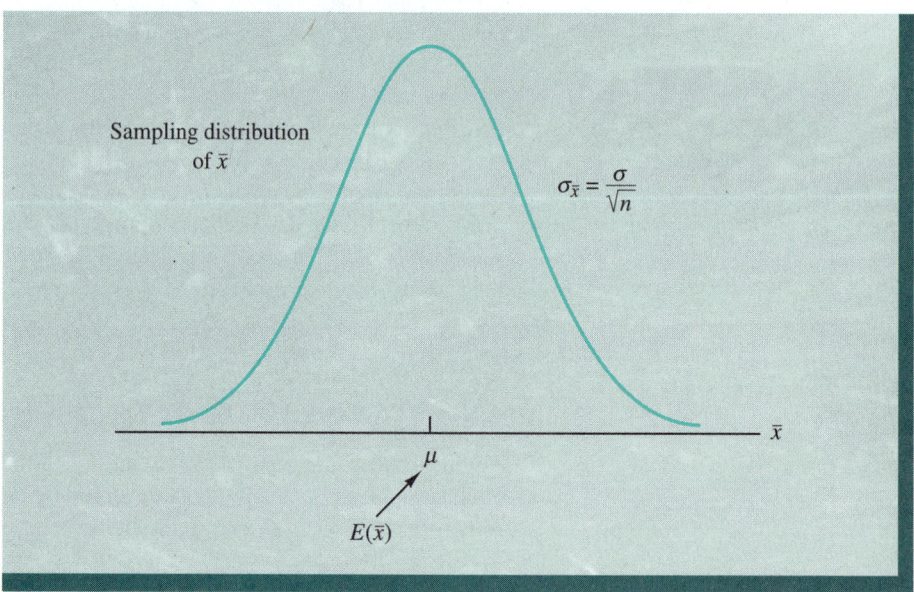

FIGURE 20.3 Sampling Distribution of $\bar{x}$

probability distribution with mean μ and standard deviation $\sigma_{\bar{x}}$. This distribution is shown in Figure 20.3.

The sampling distribution of $\bar{x}$ is used to determine what values of $\bar{x}$ are reasonable if the process is in control. The general practice in quality control is to define as reasonable any value of $\bar{x}$ that is within 3 standard deviations above or below the mean value. Recall from the study of the normal probability distribution that approximately 99.7% of the values of a normally distributed random variable are within ± 3 standard deviations of its mean value. Thus, if a value of $\bar{x}$ is within the interval $\mu - 3\sigma_{\bar{x}}$ to $\mu + 3\sigma_{\bar{x}}$, we will assume that the process is in control. In summary, then, the control limits for an $\bar{x}$ chart are as follows.

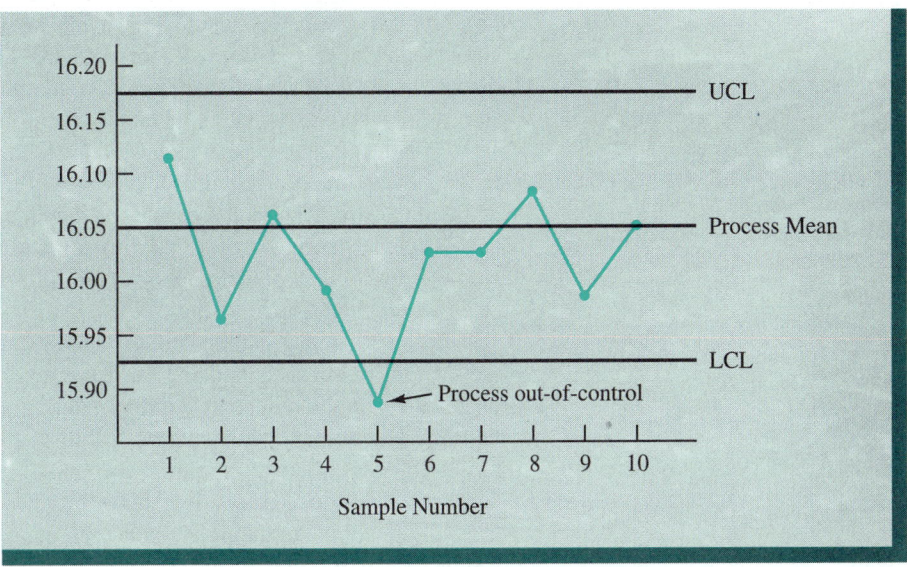

FIGURE 20.4 The $\bar{x}$ Chart for the Cereal-Carton Filling Process

> **CONTROL LIMITS FOR AN $\bar{x}$ CHART: PROCESS MEAN AND STANDARD DEVIATION KNOWN**
>
> $$UCL = \mu + 3\sigma_{\bar{x}} \qquad (20.2)$$
>
> $$LCL = \mu - 3\sigma_{\bar{x}} \qquad (20.3)$$

Reconsider the KJW Packaging example with the process distribution of filling weights shown in Figure 20.2 and the sampling distribution of $\bar{x}$ shown in Figure 20.3. Assume that a quality-control inspector periodically samples six cartons and uses the sample mean filling weight to determine whether the process is in control or out of control. Using (20.1), we find that the standard error of the mean is $\sigma_{\bar{x}} = \sigma/\sqrt{n} = .10/\sqrt{6} = .04$. Thus, with the process mean at 16.05, the control limits are UCL=16.05+3(.04)=16.17 and LCL=16.05−3(.04)=15.93. Figure 20.4 is the control chart with the results of 10 samples taken over a 10-hour period. For ease of reading, the sample numbers 1 through 10 are listed below the chart.

Note that the mean for the fifth sample in Figure 20.4 shows that the process was out of control. In other words, the sample mean $\bar{x} = 15.89$ provides an indication that assignable causes of output variation were present and that underfilling was occurring. As a result, corrective action was taken at this point to bring the process back into control. The fact that the remaining points on the $\bar{x}$ chart are within the upper and lower control limits indicates that the corrective action was successful.

$\bar{x}$ CHART: PROCESS MEAN AND STANDARD DEVIATION UNKNOWN

In the KJW Packaging example, we showed how an $\bar{x}$ chart can be developed when the mean and standard deviation of the process are known. In most situations, those values must be estimated by using samples that are selected from the process when it is known to be operating in control. For instance, KJW might select a random sample of five boxes each morning and five boxes each afternoon for 10 days of in-control operation.

For each subgroup, or sample, the mean and standard deviation of the sample are computed. The overall averages of both the sample means and the sample standard deviations are used to construct control charts for both the process mean and the process standard deviation.

In practice, it is more common to monitor the variability of the process by using the range instead of the standard deviation because the range is easier to compute. In addition to providing good estimates of the process standard deviation when the sample size is small, the range can be used to construct upper and lower control limits for the $\bar{x}$ chart with little computational effort. To illustrate, let us consider the problem facing Jensen Computer Supplies, Inc.

Jensen Computer Supplies (JCS) manufactures 3.5-inch-diameter floppy disks that are used in personal computers. For example, random samples of five disks could be taken during the first hour of operation, during the second hour of operation, and so on, until 20 samples have been selected. Table 20.2 lists the data, including the mean $\bar{x}_j$ and range R_j for each of the samples.

Assume that the diameter of disks produced when the process is in control is a normally distributed random variable with mean μ and standard deviation σ, and that k samples, each of size n, have been selected. The estimate of the process mean μ is given by the overall sample mean.

OVERALL SAMPLE MEAN

$$\bar{\bar{x}} = \frac{\bar{x}_1 + \bar{x}_2 + \cdots + \bar{x}_k}{k} \tag{20.4}$$

where

$$\bar{x}_j = \text{mean of the } j\text{th sample } j = 1, 2, \ldots, k$$

$$k = \text{number of samples}$$

For the JCS data in Table 20.2, the overall sample mean is $\bar{\bar{x}} = 3.4995$. This value will be the center line for the $\bar{x}$ chart. The range of each sample, denoted R_j, is simply the difference between the largest and smallest values in each sample. The average range follows.

AVERAGE RANGE

$$\bar{R} = \frac{R_1 + R_2 + \cdots + R_k}{k} \tag{20.5}$$

where

$$R_j = \text{range of the } j\text{th sample, } j = 1, 2, \ldots, k$$

$$k = \text{number of samples}$$

For the JCS data in Table 20.2, the average range is $\bar{R} = .0253$.

In the preceding section we showed that the upper and lower control limits for the $\bar{x}$ chart are

$$\bar{x} \pm 3 \frac{\sigma}{\sqrt{n}} \tag{20.6}$$

TABLE 20.2 Data for the Jensen Computer Supplies Problem

Sample Number	Observations					Sample Mean $\bar{x}_j$	Sample Range R_j
1	3.5056	3.5086	3.5144	3.5009	3.5030	3.5065	.0135
2	3.4882	3.5085	3.4884	3.5250	3.5031	3.5026	.0368
3	3.4897	3.4898	3.4995	3.5130	3.4969	3.4978	.0233
4	3.5153	3.5120	3.4989	3.4900	3.4837	3.5000	.0316
5	3.5059	3.5113	3.5011	3.4773	3.4801	3.4951	.0340
6	3.4977	3.4961	3.5050	3.5014	3.5060	3.5012	.0099
7	3.4910	3.4913	3.4976	3.4831	3.5044	3.4935	.0213
8	3.4991	3.4853	3.4830	3.5083	3.5094	3.4970	.0264
9	3.5099	3.5162	3.5228	3.4958	3.5004	3.5090	.0270
10	3.4880	3.5015	3.5094	3.5102	3.5146	3.5047	.0266
11	3.4881	3.4887	3.5141	3.5175	3.4863	3.4989	.0312
12	3.5043	3.4867	3.4946	3.5018	3.4784	3.4932	.0259
13	3.5043	3.4769	3.4944	3.5014	3.4904	3.4935	.0274
14	3.5004	3.5030	3.5082	3.5045	3.5234	3.5079	.0230
15	3.4846	3.4938	3.5065	3.5089	3.5011	3.4990	.0243
16	3.5145	3.4832	3.5188	3.4935	3.4989	3.5018	.0356
17	3.5004	3.5042	3.4954	3.5020	3.4889	3.4982	.0153
18	3.4959	3.4823	3.4964	3.5082	3.4871	3.4940	.0259
19	3.4878	3.4864	3.4960	3.5070	3.4984	3.4951	.0206
20	3.4969	3.5144	3.5053	3.4985	3.4885	3.5007	.0259

Hence, to construct the control limits for the $\bar{x}$ chart, we need to estimate σ, the standard deviation of the process. An estimate of σ can be developed by using the range of each sample.

It can be shown that an estimator of the process standard deviation σ is the average range divided by d_2, a constant that depends on the sample size n. That is,

$$\text{Estimator of } \sigma = \frac{\bar{R}}{d_2} \tag{20.7}$$

The American Society for Testing and Materials Manual on Presentation of Data and Control Chart Analysis provides values for d_2 as shown in Table 12 of Appendix B. For instance, when $n = 5$, $d_2 = 2.326$ and the estimate of σ is the average range divided by 2.326. If we substitute $\bar{R}/d_2$ for σ in (20.6), we can write the control limits for the $\bar{x}$ chart as

$$\bar{\bar{x}} \pm 3\frac{\bar{R}/d_2}{\sqrt{n}} = \bar{\bar{x}} \pm \frac{3}{d_2\sqrt{n}}\bar{R} = \bar{\bar{x}} \pm A_2\bar{R} \tag{20.8}$$

Note that $A_2 = 3/(d_2\sqrt{n})$ is a constant that depends only on the sample size. Values for A_2 are provided in Table 12 in Appendix B. For $n = 5$, $A_2 = .577$; thus, the control limits for the $\bar{x}$ chart are

$$3.4995 \pm (.577)(.0253) = 3.4995 \pm .0146$$

Hence, LCL = 3.4849 and UCL = 3.5141.

R CHART

Let us now consider the use of a range chart (*R* chart) which can be used to control the variability of a process. To develop the *R* chart, we need to think of the range of a sample as a random variable with its own mean and standard deviation. The average range $\bar{R}$ provides an estimate of the mean of this random variable. Moreover, it can be shown that an estimate of the standard deviation of the range is

$$\hat{\sigma}_R = d_3 \frac{\bar{R}}{d_2} \qquad \text{(20.9)}$$

where d_2 and d_3 are constants that depend on the sample size; values of d_2 and d_3 are also provided in Table 12 of Appendix B. Thus, the UCL for the R chart is given by

$$\bar{R} + 3\hat{\sigma}_R = \bar{R} + 3\,d_3\,\frac{\bar{R}}{d_2} \qquad \text{(20.10)}$$

and the LCL is

$$\bar{R} - 3\hat{\sigma}_R = \bar{R} - 3\,d_3\,\frac{\bar{R}}{d_2} \qquad \text{(20.11)}$$

If we let

$$D_4 = 1 + 3\,\frac{d_3}{d_2} \qquad \text{(20.12)}$$

$$D_3 = 1 - 3\,\frac{d_3}{d_2} \qquad \text{(20.13)}$$

we can write the control limits for the R chart as

$$\text{UCL} = \bar{R}D_4 \qquad \text{(20.14)}$$

$$\text{LCL} = \bar{R}D_3 \qquad \text{(20.15)}$$

Values for D_3 and D_4 are also provided in Table 12 of Appendix B. Note that for $n = 5, D_3 = 0$ and $D_4 = 2.115$. Thus, with $\bar{R} = .0253$, the control limits are

$$\text{UCL} = .0253(2.115) = .0535$$

$$\text{LCL} = .0253(0) = 0$$

Figure 20.5 is the R chart. The 20 ranges plotted on the chart do not indicate that the process is out of control. Figure 20.6 is the $\bar{x}$ chart with the 20 sample means for the JCS data; we note that these points show no indication of an out-of-control condition. These data confirm our assumption that during the time period in which the data were collected, the process was in control both in terms of its mean and its variation.

p CHART

Let us consider the case in which the output quality is measured in terms of the items being either nondefective or defective. The decision to continue or to adjust the production process will be based on $\bar{p}$, the proportion of defective items found in a sample of the output. The control chart used for proportion-defective data is called a p chart.

To illustrate the construction of a p chart, consider the use of automated mail-sorting machines in a post office. These automated machines scan the zip codes on letters and divert each letter to its proper carrier route. Even when a machine is operating properly, some letters are diverted to incorrect routes. Assume that when a machine is operating

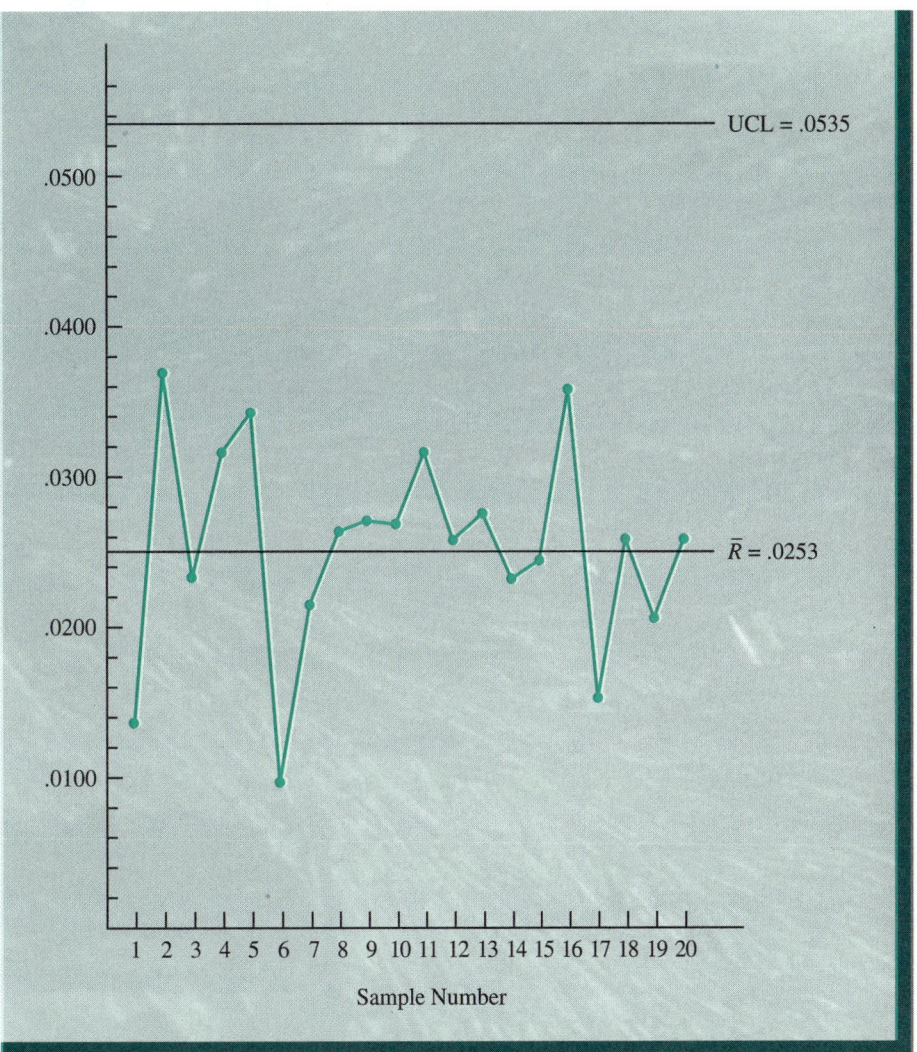

FIGURE 20.5   *R* Chart for the Jensen Computer Supplies Problem

correctly, or in a state of control, 3% of the letters are incorrectly diverted. Thus *p,* the proportion of letters incorrectly diverted when the process is in control, is .03.

The sampling distribution of $\bar{p}$, as presented in Chapter 7, can be used to determine the variation that can be expected in $\bar{p}$ values for a process that is in control. Recall that the expected value or mean of $\bar{p}$ is *p,* the proportion defective when the process is in control. With samples of size *n,* the formula for the standard deviation of $\bar{p}$, called the standard error of the proportion, is

$$\sigma_{\bar{p}} = \sqrt{\frac{p(1 - p)}{n}}$$ **(20.16)**

We also learned in Chapter 7 that the sampling distribution of $\bar{p}$ can be approximated by a normal probability distribution whenever the sample size is large. With $\bar{p}$, the sample size can be considered large whenever the following two conditions are satisfied.

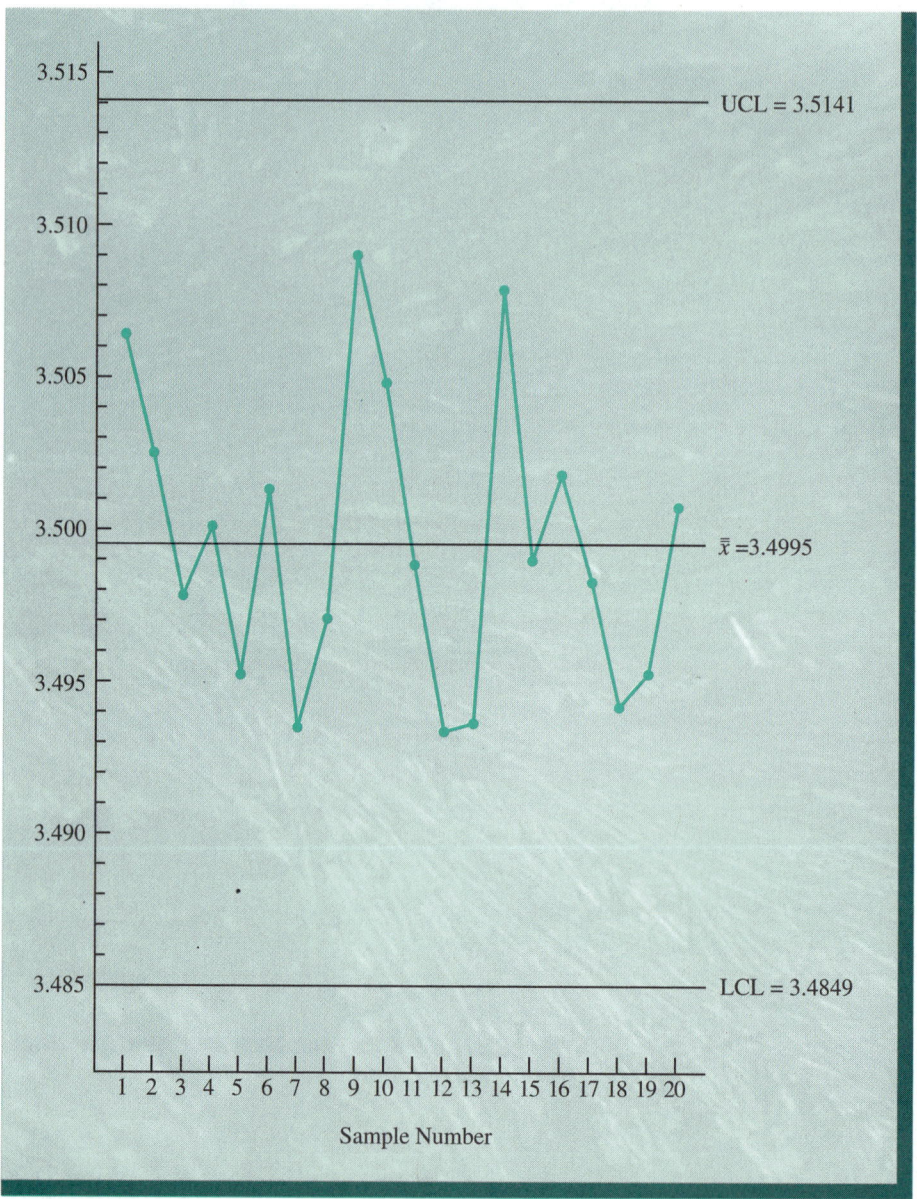

FIGURE 20.6 $\bar{x}$ Chart for the Jensen Computer Supplies Problem

$$np \geq 5$$

$$n(1 - p) \geq 5$$

In summary, whenever the sample size is large, the sampling distribution of $\bar{p}$ can be approximated by a normal probability distribution with mean p and standard deviation $\sigma_{\bar{p}}$. This distribution is shown in Figure 20.7.

To establish control limits for a p chart, we follow the same procedure we used to establish control limits for an $\bar{x}$ chart. That is, the limits for the control chart are set at 3 standard deviations, or standard errors, above and below the proportion defective when the process is in control. Thus, we have the following control limits.

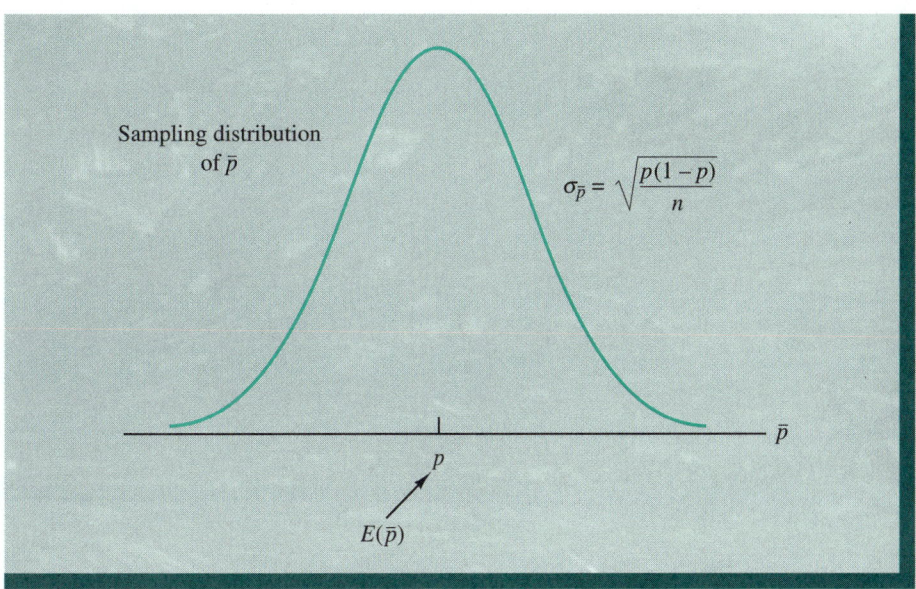

FIGURE 20.7 Sampling Distribution of $\bar{p}$

CONTROL LIMITS FOR A p CHART

$$\text{UCL} = p + 3\sigma_{\bar{p}} \qquad (20.17)$$

$$\text{LCL} = p - 3\sigma_{\bar{p}} \qquad (20.18)$$

With $p = .03$ and samples of size $n = 200$, (20.16) shows that the standard error is

$$\sigma_{\bar{p}} = \sqrt{\frac{.03(1 - .03)}{200}} = .0121$$

Hence, the control limits are UCL $= .03 + 3(.0121) = .0663$ and LCL $= .03 - 3(.0121) = -.0063$. Since LCL is negative, LCL is set equal to zero in the control chart.

Figure 20.8 is the control chart for the mail-sorting process. The points plotted show the proportions defective found in samples of 200 letters taken from the process. Since all points are within the control limits, there is no evidence to conclude that the sorting process is out of control. In fact, the p chart indicates that the process should continue to operate.

If the proportion of defective items for a process that is in control is not known, that value is first estimated by using sample data. Suppose, for example, that M different samples, each of size n, are selected from a process that is in control. The fraction or proportion of defective items in each sample is then determined. Treating all the data collected as one large sample, we can determine the average number of defective items for all the data; that value can then be used to provide an estimate of p, the proportion of defective items observed when the process is in control. Note that this estimate of p also enables us to estimate the standard error of the proportion; upper and lower control limits can then be established.

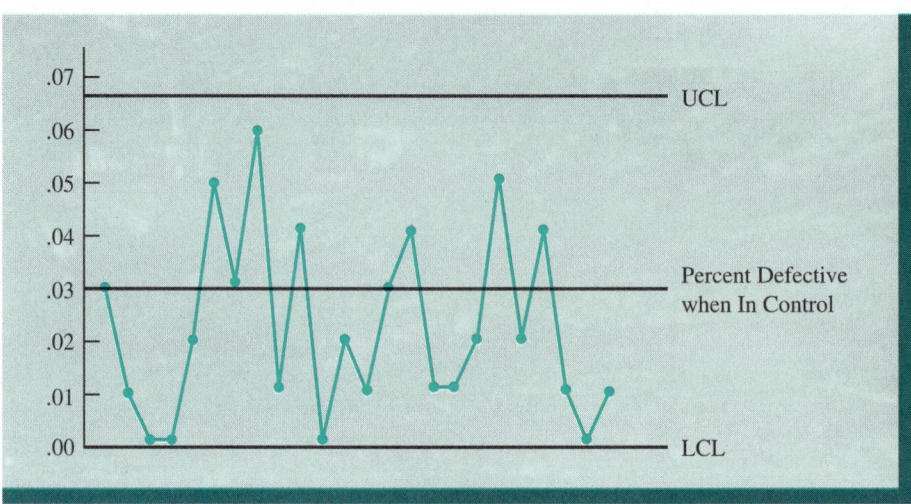

FIGURE 20.8 *p* Chart for the Proportion Defective in a Mail-Sorting Process

np CHART

An *np* chart is a control chart developed for the number of defective items observed in a sample. With *p* denoting the probability of observing a defective item when the process is in control, the binomial probability distribution, as presented in Chapter 5, can be used to determine the probability of observing *x* defective items in a sample of size *n*. The expected value or mean of a binomial distribution is *np* and the standard deviation is $\sqrt{np(1-p)}$.

In Chapter 7 we learned that the normal probability distribution can be used to approximate the binomial probability distribution whenever the sample size is large. The sample size can be considered large whenever the following two conditions are satisfied.

$$np \geq 5$$

$$n(1-p) \geq 5$$

In summary, whenever the sample size is large, the distribution of the number of defective items observed in a sample of size *n* can be approximated by a normal probability distribution with mean *np* and standard deviation $\sqrt{np(1-p)}$. Thus, for the mail-sorting example, with *n* = 200 and *p* = .03, the number of defective items observed in a sample of 200 letters can be approximated by a normal probability distribution with a mean of 200(.03) = 6 and a standard deviation of $\sqrt{200(.03)(.97)}$ = 2.4125.

The control limits for an *np* chart are set at 3 standard deviations above and below the expected number of defective items observed when the process is in control. Thus, we have the following control limits.

CONTROL LIMITS FOR AN *np* CHART

$$\text{UCL} = np + 3\sqrt{np(1-p)} \tag{20.19}$$

$$\text{LCL} = np - 3\sqrt{np(1-p)} \tag{20.20}$$

For the mail-sorting process example, with $p = .03$ and $n = 200$, the control limits are UCL $= 6 + 3(2.4125) = 13.2375$ and LCL $= 6 - 3(2.4125) = -1.2375$. Since LCL is negative, LCL is set equal to zero in the control chart. Hence, if the number of letters diverted to incorrect routes is greater than 13, the process is concluded to be out of control.

The information provided by an *np* chart is equivalent to the information provided by the *p* chart; the only difference is that the *np* chart is a plot of the number of defective items observed whereas the *p* chart is a plot of the proportion of defective items observed. Thus, if we were to conclude that a particular process is out of control on the basis of a *p* chart, the process would also be concluded to be out of control on the basis of an *np* chart.

INTERPRETATION OF CONTROL CHARTS

The location and pattern of points in a control chart enable us to determine, with a small probability of error, whether a process is in statistical control. A primary indication that a process may be out of control is a data point outside the control limits, such as point 5 in Figure 20.4. Finding such a point is statistical evidence that the process is out of control; in such cases, corrective action should be taken as soon as possible.

In addition to points outside the control limits, certain patterns of the points within the control limits can be warning signals of quality-control problems. For example, assume that all the data points are within the control limits but that a large number of points are on one side of the center line. This pattern may indicate that an equipment problem, a change in materials, or some other assignable cause of a shift in quality has occurred. Careful investigation of the production process should be undertaken to determine whether quality has changed.

Another pattern to watch for in control charts is a gradual shift, or trend, over time. For example, as tools wear out, the dimensions of machined parts will gradually deviate from their designed levels. Gradual changes in temperature or humidity, general equipment deterioration, dirt buildup, or operator fatigue may also result in a trend pattern in control charts. Six or seven points in a row that indicate either an increasing or decreasing trend should be cause for concern, even if the data points are all within the control limits. When such a pattern occurs, the process should be reviewed for possible changes or shifts in quality. Corrective action to bring the process back into control may be necessary.

NOTES AND COMMENTS

1. Since the control limits for the $\bar{x}$ chart depend on the value of the average range, these limits will not have much meaning unless the process variability is in control. In practice, the R chart is usually constructed before the $\bar{x}$ chart; if the R chart indicates that the process variability is in control, then the $\bar{x}$ chart is constructed.

2. An *np* chart is used to monitor a process in terms of the number of defects. The Motorola Six Sigma (6σ) Quality Level sets a goal of producing no more than 3.4 defects per million operations (*American Production and Inventory Control Society,* July 1991); this goal implies $p = .0000034$.

EXERCISES

METHODS

1. A process that is in control has a mean of $\mu = 12.5$ and a standard deviation of $\sigma = .8$.
   a. Construct an $\bar{x}$ chart if samples of size four are to be used.
   b. Repeat (a) for samples of size eight and 16.
   c. What happens to the limits of the control chart as the sample size is increased? Discuss why this is reasonable.

2. Twenty-five samples, each of size five, were selected from a process that was in control. The sum of all the data collected was 677.5 pounds.
   a. What is an estimate of the process mean (in terms of pounds per unit) when the process is in control?
   b. Develop the control chart for this process if samples of size five will be used. Assume that the process standard deviation is .5 when the process is in control, and that the mean of the process is the estimate developed in (a).

3. Twenty-five samples of 100 items each were inspected when a process was considered to be operating satisfactorily. In the 25 samples, a total of 135 items were found to be defective.
   a. What is an estimate of the proportion defective when the process is in control?
   b. What is the standard error of the proportion if samples of size 100 will be used for statistical process control?
   c. Compute the upper and lower control limits for the control chart.

4. A process sampled 20 times with a sample of size eight resulted in $\bar{\bar{x}} = 28.5$ and $\bar{R} = 1.6$. Compute the upper and lower control limits for the $\bar{x}$ and R charts for this process.

APPLICATIONS

5. Temperature is used to measure the output of a production process. When the process is in control, the mean of the process is $\mu = 128.5$ and the standard deviation is $\sigma = .4$.
   a. Construct an $\bar{x}$ chart if samples of size six are to be used.
   b. Is the process in control for a sample providing the following data?

   $$128.8 \quad 128.2 \quad 129.1 \quad 128.7 \quad 128.4 \quad 129.2$$

   c. Is the process in control for a sample providing the following data?

   $$129.3 \quad 128.7 \quad 128.6 \quad 129.2 \quad 129.5 \quad 129.0$$

6. A quality control process monitors the weight per carton of laundry detergent. Control limits are set at UCL=20.12 ounces and LCL=19.90 ounces. Samples of size five are used for the sampling and inspection process. What are the process mean and process standard deviation for the manufacturing operation?

7. The Goodman Tire and Rubber Company periodically tests its tires for tread wear under simulated road conditions. To study and control the manufacturing process, 20 samples, each containing three radial tires, were chosen from different shifts over several days of operation. The results are reported in Table 20.3. Assuming that these data were collected when the manufacturing process was believed to be operating in control, develop the R and $\bar{x}$ charts.

8. Over several weeks of normal, or in-control, operation, 20 samples of 150 packages each of synthetic-gut tennis strings were tested for breaking strength. A total of 141 packages of the 3000 tested failed to conform to the manufacturer's specifications.
   a. What is an estimate of the process proportion defective when the system is in control?
   b. Compute the upper and lower control limits for a p chart.
   c. With the results of part (b), what conclusion should be made about the process if tests on a new sample of 150 packages find 12 defective? Do there appear to be assignable causes in this situation?

TABLE 20.3 Exercise 7

Sample	Tread Wear*		
1	31	42	28
2	26	18	35
3	25	30	34
4	17	25	21
5	38	29	35
6	41	42	36
7	21	17	29
8	32	26	28
9	41	34	33
10	29	17	30
11	26	31	40
12	23	19	25
13	17	24	32
14	43	35	17
15	18	25	29
16	30	42	31
17	28	36	32
18	40	29	31
19	18	29	28
20	22	34	26

*Hundredths of an inch

d. Compute the upper and lower control limits for an *np* chart.

e. Answer part (c) using the results of part (d).

f. Which control chart would be preferred in this situation? Explain.

9. An automotive industry supplier produces pistons for several models of automobiles. Twenty samples, each consisting of 200 pistons, were selected when the process was known to be operating correctly. The numbers of defective pistons found in the samples follow.

8	10	6	4	5	7	8	12	8	15
14	10	10	7	5	8	6	10	4	8

a. What is an estimate of the proportion defective for the piston-manufacturing process when it is in control?

b. Construct a *p* chart for the manufacturing process, assuming each sample has 200 pistons.

c. With the results of part (b), what conclusion should be made if a sample of 200 has 20 defective pistons?

d. Compute the upper and lower control limits for an *np* chart.

e. Answer part (c) using the results of part (d).

20.2   ACCEPTANCE SAMPLING

In acceptance sampling, the items of interest can be incoming shipments of raw materials or purchased parts as well as finished goods from final assembly. Suppose we want to decide whether to accept or reject a group of items on the basis of specified quality characteristics. In quality-control terminology, the group of items is a *lot,* and *acceptance sampling* is a statistical method that enables us to base the accept-reject decision on the inspection of a sample of items from the lot.

The general steps of acceptance sampling are shown in Figure 20.9. After a lot is received, a sample of items is selected for inspection. The results of the inspection are compared to specified quality characteristics. If the quality characteristics are satisfied, the lot is accepted and sent to production or shipped to customers. If the lot is rejected, managers must decide on its disposition. In some cases, the decision may be to keep the lot and remove the unacceptable or nonconforming items during production. In other cases, the lot may be returned to the supplier at the supplier's expense; the extra work and cost placed on the supplier can motivate the supplier to provide high-quality lots. Finally, if the rejected lot consists of finished goods, the goods must be scrapped or reworked to meet acceptable quality standards.

The statistical procedure of acceptance sampling is based on the hypothesis-testing methodology presented in Chapter 9. The null and alternative hypotheses are stated as follows.

$$H_0: \text{Good-quality lot}$$

$$H_a: \text{Poor-quality lot}$$

Table 20.4, like the one in Chapter 9, shows the results of the hypothesis-testing procedure. Note that correct decisions correspond to accepting a good-quality lot and rejecting a poor-quality lot. However, as with other hypothesis-testing procedures, we need to be aware of the possibilities of making a Type I error (rejecting a good-quality lot) or a Type II error (accepting a poor-quality lot).

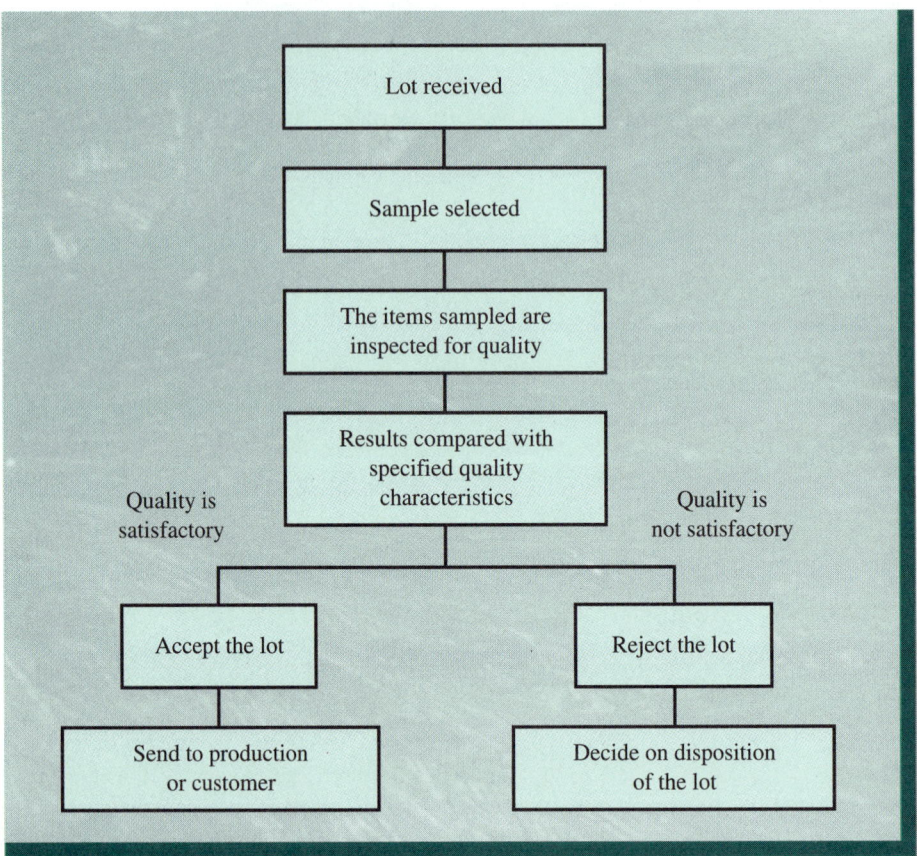

FIGURE 20.9   Acceptance Sampling Procedure

TABLE 20.4   The Outcomes of Acceptance Sampling

		State of the Lot	
		H_0 True Good-Quality Lot	H_0 False Poor-Quality Lot
Decision	Accept the Lot	Correct decision	Type II error (accepting a poor-quality lot)
	Reject the Lot	Type I error (rejecting a good-quality lot)	Correct decision

Since the probability of a Type I error creates a risk for the producer of the lot, it is known as the *producer's risk*. For example, a producer's risk of .05 indicates that there is a 5% chance that a good-quality lot will be erroneously rejected. Since the probability of a Type II error creates a risk for the consumer of the lot, it is known as the *consumer's risk*. For example, a consumer's risk of .10 means that there is a 10% chance that a poor-quality lot will be erroneously accepted and thus used in production or shipped to the customer. Specific values for the producer's risk and the consumer's risk can be controlled by the person designing the acceptance sampling procedure. To illustrate how this is done, let us consider the problem faced by KALI, Inc.

KALI, INC.: AN EXAMPLE OF ACCEPTANCE SAMPLING

KALI, Inc., manufactures home appliances that are marketed under a variety of trade names. However, KALI does not manufacture every component used in its products. Several components are purchased directly from suppliers. For example, one of the components that KALI purchases for use in home air conditioners is an overload protector, a device that turns off the compressor if it overheats. Since the compressor can be seriously damaged if the overload protector does not function properly, KALI is very concerned about the quality of the overload protectors. One way to ensure quality would be to test every component received; that approach is known as 100% inspection. However, to determine proper functioning of an overload protector, the device must be subjected to time-consuming and expensive tests, and KALI cannot justify testing every overload protector it receives.

Instead, KALI uses an acceptance sampling plan to monitor the quality of the overload protectors. The acceptance sampling plan requires that KALI's quality-control inspectors select and test a sample of overload protectors from each shipment. If very few defective units are found in the sample, the lot is probably of good quality and should be accepted. However, if a large number of defective units are found in the sample, the lot is probably of poor quality and should be rejected.

An *acceptance sampling plan* consists of a sample size n and an acceptance criterion c. The *acceptance criterion* is the maximum number of defective items that can be found in the sample and still indicate an acceptable lot. For example, for the KALI problem let us assume that a sample of 15 items will be selected from each incoming shipment or lot. Furthermore, assume that the manager of quality control states that the lot can be accepted only if no defective items are found. In this case, the acceptance sampling plan established by the quality-control manager is $n = 15$ and $c = 0$.

This acceptance sampling plan is easy for the quality-control inspector to implement. The inspector simply selects a sample of 15 items, performs the tests, and reaches a conclusion based on the following decision rule.

- *Accept the lot* if zero defective items are found.
- *Reject the lot* if one or more defective items are found.

Before implementing this acceptance sampling plan, the quality-control manager wants to evaluate the risks or errors possible under the plan. The plan will be implemented only if both the producer's risk (Type I error) and the consumer's risk (Type II error) are controlled at reasonable levels.

COMPUTING THE PROBABILITY OF ACCEPTING A LOT

The key to analyzing both the producer's risk and the consumer's risk is a "What-if?" type of analysis. That is, we will assume that a lot has some known percentage of defective items and compute the probability of accepting the lot for a given sampling plan. By varying the assumed percentage of defective items, we can examine the effect of the sampling plan on both types of risks.

Let us begin by assuming that a large shipment of overload protectors has been received and that 5% of the overload protectors in the shipment are defective. For a shipment or lot with 5% of the items defective, what is the probability that the $n = 15$, $c = 0$ sampling plan will lead us to accept the lot? Since each overload protector tested will be either defective or nondefective and since the lot size is large, the number of defective items in a sample of 15 has a *binomial probability distribution*. The binomial probability function, which was presented in Chapter 5, follows.

BINOMIAL PROBABILITY FUNCTION FOR ACCEPTANCE SAMPLING

$$f(x) = \frac{n!}{x!(n-x)!} p^x (1-p)^{(n-x)} \qquad (20.21)$$

where

n = the sample size

p = the proportion of defective items in the lot

x = the number of defective items in the sample

$f(x)$ = the probability of x defective items in the sample

For the KALI acceptance sampling plan, $n = 15$; thus, for a lot with 5% defective ($p = .05$), we have

$$f(x) = \frac{15!}{x!(15-x)!} (.05)^x (1-.05)^{(15-x)} \qquad (20.22)$$

Using (20.22), $f(0)$ will provide the probability that zero overload protectors will be defective and the lot will be accepted. In using (20.22), recall that $0! = 1$. Thus, the probability computation for $f(0)$ is

$$f(0) = \frac{15!}{0!(15-0)!} (.05)^0 (1-.05)^{(15-0)}$$

$$= \frac{15!}{0!(15)!} (.05)^0 (.95)^{15} = (.95)^{15} = .4633$$

We now know that the $n = 15$, $c = 0$ sampling plan has a .4633 probability of accepting a lot with 5% defective items. Hence, there must be a corresponding $1 - .4633 = .5367$ probability of rejecting a lot with 5% defective items.

In Table 20.5 we show the probability that the $n = 15$, $c = 0$ sampling plan will lead to the acceptance of lots with 1%, 2%, 3%, . . . defective items. The probabilities in the table were computed by using $p = .01$, $p = .02$, $p = .03$, . . . in the binomial probability function (20.1).

Tables of binomial probabilities (see Table 5, Appendix B) can help reduce the computational effort in determining the probabilities of accepting lots. Selected binomial probabilities for $n = 15$ and $n = 20$ are listed in Table 20.6, and it can be used to verify that if the lot contains 10% defective items, there would be a .2059 probability that the $n = 15$, $c = 0$ sampling plan would indicate an acceptable lot.

With the data in Table 20.5, a graph of the probability of accepting the lot versus the percent defective in the lot can be drawn as shown in Figure 20.10. This graph, or curve, is called the *operating characteristic* (OC) *curve* for the $n = 15$, $c = 0$ acceptance sampling plan.

Perhaps we should consider other sampling plans, ones with different sample sizes n and/or different acceptance criteria c. First consider the case in which the sample size remains $n = 15$ but the acceptance criterion increases from $c = 0$ to $c = 1$. That is, we will now accept the lot if zero or one defective component is found in the sample. For a lot with 5% defective items ($p = .05$), the binomial probability function in (20.21) can be used to compute $f(0)$ and $f(1)$. Summing these two probabilities provides the probability that the $n = 15$, $c = 1$ sampling plan will accept the lot. Alternatively, using

TABLE 20.5 Probability of Accepting the Lot for the KALI Problem with $n = 15$ and $c = 0$

Percent Defective in the Lot	Probability of Accepting the Lot
1	.8601
2	.7386
3	.6333
4	.5421
5	.4633
10	.2059
15	.0874
20	.0352
25	.0134

TABLE 20.6 Selected Binomial Probabilities for Samples of Sizes 15 and 20

n	x	.05	.10	.15	.20	.25	.30	.35	.40	.45	.50
15	0	.4633	.2059	.0874	.0352	.0134	.0047	.0016	.0005	.0001	.0000
	1	.3658	.3432	.2312	.1319	.0668	.0305	.0126	.0047	.0016	.0005
	2	.1348	.2669	.2856	.2309	.1559	.0916	.0476	.0219	.0090	.0032
	3	.0307	.1285	.2184	.2501	.2252	.1700	.1110	.0634	.0318	.0139
	4	.0049	.0428	.1156	.1876	.2252	.2186	.1792	.1268	.0780	.0417
	5	.0006	.0105	.0449	.1032	.1651	.2061	.2123	.1859	.1404	.0916
	6	.0000	.0019	.0132	.0430	.0917	.1472	.1906	.2066	.1914	.1527
	7	.0000	.0003	.0030	.0138	.0393	.0811	.1319	.1771	.2013	.1964
	8	.0000	.0000	.0005	.0035	.0131	.0348	.0710	.1181	.1647	.1964
	9	.0000	.0000	.0001	.0007	.0034	.0116	.0298	.0612	.1048	.1527
	10	.0000	.0000	.0000	.0001	.0007	.0030	.0096	.0245	.0515	.0916
	11	.0000	.0000	.0000	.0000	.0001	.0006	.0024	.0074	.0191	.0417
	12	.0000	.0000	.0000	.0000	.0000	.0001	.0004	.0016	.0052	.0139
	13	.0000	.0000	.0000	.0000	.0000	.0000	.0001	.0003	.0010	.0032
	14	.0000	.0000	.0000	.0000	.0000	.0000	.0000	.0000	.0001	.0005
	15	.0000	.0000	.0000	.0000	.0000	.0000	.0000	.0000	.0000	.0000
20	0	.3585	.1216	.0388	.0115	.0032	.0008	.0002	.0000	.0000	.0000
	1	.3774	.2702	.1368	.0576	.0211	.0068	.0020	.0005	.0001	.0000
	2	.1887	.2852	.2293	.1369	.0669	.0278	.0100	.0031	.0008	.0002
	3	.0596	.1901	.2428	.2054	.1339	.0716	.0323	.0123	.0040	.0011
	4	.0133	.0898	.1821	.2182	.1897	.1304	.0738	.0350	.0139	.0046
	5	.0022	.0319	.1028	.1746	.2023	.1789	.1272	.0746	.0365	.0148
	6	.0003	.0089	.0454	.1091	.1686	.1916	.1712	.1244	.0746	.0370
	7	.0000	.0020	.0160	.0545	.1124	.1643	.1844	.1659	.1221	.0739
	8	.0000	.0004	.0046	.0222	.0609	.1144	.1614	.1797	.1623	.1201
	9	.0000	.0001	.0011	.0074	.0271	.0654	.1158	.1597	.1771	.1602
	10	.0000	.0000	.0002	.0020	.0099	.0308	.0686	.1171	.1593	.1762
	11	.0000	.0000	.0000	.0005	.0030	.0120	.0336	.0710	.1185	.1602
	12	.0000	.0000	.0000	.0001	.0008	.0039	.0136	.0355	.0727	.1201
	13	.0000	.0000	.0000	.0000	.0002	.0010	.0045	.0146	.0366	.0739
	14	.0000	.0000	.0000	.0000	.0000	.0002	.0012	.0049	.0150	.0370
	15	.0000	.0000	.0000	.0000	.0000	.0000	.0003	.0013	.0049	.0148
	16	.0000	.0000	.0000	.0000	.0000	.0000	.0000	.0003	.0013	.0046
	17	.0000	.0000	.0000	.0000	.0000	.0000	.0000	.0000	.0002	.0011
	18	.0000	.0000	.0000	.0000	.0000	.0000	.0000	.0000	.0000	.0002
	19	.0000	.0000	.0000	.0000	.0000	.0000	.0000	.0000	.0000	.0000
	20	.0000	.0000	.0000	.0000	.0000	.0000	.0000	.0000	.0000	.0000

Table 20.6, we find that with $n = 15$ and $p = .05$, $f(0) = .4633$ and $f(1) = .3658$. Thus, there is a $.4633 + .3658 = .8291$ probability that the $n = 15$, $c = 1$ plan will lead to the acceptance of a lot with 5% defective items.

Figure 20.11 shows the operating characteristic curves for four alternative acceptance sampling plans for the KALI problem. Samples of size 15 and 20 are considered. Note that regardless of the proportion defective in the lot, the $n = 15$, $c = 1$ sampling plan

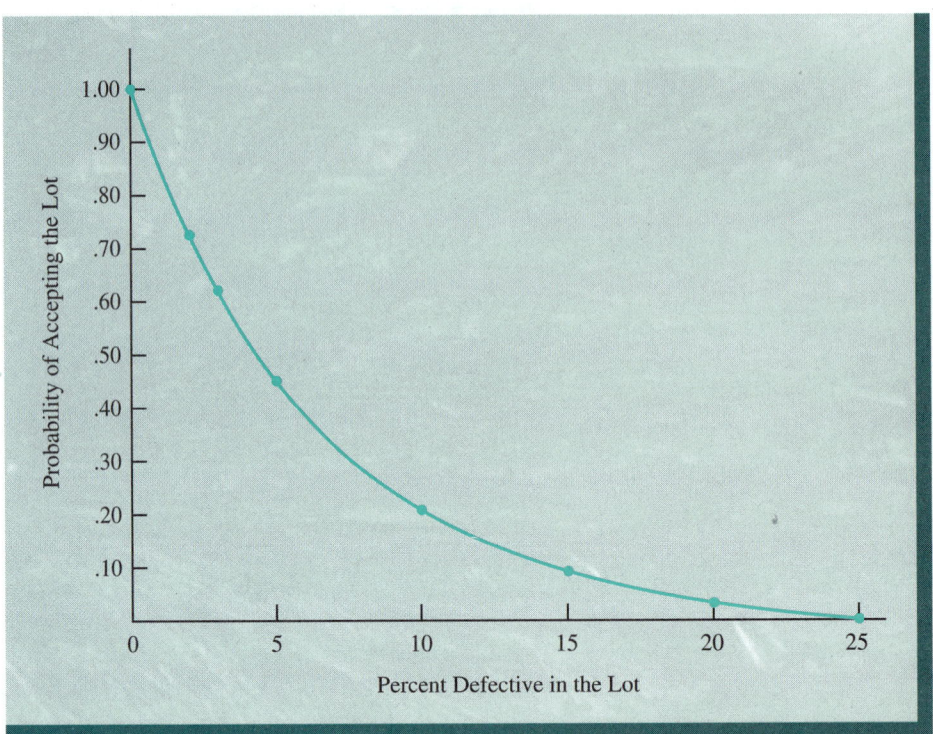

FIGURE 20.10   Operating Characteristic Curve for the $n = 15$, $c = 0$ Acceptance Sampling Plan

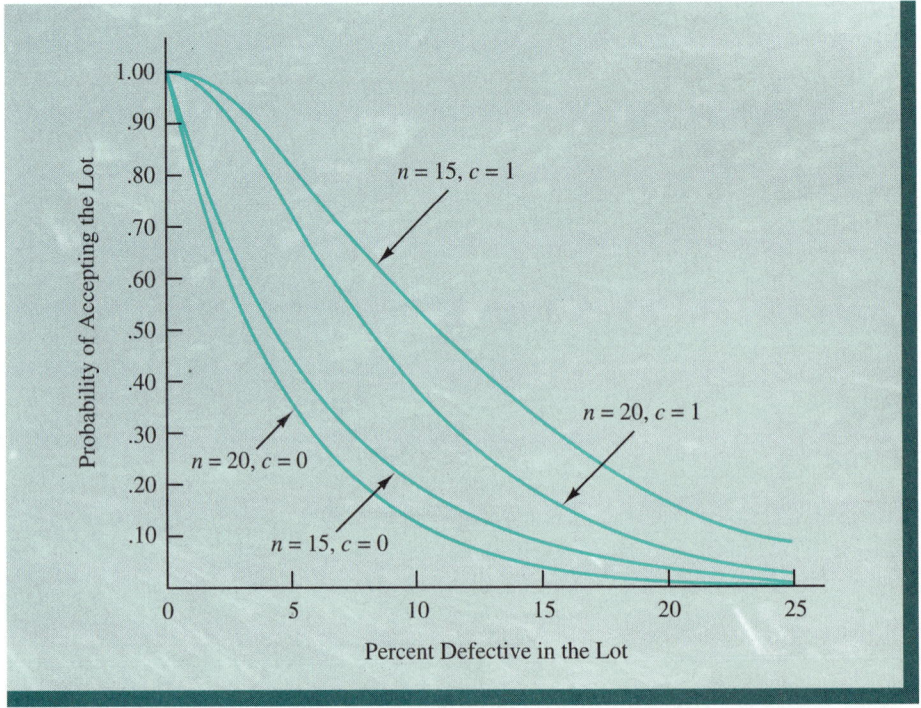

FIGURE 20.11   Operating Characteristic Curves for Four Acceptance Sampling Plans

provides the highest probabilities of accepting the lot. The $n = 20$, $c = 0$ sampling plan provides the lowest probabilities of accepting the lot; however, that plan also provides the highest probabilities of rejecting the lot.

SELECTING AN ACCEPTANCE SAMPLING PLAN

Now that we know how to use the binomial probability distribution to compute the probability of accepting a lot with a given proportion defective, we are ready to select the values of n and c that determine the desired acceptance sampling plan for the application being studied. To do this, managers must specify two values for the fraction defective in the lot. One value, denoted p_0, will be used to control for the producer's risk, and the other value, denoted p_1, will be used to control for the consumer's risk.

In showing how this can be done, we will use the following notation.

α = the producer's risk; the probability that a lot with p_0 defective will be rejected

β = the consumer's risk; the probability that a lot with p_1 defective will be accepted

Suppose that for the KALI problem, the managers specify that $p_0 = .03$ and $p_1 = .15$. From the OC curve for $n = 15$, $c = 0$ in Figure 20.12, we see that $p_0 = .03$ provides a producer's risk of approximately $1 - .63 = .37$, and $p_1 = .15$ provides a consumer's risk of approximately .09. Thus, if the managers are willing to tolerate both a .37 probability of rejecting a lot with 3% defective items (producer's risk) and a .09 probability of accepting a lot with 15% defective items (consumer's risk), the $n = 15$, $c = 0$ acceptance sampling plan would be acceptable.

Suppose, however, that the managers request a producer's risk of $\alpha = .10$ and a consumer's risk of $\beta = .20$. We see that now the $n = 15$, $c = 0$ sampling plan has a

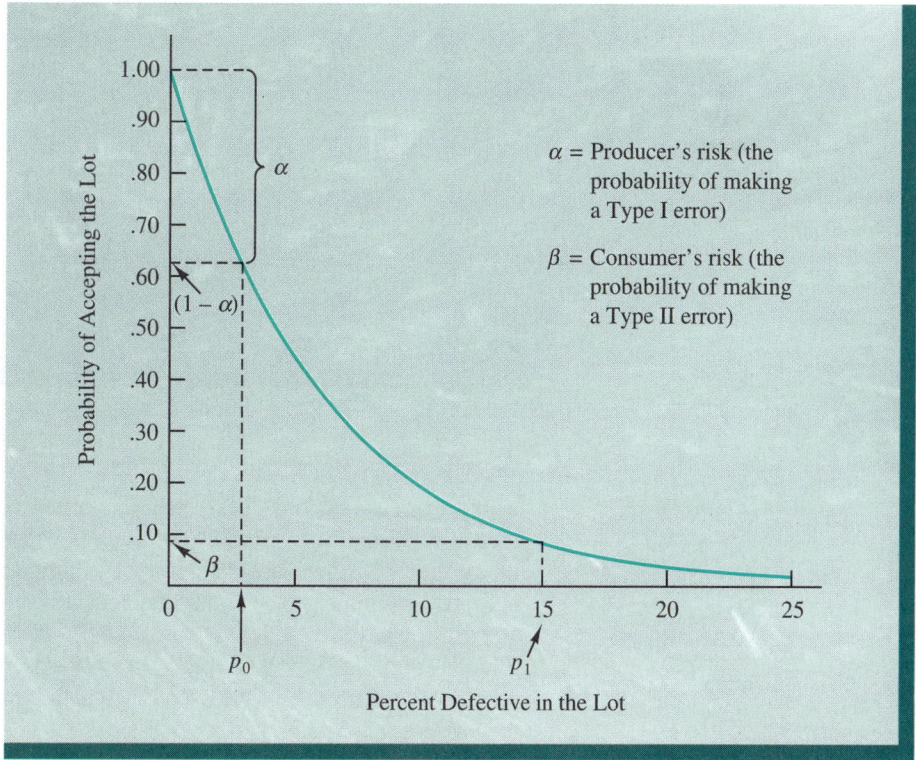

FIGURE 20.12 Operating Characteristic Curve for $n = 15$, $c = 0$ with $p_0 = .03$ and $p_1 = .15$

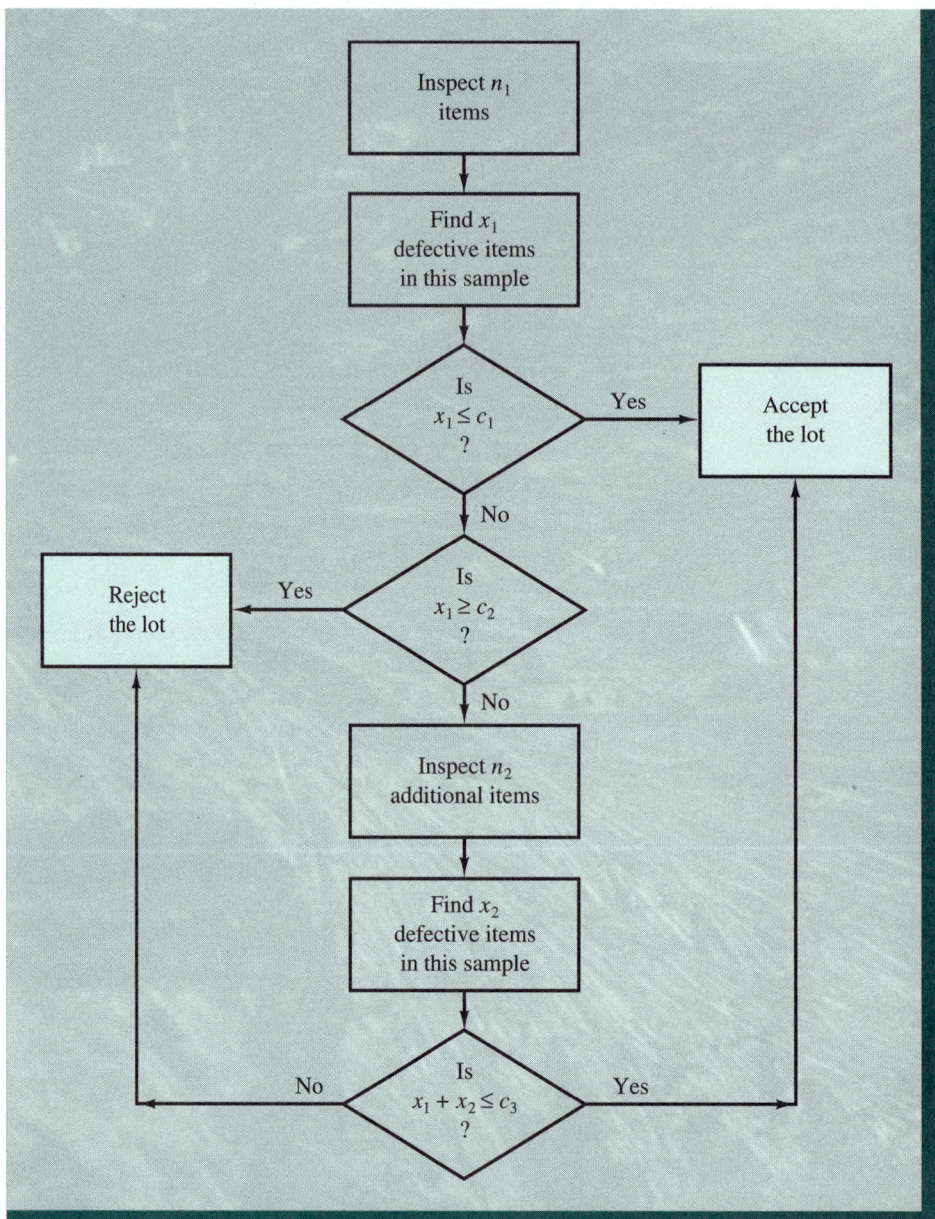

FIGURE 20.13   A Two-Stage Acceptance Sampling Plan

better-than-desired consumer's risk but an unacceptably large producer's risk. The fact that $\alpha = .37$ indicates that 37% of the lots will be erroneously rejected when only 3% of the items in them are defective. The producer's risk is too high, and a different acceptance sampling plan should be considered.

Using $p_0 = .03$, $\alpha = .10$, $p_1 = .15$, and $\beta = .20$ in Figure 20.11 shows that the acceptance sampling plan with $n = 20$ and $c = 1$ comes closest to meeting both the producer's and the consumer's risk requirements. Exercise 13 at the end of this section will ask you to compute the producer's risk and the consumer's risk for the $n = 20$, $c = 1$ sampling plan.

As shown in this section, several computations and several operating characteristic curves may need to be considered to determine the sampling plan with the desired producer's and consumer's risk. Fortunately, tables of sampling plans are published. For example, the American Military Standard Table, MIL-STD-105D, provides information helpful in designing acceptance sampling plans. More advanced texts on quality control, such as those listed in the bibliography, describe the use of such tables. The advanced texts also discuss the role of sampling costs in determining the optimal sampling plan.

MULTIPLE SAMPLING PLANS

The acceptance sampling procedure that we have presented for the KALI problem is a *single-sample* plan. It is called a single-sample plan because only one sample or sampling stage is used. After the number of defective components in the sample is determined, a decision must be made to accept or reject the lot. An alternative to the single-sample plan is a multiple sampling plan, in which two or more stages of sampling are used. At each stage a decision is made among three possibilities: stop sampling and accept the lot, stop sampling and reject the lot, or continue sampling. Although more complex, multiple sampling plans often result in a smaller total sample size than single-sample plans with the same α and β probabilities.

The logic of a two-stage, or double-sample, plan is shown in Figure 20.13. Initially a sample of n_1 items is selected. If the number of defective components x_1 is less than or equal to c_1, accept the lot. If x_1 is greater than or equal to c_2, reject the lot. If x_1 is between c_1 and c_2 $(c_1 < x_1 < c_2)$, select a second sample of n_2 items. Determine the combined, or total, number of defective components from the first sample (x_1) and the second sample (x_2). If $x_1 + x_2 \leq c_3$, accept the lot; otherwise reject the lot. The development of the double-sample plan is more difficult because the sample sizes n_1 and n_2 and the acceptance numbers c_1, c_2, and c_3 must meet both the producer's and consumer's risks desired.

NOTES AND COMMENTS

1. The use of the binomial probability distribution for acceptance sampling is based on the assumption of large lots. If the lot size is small, the hypergeometric probability distribution is the appropriate distribution. Experts in the field of quality control indicate that the Poisson distribution provides a good approximation for acceptance sampling when the sample size is at least 16, the lot size is at least 10 times the sample size, and p is less than .1.* For larger sample sizes, the normal approximation to the binomial probability distribution can be used.

2. In the MIL-ST-105D sampling tables, p_0 is called the acceptable quality level (AQL). In some sampling tables, p_1 is called the lot tolerance percent defective (LTPD) or the rejectable quality level (RQL). Many of the published sampling plans also use quality indexes such as the indifference quality level (IQL) and the average outgoing quality limit (AOQL). The more advanced texts listed in the bibliography provide a complete discussion of these other indexes.

3. In this section we provided an introduction to *attributes sampling plans.* In these plans each item sampled is classified as nondefective or defective. In *variables sampling plans,* a sample is taken and a measurement of the quality characteristic is taken. For example, for gold jewelry a measurement of quality may be the amount of gold it contains. A simple statistic such as the average amount of gold in the sample jewelry is computed and compared with an allowable value to determine whether to accept or reject the lot.

*J. M. Juran and Frank M. Gryna, Jr., *Quality Planning and Analysis,* McGraw-Hill, New York, 1980, p. 412.

EXERCISES

METHODS

Self-Test

10. For an acceptance sampling plan with $n = 25$ and $c = 0$, find the probability of accepting a lot that has a defect rate of 2%. What is the probability of accepting the lot if the defect rate is 6%?

11. Consider an acceptance sampling plan with $n = 20$ and $c = 0$. Compute the producer's risk for each of the following cases.
   a. The lot has a defect rate of 2%.
   b. The lot has a defect rate of 6%.

12. Repeat Exercise 11 for the acceptance sampling plan with $n = 20$ and $c = 1$. What happens to the producer's risk as the acceptance number c is increased? Explain.

APPLICATIONS

13. Refer to the KALI problem presented in this section. The quality-control manager requested a producer's risk of .10 when p_0 was .03 and a consumer's risk of .20 when p_1 was .15. Consider the acceptance sampling plan based on a sample size of 20 and an acceptance number of 1. Answer the following questions.
   a. What is the producer's risk for the $n = 20$, $c = 1$ sampling plan?
   b. What is the consumer's risk for the $n = 20$, $c = 1$ sampling plan?
   c. Does the $n = 20$, $c = 1$ sampling plan satisfy the risks requested by the quality-control manager? Discuss.

14. To inspect incoming shipments of raw materials, a manufacturer is considering samples of sizes 10, 15, and 20. Use the binomial probabilities from Table 5 of Appendix B to select a sampling plan that provides a producer's risk of $\alpha = .03$ when p_0 is .05 and a consumer's risk of $\beta = .12$ when p_1 is .30.

15. A domestic manufacturer of watches purchases quartz crystals from a Swiss firm. The crystals are shipped in lots of 1000. The acceptance sampling procedure uses 20 randomly selected crystals.
   a. Construct operating characteristic curves for acceptance numbers of 0, 1, and 2.
   b. If p_0 is .01 and $p_1 = .08$, what are the producer's and consumer's risks for each sampling plan in (a)?

SUMMARY

In this chapter we discussed how statistical methods can be used to assist in the control of quality. We first presented the $\bar{x}$, R, p and np control charts as graphical aids in monitoring process quality. Control limits are established for each chart; samples are selected periodically and the data points plotted on the control chart. Data points outside the control limits indicate that the process is out of control and that corrective action should be taken. Patterns of data points within the control limits can also indicate potential quality-control problems and suggest that corrective action may be warranted.

We also considered the technique known as acceptance sampling. With this procedure, a sample is selected and inspected. The number of defective items in the sample provides the basis for accepting or rejecting the lot. The sample size and the acceptance criterion can be adjusted to control both the producer's risk (Type I error) and the consumer's risk (Type II error).

GLOSSARY

Quality control   A series of inspections and measurements that determine whether quality standards are being met.

Common causes   Normal or natural variations in process outputs that are due purely to chance. No corrective action is necessary when output variations are due to common causes.

Assignable causes   Variations in process outputs that are due to factors such as machine tools wearing out, incorrect machine settings, poor-quality raw materials, operator error, and so on. Corrective action should be taken when assignable causes of output variation are detected.

Control chart   A graphical tool used to help determine whether a process is in control or out of control.

$\bar{x}$ chart   A control chart used when the output of a process is measured in terms of the mean value of a variable such as a length, weight, temperature, and so on.

R chart   A control chart used when the output of a process is measured in terms of the range of a variable.

p chart   A control chart used when the output of a process is measured in terms of the proportion defective.

np chart   A control chart used to monitor the output of a process in terms of the number of defective items.

Lot   A group of items such as incoming shipments of raw materials or purchased parts as well as finished goods from final assembly.

Acceptance sampling   A statistical procedure in which the number of defective items found in a sample is used to determine whether a lot should be accepted or rejected.

Producer's risk   The risk of rejecting a good-quality lot. This is the Type I error.

Consumer's risk   The risk of accepting a poor-quality lot. This is the Type II error.

Acceptance criterion   The maximum number of defective items that can be found in the sample and still allow acceptance of the lot.

Operating characteristic curve   A graph showing the probability of accepting the lot as a function of the percentage defective in the lot. This curve can be used to help determine whether a particular acceptance sampling plan meets both the producer's and the consumer's risk requirements.

Multiple sampling plan   A form of acceptance sampling in which more than one sample or stage is used. On the basis of the number of defective items found in a sample, a decision will be made to accept the lot, reject the lot, or continue sampling.

KEY FORMULAS

Standard Error of the Mean

$$\sigma_{\bar{x}} = \frac{\sigma}{\sqrt{n}} \qquad\qquad \text{(20.1)}$$

Control Limits for an $\bar{x}$ Chart: Process Mean and Standard Deviation Known

$$\text{UCL} = \mu + 3\sigma_{\bar{x}} \tag{20.2}$$

$$\text{LCL} = \mu - 3\sigma_{\bar{x}} \tag{20.3}$$

Overall Sample Mean

$$\bar{\bar{x}} = \frac{\bar{x}_1 + \bar{x}_2 + \cdots + \bar{x}_k}{k} \tag{20.4}$$

Average Range

$$\bar{R} = \frac{R_1 + R_2 + \cdots + R_k}{k} \tag{20.5}$$

Control Limits for an $\bar{x}$ Chart: Process Mean and Standard Deviation Unknown

$$\bar{\bar{x}} \pm A_2\bar{R} \tag{20.8}$$

Control Limits for an R Chart

$$\text{UCL} = \bar{R}D_4 \tag{20.14}$$
$$\text{LCL} = \bar{R}D_3 \tag{20.15}$$

Standard Error of the Proportion

$$\sigma_{\bar{p}} = \sqrt{\frac{p(1 - p)}{n}} \tag{20.16}$$

Control Limits for a p Chart

$$\text{UCL} = p + 3\sigma_{\bar{p}} \tag{20.17}$$
$$\text{LCL} = p - 3\sigma_{\bar{p}} \tag{20.18}$$

Control Limits for an np Chart

$$\text{UCL} = np + 3\sqrt{np\,(1 - p)} \tag{20.19}$$

$$\text{LCL} = np - 3\sqrt{np\,(1 - p)} \tag{20.20}$$

Binomial Probability Function for Acceptance Sampling

$$f(x) = \frac{n!}{x!(n - x)!}p^x(1 - p)^{(n - x)} \tag{20.21}$$

TABLE 20.7   Exercise 16

95.72	95.24	95.18
95.44	95.46	95.32
95.40	95.44	95.08
95.50	95.80	95.22
95.56	95.22	95.04
95.72	94.82	95.46
95.60	95.78	

SUPPLEMENTARY EXERCISES

16. Samples of size five provided the 20 sample means listed in Table 20.7 for a production process that is believed to be in control.
   a. Based on these data, what is an estimate of the mean when the process is in control?
   b. Assuming that the process standard deviation is $\sigma = .50$, develop a control chart for this production process. Assume that the mean of the process is the estimate developed in (a).
   c. Do any of the 20 sample means indicate that the process was out of control?

17. Product filling weights are normally distributed with a mean of 350 grams and a standard deviation of 15 grams.
    a. Develop the control limits for samples of size 10, 20, and 30.
    b. What happens to the control limits as the sample size is increased?
    c. What happens when a Type I error is made?
    d. What happens when a Type II error is made?
    e. What is the probability of a Type I error for samples of size 10, 20, and 30?
    f. What is the advantage of increasing the sample size for control-chart purposes? What error probability is reduced as the sample size is increased?

18. Twenty-five samples of size five resulted in $\bar{\bar{x}} = 5.42$ and $\bar{R} = 2.0$. Compute control limits for the $\bar{x}$ and R charts, and estimate the standard deviation of the process.

19. Construct $\bar{x}$ and R charts for the following sample data. Assume that a sample of size five was used.

Sample	$\bar{x}$	R	Sample	$\bar{x}$	R
1	95.72	1.0	11	95.80	.6
2	95.24	.9	12	95.22	.2
3	95.18	.8	13	95.56	1.3
4	95.44	.4	14	95.22	.5
5	95.46	.5	15	95.04	.8
6	95.32	1.1	16	95.72	1.1
7	95.40	.9	17	94.82	.6
8	95.44	.3	18	95.46	.5
9	95.08	.2	19	95.60	.4
10	95.50	.6	20	95.74	.6

20. Develop $\bar{x}$ and R charts for the following data.

Sample	Observations				
	1	2	3	4	5
1	3.05	3.08	3.07	3.11	3.11
2	3.13	3.07	3.05	3.10	3.10
3	3.06	3.04	3.12	3.11	3.10
4	3.09	3.08	3.09	3.09	3.07
5	3.10	3.06	3.06	3.07	3.08
6	3.08	3.10	3.13	3.03	3.06
7	3.06	3.06	3.08	3.10	3.08
8	3.11	3.08	3.07	3.07	3.07
9	3.09	3.09	3.08	3.07	3.09
10	3.06	3.11	3.07	3.09	3.07

21. Consider the following situations. For each, comment on whether there is reason for concern about the quality of the process.
    a. A p chart has LCL=0 and UCL=.068. When the process is in control, the proportion defective is .033. Plot the following seven sample results: .035, .062, .055, .049, .058, .066, and .055. Discuss.
    b. An $\bar{x}$ chart has LCL=22.2 and UCL=24.5. The mean is $\mu = 23.35$ when the process is in control. Plot the following seven sample results: 22.4, 22.6, 22.65, 23.2, 23.4, 23.85, and 24.1. Discuss.

22. Managers of 1200 different retail outlets make twice-a-month restocking orders from a central warehouse. Past experience has shown that 4% of the orders have one or more errors such as wrong item shipped, wrong quantity shipped, and item requested but not shipped. Random samples of 200 orders are selected monthly and checked for accuracy.
    a. Construct a control chart for this situation.
    b. Six months of data show the following numbers of orders with one or more errors: 10, 15, 6, 13, 8, and 17. Plot the data on the control chart. What does your plot indicate about the order process?

23. An $n = 10$, $c = 2$ acceptance sampling plan is being considered; assume that $p_0 = .05$ and $p_1 = .20$.
    a. Compute both the producer's and the consumer's risk for this acceptance sampling plan.
    b. Would either the producer, the consumer, or both be unhappy with the proposed sampling plan?
    c. What change in the sampling plan, if any, would you recommend?

24. An acceptance sampling plan with $n = 15$ and $c = 1$ has been designed with a producer's risk of .075.
    a. Was the value of p_0 .01, .02, .03, .04, or .05? What does this value mean?
    b. What is the consumer's risk associated with this plan if p_1 is .25?

25. A manufacturer produces lots of a canned food product. Let p denote the proportion of the lots that do not meet the product quality specifications. An $n = 25$, $c = 0$ acceptance sampling plan will be used.
    a. Compute points on the operating characteristic curve when $p = .01, .03, .10$, and .20.
    b. Plot the operating characteristic curve.
    c. What is the probability that the acceptance sampling plan will reject a lot that has .01 defective?

26. Sometimes an acceptance sampling plan will be based on a large sample. In this case, the normal approximation to the binomial probability distribution can be used to compute the producer's and the consumer's risk associated with the plan. Referring to Chapter 6, we know that the normal distribution used to approximate binomial probabilities has a mean of np and a standard deviation of $\sqrt{np(1-p)}$. Assume that an acceptance sampling plan is $n = 250$, $c = 10$.
    a. What is the producer's risk if p_0 is .02? As discussed in Chapter 6, a continuity correction factor should be used in this case. Thus, the probability of acceptance is based on the normal probability of the random variable being less than or equal to 10.5.
    b. What is the consumer's risk if p_1 is .08?
    c. What is an advantage of a large sample size for acceptance sampling? What is a disadvantage?

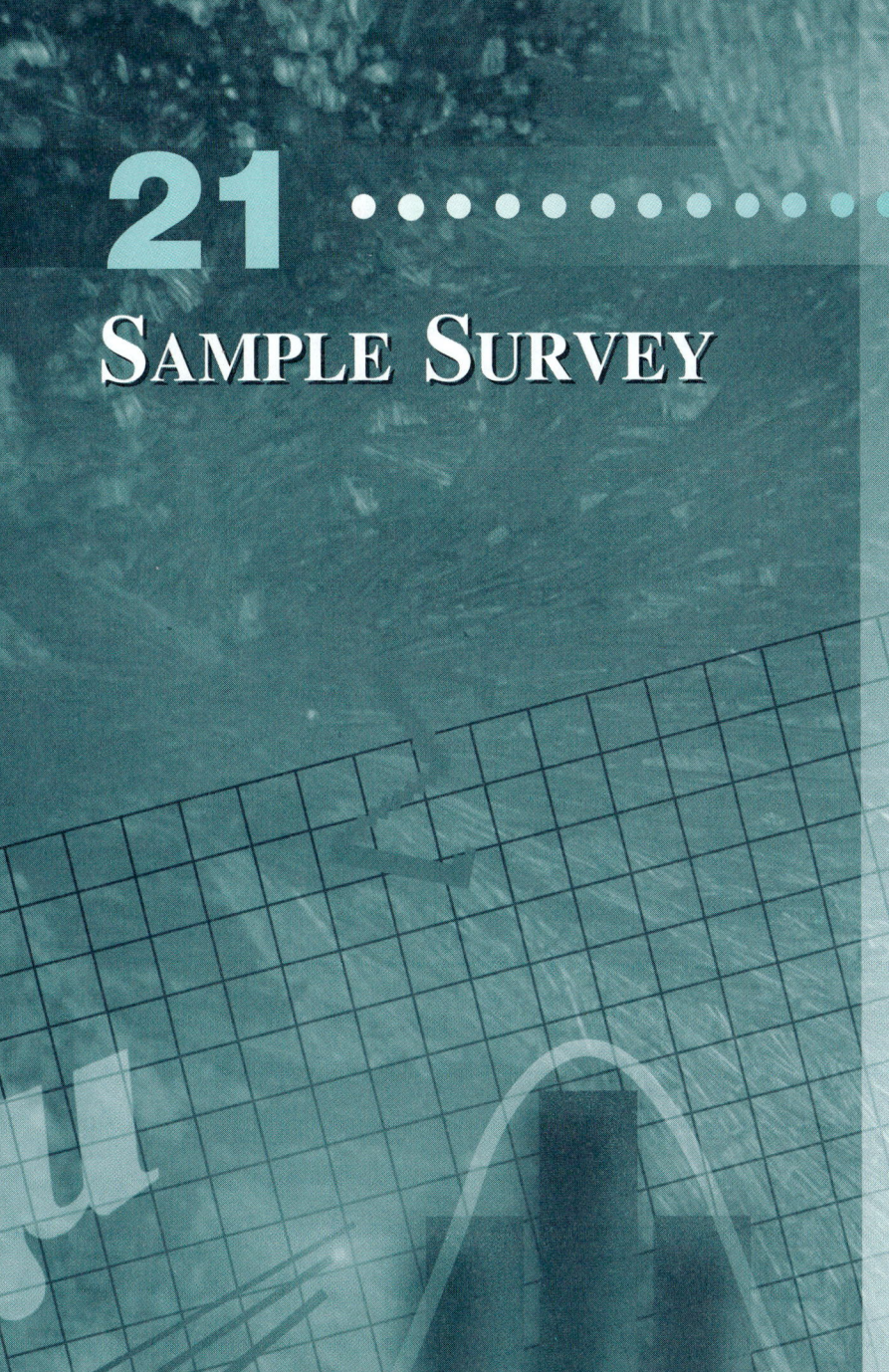

21

SAMPLE SURVEY

CONTENTS

STATISTICS IN PRACTICE ● ● ● ● ● ● ● ● ● ● ● ● ● ● ● ● ● ●

Cincinnati Gas & Electric Company*
Cincinnati, Ohio

The Cincinnati Gas & Electric Company (CG&E) is a public utility which provides gas and electric power to customers in the Greater Cincinnati area. To improve service to its customers, CG&E continually strives to stay up-to-date with its customers' needs. In 1991, CG&E undertook a sample survey, the Building Characteristics Survey, to learn about the energy requirements of commercial buildings in its service area.

A variety of information concerning commercial buildings was sought, such as the floor space, number of employees, energy end-use, age of the building, type of building materials, and energy conservation measures. During preparations for the survey, CG&E analysts found that there were approximately 27,000 commercial buildings in the CG&E service area. Based on available funds and the precision desired in the results, they recommended that a sample of 616 commercial buildings be surveyed.

The sample design chosen was stratified simple random sampling. Total electrical usage over the past year for each commercial building in the service area was available from company records, and because many of the building characteristics of interest (size, number of employees, etc.) were related to usage, it was the criteria used to divide the population of buildings into six strata.

The first stratum contained the commercial buildings for the 100 largest energy users; each building in this stratum was included in the sample. Although these build-

---

*The authors are indebted to Mr. Jim Riddle of Cincinnati Gas & Electric for providing this Statistics in Practice.

ings constituted only .2% of the population, they accounted for 14.4% of the total electrical usage. For the other strata, the number of buildings sampled was determined on the basis of obtaining the greatest precision possible per unit cost.

A questionnaire was carefully developed and pretested before the actual survey was conducted. Data were collected through personal interviews. Completed surveys totaled 526 out of the sample of 616 commercial buildings. This response rate of 85.4% was considered to be excellent. Currently, CG&E is using the survey results to improve the forecasts of energy demand and to improve service to its commercial customers.

In this chapter you will learn about the issues that statisticians consider in the design and execution of a sample survey such as the one conducted by CG&E. Sample surveys are often used to develop profiles of a company's customers; they are also used by the government and other agencies to learn about various segments of the population.

A Cincinnati Gas & Electric Company line worker fixes an electric high-voltage transmission tower.

21.1   TERMINOLOGY USED IN SAMPLE SURVEYS

In Chapter 1 we gave the following definitions of an element, a population, and a sample.

- An *element* is the entity on which data are collected.
- A *population* is the collection of all the elements of interest.
- A *sample* is a subset of the population.

To illustrate these concepts, consider the following situation. Dunning Microsystems, Inc. (DMI), a manufacturer of personal computers and peripherals, would like to collect data about the characteristics of individuals who have purchased a DMI personal computer. To obtain such data, a sample survey of DMI personal computer owners could be conducted. The *elements* in this sample survey would be individuals who have purchased a DMI personal computer. The *population* would be the collection of all people who have purchased a DMI personal computer, and the *sample* would be the subset of DMI personal computer owners who are surveyed.

In sample surveys it is necessary to distinguish between the *target population* and the *sampled population*. The target population is the population we want to make inferences about, while the sampled population is the population from which the sample is actually selected. It is important to understand that these two populations are not always the same. In the DMI example, the target population consists of all people who have purchased a DMI personal computer. The sampled population, however, might be all owners who have sent warranty registration cards back to DMI. Since every person who buys a DMI personal computer does not send in the warranty card, the sampled population would differ from the target population.

Conclusions drawn from a sample survey apply only to the sampled population. Whether these conclusions can be extended to the target population depends on the judgment of the analyst. The key issue is whether the correspondence between the sampled population and the target population on the elements of interest is close enough to allow this extension.

Before sampling, the population must be divided into *sampling units*. In some cases, the sampling units are simply the elements. In other cases, the sampling units are groups of the elements. For example, suppose we want to survey certified professional engineers who are involved in the design of heating and air conditioning systems for commercial buildings. If a list of all professional engineers involved in such work were available, the sampling units would be the professional engineers we want to survey. If such a list is not available, we must find an alternative approach. A business telephone directory might provide a list of all engineering firms involved in the design of heating and air conditioning systems. Given this list, we could select a sample of the engineering firms to survey; then, for each firm surveyed, we might interview all the professional engineers. In this case, the engineering firms would be the sampling units and the engineers interviewed would be the elements.

A list of the sampling units for a particular study is called a *frame*. In the sample survey of professional engineers, the frame is defined as all engineering firms listed in the business telephone directory; the frame is not a list of all professional engineers because no such list is available. The choice of a particular frame and hence the definition of the sampling units is often determined by the availability and reliability of a list. In practice, the development of the frame can be one of the most difficult and important steps in conducting a sample survey.

21.2 TYPES OF SURVEYS AND SAMPLING METHODS

The three most common types of surveys are mail surveys, telephone surveys, and personal interview surveys; each of these types involves the design and administration of a questionnaire. Other types of surveys used to collect data do not involve questionnaires. For example, auditing firms are often hired to sample a company's inventory of goods to estimate the value of inventory on the company's balance sheet. In such surveys, someone simply counts the items and records the results.

In surveys that use questionnaires, the design of the questionnaire is critical. The designer must resist the temptation to include questions that *might* be of interest, since every question adds to the length of the questionnaire. Long questionnaires lead not only to respondent fatigue, but also to interviewer fatigue, especially in mail and telephone surveys. However, if personal interviews are to be used, a longer and more complex questionnaire is feasible. A large body of knowledge exists concerning the phrasing, sequencing, and grouping of questions for a questionnaire. These issues are discussed in more comprehensive books on survey sampling; several good sources for this type of information are listed in the bibliography.

Sample surveys can also be classified in terms of the sampling method used. With a *probabilistic sampling method,* the probability of obtaining each possible sample can be computed; with a *nonprobabilistic sampling method,* this probability is unknown. Nonprobabilistic sampling methods should not be used if the researcher wants to make statements about the precision of the estimates. In contrast, probabilistic sampling methods can be used to develop confidence intervals which provide bounds on the sampling error. In the following sections, four of the most popular probabilistic sampling methods are discussed: simple random sampling, stratified simple random sampling, cluster sampling, and systematic sampling.

Although statisticians prefer to use a probabilistic sampling method, nonprobabilistic sampling methods often are necessary. The advantages of nonprobabilistic sampling methods are their low expense and ease of implementation. The disadvantage is that statistically valid statements cannot be made about the precision of the estimates. Two of the more common nonprobabilistic methods are convenience sampling and judgment sampling.

With *convenience sampling,* the units included in the sample are chosen because of accessibility. For example, a professor conducting a research study at a university may ask student volunteers to participate in the study simply because they are in the professor's class; in this case, the sample of students is referred to as a convenience sample. In some situations, convenience sampling is the only practical approach. For example, to sample a shipment of oranges, an inspector might select oranges haphazardly from several crates since labeling each orange in the entire shipment to create a frame and employing a probabilistic sampling method would be impractical. Wildlife captures and volunteer panels for consumer research are other examples of convenience samples.

Although convenience sampling is a relatively easy approach to sample selection and data gathering, it is impossible to evaluate the "goodness" of the sample statistics obtained in terms of their ability to estimate the population parameters of interest. A convenience sample may provide good results or it may not; there is no statistically justified procedure for making any statistical inferences from the sample results. Nevertheless, at times some researchers apply a statistical method designed for a probability sample to the data gathered from a convenience sample. In doing so, the researcher may argue that the convenience sample can be treated as though it were a random sample in the sense that it is representative of the population. However, this argument should be questioned; one should be very cautious in using a convenience sample to make statistical inferences about population parameters.

In using the nonprobability sampling technique referred to as *judgment sampling,* a person knowledgeable on the subject of the study selects sampling units that he or she feels are most representative of the population. Although judgment sampling is often a relatively easy way to select samples, users of the survey results must recognize that the quality of the results is dependent on the judgment of the person selecting the sample. Consequently, caution must be exercised in using judgment samples to make statistical inferences about a population parameter. In general, no statistical statements should be made about the precision of the results from a judgment sample.

Both probabilistic and nonprobabilistic sampling methods can be used to select a sample. The advantage of nonprobabilistic methods is that they are generally inexpensive and easy to use. However, if it is necessary to provide statements about the precision of the estimates, a probabilistic sampling method must be used. Almost all large sample surveys employ probabilistic sampling methods.

21.3 SURVEY ERRORS

Two types of errors can occur in conducting a survey. One type, *sampling error,* is defined as the magnitude of the difference between the point estimator developed from the sample and the population parameter. In other words, sampling error is the error that occurs because not every element in the population is surveyed. The second type, *nonsampling error,* refers to all other types of errors that can occur when a survey is conducted such as measurement error, interviewer error, and processing error. Although sampling error can occur only in a sample survey, nonsampling errors can occur in both a census and a sample survey.

NONSAMPLING ERROR

One of the most common types of nonsampling error occurs whenever we incorrectly measure the characteristic of interest. Measurement error can occur in a census or a sample survey. For either type of survey, the researcher must exercise care to ensure that any measuring instruments (e.g., the questionnaire) are properly calibrated and that the people who take the measurements are properly trained. Attention to detail is the best precaution in most situations.

Errors due to nonresponse are a concern to both the statistician responsible for designing the survey and the manager using the results. This type of nonsampling error occurs when data cannot be obtained for some of the units surveyed or when only partial data are obtained. The problem is most serious when a bias is created. For example, if interviews were conducted to assess women's attitudes toward working outside the home, making housecalls only during the daytime would create an obvious bias since women who work outside the home would be excluded from the sample.

Nonsampling errors due to lack of respondent knowledge are common in technical surveys. For example, suppose building managers were surveyed to obtain detailed information about the types of ventilation systems used in office buildings. Managers of large office buildings may be very knowledgeable about such systems because they may attend training seminars and have support staff to help keep them current. In contrast, managers of smaller office buildings may be less knowledgeable about such systems because of the wide variety of duties they must perform. This difference in knowledge can significantly affect the survey results.

Two other types of nonsampling error are selection error and processing error. Selection errors occur when an inappropriate item is included in the survey. Suppose a sample survey was designed to develop a profile of men with beards; if some interviewers interpreted the statement "men with beards" to include men with mustaches while other interviewers did not, the resulting data would be flawed. Processing errors occur whenever data are incorrectly recorded or incorrectly transferred from recording forms, such as from questionnaires to computer files.

Although some nonsampling errors will occur in most surveys, they can be minimized by careful planning. Care should be taken to ensure that the sampled population corresponds closely to the target population, good questionnaire design principles are followed, interviewers are well trained, and so on. The final report on a survey should include some discussion of the likely impact of nonsampling errors on the results.

SAMPLING ERROR

Recall the Dunning Microsystems (DMI) sample survey introduced in Section 21.1. Suppose DMI wants to estimate the mean age of people who have purchased a DMI personal computer. If the entire population of DMI personal computer owners could be surveyed (a census) and nonsampling errors were not present, we could determine the mean age exactly. But what if less than 100% of the population of DMI owners can be surveyed? In this case, there will most likely be a difference between the sample mean and the population mean; the absolute value of this difference is the sampling error. In practice, it is not possible to know what the sampling error will be for any one particular sample because the population mean is unknown; however, it is possible to provide probability statements about the size of the sampling error.

As stated, sampling error occurs because a sample, and not the entire population, is surveyed. Even though sampling error cannot be avoided, it can be controlled. Selecting an appropriate sampling method or design is one important way to control this type of error. In the following sections we will discuss four probabilistic sampling methods: simple random sampling, stratified simple random sampling, cluster sampling, and systematic sampling.

21.4 SIMPLE RANDOM SAMPLING

Recall the definition of simple random sampling from Chapter 7:

A simple random sample of size n from a finite population of size N is a sample selected such that every possible sample of size n has the same probability of being selected.

To conduct a sample survey using simple random sampling, we begin by developing a frame or list of all elements in the sampled population. Then a selection procedure, based on the use of random numbers, is used to ensure that each element in the sampled population has the same probability of being selected. In this section we show how estimates of a population mean, total, and proportion are made for sample surveys that use simple random sampling.

POPULATION MEAN

In most sample surveys, the form of the probability distribution for the population is unknown. For example, in the DMI sample survey, management wants to estimate μ, the mean age of people who have purchased a DMI personal computer. Most likely, DMI would not know the form of the probability distribution of age for the population of all DMI owners. This is usually not a problem because the properties of the sampling distribution of $\bar{x}$, the point estimator of μ, depend primarily on the choice of the sample design.

In Chapter 7 we indicated that if a *large* ($n \geq 30$) *simple random sample* is selected, the central limit theorem enables us to conclude that the sampling distribution of $\bar{x}$ can be approximated by a normal probability distribution. In Chapter 8 we showed that for cases where the sampling distribution of $\bar{x}$ can be approximated by a normal probability distribution, an interval estimate of μ is given by

$$\bar{x} \pm z_{\alpha/2}\sigma_{\bar{x}} \tag{21.1}$$

where

$$\sigma_{\bar{x}} = \text{standard error of the mean.}$$

Recall that $1 - \alpha$ is the confidence coefficient and $z_{\alpha/2}$ is the z value providing an area of $\alpha/2$ in the upper tail of the standard normal probability distribution. For example, for a 95% confidence interval, $z_{.025} = 1.96$. Note also that the standard error of the mean, $\sigma_{\bar{x}}$, is just the standard deviation of the sampling distribution of $\bar{x}$. In general, whenever we use the term *standard error* in this chapter, we will be referring to the standard deviation of the sampling distribution for the point estimator being considered.

When a simple random sample of size n is selected from a finite population of size N, an estimate of the standard error of the mean is

$$s_{\bar{x}} = \sqrt{\frac{N-n}{N}}\left(\frac{s}{\sqrt{n}}\right) \tag{21.2}$$

In this case, the interval estimate of the population mean becomes

$$\bar{x} \pm z_{\alpha/2}s_{\bar{x}} \tag{21.3}$$

In a sample survey it is common practice to use a value of $z = 2$ when developing interval estimates. Thus, when simple random sampling is used, an approximate 95% confidence interval estimate of the population mean is given by the following expression.

APPROXIMATE 95% CONFIDENCE INTERVAL ESTIMATE OF THE POPULATION MEAN

$$\bar{x} \pm 2s_{\bar{x}} \tag{21.4}$$

As an example, consider the situation of the publisher of *Great Lakes Recreation,* a regional magazine specializing in articles on boating and fishing. The magazine currently has $N = 8000$ subscribers. A simple random sample of $n = 484$ subscribers shows mean annual income to be $30,500 with a standard deviation of $7040. An unbiased estimate of the mean annual income of all subscribers is given by $\bar{x} = $30,500$.

Using the sample results and (21.2), we obtain the following estimate of the standard error of the mean.

$$s_{\bar{x}} = \sqrt{\frac{8000 - 484}{8000}} \left(\frac{7040}{\sqrt{484}}\right) = 310$$

Therefore, using (21.4), we find that an approximate 95% confidence interval estimate of the mean annual income for the magazine subscribers is

$$30{,}500 \pm 2(310) = 30{,}500 \pm 620$$

or $29,880 to $31,120.

The above procedure can be used to compute an interval estimate for other population parameters such as the population total or the population proportion. In all cases where the sampling distribution of the point estimator can be approximated by a normal probability distribution, the approximate 95% confidence interval can be written as

Point Estimator ± 2(Estimate of the Standard Error of the Point Estimator).

For example, in the *Great Lakes Recreation* sample survey, an estimate of the standard error of the point estimator is $s_{\bar{x}} = \$310$, and the bound on the sampling error is 2 ($310) = $620.

POPULATION TOTAL

Consider the problem facing Northeast Electric and Gas (NEG). As part of an energy usage study, NEG needs to estimate the *total* square footage for the 500 public schools in its service area. We will denote the total square footage for the 500 schools as X; in other words, X denotes the population total. Note that if μ, the mean square footage for the 500 public schools, were known, the value of X could be computed by multiplying N times μ. However, since μ is unknown, a point estimate of X is obtained by multiplying N times $\bar{x}$. We will denote the point estimator of X as $\hat{X}$.

POINT ESTIMATOR OF A POPULATION TOTAL

$$\hat{X} = N\bar{x} \tag{21.5}$$

An estimate of the standard error of this point estimator is given by

$$s_{\hat{X}} = Ns_{\bar{x}} \tag{21.6}$$

where

$$s_{\bar{x}} = \sqrt{\frac{N - n}{N}} \left(\frac{s}{\sqrt{n}}\right) \tag{21.7}$$

Note that (21.7) is just the formula for the estimated standard error of the mean. With the above standard error, an approximate 95% confidence interval for the population total is given by the following expression.

Suppose that in the NEG study a simple random sample of $n = 50$ public schools is selected from the population of $N = 500$ schools; the sample mean is $\bar{x} = 22{,}000$ square feet and the sample standard deviation is $s = 4000$ square feet. Using (21.5), we find that the point estimator of the population total is

$$\hat{X} = (500)(22{,}000) = 11{,}000{,}000.$$

Equation (21.7) can be used to compute an estimate of the standard error of the mean.

$$s_{\bar{x}} = \sqrt{\frac{500 - 50}{500}} \left(\frac{4000}{\sqrt{50}}\right) = 536.66$$

Then, using (21.6), we can obtain an estimate of the standard error of $\hat{X}$.

$$s_{\hat{X}} = (500)(536.66) = 268{,}330$$

Therefore, using (21.8), we find that an approximate 95% confidence interval estimate of the total square footage for the 500 public schools in NEG's service area is

$$11{,}000{,}000 \pm 2(268{,}330) = 11{,}000{,}000 \pm 536{,}660$$

or 10,463,340 to 11,536,660 square feet.

POPULATION PROPORTION

The population proportion p is the fraction of the elements in the population with some characteristic of interest. In a market research study, for example, one might be interested in the proportion of consumers preferring a certain brand of product. The sample proportion $\bar{p}$ is an unbiased point estimator of the population proportion. An estimate of the standard error of the proportion is given by

$$s_{\bar{p}} = \sqrt{\left(\frac{N - n}{N}\right)\left(\frac{\bar{p}(1 - \bar{p})}{n - 1}\right)} \qquad \text{(21.9)}$$

An approximate 95% confidence interval estimate of the population proportion is given by the following expression.

As an illustration, suppose that in the Northeast Electric and Gas sampling problem, NEG would also like to estimate the proportion of the 500 public schools in its service area that use natural gas as fuel for heating. If 35 of the 50 sampled schools indicate that they use natural gas, the point estimate of the proportion of the 500 schools in the population that use natural gas is $\bar{p} = 35/50 = .70$. Using (21.9), we can compute an estimate of the standard error of the proportion.

$$s_{\bar{p}} = \sqrt{\left(\frac{500 - 50}{500}\right)\left(\frac{.7(1 - .7)}{50 - 1}\right)} = .062$$

Therefore, using (21.10), we find that an approximate 95% confidence interval for the population proportion is

$$.7 \pm 2(.062) = .7 \pm .124$$

or .576 to .824.

As this example has shown, the width of the confidence interval can be rather large when one is estimating a population proportion. In general, large sample sizes are needed to obtain precise estimates of population proportions. A report of a sample survey of 529 mutual-fund investors conducted by Louis Harris & Associates stated, "Results should be accurate to within 4.3 percentage points" (*Business Week,* August 15, 1994). This implies an approximate 95% confidence interval with width of .086. For large populations, samples of $n = 1200$ or more are often used.

DETERMINING THE SAMPLE SIZE

An important consideration in sample design is the choice of sample size. The best choice usually involves a trade-off between cost and precision. Larger samples provide greater precision (tighter bounds on the sampling error), but are more costly. Often the budget for a study will dictate how large the sample can be. In other cases, the size of the sample must be large enough to provide a specified level of precision.

A common approach to choosing the sample size is to first specify the precision desired and then determine the smallest sample size providing that precision. In this context, the term *precision* refers to the size of the approximate confidence interval; smaller confidence intervals provide more precision. Since the size of the approximate confidence interval depends on the bound B on the sampling error, choosing a level of precision amounts to choosing a value for B. Let us see how this approach works in choosing the sample size necessary to estimate the population mean.

Equation (21.2) showed that the estimate of the standard error of the mean is

$$s_{\bar{x}} = \sqrt{\frac{N - n}{N}}\left(\frac{s}{\sqrt{n}}\right)$$

Recall that the bound on the sampling error is "2 times the estimate of the standard error of the point estimator." Thus,

$$B = 2\sqrt{\frac{N - n}{N}}\left(\frac{s}{\sqrt{n}}\right) \qquad \textbf{(21.11)}$$

Solving (21.11) for n will provide a bound on the sampling error equal to B. Doing so yields

$$n = \frac{Ns^2}{N\left(\dfrac{B^2}{4}\right) + s^2} \qquad \textbf{(21.12)}$$

Once a desired level of precision has been selected (by choosing a value for B), (21.12) can be used to find the value of n that will provide the desired level of precision. Using (21.12) to choose n for a practical study presents problems, however. In addition to specifying the desired bound on the sampling error B, one must know the sample variance s^2. But, s^2 will not be known until the sample is actually taken.

Cochran* suggests several ways to develop an estimate of s^2 in practice. Three of them are stated below.

1. Take the sample in two stages. Use the value of s^2 found in stage 1 in (21.12); the resulting value of n is what the size of the total sample must be. Then, select the number of additional units needed at stage 2 to provide the total sample size determined in stage 1.
2. Use the results of a pilot survey or pretest to estimate s^2.
3. Use information from a previous sample.

Let us now consider an example involving the estimate of the population mean for starting salaries of graduates of a particular university. Suppose there are $N = 5000$ graduates, and we want to develop an approximate 95% confidence interval with a width of at most $1000. To provide such a confidence interval, $B = 500$. Before using (21.12) to determine the sample size, we need an estimate of s^2. Suppose a study of starting salaries conducted last year found that $s = \$3000$. We can use the data from this previous sample to estimate s^2. Using $B = 500$, $s = 3000$, and $N = 5000$, we can now use (21.12) to determine the sample size.

$$n = \frac{5000(3000)^2}{5000\left(\dfrac{(500)^2}{4}\right) + (3000)^2}$$

$$= 139.9689$$

Rounding up, we see that a sample size of 140 will provide an approximate 95% confidence interval of width $1000. Keep in mind, however, that this calculation is based on our initial estimate of $s = \$3000$. If s turns out to be larger in this year's sample survey, the resulting approximate confidence interval will have a width greater than $1000. Consequently, if cost considerations permit, the survey designer might choose a sample size of, say, 150 to provide added assurance that the final approximate 95% confidence interval will have a width less than $1000.

The formula for determining the sample size necessary for estimating a population total with a bound B on the error of estimate is similar to that for the sample mean.

$$n = \frac{Ns^2}{\left(\dfrac{B^2}{4N}\right) + s^2} \qquad \textbf{(21.13)}$$

In our previous example, we wanted to estimate the mean starting salary with a bound on the sampling error of $B = 500$. Suppose we are also interested in estimating the total salary of all 5000 graduates with a bound of $2 million. We can use (21.13) with $B = 2,000,000$ to find the sample size needed to provide such a bound on the population total.

$$n = \frac{5000(3000)^2}{\dfrac{(2,000,000)^2}{4(5000)} + (3000)^2}$$

$$= 215.311$$

---

*William G. Cochran, *Sampling Techniques,* 3rd ed., Wiley, 1977.

Rounding up, we see that a sample size of 216 is necessary to provide an approximate 95% confidence interval with a bound of $2 million. We note here that if the same survey is expected to provide a bound of $500 on the population mean and a bound of $2 million on the population total, a sample size of at least 216 must be used. This size will provide a tighter bound than necessary on the population mean, while providing the minimum desired precision for the population total.

To choose the sample size for estimating a population proportion, we use a formula very similar to the one for the population mean. We simply substitute $\bar{p}(1 - \bar{p})$ for s^2 in (21.12) to obtain

$$n = \frac{N\bar{p}(1 - \bar{p})}{N\left(\dfrac{B^2}{4}\right) + \bar{p}(1 - \bar{p})} \qquad \text{(21.14)}$$

To use (21.14), we must specify the desired bound B and provide an estimate of $\bar{p}$. If a good estimate of $\bar{p}$ is not available, we can use $\bar{p} = .5$; this will ensure that the resulting approximate confidence interval will have a bound on the sampling error at least as small as desired.

EXERCISES

METHODS

Self-Test ▶

1. Simple random sampling has been used to obtain a sample of $n = 50$ elements from a population of $N = 800$. The sample mean was $\bar{x} = 215$, and the sample standard deviation was found to be $s = 20$.
   a. Estimate the population mean.
   b. Estimate the standard error of the mean.
   c. Develop an approximate 95% confidence interval for the population mean.

2. Simple random sampling has been used to obtain a sample of $n = 80$ elements from a population of $N = 400$. The sample mean was $\bar{x} = 75$, and the sample standard deviation was found to be $s = 8$.
   a. Estimate the population total.
   b. Estimate the standard error of the population total.
   c. Develop an approximate 95% confidence interval for the population total.

3. Simple random sampling has been used to obtain a sample of $n = 100$ elements from a population of $N = 1000$. The sample proportion was $\bar{p} = .30$.
   a. Estimate the population proportion.
   b. Estimate the standard error of the proportion.
   c. Develop an approximate 95% confidence interval for the population proportion.

4. A sample is to be taken to develop an approximate 95% confidence interval estimate of the population mean. The population consists of 450 elements, and a pilot study has resulted in $s = 70$. How large must the sample be if we want to develop an approximate 95% confidence interval with a width of 30?

APPLICATIONS

Self-Test ▶

5. In 1992, there were 361 cases of a foreign company acquiring a U.S. company (*Statistical Abstract of the United States, 1994*). Suppose a sample of 30 acquisitions showed an average value of $48.842 million with a standard deviation of $8.1 million and that 13 of the acquisitions in the sample were manufacturing companies.
   a. Develop an approximate 95% confidence interval for the mean value of an acquisition.
   b. Develop an approximate 95% confidence interval for the total value of all acquisitions.

c. In the sample, 13 of the acquired companies were involved in manufacturing. Develop an approximate 95% confidence interval for the proportion of acquisitions involving manufacturing companies.

6. A county in California had 724 corporate tax returns filed. The mean annual income reported was $161.22 thousand with a standard deviation of $31.3 thousand. How large a sample will be necessary next year to develop an approximate 95% confidence interval for mean annual corporate earnings? The precision required is an interval width of no more than $5000.

21.5   STRATIFIED SIMPLE RANDOM SAMPLING

In stratified simple random sampling, the population is first divided into H groups, called strata. Then for stratum h a simple random sample of size n_h is selected. The data from the H simple random samples are combined to develop an estimate of a population parameter such as the population mean, total, or proportion.

If the variability within each stratum is smaller than the variability across the strata, a stratified simple random sample can lead to greater precision (narrower interval estimates of the population parameters). The basis for forming the various strata depends on the judgment of the designer of the sample. Depending on the application, a population might be stratified by department, location, age, product type, industry type, sales levels, and so on.

As an example, suppose the College of Business at Lakeside College wants to conduct a survey of this year's graduating class to learn about their starting salaries. There are five majors in the college: accounting, finance, information systems, marketing, and operations management. Of the $N = 1500$ students who graduated this year, there were $N_1 = 500$ accounting majors, $N_2 = 350$ finance majors, $N_3 = 200$ information systems majors, $N_4 = 300$ marketing majors, and $N_5 = 150$ operations management majors. Analysis of previous salary data suggests that there would be more variability in starting salaries across majors than within each major. As a result, a stratified simple random sample of $n = 180$ students is selected; 45 of the 180 students majored in accounting ($n_1 = 45$), 40 majored in finance ($n_2 = 40$), 30 majored in information systems ($n_3 = 30$), 35 majored in marketing ($n_4 = 35$), and 30 majored in operations management ($n_5 = 30$).

POPULATION MEAN

In stratified sampling an unbiased estimate of the population mean is obtained by computing a weighted average of the sample means for each stratum. The weights used are the fraction of the population in each stratum. The resulting point estimator, denoted $\bar{x}_{st}$, is defined as follows.

POINT ESTIMATOR OF THE POPULATION MEAN

$$\bar{x}_{st} = \sum_{h=1}^{H} \left(\frac{N_h}{N}\right)\bar{x}_h \qquad (21.15)$$

H = number of strata

$\bar{x}_h$ = sample mean for stratum h

N_h = number of elements in the population in stratum h

N = total number of elements in the population; $N = N_1 + N_2 + \cdots + N_H$

TABLE 21.1   Lakeland College Sample Survey of Starting Salaries of Graduates

Major (h)	$\bar{x}_h$	s_h	N_h	n_h
Accounting	$30,000	2000	500	45
Finance	$28,500	1700	350	40
Information systems	$31,500	2300	200	30
Marketing	$27,000	1600	300	35
Operations management	$31,000	2250	150	30

For stratified simple random sampling, the formula for computing an estimate of the standard error of the mean is

$$s_{\bar{x}_{st}} = \sqrt{\frac{1}{N^2} \sum_{h=1}^{H} N_h(N_h - n_h)\frac{s_h^2}{n_h}} \qquad (21.16)$$

Using the above results, we see that an approximate 95% confidence interval estimate of the population mean is given by the following expression.

APPROXIMATE 95% CONFIDENCE INTERVAL ESTIMATE OF THE POPULATION MEAN

$$\bar{x}_{st} \pm 2s_{\bar{x}_{st}} \qquad (21.17)$$

Suppose the survey of 180 graduates of the College of Business at Lakeland College provided the sample results shown in Table 21.1. The sample means for each major, or stratum, are: $30,000 for accounting, $28,500 for finance, $31,500 for information systems, $27,000 for marketing, and $31,000 for operations management. Using these results and (21.15), we can compute a point estimate of the population mean.

$$\bar{x}_{st} = \left(\frac{500}{1500}\right)(30,000) + \left(\frac{350}{1500}\right)(28,500) + \left(\frac{200}{1500}\right)(31,500)$$

$$+ \left(\frac{300}{1500}\right)(27,000) + \left(\frac{150}{1500}\right)(31,000) = \$29,350$$

In Table 21.2 we show a portion of the calculations needed to estimate the standard error; note that

$$\sum_{h=1}^{5} N_h(N_h - n_h)\frac{s_h^2}{n_h} = 42,909,037,698$$

Thus,

$$s_{\bar{x}_{st}} = \sqrt{\left(\frac{1}{(1500)^2}\right)(42,909,037,698)} = \sqrt{19,070.68} = 138$$

Hence, using (21.17), we find that an approximate 95% confidence interval estimate of the population mean is $29,350 \pm 2(138) = 29,350 \pm 276$, or $29,074 to $29,626.

TABLE 21.2 Partial Calculations for the Estimate of the Standard Error of the Mean for the Lakeland College Sample Survey

Major	h	$N_h(N_h - n_h)\dfrac{s_h^2}{n_h}$
Accounting	1	$500(500 - 45)\dfrac{(2000)^2}{45} = 20{,}222{,}222{,}222$
Finance	2	$350(350 - 40)\dfrac{(1700)^2}{40} = 7{,}839{,}125{,}000$
Information systems	3	$200(200 - 30)\dfrac{(2300)^2}{30} = 5{,}995{,}333{,}333$
Marketing	4	$300(300 - 35)\dfrac{(1600)^2}{35} = 5{,}814{,}857{,}143$
Operations management	5	$150(150 - 30)\dfrac{(2250)^2}{30} = \underline{3{,}037{,}500{,}000}$
		$42{,}909{,}037{,}698$

$$\sum_{h=1}^{5} N_h(N_h - n_h)\frac{s_h^2}{n_h}$$

POPULATION TOTAL

The point estimator of the population total (X) is obtained by multiplying N times $\bar{x}_{st}$.

POINT ESTIMATOR OF THE POPULATION TOTAL

$$\hat{X} = N\bar{x}_{st} \qquad \text{(21.18)}$$

An estimate of the standard error of this point estimator is

$$s_{\hat{X}} = Ns_{\bar{x}_{st}} \qquad \text{(21.19)}$$

Thus, an approximate 95% confidence interval for the population total is given by the following expression.

APPROXIMATE 95% CONFIDENCE INTERVAL ESTIMATE OF THE POPULATION TOTAL

$$N\bar{x}_{st} \pm 2s_{\hat{X}} \qquad \text{(21.20)}$$

Now suppose the College of Business at Lakeland College would also like to estimate the total earnings of the 1500 business graduates in order to estimate their impact on the economy. Using (21.18), we obtain an unbiased estimate of the total earnings.

$$\hat{X} = (1500)29{,}350 = \$44{,}025{,}000$$

Using (21.19), we obtain an estimate of the standard error of the population total.

$$s_{\hat{X}} = 1500(138) = \$207,000$$

Thus, using (21.20), we find that an approximate 95% confidence interval estimate of the total earnings of the 1500 graduates is $44,025,000 \pm 2(207,000) = 44,025,000 \pm 414,000$ or \$43,611,000 to \$44,439,000.

POPULATION PROPORTION

An unbiased estimate of the population proportion, p, for stratified simple random sampling is a weighted average of the proportions for each stratum. The weights used are the fraction of the population in each stratum. The resulting point estimator, denoted $\bar{p}_{st}$, is defined as follows.

POINT ESTIMATOR OF THE POPULATION PROPORTION

$$\bar{p}_{st} = \sum_{h=1}^{H} \left(\frac{N_h}{N}\right)\bar{p}_h \tag{21.21}$$

where

    H = the number of strata

    $\bar{p}_h$ = the sample proportion for stratum h

    N_h = the number of elements in the population in stratum h

    N = the total number of elements in the population: $N = N_1 + N_2 + \cdots + N_H$

An estimate of the standard error of $\bar{p}_{st}$ is given by

$$s_{\bar{p}_{st}} = \sqrt{\frac{1}{N^2} \sum_{h=1}^{H} N_h(N_h - n_h)\left[\frac{\bar{p}_h(1 - \bar{p}_h)}{n_h - 1}\right]} \tag{21.22}$$

Thus, an approximate 95% confidence interval estimate of the population proportion is given by the following expression.

APPROXIMATE 95% CONFIDENCE INTERVAL ESTIMATE OF THE POPULATION PROPORTION

$$\bar{p}_{st} \pm 2s_{\bar{p}_{st}} \tag{21.23}$$

In the Lakeland College survey, the college wants to know the proportion of graduates receiving a starting salary of $36,000 or more. The results of the sample survey of 180 graduates show that 20 received starting salaries of $36,000 or more and that 4 of the 20 majored in accounting, 2 majored in finance, 7 majored in information systems, 1 majored in marketing, and 6 majored in operations management.

Using (21.21), we can compute the point estimate of the proportion receiving starting salaries of $36,000 or more.

TABLE 21.3 Partial Calculations for the Estimate of the Standard Error of $\bar{p}_{st}$ for the Lakeland College Sample Survey

Major	h	$N_h(N_h - n_h)\left[\dfrac{\bar{p}_h(1 - \bar{p}_h)}{n_h - 1}\right]$
Accounting	1	$500(500 - 45)\left[\dfrac{(4/45)(41/45)}{45 - 1}\right] = 418.7430$
Finance	2	$350(350 - 40)\left[\dfrac{(2/40)(38/40)}{40 - 1}\right] = 132.1474$
Information systems	3	$200(200 - 30)\left[\dfrac{(7/30)(23/30)}{30 - 1}\right] = 209.7318$
Marketing	4	$300(300 - 35)\dfrac{(1/35)(34/35)}{35 - 1}] = 64.8980$
Operations management	5	$150(150 - 30)\left[\dfrac{(6/30)(24/30)}{30 - 1}\right] = \underline{99.3103}$
		924.8305

$$\sum_{h=1}^{5} N_h(N_h - n_h)\left[\frac{\bar{p}_h(1 - \bar{p}_h)}{n_h - 1}\right]$$

$$\bar{p}_{st} = \left(\frac{500}{1500}\right)\left(\frac{4}{45}\right) + \left(\frac{350}{1500}\right)\left(\frac{2}{40}\right) + \left(\frac{200}{1500}\right)\left(\frac{7}{30}\right) + \left(\frac{300}{1500}\right)\left(\frac{1}{35}\right) + \left(\frac{150}{1500}\right)\left(\frac{6}{30}\right)$$

$$= .0981$$

In Table 21.3 we show a portion of the calculations needed to estimate the standard error; note that

$$\sum_{h=1}^{5} N_h(N_h - n_h)\left[\frac{\bar{p}_h(1 - \bar{p}_h)}{n_h - 1}\right] = 924.8305$$

Thus,

$$s_{\bar{p}_{st}} = \sqrt{\frac{1}{(1500)^2}(924.8305)}$$

$$= .0203$$

Using (21.23), we find that an approximate 95% confidence interval for the proportion of graduates receiving starting salaries of \$36,000 or more is .0981 ± 2(.0203) = .0981 ± .0406, or .0575 to .1387.

DETERMINING THE SAMPLE SIZE

With stratified simple random sampling we can think of choosing a sample size as a two-step process. First, a total sample size n must be chosen. Second, we must decide how to assign the sampled units to the various strata. Alternatively, we could first decide how large a sample to take in each stratum and then sum the stratum sample sizes to obtain the total sample size. Since it is often of interest to develop estimates of the mean, total, and proportion for the individual strata, a combination of these two approaches is often employed. An overall sample size n and an allocation that will provide the necessary precision for the overall population parameter of interest are found. Then, if the sample sizes in some of the strata are not large enough to provide the precision necessary for the estimates within the strata, the sample sizes for those strata are adjusted upward as necessary. In this section we discuss some of the issues pertinent to allocating the total sample to the various strata and present a method for choosing the total sample size and making the allocation.

The allocation task is to decide what fraction of the total sample should be assigned to each stratum. This fraction determines how large the simple random sample will be in each stratum. The factors considered most important in making the allocation are:

1. The number of elements in each stratum.
2. The variance of the elements within each stratum.
3. The cost of selecting elements within each stratum.

Generally, larger samples should be assigned to the larger strata and to the strata with larger variances. Conversely, to get the most information for a given cost, smaller samples should be allocated to the strata where the cost per unit of sampling is greatest.

The individual stratum variances often differ greatly. For example, suppose that in a particular study we are interested in determining the mean number of employees per building; since variability is greater in a stratum with larger buildings than in one with smaller buildings, a proportionately larger sample should be taken in such a stratum. The cost of selection can be an important consideration when significant interviewer travel between sampled units is necessary in some of the strata but not in others; this frequently occurs when some of the strata involve rural areas and others involve cities.

In many surveys the cost per unit of sampling is approximately the same for each stratum (e.g., mail and telephone surveys); in such cases, the cost of sampling can be ignored in making the allocation. We present here the appropriate formulas for choosing the sample size and making the allocation in such cases. More advanced texts on sampling provide formulas for the case when sampling costs vary significantly across strata. The formulas we present in this section will minimize the total sampling cost for a given level of precision. This method, known as *Neyman allocation,* allocates the total sample n to the various strata as follows.

$$n_h = n \left(\frac{N_h s_h}{\displaystyle\sum_{h=1}^{H} N_h s_h} \right) \qquad \text{(21.24)}$$

Equation (21.24) shows that the number of units allocated to a stratum increases with the stratum size and standard deviation. Note that to make this allocation, we need to first determine the total sample size n. Given a specified level of precision B, we can use the following formulas to choose the total sample size when estimating the population mean and the population total.

SAMPLE SIZE WHEN ESTIMATING THE POPULATION MEAN

$$n = \frac{\left(\displaystyle\sum_{h=1}^{H} N_h s_h \right)^2}{N^2 \left(\dfrac{B^2}{4} \right) + \displaystyle\sum_{h=1}^{H} N_h s_h^2} \qquad \text{(21.25)}$$

SAMPLE SIZE WHEN ESTIMATING THE POPULATION TOTAL

$$n = \frac{\left(\sum_{h=1}^{H} N_h s_h \right)^2}{\dfrac{B^2}{4} + \sum_{h=1}^{H} N_h s_h^2} \tag{21.26}$$

As an example, suppose a Chevrolet dealer wants to survey the customers who have purchased a Corvette, Geo Prizm, or Cavalier to obtain information the dealer feels will be helpful in determining future advertising. In particular, suppose the dealer wants to estimate the mean monthly income for these customers with a bound on the sampling error of $100. The dealer's 600 Corvette, Geo Prizm, and Cavalier customers have been divided into three strata: 100 Corvette owners, 200 Geo Prizm owners, and 300 Cavalier owners. A pilot survey was used to estimate the standard deviation in each stratum; the results are $s_1 = \$1300$, $s_2 = \$900$, and $s_3 = \$500$ for the Corvette, Geo Prizm, and Cavalier owners, respectively.

The first step in choosing a sample size for this survey is to use (21.25) to determine the total sample size necessary to provide a bound of $B = \$100$ on the estimate of the population mean. First, we compute

$$\sum_{h=1}^{3} N_h s_h = 100(1300) + 200(900) + 300(500) = 460{,}000$$

Next, we compute

$$\sum_{h=1}^{3} N_h s_h^2 = 100(1300)^2 + 200(900)^2 + 300(500)^2 = 406{,}000{,}000$$

Substituting these values into (21.25), we can determine the total sample size needed to provide a bound on the sampling error of $B = \$100$.

$$n = \frac{(460{,}000)^2}{\dfrac{(600)^2(100)^2}{4} + 406{,}000{,}000} = 162$$

Thus, a total sample size of 162 will provide the precision desired. To allocate the total sample to the three strata, we use (21.24).

$$n_1 = 162\left(\frac{100(1300)}{460{,}000} \right) = 46$$

$$n_2 = 162\left(\frac{200(900)}{460{,}000} \right) = 63$$

$$n_3 = 162\left(\frac{300(500)}{460{,}000} \right) = 53$$

We would therefore recommend sampling 46 Corvette owners, 63 Geo Prizm owners, and 53 Cavalier owners for a total sample size of 162 customers.

To determine the sample size when estimating a population proportion, we simply substitute $\sqrt{\bar{p}_h(1-\bar{p}_h)}$ for s_h in (21.25); the result is

$$n = \frac{\left(\displaystyle\sum_{h=1}^{H} N_h \sqrt{\bar{p}_h(1-\bar{p}_h)}\right)^2}{N^2\left(\dfrac{B^2}{4}\right) + \displaystyle\sum_{h=1}^{H} N_h \bar{p}_h(1-\bar{p}_h)} \qquad\qquad \textbf{(21.27)}$$

Once the total sample size for the population proportion estimate has been determined, allocation to the various strata is again made by using (21.24) with $\sqrt{\bar{p}_h(1-\bar{p}_h)}$ substituted for s_h.

NOTES AND COMMENTS

1. An advantage of stratified simple random sampling is that estimates of population parameters for each stratum are automatically available as a byproduct of the sampling procedure. For example, besides obtaining an estimate of the average starting salary for all graduates in the Lakeland College sampling problem, we obtained an estimate of the average starting salary for each major. Since each of the starting salary estimates was based on a simple random sample from each stratum, the procedure for developing an approximate confidence interval estimate when a simple random sample is selected (see Equation (21.4)) can be used to compute an approximate 95% confidence interval estimate for the mean in each stratum. In a similar manner, interval estimates for the population total and the population proportion for each stratum can be developed by using (21.8) and (21.10), respectively.

2. Another type of allocation that is sometimes used with stratified simple random sampling is called *proportional allocation*. In this approach, the sample size allocated to each stratum is given by the following formula.

$$n_h = n\left(\frac{N_h}{N}\right) \qquad\qquad \textbf{(21.28)}$$

Proportional allocation is appropriate when the stratum variances are approximately equal and the cost per unit of sampling is about the same across strata. In the case where the stratum variances are equal, proportional allocation and the Neyman procedure result in the same allocation.

EXERCISES

METHODS

Self-Test

7. A stratified simple random sample has been taken with the following results.

Stratum (h)	$\bar{x}_h$	s_h	$\bar{p}_h$	N_h	n_h
1	138	30	.50	200	20
2	103	25	.78	250	30
3	210	50	.21	100	25

a. Develop an estimate of the population mean for each stratum.
b. Develop an approximate 95% confidence interval for the population mean in each stratum.
c. Develop an approximate 95% confidence interval for the overall population mean.

8. Reconsider the sample results in Exercise 7.
a. Develop an estimate of the population total for each stratum.
b. Develop a point estimate of the total for all 550 elements in the population.
c. Develop an approximate 95% confidence interval for the population total.

9. Reconsider the sample results in Exercise 7.
a. Develop an approximate 95% confidence interval for the proportion in each stratum.
b. Develop a point estimate of the population proportion for the 550 elements in the population.
c. Estimate the standard error of the population proportion.
d. Develop an approximate 95% confidence interval for the population proportion.

10. A population has been divided into three strata with $N_1 = 300$, $N_2 = 600$, and $N_3 = 500$. From a past survey, the following estimates for the standard deviations in the three strata are available: $s_1 = 150$, $s_2 = 75$, $s_3 = 100$.
a. Suppose an estimate of the population mean with a bound on the error of estimate of $B = 20$ is required. How large must the sample be? How many elements should be allocated to each stratum?
b. Suppose a bound of $B = 10$ is desired. How large must the sample be? How many elements should be allocated to each stratum?
c. Suppose an estimate of the population total with a bound of $B = 15,000$ is requested. How large must the sample be? How many elements should be allocated to each stratum?

APPLICATIONS

11. A drug store chain has stores in four cities: 38 stores in Indianapolis, 45 in Louisville, 80 in St. Louis, and 70 in Memphis. Pharmacy sales in the four cities vary considerably because of the competition. The following sales data (in $1000s) are available from a sample survey. Each of the cities was considered a separate stratum, and a stratified simple random sample was taken.

Indianapolis	Louisville	St. Louis	Memphis
50.3	48.7	16.7	14.7
41.2	59.8	38.4	88.3
15.7	28.9	51.6	94.2
22.5	36.5	42.7	76.8
26.7	89.8	45.0	35.1
20.8	96.0	59.7	48.2
	77.2	80.0	57.9
	81.3	27.6	18.8
			22.0
			74.3

a. Estimate the mean sales for each city (stratum).
b. Develop an approximate 95% confidence interval for the mean sales in each city.
c. Estimate the proportion of stores with sales of $50,000 or more.
d. Develop an approximate 95% confidence interval for the proportion of stores with sales of $50,000 or more.

12. Reconsider the sample survey results in Exercise 11.
a. Estimate the population total for St. Louis.
b. Estimate the population total for Indianapolis.

   c. Develop an approximate 95% confidence interval for mean pharmacy sales for the drug store chain.

   d. Develop an approximate 95% confidence interval for total pharmacy sales for the drug store chain.

13. An accounting firm has a number of clients in the banking, insurance, and brokerage industries. There are $N_1 = 50$ banks, $N_2 = 38$ insurance companies, and $N_3 = 35$ brokerage firms. A marketing research firm has been hired to survey the accounting firm's clients in these three industries. The survey will ask a variety of questions about both the clients' businesses and their satisfaction with services provided by the accounting firm. Suppose an approximate 95% confidence interval is requested for the mean number of employees for the 123 clients with a bound on the error of estimation of $B = 30$.

   a. Suppose a pilot study finds $s_1 = 80$, $s_2 = 150$, and $s_3 = 45$. Choose a total sample size, and explain how the sample size should be allocated to the three strata.

   b. Suppose the pilot test is called into question and a decision is made to assume the stratum standard deviations are all equal to 100 in choosing the sample size. Choose a total sample size, and determine how many elements should be sampled in each stratum.

21.6 CLUSTER SAMPLING

Cluster sampling requires that the population be divided into N groups of elements called clusters such that each element in the population belongs to one and only one cluster. For example, suppose we want to survey registered voters in the state of Ohio. One approach would be to develop a frame consisting of all registered voters in the state of Ohio and then select a simple random sample of voters from this frame. Alternatively, in cluster sampling, we might choose to define the frame as the list of the $N = 88$ counties in the state (see Figure 21.1). In this approach, each county or cluster would consist of a group of registered voters, and each registered voter in the state would belong to one and only one cluster.

Suppose we select a simple random sample of $n = 12$ of the 88 counties. At this point, we could collect data for *all* registered voters in each of the 12 sampled clusters, an approach referred to as *single-stage cluster sampling,* or we could select a simple random sample of registered voters from each of the 12 sampled clusters, an approach referred to as *two-stage cluster sampling.* In either case, formulas are available for using the sample results to develop point and interval estimates of population parameters such as the population mean, total, or proportion. In this chapter, however, we consider only single-stage cluster sampling; more advanced texts on sampling present results for two-stage cluster sampling.

In the sense that both stratified and cluster sampling divide the population into groups of elements, the two sampling procedures are similar. The reasons for choosing cluster sampling, however, differ from the reasons for choosing stratified sampling. Cluster sampling tends to provide better results when the elements within the clusters are heterogeneous (not alike). In the ideal case, each cluster would be a small-scale version of the entire population. In this case, sampling a small number of clusters would provide good information about the characteristics of the entire population.

One of the primary applications of cluster sampling involves area sampling, where the clusters are counties, townships, city blocks, or other well-defined geographic sections of the population. Since data are collected from only a sample of the total geographic areas or clusters available, and since the elements within the clusters are typically close to one another, significant savings in time and cost can be realized when a data collector or interviewer is sent to a sampled unit. As a result, even if a larger total sample size is required, cluster sampling may be less costly than either simple random

FIGURE 21.1 Counties of the State of Ohio Used as Clusters of Registered Voters

sampling or stratified simple random sampling. In addition, cluster sampling can minimize the time and cost associated with developing the frame or list of elements to be sampled, since cluster sampling does not require that a list of every element in the population be developed. One needs only a list of the elements in the clusters sampled.

To illustrate cluster sampling, let us consider a survey conducted by the CPA (certified public accountant) Society of the 12,000 practicing CPAs in a particular state. As part of the survey, the CPA Society collected information on income, gender, and factors related to the CPA's life-style. Because personal interviews were needed to obtain all the desired information, the CPA Society used a cluster sample to minimize the total travel and interviewing cost. The frame consisted of all CPA firms that were registered to practice accounting in the state. Suppose, there are $N = 1000$ clusters, or CPA firms registered to practice accounting in the state, and that a simple random sample of $n = 10$ CPA firms is to be selected.

In presenting the formulas for cluster sampling that are needed to develop approximate 95% confidence interval estimates of the population mean, total, and proportion, we will use the following notation.

N = number of clusters in the population

n = number of clusters selected in the sample

M_i = number of elements in cluster i

M = number of elements in the population; $M = M_1 + M_2 + \cdots + M_N$

$\bar{M} = M/N$ = average number of elements in a cluster

x_i = total of all observations in cluster i

a_i = number of observations in cluster i with a certain characteristic

For the CPA Society sample survey we have the following information.

$$N = 1000$$
$$n = 10$$
$$M = 12,000$$
$$\bar{M} = 12,000/1000 = 12$$

Note that Table 21.4 shows the values of M_i and x_i for each of the sampled clusters as well as the number of female CPAs in the sampled firms (a_i).

POPULATION MEAN

The point estimator of the population mean obtained from cluster sampling is given by the following formula.

POINT ESTIMATOR OF THE POPULATION MEAN

$$\bar{x}_c = \frac{\sum_{i=1}^{n} x_i}{\sum_{i=1}^{n} M_i} \qquad (21.29)$$

TABLE 21.4   Results of CPA Sample Survey

Firm (i)	CPAs (M_i)	Total Salary ($1000s) for Firm i (x_i)	Female CPAs (a_i)
1	8	320	2
2	25	1125	8
3	4	115	0
4	17	714	6
5	7	247	1
6	3	94	2
7	15	634	2
8	4	147	0
9	12	481	5
10	33	1567	9
Totals	128	5444	35

An estimate of the standard error of this point estimator is

$$s_{\bar{x}_c} = \sqrt{\left(\frac{N-n}{Nn\bar{M}^2}\right) \frac{\sum_{i=1}^{n} (x_i - \bar{x}_c M_i)^2}{n-1}} \tag{21.30}$$

Thus, the following expression gives an approximate 95% confidence interval estimate of the population mean.

Using the data in Table 21.4, we obtain an estimate of the mean salary for practicing certified public accountants.

$$\bar{x}_c = \frac{5444}{128} = 42.531$$

Since the salary data in Table 21.4 are in thousands of dollars, an estimate of the mean salary for practicing certified public accountants in the state is $42,531.

In Table 21.5, we show a portion of the calculations needed to estimate the standard error; note that

$$\sum_{i=1}^{n} (x_i - \bar{x}_c M_i)^2 = 39,178.688$$

Thus,

$$s_{\bar{x}_c} = \sqrt{\left[\frac{1000-10}{(1000)(10)(12)^2}\right] \frac{39,178.688}{10-1}} = 1.730$$

TABLE 21.5 Partial Calculations for the Estimate of the Standard Error of the Mean for the CPA Sample Survey where $\bar{x}_c = 42.531$

Firm (i)	M_i	x_i	$(x_i - 42.531M_i)^2$	
1	8	320	$[320 - 42.531(8)]^2 =$	409.982
2	25	1125	$[1125 - 42.531(25)]^2 =$	3,809.976
3	4	115	$[115 - 42.531(4)]^2 =$	3,038.655
4	17	714	$[714 - 42.531(17)]^2 =$	81.487
5	7	247	$[247 - 42.531(7)]^2 =$	2,572.214
6	3	94	$[94 - 42.531(3)]^2 =$	1,128.490
7	15	634	$[634 - 42.531(15)]^2 =$	15.721
8	4	147	$[147 - 42.531(4)]^2 =$	534.719
9	12	481	$[481 - 42.531(12)]^2 =$	862.714
10	33	1567	$[1567 - 42.531(33)]^2 =$	26,724.730
Totals	128	5444		39,178.688

$$\sum_{i=1}^{n} (x_i - \bar{x}_c M_i)^2$$

Hence, the standard error is $1730. Using (21.31), we find that an approximate 95% confidence interval estimate for the mean annual salary is $42{,}531 \pm 2(1730) = 42{,}531 \pm 3460$ or \$39,071 to \$45,991.

POPULATION TOTAL

The point estimator of the population total X is obtained by multiplying M times $\bar{x}_c$.

POINT ESTIMATOR OF THE POPULATION TOTAL

$$\hat{X} = M\bar{x}_c \tag{21.32}$$

An estimate of the standard error of this point estimator is

$$s_{\hat{X}} = Ms_{\bar{x}_c} \tag{21.33}$$

Thus, an approximate 95% confidence interval estimate for the population total is given by the following expression.

APPROXIMATE 95% CONFIDENCE INTERVAL ESTIMATE OF THE POPULATION TOTAL

$$M\bar{x}_c \pm 2s_{\hat{X}} \tag{21.34}$$

For the CPA sample survey,

$$\hat{X} = M\bar{x}_c = 12{,}000(42{,}531) = \$510{,}372{,}000$$

$$s_{\hat{X}} = Ms_{\bar{x}_c} = 12{,}000(1730) = \$20{,}760{,}000$$

Thus, using (21.34), we find that an approximate 95% confidence interval is $\$510{,}372{,}000 \pm 2(\$20{,}760{,}000) = \$510{,}372{,}000 \pm \$41{,}520{,}000$ or \$468,852,000 to \$551,892,000.

POPULATION PROPORTION

The point estimator of the population proportion obtained from cluster sampling follows.

POINT ESTIMATOR OF THE POPULATION PROPORTION

$$\bar{p}_c = \frac{\displaystyle\sum_{i=1}^{n} a_i}{\displaystyle\sum_{i=1}^{n} M_i} \tag{21.35}$$

where

a_i = number of elements in cluster i with the characteristic of interest

An estimate of the standard error of this point estimator is

$$s_{\bar{p}_c} = \sqrt{\left(\frac{N-n}{Nn\bar{M}^2}\right)\frac{\sum\limits_{i=1}^{n}(a_i - \bar{p}_c M_i)^2}{n-1}}$$ (21.36)

Thus, an approximate 95% confidence interval estimate for the population proportion is given by the following expression.

APPROXIMATE 95% CONFIDENCE INTERVAL ESTIMATE OF THE POPULATION PROPORTION

$$\bar{p}_c \pm 2s_{\bar{p}_c}$$ (21.37)

For the CPA sample survey, we can use (21.35) and the data in Table 21.4 to develop an estimate of the number of practicing certified public accountants who are women.

$$\bar{p}_c = \frac{2+8+\cdots+9}{8+25+\cdots+33} = \frac{35}{128} = .2734$$

In Table 21.6 we show a portion of the calculations needed to estimate the standard error; note that

$$\sum_{i=1}^{n}(a_i - \bar{p}_c M_i)^2 = 15.2098$$

Thus,

TABLE 21.6 Partial Calculations for the Estimate of the Standard Error of $\bar{p}_c$ for the CPA Sample Survey where $\bar{p}_c = .2734$

Firm (i)	M_i	a_i	$(a_i - .2734 M_i)^2$	
1	8	2	$[2 - .2734(8)]^2$ =	.0350
2	25	8	$[8 - .2734(25)]^2$ =	1.3572
3	4	0	$[0 - .2734(4)]^2$ =	1.1960
4	17	6	$[6 - .2734(17)]^2$ =	1.8284
5	7	1	$[1 - .2734(7)]^2$ =	.8350
6	3	2	$[2 - .2734(3)]^2$ =	1.3919
7	15	2	$[2 - .2734(15)]^2$ =	4.4142
8	4	0	$[0 - .2734(4)]^2$ =	1.1960
9	12	5	$[5 - .2734(12)]^2$ =	2.9556
10	33	9	$[9 - .2734(33)]^2$ =	.0005
Totals	128	35		15.2098

$$\sum_{i=1}^{n}(a_i - \bar{p}_c M_i)^2$$

$$s_{\bar{p}_c} = \sqrt{\left[\frac{1000 - 10}{(1000)(10)(12)^2}\right]\frac{15.2098}{10 - 1}} = .0341$$

Hence, using (21.37), we find that an approximate 95% confidence interval for the proportion of practicing CPAs who are women is $.2734 \pm 2(.0341) = .2734 \pm .0682$ or .2052 to .3416.

DETERMINING THE SAMPLE SIZE

Once the clusters have been formed, the primary issue in choosing a sample size is selecting the number of clusters n. The procedure for cluster sampling is similar to that for other methods of sampling. An acceptable level of precision is specified by choosing a value for B, the bound on the sampling error. Then a formula is developed for finding the value of n that will provide the desired precision.

The average cluster size and the variance between clusters are key factors in deciding how many clusters to include in the sample. If the clusters are similar, there will be a small variance between them and the number of clusters sampled can be smaller. Also, if the average number of elements per cluster is larger, the number of clusters sampled can be smaller. The formulas for making an exact determination of sample size are included in more advanced texts on sampling.

EXERCISES

METHODS

Self-Test ▶

14. A sample of four clusters is to be taken from a population with $N = 25$ clusters and $M = 300$ elements. The values of M_i, x_i, and a_i for each cluster in the sample are given in Table 21.7.
   a. Develop point estimates of the population mean, total, and proportion.
   b. Estimate the standard error for the estimates in (a).
   c. Develop an approximate 95% confidence interval for the population mean.
   d. Develop an approximate 95% confidence interval for the population total.
   e. Develop an approximate 95% confidence interval for the population proportion.

TABLE 21.7 Exercise 14

Cluster (i)	M_i	x_i	a_i
1	7	95	1
2	18	325	6
3	15	190	6
4	10	140	2
Totals	50	750	15

15. A sample of six clusters is to be taken from a population with $N = 30$ clusters and $M = 600$ elements. The values of M_i, x_i, and a_i for each cluster in the sample are given in Table 21.8.
   a. Develop point estimates of the population mean, total, and proportion.
   b. Develop an approximate 95% confidence interval for the population mean.
   c. Develop an approximate 95% confidence interval for the population total.
   d. Develop an approximate 95% confidence interval for the population proportion.

TABLE 21.8 Exercise 15

Cluster (i)	M_i	x_i	a_i
1	35	3,500	3
2	15	965	0
3	12	960	1
4	23	2,070	4
5	20	1,100	3
6	25	1,805	2
Totals	130	10,400	13

APPLICATIONS

16. A public utility is conducting a survey of mechanical engineers to learn more about the factors influencing the choice of heating, ventilation, and air conditioning (HVAC) equipment for new commercial buildings. A total of 120 firms in the utility's service area are engaged in designing HVAC systems. The sampling plan is to use cluster sampling with each firm representing a cluster. For each firm in the sample, all of the mechanical engineers will be interviewed. Approximately 500 mechanical engineers are believed to be employed by the 120 firms.

A sample of 10 firms was taken. Among other things, the age of each respondent was recorded as well as whether or not the respondent had attended the local university.

Cluster (i)	M_i	Total of Respondents' Ages	Number Attending Local University
1	12	520	8
2	1	33	0
3	2	70	1
4	1	29	1
5	6	270	3
6	3	129	2
7	2	102	0
8	1	48	1
9	9	337	7
10	13	462	12
Totals	50	2000	35

a. Estimate the mean age of mechanical engineers engaged in this type of work.
b. Estimate the proportion of mechanical engineers in the utility's service area who attended the local university.
c. Develop an approximate 95% confidence interval for the mean age of mechanical engineers designing HVAC systems for commercial buildings.
d. Develop an approximate 95% confidence interval for the proportion of mechanical engineers in the utility's service area who attended the local university.

17. A national real estate company has just acquired a smaller firm that has 150 offices and 6000 agents in Los Angeles and other parts of Southern California. The national firm has conducted a sample survey to learn about attitudes and other characteristics of its new employees. A sample of eight offices has been taken, and all of the agents at these offices have completed the questionnaire. Results of the survey for the eight offices follow.

Office	Agents	Average Age	College Graduates	Male Agents
1	17	37	3	4
2	35	32	14	12
3	26	36	8	7
4	66	30	38	28
5	43	41	18	12
6	12	52	2	6
7	48	35	20	17
8	57	44	25	26

a. Estimate the mean age of the agents.
b. Estimate the proportion of agents who are college graduates and the proportion who are male.
c. Develop an approximate 95% confidence interval for the mean age of the agents.
d. Develop an approximate 95% confidence interval for the proportion of agents who are college graduates.
e. Develop an approximate 95% confidence interval for the proportion of agents who are male.

21.7 SYSTEMATIC SAMPLING

Systematic sampling is often used as an alternative to simple random sampling. In some sampling situations, especially those with large populations, it can be time-consuming to select a simple random sample by first finding a random number and then counting or searching through the frame until the corresponding element is found. Systematic sampling offers an alternative to simple random sampling in such cases. For example, if a sample size of 50 from a population containing 5000 elements is desired, we might sample one element for every 5000/50 = 100 elements in the population. A systematic sample for this case would involve randomly selecting one of the first 100 elements from the frame. The remaining sample elements are identified by starting with the first sampled element and then selecting every 100th element that follows in the frame. In effect, the sample of 50 is identified by moving systematically through the population and identifying every 100th element after the first randomly selected element. The sample of 50 will often be easier to select in this manner than it would be if simple random sampling were used. Since the first element selected is a random choice, a systematic sample is often assumed to have the properties of a simple random sample. This assumption is usually appropriate when the frame is a random ordering of the elements in the population.

SUMMARY

We have provided a brief introduction to the field of survey sampling in this chapter. The purpose of survey sampling is to collect data for the purpose of making estimates of population parameters such as the population mean, total, or proportion. Survey sampling as a method of data collection can be contrasted with conducting experiments to generate data. When survey sampling is used, the design of the sampling plan is of critical importance in determining which existing data will be collected. When experiments are employed, experimental design issues are of critical importance in determining which data will be generated, or created.

Two types of errors can occur with sample surveys: sampling error and nonsampling error. Sampling error is the error that occurs because a sample, and not the entire population, is used to estimate a population parameter. Nonsampling error refers to all the other types of errors that can occur, such as measurement, interviewer, nonresponse, and processing error. Nonsampling errors are controlled by proper questionnaire design, thorough training of interviewers, careful verification of data, and so on. Sampling errors are minimized by a proper choice of sample design and by selecting an appropriate sample size.

We discussed four commonly used sample designs in this chapter: simple random sampling, stratified simple random sampling, cluster sampling, and systematic sampling. The objective of sample design is to get the most precise estimates for the least cost. When the population can be divided into strata so that the elements within each stratum are relatively homogeneous, stratified simple random sampling will provide more precision (smaller approximate confidence intervals) than simple random sampling. When the elements can be grouped in clusters so that all the elements in a cluster are close together geographically, cluster sampling often reduces interviewer cost; in these situations, cluster sampling will often provide the most precision per dollar. Systematic random sampling was presented as an alternative to simple random sampling.

GLOSSARY

Element   The entity on which data are collected.

Population   The collection of all elements of interest.

Sample   A subset of the population.

Sampled population   The population from which the sample is taken.

Target population   The population about which inferences are made.

Sampling unit   The units selected for sampling. A sampling unit may include several elements.

Frame   A list of the sampling units for a study. The sample is drawn by selecting units from the frame.

Probabilistic sampling   Any method of sampling for which the probability of each possible sample can be computed.

Nonprobabilistic sampling   Any method of sampling for which the probability of selecting a sample cannot be computed.

Convenience sampling   A nonprobabilistic method of sampling whereby elements are selected on the basis of convenience.

Judgment sampling   A nonprobabilistic method of sampling whereby element selection is based on the judgment of the person doing the study.

Sampling error   The error that occurs because a sample, and not the entire population, is used to estimate a population parameter.

Nonsampling error   All types of errors other than sampling error, such as measurement error, interviewer error, and processing error.

Simple random sample   A sample selected in such a manner that each sample of size n has the same probability of being selected.

Bound on sampling error   A number added to and subtracted from a point estimate to create an approximate 95% confidence interval. It is given by two times the standard error of the point estimator.

Stratified simple random sampling   A probabilistic method of selecting a sample in which the population is first divided into strata and a simple random sample is then taken from each stratum.

Cluster sampling   A probabilistic method of sampling in which the population is first divided into clusters and then one or more clusters is selected for sampling. In single-stage cluster sampling, every element in each selected cluster is sampled; in two-stage cluster sampling, a sample of the elements in each selected cluster is collected.

Systematic sampling   A method of choosing a sample by randomly selecting the first element and then selecting every kth element thereafter.

KEY FORMULAS

SIMPLE RANDOM SAMPLING

Interval Estimate of the Population Mean

$$\bar{x} \pm z_{\alpha/2}\sigma_{\bar{x}} \qquad (21.1)$$

Estimate of the Standard Error of the Population Mean

$$s_{\bar{x}} = \sqrt{\frac{N-n}{N}}\left(\frac{s}{\sqrt{n}}\right) \qquad (21.2)$$

Interval Estimate of the Population Mean

$$\bar{x} \pm z_{\alpha/2} s_{\bar{x}} \tag{21.3}$$

Approximate 95% Confidence Interval Estimate of the Population Mean

$$\bar{x} \pm 2 s_{\bar{x}} \tag{21.4}$$

Point Estimator of a Population Total

$$\hat{X} = N\bar{x} \tag{21.5}$$

Estimate of the Standard Error of $\hat{X}$

$$s_{\hat{X}} = N s_{\bar{x}} \tag{21.6}$$

Approximate 95% Confidence Interval Estimate of the Population Total

$$N\bar{x} \pm 2 s_{\hat{X}} \tag{21.8}$$

Estimate of the Standard Error of the Population Proportion

$$s_{\bar{p}} = \sqrt{\left(\frac{N-n}{N}\right)\left(\frac{\bar{p}(1-\bar{p})}{n-1}\right)} \tag{21.9}$$

Approximate 95% Confidence Interval Estimate of the Population Proportion

$$\bar{p} \pm 2 s_{\bar{p}} \tag{21.10}$$

Sample Size for an Estimate of the Population Mean

$$n = \frac{N s^2}{N\left(\dfrac{B^2}{4}\right) + s^2} \tag{21.12}$$

Sample Size for an Estimate of the Population Total

$$n = \frac{N s^2}{\left(\dfrac{B^2}{4N}\right) + s^2} \tag{21.13}$$

Sample Size for an Estimate of the Population Proportion

$$n = \frac{N\bar{p}(1-\bar{p})}{N\left(\dfrac{B^2}{4}\right) + \bar{p}(1-\bar{p})} \tag{21.14}$$

STRATIFIED SIMPLE RANDOM SAMPLING

Point Estimator of the Population Mean

$$\bar{x}_{\mathrm{st}} = \sum_{h=1}^{H} \left(\frac{N_h}{N}\right) \bar{x}_h \tag{21.15}$$

Estimate of the Standard Error of the Population Mean

$$s_{\bar{x}_{st}} = \sqrt{\frac{1}{N^2}\sum_{h=1}^{H} N_h(N_h - n_h)\frac{s_h^2}{n_h}}$$

(21.16)

Approximate 95% Confidence Interval Estimate of the Population Mean

$$\bar{x}_{st} \pm 2s_{\bar{x}_{st}}$$

(21.17)

Point Estimator of the Population Total

$$\hat{X} = N\bar{x}_{st}$$

(21.18)

Estimate of the Standard Error of $\hat{X}$

$$s_{\hat{X}} = Ns_{\bar{x}_{st}}$$

(21.19)

Approximate 95% Confidence Interval Estimate of the Population Total

$$N\bar{x}_{st} \pm 2s_{\hat{X}}$$

(21.20)

Point Estimator of the Population Proportion

$$\bar{p}_{st} = \sum_{h=1}^{H} \left(\frac{N_h}{N}\right)\bar{p}_h$$

(21.21)

Estimate of the Standard Error of $\bar{p}_{st}$

$$s_{\bar{p}_{st}} = \sqrt{\frac{1}{N^2}\sum_{h=1}^{H} N_h(N_h - n_h)\left[\frac{\bar{p}_h(1-\bar{p}_h)}{n_h - 1}\right]}$$

(21.22)

Approximate 95% Confidence Interval Estimate of the Population Proportion

$$\bar{p}_{st} \pm 2s_{\bar{p}_{st}}$$

(21.23)

Allocating the Total Sample n to the Strata: Neyman Allocation

$$n_h = n\left(\frac{N_h s_h}{\sum_{h=1}^{H} N_h s_h}\right)$$

(21.24)

Sample Size When Estimating the Population Mean

$$n = \frac{\left(\sum_{h=1}^{H} N_h s_h\right)^2}{N^2\left(\frac{B^2}{4}\right) + \sum_{h=1}^{H} N_h s_h^2}$$

(21.25)

Sample Size When Estimating the Population Total

$$n = \frac{\left(\sum_{h=1}^{H} N_h s_h\right)^2}{\frac{B^2}{4} + \sum_{h=1}^{H} N_h s_h^2} \tag{21.26}$$

Sample Size for the Estimate of the Population Proportion

$$n = \frac{\left(\sum_{h=1}^{H} N_h \sqrt{\bar{p}_h(1 - \bar{p}_h)}\right)^2}{N^2\left(\frac{B^2}{4}\right) + \sum_{h=1}^{H} N_h \bar{p}_h(1 - \bar{p}_h)} \tag{21.27}$$

Proportional Allocation of Sample n to the Strata

$$n_h = n\left(\frac{N_h}{N}\right) \tag{21.28}$$

CLUSTER SAMPLING

Point Estimator of the Population Mean

$$\bar{x}_c = \frac{\sum_{i=1}^{n} x_i}{\sum_{i=1}^{n} M_i} \tag{21.29}$$

Estimate of the Standard Error of the Population Mean

$$s_{\bar{x}_c} = \sqrt{\left(\frac{N-n}{Nn\bar{M}^2}\right)\frac{\sum_{i=1}^{n}(x_i - \bar{x}_c M_i)^2}{n-1}} \tag{21.30}$$

Approximate 95% Confidence Interval Estimate of the Population Mean

$$\bar{x}_c \pm 2s_{\bar{x}_c} \tag{21.31}$$

Point Estimator of the Population Total

$$\hat{X} = M\bar{x}_c \tag{21.32}$$

Estimate of the Standard Error of $\hat{X}$

$$s_{\hat{X}} = Ms_{\bar{x}_c} \tag{21.33}$$

Approximate 95% Confidence Interval Estimate of the Population Total

$$M\bar{x}_c \pm 2s_{\hat{X}} \tag{21.34}$$

Point Estimator of the Population Proportion

$$\bar{p}_c = \frac{\sum\limits_{i=1}^{n} a_i}{\sum\limits_{i=1}^{n} M_i}$$

(21.35)

Estimate of the Standard Error of $\bar{p}_c$

$$s_{\bar{p}_c} = \sqrt{\left(\frac{N-n}{Nn\bar{M}^2}\right)\frac{\sum\limits_{i=1}^{n}(a_i - \bar{p}_c M_i)^2}{n-1}}$$

(21.36)

**Approximate 95% Confidence Interval Estimate
of the Population Proportion**

$$\bar{p}_c \pm 2 s_{\bar{p}_c}$$

(21.37)

SUPPLEMENTARY EXERCISES

18. A *USA Today*/CNN/Gallup telephone poll of 1421 adults nationwide (*USA Today,* January 16, 1992) concerned issues that were likely to influence voters. The following questions are based on that survey. (Note: Since the survey sampled a very small fraction of all adults, assume $N - n/N = 1$ in any formulas involving standard error.)
   a. Eighty percent indicated they would be more likely to vote for a candidate in favor of "requiring all able-bodied people on welfare to do work for their welfare checks." Develop an approximate 95% confidence interval for the population proportion.
   b. Sixty percent indicated they would be more likely to vote for a candidate in favor of "a national health care system paid for by new taxes." Develop an approximate 95% confidence interval for the population proportion.
   c. Forty-four percent indicated they would be more likely to vote for a candidate in favor of "giving families a tax credit for each child attending a private or parochial school" while 40% were less likely to vote for such a candidate and 16% did not express a preference. Develop an approximate 95% confidence interval for the proportion of adults more likely to vote for such a candidate.
   d. *USA Today* reported that the "margin of sampling error is plus or minus 3 percentage points" for the survey. What does this mean, and how do you think they arrived at this number?
   e. How might nonsampling error bias the results of such a survey? The actual polling was done by the Gallup organization.

19. The National Association of Children's Hospitals and Related Institutions and the new Coalition for America's Children (*Cincinnati Enquirer,* January 8, 1992) commissioned a nationwide telephone survey of 1083 registered voters concerning children's issues.
   a. Seventy-one percent of respondents worried that "the quality of education is declining for children in public schools." Develop an approximate 95% confidence interval for the population proportion.
   b. Sixty-two percent worried that "children are not provided with the basics that they need in health care, food and education." Develop an approximate 95% confidence interval for the population proportion.
   c. Thirty-four percent worried that "pregnant mothers aren't getting the health care they need to make sure their child is healthy." Develop an approximate 95% confidence interval for this estimate.
   d. It was reported that the "percent of error is plus or minus 3.1%." Interpret this statement.

20. A quality of life survey was conducted with employees of a manufacturing firm. Of the firm's 3000 employees, a sample of 300 were sent questionnaires. Two hundred usable questionnaires were obtained for a response rate of 67%.

    a. The mean annual salary for the sample was $\bar{x} = \$23,200$ with $s = 3000$. Develop an approximate 95% confidence interval for the mean annual salary of the population.

    b. Using the information in (a), develop an approximate 95% confidence interval for the total salary of all 3000 employees.

    c. Seventy-three percent of respondents reported that they were "generally satisfied" with their job. Develop an approximate 95% confidence interval for the population proportion.

    d. Comment on whether or not you think the results in (c) might be biased. Would your opinion change if you knew the respondents were guaranteed anonymity?

21. A U.S. Senate Judiciary Committee report showed the number of homicides in each state for 1991. In Indiana, Ohio, and Kentucky, the number of homicides was, respectively, 380, 760, and 260. Suppose a stratified random sample with the following results was taken to learn more about the victims and the cause of death.

Stratum	Sample Size	Shootings	Beatings	Black Victims
Indiana	30	10	9	21
Ohio	45	19	12	34
Kentucky	25	7	11	15

    a. Develop an approximate 95% confidence interval for the proportion of shooting deaths in Indiana.

    b. Develop an estimate for the total number of shooting deaths in Ohio.

    c. Develop an approximate 95% confidence interval for the proportion of shooting deaths in Ohio.

    d. Develop an approximate 95% confidence interval for the proportion of shooting deaths across all three states.

22. Refer again to the data in Exercise 21.

    a. Develop an estimate of the total number of deaths (in the three states) due to beatings.

    b. Develop an approximate 95% confidence interval for the proportion of deaths across all three states due to beatings.

    c. Develop an approximate 95% confidence interval for the proportion of victims who are black.

    d. Develop an estimate of the total number of victims who are black.

23. A stratified simple random sample is to be taken of a bank's customers to learn about a variety of attitudinal and demographic issues. The stratification is to be based on savings account balances as of June 30, 1995. A frequency distribution showing the number of accounts in each stratum, together with the standard deviation of account balances by stratum, follows.

Stratum ($)	Accounts	Standard Deviation of Account Balances
0.00–1,000.00	3000	80
1,000.01–2,000.00	600	150
2,000.01–5,000.00	250	220
5,000.01–10,000.00	100	700
over 10,000.00	50	3000

a. Assuming the cost per unit sampled is approximately equal across strata, determine the total number of persons to include in the sample. Assume we want a bound on the error of estimate of the population mean for savings account balances of $B = \$20$.

b. Use the Neyman allocation procedure to determine the number to be sampled for each stratum.

24. A public agency is interested in learning more about the persons living in nursing homes in a particular city. A total of 100 nursing homes are caring for 4800 people in the city and a cluster sample of six homes has been taken. Each person in the six homes has been interviewed. A portion of the sample results follows.

Home	Residents	Average Age of Residents	Disabled Residents
1	14	61	12
2	7	74	2
3	96	78	30
4	23	69	8
5	71	73	10
6	29	84	22

a. Develop an estimate of the mean age of nursing home residents in this city.

b. Develop an approximate 95% confidence interval for the proportion of disabled persons in the city's nursing homes.

c. Estimate the total number of disabled persons residing in nursing homes in this city.

22

DECISION ANALYSIS

CONTENTS

$\overline{x}$

STATISTICS IN PRACTICE ●

Ohio Edison Company*
Akron, Ohio

Ohio Edison Company, an investor-owned electric utility headquartered in northeastern Ohio, provides electrical service to more than two million people. Most of the electricity is generated by coal-fired power plants. Because of evolving pollution-control requirements, Ohio Edison embarked on a program to replace the existing pollution-control equipment at most of its generating plants.

To meet new emission limits for sulfur dioxide at one of its largest power plants, Ohio Edison decided to burn low-sulfur coal in four of the smaller units at the plant and to install fabric filters on those units to control particulate emissions. Fabric filters use thousands of fabric bags to filter out particles and function in much the same way as a household vacuum cleaner.

It was considered likely, although not certain, that the three larger units at the plant would burn medium- to high-sulfur coal. Preliminary studies narrowed the particulate equipment choice for these larger units to fabric filters and electrostatic precipitators (which remove particles suspended in the flue gas by passing it through a strong electrical field). Among the uncertainties that would affect the final choice were the way some air-quality laws and regulations might be interpreted, potential future changes in air-quality laws and regulations, and fluctuations in construction costs.

Because of the complexity of the problem, the high degree of uncertainty associated with factors affecting the decision, and the cost impact on Ohio Edison, decision analysis was used in the selection process. A graphical description of the problem, referred to as a decision tree, was developed. The measure used to evaluate the outcomes depicted on the decision tree was the annual revenue requirements for the three large units over their

remaining lifetime. Revenue requirements were the monies that would have to be collected from the utility customers to recover costs resulting from the installation of the new pollution-control equipment. An analysis of the decision tree led to the following conclusions.

- The expected value of annual revenue requirements for the electrostatic precipitators was approximately $1 million less than that for the fabric filters.
- The fabric filters had a higher probability of high revenue requirements than the electrostatic precipitators.
- The electrostatic precipitators had nearly a .8 probability of having lower annual revenue requirements.

These results led Ohio Edison to select the electrostatic precipitators for the generating units in question. Had the decision analysis not been performed, the particulate-control decision might have been based chiefly on capital cost, a decision measure that favored the fabric filter equipment. It was felt that the use of decision analysis resulted in both lower expected revenue requirements and lower risk.

In this chapter we will introduce the methodology of decision analysis that Ohio Edison used. The focus will be on showing how decision analysis can identify the best decision alternative given an uncertain or risk-filled pattern of future events.

Some utility companies generate electric power by using modern hydroelectric plants.

---

*The authors are indebted to Thomas J. Madden and M. S. Hyrnick of Ohio Edison Company, Akron, Ohio, for providing this Statistics in Practice.

● Decision analysis can be used to determine optimal strategies when a decision maker is faced with several decision alternatives and an uncertain or risk-filled pattern of future events. For example, a manufacturer of a new line of seasonal clothing would like to manufacture large quantities if consumer acceptance and consequently demand for the product are going to be high. However, the manufacturer would like to produce much smaller quantities if consumer acceptance and demand for the product are going to be low. Unfortunately, seasonal clothing items require the manufacturer to make a production–volume decision before the demand is known. Actual consumer acceptance of the product will not be determined until the items have been placed in the stores and customers have had an opportunity to purchase them. Selection of the best production–volume decision from among several alternatives when the decision maker is faced with the uncertainty of future demand is a problem suited for decision analysis.

We begin the study of decision analysis by considering problems involving reasonably few decision alternatives and reasonably few future events. We introduce the concepts of a payoff table and a decision tree to provide a structure for this type of decision situation and to illustrate the fundamentals of decision analysis. We then extend the discussion to show how additional information obtained through experimentation can be combined with the decision maker's preliminary information to develop an optimal decision strategy.

22.1   STRUCTURING THE DECISION PROBLEM

Pittsburgh Development Corporation (PDC) has purchased land for a luxury riverfront condominium complex. The site provides a spectacular view of downtown Pittsburgh and the Golden Triangle where the Allegheny and Monongahela rivers meet to form the Ohio River. The individual units will be priced from $300,000 to $1,200,000, depending on the floor, the square footage of the unit, and optional features such as fireplaces and large balconies.

The company has had preliminary architectural drawings developed for projects of three different sizes: six floors with 30 units, 12 floors with 60 units, and 18 floors with 90 units. The financial success of the project will depend heavily on PDC's decision about the size of the condominium project. Let us consider how decision analysis can help PDC determine which size project to develop.

The first step in the decision analysis approach is to identify the decision alternatives that are being considered. For PDC, there are three.

d_1 = a small condominium complex with six floors and 30 units

d_2 = a medium condominium complex with 12 floors and 60 units

d_3 = a large condominium complex with 18 floors and 90 units

A key factor in selecting one of these decision alternatives is PDC's assessment of the demand for the condominiums.

When asked about possible market acceptance of the condominium project, PDC managers viewed acceptance as an all-or-nothing situation. That is, they saw only two possibilities: high market acceptance of the project and hence a substantial demand for the condominiums, or low market acceptance of the project and hence a limited demand for the condominiums. Although PDC can exercise some influence over market acceptance with advertising, the prices of the units suggest that demand is likely to depend on a variety of factors over which PDC will have no control.

TABLE 22.1 Payoff Table for the PDC Condominium Project
(Profit in $Millions)

	State of Nature	
Decision Alternative	High Acceptance s_1	Low Acceptance s_2
Small complex, d_1	8	7
Medium complex, d_2	14	5
Large complex, d_3	20	-9

In decision analysis, events that might occur but which the decision maker cannot control are called *states of nature*. The list of possible states of nature includes everything that can happen, and individual states of nature are defined so that only one of them will actually occur. For the PDC condominium project, the two states of nature are

s_1 = high market acceptance and hence a substantial demand for the units and

s_2 = low market acceptance and hence a limited demand for the units.

PAYOFF TABLES

Given the three decision alternatives and the two states of nature, which condominium design should PDC select? To answer this question, PDC will need information on the profit associated with each combination of a decision alternative and a state of nature. For example, what profit would be realized if PDC constructs a large condominium complex (d_3) and market acceptance turns out to be high (s_1)? What would happen to profit if PDC constructs a large condominium complex (d_3) and market acceptance turns out to be low (s_2)? In decision analysis, we refer to the outcome that results from a specific decision alternative and the occurrence of a particular state of nature as a *payoff*. A table showing the payoffs for all combinations of the decision alternatives and states of nature is called a *payoff table*.

Using the best information available, managers have estimated the payoffs, or profits, for the PDC condominium project. These estimates, with profits expressed in millions of dollars, are listed in Table 22.1. In general, entries in a payoff table can be stated in terms of profits, costs, time, distance, or any other measure of output that may be appropriate for the situation being analyzed. We will refer to the payoff associated with decision alternative i and state of nature j as V_{ij}. For example Table 22.1 shows that $V_{31} = 20$, indicating that a $20 million profit is anticipated if the large complex is constructed (d_3) and market acceptance is high (s_1). However, $V_{32} = -9$ shows an anticipated loss of $9 million if the large complex is constructed (d_3) and market acceptance is low (s_2).

DECISION TREES

A *decision tree* is a graphical representation of the decision-making process. Figure 22.1 is a decision tree for the PDC problem. Note that it shows the natural or logical progression that will occur over time. First, PDC must make a decision about the size of the condominium complex (d_1, d_2, or d_3). Then, after the decision is implemented, either state of nature s_1 or s_2 will occur. The number at each end point of the tree indicates the payoff associated with a particular sequence. For example, the topmost payoff of 8 indicates that an $8 million profit is anticipated if PDC constructs a small condominium

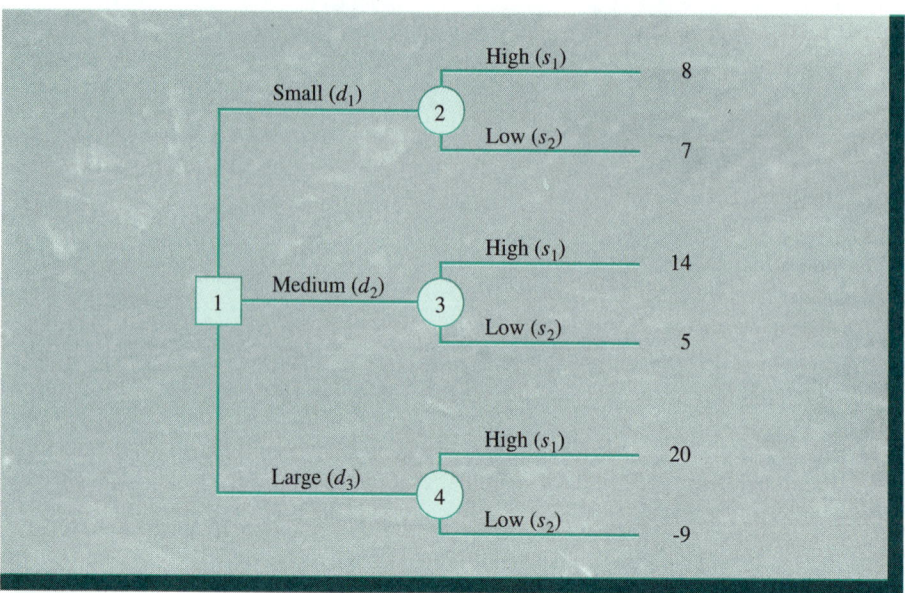

FIGURE 22.1   Decision Tree for the PDC Condominium Project (Payoffs in $Millions)

complex (d_1) and market acceptance turns out to be high (s_1). The next payoff of 7 indicates an anticipated profit of $7 million if PDC constructs a small condominium complex (d_1) and market acceptance turns out to be low (s_2). Thus, the decision tree shows graphically the sequences of decision alternatives and states of nature that provide the six possible payoffs for PDC.

We refer to an intersection or junction point of the decision tree as a *node* and the arc or connector between nodes as a *branch*. Figure 22.1 is the PDC decision tree with the nodes numbered 1 through 4. When the branches *leaving* a node are decision branches, we refer to the node as a *decision node* and represent it by a square. Similarly, when the branches leaving a node are state-of-nature branches, we refer to the node as a *state-of-nature node* and represent it by a circle. Hence, node 1 is a decision node, whereas nodes 2, 3, and 4 are state-of-nature nodes.

The identification of the decision alternatives, the states of nature, and the payoff associated with each decision alternative and state-of-nature combination is the first step in the decision analysis process. The question we now turn to is: How can the decision maker best utilize the information presented in the payoff table or the decision tree to arrive at a decision?

NOTES AND COMMENTS

1. Experts in problem solving agree that the first step in solving a complex problem is to decompose it into a series of smaller subproblems. Decision trees provide a useful way to show how the problem can be decomposed and the sequential nature of the decision process.

2. People often view the same problem from different perspectives. Hence, there is no one correct way to develop a decision tree for a problem. Often the discussion about the most appropriate decision tree provides additional insight about the problem.

22.2 DECISION MAKING WITH PROBABILITIES

In many decision-making situations, we can obtain probability estimates for each of the states of nature. When such probabilities are available, we can use the *expected value approach* to identify the best decision alternative. Let us first define the expected value of a decision alternative and then apply it to the PDC problem.

Let

$$N = \text{the number of states of nature and}$$

$$P(s_j) = \text{the probability of state of nature } s_j, \ j = 1, 2, \ldots, N$$

Since one and only one of the N states of nature can occur, the probabilities must satisfy two conditions.

$$P(s_j) \geq 0 \quad \text{for all states of nature} \tag{22.1}$$

$$\sum_{j=1}^{N} P(s_j) = P(s_1) + P(s_2) + \cdots + P(s_N) = 1 \tag{22.2}$$

The *expected value* (EV) of decision alternative d_i is defined as follows.

EXPECTED VALUE OF DECISION ALTERNATIVE d_i

$$\text{EV}(d_i) = \sum_{j=1}^{N} P(s_j) V_{ij} \tag{22.3}$$

In words, the expected value of a decision alternative is the sum of weighted payoffs for the decision alternative. The weight for a payoff is the probability of the associated state of nature and therefore the probability that the payoff will occur. Let us return to the PDC problem to see how the expected value approach can be applied.

PDC is very optimistic about the potential for the luxury high-rise condominium complex. Suppose this optimism has been translated into an initial subjective probability assessment of .8 that market acceptance will be high (s_1) and a corresponding probability of .2 that market acceptance will be low (s_2). Thus, $P(s_1) = .8$ and $P(s_2) = .2$. Using the payoffs in Table 22.1 and (22.3), we compute the expected value for each of the three decision alternatives as follows.

$$\text{EV}(d_1) = .8(8) + .2(7) = 7.8$$

$$\text{EV}(d_2) = .8(14) + .2(5) = 12.2$$

$$\text{EV}(d_3) = .8(20) + .2(-9) = 14.2$$

Hence, using the expected value approach, we find that the large condominium complex, with an expected value of $14.2 million, is the recommended decision.

The calculations required to identify the decision alternative with the best expected value can be carried out conveniently on a decision tree. Figure 22.2 is the decision tree for the PDC problem with state-of-nature branch probabilities. Working backward through the decision tree, we first compute the expected value at each state-of-nature node. That is, at each state-of-nature node, we weight each possible payoff by its chance

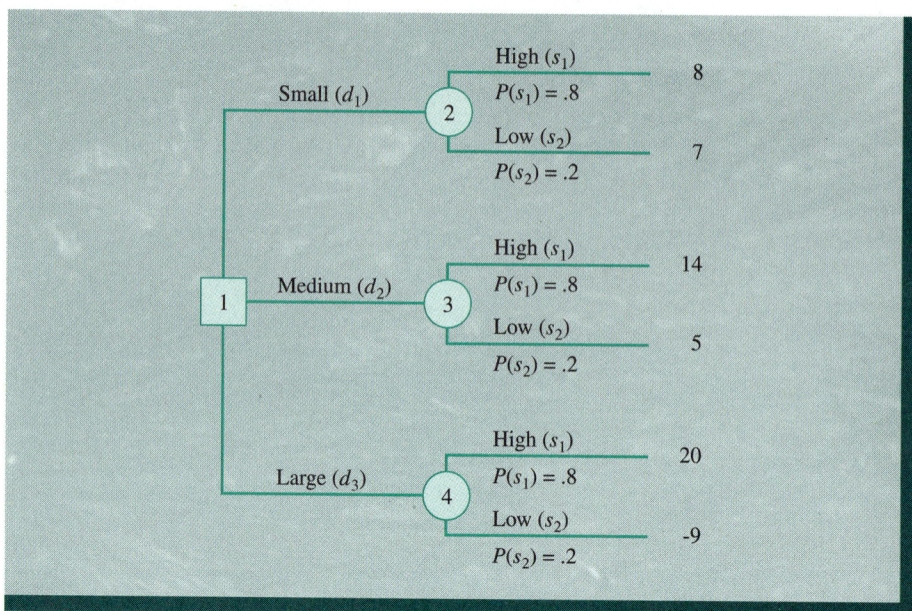

FIGURE 22.2   PDC Decision Tree with State-of-Nature Branch Probabilities

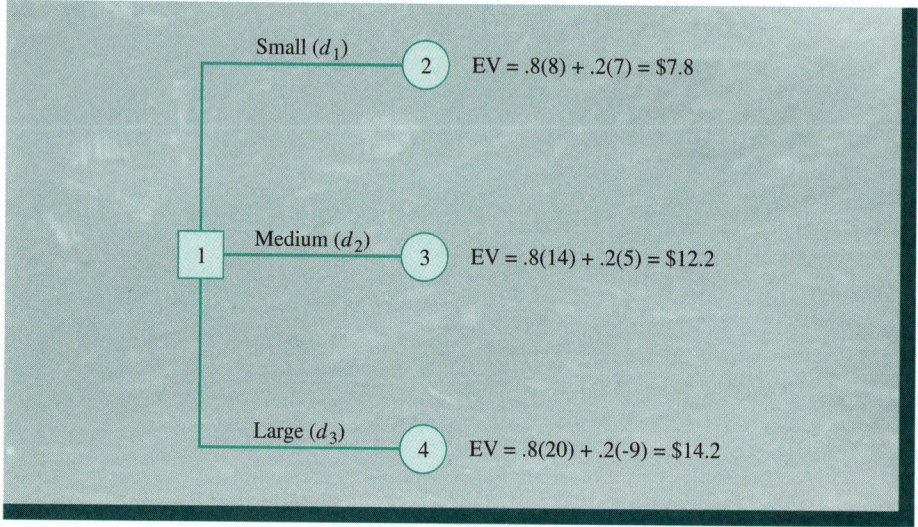

FIGURE 22.3   Applying the Expected Value Approach by Using a Decision Tree

of occurrence. By doing so, we obtain the expected values for nodes 2, 3, and 4, as shown in Figure 22.3.

Since the decision maker controls the branch leaving decision node 1 and since we are trying to maximize the expected profit, the best decision branch at node 1 is d_3. Thus, the decision tree analysis leads to a recommendation of d_3 with an expected value of $14.2 million. Note that this is the same recommendation obtained with the expected value approach in conjunction with the payoff table.

Other decision problems may be substantially more complex than the PDC problem, but if the number of decision alternatives and states of nature is reasonable, we can use the decision tree approach outlined here. First, we draw a decision tree consisting of decision and state-of-nature nodes and branches that describe the sequential nature of the problem. If we use the expected value approach, the next step is to determine the probabilities for each of the state-of-nature branches and compute the expected value at each state-of-nature node. Then we select the decision branch leading to the state-of-nature node with the best expected value. The decision alternative associated with this branch is the recommended decision.

EXERCISES

METHODS

Self-Test

1. Consider the following profit payoff table.

		States of Nature		
		s_1	s_2	s_3
Decision Alternatives	d_1	250	100	25
	d_2	100	100	75

Suppose the decision maker has obtained three probability estimates: $P(s_1) = .65$, $P(s_2) = .15$, and $P(s_3) = .20$. Use the expected value approach to determine the optimal decision.

2. Consider the following profit payoff table.

		States of Nature			
		s_1	s_2	s_3	s_4
Decision Alternatives	d_1	14	9	10	5
	d_2	11	10	8	7
	d_3	9	10	10	11
	d_4	8	10	11	13

Suppose the decision maker obtains information that leads to four probability estimates: $P(s_1) = .5$, $P(s_2) = .2$, $P(s_3) = .2$, and $P(s_4) = .1$.

a. Use the expected value approach to determine the optimal decision.
b. Now assume that the entries in the payoff table are costs; use the expected value approach to determine the optimal decision.

APPLICATIONS

3. Hale's TV Productions is considering producing a pilot for a comedy series for a major television network. The network may reject the pilot and the series or it may purchase the program for one or two years. Hale may decide to produce the pilot or transfer the rights for the series to a competitor for $100,000. Hale's profits are summarized in the following profit ($1000s) payoff table:

		States of Nature		
		Reject	*1 Year*	*2 Years*
Produce pilot	d_1	−100	50	150
Sell to competitor	d_2	100	100	100

If the probability estimates for the states of nature are P(reject) = .2, P(1 year) = .3, and P(2 years) = .5, what should the company do?

Self-Test

4. McHuffter Condominiums, Inc., of Pensacola, Florida, recently purchased land near the Gulf of Mexico and is attempting to determine the size of the condominium development it should build. Three sizes are being considered: small, d_1; medium, d_2; and large, d_3. An uncertain economy makes it difficult to ascertain the demand for the new condominiums. McHuffter's managers realize that a large development followed by a low demand could be very costly to the company. However, if McHuffter makes a conservative small-development decision and then finds a high demand, the firm's profits will be lower than they might have been. With three levels of demand—low, medium, and high—McHuffter's managers have prepared the following profit ($1000s) payoff table.

		Demand		
		Low	*Medium*	*High*
Decision Alternatives	*Small*	400	400	400
	Medium	100	600	600
	Large	−300	300	900

If P(low) = .20, P(medium) = .35, and P(high) = .45, what is the recommended decision with the expected value approach?

5. Martin's Service Station is considering investing in a heavy-duty snowplow this fall. Martin has analyzed the situation carefully and feels that the investment would be very profitable if the snowfall is heavy. A small profit could still be made if the snowfall is moderate, but Martin would lose money if the snowfall is light. Specifically, Martin forecasts a profit of $7000 if the snowfall is heavy and $2000 if it is moderate, and a $9000 loss if it is light. On the basis of the weather bureau's long-range forecast, Martin estimates that P(heavy snowfall) = .4, P(moderate snowfall) = .3, and P(light snowfall) = .3.
   a. Prepare a decision tree for Martin's problem.
   b. What is the expected value for each state-of-nature node?
   c. Using the expected value approach, would you recommend that Martin invest in the snowplow?

6. Joseph Software, Inc. (JSI), has been investigating the possibility of developing a grammar-and-style checker for use on microcomputers. From experience with other software projects, JSI estimates that the total cost to develop a prototype of the software is $200,000. If the performance of the prototype is somewhat better than that of existing software, referred to as a *moderate success,* JSI believes it could sell the rights to the software to a larger software developer for $600,000. If the performance of the prototype is significantly better than that of existing software, referred to as a *major success,* JSI believes it can sell the software for $1.2 million. However, if the performance of the prototype does not exceed the performance of existing software, referred to as a *failure,* JSI will not be able to sell the software and hence will lose all of its development costs.

a. Prepare a decision tree for JSI.

b. If the best estimates of the states of nature are $P(\text{failure}) = .70$, $P(\text{moderate success}) = .20$, and $P(\text{major success}) = .10$, what should JSI do if it uses the expected value approach?

7. Six months ago, Doug Reynolds paid $25,000 for an option to purchase a tract of land that he is considering developing. Another investor has offered to purchase Doug's option for $275,000. If Doug does not accept the investor's offer, he will purchase the property, clear the land, and prepare the site for building. He believes that once the site is prepared he can sell the land to a home builder. However, the success of the investment depends on the real estate market at the time he sells the property. If the real estate market is down, Doug feels that he will lose $1.5 million. If market conditions stay at their current level, he estimates that his profit will be $1 million; if market conditions are up at the time he sells, he estimates that his profit will be $4 million. Because of other commitments Doug does not consider it feasible to hold the land once he has developed it; hence, the only two alternatives are to sell the option or to develop the land. Suppose the probability of the real estate market being down, at the current level, or up is .6, .3, and .1, respectively. What decision should Doug make if he follows the expected value approach?

22.3 EXPECTED VALUE OF PERFECT INFORMATION

Suppose PDC has an opportunity to conduct a market research study that would help evaluate buyer interest in the condominium project and provide information that managers could use to improve the probability assessments for the states of nature. To determine the potential value of this information, we begin by assuming that the study could provide *perfect information* about the states of nature; that is, we assume that PDC could determine with certainty which state of nature is going to occur. To make use of this perfect information, we will develop a decision strategy that PDC should follow once it knows which state of nature will occur. As we will show, a decision strategy is simply a decision rule that specifies the decision alternative to be selected after new information becomes available.

To help determine the decision strategy for PDC, we have reproduced PDC's payoff table as Table 22.2. Note that if PDC knew for sure that state of nature s_1 would occur, the best decision alternative would be d_3, with a payoff of $20 million. Similarly, if PDC knew for sure that state of nature s_2 would occur, the best decision alternative would be d_1, with a payoff of $7 million. Thus, we can state PDC's optimal decision strategy based on perfect information as follows.

$$\text{If } s_1\text{, select } d_3$$

$$\text{If } s_2\text{, select } d_1$$

TABLE 22.2 Payoff Table for the PDC Condominium Project (Profit in $Millions)

	State of Nature	
Decision Alternative	**High Acceptance, s_1**	**Low Acceptance, s_2**
Small complex, d_1	8	7
Medium complex, d_2	14	5
Large complex, d_3	20	−9

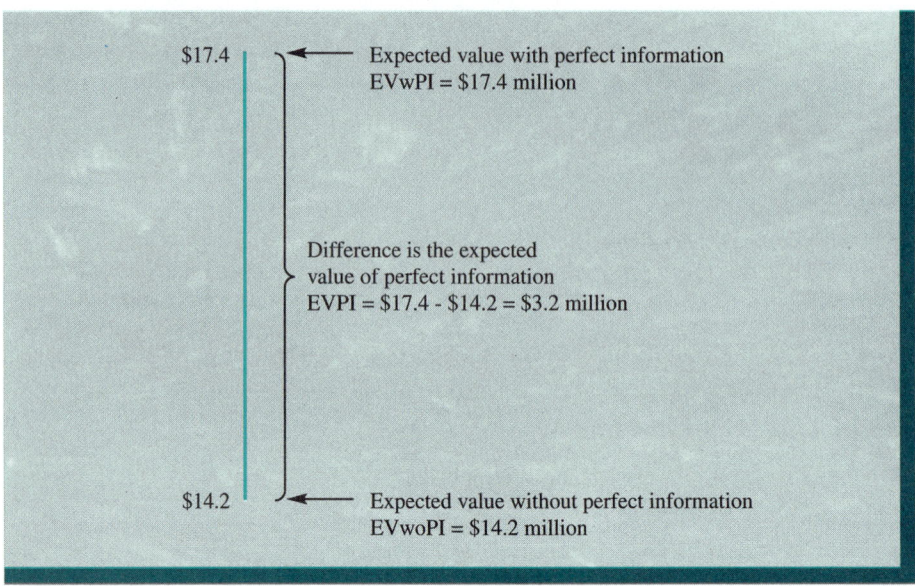

FIGURE 22.4 The Expected Value of Perfect Information

What is the expected value for this decision strategy? To compute the expected value with perfect information, we return to the original probability estimates for the states of nature: $P(s_1) = .8$ and $P(s_2) = .2$. There is a .8 probability that the perfect information will indicate state of nature s_1. In this case, the resulting decision alternative d_3 will provide a $20 million profit. Similarly, with a .2 probability for state of nature s_2, the resulting decision alternative d_1 will provide a $7 million profit. Thus, the expected value of the decision strategy that uses perfect information is

$$.8(20) + .2(7) = 17.4$$

We refer to the expected value of $17.4 million as the *expected value with perfect information* (EVwPI).

Recall from Section 22.2 that the recommended decision using the expected value approach is decision alternative d_3, with an expected value of $14.2 million. Because this decision recommendation and the expected value computation were made without the benefit of perfect information, $14.2 million is referred to as the *expected value without perfect information* (EVwoPI).

The expected value with perfect information is $17.4 million and the expected value without perfect information is $14.2, so the expected value of the perfect information (EVPI) is $17.4 − $14.2 = $3.2 million. In other words, $3.2 million is the additional expected value that would be obtained if perfect information were available about the states of nature. Figure 22.4 provides a summary of the computation of EVPI for the PDC problem.

Generally a market research study will not provide "perfect" information; however, if the study is a good one, the information gathered might be worth a sizable portion of the $3.2 million. Given the EVPI of $3.2 million, PDC should certainly consider the market survey as a way to obtain more information about the states of nature. In general, the expected value of perfect information is computed as follows.

EXPECTED VALUE OF PERFECT INFORMATION

$$EVPI = |\, EVwPI - EVwoPI \,| \qquad (22.4)$$

where

$$EVPI = \text{expected value of perfect information}$$

$$EVwPI = \text{expected value } \textit{with } \text{perfect information} \\ \text{about the states of nature}$$

$$EVwoPI = \text{expected value } \textit{without } \text{perfect information} \\ \text{about the states of nature}$$

Note the role of the absolute value in (22.4). That is, for minimization problems the expected value with perfect information is always less than or equal to the expected value without perfect information. In this case, EVPI is the magnitude of the difference between EVwPI and EVwoPI, or the absolute value of the difference as shown in (22.4).

EXERCISES

METHODS

Self-Test

8. The payoff table presented in Exercise 1 is repeated here.

		States of Nature		
		s_1	s_2	s_3
Decision Alternatives	d_1	250	100	25
	d_2	100	100	75

The probabilities for the states of nature are $P(s_1) = .65$, $P(s_2) = .15$, and $P(s_3) = .20$.

a. What is the optimal decision strategy if perfect information were available?

b. What is the expected value for the decision strategy developed in (a)?

c. With the expected value approach, what is the recommended decision? What is its expected value?

d. What is the expected value of perfect information?

9. The profit payoff table presented in exercise 2 is repeated here.

		States of Nature			
		s_1	s_2	s_3	s_4
Decision Alternatives	d_1	14	9	10	5
	d_2	11	10	8	7
	d_3	9	10	10	11
	d_4	8	10	11	13

The probabilities of the states of nature are $P(s_1) = .5$, $P(s_2) = .2$, $P(s_3) = .2$, and $P(s_4) = .1$.

a. What is the optimal decision strategy if perfect information were available?

b. What is the expected value for the decision strategy developed in (a)?

c. With the expected value approach, what is the recommended decision? What is its expected value?

d. What is the expected value of perfect information?

APPLICATIONS

10. Consider the Hale's TV Productions problem (Exercise 3). What is the maximum that Hale should be willing to pay for inside information on what the network will do?

Self-Test

11. Consider the McHuffter Condominiums problem (Exercise 4). What is the expected value of perfect information?

12. Refer again to the investment problem faced by Martin's Service Station (Exercise 5). Martin can purchase a blade to attach to his service truck that can be used to plow driveways and parking lots. Since this truck must also be available to start cars, Martin will not be able to generate as much revenue plowing snow if he elects this alternative, but his loss will be smaller if snowfall is light. Under this alternative, Martin forecasts a profit of $3500 if snowfall is heavy and $1000 if it is moderate, and a $1500 loss if snowfall is light.

a. Prepare a new decision tree showing all three alternatives.

b. With the expected value approach, what is the optimal decision?

c. What is the expected value of perfect information?

22.4   DECISION ANALYSIS WITH SAMPLE INFORMATION

In applying the expected value approach, we have shown how probability information about the states of nature affects the expected value calculations and thus the decision recommendation. Frequently, decision makers have preliminary or prior probability estimates for the states of nature that are the best probability values available. However, to make the best possible decision, the decision maker may want to seek additional information about the states of nature. This new information can be used to revise or update the prior probabilities so that the final decision is based on better probability estimates for the states of nature.

Most often, additional information is obtained through experiments designed to provide sample information about the states of nature. Raw material sampling, product testing, and market research are examples of experiments that may enable managers to revise or update the state-of-nature probabilities. In the following discussion, we will reconsider the PDC problem and show how to use sample information to revise the state-of-nature probabilities. We will then show how to use the revised probabilities to develop an optimal decision strategy for PDC.

Recall that PDC's managers provided initial subjective probability estimates of .8 for high market acceptance and .2 for low market acceptance. Since $P(s_1) = .8$ and $P(s_2) = .2$ were estimates developed prior to the collection of any sample information, they are called the *prior probabilities* for the states of nature. Recall that, using these prior probabilities, we determined that d_3, the decision to construct the large condominium complex was optimal, yielding an expected value of $14.2 million. Calculation of the expected value of perfect information showed that new information about the states of nature could potentially be worth as much as $3.2 million.

Suppose PDC considers undertaking a six-month market research study designed to evaluate market acceptance and ultimately buyer interest in purchasing the condo-

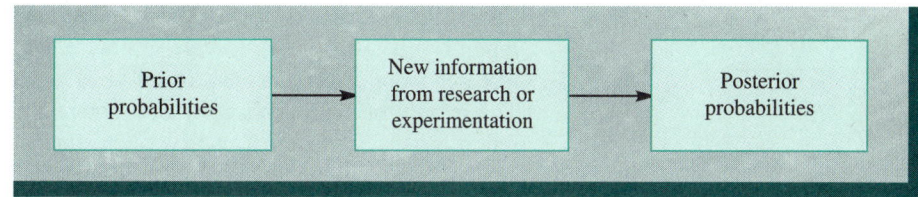

FIGURE 22.5 Probability Revision Based on New Information

minium units. The market research will provide new information that can be combined with the prior probabilities through a Bayesian procedure to obtain updated or revised probability estimates for the states of nature. These *revised* probabilities are called *posterior probabilities*. Figure 22.5 summarizes the process of revising probabilities.

We will refer to the new information obtained through research or experimentation as an *indicator*. In many cases the experiment conducted to obtain the additional information consists of taking a statistical sample, so the new information is also called *sample information*.

Using the indicator terminology, we can denote the outcomes of the PDC market research study as

I_1 = favorable market research report (i.e., the individuals contacted generally express interest in PDC's condominiums)

I_2 = unfavorable market research report (i.e., the individuals contacted generally express little interest in PDC's condominiums)

Given one of these possible indicators, the objective is to develop improved estimates of the probabilities of the two states of nature. The end result of the *Bayesian revision* process depicted in Figure 22.5 is a set of posterior probabilities of the form $P(s_j \mid I_k)$, where $P(s_j \mid I_k)$ represents the conditional probability that state of nature s_j will occur given that the outcome of the market research study is indicator I_k.

To make effective use of this indicator information, we must know something about the probability relationships between the indicators and the states of nature. For example, in the PDC problem, if the state of nature ultimately turns out to be high acceptance, what is the probability that the market research study will result in a favorable report? In this case, we are asking about the conditional probability of indicator I_1 given state of nature s_1, written $P(I_1 \mid s_1)$. To carry out the analysis, we will need conditional probabilities for all indicators given all states of nature, that is, $P(I_1 \mid s_1)$, $P(I_1 \mid s_2)$ $P(I_2 \mid s_1)$, and $P(I_2 \mid s_2)$.

In the PDC problem, we assume that the following estimates are available for the conditional probabilities.

	Market Research Report	
	Favorable	**Unfavorable**
State of Nature	I_1	I_2
High acceptance, s_1	$P(I_1 \mid s_1) = .90$	$P(I_2 \mid s_1) = .10$
Low acceptance, s_2	$P(I_1 \mid s_2) = .25$	$P(I_2 \mid s_2) = .75$

Note that these probability estimates provide a reasonable degree of confidence in the market research study. If the true state of nature is s_1, the probability of a favorable market research report (I_1) is .90 and the probability of an unfavorable market research report (I_2) is .10. If the true state of nature is s_2, the probability of a favorable market research report is .25 and the probability of an unfavorable market research report is .75. The reason for a .25 probability of a potentially misleading favorable market research report for state of nature s_2 is that when some potential buyers first hear about the new condominium project, their enthusiasm may lead them to overstate their real interest in it. A potential buyer's initial favorable response can reverse quickly once the individual is faced with the reality of signing a purchase contract and making a down payment.

22.5   DEVELOPING A DECISION STRATEGY

As we indicated in Section 22.3, a decision strategy is a decision rule that specifies the decision alternatives to be selected after new information becomes available. In the PDC problem, a decision strategy is a rule that recommends a particular decision based on whether the market research report is favorable or unfavorable. We will use a decision tree analysis to find the optimal decision strategy for PDC.

Figure 22.6 is the decision tree for the PDC problem if a market research study is conducted. Note that, from left to right, the tree shows the natural or logical order that will occur in the decision-making process. First, the firm will obtain the market research report indicator (I_1 or I_2); then a decision (d_1, d_2, or d_3) will be made; finally, the state of nature (s_1 or s_2) will occur. The decision and the state of nature combine to provide the final profit or payoff.

Using decision tree terminology, we have now introduced an *indicator node,* node 1, and *indicator branches,* I_1 and I_2. Since the branches emanating from indicator nodes are not under the control of the decision maker, but are determined by chance, we represent these nodes by a circle as we did the state-of-nature nodes. Nodes 2 and 3 are decision nodes, whereas nodes 4, 5, 6, 7, 8, and 9 are state-of-nature nodes. For decision nodes, the decision maker must select the specific branch d_1, d_2, or d_3 that will be taken. Selecting the best decision branch is equivalent to making the best decision. However, as the indicator and state-of-nature branches are not controlled by the decision maker, the specific branch leaving an indicator or a state-of-nature node will depend on the probability associated with the branch. Thus, before we can carry out an analysis of the decision tree and develop a decision strategy, we must compute the probability of each indicator branch and the probability of each state-of-nature branch. Note from the decision tree that the state-of-nature branches occur *after* the indicator branches. Hence, when we attempt to compute state-of-nature branch probabilities, we will need to consider which indicator was previously observed. That is, we will express the state-of-nature probabilities in terms of the probability of state of nature s_j *given* that indicator I_k was observed. Thus, all state-of-nature probabilities will be expressed in a $P(s_j \mid I_k)$ form.

COMPUTING BRANCH PROBABILITIES

Recall that the prior probabilities for the states of nature in the PDC problem are $P(s_1) = .8$ and $P(s_2) = .2$. In Section 22.4 we identified the relationships between the market research indicators and states of nature with the following conditional probabilities

$$P(I_1 \mid s_1) = .90 \quad P(I_2 \mid s_1) = .10$$

$$P(I_1 \mid s_2) = .25 \quad P(I_2 \mid s_2) = .75$$

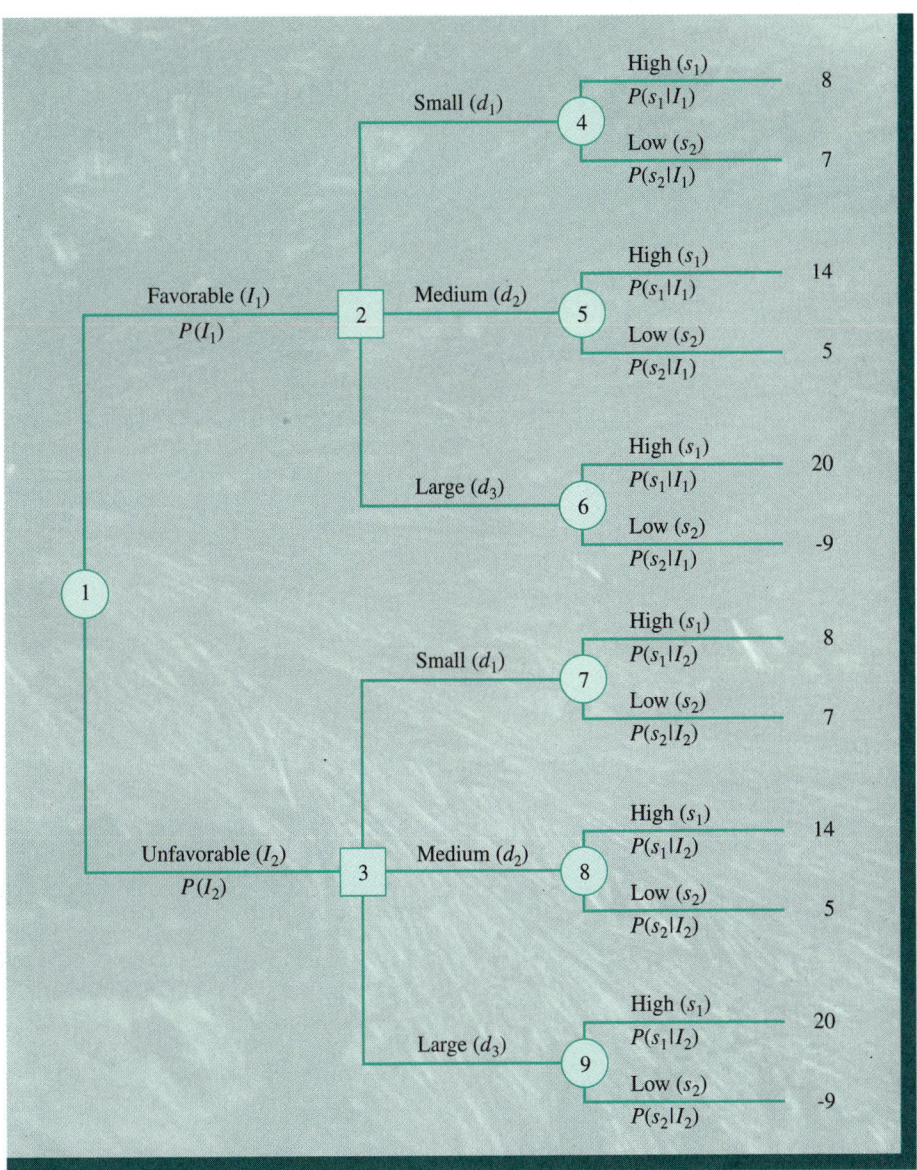

FIGURE 22.6 PDC Decision Tree Incorporating the Results of the Market Research Study (Payoffs in $Millions)

To develop a decision strategy by using the decision tree in Figure 22.6, we need indicator branch probabilities $P(I_k)$ and state-of-nature branch probabilities $P(s_j \mid I_k)$. The problem now is to determine how to use the prior probability estimates $P(s_j)$ and the conditional probability estimates $P(I_k \mid s_j)$ to calculate the branch probabilities $P(I_k)$ and $P(s_j \mid I_k)$. In this section we will show how to use the Bayesian revision process to calculate the branch probabilities $P(I_k)$ and $P(s_j \mid I_k)$.

In Section 4.5 we showed how to use Bayes' Theorem to revise or update prior probability values on the basis of new information from research or experimentation. We presented a tabular approach as a convenient method for carrying out the computations needed to obtain the revised or posterior probabilities. We will use this tabular approach to compute the branch probabilities for the PDC decision tree. The

TABLE 22.3 Branch Probabilities for the PDC Condominium Project Based on Indicator I_1, a Favorable Market Research Report

States of Nature s_j	Prior Probabilities $P(s_j)$	Conditional Probabilities $P(I_1 \mid s_j)$	Joint Probabilities $P(I_1 \cap s_j)$	Posterior Probabilities $P(s_j \mid I_1)$
s_1	.8	.90	.72	.9351
s_2	.2	.25	.05	.0649
			$P(I_1) = .77$	

TABLE 22.4 Branch Probabilities for the PDC Condominium Project Based on Indicator I_2, an Unfavorable Market Research Report

States of Nature s_j	Prior Probabilities $P(s_j)$	Conditional Probabilities $P(I_2 \mid s_j)$	Joint Probabilities $P(I_2 \cap s_j)$	Posterior Probabilities $P(s_j \mid I_2)$
s_1	.8	.10	.08	.3478
s_2	.2	.75	.15	.6522
			$P(I_2) = .23$	

computations for the PDC problem based on a favorable market research report (I_1) are summarized in Table 22.3. The steps used to develop this table follow.

Step 1. Enter the states of nature in column 1, the prior probabilities for the states of nature in column 2, and the conditional probabilities of indicator I_1 for each state of nature in column 3.

Step 2. In column 4 compute the joint probabilities for each state of nature-indicator combination by multiplying the prior probability entry in column 2 by the corresponding conditional probability entry in column 3.

Step 3. Sum the joint probabilities in column 4 to obtain $P(I_1)$, the probability of indicator I_1.

Step 4. Compute the posterior probabilities in column 5 by dividing each joint probability entry in column 4 by $P(I_1) = .77$.

Table 22.3 shows that the probability of obtaining a favorable market research report is $P(I_1) = .77$. The posterior probabilities of the states of nature based on a favorable market report are $P(s_1 \mid I_1) = .9351$ and $P(s_2 \mid I_1) = .0649$. In particular, note that if the market report is favorable, there is a .9351 probability of high market acceptance (s_1) of the condominium project; thus, a favorable market research report will encourage PDC to go ahead with plans to build the large condominium complex.

The tabular procedure must be repeated for each possible indicator. Table 22.4 shows the computations of the branch probabilities for the PDC problem based on an unfavorable market research report (I_2). Note that the probability of obtaining an unfavorable market research report is $P(I_2) = .23$. If an unfavorable report is obtained, the posterior probability of high market acceptance (s_1) is .3478 and that of low market acceptance (s_2) is .6522. The branch probabilities from Table 22.3 and 22.4 are shown on the PDC decision tree in Figure 22.7.

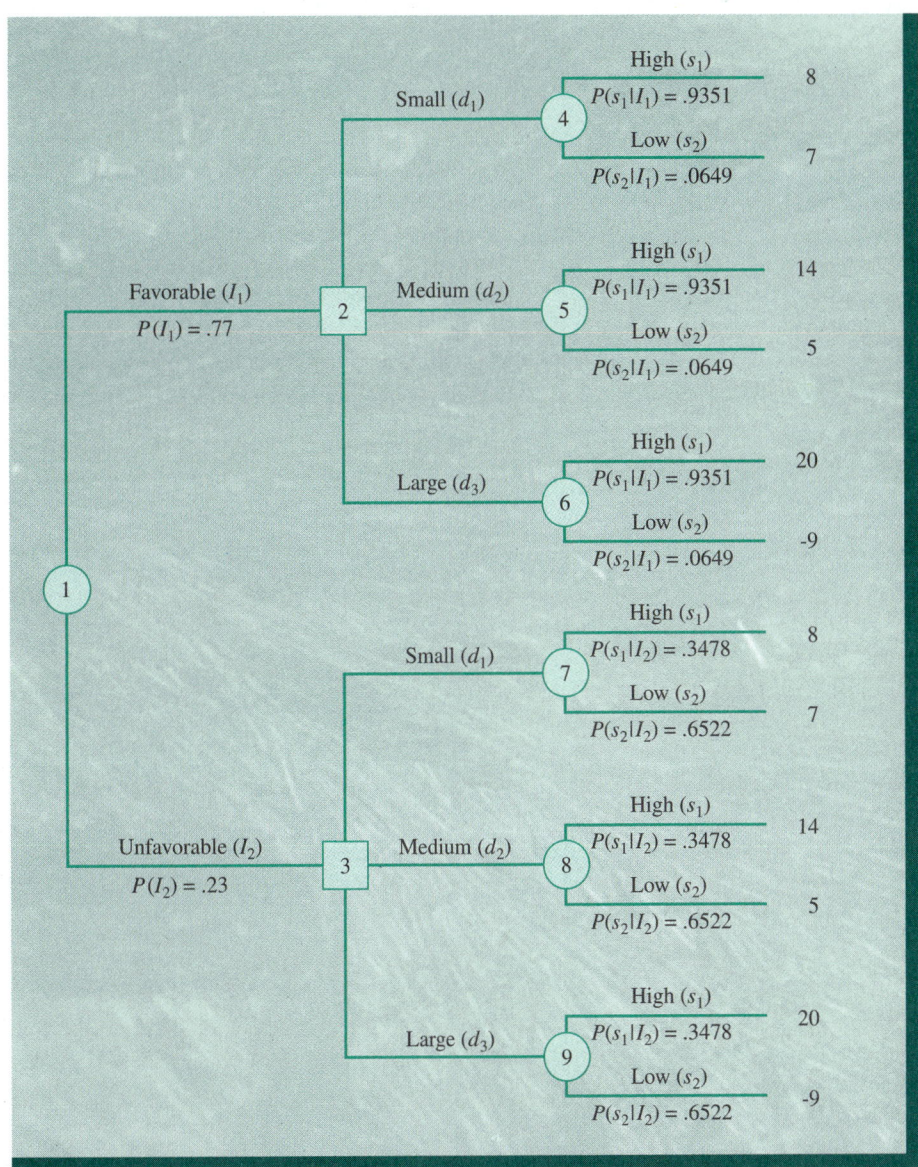

FIGURE 22.7 PDC Decision Tree with Branch Probabilities

• • • • • • • • • • • • • • • • • • **AN OPTIMAL DECISION STRATEGY**

After we have computed the branch probabilities, we can use the expected value approach to determine the optimal decision strategy. Working *backward* through the decision tree in Figure 22.7, we first compute the expected value at each state-of-nature node. That is, at each state-of-nature node, we weight the possible payoffs by their chance of occurring. Thus, we obtain the following expected values for nodes 4 through 9.

$$EV(\text{node } 4) = .9351(8) \ + .0649(7) \ = 7.935$$

$$EV(\text{node } 5) = .9351(14) + .0649(5) \ = 13.416$$

$$EV(\text{node } 6) = .9351(20) + .0649(-9) = 18.118$$

$$EV(\text{node } 7) = .3478(8) + .6522(7) = 7.348$$

$$EV(\text{node } 8) = .3478(14) + .6522(5) = 8.130$$

$$EV(\text{node } 9) = .3478(20) + .6522(-9) = 1.086$$

Figure 22.8 shows these calculations on the decision tree. Since the decision maker controls the branch leaving a decision node and is trying to maximize expected profit, the optimal decision at node 2 is d_3, with an expected value of 18.118. Thus, we write $EV(\text{node } 2)$ as 18.118. A similar analysis at node 3 shows that the optimal decision branch is d_2, with an expected value of 8.130. Thus, $EV(\text{node } 3) = 8.130$.

We continue working backward to determine the expected value of node 1. Node 1 has two probability branches, corresponding to indicators I_1 and I_2. We must use the branch probabilities, $P(I_1)$ and $P(I_2)$, to compute the overall expected value.

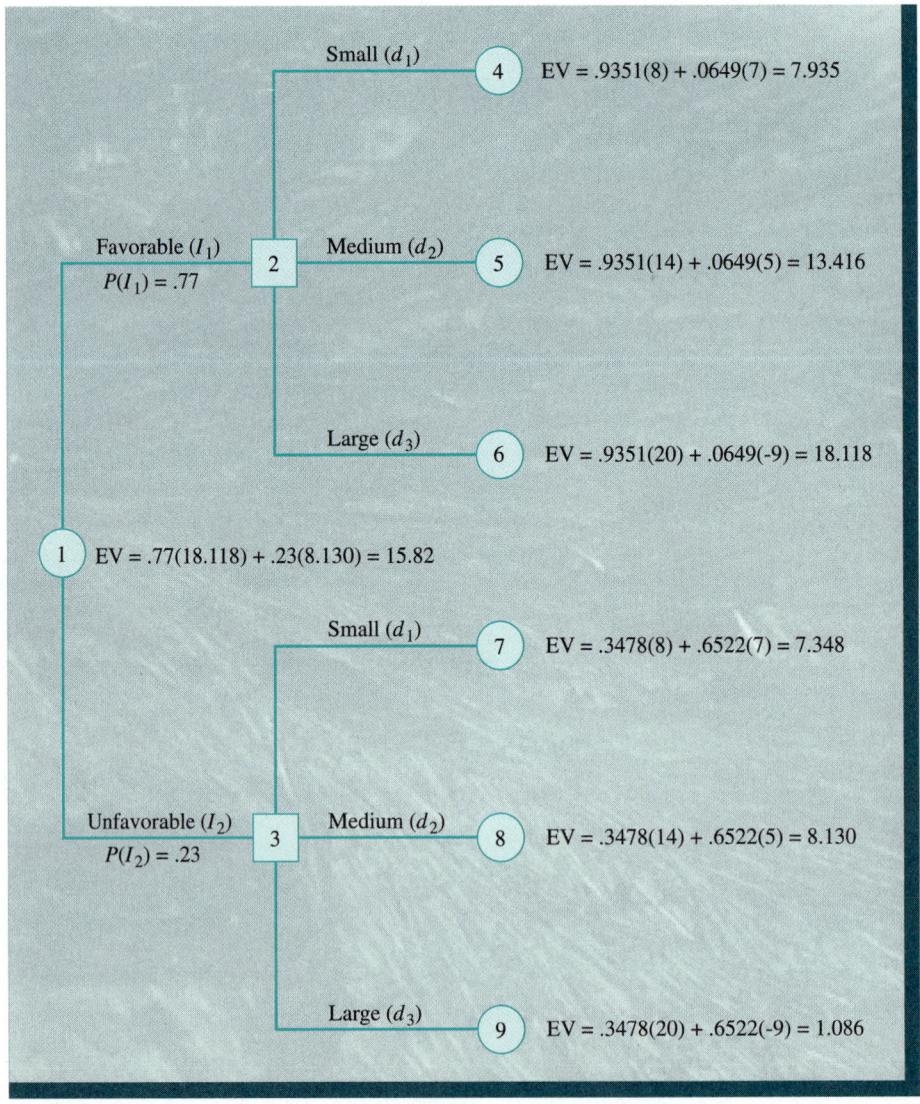

FIGURE 22.8   Developing a Decision Strategy for the PDC Problem

$$EV(\text{node } 1) = .77EV(\text{node } 2) + .23EV(\text{node } 3)$$

$$= (.77)(18.118) + (.23)(8.130) = 15.82$$

The value $15.82 million is the expected value of the optimal decision strategy if PDC conducts the market research study and uses the resulting information to determine a recommended size for the condominium complex.

Note that PDC has not yet determined the size of the complex. Managers will need to know the results of the market research study before deciding whether to construct the large complex (d_3) or the medium complex (d_2). The results of the decision analysis at this point, however, provide the following optimal decision strategy.

If	Then
Market report is favorable (I_1)	Construct the large condominium complex (d_3)
Market report is unfavorable (I_2)	Construct the medium condominium complex (d_2)

Although other problem, the optimal decision strategy approach outlined is still applicable. First, draw a decision tree consisting of indicator, decision, and state-of-nature nodes and branches so that the tree describes the specific sequence of decisions and chance outcomes. Make posterior probability calculations to establish indicator and state-of-nature branch probabilities. Then, by working backward through the tree, computing expected values at state-of-nature and indicator nodes, and selecting the best decision branch at decision nodes, determine an optimal decision strategy and its associated expected value.

EXERCISES

METHODS

Self-Test ·········▶

13. Suppose you are given a decision situation with three possible states of nature: s_1, s_2, and s_3. The prior probabilities are $P(s_1) = .2$, $P(s_2) = .5$, and $P(s_3) = .3$. Indicator information I is obtained, and it is known that $P(I \mid s_1) = .1$, $P(I \mid s_2) = .05$, and $P(I \mid s_3) = .2$. Compute the revised or posterior probabilities $P(s_1 \mid I)$, $P(s_2 \mid I)$, and $P(s_3 \mid I)$.

TABLE 22.5
Exercise 14

	s_1	s_2
d_1	15	10
d_2	10	12
d_3	8	20

14. Table 22.5 is a payoff table showing profit for a decision problem with two states of nature and three decision alternatives. The prior probabilities for s_1 and s_2 are $P(s_1) = .8$ and $P(s_2) = .2$.
   a. Using only the prior probabilities and the expected value approach, find the optimal decision.
   b. Find the EVPI.
   c. Suppose some indicator information I is obtained with $P(I \mid s_1) = .2$ and $P(I \mid s_2) = .75$. Find the posterior probabilities $P(s_1 \mid I)$ and $P(s_2 \mid I)$. Recommend a decision alternative based on these probabilities.

15. Consider the following decision tree representation of a decision analysis problem with two indicators, two decision alternatives, and two states of nature.

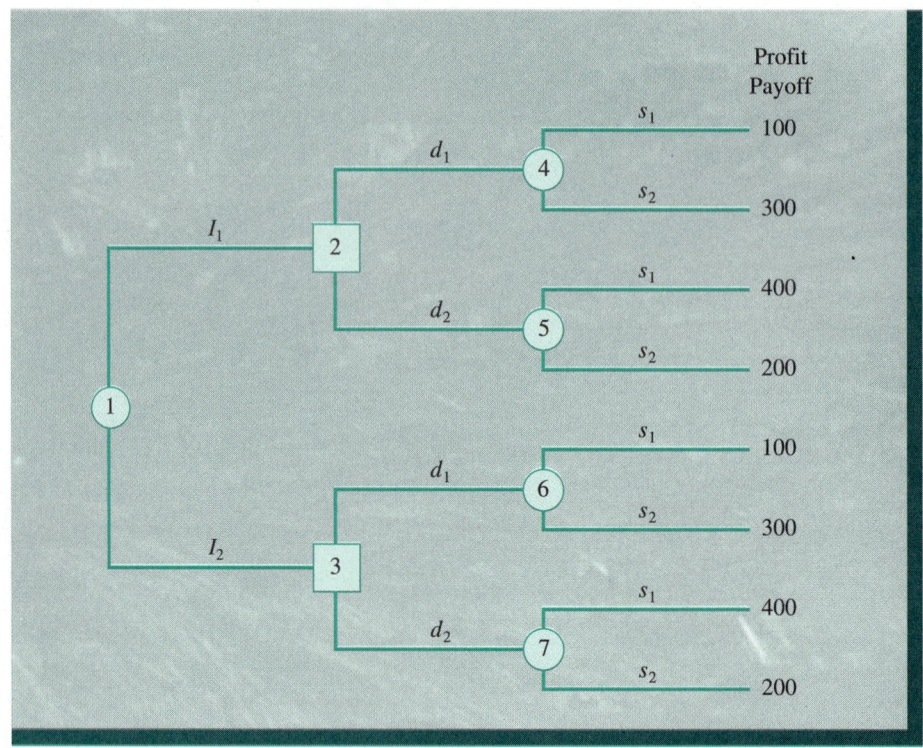

Assume that the following probability information is given.

$$P(s_1) = .4 \quad P(I_1 \mid s_1) = .8 \quad P(I_2 \mid s_1) = .2$$
$$P(s_2) = .6 \quad P(I_1 \mid s_2) = .4 \quad P(I_2 \mid s_2) = .6$$

a. What are the values for $P(I_1)$ and $P(I_2)$?
b. What are the values of $P(s_1 \mid I_1)$, $P(s_2 \mid I_1)$, $P(s_1 \mid I_2)$, and $P(s_2 \mid I_2)$?
c. Use the decision tree approach and determine the optimal decision strategy. What is the expected value of your solution?

22.6   EXPECTED VALUE OF SAMPLE INFORMATION

The optimal decision strategy developed in the preceding section shows that if the market research report is favorable, PDC should construct the large condominium complex. However, if the market research report is unfavorable, PDC should construct the medium condominium complex. The expected value of this optimal decision strategy, $15.82 million, is the *expected value with sample information* (EVwSI).

In Section 22.2 we used the expected value to recommend a decision alternative based on PDC's original probability estimates of $P(s_1) = .8$ and $P(s_2) = .2$. That analysis showed that d_3, with an expected value of $14.2 million, is the best decision. However, that recommendation lacked the benefit of sample information, so the $14.2 million result is the *expected value without sample information* (EVwoSI).

Since the expected value with sample information is $15.82 million and the expected value without sample information is $14.2 million, the expected value of the sample information (EVSI) is $15.82 − $14.2 = $1.62 million. In other words, $1.62 million is the increase in the expected value based on the sample information. In general, the expected value of sample information is computed as follows.

EXPECTED VALUE OF SAMPLE INFORMATION

$$EVSI = |\,EVwSI - EVwoSI\,|$$ (22.5)

where

$EVSI$ = expected value of sample information

$EVwSI$ = expected value with sample information about the states of nature

$EVwoSI$ = expected value *without* sample information about the states of nature

Note the role of the absolute value in (22.5). That is, for minimization problems the expected value with sample information always is less than or equal to the expected value without sample information. In this case, EVSI is the magnitude of the difference between EVwSI and EVwoSI; thus, by taking the absolute value of the difference as shown in (22.5), we can handle both the maximization and minimization cases with one equation.

Using (22.5) for the PDC problem, we have EVSI = | $15.82 − $14.2 | = $1.62 million. With this EVSI, PDC should consider undertaking the market research study.

EFFICIENCY OF SAMPLE INFORMATION

In Section 22.3 we showed that the expected value of perfect information (EVPI) for the PDC problem is $3.2 million. We did not expect the market research study to obtain perfect information, but we can use an *efficiency* measure to express the value of the market research information. With perfect information having an efficiency rating of 100%, the efficiency rating E for sample information is computed as follows.

EFFICIENCY OF SAMPLE INFORMATION

$$E = \frac{EVSI}{EVPI} \times 100$$ (22.6)

For the PDC problem,

$$E = \frac{1.62}{3.2} \times 100 = 50.6\%$$

In other words, the information from the market research study is 50.6% as efficient as perfect information.

Low efficiency ratings for sample information might lead the decision maker to look for other types of information. However, high efficiency ratings indicate that the sample information is almost as good as perfect information and that additional sources of information would not yield significantly better results.

EXERCISES

METHODS

Self-Test

16. For a particular decision problem, suppose the expected value of the optimal decision with sample information is $45,000 and the expected value of the optimal decision without sample information is $37,000. The expected value with perfect information is $60,000.
    a. Compute EVSI.
    b. What is the efficiency of the sample information?
    c. If the study to obtain the sample information had a cost of $10,000, what would you recommend?

17. Refer to Exercise 15.
    a. What is your decision without the indicator information?
    b. What is the expected value of the indicator or sample information EVSI?
    c. What is the expected value of perfect information EVPI?
    d. What is the efficiency of the indicator information?

APPLICATIONS

Self-Test

18. The payoff table (profit in $1000s) for Hale's TV Productions (Exercise 3) follows.

			States of Nature		
			s_1	s_2	s_3
	Produce pilot	d_1	−100	50	150
Decision Alternatives					
	Sell to competitor	d_2	100	100	100
Probability of States of Nature			.2	.3	.5

For a consulting fee of $2500, an agency will review the plans for the comedy series and indicate the overall chance of a favorable network reaction to the series. If the special agency review results in a favorable (I_1) or an unfavorable (I_2) evaluation, what should Hale's decision strategy be? Assume that Hale believes the following conditional probabilities are realistic appraisals of the agency's evaluation accuracy.

$$P(I_1 \mid s_1) = .3 \quad P(I_2 \mid s_1) = .7$$

$$P(I_1 \mid s_2) = .6 \quad P(I_2 \mid s_2) = .4$$

$$P(I_1 \mid s_3) = .9 \quad P(I_2 \mid s_3) = .1$$

a. Show the decision tree for this problem.
b. What is the recommended decision strategy and the expected value, assuming the agency information is obtained?
c. What is the EVSI? Is the $2500 consulting fee worth the information? What is the maximum that Hale should be willing to pay for the consulting information?

19. McHuffter Condominiums (exercise 4) is conducting a survey that will help evaluate the demand for the new condominium development. McHuffter's payoff table (profit in $1000s) follows.

		States of Nature		
		Low s_1	Medium s_2	High s_3
	Small d_1	400	400	400
Decision Alternatives Medium d_2		100	600	600
	Large d_3	-300	300	900
Probability of States of Nature		.20	.35	.45

TABLE 22.6
Exercise 19

$P(I_k|s_j)$			
	I_1	I_2	I_3
s_1	.6	.3	.1
s_2	.4	.4	.2
s_3	.1	.4	.5

The survey will result in three indicators of demand: weak (I_1), average (I_2), or strong (I_3). The conditional probabilities are as shown in Table 22.6.

a. What is McHuffter's optimal strategy?
b. What is the value of the survey information?
c. What are the EVPI and the efficiency of the survey information?

20. The payoff table ($) for Martin's Service Station (Exercises 5 and 12) follows.

		Snowfall		
		Heavy s_1	Moderate s_2	Light s_3
	Purchase snowplow d_1	7000	2000	-9000
Decision Alternatives	Do not invest d_2	0	0	0
	Purchase blade d_3	3500	1000	-1500
Probability of States of Nature		.4	.3	.3

Suppose Martin decides to wait to check the September temperature pattern before making a final decision. Estimates of the probabilities associated with an unseasonably cold September (I_1) are $P(I_1 \mid s_1) = .30$, $P(I_1 \mid s_2) = .20$, $P(I_1 \mid s_3) = .05$. If Martin observes an unseasonably cold September, what is the recommended decision? If Martin does not observe an unseasonably cold September (I_2), what is the recommended decision?

21. Suppose Joseph Software, Inc. (exercise 6) can hire an independent consultant to review its ideas for the new software. For a fee of $5000, the consultant will make a recommendation as to whether or not JSI should develop a prototype. On the basis of previous experience with this consultant, JSI has assigned the following conditional probabilities.

$$P(I_1 \mid s_1) = .2$$

$$P(I_1 \mid s_2) = .6$$

$$P(I_1 \mid s_3) = .9$$

where

$$I_1 = \text{recommendation to develop a prototype}$$

$$s_1 = \text{failure}$$

$$s_2 = \text{moderate success}$$

$$s_3 = \text{major success}$$

Should JSI hire the consultant? Explain.

22. Milford Trucking has the following payoff table.

			Return Shipment from Detroit	No Return Shipment from Detroit
			s_1	s_2
Shipment	St. Louis	d_1	2000	2000
	Detroit	d_2	2500	1000
Probabilities			.40	.60

a. Milford can phone a Detroit truck dispatch center and determine whether general Detroit shipping activity is busy (I_1) or slow (I_2). If the activity is busy, the chances of obtaining a return shipment will increase. Suppose the following conditional probabilities are given.

$$P(I_1 \mid s_1) = .6 \quad P(I_2 \mid s_1) = .4$$

$$P(I_1 \mid s_2) = .3 \quad P(I_2 \mid s_2) = .7$$

What should Milford do?

b. If the Detroit activity is busy (I_1), what is the probability that Milford will obtain a return shipment if it makes the trip to Detroit?

c. What is the efficiency of the phone information?

SUMMARY

In this chapter we showed how decision analysis can be used to solve problems with a limited number of decision alternatives and a limited number of states of nature. The goal of decision analysis is to identify the best decision alternative in the face of uncertain or risk-filled future events (i.e., states of nature).

We presented the use of expected value for decision making based on probabilities for the states of nature. Then we showed how to use additional information about the states of nature to revise or update the probability estimates and develop an optimal decision strategy. We applied the concepts of expected value of sample information, expected value of perfect information, and efficiency of information to measure the value of the sample information.

GLOSSARY

States of nature   The uncontrollable future events that affect the payoff associated with a decision alternative.

Payoff   The outcome measure, such as profit, cost, and time. Each combination of a decision alternative and a state of nature has an associated payoff.

Payoff table   A tabular representation of the payoffs for a decision problem.

Decision tree   A graphical representation of the decision problem that shows the sequential nature of the decision-making process.

Node   An intersection or junction point of the decision tree.

Branch   A line or arc connecting nodes of the decision tree.

Expected value (EV)   The weighted average of the payoffs for a decision alternative. The weights are the state-of-nature probabilities.

Expected value of perfect information (EVPI)   The expected value of information that would tell the decision maker exactly which state of nature is going to occur (i.e., perfect information).

Prior probabilities   The probabilities of the states of nature prior to obtaining sample information.

Posterior (revised) probabilities   The probabilities of the state of nature after revising the prior probabilities on the basis of sample information.

Indicator   Information about a state of nature. An indicator may be the result of a sample.

Bayesian revision   The process of revising prior probabilities to create the posterior probabilities based on sample information.

Expected value of sample information (EVSI)   The difference between the expected value of an optimal strategy based on sample information and the "best" expected value without any sample information.

Efficiency   The ratio of EVSI to EVPI; perfect information is 100% efficient.

KEY FORMULAS

Expected Value of Decision Alternative d_i

$$\text{EV}(d_i) = \sum_{j=1}^{N} P(s_j)V_{ij} \tag{22.3}$$

Expected Value of Perfect Information

$$\text{EVPI} = |\,\text{EVwPI} - \text{EVwoPI}\,| \tag{22.4}$$

Expected Value of Sample Information

$$\text{EVSI} = |\,\text{EVwSI} - \text{EVwoSI}\,| \tag{22.5}$$

Efficiency of Sample Information

$$\text{E} = \frac{\text{EVSI}}{\text{EVPI}}(100) \tag{22.6}$$

SUPPLEMENTARY EXERCISES

23. To save on gasoline expenses, Rona and Jerry agreed to form a carpool for traveling to and from work. After limiting the travel routes to two alternatives, Rona and Jerry could not agree on the best way to travel to work. Jerry preferred the expressway, since it was usually the fastest; however, Rona pointed out that traffic jams on the expressway sometimes led to long delays. Rona preferred the somewhat longer but more consistent Queen City Avenue. While Jerry still preferred the expressway, he agreed with Rona that they should take Queen City Avenue if the expressway had a traffic jam. Unfortunately, they do not know the state of the expressway in advance. The following payoff table provides the one-way time estimates in minutes for traveling to or from work.

			States of Nature	
			Expressway Open s_1	Expressway Jammed s_2
Route	Expressway	d_1	25	45
	Queen City Avenue	d_2	30	30

a. After driving to work on the expressway for one month (20 days), they found the expressway jammed three times. If these days are representative of future days, should they continue to use the expressway for traveling to work? Explain.

b. Would it make sense to not use the expected value approach for this particular problem? Explain.

After a period of time Rona and Jerry noted that the weather seemed to affect the traffic conditions on the expressway. They identified three weather conditions (indicators) with the following conditional probabilities.

$$I_1 = \text{clear} \quad I_2 = \text{overcast} \quad I_3 = \text{rain}$$

$$P(I_1 \mid s_1) = .8 \quad P(I_2 \mid s_1) = .2 \quad P(I_3 \mid s_1) = 0$$

$$P(I_1 \mid s_2) = .1 \quad P(I_2 \mid s_2) = .3 \quad P(I_3 \mid s_2) = .6$$

c. Show the decision tree for the problem of traveling to work.

d. What is the optimal decision strategy and the expected travel time?

e. What is the efficiency of the weather information?

24. The Gorman Manufacturing Company must decide whether it should purchase a component from a supplier or manufacture the component at its Milan, Michigan, plant. If demand is high, it would be to Gorman's advantage to manufacture the component. However, if demand is low, Gorman's unit manufacturing cost will be high due to underutilization of equipment. The projected profit figures in thousands of dollars for Gorman's make-or-buy decision follow.

		Demand		
		Low	Medium	High
Decision Alternatives	Manufacture component	−20	40	100
	Purchase component	10	45	70

The states of nature have the following probabilities: $P(\text{low demand}) = .35$, $P(\text{medium demand}) = .35$, and $P(\text{high demand}) = .30$.

a. Use a decision tree to recommend a decision.

b. Use EVPI to determine whether Gorman should attempt to obtain a better estimate of demand.

A test market study of the potential demand for the product is expected to indicate either a favorable (I_1) or unfavorable (I_2) condition. The relevant conditional probabilities follow.

$$P(I_1 \mid s_1) = .10 \quad P(I_2 \mid s_1) = .90$$

$$P(I_1 \mid s_2) = .40 \quad P(I_2 \mid s_2) = .60$$

$$P(I_1 \mid s_3) = .60 \quad P(I_2 \mid s_3) = .40$$

c. What is the probability that the market research report will be favorable?

d. What is Gorman's optimal decision strategy?

e. What is the expected value of the market research information?

f. What is the efficiency of the information?

25. A firm produces a perishable food product at a cost of $10 per case. The product sells for $15 per case. For planning purposes, the company is considering possible demand of 100, 200, or 300 cases. If the demand is less than production, the excess production is lost. If demand is more than production, the firm, in an attempt to maintain a good service image, will satisfy the excess demand with a special production run at a cost of $18 per case. The product always sells at $15 per case.

a. Set up the payoff table for this problem.

b. If $P(100) = .2$, $P(200) = .2$, and $P(300) = .6$, should the company produce 100, 200, or 300 cases?

c. What is the EVPI?

26. Sealcoat, Inc., has a contract with one of its customers to supply a unique liquid chemical product that will be used by the customer in the manufacture of a lubricant for airplane engines. Because of the chemical process used by Sealcoat, batch size for the liquid chemical product must be 1000 pounds. The customer has agreed to adjust manufacturing to the full batch quantities and will order either one, two, or three batches every three months. Since an aging process of one month is necessary for the product, Sealcoat will have to make its production (how much to make) decision before the customer places an order. Thus, Sealcoat can list the product demand alternatives of 1000, 2000, or 3000 pounds, but the exact demand is unknown.

Sealcoat's manufacturing costs are $150 per pound, and the product sells at the fixed contract price of $200 per pound. If the customer orders more than Sealcoat has produced, Sealcoat has agreed to absorb the added cost of filling the order by purchasing a higher quality substitute product from another chemical firm. The substitute product, including transportation expenses, will cost Sealcoat $240 per pound. Since the product cannot be stored more than two months without spoilage, Sealcoat cannot inventory excess production until the customer's next three-month order. Therefore, if the customer's current order is less than Sealcoat has produced, the excess production will be reprocessed and valued at $50 per pound.

The inventory decision in this problem is how much Sealcoat should produce given the costs and the possible demands of 1000, 2000, or 3000 pounds. From historical data and an analysis of the customer's future demands, Sealcoat has assessed the probability distribution for demand shown in Table 22.7.

a. Develop a payoff table for the Sealcoat problem.

b. How many batches should Sealcoat produce every three months?

c. How much of a discount should Sealcoat be willing to allow the customer for specifying in advance exactly how many batches will be purchased?

Sealcoat has identified a pattern in the demand for the product based on the customer's previous order quantity. Let

TABLE 22.7 Exercise 26

Demand	Probability
1000	.3
2000	.5
3000	.2

$$I_1 = \text{customer's last order was 1000 pounds}$$

$$I_2 = \text{customer's last order was 2000 pounds}$$

$$I_3 = \text{customer's last order was 3000 pounds.}$$

The conditional probabilities follow.

$P(I_1 \mid s_1) = .10$	$P(I_2 \mid s_1) = .40$	$P(I_3 \mid s_1) = .50$
$P(I_1 \mid s_2) = .22$	$P(I_2 \mid s_2) = .68$	$P(I_3 \mid s_2) = .10$
$P(I_1 \mid s_3) = .80$	$P(I_2 \mid s_3) = .20$	$P(I_3 \mid s_3) = .00$

   d. Develop an optimal decision strategy for Sealcoat.
   e. What is the EVSI?
   f. What is the efficiency of the information for the most recent order?

TABLE 22.8 Exercise 27

Percent Defective	Probability
0	.15
1	.25
2	.40
3	.20

27. A quality-control procedure involves 100% inspection of parts received from a supplier. Historical records indicate that the defect rates in Table 22.8 have been observed. The cost to inspect 100% of the parts received is $250 for each shipment of 500 parts. If the shipment is not 100% inspected, defective parts will cause rework problems later in the production process. The rework cost is $25 for each defective part.

   a. Complete the following payoff table, where the entries represent the total cost of inspection and reworking.

		Percent Defective			
		0	1	2	3
Inspection	100% inspection	$250	$250	$250	$250
	No inspection				

   b. The plant manager is considering eliminating the inspection process to save the $250 inspection cost per shipment. Do you support this action? Use expected value to justify your answer.
   c. Show the decision tree for this problem.
   d. Suppose a sample of five parts is selected from the shipment and one defect is found. Let $I = 1$ defect in a sample of five. Use the binomial probability distribution to compute $P(I \mid s_1)$, $P(I \mid s_2)$, $P(I \mid s_3)$, and $P(I \mid s_4)$ where the state of nature identifies the value for p. The binomial probability function follows.

$$f(x) = \frac{n!}{x!(n-x)!} p^x (1-p)^{n-x}$$

where

$$n = \text{the sample size}$$

$$x = \text{the number of defects}$$

$$p = \text{the proportion defective}$$

In this problem, $n = 5$, $x = 1$, and $p = 0$, .01, .02, and .03.

   e. If I occurs, what are the revised probabilities for the states of nature?
   f. Should the entire shipment be 100% inspected whenever one defect is found in a sample of size five?
   g. What is the cost savings associated with the sample information?

28. A food processor considers daily production runs of 100, 200, and 300 cases. Possible demand for the product is 100, 200, and 300 cases. The payoff table follows.

			Demand		
			100	200	300
			s_1	s_2	s_3
	100	d_1	500	200	−100
Production	200	d_2	−400	800	700
	300	d_3	−1000	−200	1600

a. If $P(s_1) = .2$, $P(s_2) = .2$, and $P(s_3) = .6$, what is your recommended production quantity?

b. On some days the firm receives phone calls for advance orders, and on some days it does not. Suppose I_1 = advance orders are received and I_2 = no advance orders are received. If $P(I_2 \mid s_1) = .8$, $P(I_2 \mid s_2) = .4$, and $P(I_2 \mid s_3) = .1$, what is your recommended production quantity for days when the company does not receive any advance orders?

29. The research and development manager for Beck Company is trying to decide whether to fund the development of a new lubricant. The assumption is that the project will be either a major technical success, a minor success, or a failure. The company has estimated that the value of a major success is $150,000, since the lubricant can be used in a number of products the company is making. If the project is a minor success, its value is $10,000, since Beck feels the knowledge gained will benefit some other ongoing projects. If the project is a failure, it will cost the company $100,000.

The opinion of the scientists involved and the manager's own subjective assessment led to the following prior probabilities.

$$P(\text{major success}) = .15$$

$$P(\text{minor success}) = .45$$

$$P(\text{failure}) = .40$$

a. Does the expected value approach show that the project should be funded?

b. Suppose a group of expert scientists from a research institute could be hired as consultants to study the project and make a recommendation. If this study will cost $30,000, should the Beck Company consider hiring the consultants?

Suppose an experiment can be conducted to shed some light on the technical feasibility of the project. There are three possible outcomes for the experiment.

$$I_1 = \text{prototype lubricant works well at all temperatures}$$

$$I_2 = \text{prototype lubricant works well only at temperatures above } 10°F$$

$$I_3 = \text{prototype lubricant does not work well at any temperature}$$

Assume that we can determine the following conditional probabilities.

$P(I_1 \mid \text{major success}) = .70$	$P(I_2 \mid \text{major success}) = .25$	$P(I_3 \mid \text{major success}) = .05$
$P(I_1 \mid \text{minor success}) = .10$	$P(I_2 \mid \text{minor success}) = .70$	$P(I_3 \mid \text{minor success}) = .20$
$P(I_1 \mid \text{failure}) = .10$	$P(I_2 \mid \text{failure}) = .30$	$P(I_3 \mid \text{failure}) = .60$

c. If the experiment is conducted and the prototype lubricant works well at all temperatures, should the development project be funded?

d. If the experiment is conducted and the prototype lubricant works well only at temperatures above 10°F, should the project be funded?

e. Develop a decision strategy that Beck's R&D manager can use to recommend a funding decision based on the outcome of the experiment.

f. Find the EVSI for the experiment. How efficient is the information in the experiment?

Appendixes •••••••••••••

APPENDIX A

References and Bibliography

GENERAL

DuToit, S. H.C., *Graphical Exploratory Data Analysis,* New York, Springer-Verlag, 1986.

Freedman, D., R. Pisani, and R. Purves, *Statistics,* 2nd ed., New York, W. W. Norton, 1991.

Freund, J. E., and R. E. Walpole, *Mathematical Statistics,* 4th ed., Englewood Cliffs, NJ, Prentice-Hall, 1987.

Hoaglin, D. C., F. Mosteller, and J. W. Tukey, *Understanding Robust and Exploratory Data Analysis,* New York, Wiley, 1983.

Hogg, R. V., and A. T. Craig, *Introduction to Mathematical Statistics,* 4th ed., New York, Macmillian, 1978.

McClave, J. T., and G. B. Benson, *Statistics for Business and Economics,* 6th ed., New York, Dellen, 1994.

Mood, A. M., F. A. Graybill, and D. C. Boes, *Introduction to the Theory of Statistics,* 3rd ed., New York, McGraw-Hill, 1974.

Moore, D. S., and G. P. McCabe, *Introduction to the Practice of Statistics,* 2nd ed., New York, Freeman, 1992.

Neter, J., W. Wasserman, and G. A. Whitmore, *Applied Statistics,* 4th ed., Boston, Allyn & Bacon, 1993.

Roberts, H., *Data Analysis for Managers,* 2nd ed., Redwood City, CA., Scientific Press, 1991.

Ryan, T. A., B. L. Joiner, and B. F. Ryan, *Minitab Handbook,* 2nd ed., Boston, PWS-Kent, 1992.

Tanur, J. M., et al., *Statistics: A Guide to the Unknown,* 3rd ed., Pacific Grove, CA, Wadsworth, 1989.

Tukey, J. W., *Exploratory Data Analysis,* Reading, MA, Addison-Wesley, 1977.

Winkler, R. L., and W. L. Hays, *Statistics: Probability, Inference, and Decision,* 2nd ed., New York, Holt, Rinehart & Winston, 1975.

PROBABILITY

Barr, D. R., and P. W. Zehna, *Probability: Modeling Uncertainty,* Reading, MA., Addison-Wesley, 1983.

Feller, W., *An Introduction to Probability Theory and Its Applications,* Vol. I, 3rd ed., New York, Wiley, 1968.

Feller, W., *An Introduction to Probability Theory and Its Applications,* Vol. II, 2nd ed., New York, Wiley, 1971.

Hogg, R. V., and Elliott A. Tanis, *Probability and Statistical Inference,* 4th ed., New York, Macmillan, 1992.

Mendenhall, W., R. L. Scheaffer, and D. Wackerly, *Mathematical Statistics with Applications,* 4th ed., Boston, PWS-Kent, 1990.

Ross, S. M., *Introduction to Probability Models* 5 ed., San Diego, Academic Press, 1993.

EXPERIMENTAL DESIGN

Anderson, V. L., and R. A. McLean, *Design of Experiments: A Realistic Approach,* New York, Marcel Dekker, 1974.

Box, G. E. P., W. G. Hunter, and J. S. Hunter, *Statistics for Experimenters,* New York, Wiley, 1978.

Brown, S. B., and L. E. Melamed, *Experimental Design and Analysis,* Newbury Park, Sage Publications, 1990.

Cochran, W. G., and G. M. Cox, *Experimental Designs,* 2nd ed., New York, Wiley, 1992.

Hicks, C. R., *Fundamental Concepts in the Design of Experiments,* 4th ed., New York, Saunders College Publishing, 1993.

Maxwell, S. E., and H. D. Delaney, *Designing Experiments and Analyzing Data,* Belmont, CA, Wadsworth, 1990.

Montgomery, D. C., *Design and Analysis of Experiments,* 3rd ed., New York, Wiley, 1993.

Winer, B. J., *Statistical Principles in Experimental Design,* 3rd ed., New York, McGraw-Hill, 1991.

REGRESSION ANALYSIS

Belsley, D. A., E. Kuh, and R. Welsch, *Regression Diagnostics: Identifying Influential Data and Sources of Collinearity,* New York, Wiley, 1980.

Chatterjee, S., and B. Price, *Regression Analysis by Example,* New York, Wiley, 1977.

Cook, R. D., and S. Weisberg, *Residuals and Influence in Regression,* New York, Chapman and Hall, 1982.

Daniel, C., and F. Wood, *Fitting Equations to Data,* 2nd ed., New York, Wiley, 1980.

Draper, N. R., and H. Smith, *Applied Regression Analysis,* 2nd ed., New York, Wiley, 1981.

Graybill, F. A., and H. K. Iyer, *Regression Analysis: Concepts and Applications,* Belmont, CA, Duxbury, 1994.

Kleinbaum, D. G., and L. L. Kupper, *Applied Regression Analysis and Other Multivariable Methods,* 2nd ed., Boston, PWS-Kent, 1988.

Mosteller, F., and J. W. Tukey, *Data Analysis and Regression: A Second Course in Statistics,* Reading, MA, Addison-Wesley, 1977.

Myers, R. H., *Classical and Modern Regression with Applications,* 2nd ed., Boston, PWS-Kent, 1990.

Neter, J., W. Wasserman, and M. H. Kutner, *Applied Linear Statistical Models,* 2nd ed., Homewood, IL, Richard D. Irwin, 1985.

Weisberg, S., *Applied Linear Regression,* 2nd ed., New York, Wiley, 1985.

Wesolowsky, G. O., *Multiple Regression and Analysis of Variance,* New York, Wiley, 1976.

Wonnacott, T. H., and R. J. Wonnacott, *Regression: A Second Course in Statistics,* New York, Wiley, 1981.

INDEX NUMBERS

U.S. Dept. of Commerce *Survey of Current Business.*

U.S. Department of Labor, Bureau of Labor Statistics, *CPI Detailed Report.*

U.S. Department of Labor, *Producer Price Indexes.*

FORECASTING

Bowerman, B. L., and R. T. O'Connell, *Time Series Forecasting,* 3rd ed., Belmont, CA, Duxbury Press, 1993.

Box, G. E. P., G. M. Jenkins, and G. C. Reinsel, *Time Series Analysis, Forecasting and Control,* 3rd ed., Englewood Cliffs, NJ, Prentice-Hall, 1994.

Brown, R. G., *Smoothing, Forecasting, and Prediction,* Englewood Cliffs, NJ, Prentice-Hall, 1963.

Gilchrist, W. G., *Statistical Forecasting,* New York, Wiley, 1976.

Makridakis, S., and S. C. Wheelwright, *Forecasting: Methods and Applications,* New York, Wiley, 1978.

Nelson, C. R., *Applied Time Series Analysis for Managerial Forecasting,* San Francisco, Holden-Day, 1973.

Pankratz, A., *Forecasting with Univariate Box-Jenkins Models,* New York, Wiley, 1983.

Thomopoulos, N. T., *Applied Forecasting Methods,* Englewood Cliffs, NJ, Prentice-Hall, 1980.

Wheelwright, S. C., and S. Makridakis, *Forecasting Methods for Management,* 5th ed., New York, Wiley, 1989.

NONPARAMETRIC METHODS

Conover, W. J., *Practical Nonparametric Statistics,* 2nd ed., New York, Wiley, 1980.

Gibbons, J. D., *Nonparametric Statistical Inference,* 3rd ed., New York, Dekker, 1992.

Lehmann, E. L., *Nonparametrics: Statistical Methods Based on Ranks,* San Francisco, Holden-Day, 1975.

Siegel, S., *Nonparametric Statistics for the Behavioral Sciences,* New York, McGraw-Hill, 1956.

Sprent, P., *Applied Nonparametric Statistical Methods,* London, New York, Chapman and Hall, 1993.

QUALITY CONTROL

Deming, W. E., *Quality, Productivity, and Competitive Position,* Cambridge, MA, MIT Center for Advanced Engineering Study, 1982.

Duncan, A. J., *Quality Control and Industrial Statistics,* 5th ed. Homewood, IL, Irwin, 1986.

Evans, J. R., and W. M. Lindsay, *The Management and Control of Quality,* 2nd ed., St. Paul, MN, West, 1992.

Gitlow, H., S. Gitlow, A. Oppenheim, and R. Oppenheim, *Tools and Methods for the Improvement of Quality,* Homewood, IL, Irwin, 1989.

Ishikawa, Kaoru, *Guide to Quality Control,* 2nd rev. ed., New York, Quality Resources, 1986.

Juran, J. M., and F. M. Gryna, Jr., *Quality Planning and Analysis,* 2nd ed., New York, McGraw-Hill, 1980.

Montgomery, D. C., Introduction to Statistical Quality Control, 2nd ed., New York, Wiley, 1991.

SAMPLING METHODS

Cochran, W. G., *Sampling Techniques,* 3rd ed., New York, Wiley, 1977.

Deming, W. E., *Sample Design in Business Research,* New York, Wiley, 1960.

Kish, L., *Survey Sampling,* New York, Wiley, 1965.

Levy, P. S., and S. Lemeshow, *Sampling of Populations: Methods and Applications,* New York, Wiley, 1991.

Scheaffer, R. L., W. Mendenhall, and L. Ott, *Elementary Survey Sampling,* 4th ed., Boston, PWS-Kent, 1990.

Williams, B., *A Sampler on Sampling,* New York, Wiley, 1978.

Warwick, D. P., and C. Lininger, *The Sample Survey: Theory and Practice,* New York, McGraw-Hill, 1975.

DECISION ANALYSIS

Behn, R. D., and J. W. Vaupel, *Quick Analysis for Busy Decision Makers,* New York, Basic Books, 1982.

Berger, J. O., *Statistical Decision Theory and Bayesian Analysis,* 2nd ed., New York, Springer-Verlag, 1985.

Lee, P. M., *Bayesian Statistics: An Introduction,* London, Oxford University Press, 1992.

Luce, R. D., and H. Raiffa, *Games and Decisions: Introduction and Critical Survey,* New York, Wiley, 1957.

Raiffa, H., *Decision Analysis: Introductory Lectures on Choices under Uncertainty,* Reading, MA, Addison-Wesley, 1968.

Winkler, R. L., *An Introduction to Bayesian Inference and Decision,* New York, Holt, Rinehart & Winston, 1972.

APPENDIX B

Tables

TABLE 1 Standard Normal Distribution

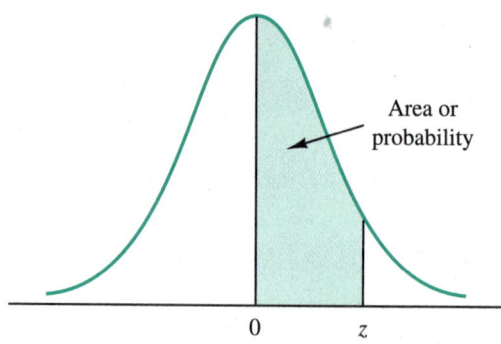

Area or probability

0　　z

Entries in the table give the area under the curve between the mean and z standard deviations above the mean. For example, for $z = 1.25$ the area under the curve between the mean and z is .3944.

z	.00	.01	.02	.03	.04	.05	.06	.07	.08	.09
.0	.0000	.0040	.0080	.0120	.0160	.0199	.0239	.0279	.0319	.0359
.1	.0398	.0438	.0478	.0517	.0557	.0596	.0636	.0675	.0714	.0753
.2	.0793	.0832	.0871	.0910	.0948	.0987	.1026	.1064	.1103	.1141
.3	.1179	.1217	.1255	.1293	.1331	.1368	.1406	.1443	.1480	.1517
.4	.1554	.1591	.1628	.1664	.1700	.1736	.1772	.1808	.1844	.1879
.5	.1915	.1950	.1985	.2019	.2054	.2088	.2123	.2157	.2190	.2224
.6	.2257	.2291	.2324	.2357	.2389	.2422	.2454	.2486	.2518	.2549
.7	.2580	.2612	.2642	.2673	.2704	.2734	.2764	.2794	.2823	.2852
.8	.2881	.2910	.2939	.2967	.2995	.3023	.3051	.3078	.3106	.3133
.9	.3159	.3186	.3212	.3238	.3264	.3289	.3315	.3340	.3365	.3389
1.0	.3413	.3438	.3461	.3485	.3508	.3531	.3554	.3577	.3599	.3621
1.1	.3643	.3665	.3686	.3708	.3729	.3749	.3770	.3790	.3810	.3830
1.2	.3849	.3869	.3888	.3907	.3925	.3944	.3962	.3980	.3997	.4015
1.3	.4032	.4049	.4066	.4082	.4099	.4115	.4131	.4147	.4162	.4177
1.4	.4192	.4207	.4222	.4236	.4251	.4265	.4279	.4292	.4306	.4319
1.5	.4332	.4345	.4357	.4370	.4382	.4394	.4406	.4418	.4429	.4441
1.6	.4452	.4463	.4474	.4484	.4495	.4505	.4515	.4525	.4535	.4545
1.7	.4554	.4564	.4573	.4582	.4591	.4599	.4608	.4616	.4625	.4633
1.8	.4641	.4649	.4656	.4664	.4671	.4678	.4686	.4693	.4699	.4706
1.9	.4713	.4719	.4726	.4732	.4738	.4744	.4750	.4756	.4761	.4767
2.0	.4772	.4778	.4783	.4788	.4793	.4798	.4803	.4808	.4812	.4817
2.1	.4821	.4826	.4830	.4834	.4838	.4842	.4846	.4850	.4854	.4857
2.2	.4861	.4864	.4868	.4871	.4875	.4878	.4881	.4884	.4887	.4890
2.3	.4893	.4896	.4898	.4901	.4904	.4906	.4909	.4911	.4913	.4916
2.4	.4918	.4920	.4922	.4925	.4927	.4929	.4931	.4932	.4934	.4936
2.5	.4938	.4940	.4941	.4943	.4945	.4946	.4948	.4949	.4951	.4952
2.6	.4953	.4955	.4956	.4957	.4959	.4960	.4961	.4962	.4963	.4964
2.7	.4965	.4966	.4967	.4968	.4969	.4970	.4971	.4972	.4973	.4974
2.8	.4974	.4975	.4976	.4977	.4977	.4978	.4979	.4979	.4980	.4981
2.9	.4981	.4982	.4982	.4983	.4984	.4984	.4985	.4985	.4986	.4986
3.0	.4986	.4987	.4987	.4988	.4988	.4989	.4989	.4989	.4990	.4990

TABLE 2 *t* Distribution

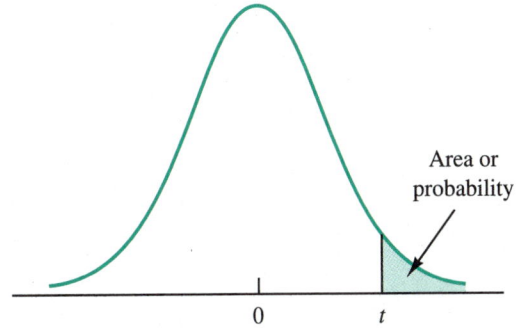

Area or probability

0   *t*

Entries in the table give *t* values for an area or probability in the upper tail of the *t* distribution. For example, with 10 degrees of freedom and a .05 area in the upper tail, $t_{.05} = 1.812$.

Degrees of Freedom	Area in Upper Tail				
	.10	.05	.025	.01	.005
1	3.078	6.314	12.706	31.821	63.657
2	1.886	2.920	4.303	6.965	9.925
3	1.638	2.353	3.182	4.541	5.841
4	1.533	2.132	2.776	3.747	4.604
5	1.476	2.015	2.571	3.365	4.032
6	1.440	1.943	2.447	3.143	3.707
7	1.415	1.895	2.365	2.998	3.499
8	1.397	1.860	2.306	2.896	3.355
9	1.383	1.833	2.262	2.821	3.250
10	1.372	1.812	2.228	2.764	3.169
11	1.363	1.796	2.201	2.718	3.106
12	1.356	1.782	2.179	2.681	3.055
13	1.350	1.771	2.160	2.650	3.012
14	1.345	1.761	2.145	2.624	2.977
15	1.341	1.753	2.131	2.602	2.947
16	1.337	1.746	2.120	2.583	2.921
17	1.333	1.740	2.110	2.567	2.898
18	1.330	1.734	2.101	2.552	2.878
19	1.328	1.729	2.093	2.539	2.861
20	1.325	1.725	2.086	2.528	2.845
21	1.323	1.721	2.080	2.518	2.831
22	1.321	1.717	2.074	2.508	2.819
23	1.319	1.714	2.069	2.500	2.807
24	1.318	1.711	2.064	2.492	2.797
25	1.316	1.708	2.060	2.485	2.787
26	1.315	1.706	2.056	2.479	2.779
27	1.314	1.703	2.052	2.473	2.771
28	1.313	1.701	2.048	2.467	2.763
29	1.311	1.699	2.045	2.462	2.756
30	1.310	1.697	2.042	2.457	2.750
40	1.303	1.684	2.021	2.423	2.704
60	1.296	1.671	2.000	2.390	2.660
120	1.289	1.658	1.980	2.358	2.617
∞	1.282	1.645	1.960	2.326	2.576

This table is reprinted by permission of Biometrika Trustees from Table 12, Percentage Points of the *t* Distribution, 3rd Edition, 1966. E. S. Pearson and H. O. Hartley, *Biometrika Tables for Statisticians*, Vol. I.

TABLE 3   Chi-Square Distribution

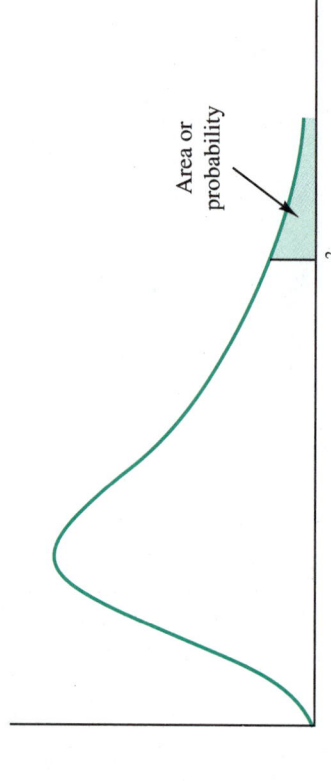

Area or probability

χ_α^2

Entries in the table give χ_α^2 values, where α is the area or probability in the upper tail of the chi-square distribution. For example, with 10 degrees of freedom and a .01 area in the upper tail, $\chi_{.01}^2 = 23.2093$.

Area in Upper Tail

Degrees of Freedom	.995	.99	.975	.95	.90	.10	.05	.025	.01	.005
1	$392,704 \times 10^{-10}$	$157,088 \times 10^{-9}$	$982,069 \times 10^{-9}$	$393,214 \times 10^{-8}$	.0157908	2.70554	3.84146	5.02389	6.63490	7.87944
2	.0100251	.0201007	.0506356	.102587	.210720	4.60517	5.99147	7.37776	9.21034	10.5966
3	.0717212	.114832	.215795	.351846	.584375	6.25139	7.81473	9.34840	11.3449	12.8381
4	.206990	.297110	.484419	.710721	1.063623	7.77944	9.48773	11.1433	13.2767	14.8602
5	.411740	.554300	.831211	1.145476	1.61031	9.23635	11.0705	12.8325	15.0863	16.7496
6	.675727	.872085	1.237347	1.63539	2.20413	10.6446	12.5916	14.4494	16.8119	18.5476
7	.989265	1.239043	1.68987	2.16735	2.83311	12.0170	14.0671	16.0128	18.4753	20.2777
8	1.344419	1.646482	2.17973	2.73264	3.48954	13.3616	15.5073	17.5346	20.0902	21.9550
9	1.734926	2.087912	2.70039	3.32511	4.16816	14.6837	16.9190	19.0228	21.6660	23.5893

10	2.15585	2.55821	3.24697	3.94030	4.86518	15.9871	18.3070	20.4831	23.2093	25.1882
11	2.60321	3.05347	3.81575	4.57481	5.57779	17.2750	19.6751	21.9200	24.7250	26.7569
12	3.07382	3.57056	4.40379	5.22603	6.30380	18.5494	21.0261	23.3367	26.2170	28.2995
13	3.56503	4.10691	5.00874	5.89186	7.04150	19.8119	22.3621	24.7356	27.6883	29.8194
14	4.07468	4.66043	5.62872	6.57063	7.78953	21.0642	23.6848	26.1190	29.1413	31.3193
15	4.60094	5.22935	6.26214	7.26094	8.54675	22.3072	24.9958	27.4884	30.5779	32.8013
16	5.14224	5.81221	6.90766	7.96164	9.31223	23.5418	26.2962	28.8454	31.9999	34.2672
17	5.69724	6.40776	7.56418	8.67176	10.0852	24.7690	27.5871	30.1910	33.4087	35.7185
18	6.26481	7.01491	8.23075	9.39046	10.8649	25.9894	28.8693	31.5264	34.8053	37.1564
19	6.84398	7.63273	8.90655	10.1170	11.6509	27.2036	30.1435	32.8523	36.1908	38.5822
20	7.43386	8.26040	9.59083	10.8508	12.4426	28.4120	31.4104	34.1696	37.5662	39.9968
21	8.03366	8.89720	10.28293	11.5913	13.2396	29.6151	32.6705	35.4789	38.9321	41.4010
22	8.64272	9.54249	10.9823	12.3380	14.0415	30.8133	33.9244	36.7807	40.2894	42.7958
23	9.26042	10.19567	11.6885	13.0905	14.8479	32.0069	35.1725	38.0757	41.6384	44.1813
24	9.88623	10.8564	12.4011	13.8484	15.6587	33.1963	36.4151	39.3641	42.9798	45.5585
25	10.5197	11.5240	13.1197	14.6114	16.4734	34.3816	37.6525	40.6465	44.3141	46.9278
26	11.1603	12.1981	13.8439	15.3791	17.2919	35.5631	38.8852	41.9232	45.6417	48.2899
27	11.8076	12.8786	14.5733	16.1513	18.1138	36.7412	40.1133	43.1944	46.9630	49.6449
28	12.4613	13.5648	15.3079	16.9279	18.9392	37.9159	41.3372	44.4607	48.2782	50.9933
29	13.1211	14.2565	16.0471	17.7083	19.7677	39.0875	42.5569	45.7222	49.5879	52.3356
30	13.7867	14.9535	16.7908	18.4926	20.5992	40.2560	43.7729	46.9792	50.8922	53.6720
40	20.7065	22.1643	24.4331	26.5093	29.0505	51.8050	55.7585	59.3417	63.6907	66.7659
50	27.9907	29.7067	32.3574	34.7642	37.6886	63.1671	67.5048	71.4202	76.1539	79.4900
60	35.5346	37.4848	40.4817	43.1879	46.4589	74.3970	79.0819	83.2976	88.3794	91.9517
70	43.2752	45.4418	48.7576	51.7393	55.3290	85.5271	90.5312	95.0231	100.425	104.215
80	51.1720	53.5400	57.1532	60.3915	64.2778	96.5782	101.879	106.629	112.329	116.321
90	59.1963	61.7541	65.6466	69.1260	73.2912	107.565	113.145	118.136	124.116	128.299
100	67.3276	70.0648	74.2219	77.9295	82.3581	118.498	124.342	129.561	135.807	140.169

TABLE 4 *F* Distribution

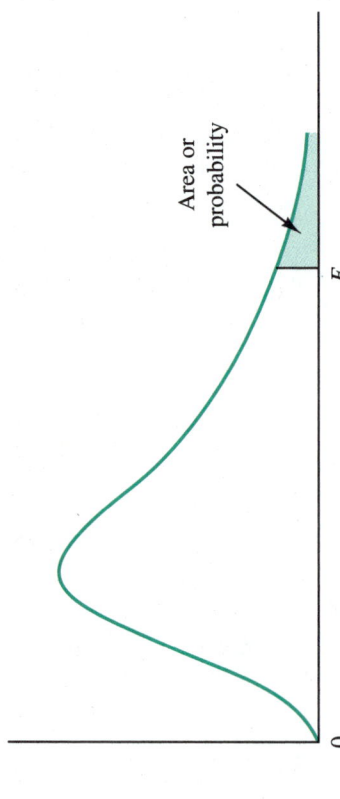

Area or probability

F_α

0

Entries in the table give F_α values, where α is the area or probability in the upper tail of the *F* distribution. For example, with 12 numerator degrees of freedom, 15 denominator degrees of freedom, and a .05 area in the upper tail, $F_{.05} = 2.48$.

Table of $F_{.05}$ Values

Denominator Degrees of Freedom	Numerator Degrees of Freedom																		
	1	2	3	4	5	6	7	8	9	10	12	15	20	24	30	40	60	120	∞
1	161.4	199.5	215.7	224.6	230.2	234.0	236.8	238.9	240.5	241.9	243.9	245.9	248.0	249.1	250.1	251.1	252.2	253.3	254.3
2	18.51	19.00	19.16	19.25	19.30	19.33	19.35	19.37	19.38	19.40	19.41	19.43	19.45	19.45	19.46	19.47	19.48	19.49	19.50
3	10.13	9.55	9.28	9.12	9.01	8.94	8.89	8.85	8.81	8.79	8.74	8.70	8.66	8.64	8.62	8.59	8.57	8.55	8.53
4	7.71	6.94	6.59	6.39	6.26	6.16	6.09	6.04	6.00	5.96	5.91	5.86	5.80	5.77	5.75	5.72	5.69	5.66	5.63
5	6.61	5.79	5.41	5.19	5.05	4.95	4.88	4.82	4.77	4.74	4.68	4.62	4.56	4.53	4.50	4.46	4.43	4.40	4.36

6	5.99	5.14	4.76	4.53	4.39	4.28	4.21	4.15	4.10	4.06	4.00	3.94	3.87	3.84	3.81	3.77	3.74	3.70	3.67
7	5.59	4.74	4.35	4.12	3.97	3.87	3.79	3.73	3.68	3.64	3.57	3.51	3.44	3.41	3.38	3.34	3.30	3.27	3.23
8	5.32	4.46	4.07	3.84	3.69	3.58	3.50	3.44	3.39	3.35	3.28	3.22	3.15	3.12	3.08	3.04	3.01	2.97	2.93
9	5.12	4.26	3.86	3.63	3.48	3.37	3.29	3.23	3.18	3.14	3.07	3.01	2.94	2.90	2.86	2.83	2.79	2.75	2.71
10	4.96	4.10	3.71	3.48	3.33	3.22	3.14	3.07	3.02	2.98	2.91	2.85	2.77	2.74	2.70	2.66	2.62	2.58	2.54
11	4.84	3.98	3.59	3.36	3.20	3.09	3.01	2.95	2.90	2.85	2.79	2.72	2.65	2.61	2.57	2.53	2.49	2.45	2.40
12	4.75	3.89	3.49	3.26	3.11	3.00	2.91	2.85	2.80	2.75	2.69	2.62	2.54	2.51	2.47	2.43	2.38	2.34	2.30
13	4.67	3.81	3.41	3.18	3.03	2.92	2.83	2.77	2.71	2.67	2.60	2.53	2.46	2.42	2.38	2.34	2.30	2.25	2.21
14	4.60	3.74	3.34	3.11	2.96	2.85	2.76	2.70	2.65	2.60	2.53	2.46	2.39	2.35	2.31	2.27	2.22	2.18	2.13
15	4.54	3.68	3.29	3.06	2.90	2.79	2.71	2.64	2.59	2.54	2.48	2.40	2.33	2.29	2.25	2.20	2.16	2.11	2.07
16	4.49	3.63	3.24	3.01	2.85	2.74	2.66	2.59	2.54	2.49	2.42	2.35	2.28	2.24	2.19	2.15	2.11	2.06	2.01
17	4.45	3.59	3.20	2.96	2.81	2.70	2.61	2.55	2.49	2.45	2.38	2.31	2.23	2.19	2.15	2.10	2.06	2.01	1.96
18	4.41	3.55	3.16	2.93	2.77	2.66	2.58	2.51	2.46	2.41	2.34	2.27	2.19	2.15	2.11	2.06	2.02	1.97	1.92
19	4.38	3.52	3.13	2.90	2.74	2.63	2.54	2.48	2.42	2.38	2.31	2.23	2.16	2.11	2.07	2.03	1.98	1.93	1.88
20	4.35	3.49	3.10	2.87	2.71	2.60	2.51	2.45	2.39	2.35	2.28	2.20	2.12	2.08	2.04	1.99	1.95	1.90	1.84
21	4.32	3.47	3.07	2.84	2.68	2.57	2.49	2.42	2.37	2.32	2.25	2.18	2.10	2.05	2.01	1.96	1.92	1.87	1.81
22	4.30	3.44	3.05	2.82	2.66	2.55	2.46	2.40	2.34	2.30	2.23	2.15	2.07	2.03	1.98	1.94	1.89	1.84	1.78
23	4.28	3.42	3.03	2.80	2.64	2.53	2.44	2.37	2.32	2.27	2.20	2.13	2.05	2.01	1.96	1.91	1.86	1.81	1.76
24	4.26	3.40	3.01	2.78	2.62	2.51	2.42	2.36	2.30	2.25	2.18	2.11	2.03	1.98	1.94	1.89	1.84	1.79	1.73
25	4.24	3.39	2.99	2.76	2.60	2.49	2.40	2.34	2.28	2.24	2.16	2.09	2.01	1.96	1.92	1.87	1.82	1.77	1.71
26	4.23	3.37	2.98	2.74	2.59	2.47	2.39	2.32	2.27	2.22	2.15	2.07	1.99	1.95	1.90	1.85	1.80	1.75	1.69
27	4.21	3.35	2.96	2.73	2.57	2.46	2.37	2.31	2.25	2.20	2.13	2.06	1.97	1.93	1.88	1.84	1.79	1.73	1.67
28	4.20	3.34	2.95	2.71	2.56	2.45	2.36	2.29	2.24	2.19	2.12	2.04	1.96	1.91	1.87	1.82	1.77	1.71	1.65
29	4.18	3.33	2.93	2.70	2.55	2.43	2.35	2.28	2.22	2.18	2.10	2.03	1.94	1.90	1.85	1.81	1.75	1.70	1.64
30	4.17	3.32	2.92	2.69	2.53	2.42	2.33	2.27	2.21	2.16	2.09	2.01	1.93	1.89	1.84	1.79	1.74	1.68	1.62
40	4.08	3.23	2.84	2.61	2.45	2.34	2.25	2.18	2.12	2.08	2.00	1.92	1.84	1.79	1.74	1.69	1.64	1.58	1.51
60	4.00	3.15	2.76	2.53	2.37	2.25	2.17	2.10	2.04	1.99	1.92	1.84	1.75	1.70	1.65	1.59	1.53	1.47	1.39
120	3.92	3.07	2.68	2.45	2.29	2.17	2.09	2.02	1.96	1.91	1.83	1.75	1.66	1.61	1.55	1.50	1.43	1.35	1.25
∞	3.84	3.00	2.60	2.37	2.21	2.10	2.01	1.94	1.88	1.83	1.75	1.67	1.57	1.52	1.46	1.39	1.32	1.22	1.00

This table is reprinted by permission of the Biometrika Trustees from Table 18, Percentage Points of the *F Distribution*, by E. S. Pearson and H. O. Hartley, *Biometrika Tables for Statisticians*, Vol. I, 3rd Edition, 1966.

TABLE 4 (Continued)

Table of $F_{.01}$ Values

Denominator Degrees of Freedom	Numerator Degrees of Freedom																		
	1	2	3	4	5	6	7	8	9	10	12	15	20	24	30	40	60	120	∞
1	4,052	4,999.5	5,403	5,625	5,764	5,859	5,928	5,982	6,022	6,056	6,106	6,157	6,209	6,235	6,261	6,287	6,313	6,339	6,366
2	98.50	99.00	99.17	99.25	99.30	99.33	99.36	99.37	99.39	99.40	99.42	99.43	99.45	99.46	99.47	99.47	99.48	99.49	99.50
3	34.12	30.82	29.46	28.71	28.24	27.91	27.67	27.49	27.35	27.23	27.05	26.87	26.69	26.60	26.50	26.41	26.32	26.22	26.13
4	21.20	18.00	16.69	15.98	15.52	15.21	14.98	14.80	14.66	14.55	14.37	14.20	14.02	13.93	13.84	13.75	13.65	13.56	13.46
5	16.26	13.27	12.06	11.39	10.97	10.67	10.46	10.29	10.16	10.05	9.89	9.72	9.55	9.47	9.38	9.29	9.20	9.11	9.06
6	13.75	10.92	9.78	9.15	8.75	8.47	8.26	8.10	7.98	7.87	7.72	7.56	7.40	7.31	7.23	7.14	7.06	6.97	6.88
7	12.25	9.55	8.45	7.85	7.46	7.19	6.99	6.84	6.72	6.62	6.47	6.31	6.16	6.07	5.99	5.91	5.82	5.74	5.65
8	11.26	8.65	7.59	7.01	6.63	6.37	6.18	6.03	5.91	5.81	5.67	5.52	5.36	5.28	5.20	5.12	5.03	4.95	4.86
9	10.56	8.02	6.99	6.42	6.06	5.80	5.61	5.47	5.35	5.26	5.11	4.96	4.81	4.73	4.65	4.57	4.48	4.40	4.31
10	10.04	7.56	6.55	5.99	5.64	5.39	5.20	5.06	4.94	4.85	4.71	4.56	4.41	4.33	4.25	4.17	4.08	4.00	3.91
11	9.65	7.21	6.22	5.67	5.32	5.07	4.89	4.74	4.63	4.54	4.40	4.25	4.10	4.02	3.94	3.86	3.78	3.69	3.60
12	9.33	6.93	5.95	5.41	5.06	4.82	4.64	4.50	4.39	4.30	4.16	4.01	3.86	3.78	3.70	3.62	3.54	3.45	3.36
13	9.07	6.70	5.74	5.21	4.86	4.62	4.44	4.30	4.19	4.10	3.96	3.82	3.66	3.59	3.51	3.43	3.34	3.25	3.17
14	8.86	6.51	5.56	5.04	4.69	4.46	4.28	4.14	4.03	3.94	3.80	3.66	3.51	3.43	3.35	3.27	3.18	3.09	3.00
15	8.68	6.36	5.42	4.89	4.56	4.32	4.14	4.00	3.89	3.80	3.67	3.52	3.37	3.29	3.21	3.13	3.05	2.96	2.87
16	8.53	6.23	5.29	4.77	4.44	4.20	4.03	3.89	3.78	3.69	3.55	3.41	3.26	3.18	3.10	3.02	2.93	2.84	2.75
17	8.40	6.11	5.18	4.67	4.34	4.10	3.93	3.79	3.68	3.59	3.46	3.31	3.16	3.08	3.00	2.92	2.83	2.75	2.65
18	8.29	6.01	5.09	4.58	4.25	4.01	3.84	3.71	3.60	3.51	3.37	3.23	3.08	3.00	2.92	2.84	2.75	2.66	2.57
19	8.18	5.93	5.01	4.50	4.17	3.94	3.77	3.63	3.52	3.43	3.30	3.15	3.00	2.92	2.84	2.76	2.67	2.58	2.49
20	8.10	5.85	4.94	4.43	4.10	3.87	3.70	3.56	3.46	3.37	3.23	3.09	2.94	2.86	2.78	2.69	2.61	2.52	2.42
21	8.02	5.78	4.87	4.37	4.04	3.81	3.64	3.51	3.40	3.31	3.17	3.03	2.88	2.80	2.72	2.64	2.55	2.46	2.36
22	7.95	5.72	4.82	4.31	3.99	3.76	3.59	3.45	3.35	3.26	3.12	2.98	2.83	2.75	2.67	2.58	2.50	2.40	2.31
23	7.88	5.66	4.76	4.26	3.94	3.71	3.54	3.41	3.30	3.21	3.07	2.93	2.78	2.70	2.62	2.54	2.45	2.35	2.26
24	7.82	5.61	4.72	4.22	3.90	3.67	3.50	3.36	3.26	3.17	3.03	2.89	2.74	2.66	2.58	2.49	2.40	2.31	2.21
25	7.77	5.57	4.68	4.18	3.85	3.63	3.46	3.32	3.22	3.13	2.99	2.85	2.70	2.62	2.54	2.45	2.36	2.27	2.17
26	7.72	5.53	4.64	4.14	3.82	3.59	3.42	3.29	3.18	3.09	2.96	2.81	2.66	2.58	2.50	2.42	2.33	2.23	2.13
27	7.68	5.49	4.60	4.11	3.78	3.56	3.39	3.26	3.15	3.06	2.93	2.78	2.63	2.55	2.47	2.38	2.29	2.20	2.10
28	7.64	5.45	4.57	4.07	3.75	3.53	3.36	3.23	3.12	3.03	2.90	2.75	2.60	2.52	2.44	2.35	2.26	2.17	2.06
29	7.60	5.42	4.54	4.04	3.73	3.50	3.33	3.20	3.09	3.00	2.87	2.73	2.57	2.49	2.41	2.33	2.23	2.14	2.03
30	7.56	5.39	4.51	4.02	3.70	3.47	3.30	3.17	3.07	2.98	2.84	2.70	2.55	2.47	2.39	2.30	2.21	2.11	2.01
40	7.31	5.18	4.31	3.83	3.51	3.29	3.12	2.99	2.89	2.80	2.66	2.52	2.37	2.29	2.20	2.11	2.02	1.92	1.80
60	7.08	4.98	4.13	3.65	3.34	3.12	2.95	2.82	2.72	2.63	2.50	2.35	2.20	2.12	2.03	1.94	1.84	1.73	1.60
120	6.85	4.79	3.95	3.48	3.17	2.96	2.79	2.66	2.56	2.47	2.34	2.19	2.03	1.95	1.86	1.76	1.66	1.53	1.38
∞	6.63	4.61	3.78	3.32	3.02	2.80	2.64	2.51	2.41	2.32	2.18	2.04	1.88	1.79	1.70	1.59	1.47	1.32	1.00

TABLE 4 (Continued)

Table of $F_{.025}$ Values

Denominator Degrees of Freedom	\multicolumn{19}{c}{Numerator Degrees of Freedom}

Denominator Degrees of Freedom	1	2	3	4	5	6	7	8	9	10	12	15	20	24	30	40	60	120	∞
1	647.8	799.5	864.2	899.6	921.8	937.1	948.2	956.7	963.3	968.6	976.7	984.9	993.1	997.2	1,001	1,006	1,010	1,014	1,018
2	38.51	39.00	39.17	39.25	39.30	39.33	39.36	39.37	39.39	39.40	39.41	39.43	39.45	39.46	39.46	39.47	39.48	39.49	39.50
3	17.44	16.04	15.44	15.10	14.88	14.73	14.62	14.54	14.47	14.42	14.34	14.25	14.17	14.12	14.08	14.04	13.99	13.95	13.90
4	12.22	10.65	9.98	9.60	9.36	9.20	9.07	8.98	8.90	8.84	8.75	8.66	8.56	8.51	8.46	8.41	8.36	8.31	8.26
5	10.01	8.43	7.76	7.39	7.15	6.98	6.85	6.76	6.68	6.62	6.52	6.43	6.33	6.28	6.23	6.18	6.12	6.07	6.02
6	8.81	7.26	6.60	6.23	5.99	5.82	5.70	5.60	5.52	5.46	5.37	5.27	5.17	5.12	5.07	5.01	4.96	4.90	4.85
7	8.07	6.54	5.89	5.52	5.29	5.12	4.99	4.90	4.82	4.76	4.67	4.57	4.47	4.42	4.36	4.31	4.25	4.20	4.14
8	7.57	6.06	5.42	5.05	4.82	4.65	4.53	4.43	4.36	4.30	4.20	4.10	4.00	3.95	3.89	3.84	3.78	3.73	3.67
9	7.21	5.71	5.08	4.72	4.48	4.32	4.20	4.10	4.03	3.96	3.87	3.77	3.67	3.61	3.56	3.51	3.45	3.39	3.33
10	6.94	5.46	4.83	4.47	4.24	4.07	3.95	3.85	3.78	3.72	3.62	3.52	3.42	3.37	3.31	3.26	3.20	3.14	3.08
11	6.72	5.26	4.63	4.28	4.04	3.88	3.76	3.66	3.59	3.53	3.43	3.33	3.23	3.17	3.12	3.06	3.00	2.94	2.88
12	6.55	5.10	4.47	4.12	3.89	3.73	3.61	3.51	3.44	3.37	3.28	3.18	3.07	3.02	2.96	2.91	2.85	2.79	2.72
13	6.41	4.97	4.35	4.00	3.77	3.60	3.48	3.39	3.31	3.25	3.15	3.05	2.95	2.89	2.84	2.78	2.72	2.66	2.60
14	6.30	4.86	4.24	3.89	3.66	3.50	3.38	3.29	3.21	3.15	3.05	2.95	2.84	2.79	2.73	2.67	2.61	2.55	2.49
15	6.20	4.77	4.15	3.80	3.58	3.41	3.29	3.20	3.12	3.06	2.96	2.86	2.76	2.70	2.64	2.59	2.52	2.46	2.40
16	6.12	4.69	4.08	3.73	3.50	3.34	3.22	3.12	3.05	2.99	2.89	2.79	2.68	2.63	2.57	2.51	2.45	2.38	2.32
17	6.04	4.62	4.01	3.66	3.44	3.28	3.16	3.06	2.98	2.92	2.82	2.72	2.62	2.56	2.50	2.44	2.38	2.32	2.25
18	5.98	4.56	3.95	3.61	3.38	3.22	3.10	3.01	2.93	2.87	2.77	2.67	2.56	2.50	2.44	2.38	2.32	2.26	2.19
19	5.92	4.51	3.90	3.56	3.33	3.17	3.05	2.96	2.88	2.82	2.72	2.62	2.51	2.45	2.39	2.33	2.27	2.20	2.13
20	5.87	4.46	3.86	3.51	3.29	3.13	3.01	2.91	2.84	2.77	2.68	2.57	2.46	2.41	2.35	2.29	2.22	2.16	2.09
21	5.83	4.42	3.82	3.48	3.25	3.09	2.97	2.87	2.80	2.73	2.64	2.53	2.42	2.37	2.31	2.25	2.18	2.11	2.04
22	5.79	4.38	3.78	3.44	3.22	3.05	2.93	2.84	2.76	2.70	2.60	2.50	2.39	2.33	2.27	2.21	2.14	2.08	2.00
23	5.75	4.35	3.75	3.41	3.18	3.02	2.90	2.81	2.73	2.67	2.57	2.47	2.36	2.30	2.24	2.18	2.11	2.04	1.97
24	5.72	4.32	3.72	3.38	3.15	2.99	2.87	2.78	2.70	2.64	2.54	2.44	2.33	2.27	2.21	2.15	2.08	2.01	1.94
25	5.69	4.29	3.69	3.35	3.13	2.97	2.85	2.75	2.68	2.61	2.51	2.41	2.30	2.24	2.18	2.12	2.05	1.98	1.91
26	5.66	4.27	3.67	3.33	3.10	2.94	2.82	2.73	2.65	2.59	2.49	2.39	2.28	2.22	2.16	2.09	2.03	1.95	1.88
27	5.63	4.24	3.65	3.31	3.08	2.92	2.80	2.71	2.63	2.57	2.47	2.36	2.25	2.19	2.13	2.07	2.00	1.93	1.85
28	5.61	4.22	3.63	3.29	3.06	2.90	2.78	2.69	2.61	2.55	2.45	2.34	2.23	2.17	2.11	2.05	1.98	1.91	1.83
29	5.59	4.20	3.61	3.27	3.04	2.88	2.76	2.67	2.59	2.53	2.43	2.32	2.21	2.15	2.09	2.03	1.96	1.89	1.81
30	5.57	4.18	3.59	3.25	3.03	2.87	2.75	2.65	2.57	2.51	2.41	2.31	2.20	2.14	2.07	2.01	1.94	1.87	1.79
40	5.42	4.05	3.46	3.13	2.90	2.74	2.62	2.53	2.45	2.39	2.29	2.18	2.07	2.01	1.94	1.88	1.80	1.72	1.64
60	5.29	3.93	3.34	3.01	2.79	2.63	2.51	2.41	2.33	2.27	2.17	2.06	1.94	1.88	1.82	1.74	1.67	1.58	1.48
120	5.15	3.80	3.23	2.89	2.67	2.52	2.39	2.30	2.22	2.16	2.05	1.94	1.82	1.76	1.69	1.61	1.53	1.43	1.31
∞	5.02	3.69	3.12	2.79	2.57	2.41	2.29	2.19	2.11	2.05	1.94	1.83	1.71	1.64	1.57	1.48	1.39	1.27	1.00

TABLE 5 Binomial Probabilities

Entries in the table give the probability of x successes in n trials of a binomial experiment, where p is the probability of a success on one trial. For example, with six trials and $p = .05$, the probability of two successes is .0305.

						p				
n	x	.01	.02	.03	.04	.05	.06	.07	.08	.09
2	0	.9801	.9604	.9409	.9216	.9025	.8836	.8649	.8464	.8281
	1	.0198	.0392	.0582	.0768	.0950	.1128	.1302	.1472	.1638
	2	.0001	.0004	.0009	.0016	.0025	.0036	.0049	.0064	.0081
3	0	.9703	.9412	.9127	.8847	.8574	.8306	.8044	.7787	.7536
	1	.0294	.0576	.0847	.1106	.1354	.1590	.1816	.2031	.2236
	2	.0003	.0012	.0026	.0046	.0071	.0102	.0137	.0177	.0221
	3	.0000	.0000	.0000	.0001	.0001	.0002	.0003	.0005	.0007
4	0	.9606	.9224	.8853	.8493	.8145	.7807	.7481	.7164	.6857
	1	.0388	.0753	.1095	.1416	.1715	.1993	.2252	.2492	.2713
	2	.0006	.0023	.0051	.0088	.0135	.0191	.0254	.0325	.0402
	3	.0000	.0000	.0001	.0002	.0005	.0008	.0013	.0019	.0027
	4	.0000	.0000	.0000	.0000	.0000	.0000	.0000	.0000	.0001
5	0	.9510	.9039	.8587	.8154	.7738	.7339	.6957	.6591	.6240
	1	.0480	.0922	.1328	.1699	.2036	.2342	.2618	.2866	.3086
	2	.0010	.0038	.0082	.0142	.0214	.0299	.0394	.0498	.0610
	3	.0000	.0001	.0003	.0006	.0011	.0019	.0030	.0043	.0060
	4	.0000	.0000	.0000	.0000	.0000	.0001	.0001	.0002	.0003
	5	.0000	.0000	.0000	.0000	.0000	.0000	.0000	.0000	.0000
6	0	.9415	.8858	.8330	.7828	.7351	.6899	.6470	.6064	.5679
	1	.0571	.1085	.1546	.1957	.2321	.2642	.2922	.3164	.3370
	2	.0014	.0055	.0120	.0204	.0305	.0422	.0550	.0688	.0833
	3	.0000	.0002	.0005	.0011	.0021	.0036	.0055	.0080	.0110
	4	.0000	.0000	.0000	.0000	.0001	.0002	.0003	.0005	.0008
	5	.0000	.0000	.0000	.0000	.0000	.0000	.0000	.0000	.0000
	6	.0000	.0000	.0000	.0000	.0000	.0000	.0000	.0000	.0000
7	0	.9321	.8681	.8080	.7514	.6983	.6485	.6017	.5578	.5168
	1	.0659	.1240	.1749	.2192	.2573	.2897	.3170	.3396	.3578
	2	.0020	.0076	.0162	.0274	.0406	.0555	.0716	.0886	.1061
	3	.0000	.0003	.0008	.0019	.0036	.0059	.0090	.0128	.0175
	4	.0000	.0000	.0000	.0001	.0002	.0004	.0007	.0011	.0017
	5	.0000	.0000	.0000	.0000	.0000	.0000	.0000	.0001	.0001
	6	.0000	.0000	.0000	.0000	.0000	.0000	.0000	.0000	.0000
	7	.0000	.0000	.0000	.0000	.0000	.0000	.0000	.0000	.0000
8	0	.9227	.8508	.7837	.7214	.6634	.6096	.5596	.5132	.4703
	1	.0746	.1389	.1939	.2405	.2793	.3113	.3370	.3570	.3721
	2	.0026	.0099	.0210	.0351	.0515	.0695	.0888	.1087	.1288
	3	.0001	.0004	.0013	.0029	.0054	.0089	.0134	.0189	.0255
	4	.0000	.0000	.0001	.0002	.0004	.0007	.0013	.0021	.0031
	5	.0000	.0000	.0000	.0000	.0000	.0000	.0001	.0001	.0002
	6	.0000	.0000	.0000	.0000	.0000	.0000	.0000	.0000	.0000
	7	.0000	.0000	.0000	.0000	.0000	.0000	.0000	.0000	.0000
	8	.0000	.0000	.0000	.0000	.0000	.0000	.0000	.0000	.0000

(Table Continues)

TABLE 5 (Continued)

						p				
n	x	.01	.02	.03	.04	.05	.06	.07	.08	.09
9	0	.9135	.8337	.7602	.6925	.6302	.5730	.5204	.4722	.4279
	1	.0830	.1531	.2116	.2597	.2985	.3292	.3525	.3695	.3809
	2	.0034	.0125	.0262	.0433	.0629	.0840	.1061	.1285	.1507
	3	.0001	.0006	.0019	.0042	.0077	.0125	.0186	.0261	.0348
	4	.0000	.0000	.0001	.0003	.0006	.0012	.0021	.0034	.0052
	5	.0000	.0000	.0000	.0000	.0000	.0001	.0002	.0003	.0005
	6	.0000	.0000	.0000	.0000	.0000	.0000	.0000	.0000	.0000
	7	.0000	.0000	.0000	.0000	.0000	.0000	.0000	.0000	.0000
	8	.0000	.0000	.0000	.0000	.0000	.0000	.0000	.0000	.0000
	9	.0000	.0000	.0000	.0000	.0000	.0000	.0000	.0000	.0000
10	0	.9044	.8171	.7374	.6648	.5987	.5386	.4840	.4344	.3894
	1	.0914	.1667	.2281	.2770	.3151	.3438	.3643	.3777	.3851
	2	.0042	.0153	.0317	.0519	.0746	.0988	.1234	.1478	.1714
	3	.0001	.0008	.0026	.0058	.0105	.0168	.0248	.0343	.0452
	4	.0000	.0000	.0001	.0004	.0010	.0019	.0033	.0052	.0078
	5	.0000	.0000	.0000	.0000	.0001	.0001	.0003	.0005	.0009
	6	.0000	.0000	.0000	.0000	.0000	.0000	.0000	.0000	.0001
	7	.0000	.0000	.0000	.0000	.0000	.0000	.0000	.0000	.0000
	8	.0000	.0000	.0000	.0000	.0000	.0000	.0000	.0000	.0001
	9	.0000	.0000	.0000	.0000	.0000	.0000	.0000	.0000	.0001
	10	.0000	.0000	.0000	.0000	.0000	.0000	.0000	.0000	.0001
12	0	.8864	.7847	.6938	.6127	.5404	.4759	.4186	.3677	.3225
	1	.1074	.1922	.2575	.3064	.3413	.3645	.3781	.3837	.3827
	2	.0060	.0216	.0438	.0702	.0988	.1280	.1565	.1835	.2082
	3	.0002	.0015	.0045	.0098	.0173	.0272	.0393	.0532	.0686
	4	.0000	.0001	.0003	.0009	.0021	.0039	.0067	.0104	.0153
	5	.0000	.0000	.0000	.0001	.0002	.0004	.0008	.0014	.0024
	6	.0000	.0000	.0000	.0000	.0000	.0000	.0001	.0001	.0003
	7	.0000	.0000	.0000	.0000	.0000	.0000	.0000	.0000	.0000
	8	.0000	.0000	.0000	.0000	.0000	.0000	.0000	.0000	.0000
	9	.0000	.0000	.0000	.0000	.0000	.0000	.0000	.0000	.0000
	10	.0000	.0000	.0000	.0000	.0000	.0000	.0000	.0000	.0000
	11	.0000	.0000	.0000	.0000	.0000	.0000	.0000	.0000	.0000
	12	.0000	.0000	.0000	.0000	.0000	.0000	.0000	.0000	.0000
15	0	.8601	.7386	.6333	.5421	.4633	.3953	.3367	.2863	.2430
	1	.1303	.2261	.2938	.3388	.3658	.3785	.3801	.3734	.3605
	2	.0092	.0323	.0636	.0988	.1348	.1691	.2003	.2273	.2496
	3	.0004	.0029	.0085	.0178	.0307	.0468	.0653	.0857	.1070
	4	.0000	.0002	.0008	.0022	.0049	.0090	.0148	.0223	.0317
	5	.0000	.0000	.0001	.0002	.0006	.0013	.0024	.0043	.0069
	6	.0000	.0000	.0000	.0000	.0000	.0001	.0003	.0006	.0011
	7	.0000	.0000	.0000	.0000	.0000	.0000	.0000	.0001	.0001
	8	.0000	.0000	.0000	.0000	.0000	.0000	.0000	.0000	.0000
	9	.0000	.0000	.0000	.0000	.0000	.0000	.0000	.0000	.0000
	10	.0000	.0000	.0000	.0000	.0000	.0000	.0000	.0000	.0000
	11	.0000	.0000	.0000	.0000	.0000	.0000	.0000	.0000	.0000
	12	.0000	.0000	.0000	.0000	.0000	.0000	.0000	.0000	.0000
	13	.0000	.0000	.0000	.0000	.0000	.0000	.0000	.0000	.0000
	14	.0000	.0000	.0000	.0000	.0000	.0000	.0000	.0000	.0000
	15	.0000	.0000	.0000	.0000	.0000	.0000	.0000	.0000	.0000

(Table Continues on Next Page)

TABLE 5 (Continued)

n	x	.01	.02	.03	.04	.05	.06	.07	.08	.09
18	0	.8345	.6951	.5780	.4796	.3972	.3283	.2708	.2229	.1831
	1	.1517	.2554	.3217	.3597	.3763	.3772	.3669	.3489	.3260
	2	.0130	.0443	.0846	.1274	.1683	.2047	.2348	.2579	.2741
	3	.0007	.0048	.0140	.0283	.0473	.0697	.0942	.1196	.1446
	4	.0000	.0004	.0016	.0044	.0093	.0167	.0266	.0390	.0536
	5	.0000	.0000	.0001	.0005	.0014	.0030	.0056	.0095	.0148
	6	.0000	.0000	.0000	.0000	.0002	.0004	.0009	.0018	.0032
	7	.0000	.0000	.0000	.0000	.0000	.0000	.0001	.0003	.0005
	8	.0000	.0000	.0000	.0000	.0000	.0000	.0000	.0000	.0001
	9	.0000	.0000	.0000	.0000	.0000	.0000	.0000	.0000	.0000
	10	.0000	.0000	.0000	.0000	.0000	.0000	.0000	.0000	.0000
	11	.0000	.0000	.0000	.0000	.0000	.0000	.0000	.0000	.0000
	12	.0000	.0000	.0000	.0000	.0000	.0000	.0000	.0000	.0000
	13	.0000	.0000	.0000	.0000	.0000	.0000	.0000	.0000	.0000
	14	.0000	.0000	.0000	.0000	.0000	.0000	.0000	.0000	.0000
	15	.0000	.0000	.0000	.0000	.0000	.0000	.0000	.0000	.0000
	16	.0000	.0000	.0000	.0000	.0000	.0000	.0000	.0000	.0000
	17	.0000	.0000	.0000	.0000	.0000	.0000	.0000	.0000	.0000
	18	.0000	.0000	.0000	.0000	.0000	.0000	.0000	.0000	.0000
20	0	.8179	.6676	.5438	.4420	.3585	.2901	.2342	.1887	.1516
	1	.1652	.2725	.3364	.3683	.3774	.3703	.3526	.3282	.3000
	2	.0159	.0528	.0988	.1458	.1887	.2246	.2521	.2711	.2818
	3	.0010	.0065	.0183	.0364	.0596	.0860	.1139	.1414	.1672
	4	.0000	.0006	.0024	.0065	.0133	.0233	.0364	.0523	.0703
	5	.0000	.0000	.0002	.0009	.0022	.0048	.0088	.0145	.0222
	6	.0000	.0000	.0000	.0001	.0003	.0008	.0017	.0032	.0055
	7	.0000	.0000	.0000	.0000	.0000	.0001	.0002	.0005	.0011
	8	.0000	.0000	.0000	.0000	.0000	.0000	.0000	.0001	.0002
	9	.0000	.0000	.0000	.0000	.0000	.0000	.0000	.0000	.0000
	10	.0000	.0000	.0000	.0000	.0000	.0000	.0000	.0000	.0000
	11	.0000	.0000	.0000	.0000	.0000	.0000	.0000	.0000	.0000
	12	.0000	.0000	.0000	.0000	.0000	.0000	.0000	.0000	.0000
	13	.0000	.0000	.0000	.0000	.0000	.0000	.0000	.0000	.0000
	14	.0000	.0000	.0000	.0000	.0000	.0000	.0000	.0000	.0000
	15	.0000	.0000	.0000	.0000	.0000	.0000	.0000	.0000	.0000
	16	.0000	.0000	.0000	.0000	.0000	.0000	.0000	.0000	.0000
	17	.0000	.0000	.0000	.0000	.0000	.0000	.0000	.0000	.0000
	18	.0000	.0000	.0000	.0000	.0000	.0000	.0000	.0000	.0000
	19	.0000	.0000	.0000	.0000	.0000	.0000	.0000	.0000	.0000
	20	.0000	.0000	.0000	.0000	.0000	.0000	.0000	.0000	.0000

(Table Continues)

TABLE 5 (Continued)

n	x	.10	.15	.20	.25	.30	.35	.40	.45	.50
						p				
2	0	.8100	.7225	.6400	.5625	.4900	.4225	.3600	.3025	.2500
	1	.1800	.2550	.3200	.3750	.4200	.4550	.4800	.4950	.5000
	2	.0100	.0225	.0400	.0625	.0900	.1225	.1600	.2025	.2500
3	0	.7290	.6141	.5120	.4219	.3430	.2746	.2160	.1664	.1250
	1	.2430	.3251	.3840	.4219	.4410	.4436	.4320	.4084	.3750
	2	.0270	.0574	.0960	.1406	.1890	.2389	.2880	.3341	.3750
	3	.0010	.0034	.0080	.0156	.0270	.0429	.0640	.0911	.1250
4	0	.6561	.5220	.4096	.3164	.2401	.1785	.1296	.0915	.0625
	1	.2916	.3685	.4096	.4219	.4116	.3845	.3456	.2995	.2500
	2	.0486	.0975	.1536	.2109	.2646	.3105	.3456	.3675	.3750
	3	.0036	.0115	.0256	.0469	.0756	.1115	.1536	.2005	.2500
	4	.0001	.0005	.0016	.0039	.0081	.0150	.0256	.0410	.0625
5	0	.5905	.4437	.3277	.2373	.1681	.1160	.0778	.0503	.0312
	1	.3280	.3915	.4096	.3955	.3602	.3124	.2592	.2059	.1562
	2	.0729	.1382	.2048	.2637	.3087	.3364	.3456	.3369	.3125
	3	.0081	.0244	.0512	.0879	.1323	.1811	.2304	.2757	.3125
	4	.0004	.0022	.0064	.0146	.0284	.0488	.0768	.1128	.1562
	5	.0000	.0001	.0003	.0010	.0024	.0053	.0102	.0185	.0312
6	0	.5314	.3771	.2621	.1780	.1176	.0754	.0467	.0277	.0156
	1	.3543	.3993	.3932	.3560	.3025	.2437	.1866	.1359	.0938
	2	.0984	.1762	.2458	.2966	.3241	.3280	.3110	.2780	.2344
	3	.0146	.0415	.0819	.1318	.1852	.2355	.2765	.3032	.3125
	4	.0012	.0055	.0154	.0330	.0595	.0951	.1382	.1861	.2344
	5	.0001	.0004	.0015	.0044	.0102	.0205	.0369	.0609	.0938
	6	.0000	.0000	.0001	.0002	.0007	.0018	.0041	.0083	.0156
7	0	.4783	.3206	.2097	.1335	.0824	.0490	.0280	.0152	.0078
	1	.3720	.3960	.3670	.3115	.2471	.1848	.1306	.0872	.0547
	2	.1240	.2097	.2753	.3115	.3177	.2985	.2613	.2140	.1641
	3	.0230	.0617	.1147	.1730	.2269	.2679	.2903	.2918	.2734
	4	.0026	.0109	.0287	.0577	.0972	.1442	.1935	.2388	.2734
	5	.0002	.0012	.0043	.0115	.0250	.0466	.0774	.1172	.1641
	6	.0000	.0001	.0004	.0013	.0036	.0084	.0172	.0320	.0547
	7	.0000	.0000	.0000	.0001	.0002	.0006	.0016	.0037	.0078
8	0	.4305	.2725	.1678	.1001	.0576	.0319	.0168	.0084	.0039
	1	.3826	.3847	.3355	.2670	.1977	.1373	.0896	.0548	.0312
	2	.1488	.2376	.2936	.3115	.2965	.2587	.2090	.1569	.1094
	3	.0331	.0839	.1468	.2076	.2541	.2786	.2787	.2568	.2188
	4	.0046	.0185	.0459	.0865	.1361	.1875	.2322	.2627	.2734
	5	.0004	.0026	.0092	.0231	.0467	.0808	.1239	.1719	.2188
	6	.0000	.0002	.0011	.0038	.0100	.0217	.0413	.0703	.1094
	7	.0000	.0000	.0001	.0004	.0012	.0033	.0079	.0164	.0312
	8	.0000	.0000	.0000	.0000	.0001	.0002	.0007	.0017	.0039

(Table Continues on Next Page)

TABLE 5 (Continued)

| | | \multicolumn{9}{c}{p} | | | | | | | | |
n	x	.10	.15	.20	.25	.30	.35	.40	.45	.50
9	0	.3874	.2316	.1342	.0751	.0404	.0207	.0101	.0046	.0020
	1	.3874	.3679	.3020	.2253	.1556	.1004	.0605	.0339	.0176
	2	.1722	.2597	.3020	.3003	.2668	.2162	.1612	.1110	.0703
	3	.0446	.1069	.1762	.2336	.2668	.2716	.2508	.2119	.1641
	4	.0074	.0283	.0661	.1168	.1715	.2194	.2508	.2600	.2461
	5	.0008	.0050	.0165	.0389	.0735	.1181	.1672	.2128	.2461
	6	.0001	.0006	.0028	.0087	.0210	.0424	.0743	.1160	.1641
	7	.0000	.0000	.0003	.0012	.0039	.0098	.0212	.0407	.0703
	8	.0000	.0000	.0000	.0001	.0004	.0013	.0035	.0083	.0176
	9	.0000	.0000	.0000	.0000	.0000	.0001	.0003	.0008	.0020
10	0	.3487	.1969	.1074	.0563	.0282	.0135	.0060	.0025	.0010
	1	.3874	.3474	.2684	.1877	.1211	.0725	.0403	.0207	.0098
	2	.1937	.2759	.3020	.2816	.2335	.1757	.1209	.0763	.0439
	3	.0574	.1298	.2013	.2503	.2668	.2522	.2150	.1665	.1172
	4	.0112	.0401	.0881	.1460	.2001	.2377	.2508	.2384	.2051
	5	.0015	.0085	.0264	.0584	.1029	.1536	.2007	.2340	.2461
	6	.0001	.0012	.0055	.0162	.0368	.0689	.1115	.1596	.2051
	7	.0000	.0001	.0008	.0031	.0090	.0212	.0425	.0746	.1172
	8	.0000	.0000	.0001	.0004	.0014	.0043	.0106	.0229	.0439
	9	.0000	.0000	.0000	.0000	.0001	.0005	.0016	.0042	.0098
	10	.0000	.0000	.0000	.0000	.0000	.0000	.0001	.0003	.0010
12	0	.2824	.1422	.0687	.0317	.0138	.0057	.0022	.0008	.0002
	1	.3766	.3012	.2062	.1267	.0712	.0368	.0174	.0075	.0029
	2	.2301	.2924	.2835	.2323	.1678	.1088	.0639	.0339	.0161
	3	.0853	.1720	.2362	.2581	.2397	.1954	.1419	.0923	.0537
	4	.0213	.0683	.1329	.1936	.2311	.2367	.2128	.1700	.1208
	5	.0038	.0193	.0532	.1032	.1585	.2039	.2270	.2225	.1934
	6	.0005	.0040	.0155	.0401	.0792	.1281	.1766	.2124	.2256
	7	.0000	.0006	.0033	.0115	.0291	.0591	.1009	.1489	.1934
	8	.0000	.0001	.0005	.0024	.0078	.0199	.0420	.0762	.1208
	9	.0000	.0000	.0001	.0004	.0015	.0048	.0125	.0277	.0537
	10	.0000	.0000	.0000	.0000	.0002	.0008	.0025	.0068	.0161
	11	.0000	.0000	.0000	.0000	.0000	.0001	.0003	.0010	.0029
	12	.0000	.0000	.0000	.0000	.0000	.0000	.0000	.0001	.0002
15	0	.2059	.0874	.0352	.0134	.0047	.0016	.0005	.0001	.0000
	1	.3432	.2312	.1319	.0668	.0305	.0126	.0047	.0016	.0005
	2	.2669	.2856	.2309	.1559	.0916	.0476	.0219	.0090	.0032
	3	.1285	.2184	.2501	.2252	.1700	.1110	.0634	.0318	.0139
	4	.0428	.1156	.1876	.2252	.2186	.1792	.1268	.0780	.0417
	5	.0105	.0449	.1032	.1651	.2061	.2123	.1859	.1404	.0916
	6	.0019	.0132	.0430	.0917	.1472	.1906	.2066	.1914	.1527
	7	.0003	.0030	.0138	.0393	.0811	.1319	.1771	.2013	.1964
	8	.0000	.0005	.0035	.0131	.0348	.0710	.1181	.1647	.1964
	9	.0000	.0001	.0007	.0034	.0116	.0298	.0612	.1048	.1527
	10	.0000	.0000	.0001	.0007	.0030	.0096	.0245	.0515	.0916
	11	.0000	.0000	.0000	.0001	.0006	.0024	.0074	.0191	.0417
	12	.0000	.0000	.0000	.0000	.0001	.0004	.0016	.0052	.0139
	13	.0000	.0000	.0000	.0000	.0000	.0001	.0003	.0010	.0032
	14	.0000	.0000	.0000	.0000	.0000	.0000	.0000	.0001	.0005
	15	.0000	.0000	.0000	.0000	.0000	.0000	.0000	.0000	.0000

(Table Continues)

TABLE 5 (Continued)

n	x	.10	.15	.20	.25	.30	.35	.40	.45	.50
						p				
18	0	.1501	.0536	.0180	.0056	.0016	.0004	.0001	.0000	.0000
	1	.3002	.1704	.0811	.0338	.0126	.0042	.0012	.0003	.0001
	2	.2835	.2556	.1723	.0958	.0458	.0190	.0069	.0022	.0006
	3	.1680	.2406	.2297	.1704	.1046	.0547	.0246	.0095	.0031
	4	.0700	.1592	.2153	.2130	.1681	.1104	.0614	.0291	.0117
	5	.0218	.0787	.1507	.1988	.2017	.1664	.1146	.0666	.0327
	6	.0052	.0301	.0816	.1436	.1873	.1941	.1655	.1181	.0708
	7	.0010	.0091	.0350	.0820	.1376	.1792	.1892	.1657	.1214
	8	.0002	.0022	.0120	.0376	.0811	.1327	.1734	.1864	.1669
	9	.0000	.0004	.0033	.0139	.0386	.0794	.1284	.1694	.1855
	10	.0000	.0001	.0008	.0042	.0149	.0385	.0771	.1248	.1669
	11	.0000	.0000	.0001	.0010	.0046	.0151	.0374	.0742	.1214
	12	.0000	.0000	.0000	.0002	.0012	.0047	.0145	.0354	.0708
	13	.0000	.0000	.0000	.0000	.0002	.0012	.0045	.0134	.0327
	14	.0000	.0000	.0000	.0000	.0000	.0002	.0011	.0039	.0117
	15	.0000	.0000	.0000	.0000	.0000	.0000	.0002	.0009	.0031
	16	.0000	.0000	.0000	.0000	.0000	.0000	.0000	.0001	.0006
	17	.0000	.0000	.0000	.0000	.0000	.0000	.0000	.0000	.0001
	18	.0000	.0000	.0000	.0000	.0000	.0000	.0000	.0000	.0000
20	0	.1216	.0388	.0115	.0032	.0008	.0002	.0000	.0000	.0000
	1	.2702	.1368	.0576	.0211	.0068	.0020	.0005	.0001	.0000
	2	.2852	.2293	.1369	.0669	.0278	.0100	.0031	.0008	.0002
	3	.1901	.2428	.2054	.1339	.0716	.0323	.0123	.0040	.0011
	4	.0898	.1821	.2182	.1897	.1304	.0738	.0350	.0139	.0046
	5	.0319	.1028	.1746	.2023	.1789	.1272	.0746	.0365	.0148
	6	.0089	.0454	.1091	.1686	.1916	.1712	.1244	.0746	.0370
	7	.0020	.0160	.0545	.1124	.1643	.1844	.1659	.1221	.0739
	8	.0004	.0046	.0222	.0609	.1144	.1614	.1797	.1623	.1201
	9	.0001	.0011	.0074	.0271	.0654	.1158	.1597	.1771	.1602
	10	.0000	.0002	.0020	.0099	.0308	.0686	.1171	.1593	.1762
	11	.0000	.0000	.0005	.0030	.0120	.0336	.0710	.1185	.1602
	12	.0000	.0000	.0001	.0008	.0039	.0136	.0355	.0727	.1201
	13	.0000	.0000	.0000	.0002	.0010	.0045	.0146	.0366	.0739
	14	.0000	.0000	.0000	.0000	.0002	.0012	.0049	.0150	.0370
	15	.0000	.0000	.0000	.0000	.0000	.0003	.0013	.0049	.0148
	16	.0000	.0000	.0000	.0000	.0000	.0000	.0003	.0013	.0046
	17	.0000	.0000	.0000	.0000	.0000	.0000	.0000	.0002	.0011
	18	.0000	.0000	.0000	.0000	.0000	.0000	.0000	.0000	.0002
	19	.0000	.0000	.0000	.0000	.0000	.0000	.0000	.0000	.0000
	20	.0000	.0000	.0000	.0000	.0000	.0000	.0000	.0000	.0000

(Table Continues on Next Page)

TABLE 5 (Continued)

n	x	.55	.60	.65	.70	.75	.80	.85	.90	.95
						p				
2	0	.2025	.1600	.1225	.0900	.0625	.0400	.0225	.0100	.0025
	1	.4950	.4800	.4550	.4200	.3750	.3200	.2550	.1800	.0950
	2	.3025	.3600	.4225	.4900	.5625	.6400	.7225	.8100	.9025
3	0	.0911	.0640	.0429	.0270	.0156	.0080	.0034	.0010	.0001
	1	.3341	.2880	.2389	.1890	.1406	.0960	.0574	.0270	.0071
	2	.4084	.4320	.4436	.4410	.4219	.3840	.3251	.2430	.1354
	3	.1664	.2160	.2746	.3430	.4219	.5120	.6141	.7290	.8574
4	0	.0410	.0256	.0150	.0081	.0039	.0016	.0005	.0001	.0000
	1	.2005	.1536	.1115	.0756	.0469	.0256	.0115	.0036	.0005
	2	.3675	.3456	.3105	.2646	.2109	.1536	.0975	.0486	.0135
	3	.2995	.3456	.3845	.4116	.4219	.4096	.3685	.2916	.1715
	4	.0915	.1296	.1785	.2401	.3164	.4096	.5220	.6561	.8145
5	0	.0185	.0102	.0053	.0024	.0010	.0003	.0001	.0000	.0000
	1	.1128	.0768	.0488	.0284	.0146	.0064	.0022	.0005	.0000
	2	.2757	.2304	.1811	.1323	.0879	.0512	.0244	.0081	.0011
	3	.3369	.3456	.3364	.3087	.2637	.2048	.1382	.0729	.0214
	4	.2059	.2592	.3124	.3601	.3955	.4096	.3915	.3281	.2036
	5	.0503	.0778	.1160	.1681	.2373	.3277	.4437	.5905	.7738
6	0	.0083	.0041	.0018	.0007	.0002	.0001	.0000	.0000	.0000
	1	.0609	.0369	.0205	.0102	.0044	.0015	.0004	.0001	.0000
	2	.1861	.1382	.0951	.0595	.0330	.0154	.0055	.0012	.0001
	3	.3032	.2765	.2355	.1852	.1318	.0819	.0415	.0146	.0021
	4	.2780	.3110	.3280	.3241	.2966	.2458	.1762	.0984	.0305
	5	.1359	.1866	.2437	.3025	.3560	.3932	.3993	.3543	.2321
	6	.0277	.0467	.0754	.1176	.1780	.2621	.3771	.5314	.7351
7	0	.0037	.0016	.0006	.0002	.0001	.0000	.0000	.0000	.0000
	1	.0320	.0172	.0084	.0036	.0013	.0004	.0001	.0000	.0000
	2	.1172	.0774	.0466	.0250	.0115	.0043	.0012	.0002	.0000
	3	.2388	.1935	.1442	.0972	.0577	.0287	.0109	.0026	.0002
	4	.2918	.2903	.2679	.2269	.1730	.1147	.0617	.0230	.0036
	5	.2140	.2613	.2985	.3177	.3115	.2753	.2097	.1240	.0406
	6	.0872	.1306	.1848	.2471	.3115	.3670	.3960	.3720	.2573
	7	.0152	.0280	.0490	.0824	.1335	.2097	.3206	.4783	.6983
8	0	.0017	.0007	.0002	.0001	.0000	.0000	.0000	.0000	.0000
	1	.0164	.0079	.0033	.0012	.0004	.0001	.0000	.0000	.0000
	2	.0703	.0413	.0217	.0100	.0038	.0011	.0002	.0000	.0000
	3	.1719	.1239	.0808	.0467	.0231	.0092	.0026	.0004	.0000
	4	.2627	.2322	.1875	.1361	.0865	.0459	.0185	.0046	.0004
	5	.2568	.2787	.2786	.2541	.2076	.1468	.0839	.0331	.0054
	6	.1569	.2090	.2587	.2965	.3115	.2936	.2376	.1488	.0515
	7	.0548	.0896	.1373	.1977	.2670	.3355	.3847	.3826	.2793
	8	.0084	.0168	.0319	.0576	.1001	.1678	.2725	.4305	.6634

(Table Continues)

TABLE 5   (Continued)

					p					
n	x	.55	.60	.65	.70	.75	.80	.85	.90	.95
9	0	.0008	.0003	.0001	.0000	.0000	.0000	.0000	.0000	.0000
	1	.0083	.0035	.0013	.0004	.0001	.0000	.0000	.0000	.0000
	2	.0407	.0212	.0098	.0039	.0012	.0003	.0000	.0000	.0000
	3	.1160	.0743	.0424	.0210	.0087	.0028	.0006	.0001	.0000
	4	.2128	.1672	.1181	.0735	.0389	.0165	.0050	.0008	.0000
	5	.2600	.2508	.2194	.1715	.1168	.0661	.0283	.0074	.0006
	6	.2119	.2508	.2716	.2668	.2336	.1762	.1069	.0446	.0077
	7	.1110	.1612	.2162	.2668	.3003	.3020	.2597	.1722	.0629
	8	.0339	.0605	.1004	.1556	.2253	.3020	.3679	.3874	.2985
	9	.0046	.0101	.0207	.0404	.0751	.1342	.2316	.3874	.6302
10	0	.0003	.0001	.0000	.0000	.0000	.0000	.0000	.0000	.0000
	1	.0042	.0016	.0005	.0001	.0000	.0000	.0000	.0000	.0000
	2	.0229	.0106	.0043	.0014	.0004	.0001	.0000	.0000	.0000
	3	.0746	.0425	.0212	.0090	.0031	.0008	.0001	.0000	.0000
	4	.1596	.1115	.0689	.0368	.0162	.0055	.0012	.0001	.0000
	5	.2340	.2007	.1536	.1029	.0584	.0264	.0085	.0015	.0001
	6	.2384	.2508	.2377	.2001	.1460	.0881	.0401	.0112	.0010
	7	.1665	.2150	.2522	.2668	.2503	.2013	.1298	.0574	.0105
	8	.0763	.1209	.1757	.2335	.2816	.3020	.2759	.1937	.0746
	9	.0207	.0403	.0725	.1211	.1877	.2684	.3474	.3874	.3151
	10	.0025	.0060	.0135	.0282	.0563	.1074	.1969	.3487	.5987
12	0	.0001	.0000	.0000	.0000	.0000	.0000	.0000	.0000	.0000
	1	.0010	.0003	.0001	.0000	.0000	.0000	.0000	.0000	.0000
	2	.0068	.0025	.0008	.0002	.0000	.0000	.0000	.0000	.0000
	3	.0277	.0125	.0048	.0015	.0004	.0001	.0000	.0000	.0000
	4	.0762	.0420	.0199	.0078	.0024	.0005	.0001	.0000	.0000
	5	.1489	.1009	.0591	.0291	.0115	.0033	.0006	.0000	.0000
	6	.2124	.1766	.1281	.0792	.0401	.0155	.0040	.0005	.0000
	7	.2225	.2270	.2039	.1585	.1032	.0532	.0193	.0038	.0002
	8	.1700	.2128	.2367	.2311	.1936	.1329	.0683	.0213	.0021
	9	.0923	.1419	.1954	.2397	.2581	.2362	.1720	.0852	.0173
	10	.0339	.0639	.1088	.1678	.2323	.2835	.2924	.2301	.0988
	11	.0075	.0174	.0368	.0712	.1267	.2062	.3012	.3766	.3413
	12	.0008	.0022	.0057	.0138	.0317	.0687	.1422	.2824	.5404
15	0	.0000	.0000	.0000	.0000	.0000	.0000	.0000	.0000	.0000
	1	.0001	.0000	.0000	.0000	.0000	.0000	.0000	.0000	.0000
	2	.0010	.0003	.0001	.0000	.0000	.0000	.0000	.0000	.0000
	3	.0052	.0016	.0004	.0001	.0000	.0000	.0000	.0000	.0000
	4	.0191	.0074	.0024	.0006	.0001	.0000	.0000	.0000	.0000
	5	.0515	.0245	.0096	.0030	.0007	.0001	.0000	.0000	.0000
	6	.1048	.0612	.0298	.0116	.0034	.0007	.0001	.0000	.0000
	7	.1647	.1181	.0710	.0348	.0131	.0035	.0005	.0000	.0000
	8	.2013	.1771	.1319	.0811	.0393	.0138	.0030	.0003	.0000
	9	.1914	.2066	.1906	.1472	.0917	.0430	.0132	.0019	.0000
	10	.1404	.1859	.2123	.2061	.1651	.1032	.0449	.0105	.0006
	11	.0780	.1268	.1792	.2186	.2252	.1876	.1156	.0428	.0049
	12	.0318	.0634	.1110	.1700	.2252	.2501	.2184	.1285	.0307
	13	.0090	.0219	.0476	.0916	.1559	.2309	.2856	.2669	.1348
	14	.0016	.0047	.0126	.0305	.0668	.1319	.2312	.3432	.3658
	15	.0001	.0005	.0016	.0047	.0134	.0352	.0874	.2059	.4633

(Table Continues on Next Page)

TABLE 5 (Continued)

n	x	.55	.60	.65	.70	.75	.80	.85	.90	.95
						p				
18	0	.0000	.0000	.0000	.0000	.0000	.0000	.0000	.0000	.0000
	1	.0000	.0000	.0000	.0000	.0000	.0000	.0000	.0000	.0000
	2	.0001	.0000	.0000	.0000	.0000	.0000	.0000	.0000	.0000
	3	.0009	.0002	.0000	.0000	.0000	.0000	.0000	.0000	.0000
	4	.0039	.0011	.0002	.0000	.0000	.0000	.0000	.0000	.0000
	5	.0134	.0045	.0012	.0002	.0000	.0000	.0000	.0000	.0000
	6	.0354	.0145	.0047	.0012	.0002	.0000	.0000	.0000	.0000
	7	.0742	.0374	.0151	.0046	.0010	.0001	.0000	.0000	.0000
	8	.1248	.0771	.0385	.0149	.0042	.0008	.0001	.0000	.0000
	9	.1694	.1284	.0794	.0386	.0139	.0033	.0004	.0000	.0000
	10	.1864	.1734	.1327	.0811	.0376	.0120	.0022	.0002	.0000
	11	.1657	.1892	.1792	.1376	.0820	.0350	.0091	.0010	.0000
	12	.1181	.1655	.1941	.1873	.1436	.0816	.0301	.0052	.0002
	13	.0666	.1146	.1664	.2017	.1988	.1507	.0787	.0218	.0014
	14	.0291	.0614	.1104	.1681	.2130	.2153	.1592	.0700	.0093
	15	.0095	.0246	.0547	.1046	.1704	.2297	.2406	.1680	.0473
	16	.0022	.0069	.0190	.0458	.0958	.1723	.2556	.2835	.1683
	17	.0003	.0012	.0042	.0126	.0338	.0811	.1704	.3002	.3763
	18	.0000	.0001	.0004	.0016	.0056	.0180	.0536	.1501	.3972
20	0	.0000	.0000	.0000	.0000	.0000	.0000	.0000	.0000	.0000
	1	.0000	.0000	.0000	.0000	.0000	.0000	.0000	.0000	.0000
	2	.0000	.0000	.0000	.0000	.0000	.0000	.0000	.0000	.0000
	3	.0002	.0000	.0000	.0000	.0000	.0000	.0000	.0000	.0000
	4	.0013	.0003	.0000	.0000	.0000	.0000	.0000	.0000	.0000
	5	.0049	.0013	.0003	.0000	.0000	.0000	.0000	.0000	.0000
	6	.0150	.0049	.0012	.0002	.0000	.0000	.0000	.0000	.0000
	7	.0366	.0146	.0045	.0010	.0002	.0000	.0000	.0000	.0000
	8	.0727	.0355	.0136	.0039	.0008	.0001	.0000	.0000	.0000
	9	.1185	.0710	.0336	.0120	.0030	.0005	.0000	.0000	.0000
	10	.1593	.1171	.0686	.0308	.0099	.0020	.0002	.0000	.0000
	11	.1771	.1597	.1158	.0654	.0271	.0074	.0011	.0001	.0000
	12	.1623	.1797	.1614	.1144	.0609	.0222	.0046	.0004	.0000
	13	.1221	.1659	.1844	.1643	.1124	.0545	.0160	.0020	.0000
	14	.0746	.1244	.1712	.1916	.1686	.1091	.0454	.0089	.0003
	15	.0365	.0746	.1272	.1789	.2023	.1746	.1028	.0319	.0022
	16	.0139	.0350	.0738	.1304	.1897	.2182	.1821	.0898	.0133
	17	.0040	.0123	.0323	.0716	.1339	.2054	.2428	.1901	.0596
	18	.0008	.0031	.0100	.0278	.0669	.1369	.2293	.2852	.1887
	19	.0001	.0005	.0020	.0068	.0211	.0576	.1368	.2702	.3774
	20	.0000	.0000	.0002	.0008	.0032	.0115	.0388	.1216	.3585

TABLE 6 Values of $e^{-\mu}$

μ	$e^{-\mu}$	μ	$e^{-\mu}$	μ	$e^{-\mu}$
.00	1.0000				
.05	.9512	2.05	.1287	4.05	.0174
.10	.9048	2.10	.1225	4.10	.0166
.15	.8607	2.15	.1165	4.15	.0158
.20	.8187	2.20	.1108	4.20	.0150
.25	.7788	2.25	.1054	4.25	.0143
.30	.7408	2.30	.1003	4.30	.0136
.35	.7047	2.35	.0954	4.35	.0129
.40	.6703	2.40	.0907	4.40	.0123
.45	.6376	2.45	.0863	4.45	.0117
.50	.6065	2.50	.0821	4.50	.0111
.55	.5769	2.55	.0781	4.55	.0106
.60	.5488	2.60	.0743	4.60	.0101
.65	.5220	2.65	.0707	4.65	.0096
.70	.4966	2.70	.0672	4.70	.0091
.75	.4724	2.75	.0639	4.75	.0087
.80	.4493	2.80	.0608	4.80	.0082
.85	.4274	2.85	.0578	4.85	.0078
.90	.4066	2.90	.0550	4.90	.0074
.95	.3867	2.95	.0523	4.95	.0071
1.00	.3679	3.00	.0498	5.00	.0067
1.05	.3499	3.05	.0474	5.05	.0064
1.10	.3329	3.10	.0450	5.10	.0061
1.15	.3166	3.15	.0429	5.15	.0058
1.20	.3012	3.20	.0408	5.20	.0055
1.25	.2865	3.25	.0388	5.25	.0052
1.30	.2725	3.30	.0369	5.30	.0050
1.35	.2592	3.35	.0351	5.35	.0047
1.40	.2466	3.40	.0334	5.40	.0045
1.45	.2346	3.45	.0317	5.45	.0043
1.50	.2231	3.50	.0302	5.50	.0041
1.55	.2122	3.55	.0287	5.55	.0039
1.60	.2019	3.60	.0273	5.60	.0037
1.65	.1920	3.65	.0260	5.65	.0035
1.70	.1827	3.70	.0247	5.70	.0033
1.75	.1738	3.75	.0235	5.75	.0032
1.80	.1653	3.80	.0224	5.80	.0030
1.85	.1572	3.85	.0213	5.85	.0029
1.90	.1496	3.90	.0202	5.90	.0027
1.95	.1423	3.95	.0193	5.95	.0026
2.00	.1353	4.00	.0183	6.00	.0025
				7.00	.0009
				8.00	.000335
				9.00	.000123
				10.00	.000045

TABLE 7 Poisson Probabilities

Entries in the table give the probability of x occurrences for a Poisson process with a mean μ. For example, when $\mu = 2.5$, the probability of four occurrences is .1336.

					μ					
x	0.1	0.2	0.3	0.4	0.5	0.6	0.7	0.8	0.9	1.0
0	.9048	.8187	.7408	.6703	.6065	.5488	.4966	.4493	.4066	.3679
1	.0905	.1637	.2222	.2681	.3033	.3293	.3476	.3595	.3659	.3679
2	.0045	.0164	.0333	.0536	.0758	.0988	.1217	.1438	.1647	.1839
3	.0002	.0011	.0033	.0072	.0126	.0198	.0284	.0383	.0494	.0613
4	.0000	.0001	.0002	.0007	.0016	.0030	.0050	.0077	.0111	.0153
5	.0000	.0000	.0000	.0001	.0002	.0004	.0007	.0012	.0020	.0031
6	.0000	.0000	.0000	.0000	.0000	.0000	.0001	.0002	.0003	.0005
7	.0000	.0000	.0000	.0000	.0000	.0000	.0000	.0000	.0000	.0001

					μ					
x	1.1	1.2	1.3	1.4	1.5	1.6	1.7	1.8	1.9	2.0
0	.3329	.3012	.2725	.2466	.2231	.2019	.1827	.1653	.1496	.1353
1	.3662	.3614	.3543	.3452	.3347	.3230	.3106	.2975	.2842	.2707
2	.2014	.2169	.2303	.2417	.2510	.2584	.2640	.2678	.2700	.2707
3	.0738	.0867	.0998	.1128	.1255	.1378	.1496	.1607	.1710	.1804
4	.0203	.0260	.0324	.0395	.0471	.0551	.0636	.0723	.0812	.0902
5	.0045	.0062	.0084	.0111	.0141	.0176	.0216	.0260	.0309	.0361
6	.0008	.0012	.0018	.0026	.0035	.0047	.0061	.0078	.0098	.0120
7	.0001	.0002	.0003	.0005	.0008	.0011	.0015	.0020	.0027	.0034
8	.0000	.0000	.0001	.0001	.0001	.0002	.0003	.0005	.0006	.0009
9	.0000	.0000	.0000	.0000	.0000	.0000	.0001	.0001	.0001	.0002

					μ					
x	2.1	2.2	2.3	2.4	2.5	2.6	2.7	2.8	2.9	3.0
0	.1225	.1108	.1003	.0907	.0821	.0743	.0672	.0608	.0550	.0498
1	.2572	.2438	.2306	.2177	.2052	.1931	.1815	.1703	.1596	.1494
2	.2700	.2681	.2652	.2613	.2565	.2510	.2450	.2384	.2314	.2240
3	.1890	.1966	.2033	.2090	.2138	.2176	.2205	.2225	.2237	.2240
4	.0992	.1082	.1169	.1254	.1336	.1414	.1488	.1557	.1622	.1680

(Table Continues)

TABLE 7 (Continued)

	μ									
x	2.1	2.2	2.3	2.4	2.5	2.6	2.7	2.8	2.9	3.0
5	.0417	.0476	.0538	.0602	.0668	.0735	.0804	.0872	.0940	.1008
6	.0146	.0174	.0206	.0241	.0278	.0319	.0362	.0407	.0455	.0504
7	.0044	.0055	.0068	.0083	.0099	.0118	.0139	.0163	.0188	.0216
8	.0011	.0015	.0019	.0025	.0031	.0038	.0047	.0057	.0068	.0081
9	.0003	.0004	.0005	.0007	.0009	.0011	.0014	.0018	.0022	.0027
10	.0001	.0001	.0001	.0002	.0002	.0003	.0004	.0005	.0006	.0008
11	.0000	.0000	.0000	.0000	.0000	.0001	.0001	.0001	.0002	.0002
12	.0000	.0000	.0000	.0000	.0000	.0000	.0000	.0000	.0000	.0001

	μ									
x	3.1	3.2	3.3	3.4	3.5	3.6	3.7	3.8	3.9	4.0
0	.0450	.0408	.0369	.0344	.0302	.0273	.0247	.0224	.0202	.0183
1	.1397	.1304	.1217	.1135	.1057	.0984	.0915	.0850	.0789	.0733
2	.2165	.2087	.2008	.1929	.1850	.1771	.1692	.1615	.1539	.1465
3	.2237	.2226	.2209	.2186	.2158	.2125	.2087	.2046	.2001	.1954
4	.1734	.1781	.1823	.1858	.1888	.1912	.1931	.1944	.1951	.1954
5	.1075	.1140	.1203	.1264	.1322	.1377	.1429	.1477	.1522	.1563
6	.0555	.0608	.0662	.0716	.0771	.0826	.0881	.0936	.0989	.1042
7	.0246	.0278	.0312	.0348	.0385	.0425	.0466	.0508	.0551	.0595
8	.0095	.0111	.0129	.0148	.0169	.0191	.0215	.0241	.0269	.0298
9	.0033	.0040	.0047	.0056	.0066	.0076	.0089	.0102	.0116	.0132
10	.0010	.0013	.0016	.0019	.0023	.0028	.0033	.0039	.0045	.0053
11	.0003	.0004	.0005	.0006	.0007	.0009	.0011	.0013	.0016	.0019
12	.0001	.0001	.0001	.0002	.0002	.0003	.0003	.0004	.0005	.0006
13	.0000	.0000	.0000	.0000	.0001	.0001	.0001	.0001	.0002	.0002
14	.0000	.0000	.0000	.0000	.0000	.0000	.0000	.0000	.0000	.0001

	μ									
x	4.1	4.2	4.3	4.4	4.5	4.6	4.7	4.8	4.9	5.0
0	.0166	.0150	.0136	.0123	.0111	.0101	.0091	.0082	.0074	.0067
1	.0679	.0630	.0583	.0540	.0500	.0462	.0427	.0395	.0365	.0337
2	.1393	.1323	.1254	.1188	.1125	.1063	.1005	.0948	.0894	.0842
3	.1904	.1852	.1798	.1743	.1687	.1631	.1574	.1517	.1460	.1404
4	.1951	.1944	.1933	.1917	.1898	.1875	.1849	.1820	.1789	.1755
5	.1600	.1633	.1662	.1687	.1708	.1725	.1738	.1747	.1753	.1755
6	.1093	.1143	.1191	.1237	.1281	.1323	.1362	.1398	.1432	.1462
7	.0640	.0686	.0732	.0778	.0824	.0869	.0914	.0959	.1002	.1044
8	.0328	.0360	.0393	.0428	.0463	.0500	.0537	.0575	.0614	.0653
9	.0150	.0168	.0188	.0209	.0232	.0255	.0280	.0307	.0334	.0363

(Table Continues on Next Page)

TABLE 7 (Continued)

					μ					
x	4.1	4.2	4.3	4.4	4.5	4.6	4.7	4.8	4.9	5.0
10	.0061	.0071	.0081	.0092	.0104	.0118	.0132	.0147	.0164	.0181
11	.0023	.0027	.0032	.0037	.0043	.0049	.0056	.0064	.0073	.0082
12	.0008	.0009	.0011	.0014	.0016	.0019	.0022	.0026	.0030	.0034
13	.0002	.0003	.0004	.0005	.0006	.0007	.0008	.0009	.0011	.0013
14	.0001	.0001	.0001	.0001	.0002	.0002	.0003	.0003	.0004	.0005
15	.0000	.0000	.0000	.0000	.0001	.0001	.0001	.0001	.0001	.0002

					μ					
x	5.1	5.2	5.3	5.4	5.5	5.6	5.7	5.8	5.9	6.0
0	.0061	.0055	.0050	.0045	.0041	.0037	.0033	.0030	.0027	.0025
1	.0311	.0287	.0265	.0244	.0225	.0207	.0191	.0176	.0162	.0149
2	.0793	.0746	.0701	.0659	.0618	.0580	.0544	.0509	.0477	.0446
3	.1348	.1293	.1239	.1185	.1133	.1082	.1033	.0985	.0938	.0892
4	.1719	.1681	.1641	.1600	.1558	.1515	.1472	.1428	.1383	.1339
5	.1753	.1748	.1740	.1728	.1714	.1697	.1678	.1656	.1632	.1606
6	.1490	.1515	.1537	.1555	.1571	.1584	.1594	.1601	.1605	.1606
7	.1086	.1125	.1163	.1200	.1234	.1267	.1298	.1326	.1353	.1377
8	.0692	.0731	.0771	.0810	.0849	.0887	.0925	.0962	.0998	.1033
9	.0392	.0423	.0454	.0486	.0519	.0552	.0586	.0620	.0654	.0688
10	.0200	.0220	.0241	.0262	.0285	.0309	.0334	.0359	.0386	.0413
11	.0093	.0104	.0116	.0129	.0143	.0157	.0173	.0190	.0207	.0225
12	.0039	.0045	.0051	.0058	.0065	.0073	.0082	.0092	.0102	.0113
13	.0015	.0018	.0021	.0024	.0028	.0032	.0036	.0041	.0046	.0052
14	.0006	.0007	.0008	.0009	.0011	.0013	.0015	.0017	.0019	.0022
15	.0002	.0002	.0003	.0003	.0004	.0005	.0006	.0007	.0008	.0009
16	.0001	.0001	.0001	.0001	.0001	.0002	.0002	.0002	.0003	.0003
17	.0000	.0000	.0000	.0000	.0000	.0001	.0001	.0001	.0001	.0001

					μ					
x	6.1	6.2	6.3	6.4	6.5	6.6	6.7	6.8	6.9	7.0
0	.0022	.0020	.0018	.0017	.0015	.0014	.0012	.0011	.0010	.0009
1	.0137	.0126	.0116	.0106	.0098	.0090	.0082	.0076	.0070	.0064
2	.0417	.0390	.0364	.0340	.0318	.0296	.0276	.0258	.0240	.0223
3	.0848	.0806	.0765	.0726	.0688	.0652	.0617	.0584	.0552	.0521
4	.1294	.1249	.1205	.1162	.1118	.1076	.1034	.0992	.0952	.0912
5	.1579	.1549	.1519	.1487	.1454	.1420	.1385	.1349	.1314	.1277
6	.1605	.1601	.1595	.1586	.1575	.1562	.1546	.1529	.1511	.1490
7	.1399	.1418	.1435	.1450	.1462	.1472	.1480	.1486	.1489	.1490
8	.1066	.1099	.1130	.1160	.1188	.1215	.1240	.1263	.1284	.1304
9	.0723	.0757	.0791	.0825	.0858	.0891	.0923	.0954	.0985	.1014

(Table Continues)

TABLE 7 (Continued)

| | μ | | | | | | | | | |
x	6.1	6.2	6.3	6.4	6.5	6.6	6.7	6.8	6.9	7.0
10	.0441	.0469	.0498	.0528	.0558	.0588	.0618	.0649	.0679	.0710
11	.0245	.0265	.0285	.0307	.0330	.0353	.0377	.0401	.0426	.0452
12	.0124	.0137	.0150	.0164	.0179	.0194	.0210	.0227	.0245	.0264
13	.0058	.0065	.0073	.0081	.0089	.0098	.0108	.0119	.0130	.0142
14	.0025	.0029	.0033	.0037	.0041	.0046	.0052	.0058	.0064	.0071
15	.0010	.0012	.0014	.0016	.0018	.0020	.0023	.0026	.0029	.0033
16	.0004	.0005	.0005	.0006	.0007	.0008	.0010	.0011	.0013	.0014
17	.0001	.0002	.0002	.0002	.0003	.0003	.0004	.0004	.0005	.0006
18	.0000	.0001	.0001	.0001	.0001	.0001	.0001	.0002	.0002	.0002
19	.0000	.0000	.0000	.0000	.0000	.0000	.0000	.0001	.0001	.0001

| | μ | | | | | | | | | |
x	7.1	7.2	7.3	7.4	7.5	7.6	7.7	7.8	7.9	8.0
0	.0008	.0007	.0007	.0006	.0006	.0005	.0005	.0004	.0004	.0003
1	.0059	.0054	.0049	.0045	.0041	.0038	.0035	.0032	.0029	.0027
2	.0208	.0194	.0180	.0167	.0156	.0145	.0134	.0125	.0116	.0107
3	.0492	.0464	.0438	.0413	.0389	.0366	.0345	.0324	.0305	.0286
4	.0874	.0836	.0799	.0764	.0729	.0696	.0663	.0632	.0602	.0573
5	.1241	.1204	.1167	.1130	.1094	.1057	.1021	.0986	.0951	.0916
6	.1468	.1445	.1420	.1394	.1367	.1339	.1311	.1282	.1252	.1221
7	.1489	.1486	.1481	.1474	.1465	.1454	.1442	.1428	.1413	.1396
8	.1321	.1337	.1351	.1363	.1373	.1382	.1388	.1392	.1395	.1396
9	.1042	.1070	.1096	.1121	.1144	.1167	.1187	.1207	.1224	.1241
10	.0740	.0770	.0800	.0829	.0858	.0887	.0914	.0941	.0967	.0993
11	.0478	.0504	.0531	.0558	.0585	.0613	.0640	.0667	.0695	.0722
12	.0283	.0303	.0323	.0344	.0366	.0388	.0411	.0434	.0457	.0481
13	.0154	.0168	.0181	.0196	.0211	.0227	.0243	.0260	.0278	.0296
14	.0078	.0086	.0095	.0104	.0113	.0123	.0134	.0145	.0157	.0169
15	.0037	.0041	.0046	.0051	.0057	.0062	.0069	.0075	.0083	.0090
16	.0016	.0019	.0021	.0024	.0026	.0030	.0033	.0037	.0041	.0045
17	.0007	.0008	.0009	.0010	.0012	.0013	.0015	.0017	.0019	.0021
18	.0003	.0003	.0004	.0004	.0005	.0006	.0006	.0007	.0008	.0009
19	.0001	.0001	.0001	.0002	.0002	.0002	.0003	.0003	.0003	.0004
20	.0000	.0000	.0001	.0001	.0001	.0001	.0001	.0001	.0001	.0002
21	.0000	.0000	.0000	.0000	.0000	.0000	.0000	.0000	.0001	.0001

(Table Continues on Next Page)

TABLE 7   (Continued)

					μ					
x	8.1	8.2	8.3	8.4	8.5	8.6	8.7	8.8	8.9	9.0
0	.0003	.0003	.0002	.0002	.0002	.0002	.0002	.0002	.0001	.0001
1	.0025	.0023	.0021	.0019	.0017	.0016	.0014	.0013	.0012	.0011
2	.0100	.0092	.0086	.0079	.0074	.0068	.0063	.0058	.0054	.0050
3	.0269	.0252	.0237	.0222	.0208	.0195	.0183	.0171	.0160	.0150
4	.0544	.0517	.0491	.0466	.0443	.0420	.0398	.0377	.0357	.0337
5	.0882	.0849	.0816	.0784	.0752	.0722	.0692	.0663	.0635	.0607
6	.1191	.1160	.1128	.1097	.1066	.1034	.1003	.0972	.0941	.0911
7	.1378	.1358	.1338	.1317	.1294	.1271	.1247	.1222	.1197	.1171
8	.1395	.1392	.1388	.1382	.1375	.1366	.1356	.1344	.1332	.1318
9	.1256	.1269	.1280	.1290	.1299	.1306	.1311	.1315	.1317	.1318
10	.1017	.1040	.1063	.1084	.1104	.1123	.1140	.1157	.1172	.1186
11	.0749	.0776	.0802	.0828	.0853	.0878	.0902	.0925	.0948	.0970
12	.0505	.0530	.0555	.0579	.0604	.0629	.0654	.0679	.0703	.0728
13	.0315	.0334	.0354	.0374	.0395	.0416	.0438	.0459	.0481	.0504
14	.0182	.0196	.0210	.0225	.0240	.0256	.0272	.0289	.0306	.0324
15	.0098	.0107	.0116	.0126	.0136	.0147	.0158	.0169	.0182	.0194
16	.0050	.0055	.0060	.0066	.0072	.0079	.0086	.0093	.0101	.0109
17	.0024	.0026	.0029	.0033	.0036	.0040	.0044	.0048	.0053	.0058
18	.0011	.0012	.0014	.0015	.0017	.0019	.0021	.0024	.0026	.0029
19	.0005	.0005	.0006	.0007	.0008	.0009	.0010	.0011	.0012	.0014
20	.0002	.0002	.0002	.0003	.0003	.0004	.0004	.0005	.0005	.0006
21	.0001	.0001	.0001	.0001	.0001	.0002	.0002	.0002	.0002	.0003
22	.0000	.0000	.0000	.0000	.0001	.0001	.0001	.0001	.0001	.0001

					μ					
x	9.1	9.2	9.3	9.4	9.5	9.6	9.7	9.8	9.9	10
0	.0001	.0001	.0001	.0001	.0001	.0001	.0001	.0001	.0001	.0000
1	.0010	.0009	.0009	.0008	.0007	.0007	.0006	.0005	.0005	.0005
2	.0046	.0043	.0040	.0037	.0034	.0031	.0029	.0027	.0025	.0023
3	.0140	.0131	.0123	.0115	.0107	.0100	.0093	.0087	.0081	.0076
4	.0319	.0302	.0285	.0269	.0254	.0240	.0226	.0213	.0201	.0189
5	.0581	.0555	.0530	.0506	.0483	.0460	.0439	.0418	.0398	.0378
6	.0881	.0851	.0822	.0793	.0764	.0736	.0709	.0682	.0656	.0631
7	.1145	.1118	.1091	.1064	.1037	.1010	.0982	.0955	.0928	.0901
8	.1302	.1286	.1269	.1251	.1232	.1212	.1191	.1170	.1148	.1126
9	.1317	.1315	.1311	.1306	.1300	.1293	.1284	.1274	.1263	.1251

(Table Continues)

TABLE 7 (Continued)

x	9.1	9.2	9.3	9.4	9.5	9.6	9.7	9.8	9.9	10.0
					μ					
10	.1198	.1210	.1219	.1228	.1235	.1241	.1245	.1249	.1250	.1251
11	.0991	.1012	.1031	.1049	.1067	.1083	.1098	.1112	.1125	.1137
12	.0752	.0776	.0799	.0822	.0844	.0866	.0888	.0908	.0928	.0948
13	.0526	.0549	.0572	.0594	.0617	.0640	.0662	.0685	.0707	.0729
14	.0342	.0361	.0380	.0399	.0419	.0439	.0459	.0479	.0500	.0521
15	.0208	.0221	.0235	.0250	.0265	.0281	.0297	.0313	.0330	.0347
16	.0118	.0127	.0137	.0147	.0157	.0168	.0180	.0192	.0204	.0217
17	.0063	.0069	.0075	.0081	.0088	.0095	.0103	.0111	.0119	.0128
18	.0032	.0035	.0039	.0042	.0046	.0051	.0055	.0060	.0065	.0071
19	.0015	.0017	.0019	.0021	.0023	.0026	.0028	.0031	.0034	.0037
20	.0007	.0008	.0009	.0010	.0011	.0012	.0014	.0015	.0017	.0019
21	.0003	.0003	.0004	.0004	.0005	.0006	.0006	.0007	.0008	.0009
22	.0001	.0001	.0002	.0002	.0002	.0002	.0003	.0003	.0004	.0004
23	.0000	.0001	.0001	.0001	.0001	.0001	.0001	.0001	.0002	.0002
24	.0000	.0000	.0000	.0000	.0000	.0000	.0000	.0001	.0001	.0001

x	11	12	13	14	15	16	17	18	19	20
					μ					
0	.0000	.0000	.0000	.0000	.0000	.0000	.0000	.0000	.0000	.0000
1	.0002	.0001	.0000	.0000	.0000	.0000	.0000	.0000	.0000	.0000
2	.0010	.0004	.0002	.0001	.0000	.0000	.0000	.0000	.0000	.0000
3	.0037	.0018	.0008	.0004	.0002	.0001	.0000	.0000	.0000	.0000
4	.0102	.0053	.0027	.0013	.0006	.0003	.0001	.0001	.0000	.0000
5	.0224	.0127	.0070	.0037	.0019	.0010	.0005	.0002	.0001	.0001
6	.0411	.0255	.0152	.0087	.0048	.0026	.0014	.0007	.0004	.0002
7	.0646	.0437	.0281	.0174	.0104	.0060	.0034	.0018	.0010	.0005
8	.0888	.0655	.0457	.0304	.0194	.0120	.0072	.0042	.0024	.0013
9	.1085	.0874	.0661	.0473	.0324	.0213	.0135	.0083	.0050	.0029
10	.1194	.1048	.0859	.0663	.0486	.0341	.0230	.0150	.0095	.0058
11	.1194	.1144	.1015	.0844	.0663	.0496	.0355	.0245	.0164	.0106
12	.1094	.1144	.1099	.0984	.0829	.0661	.0504	.0368	.0259	.0176
13	.0926	.1056	.1099	.1060	.0956	.0814	.0658	.0509	.0378	.0271
14	.0728	.0905	.1021	.1060	.1024	.0930	.0800	.0655	.0514	.0387
15	.0534	.0724	.0885	.0989	.1024	.0992	.0906	.0786	.0650	.0516
16	.0367	.0543	.0719	.0866	.0960	.0992	.0963	.0884	.0772	.0646
17	.0237	.0383	.0550	.0713	.0847	.0934	.0963	.0936	.0863	.0760
18	.0145	.0256	.0397	.0554	.0706	.0830	.0909	.0936	.0911	.0844
19	.0084	.0161	.0272	.0409	.0557	.0699	.0814	.0887	.0911	.0888

(Table Continues on Next Page)

TABLE 7 (Continued)

					μ					
x	11	12	13	14	15	16	17	18	19	20
20	.0046	.0097	.0177	.0286	.0418	.0559	.0692	.0798	.0866	.0888
21	.0024	.0055	.0109	.0191	.0299	.0426	.0560	.0684	.0783	.0846
22	.0012	.0030	.0065	.0121	.0204	.0310	.0433	.0560	.0676	.0769
23	.0006	.0016	.0037	.0074	.0133	.0216	.0320	.0438	.0559	.0669
24	.0003	.0008	.0020	.0043	.0083	.0144	.0226	.0328	.0442	.0557
25	.0001	.0004	.0010	.0024	.0050	.0092	.0154	.0237	.0336	.0446
26	.0000	.0002	.0005	.0013	.0029	.0057	.0101	.0164	.0246	.0343
27	.0000	.0001	.0002	.0007	.0016	.0034	.0063	.0109	.0173	.0254
28	.0000	.0000	.0001	.0003	.0009	.0019	.0038	.0070	.0117	.0181
29	.0000	.0000	.0001	.0002	.0004	.0011	.0023	.0044	.0077	.0125
30	.0000	.0000	.0000	.0001	.0002	.0006	.0013	.0026	.0049	.0083
31	.0000	.0000	.0000	.0000	.0001	.0003	.0007	.0015	.0030	.0054
32	.0000	.0000	.0000	.0000	.0001	.0001	.0004	.0009	.0018	.0034
33	.0000	.0000	.0000	.0000	.0000	.0001	.0002	.0005	.0010	.0020
34	.0000	.0000	.0000	.0000	.0000	.0000	.0001	.0002	.0006	.0012
35	.0000	.0000	.0000	.0000	.0000	.0000	.0000	.0001	.0003	.0007
36	.0000	.0000	.0000	.0000	.0000	.0000	.0000	.0001	.0002	.0004
37	.0000	.0000	.0000	.0000	.0000	.0000	.0000	.0000	.0001	.0002
38	.0000	.0000	.0000	.0000	.0000	.0000	.0000	.0000	.0000	.0001
39	.0000	.0000	.0000	.0000	.0000	.0000	.0000	.0000	.0000	.0001

TABLE 8 Random Numbers

63271	59986	71744	51102	15141	80714	58683	93108	13554	79945
88547	09896	95436	79115	08303	01041	20030	63754	08459	28364
55957	57243	83865	09911	19761	66535	40102	26646	60147	15702
46276	87453	44790	67122	45573	84358	21625	16999	13385	22782
55363	07449	34835	15290	76616	67191	12777	21861	68689	03263
69393	92785	49902	58447	42048	30378	87618	26933	40640	16281
13186	29431	88190	04588	38733	81290	89541	70290	40113	08243
17726	28652	56836	78351	47327	18518	92222	55201	27340	10493
36520	64465	05550	30157	82242	29520	69753	72602	23756	54935
81628	36100	39254	56835	37636	02421	98063	89641	64953	99337
84649	48968	75215	75498	49539	74240	03466	49292	36401	45525
63291	11618	12613	75055	43915	26488	41116	64531	56827	30825
70502	53225	03655	05915	37140	57051	48393	91322	25653	06543
06426	24771	59935	49801	11082	66762	94477	02494	88215	27191
20711	55609	29430	70165	45406	78484	31639	52009	18873	96927
41990	70538	77191	25860	55204	73417	83920	69468	74972	38712
72452	36618	76298	26678	89334	33938	95567	29380	75906	91807
37042	40318	57099	10528	09925	89773	41335	96244	29002	46453
53766	52875	15987	46962	67342	77592	57651	95508	80033	69828
90585	58955	53122	16025	84299	53310	67380	84249	25348	04332
32001	96293	37203	64516	51530	37069	40261	61374	05815	06714
62606	64324	46354	72157	67248	20135	49804	09226	64419	29457
10078	28073	85389	50324	14500	15562	64165	06125	71353	77669
91561	46145	24177	15294	10061	98124	75732	00815	83452	97355
13091	98112	53959	79607	52244	63303	10413	63839	74762	50289
73864	83014	72457	22682	03033	61714	88173	90835	00634	85169
66668	25467	48894	51043	02365	91726	09365	63167	95264	45643
84745	41042	29493	01836	09044	51926	43630	63470	76508	14194
48068	26805	94595	47907	13357	38412	33318	26098	82782	42851
54310	96175	97594	88616	42035	38093	36745	56702	40644	83514
14877	33095	10924	58013	61439	21882	42059	24177	58739	60170
78295	23179	02771	43464	59061	71411	05697	67194	30495	21157
67524	02865	39593	54278	04237	92441	26602	63835	38032	94770
58268	57219	68124	73455	83236	08710	04284	55005	84171	42596
97158	28672	50685	01181	24262	19427	52106	34308	73685	74246
04230	16831	69085	30802	65559	09205	71829	06489	85650	38707
94879	56606	30401	02602	57658	70091	54986	41394	60437	03195
71446	15232	66715	26385	91518	70566	02888	79941	39684	54315
32886	05644	79316	09819	00813	88407	17461	73925	53037	91904
62048	33711	25290	21526	02223	75947	66466	06232	10913	75336
84534	42351	21628	53669	81352	95152	08107	98814	72743	12849
84707	15885	84710	35866	06446	86311	32648	88141	73902	69981
19409	40868	64220	80861	13860	68493	52908	26374	63297	45052
57978	48015	25973	66777	45924	56144	24742	96702	88200	66162
57295	98298	11199	96510	75228	41600	47192	43267	35973	23152
94044	83785	93388	07833	38216	31413	70555	03023	54147	06647
30014	25879	71763	96679	90603	99396	74557	74224	18211	91637
07265	69563	64268	88802	72264	66540	01782	08396	19251	83613
84404	88642	30263	80310	11522	57810	27627	78376	36240	48952
21778	02085	27762	46097	43324	34354	09369	14966	10158	76089

TABLE 9 Critical Values for the Durbin-Watson Test for Autocorrelation
Entries in the table give the critical values for a one-tailed Durbin-Watson test for autocorrelation. For a two-tailed test, the level of significance is doubled.

Significance Points of d_L and d_U: $\alpha = .05$
Number of Independent Variables

k	1		2		3		4		5	
n	d_L	d_U	d_L	d_U	d_L	d_U	d_L	d_U	d_L	d_U
15	1.08	1.36	0.95	1.54	0.82	1.75	0.69	1.97	0.56	2.21
16	1.10	1.37	0.98	1.54	0.86	1.73	0.74	1.93	0.62	2.15
17	1.13	1.38	1.02	1.54	0.90	1.71	0.78	1.90	0.67	2.10
18	1.16	1.39	1.05	1.53	0.93	1.69	0.82	1.87	0.71	2.06
19	1.18	1.40	1.08	1.53	0.97	1.68	0.86	1.85	0.75	2.02
20	1.20	1.41	1.10	1.54	1.00	1.68	0.90	1.83	0.79	1.99
21	1.22	1.42	1.13	1.54	1.03	1.67	0.93	1.81	0.83	1.96
22	1.24	1.43	1.15	1.54	1.05	1.66	0.96	1.80	0.86	1.94
23	1.26	1.44	1.17	1.54	1.08	1.66	0.99	1.79	0.90	1.92
24	1.27	1.45	1.19	1.55	1.10	1.66	1.01	1.78	0.93	1.90
25	1.29	1.45	1.21	1.55	1.12	1.66	1.04	1.77	0.95	1.89
26	1.30	1.46	1.22	1.55	1.14	1.65	1.06	1.76	0.98	1.88
27	1.32	1.47	1.24	1.56	1.16	1.65	1.08	1.76	1.01	1.86
28	1.33	1.48	1.26	1.56	1.18	1.65	1.10	1.75	1.03	1.85
29	1.34	1.48	1.27	1.56	1.20	1.65	1.12	1.74	1.05	1.84
30	1.35	1.49	1.28	1.57	1.21	1.65	1.14	1.74	1.07	1.83
31	1.36	1.50	1.30	1.57	1.23	1.65	1.16	1.74	1.09	1.83
32	1.37	1.50	1.31	1.57	1.24	1.65	1.18	1.73	1.11	1.82
33	1.38	1.51	1.32	1.58	1.26	1.65	1.19	1.73	1.13	1.81
34	1.39	1.51	1.33	1.58	1.27	1.65	1.21	1.73	1.15	1.81
35	1.40	1.52	1.34	1.58	1.28	1.65	1.22	1.73	1.16	1.80
36	1.41	1.52	1.35	1.59	1.29	1.65	1.24	1.73	1.18	1.80
37	1.42	1.53	1.36	1.59	1.31	1.66	1.25	1.72	1.19	1.80
38	1.43	1.54	1.37	1.59	1.32	1.66	1.26	1.72	1.21	1.79
39	1.43	1.54	1.38	1.60	1.33	1.66	1.27	1.72	1.22	1.79
40	1.44	1.54	1.39	1.60	1.34	1.66	1.29	1.72	1.23	1.79
45	1.48	1.57	1.43	1.62	1.38	1.67	1.34	1.72	1.29	1.78
50	1.50	1.59	1.46	1.63	1.42	1.67	1.38	1.72	1.34	1.77
55	1.53	1.60	1.49	1.64	1.45	1.68	1.41	1.72	1.38	1.77
60	1.55	1.62	1.51	1.65	1.48	1.69	1.44	1.73	1.41	1.77
65	1.57	1.63	1.54	1.66	1.50	1.70	1.47	1.73	1.44	1.77
70	1.58	1.64	1.55	1.67	1.52	1.70	1.49	1.74	1.46	1.77
75	1.60	1.65	1.57	1.68	1.54	1.71	1.51	1.74	1.49	1.77
80	1.61	1.66	1.59	1.69	1.56	1.72	1.53	1.74	1.51	1.77
85	1.62	1.67	1.60	1.70	1.57	1.72	1.55	1.75	1.52	1.77
90	1.63	1.68	1.61	1.70	1.59	1.73	1.57	1.75	1.54	1.78
95	1.64	1.69	1.62	1.71	1.60	1.73	1.58	1.75	1.56	1.78
100	1.65	1.69	1.63	1.72	1.61	1.74	1.59	1.76	1.57	1.78

This table comes from J. Durbin and G. S. Watson, "Testing for serial correlation in least square regression II," *Biometrika,* 38, 1951, 159–178.

TABLE 9 (Continued)

	Significance Points of d_L and d_U: $\alpha = .025$ Number of Independent Variables								
k	**1**		**2**		**3**		**4**		**5**	
n	d_L	d_U	d_L	d_U	d_L	d_U	d_L	d_U	d_L	d_U
15	0.95	1.23	0.83	1.40	0.71	1.61	0.59	1.84	0.48	2.09
16	0.98	1.24	0.86	1.40	0.75	1.59	0.64	1.80	0.53	2.03
17	1.01	1.25	0.90	1.40	0.79	1.58	0.68	1.77	0.57	1.98
18	1.03	1.26	0.93	1.40	0.82	1.56	0.72	1.74	0.62	1.93
19	1.06	1.28	0.96	1.41	0.86	1.55	0.76	1.72	0.66	1.90
20	1.08	1.28	0.99	1.41	0.89	1.55	0.79	1.70	0.70	1.87
21	1.10	1.30	1.01	1.41	0.92	1.54	0.83	1.69	0.73	1.84
22	1.12	1.31	1.04	1.42	0.95	1.54	0.86	1.68	0.77	1.82
23	1.14	1.32	1.06	1.42	0.97	1.54	0.89	1.67	0.80	1.80
24	1.16	1.33	1.08	1.43	1.00	1.54	0.91	1.66	0.83	1.79
25	1.18	1.34	1.10	1.43	1.02	1.54	0.94	1.65	0.86	1.77
26	1.19	1.35	1.12	1.44	1.04	1.54	0.96	1.65	0.88	1.76
27	1.21	1.36	1.13	1.44	1.06	1.54	0.99	1.64	0.91	1.75
28	1.22	1.37	1.15	1.45	1.08	1.54	1.01	1.64	0.93	1.74
29	1.24	1.38	1.17	1.45	1.10	1.54	1.03	1.63	0.96	1.73
30	1.25	1.38	1.18	1.46	1.12	1.54	1.05	1.63	0.98	1.73
31	1.26	1.39	1.20	1.47	1.13	1.55	1.07	1.63	1.00	1.72
32	1.27	1.40	1.21	1.47	1.15	1.55	1.08	1.63	1.02	1.71
33	1.28	1.41	1.22	1.48	1.16	1.55	1.10	1.63	1.04	1.71
34	1.29	1.41	1.24	1.48	1.17	1.55	1.12	1.63	1.06	1.70
35	1.30	1.42	1.25	1.48	1.19	1.55	1.13	1.63	1.07	1.70
36	1.31	1.43	1.26	1.49	1.20	1.56	1.15	1.63	1.09	1.70
37	1.32	1.43	1.27	1.49	1.21	1.56	1.16	1.62	1.10	1.70
38	1.33	1.44	1.28	1.50	1.23	1.56	1.17	1.62	1.12	1.70
39	1.34	1.44	1.29	1.50	1.24	1.56	1.19	1.63	1.13	1.69
40	1.35	1.45	1.30	1.51	1.25	1.57	1.20	1.63	1.15	1.69
45	1.39	1.48	1.34	1.53	1.30	1.58	1.25	1.63	1.21	1.69
50	1.42	1.50	1.38	1.54	1.34	1.59	1.30	1.64	1.26	1.69
55	1.45	1.52	1.41	1.56	1.37	1.60	1.33	1.64	1.30	1.69
60	1.47	1.54	1.44	1.57	1.40	1.61	1.37	1.65	1.33	1.69
65	1.49	1.55	1.46	1.59	1.43	1.62	1.40	1.66	1.36	1.69
70	1.51	1.57	1.48	1.60	1.45	1.63	1.42	1.66	1.39	1.70
75	1.53	1.58	1.50	1.61	1.47	1.64	1.45	1.67	1.42	1.70
80	1.54	1.59	1.52	1.62	1.49	1.65	1.47	1.67	1.44	1.70
85	1.56	1.60	1.53	1.63	1.51	1.65	1.49	1.68	1.46	1.71
90	1.57	1.61	1.55	1.64	1.53	1.66	1.50	1.69	1.48	1.71
95	1.58	1.62	1.56	1.65	1.54	1.67	1.52	1.69	1.50	1.71
100	1.59	1.63	1.57	1.65	1.55	1.67	1.53	1.70	1.51	1.72

TABLE 9 (Continued)

Significance Points of d_L and d_U: $\alpha = .01$
Number of Independent Variables

	k	1		2		3		4		5	
n	d_L	d_U	d_L	d_U	d_L	d_U	d_L	d_U	d_L	d_U	
15	0.81	1.07	0.70	1.25	0.59	1.46	0.49	1.70	0.39	1.96	
16	0.84	1.09	0.74	1.25	0.63	1.44	0.53	1.66	0.44	1.90	
17	0.87	1.10	0.77	1.25	0.67	1.43	0.57	1.63	0.48	1.85	
18	0.90	1.12	0.80	1.26	0.71	1.42	0.61	1.60	0.52	1.80	
19	0.93	1.13	0.83	1.26	0.74	1.41	0.65	1.58	0.56	1.77	
20	0.95	1.15	0.86	1.27	0.77	1.41	0.68	1.57	0.60	1.74	
21	0.97	1.16	0.89	1.27	0.80	1.41	0.72	1.55	0.63	1.71	
22	1.00	1.17	0.91	1.28	0.83	1.40	0.75	1.54	0.66	1.69	
23	1.02	1.19	0.94	1.29	0.86	1.40	0.77	1.53	0.70	1.67	
24	1.04	1.20	0.96	1.30	0.88	1.41	0.80	1.53	0.72	1.66	
25	1.05	1.21	0.98	1.30	0.90	1.41	0.83	1.52	0.75	1.65	
26	1.07	1.22	1.00	1.31	0.93	1.41	0.85	1.52	0.78	1.64	
27	1.09	1.23	1.02	1.32	0.95	1.41	0.88	1.51	0.81	1.63	
28	1.10	1.24	1.04	1.32	0.97	1.41	0.90	1.51	0.83	1.62	
29	1.12	1.25	1.05	1.33	0.99	1.42	0.92	1.51	0.85	1.61	
30	1.13	1.26	1.07	1.34	1.01	1.42	0.94	1.51	0.88	1.61	
31	1.15	1.27	1.08	1.34	1.02	1.42	0.96	1.51	0.90	1.60	
32	1.16	1.28	1.10	1.35	1.04	1.43	0.98	1.51	0.92	1.60	
33	1.17	1.29	1.11	1.36	1.05	1.43	1.00	1.51	0.94	1.59	
34	1.18	1.30	1.13	1.36	1.07	1.43	1.01	1.51	0.95	1.59	
35	1.19	1.31	1.14	1.37	1.08	1.44	1.03	1.51	0.97	1.59	
36	1.21	1.32	1.15	1.38	1.10	1.44	1.04	1.51	0.99	1.59	
37	1.22	1.32	1.16	1.38	1.11	1.45	1.06	1.51	1.00	1.59	
38	1.23	1.33	1.18	1.39	1.12	1.45	1.07	1.52	1.02	1.58	
39	1.24	1.34	1.19	1.39	1.14	1.45	1.09	1.52	1.03	1.58	
40	1.25	1.34	1.20	1.40	1.15	1.46	1.10	1.52	1.05	1.58	
45	1.29	1.38	1.24	1.42	1.20	1.48	1.16	1.53	1.11	1.58	
50	1.32	1.40	1.28	1.45	1.24	1.49	1.20	1.54	1.16	1.59	
55	1.36	1.43	1.32	1.47	1.28	1.51	1.25	1.55	1.21	1.59	
60	1.38	1.45	1.35	1.48	1.32	1.52	1.28	1.56	1.25	1.60	
65	1.41	1.47	1.38	1.50	1.35	1.53	1.31	1.57	1.28	1.61	
70	1.43	1.49	1.40	1.52	1.37	1.55	1.34	1.58	1.31	1.61	
75	1.45	1.50	1.42	1.53	1.39	1.56	1.37	1.59	1.34	1.62	
80	1.47	1.52	1.44	1.54	1.42	1.57	1.39	1.60	1.36	1.62	
85	1.48	1.53	1.46	1.55	1.43	1.58	1.41	1.60	1.39	1.63	
90	1.50	1.54	1.47	1.56	1.45	1.59	1.43	1.61	1.41	1.64	
95	1.51	1.55	1.49	1.57	1.47	1.60	1.45	1.62	1.42	1.64	
100	1.52	1.56	1.50	1.58	1.48	1.60	1.46	1.63	1.44	1.65	

TABLE 10 T_L Values for the Mann-Whitney-Wilcoxon Test
Reject the hypothesis of identical populations if the sum of the ranks for the n_1 items is *less* than the value T_L shown in the following table or if the sum of the ranks for the n_1 items is *greater* than the value T_U where

$$T_U = n_1(n_1 + n_2 + 1) - T_L$$

$\alpha = .05$	n_2								
n_1	2	3	4	5	6	7	8	9	10
2	3	3	3	3	3	3	4	4	4
3	6	6	6	7	8	8	9	9	10
4	10	10	11	12	13	14	15	15	16
5	15	16	17	18	19	21	22	23	24
6	21	23	24	25	27	28	30	32	33
7	28	30	32	34	35	37	39	41	43
8	37	39	41	43	45	47	50	52	54
9	46	48	50	53	56	58	61	63	66
10	56	59	61	64	67	70	73	76	79

$\alpha = .10$	n_2								
n_1	2	3	4	5	6	7	8	9	10
2	3	3	3	4	4	4	5	5	5
3	6	7	7	8	9	9	10	11	11
4	10	11	12	13	14	15	16	17	18
5	16	17	18	20	21	22	24	25	27
6	22	24	25	27	29	30	32	34	36
7	29	31	33	35	37	40	42	44	46
8	38	40	42	45	47	50	52	55	57
9	47	50	52	55	58	61	64	67	70
10	57	60	63	67	70	73	76	80	83

TABLE 11 Critical Values of the Studentized Range Distribution

$\alpha = .05$

Degrees of Freedom	Number of Populations																		
	2	3	4	5	6	7	8	9	10	11	12	13	14	15	16	17	18	19	20
1	18.0	27.0	32.8	37.1	40.4	43.1	45.4	47.4	49.1	50.6	52.0	53.2	54.3	55.4	56.3	57.2	58.0	58.8	59.6
2	6.08	8.33	9.80	10.9	11.7	12.4	13.0	13.5	14.0	14.4	14.7	15.1	15.4	15.7	15.9	16.1	16.4	16.6	16.8
3	4.50	5.91	6.82	7.50	8.04	8.48	8.85	9.18	9.46	9.72	9.95	10.2	10.3	10.5	10.7	10.8	11.0	11.1	11.2
4	3.93	5.04	5.76	6.29	6.71	7.05	7.35	7.60	7.83	8.03	8.21	8.37	8.52	8.66	8.79	8.91	9.03	9.13	9.23
5	3.64	4.60	5.22	5.67	6.03	6.33	6.58	6.80	6.99	7.17	7.32	7.47	7.60	7.72	7.83	7.93	8.03	8.12	8.21
6	3.46	4.34	4.90	5.30	5.63	5.90	6.12	6.32	6.49	6.65	6.79	6.92	7.03	7.14	7.24	7.34	7.43	7.51	7.59
7	3.34	4.16	4.68	5.06	5.36	5.61	5.82	6.00	6.16	6.30	6.43	6.55	6.66	6.76	6.85	6.94	7.02	7.10	7.17
8	3.26	4.04	4.53	4.89	5.17	5.40	5.60	5.77	5.92	6.05	6.18	6.29	6.39	6.48	6.57	6.65	6.73	6.80	6.87
9	3.20	3.95	4.41	4.76	5.02	5.24	5.43	5.59	5.74	5.87	5.98	6.09	6.19	6.28	6.36	6.44	6.51	6.58	6.64
10	3.15	3.88	4.33	4.65	4.91	5.12	5.30	5.46	5.60	5.72	5.83	5.93	6.03	6.11	6.19	6.27	6.34	6.40	6.47
11	3.11	3.82	4.26	4.57	4.82	5.03	5.20	5.35	5.49	5.61	5.71	5.81	5.90	5.98	6.06	6.13	6.20	6.27	6.33
12	3.08	3.77	4.20	4.51	4.75	4.95	5.12	5.27	5.39	5.51	5.61	5.71	5.80	5.88	5.95	6.02	6.09	6.15	6.21
13	3.06	3.73	4.15	4.45	4.69	4.88	5.05	5.19	5.32	5.43	5.53	5.63	5.71	5.79	5.86	5.93	5.99	6.05	6.11
14	3.03	3.70	4.11	4.41	4.64	4.83	4.99	5.13	5.25	5.36	5.46	5.55	5.64	5.71	5.79	5.85	5.91	5.97	6.03
15	3.01	3.67	4.08	4.37	4.59	4.78	4.94	5.08	5.20	5.31	5.40	5.49	5.57	5.65	5.72	5.78	5.85	5.90	5.96
16	3.00	3.65	4.05	4.33	4.56	4.74	4.90	5.03	5.15	5.26	5.35	5.44	5.52	5.59	5.66	5.73	5.79	5.84	5.90
17	2.98	3.63	4.02	4.30	4.52	4.70	4.86	4.99	5.11	5.21	5.31	5.39	5.47	5.54	5.61	5.67	5.73	5.79	5.84
18	2.97	3.61	4.00	4.28	4.49	4.67	4.82	4.96	5.07	5.17	5.27	5.35	5.43	5.50	5.57	5.63	5.69	5.74	5.79
19	2.96	3.59	3.98	4.25	4.47	4.65	4.79	4.92	5.04	5.14	5.23	5.31	5.39	5.46	5.53	5.59	5.65	5.70	5.75
20	2.95	3.58	3.96	4.23	4.45	4.62	4.77	4.90	5.01	5.11	5.20	5.28	5.36	5.43	5.49	5.55	5.61	5.66	5.71
24	2.92	3.53	3.90	4.17	4.37	4.54	4.68	4.81	4.92	5.01	5.10	5.18	5.25	5.32	5.38	5.44	5.49	5.55	5.59
30	2.89	3.49	3.85	4.10	4.30	4.46	4.60	4.72	4.82	4.92	5.00	5.08	5.15	5.21	5.27	5.33	5.38	5.43	5.47
40	2.86	3.44	3.79	4.04	4.23	4.39	4.52	4.63	4.73	4.82	4.90	4.98	5.04	5.11	5.16	5.22	5.27	5.31	5.36
60	2.83	3.40	3.74	3.98	4.16	4.31	4.44	4.55	4.65	4.73	4.81	4.88	4.94	5.00	5.06	5.11	5.15	5.20	5.24
120	2.80	3.36	3.68	3.92	4.10	4.24	4.36	4.47	4.56	4.64	4.71	4.78	4.84	4.90	4.95	5.00	5.04	5.09	5.13
∞	2.77	3.31	3.63	3.86	4.03	4.17	4.29	4.39	4.47	4.55	4.62	4.68	4.74	4.80	4.85	4.89	4.93	4.97	5.01

TABLE 11 (Continued)

Degrees of Freedom	$\alpha = .01$ Number of Populations																		
	2	3	4	5	6	7	8	9	10	11	12	13	14	15	16	17	18	19	20
1	90.0	135.	164.	186.	202.	216.	227.	237.	246.	253.	260.	266.	272.	277.	282.	286.	290.	294.	298.
2	14.0	19.0	22.3	24.7	26.6	28.2	29.5	30.7	31.7	32.6	33.4	34.1	34.8	35.4	36.0	36.5	37.0	37.5	37.9
3	8.26	10.6	12.2	13.3	14.2	15.0	15.6	16.2	16.7	17.1	17.5	17.9	18.2	18.5	18.8	19.1	19.3	19.5	19.8
4	6.51	8.12	9.17	9.96	10.6	11.1	11.5	11.9	12.3	12.6	12.8	13.1	13.3	13.5	13.7	13.9	14.1	14.2	14.4
5	5.70	6.97	7.80	8.42	8.91	9.32	9.67	9.97	10.2	10.5	10.7	10.9	11.1	11.2	11.4	11.6	11.7	11.8	11.9
6	5.24	6.33	7.03	7.56	7.97	8.32	8.61	8.87	9.10	9.30	9.49	9.65	9.81	9.95	10.1	10.2	10.3	10.4	10.5
7	4.95	5.92	6.54	7.01	7.37	7.68	7.94	8.17	8.37	8.55	8.71	8.86	9.00	9.12	9.24	9.35	9.46	9.55	9.65
8	4.74	5.63	6.20	6.63	6.96	7.24	7.47	7.68	7.87	8.03	8.18	8.31	8.44	8.55	8.66	8.76	8.85	8.94	9.03
9	4.60	5.43	5.96	6.35	6.66	6.91	7.13	7.32	7.49	7.65	7.78	7.91	8.03	8.13	8.23	8.32	8.41	8.49	8.57
10	4.48	5.27	5.77	6.14	6.43	6.67	6.87	7.05	7.21	7.36	7.48	7.60	7.71	7.81	7.91	7.99	8.07	8.15	8.22
11	4.39	5.14	5.62	5.97	6.25	6.48	6.67	6.84	6.99	7.13	7.25	7.36	7.46	7.56	7.65	7.73	7.81	7.88	7.95
12	4.32	5.04	5.50	5.84	6.10	6.32	6.51	6.67	6.81	6.94	7.06	7.17	7.26	7.36	7.44	7.52	7.59	7.66	7.73
13	4.26	4.96	5.40	5.73	5.98	6.19	6.37	6.53	6.67	6.79	6.90	7.01	7.10	7.19	7.27	7.34	7.42	7.48	7.55
14	4.21	4.89	5.32	5.63	5.88	6.08	6.26	6.41	6.54	6.66	6.77	6.87	6.96	7.05	7.12	7.20	7.27	7.33	7.39
15	4.17	4.83	5.25	5.56	5.80	5.99	6.16	6.31	6.44	6.55	6.66	6.76	6.84	6.93	7.00	7.07	7.14	7.20	7.26
16	4.13	4.78	5.19	5.49	5.72	5.92	6.08	6.22	6.35	6.46	6.56	6.66	6.74	6.82	6.90	6.97	7.03	7.09	7.15
17	4.10	4.74	5.14	5.43	5.66	5.85	6.01	6.15	6.27	6.38	6.48	6.57	6.66	6.73	6.80	6.87	6.94	7.00	7.05
18	4.07	4.70	5.09	5.38	5.60	5.79	5.94	6.08	6.20	6.31	6.41	6.50	6.58	6.65	6.72	6.79	6.85	6.91	6.96
19	4.05	4.67	5.05	5.33	5.55	5.73	5.89	6.02	6.14	6.25	6.34	6.43	6.51	6.58	6.65	6.72	6.78	6.84	6.89
20	4.02	4.64	5.02	5.29	5.51	5.69	5.84	5.97	6.09	6.19	6.29	6.37	6.45	6.52	6.59	6.65	6.71	6.76	6.82
24	3.96	4.54	4.91	5.17	5.37	5.54	5.69	5.81	5.92	6.02	6.11	6.19	6.26	6.33	6.39	6.45	6.51	6.56	6.61
30	3.89	4.45	4.80	5.05	5.24	5.40	5.54	5.65	5.76	5.85	5.93	6.01	6.08	6.14	6.20	6.26	6.31	6.36	6.41
40	3.82	4.37	4.70	4.93	5.11	5.27	5.39	5.50	5.60	5.69	5.77	5.84	5.90	5.96	6.02	6.07	6.12	6.17	6.21
60	3.76	4.28	4.60	4.82	4.99	5.13	5.25	5.36	5.45	5.53	5.60	5.67	5.73	5.79	5.84	5.89	5.93	5.98	6.02
120	3.70	4.20	4.50	4.71	4.87	5.01	5.12	5.21	5.30	5.38	5.44	5.51	5.56	5.61	5.66	5.71	5.75	5.79	5.83
∞	3.64	4.12	4.40	4.60	4.76	4.88	4.99	5.08	5.16	5.23	5.29	5.35	5.40	5.45	5.49	5.54	5.57	5.61	5.65

TABLE 12 Factors for $\bar{x}$ and R Control Charts

Observations in Sample, n	d_2	A_2	d_3	D_3	D_4
2	1.128	1.880	0.853	0	3.267
3	1.693	1.023	0.888	0	2.574
4	2.059	0.729	0.880	0	2.282
5	2.326	0.577	0.864	0	2.114
6	2.534	0.483	0.848	0	2.004
7	2.704	0.419	0.833	0.076	1.924
8	2.847	0.373	0.820	0.136	1.864
9	2.970	0.337	0.808	0.184	1.816
10	3.078	0.308	0.797	0.223	1.777
11	3.173	0.285	0.787	0.256	1.744
12	3.258	0.266	0.778	0.283	1.717
13	3.336	0.249	0.770	0.307	1.693
14	3.407	0.235	0.763	0.328	1.672
15	3.472	0.223	0.756	0.347	1.653
16	3.532	0.212	0.750	0.363	1.637
17	3.588	0.203	0.744	0.378	1.622
18	3.640	0.194	0.739	0.391	1.608
19	3.689	0.187	0.734	0.403	1.597
20	3.735	0.180	0.729	0.415	1.585
21	3.778	0.173	0.724	0.425	1.575
22	3.819	0.167	0.720	0.434	1.566
23	3.858	0.162	0.716	0.443	1.557
24	3.895	0.157	0.712	0.451	1.548
25	3.931	0.153	0.708	0.459	1.541

Adapted from Table 27 of ASTM STP 15D *ASTM Manual on Presentation of Data and Control Chart Analysis.* Copyright 1976 American Society for Testing and Materials, Philadelphia, PA.

APPENDIX C

Summation Notation

SUMMATIONS

Definition

$$\sum_{i=1}^{n} x_i = x_1 + x_2 + \cdots + x_n \tag{C.1}$$

Example for $x_1 = 5$, $x_2 = 8$, $x_3 = 14$:

$$\sum_{i=1}^{3} x_i = x_1 + x_2 + x_3$$

$$= 5 + 8 + 14$$

$$= 27$$

Result 1

For a constant c:

$$\sum_{i=1}^{n} c = \underbrace{(c + c + \ldots + c)}_{n \text{ times}} = nc \tag{C.2}$$

Example for $c = 5$, $n = 10$:

$$\sum_{i=1}^{10} 5 = 10(5) = 50$$

Example for $c = \bar{x}$:

$$\sum_{i=1}^{n} \bar{x} = n\bar{x}$$

Result 2

$$\sum_{i=1}^{n} cx_i = cx_1 + cx_2 + \cdots + cx_n$$

$$= c(x_1 + x_2 + \cdots + x_n) = c \sum_{i=1}^{n} x_i \tag{C.3}$$

Example for $x_1 = 5$, $x_2 = 8$, $x_3 = 14$, $c = 2$:

$$\sum_{i=1}^{3} 2x_i = 2 \sum_{i=1}^{3} x_i = 2(27) = 54$$

Result 3

$$\sum_{i=1}^{n} (ax_i + by_i) = a \sum_{i=1}^{n} x_i + b \sum_{i=1}^{n} y_i \qquad \textbf{(C.4)}$$

Example for $x_1 = 5$, $x_2 = 8$, $x_3 = 14$, $a = 2$, $y_1 = 7$, $y_2 = 3$, $y_3 = 8$, $b = 4$:

$$\sum_{i=1}^{3} (2x_i + 4y_i) = 2 \sum_{i=1}^{3} x_i + 4 \sum_{i=1}^{3} y_i$$

$$= 2(27) + 4(18)$$

$$= 54 + 72$$

$$= 126$$

DOUBLE SUMMATIONS

Consider the following data involving the variable x_{ij}, where i is the subscript denoting the row position and j is the subscript denoting the column position:

		Column		
		1	2	3
Row	1	$x_{11} = 10$	$x_{12} = 8$	$x_{13} = 6$
	2	$x_{21} = 7$	$x_{22} = 4$	$x_{23} = 12$

Definition

$$\sum_{i=1}^{n} \sum_{j=1}^{m} x_{ij} = (x_{11} + x_{12} + \cdots + x_{1m}) + (x_{21} + x_{22} + \cdots + x_{2m})$$

$$+ (x_{31} + x_{32} + \cdots + x_{3m}) + \cdots + (x_{n1} + x_{n2} + \cdots + x_{nm}) \qquad \textbf{(C.5)}$$

Example:

$$\sum_{i=1}^{2} \sum_{j=1}^{3} x_{ij} = x_{11} + x_{12} + x_{13} + x_{21} + x_{22} + x_{23}$$

$$= 10 + 8 + 6 + 7 + 4 + 12$$

$$= 47$$

Definition

$$\sum_{i=1}^{n} x_{ij} = x_{1j} + x_{2j} + \cdots + x_{nj} \qquad \textbf{(C.6)}$$

Example:

$$\sum_{i=1}^{2} x_{i2} = x_{12} + x_{22}$$

$$= 8 + 4$$

$$= 12$$

SHORTHAND NOTATION

Sometimes when a summation is for all values of the subscript, we use the following shorthand notations:

$$\sum_{i=1}^{n} x_i = \Sigma x_i \qquad \text{(C.7)}$$

$$\sum_{i=1}^{n} \sum_{j=1}^{m} x_{ij} = \Sigma \Sigma x_{ij} \qquad \text{(C.8)}$$

$$\sum_{i=1}^{n} x_{ij} = \sum_{i} x_{ij} \qquad \text{(C.9)}$$

APPENDIX D

The Data Disk

The Data Disk contains most of the larger data sets presented in the text. The Data Disk is available in formats that will enable you to retrieve any data set listed using Minitab, Excel, or The Data Analyst software package. A list of the data set filenames that appear in each chapter is shown below. In addition, each data set on The Data Disk is also identified in the text with a logo that appears in the margin.

Chapter 2

RETURN	Exercise 16
RETAIL	Exercise 18
COMPUTER	Exercise 21
APTEST	Table 2.13
JOBSAT	Exercise 27
PEFORCST	Exercise 28
SCATTER	Exercise 30
FINANCE	Table 2.18
LAWAGES	Exercise 40
COMSTOCK	Exercise 42
GRADEAVE	Exercise 43
SHADOW	Exercise 45
STATES	Exercise 46
CITIES	Exercise 48
BWDATA	Exercise 50
CONSOLID	Computer Case

Chapter 3

ENTRYSAL	Exercise 5
LAWAGES	Exercise 26
CHAINSAL	Exercise 35
GROWTH	Exercise 44
INJURY	Exercise 47
UTILITY	Exercise 54
CITIES	Exercise 55
PRICES	Exercise 62
MORTGAGE	Exercise 65
EXAM	Exercise 69
DUKE	Exercise 76
CONSOLID	Computer Case
HEALTH1	Computer Case
HEALTH2	Computer Case

Chapter 8

LIFEINS	Table 8.1
MIAMI	Exercise 14
BOCK	Computer Case
AUTO	Computer Case

Chapter 9

DISTANCE	Table 9.2
QUALITY	Computer Case

Chapter 10

AIRPORT	Exercise 6
UNION	Exercise 10
EXAMDATA	Table 10.7
GOLF	Computer Case

Chapter 11

BAGS	Exercise 19
DOWJONES	Exercise 21
TRAINING	Computer Case

Chapter 13

MACHINES	Exercise 9
MKTVALUE	Exercise 10
SNOW	Exercise 40
ASSEMBLY	Exercise 52
MKTCAP	Exercise 53
MKTPERF	Exercise 56
MEDICAL1	Computer Case
MEDICAL2	Computer Case

Chapter 14

HOME1	Exercise 44
PRESCRIP	Exercise 43
HOME2	Exercise 53
TEMPSC	Exercise 54
SAFETY	Computer Case

Chapter 15

BUTLER	Table 15.2
SHOWTIME	Exercise 5
AUTO1	Exercise 6
MOWER	Exercise 7
PHARMACY	Exercise 8
SCHOOLS1	Exercise 9
HOUSING	Exercise 10
FORBES1	Exercise 25
JOHNSON	Table 15.6
REPAIR	Exercise 35
MONITOR1	Exercise 37
STROKE	Exercise 38
JOBS	Exercise 52

AUTO2	Exercise 54
CONSUMER	Computer Case

Chapter 16

REYNOLDS	Table 16.1
TYLER	Table 16.2
MPG	Table 16.4
SMOKE	Exercise 8
FOOTBALL	Exercise 12
STROKE	Exercise 14
CRAVENS	Table 16.8
SCHOOLS2	Exercise 15
STKPRICE	Exercise 16
PGA	Exercise 18
FORBES2	Exercise 19
MONITOR2	Exercise 30
AUDIT	Exercise 31
JOBS	Exercise 32
LAYOFFS	Computer Case

APPENDIX E

Answers to Even-Numbered Exercises

Chapter 1

2. a. 10
   b. 4
   c. Industry and Comp. vs. Shareholder Return qualitative
      CEO Compensation and Sales quantitative
4. a. 10
   b. *Fortune 500* Corporations, April 1994.
   c. $3,756 million
   d. $3,756 million
6. a, c, and d are quantitative
   b and e are qualitative
8. a. 1000
   b. Qualitative
   c. Percentages
   d. 17%
10. a and e are quantitative
    b, c, and d are qualitative
12. a. Visitors to Hawaii
    b. Yes; vast majority travel to Hawaii by air
    c. 1 and 4 are quantitative; 2 and 3 are qualitative
14. a. 4
    b. All variables are quantitative
    c. Times series for 1990 to 1993
16. a. Product taste and preference data
    b. Actual test data from young adults
18. a. 40% in the sample died of heart disease
    b. Qualitative
20. a. 56% food manufacturers; 12% HBA manufacturers; 3.6
       average satisfaction.
    b. 3.6
    c. 12%
22. a. All adult viewers reached by the television station
    b. The viewers contacted by the telephone survey
    c. A sample requires less time and a lower cost compared
       to contacting all viewers in the population
24. a and c are correct
    b, d and e should be challenged

Chapter 2

2. a. .20
   b. 40
   c/d.

Class	Frequency	Percent Frequency
A	44	22
B	36	18
C	80	40
D	40	20
Total	200	100

4. a. Names of trucks
   b.

Truck	Frequency	Percent Frequency
C/K Pickup	13	26
Caravan	7	14
Explorer	7	14
F-Series	14	28
Ranger	9	18
Total	50	100

   d. Ford F-Series pickup; Chevy C/K pickup
      is a close second.
6. a.

Book	Frequency	Percent Frequency
C	9	20.0
D	6	13.3
I	7	15.6
L	5	11.1
P	8	17.8
W	10	22.2
Total	45	100.0

   b. W, C, P, I, D and L

c. D - 13.3%; L - 11.1%; Combined 24.4%

8. a.

Position	Frequency	Relative Frequency
P	17	.309
H	4	.073
1	5	.091
2	4	.073
3	2	.036
S	5	.091
L	6	.109
C	5	.091
R	7	.127
Totals	55	1.000

b. Pitcher
c. 3rd base
d. Rightfield
e. Infielders 16 to outfielders 18

10. a. Quality classifications
b.

Rating	Frequency	Relative Frequency
Poor	2	.03
Fair	4	.07
Good	12	.20
Very good	24	.40
Excellent	18	.30
Totals	60	1.00

12.

Class	Cumulative Frequency	Cumulative Relative Frequency
≤19	10	.20
≤29	24	.48
≤39	41	.82
≤49	48	.96
≤59	50	1.00

14. b, c.

Class	Frequency	Percent Frequency
6.0–7.9	4	20
–9.9	2	10
11.9	8	40
3.9	3	15
9	3	15
	20	100

16. a.

12 Month Return	Frequency	Relative Frequency	Percent Frequency
1–5	2	.071	7.1
6–10	5	.179	17.9
11–15	13	.464	46.4
16–20	5	.179	17.9
21–25	2	.071	7.1
26–30	1	.036	3.6
Total	28	1.000	100.0

b.

5-Year Return	Frequency	Relative Frequency	Percent Frequency
1–5	2	.071	7.1
6–10	8	.286	28.6
11–15	10	.357	35.7
16–20	5	.179	17.9
21–25	2	.071	7.1
26–30	1	.036	3.6
Total	28	1.000	100.0

c. Very similar, with 12-Month having slightly more in the 11–15% class.

18. a. $31,000, $57,000
b.

Salary	Frequency	Relative Frequency	Percent Frequency
31–35	2	.050	5.0
36–40	4	.100	10.0
41–45	13	.325	32.5
46–50	11	.275	27.5
51–55	8	.200	20.0
56–60	2	.050	5.0
Total	40	1.000	100.0

c. .05
d. 25%

20. a. 38%
b. 33%
c. 29%
d. 163
e. 310

22.

5	7	8				
6	4	5	8			
7	0	2	2	5	5	6	8
8	0	2	3	5		

24.

```
11 | 6
12 | 0 2
13 | 0 6 7
14 | 2 2 7
15 | 5
16 | 0 2 8
17 | 0 2 3
```

26.

```
-3 | 0
-2 |
-1 | 1 1 7
-0 | 3 3 9
 0 | 5 7
 1 | 4
 2 | 0 1 3 5 6
 3 | 9
 4 | 6 8
 5 | 4 5
14 | 0
```

28.

```
 4 | 7
 5 | 2
 6 |
 7 |
 8 | 0 0 1
 9 | 1 4 5 8 8
10 | 4
11 | 3 3 5 7
12 | 0 8
13 | 5 6 8 8
14 | 0 6 7 8 9
15 | 4
16 | 8
17 |
18 |
19 |
20 |
21 | 6
22 | 7
```

Forecast	Frequency	Percent Frequency
4–6	2	6.67
7–9	8	26.67
10–12	7	23.33
13–15	10	33.33
16–18	1	3.33
19–21	1	3.33
22–25	1	3.33
Total	30	100.00

30. Negative relationship

32.

Earn/share	Book value/share				
	0.00–4.99	5.00–9.99	10.00–14.99	15.00–19.99	Total
0.00–0.99	7	4	1	0	12
1.00–1.99	2	7	1	1	11
2.00–2.99	0	1	4	2	7
Total	9	12	6	3	30

Lower earning per share tends to have a lower book value per share.

34. Positive relationship

36. a/b.

Sport	Frequency	Relative Frequency
Baseball	7	.175
Basketball	6	.150
Football	14	.350
Ice Hockey	1	.025
Tennis	1	.025
Other	11	.275
Total	40	1.000

38. a.

Party Affiliation	Frequency	Relative Frequency
Democrat	17	.425
Republican	17	.425
Independent	6	.150
Totals	40	1.000

40.

Hourly Wage	Freq.	Rel. Freq.	Cum. Freq.	Cum. Rel. Freq.
4.00–5.99	1	.04	1	.04
6.00–7.99	3	.12	4	.16
8.00–9.99	8	.32	12	.48
10.00–11.99	6	.24	18	.72
12.00–13.99	5	.20	23	.92
14.00–15.99	2	.08	25	1.00
Totals	25	1.00		

42.

Closing Price	Freq.	Rel. Freq.	Cum. Freq.	Cum. Rel. Freq.
0–9⅞	9	.225	9	.225
10–19⅞	10	.250	19	.475
20–29⅞	5	.125	24	.600
30–39⅞	11	.275	35	.875
40–49⅞	2	.050	37	.925
50–59⅞	2	.050	39	.975
60–69⅞	0	.000	39	.975
70–79⅞	1	.025	40	1.000
Totals	40	1.000		

44.

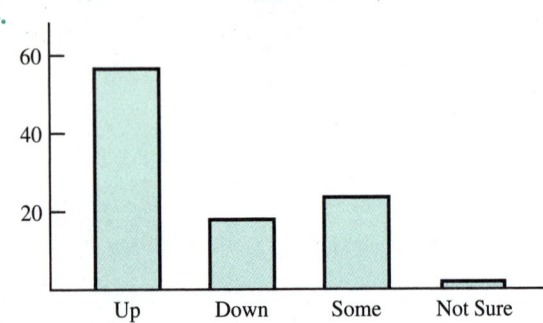

46.

Income	Frequency	Relative Frequency
12,000–13,999	1	.020
14,000–15,999	10	.196
16,000–17,999	17	.333
18,000–19,999	11	.216
20,000–21,999	6	.118
22,000–23,999	3	.059
24,000–25,999	3	.059
Totals	51	1.000

48. a.

```
1 | 7
2 | 5 6 7 7
3 | 1 7 7 8
4 | 2 3 9
5 | 1 1 2 2 4 4 8
6 | 6 8
7 | 2 5
```

b.

```
0 | 9
1 | 0 0 2 3 6 9
2 | 4 6 8 8
3 | 3 4 4 5 5 9
4 | 1 5 8 8 9
5 | 7 9
```

d. 11

e.

Temperature	Frequency High Temp.	Frequency Low Temp.
0–9	0	1
10–19	1	6
20–29	4	4
30–39	4	6
40–49	3	5
50–59	8	2
60–69	2	0
70–79	2	0
	24	24

50. a.

Industry	P/E Ratio 5-9	10-14	15-19	20-24	25-29	Total
Consumer	0	3	5	1	1	10
Banking	4	4	2	0	0	10
Total	4	7	7	1	1	20

b.

Industry	P/E Ratio 5-9	10-14	15-19	20-24	25-29	Total
Consumer	0	30	50	10	10	100
Banking	40	40	20	0	0	100

c. Consumer tends to have higher P/E ratios.

52. b.

Year	Freq.
1973 or before	247
1974–79	54
1980–86	82
1981–91	121
Total	504

Fuel	Freq.
Elect.	149
Nat Gas	317
Oil	17
Propane	7
Other	14
Total	504

Chapter 3

2. 16, 16.5
4. 2 from each end
6. a. $103.90, $97.50, $75.00
   b. $59.50, $149.50
8. a. 38.75, 29
   b. 38.61, 38.38
   c. 38.5
   d. 29.5, 47.5
   e. 31

10. a. 178
   b. 178
   c. Do not report a mode
   d. 184
12. a. 48.33, 49; do not report a mode
   b. 45, 55
   c. 45, 55
14. *City:*   mean = 15.58, median = 15.9,
                 mode = 15.3
   Country: mean = 18.92, median = 18.7,
                 mode = 18.6 and 19.4
16. a. 4.44, 4.25, 4.20
   b. 4.10, 5.10
   c. 4.15, 4.80
18. 6, 4
20. a. Mainland
            115,130 111,560
         Asia
            36,620 36,695
   b. Mainland
            86,240 26,820 23.4%
            42,970 11,400 31.1%
   c. More visitors and more variation from Mainland
22. a. Range = 32, IQR = 10
   b. 92.75, 9.63
24. *Dawson:* range = 2, $s = .67$
       Clark: range = 8, $s = 2.58$
26. a. 10.40
   b. 10.05
   c. 9.50
   d. 3.60
   e. 6.75
   f. 2.60
28. *Quarter milers:* $s = .056$, Coef. of Var. = 5.8
         Milers: $s = .130$, Coef. of Var. = 2.9
30. .20, 1.50, 0, $-.50$, -2.20
32. a. 95%
   b. Almost all
   c. 68%
34. a. 73.2, 13.71
   b. $z = 2.54$; No
   c. 16%, 2.5%
36. a. At least 75%
   b. At least 81%
38. a. 75%, 84%, 89%
   b. 95%; almost all
40. 15, 22.5, 26, 29, 34
42. 5, 8, 10, 15, 18
44. a. 1.9, 10.0, 14.5, 20.4, 55.9
   b. *Inner fences:* -5.6, 36.0
       Outer fences: -21.2, 51.6
   c. 46.1 and 49.9 are mild outliers;
       55.9 is an extreme outlier
46. a. 79.31, 78.5
   b. 76.5, 80.5
   c. 72, 76.5, 78.5, 80.5, 90

   d. Camcorders have higher variation
   e. Yes; Hitachi and Mitsubishi are mild outliers
48. a. 9.32, 9.8
   b. 6.5, 14.6
   c. *Inner fences:* -5.65, 26.75
       Outer fences: -17.8, 38.9
       Six mild outliers plus
       Hong Kong is an extreme outlier
50. b. There appears to be a linear relationship between x
       and y
   c. $s_{xy} = 26.5$
   d. $r_{xy} = .69$
52. $-.91$; negative relationship
54. b. 4.14
   c. $+.697$
56. 13
58. 74.02, 158.78, 12.6
60. 10.74, 25.63, 5.06
62. a. 3.19, 3.30, 3.70
   b. 2.90, 3.50
   c. 2.80, .60
   d. .30, .54
   e. *Inner fences:* 2.00, 4.40
       Two mild outliers
64. a. $\bar{x} = 1028.18$, median = 1000, no mode
   b. Range = 510, IQR = 220
   c. $s^2 = 24,256.36$, $s = 155.74$
   d. No outliers
66. 6.1, 6, 4
       8, 6.32, 2.51
68. a. Public: 32; auto: 32
   b. Public: 4.64; auto: 1.83
   c. Auto has less variability
70. a. 400, 624, 836, 999, 1278
   c. *Inner fences:* 61.5, 1561.5
       No outliers
72. 51.50, 227.37, 15.08
74. a.   *Duke:* 87.97, 88.50
       Opponent: 72.64, 71.50
   b.   *Duke:* 50, 21.5
       Opponent: 52, 15.5

Chapter 4

2. 20
4. a. 9
6. a. 9
   c. 5
   d. 1
8. 2,598,960
10. 35
12. a. 1,000,000
   b. 5,760,000
14. .40, .26, .34; relative frequency method
16. a. 52
   b. Classical
   c. $1/52$

18. a. 6
  b. Relative frequency
  c. .12, .24, .30, .20, .10, .04; requirements are satisfied.
20. No, probabilities do not sum to 1
22. No
24. a. ¼
  b. ½
  c. ¾
26. a. 36
  c. ⅙
  d. ⁵⁄₁₈
  e. No; $P(\text{odd}) = P(\text{even}) = \dfrac{1}{2}$
  f. Classical
28. a. $P(0) = .05$
  b. $P(4 \text{ or } 5) = .20$
  c. $P(0, 1, \text{ or } 2) = .55$
30. a. .152
  b. .340
  c. .508
32. a. .40, .40, .60
  b. .80, yes
  c. $A^c = \{E_3, E_4, E_5\}$; $C^c = \{E_1, E_4\}$;
    $P(A^c) = .60$; $P(C^c) = .40$
  d. $\{E_1, E_2, E_5\}$; .60
  e. .80
34. .26
36. a. $P(V) = .7197$, $P(Q) = .4498$, $P(V \cap Q) = .2699$
  b. .8996
  c. .1004
38. a. .698
  b. .302
40. a. $A =$ first car starts, $B =$ second car starts
    $P(A) = .80$, $P(B) = .40$,
    $P(A \cap B) = .30$.
  b. .90
  c. .10
42. a. .67
  b. .80
  c. No
44. a.

	Single	Married	Total
Under 30	.55	.10	.65
30 or over	.20	.15	.35
Total	.75	.25	1.00

  b. Higher probability of under 30
  c. Higher probability of single
  d. .55
  e. .8462
  f. No

46. a.

		U.S. Car		
		Yes	No	Total
Foreign Car	Yes	.386	.226	.612
	No	.369	.019	.388
Total		.755	.245	1.000

  b. $P(U) = .755$, $P(F) = .612$
    Higher probability for U.S.
  c. .386
  d. .981
  e. .511
  f. .631
  g. No
48. c. .72
  d. .40
  e. No
50. a. .5541
  c. .67
52. a. .197
  b. .121
  c. No
54. a. .10, .20, .09
  b. .51
  c. .26, .51, .23
56. a. .21
  b. Yes
58. .6754
60. a. 4
  b. .61, .19, .10, .10
62. a. $\{E_1, E_2, E_3, E_4\}$
  b. $\{E_1, E_5, E_6, E_7, E_8\}$
  c. $\{E_2\}$
  d. $\{E_7, E_8\}$
  e. Empty
  f. $\{E_4, E_5, E_6, E_7, E_8\}$
  g. $\{E_1, E_2, E_3, E_4\}$
  h. $\{E_1, E_2, E_3, E_4\}$
  i. $\{E_1, E_2, E_3\}$
  j. No
  k. Yes
64. a. .4642
  b. .3458
  c. .1498
66. a. .76
  b. .24
68. b. .2022
  c. .4618
  d. .4005
70. b. $1 million – $2 million
  c. $P(2M) = .2286$, $P(2M\,|\,T) = .1556$, $P(2M\,|\,F) = .2833$
  d. No

72. a. .25
  b. Yes
  c. No
74. a. .25, .40, .10
  b. .25
  c. B and S are independent; program appears to have no effect
76. a. .20
  b. .35
  c. 65%
78. Call back since P(sale | call back) = .21
80. 3.44%
82. a. .12
  b. .625
  c. .305
84. a. .0625
  b. .0132
  c. Three

Chapter 5

2. a. x = time in minutes to assemble product
  b. Any positive value: $x > 0$
  c. Continuous
4. $x = 0, 1, 2, \ldots, 12$
6. a. 0, 1, 2, . . . , 20; discrete
  b. 0, 1, 2, . . . ; discrete
  c. 0, 1, 2, . . . , 50; discrete
  d. $0 \leq x \leq 8$; continuous
  e. $x > 0$; continuous
8. a.

x	1	2	3	4
$f(x)$	.15	.25	.40	.20

  c. $f(x) \geq 0, \Sigma f(x) = 1$
10. a. It is a proper probability distribution
  b. .60
12. a. Yes
  b. .65
14. a. .05
  b. .70
  c. .40
16. a. 5.20
  b. 4.56, 2.14
18. a. $E(x) = 2.2$, same
  b. Var(x) = 1.16, $\sigma = 1.08$
20. a. 166
  b. −94; concern is to protect against the expense of a big accident
22. a. 445
  b. 1250 loss
24. a. Medium: 145; large: 140
  b. Medium: 2725; large: 12,400
26. a. $f(0) = .3487$
  b. $f(2) = .1937$
  c. .9298
  d. .6513

e. 1
  f. $\sigma^2 = .9000, \sigma = .9487$
28. a. .2301
  b. .3410
  c. .8784
30. a. Probability of a defective part must be .03 for each trial; trials must be independent
  c. 2
  d.

Number of defects	0	1	2
Probability	.9409	.0582	.0009

32. a. $P(x \geq 8) = .2402$
  b. $f(1) = .2488$
34. a. .90
  b. .99
  c. .999
  d. Yes
36. a. .2547
  b. .9566
  c. .8009
40. 212.5, 31.88
42. a. $f(x) = \dfrac{3^x e^{-3}}{x!}$
  b. .2241
  c. .1494
  d. .8008
44. a. .1952
  b. .1048
  c. .0183
  d. .0907
46. a. .2001
  b. 7.8
  c. .9996
48. a. .000045
  b. .010245
  c. .0821
  d. .9179
50. a. $\mu = 1$
  b. .3679
  c. .3679
  d. .2642
52. a. 50
  b. .067
  c. .4667
  d. .30
54. a. .50
  b. .3333
56. a. .01
  b. .07
  c. .92
  d. .07
58. a. .5333
  b. .6667
  c. .7778
  d. $n = 7$

60. a. 1.6
   b. $120
62. a. 2.2
   b. 1.16
64. a. $f(x) \geq 0$ and $\Sigma f(x) = 1$
   b. $17.25
   c. $1.25, 7.8%
   d. 1.3875
66. a. 3 hours
   b. 1
68. a. .2793
   b. .7762
   c. .1496
70. a. .2785
   b. .3417
72. a. .9510
   b. .0480
   c. .0490
74. a. 1912
76. a. .2240
   b. .5767
78. a. .5333
   b. .1333
   c. .3333

Chapter 6

2. b. .50
   c. .60
   d. 15
   e. 8.33
4. b. .50
   c. .30
   d. .40
6. a. .40
   b. .64
   c. .68
10. a. .3413
   b. .4332
   c. .4772
   d. .4938
12. a. .2967
   b. .4418
   c. .3300
   d. .5910
   e. .8849
   f. .2388
14. a. $z = 1.96$
   b. $z = .61$
   c. $z = 1.12$
   d. $z = .44$
16. a. $z = 2.33$
   b. $z = 1.96$
   c. $z = 1.645$
   d. $z = 1.28$

18. a. .1814
   b. .9656
   c. $12,816 or more
20. a. 50.77%
   b. 15.87%
   c. 23.88%
22. a. .7295
   b. $19.49 per hour
   c. .0110
24. a. .2266
   b. .7745
   c. 31.12 years
26. a. $\mu = 20, \sigma = 4$
   b. yes
   c. .0602
   d. .4714
   e. .1292
28. a. .7910
   b. .9616
   c. .1066
30. a. .1151
   b. .2852
   c. 49 or less
32. a. .8336
   b. .0049
34. a. $1 - e^{-x_0/3}$
   b. .4866
   c. .3679
   d. .8111
   e. .3245
36. b. .6321
   c. .3935
   d. .0821
38. a. .3935
   b. .5276
   c. .1353
40. b. .30
   c. .15
   d. .40
   e. 2.50 minutes
42. b. .25
44. a. .8106
   b. .0833
   c. .6955
   d. .9500
46. a. .3174, 317.4 defects
   b. .0028, 2.8 defects
48. .0062
50. a. .5899
   b. 30 or more
52. a. 47.06%
   b. .0475
   c. 42,480
54. a. .6068
   b. .0146

c. .0735
d. $59,815
56. a. 5.16%
   b. 57.87%
   c. 99.55%
   d. Approximately 0
58. a. 300
   b. $\sigma^2 = 120$, $\sigma = 10.95$
   c. .8008
   d. .0125
60. a. 4 hours
   b. $1/4\ e^{-x/4}$
   c. .7788
   d. .1353
62. a. 2 minutes
   b. .2212
   c. .3935
   d. .0821

Chapter 7

2. 22, 147, 229, 289
4. a. Supra, Cadillac, Lincoln, Legend and Infinity
   b. 252
6. 2782, 493, 825, 1807, 289
8. 55, 126, 36, 159, 241, 99,
   152, 45, 59, 258, 266, 105
10. a. Randomly select a page (1–853), and then randomly
      select a line (1–400) on the sampled page
    b. Skip or ignore inappropriate lines, and repeat the
      sampling procedure of part (a)
12. Finite, infinite, infinite, infinite, finite
14. a. .50
    b. .3667
16. a. .34
    b. .26
18. .09
20. a. 200
    b. 5
    c. Normal with $E(\bar{x}) = 200$ and $\sigma_{\bar{x}} = 5$
    d. The probability distribution of $\bar{x}$
22. a. .6826
    b. .9544
24. 3.54, 2.50, 2.04, 1.77
    $\sigma_{\bar{x}}$ decreases as n increases
26. a. Only for $n = 30$ and $n = 40$
    b. $n = 30$; normal with $E(\bar{x}) = 400$
      and $\sigma_{\bar{x}} = 9.13$
      $n = 40$; normal with $E(\bar{x}) = 400$
      and $\sigma_{\bar{x}} = 7.91$
28. a. Normal with $E(\bar{x}) = 51,800$ and $\sigma_{\bar{x}} = 516.40$
    b. $\sigma_{\bar{x}}$ decreases to 365.15
    c. $\sigma_{\bar{x}}$ decreases as n increases
30. a. Normal with $E(\bar{x}) = 215.60$ and $\sigma_{\bar{x}} = 13.44$
    b. .8639
    c. .5408

32. 170, 4.43
34. a. 1
    b. .8926
36. a. Normal with $E(\bar{x}) = 16,012$ and $\sigma_{\bar{x}} = 420$
    b. .9826
    c. .7660, .4514, .1896
    d. Increase the sample size
38. a. Normal with $E(\bar{x}) = 3.6$ and $\sigma_{\bar{x}} = .15$
    b. .0038
    c. .9924
40. a. Normal with $E(\bar{x}) = 320$ and $\sigma_{\bar{x}} = 13.69$
    b. 13.69
    c. .8558
    d. .3557
42. a. .6156
    b. .8530
44. a. .6156
    b. .7814
    c. .9488
    d. .9942
    e. High probability with larger n
46. a. Normal with $E(\bar{p}) = .71$ and $\sigma_{\bar{p}} = .0214$
    b. .8384
    c. .9452
48. a. .7062
    b. .1469
    c. .0025
50. a. Normal with $E(\bar{p}) = .37$ and $\sigma_{\bar{p}} = .0153$
    b. .95
    c. .8354
52. a. Normal with $E(\bar{p}) = .15$ and $\sigma_{\bar{p}} = .0505$
    b. .4448
    c. .8389
54. 4324, 2875, 318, 538, 4771
56. a. Normal with $E(\bar{x}) = 30$ and $\sigma_{\bar{x}} = 1.70$
    b. .7620
58. a. Normal with $E(\bar{x}) = 49,000$
      and $\sigma_{\bar{x}} = 1200$
    b. .5934
    c. .7620
    d. .9050
    e. 553
60. a. 67
    b. 1.5
    c. Normal with $E(\bar{x}) = 67$ and $\sigma_{\bar{x}} = 1.5$
    d. .9082
    e. .4972
62. a. No, since $n/N = .01$
    b. Use $\sigma_{\bar{x}} = .0566$
    c. .9232
64. 246
66. a. 625
    b. .7888
68. a. Assume population has a normal distribution
    b. .9266
    c. Increase n to at least 30

70. a. Normal with $E(\bar{p}) = .74$ and $\sigma_{\bar{p}} = .031$
   b. .8030
   c. .4778
72. .9525
74. .4714

Chapter 8

 2. a. 30.60 to 33.40
   b. 30.34 to 33.66
   c. 29.82 to 34.18
 4. 62
 6. 297.60 to 322.40
 8. a. 12,003 to 12,333
   b. 11,971 to 12,365
   c. 11,909 to 12,427
   d. Width increases to be more confident.
10. $162,923 to $187,077
12. 279 to 321
14. 5.74 to 6.94
16. a. 1.734
   b. -1.321
   c. 3.365
   d. -1.761 and 1.761
   e. -2.048 and 2.048
18. a. 15.97 to 18.53
   b. 15.71 to 18.79
   c. 15.14 to 19.36
20. a. 13.2
   b. 7.8
   c. 7.62 to 18.78
   d. Wide interval; larger sample desirable
22. 6.28 to 6.78
24. a. 21.15 to 23.65
   b. 21.12 to 23.68
   c. Intervals are essentially the same
26. 4.51 to 6.59
28. a. 9
   b. 35
   c. 78
30. a. 50, 89, 200
   b. Only if $E = 1$ is essential
32. 385
34. 59
36. a. 49
   b. 30 to 34
38. a. .6733 to .7267
   b. .6682 to .7318
40. 1067
42. a. .0908
   b. .0681 to .1135
44. .9366 to .9674
46. a. .7728 to .8272
   b. 1537
48. a. .9192 to .9598
   b. .2036 to .2764

50. a. 85
   b. 340
   c. 2124
   d. 8494
   e. The sample size increases.
52. 2.11 to 2.39
54. a. $234.20 to $270.70
   b. Yes since lower limit for μ is $234.20
56. a. 2196.13
   b. 785.31
   c. 1539.49 to 2852.77
58. 9.20 to 14.80
60. 710
62. 37
64. 166
66. .0438 to .2362
68. .5165 to .6035
   .2216 to .2984
   A greater proportion use recognition
70. a. 1267
   b. 1508
72. .2895 to .3719
74. a. .31
   b. .29 to .33
   c. 8318; No, this sample size is unnecessarily large

Chapter 9

 2. a. $H_0: \mu \le 14$
     $H_a: \mu > 14$
 4. a. $H_0: \mu \ge 220$
     $H_a: \mu < 220$
 6. a. $H_0: \mu \le 1$
     $H_a: \mu > 1$
   b. Claiming $\mu > 1$ when it is not true
   c. Claiming $\mu \le 1$ when it is not true
 8. a. $H_0: \mu \ge 220$
     $H_a: \mu < 220$
   b. Claiming $\mu < 220$ when it is not true
   c. Claiming $\mu \ge 220$ when it is not true
10. a. Reject H_0 if $z > 2.05$
   b. 1.36
   c. .0869
   d. Do not reject H_0
12. a. .0344; reject H_0
   b. .3264; do not reject H_0
   c. .0668; do not reject H_0
   d. Approximately 0; reject H_0
14. a. $H_0: \mu \le 6.5$; $H_a: \mu > 6.5$
   b. $z = 5.91$; reject H_0
   c. Current cars being driven longer
16. $z = 1.77$; do not reject H_0
18. $z = -2.74$; reject H_0
   p-value = .0031

20. a. Reject H_0 if $z < -1.645$
    b. $z = -1.98$; reject H_0
    c. .0239
22. a. Reject H_0 if $z < -2.33$ or $z > 2.33$
    b. 1.13
    c. .2584
    d. Do not reject H_0
24. a. .0718; do not reject H_0
    b. .6528; do not reject H_0
    c. .0404; reject H_0
    d. Approximately 0; reject H_0
    e. .3174; do not reject H_0
26. a. $z = -1.06$; do not reject H_0
    b. .2892
28. $z = 6.37$; reject H_0
30. a. 71,167 to 74,433
    b. Reject H_0 since 61,650 is not in the interval
32. a. \$8.66 or less
    b. Reject H_0
34. a. 18
    b. 1.41
    c. Reject H_0 if $t < -2.571$ or $t > 2.571$
    d. −3.47
    e. Reject H_0
36. a. .01; reject H_0
    b. .10; do not reject H_0
    c. Between .025 and .05; reject H_0
    d. Greater than .10; do not reject H_0
    e. Approximately 0; reject H_0
38. $t = 1.20$; do not reject H_0
40. a. $t = -3.33$; reject H_0
    b. p-value is less than .005
42. $\bar{x} = 2.4$, $s = .52$, $t = 2.43$
    Reject H_0
44. a. Reject H_0 if $z < -1.96$ or $z > 1.96$
    b. −1.25
    c. .2112
    d. Do not reject H_0
46. .1118; do not reject H_0
48. $z = -1.25$; do not reject H_0
    p-value = .1056
50. a. $z = 1.38$; reject H_0
    b. .0838
52. $H_0: p \geq .91$
    $H_a: p < .91$
    $z = -5.44$; reject H_0.
54. $z = 1.63$; do not reject H_0
    p-value = .0516
56. a. .2912
    b. Type II error
    c. .0031
58. a. Concluding $\mu \leq 15$ when it is not true
    b. .2676
    c. .0179

60. a. Concluding $\mu = 28$ when it is not true
    b. .0853, .6179, .6179, .0853
    c. .9147
62. .1151, .0015
    Increasing n reduces β
64. 214
66. 109
68. 324
70. $z = -1.96$; do not reject H_0.
72. $z = 2.26$; reject H_0
74. a. $z = 1.80$; do not reject H_0
    b. .0718
    c. 549 to 575
76. a. .0143
    b. Reject H_0
78. $z = -3.84$; reject H_0
80. a. Show $p < .50$
    b. $z = -6.62$; reject H_0
82. $z = 1.07$; do not reject H_0
    p-value = .1423
84. $z = 6.81$; reject H_0.
86. 219

Chapter 10

2. a. 2.4
   b. 5.27
   c. .09 to 4.71
4. a. 3.9
   b. 0.6 to 7.0
6. −.51 to 1.27
8. a. 1200
   b. 438 to 1962
   c. Populations normal with equal variances
10. a. Populations normal with equal variances
    b. 4.41
    c. 0.71 to 3.65 ($t_{.025} = 2.042$)
12. a. $z = -1.53$; do not reject H_0
    b. .1260
14. .84, Do not reject H_0
16. $z = 4.99$; reject H_0
18. $z = 2.66$; reject H_0
20. a. $t = 2.22$; reject H_0
    b. .11 to 3.27 (thousands)
22. a. 3, −1, 3, 5, 3, 0, 1
    b. 2
    c. 2.082
    d. 2
    e. .07 to 3.93
24. a. Matched sample
    b. .65 to 1.49
26. $\bar{d} = 3$; $t = 2.23$; reject H_0
28. a. $t = 5.88$; reject H_0
    b. 1.4 to 3.0

30. a. .12
  b. .0586 to .1814
  c. .0469 to .1931
32. .2122 to .2879
34. .07 to .24
36. $z = 3.94$; reject H_0
38. a. $z = 2.33$; reject H_0
  b. .02 to .22
40. 3354 to 4646
42. $t = -1.69$; do not reject H_0
44. $t = 2.29$; reject H_0
46. a. $H_0: p_1 - p_2 \leq 0$
      $H_a: p_1 - p_2 > 0$
  b. $z = 1.80$; reject H_0
      p-value = .0359
48. .0174; reject H_0

Chapter 11

2. a. 15.76 to 46.95
  b. 14.46 to 53.33
  c. 3.8 to 7.3
4. a. .22 to .71
  b. .47 to .84
6. a. 7.56 to 12.77
  b. 7.95 to 11.81
  c. 8.35 to 11.03
  d. The estimate is more precise for
      larger n
8. a. $\chi^2 = 32.39$; do not reject H_0
  b. 40.83 to 133.02
  c. 6.39 to 11.53
10. $\chi^2 = 206.22$; reject H_0
12. a. .8106
  b. $\chi^2 = 9.49$; do not reject H_0
14. $F = 2.42$; reject H_0
16. $F = 1.19$; do not reject H_0
18. $F = 1.13$; do not reject H_0
20. $F = 5.29$; reject H_0
22. a. $F = 4$; reject H_0
  b. Drive carefully on wet pavement
24. 10.72 to 24.68
26. a. $\chi^2 = 27.44$; reject H_0
  b. .00012 to .00042
28. $\chi^2 = 31.5$; reject H_0
30. a. 15
  b. 6.25 to 11.13
32. $F = 1.39$; do not reject H_0
34. $F = 2.08$; reject H_0

Chapter 12

2. $\chi^2 = 15.33$, $\chi^2_{.05} = 7.81473$; reject H_0
4. $\chi^2 = 99.50$, $\chi^2_{.01} = 13.28$; reject H_0
  opinions have changed

6. $\chi^2 = 6.24$, $\chi^2_{.10} = 4.60517$; reject H_0
8. $\chi^2 = 8.89$, $\chi^2_{.05} = 9.48773$; do not reject H_0
10. $\chi^2 = 19.78$, $\chi^2_{.05} = 9.48773$; reject H_0
12. $\chi^2 = 6.31$, $\chi^2_{.05} = 9.48773$; do not reject H_0
14. $\chi^2 = 14.72$, $\chi^2_{.05} = 5.99147$; reject H_0
16. $\chi^2 = 37.17$, $\chi^2_{.01} = 9.21034$; reject H_0
18. $\chi^2 = 7.96$ $\chi^2_{.05} = 9.48773$; do not reject H_0
20. $\chi^2 = 102.56$, $\chi^2_{.01} = 13.2767$; reject H_0
  Conclude executive opinions have changed
22. $\chi^2 = 3.20$, $\chi^2_{.025} = 9.34840$; do not reject H_0
24. $\chi^2 = 4.98$, $\chi^2_{.10} = 7.77944$; do not reject H_0
26. $\chi^2 = 11.2$, $\chi^2_{.01} = 9.21034$; reject H_0
28. $\chi^2 = 41.69$, $\chi^2_{.01} = 13.2767$; reject H_0
  Attitudes differ
30. $\chi^2 = 7.44$, $\chi^2_{.05} = 9.48773$; do not reject H_0
32. $\chi^2 = 5.26$, $\chi^2_{.05} = 5.99147$; do not reject H_0
34. $\chi^2 = 59.41$, $\chi^2_{.025} = 23.3367$; reject H_0
  They are related
36. $\chi^2 = 6.20$, $\chi^2_{.05} = 12.5916$; do not reject H_0
38. $\chi^2 = 7.78$, $\chi^2_{.05} = 7.81473$; do not reject H_0

Chapter 13

2. a. MSB = 268
  b. MSW = 92
  c. Cannot reject H_0 since $F = 2.91 < F_{.05} = 4.26$
  d.

Source of Variation	Sum of Squares	Degrees of Freedom	Mean Square	F
Between	536	2	268	2.91
Within	828	9	92	
Total	1364	11		

4. b. Reject H_0 since $F = 80 > F_{.05} = 2.76$
6. Reject H_0 since $F = 10.63 > F_{.05} = 4.26$
8. Significant difference;
  $F = 7.00 > F_{.05} = 3.68$
10. Significant difference;
  p-value = .015
12. a. Significant difference; $F = 7.87 > F_{.05} = 4.26$
  b. 1 and 2; 2 and 3
14. -8.54 to -1.46
16. Significant difference;
  $2.3 > LSD = 1.19$
18. 1 and 2: significant difference (LSD = 3.38)
  1 and 3: significant difference (LSD = 3.17)
  2 and 3: no significant difference (LSD = 3.51)

20. a.

Source of Variation	Sum of Squares	Degrees of Freedom	Mean Square	F
Treatment	1488	2	744	5.50
Error	2030	15	135.3	
Total	3518	17		

   b. Significant difference between A and C

22. a. $H_0: \mu_1 = \mu_2 = \mu_3 = \mu_4 = \mu_5$
     H_a: Not all the population means are equal
   b. Reject H_0 since $F = 14.07 > 2.69$

24. Significant difference; $F = 43.99$ exceeds the critical value, which is between 3.15 and 3.23

26. b. Significant difference; $F = 9.87 > F_{.05} = 3.35$

28. Not significant; $F = 1.78 < F_{.05} = 3.89$

30. Not significant; $F = 2.54 < F_{.05} = 3.24$

32. Means are all different (LSD = 2.53)

34. Significant; $F = 6.60 > F_{.05} = 4.46$

36. Significant; $F = 12.60 > F_{.05} = 3.07$

38. Significant; $F = 7.12 > F_{.05} = 3.26$

40. Significant difference
    $F = 22.46 > F_{.05} = 2.96$

42. Factor A is significant since $F = 3.72 > F_{.05} = 3.01$
    Factor B is significant since $F = 4.94 > F_{.05} = 3.40$
    Interaction is significant since $F = 12.52 > F_{.05} = 2.51$

44. No significant effect due to the loading and unloading method, the type of ride, or interaction

46. Factor A is not significant
    Factor B is significant
    Interaction is significant

48. Significant difference;
    $F = 4.45 > F_{.05} = 4.26$

50. Significant difference

52. Not significant;
    $F = 1.48 < F_{.05} = 3.35$

54. Significant; $F = 7.23 > F_{.05} = 4.26$

56. Not significant; $F = 1.66 < F_{.05} = 3.01$

58. Significant; $F = 5.19 > F_{.05} = 4.26$

60. Significant; $F = 6.99 > F_{.05} = 4.46$

62. Not significant; $F = 1.67 < F_{.01} = 10.92$

64. Type of machine is significant; type of loading system and interaction are not significant

Chapter 14

2. b. There appears to be a linear relationship between x and y
   d. $\hat{y} = 30.33 - 1.88x$
   e. 19.05

4. b. There appears to be a linear relationship between x and y
   d. $\hat{y} = -240.5 + 5.5x$
   e. 106 pounds

6. c. $\hat{y} = .38 + .35x$
   d. 9.13

8. a. $\hat{y} = 49.5 + 75.5x$
   b. 276

10. b. $\hat{y} = -2196.89 + 39.42x$
   e. 1350.91

12. c. $\hat{y} = -55.84 + 1.67x$
   d. 44.36%
   e. $\hat{y} = 36.01$; predicted value is almost the same as the observed value

14. b. $\hat{y} = 4.68 + .16x$
   c. deductions are excessive; audit appears justified

16. a. SSE = 6.3325, SST = 114.80,
    SSR = 108.47
   b. $r^2 = .945$
   c. $r = -.9721$

18. a. SSE = 85,135, SST = 335,000,
    SSR = 249,865
   b. $r^2 = .746$
   c. $r = +.8637$

20. a. $\hat{y} = -54.85 + 98.80x$
   b. $r^2 = .992$
   c. 38.13 mgs

22. a. $\hat{y} = 22.66 + .26x$
   b. $r^2 = .0997$
   c. $r = +.3158$

24. a. 2.11
   b. 1.453
   c. .262
   d. significant
    $t = -7.18 < -t_{.05} = -3.182$
   e. significant
    $F = 51.41 > F_{.05} = 10.13$

26. a. Significant
    $t = 3.43 > t_{.025} = 2.776$
   b. Significant
    $F = 11.74 > F_{.05} = 7.71$

28. They are related since $F = 238.42 > F_{.01} = 12.25$

32. a. 1.11
   b. 7.07 to 14.13
   c. 2.32
   d. 3.22 to 17.98

34. *Confidence interval:* $-.4$ to 4.98
   Prediction interval: -2.27 to 7.31

36. a. 1350.91
   b. 1303.02 to 1398.80
   c. 1201.42 to 1500.40

38. a. $11,740 to $14,420
   b. $9,300 to $16,860
   c. Yes

40. a. 9
   b. $\hat{y} = 20.0 + 7.21x$
   c. 1.3626
   d. Significant relationship since $F = 28 > F_{.05} = 5.59$
   e. $380,500

42. a. $\hat{y} = 80.0 + 50.0x$
   b. 30

c. Significant relationship since $F = 83.17 > F_{.05} = 4.20$

d. \$680,000

44. b. Yes

c. $\hat{y} = 17.3 + 1.32x$

d. Significant relationship; p-value $= 0.000$

e. $r^2 = .537$; not a very good fit

f. \$60,940 to \$65,903

g. \$53,493 to \$73,349

46. a. $\hat{y} = 2.32 + .64x$

b. No; the variance does not appear to be the same for all values of x

48. b. Yes

50. a. Yes; $x = 135$, $y = 145$ may be an outlier

b. Yes

c. Yes

52. a. $\hat{y} = -.23 + .049x$

b. Minitab identifies observation 10 as an influential observation; the standardized residual plot shows an unusual trend in the residuals

54. a. $\hat{y} = -10.9 + 1.04x$

b. Observation 10 is a possible outlier

58. a. $\hat{y} = .042 + .564x$

b. $r^2 = .8441$; good fit

c. 42% saving

d. \$1.90

60. a. .95

b. Woolworth has a higher risk

c. $r^2 = .4695$

62. a. $\hat{y} = 10.5 + .953x$

b. Significant relationship; p-value $= 0.000$

c. \$2874 to \$4952

d. Yes

64. a. Significant

$t = 6.58 > t_{.025} = 2.306$

b. Significant

$F = 43.28 > F_{.05} = 5.32$

c. \$.98 to \$1.34

d. \$.57 to \$1.75

66. a. Significant

$t = 2.66 > t_{.025} = 2.306$

b. Significant

$F = 7.08 > F_{.05} = 5.32$

68. a. $\hat{y} = 20.7 - .234x$

b. Not significant; p-value $= .096$

c. Linear relationship is not appropriate

70. a. $\hat{y} = 220 + 132x$

b. Significant relationship; p-value $= 0.000$

c. $r^2 = .873$; a very good fit

d. \$559.50 to \$933.90

72. a. $\hat{y} = 5.85 + .830x$

b. Significant relationship; p-value $= 0.000$

c. 84.65

d. 65.35 to 103.96

74. a. $\hat{y} = 50.43 + 1.172x$

b. $r^2 = .05$

c. 75.21

d. Not significant

$t = .65 < t_{.025} = 2.306$

e. Not significant

$F = .42 < F_{.05} = 5.32$

f. Budget is not a significant predictor of gross sales

Chapter 15

2. a. $\hat{y} = 45.06 + 1.94x_1$; $\hat{y} = 132.36$

b. $\hat{y} = 85.22 + 4.32x_2$; $\hat{y} = 150.02$

c. $\hat{y} = -18.37 + 2.01x_1 + 4.74x_2$;

$\hat{y} = 143.18$

4. a. \$255,000

6. a. PRICE $= -0.97 + 0.139$ HORSEPWR

b. PRICE $= 31.0 + 0.108$ HORSEPWR -3.80 ZEROTO6O

c. Multiple

d. \$34,068

8. a. $\hat{y} = 2.1 + .0138x_1 + .00584x_2$

b. Advertising expenditure, per capita income, store size

10. a. $\hat{y} = -5.7 + 1.54$ STARTS $+ 1.81$ INCOME

b. 96.96

12. a. .926

b. .905

c. Yes

14. a. .75

b. .68

16. a. $R^2 = .916$, $R_a^2 = .892$

18. a. $R^2 = .377$, $R_a^2 = .282$

b. The fit is not very good

20. a. Significant; p-value $= .000$

b. Significant; p-value $= .000$

c. Significant; p-value $= .000$

22. a. SSE $= 4000$, $s^2 = 571.43$,

MSR $= 6000$

b. Significant; $F = 10.50 > F_{.05} = 4.74$

24. a. Reject $H_0: \beta_1 = \beta_2 = 0$

$F = 38.26 > F_{.05} = 4.74$

b. Reject $H_0: \beta_1 = 0$

$t = 5.40 > t_{.025} = 2.365$

Reject $H_0: \beta_2 = 0$

$t = -2.82 < -t_{.025} = -2.365$

26. a. Significant; p-value $= .046 < \alpha = .05$

b. Not significant; p-value $= .219$

c. Not significant; p-value $= .099$

28. a. 132.16 to 154.15

b. 111.15 to 175.17

30. a. \$30,656

b. \$27,176 to \$34,197

c. \$22,837 to \$38,536

32. a. $x_2 = 0$ if level 1; $x_2 = 1$ if level 2

$E(y) = \beta_0 + \beta_1x_1 + \beta_2x_2$

b. $E(y) = \beta_0 + \beta_1x_1$

c. $E(y) = \beta_0 + \beta_1x_1 + \beta_2$

d. $\beta_2 = E(y \,|\, \text{level 2}) - E(y \,|\, \text{level 1})$

34. a. $15,300
  b. $56,100
  c. $41,600
36. a. $\hat{y} = 1.86 + 0.291$ MONTHS $+ 1.10$ type $- 0.609$ person
  b. Significant; p-value $= .002 < \alpha = .05$
  c. PERSON is not significant
38. a. $\hat{y} = -91.8 + 1.08$ AGE $+ .252$ PRESSURE $+ 8.74$ SMOKER
  b. Significant; p-value $= .01 < \alpha = .05$
  c. 95% prediction interval is 21.35 to 47.19 or a probability of .2135 to .4719; quit smoking and begin some type of treatment to reduce his blood pressure
40. a. $\hat{y} = -53.3 + 3.11x$
  b. $-1.40, -.15, 1.36, .47, -1.39$; no
  c. $.38, .28, .22, .20, .98$; no
  d. $.60, .00, .26, .03, 11.09$; yes, the fifth observation
42. c. No outliers
  d. No influential observations
44. b. 3.19
46. a. $R^2 = .95$, $R_a^2 = .93$
  b. Significant; $F = 57.84 > F_{.01} = 5.21$
48. a. 3.04, 3.61, 5.08
  b. Both are significant
  d. .91
50. b. Significant; $F = 22.79 > F_{.05} = 5.79$
  c. $R_a^2 = .861$; good fit
  d. Both are significant
52. a. $\hat{y} = -16.7 + 1.02$ %WOMEN
  b. $R^2 = .868$; very good fit
  c.

D_1	D_2	D_3	D_4	D_5	Industry
0	0	0	0	0	Industrial
1	0	0	0	0	Technology
0	1	0	0	0	Consumer
0	0	1	0	0	Retailing
0	0	0	1	0	Media
0	0	0	0	1	Financial

$\hat{y} = 11.5 + 7.75D_1 + 7.75D_2 + 26.7D_3 + 24.8D_4 + 33.5D_5$

  d. %WOMEN is a better predictor than the type of industry
  e. $\hat{y} = -20.0 + 1.18$ %WOMEN $- 1.96D_1 - 5.49D_2 - 8.20D_3 + 3.74D_4 - 7.99D_5$
  f. Adding type of industry to the model involving %WOMEN is not significant
54. d. Top speed is not significant
  f. No outliers
  g. No influential observations

Chapter 16

2. a. $\hat{y} = 9.32 + .424x$; p-value $= .117$ indicates that the relationship between x and y is not significant
  b. $\hat{y} = -8.10 + 2.41x - .0480x^2$ $R_a^2 = .932$, a very good fit
  c. 20.965
4. a. $\hat{y} = 943 + 8.71x$
  b. Significant; p-value $= .005 < \alpha = .01$
6. b. No, the relationship appears to be curvilinear
  c. Several possible models; e.g., $\hat{y} = 2.90 - .185x + .00351x^2$
8. b. PERCENT $= 30.6 - 1.74$ YEAR $+ 0.0605$ YEARSQ
  c. $\hat{y} = 26.92(.974)^x$
  d. Part (b) provides a better fit
  e. The percentage has been declining, but recently has stabilized at about 17–19%
10. a. Significant; $F = 49.52 > 4.24$
  b. Significant; $F = 48.3 > 3.42$
  c. Significant; $t = -4.46 < -2.069$
  d. x_2 can be dropped
12. a. $\hat{y} = 170 + 6.61$ TEAMINT
  b. $\hat{y} = 280 + 5.18$ TEAMINT $- .0037$ RUSHING $- 3.92$ OPPONINT
  c. Addition of the two independent variables is not significant
14. a. $\hat{y} = -111 + 1.32$ AGE $+ .296$ PRESSURE
  b. $\hat{y} = -123 + 1.51$ AGE $+ .448$ PRESSURE $+ 8.87$ SMOKER $- .00276$ AGEXPRES
  c. Significant
16. a. $\hat{y} = 3.332 + 25.9x_1 - 6.7x_3$
  b. Same as (a)
  c. Curvilinear relationship
18. a. ACCURACY
  b. SCORE $= 53.5 - .03$ DISTANCE $- .0755$ ACCURACY $+ 16.9$ PUTTS
  c. Yes
  d. 70.14
20. $\hat{y} = -91.8 + 1.08$ AGE $+ .252$ PRESSURE $+ 8.74$ SMOKER
22. $d = 1.60$; test is inconclusive
24.

x_1	x_2	Treatment
0	0	1
1	0	2
0	1	3

$x_3 = 0$ if block 1; $x_3 = 1$ if block 2
$E(y) = \beta_0 + \beta_1 x_1 + \beta_2 x_2 + \beta_3 x_3$

26. a.

D_1	D_2	Manufacturer
0	0	1
1	0	2
0	1	3

$E(y) = \beta_0 + \beta_1 D_1 + \beta_2 D_2$

   b. $\hat{y} = 23.0 + 5.00D_1 - 2.00D_2$

   c. $H_0: \beta_1 = \beta_2 = 0$

   d. Mean time is not the same for each manufacturer; p-value = .004

28. Significant difference between the two analyzers

30. PRICE = −881 + 38.6 FOCUS − 27.9 UNIFORM
            + 17.4 DISTORT

   $R_a^2 = .834$

32. a. $\hat{y} = -16.7 + 1.02$ %WOMEN

   b. Use %WOMEN and D4, where $D_4 = 1$ if media, $D_4 = 0$ otherwise

34. a. $\hat{y} = 70.6 + 12.7$ INDUS − 2.92 ICQUAL

   b. No obvious pattern

   c. Test is inconclusive

36. Significant differences between comfort levels for the three types of browsers

Chapter 17

2. a. 32%

   b. $8.14

4. $I_{1995} = 105$

6. $I = 125$

8. $I = 105$; portfolio is up 5%

10. a. 1980 wages: $8.82
      1993 wages: $8.14

   b. 61.8% increase

   c. 7.7% decrease

12. a. 305, 306, 300, 279, 266
      Inventories are declining in constant dollars

   b. 350, 349, 340, 320, 309

   c. PPI

14. $I_{1995} = 110$

16. $I = 83$

18. a. 151, 197, 143, 178

   b. $I = 170$

20. $I_{Jan} = 96$ $I_{Mar} = 92$

22. $I = 112$

24. $36,082; $32,528; $27,913; $34,387; $40,551; $41,522

26. $I = 143$; quantity is up 43%

Chapter 18

2. a.

Week	4-Week	5-Week
10	19.00	18.80
11	20.00	19.20
12	18.75	19.00

   b. 9.65, 7.41

   c. 5-week

4. Weeks 10, 11, and 12: 18.48, 18.63, 18.27
   MSE = 9.25; $\alpha = .2$ is better

6. a.

Year	$\alpha = .2$	$\alpha = .3$
10	2.85	2.92
11	2.91	2.99
12	2.97	3.05

   b. Using $\alpha = .3$, we obtain 2.99

8. a.

Month	3-Month	$\alpha = .2$
10	256.67	265.51
11	286.67	274.41
12	263.33	267.53

Using only the errors for months 4 to 12 for both, $\alpha = .2$ is better

   b. 260

10. a. Months 10, 11, and 12: 4478.44, 4478.75, 4489.00

   b. Months 10, 11, and 12: 4474.31, 4476.02, 4492.21

   c. MSE ($\alpha = .2$) = 1075;
      MSE ($\alpha = .3$) = 1092; use $\alpha = .2$;
      $F_{13} = 4501$

12. $T_t = 4.7 - 2.1t$; 17.3

14. $T_t = 6.96 + 2.14t$; 19.8

16. Consider a nonlinear trend

18. a. $T_t = .365 + .193t$; $2.49

   b. EPS increasing by an average of $.193 per year

20. a. $T_t = 1997.6 + 397.545t$

   b. $T_{11} = 6371$, $T_{12} = 6768$

22. a. *Four-quarter moving average:* 3.50, 4.00, 4.25, 4.75, 5.25, 5.50, 6.25, 6.50, 6.75
      Centered moving average: 3.750, 4.125, 4.500, 5.000, 5.375, 5.875, 6.375, 6.625

   b. *Adjusted seasonal indexes:* 1.2050, 0.7463, 0.8675, 1.1912
      Note: adjustment = 0.9912

24. *Adjusted seasonal indexes:* 0.707, 0.777, 0.827, 0.966, 1.016, 1.305, 1.494, 1.225, 0.976, 0.986, 0.936, 0.787
   Note: adjustment = 0.996

26. a. Yes

   b. 12−4: 166,761.13
      4−8: 146,052.99

28. *Forecast for weeks 8, 9, 10, and 11:* 258.64, 281.48, 283.61, and 292.71

30. 20.26

32. a. $\alpha = .5$

   b. $T_t = 244.778 + 22.088t$

   c. Trend projection; smaller MSE

34. $T_8 = 252.28$, $T_9 = 259.10$

36. a. Yes

   b. $T_t = -5 + 15t$

38. a. *PC:* $T_t = -31.267 + 60.314t$
      Mainframe: $T_t = 140.467 + 15.629t$

   b. *PC:* 390.93
      Mainframe: 249.87

40. b. Adjusted seasonal indexes: 0.899, 1.362, 1.118, 0.621
   Note: adjustment = 1.0101
   c. Quarter 2; seems reasonable
42. a. $T_t = 6.329 + 1.055t$
   b. 36.92, 37.98, 39.03, 40.09
   c. 33.23, 51.65, 43.71, 24.86

Chapter 19

2. $z = 3.27$; reject H_0
4. $z = 3.15$; reject H_0
6. $z = 1.90$; do not reject H_0
8. $z = 3.76$; reject H_0
10. $z = 1.27$; do not reject H_0
12. $z = 2.43$; reject H_0
14. $z = 2.31$; reject H_0
   Net income increased
16. $z = -2.05$; reject H_0
18. $T = 34$; reject H_0
20. $T = 28.5$; reject H_0
22. $z = 2.77$; reject H_0
   P/E ratios differ
24. $z = -.25$; do not reject H_0
26. $W = 10.22$; reject H_0
28. $W = 3.06$; do not reject H_0
30. $W = 8.03$; reject H_0
32. a. .68
   b. $z = 2.06$; reject H_0
34. $z = .72$; do not reject H_0
36. $r_s = .04$; $z = .12$; do not reject H_0
38. $z = .82$; do not reject H_0
40. $z = 1.81$; reject H_0
42. a. $z = -3.20$; reject H_0
   Houston is below national median
   b. $z = 2.21$; reject H_0
   Philadelphia is above national median
44. $z = -2.59$; reject H_0
46. $z = -2.97$; reject H_0
48. $W = 12.61$; reject H_0
50. $r_s = .0490$; do not reject H_0
   Sales and profits are not significantly related
52. $r_s = .76$; $z = 2.84$; reject H_0

Chapter 20

2. a. 5.42
   b. UCL = 6.09, LCL = 4.75
4.

	R Chart	$\bar{x}$ Chart
UCL	2.98	29.10
LCL	.22	27.90

6. 20.01, .082
8. a. .0470
   b. UCL = .0989, LCL = −.0049 (use LCL = 0)
   c. $\bar{p} = .08$; in control

d. UCL = 14.826, LCL = −0.726
   Process is out of control if more than 14 defective
e. In control since 12 defective
f. *np* chart
10. $p = .02$; $f(0) = .6035$
   $p = .06$; $f(0) = .2129$
12. $p_0 = .02$; producer's risk = .0599
   $p_0 = .06$; producer's risk = .3396
   Producer's risk decreases as the acceptance number c is increased
14. $n = 20$, $c = 3$
16. a. 95.4
   b. UCL = 96.07, LCL = 94.73
   c. No
18.

	R Chart	$\bar{x}$ Chart
UCL	4.23	6.57
LCL	0	4.27

Estimate of standard deviation = .86

20.

	R Chart	$\bar{x}$ Chart
UCL	.11	3.11
LCL	0	3.05

22. a. UCL = .0817, LCL = −.0017 (use LCL = 0)
24. a. .03
   b. $\beta = .0802$
26. a. Producer's risk = .0064
   b. Consumer's risk = .0136
   c. *Advantage:* excellent control
   Disadvantage: cost

Chapter 21

2. a. 30,000
   b. 320
   c. 29,360 to 30,640
4. 73
6. 337
8. a. *stratum 1:* 27,600
   stratum 2: 25,750
   stratum 3: 21,000
   b. 74,350
   c. 70,599.88 to 78,100.12
10. a. $n = 93$, $n_1 = 30$, $n_2 = 30$, $n_3 = 33$
   b. $n = 306$, $n_1 = 98$, $n_2 = 98$,
   $n_3 = 109$
   c. $n = 275$, $n_1 = 88$, $n_2 = 88$, $n_3 = 98$
12. a. $3,617,000
   b. $1,122,265
   c. $41,066 to $56,499
   d. $9,568,261 to $13,164,197
14. a. 15, 4500, .30
   b. 1.4708, 441.24, .0484

c. 12.0584 to 17.9416

d. 3617.52 to 5382.48

e. .2032 to .3968

16. a. 40

b. .70

c. 35.8634 to 44.1366

d. .5234 to .8766

18. a. .7788 to .8212

b. .5740 to .6260

c. .4136 to .4664

20. a. $22,790 to $23,610

b. $68,370,366 to $70,829,634

c. .6692 to .7908

22. a. 431

b. .2175 to .3983

c. .6230 to .8002

d. 996

24. a. 75.275

b. .198 to .502

c. 1680

Chapter 22

2. a. d_1

b. d_4

4. d_2 (medium)

6. b. Develop the software

8. a. If s_1, d_1; If s_2, d_1 or d_2; If s_3, d_2.

b. 192.5

c. d_1, 182.5

d. 10

10. EVPI = 25

12. b. d_3, 1250

c. 2150

14. a. d_1

b. 2

c. d_3

16. a. $8000

b. 13.13%

c. Not worth doing the study

18. b. If I_1, then d_1; if I_2, then d_2

EV(node 1) = $101.50

c. EVSI = $1500

20. If unseasonably cold, then purchase snowplow

If not unseasonably cold, then purchase blade

22. a. If I_1, then d_1

If I_2, then d_1

EV = 2000

b. .57

c. 0%

24. a. Purchase component

b. EVPI = $9000

c. .355

d. If I_1, then manufacture

If I_2, then purchase

EV = 43.9

e. EVSI = $3650

f. 40.6%

26. a.

		Demand		
		1000	*2000*	*3000*
	1000	50,000	10,000	−30,000
Amount Produced	*2000*	−50,000	100,000	60,000
	3000	−150,000	0	150,000

b. d_2 = 2000 pounds

c. $48,000

d. If I_1, then d_3

If I_2, then d_2

If I_3, then d_1

e. $10,900

f. 22.7%

28. a. d_3

b. d_1

APPENDIX F

Solutions to Self-Test Exercises

Chapter 1

2. **a.** 10
   b. 4
   c. Industry and Compensation vs. Shareholder Return Rating are qualitative; compensation vs. Shareholder Return Rating, while numeric data, is a qualitative variable because the data are used to place the company into a class based on best to worst performance in terms of Compensation vs. Shareholder Return; CEO Compensation and Sales are quantitative variables

3. **a.** Average CEO compensation = $27,580/10 = $2758 or $2,758,000
   b. 2 of 10 are in the banking industry; 20%
   c. 3 of 10 received a rating of 3; 30%

4. **a.** 10
   b. *Fortune 500* largest U.S. industrial corporations
   c. Average sales = $37,560/10 = $3756 million
   d. Using the sample results, estimate the average sales for the population of corporations at $3756 million

13. **a.** Quantitative
    b. A time series with 13 observations
    c. Volume of new equity for initial public offerings
    d. The time-series is showing a decreasing trend in the most recent June to September period

Chapter 2

3. **a.** 360° × 58/120 = 174°
   b. 360° × 42/120 = 126°
   c.

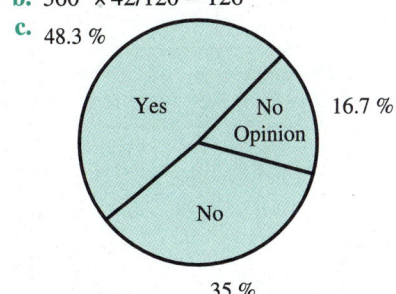

d.

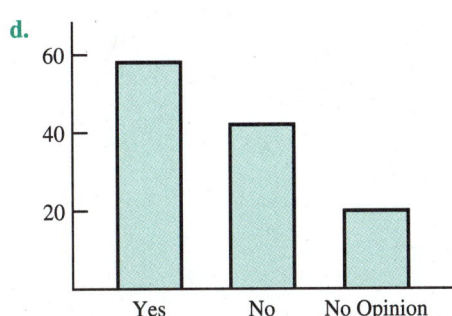

7.

Rating	Frequency	Relative Frequency
Outstanding	19	.38
Very good	13	.26
Good	10	.20
Average	6	.12
Poor	2	.04

Management should be pleased with these results: 64% of the ratings are very good to outstanding, and 84% of the ratings are good or better; comparing these ratings to previous results will show whether or not the restaurant is making improvements in its customers' ratings of food quality

12.

Class	Cumulative Frequency	Cumulative Relative Frequency
≤ 19	10	.20
≤ 29	24	.48
≤ 39	41	.82
≤ 49	48	.96
≤ 59	50	1.00

15. a, b.

Waiting Time	Frequency	Relative Frequency
0–4	4	.20
5–9	8	.40
10–14	5	.25
15–19	2	.10
20–24	1	.05
Totals	20	1.00

c, d.

Waiting Time	Cumulative Frequency	Cumulative Relative Frequency
≤ 4	4	.20
≤ 9	12	.60
≤ 14	17	.85
≤ 19	19	.95
≤ 24	20	1.00

e. $^{12}/_{20} = .60$

23.

6	3		
7	5	5	7
8	1	3	4	8
9	3	6	
10	0	4	5
11	3		

25.

9	8	9			
10	2	4	6	6	
11	4	5	7	8	8	9
12	2	4	5	7
13	1	2		
14	4			
15	1			

29. a.

		y		
		1	2	Total
	A	5	0	5
x	B	11	2	13
	C	2	10	12
Total		18	12	30

b.

		y		
		1	2	Total
	A	100.0	0.0	100.0
x	B	84.6	15.4	100.0
	C	16.7	83.3	100.0

c.

		y	
		1	2
	A	27.8	0.0
x	B	61.1	16.7
	C	11.1	83.3
Total		100.0	100.0

d. A values are alway in y = 1
B values are most often in y = 1
C values are most often in y = 2

32. a.

		Bookvalue/share				
		0.00-4.99	5.00-9.99	10.00-14.99	15.00-19.99	Total
Earn/share	0.00-0.99	7	4	1	0	12
	1.00-1.99	2	7	1	1	11
	2.00-2.99	0	1	4	2	7
Total		9	12	6	3	30

b.

		Bookvalue/share				
		0.00-4.99	5.00-9.99	10.00-14.99	15.00-19.99	Total
Earn/share	0.00-0.99	58.3	33.3	8.4	0.0	100.0
	1.00-1.99	18.2	63.6	9.1	9.1	100.0
	2.00-2.99	0.0	14.3	57.1	28.6	100.0

When book value is low, earnings per share tends to be low; when book value is high, earnings per share tends to be high

Chapter 3

3. Arrange data in order: 15, 20, 25, 25, 27, 28, 30, 34.

$i = \dfrac{20}{100}(8) = 1.6$; round up to position 2

20th percentile = 20

$i = \dfrac{25}{100}(8) = 2$; use positions 2 and 3

25th percentile = $\dfrac{20 + 25}{2} = 22.5$

$i = \dfrac{65}{100}(8) = 5.2$; round up to position 6

65th percentile = 28

$i = \dfrac{75}{100}(8) = 6$; use positions 6 and 7

75th percentile = $\dfrac{28 + 30}{2} = 29$

8. a. $\bar{x} = \dfrac{\Sigma x_i}{n} = \dfrac{775}{20} = 38.75$

Mode = 29 (appears three times)

b. $.05(20) = 1$; trim lowest (22) and highest (58) values

5% trimmed mean = $\dfrac{695}{18} = 38.61$

$.10(20) = 2$; trim two lowest (22, 24) and two highest (57, 58) values

10% trimmed mean = $\dfrac{614}{16} = 38.38$

c. Data in order: 22, 24, 29, 29, 29, 30, 31, 31, 32, 37, 40, 41, 44, 44, 46, 49, 50, 52, 57, 58

Median (10th and 11th positions)

$\dfrac{37 + 40}{2} = 38.5$

At home workers are slightly younger

d. $i = \dfrac{25}{100}(20) = 5$; use positions 5 and 6

$Q_1 = \dfrac{29 + 30}{2} = 29.5$

$i = \dfrac{75}{100}(20) = 15$; use positions 15 and 16

$Q_3 = \dfrac{46 + 49}{2} = 47.5$

e. $i = \dfrac{32}{100}(20) = 6.4$; round up to position 7

32nd percentile = 31

At least 32% of the people are 31 or younger

19. Range = $34 - 15 = 19$

Arrange data in order: 15, 20, 25, 25, 27, 28, 30, 34

$i = \dfrac{25}{100}(8) = 2$; $Q_1 = \dfrac{20 + 25}{2} = 22.5$

$i = \dfrac{75}{100}(8) = 6$; $Q_3 = \dfrac{28 + 30}{2} = 29$

IQR $= Q_3 - Q_1 = 29 - 22.5 = 6.5$

$\bar{x} = \dfrac{\Sigma x_i}{n} = \dfrac{204}{8} = 25.5$

x_i	$(x_i - \bar{x})$	$(x_i - \bar{x})^2$
27	1.5	2.25
25	−.5	.25
20	−5.5	30.25
15	−10.5	110.25
30	4.5	20.25
34	8.5	72.25
28	2.5	6.25
25	−.5	.25
		242.00

$s^2 = \dfrac{\Sigma(x_i - \bar{x})^2}{n - 1} = \dfrac{242}{8 - 1} = 34.57$

$s = \sqrt{34.57} = 5.88$

25. a. Range = $190 - 168 = 22$

b. $\bar{x} = \dfrac{\Sigma x_i}{n} = \dfrac{1068}{6} = 178$

$s^2 = \dfrac{\Sigma(x_i - \bar{x})^2}{n - 1}$

$= \dfrac{4^2 + (-10)^2 + 6^2 + 12^2 + (-8)^2 + (-4)^2}{6 - 1}$

$= \dfrac{376}{5} = 75.2$

c. $s = \sqrt{75.2} = 8.67$

d. $\dfrac{s}{\bar{x}}(100) = \dfrac{8.67}{178}(100) = 4.87$

31. Chebyshev's theorem: *at least* $(1 - 1/k^2)$

a. $k = \dfrac{40 - 30}{5} = 2$; $(1 - \frac{1}{2}^2) = .75$

b. $k = \dfrac{45 - 30}{5} = 3$; $(1 - \frac{1}{3}^2) = .89$

c. $k = \dfrac{38 - 30}{5} = 1.6$; $(1 - \frac{1}{1.6}^2) = .61$

d. $k = \dfrac{42 - 30}{5} = 2.4$; $(1 - \frac{1}{2.4}^2) = .83$

e. $k = \dfrac{48 - 30}{5} = 3.6$; $(1 - \frac{1}{3.6}^2) = .92$

34. a.

$\bar{x} = 73.2$, $s = \sqrt{\dfrac{\Sigma(x_i - \bar{x})^2}{n - 1}} = 13.71$

b. $z = \dfrac{x_i - \bar{x}}{s} = \dfrac{108 - 73.2}{13.71} = 2.54$

It is a high score, but does not exceed 3 so is not an outlier

c. $z = \dfrac{87 - 73.2}{13.71} \approx 1$

68% within ±1, so 32%/2 = 16% 87 or more

$z = \dfrac{46 - 73.2}{13.71} \approx -2$

95% within ±2, so 5%/2 = 2.5% 46 or less

42. Arrange data in order: 5, 6, 8, 10, 10, 12, 15, 16, 18

$i = \dfrac{25}{100}(9) = 2.25$; round up to position 3

$Q_1 = 8$

Median (5th position) = 10

$i = \dfrac{75}{100}(9) = 6.75$; round up to position 7

$Q_3 = 15$

5-number summary: 5, 8, 10, 15, 18

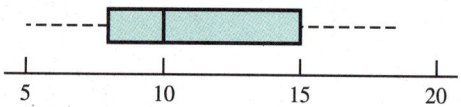

45. a. Arrange data in order low to high.

$i = \dfrac{25}{100}(21) = 5.25$; round up to 6th position

$Q_1 = 1872$

Median (11th position) = 4019

$i = \dfrac{75}{100}(21) = 15.75$; round up to 16th position

$Q_3 = 8305$

5-number summary: 608, 1872, 4019, 8305, 14,138

b. IQR = $Q_3 - Q_1 = 8305 - 1872 = 6433$

Inner Fences: $1872 - 1.5(6433) = -7777$
$ 8305 + 1.5(6433) = 17,955$

Outer Fences: $1872 - 3(6433) = -17,427$
$ 8305 + 3(6433) = 27,604$

c. No; data are within fences

d. 41,138 > 27,604. 41,138 would be an extreme outlier. Data value should be reviewed and corrected

e.

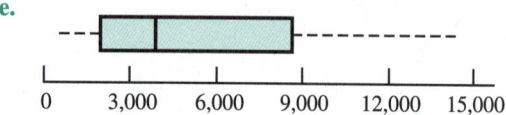

49. b. There appears to be a negative linear relationship between x and y

c.

x_i	y_i	$x_i - \bar{x}$	$y_i - \bar{y}$	$(x_i - \bar{x})(y_i - \bar{y})$
4	50	−4	4	−16
6	50	−2	4	−8
11	40	3	−6	−18
3	60	−5	14	−70
16	30	8	−16	−128
40	230	0	0	−240

$\bar{x} = 8$; $\bar{y} = 46$

$s_{xy} = \dfrac{\Sigma(x_i - \bar{x})(y_i - \bar{y})}{n - 1} = \dfrac{-240}{4} = -60$

The sample covariance indicates a negative linear association between x and y

d. $r_{xy} = \dfrac{s_{xy}}{s_x s_y} = \dfrac{-60}{(5.43)(11.40)} = -.97$

The sample correlation coefficient of −.97 is indicative of a strong negative linear relationship

56.

f_i	M_i	$f_i M_i$
4	5	20
7	10	70
9	15	135
5	20	100
25		325

$\bar{x} = \dfrac{\Sigma f_i M_i}{n} = \dfrac{325}{25} = 13$

57.

f_i	M_i	$(M_i - \bar{x})$	$(M_i - \bar{x})^2$	$f_i(M_i - \bar{x})^2$
4	5	−8	64	256
7	10	−3	9	63
9	15	2	4	36
5	20	7	49	245
25				600

$s^2 = \dfrac{\Sigma f_i(M_i - \bar{x})^2}{n - 1} = \dfrac{600}{25 - 1} = 25$

$s = \sqrt{25} = 5$

Chapter 4

2. $\dbinom{6}{3} = \dfrac{6!}{3!3!} = \dfrac{6 \cdot 5 \cdot 4 \cdot 3 \cdot 2 \cdot 1}{(3 \cdot 2 \cdot 1)(3 \cdot 2 \cdot 1)} = 20$

ABC	ACE	BCD	BEF
ABD	ACF	BCE	CDE
ABE	ADE	BCF	CDF
ABF	ADF	BDE	CEF
ACD	AEF	BDF	DEF

9. $\binom{50}{4} = \frac{50!}{4!46!} = \frac{50 \cdot 49 \cdot 48 \cdot 47}{4 \cdot 3 \cdot 2 \cdot 1} = 230,300$

14. $P(E_1) = .40$, $P(E_2) = .26$, $P(E_3) = .34$
The relative frequency method was used

17. $P(\text{never married}) = \frac{1106}{2038}$

$P(\text{married}) = \frac{826}{2038}$

$P(\text{other}) = \frac{106}{2038}$

Note that the sum of the probabilities equals 1

25. a. $S = \{$ace of clubs, ace of diamonds, ace of hearts, ace of spades$\}$
b. $S = \{$2 of clubs, 3 of clubs, ..., 10 of clubs, J of clubs, Q of clubs, K of clubs, A of clubs$\}$
c. There are 12; jack, queen, or king in each of the four suits
d. $For(a)$: 4/52 = 1/13 = .08
$For(b)$: 13/52 = 1/4 = .25
$For(c)$: 12/52 = .23

27. a. (4, 6), (4, 7), (4, 8)
b. .05 + .10 + .15 = .30
c. (2, 8), (3, 8), (4, 8)
d. .05 + .05 + .15 = .25
e. .15

33. a. $P(A) = P(E_1) + P(E_4) + P(E_6) = .05 + .25 + .10 = .40$

$P(B) = P(E_2) + P(E_4) + P(E_7) = .20 + .25 + .05 = .50$

$P(C) = P(E_2) + P(E_3) + P(E_5) + P(E_7)$

$= .20 + .20 + .15 + .05 = .60$

b. $A \cup B = \{E_1, E_2, E_4, E_6, E_7\}$

$P(A \cup B) = P(E_1) + P(E_2) + P(E_4) + P(E_6) + P(E_7)$

$= .05 + .20 + .25 + .10 + .05$

$= .65$

c. $A \cap B = \{E_4\}$, $P(A \cap B) = P(E_4) = .25$
d. Yes, they are mutually exclusive
e. $B^c = \{E_1, E_3, E_5, E_6\}$

$P(B^c) = P(E_1) + P(E_3) + P(E_5) + P(E_6)$

$= .05 + .20 + .15 + .10$

$= .50$

38. Let B = rented a car for business reasons
P = rented a car for personal reasons
a. $P(B \cup P) = P(B) + P(P) - P(B \cap P)$

$= .540 + .458 - .300$

$= .698$
b. $P(\text{Neither}) = 1 - .698 = .302$

42. a. $P(A \mid B) = \frac{P(A \cap B)}{P(B)} = \frac{.40}{.60} = .6667$

b. $P(B \mid A) = \frac{P(A \cap B)}{P(A)} = \frac{.40}{.50} = .80$

c. No, because $P(A \mid B) \neq P(A)$

45. a.

| | Reason for Applying | | | |
	Quality	Cost/Convenience	Other	Total
Full-time	.218	.204	.039	.461
Part-time	.208	.307	.024	.539
Total	.426	.511	.063	1.00

b. It is most likely a student will cite cost or convenience as the first reason (probability = .511); school quality is the first reason cited by the second largest number of students (probability = .426)
c. $P(\text{quality} \mid \text{full-time}) = .218/.461 = .473$
d. $P(\text{quality} \mid \text{part-time}) = .208/.539 = .386$
e. For independence, we must have $P(A)P(B) = P(A \cap B)$; from the table,

$P(A \cap B) = .218$, $P(A) = .461$, $P(B) = .426$
$P(A)P(B) = (.461)(.426) = .196$

Since $P(A)P(B) \neq P(A \cap B)$, the events are not independent

53. a. Yes, since $P(A_1 \cap A_2) = 0$
b. $P(A_1 \cap B) = P(A_1)P(B \mid A_1) = .40(.20) = .08$
$P(A_2 \cap B) = P(A_2)P(B \mid A_2) = .60(.05) = .03$
c. $P(B) = P(A_1 \cap B) + P(A_2 \cap B) = .08 + .03 = .11$
d. $P(A_1 \mid B) = \frac{.08}{.11} = .7273$

$P(A_2 \mid B) = \frac{.03}{.11} = .2727$

56. M = missed payment
D_1 = customer defaults
D_2 = customer does not default
$P(D_1) = .05$, $P(D_2) = .95$, $P(M \mid D_2) = .2$, $P(M \mid D_1) = 1$
a. $P(D_1 \mid M) = \dfrac{P(D_1)P(M \mid D_1)}{P(D_1)P(M \mid D_1) + P(D_2)P(M \mid D_2)}$

$= \dfrac{(.05)(1)}{(.05)(1) + (.95)(.2)}$

$= \dfrac{.05}{.24} = .21$

b. Yes, the probability of default is greater than .20

Chapter 5

1. a. Head, Head (H, H)
Head, Tail (H, T)
Tail, Head (T, H)
Tail, Tail (T, T)

b. x = number of heads on two coin tosses

c.

Outcome	Values of x
(H, H)	2
(H, T)	1
(T, H)	1
(T, T)	0

3. Let: Y = position is offered
N = position is not offered

a. $S = \{(Y, Y, Y), (Y, Y, N), (Y, N, Y), (Y, N, N), (N, Y, Y),$
$(N, Y, N), (N, N, Y), (N, N, N)\}$

b. Let N = number of offers made; N is a discrete random variable

c.

Experimental Outcome	(Y, Y, Y)	(Y, Y, N)	(Y, N, Y)	(Y, N, N)	(N, Y, Y)	(N, Y, N)	(N, N, Y)	(N, N, N)
Value of N	3	2	2	1	2	1	1	0

7. a. $f(x) \geq 0$ for all values of x
$\Sigma f(x) = 1$; therefore, it is a proper probability distribution

b. Probability $x = 30$ is $f(30) = .25$

c. Probability $x \leq 25$ is $f(20) + f(25) = .20 + .15 = .35$

d. Probability $x > 30$ is $f(35) = .40$

8. a.

x	$f(x)$
1	3/20 = .15
2	5/20 = .25
3	8/20 = .40
4	4/20 = .20
Total	1.00

b. $f(x)$

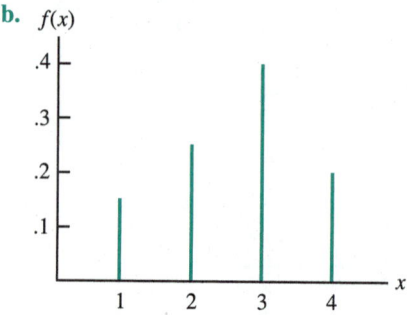

c. $f(x) \geq 0$ for $x = 1, 2, 3, 4$
$\Sigma f(x) = 1$

16. a.

y	$f(y)$	$yf(y)$
2	.20	.40
4	.30	1.20
7	.40	2.80
8	.10	.80
Totals	1.00	5.20

$E(y) = \mu = 5.20$

b.

y	$y - \mu$	$(y - \mu)^2$	$f(y)$	$(y - \mu)^2 f(y)$
2	-3.20	10.24	.20	2.048
4	-1.20	1.44	.30	.432
7	1.80	3.24	.40	1.296
8	2.80	7.84	.10	.784
			Total	4.560

$\text{Var}(y) = 4.56$
$\sigma = \sqrt{4.56} = 2.14$

18. a & b

x	$f(x)$	$xf(x)$	$(x - \mu)$	$(x - \mu)^2$	$(x - \mu)^2 f(x)$
0	.02	.00	-2.20	4.84	.0968
1	.24	.24	-1.20	1.44	.3456
2	.42	.84	-0.20	0.04	.0168
3	.20	.60	0.80	0.64	.1280
4	.08	.32	1.80	3.24	.2592
5	.04	.20	2.80	7.84	.3136
	$E(x) = 2.20$			$\text{Var}(x) = 1.1600$	
				$\sigma = 1.08$	

The expected value, $E(x) = 2.2$ of the the probability distribution is the same as the average reported in the *1994 Statistical Abstract of the United States*

$\text{Var}(x) = 1.16$ television sets squared

$\sigma = \sqrt{1.16} = 1.08$ television sets

25. a.

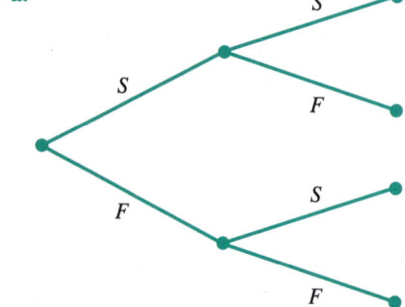

b. $f(1) = \binom{2}{1}(.4)^1(.6)^1 = \frac{2!}{1!1!}(.4)(.6) = .48$

c. $f(0) = \binom{2}{0}(.4)^0(.6)^2 = \frac{2!}{0!2!}(1)(.36) = .36$

d. $f(2) = \binom{2}{2}(.4)^2(.6)^0 = \frac{2!}{2!0!}(.16)(1) = .16$

e. $P(x \geq 1) = f(1) + f(2) = .48 + .16 = .64$

f. $E(x) = np = 2(.4) = .8$

$Var(x) = np(1-p) = 2(.4)(.6) = .48$

$\sigma = \sqrt{.48} = .6928$

30. a. Probability of a defective part being produced must be .03 for each trial; trials must be independent

b. Let: D = defective

G = not defective

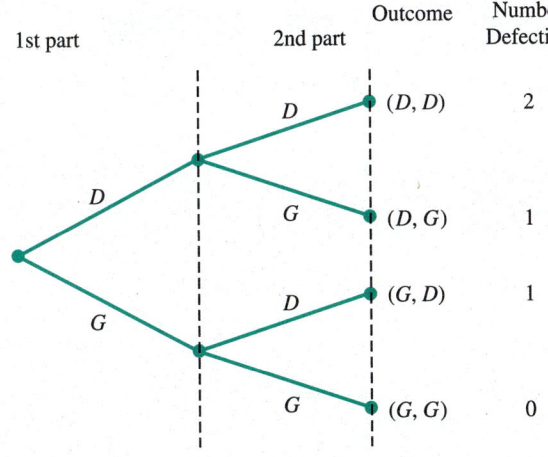

1st part	2nd part	Experimental Outcome	Number Defective
D	D	(D, D)	2
D	G	(D, G)	1
G	D	(G, D)	1
G	G	(G, G)	0

c. Two outcomes result in exactly one defect

d. $P(\text{no defects}) = (.97)(.97) = .9409$

$P(1 \text{ defect}) = 2(.03)(.97) = .0582$

$P(2 \text{ defects}) = (.03)(.03) = .0009$

43. a. $f(x) = \frac{2^x e^{-2}}{x!}$

b. $\mu = 6$ for 3 time periods

c. $f(x) = \frac{6^x e^{-6}}{x!}$

d. $f(2) = \frac{2^2 e^{-2}}{2!} = \frac{4(.1353)}{2} = .2706$

e. $f(6) = \frac{6^6 e^{-6}}{6!} = .1606$

f. $f(5) = \frac{4^5 e^{-4}}{5!} = .1563$

44. a. $\mu = 48(5/60) = 4$

$f(3) = \frac{4^3 e^{-4}}{3!} = \frac{(64)(.0183)}{6} = .1952$

b. $\mu = 48(15/60) = 12$

$f(10) = \frac{12^{10} e^{-12}}{10!} = .1048$

c. $\mu = 48(5/60) = 4$; one can expect 4 callers to be waiting after 5 minutes

$f(0) = \frac{4^0 e^{-4}}{0!} = .0183$; the probability none will be waiting after 5 minutes is .0183

d. $\mu = 48(3/60) = 2.4$

$f(0) = \frac{2.4^0 e^{-2.4}}{0!} = .0907$; the probability of no interruptions in 3 minutes is .0907

52. a. $f(1) = \frac{\binom{3}{1}\binom{10-3}{4-1}}{\binom{10}{4}} = \frac{\left(\frac{3!}{1!2!}\right)\left(\frac{7!}{3!4!}\right)}{\frac{10!}{4!6!}}$

$= \frac{(3)(35)}{210} = .50$

b. $f(2) = \frac{\binom{3}{2}\binom{10-3}{2-2}}{\binom{10}{2}} = \frac{(3)(1)}{45} = .067$

56. $N = 60, n = 10$

a. $r = 20, x = 0$

$f(0) = \frac{\binom{20}{0}\binom{40}{10}}{\binom{60}{10}} = \frac{(1)\left(\frac{40!}{10!30!}\right)}{\frac{60!}{10!50!}} = \left(\frac{40!}{10!30!}\right)\left(\frac{10!50!}{60!}\right)$

$= \frac{40 \cdot 39 \cdot 38 \cdot 37 \cdot 36 \cdot 35 \cdot 34 \cdot 33 \cdot 32 \cdot 31}{60 \cdot 59 \cdot 58 \cdot 57 \cdot 56 \cdot 55 \cdot 54 \cdot 53 \cdot 52 \cdot 51}$

$\approx .01$

b. $r = 20, x = 1$

$f(1) = \frac{\binom{20}{1}\binom{40}{9}}{\binom{60}{10}} = 20\left(\frac{40!}{9!31!}\right)\left(\frac{10!50!}{60!}\right)$

$\approx .07$

c. $1 - f(0) - f(1) = 1 - .08 = .92$

d. Same as the probability one will be from Hawaii; in part (b) that was found to equal approximately .07

Chapter 6

1. a.

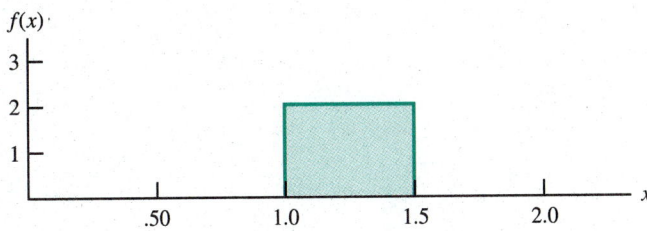

b. $P(x = 1.25) = 0$; the probability of any single point is zero since the area under the curve above any single point is zero

c. $P(1.0 \le x \le 1.25) = 2(.25) = .50$

d. $P(1.20 < x < 1.5) = 2(.30) = .60$

4. a.

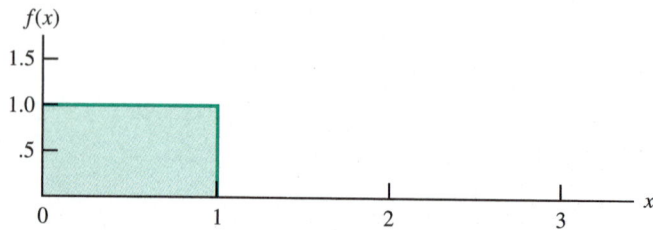

b. $P(.25 < x < .75) = 1(.50) = .50$

c. $P(x \le .30) = 1(.30) = .30$

d. $P(x > .60) = 1(.40) = .40$

13. a. $.4761 + .1879 = .6640$

b. $.3888 - .1985 = .1903$

c. $.4599 - .3508 = .1091$

15. a. Look in the table for an area of $.5000 - .2119 = .2881$; since the value we are seeking is below the mean, the z value must be negative; thus, for an area of $.2881$, $z = -.80$

b. Look in the table for an area of $.9030/2 = .4515$; $z = 1.66$

c. Look in the table for an area of $.2052/2 = .1026$; $z = .26$

d. Look in the table for an area of $.9948 - .5000 = .4948$; $z = 2.56$

e. Look in the table for an area of $.6915 - .5000 = .1915$; since the value we are seeking is below the mean, the z value must be negative; thus, $z = -.50$

18. a. With $z = \dfrac{(12{,}000 - 10{,}000)}{2200} = .91$,

$P(x \le 12{,}000) = P(z \le .91) = .5000 + .3186 = .8186$

$P(x \ge 12{,}000) = 1 - P(x \le 12{,}000) = 1 - .8186 = = .1814$

So, the probability that a rehabilitation program will cost at least \$12,000 is .1814

b. With $z = \dfrac{(6000 - 10{,}000)}{2200} = -1.82$,

$P(x \ge 6000) = P(z \ge -1.82) = .4656 + .5000 = .9656$

The probability that a rehabilitation program will cost at least \$6000 is .9656

c. First, find the value of z that cuts off an area of .10 in the upper tail of the standard normal distribution; a value of $z = 1.28$ does this

Now find the value of x corresponding to $z = 1.28$

$\dfrac{x - 10{,}000}{2200} = 1.28$

$x = 10{,}000 + 1.28(2200) = 12{,}816$

The cost range for the 10% most expensive programs is \$12,816 or more

26. a. $\mu = np = 100(.20) = 20$

$\sigma^2 = np(1 - p) = 100(.20)(.80) = 16$

$\sigma = \sqrt{16} = 4$

b. Yes, since $np = 20$ and $n(1 - p) = 80$

c. Compute $P(23.5 \le x \le 24.5)$

$z = \dfrac{24.5 - 20}{4} = 1.13 \rightarrow$ Area $= .3708$

$z = \dfrac{23.5 - 20}{4} = .88 \rightarrow$ Area $= .3106$

$P(23.5 \le x \le 24.5) = .3708 - .3106 = .0602$

d. Compute $P(17.5 \le x \le 22.5)$

$z = \dfrac{17.5 - 20}{4} = -.63 \rightarrow$ Area $= .2357$

$z = \dfrac{22.5 - 20}{4} = .63 \rightarrow$ Area $= .2357$

$P(17.5 \le x \le 22.5) = .2357 + .2357 = .4714$

e. Compute $P(x \le 15.5)$

$z = \dfrac{15.5 - 20}{4} = -1.13 \rightarrow$ Area $= .3708$

$P(x \le 15.5) = .5000 - .3708 = .1292$

28. Use the normal approximation of binomial probabilities with $\mu = np = 250(.04) = 10$ and

$\sigma = \sqrt{np(1 - p)} = \sqrt{250(.04)(.96)} = 3.1$

a. Compute $P(x \le 12.5)$

$z = \dfrac{12.5 - 10}{3.1} = .81 \rightarrow$ Area $= .2910$

$P(x \le 12.5) = .5000 + .2910 = .7910$

b. Compute $P(x \ge 4.5)$

$z = \dfrac{4.5 - 10}{3.1} = -1.77 \rightarrow$ Area $= .4616$

$P(x \ge 4.5) = .5000 + .4616 = .9616$

c. Compute $P(7.5 \le x \le 8.5)$

$z = \dfrac{7.5 - 10}{3.1} = -.81 \rightarrow$ Area $= .2910$

$z = \dfrac{8.5 - 10}{3.1} = -.48 \rightarrow$ Area $= .1844$

$P(7.5 \le x \le 8.5) = .2910 - .1844 = .1066$

34. a. $P(x \le x_0) = 1 - e^{-x_0/3}$

b. $P(x \le 2) = 1 - e^{-2/3} = 1 - .5134 = .4866$

c. $P(x \ge 3) = 1 - P(x \le 3) = 1 - (1 - e^{-3/3}) = e^{-1} = .3679$

d. $P(x \le 5) = 1 - e^{-5/3} = 1 - .1889 = .8111$

e. $P(2 \le x \le 5) = P(x \le 5) - P(x \le 2) = .8111 - .4866 = .3245$

36. a.

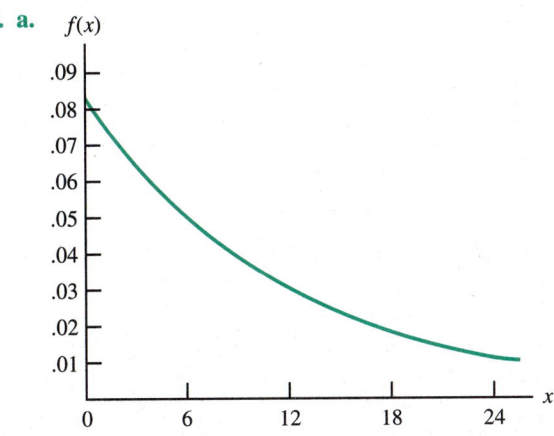

b. $P(x \le 12) = 1 - e^{-12/12} = 1 - .3679 = .6321$
c. $P(x \le 6) = 1 - e^{-6/12} = 1 - .6065 = .3935$
d. $P(x \ge 30) = 1 - P(x < 30)$
$$= 1 - (1 - e^{-30/12})$$
$$= .0821$$

Chapter 7

1. a. AB, AC, AD, AE, BC, BD, BE, CD, CE, DE
b. With 10 samples, each has a $\frac{1}{10}$ probability
c. E and C because 8 and 0 do not apply; 5 identifies E; 7 does not apply; 5 is skipped since E is already in the sample; 3 identifies C; 2 is not needed since the sample of size 2 is complete

3. 554, 459, 147, 385, 689, 640, 113, 340, 756, 953, 401, 827

13. a. $\bar{x} = \dfrac{\Sigma x_i}{n} = \dfrac{54}{6} = 9$

b. $s^2 = \sqrt{\dfrac{\Sigma(x_i - \bar{x})^2}{n-1}}$

$\Sigma(x_i - \bar{x})^2 = (-4)^2 + (-1)^2 + 1^2 + (-2)^2 + 1^2 + 5^2 = 48$

$s = \sqrt{\dfrac{48}{6-1}} = 3.1$

15. a. $\bar{x} = \dfrac{\Sigma x_i}{n} = \dfrac{465}{5} = 93$

b.

x_i	$(x_i - \bar{x})$	$(x_i - \bar{x})^2$
94	+1	1
100	+7	49
85	−8	64
94	+1	1
92	−1	1
Totals 465	0	116

$s = \sqrt{\dfrac{\Sigma(x_i - \bar{x})^2}{n-1}} = \sqrt{\dfrac{116}{4}} = 5.39$

22. a. The sampling distribution is normal with:

$$E(\bar{x}) = \mu = 200$$
$$\sigma_{\bar{x}} = \frac{\sigma}{\sqrt{n}} = \frac{50}{\sqrt{100}} = 5$$

For ± 5, $(\bar{x} - \mu) = 5$,
$$z = \frac{\bar{x} - \mu}{\sigma_{\bar{x}}} = \frac{5}{5} = 1$$
$$\text{Area} = .3413 \times 2 = .6826$$

b. For ± 10, $(\bar{x} - \mu) = 10$,

$$z = \frac{\bar{x} - \mu}{\sigma_{\bar{x}}} = \frac{10}{5} = 2$$
$$\text{Area} = .4772 \times 2 = .9544$$

29. a.

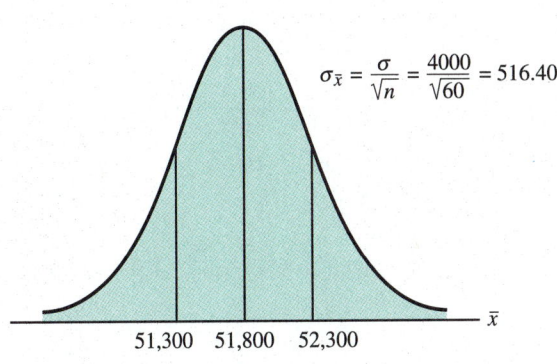

$\sigma_{\bar{x}} = \dfrac{\sigma}{\sqrt{n}} = \dfrac{4000}{\sqrt{60}} = 516.40$

$$z = \frac{52,300 - 51,800}{516.40} = +.97$$
$$\text{Area} = .3340 \times 2 = .6680$$

b. $\sigma_{\bar{x}} = \dfrac{\sigma}{\sqrt{n}} = \dfrac{4000}{\sqrt{120}} = 365.15$

$$z = \frac{52,300 - 51,800}{365.15} = +1.37$$
$$\text{Area} = .4147 \times 2 = .8294$$

42. a. $E(\bar{p}) = .40$

$$\sigma_{\bar{p}} = \sqrt{\frac{p(1-p)}{n}} = \sqrt{\frac{(.40)(.60)}{200}} = .0346$$
$$z = \frac{\bar{p} - p}{\sigma_{\bar{p}}} = \frac{.03}{.0346} = .87$$
$$\text{Area} = .3078 \times 2 = .6156$$

b. $z = \dfrac{\bar{p} - p}{\sigma_{\bar{p}}} = \dfrac{.05}{.0346} = 1.45$

$$\text{Area} = .4265 \times 2 = .8530$$

45. a.

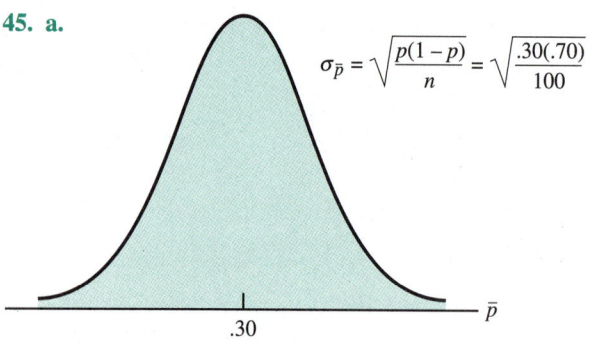

$$\sigma_{\bar{p}} = \sqrt{\frac{p(1-p)}{n}} = \sqrt{\frac{.30(.70)}{100}} = .0458$$

The normal distribution is appropriate because $np = 100(.30) = 30$ and $n(1-p) = 100(.70) = 70$ are both greater than 5

b. $P(.20 \leq \bar{p} \leq .40) = ?$

$$z = \frac{.40 - .30}{.0458} = 2.18$$

$$\text{Area} = .4854 \times 2 = .9708$$

c. $P(.25 \leq \bar{p} \leq .35) = ?$

$$z = \frac{.35 - .30}{.0458} = 1.09$$

$$\text{Area} = .3621 \times 2 = .7242$$

Chapter 8

2. Use $\bar{x} \pm z_{\alpha/2}(\sigma/\sqrt{n})$ with the sample standard deviation s used to estimate σ

a. $32 \pm 1.645 \ (6/\sqrt{50})$
   32 ± 1.4; (30.6 to 33.4)
b. $32 \pm 1.96(6/\sqrt{50})$
   32 ± 1.66; (30.34 to 33.66)
c. $32 \pm 2.576(6/\sqrt{50})$
   32 ± 2.18; (29.82 to 34.18)

5. a. $\sigma_{\bar{x}} = \sigma/\sqrt{n} = 2.50/\sqrt{49} = .3571$
b. Sampling error less than or equal to $1.96\sigma_{\bar{x}} = .70$
c. $22.60 \pm .70 \ or \ (21.90 \ to \ 23.30)$

17. a. $\bar{x} = \dfrac{\Sigma x_i}{n} = \dfrac{80}{8} = 10$

b. $s = \sqrt{\dfrac{\Sigma(x_i - \bar{x})^2}{n-1}} = \sqrt{\dfrac{84}{8-1}} = 3.46$

c. With 7 degrees of freedom, $t_{.025} = 2.365$

$$\bar{x} \pm t_{.025} \frac{s}{\sqrt{n}}$$

$$10 \pm 2.365 \frac{3.464}{\sqrt{8}}$$

$$10 \pm 2.89; (7.11 \ to \ 12.89)$$

19. At 90%, $80 \pm t_{.05}(s/\sqrt{n})$ with degrees of freedom = 17
$$t_{.05} = 1.740$$
$$80 \pm 1.740(10/\sqrt{18})$$
$$80 \pm 4.10; (75.90 \ to \ 84.10)$$

At 95%, $80 \pm t_{.025}(10/\sqrt{18})$ with degrees of freedom = 17
$$t_{.025} = 2.110$$
$$80 \pm 4.97; (75.03 \ to \ 84.97)$$

28. a. Planning value of $\sigma = \dfrac{\text{Range}}{4} = \dfrac{36}{4} = 9$

b. $n = \dfrac{z_{.025}^2 \sigma^2}{E^2} = \dfrac{(1.96)^2(9)^2}{(3)^2} = 34.6 \approx 35$

c. $n = \dfrac{(1.96)^2(9)^2}{(2)^2} = 77.8 \approx 78$

29. Use $n = \dfrac{z_{\alpha/2}^2 \sigma^2}{E^2}$,

$$n = \frac{(1.96)^2(6.82)^2}{(1.5)^2} = 79.4 \ or \ 80$$

$$n = \frac{(1.645)^2(6.82)^2}{(2)^2} = 31.5 \ or \ 32$$

37. a. $\bar{p} = \dfrac{100}{400} = .25$

b. $\sqrt{\dfrac{\bar{p}(1-\bar{p})}{n}} = \sqrt{\dfrac{.25(.75)}{400}} = .0217$

c. $\bar{p} \pm z_{.025}\sqrt{\dfrac{\bar{p}(1-\bar{p})}{n}}$

$$.25 \pm 1.96(.0217)$$
$$.25 \pm .0425; (.2075 \ to \ .2925)$$

41. a. $\bar{p} = 248/400 = .62$

b. $\bar{p} \pm 1.645\sqrt{\dfrac{.62(.38)}{400}}$

$$.62 \pm .04; (.58 \ to \ .66)$$

Chapter 9

2. a. $H_0: \mu \leq 14$
   $H_a: \mu > 14$
b. No evidence that the new plan increases sales
c. The research hypothesis $\mu > 14$ is supported; the new plan increases sales

5. a. Rejecting $H_0: \mu \leq 8.6$ when it is true
b. Accepting $H_0: \mu \leq 8.6$ when it is false

10. a. $z = 2.05$

   Reject H_0 if $z > 2.05$
b. $z = \dfrac{\bar{x} - \mu}{s/\sqrt{n}} = \dfrac{16.5 - 15}{7/\sqrt{40}} = 1.36$

c. Area for $z = 1.36 = .4131$
p-value $= .5000 - .4131 = .0869$

d. Do not reject H_0

13. a. $H_0: \mu \geq 1056$

$H_a: \mu < 1056$

b. Reject H_0 if $z < -1.645$

$$z = \frac{\bar{x} - \mu}{s/\sqrt{n}} = \frac{910 - 1056}{1600/\sqrt{400}} = -1.83$$

Reject H_0.

c. p-value $= .5000 - .4664 = .0336$

22. a. Reject H_0 if $z < -2.33$ or $z > 2.33$

b. $z = \dfrac{\bar{x} - \mu}{\sigma/\sqrt{n}} = \dfrac{14.2 - 15}{5/\sqrt{50}} = 1.13$

c. p-value $= 2(.5000 - .3708) = .2584$

d. Do not reject H_0

25. a. $H_0: \mu = 18,688$
$H_a: \mu \neq 18,688$

Reject H_0 if $z < -1.96$ or $z > 1.96$

$$z = \frac{\bar{x} - \mu_0}{s/\sqrt{n}} = \frac{16,860 - 18,688}{14,624/\sqrt{400}} = -2.50$$

Reject H_0 and conclude S.C. $\mu \neq 18,688$.

b. p-value $= 2(.5000 - .4938) = .0124$

34. a. $\bar{x} = \dfrac{\Sigma x_i}{n} = \dfrac{108}{6} = 18$

b. $s = \sqrt{\dfrac{\Sigma(x_i - \bar{x})}{n-1}} = \sqrt{\dfrac{10}{6-1}} = 1.41$

c. Reject H_0 if $t < -2.571$ or $t > 2.571$

d. $t = \dfrac{\bar{x} - \mu}{s/\sqrt{n}} = \dfrac{18 - 20}{1.41/\sqrt{6}} = -3.47$

e. Reject H_0; conclude H_a is true

37. a. $\bar{x} = \Sigma x_i/n = 270$

b. $s = \sqrt{\dfrac{\Sigma(x_i - \bar{x})^2}{n-1}} = 24.78$

c.
$H_0: \mu \leq 258$
$H_a: \mu > 258$
Reject H_0 if $t > 1.761$

$$t = \frac{\bar{x} - \mu_0}{s/\sqrt{n}} = \frac{270 - 258}{24.78/\sqrt{15}} = 1.88$$

Reject H_a; mean has increased

d. Between .05 and .025

44. a. Reject H_0 if $z < -1.96$ or $z > 1.96$

b. $\sigma_{\bar{p}} = \sqrt{\dfrac{.20(.80)}{400}} = .02$

$$z = \frac{\bar{p} - p}{\sigma_{\bar{p}}} = \frac{.175 - .20}{.02} = -1.25$$

c. p-value $= 2(.5000 - .3944) = .2112$

d. Do not reject H_0

47. $H_0: p > .64$
$H_a: p < .64$

Reject H_0 if $z < -1.645$
$\bar{p} = 52/100 = .52$

$$z = \frac{.52 - .64}{\sqrt{\dfrac{.64(.36)}{100}}} = -2.5$$

Reject H_0

56.

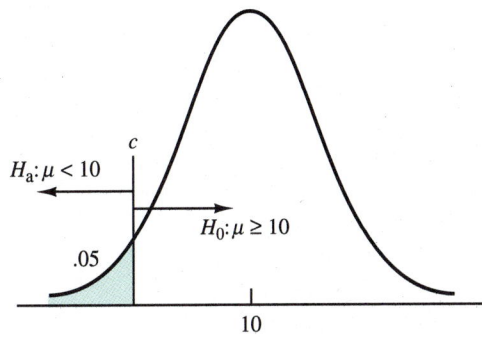

$$c = 10 - 1.645(5/\sqrt{120}) = 9.25$$
Reject H_0 if $\bar{x} < 9.25$

a. When $\mu = 9$,

$$z = \frac{9.25 - 9}{5/\sqrt{120}} = .55$$
$$P(H_0) = (.5000 - .2088) = .2912$$

b. Type II error

c. When $\mu = 8$,

$$z = \frac{9.25 - 8}{5/\sqrt{120}} = 2.74$$
$$\beta = (.5000 - .4969) = .0031$$

59. a. $H_0: \mu \geq 25$
$H_a: \mu < 25$
Reject H_0 if $z < -2.05$

$$z = \frac{\bar{x} - \mu_0}{\sigma/\sqrt{n}} = \frac{\bar{x} - 25}{3/\sqrt{30}} = -2.05$$

Solve for $\bar{x} = 23.88$
Decision Rule: Accept H_0 if $\bar{x} \geq 23.88$
Reject H_0 if $\bar{x} < 23.88$

b. For $\mu = 23$,

$$z = \frac{23.88 - 23}{3/\sqrt{30}} = 1.61$$

$$\beta = .5000 - .4463 = .0537$$

c. For $\mu = 24$,

$$z = \frac{23.88 - 24}{3/\sqrt{30}} = -.22$$

$$\beta = .5000 + .0871 = .5871$$

d. The Type II error cannot be made in this case; note that when $\mu = 25.5$, H_0 is true: the Type II error can only be made when H_0 is false

64. $n = \dfrac{(z_\alpha + z_\beta)\sigma^2}{(\mu_0 - \mu_a)^2} = \dfrac{(1.645 + 1.28)^2(5)^2}{(10 - 9)^2} = 214$

67. At $\mu_0 = 400$, $\alpha = .02$; $z_{.02} = 2.05$
At $\mu_a = 385$, $\beta = .10$; $z_{.10} = 1.28$
With $\sigma = 30$,

$$n = \frac{(z_\alpha + z_\beta)^2\sigma^2}{(\mu_0 - \mu_a)^2} = \frac{(2.05 + 1.28)^2(30)^2}{(400 - 385)^2} = 44.4 \text{ or } 45$$

Chapter 10

1. a. $\bar{x}_1 - \bar{x}_2 = 13.6 - 11.6 = 2$

b. $s_{\bar{x}_1 - \bar{x}_2} = \sqrt{\dfrac{s_1^2}{n_1} + \dfrac{s_2^2}{n_2}} = \sqrt{\dfrac{(2.2)^2}{50} + \dfrac{3^2}{35}} = .595$

$2 \pm 1.645(.595)$

$2 \pm .98$ or 1.02 to 2.98

c. $2 \pm 1.96(.595)$

2 ± 1.17 or $.83$ to 3.17

8. a. $\bar{x}_1 - \bar{x}_2 = 15{,}700 - 14{,}500 = 1200$

b. Pooled variance

$$s^2 = \frac{7(700)^2 + 11(850)^2}{18} = 632{,}083$$

$$s_{\bar{x}_1 - \bar{x}_2} = \sqrt{632{,}083\left(\frac{1}{8} + \frac{1}{12}\right)} = 362.88$$

With 18 degrees of freedom $t_{.025} = 2.101$,

$$1200 \pm 2.101(362.88)$$
$$1200 \pm 762, \text{ or } 438 \text{ to } 1962$$

c. Populations are normally distributed with equal variances

11. a. $s_{\bar{x}_1 - \bar{x}_2} = \sqrt{\dfrac{s_1^2}{n_1} + \dfrac{s_2^2}{n_2}} = \sqrt{\dfrac{(5.2)^2}{40} + \dfrac{6^2}{50}} = 1.18$

$$z = \frac{(\bar{x}_1 - \bar{x}_2) - (\mu_1 - \mu_2)}{s_{\bar{x}_1 - \bar{x}_2}} = \frac{(25.2 - 22.8)}{1.18} = 2.03$$

Reject H_0 if $z > 1.645$; therefore reject H_0; conclude H_a is true and $\mu_1 > \mu_2$

b. p-value $= .5000 - .4788 = .0212$

15. H_0: $\mu_1 - \mu_2 = 0$
H_a: $\mu_1 - \mu_2 \neq 0$
Reject H_0 if $z < -1.96$ or if $z > 1.96$

$$z = \frac{(\bar{x}_1 - \bar{x}_2) - 0}{\sqrt{\sigma_1^2/n_1 + \sigma_2^2/n_2}} = \frac{40 - 35}{\sqrt{(9)^2/36 + (10)^2/49}}$$

$$= 2.41$$

Reject H_0; customers at the two stores differ in terms of mean ages

21. a. 1, 2, 0, 0, 2

b. $\bar{d} = \dfrac{\Sigma d_i}{n} = \dfrac{5}{5} = 1$

c. $s_d = \sqrt{\dfrac{\Sigma(d_i - \bar{d})^2}{n - 1}} = \sqrt{\dfrac{4}{5 - 1}} = 1$

d. With 4 degrees of freedom, $t_{.05} = 2.132$; reject H_0 if $t > 2.132$

$$t = \frac{\bar{d} - \mu_d}{s_d/\sqrt{n}} = \frac{1 - 0}{1/\sqrt{5}} = 2.24$$

Reject H_0; conclude $\mu_d > 0$

23. $d = $ rating after – rating before
H_0: $\mu_d \leq 0$
H_a: $\mu_d > 0$
With 7 degrees of freedom, reject H_0 if $t > 1.895$; when $\bar{d} = .63$ and $s_d = 1.3025$,

$$t = \frac{\bar{d} - \mu_d}{s_d/\sqrt{n}} = \frac{.63 - 0}{1.3025/\sqrt{8}} = 1.36$$

Do not reject H_0; we cannot conclude that seeing the commercial improves the potential to purchase

31. a. $\bar{p} = \dfrac{n_1\bar{p}_1 + n_2\bar{p}_2}{n_1 + n_2} = \dfrac{200(.22) + 300(.16)}{200 + 300} = .184$

$$s_{\bar{p}_1 - \bar{p}_2} = \sqrt{(.184)(.816)\left(\frac{1}{200} + \frac{1}{300}\right)} = .0354$$

Reject H_0 if $z > 1.645$

$$z = \frac{(.22 - .16) - 0}{.0354} = 1.69$$

Reject H_0

b. p-value = $(.5000 - .4545) = .0455$

Chapter 11

2. $s^2 = 25$

a. With 19 degrees of freedom, $\chi^2_{.05} = 30.1435$ and $\chi^2_{.95} = 10.1170$

$$\frac{19(25)}{30.1435} \le \sigma^2 \le \frac{19(25)}{10.1170}$$

$$15.76 \le \sigma^2 \le 46.95$$

b. With 19 degrees of freedom, $\chi^2_{.025} = 32.8523$ and $\chi^2_{.975} = 8.90655$

$$\frac{19(25)}{32.8523} \le \sigma^2 \le \frac{19(25)}{8.90655}$$

$$14.46 \le \sigma^2 \le 53.33$$

c. $3.8 \le \sigma \le 7.3$

9. H_0: $\sigma^2 \le .0004$

H_a: $\sigma^2 > .0004$
$n = 30$

$$\chi^2_{.05} = 42.5569 \text{ (29 degrees of freedom)}$$

$$\chi^2 = \frac{(29)(.0005)}{.0004} = 36.25$$

Do not reject H_0; the product specification does not appear to be violated

15. We recommend placing the larger sample variance in the numerator; with $\alpha = .05$, $F_{.025,20,24} = 2.33$: reject H_0 if $F > 2.33$

$$F = \frac{8.2}{4.0} = 2.05; \text{ do not reject } H_0$$

Or, had we used the lower tail F value,

$$F_{.025,20,24} = \frac{1}{F_{.025,24,20}} = \frac{1}{2.46} = .41$$

$$F = \frac{4.0}{8.2} = .49$$

$$F > .41; \text{ do not reject } H_0$$

17. a. Let: σ_1^2 = variance in repair costs (4-year-old automobiles)

σ_2^2 = variance in repair costs (2-year-old automobiles)

H_0: $\sigma_1^2 \le \sigma_2^2$

H_a: $\sigma_1^2 > \sigma_2^2$

b. $s_1^2 = (170)^2 = 28,900$

$s_2^2 = (100)^2 = 10,000$

$$F = \frac{s_1^2}{s_2^2} = \frac{28,900}{10,000} = 2.89$$

$$F_{.01,24,24} = 2.66$$

Reject H_0; conclude that automobiles 4 years old have a larger variance in annual repair costs compared to automobiles 2 years old; this is expected due to the fact that older automobiles are more likely to have some very expensive repairs that lead to greater variance in the annual repair costs

Chapter 12

1. *Expected frequencies:* $e_1 = 200(.40) = 80$,
$$e_2 = 200(.40) = 80,$$
$$e_3 = 200(.20) = 40$$

Actual frequencies: $f_1 = 60, f_2 = 120, f_3 = 20$

$$\chi^2 = \frac{(60 - 80)^2}{80} + \frac{(120 - 80)^2}{80} + \frac{(20 - 40)^2}{40}$$

$$= \frac{400}{80} + \frac{1600}{80} + \frac{400}{40}$$

$$= 5 + 20 + 10 = 35$$

$\chi^2_{.01} = 9.21034$ with $k - 1 = 3 - 1 = 2$ degrees of freedom

Since $\chi^2 = 35 > 9.21034$, reject the null hypothesis; that is, the population proportions are not as stated in the null hypothesis

3. H_0: $p_{ABC} = .29$, $p_{CBS} = .28$, $p_{NBC} = .25$, $p_{IND} = .18$

H_a: The proportions are not
$$p_{ABC} = .29, p_{CBS} = .28, p_{NBC} = .25, p_{IND} = .18$$

Expected frequencies: $300(.29) = 87, 300(.28) = 84$,
$$300(.25) = 75, 300(.18) = 54$$

$$e_1 = 87, e_2 = 84, e_3 = 75, e_4 = 54$$

Actual frequencies: $f_1 = 95, f_2 = 70, f_3 = 89, f_4 = 46$

$$\chi^2_{.05} = 7.81 \text{ (3 degrees of freedom)}$$

$$\chi^2 = \frac{(95 - 87)^2}{87} + \frac{(70 - 84)^2}{84} + \frac{(89 - 75)^2}{75}$$

$$+ \frac{(46 - 54)^2}{54} = 6.87$$

Do not reject H_0; there is no significant change in the viewing audience proportions

9. H_0: The column factor is independent of the row factor

H_a: The column factor is not independent of the row factor

Expected frequencies:

	A	B	C
P	28.5	39.9	45.6
Q	21.5	30.1	34.4

$$\chi^2 = \frac{(20-28.5)^2}{28.5} + \frac{(44-39.9)^2}{39.9} + \frac{(50-45.6)^2}{45.6} +$$
$$\frac{(30-21.5)^2}{21.5} + \frac{(26-30.1)^2}{30.1} + \frac{(30-34.4)^2}{34.4}$$

$$= 7.86$$

$\chi^2_{.025} = 7.37776$ with $(2-1)(3--1) = 2$ degrees of freedom

Since $\chi^2 = 7.86 > 7.37776$, reject H_0; that is, conclude that the column factor is not independent of the row factor

11. H_0: There is no difference in shooting percentage among the teams

H_a: There is a difference in shooting percentage among the teams

Row 1 total = 629; row 2 total = 988
Column 1 total = 374; column 2 total = 341
Column 3 total = 369; column 4 total = 533

Overall total = 1617

Using these totals, we compute the expected frequencies

Expected frequencies:

	Duke	Mich.	Ind.	Cin.
Made	145.4830	132.6463	143.5380	207.3327
Missed	228.5170	208.3537	225.4620	325.6673

$$\chi^2 = \frac{(160-145.4830)^2}{145.4830} + \frac{(113-132.6463)^2}{132.6463} + \cdots$$

$$+ \frac{(331-325.6673)^2}{325.6673}$$

$$= 1.4486 + 2.9098 + .7625$$

$$+ .1372 + .9222 + 1.8525 + .4855 + .0873$$

$$= 8.6056$$

$\chi^2_{.05} = 7.81473$ with 3 degrees of freedom

Since $\chi^2 = 8.6056 > 7.81473$, reject H_0; that is, conclude that there is a difference in 3-point shooting ability for the teams

21. First estimate μ from the sample data (sample size = 120)

$$\mu = \frac{0(39) + 1(30) + 2(30) + 3(18) + 4(3)}{120}$$

$$= \frac{156}{120} = 1.3$$

Therefore, we use Poisson probabilities with $\mu = 1.3$ to compute expected frequencies

x	Observed Frequency	Poisson Probability	Expected Frequency	Difference $(f_i - e_i)$
0	39	.2725	32.700	6.300
1	30	.3543	42.516	−12.516
2	30	.2303	27.636	2.364
3	18	.0998	11.976	6.024
4 or more	3	.0430	5.160	−2.160

$$\chi^2 = \frac{(6.300)^2}{32.700} + \frac{(-12.516)^2}{42.516} + \frac{(2.364)^2}{27.636} + \frac{(6.024)^2}{11.976}$$

$$+ \frac{(-2.160)^2}{5.160} = 9.0348$$

$\chi^2_{.05} = 7.81473$ with $5-1-1 = 3$ degrees of freedom

Since $\chi^2 = 9.0348 > 7.81473$, reject H_0; that is, conclude that the data do not follow a Poisson probability distribution

22. With $N = 30$ we will use six classes with $16\frac{2}{3}\%$ of the probability associated with each class

$$\bar{x} = 22.80 \quad s = 6.2665$$

The z values that create 6 intervals, each with probability .1667 are $-.98, -.43, 0, .43, .98$

z	Cut off value of x
−.98	22.8 − .98 (6.2665) = 16.66
−.43	22.8 − .43 (6.2665) = 20.11
0	22.8 + .00 (6.2665) = 22.80
.43	22.8 + .43 (6.2665) = 25.49
.98	22.8 + .98 (6.2665) = 28.94

Interval	Observed Frequency	Expected Frequency	Difference
less than 16.66	3	5	−2
16.66–20.11	7	5	2
20.11–22.80	5	5	0
22.80–25.49	7	5	2
25.49–28.94	3	5	−2
28.94 and up	5	5	0

$$\chi^2 = \frac{(-2)^2}{5} + \frac{(2)^2}{5} + \frac{(0)^2}{5} + \frac{(2)^2}{5} + \frac{(-2)^2}{5} + \frac{(0)^2}{5}$$

$$= \frac{16}{5} = 3.20$$

$\chi^2_{.025} = 9.34840$ with $6-2-1 = 3$ degrees of freedom

Since $\chi^2 = 3.20 \le 9.34840$ Do not reject H_0
The claim that the data comes from a normal distribution cannot be rejected

FIGURE F13.1a

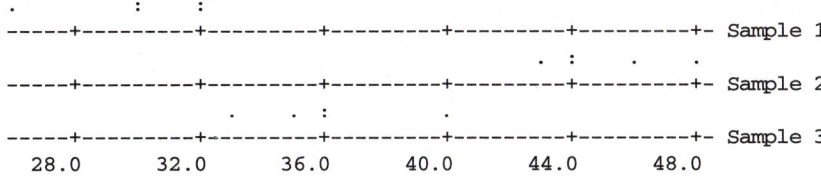

```
               .            :    :
     ----+---------+---------+---------+---------+---------+-- Sample 1
                                                   . :    .    .
     ----+---------+---------+---------+---------+---------+-- Sample 2
                            .     . :       .
     ----+---------+---------+---------+---------+---------+-- Sample 3
       28.0      32.0      36.0      40.0      44.0      48.0
```

Chapter 13

1. a. See Figure F13.1a

b. $\bar{\bar{x}} = (30 + 45 + 36)/3 = 37$

$$\text{SSB} = \sum_{j=1}^{k} n_j(\bar{x}_j - \bar{\bar{x}})^2$$

$$= 5(30 - 37)^2 + 5(45 - 37)^2 + 5(36 - 37)^2 = 570$$

$$\text{MSB} = \frac{\text{SSB}}{k-1} = \frac{570}{2} = 285$$

c. $\text{SSW} = \sum_{j=1}^{k} (n_j - 1)s_j^2$

$$= 4(6) + 4(4) + 4(6.5) = 66$$

$$\text{MSW} = \frac{\text{SSW}}{n_T - k} = \frac{66}{15 - 3} = 5.5$$

d. $F = \frac{\text{MSB}}{\text{MSW}} = \frac{285}{5.5} = 51.82$

$F_{.05} = 3.89$ (2 degrees of freedom numerator and 12 denominator)

Since $F = 51.82 > F_{.05} = 3.89$, we reject the null hypothesis that the means of the three populations are equal

e.

Source of Variation	Sum of Squares	Degrees of Freedom	Mean Square	F
Between	570	2	285	51.82
Within	66	12	5.5	
Total	636	14		

6.

	Manufacturer 1	Manufacturer 2	Manufacturer 3
Sample mean	23	28	21
Sample variance	6.67	4.67	3.33

$$\bar{\bar{x}} = (23 + 28 + 21)/3 = 24$$

$$\text{SSB} = \sum_{j=1}^{k} n_j(\bar{x}_j - \bar{\bar{x}})^2$$

$$= 4(23 - 24)^2 + 4(28 - 24)^2$$

$$+ 4(21 - 24)^2 = 104$$

$$\text{MSB} = \frac{\text{SSB}}{k-1} = \frac{104}{2} = 52$$

$$\text{SSW} = \sum_{j=1}^{k} (n_j - 1)s_j^2$$

$$= 3(6.67) + 3(4.67) + 3(3.33) = 44.01$$

$$\text{MSW} = \frac{\text{SSW}}{n_T - k} = \frac{44.01}{12 - 3} = 4.89$$

$$F = \frac{\text{MSB}}{\text{MSW}} = \frac{52}{4.89} = 10.63$$

$F_{.05} = 4.26$ (2 degrees of freedom numerator and 9 denominator)

Since $F = 10.63 > F_{.05} = 4.26$, we reject the null hypothesis that the mean time needed to mix a batch of material is the same for each manufacturer

11. a. $\text{LSD} = t_{\alpha/2}\sqrt{\text{MSW}\left(\frac{1}{n_i} + \frac{1}{n_j}\right)}$

$$= t_{.025}\sqrt{5.5\left(\frac{1}{5} + \frac{1}{5}\right)}$$

$$= 2.776\sqrt{2.2} = 4.12$$

$|\bar{x}_1 - \bar{x}_2| = |30 - 45| = 15 > \text{LSD}$; significant difference
$|\bar{x}_1 - \bar{x}_3| = |30 - 36| = 6 > \text{LSD}$; significant difference
$|\bar{x}_2 - \bar{x}_3| = |45 - 36| = 9 > \text{LSD}$; significant difference

b. $\bar{x}_1 - \bar{x}_2 \pm t_{\alpha/2}\sqrt{\text{MSW}\left(\frac{1}{n_1} + \frac{1}{n_2}\right)}$

$$(30 - 45) \pm 2.776\sqrt{5.5\left(\frac{1}{n_1} + \frac{1}{n_2}\right)}$$

$$-15 \pm 4.12 = -19.12 \text{ to } -10.88$$

13. $\text{LSD} = t_{\alpha/2}\sqrt{\text{MSW}\left(\frac{1}{n_1} + \frac{1}{n_3}\right)}$

$$= t_{.025}\sqrt{4.89\left(\frac{1}{4} + \frac{1}{4}\right)}$$

$$= 2.262\sqrt{2.45} = 3.54$$

Since $|\bar{x}_1 - \bar{x}_3| = |23 - 21| = 2 < 3.54$, there does not appear to be any significant difference between the means of populations 1 and 3

TABLE F13.41

		Factor B			Factor A
		Level 1	Level 2	Level 3	Means
Factor B	Level 1	$\bar{x}_{11} = 150$	$\bar{x}_{12} = 78$	$\bar{x}_{13} = 84$	$\bar{x}_{1.} = 104$
	Level 2	$\bar{x}_{21} = 110$	$\bar{x}_{22} = 116$	$\bar{x}_{23} = 128$	$\bar{x}_{2.} = 118$
Factor B Means		$\bar{x}_{.1} = 130$	$\bar{x}_{.2} = 97$	$\bar{x}_{.3} = 106$	$\bar{\bar{x}} = 111$

14. $\bar{x}_1 - \bar{x}_2 \pm \text{LSD}$

$23 - 28 \pm 3.54$

$-5 \pm 3.54 = -8.54 \text{ to } -1.46$

19. a. $\bar{\bar{x}} = (156 + 142 + 134)/3 = 144$

$$\text{SSTR} = \sum_{j=1}^{k} n_j(\bar{x}_j - \bar{\bar{x}})^2$$

$= 6(156 - 144)^2 + 6(142 - 144)^2 + 6(134 - 144)^2 = 1488$

b. $\text{MSTR} = \dfrac{\text{SSTR}}{k-1} = \dfrac{1488}{2} = 744$

c. $s_1^2 = 164.4, \quad s_2^2 = 131.2, \quad s_3^2 = 110.4$

$$\text{SSE} = \sum_{j=1}^{k} (n_j - 1)s_j^2$$

$= 5(164.4) + 5(131.2) + 5(110.4)$

$= 2030$

d. $\text{MSE} = \dfrac{\text{SSE}}{n_T - k} = \dfrac{2030}{18 - 3} = 135.3$

e. $F = \dfrac{\text{MSTR}}{\text{MSE}} = \dfrac{744}{135.3} = 5.50$

$F_{.05} = 3.68$ (2 degrees of freedom numerator and 15 denominator)

Since $F = 5.50 > F_{.05} = 3.68$, we reject the hypothesis that the means for the three treatments are equal

34. Treatment Means

$\bar{x}_{.1} = 13.6 \quad \bar{x}_{.2} = 11.0 \quad \bar{x}_{.3} = 10.6$

Block Means

$\bar{x}_{1.} = 9 \quad \bar{x}_{2.} = 7.67 \quad \bar{x}_{3.} = 15.67 \quad \bar{x}_{4.} = 18.67$

$\bar{x}_{5.} = 7.67$

Overall Mean

$\bar{\bar{x}} = 176/15 = 11.73$

Step 1

$$\text{SST} = \sum_i \sum_j (x_{ij} - \bar{\bar{x}})^2$$

$= (10 - 11.73)^2 + (9 - 11.73)^2 + \cdots + (8 - 11.73)^2$

$= 354.93$

Step 2

$$\text{SSTR} = b \sum_j (\bar{x}_{.j} - \bar{\bar{x}})^2$$

$= 5[(13.6 - 11.73)^2 + (11.0 - 11.73)^2$
$+ (10.6 - 11.73)^2] = 26.53$

Step 3

$$\text{SSBL} = k \sum_i (\bar{x}_{i.} - \bar{\bar{x}})^2$$

$= 3[(9 - 11.73)^2 + (7.67 - 11.73)^2 + (15.67 - 11.73)^2$
$+ (18.67 - 11.73)^2 + (7.67 - 11.73)^2] = 312.32$

Step 4

$\text{SSE} = \text{SST} - \text{SSTR} - \text{SSBL}$

$= 354.93 - 26.53 - 312.32 = 16.08$

Source of Variation	Sum of Squares	Degrees of Freedom	Mean Square	F
Treatments	26.53	2	13.27	6.60
Blocks	312.32	4	78.08	
Error	16.08	8	2.01	
Total	354.93	14		

$F_{.05} = 4.46$ (2 numerator degrees of freedom and 8 denominator)

Since $F = 6.60 > F_{.05} = 4.46$, we reject the null hypothesis that the means of the three treatments are equal

41. See Table F13.41

Step 1

$$\text{SST} = \sum_i \sum_j \sum_k (x_{ijk} - \bar{\bar{x}})^2$$

$= (135 - 111)^2 + (165 - 111)^2 + \cdots$
$+ (136 - 111)^2 = 9028$

Step 2

$$\text{SSA} = br \sum_i (\bar{x}_{i.} - \bar{\bar{x}})^2$$

$= 3(2)[(104 - 111)^2 + (118 - 111)^2] = 588$

Step 3

$$SSB = ar \sum_j (\bar{x}_{\cdot j} - \bar{\bar{x}})^2$$

$$= 2(2)[(130 - 111)^2 + (97 - 111)^2$$
$$+ (106 - 111)^2] = 2328$$

Step 4

$$SSAB = r \sum_i \sum_j (\bar{x}_{ij} - \bar{x}_{i\cdot} - \bar{x}_{\cdot j} + \bar{\bar{x}})^2$$

$$= 2[(150 - 104 - 130 + 111)^2$$
$$+ (78 - 104 - 97 + 111)^2 + \cdots$$
$$+ (128 - 118 - 106 + 111)^2] = 4392$$

Step 5

$$SSE = SST - SSA - SSB - SSAB$$

$$= 9028 - 588 - 2328 - 4392 = 1720$$

Source of Variation	Sum of Squares	Degrees of Freedom	Mean Square	F
Factor A	588	1	588	2.05
Factor B	2328	2	1164	4.06
Interaction	4392	2	2196	7.66
Error	1720	6	286.67	
Total	9028	11		

$F_{.05} = 5.99$ (1 degree of freedom numerator and 6 denominator)

$F_{.05} = 5.14$ (2 degrees of freedom numerator and 6 denominator)

Since $F = 2.05 < F_{.05} = 5.99$, factor A is not significant
Since $F = 4.06 < F_{.05} = 5.14$, factor B is not significant
Since $F = 7.66 > F_{.05} = 5.14$, interaction is significant

Chapter 14

1. a.

b. There appears to be a linear relationship between x and y
c. Many different straight lines can be drawn to provide a linear approximation of the relationship between x and

y; in part (d) we will determine the equation of a straight line that "best" represents the relationship according to the least squares criterion
d. $\Sigma x_i = 15$, $\Sigma y_i = 40$, $\Sigma x_i y_i = 146$, $\Sigma x_i^2 = 55$

$$b_1 = \frac{\Sigma x_i y_i - (\Sigma x_i \Sigma y_i)/n}{\Sigma x_i^2 - (\Sigma x_i)^2/n}$$

$$= \frac{146 - (15)(40)/5}{55 - (15)^2/5} = 2.6$$

$$b_0 = \bar{y} - b_1 \bar{x}$$
$$= 8 - 2.6(3) = .2$$
$$\hat{y} = .2 + 2.6x$$

e. $\hat{y} = .2 + 2.6x = .2 + 2.6(4) = 10.6$

4. a.

b. It indicates there may be a linear relationship between the variables
c. Many different straight lines can be drawn to provide a linear approximation of the relationship between x and y; in part (d) we will determine the equation of a straight line that "best" represents the relationship according to the least squares criterion
d. $\Sigma x_i = 325$, $\Sigma y_i = 585$; $\Sigma x_i y_i = 38,135$, $\Sigma x_i^2 = 21,145$

$$b_1 = \frac{\Sigma x_i y_i - (\Sigma x_i \Sigma y_i)/n}{\Sigma x_i^2 - (\Sigma x_i)^2/n}$$

$$= \frac{38,135 - (325)(585)/5}{21,145 - (325)^2/5} = 5.5$$

$$b_0 = \bar{y} - b_1 \bar{x}$$
$$= 117 - 5.5(65) = -240.5$$
$$\hat{y} = -240.5 + 5.5x$$

e. $\hat{y} = -240.5 + 5.5(63) = 106$
The estimate of weight is 106 pounds

15. a. $\hat{y}_i = .2 + 2.6x_i$ and $\bar{y} = 8$

x_i	y_i	$\hat{y}_i$	$y_i - \hat{y}_i$	$(y_i - \hat{y}_i)^2$	$y_i - \bar{y}$	$(y_i - \bar{y})^2$
1	3	2.8	.2	.04	−5	25
2	7	5.4	1.6	2.56	−1	1
3	5	8.0	−3.0	9.00	−3	9
4	11	10.6	.4	.16	3	9
5	14	13.2	.8	.64	6	36
				SSE = 12.40		SST = 80

$$\text{SSR} = \text{SST} - \text{SSE} = 80 - 12.4 = 67.6$$

b. $r^2 = \dfrac{\text{SSR}}{\text{SST}} = \dfrac{67.6}{80} = .845$

The least squares line provided a very good fit; 84.5% of the variability in y has been explained by the least squares line

c. $\Sigma x_i = 15, \Sigma y_i = 40, \Sigma x_i y_i = 146,$

$$\Sigma x_i^2 = 55, \Sigma y_i^2 = 400$$

$$\text{SSR} = \frac{[\Sigma x_i y_i - (\Sigma x_i \Sigma y_i)/n]^2}{\Sigma x_i^2 - (\Sigma x_i)^2/n}$$

$$= \frac{[146 - (15)(40)/5]^2}{55 - (15)^2/5} = 67.6$$

$$\text{SST} = \Sigma y_i^2 - \frac{(\Sigma y_i)^2}{n}$$

$$= 400 - \frac{(40)^2}{5} = 80$$

Note that these are the same values shown in part (a)

d. $r = \sqrt{.845} = +.9192$

18. a. $\Sigma x_i = 19.2, \Sigma y_i = 12,900, \Sigma x_i y_i = 41,710$
$\Sigma x_i^2 = 62.18, \Sigma y_i^2 = 28,070,000$

$$\text{SST} = \Sigma y_i^2 - \frac{(\Sigma y_i)^2}{n}$$

$$= 28,070,000 - \frac{(12,900)^2}{6} = 335,000$$

$$\text{SSR} = \frac{[\Sigma x_i y_i - (\Sigma x_i \Sigma y_i)/n]^2}{\Sigma x_i^2 - (\Sigma x_i)^2/n}$$

$$= \frac{[41,710 - (19.2)(12,900)/6]^2}{62.18 - (19.2)^2/6} = 249,865$$

$$\text{SSE} = \text{SST} - \text{SSR} = 335,000 - 249,865$$

$$= 85,135$$

b. $r^2 = \dfrac{\text{SSR}}{\text{SST}} = \dfrac{249,865}{335,000} = .746$

The least squares line accounted for 74.6% of the total sum of squares

c. $r = \sqrt{.746} = +.8637$

23. a. $s^2 = \text{MSE} = \dfrac{\text{SSE}}{n-2} = \dfrac{12.4}{3} = 4.133$

b. $s = \sqrt{\text{MSE}} = \sqrt{4.133} = 2.033$

c. $\Sigma x_i = 15, \Sigma x_i^2 = 55$

$$s_{b_1} = \frac{s}{\sqrt{\Sigma x_i^2 - (\Sigma x_i)^2/n}}$$

$$= \frac{2.033}{\sqrt{55 - (15)^2/5}} = .643$$

d. $t = \dfrac{b_1 - \beta_1}{s_{b_1}} = \dfrac{2.6 - 0}{.643} = 4.04$

$t_{.025} = 3.182$ (3 degrees of freedom)
Since $t = 4.04 > t_{.05} = 3.182$, we reject $H_0: \beta_1 = 0$

e. $\text{MSR} = \dfrac{\text{SSR}}{1} = 67.6$

$$F = \frac{\text{MSR}}{\text{MSE}} = \frac{67.6}{4.133} = 16.36$$

$F_{.05} = 10.13$ (1 degree of freedom numerator and 3 denominator)
Since $F = 16.36 > F_{.05} = 10.13$, we reject $H_0: \beta_1 = 0$

Source of Variation	Sum of Squares	Degrees of Freedom	Mean Square	F
Regression	67.6	1	67.6	16.36
Error	12.4	3	4.133	
Total	80	4		

26. a. $s^2 = \text{MSE} = \dfrac{\text{SSE}}{n-2} = \dfrac{85,135.14}{4} = 21,283.79$

$$s = \sqrt{\text{MSE}} = \sqrt{21,283.79} = 145.89$$

$$\Sigma x_i = 19.2, \Sigma x_i^2 = 62.18$$

$$s_{b_1} = \frac{s}{\sqrt{\Sigma x_i^2 - (\Sigma x_i)^2/n}}$$

$$= \frac{145.89}{\sqrt{62.18 - (19.2)^2/6}} = 169.59$$

$$t = \frac{b_1 - \beta_1}{s_{b_1}} = \frac{581.08 - 0}{169.59} = 3.43$$

$t_{.025} = 2.776$ (4 degrees of freedom)

Since $t = 3.43 > t_{.025} = 2.776$, we reject $H_0: \beta_1 = 0$

b. $\text{MSR} = \dfrac{\text{SSR}}{1} = \dfrac{249,864.86}{1} = 249,864.86$

$$F = \frac{\text{MSR}}{\text{MSE}} = \frac{249,864.86}{21,283.79} = 11.74$$

$F_{.05} = 7.71$ (1 degree of freedom numerator and 4 denominator)

Since $F = 11.74 > F_{.05} = 7.71$, we reject $H_0: \beta_1 = 0$

c.

Source of Variation	Sum of Squares	Degrees of Freedom	Mean Square	F
Regression	1543.84	1	1543.84	48.17
Error	96.16	3	32.05	
Total	1640.00	4		

32. a. $s = 2.033$

$\Sigma x_i = 15, \quad \Sigma x_i^2 = 55$

$$s_{\hat{y}_p} = s\sqrt{\frac{1}{n} + \frac{(x_p - \bar{x})^2}{\Sigma x_i^2 - (\Sigma x_i)^2/n}}$$

$$= 2.033\sqrt{\frac{1}{5} + \frac{(4-3)^2}{55 - (15)^2/5}} = 1.11$$

b. $\hat{y} = .2 + 2.6x = .2 + 2.6(4) = 10.6$

$\hat{y}_p \pm t_{\alpha/2}s_{\hat{y}_p}$

$10.6 \pm 3.182(1.11)$

10.6 ± 3.53 or 7.07 to 14.13

c. $s_{ind} = s\sqrt{1 + \frac{1}{n} + \frac{(x_p - \bar{x})^2}{\Sigma x_i^2 - (\Sigma x_i)^2/n}}$

$$= 2.033\sqrt{1 + \frac{1}{5} + \frac{(4-3)^2}{55 - (15)^2/5}} = 2.32$$

d. $\hat{y}_p \pm t_{\alpha/2}s_{ind}$

$10.6 \pm 3.182(2.32)$

10.6 ± 7.38 or 3.22 to 17.98

35. a. $s = 145.89, \quad \Sigma x_i = 19.2, \quad \Sigma x_i^2 = 62.18$

$\hat{y} = 290.54 + 581.08x = 290.54 + 581.08(3)$

$= 2033.78$

$$s_{\hat{y}_p} = s\sqrt{\frac{1}{n} + \frac{(x_p - \bar{x})^2}{\Sigma x_i^2 - (\Sigma x_i)^2/n}}$$

$$= 145.89\sqrt{\frac{1}{6} + \frac{(3-3.2)^2}{62.18 - (19.2)^2/6}} = 68.54$$

$\hat{y}_p \pm t_{\alpha/2}s_{\hat{y}_p}$

$2033.78 \pm 2.776(68.54)$

2033.78 ± 190.27 or 1843.51 to 2224.05

b. $\hat{y} = 290.54 + 581.08x = 290.54 + 581.08(3)$

$= 2033.78$

$$s_{ind} = s\sqrt{1 + \frac{1}{n} + \frac{(x_p - \bar{x})^2}{\Sigma x_i^2 - (\Sigma x_i)^2/n}}$$

$$= 145.89\sqrt{1 + \frac{1}{6} + \frac{(3-3.2)^2}{62.18 - (19.2)^2/6}} = 161.19$$

$\hat{y}_p \pm t_{\alpha/2}s_{ind}$

$2033.78 \pm 2.776(161.19)$

2033.78 ± 447.46 or 1586.32 to 2481.24

40. a. 9

b. $\hat{y} = 20.0 + 7.21x$

c. 1.3626

d. $SSE = SST - SSR = 51{,}984.1 - 41{,}587.3 = 10{,}396.8$

$MSE = 10{,}396.8/7 = 1485.3$

$$F = \frac{MSR}{MSE} = \frac{41{,}587.3}{1485.3} = 28.0$$

$F_{.05} = 5.59$ (1 degree of freedom numerator and 7 denominator)

Since $F = 28 > F_{.05} = 5.59$, we reject $H_0: \beta_1 = 0$

e. $\hat{y} = 20.0 + 7.21(50) = 380.5$ or $\$380{,}500$

45. a. $\Sigma x_i = 70, \Sigma y_i = 76, \Sigma x_i y_i = 1264, \Sigma x_i^2 = 1106$

$$b_1 = \frac{\Sigma x_i y_i - (\Sigma x_i \Sigma y_i)/n}{\Sigma x_i^2 - (\Sigma x_i)^2/n}$$

$$= \frac{1264 - (70)(65)/5}{1106 - (70)^2/5} = 1.5873$$

$b_0 = \bar{y} - b_1\bar{x}$

$= 15.2 - 1.5873(14) = -7.0222$

$\hat{y} = -7.02 + 1.59x$

b.

x_i	y_i	$\hat{y}_i$	$y_i - \hat{y}_i$
6	6	2.52	3.48
11	8	10.47	-2.47
15	12	16.83	-4.83
18	20	21.60	-1.60
20	30	24.78	5.22

c. $y - \hat{y}$

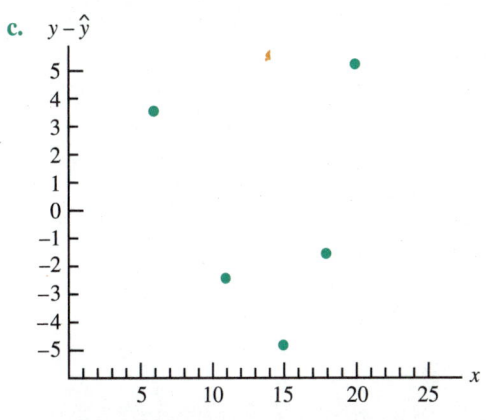

With only five observations, it is difficult to determine whether the assumptions are satisfied; however, the plot does suggest curvature in the residuals, which would indicate that the error term assumptions are not satisfied; the scatter diagram for these data also indicates that the underlying relationship between x and y may be curvilinear

d. $s^2 = 23.78$

$$h_i = \frac{1}{n} + \frac{(x_i - \bar{x})^2}{\Sigma x_i^2 - (\Sigma x_i)^2/n}$$

$$= \frac{1}{5} + \frac{(x_i - 14)^2}{1106 - (70)^2/5} = \frac{1}{5} + \frac{(x_i - 14)^2}{126}$$

x_i	h_i	$s_{y_i - \hat{y}_i}$	$y_i - \hat{y}_i$	Standardized Residuals
6	.7079	2.64	3.48	1.32
11	.2714	4.16	−2.47	−.59
15	.2079	4.34	−4.83	−1.11
18	.3270	4.00	−1.60	−.40
20	.4857	3.50	5.22	1.49

e. The plot of the standardized residuals against $\hat{y}$ has the same shape as the original residual plot; as stated in part (c), the curvature observed indicates that the assumptions regarding the error term may not be satisfied

47. $\Sigma x_i = 57$, $\Sigma y_i = 294$, $\Sigma x_i y_i = 2841$,

$\Sigma x_i^2 = 753$, $\Sigma y_i^2 = 13{,}350$

$$b_1 = \frac{\Sigma x_i y_i - (\Sigma x_i \Sigma y_i)/n}{\Sigma x_i^2 - (\Sigma x_i)^2/n}$$

$$= \frac{2841 - (57)(294)/7}{753 - (57)^2/7} = 1.5475$$

$b_0 = \bar{y} - b_1 \bar{x}$

$\quad = 42 - (1.5475)(8.1492) = 29.3989$

$\hat{y} = 29.40 + 1.55x$

b. From Exercise 19 we have SSR = 691.72 and SST = 1002; therefore SSE = 1002 − 691.72 = 310.28

$$F = \frac{MSR}{MSE} = \frac{691.72}{310.28/5} = 11.15$$

$F_{.05} = 6.61$ (1 degree of freedom numerator and 5 denominator)

Since $F = 11.47 > F_{.05} = 6.61$, we reject H_0: $\beta_1 = 0$; the relationship is significant at the .05 level

c.

x_i	y_i	$\hat{y}_i = 29.40 + 1.55x_i$	$y_i - \hat{y}_i$
1	19	30.95	−11.95
2	32	32.50	−.50
4	44	35.60	8.40
6	40	38.70	1.30
10	52	44.90	7.10
14	53	51.10	1.90
20	54	60.40	−6.40

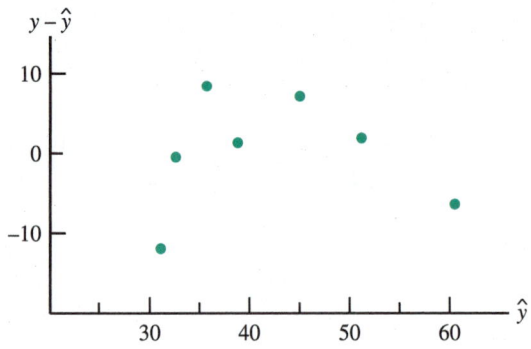

d. The residual plot leads us to question the assumption of a linear relationship between x and y; even though the relationship is significant at the $\alpha = .05$ level, it would be extremely dangerous to extrapolate beyond the range of the data (e.g., $x > 20$)

50. a. Using Minitab, we obtained the estimated regression equation $\hat{y} = 66.1 + .4023x$; a portion of the Minitab output is shown in Figure F14.50a

The fitted values and standardized residuals are shown below:

x_i	y_i	$\hat{y}_i$	Standardized Residuals
135	145	120.41	2.11
110	100	110.35	−1.08
130	120	118.40	.14
145	120	124.43	−.38
175	130	136.50	−.78
160	130	130.47	−.04
120	110	114.38	−.41

FIGURE F14.50a

```
The regression equation is
Y = 66.1 + 0.402 X

Predictor        Coef       Stdev      t-ratio         p
Constant        66.10       32.06         2.06     0.094
X              0.4023      0.2276         1.77     0.137

s = 12.62      R-sq = 38.5%      R-sq(adj) = 26.1%

Analysis of Variance

SOURCE          DF          SS          MS          F          p
Regression       1       497.2       497.2       3.12      0.137
Error            5       795.7       159.1
Total            6      1292.9

Unusual Observations
Obs.       X          Y       Fit Stdev.Fit   Residual    St.Resid
  1      135     145.00    120.42      4.87      24.58       2.11R
```

FIGURE F14.52b

```
The regression equation is
Y = -0.230 + 0.0490 X

Predictor        Coef       Stdev      t-ratio         p
Constant      -0.2303      0.1138        -2.02     0.078
X            0.048987    0.002769        17.69     0.000

s = 0.1086      R-sq = 97.5%      R-sq(adj) = 97.2%

Analysis of Variance

SOURCE          DF          SS          MS          F          p
Regression       1      3.6946      3.6946     313.04     0.000
Error            8      0.0944      0.0118
Total            9      3.7890

Unusual Observations
Obs.       X          Y       Fit Stdev.Fit   Residual    St.Resid
 10      67.0    3.0000    3.0518    0.0843     -0.0518      -0.76 X
```

b. Standardized
   Residuals

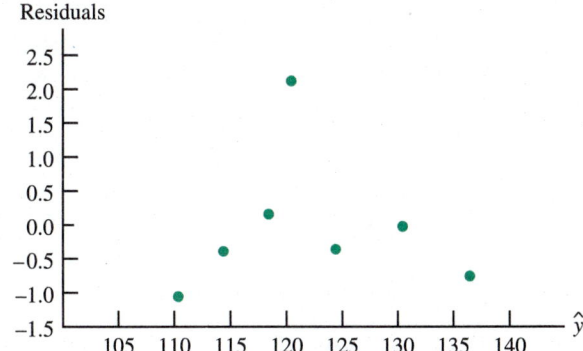

The standardized residual plot indicates that the observation $x = 135$, $y = 145$ may be an outlier; note that this observation has a standardized residual of 2.11

c. The scatter diagram is shown below:

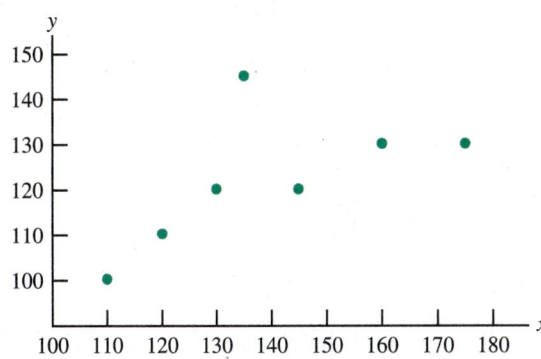

The scatter diagram also indicates that the observation $x = 135$, $y = 145$ may be an outlier; the implication is that for simple linear regression outliers can be identified by looking at the scatter diagram

FIGURE F15.5a

```
The regression equation is
REVENUE = 88.6 + 1.60 TVADV

Predictor      Coef       Stdev      t-ratio        p
Constant       88.638     1.582      56.02      0.000
TVADV          1.6039     0.4778      3.36      0.015

s = 1.215      R-sq = 65.3%      R-sq(adj) = 59.5%

Analysis of Variance

SOURCE         DF        SS         MS          F         p
Regression     1      16.640     16.640      11.27     0.015
Error          6       8.860      1.477
Total          7      25.500
```

FIGURE F15.5b

```
The regression equation is
REVENUE = 83.2 + 2.29 TVADV + 1.30 NEWSADV

Predictor      Coef       Stdev      t-ratio        p
Constant       83.230     1.574      52.88      0.000
TVADV          2.2902     0.3041      7.53      0.001
NEWSADV        1.3010     0.3207      4.06      0.010

s = 0.6426     R-sq = 91.9%      R-sq(adj) = 88.7%

Analysis of Variance

SOURCE         DF        SS         MS          F         p
Regression     2      23.435     11.718      28.38     0.002
Error          5       2.065      0.413
Total          7      25.500
```

52. a. Using Minitab, we obtained the estimated regression equation $\hat{y} = -.23 + .049x$

b. A portion of the Minitab output is shown in Figure F14.52b.
Note that Minitab identifies observation 10 as an influential observation; the standardized residual plot for these data also shows a very unusual trend in the residuals, an indication that the assumptions for ϵ may not be satisfied for these data

Chapter 15

2. a. The estimated regression equation is

$$\hat{y} = 45.06 + 1.94x_1$$

An estimate of y when $x_1 = 45$ is

$$\hat{y} = 45.06 + 1.94(45) = 132.36$$

b. The estimated regression equation is

$$\hat{y} = 85.22 + 4.32x_2$$

An estimate of y when $x_2 = 15$ is

$$\hat{y} = 85.22 + 4.32(15) = 150.02$$

c. The estimated regression equation is

$$\hat{y} = -18.37 + 2.01x_1 + 4.74x_2$$

An estimate of y when $x_1 = 45$ and $x_2 = 15$ is

$$\hat{y} = -18.37 + 2.01(45) + 4.74(15) = 143.18$$

5. a. The Minitab output is shown in Figure F15.5a
b. The Minitab output is shown in Figure F15.5b
c. It is 1.60 in (a) and 2.29 in (b). In (a) the coefficient is an estimate of the change in revenue due to a one-unit change in television advertising expenditures. In (b) it represents an estimate of the change in revenue due to a one unit change in television advertising expenditures when the amount of newspaper advertising is held constant.
d. Revenue $= 83.2 + 2.29(3.5) + 1.30(1.8) = 93.56$ or $\$93,560$.

12. a. $R^2 = \dfrac{SSR}{SST} = \dfrac{14{,}052.2}{15{,}182.9} = .926$

b. $R_a^2 = 1 - (1 - R^2)\dfrac{n-1}{n-p-1}$

$$= 1 - (1 - -.926)\dfrac{10-1}{10-2-1} = .905$$

c. Yes; after adjusting for the number of independent variables in the model, we see that 90.5% of the variability in y has been accounted for

FIGURE F15.39a

```
The regression equation is
Y = 0.20 + 2.60 X

Predictor        Coef        Stdev      t-ratio         p
Constant        0.200        2.132         0.09       0.931
X               2.6000       0.6429        4.04       0.027

s = 2.033          R-sq = 84.5%       R-sq(adj) = 79.3%

Analysis of Variance

SOURCE          DF           SS           MS          F          p
Regression       1        67.600       67.600      16.35      0.027
Error            3        12.400        4.133
Total            4        80.000
```

15. a. $R^2 = \dfrac{SSR}{SST} = \dfrac{23.435}{25.5} = .919$

$R_a^2 = 1 - (1 - R^2)\dfrac{n-1}{n-p-1}$

$= 1 - -(1 - .919)\dfrac{8-1}{8-2-1} = .887$

b. Multiple regression analysis is preferred since both R^2 and R_a^2 show an increased percentage of the variability of y explained when both independent variables are used

19. a. $MSR = \dfrac{SSR}{p} = \dfrac{6216.375}{2} = 3108.188$

$MSE = \dfrac{SSE}{n-p-1} = \dfrac{507.75}{10-2-1} = 72.536$

b. $F = \dfrac{MSR}{MSE} = \dfrac{3108.188}{72.536} = 42.85$

$F_{.05} = 4.74$ (2 degrees of freedom numerator and 7 denominator)

Since $F = 42.85 > F_{.05} = 4.74$, the overall model is significant

c. $t = \dfrac{b_1}{s_{b_1}} = \dfrac{.5906}{.0813} = 7.26$

$t_{.025} = 2.365$ (7 degrees of freedom)

Since $t = 7.26 > t_{.025} = 2.365$, β_1 is significant

d. $t = \dfrac{b_2}{s_{b_2}} = \dfrac{.4980}{.0567} = 8.78$

Since $t = 8.78 > t_{.025} = 2.365$, β_2 is significant

23. a. $F = 28.38$

$F_{.01} = 13.27$ (2 degrees of freedom numerator and 1 denominator)

Since $F > F_{.01} = 13.27$, reject H_0.

Alternatively, the p-value of .002 leads to the same conclusion.

b. $t = 7.53$

$t_{.025} = 2.571$

Since $t > t_{.025} = 2.571$, β_1 is significant and x_1 should not be dropped from the model.

c. $t = 4.06$

$t_{.025} = 2.571$

Since $t > t_{.025} = 2.571$, β_2 is significant and x_2 should not be dropped from the model.

28. a. Using Minitab, the 95% confidence interval is 132.16 to 154.15

b. Using Minitab, the 95% prediction interval is 111.15 to 175.17

29. a. See Minitab output in Figure F15.5b.

$\hat{y} = 83.230 + 2.2902(3.5) + 1.3010(1.8) = 93.588$

or \$93,588

b. Using Minitab: 92.840 to 94.335 or \$92,840 to \$94,335

c. Using Minitab: 91.774 to 95.401 or \$91,774 to \$95,401

32. a. $E(y) = \beta_0 + \beta_1 x_1 + \beta_2 x_2$

where $x_2 = \begin{cases} 0 \text{ if level 1} \\ 1 \text{ if level 2} \end{cases}$

b. $E(y) = \beta_0 + \beta_1 x_1 + \beta_2(0) = \beta_0 + \beta_1 x_1$

c. $E(y) = \beta_0 + \beta_1 x_1 + \beta_2(1) = \beta_0 + \beta_1 x_1 + \beta_2$

d. $\beta_2 = E(y \mid \text{level 2}) - E(y \mid \text{level 1})$

β_1 is the change in $E(y)$ for a 1-unit change in x_1 holding x_2 constant

34. a. \$15,300, since $b_3 = 15.3$

b. $\hat{y} = 10.1 - 4.2(2) + 6.8(8) + 15.3(0)$

$= 10.1 - 8.4 + 54.4$

$= 56.1$

Sales prediction: \$56,100

c. $\hat{y} = 10.1 - 4.2(1) + 6.8(3) + 15.3(1)$

$= 10.1 - 4.2 + 20.4 + 15.3$

$= 41.6$

Sales prediction: \$41,600

39. a. The Minitab output is shown in Figure F15.39a.

b. Using Minitab, we obtained the following values:

x_i	y_i	$\hat{y}_i$	Standardized Residual
1	3	2.8	.16
2	7	5.4	.94
3	5	8.0	−1.65
4	11	10.6	.24
5	14	13.2	.62

$\hat{y}_i$	Standardized Residual	$\hat{y}_i$	Standardized Residual
96.63	−1.62	94.39	1.10
90.41	−1.08	94.24	−.40
94.34	1.22	94.42	−1.12
92.21	−.37	93.35	1.08

Standardized Residuals

Standardized Residuals

The point (3,5) does not appear to follow the trend of the remaining data; however, the value of the standardized residual for this point, −1.65, is not large enough for us to conclude that (3,5) is an outlier

c. Using Minitab, we obtained the following values:

x_i	y_i	Studentized Deleted Residual
1	3	.13
2	7	.92
3	5	−4.42
4	11	.19
5	14	.54

$t_{.025} = 4.303$ ($n − p − 2 = 5 − 1 − 2 = 2$ degrees of freedom)

Since the studentized deleted residual for (3,5) is $−4.42 < −4.303$, we conclude that the 3rd observation is an outlier

41. a. The Minitab output appears in Figure F15.6a; the estimated regression equation is

$$\text{REVENUE} = 83.2 + 2.29 \text{ TVADV} + 1.30 \text{ NEWSADV}$$

b. Using Minitab, we obtained the following values:

With relatively few observations, it is difficult to determine if any of the assumptions regarding ϵ have been violated; for instance, an argument could be made that there does not appear to be any pattern in the plot; alternatively, an argument could be made that there is a curvilinear pattern in the plot

c. The values of the standardized residuals are greater than $−2$ and less than $+2$; thus, using this test, there are no outliers

As a further check for outliers, we used Minitab to compute the following studentized deleted residuals:

Observation	Studentized Deleted Residual	Observation	Studentized Deleted Residual
1	−2.11	5	1.13
2	−1.10	6	−.36
3	1.31	7	−1.16
4	−.33	8	1.10

$t_{.025} = 2.776$ ($n − p − 2 = 8 − 2 − 2 = 4$ degrees of freedom)

Since none of the studentized deleted residuals is less than $−2.776$ or greater than 2.776, we conclude that there are no outliers in the data

d. Using Minitab, we obtained the following values:

Observation	h_i	D_i
1	.63	1.52
2	.65	.70
3	.30	.22
4	.23	.01
5	.26	.14
6	.14	.01
7	.66	.81
8	.13	.06

The critical leverage value is

$$\frac{3(p+1)}{n} = \frac{3(2+1)}{8} = 1.125$$

Since none of the values exceed 1.125, we conclude that there are no influential observations

However, using Cook's distance measure, we see that $D_1 > 1$ (rule of thumb critical value); thus, we conclude that the first observation is influential

Final conclusion: observation 1 is an influential observation

Chapter 16

1. **a.** The Minitab output is shown in Figure F16.1a
   b. Since the *p*-value corresponding to $F = 6.85$ is $.059 > \alpha = .05$, the relationship is not significant
   c.

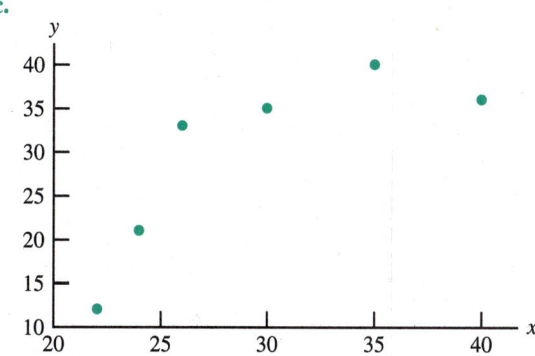

The scatter diagram suggests that a curvilinear relationship may be appropriate
   d. The Minitab output is shown in Figure F16.1d
   e. Since the *p*-value corresponding to $F = 25.68$ is $.013 < \alpha = .05$, the relationship is significant

FIGURE F16.1a

```
The regression equation is
Y = - 6.8 + 1.23 X

Predictor      Coef      Stdev    t-ratio       p
Constant      -6.77      14.17      -0.48    0.658
X            1.2296     0.4697       2.62    0.059

s = 7.269      R-sq = 63.1%     R-sq(adj) = 53.9%

Analysis of Variance

SOURCE        DF         SS         MS        F       p
Regression     1     362.13     362.13     6.85   0.059
Error          4     211.37      52.84
Total          5     573.50
```

FIGURE F16.1d

```
The regression equation is
Y = - 169 + 12.2 X - 0.177 XSQ

Predictor       Coef      Stdev    t-ratio       p
Constant     -168.88      39.79      -4.24    0.024
X             12.187      2.663       4.58    0.020
XSQ         -0.17704    0.04290      -4.13    0.026

s = 3.248      R-sq = 94.5%     R-sq(adj) = 90.8%

Analysis of Variance

SOURCE        DF         SS         MS        F       p
Regression     2     541.85     270.92    25.68   0.013
Error          3      31.65      10.55
Total          5     573.50
```

FIGURE F16.5a

```
The regression equation is
Y = 433 + 37.4 X -0.383 XSQ

Predictor       Coef       Stdev     t-ratio        p
Constant       432.6       141.2        3.06     0.055
X             37.429       7.807        4.79     0.017
XSQ          -0.3829      0.1036       -3.70     0.034

s = 15.83      R-sq = 98.0%      R-sq(adj) = 96.7%

Analysis of Variance

SOURCE         DF          SS          MS         F         p
Regression      2       36643       18322     73.15     0.003
Error           3         751         250
Total           5       37395
```

FIGURE F16.5C

```
     Fit    Stdev.Fit           95% C.I.                95% P.I.
  1302.01        9.93   (1270.41, 1333.61)    (1242.55, 1361.47)
```

FIGURE F16.12A

```
The regression equation is
POINTS = 170 + 6.61 TEAMINT

Predictor       Coef       Stdev     t-ratio        p
Constant      170.13       44.02        3.86     0.002
TEAMINT        6.613       2.258        2.93     0.013

s = 43.93      R-sq = 41.7%      R-sq(adj) = 36.8%

Analysis of Variance

SOURCE         DF          SS          MS         F         p
Regression      1       16546       16546      8.57     0.013
Error          12       23157        1930
Total          13       39703

Unusual Observations
Obs. TEAMINT     POINTS      Fit Stdev.Fit  Residual    St.Resid
 13     33.0      340.0    388.4      34.2     -48.4       -1.75 X

X denotes an obs. whose X value gives it large influence.
```

f. $\hat{y} = -168.88 + 12.187(25) - .17704(25)^2 = 25.145$

5. a. The Minitab output is shown in Figure F16.5a

b. Since the relationship between x and y was significant in Exercise 4, the relationship which includes x^2 must also be significant; looking at the p-value, we see that $.003 < .01$, and thus we would reject H_0: $\beta_1 = \beta_2 = 0$

c. See Figure F16.5c

11. a. SSE = $1805 - 1760 = 45$

$$F = \frac{MSR}{MSE} = \left(\frac{1760/4}{45/25}\right) = 244.44$$

$F_{.05} = 2.76$ (4 degrees of freedom numerator and 25 denominator)

Since $244.44 > 2.76$, reject H_0, and conclude that the relationship is significant

b. SSE$(x_1, x_2, x_3, x_4) = 45$

c. SSE$(x_2, x_3) = 1805 - 1705 = 100$

d. $F = \dfrac{(100 - 45)/2}{1.8} = 15.28$ $F_{.05} = 3.39$

Since $F = 15.28 > 3.39$, x_1 and x_2 are significant

12. a. The Minitab output is shown in Figure F16.12a

b. The Minitab output is shown in Figure F16.12b

c. $F = \dfrac{[SSE(\text{reduced}) - SSE(\text{full})]/(\text{\# extra terms})}{MSE(\text{full})}$

FIGURE F16.12b

```
The regression equation is
POINTS = 280 + 5.18 TEAMINT - 0.0037 RUSHING - 3.92 OPPONINT


Predictor        Coef       Stdev     t-ratio        p
Constant       280.34       81.42        3.44    0.006
TEAMINT         5.176        2.073       2.50    0.032
RUSHING        -0.00373      0.03336    -0.11    0.913
OPPONINT       -3.918        1.651      -2.37    0.039


s = 37.84       R-sq = 63.9%      R-sq(adj) = 53.1%

Analysis of Variance

SOURCE         DF          SS          MS          F        p
Regression      3        25386        8462       5.91    0.014
Error          10        14317        1432
Total          13        39703


SOURCE         DF        SEQ SS
Regression      1        16546
Error           1          776
Total           1         8064
```

FIGURE F16.12c

```
The regression equation is
POINTS = 274 + 5.23 TEAMINT - 3.96 OPPONINT


Predictor        Coef       Stdev     t-ratio        p
Constant       273.77       53.81        5.09    0.000
TEAMINT         5.227        1.931       2.71    0.020
OPPONINT       -3.965        1.524      -2.60    0.025


s = 36.10       R-sq = 63.9%      R-sq(adj) = 57.3%

Analysis of Variance

SOURCE         DF          SS          MS          F        p
Regression      2        25386       12684       9.73    0.004
Error          11        14335        1303
Total          13        39703


SOURCE         DF        SEQ SS
TEAMINT         1        16546
OPPONINT        1         8822
```

$$= \frac{(23{,}157 - 14{,}317)/2}{1432} = 3.09$$

$F_{.05} = 4.10$ (2 degrees of freedom numerator and 10 denominator)

Since $F = 3.09 < F_{.05} = 4.10$, the addition of the two independent variables is not significant

Note: Suppose that we consider adding only the number of interceptions made by the opponents; the corresponding Minitab output is shown in Figure F16.12c; in this case,

$$F = \frac{(23{,}157 - 14{,}335)/1}{1303} = 6.77$$

$F_{.05} = 4.84$ (1 degree of freedom numerator and 11 denominator)

Since $F = 6.77 > F_{.05} = 4.84$, the addition of the number of interceptions made by the opponents is significant

15. **a.** The Minitab output is shown in Figure F16.15a

   b. Stepwise procedure (see Figure F16.15b)

   c. Backward elimination procedure (see Figure F16.15c)

   d. Best subsets regression (see Figure F16.15d)

FIGURE F16.15a

```
The regression equation is
%COLLEGE = -26.6 + 0.0970 SATSCORE

Predictor       Coef       Stdev     t-ratio        p
Constant       -26.61      37.22      -0.72       0.485
SATSCORE       0.09703     0.03734     2.60       0.019

s = 12.83      R-sq = 29.7%      R-sq(adj) = 25.3%

Analysis of Variance

SOURCE        DF       SS          MS         F         p
Regression     1      1110.8     1110.8      6.75      0.019
Error         16      2632.3      164.5
Total         17      3743.1
```

FIGURE F16.15b

```
STEP              1          2
CONSTANT        -26.61     -26.93

SATSCORE         0.097      0.084
t-RATIO          2.60       2.46

%TAKESAT                    0.204
t-RATIO                     2.21

s               12.8       11.5
R-sq            29.68      46.93
```

FIGURE F16.15c

```
STEP              1          2          3          4
CONSTANT        33.71      17.46     -32.47     -26.93

SIZE            -1.56      -1.39
t-RATIO         -1.43      -1.42

STUDENT$       -0.0024    -0.0026    -0.0019
t-RATIO         -1.47      -1.75      -1.31

SALARY         -0.00026
t-RATIO         -0.40

SATSCORE         0.077      0.081      0.095      0.084
t-RATIO          2.06       2.36       2.77       2.46

%TAKESAT         0.285      0.274      0.291      0.204
t-RATIO          2.47       2.53       2.60       2.21

s               11.2       10.9       11.2       11.5
R-sq            59.65      59.10      52.71      46.93
```

FIGURE F16.15d

		Adj.		S T U D S I Z E $	S A T A S L N A T R S	S T A S C O R R Y E	S % A T A K C E O A S R E T
Vars	R-sq	R-sq	S				
1	29.7	25.3	12.826			X	
1	25.5	20.8	13.203				X
2	46.9	39.9	11.508			X	X
2	38.2	30.0	12.417	X		X	
3	52.7	42.6	11.244		X	X	X
3	49.5	38.7	11.618	X		X	X
4	59.1	46.5	10.852	X	X	X	X
4	52.8	38.3	11.660		X X	X	X
5	59.6	42.8	11.219	X	X X	X	X

FIGURE F16.21a

```
The regression equation is
P/E = 6.51 + 0.569 %PROFIT

Predictor        Coef       Stdev      t-ratio         p
Constant        6.507       1.509        4.31      0.000
%PROFIT        0.5691      0.1281        4.44      0.000

s = 2.580      R-sq = 53.7%      R-sq(adj) = 51.0%

Analysis of Variance

SOURCE          DF          SS          MS          F         p
Regression       1      131.40      131.40      19.74     0.000
Error           17      113.14        6.66
Total           18      244.54
```

21. **a.** The Minitab output is shown in Figure F16.21a

b. Residual plot as a function of the order in which the data are presented is shown below; there does not appear to be any pattern indicative of positive autocorrelation

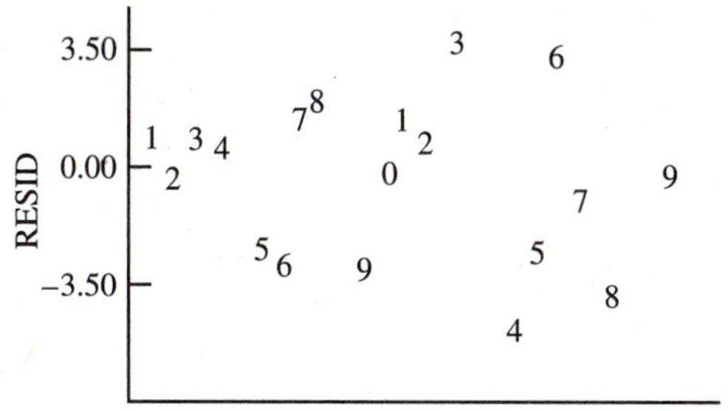

c. The Durban-Watson statistic (obtained from Minitab) is $d = 2.34$; at $\alpha = .05$, $d_L = 1.18$ and $d_U = 1.39$; since $d > d_U$, there is no significant positive autocorrelation

23.

x_1	x_2	x_3	Treatment
0	0	0	A
1	0	0	B
0	1	0	C
0	0	1	D

$E(y) = \beta_0 + \beta_1 x_1 + \beta_2 x_2 + \beta_3 x_3$

26. **a.**

D_1	D_2	Manufacturer
0	0	1
1	0	2
0	1	3

$E(y) = \beta_0 + \beta_1 D_1 + \beta_2 D_2$

b. See Figure F16.26b

c. $H_0: \beta_1 = \beta_2 = 0$

d. Since the p-value is $.004 < \alpha = .05$, we conclude that the mean time to mix a batch of material is not the same for each manufacturer

FIGURE F16.26b

```
The regression equation is
Time = 23.0 + 5.00 D1 - 2.00 D2

Predictor        Coef       Stdev     t-ratio        p
Constant       23.000       1.106      20.80      0.000
D1              5.000       1.563       3.20      0.011
D2             -2.000       1.563      -1.28      0.233

s = 2.211      R-sq = 70.3%      R-sq(adj) = 63.7%

Analysis of Variance

SOURCE        DF         SS         MS         F         p
Regression     2     104.000     52.000     10.64     0.004
Error          9      44.000      4.889
Total         11     148.000
```

Chapter 17

1. a.

Item	Price Relative
A	103=(7.75/7.50)
B	238=(1500/630)

b. $I_{1995} = \dfrac{7.75 + 1500.00}{7.50 + 630.00}(100) = \dfrac{1507.75}{637.50}(100) = 237$

c. $I_{1995} = \dfrac{7.75(1500) + 1500.00(2)}{7.50(1500) + 630.00(2)}(100)$

$= \dfrac{14,625.00}{12,510.00}(100) = 117$

d. $I_{1995} = \dfrac{7.75(1800) + 1500.00(1)}{7.50(1800) + 630.00(1)}(100)$

$= \dfrac{15,450.00}{14,130.00}(100) = 109$

3. a. Price relatives for $A = (6.00/5.45)100 = 110$
$B = (5.95/5.60)100 = 106$
$C = (6.20/5.50)100 = 113$

b. $I_{1995} = \dfrac{6.00 + 5.95 + 6.20}{5.45 + 5.60 + 5.50}(100) = 110$

c. $I_{1995} = \dfrac{6.00(150) + 5.95(200) + 6.20(120)}{5.45(150) + 5.60(200) + 5.50(120)}(100) = 109$

9% increase over the two year period.

6.

	Price	Base Period			Weighted
Item	Relative	Price	Usage	Weight	Price Relative
A	150	22.00	20	440	66,000
B	90	5.00	50	250	22,500
C	120	14.00	40	560	67,200
			Totals	1250	155,700

$I = \dfrac{155,700}{1250} = 125$

7. a. Price relatives for $A = (3.95/2.50)100 = 158$
$B = (9.90/8.75)100 = 113$
$C = (.95/.99)100 = 96$

b.

Item	Price Relative	Base Price	Quantity	Weight $P_{i0}Q_i$	Weighted Price Relative
A	158	2.50	25	62.5	9,875
B	113	8.75	15	131.3	14,837
C	96	.99	60	59.4	5,702
			Totals	253.2	30,414

$I = \dfrac{30414}{253.2} = 120$

Cost of raw materials is up 20% for the chemical

10. a. Deflated 1980 wages: $\dfrac{\$7.27}{82.4}(100) = \$8.82$

Deflated 1993 Wages: $\dfrac{\$11.76}{144.5}(100) = \$8.14$

b. $\dfrac{11.76}{7.27}(100) = 161.8$ The percentage increase in actual wages is 61.8%

c. $\dfrac{8.14}{8.82}(100) = 92.3$ The change in real wages is a decrease of 7.7%

14. $I_{1995} = \dfrac{300(18.00) + 400(4.90) + 850(15.00)}{350(18.00) + 220(4.90) + 730(15.00)}(100)$

$= \dfrac{20,110}{18,328}(100) = 110$

15. $I = \dfrac{95(1200) + 75(1800) + 50(2000) + 70(1500)}{120(1200) + 86(1800) + 35(2000) + 60(1500)}(100) = 99$

Quantities are down slightly

Chapter 18

1. a.

Week	Time Series Value	Forecast	Forecast Error	Squared Forecast Error
1	8			
2	13			
3	15			
4	17	12	5	25
5	16	15	1	1
6	9	16	−7	49
			Total	75

Forecast for week 7 is $(17 + 16 + 9)/3 = 14$

b. MSE = 75/3 = 25

c.

Week (t)	Time Series Value (Y_t)	Forecast F_t	Forecast Error $Y_t - F_t$	Squared Error $(Y_t - F_t)^2$
1	8			
2	13	8.00	5.00	25.00
3	15	9.00	6.00	36.00
4	17	10.20	6.80	46.24
5	16	11.56	4.44	19.71
6	9	12.45	−3.45	11.90
			Total	138.85

Forecast for week 7 is $.2(9) + .8(12.45) = 11.76$

d. For the $\alpha = .2$ exponential smoothing forecast

$$\text{MSE} = \frac{138.85}{5} = 27.77$$

Since the 3-week moving average has a smaller MSE, it appears to provide the better forecasts

e.

Week (t)	Time Series Value (Y_t)	Forecast F_t	Forecast Error $Y_t - F_t$	Squared Error $(Y_t - F_t)^2$
1	8			
2	13	8.0	5.0	25.00
3	15	10.0	5.0	25.00
4	17	12.0	5.0	25.00
5	16	14.0	2.0	4.00
6	9	14.8	−5.8	33.64
			Total	112.64

$$\text{MSE} = \frac{112.64}{5} = 22.53$$

A smoothing constant of .4 appears to provide the better forecasts; for week 7 the forecast using $\alpha = .4$ is $.4(9) + .6(14.8) = 12.48$

8. a.

Month	Time Series Value	3-Month Moving Average Forecast	(Error)^2	$\alpha = .2$ Forecast	(Error)^2
1	240				
2	350			240.00	12,100.00
3	230			262.00	1,024.00
4	260	273.33	177.69	255.60	19.36
5	280	280.00	0.00	256.48	553.19
6	320	256.67	4,010.69	261.18	3,459.79
7	220	286.67	4,444.89	272.95	2,803.70
8	310	273.33	1,344.69	262.36	2,269.57
9	240	283.33	1,877.49	271.89	1,016.97
10	310	256.67	2,844.09	265.51	1,979.36
11	240	286.67	2,178.09	274.41	1,184.05
12	230	263.33	1,110.89	267.53	1,408.50
		Totals	17,988.52		27,818.49

MSE (3-month) = 17,988.52/9 = 1998.72

MSE ($\alpha = .2$) = 27,818.49/11 = 2528.95

Based on the above MSE values, the 3-month moving average appears better; however, exponential smoothing was penalized by including month 2, which was difficult for any method to forecast. Using only the errors for months 4–12, the MSE for exponential smoothing is revised to

$$\text{MSE}(\alpha = .2) = 14,694.49/9 = 1632.72$$

Thus, exponential smoothing was better considering months 4–12

b. Using exponential smoothing,

$$F_{13} = \alpha Y_{12} + (1 - \alpha)F_{12}$$
$$= .20(230) + .80(267.53) = 260$$

12. $\Sigma t = 15$, $\Sigma t^2 = 55$, $\Sigma Y_t = 55$, $\Sigma t Y_t = 186$

$$b_1 = \frac{\Sigma t Y_t - (\Sigma t \, \Sigma Y_t)/n}{\Sigma t^2 - (\Sigma t)^2/n}$$

$$= \frac{186 - (15)(55)/5}{55 - (15)^2/5} = 2.1$$

$$b_0 = \overline{Y} - b_1 \bar{t} = 11 - 2.1(3) = 4.7$$

$$T_t = 4.7 + 2.1t$$

$$T_6 = 4.7 + 2.1(6) = 17.3$$

14. $\Sigma t = 15$, $\Sigma t^2 = 55$, $\Sigma Y_t = 66.9$, $\Sigma t Y_t = 222.1$

$$b_1 = \frac{\Sigma t Y_t - (\Sigma t \, \Sigma Y_t)/n}{\Sigma t^2 - (\Sigma t)^2/n}$$

$$= \frac{222.1 - (15)(66.9)/5}{55 - (15)^2/5} = 2.14$$

$b_0 = \overline{Y} - b_1\overline{t} = 13.38 - 2.14(3) = 6.96$

$T_t = 6.96 + 2.14t$

$T_6 = 6.96 + 2.14(6) = 19.8$ or 19.8 million
working couples

22. a.

Year	Quarter	Y_t	Four-Quarter Moving Average	Centered Moving Average
1	1	4		
	2	2		
			3.50	
	3	3		3.750
			4.00	
	4	5		4.125
			4.25	
2	1	6		4.500
			4.75	
	2	3		5.000
			5.25	
	3	5		5.375
			5.50	
	4	7		5.875
			6.25	
3	1	7		6.375
			6.50	
	2	6		6.625
			6.75	
	3	6		
	4	8		

b.

Year	Quarter	Y_t	Centered Moving Average	Seasonal—Irregular Component
1	1	4		
	2	2		
	3	3	3.750	.8000
	4	5	4.125	1.2121
2	1	6	4.500	1.3333
	2	3	5.000	.6000
	3	5	5.375	.9302
	4	7	5.875	1.1915
3	1	7	6.375	1.0980
	2	6	6.625	.9057
	3	6		
	4	8		

Quarter	Seasonal—Irregular Component Values	Seasonal Index
1	1.3333, 1.0980	1.2157
2	.6000, .9057	.7529
3	.8000, .9302	.8651
4	1.2121, 1.1915	1.2018
	Total	4.0355

Adjustment for seasonal index $= \dfrac{4}{4.0355} = .9912$

Quarter	Adjusted Seasonal Index
1	1.2050
2	.7463
3	.8575
4	1.1912

Chapter 19

1. Binomial probabilities for $n = 10, p = .50$

x	Probability	x	Probability
0	.0010	6	.2051
1	.0098	7	.1172
2	.0439	8	.0439
3	.1172	9	.0098
4	.2051	10	.0010
5	.2461		

$P(0) + P(1) = .0108$; Adding $P(2)$, exceeds .025 required in the tail; therefore, reject H_0 if the number of plus signs is less than 2 or greater than 8;
Number of plus signs is 7
Do not reject H_0; conclude that there is no indication that a difference exists

2. $n = 27$ cases in which a value different from 150 is obtained
Use normal approximation with $\mu = np = .5(27) = 13.5$ and $\sigma = \sqrt{.25n} = \sqrt{.25(27)} = 2.6$
Use $x = 22$ as the number of plus signs and obtain the following test statistic:

$$z = \frac{x - \mu}{\sigma} = \frac{22 - 13.5}{2.6} = 3.27$$

With $\alpha = .01$, we reject if $z > 2.33$;
Since $z = 3.27 > 2.33$, reject H_0 and, conclude the median is greater than 150

4. We need to determine the number of "better" responses and the number of "worse" responses; the sum of the two is the sample size used for the study

$$n = .34(1253) + .29(1253) = 789.4$$

Use the large-sample test using the normal distribution; this means the value of $n(n = 789.4$ above) need not be integer. Use

$$\mu = .5n = .5(789.4) = 394.7$$

$$\sigma = \sqrt{.25n} = \sqrt{.25(789.4)} = 14.05$$

Let: $p =$ proportion of adults who feel children will have a better future

$H_0: p \leq .50$

$H_a: p > .50$

$$x = .34(1253) = 426.0$$

$$z = \frac{x - \mu}{\sigma} = \frac{426.0 - 394.7}{14.05} = 2.23$$

With $\alpha = .05$, we reject if $z > 1.645$;
Since $z = 2.23 > 1.645$, reject H_0 and, conclude that more than half of the adults feel their children will have a better future

12. H_0: The populations are identical
    H_a: The populations are not identical

Additive			Absolute		Signed
1	2	Difference	Value	Rank	Rank
20.12	18.05	2.07	2.07	9	+9
23.56	21.77	1.79	1.79	7	+7
22.03	22.57	−.54	.54	3	−3
19.15	17.06	2.09	2.09	10	+10
21.23	21.22	.01	.01	1	+1
24.77	23.80	.97	.97	4	+4
16.16	17.20	−1.04	1.04	5	−5
18.55	14.98	3.57	3.57	12	+12
21.87	20.03	1.84	1.84	8	+8
24.23	21.15	3.08	3.08	11	+11
23.21	22.78	.43	.43	2	+2
25.02	23.70	1.32	1.32	6	+6
					$T = 62$

$\mu_T = 0$

$$\sigma_T = \sqrt{\frac{n(n + 1)(2n + 1)}{6}} = \sqrt{\frac{12(13)(25)}{6}} = 25.5$$

$$z = \frac{T - \mu_T}{\sigma_T} = \frac{62 - 0}{25.5} = 2.43$$

Two-tailed test; reject H_0 if $z < -1.96$ or $z > 1.96$
Since $z = 2.43 > 1.96$, reject H_0 and, conclude that there is a significant difference in the additives

13.

Without Relaxant	With Relaxant	Difference	Rank of Absolute Difference	Signed Rank
15	10	5	9	9
12	10	2	3	3
22	12	10	10	10
8	11	−3	6.5	−6.5
10	9	1	1	1
7	5	2	3	3
8	10	−2	3	−3
10	7	3	6.5	6.5
14	11	3	6.5	6.5
9	6	3	6.5	6.5
				$T = 36$

$\mu_T = 0$

$$\sigma_T = \sqrt{\frac{n(n + 1)(2n + 1)}{6}} = \sqrt{\frac{10(11)(21)}{6}} = 19.62$$

$$z = \frac{T - \mu_T}{\sigma_T} = \frac{36}{19.62} = 1.83$$

One-tailed test; reject H_0 if $z > 1.645$
Reject H_0; there is a significant difference in favor of the relaxant

18. Rank the combined samples and find rank sum for each sample; this is a small-sample test since $n_1 = 7$ and $n_2 = 9$

Additive 1		Additive 2	
MPG	Rank	MPG	Rank
17.3	2	18.7	8.5
18.4	6	17.8	4
19.1	10	21.3	15
16.7	1	21.0	14
18.2	5	22.1	16
18.6	7	18.7	8.5
17.5	3	19.8	11
	34	20.7	13
		20.2	12
			102

$T = 34$
With $\alpha = .05$, $n_1 = 7$, and $n_2 = 9$

$$T_L = 41 \text{ and } T_U = 7(7 + 9 + 1) - 41 = 78$$

Since $T = 34 < 41$, reject H_0; and, conclude that there is a significant difference in gasoline mileage

19. a. Rank the combined samples, and find rank sum for each sample; with $n_1 = 12$ and $n_2 = 12$, this is a large-sample case

H_0: There are no differences in the distribution of starting salaries

H_a: There is a difference between the distributions of starting salaries

We reject H_0 if $z < -1.96$ or $z > 1.96$

	Accounting		Finance	
	Salary	*Rank*	*Salary*	*Rank*
	28.8	20	26.3	13
	25.3	9	23.6	3
	26.2	11	25.0	7
	27.9	17.5	23.0	1
	27.0	15	27.9	17.5
	26.2	11	24.5	5
	28.1	19	29.0	21
	24.7	6	27.4	16
	25.2	8	23.5	2
	29.2	22	26.9	14
	29.7	24	26.2	11
	29.3	23	24.0	4
Totals	327.6	185.5	307.3	114.5

$\mu_T = \frac{1}{2}n_1(n_1 + n_2 + 1) = \frac{1}{2}12(12 + 12 + 1) = 150$

$\sigma_T = \sqrt{\frac{1}{12}n_1 n_2(n_1 + + n_2 + 1)} = \sqrt{\frac{1}{12}(12)(12)(25)} = 17.32$

$T = 185.5$

$z = \dfrac{T - \mu_T}{\sigma_T} = \dfrac{185.5 - 150}{17.32} = 2.05$

Since $z = 2.05 > 1.96$, reject H_0; and, conclude that there is a difference in starting salaries

26. Rankings:

	Product A	Product B	Product C
	4	11	7
	8	14	2
	10	15	1
	3	12	6
	9	13	5
Sums	34	65	21

$W = \dfrac{12}{(15)(16)}\left[\dfrac{(34)^2}{5} + \dfrac{(65)^2}{5} + \dfrac{(21)^2}{5}\right] - 3(16)$

$= 58.22 - 48 = 10.22$

$\chi^2_{.05} = 5.99147$ (2 degrees of freedom)

Reject H_0; and conclude the ratings for the products differ

28. Specialty rankings:

Surgery	Radiology	Obstetrics
16	17	7.5
10.5	2	1
18	12	3
7.5	15	14
6	5	4
10.5	13	9
Totals 68.5	64	38.5

$W = \dfrac{12}{(18)(19)}\left[\dfrac{(68.5)^2}{6} + \dfrac{(64)^2}{6} + \dfrac{(38.5)^2}{6}\right] - 3(19)$

$= 60.06 - 57 = 3.06$

$\chi^2_{.05} = 5.99147$ (2 degrees of freedom)

Since $3.06 \leq 5.99147$, do not reject H_0; for these three specialties, we cannot conclude that there are significant differences in salary

32. a. $\Sigma d_i^2 = 52$

$r_s = 1 - \dfrac{6\Sigma d_i^2}{n(n^2 - 1)} = 1 - \dfrac{6(52)}{10(99)} = .68$

b. $\sigma_{r_s} = \sqrt{\dfrac{1}{n-1}} = \sqrt{\dfrac{1}{9}} = .33$

$z = \dfrac{r_s - 0}{\sigma_{r_s}} = \dfrac{.68}{.33} = 2.06$

Reject H_0 if $z < -1.96$ or $z > 1.96$;

Since $z = 2.06 > 1.96$, reject H_0 and conclude that significant rank correlation exists

34. $\Sigma d_i^2 = 250$

$r_s = 1 - \dfrac{6\Sigma d_i^2}{n(n^2 - 1)} = 1 - \dfrac{6(250)}{11(120)} = -.136$

$\sigma_{r_s} = \sqrt{\dfrac{1}{n-1}} = \sqrt{\dfrac{1}{10}} = .32$

$z = \dfrac{r_s - 0}{\sigma_{r_s}} = \dfrac{-.136}{.32} = -.425$

Reject H_0 if $z < -1.96$ or $z > 1.96$; since $z = -.425$, do not reject H_0; we cannot conclude that there is a significant relationship between the rankings

Chapter 20

4. *R chart:*

UCL $= \bar{R}D_4 = 1.6(1.864) = 2.98$

LCL $= \bar{R}D_3 = 1.6(.136) = .22$

$\bar{x}$ *chart:*

UCL $= \bar{\bar{x}} + A_2\bar{R} = 28.5 + .373(1.6) = 29.10$

LCL $= \bar{\bar{x}} - A_2\bar{R} = 28.5 - .373(1.6) = 27.90$

10. $f(x) = \dfrac{n!}{x!(n-x)!} p^x(1-p)^{n-x}$

When $p = .02$, the probability of accepting the lot is

$$f(0) = \frac{25!}{0!(25-0)!}(.02)^0(1-.02)^{25} = .6035$$

When $p = .06$, the probability of accepting the lot is

$$f(0) = \frac{25!}{0!(25-0)!}(.06)^0(1-.06)^{25} = .2129$$

Chapter 21

1. a. $\bar{x} = 215$ is an estimate of the population mean

b. $s_{\bar{x}} = \dfrac{20}{\sqrt{50}}\sqrt{\dfrac{800-50}{800}} = 2.7386$

c. $215 \pm 2(2.7386)$ or 209.5228 to 220.4772

5. a. $\bar{x} = 48.842$ and $s = 8.1$

$$s_{\bar{x}} = \sqrt{\left(\frac{361-30}{361}\right)}\frac{8.1}{\sqrt{30}} = 1.416$$

Approximate 95% confidence interval:

$$48.842 \pm 2(1.416)$$

or

46.010 million to 51.674 billion

b. $\hat{X} = N\bar{x} = 361(48.842) = 17,632$

$s_{\hat{X}} = Ns_{\bar{x}} = 361(1.416) = 511.176$

Approximate 95% confidence interval:

$$17,632 \pm 2(511.176)$$

or

$16,610$ million to $18,654$ million

c. $\bar{p} = {}^{13}/_{30} = .4333$ and

$$s_{\bar{p}} = \sqrt{\left(\frac{361-30}{361}\right)\frac{(^{13}/_{30})(^{17}/_{30})}{29}} = .0881$$

Approximate 95% confidence interval:

$$.4333 \pm 2(.0881)$$

or

$.2571$ to $.6095$

This is a rather large interval; sample sizes must be rather large to obtain tight confidence intervals on a population proportion

7. a. Stratum *1*: $\bar{x}_1 = 138$
   Stratum *2*: $\bar{x}_2 = 103$
   Stratum *3*: $\bar{x}_3 = 210$

b. Stratum *1*

$$\bar{x}_1 = 138; \; s_{\bar{x}_1} = \left(\frac{30}{\sqrt{20}}\right)\sqrt{\frac{200-20}{200}} = 6.3640$$

Approximate 95% confidence interval:

$$138 \pm 2(6.3640)$$

or 125.272 to 150.728

Stratum *2*

$$\bar{x}_2 = 103; \; s_{\bar{x}_2} = \left(\frac{25}{\sqrt{30}}\right)\sqrt{\frac{250-30}{250}} = 4.2817$$

Approximate 95% confidence interval:

$$103 \pm 2(4.2817)$$

or 94.4366 to 111.5634

Stratum *3*

$$\bar{x}_3 = 210; \; s_{\bar{x}_3} = \left(\frac{50}{\sqrt{25}}\right)\sqrt{\frac{100-25}{100}} = 8.6603$$

Approximate 95% confidence interval:

$$210 \pm 2(8.6603)$$

or 192.6794 to 227.3206

c. $\bar{x}_{st} = \left(\dfrac{200}{550}\right)138 + \left(\dfrac{250}{550}\right)103 + \left(\dfrac{100}{550}\right)210$

$= 50.1818 + 46.8182 + 38.1818 = 135.1818$

$$s_{\bar{x}_{st}} = \sqrt{\left(\frac{1}{(550)^2}\right)\left(200(180)\frac{(30)^2}{20} + 250(220)\frac{(25)^2}{30} + 100(75)\frac{(50)^2}{25}\right)}$$

$$= \sqrt{\left(\frac{1}{(550)^2}\right)3,515,833.3} = 3.4092$$

Approximate 95% confidence interval:

$$135.1818 \pm 2(3.4092)$$

or 128.3634 to 142.0002

14. a. $\bar{x}_c = \dfrac{\Sigma x_i}{\Sigma M_i} = \dfrac{750}{50} = 15$

$\hat{X} = M\bar{x}_c = 300(15) = 4500$

$\bar{p}_c = \dfrac{\Sigma a_i}{\Sigma M_i} = \dfrac{15}{50} = .30$

b. $\Sigma(x_i - \bar{x}_c M_i)^2 = [95 - 15(7)]^2 + [325 - 15(18)]^2$

$+ [190 - 15(15)]^2 + [140 - 15(10)]^2$

$= (-10)^2 + (55)^2 + (-35)^2 + (-10)^2 = 4450$

$$s_{\bar{x}_c} = \sqrt{\left(\frac{25-4}{(25)(4)(12)^2}\right)\left(\frac{4450}{3}\right)} = 1.4708$$

$s_{\hat{X}} = Ms_{\bar{x}_c} = 300(1.4708) = 441.24$

$$\Sigma\,(a_i - \bar{p}_c M_i)^2 = [1 - .3(7)]^2 + [6 - .3(18)]^2$$
$$+ [6 - .3(15)]^2 + [2 - .3(10)]^2$$
$$= (-1.1)^2 + (.6)^2 + (1.5)^2 + (-1)^2 = 4.82$$

$$s_{\bar{p}_c} = \sqrt{\left(\frac{25-4}{(25)(4)(12)^2}\right)\left(\frac{4.82}{3}\right)} = .0484$$

c.

Approximate 95% confidence interval for population mean:

$$15 \pm 2(1.4708)$$

or 12.0584 to 17.9416

d.   **Approximate 95% confidence interval for population total:**

$$4500 \pm 2(441.24)$$

or 3617.52 to 5382.48

e.   **Approximate 95% confidence interval for population proportion:**

$$.30 \pm 2(.0484)$$

or .2032 to .3968

Chapter 22

1. $EV(d_1) = .65(250) + .15(100) + .20(25) = 182.5$
$EV(d_2) = .65(100) + .15(100) + .20(75) = 95$
The optimal decision is d_1

4. a. $EV(d_1) = .20(400) + .35(400) + .45(400) = 400$

$EV(d_2) = .20(100) + .35(600) + .45(600) = 500$

$EV(d_3) = .20(-300) + .35(300) + .45(900) = 450$

Recommended decison: d_2 (medium)

8. a. If s_1, then d_1; if s_2, then d_1 or d_2; if s_3, then d_2
b. $EVwPI = .65(250) + .15(100) + .20(75) = 192.5$
c. From the solution to Exercise 5, we know that $EV(d_1) = 182.5$ and $EV(d_2) = 95$; thus, the recommended decision is d_1; hence, $EVwoPI = 182.5$
d. $EVPI = EVwPI - EVwoPI$
$$= 192.5 - 182.5 = 10$$

11. Optimal decision with perfect information:
If s_1, then d_1
If s_2, then d_2
If s_3, then d_3
Expected value of this strategy is

$$.2(400) + .35(600) + .45(900) = 695$$

$EVPI = 695 - 500 = 195$

13.

State of Nature	$P(s_j)$	$P(I\mid s_j)$	$P(I \cap s_j)$	$P(s_j\mid I)$
s_1	.2	.10	.020	.1905
s_2	.5	.05	.025	.2381
s_3	.3	.20	.060	.5714
	1.0		$P(I) = .105$	1.0000

16. a. $EVSI = EVwSI - EVwoSI$
$$= 45,000 - 37,000 = \$8000$$

b. $E = \dfrac{EVSI}{EVPI} \times 100$

$$= \frac{8000}{60,000} \times 100 = 13.13\%$$

c. Since the cost required to obtain the sample information exceeds the expected value of the sample information, the study should not be conducted

18. a.

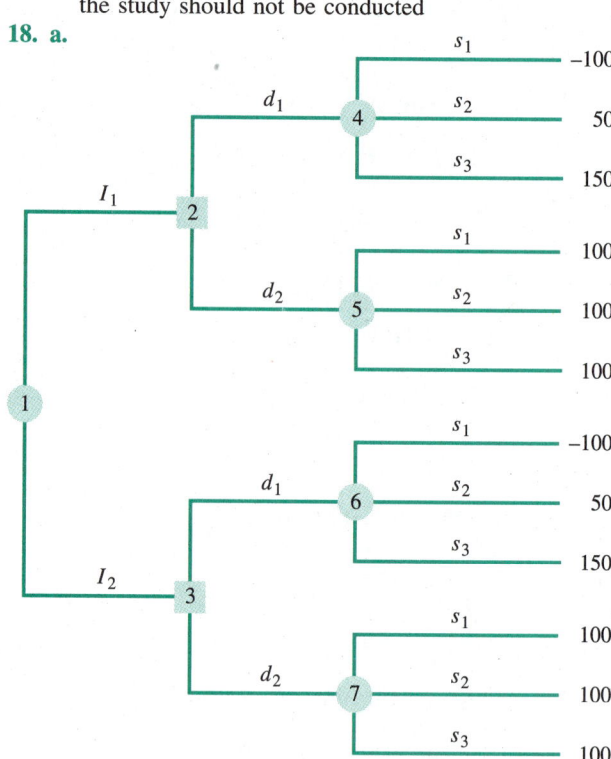

b. For I_1—favorable,

States of Nature	$P(s_j)$	$P(I_1\mid s_j)$	$P(I_1 \cap s_j)$	$P(s_j\mid I_1)$
s_1	.2	.3	.06	.0870
s_2	.3	.6	.18	.2609
s_3	.5	.9	.45	.6522
			$P(I_1) = .69$	

For I_2—unfavorable,

States of Nature	$P(s_j)$	$P(I_2 \mid s_j)$	$P(I_2 \cap s_j)$	$P(s_j \mid I_2)$
s_1	.2	.7	.14	.4516
s_2	.3	.4	.12	.3871
s_3	.5	.1	.05	.1613
			$P(I_2) = .31$	

$$\text{EV(node 4)} = .0870(-100) + .2609(50) + .6522(150)$$

$$= 102.17$$

$$\text{EV(node 5)} = 100$$

$$\text{EV(node 6)} = .4516(-100) + .3871(50) + .1613(150)$$

$$= -1.61$$

$$\text{EV(node 7)} = 100$$

Decision strategy:

If I_1, then select d_1 since EV(node 4) > EV(node 5)

If I_2, then select d_2 since EV(node 7) > EV(node 6)

c. From exercise 7, we know that the expected value of the best decision (d_2) is $100; thus,

EVSI = 101.5 − 100 = 1.5, or $1500; the consulting information is not worthwhile since the cost of $2500 is worth more than the expected gain

INDEX